# 1999 STATE by STATE GUIDE to HUMAN RESOURCES LAW

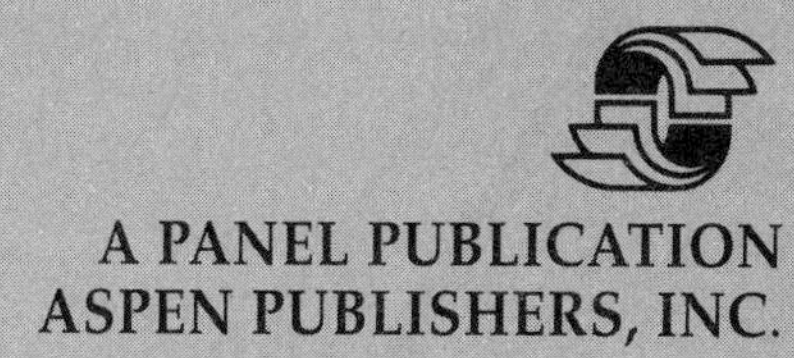

A PANEL PUBLICATION
ASPEN PUBLISHERS, INC.

JOHN F. BUCKLEY

RONALD M. GREEN

A division of Aspen Publishers, Inc.
*A Wolters Kluwer Company*
1185 Avenue of the Americas
New York, NY 10036
(212) 597-0200

All Panel publications are supplemented periodically to ensure that the information presented is accurate and up to date. If you would like to obtain more information about Panel publications or to receive updates for this volume, please contact our Customer Service Department at 1-800-234-1660.

ISBN: 0-7355-0409-1



Printed in the United States of America

# About Panel Publishers

Panel Publishers derives its name from a panel of business professionals who organized in 1964 to publish authoritative and timely books, information services, and journals written by specialists to assist business professionals in the areas of human resources administration, compensation and benefits management, and pension planning and compliance. Our mission is to provide practical, solution-based "how-to" information to business professionals.

Also available from Panel Publishers:

Employment Law Answer Book
Mandated Benefits: 1999 Compliance Guide
Multistate Payroll Guide
State by State Guide to Managed Care Law
Multistate Guide to Benefits Law
COBRA Handbook
Employee Benefits Answer Book*
Employment Relationships: Law & Practice
The Pension Answer Book*
401(k) Answer Book*
Executive Compensation Answer Book*
Officer Compensation Report
Managed Care Answer Book*
On Managed Care
Health Insurance Answer Book
Flexible Benefits Answer Book*

If you would like to obtain more information about these or any other Panel products, please contact our Customer Service Department at 1-800-234-1660.

*A companion volume of forms and worksheets is also available.

**PANEL PUBLISHERS**
**Aspen Publishers, Inc.**
**Practical Solutions for Business Professionals**

## SUBSCRIPTION NOTICE

This Panel product is updated on a periodic basis with supplements to reflect important changes in the subject matter. If you purchased this product directly from Panel Publishers, we have already recorded your subscription for this update service.

If, however, you purchased this product from a bookstore and wish to receive future updates and revised or related volumes billed separately with a 30-day examination review, please contact our Customer Service Department at 1-800-234-1660, or send your name, company name (if applicable), address, and the title of the product to:

PANEL PUBLISHERS
A division of Aspen Publishers, Inc.
*A Wolters Kluwer Company*

7201 McKinney Circle
Frederick, MD 21701

# About the Authors

The *1999 State by State Guide to Human Resources Law* was prepared by the attorneys of the National Legal Research Group. Founded in 1969, the National Legal Research Group has provided consulting and research services to attorneys on more than 100,000 cases.

**JOHN F. BUCKLEY IV** serves as editor and contributing author to the *1999 State by State Guide to Human Resources Law.* Mr. Buckley is a senior attorney on the Public Law team of the National Legal Research Group, where he specializes in civil rights, employment discrimination, and local and state government law; in this capacity, he has advised attorneys throughout the country on legal issues related to equal employment. In addition to his work on the *State by State Guide to Human Resources Law,* Mr. Buckley has served as editor and contributing author for Panel's *Multistate Payroll Guide* and the *Multistate Guide to Benefits Law.* He is also the co-author of the second edition of Shepard's/McGraw-Hill's *Defense of Equal Employment Claims.*

Mr. Buckley received his Bachelor of Arts degree in History from the University of North Carolina at Chapel Hill in 1983. In 1987 he received his Juris Doctor degree from the University of North Carolina School of Law, where he was a member of the Board of Editors of the Law Review.

**RONALD M. GREEN** is a partner in Epstein Becker & Green, P.C. A lawyer of national reputation, he is actively engaged in the private practice of employment and labor law on behalf of multinational and domestic corporations. Mr. Green has lectured extensively throughout the United States on behalf of public and private institutions, trade associations, and corporations. He is also on the Labor Panel of Arbitrators of the American Arbitration Association and the American Bar Association's Committee on Equal Employment Law and Its Impact on Collective Bargaining.

Mr. Green received a Bachelor of Science degree in Business Management from New York University School of Commerce in 1965. He was graduated from Brooklyn Law School in 1968 with a Juris Doctor degree, having served on the Law Review and participated in the Honors Program. He also earned an LL.M. degree in Labor Law from George Washington University School of Law.

---

The authors wish to acknowledge and thank the following attorneys and law clerks who served as contributing authors to the 1999 edition:

Joan C. McKenna, J.D.

Nicole D. Prysby, J.D.

Dwight D. Wilkerson

C. Edward Cather III

John K. Dickinson

The authors also wish to thank Laura Greeney, our editor at Panel Publishers, and the many state labor officials and members of their legal staffs for their assistance in keeping the Guide accurate and current.

Please contact the Editorial Department, Panel Publishers, (212) 597-0200, with comments or suggestions.

# Preface

The *1999 State by State Guide to Human Resources Law* is the only comprehensive authoritative guide to the employment laws of the 50 United States and the District of Columbia. The purpose of the Guide is to serve human resources, compensation, and benefits professionals who work in multijurisdictional environments. Thousands of research hours have been spent to develop this quick-reference chart format, which allows the user to compare and contrast how the various states address any single issue. Assignments that cut across state lines are made easier because the reader at a glance will be able to ascertain whether various states treat an issue in a consistent or incongruous manner.

The 1999 edition incorporates a significant number of substantive changes and valuable additions, as follows:

- Included in the continuing coverage of Trends and Controversies in Human Resources Law is a discussion of recent major U.S. Supreme Court pronouncements relating to employment discrimination.
  - — The Supreme Court recently handed down two landmark cases on sexual harassment. Although these cases both deal primarily with the issue of employer liability for sexual harassment by supervisors, the cases also address the difficult distinction between quid pro quo and hostile environment sexual harassment. In addition to explaining the impact of these decisions on federal law and the implications for human resources professionals, this section discusses how these cases will be applied by the state courts in construing their own fair employment practices laws.
  - — The Supreme Court also handed down a decision that resolved a conflict in the lower courts regarding whether persons suffering from AIDS and those infected with the HIV virus were protected by federal prohibitions against disability discrimination. Another issue that had been the subject of some conflict in the courts was whether infertility or other reproductive limitations met the ADA's requirement that a disability affect a major life activity. The Supreme Court recently resolved both of these questions in a single decision. The impact of this decision on state fair employment laws is already apparent, as evidenced by a recent decision from the Michigan Supreme Court.

Also in the Trends and Controversies section:

— A new section has been added on state subminimum wage provisions. A notable recent trend that has gained significant political support at both the state and federal levels has been the use of "training" or "opportunity" wages. These subminimum wage provisions are generally directed at minors, students, handicapped employees, and, in some cases, all new hires. New Table II sets out the specific provisions of state law relating to subminimum or training wage exceptions to state minimum wage laws.

- In Part 1, Exhibit 1.4-1 has been expanded and updated to include recent state decisions on the validity and enforceability of noncompetition clauses in employment agreements.
- Part 2 has been revised to reflect changes in the law of sexual harassment brought about by recent Supreme Court decisions.
- New tables have been added to Part 4. Table 4.7-1 sets out specific provisions of state right-to-work and other employee rights under organized labor laws. Table 4-7.2 deals with state provisions regarding prohibited employer practices under state organized labor laws. Part 4 has also been revised to reflect state law decisions on wrongful discharge and exceptions to the at-will rule.
- In Part 7, Exhibit 7.2-1, dealing with employee drug testing, has been expanded to cover state law provisions regarding whether the employer or employee must pay for drug testing and whether the employer is under any obligation to provide employee assistance benefits designed to assist employees whose performance level at work is being adversely affected by drug abuse or other personal problems. A new text section has also been added explaining how to develop an employee assistance plan (EAP). Included within this section is a discussion of the elements that should be included in such a plan, as well as a sample EAP.
- Part 8 includes expanded coverage in Table 8.1-3 regarding whether employees are entitled to wages while participating in state OSHA inspections.

Business executives and their professional advisors today face an increasingly complex web of law and regulation with regard to the human resources function. Actions of both the federal and state governments have placed increasing burdens and responsibilities on business relating to the treatment of applicants and employees. And the courts, both federal and state, have also involved themselves in how employers may deal with applicants and employees, importing legal concepts and doctrines of long standing into the domain of the employer-employee relationship.

The information in this book is, for the most part, presented in a tabular format, which is meant to give the reader easy access to information on discrete topics. This Guide is, first and foremost, a reference tool for the professional who needs to put his or her finger on the particulars of personnel law on a state-by-state basis quickly without wading through large amounts of extraneous data. Liberal cross-referencing and two indexes help the user locate exactly what he or she may need.

What follows is a summary of the information that can be found in each of the parts of this Guide.

## Defining the Employment Relationship

This section introduces and describes the major types of employment relationships (i.e., employer and employee, employer and independent contractor, and principal and agent) so that the application of statutory and common-law concepts to the employer-employee relationship can be distinguished.

General information is provided on aspects of the offer and acceptance of employment, including written and oral contracts, the nature of the relationship in the absence of a contract, and the role played by employee manuals. Exhibit 1.2-1, based on Equal Employment Opportunity Guidelines, generally sets forth permitted and prohibited topics of preemployment inquiry; Exhibit 1.2-2 provides a closer look at each state's specific statutory provisions.

Also discussed are two important aspects of the dissolution of an employment relationship: breach of contract and alternative dispute resolution.

## Fair Employment Practices

Forty-seven states and the District of Columbia have enacted state analogues to Title VII, barring private-sector discrimination on the basis of race, color, national origin, religion, and sex. (The states that have not enacted comprehensive statutes are Alabama, Arkansas, and Mississippi; Georgia's statute applies only to public employment.) A majority of these states have also used their general fair employment statutes to prohibit age and handicap discrimination. States with separate nondiscrimination statutes addressing particular areas—for example, age or handicap—are also identified. In addition, various states have determined that other bases for making employment decisions should be prohibited; for example, political affiliation, sexual orientation, nonsmoker status, or veteran status. The tables in this part make it easy to identify what may be prohibited in a particular jurisdiction.

Other tables indicate who is covered and what actions are prohibited or excepted by the statute; set forth the procedures for bringing and litigating a charge before an administrative agency and a court; identify the time constraints for alleging statutory violations; indicate what statutory defenses may be provided; note the relief available by law, including the penalties and sanctions that may be imposed; and describe in some detail the powers of the state enforcement and regulatory agencies. This part also includes a table that describes any affirmative action obligations the state imposes on employers generally or on those that contract with the state to provide goods or services.

## Wages, Hours, and Holidays

The federal government has established certain baseline standards governing employee wages and hours. Minimum wage and maximum hour standards and methods for determining overtime are the most evident and pervasive of the federal rules.

Employers must also know of and comply with myriad state laws governing these same issues. Most states have enacted wage and hour laws that are both consistent with and different from the federal rules, and knowing where the differences are is essential. Tables in this part identify which states have laws setting minimum wage and overtime standards. The tables also note state law recordkeeping requirements for wage and hour matters and the penalties for violating the state statutes.

Most states regulate the ages at which children may work and the types of jobs that children may hold at various ages. A separate series of tables describe state laws pertaining to child labor, recordkeeping rules for both minors and adults, and the penalties for violating the state laws.

A final table addresses state holidays. The listing in the table does not reflect holidays that private-sector employers must give their employees. Rather, it notes those holidays that a state recognizes for its employees. Many private employers follow their host state's lead, however, in granting holidays to employees, which makes this information of some value to those practicing in the private sector.

## Employment at Will

Although the Guide generally is concerned with statutory provisions affecting the employment relationship, issues attendant to employee termination and employment at will, and the various standards and rules applicable in the states, require discussion in this volume. Matters affecting the severing of an employment relationship are among the most troublesome employers face. Challenges to a termination almost always raise issues such as breach of contract or violation of an important public policy concern.

The traditional rule relative to the employer-employee relationship had been (and, in a few states, remains) that either party could terminate the relationship at any time and for any reason. Since the nineteenth century, however, employees have gained a number of important statutory protections, such as those noted in the state fair employment law part. This, in turn, has made it easier for the courts to impose additional obligations on employers seeking to discharge employees. Part 3 identifies the states that have recognized exceptions to the traditional employment-at-will rule. One table notes which states have recognized contractual causes of action as defenses to discharge: for example, statements printed in handbooks or manuals or oral promises of job security.

Another table explains the public policy exception. Specifically, it notes which states have limited an employer's right to discharge employees for serving on juries, exercising a right to seek workers' compensation, informing state officials of health or safety violations, and so forth.

Other tables in this part note several other nonstatutory causes of action an employee may either file to challenge a discharge, such as interference with contractual relations, or include as a separate issue, such as infliction of emotional distress or defamation; defenses that courts have recognized in discharge lawsuits; statutory restrictions on discharging employees; and the remedies available to employees who prevail. This table is especially important because employees are often able to recover compensatory and punitive damages against an employer deemed to have engaged in an improper termination.

Because the body of law governing wrongful termination is developed almost exclusively by the state courts, the authors have attempted to include citations to the most recent relevant state court decisions; however, inasmuch as this area is one of the fastest changing in employment law, employers will need to consistently monitor judicial determinations concerning contractual and tort theories in the wrongful discharge area.

## Employee Benefits

A number of states have enacted statutes requiring that employers offer certain types of benefits to employees. This part identifies those states and describes the benefits.

The part begins, however, with a brief description of the issue of a legal doctrine known as "preemption." By and large, the federal government regulates what employers are required to do for employees in the benefits area. Under a federal law, the Employee Retirement Income Security Act of 1974, as amended (ERISA), Congress states that all state and local laws that relate to employee benefits plans are preempted by the federal law. That is to say, the state and local laws are rendered null and void, and employee benefits plans are governed by a single set of regulations. Unlike unemployment and workers' compensation programs, in which the states are free to set their own standards, employers here are protected from conflicting and inconsistent state requirements. There are limits to the reach of the preemption rule, and, as the introduction to the part notes, employers subject to state regulation on a benefits plan issue may need to seek assistance in determining whether it must comply with the state provision.

This part describes types of benefits that states may require employers to provide to employees. The principal benefit is group health insurance, covered in nine separate tables. Most states do not directly require employers to offer certain health insurance benefits, but rather require insurers offering group policies to include certain benefits. Additional tables describe health insurance continuation and conversion rules, regulation of health maintenance organizations, group life insurance and legal expenses insurance provisions, wage payment laws (requiring employers to make certain payments to terminating employees either immediately on termination or within a defined period), and "parental leave" laws. The issue of parental leave for purposes related to childbirth or adoption or illness of close family members is one that has just begun to make its way into the social consciousness. A federal law, the Family and Medical Leave Act, now requires most employers to allow employees up to 12 weeks of leave for certain specified reasons, and many states have enacted legislation giving employees even greater leave rights.

## Unemployment Compensation

An unemployment compensation program is also like insurance. Here, the employer is insuring its employees against the loss of income associated with termination of employment. A state-mandated Social Security program, unemployment compensation provides terminated employees with weekly cash benefits for a period of time, giving employees a cushion during the period they are seeking new positions. States require that employers pay into a state fund (not a private insurance carrier as in workers' compensation) a certain amount per employee. Terminated employees who meet qualification standards are entitled to draw out of the employer's fund for a statutorily defined period. (Also like an insurance program, an employer's unemployment compensation payments are affected by the number of claims made on its account by terminated employees.)

The tables in this part set forth the state requirements. They define who is covered and who is exempted. Most states require that all employers participate in the unemployment compensation program, although a few set different standards for employers in certain industries. Also described are how benefits are calculated, how long an employee must wait before becoming eligible for benefits, the maximum number of weeks one may collect, the weekly benefit amount, the disqualifications for benefits, tax (or premium) rates, and the reporting and recordkeeping requirements.

## Workplace Privacy

At common law, the right of privacy has involved four distinct concerns: the right to control and limit the commercial appropriation of one's identity by another; the right to be free from intrusion; the right to control the disclosure of private information about oneself; and the right to avoid being placed in a "false light" in the public eye. Each of these has a relationship to the workplace and the employer-employee relationship. For example, an employer that uses employees in advertising may be violating the first noted right, that of commercial misappropriation, unless it obtains the employees' consent. The right to be free from the public disclosure of private information may be violated when an employer fails to limit the dissemination of private information about the employee to a "need-to-know" group. An intrusion into an employee's seclusion may result from a search of an employee's desk or locker when the employer failed to reserve the right to conduct such searches or failed to limit the employee's right to the privacy of employer-provided furniture. And the "false light" protection may be violated by an employer that makes statements on behalf of employees without the employees' consent. Because these privacy concepts involve the common law and, as a rule, are not statutory in nature, they are not addressed in this part.

There are, however, a number of discrete issues that are statutory and involve concerns that have a nexus to privacy. Specifically, this part includes tables concerning various types of applicant or employee testing, including tests for use of drugs; exposure to the AIDS virus; and polygraph tests. Additional tables address employer use of consumer credit reporting agencies to conduct background checks, generally of applicants, and an employer's right to use arrest or conviction information about applicants in making employment decisions. Also listed are states with so-called anti-blacklisting statutes, which prohibit employers from blacklisting "troublemaking" employees. These statutes may also contain requirements for employers relative to providing references for former employees. Finally, states that make provisions for employee access to personnel records are also listed.

### Safety and Health

This part includes a discussion of state occupational safety and health statutes. Some states require employees to provide certain health and safety related equipment and, in some instances, medical examinations. The various state requirements in this area are covered in this chapter. The increasing amount of regulation in the area of workplace smoking is also covered in this part.

### Summary of Federal Legislation, Guidelines, and Policy on Human Resources Law

Although the function of this Guide is to provide a quick reference to state laws in a number of important areas, it would nonetheless be incomplete if it failed to address the federal statutes applicable to the employment relationship. Therefore, this part summarizes the major legislation on the federal level affecting personnel law.

Title VII of the Civil Rights Act of 1964, as amended, is the primary federal law prohibiting discrimination on the basis of race, color, national origin, religion, and sex. Although a number of federal statutes preceded it, most notably the National Labor Relations Act (NLRA) and the Equal Pay Act, Title VII marked the beginning of an era in which the U.S. Congress enacted a number of far-reaching laws designed to extend various protections against discrimination to employees in the workplace. The Civil Rights Act of 1991 has not only expanded the remedies available under Title VII, but has also made jury trials available in such cases. Further, the Americans With Disabilities Act, effective for most employers on July 26, 1992, now provides a vehicle for employees with disabilities to seek redress for discrimination. Both new statutes are discussed in detail. Other statutes include the Age Discrimination in Employment Act (ADEA), the Rehabilitation Act, and the Vietnam Era Veterans Readjustment Assistance Act. The federal government also attacked discrimination through its power of the purse: Executive Order 11246 prohibits government contractors from discriminating on the same bases as Title VII and further requires development of affirmative action plans, which have created a certain amount of controversy related to issues of reverse discrimination.

Other federal statutes with principal purposes other than preventing discrimination also contain components that bar the use of certain criteria to make employment-related decisions. These statutes include the Employee Retirement Income Security Act of 1974 (ERISA) (prohibiting discrimination on the basis of an individual's entitlement to covered benefits), the Immigration Reform and Control Act (IRCA) (citizenship), the Consumer Credit Protection Act (garnishment), and the Jury System Improvement Act (jury service).

Finally, this overview of federal law describes a host of statutes affecting the employment relationship beyond issues of discrimination. For example, the Occupational Safety and Health Act requires that employers establish and maintain safe working environments for employees and sets certain standards for employers to follow in various workplace settings; the Worker Adjustment and Retraining Notification Act (WARN) requires that employers notify employees of large-scale layoffs or business closings; the Fair Credit Reporting Act requires that employers inform employees or applicants of certain efforts to obtain information about them through use of third parties; and the Drug-Free Workplace Act requires that government contractors and recipients of federal grants implement policies barring the use, sale, and manufacture of controlled substances by employees assigned to work on the contract or grant and develop "drug-free awareness" programs to inform such employees of the dangers of drugs in the workplace and where drug-involved employees may obtain assistance.

### Finding Aids

A glossary of legal terms that have been used in the tables and text can be found at the back of the Guide. This Guide also maintains a traditional index, which should prove helpful in locating information.

We have again labored to make this book as fresh and as timely as possible; however, inasmuch as state laws are constantly changing, we apologize—in advance—for any omission that may occur. We welcome your suggestions for making the Guide even more useful.

John F. Buckley
Ronald M. Green

January 1999

# How to Use This Guide

The *1999 State by State Guide to Human Resources Law* is designed to provide quick access to each state's laws on the expanding number of issues and concerns facing business executives and their advisors. The easy-to-use tabular format enables the reader to quickly locate the laws of a specific state, to determine their applicability to specific situations, and to compare how the states approach numerous aspects of personnel law.

Topics that require more extensive discussion appear as two-column text exhibits.

## Organization

The annual edition of this Guide is organized into eight major parts. Each part has an overview that introduces the subject area as a whole; within each part, tables are grouped in topical sections, each with its own brief introduction.

Tables and exhibits appear in Parts 1 through 8. Part 9 is a narrative summary of the federal regulation of personnel law.

Part 1 Defining the Employment Relationship
Part 2 Fair Employment Practices
Part 3 Wages, Hours, and Holidays
Part 4 Employment at Will
Part 5 Benefits
Part 6 Unemployment Compensation
Part 7 Workplace Privacy
Part 8 Health and Safety
Part 9 Summary of Federal Legislation, Guidelines, and Policies on Human Resources Law

A supplement to the Guide is produced each year, following the publication of the annual edition by approximately six months. In addition to updating changes in state legislation, the supplement features a special comprehensive section on statewide workers' compensation laws. The section on state workers' compensation laws is prepared by the Chamber of Commerce of the United States.

## Table and Exhibit Formats

Each table and exhibit lists in alphabetical order, by state, the provisions of law under discussion. States are listed by standard postal abbreviation. In a handful of instances, where only a few state laws address a particular topic, only those states are listed. Finally, every table is cross-referenced to the text that discusses its content. The cross-reference appears under the table title.

## Citation System

Each table and exhibit contains a column titled "Citations to Authority." The information contained within the table is referenced to the state statutes and federal and state court cases that provide the basis for such information. The citations permit immediate access to original sources.

## Reference System

Each part has a number, 1 through 9. Within each part, text is identified consecutively by section number; for example, § 1.1, § 1.2, § 1.3, and so forth.

Tables and exhibits are numbered consecutively, but carry the number of the section in which they appear. For example, the tables in § 3.2 are numbered Table 3.2-1, Table 3.2-2, Table 3.2-3, whereas the exhibits in § 1.2 are numbered Exhibit 1.2-1 and Exhibit 1.2-2. For ease of access from the indexes, table, exhibit, and section numbers appear at the top of each page.

## Special Reference Features

The *1999 State by State Guide to Human Resources Law* offers a number of special reference features to assist the reader in locating sought-after material of various kinds. These reference guides include the following tables:

- **Glossary of Legal Terms.** The glossary provides definitions of legal terms that have been used in the Guide.
- **Topical Index.** The traditional topical index provides another way to locate specific information. References in this index are to section number, table number, or exhibit number.

# Summary of Contents

# Table of Contents

# Trends and Controversies in Human Resources Law

The laws that define and regulate the relationship between employer and employee are constantly evolving. The rapidity of this evolution has been driven, to a large extent, by the overall pace of social change in this country during the last 30 years. For instance, the media's treatment of issues related to sexual harassment and assault in a variety of settings and evolving social attitudes toward sexual harassment have directly affected legislation defining prohibited workplace conduct. The increasing amount of employment-related litigation has also fueled rapid changes in procedural issues relating to how workplace claims are resolved.

In many instances, judges and legislators may have reached different conclusions regarding the appropriate resolution of these issues, leaving an employer's long-term potential exposure to claims involving these issues somewhat uncertain. This section examines recent and evolving issues in human resources law. Familiarity with these issues will enable employers and human resources professionals to anticipate future changes and to formulate appropriate personnel policies.

## [a] Recent Supreme Court Pronouncements on Sexual Harassment

The Supreme Court recently handed down two landmark cases on sexual harassment. Although both these cases dealt primarily with the issue of employer liability for sexual harassment by supervisors, the cases also addressed the difficult distinction between quid pro quo and hostile environment sexual harassment.

The courts and the Equal Employment Opportunity Commission (EEOC) have recognized two basic types of sexual harassment: (1) harassment in which tangible job benefits are granted or denied based on submission to or rejection of unwelcome sexual advances or conduct; and (2) harassment in which the conduct of others creates an intimidating, hostile, or offensive working environment. These two distinct types of harassment are referred to, respectively, as *quid pro quo harassment* and *hostile environment harassment.* The distinction between these two types of sexual harassment is central to both the determination of whether there has been actionable harassment and whether the employer can be held liable for that harassment.

**Quid Pro Quo Harassment.** There had been some question regarding whether the mere threat of an adverse employment consequence could support a claim of quid pro quo harassment. The Supreme Court has now made it clear that a claim based solely on unfulfilled threats should be categorized as a hostile work environment claim that requires a showing of severe or pervasive conduct. To support a claim of quid pro quo harassment, an employee must show that a tangible employment action resulted from the employee's refusal to submit to a supervisor's sexual demands.[1] Thus, if no tangible employment action results from the employee's refusal, the claim must be characterized as hostile environment sexual harassment.

**Employer Liability for Sexual Harassment.** If an employee establishes that he or she was sexually harassed by a supervisor or other employee, the question

1. Ellerth v. Burlington Industries, Inc., 118 S. Ct. 2275 (1998).

remains whether the employer can be held liable for the harassment. Although there had been some disagreement among the courts regarding the precise standard to be applied, the Supreme Court has now provided some clarification.[2] Under the Supreme Court's standard, the question of employer liability turns on whether the harassment was committed by a co-worker or a supervisor and whether the harassment—or the employee's response to the harassment—resulted in a tangible job action. Although the Supreme Court's decision clarifies the basic standard, the decision also raises a number of uncertainties for employers.

Although the Supreme Court did not address precisely what constitutes a tangible job action, the Court did provide some guidance in this area. Examples given by the court of sufficiently tangible employment actions include:

- Hiring
- Firing
- Failing to promote
- Reassignment with significantly different responsibilities
- A decision causing a significant change in benefits

Employment actions that may not be sufficient to trigger vicarious liability, the Court indicated, include:

- A "bruised ego"
- Demotion without change in pay, benefits, duties, or prestige
- Reassignment to a less convenient job

**Liability for Harassment by Supervisory Personnel.** The stated position of the EEOC is that an employer is responsible for the sexual harassment of its supervisory employees, regardless of whether the specific acts complained of were authorized or even forbidden by the employer, and regardless of whether the employer knew or should have known of the acts.[3] Although, as stated, the position seems to suggest automatic liability for harassment by supervisors in every case, the EEOC has indicated that an employer who has an explicit policy prohibiting sexual harassment will be held liable for hostile environment sexual harassment only if it knew or should have known of the harassment and failed to take prompt remedial action. Although many courts had accepted the EEOC's position with respect to quid pro quo harassment by supervisors, most courts rejected the EEOC's position to the extent that it applied to hostile environment harassment by supervisors. The Supreme Court's decisions in *Ellerth* and *Faragher,* however, appear to adopt the EEOC's position in many respects.

Under the Supreme Court's recent pronouncements, in cases in which a tangible employment action results from a refusal to submit to a supervisor's sexual demands, the employer is automatically liable, and no defense is available to the employer. In cases in which no tangible employment action is taken, the employer will still be held liable unless it can prove as a matter of defense that:

1. The employer exercised reasonable care to prevent and correct promptly any sexually harassing behavior; and
2. The plaintiff employee unreasonably failed to take advantage of any preventive or corrective opportunities provided by the employer or to avoid harm otherwise.

The Court's decision, while providing some needed guidance to employers, leaves a number of questions unanswered. First, the Court does not address the situation in which an employee accedes to the sexual demands of a supervisor. Strictly speaking, the Court's opinion would suggest that such cases be considered hostile environment cases, since the threats remain unfulfilled and no tangible job detriment is involved. It is more likely, however, that such cases will continue to result in automatic liability for employers because the supervisor in such cases is clearly using the authority conferred upon him to make the sexual demands. Second, the court did not indicate whether the employer liability standard it enunciated for harassment by supervisors should also be applied to harassment by fellow employees. It is likely, however, that courts will continue to apply the standard previously applicable to employer liability for harassment by fellow employees and will not apply the standard set out in *Faragher* and *Ellerth* when no supervisory harassment is involved.

**Application to State Fair Employment Laws.** The Supreme Court's *Faragher* and *Ellerth* holdings affect state courts as well as federal courts. So far, only a few state courts have explicitly discussed the application of these decisions to state fair employment laws; a number of state courts have cited *Faragher* or *Ellerth,* however, indicating that these decisions may be applied in the future to state statutes.

2. Faragher v. City of Boca Raton, 118 S. Ct. 2275 (1998).
3. 29 C.F.R. § 1604.11(c).

The Court of Appeals of Kentucky has applied the *Faragher* and *Ellerth* holdings in declaring that an employer may be liable for the acts of a supervisory employee in a hostile environment case under the Kentucky Civil Rights Act,[4] reversing summary judgment for the employer on grounds that the supervisor had acted outside the scope of employment.[5] Applying *Faragher* where no tangible adverse action had been taken, the court also recognized the employer's affirmative defense that it had exercised reasonable care to prevent or correct harassment, and that the plaintiff had unreasonably failed to take advantage of any preventive or corrective opportunities provided by the employer.[6]

Likewise, the Court of Appeals of Texas has applied the *Ellerth* and *Faragher* holdings in a sexual harassment case brought under the Texas Commission on Human Rights Act.[7] The Texas court applied the reasoning of the Supreme Court's decisions to hold that once the employee had established a prima facie case of hostile environment by a supervisor's harassment where no tangible employment action was taken, the employee had established liability of the employer for the supervisor's action, subject only to the employer raising the two-pronged affirmative defense articulated by the U.S. Supreme Court.[8] Since the employer failed to do so, the appeals court upheld the jury verdict for the employee.[9]

Although the California courts have not expressly applied *Faragher* and *Ellerth* in construing the state's fair employment law, one justice of the California Supreme Court noted in a concurrence to a recent decision that the effect of the California court's holding—that plaintiffs under the state law cannot hold supervisors individually liable for employment discrimination, and conversely that employers will always be liable for such discrimination—is consistent with the principle articulated in *Faragher* and *Ellerth,* "that claims against employers for discriminatory employment actions with tangible results . . . have resulted in employer liability once discrimination is shown."[10]

A number of courts in other states have cited *Faragher* and *Ellerth* with approval.[11] Although these decisions did not explicitly discuss how *Faragher* and *Ellerth* would be applied to actions brought under state fair employment laws, they indicate that the principles enunciated in those decisions will have a profound effect on how state fair employment laws will be applied.

It is clear, therefore, that successful compliance with both state and federal law requires that human resources professionals be familiar with the *Faragher* and *Ellerth* decisions. Furthermore, all nondiscrimination policies should be reviewed and revised, if necessary, to ensure that the employer has made reasonable efforts to prevent and remedy discrimination, as required by *Faragher* and *Ellerth.*

**Assessing the Impact of *Faragher* and *Ellerth*.** By setting out the definitive standard for employer liability for sexual harassment, these decisions can be viewed as helpful to employers in that they provide some guidance regarding how to avoid liability. There are, however, several troubling aspects of the Court's decisions. First, an employer may be automatically liable for any tangible employment action that was preceded by and was the result of a rejected sexual advance. Second, even if the employer takes prompt remedial action upon learning of

4. Ky. Rev. Stat. Ann. §§ 344.010 *et seq.* (Michie 1997).

5. Hill v. Gateway Regional Health System, Inc., 1998 WL 412623 (Ky. App., July 24, 1998).

6. Hill at *10.

7. Tex. Lab. Code Ann. § 21.051 (West 1996).

8. Wal-Mart Stores, Inc. v. Davis, 1998 WL 655497 at *9–*10 (Tex. App. Sept. 24, 1998).

9. *Id.*

10. Reno v. Baird, 76 Cal. Rptr. 2d 499, 514 (Cal. 1998).

11. *See, e.g.,* Adams v. County of King, 1998 WL 568693 (Wash. App. Div. 1, Aug. 17, 1998) (looking to federal case in construing state anti-discrimination law, and citing *Faragher* for its statement that it is appropriate for sex and race harassment cases to draw on one another, and that conduct must be extreme to amount to a change in the terms and conditions of employment); Beyda v. City of Los Angeles, 76 Cal. Rptr. 2d 547 (Cal. App. 2 Dist. 1998) (considering federal law in deciding claim brought under the California Fair Employment and Housing Act, and citing *Faragher* for proposition that in order to be actionable, a sexually hostile environment must be both objectively and subjectively offensive); Brittell v. Department of Correction, 1998 WL 643607 (Conn., Sept. 22, 1998) (in deciding claim of co-worker harassment under the state's Fair Employment Practices Act, mentioning holdings of *Ellerth* and *Faragher* in dissent, but that they did not affect outcome of decision); Carrisales v. Department of Corrections, 77 Cal. Rptr. 2d 517 (Cal. App. 4 1998) (looking to federal law in construing state fair employment law, and citing *Faragher* for its statement that to establish employer liability for harassment by nonsupervisory personnel under Title VII, the courts have uniformly applied a negligence standard); Massey v. Connecticut Mental Health Center, 1998 WL 470590 (Conn. Super. July 31, 1998) (remarking, in decision under Connecticut's fair employment law, that federal case law gave guidance in such decisions, and that the court's analysis in its decision was "not in derogation" of the *Ellerth* holding).

harassment that did not culminate in a tangible employment action, the employer may still be unable to avoid liability, unless the employee was somehow negligent in using the available grievance procedure to report the harassment.

It is difficult to predict precisely how the second element of the affirmative defense will be applied. On the one hand, it could be applied in such a way that the affirmative defense is available only when an employee completely fails to invoke the grievance procedure, or where the employee unreasonably delays in invoking the grievance procedure. Obviously, such an application of this element of the defense would make things more difficult for employers who could heretofore avoid liability by taking prompt remedial action after learning of harassment. On the other hand, it could be applied in such a way that employees who do not promptly report incidents of harassment will not be able to rely on those incidents to establish employer liability.

At the very least, the Supreme Court's analysis will make it more difficult for employers to obtain a summary adjudication of sexual harassment liability, for the analysis requires an additional fact to be determined: whether the employee acted reasonably in reporting the harassment. Because the matter is an affirmative defense, the employer will bear the burden of proof with respect to this fact.

### [b] HIV and Reproduction Under the ADA: The Supreme Court Resolves Lower Court Conflicts

For over a decade, the federal courts had struggled with the question of whether persons suffering from AIDS and those infected with the HIV virus were protected by federal prohibitions against disability discrimination. Some courts had concluded that, while persons suffering from the symptoms of AIDS were protected, those who were infected with HIV, but who were asymptomatic, were not.[12] Another issue that had been the subject of some conflict in the courts was whether infertility, or other reproductive limitations, met the ADA's requirement that a disability affect a major life activity.[13] The Supreme Court recently resolved both of these questions in a single decision.

The Supreme Court's decision in *Bragdon v. Abbott,*[14] stemmed from a suit by a dental patient infected with the human immunodeficiency virus (HIV), who was in the phase of the infection in which no physical symptoms had yet manifested themselves. She brought suit, under the public accommodations Title of the ADA, against a dentist who refused to treat her in his office because of her HIV status. The patient argued that her asymptomatic infection was a disability because it substantially limited her in her ability to reproduce.

Finding that reproduction and the sexual dynamics surrounding it are central to the life process, the Supreme Court held that reproduction is a major life activity under the ADA. In so holding, the Court rejected the notion that activities that lack a public, economic, or daily character are not "major," finding that nothing in the statutory definition of major life activities supported such a position. The Court further found that the plaintiff's HIV infection affected her ability to reproduce and bear children because, if she tried to conceive a child: (1) she would impose on her male partner a statistically significant risk of becoming infected; and (2) she would risk infecting her child during gestation and childbirth, i.e., would risk perinatal transmission.

Although the Court acknowledged that, in some cases, persons with HIV or AIDS would not be protected under the ADA if they pose a direct threat to others, the Court indicated that this exception would be construed somewhat narrowly. Specifically, the Court stated that, under the "direct threat" doctrine, the existence or nonexistence of a significant health risk from accommodation of a person with disabilities must be analyzed from the standpoint of the person who refused the accommodation. To successfully invoke the doctrine, however, the risk assessment must be based on medical or other objective evidence and not simply on that person's good-faith belief that a significant risk existed.

12. See e.g. Runnebaum v. NationsBank of Maryland N.A., 123 F.3d 156 (4th. Cir. 1997) (holding that, in the absence of symptoms, HIV infection was not a disability under the Americans with Disabilities Act and did not substantially limit the major life activities of procreation or intimate sexual relations).

13. Pacourek v. Inland Steel Co., 916 F. Supp. 797 (N.D. Ill. 1996) (finding that firing an employee for absences from work for infertility treatment violated the ADA); Krauel v. Iowa Methodist Medical Center, 95 F.3d 674 (8th Cir. 1996) (holding that an employer's refusal to pay for fertility treatment was not a violation of the ADA, because reproduction was not a major life activity, and that the employee therefore failed to meet the requirement that she be a person with a disability).

14. Bragdon v. Abbott, 118 S. Ct. 2196 (1998).

The application of the direct threat doctrine, as explained in *Bragdon,* was recently addressed by the Michigan Supreme Court in construing the Michigan Handicappers' Civil Rights Act. In *Sanchez v. Lagoudakis,*[15] the Supreme Court of Michigan interpreted the Supreme Court's ruling in *Bragdon v. Abbott* to allow employers in the food service industry to require employees to be tested for communicable diseases on the basis of a "reasonable suspicion" of the presence of AIDS.

The plaintiff, Dorene Sanchez, was a waitress at a restaurant. A rumor circulated in late 1987 that she had AIDS. Although it is unclear how the rumor originated, the defendant testified and offered the corroborating testimony of a customer that the plaintiff herself started the rumor. After her employer became aware of the rumor, he directed Sanchez to prove that she was healthy enough to continue working in the restaurant. Sanchez returned with medical evidence to prove that she did not have AIDS, and her employer allowed her to continue working. However, Sanchez alleged that her employer's action constituted a discharge and violated the Michigan Handicappers' Civil Rights Act (HCRA).

The Supreme Court of Michigan ruled in favor of the defendant, holding that

> where a food-service employer has reasonable suspicion that a food-service employee has AIDS, which by definition is a syndrome that involves a compromised immune system that renders the employee highly susceptible to diseases that might be communicable in a manner described under the relevant regulations, the food-service employer may refuse to continue to assign the employee, pending testing for such communicable diseases.
>
> * * *
>
> Thus, to the extent that a food-service employee with AIDS suffers from an opportunistic infection that is a communicable disease, and reasonable accommodation will not eliminate the likelihood of contamination of food or food-contact surfaces, or transmission of the disease to another person, the food service industry employee is not protected under the HCRA from exclusion.[16]

In its holding, the court emphasized that its "focus here is limited and does not concern the transmission of AIDS. Rather, our decision addresses the obligations of food-service employers and employees in the presence of the potential spread of underlying communicable diseases that may be associated with AIDS."[17] The court also noted that had the plaintiff been diagnosed with AIDS but did not have a communicable disease, or had a condition that could reasonably be accommodated under the circumstances, "the case would be entirely different."[18]

In attempting to balance the food service employer's obligation under the HCRA not to discriminate against employees with the employer's concurrent obligation to provide a healthy environment for diners and other patrons of a food service establishment, the Supreme Court of Michigan applied the "objective reasonableness in light of current medical knowledge" standard that was set forth in *Bragdon.* In applying *Bragdon,* the court noted that "objective reasonableness" may be defined differently for health care professionals than for lay employers. In *Sanchez,* the court held that due to the unique facts of the case, the employer's suspicions, which were based upon rumors, were nonetheless sufficiently reliable to support his decision to order that Sanchez be tested for AIDS.

As noted in Parts 2 and 7, the *Bragdon* decision will influence the interpretation of many other state fair employment laws. This influence may be particularly apparent in states in which AIDS or HIV infection has not previously been recognized as a disability.

### [c] State Subminimum Wage Provisions

A notable recent trend that has gained significant political support at both the state and federal levels has been the use of "training," or "opportunity" wages. These subminimum wage provisions are generally directed at minors, students, handicapped employees, and in some cases, all new hires. The provisions take the form of statutes passed by the legislature or regulations adopted by the state department of labor. Some of the provisions are targeted at specific groups in the work force, as is the case in Alaska, where persons enrolled in substance abuse programs involving work therapy are targeted, or Hawaii, where paroled youth offenders from youth correctional facilities are covered by the provision. More typically, a broad class of workers, such as minors or handicapped employees will be covered by the provision.

The reasoning given for adopting these provisions is that the lower wages will encourage employers to hire

15. 458 Mich. 704, 581 N.W.2d 257 (Mich. 1998).
16. 581 N.W.2d at 259, 263.
17. Id.
18. Id. at 260.

young and inexperienced workers. The theory is that employers might otherwise hesitate to offer such workers jobs because the employer might be put off at the prospect of paying a new, young, or inexperienced employee the minimum wage. If the employer is permitted to hire the same worker at the reduced rate, the employer may be willing to risk hiring the new employee and, when appropriate, train the employee to perform the work required.

Most subminimum wage provisions prohibit displacing current employees with workers earning the subminimum wage. These restrictions are intended to address the concerns of labor groups who have opposed allowing employers to pay less than the minimum wage.

While each of the provisions adopted by the several states reflects the unique concerns of that state, there are common elements shared by many of these provisions. Minors and workers with disabilities are the most commonly included groups. Most subminimum wage provisions also typically require employers to obtain a special certificate authorizing the payment of the subminimum wage to minors and employees with disabilities. In some states, it is the workers who must apply to the department of labor for the certificate authorizing payment of the subminimum wage. A worker with such a certificate is eligible for employment at the reduced rate for the duration of the validity of the certificate. The certificate is usually obtained by application to the commissioner of labor, or the state department of labor. In states where the provisions apply to minors or all new hires, and are referred to as "training wages" or "opportunity wages," a cap is placed on the length of time the employee may be paid the subminimum wage, usually in the range of 90 days. Other states authorize employers to pay all minors the subminimum wage. Some states also include persons who are "impaired by age" under the coverage of the subminimum wage provision, with wages to be set by the same standards applied to employees with disabilities. These provisions are classified under the "Other Provisions" heading in Table II, though they will typically be found in the statutes with the states' provisions for employees with disabilities.

This table does not reflect exemptions from the applicable minimum wage laws of the various states, only those persons specifically covered by statutes and regulations authorizing the payment of wages below the established minimum wage. For information on exemptions, consult Table 3.3-1, "Minimum Wage Requirements and Exemptions." Persons not covered by a state's subminimum wage provision may be exempt by statute from the minimum wage law.

# Table I

## STATE SUBMINIMUM WAGE PROVISIONS

**KEY:** "Learners and Apprentices" refers to persons enrolled in formal apprenticeship programs or cooperative education programs associated with vocational education programs.
"Students" refers to any persons enrolled in an accredited academic institution. Any more restricted application of the term "student" is noted under this column.
"Training/Opportunity Wage" refers to a subminimum wage paid to *all* new hires, unless otherwise indicated.
"Handicapped Workers" refers to an individual defined as a handicapped employee or employee with a disability under the state's wage statutes.

| | | *Coverage* | | | | | | | |
|---|---|---|---|---|---|---|---|---|---|
| | *Does State Have Subminimum Wage Provision?* | *Are Learners and Apprentices Covered?* | *Are Handicapped Workers Covered?* | *Are Students Covered?* | *Are Minors/ Workers Under Age 21 Covered?* | *Is a Training/ Opportunity Wage Paid to New Hires?* | *Other Provisions* | *Citations to Authority* | *Comments* |
| AL | No. | — | — | — | — | — | — | — | State has no minimum wage law. |
| AK | Yes. | Yes. | Yes. | No. | No. | No. | Yes, persons in residential drug/alcohol abuse treatment programs where the program is designed to last more than 120 days if receiving wages as part of work therapy. | Alaska Stat. §§ 23.10.070; 23.10.071. | Wage set by labor commissioner. |
| AZ | Yes. | Yes. Although statute provides for subminimum wage for learners and apprentices, note that statutes authorizing the employment of *(cont'd)* | No. | No. | No. | No. | No. | Ariz. Rev. Stat. Ann. § 23-221 *et seq.*; 23-317. | Subminimum wage set by wage board. |

*(Table continues.)*

# Table I *(cont'd)*

## STATE SUBMINIMUM WAGE PROVISIONS

**KEY:** "Learners and Apprentices" refers to persons enrolled in formal apprenticeship programs or cooperative education programs associated with vocational education programs.
"Students" refers to any persons enrolled in an accredited academic institution. Any more restricted application of the term "student" is noted under this column.
"Training/Opportunity Wage" refers to a subminimum wage paid to *all* new hires, unless otherwise indicated.
"Handicapped Workers" refers to an individual defined as a handicapped employee or employee with a disability under the state's wage statutes.

| | | *Coverage* | | | | | | | |
|---|---|---|---|---|---|---|---|---|---|
| | *Does State Have Subminimum Wage Provision?* | *Are Learners and Apprentices Covered?* | *Are Handicapped Workers Covered?* | *Are Students Covered?* | *Are Minors/ Workers Under Age 21 Covered?* | *Is a Training/ Opportunity Wage Paid to New Hires?* | *Other Provisions* | *Citations to Authority* | *Comments* |
| AZ *(cont'd)* | | apprentices were repealed, effective 1/1/98. | | | | | | | |
| AR | Yes. | Yes. | Yes. | Yes. Full-time students must be paid 85% of minimum wage if working not more than 20 hours per week while school is in session, or 40 hours per week when school is not in session. | No. | No. | No. | Ark. Code Ann. §§ 11-4-210, 11-4-214, 11-4-215. | Exemptions provided by labor board. |
| CA | Yes. | Yes, may be paid for fixed time under special license issued by Industrial Welfare Commission. Under all wage orders, learn- | Yes. Special one-year license may be issued to individual; special license may be issued to nonprofit organizations to pay lower rates | Yes, organized camp employees and camp or program counselors must be paid at least 85% of minimum wage for a 40-hour | Yes. Minors may be paid less than minimum wage under wage orders; minors who have graduated from high school or equivalent must be paid at the | No. | No. | Cal. Lab. Code §§ 1182.4, 1191, 1191.5, 1192, 1193, 1391.2. | Licenses from Industrial Welfare Commission. |

| | | | |
|---|---|---|---|
| ers age 18 and over may be paid 85% of minimum wage for the first 160 hours of employment. | without individual licenses. | week, even if working more than 40 hours; if working fewer than 40 hours, must be paid 85% of hourly rate for hours worked. | adult rate, unless variations are based on seniority, length of service, ability, skill, duties, shift or time of day worked, or hours worked. Minors may be paid 85% of minimum wage (rounded to nearest nickel), provided that no more than 25% of employees are minors (except during school vacations). Minors ages 16 and 17 enrolled in approved work experience programs who work between 10:00 P.M. and 12:30 A.M. must be paid adult minimum wage (except under Wage Order 15-86, covering household occupations), and under wage orders 8-80 and 13-80 (covering agricultural workers), minors working more than 40 hours in a week must be paid adult minimum wage for all hours worked that week. Under wage order 14-80 (Agricultural Occupations) at least 80% of minors employed on a piece-rate basis must be paid at *(cont'd)* |

*(Table continues.)*

# Table I *(cont'd)*

## STATE SUBMINIMUM WAGE PROVISIONS

**KEY:** "Learners and Apprentices" refers to persons enrolled in formal apprenticeship programs or cooperative education programs associated with vocational education programs.
"Students" refers to any persons enrolled in an accredited academic institution. Any more restricted application of the term "student" is noted under this column.
"Training/Opportunity Wage" refers to a subminimum wage paid to *all* new hires, unless otherwise indicated.
"Handicapped Workers" refers to an individual defined as a handicapped employee or employee with a disability under the state's wage statutes.

| | | *Coverage* | | | | | | | |
|---|---|---|---|---|---|---|---|---|---|
| | *Does State Have Subminimum Wage Provision?* | *Are Learners and Apprentices Covered?* | *Are Handicapped Workers Covered?* | *Are Students Covered?* | *Are Minors/ Workers Under Age 21 Covered?* | *Is a Training/ Opportunity Wage Paid to New Hires?* | *Other Provisions* | *Citations to Authority* | *Comments* |
| CA *(cont'd)* | | | | | least 85% of the minimum wage; the remainder must be paid at least 80% of the minimum wage. | | | | |
| CO | Yes. | Yes. | Yes. | No. | Yes. Minors living at home may be paid 85% of minimum wage; emancipated minors shall receive the full minimum wage. | No. | No. | Colo. Rev. Stat. §§ 8-6-104 through 8-6-108.5. | Wage Order 21 lists exemptions. |
| CT | Yes. | Yes. Learners and apprentices may be paid 85% of the minimum wage for the first 200 hours of employment; after the first 200 hours, if in an institutional training program, they may be ex- | Yes, by special license issued by commissioner. | No. | Yes. Minors ages 16 to 18 employed by state or one of its political subdivisions, and minors ages 14 to 18 employed as agricultural laborers may be paid 85% of minimum wage; minors employed as agricultural laborers can be | No. | No. | Conn. Gen. Stat. Ann. §§ 31-58(a); 31-60(b); 31-67. | — |

| | | | | | | | | | |
|---|---|---|---|---|---|---|---|---|---|
| | | empted by labor commissioner. | | | paid 70% of minimum wage if employer did not employ 8 or more workers at the same time the previous year. | | | | |
| DE | Yes. | Yes. | Yes. | No. | No. | No. | No. | Del. Code Ann. tit. 19 §§ 905; 906. | Exemptions provided for by department of labor. |
| DC | Yes. | Yes. | Yes, when certificate issued by U.S. Department of Labor. | Yes. Students at institutions of higher learning may be paid the federal minimum wage for 90 days. | Yes, may be paid the federal minimum wage for 90 days. | Yes. New hires 18 and over may be paid the federal minimum wage for 90 days. | Senior citizens may also be paid subminimum wage. | D.C. Code Ann. §§ 36-220.2(d), 36-220.5(c), Reg. Title 7 § 902.4. | Amount and duration of the subminimum wage is set by regulation. Apprentices, those employed under the Job Training Partnership Act, the Youth Employment Act, and the Older Americans Act may be paid lower wages. |
| FL | No. | — | — | — | — | — | — | — | State has no minimum wage law. |
| GA | Yes. | No. | Yes, may be exempted by the commissioner. | No. | No. | No. | — | Ga. Code Ann. § 34-4-4. | Exemptions granted to employers by labor commissioner. |
| HI | Yes. | Yes. | Yes. | Yes. High school and vocational education students, but not college and university students. | No. | No. | — | Haw. Rev. Stat. Ann. § 387-9. | Subminimum wage is authorized by special certificates; may include persons impaired by age and paroled youth offenders from Hawaii Youth Correctional Facility. |
| ID | Yes. | Yes. | Yes. | Yes, if enrolled in a bona fide school program adminis- *(cont'd)* | Yes. New employees under age 20 may be paid $4.25/hour for first 90 calen- *(cont'd)* | No. | No employee may be displaced or have wages, hours, or ben- *(cont'd)* | Idaho Code §§ 44-1502(3), 44-1505, 44-1506. | Other than employees under age 20, labor commissioner issues special li- *(cont'd)* |

*(Table continues.)*

## Table I *(cont'd)*

## STATE SUBMINIMUM WAGE PROVISIONS

**KEY:** "Learners and Apprentices" refers to persons enrolled in formal apprenticeship programs or cooperative education programs associated with vocational education programs.
"Students" refers to any persons enrolled in an accredited academic institution. Any more restricted application of the term "student" is noted under this column.
"Training/Opportunity Wage" refers to a subminimum wage paid to *all* new hires, unless otherwise indicated.
"Handicapped Workers" refers to an individual defined as a handicapped employee or employee with a disability under the state's wage statutes.

| | | *Coverage* | | | | | | | |
|---|---|---|---|---|---|---|---|---|---|
| | *Does State Have Subminimum Wage Provision?* | *Are Learners and Apprentices Covered?* | *Are Handicapped Workers Covered?* | *Are Students Covered?* | *Are Minors/ Workers Under Age 21 Covered?* | *Is a Training/ Opportunity Wage Paid to New Hires?* | *Other Provisions* | *Citations to Authority* | *Comments* |
| ID *(cont'd)* | | | | tered by an accredited school district that includes work training experience. | dar days of employment. | | efits reduced in order to hire a new employee at the subminimum wage. | | censes for employees to be employed at less than regular minimum wage. |
| IL | Yes. | Yes, for up to 6 months at not lower than 70% of minimum wage. | Yes. | No. | Yes. Workers under age 18 may be paid 50 cents less than minimum wage paid to adults. | No. | Lower wage may be authorized on the basis of age. | Ill. Comp. Stat. Ann. 820 §§ 105/4, 105/5, 105/6. | Director authorizes lower wages for those other than employees under 18; may authorize lower wages for persons impaired by age or physical or mental handicap. |
| IN | Yes (effective 3/1/99). | No. | No. | No. | Yes. Employees under the age of 20 may be paid $4.25/hour for first 90 consecutive calendar days of employment. | No. | No employer may displace an employee or reduce an employee's wages, hours, or benefits in order to hire an individual at the subminimum wage. | Ind. Code. Ann. § 22-2-2-4(i). | — |

| | | | | | | | | | | |
|---|---|---|---|---|---|---|---|---|---|---|
| IA | Yes. | No. | No. | No. | No. | Yes. All new hires may be paid $4.25/hr for first 90 days of service. | No. | Iowa Code Ann. § 91D.1; r347–215.1. | — |
| KS | Yes. | Yes. Employers may apply for special permit to allow first 2 months at 80% of minimum wage; after 2 months, 90%; after 3 months, minimum wage. | Yes. Employers may make written application to employ at 85% of minimum wage. | No. | No. | No. | — | Kan. Stat. Ann. §§ 44-1207; r49-31-5. | Employers may hire only one learner/apprentice per 5 regular employees; no learner or apprentice may be hired part time (fewer than 40 hours/week). |
| KY | Yes. | Yes. | Yes. | No. | No. | No. | — | Ky. Rev. Stat. Ann. § 337.010; 803 1:090. | Subminimum wage may be paid for fixed period under certificate issued by the commissioner of labor. |
| LA | No. | — | — | — | — | — | — | — | State has no minimum wage law. |
| ME | Yes. | Yes. | Yes, if authorized by certificate. | Yes. | No. | No. | No. | Me. Rev. Stat. Ann. tit. 26 §§ 666; 667. | Subminimum wages may be paid for limited periods under special certificates. |
| MD | Yes. | Yes. Commissioner of labor and industry may issue rates not less than 80% of minimum wage. | Yes. Commissioner of labor and industry may issue subminimum rates; does not apply to blind workers in sheltered workshops of the blind industries and services of Maryland; commissioner can accept federal certifi- *(cont'd)* | No. | Yes. Employees under age 20 may be paid $4.25/hr during first 90 consecutive calendar days of employment (set by regulation). | No. | No employer may displace an employee or reduce an employee's wages, hours, or benefits in order to hire an individual at the subminimum wage. | Md. Code Ann. Lab. & Emp. §§ 3-410; 3-413; 3-414; MD Code Admin. Reg. §§ 09.12.42.01–09.12.42.14. | — |

*(Table continues.)*

# Table I *(cont'd)*

## STATE SUBMINIMUM WAGE PROVISIONS

**KEY:** "Learners and Apprentices" refers to persons enrolled in formal apprenticeship programs or cooperative education programs associated with vocational education programs.
"Students" refers to any persons enrolled in an accredited academic institution. Any more restricted application of the term "student" is noted under this column.
"Training/Opportunity Wage" refers to a subminimum wage paid to *all* new hires, unless otherwise indicated.
"Handicapped Workers" refers to an individual defined as a handicapped employee or employee with a disability under the state's wage statutes.

| | | *Coverage* | | | | | | | |
|---|---|---|---|---|---|---|---|---|---|
| | *Does State Have Subminimum Wage Provision?* | *Are Learners and Apprentices Covered?* | *Are Handicapped Workers Covered?* | *Are Students Covered?* | *Are Minors/ Workers Under Age 21 Covered?* | *Is a Training/ Opportunity Wage Paid to New Hires?* | *Other Provisions* | *Citations to Authority* | *Comments* |
| MD *(cont'd)* | | | cates issued by the federal Department of Labor, or certificates issued by the state commissioner to be filed within 10 days of receipt. | | | | | | |
| MA | Yes. | Yes. | Yes, includes employees certified by the Secretary of Human Services as handicapped persons. | Yes. Special student workers may be issued special licenses authorizing employment at 80% of minimum wage. | Yes. Minors attending secondary schools may be issued special licenses authorizing employment at 80% of minimum wage. | Yes. 80% of minimum wage may be paid to retail, merchandising, or laundry employees with fewer than 80 experience hours in occupation; 80% of minimum wage for licensed personal service employees with fewer than 1,040 hours in occupation. | — | Mass. Gen. Laws Ann. ch. 151 § 7; Regulation Filing 455 r 2.01. | Labor commissioner may not establish rates below the following: $1.25/hr for ushers, ticket sellers, and ticket takers; $1.60/hr for agricultural employees; and $36/week for janitors and caretakers of residences if they are provided with living quarters. |

| | | | | | | | | | |
|---|---|---|---|---|---|---|---|---|---|
| MI | Yes. | Yes. | Yes, if clearly unable to meet production standards. | No. | Yes. Employees under age 20 may receive training wage of $4.25/hr for first 90 days of employment. | No. | Director of Department of Consumer and Industry Services must establish piece-rate scales for certain agricultural commodities. No employer may displace an employee or reduce an employee's wages, hours, or benefits in order to hire an individual at the subminimum wage. | Mich. Comp. Laws §§ 408.384; 408.384b; 408.387; Mich. Stat. Ann. §§ 17.255(4); 17.255(4b); 17.255(7). | Employers may not displace an employee to hire an individual at the subminimum wage; Director of Department of Consumer and Industry Services establishes rate of pay for apprentices, learners, and handicapped employees. |
| MN | Yes. | Yes. | Yes. | No. | Yes. Employees under age 20 may be paid $4.25/hr for first 90 consecutive days of employment. | Yes. Employees under age 20 may be paid $4.25/hr for first 90 consecutive days of employment. | — | Minn. Stat. Ann. §§ 177.24, 177.28. | Department must issue rules providing for subminimum wage for apprentices, learners, and handicapped employees; no employer may displace any employee to hire an employee at subminimum wage. |
| MS | No. | — | — | — | — | — | — | — | State has no minimum wage law. |
| MO | Yes. | Yes. Rate is tied to Fair Labor Standards Act. No worker may be considered an apprentice or learner for more than 6 months. | Yes, but no individual who maintains production rate within the limits of the other employees may be paid less than the minimum wage rate. | No. | No. | No. | — | Mo. Ann. Stat. §§ 290.500(5); 290.502; 290.515; 290.517. | Director of labor and industries sets subminimum rate for handicapped workers, learners, and apprentices. |
| MT | Yes. | Yes, if exempted by labor commis- *(cont'd)* | Yes, but only persons with disabilities who *(cont'd)* | No. | Yes. Farm workers under age 18 may be paid *(cont'd)* | No. | — | Mont. Code Ann. §§ 39-3-404, 39-3-406. | — |

*(Table continues.)*

## Table I (cont'd)

# STATE SUBMINIMUM WAGE PROVISIONS

**KEY:** "Learners and Apprentices" refers to persons enrolled in formal apprenticeship programs or cooperative education programs associated with vocational education programs.
"Students" refers to any persons enrolled in an accredited academic institution. Any more restricted application of the term "student" is noted under this column.
"Training/Opportunity Wage" refers to a subminimum wage paid to *all* new hires, unless otherwise indicated.
"Handicapped Workers" refers to an individual defined as a handicapped employee or employee with a disability under the state's wage statutes.

| | | *Coverage* | | | | | | | |
|---|---|---|---|---|---|---|---|---|---|
| | *Does State Have Subminimum Wage Provision?* | *Are Learners and Apprentices Covered?* | *Are Handicapped Workers Covered?* | *Are Students Covered?* | *Are Minors/ Workers Under Age 21 Covered?* | *Is a Training/ Opportunity Wage Paid to New Hires?* | *Other Provisions* | *Citations to Authority* | *Comments* |
| MT *(cont'd)* | | sioner, may be paid subminimum for 30 days. | are engaged in work that is incidental to training or evaluation programs or whose earning capacity is so severely impaired that they are unable to engage in competitive employment may be paid subminimum wage. | | 50% of minimum for 180 days. | | | | |
| NE | Yes. | Yes. Student learners in bona fide vocational training programs may be paid 75% of minimum wage. | No. | No. | Yes. Employees under age 20 who are not migrant or seasonal workers may be paid $4.25/hr for 90 days from date of hire; such employees may be paid subminimum wage for | Yes. Employees under age 20 may be paid $4.25/hr for first 90 days. | No. | Neb. Rev. Stat. Ann. §§ 48-1203; 48-1203.01. | Employer may not dismiss other employees in order to hire an employee at the training wage; not more than one fourth of the total hours paid by the employer shall be at the training wage. |

| | | | | | | | | | |
|---|---|---|---|---|---|---|---|---|---|
| | | | | | an additional 90 days while participating in on-the-job training programs that (1) require technical, personal, or other skills that are necessary for his or her employment, and (2) are approved by the commissioner of labor. | | | | |
| NV | Yes. | No. | Yes. Severely handicapped persons whose disabilities have diminished their productive capacity in a specific job and who are specified in certificates issued by the Rehabilitation Division of the Department of Employment, Training, and Rehabilitation may be paid a subminimum wage. | No. | Yes. Employees under age 18 are paid at 85% of the minimum wage. | No. | No. | Nev. Rev. Stat. Ann. § 608.250. | — |
| NH | Yes. | Yes. Beginners with less than 6 months' experience may be paid 75% of minimum wage. | Yes. Labor commissioner may exempt sheltered workshop programs, or person whose earning capacity is impaired by age or physical or mental deficiency. | Yes. Commissioner may establish subminimum rate, or no rate for high school students and for post secondary students working for experience. | Yes. Minors ages 16 and under may be paid 75% of minimum wage. | Yes. Beginners with less than 6 months' experience may be paid 75% of minimum wage. | — | N.H. Rev. Stat. Ann. §§ 279:21, 279:22, 279:22a, 279:22aa. | Employers may not replace an existing or laid-off worker with a student; subminimum wage for beginners requires that employer file application with labor commissioner within 10 days of hire. |
| NJ | Yes. | Yes, commissioner of labor can authorize rates below the (cont'd) | Yes, employers may apply for special permit. | Yes, full-time students may be employed by the college or university in (cont'd) | Yes. Employees under the age of 18 not possessing a special vocational school (cont'd) | No. | — | N.J. Stat. Ann. §§ 34:11-56a4, 34:11-56a5, r 12:56-9.2 | — |

*(Table continues.)*

# Table I *(cont'd)*

## STATE SUBMINIMUM WAGE PROVISIONS

**KEY:** "Learners and Apprentices" refers to persons enrolled in formal apprenticeship programs or cooperative education programs associated with vocational education programs.
"Students" refers to any persons enrolled in an accredited academic institution. Any more restricted application of the term "student" is noted under this column.
"Training/Opportunity Wage" refers to a subminimum wage paid to *all* new hires, unless otherwise indicated.
"Handicapped Workers" refers to an individual defined as a handicapped employee or employee with a disability under the state's wage statutes.

| | | *Coverage* | | | | | | | |
|---|---|---|---|---|---|---|---|---|---|
| | *Does State Have Subminimum Wage Provision?* | *Are Learners and Apprentices Covered?* | *Are Handicapped Workers Covered?* | *Are Students Covered?* | *Are Minors/ Workers Under Age 21 Covered?* | *Is a Training/ Opportunity Wage Paid to New Hires?* | *Other Provisions* | *Citations to Authority* | *Comments* |
| NJ *(cont'd)* | | statutory minimum. | | which they enrolled at 85% of the minimum wage. | graduate permit may be paid a subminimum wage if authorized by the Commissioner of Labor. | | | | |
| NM | Yes. | Yes, state labor commissioner may set rates for trainees in equal opportunity skill training programs in connection with federally aided highway construction. | Yes, labor commissioner may issue special certificates allowing payment of less than the minimum wage to workers whose earning or productive capacity is impaired by physical or mental handicap, or injury. | No. | No. | No. | No. | N.M. Stat. Ann. §§ 50-4-21; 50-4-23; OAG, 9/8/70 | Apprentices, learners, minors, and students are covered by statutory exemptions from the minimum wage law, but not by a specific subminimum wage provision. |
| NY | Yes. | Yes, if employer is issued special certificate by commissioner of labor. | Yes, if employer is issued special certificate by commissioner of labor. | Yes, in resort hotels or camps for periods of up to 17 consecutive weeks, if | Yes, under wage order 190, 1/1/85, as amended 1/1/91 (Farm Workers), 16 | No. | Special certification may be issued to allow subminimum wage payments to | N.Y. Lab. Law § 655.5(c); Wage Order 190, 1/1/85, as amended | — |

| | | | | | | | | | |
|---|---|---|---|---|---|---|---|---|---|
| | | | | employer is issued special certificate by commissioner of labor. | and 17 year-old harvest workers in their first season may be paid $3.60/hr; during their second season with the same employer, $3.80/hr; during their third season, they must be paid minimum wage. Non-harvest workers age 16 and 17 must be paid $3.60/hr for first 300 hours; $3.80/hr for next 300 hours; after 600 hours must receive minimum wage. Workers under 16 must have a farm work permit and may be paid $3.20/hr. | | residential employees of nonprofit religious, charitable, or educational organizations. | 1/1/91 (Farm Workers). | |
| NC | Yes. | Yes, 90% of minimum wage. | Yes, 90% of minimum wage, if earning capacity is impaired by physical or mental deficiency or injury. | Yes, full time students at 90% of minimum wage. | No. | Yes, by special certificate of eligibility from Employment Security Commission, 85% of minimum wage may be paid for up to 52 weeks to persons unemployed for 15 weeks, or economically disadvantaged; persons who receive, or whose families receive Work First Family Assistance, or persons who receive supplemental security benefits. | Specified seasonal employees may be compensated at a subminimum wage rate. | N.C. Gen. Stat. §§ 95-25.3; 95-25.3A. | — |

*(Table continues.)*

# Table I *(cont'd)*

## STATE SUBMINIMUM WAGE PROVISIONS

**KEY:** "Learners and Apprentices" refers to persons enrolled in formal apprenticeship programs or cooperative education programs associated with vocational education programs.
"Students" refers to any persons enrolled in an accredited academic institution. Any more restricted application of the term "student" is noted under this column.
"Training/Opportunity Wage" refers to a subminimum wage paid to *all* new hires, unless otherwise indicated.
"Handicapped Workers" refers to an individual defined as a handicapped employee or employee with a disability under the state's wage statutes.

| | | *Coverage* | | | | | | | |
|---|---|---|---|---|---|---|---|---|---|
| | *Does State Have Subminimum Wage Provision?* | *Are Learners and Apprentices Covered?* | *Are Handicapped Workers Covered?* | *Are Students Covered?* | *Are Minors/ Workers Under Age 21 Covered?* | *Is a Training/ Opportunity Wage Paid to New Hires?* | *Other Provisions* | *Citations to Authority* | *Comments* |
| ND | Yes. | Yes, learners and apprentices are covered if enrolled in vocational or related program and issued certificate by commissioner of labor. | Yes. Commissioner may authorize less than minimum wages for persons with mental or physical disabilities. | Yes. Under wage orders, students may be paid $3.60/hr if enrolled in vocational education or related programs. | No. | No. | — | N.D. Cent. Code § 34-06-15. | — |
| OH | Yes. | Yes. Under special licenses, apprentices may be paid 85% of minimum wage for no more than 90 days. | Yes, under special license. | Yes, students in cooperative vocational education program approved by the state may be paid 80% of minimum wage for 180 days each year. | No. | No. | — | Ohio Rev. Code Ann. §§ 4111.02, 4111.06, 4111.07. | — |
| OK | Yes. | Yes. | Yes, if employee has been issued special certificate. | Yes. | No. | No. | Yes. Employees of state, county, city, town, municipal, or quasi- | Okla. Stat. Ann. tit. 40 § 197.11. | — |

| | | | | | | | | | |
|---|---|---|---|---|---|---|---|---|---|
| | | | | | | | municipal corporation, political subdivision, or any of their instrumentalities may be paid subminimum wage when permitted by labor commissioner. Subminimum rates are also permitted for messengers. | | |
| OR | Yes. | Yes. Student learners may be paid 75% of minimum wage; work hours are limited in combination with school to 8 hours per day and 40 hours per week (i.e., school + work hours = 8 per day or 40 per week). | Yes. | No. | No. | No. | No. | Or. Rev. Stat. §§ 653.030; 653.070. | Commissioner of the bureau of labor and industry sets rates for subminimum wages. |
| PA | Yes. | Learners are covered. | Yes. Requires joint application (employee and employer) for special certificate from secretary of labor that pay will be commensurate with employees' productive capacity; or federal certificate under Fair Labor Standards Act. | Yes. For 6 or fewer students, employment must be part-time (not more than 20 hours/ week). Special certification required if 7 or more students employed. | No. | No. | — | Pa. Stat. Ann. tit. 43 § 333.104. | Students and learners may be paid 85% of minimum wage under special certificates from the state secretary of labor. |
| RI | Yes. | Yes, with special permit for up to 90 days. | Yes, under special license. | Yes. Full-time students under 19 and employed by *(cont'd)* | Yes. Employees ages 14 and 15 may be paid 75% of mini- *(cont'd)* | No. | — | R.I. Gen. Laws §§ 28-12-3.1; 28-12-5; *(cont'd)* | — |

*(Table continues.)*

# Table I *(cont'd)*

## STATE SUBMINIMUM WAGE PROVISIONS

**KEY:** "Learners and Apprentices" refers to persons enrolled in formal apprenticeship programs or cooperative education programs associated with vocational education programs.
"Students" refers to any persons enrolled in an accredited academic institution. Any more restricted application of the term "student" is noted under this column.
"Training/Opportunity Wage" refers to a subminimum wage paid to *all* new hires, unless otherwise indicated.
"Handicapped Workers" refers to an individual defined as a handicapped employee or employee with a disability under the state's wage statutes.

| | | *Coverage* | | | | | | | |
|---|---|---|---|---|---|---|---|---|---|
| | *Does State Have Subminimum Wage Provision?* | *Are Learners and Apprentices Covered?* | *Are Handicapped Workers Covered?* | *Are Students Covered?* | *Are Minors/ Workers Under Age 21 Covered?* | *Is a Training/ Opportunity Wage Paid to New Hires?* | *Other Provisions* | *Citations to Authority* | *Comments* |
| RI *(cont'd)* | | | | nonprofit associations or corporations whose aims and objectives are of a religious, educational, librarian, or community service nature may be paid 90% of minimum wage. | mum wage for a workweek of 24 hours or less; over 24 hours must be paid regular minimum wage. | | | 28-12-9; 28-12-10. | |
| SC | No. | — | — | — | — | — | — | — | State has no minimum wage law. |
| SD | Yes. | Yes. | Yes. | No. | Yes. Employees ages 18 and 19 may be paid opportunity wage of $4.25/hr for first 90 days of employment; employees under age 18 may be paid 75% of | No, unless employee is age 19 or under (see previous column). | — | S.D. Codified Laws §§ 60-11-4.1; 60-11-5; 60-12-1; 60-12-3. | Commissioner of labor and management relations must issue a permit for apprentices, learners, and handicapped employees to be paid subminimum wage. |

| | | | | | | | | | |
|---|---|---|---|---|---|---|---|---|---|
| | | | | | the minimum wage. | | | | |
| TN | No. | — | — | — | — | — | — | — | State has no minimum wage law. |
| TX | Yes. | No. | Yes. Handicapped workers may be employed at 60% of the minimum wage if employer obtains a medical certificate. | No. | No. | No. | Yes. Persons over 65 may be employed at 60% of the minimum wage if employer obtains a medical certificate. | Tex. Code Ann. Lab. §§ 62.055; 62.056; 62.102. | Piece-rate workers are excluded from these provisions. |
| UT | Yes. | No. | Yes. Wage must be related to employee's productivity. | No. | Yes. Minors may be paid $4.25/hr for first 90 days of employment. | No. | — | Utah Code Ann. § 34-40-104; Utah Admin. Code 487-1-3. | — |
| VT | No; abolished in 1997. | — | — | — | — | — | — | Vt. Stat. Ann. tit. 21 §§ 384(a); 385. | Wage board may recommend reduced wages; see Wage Order No. 1; commissioner of labor may grant permits for reduced wages for handicapped employees. |
| VA | No. | — | — | — | — | — | — | — | Note specific exemptions to minimum wage law. |
| WA | Yes. | Yes, if employee has been issued special certificate. | Yes, if employee has been issued special certificate. | No. | Yes. Employees under age 16 may be paid 85% of the minimum wage, or $4.17/hr. If minor is employed by employer covered by Fair Labor Standards Act, then the subminimum wage does not apply, and the employee should receive the federal minimum wage. | No. | Workers in seasonal recreational camps. | Wash. Rev. Code Ann. §§ 49.12.110; 49.46.060; Wash. Admin. Code 296-125-043; 296-126-020; 296-126-204. | Director of labor and industries may authorize subminimum rates for apprentices, learners, handicapped persons, and messengers. |

*(Table continues.)*

# Table I *(cont'd)*

## STATE SUBMINIMUM WAGE PROVISIONS

**KEY:** "Learners and Apprentices" refers to persons enrolled in formal apprenticeship programs or cooperative education programs associated with vocational education programs.
"Students" refers to any persons enrolled in an accredited academic institution. Any more restricted application of the term "student" is noted under this column.
"Training/Opportunity Wage" refers to a subminimum wage paid to *all* new hires, unless otherwise indicated.
"Handicapped Workers" refers to an individual defined as a handicapped employee or employee with a disability under the state's wage statutes.

| | | *Coverage* | | | | | | | |
|---|---|---|---|---|---|---|---|---|---|
| | *Does State Have Subminimum Wage Provision?* | *Are Learners and Apprentices Covered?* | *Are Handicapped Workers Covered?* | *Are Students Covered?* | *Are Minors/ Workers Under Age 21 Covered?* | *Is a Training/ Opportunity Wage Paid to New Hires?* | *Other Provisions* | *Citations to Authority* | *Comments* |
| WV | Yes. | No. | No. | No. | Yes. Employees age 19 and under may be paid $4.25 per hour (85% of current minimum wage); if the employer has been operating for less than 90 days at the time the employee is hired, the employer may pay the subminimum wage for an additional 90 days. Employees under age 21 may be paid $4.25 per hour for up to 90 days. | No. | No. | W. Va. Code § 21-5C-2(b). | — |
| WI | Yes. | Yes. Students in bona fide school training programs may be paid 75% of the minimum wage. | Yes. Handicapped workers may be paid 75% of the minimum wage; handicapped workers in shel- | No. | Yes. "Opportunity employees," those under age 20 for first 90 days of employment, may be paid $4.25/hr; minors em- | No. | Summer camp employees are covered under DWD r 272.07; adult agricultural workers may receive $4.05/ | Wis. Stat. Ann. §§ 104.07; 104.08; DWD r 272.07; DWD r 272.05(1); DWD | — |

| | | | | | | | | | |
|---|---|---|---|---|---|---|---|---|---|
| | | | tered workshops may be paid 50% of minimum wage; severely impaired workers may be paid 25% of minimum wage. | | ployed in agriculture may receive $3.70/hr. | | hr; caddies may be paid $3.35 for 9 holes, and $5.95 for 18 holes. | r 272.08; DWD r 272.09. | |
| WY | No. | — | — | — | — | — | — | — | — |

### [d] The Personal Responsibility and Work Opportunity Reconciliation Act of 1996 and State New Hire Reporting Requirements

Federally mandated new-hire reporting is one measure the 104th Congress employed in the effort to reform the welfare system. Though new-hire reporting requirements make up a relatively small part of the Personal Responsibility and Work Opportunity Reconciliation Act, Congress viewed new-hire reporting as an important tool in eliminating the cycle of welfare dependency. The introduction to the act cites the pre-1996 welfare system as a failure and states that the system's single greatest failure was the way in which it harmed the nation's children.

The new-hire reporting requirements are designed to provide information to state agencies administering Medicaid, Food Stamps, Unemployment Compensation, and Temporary Assistance for Needy Families, in order to facilitate the identification of those most in need. The information gathered through the new-hire reporting requirements is also designed to identify individuals who are delinquent in child support obligations and to enable greater enforcement of support orders.

Many states had enacted new-hire reporting laws prior to the Personal Responsibility and Work Opportunity Reconciliation Act. In fact, state experimentation with reporting requirements as part of an effort to identify noncustodial parents who have not met their child support obligations inspired that section of the federal legislation.

The federal law will require that states establish a Directory of New Hires to which all employers in the state must furnish a report concerning all of their employees. Connecticut, Hawaii, and South Dakota are among the states that already require such reporting under state law. However, many states will have to modify their reporting requirements. California, Ohio, and Washington, for example, require only employers in certain industries to report new hires. In Alaska, on the other hand, only employers with a certain number of employees must submit reports. Some states, such as West Virginia, permit reporting exceptions for new hires who earn less than $300 a month or work fewer than 350 hours in a 6-month period. Furthermore, several states, including New Jersey, Texas, and Vermont, have voluntary reporting policies.

Federally mandated new-hire reporting also requires all employers to include specific information in their reports. A report must contain the employer's name, address, and employer identification number, as well as the employee's name, address, and Social Security number. Individual state Directories of New Hires may require employers to report additional information, such as the employee's salary. Iowa requires reports to state whether dependent health care coverage is available to employees through their employers.

The information to be reported must be delivered to the state Directory of New Hires within 20 days of the date of hire under the new federal law. States may elect to shorten the 20-day deadline but may not extend it. California, Connecticut, Ohio, and Washington will have to alter their reporting requirements, for, at present, each allows employers at least 30 days to deliver a report. Hawaii, however, is safely within the federal guidelines with its 5-day deadline. Under the federal guidelines, reports may be made by employers on W-4 forms or equivalent documents, and this requirement is in keeping with the applicable requirements in most states.

The Personal Responsibility and Work Opportunity Reconciliation Act also gives the option to each state to set a civil penalty for noncompliance with the new-hire reporting law. The act states, however, that the penalty may not be less than $25. If noncompliance is the result of a conspiracy between an employer and an employee, however, the penalty may not be less than $500.

The federal new-hire reporting guidelines became effective on October 1, 1997, in states that previously had no new-hire requirements. States that had already implemented new-hire reporting requirements before the welfare reform act were required to conform to federal guidelines by October 1, 1998.

# Table II
## STATE LAWS REQUIRING NEW HIRE REPORTING

**NOTE:** Employer Identification Number is abbreviated EIN; Social Security Number is abbreviated SSN.

| | *Which Employers Must Report?* | *Which Employees Must Be Reported?* | *Which Employees Need Not Be Reported?* | *How May Report Be Filed with State Agency?* | *When Must Report Be Filed?* | *What Employer Information Must Be Included in Report?* | *What Employee Information Must Be Included in Report?* | *Failure to Report* | *Citations to Authority* |
|---|---|---|---|---|---|---|---|---|---|
| AL | All employers. | All new employees and rehires. | — | W-4 form or other authorized means. | Within 7 days of hiring. | Name, address, and state and federal EIN. | Name, address, SSN, and date employee began work. | Administrative penalty up to $25 per violation. | Ala. Code § 25-11-5. |
| AK | All employers. | All new employees and rehires. | — | W-4 form or mutually agreeable method. Information may be submitted electronically or magnetically. | Within 20 days of hiring. | Name, address, and federal EIN. | Name, address, SSN, and date of birth. | Fine of $10 per employee ($100 if conspiracy) may be imposed. | Alaska Stat. § 25.27.075. |
| AZ | All employers. | New employees and rehires. | — | State form or W-4. Information may be submitted by mail, magnetic tape, telefax, or any other means that are authorized by the state. | Within 20 days of hiring. | Name, address, and federal EIN. | Name, address, SSN, and date of birth. | — | Ariz. Rev. Stat. Ann. § 23-722.01. |
| AR | All employers. | All new employees and rehires. | — | Employer may develop own report or use W-4 form. Information may be submitted electronically, magnetically, or by first class mail. | Within 20 days of hiring. | Name, address, and federal EIN. | Name, address, and SSN. | — | Ark. Code Ann. § 11-10-902. |

*(Table continues.)*

## Table II *(cont'd)*
## STATE LAWS REQURING NEW HIRE REPORTING

**NOTE:** Employer Identification Number is abbreviated EIN; Social Security Number is abbreviated SSN.

| | *Which Employers Must Report?* | *Which Employees Must Be Reported?* | *Which Employees Need Not Be Reported?* | *How May Report Be Filed with State Agency?* | *When Must Report Be Filed?* | *What Employer Information Must Be Included in Report?* | *What Employee Information Must Be Included in Report?* | *Failure to Report* | *Citations to Authority* |
|---|---|---|---|---|---|---|---|---|---|
| CA | All employers. | New and rehired employees. | — | State form, W-4 form, any other hiring document or by any other means authorized by the state. Information may be submitted electronically, magnetically, or by first class mail. | Within 20 days of hiring. | Name, address, and federal EIN. | Name, address, SSN, and date employee began work. | Fines of $24 will be imposed for each failure to report; failure resulting from conspiracy between employer and employee subject to $490 fine per failure to report. | Cal. Unemp. Ins. Code § 1088.5. |
| CO | All employers. | All new employees and rehires. | Employees hired for fewer than 30 days. | A copy of the W-4 or, if the employer prefers, an equivalent form. The report may be transmitted by first class mail, magnetically, or electronically. | Within 20 days of hiring or at time of first regularly scheduled payroll following the date of hire. | Name, address, and federal EIN. | Name, address, and SSN. | — | Colo. Rev. Stat. § 26-13-125. |
| CT | All employers. | All new employees and rehires. | — | CT-W4 Income Tax Withholding form or Exemption Certificate. | Within 35 days of hiring. | Name, address, and tax registration number. | Name, address, and SSN. | — | Conn. Gen. Stat. Ann. § 31-2c. |
| DE | All employers. | All new hires and rehires. | — | W-4 or, if the employer prefers, an equivalent form. Reports may be submitted using any form of | Within 20 days of hiring. | Name, address, and federal EIN. | Name, address, and SSN. | Fine of $25 per employee ($500 if conspiracy) may be imposed. | Del. Code Ann. tit. 13, § 2208; tit. 30, § 1156A. |

| | | | | | | | | |
|---|---|---|---|---|---|---|---|---|
| | | | | electronic or magnetic media or by first class mail. | | | | | |
| DC | All employers. | All new hires and rehires. | — | W-4 or D.C. New Hire Registry Reporting Form. Information can be transmitted by mail, by telefax, electronically, or by telephone. | Within 20 days of employee's first day of work. | Name, address, and EIN. | Names, address, and SSN, date of birth, date of hire, availability of dependent healthcare coverage, and salary. | Fine of $25 per employee ($500 if conspiracy) may be imposed. | D.C. Code Ann. § 30-526.5. |
| FL | All employers. | All new and rehired employees. | — | W-4 Form or equivalent may be submitted magnetically, electronically, by first-class mail, or other state approved method. | Within 20 days of hiring or rehiring. | Name, address, unemployment compensation identification number, and employer's federal EIN. | Name, SSN, date employee began work, and employee's address. If available, the employer may also include employee's date of birth. | — | Fla. Stat. Ann. § 409.2576. |
| GA | All employers. | All new employees and rehires. | — | Employer may develop own report or W-4 form. | Within 10 days of hiring or rehiring. | Name, address, employment security number, or unified business identifier number. | Name, address, SSN, and date of birth. | Written warning. | Ga. Code Ann. § 19-11-9.2. |
| HI | All employers. | All new employees and rehires. | — | W-4 form or equivalent. Information may be submitted electronically, magnetically, or by first-class mail. | Within 20 days of hiring. | Name, address, and federal EIN. | Name, address, and SSN. | Fine of $25 per employee ($500 if conspiracy) may be imposed. | Haw. Rev. Stat. §§ 383-94, 576D-16. |
| ID | All employers. | All new employees and rehires. | — | W-4 form, or by any other means authorized by the state. Information may be submitted by first class mail, telefax, or other authorized means. | Within 20 days of hiring. | Name, address, EIN, and state unemployment insurance account number. | Name, address, SSN, and date of hire. | — | Idaho Code §§ 72-1601-72-1607. |

*(Table continues.)*

## Table II *(cont'd)*
## STATE LAWS REQURING NEW HIRE REPORTING

**NOTE:** Employer Identification Number is abbreviated EIN; Social Security Number is abbreviated SSN.

| | *Which Employers Must Report?* | *Which Employees Must Be Reported?* | *Which Employees Need Not Be Reported?* | *How May Report Be Filed with State Agency?* | *When Must Report Be Filed?* | *What Employer Information Must Be Included in Report?* | *What Employee Information Must Be Included in Report?* | *Failure to Report* | *Citations to Authority* |
|---|---|---|---|---|---|---|---|---|---|
| IL | All employers. | All employees and rehires. | — | W-4, or employer's own form if it contains all required information. May be submitted by mail, fax, electronically, or magnetically. | Within 20 days of the date of hire. | Employer's name, address, EIN; address to which child support orders should be sent if different from employer's address is optional. | Employee's name, address, SSN; date of hire is optional. | Late fee of $15. Failure-to-report fee of $15; knowing conspiracy is a class B misdemeanor with a fine up to $500. | SB 1024. |
| IN | All employers. | All employees. | — | By W-4 form or, at the employer's option, its equivalent. Information may be submitted by first class mail, fax, electronically, or magnetically. | Within 20 days of hire. | Employer's name, address, and federal tax identification number. | Employer's name, address, and SSN. | — | Ind. Code § 22-4.1–4.2. |
| IA | All employers. | New employees and rehires. | — | Employee's withholding allowance certificate form, or by submitting electronic media in a format approved in advance by the state, mailing, faxing, or by any other means authorized by the state. | Within 15 days of hiring. | Name, address, federal EIN, and employer's address to which income withholding orders and garnishments should be sent. | Name, address, SSN, date of birth, whether employee has dependent health care coverage available, and date on which employee qualifies for coverage. | Employer will be subject to court action, and willful failure to provide the information will be punishable as contempt. | Iowa Code Ann. §§ 252G.2–252G.3 |

| | | | | | | | | | |
|---|---|---|---|---|---|---|---|---|---|
| KS | All employers. | All new hires required to complete a federal I-9 form who answer in the affirmative an additional, mandatory form regarding whether the employee's income is subject to child support orders. | — | W-4 form. | Within 20 days of the date the employee is first paid. | Name, address, and EIN. | Name, address, and SSN. | — | Kan. Stat. Ann. §§ 75-5742 *et seq.* |
| KY | All employers. | All new employees, rehires, and potential employees refusing employment. | — | W-4 form or state form. | Within 7 days of hiring. | Name, address, unemployment insurance number, and signature of employer representative. | Name, SSN, date on which employment was accepted or refused, and if employment was accepted, signature of employee. | — | Ky. Rev. Stat. Ann. § 341.190 |
| LA | All employers. | All new employees. | — | W-4, or employer's own form if it contains all required information. Information may be submitted by first class mail, magnetically, or electronically. | Within 20 days of hiring. | Name, address, and federal EIN. | Name, address, and SSN. | $25 for each failure to report; if conspiracy, fines may be up to $500. | La. Rev. Stat. § 46:236.14. |
| ME | All employers. | All new employees and rehires. | — | W-4 form or other mutually agreeable means. Information may be submitted by first class mail, fax, or magnetically. | Within 7 days of beginning of employment. | Name, address, and employment security reference number. | Name, address, SSN, and date of birth. | Written notice of delinquency in filing will be followed by a fine of up to $200 for subsequent violations. | Me. Rev. Stat. Ann. tit. 19A, § 2154. |
| MD | All employers. | All new employees and rehires. | — | W-4 form or by the employer's own form containing the required information. Information may be submitted by *(cont'd)* | Within 20 days of date on which employee begins work for employer. | Name, address, federal EIN, and state unemployment insurance account number. | Name, address, SSN, and date of hire. | Written notice of delinquency in filing for the first violation will be followed by fine of $20 per month for *(cont'd)* | Md. Code Ann., Lab. & Empl. § 8-626.1. |

*(Table continues.)*

# Table II *(cont'd)*

## STATE LAWS REQURING NEW HIRE REPORTING

**NOTE:** Employer Identification Number is abbreviated EIN; Social Security Number is abbreviated SSN.

| | *Which Employers Must Report?* | *Which Employees Must Be Reported?* | *Which Employees Need Not Be Reported?* | *How May Report Be Filed with State Agency?* | *When Must Report Be Filed?* | *What Employer Information Must Be Included in Report?* | *What Employee Information Must Be Included in Report?* | *Failure to Report* | *Citations to Authority* |
|---|---|---|---|---|---|---|---|---|---|
| MD *(cont'd)* | | | | first class mail, electronically, magnetically, or by other approved means. | | | | each month in which subsequent violations occur, or $500 if the failure is the result of a conspiracy between the employer and the employee. | |
| MA | All employers. | All new employees and rehires. | — | W-4 form. | Within 14 days of hiring. | Name, address, and federal EIN. | Name, address, and SSN. | Fines from $25 to $100 may be imposed. | Mass. Gen. Laws Ann. ch. 30A, § 6. |
| MI | All employers. | All new hires and rehires. | — | W-4 or state form, by hard copy, magnetically, or electronically. | Within 20 days of hire or return to work. | Name, address, and federal EIN. | Name, address, and SSN. | — | Mich. Stat. Ann. § 25.176(18); Mich. Comp. Laws Ann. § 552.518. |
| MN | All employers. | All new employees and rehires who will earn more than $250 a month and who will be employed for at least 2 months' duration. | Employees earning less than $250 a month, domestic servants in a private home, and employees working for less than 2 months. | W-4 form, W-9 form or similar form. Information may be submitted by first-class mail, fax, electronically, or by other authorized means. | Within 15 days of hiring. | Name, address, and federal EIN. | Name, address, SSN, and date of birth. | Written notice of delinquency in filing will be followed by fines of $25 per employee, and $500 if the failure to report is the result of a conspiracy. | Minn. Stat. Ann. § 256.988. |

| | | | | | | | | | |
|---|---|---|---|---|---|---|---|---|---|
| MS | All employers. | All new employees and rehires. | — | W-4 form or equivalent. | Within 15 days of hiring or return to work. | Name, address, and state and federal withholding tax identification numbers. | Name, address, SSN, date of birth, and date on which employee began or resumed employment or is scheduled to begin. | Fine of $25 ($500 if conspiracy) may be imposed. | Miss. Code Ann. § 43-19-46. |
| MO | All employers. | All employees and new hires. | — | W-4 form or equivalent. | Within 30 days of the date of hire. | Name, address, and EIN. | Name, address, and SSN. If form other than W-4 is used, include date of hire or date W-4 is signed. | $25 for each time the employer fails to submit the required information; $350 for each failure to report information due to conspiracy. | Mo. Ann. Stat. §§ 285.300–285.304. |
| MT | All employers. | All employees and rehires. | — | W-4, state-provided form, or in any other form with the required information. Information may be submitted by first-class mail, electronically, magnetically, or by other agreed-upon format. | Within 20 days of hire. | Name, address, and federal EIN. | Name, date of hire, residential and mailing address, SSN, and date of hire. Employer may also provide employee's home phone number, date of birth, and insurance information. | — | Mont. Code Ann. § 40-5-922. |
| NE | All employers. | All new employees and rehires. | — | W-4 form, employer report listing the elements required by law. Information may be submitted by first class mail, fax, tape, disk, electronically, magnetically, or by other authorized means. | Within 20 days of hiring. | Name, address, and federal EIN. | Name, address, and SSN. | Fines of $25 may be imposed, and a maximum fine of $500 may be imposed where an employer and employee have conspired not to report. | Neb. Rev. Stat. Ann. §§ 48-2301–48-2308 |
| NV | All employers. | All new hires and rehires. | — | W-4, or other form containing required information. | Within 20 days of hire. | Name, address, and federal tax number EIN. | Name, address, and SSN. | $25 for each offense. | Nev. Rev. Stat. §§ 606.010–606.120. |

*(Table continues.)*

## **Table II** *(cont'd)*

## STATE LAWS REQURING NEW HIRE REPORTING

**NOTE:** Employer Identification Number is abbreviated EIN; Social Security Number is abbreviated SSN.

| | *Which Employers Must Report?* | *Which Employees Must Be Reported?* | *Which Employees Need Not Be Reported?* | *How May Report Be Filed with State Agency?* | *When Must Report Be Filed?* | *What Employer Information Must Be Included in Report?* | *What Employee Information Must Be Included in Report?* | *Failure to Report* | *Citations to Authority* |
|---|---|---|---|---|---|---|---|---|---|
| NH | All employers. | All new employees, rehires, and contractors for services expected to exceed $2,500. | — | W-4 form, or the equivalent. Reports may be mailed, submitted magnetically, or filed electronically. | Within 20 days of hire. | Name, address, and EIN. | Name, address, and SSN. | Fines from $25 to $500 may be imposed. | N.H. Rev. Stat. Ann. § 282-A:117. |
| NJ | All employers. | All employees and rehires. | — | W-4 or equivalent including the required information. | Within 20 days of the date of hiring. | Employer's name, address, and federal EIN. | Employee's name, address, SSN, and date of birth. | Fine of $25 per employee not reported; $500 if failure is result of conspiracy between employer and employee. | N.J. Stat. Ann. § 2A:17—56.61. |
| NM | All employers. | All new employees and rehires. | — | Employer may develop own report or W-4 form. Information may be submitted by first class mail, electronically, or magnetically. | Within 20 days of hiring. | Name, address, and EIN. | Name, address, and SSN. | Fines of $20 ($500 if conspiracy) may be imposed. | N.M. Stat. Ann. §§ 50-13-1 to 50-13-4. |
| NY | All employers. | All new employees and rehires. | — | W-4 form or, at the employer's option, an equivalent form. Employers may file by mail, fax, or magnetically. | Within 20 days from date of hire or rehire. | Name, address, and EIN. | Name, address, and SSN. | Fine of $20 per employee for each failure to report; if failure to report is result of conspiracy between employer and employee, | N.Y. Tax Law § 171-h. |

| | | | | | | | | | |
|---|---|---|---|---|---|---|---|---|---|
| | | | | | | | | $450 per employee for each occurrence. | |
| NC | All employers. | All employees and new hires. | — | W-4 form or equivalent. | Within 20 days of hiring. | Name, address, federal EIN, and state unemployment insurance number. | Name, address, and SSN. | Fine of $25 per employee not reported; $500 if failure is result of conspiracy between employee and employer. | N.C. Gen. Stat. § 11D-129.2 (expired 6/30/98). |
| ND | All employers. | All new employees and rehires. | — | W-4 form or equivalent. Information may be submitted by mail or any magnetic or electronic means, including fax, e-mail, and modem transfer. | Within 20 days of hiring. | Name, address, and EIN. | Name, address, and SSN. | Written notice of delinquency in filing may be followed by fines of $20 ($250 if conspiracy) for subsequent violations. | N.D. Cent. Code §§ 34-15-01–34-15-08. |
| OH | All employers. | All new employees and rehires. | — | State form, W-4 form, or other mutually agreeable method. Information may be submitted by mail, fax, magnetically, electronically, or by other authorized means. | Within 20 days of hiring. | Name, address, and EIN. | Name, address, SSN, date of birth, and date of hire. | Fines of $25 per employee may be imposed for an unintentional failure to report; a $500 fine per employee may be imposed for intentional failure to report. | Ohio Rev. Code Ann. § 5101.312. |
| OK | All employers. | Employees and new hires. | — | W-4 form. Information may be submitted by mail, fax, electronically, or by other authorized means. | Within 20 days of the date of hire. | Name, address, and federal EIN. | Name, address, SSN, and date of hire. | — | Okla. Stat. Ann. tit. 40, § 2-802. |
| OR | All employers. | All new employees and rehires. | — | State form or W-4 Form. | Within 20 days of hiring. | Name, address, and federal EIN. | Name, address, and SSN. | — | Or. Rev. Stat. Ann. Sec. 21, ch 746 of Laws 1997. See note following § 25.790. |

*(Table continues.)*

## Table II *(cont'd)*
## STATE LAWS REQURING NEW HIRE REPORTING

**NOTE:** Employer Identification Number is abbreviated EIN; Social Security Number is abbreviated SSN.

| | *Which Employers Must Report?* | *Which Employees Must Be Reported?* | *Which Employees Need Not Be Reported?* | *How May Report Be Filed with State Agency?* | *When Must Report Be Filed?* | *What Employer Information Must Be Included in Report?* | *What Employee Information Must Be Included in Report?* | *Failure to Report* | *Citations to Authority* |
|---|---|---|---|---|---|---|---|---|---|
| PA | All employers. | All employees. | — | Form provided by the state, or by W-4 with the additional required information. Information may be submitted by mail, electronically, magnetically, or by other authorized means. | Within 20 days of hiring. | Employer's name, address, and EIN, the name of an employer representative, and telephone number. | Employee's name, address, SSN, date of birth, and date of hire. | $25 per employee not reported per month; $500 if failure to report is the result of a conspiracy. | Pa. Stat. Ann. tit. 23 §§ 4392, 4396. |
| RI | All employers. | All new hires and rehires. | — | W-4 with the additional required information, or state form. Information may be submitted by first class mail, fax, magnetically, or electronically. | Within 14 days of hiring. | Employer's name, address, and federal EIN. | Employee's name, address, SSN, availability of health insurance for dependents, date of eligibility for such insurance, and address to which garnishment orders should be sent. | $20 per day for each failure to report; $500 if the failure is the result of a conspiracy between employee and employer. | R.I. Gen. Laws §§ 2415-24-1–2415-24-9. |
| SC | All employers. | New employees and rehires. | — | W-4 form or equivalent. Information may be submitted by mail, fax, electronically, or magnetically. | Within 20 days of hiring. | Name, address, and EIN. | Name, address, and SSN. | $25 for the second offense and every offense thereafter unless the employer can demonstrate good cause for failure; | S.C. Code Ann. § 43-5-598. |

| | | | | | | | | | |
|---|---|---|---|---|---|---|---|---|---|
| | | | | | | | | $500 for each failure to report resulting from a conspiracy. | |
| SD | All employers. | All new employees and rehires. | — | W-4 form or equivalent. Information may be submitted by first class mail, magnetically, or electronically. | Within 20 days of hiring. | Name, address, and EIN. | Name, address, and SSN. | Intentional failure to comply is a petty offense. | S.D. Codified Laws Ann. § 25-7A-3.3. |
| TN | All employers. | All employees and new hires. | — | W-4 or, at the option of the employer, an equivalent form containing the same data. Report may be transmitted by first class mail, magnetically, or electronically in a format approved by the state. | Within 20 business days of hiring. | Name, address, and federal EIN. | Name, address, and SSN. | After notice, fine of $20 may be imposed, and if the failure is due to a conspiracy, a $400 fine may be imposed. | Tenn. Code Ann. §§ 36-5-1101 *et seq.* |
| TX | All employers. | New employees and rehires. | — | W-4 form, or any other means authorized by the state. May be submitted electronically or magnetically. | No later than the 20th working day after hire. | Name, address, and EIN. | Name, address, and SSN. | — | Tex. Fam. Code Ann. §§ 234.101–234.104. |
| UT | All employers. | All new employees and rehires. | — | Utah New Hire Registry Reporting Form, W-4, or any other form containing the required information. May be submitted electronically, magnetically, or by voice-activated transmissions. | Within 20 days of hiring. | Name, address, and federal EIN. | Name, address, and SSN. Employer may, but is not required to, provide date of hire, occupational title, and whether employee is full-time or part-time. | Fine of $25 per employee ($500 if conspiracy) may be imposed. | Utah Code Ann. § 35A-7-101-108. |
| VT | All employers. | All employees and new hires. | — | Employer may develop own report or W-4 form. Information may be sub- *(cont'd)* | Within 20 days of hiring. | Name, address, and federal EIN. | Name, address, and SSN. | Fine of $500 may be imposed if employer and employee *(cont'd)* | Vt. Stat. Ann. tit. 33, § 4110(B). |

*(Table continues.)*

# Table II *(cont'd)*
## STATE LAWS REQURING NEW HIRE REPORTING

**NOTE:** Employer Identification Number is abbreviated EIN; Social Security Number is abbreviated SSN.

| | *Which Employers Must Report?* | *Which Employees Must Be Reported?* | *Which Employees Need Not Be Reported?* | *How May Report Be Filed with State Agency?* | *When Must Report Be Filed?* | *What Employer Information Must Be Included in Report?* | *What Employee Information Must Be Included in Report?* | *Failure to Report* | *Citations to Authority* |
|---|---|---|---|---|---|---|---|---|---|
| VT *(cont'd)* | | | | mitted by mail, fax, input of data, by telephone, magnetically, or electronically. | | | | conspire in not reporting. | |
| VA | All employers. | All new employees and rehires. | — | W-4 form, or mutually agreeable method. Information may be submitted by mail, magnetically, electronically, or by other authorized means. | Within 20 days of hiring. | Name, address, and federal EIN. | Name, address, date of birth, and SSN. | — | Va. Code Ann. §§ 60.2-114; 60.2-114.1; 63.1-274.11. |
| WA | All employers. | All new employees and rehires. | — | W-4 form or other authorized means. Information may be submitted by mail or other authorized means. | Within 20 days of employment. | Name, address, and employment security reference number or unified business number and federal EIN. | Name, address, SSN, and date of birth. | Written warning will be followed by fines of up to $200 per month for subsequent violations. | Wash. Rev. Code Ann. § 26.23.040. |
| WV | All employers. | New employees and rehires. | — | W-4 form or other mutually agreeable method. Information may be submitted by mail or means authorized in writing. | Within 14 days of hiring. | Name, address, address of payroll office, and federal EIN. | Name, address, SSN, and date of birth. If requested in writing employer must also furnish information on wage/ salary, medical | Fine of $25 per employee ($500 if conspiracy) may be imposed. | W. Va. Code § 48A-2-34. |

| | | | | | | | | | |
|---|---|---|---|---|---|---|---|---|---|
| | | | | | | | insurance, and location of employment. | | |
| WI | All employers. | All employees and new hires. | — | State tax withholding form (WT-4); information may be submitted by fax, magnetically, or electronically. | Within 20 days of hiring. | Name, address, and federal EIN. | Name, address, SSN, date of birth, and date of hire. | Fines of $25 ($500 if conspiracy) may be imposed. | Wis. Stat. Ann. § 103.05 and accompanying regulations. |
| WY | All employers. | All employees and new hires. | Employees under 18 years of age unless required for federal new hire law. | W-4 form, or mutually agreeable method. Information may be submitted by mail, magnetically, or electronically. | Within 20 days of hiring. | Name, address, and federal EIN. | Name, address, and SSN. | — | Wyo. Stat. Ann. § 27-1-115. |

### [e] Domestic Partner Benefits

In recent years, companies have begun extending benefits, such as health insurance, to domestic partners of employees. Hundreds of companies—municipalities, colleges, and universities—and other organizations currently allow employees to obtain benefits for domestic partners. One 1996 study found that 10 percent of firms extended such benefits. Some companies extend the benefits to both same-sex and opposite-sex domestic partners, although other companies include only one of these classifications.

The number of employers providing benefits to the domestic partners of employees may increase in light of recent indications from the IRS that the payment of benefits to domestic partners may receive favorable tax treatment. In two private letter rulings, the IRS has indicated that payments for benefits to the domestic partners of employees may be entitled to favorable tax treatment if the domestic partner qualifies as a dependent under Section 152(9) of the Internal Revenue Code.[19] Under Section 152(9), a dependent is an individual who resides with the taxpayer as a member of the household and who receives over half of his or her support from the taxpayer.

Generally, the decision of whether to extend benefits to domestic partners is one that is made by the individual firm. In some jurisdictions, however, such benefits may be mandated by legislation or judicial decision.

Legislation was passed in San Francisco in late 1996 that requires firms doing business with the city to offer benefits to domestic partners. To the extent that they wish to bid on city contracts, private employers are therefore affected by the legislation. Other cities, including Los Angeles, have considered such legislation. A bill has also been introduced in the California State Senate that would require domestic-partner benefits for firms contracting for state or local government work throughout California.

In a court challenge by the airline industry, however, the San Francisco legislation passed in 1996 was found to be partially preempted by ERISA. In 1998, the United States District Court for the Northern District of California, in the case of *Air Transport Association of America v. City and County of San Francisco,*[20] determined that the San Francisco domestic partner ordinance had a direct connection with ERISA plans because it mandated "employee benefit structures" for city contractors. Therefore, ERISA preempted the ordinance, but only to the extent that the ordinance addressed ERISA benefits under ERISA plans. In other words, ERISA did not preempt the ordinance with respect to non-ERISA benefits, such as travel benefits or moving expenses.

In *Air Transport,* the court further held that, regardless of semantics, an employer establishes an ERISA plan when it makes a commitment to pay benefits systematically and to undertake various obligations relating to such benefits. Even though employers may establish separate plans to provide benefits for domestic partners, these plans would nonetheless constitute an "employee welfare benefit plan" and would not be exempt from ERISA coverage. Finally, the court held that the San Francisco ordinance, with its nationwide reach, impermissibly regulated out-of-state conduct that was not related to contracts with the city.

In July of 1997, legislation was passed in Hawaii that could require employers to extend health coverage to the domestic partners and dependents of employees. The legislation essentially grants rights normally recognized only in favor of married couples to unmarried couples who register with the state as reciprocal beneficiaries. Employers who offer family health care coverage would be required to extend such benefits to registered partners. A group of employers in Hawaii has brought suit to block enforcement of the legislation.

The issue has also been raised in the judicial forum with some interesting results.

The Oregon Court of Appeals held that the denial of health and life insurance benefits to the unmarried domestic partners of the University's homosexual employees violated Article I, section 20, of the Oregon Constitution.[21] The court held that the denial of domestic partner benefits did not violate Oregon's fair employment practices act, which prohibits discrimination in employment on the basis of the sex of an employee or the sex of any other person with whom the employee associates. The University maintained that it determined insurance on the basis of marital status, not sexual orientation, and that the unintentional effect on homosexuals did not violate either the fair employment practices act or the state constitution. The court disagreed, holding that Article I, section 20, of the Oregon constitution,

---

19. Private Letter Ruling 9717018 (April 25, 1997); Private Letter Ruling 9231062 (July 31, 1992). Note that these private letter rulings are not binding precedent; they do, however, indicate the position taken by the IRS with respect to specific taxpayers.

20. No. 97-1763 CW (N.D. Cal. April 10, 1998).

21. Tanner v. Oregon Health Sciences University, P.2d 1998 WL 869976 (Ore. App. Dec. 9, 1998).

which prohibits granting privileges or immunities not equally belonging to all citizens, applied whether the effect was intended or not. Therefore, the court held that the University could not refuse to provide the same benefits to the lesbian partners of its employees that it provided to the married partners of employees.

In early 1997, this issue was addressed in a significant opinion from the Alaska Supreme Court.[22] In the Alaska case, two employees of the University of Alaska requested health insurance benefits for their same-sex domestic partners, and the university refused. The employees claimed that the denial violated the Alaska Human Rights Act, which bars discrimination in employment on the basis of marital status. The university admitted that the denial was discriminatory but denied that the Act was violated.

Although the Alaska Human Rights Act was amended during the course of the litigation to provide that an employer could, without violating the Act, provide greater health and retirement benefits on the basis of marital status, the Court found that the question was not moot, due to potential recovery of back benefits. The Court decided that the policy of the university did in fact violate the Alaska Human Rights Act.

In a New Jersey case involving the same issue, the court reached a a different conclusion.[23] A Superior Court in New Jersey found that Rutgers' denial of health insurance to same-sex domestic partners did not violate the New Jersey Law Against Discrimination, nor did it violate rights to equal protection under the state constitution. The court also found that an executive order banning discrimination on the basis of sexual orientation was not violated by the refusal to extend benefits. As of the time of this writing, the plaintiffs intended to appeal the case to the New Jersey Supreme Court.

Currently, marital status is a protected classification under the fair employment laws of 26 jurisdictions (Alaska, California, Connecticut, Delaware, District of Columbia, Florida, Hawaii, Illinois, Kentucky, Maryland, Massachusetts, Michigan, Minnesota, Montana, Nebraska, New Hampshire, New Jersey, New Mexico, New York, North Dakota, Oklahoma, Oregon, South Dakota, Virginia, Washington, and Wisconsin). Given the prevalence of such laws, it is likely that there will be further litigation over whether these statutes prohibit the denial of benefits to domestic partners.

22. University of Alaska v. Tumeo, 933 P.2d 1147 (Alaska 1997).

23. Rutgers Council of AAUP Chapters v. Rutgers, 298 N.J. Super. 442, 689 A.2d 828 (App. Div. 1997).

### [f] Does an Employee's Application for Social Security or Other Disability Benefits Preclude a Claim of Disability Discrimination?

In order to bring a claim of disability discrimination, an employee is generally required to show that he or she is otherwise qualified to perform the job, taking into account any reasonable accommodation that can be made by the employer. A number of courts have held that an individual who represents that he or she is totally disabled in order to receive Social Security or private-insurance disability payments is precluded from later claiming that he or she is a qualified individual with a disability for purposes of bringing a disability discrimination claim.[24]

For example, in one case, an employee had executed sworn statements five weeks before his discharge claiming that he was totally and permanently disabled in order to obtain state and Social Security disability benefits and a loan-repayment exemption. When the employee was discharged, he brought suit, claiming that he had been discriminated against because of his disability. The court held that, in light of his sworn statements, the employee could not maintain in court that he was a qualified individual with a disability for purposes of maintaining a claim under the New Jersey Law Against Discrimination.[25]

In another case, the court reached the opposite result, holding that the plaintiff was not prevented from bringing a case under the ADA because of her application for total disability benefits.[26] In that case, the plaintiff applied for Social Security disability benefits after she was forced to quit her former job because of back problems

24. See, e.g., Weigel v. Target Stores, 122 F.3d 461 (7th Cir. 1997); Dusch v. Appelton Elec. Co., 1997 WL 530542, 7 A.D. Cases 183 (8th Cir. 1997); Griffith v. Wal-Mart Stores, Inc., 930 F. Supp. 1167 (E.D. Ky. 1996) (employee's representations in his application for long-term Social Security disability benefits, that he was unable to do his job, precluded him from asserting in ADA action that he was otherwise qualified to perform essential functions of position as store sales associate); Cline v. Western Horseman, Inc., 922 F. Supp. 442 (D. Colo. 1996) (former employee was estopped from claiming that she was a qualified individual with a disability within meaning of the ADA by virtue of fact that she had been receiving numerous disability benefits from date of her termination that required that she affirm and be adjudged totally disabled).

25. McNemar v. Disney Store, Inc., 91 F.3d 610 (3d Cir. 1996).

26. Talavera v. School Bd. Of Palm Beach County, 129 F.3d 1214 (11th Cir. 1997).

that prevented her from standing for long periods. Her former employer had been unable or unwilling to provide an effective accommodation to the plaintiff. On her application for benefits, she wrote that she had skills that made her employable, but that potential employers regarded her as totally disabled because of her problems with walking and standing.

When the plaintiff subsequently sued her former employer for refusing to accommodate her disability, the court dismissed the complaint because of her representations of total disability on her application for benefits. The plaintiff appealed, however, and the appellate court held that her claim under the ADA was not barred by her application for disability benefits, because the representations made in support of her application for benefits were not inconsistent with her claim that she could have continued working had her former employer provided reasonable accommodation to her disability.

In some cases, although the courts have not adopted an absolute rule on the issue, they have nonetheless dismissed discrimination claims of plaintiffs who have applied for long-term disability benefits or who have represented that they are totally disabled. Thus, a federal court in Oregon held that an employee was not qualified to perform the essential functions of her job, for purposes of establishing a case of disability discrimination under Oregon's fair employment law where she had represented, both to her employer and the Social Security Administration (SSA), that she was permanently and totally disabled.[27] In a similar ruling, another court held that an employee who, in connection with a long-term disability benefits claim, represented that he could not perform the material duties of his job and who received and cashed benefit checks did not qualify for protection under the Minnesota Human Rights Act (MHRA).[28]

The decisions appear to establish three approaches to the determination of whether an employee's ADA claim is barred by a previous application for total disability benefits:

1. The "per se rule," which holds that the mere application for benefits prevents an ADA claim;[29]
2. The "rebuttable presumption rule," which holds that an employee's ADA claim is presumed to be barred by the application for disability benefits, but that an employee may present evidence to overcome this presumption;[30] and
3. The "application as evidence rule," which treats the employee's application for total disability benefits merely as one piece of evidence bearing on the determination of whether the employee can be considered to be otherwise qualified or able to perform the essential functions of the position.[31]

The EEOC has taken the position that representations made in applications for disability benefits are not necesssarily a bar to a claim under the federal Americans with Disabilities Act, due to the different purposes and standards of other statutory schemes, disability benefits programs, and contracts.[32] The Commission may give some weight to such representations, however, depending on their context and timing.

### [g] Same-Sex Harassment

It is generally recognized that Title VII of the Civil Rights Act of 1964 does not prohibit discrimination based on an individual's homosexuality or sexual orientation, although it does prohibit discrimination based on sex. (See "Trends and Controversies," [m] of this Guide for a discussion of discrimination based on homosexuality or sexual orientation.) The federal courts disagreed, however, on the issue of whether harassment by a person of the same sex is actionable under Title VII. Several courts held that Title VII does not cover sexual harassment of an employee by a supervisor or other employee of the same sex.[33]

Other courts, although not squarely holding that Title VII had been violated in the cases before them, acknowledged the potential viability of same-sex sexual harassment claims. In *Morgan v. Massachusetts General Hospital*,[34] a hospital janitorial employee filed a claim of

27. Miller v. U.S. Bancorp., 926 F. Supp. 994 (D. Or. 1996).

28. Reiff v. Interim Personnel, Inc., 906 F. Supp. 1280 (D. Minn. 1995).

29. McNemar v. Disney Store, Inc., 91 F.3d 610 (3d Cir. 1996).

30. Dush v. Appleton Electric Co., 124 F.3d 957 (8th Cir. 1997).

31. Swanks v. Washington Metropolitan Area Transit Authority, 116 F.3d 582 (D.C. Cir. 1997).

32. EEOC Notice No. 915.002 (February 12, 1997).

33. Garcia v. Elf Atochem N. Am., 28 F.3d 446 (5th Cir. 1994). *See also* Benekritis v. Johnson, 882 F. Supp. 521 (D.S.C. 1995) (male teacher's same-sex harassment action is not cognizable under Title VII); Fredette v. BVP Management Associates, 905 F. Supp. 1034, 1037 (M.D. Fla. 1995); Ashworth v. Roundup Co., 897 F. Supp. 489, 494 (W.D. Wash. 1995); Myers v. City of El Paso, 874 F. Supp. 1546, 1548 (W.D. Tex. 1995).

34. Morgan v. Massachusetts Gen'l Hosp., 901 F.2d 186 (1st Cir. 1990).

sexual harassment alleging that a fellow employee stood behind him while he mopped, stood next to him in the restroom while making sexual comments, and asked him to dance at a Christmas party. Both the district court and the court of appeals assumed that sexual harassment by a homosexual would be actionable under Title VII if sufficiently severe and pervasive. Based on the facts before them, however, both courts held that the plaintiff had not established the requisite pervasiveness or severity.

The Fourth Circuit Court of Appeals acknowledged that sexual harassment of a male by another male would be covered by Title VII, but held that a series of incidents that were merely vulgar and did not rise to the level of severity or pervasiveness necessary to create a hostile environment did not violate Title VII.[35] The incidents occurred over a period of seven years, were sexually neutral, and often were not directed solely at the employee and so did not rise to the level of a hostile environment.

In *Wrightson,* a decision subsequent to *Hopkins*, the Fourth Circuit Court of Appeals squarely addressed the issue, holding that harassment of a heterosexual male by a homosexual male violated Title VII.[36] The decision in *Wrightson* essentially followed the rationale set out in a previous Fourth Circuit case, in which the court made the distinction between same-sex harassment perpetrated by homosexuals, and same-sex harassment perpetrated by heterosexuals.[37] Only the former type of harassment has been held to violate Title VII.[38]

A number of courts allowed plaintiffs to pursue claims under Title VII based on retaliation for reporting incidents of same-sex harassment.[39]

The Supreme Court has now resolved this conflict among the federal courts in a decision that will alter the law previously recognized in a number of jurisdictions. In *Oncale v. Sundowner Offshore Services, Inc.,*[40] the Supreme Court held that same-sex harassment creating a hostile work environment may be actionable under Title VII regardless of whether the harasser is homosexual or heterosexual. To be actionable, the plaintiff must prove, however, that the discrimination was because of sex. The court stated that a trier of fact may reasonably find actionable discrimination if, for example, a female victim is harassed in such sex-specific and derogatory terms by another woman as to make it clear that the harasser is motivated by general hostility to the presence of women in the workplace. Actionable discrimination could also be shown, the Court stated, by direct comparative evidence about how the alleged harasser treated members of both sexes in a mixed-sex workplace.

The Supreme Court defended its decision against the anticipated criticism that it would transform Title VII into a "general civility code," stating that the employee's burden to prove that the harassment was based on sex would prevent such a result. The Fourth Circuit Court of Appeals may prove to be correct, however, with respect to its observation in the *Wrightson* case that the "expanded interpretation of Title VII will result in a significant increase in litigation."

It should be noted that, under the Supreme Court's analysis, to be actionable under Title VII, same-sex harassment must be because of sex, *not* because of sexual orientation. Thus, in *Dillon,*[41] the court held that verbal and physical harassment of an employee because of a belief that he is homosexual does not constitute discrimination based on sex or establish hostile environment sexual harassment under Title VII.

**Same-Sex Harassment Under State Laws.** Although the cases set out above analyze this issue in the context of harassment claims brought under federal law, the reasoning of these cases may be applied to claims under state fair employment statutes with similar language. As the discussion below shows, however, differences between state and federal law may render the

35. Hopkins v. Baltimore Gas and Electric Co., 77 F.3d 745 (4th Cir. 1996).

36. Wrightson v. Pizza Hut of America, Inc., 99 F.3d 138 (4th Cir. 1996).

37. McWilliams v. Fairfax County Bd. of Supervisors, 72 F.3d 1191 (4th Cir. 1996).

38. *See* Quick v. Donaldon Co., 90 F.3d 1372 (8th Cir. 1996); EEOC v. Walden Book, 885 F. Supp. 1100 (M.D. Tenn. 1995) (holding same sex harassment actionable under Title VII); Tietgen v. Brown's Westminster Motors Inc., 921 F. Supp. 1495 (E.D. Va. 1996); Torres v. National Precision Blanking, 943 F. Supp. 952 (N.D. Ill. 1996).

39. Benekritis v. Johnson, 882 F. Supp. 521 (D.S.C. 1995) (male teacher's same-sex harassment action is not cognizable under Title VII; the court in this instance allowed the plaintiff to pursue a retaliation claim based on his discharge after complaining of harassment by a male because he held a reasonable, although mistaken, belief that the conduct violated Title VII); King v. M.R. Brown Inc., 911 F. Supp. 161 (E.D. Pa. 1995) (employee who alleged that she was subjected to retaliatory discharge for filing a discrimination complaint concerning unwelcome sexual overtures and harassment by a female lesbian co-worker stated a claim under Title VII for sexual harassment).

40. 66 U.S.L.W. 4172 (1998).

41. Dillon v. Frank, 952 F.2d 403 (Table), 58 FEP Cases 144 (6th Cir. 1992).

analysis found in federal cases inapplicable in certain states.

A same-sex harassment claim was recently presented to a court in New York, which does not have a statute prohibiting discrimination based on sexual orientation. In a decision that essentially mirrors the analysis applied by the federal courts, the court noted that, to make out a claim of sexual harassment under New York law, the employee must show that the harassment was "based on his or her gender." After reviewing the evidence, the court held that in the case before it the male employee failed to establish harassment actionable under New York's Human Rights Law, because the employee's deposition testimony indicated he believed he was targeted due to his marital status and the group's perception he was homosexual; there was no evidence, however, that he was "targeted due to his gender."[42]

As indicated in Table 2.3-1 Part B, a number of state fair employment practices laws specifically prohibit discrimination based on homosexuality or sexual orientation. In these states, a broader range of same-sex sexual harassment claims have been held to come within the state's prohibition of discrimination. The Minnesota Court of Appeals, for example, has held that a same-sex harassment claim may be brought under the Minnesota Human Rights Act regardless of the sex or sexual orientation of either the harasser or the victim.[43] Likewise, a Massachusetts court has held that under the Massachusetts statute, harassment is not limited to conduct of a supervisor aimed at a subordinate of the opposite sex, nor is it limited to same sex conduct only where the harasser is homosexual. Rather, any physical or verbal conduct of a sexual nature that interferes unreasonably with an employee's work performance through the creation of a humiliating or sexually offensive work environment is sexual harassment.[44]

### [h] Part-Time Employees: Do They Count Under Fair Employment Practices Laws?

As shown in Table 2.3-4, an employer is subject to the provisions of many state fair employment practices laws only if it employs a specified minimum number of employees. Thus, for example, an employer with fewer than four employees is not subject to the New York Human Rights Law. Likewise under federal law, an employer is not subject to Title VII of the Civil Rights Act of 1964 unless it employs 15 or more employees.

Because the viability of a discrimination suit against an employer may turn on the number of employees, it should come as no surprise that the method by which employees are counted has been the subject of some disagreement in the federal courts. This disagreement is particularly evident with respect to the treatment of part-time employees.

The Equal Employment Opportunity Commission and a majority of courts have taken the position that all part-time employees are counted whether they work part of each day or part of each week, as long as they are on the payroll. Under this analysis, referred to as the payroll method, if the number of employees on the employer's payroll for the statutory 20-week period is 15 or more, the employer is subject to Title VII.[45] The Seventh Circuit and a number of other courts rejected the payroll method of counting employees for the purposes of Title VII determinations of who is an "employer" and instead chose to follow the counting system. Under the counting method, all salaried employees are counted for each day, but hourly and part-time workers are counted only for the days they are present at work or on paid leave.[46]

In a decision handed down on January 14, 1997, the Supreme Court of the United States reversed the Seventh Circuit's decision and adopted the payroll method in counting part-time employees under Title VII. Noting that, in the absence of an indication to the contrary, words in a statute are assumed to bear their ordinary, contemporary, and common meaning, the Court stated that, in common parlance, an employer "has" an employee if he maintains an employment relationship with that individual. The employee's appearance on payroll records would be evidence of such an employment relationship, the Court stated, but if the other indicia of the employment relationship did not exist, the payroll records would not be conclusive. (For a discussion of the indicia of an employer-employee relationship, see § 1.1.)

---

42. Yukoweic v. International Business Machines Inc., 643 N.Y.S.2d 747 (3 Dept. 1996).

43. Cummings v. Koehnen, 556 N.W.2d 586 (Minn. App. 1996).

44. Melnychenko v. 84 Lumber Co., 424 Mass. 285, 676 N.E.2d 45 (1997). *See also* Fiol v. Doellstedt, 50 Cal. App. 4th 1318, 58 Cal. Rptr. 2d 308 (1996) (holding that gender harassment prohibited by Fair Employment and Housing Act (FEHA) includes sexual harassment by member of same sex).

45. *See* Thurber v. Jack Reilly's, Inc., 717 F.2d 633, 634 (1st Cir. 1983), *cert. denied,* 466 U.S. 904 (1984).

46. Equal Employment Opportunity Commission v. Metropolitan Educational Enterprises, Inc., 60 F.3d 1225 (7th Cir. 1995); Richardson v. Bedford Place Housing Phase I Associates, 855 F. Supp. 366 (N.D. Ga. 1994).

Although the Supreme Court's decision applied only to Title VII, it is likely that many state courts will apply the reasoning of the Court's decision in construing state fair employment practices laws.

### [i] The Small Business Job Protection Act: Changes to Minimum Wage, Pension, and 401(k) Provisions

Signed into law on August 20, 1996, the Small Business Job Protection Act makes a number of changes to federal compensation, benefits, and pension laws.[47] The Act also contains provisions for tax breaks directed primarily at small businesses that will clearly impact state law in several ways. For example, with respect to the minimum wage provisions, the federal law establishes a floor for state minimum wage laws applicable to employees covered by the Fair Labor Standards Act. In addition, many state laws relating to the payroll implications of benefits are directly tied to federal laws, and therefore, even without parallel state law amendments, certain state laws will be immediately affected.

**Minimum Wage Provisions.** The Act amends paragraph (1) of Section 6(a) of the Fair Labor Standards Act of 1938, which sets out the federal minimum wage. The minimum wage, which was $4.25 per hour, is increased to $4.75 per hour effective October 1, 1996. On September 1, 1997, the minimum wage increased to $5.15 per hour. Although this minimum wage applies to most workers, an exception is created for newly hired teenage workers. For these workers, a subminimum wage of $4.25 per hour applies during the first 90 days of their employment. For tipped employees, the minimum wage remains $2.13 per hour.

**Pensions and Benefits Changes.** In addition to the minimum wage provisions, the Act contains changes to federal law relating to pensions, 401(k) plans, and other benefits. These changes range from minor changes in allowable tax deductions to the creation of a new kind of retirement plan for small employers.

*The Savings Incentive Match Plan for Employees* (SIMPLE). The Act creates a simplified retirement plan for small businesses known by the acronym SIMPLE. SIMPLE plans can be adopted by employers who do not sponsor another retirement plan and have no more than 100 employees who were paid more than $5,000 each annually. The law becomes effective for tax years that begin on or after January 1, 1997. A SIMPLE plan may take either of two forms:

1. An IRA with a $6,000 maximum contribution for each employee; or
2. A 401(k) qualified cash or deferred arrangement.

Unlike other 401(k) plans, a SIMPLE plan is not subject to the nondiscrimination rules that generally prohibit top-heavy plans from favoring highly compensated employees.

The IRS has recently released Form 5304-SIMPLE, which sets out a model plan form for use by small employers in implementing a SIMPLE plan.

*Changes to qualified pension plans.* The Act changes the definition of "highly compensated employees" for purposes of nondiscrimination provisions prohibiting top-heavy qualified pension plans. Under the Act, a highly compensated employee is:

1. An employee who had an ownership interest of 5 percent at any time during the current or preceding year; or
2. An employee who received more than $80,000 during the preceding year and was in the top one-fifth of employees in terms of compensation.

This new simplified definition is a significant improvement over its more complicated predecessor. The Act also repeals the family aggregation rules. Thus, family members of all highly compensated employees will be able to accrue retirement benefits in the same manner as unrelated employees.

*401(k) safe harbor.* Under current law, a 401(k) plan will be considered discriminatory if highly compensated employees contribute to the plan at a rate that is more than 1¼ the rate for non–highly compensated employees. The Act allows employers to meet the nondiscrimination requirements by matching all of the first 3 percent of a non–highly compensated employee's contribution, and half of any additional contributions up to 5 percent. The employer may also take advantage of this "safe-harbor" provision by simply making a 3 percent contribution for all eligible non–highly compensated employees.

**Tax Credits and Deductions.** The Act restores both the targeted jobs credit and the employer-reimbursed tuition exemption.

*Work opportunity tax credit.* The Act restores the targeted jobs credit that expired at the end of 1994, effective for individuals who begin work after September 30, 1996, and before October 1, 1997. Employers

47. Pub. L. No. 104-188, 110 Stat. 1755 (Aug. 10, 1996).

may receive a credit of 35 percent of the first year's wages for an employee in one of seven targeted groups, provided the employee is employed for at least 180 days or 400 hours.

*Employer-reimbursed tuition exemption.* The Section 127 exemption for employer-reimbursed educational expenses is reinstated under the Act for a limited period. The exemption is effective retroactively from January 1, 1995, to May 31, 1997.

### [j] IRS Training Manual: Employee or Independent Contractor

As discussed in Part 1, the distinction between an employee and an independent contractor can have significant consequences for employers. Generally, an employer must withhold income taxes, withhold and pay Social Security and Medicare taxes, and pay unemployment taxes on wages paid to an employee. No such withholding or payment of taxes is required for payments to independent contractors. The 20-factor test applied by the Internal Revenue Service (IRS) focuses on the amount of control that an employer exercises over a worker. The greater the amount of control, the more likely it is that the scales will tip in favor of finding an employer/employee relationship. Although the 20-factor test provides some guidance, determining whether a worker is an employee or independent contractor is not as simple as tallying up how many factors fall in each column. The factors are only guidelines, and not every factor applies to every type of job. Moreover, not all factors are created equal, and the importance attached to each factor varies according to the type of work and individual circumstances.

It is clear that the business community is not alone in its confusion and uncertainty over the independent contractor versus employee distinction. In fact, sufficient confusion over the distinction exists in the ranks of IRS auditors that the agency created an extensive training manual covering in great detail the appropriate analysis to be used in determining whether a worker is an employee or independent contractor. Although a manual of this kind does not constrain the IRS, it is a reliable indicator of IRS policy. The cumulative effect of the manual's guidance is to make it somewhat easier to show independent contractor status, thereby avoiding obligations owed only for employees.

For example, all other factors being equal, the IRS is likely to give weight to a statement in a written contract designating a worker as a contractor. In light of the evolving conditions of the modern workplace, the timing and location of a particular work activity are not necessarily indicators of employee status. If a company gives a worker suggestions as to how the work should be done, but not instructions, this may indicate that insufficient control exists to determine employee status. According to the manual, the wearing of company uniforms, once regarded as an important sign of employee status, has little if any significance.

Some of the manual's provisions will make it more difficult for some professionals to claim the status of independent contractor. For example, many professionals who are paid on an hourly basis think of themselves as independent contractors; however, the manual refers to an hourly wage as evidence of an employer/employee relationship. A worker's own significant investment in facilities or equipment generally is an indicator of contractor status, but if the item also has a personal use—like the home computers increasingly used by today's professionals—the IRS will discount it in applying the 20-part test.

Significantly, the training manual recognizes that a good-faith but erroneous characterization of a worker's status may not be an appropriate basis for imposing penalties. Businesses will benefit from the part of the manual that will give them a break when they accidentally mischaracterize a worker's status. If a company's classification of a worker had a reasonable basis, such as approval by an attorney or accountant with expertise, penalties are less likely.

### [k] Interplay Between the ADA and Workers' Compensation Statutes

The Americans With Disabilities Act (ADA) and many state statutes prohibit employers from discriminating against persons with physical and mental disabilities as long as those persons can perform the essential functions of their jobs with reasonable accommodations. Under the ADA, employers have an affirmative duty to reasonably accommodate persons with disabilities.

The obligation to provide reasonable accommodation may vary from employer to employer because, in assessing what is *reasonable,* courts look at the size of the employer, the financial resources of the employer, and the impact of the accommodation on the employer's primary function. Reasonable accommodation may, however, include job restructuring, part-time or modified work schedules, provision or modification of equipment, and, if necessary, reassignment to a vacant position.

A conflict may arise between the ADA and state workers' compensation statutes. It is possible, for example, for a person to be considered "permanently and partially disabled" for purposes of a state workers' compensation statute, while coming within the definition of a "qualified individual with a disability" under the ADA.[48] On September 3, 1996, the EEOC issued an Enforcement Guidance on Workers' Compensation and the ADA.[49] This notice provides guidance for many of the issues that have entrapped employers and injured employees.

Under the typical workers' compensation law, an employer is not required to consider whether a worker can perform a job's "essential functions" or to provide a "reasonable accommodation." An injured worker may therefore be legally entitled to receive workers' compensation benefits and may also be able to demand that he be employed through reasonable accommodation of his disability.

As a threshold matter, however, the employee must demonstrate that he or she is disabled. There are essentially three aspects to the definition of a disability under the ADA. A "disability" is defined as

1. A physical or mental impairment that substantially limits a major life activity;
2. A record of such an impairment; or
3. Being regarded as having such an impairment.

The guidance makes clear that not every person with an occupational injury is a person with a disability under the ADA.

Impairments resulting from occupational injury will not come within the first portion of the ADA's definition of disability if they are not severe enough to substantially limit a major life activity, or they may be only temporary, nonchronic, and have little or no long-term impact. Moreover, the mere filing of a workers' compensation claim does not, by itself, establish a record of impairment sufficient to come within the second portion of the definition. With respect to the third portion of the ADA definition—when a person with an occupational injury is considered to have a disability—the guidance states as follows:

> A person with an occupational injury has a disability under the "regarded as" portion of the ADA definition if s/he: (1) has an impairment that does not substantially limit a major life activity but is treated by an employer as if it were substantially limiting, (2) has an impairment that substantially limits a major life activity because of the attitude of others towards the impairment, or (3) has no impairment but is treated as having a substantially limiting impairment.[50]

If an employee has a substantially limiting impairment, an employer will be required to make reasonable accommodation. An employer's obligation to provide reasonable accommodation may include job restructuring, part-time or modified work scheduling, provision or modification of equipment, and if necessary, reassignment to a vacant position. Thus, an employer who tells an injured worker that he or she may not return to work until he or she is 100 percent better may be in violation of the ADA. In such a situation, it is in the employer's best interest to attempt accommodation if possible; the EEOC has taken the position that failure to make reasonable accommodation in this situation may violate the ADA.[51]

An example provided by the EEOC is helpful in understanding the employer's obligation. Suppose an employer has a sack-handler position that requires that the employee pick up 50-pound sacks from a loading dock and carry them to a storage room. The employee who holds this position is disabled by a work-related back impairment and requests an accommodation. The employer analyzes the job and finds that the essential function of the position is to *move* the sacks from the loading dock to the storage room, not necessarily to lift and carry the sacks. After consulting with the employee to determine his exact physical abilities and limitations, it is determined, with medical documentation, that the employee can lift 50-pound sacks to waist level, but cannot carry them to the storage room. A number of potential accommodations may be implemented, including the use of a dolly, a handtruck, or a cart.

Another example concerns a construction worker who falls from a ladder and breaks her leg. The leg heals normally within a few months. Although this worker may be awarded workers' compensation benefits for the injury, she would not be considered a person with a disability under the ADA, because the impairment did not "substantially limit" a major life activity and because the injury healed within a short period without long-term impact. By way of contrast, if the worker's leg took significantly longer to heal than is usual for the type of injury and during this period the worker could not walk, she would be considered to have a disability under the ADA. Or, if the injury caused a permanent limp, the worker might be considered disabled under the ADA if the limp substantially

48. For a discussion of whether an application for social security or other disability benefits precludes a claim of disability discrimination, see part [f].

49. Notice No. 915.002 (Sept. 3, 1996).

50. EEOC Enforcement Guidance No. 915.002 at 3.

51. EEOC Technical Assistance Manual §§ 3.8, 9.2 (1992).

limited her walking as compared to the average person in the general population. If so, the employer could not refuse to make reasonable accommodations.

Where such a conflict was presented, the Tenth Circuit Court of Appeals held that an employee was not the victim of discrimination despite the fact that he was not allowed to return to work after a work-related injury. Inconsistent medical opinions were given concerning permanent partial disabilities to his feet: one opinion was that he could not return to work at all; the other opinion was that he could return to work with restrictions only on standing. The court held that the employee could not be considered to be handicapped or disabled, because he failed to demonstrate a significant restriction in his ability to perform a *class* of jobs, rather than just the particular job in question.[52]

In another case, the court held that an employer violated the Rehabilitation Act by summarily discharging an employee who sustained a back injury at work that restricted her ability to walk, sit, stand, drive, care for her home, and engage in recreational activities.[53] In the court's view, the employee was a person with a disability and was qualified to perform her job as a receptionist-clerk with reasonable accommodation. The employer's failure to allow the employee to continue working with accommodations such as providing her with a wooden straight-backed chair, allowing her to use the elevator, and allowing her to take regular breaks, violated the Act.

An issue that has caused some confusion and is addressed by the EEOC guidance is whether disability discrimination claims are precluded by state statutes requiring that workers' compensation laws are the exclusive remedy for workplace injuries. The EEOC's Enforcement Guidance states that such exclusive remedy provisions do not bar federal civil rights actions for disability discrimination.[54]

States have split on how they treat the interplay between their workers' compensation statutes and their disability discrimination statutes (whether in the state FEP or in a separate statute). For example, California, Minnesota, and Michigan find that the remedy for discrimination for a disability that occurred on the job is exclusive to the workers' compensation statute.[55] Louisiana, Washington, and Maine take the opposite approach and allow remedies under both the workers' compensation statute and the statute prohibiting disability discrimination.[56]

Until this issue is resolved, employers in all states would be wise to avoid potential liability by instructing their human resources professionals and supervisory personnel to revise job descriptions, develop reasonable accommodations policies, and adopt return-to-work policies that comply with ADA requirements.

## [I] Revival of Health Care Reform

In the summer of 1994, many politicians and news analysts predicted that Congress would pass some kind of health care reform measure. However, as a result of the Republican victories in the November elections, and the apparent slowing in the rate of growth in national health care spending, health care reform became what one editorialist termed a "Ghost of an Issue."[57] It now appears that reports of the death of health care reform may have been exaggerated.

In August 1996, the Health Insurance Portability and Accountability Act of 1996 was passed. Rather than the sweeping health insurance reform discussed in 1994, the new legislation is targeted at a few specific areas. The Act provides for nondiscrimination, provisions to combat medical care fraud, and provisions to implement medical savings accounts. Of particular interest to employers are the eligibility, continuation coverage, and tax provisions of Titles I and III.

Title I contains the provisions for preexisting conditions and nondiscrimination. The Act provides that when an employee has been insured under an employer's health insurance plan, the employee may carry that insurability when moving to another group health plan. Group insurance plans may continue to exclude individuals with preexisting conditions for up to 12 months, but the new legislation changes how that 12 months is calculated. Under the Act, any "creditable prior coverage" may count toward the 12-month period. "Creditable cov-

52. Bolton v. Scrivner, Inc., 36 F.3d 939 (10th Cir. 1994).

53. Perez v. Philadelphia Hous. Auth., 677 F. Supp. 357 (E.D. Pa. 1987), *aff'd,* 841 F.2d 1120 (3d Cir. 1988).

54. EEOC Enforcement Guidance Notice No. 915.002 at 23–24.

55. *See* Usher v. American Airlines, 20 Cal. App. 4th 1520, 25 Cal. Rptr. 2d 335 (1993); Karst v. F.C. Hayer Co., 447 N.W. 2d 180 (Minn. 1989).

56. *See* Cox v. Glazer Steel Corp., 606 So. 2d 518 (La. 1992) (stating that the Civil Rights Act for Handicapped Persons provides a distinct statutory remedy for the handicapped not within the scope of the workers' compensation law, and its application is not barred by that law); Beauchamp v. Columbia Lighting, Inc., 107 Wash. 2d 563, 731 P.2d 497 (1987); Pacheo v. Clifton, 40 Mich. 308, 362 N.W.2d 642 (1984); King v. Bangor Federal Credit Union, 568 A.2d 507 (Me. 1989) *appeal after remand,* 611 A.2d 80 (1992).

57. *The Washington Post,* Nov. 28, 1994, Final Edition, Op. Ed., at A24.

erage" means any coverage under any plan such as group insurance, COBRA, Medicare, and Medicaid. Any such coverage may be counted toward the 12-month period unless there is a break in coverage for longer than 63 days. Any waiting period imposed by the new employer does not count toward the 63-day limit.

The nondiscrimination provision prohibits insurers from imposing certain conditions on eligibility under group health plans. For example, a group health insurer may not base eligibility decisions on a certain health status, claims history, medical history, genetic information, or medical condition. Group insurers also may not discriminate on the basis of disability or evidence of insurability. The provision for evidence of insurability would apply, for example, to motorcyclists or victims of domestic violence. (A similar provision relating only to domestic abuse victims was passed by many state legislatures in the 1995–1996 sessions. These new laws prevented insurers from discriminating against an individual on the basis of that person's being a victim of domestic violence.)

In addition, Title I states that access must be given to individual coverage if an individual has at least 18 months of creditable coverage. This provision means that an insurer must offer an individual policy to a person who does not have alternate coverage if the insurer offers such policies in the state where the individual resides. No limitations on preexisting conditions may be imposed. The provisions contained in COBRA have also been amended to make the 11-month extension available to any qualified beneficiary (such as a dependent) who has a disability within the first 60 days of continuation coverage.

Title I of the Act also contains a provision that assists small employers in obtaining health insurance coverage for their employees. The Act states that health plan issuers must make any plan they offer to small employers (considered to be groups of 50 or fewer) available to all eligible small employers, despite health status or prior claims experience.

Title III of the Act contains tax provisions relevant to employers. The Act authorizes medical savings accounts for employees covered by employer-sponsored health insurance plans with high deductibles. The medical savings accounts would have a yearly maximum contribution of 65 percent of the deductible for individual coverage (at least $1,500 of deductible expenses) and 75 percent of the deductible for family coverage (at least $3,000 of deductible expenses). The medical savings accounts will be in a pilot program from 1997 until 2000. The Act also states that long-term care insurance premiums, when paid by an employer, are nontaxable to the employee, and it provides for withdrawals from IRAs for medical expenses exceeding 7.5 percent of an individual's adjusted gross income.

In a separate health care reform measure, Congress passed a federal law specifically relating to pregnancy. Under the Act (29 U.S.C. § 1185), insurers must minimally cover a post-delivery hospital stay of 48 hours. This federal provision mirrors legislation passed in many states during 1995 and 1996 that provided that for insurance plans covering maternity, a post-delivery hospital stay of a certain length must be covered. (See Table 5.2-4 for information about maternity and pregnancy coverage requirements under state law for group health insurance plans.)

It appears likely that some states will also continue to experiment with other kinds of health care reform, while other states will work from previously tested approaches. The changes to health care will be modest at first, in order to avoid the problems that caused federal health care reform to fail.[58] Plans in some states that were designed before Republicans gained control of the legislatures may not be implemented.

One possible approach to health care reform is the employer mandate, which has been in place for the longest amount of time; Hawaii has had such a mandate for over 20 years. About 98 percent of Hawaii's residents are covered by the mandate, implemented after Hawaii received an ERISA waiver. Employers are required to provide coverage for most employees, and coverage for other people is provided through Medicaid and other gap-filling coverages. Because it has not been able to obtain another ERISA waiver, however, Hawaii has been unable to make alterations in its plan to keep current with changing social and economic conditions.

Managed competition is another model that has gained attention in some states. For example, Florida attempted to create an alliance system that would group employers and also mandate certain benefits so that insurers would compete to offer less expensive services. Parts of the Florida plan have been held up due to opposition in the Florida Senate. Several other states had planned some type of health reform involving managed competition, but budget deficits and changing political goals have slowed down health care reform.

---

58. Milt Freudenheim, "States Shelving Ambitious Plans on Health Care," *N.Y. Times*, July 2, 1995, at A1.

An aspect of change that is succeeding is more stringent state regulation of managed care systems. Issues of patient privacy and access to care are being addressed by state legislators. These regulations have the potential benefit of improving the system while not requiring significant state expenditures, and the majority of the states have enacted some type of law regulating access to care. These regulations usually require that managed care insurers provide some sort of appeals process for patients who are denied coverage for a procedure through the insurer's utilization review process. Statutes may also provide that insurers must respond to appeals within a certain amount of time, frequently 48 hours. (See Table 5.2-10 for information on which states have enacted some sort of regulation of the utilization review process.) As managed care becomes more and more popular, additional limits may be placed on the insurers' ability to deny treatments prescribed by doctors.

Finally, some focus has been placed recently on issues of patient privacy. Some states have enacted laws protecting the confidentiality of certain records, frequently those of patients with AIDS or of patients being tested for AIDS. Congress has also begun to consider laws protecting patient privacy by restricting access to medical records.

### [m] Legislation Barring Sexual Orientation from "Protected Class" Status

Federal laws, most notably Title VII of the Civil Rights Act of 1964, do not expressly prohibit employment discrimination on the basis of an employee's sexual orientation. (For a general discussion of Title VII and other federal laws relating to employment, see chapter 9.) Title VII claims brought by homosexuals, bisexuals, transsexuals who undergo reassignment surgery, and effeminate men have routinely failed. By contrast, the laws in a number of states and local jurisdictions do prohibit employment discrimination on the basis of sexual orientation (see Tables 2.3-1 and 2.3-2).

A large number of these jurisdictions have elected to prohibit discrimination against homosexuals in public employment, while others have made protected status for homosexuals a requirement for private businesses who wish to do business with the local government. A substantial number of localities require all businesses of a certain size within the jurisdiction, for example, those with 20 or more employees, to treat homosexuals as a protected class. A few jurisdictions, such as San Francisco and Berkeley, California, require compliance by all employers located therein.

In recent years, however, countermeasures to laws extending protected class status to homosexuals have been taken in the state and local legislative arenas. Oregon and Colorado are two states that have taken steps to *exclude* sexual orientation from protected class status. In 1988, Oregon voters adopted a measure providing that "[n]o state official shall forbid the taking of any personnel action against any state employee based on the sexual orientation of such employee."[59] In 1992, the voters in Colorado adopted an amendment to the state's constitution providing that neither the state nor any municipalities "shall enact, adopt or enforce any statute, regulation, ordinance or policy whereby homosexual, lesbian or bisexual orientation, conduct, practices or relationships shall constitute or otherwise be the basis of or entitle any person or class of persons to have or claim any minority status quota preferences, protected status or claim of discrimination."[60]

Although these statutes were approved by voters, both have been the subjects of constitutional challenges. Upon judicial challenge, the Oregon statute was declared to be in violation of the state constitutional provision protecting free speech.[61] The court reasoned that although the statute did not directly deal with speech or expression, fear of reprisal under the statute would have an unconstitutional "chilling" effect on a homosexual employee's right to speak freely about sexual orientation or to join a gay rights advocacy group. As discussed, infra, the Colorado constitutional provision was also struck down as unconstitutional.

Despite the constitutional challenge to the 1988 provision, efforts continued in Oregon to enact constitutional provisions banning the extension of protected class status to homosexuals. The Oregon Supreme Court certified a ballot title for a proposed initiative measure that sought to bar governments from spending public funds in a manner expressing approval of homosexuality.[62] This initiative was defeated by voters in the 1994 elections. In 1995, however, Oregon succeeded in enacting legislation prohibiting local governments from singling out individuals for special protections on the

59. Or. Rev. Stat. § 236.380.

60. Colo. Const. art. II, § 30b.

61. Merrick v. Board of Higher Education, 116 Or. App. 258, 841 P.2d 646 (1992).

62. Mabon v. Keisling, 317 Or. 406, 856 P.2d 1023 (1993).

basis of sexual orientation.[63] More recently, a Portland, Oregon, ordinance protecting homosexuals from discrimination was held to be unenforceable because the ordinance purported to create a private cause of action, something the court said Portland had no authority to do.[64]

A similar initiative circulated in Idaho. Unlike the Oregon initiative, however, which sought to amend the state constitution, the Idaho initiative would have enacted a new statutory provision. The short title for the Idaho initiative was "An act establishing state policies regarding homosexuality." Like the Oregon measure, the Idaho initiative was defeated by voters in the November 1994 elections.

Maine was host to the only statewide homosexual rights measure in the November 1995 elections. The Maine measure differed from its predecessors in an important respect; it did not mention homosexuality or gay rights in the text of the measure, but instead sought to limit classes of individuals entitled to protection under the Maine Human Rights Act to race, sex, physical or mental disability, religion, age, ancestry, national origin, family status, and marital status. In effect, however, the measure would have preempted local laws prohibiting discrimination against homosexuals. Two Maine localities, Portland and Long Island, had passed such laws.

The measure became the focus of many gay rights groups, which spent approximately $1.2 million in a successful effort to defeat it. Supporters of the measure were reported to have spent $100,000.[65] The measure was defeated with 53 percent voting against and 47 percent voting for it.

Gay rights organizations capitalized on their successful 1995 effort by persuading the Maine Legislature to enact a provision outlawing sexual orientation discrimination statewide. Their success was short lived, however. In February 1998, Maine voters rejected the new statute outright.

In 1997, voters in the state of Washington also overwhelmingly rejected a ballot initiative granting protected class status to homosexuals.

There have also been several local efforts to roll back antidiscrimination provisions favoring homosexuals. In *Citizens for Responsible Behavior v. Superior Court,*[66] the City of Riverside, California, refused to place on the ballot a citizens' initiative that, among other things, would have created an amendment deleting from an existing ordinance a provision banning discrimination based on sexual orientation. The court held that the amendment would have the effect of promoting or encouraging private discrimination against homosexuals and was therefore unconstitutional.

An ordinance prohibiting employment discrimination based on sexual orientation also came under attack in the City of Cincinnati, Ohio. Subsequent to the passage of that ordinance, Cincinnati voters passed Article XII to amend the Cincinnati City Charter. The amendment provided in part that no special class status could be granted based on sexual orientation and that any ordinance that had been previously enacted was null and void. The desired effect of Article XII was to repeal the protections against sexual orientation discrimination in employment that were already in place and to prevent any new protection from being enacted.

A federal district court, however, granted a preliminary injunction preventing the implementation of Article XII.[67] The court relied heavily on the analysis of the Colorado Supreme Court's decision in *Evans v. Romer,*[68] and the cases cited therein, in holding that the plaintiffs had a substantial likelihood of prevailing on the merits of their claim that Article XII violated their constitutional rights to equal protection and free speech. Following a bench trial in June, the court struck down Article XII as unconstitutional and granted a permanent injunction against enforcement of the measure.[69] The Sixth Circuit Court of Appeals reversed the district court's decision and reinstated the Cincinnati charter provision, with the effect that any ordinance prohibiting discrimination based on sexual orientation is barred.[70]

Although the decision of the Sixth Circuit Court of Appeals was vacated by the U.S. Supreme Court, the Court of Appeals revisited its earlier decision after re-

63. Or. Rev. Stat. § 659.165.

64. *Sims v. Besaw's Cafe,* Ore Cir. Ct. No. 9611-08970 (Sept. 22, 1998).

65. Christopher B. Daly, "Diverse Coalition Defeats Anti-Gay Rights Measure," *Washington Post,* Nov. 9, 1995, at A28.

66. 2 Cal. Rptr. 2d 648 (1991).

67. Equality Foundation of Greater Cincinnati, Inc. v. City of Cincinnati, 838 F. Supp. 1235 (S.D. Ohio, Nov. 19, 1993).

68. 854 P.2d 1270 (Colo.), *cert. denied,* 114 S. Ct. 419 (1993).

69. Equality Foundation of Greater Cincinnati, Inc. v. City of Cincinnati, 860 F. Supp. 417 (S.D. Ohio 1994).

70. Equality Foundation v. Cincinnati, 54 F.3d 261 (6th Cir. 1995), *vacated and remanded,* 116 S.Ct. 2519 (1996) (6th Cir. 1995).

mand and, once again, upheld the Cincinnati measure.[71] Although a petition for certiorari was also filed in the United States Supreme Court after this decision, the Supreme Court denied the petition, letting stand the most recent decision by the Sixth Circuit Court of Appeals.

Although the broader issue is certainly not completely settled, the United States Supreme Court has handed down a decision upholding the invalidation of Colorado's constitutional amendment.[72] The Court rejected the contention that the amendment merely puts gays and lesbians in the same position as all other persons, finding instead that, by withdrawing from homosexuals specific legal protection from the injuries caused by discrimination, the amendment puts homosexuals in a solitary class with respect to transactions and relations in both the private and governmental spheres.[73] The Court further held that the amendment lacked a rational relationship to a legitimate state interest. First, the Court stated that the amendment "has the peculiar property of imposing a broad and undifferentiated disability on a single named group." Second, the Court found that "its sheer breadth is so discontinuous with the reasons offered for it that the amendment seems inexplicable by anything but animus toward the class that it affects."[74]

The Court's decision clearly invalidates broad legislation prohibiting the recognition of protected status for homosexuals. It does not, however, necessarily preclude more narrow legislation restricting the power of governmental entities to enact provisions prohibiting discrimination against homosexuals. Moreover, it is consistent with a body of law recognizing that, although the equal protection clause prohibits arbitrary governmental discrimination against homosexuals, it does not preclude discrimination for which a legitimate and rational governmental objective can be advanced.[75] Thus, even before the Supreme Court's decision in *Romer v. Evans, supra,* public entities were not necessarily free to discriminate against individuals because of their status as homosexuals.

71. Equality Foundation of Greater Cincinnati, Inc. v. City of Cincinnati, 1997 WL 656228 (6th Cir. 1997).

72. Romer v. Evans, 116 S. Ct. 1620 (1996).

73. Id., slip op. at 3.

74. Id. at 1627.

75. *See, e.g.,* Meinhold v. Department of Defense, 34 F.3d 1469 (9th Cir. 1994); Steffan v. Perry, 41 F.3d 677 (D.C. Cir. 1994); Ben-Shalom v. Marsh, 881 F.2d 454 (7th Cir. 1989); Padula v. Webster, 822 F.2d 97 (D.C. Cir. 1987); Shahar v. Bowers, 114 F.3d 1097 (11th Cir. 1997).

Although there is no federal statute applicable to private employers, or to state or local government employers, the Clinton administration has issued a directive applicable to federal employees mandating that sexual orientation receive the same protected status traditionally provided to classifications based on race, color, religion, sex, national origin and age.[76]

It is therefore clear that although there is no federal statute prohibiting discrimination against homosexuals, public employers must be prepared to justify adverse employment actions against homosexuals as furthering a legitimate and rational governmental interest. Furthermore, in light of the proliferation of legislation prohibiting discrimination based on sexual orientation and the Supreme Court's removal of a potential obstacle to this trend, human resources professionals for private employers would be well advised to consult the laws of each state and locality in which the employer does business in order to avoid potential liability.

### [n] English-Only Rules and National Origin Discrimination

There is obviously a relationship between language and national origin. This relationship led the Equal Employment Opportunity Commission (EEOC) to classify discrimination based on "linguistic characteristics" as unlawful under Title VII. A number of recent cases have struggled with the issue of whether workplace rules that require employees to speak only English violate laws prohibiting national origin discrimination in employment.

An English-only rule in court offices, for example, was held to violate Title VII's prohibition against national origin discrimination.[77] The court followed the EEOC's guidelines on English-only rules, holding that "no such rule will be deemed lawful unless the employer can show that it is justified by *business necessity.*"[78]

On the other hand, it has been held that the ability to communicate in English is a valid, bona fide occupational qualification (BFOQ) for a position as a clerk and that the employer could permissibly reject an applicant because his pronounced accent would materially affect the required ability to communicate with the public.[79]

76. Further Amendment to Exec. Order No. 11478 (May 28, 1998).

77. Gutierrez v. Municipal Court, 838 F.2d 1031 (9th Cir. 1988), *vacated as moot,* 490 U.S. 1016 (1989).

78. Id. at 1039 (citing 29 C.F.R. § 1606.7(b), (c) (1993) (emphasis in original).

79. Fragante v. City & County of Honolulu, 888 F.2d 591 (9th Cir. 1989).

The Equal Employment Opportunity Guidelines referred to above have, for the most part, been followed by the courts in analyzing English-only rules. The applicable EEOC guidelines are broken into three components. With respect to rules requiring employees to speak only English at all times, the guidelines provide as follows:

> A rule requiring employees to speak only English at all times in the workplace is a burdensome term and condition of employment. The primary language of an individual is often an essential national origin characteristic. Prohibiting employees at all times, in the workplace, from speaking their primary language or the language they speak most comfortably, disadvantages an individual's employment opportunities on the basis of national origin. It may also create an atmosphere of inferiority, isolation and intimidation based on national origin which could result in a discriminatory working environment. Therefore, the Commission will presume that such a rule violates title VII and will closely scrutinize it.[80]

With respect to English-only rules that are applied only at certain times, the guidelines provide that "[a]n employer may have a rule requiring that employees speak only in English at certain times where the employer can show that the rule is justified by business necessity."[81]

The guidelines note that individuals whose primary language is not English commonly revert to speaking their primary language at certain times. Therefore, the guidelines address the notice required in order to enforce an English-only rule:

> [I]f an employer believes it has a business necessity for a speak-English-only rule at certain times, the employer should inform its employees of the general circumstances when speaking only in English is required and of the consequences of violating the rule.[82]

Failure to effectively notify employees of the rule has the consequence, under the guidelines, of making any attempted enforcement of the rule "evidence of discrimination on the basis of national origin."[83]

The crux of the EEOC's position, with regard to English-only rules, is that they per se violate Title VII. In essence, a plaintiff need only prove the existence of such a rule to prevail in the absence of proof by the employer that the rule was justified by a business necessity.

Although several courts have followed the EEOC guidelines, the Ninth Circuit Court of Appeals recently rejected the EEOC's position on English-only rules. In *Garcia,* the employer had received complaints that some Hispanic workers were using their bilingual capabilities to harass and to insult other workers in a language they could not understand.[84] Specifically, the employer received complaints that two employees had made derogatory, racist comments in Spanish about two co-workers, one of whom was African-American and the other Chinese-American.

In response, the company instituted an English-only rule, contending that it would promote racial harmony. The employer also concluded that such a rule would promote worker safety in light of the fact that some employees claimed that the use of Spanish distracted them while they were operating machinery.

Accordingly, the employer adopted the following rule:

> [I]t is hereafter the policy of this Company that only English will be spoken in connection with work. During lunch, breaks, and employees' own time, they are obviously free to speak Spanish if they wish. However, we urge all of you not to use your fluency in Spanish in a fashion which may lead other employees to suffer humiliation.[85]

Two employees of the company challenged the policy, claiming that the English-only policy had a discriminatory impact on them because it imposed a burdensome term or condition of employment exclusively upon Hispanic workers and denied them a privilege of employment—speaking in their native language—that non-Spanish-speaking workers enjoyed.

The court stated, however, that Title VII does not provide a basis for imposing liability in the absence of proof of discriminatory effect. In addition, the court stated that to prevail on a claim under Title VII, the plaintiffs must prove that the adverse effect is significant. By adopting this standard in the context of an English-only rule, the court rejected the EEOC's guidelines.

In the court's view, the EEOC's guidelines impermissibly impose liability on an employer without requiring the plaintiff to present any evidence of discriminatory effect. The EEOC guidelines, the court

80. 29 C.F.R. § 1606.7(a).
81. 29 C.F.R. § 1606.7(b).
82. 29 C.F.R. § 1606.7(c).
83. Id.

84. Garcia v. Spun Steak Co., 998 F.2d 1480, *rehearing denied,* 13 F.3d 296 (9th Cir. 1993), *cert. denied,* 114 S. Ct. 2726 (1994).
85. 998 F.2d at 1483.

noted, presume that English-only policies are discriminatory without requiring any evidence to be produced regarding their effect on employees.

To meet the burden of proving that the policy had a significant adverse effect on Hispanic employees, the plaintiffs contended that the policy denied them the right to cultural expression. Noting that Title VII does not confer any substantive privileges, the court held that the employees did not have any right protected by Title VII to express their cultural heritage in the workplace. An employer retains the right to restrict certain types of self-expression, the court stated, and there is nothing in Title VII that requires an employer to allow employees to express their cultural identity.

The plaintiffs also argued that the policy deprived them of a privilege given by the employer to native English speakers: the ability to converse on the job in the language with which they feel most comfortable. Although the court recognized that the ability to converse on the job may in fact be a significant privilege of employment, it stated that the employer has the right to define the contours of such a privilege. The court further noted that "[t]he bilingual employee can readily comply with the English-only rule and still enjoy the privilege of speaking on the job."[86] Thus, the court concluded that the employer's English-only rule did not have a significant adverse effect on the plaintiffs.

A final argument advanced by the plaintiffs in *Garcia* was that the English-only policy created an atmosphere of inferiority, isolation, and intimidation. Although the court ultimately rejected this argument, it illustrates the difficulties employers face in dealing with a bilingual workforce.

That the employer has little room for error in dealing with these issues is further underscored by a recent federal case from New York. In *McNeil v. Aguilos & Bellevue Hospital Corp.,*[87] an English-speaking plaintiff brought suit alleging that Filipina-American nurses spoke Tagalog in her hospital workplace in order to isolate and harass her and that their communication in Tagalog impeded her ability to perform her job effectively. In addition to seeking damages against the employer, the plaintiff sought the institution of a policy requiring employees to speak in English while performing job duties.

As an illustration of the plaintiff's complaints regarding the use of Tagalog in the workplace, the court set out the following excerpt from local news reports:

> Juanita McNeil was checking a patient's chart in a pediatric intensive care unit when two nurses sitting at the desk next to her starting talking loudly. "Loka, Loka," the nurses said over and over.
>
> McNeil, a clerk, did not ask what they meant [thinking it to be a private conversation]. . . . the nurses left and a woman came in and asked to see her baby.
>
> "She was acting very strange, but it was her baby, so I said, 'Come on mommy, let's go see your baby,'" she said. But the woman's demeanor made McNeil go find the nurses.
>
> "They said, 'Oh, no, you didn't leave her alone with the baby, did you? We forgot to tell you, but OB/GYN just called and said she was coming down, but not to leave her alone with the baby, she's crazy.'"
>
> In Tagalog, the main language of the Philippines, "loka-loka" means crazy woman, and the nurses' phone call was a warning to watch the mother, McNeil said. (The baby was fine, after all.)[88]

Noting that the suit raised "difficult legal issues, some of first impression, all of great importance," the court refused to dismiss the plaintiff's claims in their entirety and thus allowed her to proceed on her main claim of discrimination. In its opinion, the court summarized the significance of the plaintiff's claim as follows:

> The questions in this case are troubling, and the issues and problems are likely to become more pervasive as our society grows increasingly multiracial and polyglot. There is no simple solution, for just as a workplace English-only policy potentially violates the rights of non-English speakers, plaintiff here contends that allowing co-workers to communicate in a foreign language violates her rights, as a native English speaker.[89]

Thus, for now, employers will be forced to navigate between the Scylla and Charybdis of accommodating bilingual employees while simultaneously guarding against any erosion of workplace harmony and efficiency.

---

86. Id. at 1487.

87. McNeil v. Aguilos & Bellevue Hosp. Corp., 831 F. Supp. 1079 (S.D.N.Y. 1993).

88. "Language Conflicts," in *New York Newsday,* May 19, 1993, at 15. [McNeil v. Aguilos & Bellevue Hosp. Corp., 831 F. Supp. at 1082.]

89. Id. at 1081.

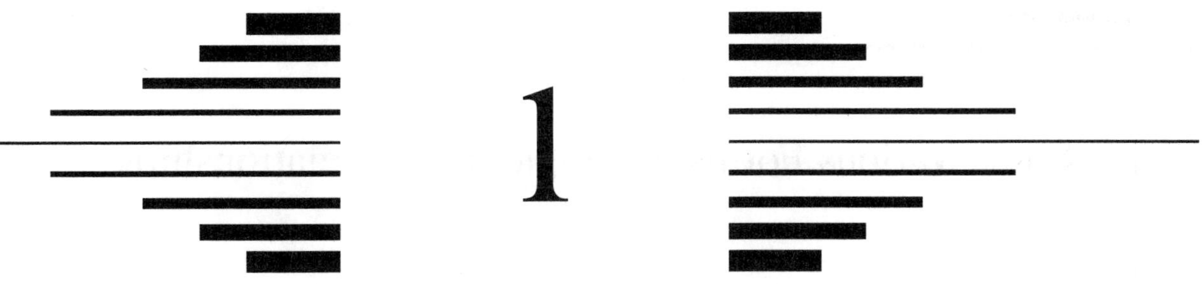

# Defining the Employment Relationship

*Part 1 covers the issues related to creating, defining, and dissolving the employment relationship.*

# § 1.1 Various Forms of Employment Relationships

Many of the statutory and common-law concepts discussed in the *State by State Guide to Human Resources Law* apply only to the employer-employee relationship. Although it is often apparent whether or not an individual is an employee, making a determination sometimes can be difficult. For example, many employers encounter considerable difficulty in determining whether individuals hired on a part-time, temporary basis are employees or independent contractors.

The existence of the employment relationship is determined from a consideration of all the surrounding facts and circumstances. No one factor is determinative in establishing the relationship. Although the employer-employee relationship is contractual, the existence of a contract in any formal sense of the term is neither required nor determinative of the relationship; however, certain elements and attributes of the relationship must be present. Furthermore, the federal government and individual states place certain restrictions on the creation of the relationship and establish limits on its contractual terms and conditions.

There are three basic types of employment relationships and worker status:

1. Employer and employee
2. Employer and independent contractor
3. Principal and agent

## [a] Employer and Employee

An employee is one who is engaged to perform certain work in a specified manner.

Among the circumstances to be considered in determining the existence of an employer-employee relationship are the following: (1) the selection and engagement of the worker; (2) the method of payment for the work; (3) the right to discharge the worker; and (4) the right to control the performance of the work.

Although no single factor is conclusive on the issue, the right to control the worker's conduct in relation to the performance of the work is the most crucial element of an employer-employee relationship. Thus, an employer-employee relationship will generally be found to exist where an employer has the right to direct the manner and means of accomplishing the work.

## [b] Employer and Independent Contractor

An independent contractor is one who contracts to do work for an employer without being subject to the control of the employer with respect to the manner in which the work is to be performed.[1]

This definition is applied in virtually every state, with only minor variations.[2] Although there is little dis-

**§ 1.1**

1. Restatement 2d, Agency § 2(3).

2. *See, e.g.,* Alp Federal Credit Union v. Ashborn, 477 P.2d 348 (Alaska 1970); Green Acres Trust v. London, 142 Ariz. 12, 688 P.2d 658 (Ariz. App. 1983); Huddleston by Huddleston v. Union Rural Elec. Ass'n, 841 P.2d 282 (Colo. 1992); Rosenblit v. Danaher, 206 Conn. 125, 537 A.2d 145 (Conn. 1988); E. I. Du Pont De Nemours & Co. v. I. D. Griffith, Inc., 11 Terry 348, 50 Del. 348, 130 A.2d 783 (Del. Supr. 1957); Dupuis v. Federal Home Loan Mortg. Corp., 879 F. Supp. 139 (D. Me. 1995); Douglas v. Pontiac General Hosp., 473 N.W.2d 68 (Mich. 1991); Union Elec. Co. v. Pacific Indem. Co., 422 S.W.2d 87 (Mo. App. 1967); Teng v. Metropolitan Retail Recovery Inc., 851 F. Supp. 61 (E.D.N.Y. 1994); Bernard Screen Printing Corp. v. Meyer Line, 328 F. Supp. 288 (S.D.N.Y. 1971), cert. denied, 410 U.S. 910

agreement on the basic definition, it is clear that no specific formulation has emerged that will govern all cases.

Other factors to be considered in determining the existence of independent contractor status are: (1) the existence of a contract between the worker and employer for a particular piece of work at a fixed price; (2) the independent nature of the worker's business; (3) the worker's obligation to furnish personnel, tools, supplies, and other necessaries for the work; and (4) the worker's right to select and supervise assistants to perform the work.

The most important element of independent contractor status is the employer's lack of power to control the performance of the work. Although an independent contractor must perform to the satisfaction of the employer by producing a specific result, he is free to use whatever methods he deems best for achieving the result.

Incorrectly classifying a worker as an independent contractor can result in the imposition of extensive damages or penalties. For example, a corporation that classified certain workers as independent contractors had them sign a form waiving rights to all benefits; however, when the IRS determined that the workers were actually employees, a court allowed the workers to sue for back benefits.[3]

### [c] Principal and Agent

A principal-agent relationship, also referred to as "an agency," exists where one individual, an agent, consents to act on behalf of another individual, a principal, in the transaction of the principal's business. The agent acts for and represents the principal pursuant to the authority vested in him by the principal. Thus, in an agency relationship, the principal always maintains a certain degree of control over the agent's conduct and activities.

It is the existence of authority in the worker which is the distinguishing factor between an agency and an employer-employee relationship. In an agency relationship, the agent is generally authorized to make contracts with third persons on behalf of the principal and to otherwise represent the principal in the principal's business dealings. An employee, by definition, does not possess this kind of authority.

The distinction between an agent and independent contractor can be difficult to determine; however, many cases point to the principal's right of control over the agent's conduct and activities as the distinguishing feature. An agent is said to be subject to his principal's control with respect to the manner of his performance; whereas, an independent contractor is merely subject to his employer's control with respect to the result, not the manner, of his performance.

For employers doing business in more than one state, the difficulties are compounded. Not only must an employer seek to comply with the many federal statutes and decisions affecting its day-to-day operations, but it must seek to comply with the statutes in the various states as well. Where the state laws are similar or consistent, this poses few problems. But where the laws diverge, and they often differ quite markedly, the task of achieving compliance becomes quite daunting. The greater the number of states in which a business operates, the more difficult the task is; challenges seem to grow geometrically.

Even for an employer that operates within a single state, the problems associated with managing the personnel function often involve addressing conflicts between federal and state requirements.

---

(1973); Lane-Hill v. Ruth, 910 P.2d 360 (Okla. App. 1995); McDermott v. Goodman, 1985 WL 15437, 1985-2 Trade Cases ¶ 66,728 (Pa. Com. Pl. 1985); Haufle v. Svoboda, 416 N.W.2d 879 (S.D. 1987); Maryland Ins. Co. v. Head Indus. Coatings and Services, Inc., 938 S.W.2d 27 (Tex. 1996); Breslauer v. Fayston School Dist., 659 A.2d 1129, 101 Ed. Law Rep. 306 (Vt. 1995); Schleit v. Warren, 693 F. Supp. 416 (E.D. Va. 1988); Freeman v. Navarre, 47 Wash. 2d 760, 289 P.2d 1015 (Wash. 1955); Select Creations, Inc. v. Paliafito America, Inc., 911 F. Supp. 1130 (D. Wis. 1995)

3. Vizcaino v. Microsoft Corp., 97 F.3d 1187 (9th Cir. 1996).

# § 1.2 Offer and Acceptance of Employment

## [a] In General

The relationship between employer and employee is a contractual one and similar to other contractual relationships in its formation. The employment contract, however, need not be a formal, written contract. The essence of an employment contract is the agreement of one party to render services or labor for the benefit of another, in exchange for payment or something else of value.

## [b] Form

Except as may be required by a state's statute of frauds, discussed below, at § 1.3[d], the form of an employment contract is not specified. Contracts for employment may be either written or oral, express or implied, bilateral or unilateral, and may be demonstrated by circumstantial as well as direct evidence.

Like any other contract, a contract for employment arises out of a meeting of the minds of the parties, with an offer on the part of one and an acceptance by the other, involving the exchange of something of value. The agreement must be mutual, as no contract for employment can arise against the will or without the consent of one of the parties.

An offer may be either written or oral[1] and can be communicated in a variety of ways, including by letter, facsimile, telephone, or employment manual.[2] (See § 1.3[c] for a discussion of employee manuals.) An offer of employment may also be implied by an employer's conduct.[3] Normally there must be some certainty as to the nature and extent of the employment, location of employment, and compensation.

Acceptance of the relationship may also be written or oral, and it need not be made in the same form as the offer. Often the acceptance will be found in the surrounding circumstances and the parties' affirmative actions manifesting an intent to be bound by the terms of the offer. It should be noted, however, that a potential employee who attempts to change the terms of the offer presents a counteroffer, not an acceptance.

## [c] Relationship in Absence of Contract

If there is no contract for employment, the relationship is usually considered to be terminable at the will of either party. In a so-called "at-will" relationship, either party may terminate the relationship for any reason, or for no reason at all. Thus, although an employment relationship may exist in the absence of a contract, the relationship may be ended by either party at any time.

To alter the at-will employment relationship, the parties must have stated clearly their intentions to limit the employer's right to terminate the relationship.[4] In this regard, a contract for employment that does not state a duration creates only an at-will relationship.[5]

---

**§ 1.2**

1. Rowe v. Noren Pattern & Foundry Co., 91 Mich. App. 254, 283 N.W.2d 713 (1979) (oral contract).

2. Rand v. CF Industries, Inc., 797 F. Supp. 643 (N.D. Ill. 1992) (employee handbook).

3. Coto v. Anipecu, Inc., 371 So. 2d 183 (Fla. App. 1979) (relationship may arise from conduct of employer).

4. Perkins v. District Gov't Employees Fed. Credit Union, 653 A.2d 842 (D.C. 1995); Littell v. Evening Star Newspaper Co., 120 F.2d 36, 37 (D.C. Cir. 1941).

5. Wheeling v. Ring Radio Co., 213 Ga. App. 210, 444 S.E.2d 144 (1994); Wiggins v. District Cablevision, Inc., 853 F. Supp. 484 (D.D.C. 1994).

### [d] Preemployment Inquiries

Employers are required to conduct the applicant screening process in a nondiscriminatory manner. Therefore, some states have placed restrictions on the types of questions that can be asked of applicants during an interview or other prehire information gathering process.

A preemployment inquiry can be any question asked of a job applicant, whether in an employment application, a preemployment interview, or in other areas of interaction between the employer and potential employee. Because preemployment inquiries can potentially give rise to a claim of job discrimination, an employer should be wary of problem questions that address issues of sex, race, citizenship, religious affiliation, disability, age, or other protected characteristics. Generally, an employer should limit itself to inquiries seeking information necessary to evaluate an applicant's ability to perform the requirements of the position.

*Federal Fair Employment Laws.* According to Guidelines issued by the EEOC, preemployment inquiries that express any limitation, specification, or discrimination as to sex are unlawful unless based on a bona fide occupational qualification;[6] however, these Guidelines do allow the employer to ask on its application whether the applicant is male or female and whether the applicant prefers to be known as "Mr., Mrs., or Ms."[7] Similarly, questions relating to family circumstances, such as child care or conflicts between job and family responsibilities are questionable, if not per se evidence of discriminatory intent.[8]

The EEOC Guidelines on religion also restrict preemployment inquiries regarding availability to work during the employer's scheduled working hours.[9] Such inquiries are permissible only if the employer shows that these inquiries do not have an adverse or exclusionary impact or that they are justified by business necessity.

With respect to questions about age, the EEOC Guidelines state that requests for information about date of birth or age are not, in themselves, violative of federal prohibitions on age discrimination.[10] The Guidelines state, however, that applications containing such inquiries will be closely scrutinized. The Guidelines further state that any such inquiries should be accompanied by a statement referring to the Age Discrimination in Employment Act, designed to convey to the applicant that the purpose of the inquiry is not one proscribed by the statute.

The EEOC Guidelines on national origin discrimination contain specific provisions regarding the use of selection criteria involving fluency in English, training and education, and height and weight requirements.[11] The Immigration Reform and Control Act also prohibits discrimination based on citizenship and states that employers cannot request more or different documents than are needed to comply with that Act.[12]

Under the Americans With Disabilities Act (ADA), employers are specifically prohibited from making preemployment inquiries into the existence, nature, or severity of an applicant's disabilities before the employer has extended a conditional offer of employment.[13] An inquiry is not unlawful merely because the applicant may volunteer information about a disability in his or her response, but inquiries that are likely to elicit information about a disability are prohibited. Certain preemployment disability-related inquiries are also prohibited under Sections 503 (applicable to government contractors) and 504 (applicable to recipients of federal financial assistance) of the Rehabilitation Act of 1970.[14] The regulations promulgated under Section 504 have been interpreted to bar any inquiry concerning past or present mental or physical conditions that do not have direct bearing on the applicant's current ability to perform the job.[15]

*Advertisements.* Advertisements for a position may also involve discrimination issues. Title VII prohibits an employer from publishing an employment advertisement that expresses a preference for applicants based on

6. 29 C.F.R. § 1604.7.

7. Id.

8. *Cf.* Bruno v. Crown Point, 950 F.2d 355 (7th Cir. 1991), cert. denied, 112 S.Ct. 2998 (1992) (rejecting sex discrimination claim), with Barbano v. Madison County, 47 BNA FEP Cas. 1872 (N.D.N.Y.), *aff'd,* 922 F.2d 139 (2d Cir. 1988) (employer's questions about family plans were evidence of sex discrimination).

9. 29 C.F.R. § 1605.3.

10. 29 C.F.R. § 1625.5.

11. 29 C.F.R. § 1606.6.

12. 8 U.S.C. § 1324b(a)(6).

13. 42 U.S.C. §12112(d)(2)(A).

14. For further discussion of the Rehabilitation Act of 1973, see § 9.2[i].

15. Doe v. Syracuse School Dist., 508 F. Supp. 333, 25 FEP Cases 534, 25 Empl. Prac. Dec. ¶ 31, 696 (N.D.N.Y. 1981) (Department of Health, Education, and Welfare regulations were violated by inquiring whether applicant for teaching position has ever experienced migraine, neuralgia, nervous breakdown, or psychiatric treatment, since a history of such a condition is not an indicator of fitness to teach; a proper inquiry would have been whether the applicant was capable of dealing with various emotionally demanding situations).

race, color, religion, sex, or national origin, unless a bona fide occupational qualification exists for the position.[16] The Age Discrimination in Employment Act (ADEA) also prohibits age discrimination in advertisements for employment.[17]

*Exceptions.* The EEOC, as well as state agencies charged with enforcing fair employment laws, recognizes that there are exceptions to the policy of discouraging preemployment inquiries that solicit information on an applicant's protected status. One such exception is for a bona fide occupational qualification (BFOQ). Essentially, a BFOQ is a condition required for the performance of a job and is necessary to the normal operation of a business. For example, a stage or television production company may inquire into an applicant's sex for a particular male or female role in a play or television show. The EEOC and state definitions of BFOQs and business necessities are usually extremely narrow and sometimes require advance written certification from the agency.

16. 42 U.S.C. § 2000e-3(b).

17. 29 U.S.C. § 623(e).

Another exception is granted to employers who ask otherwise unlawful questions pursuant to an affirmative action plan or the directives of the EEOC or any other state agency that administers fair employment laws. For example, an employer may inquire into an applicant's race, sex, disability, or other protected class in order to properly comply with EEOC orders on hiring. An employer may also ask such questions to properly record applicants' membership in protected classes and to ensure balanced workforce hiring.

*State Guidelines.* Many states have created their own guides on permitted and prohibited inquiries. Many of these state guides are based in large part on the EEOC Guide, published in 1981, and the EEOC Guidelines. These state guides are therefore, not surprisingly, very similar in regard to what is permitted and what is prohibited in relation to common preemployment inquiries. Of course, in those states that have preemployment guidelines, the specific provisions may vary from one state to another. Exhibit 1.2-1 sets out the general subjects addressed by regulations or guidelines relating to preemployment inquiries. Exhibit 1.2-2 sets out specific state statutory provisions addressing preemployment inquiries.

# Exhibit 1.2-1

## SUBJECTS COMMONLY COVERED BY STATUTES AND REGULATIONS GOVERNING PREEMPLOYMENT INQUIRIES

*Note: This exhibit is* not *exhaustive but rather is representative of the types of inquiries that are permitted or prohibited before hiring. Specific provisions may vary.*

**These inquiries are unlawful unless made pursuant to a BFOQ or other recognized exception (see text at main volume, § 2.2).*

**Subject of Inquiry.** NAME

**Lawful Inquiries.** Name. Previous name (for purposes of checking past work record).

**Unlawful Inquiries.*** Inquiry into name or title that indicates race, religion, ancestry, national origin, marital status (e.g., Mr., Mrs., Miss, or Ms.).

**Subject of Inquiry.** ADDRESS OR DURATION OF RESIDENCE

**Lawful Inquiries.** Inquiry into place and length of current or previous address.

**Unlawful Inquiries.*** Specific inquiry into foreign addresses which would indicate national origin.

**Subject of Inquiry.** BIRTHPLACE, ANCESTRY, OR NATIONAL ORIGIN

**Lawful Inquiries.** Languages applicant reads, speaks, or writes fluently.

**Unlawful Inquiries.*** Birthplace of applicant, his or her parents, spouse, or other relatives; direct inquiry into national origin or ancestry of applicant or relatives; language commonly spoken by applicant; how applicant acquired any foreign language ability.

**Subject of Inquiry.** AGE

**Lawful Inquiries.** Inquiry into whether or not the applicant meets the minimum age requirement set by law; requirement of proof of age by birth certificate after hiring.

**Unlawful Inquiries.*** Direct inquiry into applicant's age or date of birth; requirement of a birth certificate or baptismal record before hiring; use of phrases indicating age preference, such as "young," "girl," "boy," "college student," "retired person," etc.

**Subject of Inquiry.** RACE OR COLOR

**Lawful Inquiries.** N/A

**Unlawful Inquiries.*** Applicant's race, or color of his or her skin, hair, eyes, etc.; any inquiry indirectly indicating race or color.

**Subject of Inquiry.** RELIGION

**Lawful Inquiries.** An applicant may be advised concerning normal hours and days of work (e.g., "Apart from absences for religious observances, will you be available for work at the following times . . . ?"); post-hire religious accommodation inquiries are appropriate.

**Unlawful Inquiries.*** Inquiry into applicant's religious affiliation, church, pastor, or any religious holidays observed; applicant may not be told of any religious identity or preference of the employer, nor requested to provide a pastor's recommendation.

**Subject of Inquiry.** DISABILITY

**Lawful Inquiries.** Inquiry into any physical or mental impairment that may interfere with applicant's ability to perform essential tasks of the job.

**Unlawful Inquiries.*** Any inquiry into past or current medical conditions not related to the position applied for; whether applicant has a physical or mental impairment or disability; any inquiry into prior on-the-job injuries or workers' compensation claims.

**Subject of Inquiry.** SEX

**Lawful Inquiries.** Inquiries required by "business necessity."

[Note: The United States Equal Employment Opportunity Commission's Guidelines on sex state that "[a] pre-employment inquiry may ask 'Male . . . ., Female . . . .'; or 'Mr. Mrs. Miss,' provided that the inquiry is made in good faith for a nondiscriminatory purpose." 29 C.F.R. § 1604.7 (1994).]

**Unlawful Inquiries.*** Inquiry that would indicate applicant's sex; any inquiry made of one sex but not another (e.g., "Are you expecting?" "Are you pregnant?").

[Note: The United States Equal Employment Opportunity Commission's Guidelines on sex state that "[a]ny preemployment inquiry in connection with prospective employment which expresses directly or indirectly any limitation, specification, or discrimination as to sex shall be unlawful unless based upon a bona fide occupational qualification" 29 C.F.R. § 1604.7.]

**Subject of Inquiry.** CITIZENSHIP

**Lawful Inquiries.** Whether applicant is, or intends to become, a United States citizen; whether applicant is a legal United States resident; any inquiry required by the Federal Immigration Reform and Control Act of 1986, as amended.

**Unlawful Inquiries.*** Whether applicant is a native-born or naturalized citizen; whether parents or spouse are native born or naturalized; when applicant became a citizen; proof of citizenship or naturalization before hiring.

**Subject of Inquiry.** HEIGHT AND WEIGHT

**Lawful Inquiries.** Inquiries into abilities to perform actual job requirements.

**Unlawful Inquiries.*** Unless employer can demonstrate that employee of a certain height or weight cannot perform tasks of the job, such inquiries are prohibited.

**Subject of Inquiry.** PHOTOGRAPH

**Lawful Inquiries.** May be required after hiring for identification.

**Unlawful Inquiries.*** Require or request a photograph before hiring.

**Subject of Inquiry.** EDUCATION

**Lawful Inquiries.** Inquiry into applicant's academic, vocational, or professional education and schools attended.

**Unlawful Inquiries.*** Specific inquiries into the nationality, racial, or religious affiliation of the school; dates of attendance and/or graduation from school.

**Subject of Inquiry.** RELATIVES/EMERGENCY NOTIFICATION

**Lawful Inquiries.** Inquiry into name and address of person to be notified in an emergency; name of applicant's relatives who work for the employer (if any); names and addresses of guardians of a minor applicant.

**Unlawful Inquiries.*** Relationship of person to be notified in an emergency; names and addresses of any relative of an adult applicant; any inquiry about a relative which would be unlawful if it were asked of the applicant.

**Subject of Inquiry.** ARRESTS AND CONVICTIONS

**Lawful Inquiries.** Inquiry into specific *convictions* of crimes related to qualifications of the job.

**Unlawful Inquiries.*** Any inquiry that would reveal arrests without convictions.

**Subject of Inquiry.** ORGANIZATIONS

**Lawful Inquiries.** Inquiry into membership and offices held in organizations, excluding any organization the name or character of which reveals race, color, religion, sex, national origin, disability, age, or ancestry of its members.

**Unlawful Inquiries.*** Inquiry into every club or organization of which the applicant is a member.

**Subject of Inquiry.** REFERENCES

**Lawful Inquiries.** Names of persons willing to provide personal or professional references for applicant; inquiry into who referred the applicant to the position.

**Unlawful Inquiries.*** Specific request of a religious reference or a reference from any other person which might reflect race, religion, color, sex, national origin, age, or disability of applicant.

**Subject of Inquiry.** MILITARY SERVICE

**Lawful Inquiries.** Inquiry into service in the United States Armed Forces; requirement of a military discharge certificate after hiring.

**Unlawful Inquiries.*** Inquiry into military service for countries other than United States; request of service records; inquiry into type of discharge.

**Subject of Inquiry.** MARITAL STATUS

**Lawful Inquiries.** N/A

**Unlawful Inquiries.*** Whether single, married, divorced, separated, etc.; names and ages of spouse and children; spouse's place of employment.

**Subject of Inquiry.** WORK SCHEDULE

**Lawful Inquiries.** Inquiry into willingness to work required work schedule.

**Unlawful Inquiries.*** Inquiry into ability or willingness to work any particular religious holiday.

**Subject of Inquiry.** ECONOMIC STATUS

**Lawful Inquiries.** N/A

**Unlawful Inquiries.*** Questions regarding applicant's current or past assets, liabilities, or credit rating, including bankruptcy or garnishment.

**Subject of Inquiry.** MISCELLANEOUS

**Lawful Inquiries.** Any question that reveals qualifications for the job applied for; notice to applicants that misstatements or omissions of material facts in the prehire process may be cause for dismissal.

**Unlawful Inquiries.*** Request or requirement of a resume containing any information about which it is unlawful to inquire; any non-job-related inquiry that may elicit information concerning applicant's membership in a "protected class."

# Exhibit 1.2-2

## SPECIFIC STATE STATUTORY PROVISIONS ADDRESSING PREEMPLOYMENT INQUIRIES

***Note:*** *This exhibit addresses only state statutes relating to preemployment inquiries; regulations promulgated by state fair employment practices or agencies may also apply, and federal law may impose stricter standards.*

### ALABAMA

**Covered Entities.** No provision.

**Prohibited Inquiries.** No provision.

**Prohibited Advertisements.** No provision.

**Exceptions.** No provision.

**Additional Provisions.** None.

**Citations to Authority.** None.

### ALASKA

**Covered Entities.** Employers, employment agencies, and other persons.

**Prohibited Inquiries.** Any application or inquiry in connection with prospective employment expressing a discriminatory limitation, or intent to make the limitation, based on sex, physical or mental disability, marital status, pregnancy, parenthood, age, race, creed, color, or national origin.

**Prohibited Advertisements.** Printing, publishing, broadcasting, or otherwise circulating a statement, advertisement, or publication expressing such a discriminatory limitation.

**Exceptions.** Such limitation can be expressed if justified by BFOQ.

**Additional Provisions.** None.

**Citations to Authority.** Alaska Stat. §§ 18.80.220(a)(3), 18.80.220(a)(6).

### ARIZONA

**Covered Entities.** Employers, employment agencies, labor organizations, and joint labor-management committees.

**Prohibited Inquiries.** Employer may not discriminate on the basis of race, color, religion, sex, age, or national origin.

**Prohibited Advertisements.** Printing or publishing any employment-related notice or advertisement expressing a preference, limitation, specification, or discrimination based on protected classification.

**Exceptions.** Limitation can be expressed with respect to religion, sex, age, or national origin if justified by BFOQ.

**Additional Provisions.** None.

**Citations to Authority.** Ariz. Rev. Stat. Ann. §§ 41-1464(B), 41-1464(C).

### ARKANSAS

**Covered Entities.** Employers.

**Prohibited Inquiries.** The Civil Rights Act provides that an otherwise qualified person has the right to obtain and hold employment without discrimination on the basis of race, religion, ancestry, national origin, gender, or the presence of any sensory, mental, or physical disability.

**Prohibited Advertisements.** No provision.

**Exceptions.** None.

**Additional Provisions.** None.

**Citations to Authority.** Ark. Code Ann. § 16-123-105.

**CALIFORNIA**

**Covered Entities.** Employers and employment agencies.

**Prohibited Inquiries.** Employers may not make non-job-related inquiry, verbally or through application form, expressing any limitation, specification, or discrimination as to race, religion, color, national origin, ancestry, physical or mental disability, medical condition, marital status, or sex.

**Prohibited Advertisements.** Printing or circulating a publication expressing such a limitation.

**Exceptions.** Employers may, if related to business needs and not a pretext for discrimination, ask about an applicant's availability for weekend and evening work, an applicant's age for recordkeeping purposes, the physical fitness, medical condition, physical condition, or medical history of an applicant, if such information is directly related and pertinent to the position or determination of whether the applicant would endanger his own health and safety or the health and safety of others, the physical fitness or medical condition of an applicant if in compliance with the Americans With Disabilities Act, and an applicant's use of other names or an applicant's spouse's names.

**Additional Provisions.** Employers may not inquire about arrests or detentions that have not resulted in convictions for which the record has been sealed or eradicated, misdemeanor convictions for which probation has been completed or discharged, or arrests for which pretrial diversion programs have been completed.

**Citations to Authority.** Cal. Gov't Code § 12940(d); 2 Cal. AC Div. 4 §§ 7287.4(d)(1), 7292.4(b), 7292.4(c), 7293.4, 7295.5(a).

**COLORADO**

**Covered Entities.** Employers and other covered entities.

**Prohibited Inquiries.** Prohibits use of an application form or other inquiry connected with prospective employment expressing a limitation, specification, or discrimination on the basis of disability, race or color, creed, sex, age, national origin, or ancestry.

**Prohibited Advertisements.** Printing or circulating any statement, advertisement, or publication expressing such a limitation.

**Exceptions.** Inquiry permitted if based upon a BFOQ or if required by and given to a government agency for security reasons.

**Additional Provisions.** None.

**Citations to Authority.** Colo. Rev. Stat. §§ 24-34-402(1)(d), 24-34-402(1)(f)(III).

**CONNECTICUT**

**Covered Entities.** Person, employer, employment agency, or labor organization.

**Prohibited Inquiries.** Requesting or requiring information relating to a job applicant's child-bearing age or plans, pregnancy, function of the individual's reproductive system, use of birth control methods, or the individual's familial responsibilities.

**Prohibited Advertisements.** Advertising employment opportunities in a manner that restricts employment so as to discriminate against individuals because of their race, color, religious creed, age, sex, marital status, national origin, ancestry, sexual orientation, or present or past history of mental disorder, mental retardation, learning disability, or physical disability.

**Exceptions.** Inquiry permissible if justified by BFOQ; the employer, through a physician, may request such information as is directly related to workplace exposure to substances that may cause birth defects or constitute a hazard to a person's reproductive system or fetus.

**Additional Provisions.** None.

**Citations to Authority.** Conn. Gen. Stat. Ann. §§ 46a-60(6), 46a-60(9), 46a-81c.

**DELAWARE**

**Covered Entities.** Employers.

**Prohibited Inquiries.** None.

**Prohibited Advertisements.** None.

**Exceptions.** None.

**Additional Provisions.** Under the Delaware Handicapped Persons Employment Protections Act, employers are forbidden from requiring applicants to identify themselves as disabled before a conditional offer of employment, unless inquiries are made for affirmative action purposes or are directly related to essential job functions. Employers are also limited in their use of employment tests that tend to screen out persons with disabilities.

**Citations to Authority.** Del. Code Ann. tit. 19, §§ 711(a)(1), 724(a)(1), 724(a)(4), 724(e)(1), 724(f)(2).

**DISTRICT OF COLUMBIA**

**Covered Entities.** Employers.

**Prohibited Inquiries.** Use of any publication form relating to employment that indicates any preference, limitation, specification, or distinction based on race, color, religion, national origin, sex, age, marital status, personal appearance, sexual orientation, family responsibilities, matriculation, physical and mental disability, or political affiliation.

**Prohibited Advertisements.** Printing or publishing any notice or advertisement expressing such a limitation.

**Exceptions.** None.

**Additional Provisions.** None.

**Citations to Authority.** D.C. Code Ann. § 1-2512(a)(4)(B). As interpreted by the D.C. Office of Human Resources.

### FLORIDA

**Covered Entities.** Employers, labor organizations, employment agencies, and joint labor-management committees.

**Prohibited Inquiries.** None specified.

**Prohibited Advertisements.** Printing or publishing a notice or advertisement relating to employment, membership, classification, referral for employment or apprenticeship or other training indicating a preference, limitation, specification, or discrimination based on race, color, religion, sex, national origin, age, absence of disability, or marital status.

**Exceptions.** None stated.

**Additional Provisions.** None.

**Citations to Authority.** Fla. Stat. Ann. § 760.10(6).

### GEORGIA

**Covered Entities.** Employers.

**Prohibited Inquiries.** None stated.

**Prohibited Advertisements.** No statutory requirements.

**Exceptions.** An employer may make a job-related inquiry concerning the existence of an applicant's disability and the extent to which the disability has been overcome by treatment, medication, appliances, or other rehabilitation.

**Additional Provisions.** None.

**Citations to Authority.** Ga. Code Ann. § 34-6A-3(a).

### HAWAII

**Covered Entities.** Employers, employment agencies, labor organizations.

**Prohibited Inquiries.** Use of an employment application form, or a preemployment inquiry, that expresses any limitation, specification, or discrimination as to race, sex, sexual orientation, age, religion, color, ancestry, disability, marital status, or arrest or court record; assignment of income for child support or National Guard participation; or any inquiry that results in disproportionate screening-out of members of protected groups or that is not relevant to successful job performance.

**Prohibited Advertisements.** Printing or circulating a statement, advertisement, or publication expressing such a limitation.

**Exceptions.** An employer may inquire whether an applicant meets the statutory age requirements or has used another name, so as to check the applicant's work history, or may ask about the applicant's availability for work, if justified by business necessity. The state, a country, a private school, the board of directors of an association of apartment owners, or the manager of a condominium project may check records of conviction and related arrests. Financial institutions insured by a federal agency may consider criminal convictions involving dishonesty or breach of trust. Employers may inquire about age, ancestry, sex, or marital status, if justified as a BFOQ.

**Additional Provisions.** None.

**Citations to Authority.** Haw. Rev. Stat. Ann. § 378-2(1)(C); Haw. AR §§ 12-46-133(d)(1), 12-46-123(c), 12-46-152(b). As interpreted by the Hawaii Civil Rights Commission.

### IDAHO

**Covered Entities.** Employers.

**Prohibited Inquiries.** No provision.

**Prohibited Advertisements.** Printing or publishing a notice or advertisement relating to employment that indicates a preference, limitation, specification, or discrimination on the basis of race, color, religion, sex, national origin, age, or disability.

**Exceptions.** Prohibition against disability discrimination does not apply if the particular disability, even with a reasonable accommodation by the employer, prevents the performance of the work required by the employer.

**Additional Provisions.** None.

**Citations to Authority.** Idaho Code §§ 67-5909, 67-5909(4).

### ILLINOIS

**Covered Entities.** Employers.

**Prohibited Inquiries.** Inquiries as to whether an applicant has ever been arrested; also prohibits requiring applicants to disclose their national origin, ancestry, citizenship, parental status, or to list all of their conditions.

**Prohibited Advertisements.** No provision.

**Exceptions.** All employers may utilize conviction information; and applicants may be required to list physical and mental conditions that may impair their ability to perform the particular duties of the job.

**Additional Provisions.** Preemployment inquiries of prospective employees or their former employers concerning their previous claims and benefits under workers' compensation or occupational disease acts are prohibited.

**Citations to Authority.** 820 Ill. Comp. Stat. Ann. § 55/10, 775 Ill. Comp. Stat. Ann. § 5/2-101–105; Ill. Admin. Code tit. 56, §§ 2500.60(a), 5220.500, as interpreted by the Illinois Human Rights Commission.

**INDIANA**

**Covered Entities.** Employers.

**Prohibited Inquiries.** Preemployment inquiries concerning whether an applicant is disabled or the nature or severity of a disability.

**Prohibited Advertisements.** No provision.

**Exceptions.** Employer may make preemployment inquiries into the ability of an applicant to perform job-related functions.

**Additional Provisions.** None.

**Citations to Authority.** Ind. Code Ann. §§ 22-9-5-20(a), 22-9-5-20(b).

**IOWA**

**Covered Entities.** No provision.

**Prohibited Inquiries.** Iowa does not have any laws or regulations that specifically regulate or prohibit preemployment inquiries or advertisements. However, if an employer asks an applicant any questions concerning age, color, creed, national origin, disability, race, religion, sex, parental status, or retaliation (whether the applicant previously filed a Civil Rights complaint, witnessed a Civil Rights proceeding, or complained about discriminatory circumstances in the workplace) and subsequently declines to offer the applicant the position, the employer may be in violation of Iowa's civil rights laws and regulations. The applicant may file a complaint with the Iowa Civil Rights Commission if the applicant believes that he or she was not offered a job due to the answer given to any of these questions or due to his or her status with respect to any limitation.

**Prohibited Advertisements.** Employers are prohibited from publishing advertisements expressing such discriminatory limitation, unless the limitation is justified by a BFOQ.

**Exceptions.** No provision.

**Additional Provisions.** None.

**Citations to Authority.** None. As enforced by the Iowa Civil Rights Commission.

**KANSAS**

**Covered Entities.** Employers.

**Prohibited Inquiries.** Using any employment application form or making any inquiry in connection with prospective employment that expresses any limitation, specification, or discrimination as to race, religion, color, sex, physical disability, national origin, or ancestry.

**Prohibited Advertisements.** Employers may not print or circulate any statement, advertisement, or publication expressing such limitations.

**Exceptions.** Permissible if justified by BFOQ.

**Additional Provisions.** None.

**Citations to Authority.** Kan. Stat. Ann. § 44-1009(a)(3).

**KENTUCKY**

**Covered Entities.** Employers.

**Prohibited Inquiries.** No provision.

**Prohibited Advertisements.** Printing or publishing a notice or advertisement relating to employment that indicates a preference, limitation, specification, or discrimination based on race, color, religion, national origin, sex, or age.

**Exceptions.** With respect to religion, national origin, sex, or age, notices or advertisements acceptable if justified by BFOQ; permits preemployment inquiries about the existence of applicants' disabilities and about the extent to which the disabilities have been overcome by treatment, medication, or other rehabilitation.

**Additional Provisions.** None.

**Citations to Authority.** Ky. Rev. Stat. Ann. §§ 207.140(1), 344.010(4), 344.080.

**LOUISIANA**

**Covered Entities.** Employers, labor organizations, and employment agencies.

**Prohibited Inquiries.** Written or oral inquiries or use of application forms that request information about applicants' disabilities, or that express preferences or limitations with regard to disabilities, for discriminatory purposes.

**Prohibited Advertisements.** Printing, publishing, or circulating any statement, advertisement, or publication relating to employment that indicates any preference, limitation, specification, or discrimination based on race, creed, color, religion, sex, age, or national origin.

**Exceptions.** With respect to religion, sex, or age, advertisements acceptable if justified by BFOQ.

**Additional Provisions.** It is unlawful to fail or refuse to hire otherwise qualified individuals on the basis of preemployment interviews that are not directly related to the actual requirements of specific jobs.

**Citations to Authority.** La. Rev. Stat. Ann. §§ 301–354.

## MAINE

**Covered Entities.** Employers.

**Prohibited Inquiries.** Before employment, employer may not elicit, or use an application form containing questions eliciting, any information regarding race or color, sex, physical or mental disability, religion, age, ancestry, national origin, having filed a workers' compensation claim, or having engaged in protected activity under state whistle-blower statute.

**Prohibited Advertisements.** Printing or publishing a notice or advertisement relating to employment that indicates a preference, limitation, specification, or discrimination based on race or color, sex, physical or mental disability, religion, age, ancestry or national origin, having filed a workers' compensation claim, or having engaged in protected activity under the state whistle-blower statute.

**Exceptions.** Employer may ask whether applicant can perform the job with or without reasonable accommodation.

**Additional Provisions.** Employers may not use any employment agency that the employer knows or has reasonable cause to know discriminates against individuals based on the protected factors.

**Citations to Authority.** Me. Rev. Stat. Ann. tit. 5, §§ 4551, 4572.1(A), 4572.1(D)(1), 4572.1(D)(3), 4572.1(D)(4); Me. RR § 3.08(E)(2). As interpreted by the Maine Human Rights Commission.

## MARYLAND

**Covered Entities.** Employers, labor organizations, and employment agencies.

**Prohibited Inquiries.** Written or oral questions pertaining to a physical, psychological, or psychiatric illness, disability, or treatment that does not bear a direct, material, and timely relationship to the applicant's fitness or capacity properly to perform the activities or responsibilities of the desired position.

**Prohibited Advertisements.** Printing or publishing a notice or advertisement relating to employment if it indicates any preference, limitation, specification, or discrimination based on race, color, religion, sex, age, national origin, or physical or mental qualification.

**Exceptions.** Notices and advertisements acceptable, with respect to religion, sex, age, national origin, or physical or mental qualification, if justified by BFOQ.

**Additional Provisions.** None.

**Citations to Authority.** Md. Ann. Code of 1957 Art. 49B § 16(e); Md. Code Ann., Labor & Emp. § 3-701(b).

## MASSACHUSETTS

**Covered Entities.** Employers with more than 6 employees.

**Prohibited Inquiries.** Use of employment applications or preemployment inquiries concerning race, color, religion, national origin, sex, sexual orientation, age (over 40), ancestry, criminal record, or maternity, and whether the applicant is a disabled individual, or the nature and severity of the disability.

**Prohibited Advertisements.** Printing or circulating a statement, advertisement, or publication that expresses any limitation, specification, or discrimination as to race, color, religion, national origin, sex, sexual orientation, age, ancestry, disability, criminal record, or maternity.

**Exceptions.** Inquiries acceptable if justified by BFOQ or if in connection with affirmative action efforts. Employer may invite voluntary disclosure of disability. Inquiries concerning felony convictions are also permitted.

**Additional Provisions.** Applicant may be questioned as to citizenship, education, work experience, or character, and relatives who are to be notified in case of an accident.

**Citations to Authority.** Mass. Gen. Laws Ann. ch. 151B §§ 4.3, 4.16; Mass. Regs. Code §§ 3.01 *et seq.*

## MICHIGAN

**Covered Entities.** Employers, labor organizations, and employment agencies.

**Prohibited Inquiries.** Making a written or oral inquiry or use of an application form that elicits information or expresses preferences concerning the religion, race, color, national origin, age, sex, height, weight, disability, or marital status of a prospective employee.

**Prohibited Advertisements.** Printing, circulating, posting, or mailing a statement, advertisement, notice, or sign that indicates a preference, limitation, or specification based on religion, race, color, national origin, age, sex, height, weight, disability, or marital status.

**Exceptions.** Inquiries concerning arrest records are permitted.

**Additional Provisions.** None.

**Citations to Authority.** Mich. Comp. Laws Ann. §§ 37.1206(1), 37.1206(2)(a), 37.1206(2)(c), 37.2206(1), 37.2206(2)(a), 37.2206(2)(c).

**MINNESOTA**

**Covered Entities.** Employers.

**Prohibited Inquiries.** Requiring a job applicant to furnish information regarding race, color, creed, religion, national origin, sex, marital status, status with regard to public assistance, disability, sexual orientation, or age.

**Prohibited Advertisements.** Printing or publishing a notice or advertisement relating to employment that discloses a preference, limitation, specification, or discrimination based on race, color, creed, religion, national origin, sex, sexual orientation, marital status, or status with regard to public assistance, disability, or age.

**Exceptions.** Inquiries acceptable if justified by BFOQ; questions eliciting national origin are permitted if required by the federal government, the state or political subdivision for security reasons; information on any of the protected characteristics may be obtained to comply with state law regulating public contracts or a federal or state law or regulation.

**Additional Provisions.** None.

**Citations to Authority.** Minn. Stat. Ann. §§ 363.03.1(4)(a), 363.03.1(4)(c).

**MISSISSIPPI**

**Covered Entities.** No provision.

**Prohibited Inquiries.** No provision.

**Prohibited Advertisements.** No provision.

**Exceptions.** No provision.

**Additional Provisions.** None.

**Citations to Authority.** None.

**MISSOURI**

**Covered Entities.** Employers.

**Prohibited Inquiries.** Use of any application form or any inquiry in connection with prospective employment that expresses any limitation, specification, or discrimination because of race, color, religion, national origin, sex, ancestry, age, disability, or HIV, AIDS, or ARC status.

**Prohibited Advertisements.** Printing or circulating any statement, advertisement, or publication in connection with prospective employment that expresses any limitation, specification, or discrimination because of race, color, religion, national origin, sex, ancestry, age, disability, or HIV, AIDS, or ARC status.

**Exceptions.** Inquiries acceptable if justified by BFOQ.

**Additional Provisions.** None.

**Citations to Authority.** Mo. Ann. Stat. §§ 191.665, 213.055(1)(3).

**MONTANA**

**Covered Entities.** Employers.

**Prohibited Inquiries.** Use of any employment application expressing a limitation, specification, or discrimination as to sex, marital status, age, physical or mental disability, race, creed, religion, color, or national origin.

**Prohibited Advertisements.** Printing or circulating a statement, advertisement, or publication that expresses a limitation, specification, or discrimination as to sex, marital status, age, physical or mental disability, race, creed, religion, color, or national origin.

**Exceptions.** Inquiries are acceptable, with respect to disability, age, marital status, or sex, if justified by BFOQ, or for implementation of an affirmative action program, or for court-ordered reporting or recordkeeping requirements.

**Additional Provisions.** None.

**Citations to Authority.** Mont. Code Ann. § 49-2-303; Mont. Admin. R. §§ 24.9.1406(1)(a)–(c), 24.9.1406(2)(j), 24.9.1406(2)(m). As interpreted by the Montana Human Rights Commission.

**NEBRASKA**

**Covered Entities.** Employers.

**Prohibited Inquiries.** Solicitation of employees in any way that would deprive an individual of employment opportunities or otherwise adversely affect employee status because of race, color, religion, sex, disability, marital status, or national origin.

**Prohibited Advertisements.** Printing or publishing any advertisement or notice relating to employment that indicates a preference, limitation, specification, or discrimination based on race, color, religion, sex, disability, marital status, or national origin.

**Exceptions.** Advertisements and notices expressing a preference as to religion, sex, disability, marital status, or national origin are acceptable if justified by BFOQ.

**Additional Provisions.** Employers are prohibited from participating in contractual or other arrangements that have the effect of subjecting qualified individuals with disabilities to discrimination in the application or employment process, including a relationship with an employment agency or labor organization.

**Citations to Authority.** Neb. Rev. Stat. Ann. §§ 48-1104(2), 1115.

## NEVADA

**Covered Entities.** Employers.

**Prohibited Inquiries.** No provision.

**Prohibited Advertisements.** Printing or publishing any notice or advertisement that relates to employment if it indicates any preference, limitation, specification, or discrimination based on race, color, religion, sex, age, physical, mental, or visual disability, or national origin.

**Exceptions.** Religion, sex, age, physical, mental, or visual disability, or national origin may be BFOQs.

**Additional Provisions.** None.

**Citations to Authority.** Nev. Rev. Stat. Ann. § 613.340(2).

## NEW HAMPSHIRE

**Covered Entities.** Employers.

**Prohibited Inquiries.** Making any inquiry or using any application form in connection with employment that expresses any limitation, specification, or discrimination as to age, sex, race, color, marital status, physical or mental disability, religion, or national origin. Inquiry is unlawful if it discourages the applicant or is used to disqualify.

**Prohibited Advertisements.** Printing or circulating any statement, advertisement, or publication in connection with employment that expresses any limitation, specification, or discrimination as to age, sex, race, color, marital status, physical or mental disability, religion, or national origin.

**Exceptions.** Inquiries are acceptable if based on a BFOQ; employment advertising specifying an age limit lower than 18 is not unlawful if based on a BFOQ.

**Additional Provisions.** None.

**Citations to Authority.** N.H. Rev. Stat. Ann. § 354-A:7, III. As interpreted by the New Hampshire Commission for Human Rights.

## NEW JERSEY

**Covered Entities.** Employers.

**Prohibited Inquiries.** Use of any employment application or any inquiry in connection with prospective employment that expresses any limitation, specification, or discrimination as to race, creed, color, national origin, ancestry, age, marital status, sex, sexual orientation, or the liability of an applicant for service in the U.S. Armed Forces.

**Prohibited Advertisements.** Printing or circulating any statement, advertisement, or publication in connection with prospective employment that expresses any limitation, specification, or discrimination as to race, creed, color, national origin, ancestry, age, marital status, sex, sexual orientation, or the liability of an applicant for service in the U.S. Armed Forces.

**Exceptions.** Inquiries are acceptable if justified by BFOQ.

**Additional Provisions.** Public works contractor or subcontractor, in all solicitations or advertisements for employees, must state that all qualified applicants will receive consideration for employment without regard to age, race, color, creed, national origin, ancestry, marital status, sexual orientation, or sex.

**Citations to Authority.** N.J. Stat. Ann. §§ 10:5-12(c), 10:5-33(b).

## NEW MEXICO

**Covered Entities.** Employers.

**Prohibited Inquiries.** Use of an employment application or inquiry regarding prospective employment that expresses a limitation, specification, or discrimination as to race, color, religion, national origin, ancestry, sex, physical or mental disability, or serious medical condition.

**Prohibited Advertisements.** Printing or circulating a statement, advertisement, or publication regarding prospective employment that expresses a limitation, specification, or discrimination as to race, color, religion, national origin, ancestry, sex, physical or mental disability, or serious medical condition.

**Exceptions.** Inquiries are acceptable if justified by BFOQ.

**Additional Provisions.** New Mexico Human Rights Act prohibits age discrimination in all terms and conditions of employment.

**Citations to Authority.** N.M. Stat. Ann. § 28-1-7, D.

## NEW YORK

**Covered Entities.** Employers.

**Prohibited Inquiries.** Use of any employment application or inquiry in connection with prospective employment that expresses any limitation, specification, or discrimination as to age, race, creed, color, national origin, sex, marital status, disability, genetic predisposition or carrier status, or arrest record.

**Prohibited Advertisements.** Printing or circulating any statement, advertisement, or publication in connection with prospective employment that expresses any limitation, specification, or discrimination as to age, race, creed, color, national origin, sex, marital status, genetic predisposition or disability.

**Exceptions.** Inquiries are acceptable if justified by BFOQ; age prohibitions apply to those over 18.

**Additional Provisions.** None.

**Citations to Authority.** N.Y. Exec. Law §§ 296(1)(d), 296(3-a), 296(16).

### NORTH CAROLINA

**Covered Entities.** Employers.

**Prohibited Inquiries.** Employers are prohibited from requiring applicants to identify themselves as disabled before employment offers.

**Prohibited Advertisements.** No provision.

**Exceptions.** Employers may invite applicants to identify themselves as disabled in order to act affirmatively on their behalf and may inquire whether people with disabilities have the ability to perform the duties of particular jobs.

**Additional Provisions.** None.

**Citations to Authority.** N.C. Gen. Stat. §§ 168A-5(a)(4), 168A-5(b)(5).

### NORTH DAKOTA

**Covered Entities.** Employers and their agents.

**Prohibited Inquiries.** Use of application or inquiries that cause or facilitate unlawful discrimination.

**Prohibited Advertisements.** An employer is prohibited from advertising or in any way indicating or publicizing that persons of a particular race, color, sex, national origin, religion, age, physical or mental disability, or status with respect to marriage or public assistance, or who participate in lawful off-premise, nonworking-hour activity are unwelcome, objectionable, not acceptable, or not solicited for employment.

**Exceptions.** An employer may advertise in a manner indicating that individuals who participate in lawful, off-premise, nonworking-hour activities that are in direct conflict with the employer's essential business-related interests are unwelcome, objectionable, or not solicited.

**Additional Provisions.** None.

**Citations to Authority.** N.D. Cent. Code. §§ 14-02.4-03, 14-02.4-06, 14-02.4-18.

### OHIO

**Covered Entities.** Employers.

**Prohibited Inquiries.** Asking an applicant for, or using an application or personnel form asking for, information concerning race, color, religion, sex, national origin, disability, age, or ancestry.

**Prohibited Advertisements.** Printing or publishing any notice or advertisement relating to employment that indicates any preference, limitation, specification, or discrimination based on race, color, religion, sex, national origin, disability, age, or ancestry.

**Exceptions.** Inquiries are acceptable if justified by BFOQ; preemployment inquiries concerning disabilities that are preceded by statements of commitment to nondiscrimination are permitted if designed to determine whether applicants would require reasonable accommodation and can perform job without increasing occupational hazard. Employers who have federal contracts with nondiscrimination clauses may require proof of citizenship.

**Additional Provisions.** The use, in recruiting or hiring, of an employment agency, personnel placement service, training school or center, labor organization, or any other employee-referring source known to discriminate against persons because of these characteristics is prohibited.

**Citations to Authority.** Ohio Rev. Code Ann. §§ 4112.02(E)(1), 4112.02(E)(3), 4112.02(E)(4), 4112.02(E)(6); Ohio Admin. Code § 4112.02(E)(1)-(2). As interpreted by the Ohio Civil Rights Commission.

### OKLAHOMA

**Covered Entities.** Employers.

**Prohibited Inquiries.** Inquiries about whether an applicant is disabled, or the extent of any disability.

**Prohibited Advertisements.** Printing or publishing a notice or advertisement relating to employment that indicates a preference, limitation, specification, or discrimination based on race, color, religion, sex, national origin, age, or disability.

**Exceptions.** With respect to religion, sex, national origin, or age, advertisement permissible if justified by BFOQ; inquiries about whether applicant is able to perform job-related functions.

**Additional Provisions.** Inquiries permissible if made necessary for affirmative action programs or for compliance with federal contract requirements.

**Citations to Authority.** Okla. Stat. Ann. tit. 25, § 1306; Okla. Admin. Code § 335.15-9-4(1). As interpreted by the Human Rights Commission of Oklahoma.

## OREGON

**Covered Entities.** Employers.

**Prohibited Inquiries.** Use of any application or any inquiry in connection with prospective employment that expresses any limitation, specification, or discrimination on the basis of race, religion, color, sex, national origin, marital status, age, or an expunged juvenile record.

**Prohibited Advertisements.** Printing or circulating any statement, advertisement, or publication in connection with prospective employment that expresses any limitation, specification, or discrimination on the basis of race, religion, color, sex, national origin, marital status, age, or an expunged juvenile record.

**Exceptions.** Inquiries are acceptable if justified by BFOQ.

**Additional Provisions.** None.

**Citations to Authority.** Or. Rev. Stat. § 659.030(1)(d).

## PENNSYLVANIA

**Covered Entities.** Employers.

**Prohibited Inquiries.** Employer may not elicit preemployment information about, keep a record of, or use any application form containing questions about the race, color, religion, ancestry, sex, national origin, severity of disability, past disability of an applicant, or use of guide animal for disability.

**Prohibited Advertisements.** Publishing or printing any employment notice or advertisement indicating any preference, limitation, specification, or discrimination based on race, color, religion, ancestry, age, sex, national origin, non-job related disability, or use of guide animal for disability.

**Exceptions.** Conduct is acceptable if based on (1) a BFOQ, (2) membership, in the case of a fraternal organization or association, or (3) applicable federal or state security regulations. As to disability, an employer may inquire about the person's ability to perform the essential functions of the job.

**Additional Provisions.** Prohibit substantially confining or limiting recruitment or hiring with the intent to circumvent the statute's spirit and purpose, with respect to using any employment agency, employment service, labor organization, training school, or referring source that serves individuals who have predominantly the same characteristics.

**Citations to Authority.** Pa. Stat. Ann. tit. 43, §§ 955(b)(1), 955(b)(2), 955(b)(4).

## PUERTO RICO

**Covered Entities.** Employers.

**Prohibited Inquiries.** No provision.

**Prohibited Advertisements.** Publishing or disseminating advertisements, notices, or other forms of information denying employment opportunities to any person, indiscriminately, on the basis of race, color, sex, social or national origin, social position, political affiliation, religious belief, or age, without just cause.

**Exceptions.** None.

**Additional Provisions.** None.

**Citations to Authority.** P.R. Laws Ann. tit. 29, § 146a.

## RHODE ISLAND

**Covered Entities.** Employers.

**Prohibited Inquiries.** Eliciting or attempting to elicit any information or using any form of application, or personnel form, containing questions or entries pertaining to race, color, religion, sex, disability, age, ancestry, or arrest records.

**Prohibited Advertisements.** Printing or publishing any employment notice or advertisement that indicates any preference, limitation, specification, or discrimination based on race, color, religion, sex, sexual orientation, disability, age, or ancestry.

**Exceptions.** Inquiries are acceptable if justified by BFOQ or needed to comply with federally mandated affirmative action program; employers may inquire about conviction records, and employers may ask whether applicant has been arrested or charged with any crime, when attempting to fill law enforcement agency positions.

**Additional Provisions.** Prohibit using any employment agency, placement service, training school or center, labor organization, or any other employee-referring source in recruiting or hiring that it knows, or has reasonable cause to know, discriminates against individuals on the basis of race, color, religion, sex, disability, age, or ancestry.

**Citations to Authority.** R.I. Gen. Laws §§ 28-5-7(1), 28-5-7(4), 28-5-7(7).

### SOUTH CAROLINA

**Covered Entities.** Employers.

**Prohibited Inquiries.** No provision.

**Prohibited Advertisements.** Printing or publishing any employment notice or advertisement that indicates a preference, limitation, specification, or discrimination based on race, color, religion, sex, age, disability, or national origin.

**Exceptions.** With respect to religion, sex, or national origin, inquiries permissible if justified by BFOQ.

**Additional Provisions.** None.

**Citations to Authority.** S.C. Code Ann. §§ 1-13-80(F), 1-13-80(G).

### SOUTH DAKOTA

**Covered Entities.** Employers, their employees and agents.

**Prohibited Inquiries.** Covered entity may not bring about or facilitate discrimination through the use of any application form or inquiry.

**Prohibited Advertisements.** Advertising, indicating, or publicizing that individuals of any particular race, color, creed, religion, sex, ancestry, disability, or national origin are unwelcome, objectionable, not acceptable, or not solicited for employment.

**Exceptions.** None.

**Additional Provisions.** None.

**Citations to Authority.** S.D. Codified Laws §§ 3-6A-15, 20-13-10, 20-13-10.1, 20-13-13, 20-13-26.

### TENNESSEE

**Covered Entities.** Employers.

**Prohibited Inquiries.** No provision.

**Prohibited Advertisements.** Printing, publishing, or circulating any statement, advertisement, or publication that indicates a preference, limitation, specification, or discrimination based on race, creed, color, religion, sex, or national origin.

**Exceptions.** Religion, age, and sex may be BFOQs.

**Additional Provisions.** None.

**Citations to Authority.** Tenn. Code Ann. §§ 4-21-404(2), 4-21-407.

### TEXAS

**Covered Entities.** Employers.

**Prohibited Inquiries.** No provision.

**Prohibited Advertisements.** Printing or publishing an employment notice or advertisement indicating a preference, limitation, specification, or discrimination based on race, color, disability, religion, sex, national origin, or age, if the notice or advertisement concerns an employee's status, employment, or admission to or participation in an apprenticeship, on-the-job, or other training program.

**Exceptions.** Disability, religion, sex, national origin, or age may be BFOQs.

**Additional Provisions.** None.

**Citations to Authority.** Tex. Labor Code Ann. § 21.059.

### UTAH

**Covered Entities.** Employers.

**Prohibited Inquiries.** Use of any employment application or inquiry in connection with prospective employment that expresses any limitation, specification, or discrimination as to race, color, sex, pregnancy, childbirth or pregnancy-related conditions, national origin, disability, religion, or age.

**Prohibited Advertisements.** Printing or circulating any statement, advertisement, or publication in connection with prospective employment that expresses any limitation, specification, or discrimination as to race, color, sex, pregnancy, childbirth or pregnancy-related conditions, national origin, disability, religion, or age.

**Exceptions.** Inquiries permitted if justified by BFOQ or required by a government agency for security reasons.

**Additional Provisions.** None.

**Citations to Authority.** Utah Code Ann. § 34A-5-106(1)(d).

### VERMONT

**Covered Entities.** Persons seeking employees.

**Prohibited Inquiries.** No provision.

**Prohibited Advertisements.** Printing, publishing, or circulating any employment notice or advertisement indicating a preference, limitation, specification, or discrimination based on race, color, religion, ancestry, national origin, sex, sexual orientation, birth place, age, or disability.

**Exceptions.** None.

**Additional Provisions.** None.

**Citations to Authority.** Vt. Stat. Ann. tit. 21 § 495(a)(2).

## VIRGIN ISLANDS

**Covered Entities.** Employers.

**Prohibited Inquiries.** Use of any employment application or inquiry in connection with prospective employment that expresses any limitation, specification, or discrimination as to age, race, creed, color, national origin, sex (including pregnancy, childbirth, or related medical conditions), sexual orientation, or political affiliation.

**Prohibited Advertisements.** Printing or circulating any statement, advertisement, or publication in connection with prospective employment that expresses any limitation, specification, or discrimination as to age, race, creed, color, national origin, sex (including pregnancy, childbirth, or related medical conditions), sexual orientation, or political affiliation.

**Exceptions.** Inquiries are acceptable if based on BFOQ.

**Additional Provisions.** None.

**Citations to Authority.** V.I. Code Ann. tit. 10 § 64(1)(d), tit. 24 § 451(a)(3).

## VIRGINIA

**Covered Entities.** No provision.

**Prohibited Inquiries.** No provision.

**Prohibited Advertisements.** No provision.

**Exceptions.** No provision.

**Additional Provisions.** None.

**Citations to Authority.** None.

## WASHINGTON

**Covered Entities.** Employers.

**Prohibited Inquiries.** Use of any employment application or inquiry in connection with prospective employment that expresses any limitation, specification, or discrimination as to age, sex, marital status, race, creed, color, national origin, use of trained guide animal by disabled, or the presence of any sensory, mental, or physical disability. Inquiries about criminal history prohibited if connected to protected class. Note: In *Gugin v. Sonico, Inc.*, 68 Wash App. 826, 846 P.2d 571 (1993), the court held that the Human Rights Commission exceeded its statutory authority by enacting a regulation that prohibited employers from discriminating against persons who had been convicted of a crime.

**Prohibited Advertisements.** Printing or circulating any statement, advertisement, or publication in connection with prospective employment that expresses any limitation, specification, or discrimination as to age, sex, marital status, race, creed, color, national origin, use of trained guide animal by disabled, or the presence of any sensory, mental, or physical disability.

**Exceptions.** Inquiries may be justified by BFOQ; employer may request evidence of the applicant's age.

**Additional Provisions.** None.

**Citations to Authority.** Wash. Rev. Code Ann. §§ 49.44.090(2), 49.60.180(4), 49.60.205; Wash. Admin. Code §§ 162-12, 162-16. As interpreted by the Washington State Human Rights Commission.

## WEST VIRGINIA

**Covered Entities.** Employers.

**Prohibited Inquiries.** Before employment, employer may not elicit any information about, make or keep a record of, or use any application form containing questions about the race, religion, color, national origin, ancestry, sex, physical or mental impairment, or age of any applicant.

**Prohibited Advertisements.** Printing or publishing any notice or advertisement relating to employment indicating a preference, limitation, specification, or discrimination based on race, religion, color, national origin, ancestry, sex, or age.

**Exceptions.** Inquiries are permissible if justified by BFOQ or other exception.

**Additional Provisions.** The same restrictions apply to guidance programs, apprenticeship training programs, on-the-job training programs, or other occupational training or retraining programs.

**Citations to Authority.** W. Va. Code §§ 5-11-9(2)(A), 5-11-9(2)(B), 5-11-9(4)(D).

## WISCONSIN

**Covered Entities.** Employers.

**Prohibited Inquiries.** Use of an employment application or inquiry in connection with prospective employment that implies or expresses any limitation, specification, or discrimination with respect to an individual because of age (over 40), race, creed, color, disability, marital status, sex, sexual orientation, national origin, ancestry, membership in National Guard (or other reserve force), use or non-use of lawful products off employer's premises during nonworking hours, or arrest or conviction record.

**Prohibited Advertisements.** Printing or circulating any statement, advertisement, or publication in connection with prospective employment that implies or expresses any limitation, specification, or discrimination with respect to an individual because of age (over 40), race, creed, color, disability, marital status, sex, sexual orientation, national origin, ancestry, membership in National Guard (or other reserve force), use or non-use of lawful products off employer's premises during non-working hours, or arrest or conviction record.

**Exceptions.** An employer may reject an applicant whose conviction is substantially related to the job, set maximum age requirements for certain physically hazardous jobs, and determine, in limited cases, that employment of a person with a disability may present a significant risk of real harm to the safety or health of the individual or others.

**Additional Provisions.** None.

**Citations to Authority.** Wis. Stat. Ann. §§ 111.321, 111.322(2), 111.335(1)(a), 111.335(1)(d); Wis. Admin. Code § Ind. 88.20. As interpreted by the Equal Rights Division of the Wisconsin Department of Workforce Development.

### WYOMING

**Covered Entities.** No provision.

**Prohibited Inquiries.** No provision.

**Prohibited Advertisements.** No provision.

**Exceptions.** No provision.

**Additional Provisions.** None.

**Citations to Authority.** None.

# § 1.3 Oral Contracts for Employment

## [a] Implied Oral Contracts

Even in the absence of any formal contractual employment agreement, courts may imply a contractual obligation from the parties' overall conduct. Such implied-in-fact employment contracts may arise from oral representations, employee handbooks or manuals, or specific actions or performance that suggest an employer-employee relationship. For example, one court found that a statement that the employer "hoped the employee would stay forever" along with similar comments created an implied contract such that the employee could be terminated only for cause.[1] (See § 1.4 for more detailed analysis of implied contracts and the at-will rule.)

## [b] Express Oral Contracts

Of course, an employment contract need not be reduced to writing in order to be enforceable. As long as the relationship is a product of mutual assent, with an offer of one party followed by the acceptance of the other, an express oral contract for employment will be valid, provided it is not prohibited by the statute of frauds.

It should be noted, however, that not every verbal exchange relating to the employee's future in the company will lead to a finding that permanent employment has been created. Statements by the employer that the employee will have employment as long as things are going well have been found to be too vague to create an express employment contract.[2]

## [c] Employee Manuals

Employee manuals or handbooks have salutary purposes that serve both the employer's and employees' interests; however, the failure to carefully draft the contents of employee manuals can inadvertently create enforceable contractual rights in favor of employees. For example, Illinois courts have held that an employee manual may constitute a contract if three criteria are met:

1. Policy statements contain a clear promise that an offer has been made,
2. The manual is disseminated by the employer so that the employee is aware of its contents and reasonably believes it to be an offer, and
3. The employee continues to work after receiving the policy statement that serves as the basis for consideration.[3]

Some courts recognize a narrower exception. A North Carolina court recently held that to be enforceable, an employment agreement must contain a specific

**§ 1.3**

1. Torosyan v. Boehringer Ingelheim Pharmaceutical, 662 A.2d 89 (Conn. 1995).

2. *See* Wright v. Dothan Chrysler Plymouth Dodge, 658 So. 2d 428 (Ala. 1995) (words to the effect that the employment would last "as long as everything was smooth" not enough to create employment contract); Ruud v. Great Plains Supply, 526 N.W.2d 369 (Minn. 1995) (statements such as "good employees are taken care of" not definite enough to create an express or implied contract).

3. *See, e.g.,* Gaiser v. Village of Skokie, 648 N.E.2d 205 (Ill. Ct. App. 1995).

term of employment or a statement that the employee can be discharged only for cause.[4]

In many instances, courts have found that provisions in employee manuals implied contracts that the employee would be discharged only for cause, or that the employer would follow certain procedures before discharging an employee.[5] In the majority of states (43 at the time of this writing), courts have found public policy exceptions to the at-will employment rule based on an implied contract formed by provisions in employee manuals or handbooks. Furthermore, Montana passed a statute in 1987 stating that at-will employees would be protected from discharge without cause when the employer fails to follow manual or handbook policies (for example, the disciplinary procedures stated in the manual).

Despite its potential pitfalls, a well-drafted employee manual can have many benefits. The manual can be a reference guide for employment information and employment policies. It may also be used in a public relations context to promote hiring for the employer or to help encourage good employee-management relations. It will also ensure that all employees have identical information on company policies and procedures.

To avoid the traps inherent in promulgating an employee manual, human resources professionals and counsel for employers should take the following precautions:

1. The terms of the manual should be expressed in clear language, avoiding legal terms.
2. The manual should avoid making any references to permanent employment or to employment that is contingent upon work being satisfactory. Such statements are frequently cited as the basis for a judicial finding that an employee may be discharged only for cause.
3. The manual should not define policies that will not be consistently applied. For example, if the manual states that particular disciplinary procedures will be followed, a court may hold that the employer's failure to follow the procedures is a violation of an implied contract and therefore that the employee was wrongfully discharged.
4. The manual should clearly state in its introductory paragraphs that the employment is at-will and may be terminated at the option of either the employee or the employer.

This final element is perhaps the most important. Without such a disclaimer, provisions of an employee handbook may be held by a court to alter the at-will relationship.[6] Following is a sample disclaimer:

> The contents of this employee handbook present the company's programs and policies and are intended as guidelines only. The employee should be aware that these policies and programs may be amended at any time, and depending upon the particular circumstances of a given situation, the company's actions may vary from written policy. The contents of this handbook **do not constitute the terms of a contract of employment**. Nothing contained in this handbook should be construed as a guarantee of continued employment, but rather, employment with the company is on an **"at-will"** basis. This means that the employment relationship may be terminated at any time by either the employee or the company for any reason not expressly prohibited by law. Any written or oral statement to the contrary by a supervisor, corporate officer, or other agent of the company is invalid and should not be relied upon by any prospective or existing employee.[7]

The disclaimer may be underscored by accompanying each distributed manual with an acknowledgment signed by the employee at the time the employee receives the handbook. Such an acknowledgment should contain the following provisions:

> **Employee's Acknowledgment**
>
> I have received a copy of the employee manual, and I understand that it is my responsibility to read and comply with the policies and procedures of this manual. I also acknowledge that this manual is not a contract of employment and that either [employer] or I may terminate my employment at any time with or without cause and with or without notice.

---

4. Morlensen v. Magne Marelli, USA, 470 S.E.2d 354 (N.C. 1996).

5. *See* Bott v. Rockwell Int'l, 908 P.2d 909 (Wash. Ct. App. 1996) (court allowed wrongful discharge action where manual's job evaluation and grievance procedures were violated by the employer); *but see* Walpus v. Milwaukee Elec. Tool, 532 N.W.2d 316 (Neb. 1995) (handbook list of grounds for dismissal not enough to prevent firing for other than good cause; the list did not state that it was exclusive).

6. *See* Duncan v. St. Joseph's Hosp. and Med. Ctr., 903 P.2d 1107 (Ariz. Ct. App. 1995) (policy statements in handbook may give rise to an implication of job security, but the disclaimer prevented such an implication).

7. This language was held to be sufficient to prevent terms of a manual and handbook from becoming part of an employment contract in Chambers v. Valley National Bank of Arizona, 721 F. Supp. 1128 (D. Ariz. 1988). For similar disclaimer language, *see* Solomon v. Walgreen Co., 975 F.2d 1086 (5th Cir. 1992).

The employer should require the employee to sign the acknowledgment upon receipt of the manual and to sign similar statements if and when the manual is updated.

### [d] Statute of Frauds: When a Written Contract Is Required

As noted above, the general presumption is that an employment contract of unspecified duration creates only at-will employment, which is terminable by either party at any time. Under the statute of frauds in most states, an oral employment contract for a specific duration of over one year is not enforceable. Most states have enacted a statute of frauds provision that renders unenforceable any agreement not to be performed within one year and not expressed in a written document and signed by the party sought to be bound by it.

Some courts have recognized exceptions to prevent employers from defeating otherwise valid worker claims. Because so many oral contracts are at-will employment agreements for an unspecified duration, courts have constructed theories that permit these contracts to be enforced despite the statute of frauds. In some cases, courts have relied on the fact that the employment contract could be completed within one year, because the employee might resign, retire, or be discharged during the first year of employment. Other courts have enforced oral contracts under the doctrine of reliance, which applies when an employee relies to his or her detriment upon oral promises made by the employer.[8]

8. *See* Stoetzel v. Continental Textile Corp., 768 F.2d 217 (8th Cir. 1985) (employee quit other employment in reliance on oral agreement).

# § 1.4 Written Contracts

## [a] Essential Elements of Written Contracts

Although specific formalities are not normally necessary, certain general elements are essential for creating a valid employment agreement. It is essential that a contract of employment be supported by sufficient consideration. The consideration need not be in the form of wages, however, and the relationship may exist even though no monetary compensation is paid. Mutuality of obligation is also a prerequisite to a valid agreement; however, this requirement is not violated by a contract terminable at the will of either party. Certainty as to the parties and the nature and extent of the service is also generally considered essential to an employment contract. This requirement does not mean, however, that a contract must provide detail as to every aspect of the employment; a contract may still be valid even though some of its terms may become fixed at a future time or the duties are not specifically set out, and the terms may be rendered more certain by the performance of either party.

An employment contract will not necessarily be rendered unenforceable because the contract does not specify the precise duration of the employment. As noted above, a failure to specify a duration may make the employment relationship terminable at will, although specific provisions of the contract may be enforceable as long as the employment relationship continues. It should be noted, however, that a contract for permanent employment or for the duration of the employee's life must be expressed clearly and definitely. Additional terms such as hours, wages, location, and work conditions are proper subjects for the employment contract but are not considered essential.

## [b] Common Clauses in Written Contracts

Among the most common clauses found in written employment contracts are anticompetition clauses, copyright and patent clauses, release and waiver clauses, and arbitration clauses.

*Anticompetition Clauses.* As a general rule, a former employee is free to compete with his former employer after the termination of his employment or to enter into employment with a competitor of his former employer. A former employee may not compete with his former employer fraudulently, however, by misappropriating trade secrets or confidential information or by violating an enforceable anticompetition covenant.

A covenant not to compete is basically an agreement in restraint of trade. The validity of such a restrictive covenant against competition depends on whether the restrictions are reasonable under the facts and circumstances of each particular case. In determining reasonableness, courts will consider the scope of the restraint, its duration, its territorial extent, and the interest sought to be protected. If, under all the circumstances, the covenant appears to be reasonable, it will be valid and enforceable. If the covenant is deemed unreasonable under all the circumstances, it will not be enforced.

Restrictive covenants in employment contracts are subject to a rule-of-reasonableness analysis, which requires that a restrictive covenant in an employment contract be reasonable as to the employer, the employee, and the public. In ascertaining the reasonableness of a restriction in an employment contract, certain elements should be considered, including the threatened danger to the employer in the absence of such an agreement, the economic hardship imposed on the employee by such a covenant, and whether the covenant is harmful to the public interest. Many courts will also consider the nature of the employee's profession.

There is no inflexible formula for determining the reasonableness of a particular restriction. Each case must be examined in relation to the particular circumstances, and no one factor is controlling. It should be noted, however, that anticompetition covenants ancillary to employment contracts are not favored and will be strictly construed.

Finally, anticompetition clauses ancillary to a contract for the sale of a business or the dissolution of a partnership are generally judged under the same test of reasonableness. Courts will interpret such covenants more liberally, however, and with less scrutiny than anticompetition clauses ancillary to an employment contract, on the theory that there is more equality in bargaining power relating to the sale of a business or dissolution of a partnership than in the typical employer-employee context.

### [c] Tests of Reasonableness

Courts use a variety of factors to determine whether an anticompetition clause should be upheld or, in some cases, modified.

1. *Statutes.* Generally, anticompetition covenants ancillary to employment contracts are still largely governed by the reasonableness rule of judge-made law. A number of states analyze such covenants under their general antitrust statutes, however, which provide that all contracts in restraint of trade are void and unenforceable. Other states have adopted statutory provisions specifically governing anticompetition covenants in employment contracts. In these states, any covenant not conforming to the statutory requirements will be void and unenforceable. Finally, three states, California, North Dakota, and Oklahoma, have enacted statutes that have been interpreted to preclude any anticompetition clauses in employment contracts, unless such clauses are ancillary to the sale of a business or the dissolution of a partnership.
2. *Partial Enforceability.* A number of states have held that unreasonable duration or territorial restrictions in anticompetition covenants may be enforced to the extent that they can be made reasonable by application of the "blue pencil" rule, which allows a court to rewrite ambiguous provisions of a contract. Other courts have rejected the application of the blue pencil rule, but will enforce reasonable portions of a restrictive covenant if those portions are severable from the unreasonable portions. Still other courts have held that provisions in an anticompetition covenant may never be modified by a court and that therefore an unreasonable provision renders the entire covenant void and unenforceable.
3. *Duration.* One factor that courts will consider in determining the reasonableness of a covenant is its duration. Generally, covenants that are short in duration are more likely to be found reasonable than covenants restricting competition over a greater period of time. However, the duration of a restriction is never in itself determinative of the reasonableness of the covenant. Rather, the court will consider the duration of the restriction in conjunction with all other facts and circumstances. Thus, the fact that a particular duration has been found reasonable in one case does not mandate a finding that such a duration is always reasonable. Finally, a few states have created statutory durational limitations for anticompetition covenants in employment contracts.
4. *Territorial Extent.* Another factor to be considered in determining the reasonableness of a restrictive covenant is the geographic scope of the restriction. Generally, restrictions covering a specific and limited geographic area are more likely to be upheld as reasonable than those covering a wide or undefined area. Some states require that geographic restrictions may be applied only to those areas in which the employer actually does business or in areas in which the employer is likely to do business. Other states require that the area of the restriction be limited to the area in which the employee actually performed services for the employer.

   Again, the territorial extent of a restriction is never in itself determinative of the reasonableness of an anticompetition clause. Rather, the geographic scope must be considered in conjunction with the other relevant facts and circumstances of the particular situation.
5. *Protectable Interests.* In order to be valid and enforceable, anticompetition covenants in employment contracts must be no broader than necessary to protect the employer's legitimate

business interests. As a general rule, no anticompetition clause that is designed solely to prevent competition will be enforced.

Nearly all states recognize that employers have a valid and legitimate business interest in their trade secrets and other confidential information. Thus, antidisclosure covenants are more likely to be upheld. Similarly, most courts recognize a legitimate interest in protecting current customers and therefore are more likely to uphold antisolicitation covenants. Often, antidisclosure and/or antisolicitation covenants will be upheld without regard to durational or territorial limitations. Some states have also recognized other legitimate business interests that deserve protection, including unique assets or specialized training.

Exhibit 1.4-1 sets out both statutory and case law relating to the validity of anticompetition clauses in employment contracts.

*Copyright and Patent Clauses.* When employees have access to confidential information, or are involved in the research and development aspect of a business, it is common for employers to insist that employees sign agreements not to divulge trade secrets and/or give the employer first rights to any of the employees' inventions. In the absence of an agreement giving the employer first rights to employee inventions, an employee under a general employment agreement will retain ownership of his inventions, regardless of whether the employee uses the employer's property or receives assistance from other employees. However, if the employee is hired to invent, the employer has an equitable title to any inventions the employee was hired to perfect.

*Release and Waiver Clauses.* In return for some benefit to which he or she is not otherwise entitled, an employee may waive his or her right to pursue present or future legal claims against the employer. Generally, courts will uphold releases and waivers of employment rights as long as the releases are knowing and voluntary.

Although an employee may waive a cause of action under Title VII of the Civil Rights Act of 1964 as part of an existing claim, an employee's rights under Title VII may not be waived prospectively.[1] Under the Older Workers Benefit Protection Act (OWBPA), a waiver may not affect the EEOC's rights and responsibilities to enforce the Age Discrimination in Employment Act, nor may a waiver be used to interfere with the right of an employee to file a charge with or participate in an investigation by the EEOC.[2] Similarly, the Fair Labor Standards Act restricts the ability of employees to waive or settle their claims for unpaid wages.[3]

*Arbitration Clauses.* Labor contracts will commonly include some provision stating that the parties agree to submit to arbitration any labor-related dispute between the employer and union members. Agreements to arbitrate may also be included in individual employment contracts. Generally, such agreements to arbitrate labor disputes are encouraged by Congress and the courts.[4]

Agreements to arbitrate arise by contract, and therefore a party generally cannot be required to submit to arbitration any dispute that is not the subject of an arbitration agreement.[5] If an arbitration agreement does exist, however, all issues related to the dispute will generally be covered by the agreement to arbitrate unless they are specifically excluded. In fact, the Supreme Court has held that when it is unclear whether the parties agreed to arbitrate a particular issue, any doubts should be resolved in favor of arbitrability.[6]

The Supreme Court has recently held that federal discrimination claims may also be subject to a contractual obligation to submit claims first to arbitration.[7] Statutory Employment Retirement Income Security Act (ERISA) claims have also been held subject to arbitration.[8]

From the employer's perspective, an arbitration clause can be of great benefit in the event of a dispute with an employee. Arbitration is generally far less costly than litigation, and the arbitral process is also generally less disruptive to the employer's operations than litigation.

**§ 1.4**

1. Alexander v. Gardner-Denver Co., 415 U.S. 36 (1974).

2. 29 U.S.C. § 626(f)(4).

3. 29 U.S.C. § 216(b). *See also* Brooklyn Savings Bank v. O'Neil, 324 U.S. 697 (1945).

4. *See, e.g.,* International Association of Machinists v. General Electric Co., 406 F.2d 1046 (2d Cir. 1969).

5. Gateway Coal Co. v. United Mine Workers, 414 U.S. 368 (1974).

6. United Steelworkers of America v. Warrior & Gulf Navigation Co., 363 U.S. 574 (1960).

7. Gilmer v. Interstate/Johnson Lane Corp., 500 U.S. 20 (1991).

8. Bird v. Shearson Lehman/American Express, Inc., 926 F.2d 116 (2d Cir. 1991), cert. denied, 501 U.S. 1251 (1991).

# Exhibit 1.4-1

## COVENANTS NOT TO COMPETE IN EMPLOYMENT CONTRACTS

### ALABAMA

**Relevant Statute.** Ala. Code § 8-1-1 (1993). Covenants not within statutory parameters are void and unenforceable. *Construction Materials, LTD. v. Kirkpatrick Concrete, Inc.*, 631 So.2d 1006 (Ala. 1994).

**Partial Enforceability.** Yes. Unreasonable restrictions in a covenant may be stricken, leaving the balance of the revision binding on the parties. *Cullman Broadcasting Co. v. Bosley,* 373 So.2d 830 (Ala. 1979).

**Duration and Territorial Extent of Restriction.**
**General Guidelines:** Covenants of unlimited duration and limited geographic scope held reasonable. *American Laundry Co. v. E.&W. Dry-Cleaning Co.,* 199 Ala. 154, 74 So.85 (1917). Covenants of unlimited duration and unlimited territorial restriction held unreasonable. *American Laundry Co. v. E.&W. Dry-Cleaning Co.,* 199 Ala. 154, 74 So.85 (1917). Contracts restraining employment are disfavored because they tend to deprive public of efficient service and impoverish the individual. *Birmingham Television Corp. v. De Ramus*, 502 So.2d 761 (Ala. Civ. App. 1986). Covenant not to compete will be enforced if employer has protectable interest, restriction is reasonably related to that interest, restriction is reasonable in time and place, and restriction imposes no undue hardship on employee. *Romano v. Caribe, U.S.A., Inc.*, 702 So.2d 1230 (Ala. Civ. App. 1996).
**Specific Rulings:** Five-year covenant not to compete for current clients of heavy machinery servicing company coupled with territorial restriction of U.S. and Canada held reasonable. *Kershaw v. Knox Kershaw, Inc.*, 523 So.2d 351 (Ala. 1988). Two-year covenant not to compete for clients of advertising newspaper coupled with territorial restriction of 50 miles held reasonable. *Tyler v. Eufaula Tribune Publishing Co.*, 500 So.2d 1005 (Ala. 1986). "No Switching" agreement between competing companies appears to violate § 8-1-1 because agreement restrains companies' employees from exercise of lawful trade or profession. *Dyson Conveyor Maintenance, Inc. v. Young & Vann Supply Co.*, 529 So.2d 212 (Ala. 1988). Employment contract that restrained doctor from practicing within 25 miles for a one-year period after termination was unenforceable pursuant to statute providing that contract restraining person from exercising lawful profession is void. *Anniston Urologic Associates, P.C. v. Kline*, 689 So.2d 54 (Ala. 1997).

**Protectable Interests.** Trade secrets, unique assets, confidential information, customer lists, and close customer relationships. *James S. Kemper & Co. Southeast v. Cox & Associates, Inc.*, 434 So.2d 1380 (1983); *Romano v. Carbide, U.S.A., Inc.*, 702 So.2d 1242 (Ala. 1997).

### ALASKA

**Relevant Statute.** —

**Partial Enforceability.** Yes. Modification of overbroad covenant permissible if covenant was drafted in good faith. *Wiram & Cash Architects v. Cash,* 837 P.2d 692 (Alaska 1992).

**Duration and Territorial Extent of Restriction.**
**General Guidelines:** —
**Specific Rulings:** —

**Protectable Interests.** —

### ARIZONA

**Relevant Statute.** Ariz. Rev. Stat. Ann. § 44-1402 (1994).

**Partial Enforceability.** Yes. Courts may exercise "blue pencil" rule. *Amex Distributing Co. v. Mascari,* 150 Ariz. 510, 724 P.2d 596 (Ct. App. 1986).

**Duration and Territorial Extent of Restriction.**
**General Guidelines:** Perpetual or indefinite covenants are invalid. *Three Phoenix Co. v. Pace Industries, Inc.,* 135 Ariz. 126, 659 P.2d 1271 (Ct. App.), *vacated and rev'd on other grounds,* 135 Ariz. 113, 659 P.2d 1258 (1981).

**Specific Rulings:** Two-year covenant not to compete with radio station coupled with territorial restriction of 50 miles held unreasonable. *Bryceland v. Northey,* 160 Ariz. 213, 772 P.2d 36 (Ct. App. 1989). Three-year covenant not to compete for clients of employment agency coupled with territorial restriction of 35 miles held reasonable. *Snelling & Snelling, Inv. v. Dupay Enterprises, Inc.,* 125 Ariz. 362, 609 P.2d 1062 (Ct. App. 1980). Ten-year covenant not to compete with silk-screening and lettering company coupled with territorial restriction of 100-mile radius held reasonable. *Gann v. Morris,* 122 Ariz. 517, 596 P.2d 43 (Ct. App. 1979).

**Protectable Interests.** Trade secrets, confidential customer lists, means and methods of handling customers, and secret processes. *Amex Distributing Co. v. Mascari,* 150 Ariz. 510, 724 P.2d 596 (Ct. App. 1986); *Lessner Dental Laboratories, Inc. v. Kidney,* 16 Ariz. App. 159, 492 P.2d 39 (1971).

## ARKANSAS

**Relevant Statute.** —

**Partial Enforceability.** No. Courts may not rewrite covenant to make overly broad restrictions reasonable. *Federated Mutual Insurance Co. v. Bennett,* 36 Ark. App. 99, 818 S.W.2d 596 (1991).

**Duration and Territorial Extent of Restriction.**
**General Guidelines:** —
**Specific Rulings:** Five-year covenant not to compete with truck stop coupled with territorial restriction of 100 miles held reasonable. *Easley v. Sky, Inc.,* 15 Ark. App. 64, 689 S.W.2d 356 (1985). Two-year covenant not to compete for current customers of insurance agency implicitly coupled with worldwide territorial restriction held reasonable. *Girard v. Rebsamen Insurance Co.,* 14 Ark. App. 154, 685 S.W.2d 526 (1985). Five-year covenant not to compete with crop-dusting service coupled with a territorial restriction of 50 miles held unreasonable. *Brown v. Devine,* 240 Ark. 838, 402 S.W.2d 669 (1966). Five-year covenant not to compete with land-clearing service coupled with territorial restriction of four states held unreasonable. *McLeod v. Meyer,* 237 Ark. 173, 372 S.W.2d 220 (1963).

**Protectable Interests.** Trade secrets, special training, confidential information, and customer lists. *Federated Mutual Insurance Co. v. Bennett,* 36 Ark. App. 99, 818 S.W.2d 596 (1991).

## CALIFORNIA

**Relevant Statute.** Cal. Bus. & Prof. Code secs. 16600 *et seq.* (West 1997).

**Partial Enforceability.** Yes. Portions of covenants concerning protectable interests may be enforced; remainder of covenant is void and unenforceable. *Scott v. Snelling & Snelling. Inc.,* 732 F. Supp. 1034 (N.D. Cal. 1990); *Moss, Adams and Co. v. Shilling,* 179 Cal. App. 3d 124, 224 Cal. Rptr. 456 (1986); *Muggill v. Reuben H. Donnelley Corp.,* 62 Cal. 2d 239, 42 Cal. Rptr. 107 (1965); *Winston Research Corp. v. Minnesota Mining and Manufacturing Co.,* 350 F.2d 134 (9th Cir. 1965).

**Duration and Territorial Extent of Restriction.**
**General Guidelines:** —
**Specific Rulings:** All restrictions are unreasonable; covenants not to compete place unreasonable burden on employee and violate public policy. *Scott v. Snelling & Snelling. Inc.,* 732 F. Supp. 1034 (N.D. Cal. 1990); *Cerberonics, Inc. v. California Unemployment Appeals Board,* 152 Cal. App. 3d 172, 199 Cal. Rptr. 292 (1984); *Application Group, Inc. v. Hunter Group, Inc.,* 72 Cal. Rptr. 2d 73, 61 Cal. App. 4th 881 (1998).

**Protectable Interests.** Trade secrets, customer lists, and confidential information. *Scott v. Snelling & Snelling, Inc.,* 732 F. Supp. 1034 (N.D. Cal. 1990); *American Credit Indemnity Co. v. Sacks,* 213 Cal App. 3d 622, 262 Cal. Rptr. (1989); *Moss, Adams and Co. v. Shilling,* 179 Cal. App. 3d 124, 224 Cal. Rptr. 456 (1986); *Winston Research Corp. v. Minnesota Mining and Manufacturing Co.,* 350 F.2d 134 (9th Cir. 1965).

## COLORADO

**Relevant Statute.** Colo. Rev. Stat. § 8-2-113 (1986).

**Partial Enforceability.** Yes. Courts have discretion to reform unreasonable territorial restrictions to make them reasonable. *National Graphics Co. v. Dilley,* 681 P.2d 546 (Colo. Ct. App. 1984).

**Duration and Territorial Extent of Restriction.**
**General Guidelines:** Unlimited duration coupled with unlimited geographic scope held unreasonable. *National Graphics Co. v. Dilley,* 681 P.2d 546 (Colo. Ct. App. 1984).
**Specific Rulings:** Five-year covenant not to compete with electrical contracting business coupled with territorial restriction of 50 miles held reasonable. *Harrison v. Allbright,* 40 Colo. App. 227, 577 P.2d 302 (1977). Two-year covenant not to compete with insurance company coupled with territorial restriction of entire state held reasonable. *Colonial Life & Accident Insurance Co. v. Kappers,* 488 P.2d 96 (Colo. Ct. App. 1971).

**Protectable Interests.** Trade secrets. *Management Recruiters of Boulder, Inc. v. Miller,* 762 P.2d 763 (Colo. Ct. App. 1988); *Gold Messenger, Inc. v. McGuay,* 937 P.2d 907 (Colo. App. 1997).

## CONNECTICUT

**Relevant Statute.** —

**Partial Enforceability.** No. *Timenterial, Inc. v. Dagata,* 29 Conn. Supp. 180, 277 A.2d 512 (Super. Ct. 1971).

**Duration and Territorial Extent of Restriction.**
**General Guidelines:** Covenants not to compete may be evaluated by five criteria: (1) duration of restriction, (2) territorial extent of restriction, (3) degree of protection afforded one party, (4) hardship imposed on other party, and (5) public interest. *New Haven Tobacco Co. v. Perrelli,* 18 Conn. App. 531, 559 A.2d 715 (1989); *Wesley Software Development Corp. v. Burdette*, 977 F. Supp 137 (D. Conn 1997).
**Specific Rulings:** One-year covenant not to compete for customers of printing company coupled with territorial restriction of entire state held reasonable. *Van Dyek Printing Co. v. DiNicola,* 43 Conn. Supp. 191, 648 A.2d 877 (1994). Two-year covenant not to compete with automobile lubrication service coupled with territorial restriction of 50 miles held reasonable. *Grease Monkey International, Inc. v. Watkins,* 808 F. Supp. 111 (D. Conn. 1992). Five-year covenant not to compete with metal welding business coupled with territorial restriction of entire state held reasonable. *Scott v. General Iron & Welding Co.,* 171 Conn. 132, 368 A.2d 111 (1976).

**Protectable Interests.** Trade secrets, solicitation of customers, confidential information, and unique and extraordinary services. *New Haven Tobacco Co. v. Perrelli,* 118 Conn. App. 531, 559 A.2d 715 (1989); *Continental Group, Inc. v. Kensley,* 422 F. Supp. 838 (D. Conn. 1976); *Wesley Software Development Corp. v. Burdette*, 977 F. Supp 137 (D. Conn 1997).

## DELAWARE

**Relevant Statute.** —

**Partial Enforceability.** Yes. Covenants are enforceable only to the extent they are reasonable. *Knowles-Zeswitz Music, Inc. v. Cara,* 260 A.2d 171 (Del. Ch. 1987).

**Duration and Territorial Extent of Restriction.**
**General Guidelines:** —
**Specific Rulings:** Two-year covenant not to compete with envelope sales company implicitly coupled with nationwide territorial restriction held reasonable. *Curtis 100, Inc. v. Youngblade,* 878 F. Supp. 1224 (N.D. Iowa 1995) (applying Delaware law). Three-year covenant not to compete with land surveying company coupled with territorial restriction of 50 miles held reasonable. *McCann Surveyors, Inc. v. Evans,* 611 A.2d 1 (Del. Ch. 1987). Covenant not to compete with public accounting firm for indefinite duration coupled with territorial restriction of Delaware peninsula held reasonable. *Faw, Casson & Co. v. Cranston,* 375 A.2d 463 (Del. Ch. 1977).

**Protectable Interests.** —

## DISTRICT OF COLUMBIA

**Relevant Statute.** —

**Partial Enforceability.** Yes. Covenants are enforceable to extent they are reasonable. *Ellis v. James V. Hurson Associates, Inc.,* 565 A.2d 615 (D.C. 1989).

**Duration and Territorial Extent of Restriction.**
**General Guidelines:** Hardship on employer and injury to public interest are key considerations in determining reasonableness of covenant. *Mercer Management Consulting, Inc. v. Wilde,* 920 F. Supp 219 (D.D.C. 1996).

**Protectable Interests.** Solicitation of customers. *Mercer Management Consulting, Inc. v. Wilde,* 920 F. Supp 219 (D.D.C. 1996).

## FLORIDA

**Relevant Statute.** Fla. Stat. Ann. §§ 542.33 (West Supp. 1995); 542.335 (West Supp. 1997).

**Partial Enforceability.** Yes. Courts may modify duration and geographic scope of covenant. *Carnahan v. Alexander Proudfoot Co. World Headquarters,* 581 So.2d 184 (Fla. 4th DCA 1991); *Mathieu v. Old Town Flower Shops, Inc.,* 585 So.2d 1160 (Fla. 4th DCA 1991).

**Duration and Territorial Extent of Restriction.**
**General Guidelines:** —
**Specific Rulings:** One-year covenant not to compete with copier machine repair service coupled with five-county territorial restriction held reasonable. *Xerographics, Inc. v. Thomas,* 537 So.2d 140 (Fla. 2d DCA 1988). Two-year covenant not to compete with company that marketed computer software to dairy farmers coupled with nationwide territorial restriction held reasonable. *Marshall v. Gore,* 506 So.2d 91 (Fla. 2d DCA 1996).

**Protectable Interests.** Trade secrets, confidential business lists, records and information, solicitation of clients, customer goodwill, and extraordinary or specialized training that employer provided. *CYN-Co. v. Lancto,* 677 So.2d 78 (Fla. 2d DCA 1996); *Dyer v. Pioneer Concepts, Inc.,* 667 So.2d 961 (Fla. 2d 1996); *Kephart v. Hair Returns, Inc.,* 685 So.2d 959 (Fla. 4th DCA 1996); *Hapney v. Central Garage, Inc.,* 579 So.2d 127 (Fla. 2d DCA 1991).

## GEORGIA

**Relevant Statute.** Ga. Code Ann. § 13-8-2.1 (Supp. 1996).

**Partial Enforceability.** No. *Smith v. HBT, Inc.,* 213 Ga. App. 560, 445 S.E.2d 315 (1994).

**Duration and Territorial Extent of Restriction.**
**General Guidelines:** Covenants with extremely limited durations and small geographic restrictions are likely to be held reasonable. *Allen v. Hub Cap Heaven, Inc.,* 225 Ga. App. 533, 484 S.E.2d 259 (1997). Terms of covenant may not be ambiguous; covenant should address duration and territorial restrictions. *Dougherty, McKinnon & Luby, P.C. v Greenwald, Denzik & Davis, P.C.,* 213 Ga. App. 891, 447 S.E.2d 94 (1994) (concerning territory); *Stahl Headers, Inc. v. MacDonald,* 214 Ga. App. 323, 447 S.E.2d 320 (1994) (concerning territory).
**Specific Rulings:** Seven-year covenant not to compete with tax accountant group coupled with territorial restriction of all counties in which the group had satellite offices held reasonable. *Carroll v. Ralston & Associates, P.C.,* 214 Ga. App. 826, 481 S.E.2d 900 (1997). One-year covenant not to compete with food service company coupled with territorial restriction of all counties in which company had offices held reasonable. *Sysco Food Services of Atlanta, Inc. v. Chupp,* 225 Ga. App. 584, 484 S.E.2d 323 (1997). Two-year covenant not to compete with software company coupled with nationwide territorial restriction held reasonable. *American Software USA, Inc. v. Moore,* 448 S.E.2d 206 (Ga. 1994). Prohibition against "assisting others" in similar line of work prohibited employee from working for competitor in any capacity and was held unreasonable. *Johnstone v. Tom's Amusement Co., Inc.*, 228 Ga. App. 296, 491 S.E.2d 394 (1997). Restrictive covenant prohibiting sales manager from soliciting clients for one year within 11 counties where manager operated was reasonable. *Sysco Food Services of Atlanta, Inc. v. Chupp*, 484 S.E.2d 323 (Ga. App. 1997). Restrictive covenant in employment contract prohibiting employee from selling fuel to employer's customers, within 50 miles of employee's former office, for 2-year period following termination was unduly restrictive. *AmeriGas Propane, L.P. v. T-Bo Propane, Inc.*, 972 F. Supp. 685 (S.D. Ga. 1997).

**Protectable Interests.** Trade secrets, confidential business information, customer lists, marketing programs, and customer relationships. *Vortex Protective Services, Inc. v. Dempsey,* 218 Ga. App. 763, 463 S.E.2d 67 (1995); *American Software USA, Inc. v. Moore,* 448 S.E.2d 206 (Ga. 1994); *Smith v. HBT, Inc.,* 213 Ga. App. 560, 445 S.E.2d 315 (1994); *Sunstates Refrigerated Services, Inc. v. Griffin,* 215 Ga. App. 61, 449 S.E.2d 858 (1994).

## HAWAII

**Relevant Statute.** Haw. Rev. Stat. § 480-4 (1995).

**Partial Enforceability.** Yes. Portions of covenants concerning protectable interests may be enforced; remainder of covenant is void and unenforceable. *Ai v. Frank Huff Agency, Ltd.,* 57 Haw. 113, 551 P.2d 163 (1979).

**Duration and Territorial Extent of Restriction.**
**General Guidelines:** Duration, geographic restrictions, and breadth of restriction placed on activity are key considerations in determining the reasonableness of a covenant. *Technicolor, Inc. v. Traeger,* 57 Haw. 113, 551 P.2d 163 (1976).
**Specific Rulings:** Three-year covenant not to compete with photo-finish company coupled with territorial restriction of entire state held reasonable. *Technicolor, Inc. v. Traeger,* 57 Haw. 113, 551 P.2d 163 (1976).

**Protectable Interests.** —

## IDAHO

**Relevant Statute.** —

**Partial Enforceability.** Yes. Courts may apply "blue pencil" rule. *Insurance Center, Inc. v. Taylor,* 94 Idaho 896, 499 P.2d 1252 (1972).

**Duration and Territorial Extent of Restriction.**
**General Guidelines:** Restrictions unlimited in duration, geographic scope, and activity are unreasonable. *Magic Lantern Production, Inc. v. Dolsot,* 126 Idaho 805, 892 P.2d 480 (1995); *Insurance Center, Inc. v. Taylor,* 94 Idaho 896, 499 P.2d 1252 (1972).
**Specific Rulings:** —

**Protectable Interests.** —

## ILLINOIS

**Relevant Statute.** —

**Partial Enforceability.** Yes. Courts may modify covenants to make them reasonable. *Arpac Corp. v. Murray,* 168 Ill. Dec. 240, 589 N.E.2d 640 (1992).

**Duration and Territorial Extent of Restriction.**
**General Guidelines:** Covenants restricting specific activities do not need to be limited in geographic scope as long as duration of covenant is reasonable. *Agrimerica, Inc. v. Mathes,* 120 Ill. Dec. 765, 524 N.E.2d 947 (1988). Covenants unlimited in duration and territorial restrictions are unreasonable. *Akhter v. Shah,* 74 Ill. 730, 450 N.E.2d 232 (1983). Reasonableness of restrictive covenant is determined by its hardship to employee, effect upon general public, duration, geographic scope, and activity restrictions. *Lawrence and Allen, Inc. v. Cambridge Human Resource Group, Inc.*, 226 Ill. Dec. 331, 685 N.E.2d 434 (1997).
**Specific Rulings:** One-year covenant not to compete for current customers of insurance company coupled with territorial restriction of entire state held reasonable. *IDS Life Ins. Co. v. SunAmerica, Inc.,* 958 F. Supp. 1258 (N.D. Ill. 1997). Three-year covenant not to compete with real estate company coupled with territorial restriction of 75 miles held reasonable. *Hamer*

*Holding Group, Inc. v. Elmore,* 148 Ill. Dec. 310, 560 N.E.2d 907 (1990). Two-year covenant not to compete with magazine publisher coupled with nationwide territorial restriction held reasonable. *Instrumentalist Co. v. Band, Inc.,* 89 Ill. Dec. 530, 480 N.E.2d 1273 (1985).

**Protectable Interests.** Trade secrets, confidential information, and "near permanent" customer relationships. *Audio Properties, Inc. v. Kovach,* 211 Ill. Dec. 651, 655 N.E.2d 1034 (1995); *Diepholz v. Rutledge,* 213 Ill. Dec. 643, 659 N.E.2d 989 (Ill. App. 1995); *Curtis 1000, Inc. v. Suess,* 24 F.3d 941 (7th Cir. 1994); *Office Mates 5, North Shore, Inc. v. Hazen,* 175 Ill. Dec. 58, 599 N.E.2d 1072 (1992); *Lawrence and Allen, Inc. v. Cambridge Human Resource Group, Inc.*, 226 Ill. Dec. 331, 685 N.E.2d 434 (1997); *Stevens v. Rooks Pitts and Poust*, 682 N.E.2d 1125 (Ill. App. 1997).

## INDIANA

**Relevant Statute.** Ind. Code Ann. § 24-1-1-1, 24-1-2-1 (Burns 1996).

**Partial Enforceability.** Yes. Covenant may be modified to extent reasonable. *Smart Corp. v. Grider,* 650 N.E.2d 80 (Ind. Ct. App. 1995); *Licocci v. Cardinal Associates, Inc.,* 445 N.E.2d 556 (Ind. 1983); *Ackerman v. Kimball International, Inc.,* 634 N.E.2d 778 (Ind. Ct. App. 1994).

**Duration and Territorial Extent of Restriction.**
**General Guidelines:** Covenants unlimited with respect to duration and geographic scope are unreasonable. *Commercial Bankers Life Insurance Company of America v. Smith,* 516 N.E.2d 110 (Ind. Ct. App. 1987); *College Life Insurance Company of America v. Austin,* 466 N.E.2d 738 (Ind. Ct. App. 1984). Factors to be considered, in determining reasonableness of covenant not to compete, are scope of legitimate business interests of employer and geographical and temporal limits on the restraint. *Norlund v. Faust*, 675 N.E.2d 1142 (Ind. Ct. App. 1997).
**Specific Rulings:** One-year covenant not to compete with wood products manufacturer where no territorial restrictions were included was reasonable only as to trade secrets; otherwise scope limited to territory in which employee worked. *Ackerman v. Kimball International, Inc.,* 634 N.E.2d 778 (Ind. Ct. App. 1994). Ten-year covenant not to compete with cleaning business coupled with eight-county territorial restriction held unreasonable. *Frederick v. Professional Building Maintenance Industries, Inc.,* 168 Ind. App. 647, 344 N.E.2d 299 (1976). Five-year covenant not to compete with greeting service coupled with citywide territorial restriction held reasonable. *Welcome Wagon v. Haschert,* 125 Ind. App. 503, 127 N.E.2d 103 (1955). Partnership agreement between contractor and excavator prevented excavator from engaging in excavating in county for the two years following termination of agreement was not enforceable. *Wagler Excavating Corp. v. McKibben Const., Inc.*, 679 N.E.2d 155 (Ind. App. 1997).

**Protectable Interests.** Trade secrets, customer lists, confidential information, goodwill, and current client or customer relationships. *Smart Corp. v. Grider,* 650 N.E.2d 80 (Ind. Ct. App. 1995); *Brunner v. Hand Industries, Inc.,* 603 N.E.2d 157 (Ind. Ct. App. 1992); *Harvest Insurance Agency, Inc. v. Inter-Ocean Insurance Co.,* 492 N.E.2d 686 (Ind. 1086); *Seach v. Richards, Dieterle & Co.,* 439 N.E.2d 208 (Ind. 1982); *Norlund v. Faust*, 675 N.E.2d 1142 (Ind. Ct. App. 1997).

## IOWA

**Relevant Statute.** Iowa Code Ann. § 553.4 (West 1987).

**Partial Enforceability.** Yes. Courts may modify unduly restrictive covenants to make them reasonable. *Iowa Glass Depot, Inc. v. Jindrich,* 338 N.W.2d 376 (Iowa 1983).

**Duration and Territorial Extent of Restriction.**
**General Guidelines:** Covenants unlimited in duration and limited in geographic scope are unreasonable. *Brecher v. Brown,* 235 Iowa 627, 17 N.W.2d 377 (1945).
**Specific Rulings:** Ten-year covenant not to compete with boat-hoisting business coupled with 12-state territorial restriction held unreasonable. *Rasmussen Heating & Cooling, Inc. v. Idso,* 463 N.W.2d 703 (Iowa Ct. App. 1990). Ninety-day covenant not to compete with stockbroking firm coupled with territorial restriction of 30 miles held reasonable. *Dain Bosworth, Inc. v. Brandhorst,* 356 N.W.2d 590 (Iowa Ct. App. 1984). Three-year covenant not to compete with exterminating company coupled with a territorial restriction of ten miles from the city held reasonable. *Orkin Exterminating Co. (Arwell Division) v. Burnett,* 259 Iowa 218, 146 N.W.2d 320 (1966).

**Protectable Interests.** Trade secrets, peculiar knowledge gained in course of employment. *Iowa Glass Depot, Inc. v. Jindrich,* 338 N.W.2d 376 (Iowa 1983); *Baker v. Starky,* 259 Iowa 480, 144 N.W.2d 899 (1966).

## KANSAS

**Relevant Statute.** —

**Partial Enforceability.** Yes. Courts may modify covenants to make them reasonable. *Foltz v. Struxness,* 168 Kan. 714, 215 P.2d 133 (1950).

**Duration and Territorial Extent of Restriction.**
**General Guidelines:** Legitimate business interest of employer, burden on employee, and impact on public welfare are key considerations in evaluating a covenant. *Weber v. Tillman,* 913 P.2d 84 (Kan. 1996).
**Specific Rulings:** —

**Protectable Interests.** Trade secrets, expertise learned in course of employment, and customer contacts. *Eastern Distributing Co. v. Flynn,* 222 Kan. 666, 567 N.W.2d 1371 (1977).

## KENTUCKY

**Relevant Statute.** —

**Partial Enforceability.** Yes. Courts may establish reasonable limitations for covenants. *Hodges v. Todd,* 698 S.W.2d 317 (Ky. App. 1985).

**Duration and Territorial Extent of Restriction.**
**General Guidelines:** Covenants of unlimited duration and unlimited geographic scope are unreasonable. *Calhoun v. Everman,* 242 S.W.2d 100 (Ky. 1951). Covenants of limited duration and unlimited geographic scope are unreasonable. *Calhoun v. Everman,* 242 S.W.2d 100 (Ky. 1951). Covenants of unlimited duration and limited geographic scope are unreasonable. *Calhoun v. Everman,* 242 S.W.2d 100 (Ky. 1951).
**Specific Rulings:** One-year covenant not to compete with security business coupled with territorial restriction of sites at which employees in question had worked held reasonable. *Borg-Warner Protective Services Corp. v. Guardsmark, Inc.,* 946 F. Supp. 495 (E.D. Ky. 1996). Two-year covenant not to compete with adjustment company coupled with nationwide territorial restriction held reasonable. *Central Adjustment Bureau, Inc. v. Ingram Associates,* 622 S.W.2d 681 (Ky. Ct. App. 1981). One-year covenant not to compete with insurance company coupled with nationwide territorial restriction of 200 miles held reasonable. *Hammons v. Big Sandy Claims Service, Inc.* 567 S.W.2d 313 (Ky. Ct. App. 1978).

**Protectable Interests.** Confidential information and customer contacts. *Central Adjustment Bureau, Inc. v. Ingram Associates,* 622 S.W.2d 681 (Ky. Ct. App. 1981).

## LOUISIANA

**Relevant Statute.** La. Rev. Stat. Ann. sec. 23:921 (West Supp. 1997).

In order for statute prohibiting noncompetition agreements to apply, relationship between the parties must be "essentially" an employee-employer relationship, regardless of relationship contract purports to create. *L.S.P. v. Savoie Sausage,* 673 So.2d 248 (La. Ct. App. 3d Cir. 1996).

**Partial Enforceability.** No. *Comet Industries, Inc. v. Lawrence,* 600 So.2d 89 (La. Ct. App. 1992).

**Duration and Territorial Extent of Restriction.**
**General Guidelines:** Covenants unlimited in duration and geographic scope are unenforceable. *Barrera v. Ciolino,* 636 So.2d 218 (La. 1994); *Pelican Publishing Co. v. Wilson,* 626 So.2d 701 (La. Ct. App. 1993); *Comet Industries, Inc. v. Lawrence,* 600 So.2d 89 (La. Ct. App. 1992).
**Specific Rulings:** Two-year covenant not to compete with parking service coupled with territorial restriction of all parishes in which service operated held reasonable. *Dixie Parking Service, Inc. v. Hargrove,* 691 So.2d 1316 (La. Ct. App. 4th Cir. 1997). Two-year covenant not to compete with insurance company (which, due to the date of the covenant, in effect extended the duration beyond two years) coupled with territorial restriction of three parishes held unreasonable. *Millet v. Crump,* 687 So.2d 132 (La. Ct. App. 5th Cir. 1996).

**Protectable Interests.** Trade secrets, investment of substantial sums in training of employee, or the advertising of employee's connection with employer and solicitation of clients. *Walker v. Louisiana Health Management Co.,* 666 So.2d 415 (La. App. 1995); *Neeb-Kearney & Co. v. Rellstab,* 593 So.2d 741 (La. Ct. App. 1992).

## MAINE

**Relevant Statute.** —

**Partial Enforceability.** Yes. Courts may enforce only covenants to extent necessary to protect legitimate employer interest. *Chalet Suisse International, Inc. v. Mobile Oil Co.,* 597 A.2d 1350 (Me. 1991).

**Duration and Territorial Extent of Restriction.**
**General Guidelines:** —
**Specific Rulings:** Five-year covenant not to compete for current customers of insurance company implicitly coupled with nationwide territorial restriction held reasonable. *Chapman & Drake v. Harrington,* 545 A.2d 645 (Me. 1988).

**Protectable Interests.** Trade secrets, unique business methods, specialized training, customer goodwill, and confidential information. *Lord v. Lord,* 454 A.2d 830 (Me. 1983); *Roy v. Bolduc,* 140 Me. 103, 34 A.2d 479 (1943).

## MARYLAND

**Relevant Statute.** —

**Partial Enforceability.** Yes. Courts may apply "blue pencil" rule to modify unreasonable covenants. *Fowler v. Printers II, Inc.,* 89 Md. App. 448, 598 A.2d 794 (1991).

**Duration and Territorial Extent of Restriction.**
**General Guidelines:** Covenants unlimited in duration and geographic scope are unreasonable. *E.L. Cromwell & Co. v. Gutberlet,* 429 F.2d 527 (4th Cir. 1970).
**Specific Rulings:** Five-year covenant not to compete with public accounting firm coupled with a territorial restriction of 40 miles held reasonable. *Holloway v. Faw, Casson & Co.,* 319 Md. 324, 572 A.2d 510 (1990). Two-year covenant not to compete with computer company implicitly coupled with nationwide territorial restriction held reasonable. *Gill v. Com-*

*puter Equipment Corp.*, 266 Md. 170, 292 A.2d 54 (1972). Two-year covenant not to compete for clients of insurance brokerage firm implicitly coupled with nationwide territorial restriction held reasonable. *Tuttle v. Riggs-Warfield-Roloson, Inc.*, 251 Md. 45, 246 A.2d 588 (1968).

**Protectable Interests.** Trade secrets, client lists, unique services, and customer goodwill. *Holloway v. Faw, Casson & Co.*, 319 Md. 324, 572 A.2d 510 (1990); *Budget Rent A Car of Washington v. Raab*, 268 Md. 478, 302 A.2d 11 (1973).

## MASSACHUSETTS

**Relevant Statute.** Mass. Gen. Laws Ann. ch. 93, § 4 (West 1984).

**Partial Enforceability.** Yes. Overly broad duration or territorial restrictions may be enforced to the extent that they are reasonable. *Marine Contractors Co. v. Hurley*, 365 Mass. 280, 310 N.E.2d 915 (1974).

**Duration and Territorial Extent of Restriction.**
**General Guidelines:** Covenants of unlimited duration and limited geographic scope are reasonable. *Catania v. Hallisey*, 352 Mass. 327, 225 N.E.2d 368 (1967). Covenants of unlimited duration and unlimited geographic scope are unreasonable. *Abramson v. Blackman*, 340 Mass. 714, 166 N.E.2d 729 (1960).
**Specific Rulings:** Five-year covenant not to compete with construction company coupled with territorial restriction of 100 miles held reasonable. *Marine Contractors Co. v. Hurley*, 365 Mass. 280, 310 N.E.2d 915 (1974). Three-year covenant not to compete with plastics distributor coupled with 28-state territorial restriction held reasonable. *Novelty Bias Binding Co. v. Shevrin*, 342 Mass. 714, 175 N.E.2d 374 (1961).

**Protectable Interests.** Trade secrets, confidential information, goodwill, company reputation, and relationship with customers. *Marcam Corp. v. Orchard*, 885 F. Supp. 294 (D. Mass. 1995); *New England Canteen Service, Inc. v. Ashley*, 372 Mass. 671, 363 N.E.2d 526 (1977).

## MICHIGAN

**Relevant Statute.** Mich. Comp. Laws Ann. § 445.761–445.767 (West 1967), which had governed covenants not to compete, was repealed by Mich. Comp. Laws Ann. § 445.774a. However, the former statute still governs any agreements made prior to its repeal.

**Partial Enforceability.** Yes. Courts may enforce covenants to extent they are reasonable. *Follmer, Rudzeqicz & Co., P.C. v. Kosco*, 420 Mich. 394, 362 N.W.2d 676 (1984).

**Duration and Territorial Extent of Restriction.**
**General Guidelines:** —
**Specific Rulings:** Non-compete clause in employment contracts prohibiting employees from selling computer barcode systems for one year was reasonable given competitive nature of field and that employer sold systems in 48 states and in various foreign countries. *Lowry Computer Products, Inc. v. Head*, 984 F. Supp. 1111 (E.D. Mich. 1997).

**Protectable Interests.** Trade secrets and confidential information. *Follmer, Rudzeqicz & Co., P.C. v. Kosco*, 420 Mich. 394, 362 N.W.2d 676 (1984); *Structural Dynamics Research Corp. v. Engineering Mechanics Research Corp.*, 401 F. Supp. 1102 (E.D. Mich. 1975).

## MINNESOTA

**Relevant Statute.** Minn. Stat. Ann. § 325D.51 (West 1995).

**Partial Enforceability.** Yes. Courts may enforce covenants to extent they are reasonable. *Dean Van Horn Consulting Associates, Inc. v. Wold*, 395 N.W.2d 405 (Minn. Ct. App. 1986).

**Duration and Territorial Extent of Restriction.**
**General Guidelines:** Under Minnesota law covenants not to compete will not be enforced unless covenant is reasonable in time and scope to protect employer's lawful interests. *IDS Life Insurance Co. v. SunAmerica Life Insurance Co.*, 136 F.3d 537 (7th Cir. 1998).
**Specific Rulings:** Three-year covenant not to compete for current clients of tax and accounting firm implicitly coupled with nationwide territorial restriction held unreasonable. (Court modified duration of covenant from three years to one year). *Dean Van Horn Consulting Associates, Inc. v. Wold*, 395 N.W.2d 405 (Minn. Ct. App. 1986). Two-year covenant not to compete for current customers of sewage treatment plant implicitly coupled with nationwide territorial restriction held reasonable. *Cherne Industrial, Inc. v. Grounds and Associates, Inc.* 278 N.W.2d 81 (Minn. 1979). Two-year covenant not to compete with siding company coupled with a territorial restriction of six counties held reasonable. *Alside, Inc. v. Larson*, 300 Minn. 285, 220 N.W.2d 274 (1974).

**Protectable Interests.** Trade secrets, goodwill, and confidential information. *Dynamic Air, Inc. v. Bloch*, 502 N.W.2d 796 (Minn. Ct. App. 1993); *Larx Co. v. Nicol*, 224 Minn. 1, 28 N.W.2d 705 (1947).

## MISSISSIPPI

**Relevant Statute.** —

**Partial Enforceability.** Yes. Courts may modify covenants with unreasonable restrictions to make them reasonable. *Herring Gas Co. v. Magee*, 813 F. Supp. 1239 (N.D. Miss. 1993); *Hensley v. E.R. Carpenter Co.*, 633 F.2d 1106 (11th Cir. 1980).

**Duration and Territorial Extent of Restriction.**
**General Guidelines:** —
**Specific Rulings:** Six-year covenant not to compete with propane gas and accessories distributorship coupled with a territorial restriction of 50 miles from any distributorship office held reasonable. *Herring Gas Co. v. Magee,* 813 F. Supp. 1239 (N.D. Miss. 1993). Ten-year covenant not to compete with company that mined and sold dirt and gravel coupled with a territorial restriction of 100 miles held reasonable. *Cooper v. Gidden,* 515 So.2d 900 (Miss. 1987). Two-year covenant not to compete with company that sold polyester fiber coupled with territorial restriction of 300 miles held reasonable. (Court modified territorial restriction from U.S. and Canada to 300 miles). *Hensley v. E.R. Carpenter Co.,* 633 F.2d 1106 (11th Cir. 1980).

**Protectable Interests.** —

**MISSOURI**

**Relevant Statute.** Mo. Ann. Stat. § 416.031.

**Partial Enforceability.** Yes. Courts may modify unreasonable restrictions in covenants and enforce covenants to extent they are reasonable. *AEE-EMF, Inc. v. Passmore,* 906 S.W.2d 714 (Mo. Ct. App. W.D. 1995); *Superior Gearbox Co. v. Edwards,* 869 S.W.2d 239 (Mo. Ct. App. 1993).

**Duration and Territorial Extent of Restriction.**
**General Guidelines:** Covenants that are limited in duration and unlimited in geographical scope are unreasonable. *National Motor Club of Missouri, Inc. v. Noe,* 475 S.W.2d 14 (Mo. 1972). Covenants not to compete are generally enforceable if necessary to protect employer's legitimate interest and if reasonable as to time and geographical limitations. *Marion v. Hazlewood Farms Bakeries, Inc.*, 969 F. Supp. 540 (E.D. Mo. 1997). To be valid, restrictive covenants in employment contracts must be reasonable as to time and geographic limitations. *Schott v. Beussink,* 950 S.W.2d 621 (Mo. App. E.D. 1997).
**Specific Rulings:** Three-year covenant not to compete with company that repaired electronic components in aircraft control panels coupled with nationwide territorial restriction held reasonable. *AEE-EMF, Inc. v. Passmore,* 906 S.W.2d 714 (Mo. Ct. App. W.D. 1995). Eight-year covenant not to compete with athletic accessories business coupled with territorial restriction of three counties held reasonable. *Champion Sports Center, Inc. v. Peters,* 763 S.W.2d 367 (Mo. Ct. App. 1989). Two-year covenant not to compete with paint and chemical business coupled with territorial restriction of 125 miles held reasonable. *Mid-States Paint and Chemical Co. v. Herr,* 746 S.W.2d 613 (Mo. Ct. App. 1988). Two-year covenant not to compete with courier business coupled with three-state territorial restriction held reasonable. *Gelco Express Co. v. Ashby,* 689 S.W.2d 790 (Mo. Ct. App. 1985). Ten-year covenant not to compete with retail food company coupled with territorial restriction of 200 miles held reasonable. *Schnucks Twenty-Five, Inc. v. Bettendord,* 595 S.W.2d 279 (Mo. Ct. App. 1985). Three-and-one-half-year covenant not to compete with insurance adjuster company coupled with territorial restriction of 600 miles held reasonable. *Ibur & Associates Adjustment Co. v. Walsh,* 595 S.W.2d 33 (Mo. Ct. App. 1980).

**Protectable Interests.** Trade secrets, customer lists, customer contacts, goodwill, and confidential information. *Furniture Manufacturing Corp. v. Joseph,* 900 S.W.2d 642 (Mo. Ct. App. 1995); *Cape Mobile Home Mart, Inc. v. Mobley,* 780 S.W.2d 116 (Mo. Ct. App. 1989); *Mid-States Paint and Chemical Co. v. Herr,* 746 S.W.2d 613 (Mo. Ct. App. 1988); *Osage Gas, Inc. v. Donovan,* 693 S.W.2d 71 (Mo. 1985) *Renal Treatment Centers—Missouri, Inc. v. Braxton*, 945 S.W.2d 557 (E.D. Mo. 1997).

**MONTANA**

**Relevant Statute.** Mont. Code Ann. § 28-2-703 (1995).

**Partial Enforceability.** Covenant was enforceable only to extent it did not conflict with applicable statutes. *Treasure Chem., Inc. v. Team Laboratory Chem. Corp.*, 609 P.2d 285 (Mont. 1980).

**Duration and Territorial Extent of Restriction.**
**General Guidelines:** Covenant not to compete is reasonable if limited in operation as to time or place, based on good consideration, affords reasonable protection for and does not impose unreasonable burden on employer, employee, or public. *Daniels v. Thomas, Dean & Hoskins, Inc.*, 246 Mont. 125, 804 P.2d 359 (1990).
**Specific Rulings:** Five-year covenant not to compete with accounting firm coupled with territorial restriction of 100 miles held reasonable. *Dumont v. Tucker,* 250 Mont. 417, 822 P.2d 96 (1991). Ten-year covenant not to compete with radio station coupled with territorial restriction of 50 miles held reasonable. *Western Media, Inc. v. Merrick,* 224 Mont. 28, 727 P.2d 547 (1986).

**Protectable Interests.** —

**NEBRASKA**

**Relevant Statute.** —

**Partial Enforceability.** No. Courts may not reform unreasonable covenant not to compete solely to make the covenant enforceable. *CAE Vanguard, Inc. v. Newman,* 246 Neb. 334, 518 N.W.2d 652 (1994).

**Duration and Territorial Extent of Restriction.**
**General Guidelines:** —

**Specific Rulings:** One-year covenant not to compete with personnel recruiting business coupled with nationwide territorial restriction held unreasonable. *Moore v. Eggers Consulting Co., Inc.,* 252 Neb. 396, 562 N.W.2d 534 (1997). Two-year covenant not to compete with accounting firm coupled with territorial restriction of 75 miles held reasonable. *Dana F. Cole & Co. v. Byerly,* 211 Neb. 903, 320 N.W.2d 916 (1982). Fifteen-year covenant not to compete with auto dealership coupled with one-county territorial restriction held reasonable. *D.W. Trowbridge Ford v. Galyen,* 200 Neb. 103, 262 N.W.2d 442 (1978).

**Protectable Interests.** Trade secrets, goodwill, customer contacts, and confidential information. *Polly v. Ray D. Hilderman & Co.,* 225 Neb. 662, 407 N.W.2d 751 (1987); *Securities Acceptance Corp. v. Brown,* 171 Neb. 406, 106 N.W.2d 456, *clarified and rehearing denied,* 171 Neb. 701, 107 N.W.2d 540 (1961).

## NEVADA

**Relevant Statute.** Nev. Rev. Stat. Ann. § 613.200 (Michie 1996).

**Partial Enforceability.** Yes. Restrictions in covenant enforceable only if reasonable. *Hotel Riviera, Inc. v. Torres,* 97 Nev. 399, 632 P.2d 1155 (1981).

**Duration and Territorial Extent of Restriction.**
**General Guidelines:** —
**Specific Rulings:** Two-year covenant not to compete with pawnshop coupled with territorial restriction of 50 miles held unreasonable. *Camco, Inc. v. Baker,* 936 P.2d 829 (Nev. 1997). Statute treats only individuals who seek subsequent employment with others and does not cover self-employment. *Hansen v. Edwards*, 426 P.2d 792 (Nev. 1967).

**Protectable Interests.** Goodwill. *Hansen v. Edwards,* 83 Nev. 189, 426 P.2d 792 (1967).

## NEW HAMPSHIRE

**Relevant Statute.** —

**Partial Enforceability.** Covenants will be enforced only to extent necessary to protect employer interest. *Technical Aid Corp. v. Allen,* 134 N.H. 1, 591 A.2d 262 (1991).

**Duration and Territorial Extent of Restriction.**
**General Guidelines:** Contractual restraint on competition must be narrowly tailored as to both geography and time. *Concord Orthopaedics Professional Ass'n v. Forbes*, 707 A.2d 1273 (N.H. 1997).
**Specific Rulings:** One-and-one-half-year covenant not to compete with technical assistance firm implicitly coupled with national territorial restrictions held unreasonable. *Technical Aid Corp. v. Allen,* 134 N.H. 1, 591 A.2d 262 (1991). Two-year covenant prohibiting competition after termination of employment was reasonable since it was limited to existing patients within 25 miles of association's office. *Concord Orthopaedics Professional Ass'n v. Forbes*, 707 A.2d 1273 (N.H. 1997).

**Protectable Interests.** Goodwill. *Concord Orthopaedics Professional Ass'n v. Forbes*, 707 A.2d 1273 (N.H. 1997).

## NEW JERSEY

**Relevant Statute.** —

**Partial Enforceability.** Yes. Covenants are subject to total or partial enforcement to extent reasonable. *Solari Industries, Inc. v. Malady,* 5 N.J. 571, 264 A.2d 53 (1970).

**Duration and Territorial Extent of Restriction.**
**General Guidelines:** Covenants of unlimited duration and unlimited territory held unreasonable. *Mailman, Ross, Toyes & Shapiro v. Edelson,* 183 N.J. Super. 434, 444 A.2d 75 (Ch. Div. 1982). Covenants of limited duration and unlimited territory held unreasonable. *Hudson Foam Latex Products, Inc. v. Aiken,* 82 N.J. Super. 508, 198 A.2d 136 (App. Div. 1964).
**Specific Rulings:** One-year covenant not to compete for toy company distributorship clients implicitly coupled with nationwide territorial restriction held reasonable. *Platinum Management, Inc. v. Dahms,* 285 N.J. Super. 274, 666 A.2d 1028 (Law Div. 1995).

**Protectable Interests.** Trade secrets, confidential information, and customer relationships. *Mailman, Ross, Toyes & Shapiro v. Edelson,* 183 N.J. Super. 434, 444 A.2d 75 (Ch. Div. 1982); *Whitmyer Brothers, Inc. v. Doyle,* 58 N.J. 25, 274 A.2d 577 (1971).

## NEW MEXICO

**Relevant Statute.** —

**Partial Enforceability.** —

**Duration and Territorial Extent of Restriction.**
**General Guidelines:** —
**Specific Rulings:** Three-year covenant not to compete with clinic coupled with country-wide territorial restrictions held reasonable. *Lovelace Clinic v. Murphy,* 76 N.M. 645, 417 P.2d 450 (1966).

**Protectable Interests.** —

## NEW YORK

**Relevant Statute.** N.Y. Gen. Bus. Law § 340 (McKinney 1988).

**Partial Enforceability.** Yes. Courts may enforce reasonable portions of covenants and render unreasonable portions unenforceable. *Baker's Aid, A Division of M. Raubvogel Co. v. Hussman Food Service Co.,* 730 F. Supp. 1209 (E.D.N.Y. 1990); *Greenwich Mills Co. v. Barrie House Coffee Co.,* 91 A.D.2d 398, 459 N.Y.S.2d 454 (1983).

**Duration and Territorial Extent of Restriction.**
**General Guidelines:** Covenants of unlimited duration and reasonable geographic scope are enforceable. *Town Line Repairs, Inc. v. Anderson,* 90 A.D.2d 217, 455 N.Y.S.2d 28 (1982). Restrictive covenants that limit employee's ability to pursue similar employment after termination are disfavored by the law and will be enforced only if limited in duration and geographic area. *H & R Recruiters, Inc. v. Kirkpatrick,* 663 N.Y.S.2d 865 (A.D. 1997). Noncompetition agreement is enforceable only if it is reasonable in duration and geographical area, not burdensome to employee, not harmful to general public, and necessary for employer's protection. *International Paper Co. v. Suwyn,* 951 F. Supp. 445 (S.D.N.Y. 1997).
**Specific Rulings:** Two-year covenant not to compete with law bar review preparatory course coupled with nationwide territorial restriction held reasonable. *Giller v. Harcourt Brace & Co.,* 166 Misc.2d 599, 634 N.Y.S.2d 646 (Sup. Ct. 1995). Six-month covenant not to compete with mobile telephone business coupled with five-county territorial restriction held reasonable. *Rochester Telephone Mobile Communications, Inc. v. Auto Sound Systems, Inc.,* 182 A.D.2d 1119, 583 N.Y.S.2d 327 (1992). Ten-year covenant not to compete with food service company coupled with nationwide territorial restriction held unreasonable. *Baker's Aid, A Division of M. Raubvogel Co. v. Hussman Food Service Co.,* 730 F. Supp. 1209 (E.D.N.Y. 1990). Two-year covenant restricting cardiologist from working within city was harmful to the public and held unreasonable. *Muller v. N.Y. Heart Center Cardiovascular Specialists P.C.,* 656 N.Y.S.2d 464 (A.D. 3 1997). Restrictive covenant prohibiting employee from associating with individuals in the oil brokerage business in any country where employer was engaged in such business was unreasonably broad. *Crippen v. United Petroleum Feedstocks, Inc.,* 666 N.Y.S.2d 156 (A.D. 1997).

**Protectable Interests.** Trade secrets, confidential information, unique services, and goodwill. *Perfect Fit Glove Co. v. Post,* 222 A.D.2d 1025, 635 N.Y.S.2d 917 (1995); *Briskin v. All Seasons Services, Inc.,* 615 N.Y.S.2d 166 (A.D. 1994); *Ward v. Arcade Building Maintenance, Inc.,* 197 A.D.2d 856, 595 N.Y.S.2d 411 (1993); *Contempo Communications, Inc. v. MJM Creative Services, Inc.,* 182 A.D.2d 351, 582 N.Y.S.2d 667 (1992); *H & R Recruiters, Inc. v. Kirkpatrick,* 663 N.Y.S.2d 865 (A.D. 1997); *Windshield Installation Network Inc. v. Goudreau,* 654 N.Y.S.2d 442 (A.D. 1997); *International Paper Co. v. Suwyn,* 966 F. Supp. 246 (S.D.N.Y. 1997); *Inflight Newspapers, Inc. v. Magazines In-Flight,* LLC, 990 F. Supp. 119 (E.D.N.Y. 1997).

## NORTH CAROLINA

**Relevant Statute.** N.C. Gen. Stat. § 75-1 (1994).

**Partial Enforceability.** Yes. Courts may neither enforce nor reform overreaching and unreasonable covenants; however, "blue pencil" rule may be applied to strike overreaching and unreasonable portions that are distinct and easily severable from reasonable provisions of covenant. *Hartman v. W.H. Odell & Associates, Inc.,* 450 S.E.2d 912 (N.C. App. 1994).

**Duration and Territorial Extent of Restriction.**
**General Guidelines:** Covenants limited in duration and unlimited in geographic scope are unreasonable. *America Hot Rod Association, Inc. v. Carrier,* 500 F.2d 1269 (4th Cir. 1974).
**Specific Rulings:** Eight-year covenant not to compete with consulting firm implicitly coupled with nationwide territorial restriction held unreasonable. *Professional Liability Consultants, Inc. v. Todd,* 345 N.C. 176, 478 S.E.2d 201 (1996). Five-year covenant not to compete with firm coupled with eight-state territorial restriction held unreasonable. *Hartman v. W.H. Odell & Associates, Inc.,* 450 S.E.2d 912 (N.C. App. 1994). Seven-year covenant not to compete with bicycle shop coupled with two-county territorial restriction held reasonable. *Bicycle Transit Authority, Inc. v. Bell,* 314 N.C. 219, 333 S.E.2d 299 (1985).

**Protectable Interests.** Customer relationships, goodwill, business interests, unique assets, customer lists, and confidential information. *Chemimetals Processing, Inc. v. McEneny,* 124 N.C. App. 194, 476 S.E.2d 374 (1996); *Hartman v. W.H. Odell & Associates, Inc.,* 450 S.E.2d 912 (N.C. App. 1994); *Electrical South, Inc. v. Lewis,* 96 N.C. App. 160, 385 S.E.2d 352 (1989); *United Laboratories, Inc. v. Kuykendall,* 87 N.C. App. 296, 385 S.E.2d 352 (1987); *Wilmar, Inc. v. Liles,* 185 S.E.2d 278 (N.C. App. 1971).

## NORTH DAKOTA

**Relevant Statute.** N.D. Cent. Code § 9-08-06 (1987).

**Partial Enforceability.** Yes. Courts may modify and enforce covenants to the extent they are reasonable. *Herman v. Newman Signs, Inc.,* 417 N.W.2d 479 (N.D. 1987).

**Duration and Territorial Extent of Restriction.**
**General Guidelines:** —
**Specific Rulings:** Five-year covenant not to compete with pizza business coupled with territorial restriction of 60 miles held reasonable. *Lire, Inc. v. Bob's Pizza Inn Restaurants, Inc.,* 541 N.W.2d 432 (N.D. 1995). One-year covenant not to compete with insurance company coupled with territorial restriction of 25 miles held reasonable. *Werlinger v. Mutual Casualty Insurance Co.,* 496 N.W.2d 26 (N.D. 1993). Ten-year covenant not to compete with billboard advertising agency coupled with

territorial restriction of one county held reasonable. *Herman v. Newman Signs, Inc.,* 417 N.W.2d 479 (N.D. 1987).

**Protectable Interests.** Customer data and confidential information. *Kovarik v. American Family Ins. Group*, 108 F.3d 962 (8th Cir. 1997).

## OHIO

**Relevant Statute.** —

**Partial Enforceability.** Yes. Courts may modify covenants to ensure that they are no more restrictive than necessary. *Chrysalis Health Care, Inc. v. Brooks,* 65 Ohio Misc. 2d 32, 640 N.E.2d 519 (Mun. Ct. 1994).

**Duration and Territorial Extent of Restriction.**
**General Guidelines:** Covenants of limited duration and unlimited geographic scope held unreasonable. *Professional Investigations and Consulting Agency, Inc. v. Kingsland,* 69 Ohio App. 3d 753, 591 N.E.2d 1265 (1990). Covenants of unlimited duration and unlimited geographic scope held unreasonable. *Cad Cam, Inc. v. Underwood,* 36 Ohio App.3d 90, 521 N.E.2d 498 (1987).
**Specific Rulings:** Two-year covenant not to compete with equipment manufacturer coupled with statewide territorial restriction held reasonable. *Columbus Medical Equipment Company v. Watters,* 13 Ohio App.3d 149, 468 N.E.2d 343 (1983). Covenant not to compete preventing employee from providing treatment for 6 months to new patients within 5-mile radius of employer's office and current patients within 15 miles of office was reasonable and enforceable by injunction. *Wilson v. Kreusch*, 675 N.E.2d 571 (Ohio App. 2 Dist. 1996).

**Protectable Interests.** Trade secrets, confidential information, and customer lists. *HCCT, Inc. v. Walters,* 99 Ohio App.3d 472, 651 N.E.2d 25 (1995); *Hilb, Rogal and Hamilton Agency of Dayton, Inc. v. Reynolds,* 81 Ohio App.3d 330, 610 N.E.2d 1102 (1992); *Premix, Inc. v. Zappitelli,* 561 F. Supp. 269 (N.D. Ohio 1983).

## OKLAHOMA

**Relevant Statute.** Okla. Stat. Ann. tit. 15, § 217 (1993). Covenants not within statutory parameters are void and unenforceable. *Bayly, Martin & Fay, Inc. v. Pickard,* 780 P.2d 1168 (Okla. 1989).

**Partial Enforceability.** Yes. Courts may modify covenant to compete only if unreasonable portions may be remedied by imposition of reasonable limitations. *Key Temporary Personnel, Inc. v. Cox,* 884 P.2d 1213 (Okla. Ct. App. 1994).

**Duration and Territorial Extent of Restriction.**
**General Guidelines:** Key factors in assessing the reasonableness of covenant are (1) the activity addressed, (2) the duration of restriction, and (3) the geographic scope of restriction. *Key Temporary Personnel, Inc. v. Cox,* 884 P.2d 1213 (Okla. Ct. App. 1994).
**Specific Rulings:** Ten-year covenant not to compete with real estate agency implicitly coupled with nationwide territorial restriction held reasonable. *Cohen Realty, Inc. v. Marinick,* 817 P.2d 747 (Okla. Ct. App. 1991).

**Protectable Interests.** —

## OREGON

**Relevant Statute.** Or. Rev. Stat. § 653.295 (1989).

**Partial Enforceability.** Yes. Courts may enforce unreasonable covenants to extent they are reasonable. *Renzema v. Nichols,* 83 Or. App. 322, 731 P.2d 1048 (1987).

**Duration and Territorial Extent of Restriction.**
**General Guidelines:** —
**Specific Rulings:** Three-year covenant not to compete with territorial restriction of 300 miles held reasonable. *Kennedy v. Wackenhut Corp.,* 41 Or. App. 275, 599 P.2d 1126, *modified on other grounds,* 42 Or. App. 435, 601 P.2d 474 (1979). Two-year covenant not to compete with truck brokerage company coupled with a statewide territorial restriction held reasonable. *Cascade Exchange, Inc. v. Reed,* 278 Or. 749, 565 P.2d 1095 (1977).

**Protectable Interests.** Confidential information, customer contacts and access, customer lists, and specialized information. *Farmers Insurance Exchange v. Fraley,* 80 Or. App. 117, 720 P.2d 770 (1986).

## PENNSYLVANIA

**Relevant Statute.** —

**Partial Enforceability.** Yes. Courts may supply limiting terms to overly broad covenants. *Bell Fuel Corp., Inc. v. Cattolico,* 375 Pa. Super 238, 544 A.2d 450 (1988).

**Duration and Territorial Extent of Restriction.**
**General Guidelines:** Covenants of unlimited duration and unlimited geographic scope held unreasonable. *Reading Aviation Service, Inc. v. Bertolet,* 454 P. 488, 311 A.2d 628 (1973). Restrictive covenants are enforceable to extent they are incidental to employment relationship, necessary for protection of employer, and limited in duration and geographic area. *All-Pak, Inc. v. Johnston*, 694 A.2d 347 (Pa. Super. 1997).
**Specific Rulings:** Two-year covenant not to compete with insulation company coupled with territorial restriction of 300 miles held unreasonable. *Insulation Corp. of America v. Brobstein,* 446 Pa. Super 520, 667 A.2d 729 (1995). Two-year covenant not to compete with auditing business coupled with statewide territorial restriction reasonable. *Worldwide Auditing Services of America v. Richter,* 420 Pa. Super. 584, 587

A.2d 772 (1991). One-year covenant not to compete with travel agency coupled with five-state territorial restriction held reasonable. *Wainwright's Travel Service, Inc. v. Schmolk,* 347 Pa. Super. 199, 500 A.2d 476 (1985). One-year covenant not to compete with investment company coupled with territorial restriction of any city in which company had offices held reasonable. *Girard Inventory, Inc. v. Bello,* 456 Pa. 220, 318 A.2d 718 (1974).

**Protectable Interests.** Trade secrets, confidential information, customer relationships, goodwill, and specialized training. *Bell Fuel Corp., Inc. v. Cattolico,* 375 Pa. Super 238, 544 A.2d 450 (1988); *Gordon Wahls Co. v. Linde,* 306 Pa. Super. 64, 452 A.2d 4 (1982); *Boldt Machinery & Tools, Inc. v. Wallace,* 469 Pa. 504, 366 A.2d 902 (1976); *Girard Inventory, Inc. v. Bello,* 456 Pa. 220, 318 A.2d 718 (1974).

## RHODE ISLAND

**Relevant Statute.** —

**Partial Enforceability.** Yes. Courts may modify covenants and enforce them to extent reasonable. *Durapin, Inc. v. American Products, Inc.,* 559 A.2d 1051 (R.I. 1989); *Max Garelick, Inc. v. Leonardo,* 105 R.I. 142, 250 A.2d 354 (1969).

**Duration and Territorial Extent of Restriction.**
**General Guidelines:** —
**Specific Rulings:** Five-year covenant not to compete with grain merchant by agreeing not to purchase grain from sources merchant used held unreasonable. *Max Garelick, Inc. v. Leonardo,* 105 R.I. 142, 250 A.2d 354 (1969).

**Protectable Interests.** —

## SOUTH CAROLINA

**Relevant Statute.** —

**Partial Enforceability.** Generally, no. *Faces Boutique, Ltd. v. Gibbs,* 318 S.C. 39, 455 S.E.2d 707 (Ct. App. 1995); *Preferred Research, Inc. v. Reeve,* 292 S.C. 545, 357 S.E.2d 489 (Ct. App. 1987). Where there are several different restrictive agreements in a covenant, however, the Court may invalidate one and uphold another in the same document. *Oxman v. Sherman,* 239 S.C. 218, 122 S.E.2d 559 (1961).

**Duration and Territorial Extent of Restriction.**
**General Guidelines:** Covenants unlimited in duration and limited in geographic scope held unreasonable. *Sermons v. Cain & Estes Insurance Agency, Inc.,* 275 S.C. 506, 273 S.E.2d 338 (1980). Covenants unlimited in duration and unlimited in geographic scope held unreasonable. *Almers v. South Carolina National Bank of Charleston,* 265 S.C. 48, 217 S.E.2d 135 (1975).
**Specific Rulings:** Three-year covenant not to compete with hair styling salon coupled with city-wide territorial restriction held unreasonable. *Faces Boutique, Ltd. v. Gibbs,* 318 S.C. 39, 455 S.E.2d 707 (Ct. App. 1995). Three-year covenant not to compete with veterinarian practice coupled with a territorial restriction of 15 miles held unreasonable. *Stringer v. Herron,* 309 S.C. 529, 424 S.E.2d 547 (Ct. App. 1992). Four and five-year covenants not to compete for current customers of insurance company implicitly coupled with nationwide geographic scope held reasonable. *Wolf v. Colonial Life & Casualty Insurance Co.,* 309 S.C. 100, 420 S.E.2d 217 (Ct. App. 1992). Five-year covenant not to compete with restaurant chain coupled with territorial restriction of five miles from any of chain's existing restaurants held reasonable. *Cafe Assoc., Ltd. v. Gerngross,* 305 S.C. 6, 406 S.E.2d 162 (1991). State-wide territorial restriction held unreasonable where majority of company's business came from a local area. *Somerset v. Reyner,* 233 S.C. 324, 104 S.E.2d 344 (1958).

**Protectable Interests.** Trade secrets, trade lists, and confidential information. *Wolf v. Colonial Life & Casualty Insurance Co.,* 309 S.C. 100, 420 S.E.2d 217 (Ct. App. 1992). *South Carolina National Bank of Charleston,* 265 S.C. 48, 217 S.E.2d 135 (1975).

## SOUTH DAKOTA

**Relevant Statute.** S.D. Codified Laws Ann. § 53-9-11 (1990).

**Partial Enforceability.** —

**Duration and Territorial Extent of Restriction.**
**General Guidelines:** —
**Specific Rulings:** Two-year covenant not to compete with supplier of water treatment chemicals implicitly coupled with nationwide territorial restriction held reasonable. *Walling Chemical Co. v. Bigner,* 349 N.W.2d 647 (S.D. 1984).

**Protectable Interests.** Trade secrets, confidential information, and customer lists. *Walling Chemical Co. v. Bigner,* 349 N.W.2d 647 (S.D. 1984); *First American Systems, Inc. v. Rezatto,* 311 N.W.2d 51 (S.D. 1981); *Centrol, Inc. v. Morrow,* 489 N.W.2d 890 (S.D. 1992).

## TENNESSEE

**Relevant Statute.** Tenn. Code Ann. § 47-25-101 (1995).

**Partial Enforceability.** Yes. Courts may modify covenants that are unreasonably restrictive. *Central Adjustment Bureau, Inc. v. Ingram,* 678 S.W.2d 28 (Tenn. 1984).

**Duration and Territorial Extent of Restriction.**
**General Guidelines:** Covenants unlimited in duration and limited in geographic scope held reasonable. *Scott v. McReynolds,* 36 Tenn. App. 289, 255 S.W.2d 401 (1953). Covenants

unlimited in duration and unlimited in geographic scope held unreasonable. *Barner v. Boggiano,* 32 Tenn. App. 351, 222 S.W.2d 672 (1949).
**Specific Rulings:** Five-year covenant not to compete with supplier of veterinarian equipment coupled with five-state territorial restriction held reasonable. *Ramsey v. Mutual Supply Co.,* 58 Tenn. App. 164, 427 S.W.2d 849 (1968).

**Protectable Interests.** Trade secrets, goodwill, and customer relationships. *AmeriGas Propane, Inc. v. Crook,* 844 F. Supp. 379 (M.D. Tenn. 1993); *William B., Tanner Co. v. Taylor,* 530 S.W.2d 517 (Tenn. Ct. App. 1974).

## TEXAS

**Relevant Statute.** Tex. Bus. & Comm. Code Ann. § 15.50 (Vernon 1997).

**Partial Enforceability.** Yes. Courts may modify covenants that are unreasonably restrictive. *General Devices, Inc. v. Bacon,* 888 S.W.2d 497 (Tex. Ct. App. 1994).

**Duration and Territorial Extent of Restriction.**
**General Guidelines:** Covenants with unlimited duration and limited geographic scope held reasonable. *General Devices, Inc. v. Bacon,* 888 S.W.2d 497 (Tex. Ct. App. 1994). Covenants with limited duration and unlimited geographic scope held unreasonable. *Zep Manufacturing Co. v. Harthcock,* 824 S.W.2d 654 (Tex. Ct. App. 1991). Covenants with unlimited duration and unlimited geographic scope held unreasonable. *Justin Belt Co. v. Yost,* 502 S.W.2d 681 (Tex. 1973).
**Specific Rulings:** Three-year covenant not to compete with newspaper company coupled with territorial restriction of ten miles held reasonable. *Webb v. Hartman Newspapers, Inc.,* 793 S.W.2d 302 (Tex. Ct. App. 1990). One-year covenant not to compete with chemical sales company coupled with territorial restriction of 21 counties in four states held reasonable. *Wilson v. Chemco Chemical Co.,* 711 S.W.2d 265 (Tex. Ct. App. 1986). One-year covenant not to compete with financial company signed by financial advisor limited to customers the advisor served while employed by financial company was held reasonable. *American Express Financial Advisors, Inc. v. Scott,* 955 F. Supp. 688 (N.D. Tex. 1996).

**Protectable Interests.** Trade secrets, confidential information, customer lists, goodwill, and special training. *Peat Marwick Main & Co. v. Haass,* 818 S.W.2d 381 (Tex. 1991); *Tom James Co. v. Mendrop,* 819 S.W.2d 251 (Tex. Ct. App. 1991); *Murco Agency, Inc. v. Ryan,* 800 S.W.2d 600 (Tex. Ct. App. 1990); *Bertotti v. C.E. Shepherd Co.,* 752 S.W.2d 648 (Tex. Ct. App. 1988).

## UTAH

**Relevant Statute.** —

**Partial Enforceability.** —

**Duration and Territorial Extent of Restriction.**
**General Guidelines:** —
**Specific Rulings:** Two-year covenant not to compete with cable TV company coupled with territorial restriction of company's range of service held reasonable. *Systems Concepts v. Dixon,* 669 P.2d 421 (Utah 1983).

**Protectable Interests.** Trade secrets, goodwill, customer contacts, unique skills, and extraordinary training. *J & K Computer Systems v. Parrish,* 642 P.2d 732 (Utah 1982); *Robbins v. Finlay,* 645 P.2d 623 (Utah 1982).

## VERMONT

**Relevant Statute.** —

**Partial Enforceability.** Yes. Courts may modify unreasonable covenants to make them reasonable. *A.N. Deringer, Inc. v. Strough,* 103 F.3d 243 (2d Cir. 1996).

**Duration and Territorial Extent of Restriction.**
**General Guidelines:** Enforcement will be ordered unless agreement is found to be contrary to public policy, unnecessary for protection of the employer, or unnecessarily restrictive on employee's rights, with due regard being given to the subject matter of the contract and the conditions and circumstances under which it is to be performed. *Vermont Elec. Supply Co. v. Andrus,* 132 Vt. 195, 315 A.2d 456 (1974). Non-competition agreements are narrowly construed by the courts and must contain time, geographic, and/or industry limitations. *A.N. Deringer, Inc. v. Strough,* 103 F.3d 243 (2nd Cir. 1996).
**Specific Rulings:** Five-year covenant not to compete with electric company coupled with county-wide territorial restriction held reasonable. *Vermont Electric Supply Co. v. Andrus,* 132 Vt. 195, 315 A.2d 456 (1974). Ninety-day covenant not to compete with customs broker coupled with territorial restriction of 100 miles held reasonable. *A.N. Deringer, Inc. v. Strough,* 103 F.3d 243 (2d Cir. 1996).

**Protectable Interests.** —

## VIRGINIA

**Relevant Statute.** —

**Partial Enforceability.** No. *Roto-Die, Inc. v. Lesser,* 899 F. Supp. 1515 (W.D. Va. 1995).

**Duration and Territorial Extent of Restriction.**
**General Guidelines:** Covenants of limited duration and unlimited geographic scope held unreasonable. *Alston Studios, Inc. v. Lloyd V. Gress & Associates,* 492 F.2d 279 (4th Cir. 1974); *Davis-Robertson Agency v. Duke,* 119 F. Supp. 931 (E.D. Va. 1954).

**Specific Rulings:** One-year covenant not to compete coupled with territorial restriction of ten miles held reasonable. *Jackson Hewitt, Inc. v. Greene,* 865 F. Supp. 1199 (E.D. Va. 1994). One-year covenant not to compete with radio station coupled with territorial restriction of 60 miles held reasonable. *New River Media Group, Inc. v. Knighton,* 245 Va. 367, 429 S.E.2d 25 (1993). Two-year covenant not to compete with termite extermination company coupled with multi-county territorial restriction held reasonable. *Paramount Termite Control Corp. v. Rector,* 238 Va. 171, 380 S.E.2d 922 (1989). Three-year covenant not to compete with marine equipment supplier coupled with four-state territorial restriction held unreasonable. *Richardson v. Paxton Co.,* 203 Va. 790, 127 S.E.2d 113 (1962).

**Protectable Interests.** Trade secrets, confidential information, and customer contacts. *Paramount Termite Control Corp. v. Rector,* 238 Va. 171, 380 S.E.2d 922 (1989); *Meissel v. Finley,* 198 Va. 577, 95 S.E.2d 186 (1956).

## WASHINGTON

**Relevant Statute.** Wash. Rev. Code Ann. § 19.86.030 (1989).

**Partial Enforceability.** Yes. Covenants are enforceable to the extent they are reasonable. *Copier Specialists, Inc. v. Gillen,* 76 Wash. App. 771, 887 P.2d 919 (1995).

**Duration and Territorial Extent of Restriction.**
**General Guidelines:** —
**Specific Rulings:** Three-year covenant not to compete for current clients of accounting firm implicitly coupled with nationwide territorial restrictions held reasonable. *Knight, Vale & Gregory v. McDaniel,* 37 Wash. App. 366, 680 P.2d 448 (1984). Five-year covenant not to compete with horse-shoeing business coupled with territorial restrictions of 100 miles held unreasonable. *Wood v. May,* 73 Wash. 2d 307, 438 P.2d 587 (1968).

**Protectable Interests.** Goodwill. *Knight, Vale & Gregory v. McDaniel,* 37 Wash. App. 366, 680 P.2d 448 (1984).

## WEST VIRGINIA

**Relevant Statute.** W. Va. Code § 47-18-3 (1996).

**Partial Enforceability.** Yes. If covenants are reasonable, courts may narrow covenants to conform to actual requirements of parties. *Reddy v. Community Health Foundation of Man,* 171 W. Va. 368, 298 S.E.2d 906 (1982).

**Duration and Territorial Extent of Restriction.**
**General Guidelines:** Covenants of limited duration and unlimited geographic scope held unreasonable. *Pancake Realty Co. v. Harber,* 137 W. Va. 605, 73 S.E.2d 438 (1953).
**Specific Rulings:** One-year covenant not to compete with insurance company coupled with statewide territorial restriction held reasonable. *Wyckoff v. Painter,* 145 W. Va. 310, 115 S.E.2d 80 (1960).

**Protectable Interests.** Trade secrets, confidential information, and customer lists. *Torbett v. Wheeling Money Savings & Trust Co.,* 314 S.E.2d 166 (W. Va. 1983).

## WISCONSIN

**Relevant Statute.** Wis. Stat Ann. § 103. 465 (Supp. 1997).

**Partial Enforceability.** No. Wis. Stat. Ann. sec. 103.465 (Supp. 1997).

**Duration and Territorial Extent of Restriction.**
**General Guidelines:** Covenants unlimited in duration and unlimited in geographic scope held unreasonable. *Gary Van Zeeland Talent, Inc. v. Sandas,* 84 Wisc. 2d 202, 267 N.W.2d 242 (1978).
**Specific Rulings:** —

**Protectable Interests.** —

## WYOMING

**Relevant Statute.** —

**Partial Enforceability.** Yes. Courts may enforce reasonable portions of covenants. *Hopper v. All Pet Animal Clinic, Inc.,* 861 P.2d 531 (Wyo. 1993).

**Duration and Territorial Extent of Restriction.**
**General Guidelines:** —
**Specific Rulings:** —

**Protectable Interests.** —

# § 1.5 Obligations Imposed by Operation of Law—Tort Liability

The issue of tort liability within the context of the employment relationship has remained relatively unchanged and is still based on the common law of master and servant.

## [a] Liability for Employees

An employer may be liable in tort for injuries to its own employees, as well as for injuries to third parties caused by the acts of its employees. In either case, the employer's liability depends first on the existence of the employment relationship. Under the common law, the employer, or master, is that person who controls or has the right to control the details of the work or services performed by another.

Where the employment relationship exists, the employer is liable to the employee for personal injuries sustained by the employee within the scope of employment and by reason of the employer's negligence. Note, however, that in most states, workers' compensation acts and other statutes have altered or supplanted the employer's common-law liability for injuries to employees.

Generally, an employer is subject to liability for the wrongful acts of an employee when the employee commits the acts within the scope of employment. One question over which there has been frequent litigation is whether sexual harassment is within the scope of employment for purposes of tort liability. Some courts have held that employers may be liable in tort for the harassing acts of their employees, whereas other courts have found that harassment is not within the scope of employment.[1] The employer can be held vicariously liable for the tortious or negligent acts of its employee when the employee is subject to the employer's control, the employee is acting within the scope of employment, the acts were carried out in furtherance of the employer's business, the employer breached its duty to control the employee, and the employer knew or should have known of the need and opportunity to exercise control.[2]

## [b] Liability for Independent Contractors

Generally, an employer is not liable for injuries to third parties committed by independent contractors. The rationale for the employer's nonliability is that the employer has no right to control the manner in which the contractor's work is performed and the contractor's work is regarded as the contractor's own enterprise.

There are many definitions of the term "independent contractor." One of the most common definitions states that an independent contractor is one who, in exercising an independent employment, contracts to do certain work according to his or her own methods, without being

---

**§ 1.5**

1. *See* Martin v. Cavalier Hotel Corp., 48 F.3d 1343 (4th Cir. 1995) (hotel liable for harassment of employees by hotel manager because manager used his authority to accomplish the harassment); Ripberger v. Western Ohio Pizza, Inc., 908 F. Supp. 614 (S.D. Ind. 1995) (employer not liable for harassment, because it was not authorized or foreseeable by employer and was not done to serve the employer).

2. *See e.g.,* Robarge v. Bechtel Power Corp., 131 Ariz. 280, 640 P.2d 211 (App. 1982).

subject to the control of his employer, except as to the product or result of his or her work.[3] The mere retention by the employer of the right to supervise or inspect work of an independent contractor as it progresses, for the purpose of determining whether it is completed according to plans and specifications, does not operate to create the relation of master and servant between the owner and those engaged in the work.[4]

### [c] Scope of Employment

An employer will be liable for the acts of its employees only when the employee was acting within the scope of employment. The employee is within the scope of his employment when the employee acts according to an express order of the employer or under the orders of another employee with the express or implied authority to give such an order. Any act that can fairly and reasonably be deemed to be an ordinary and natural incident of the employment is said to be within the scope of employment.[5]

The scope of employment may include acts necessarily incident to the employment.[6] An employer is not liable, however, for the acts of an employee engaged in an activity wholly motivated by the employee's own interests and having no underlying purpose of furthering the employer's business.

---

3. *See, e.g.,* Millsap v. Federal Exp. Corp., 277 Cal. Rptr. 807 (1 Dist. 1991). For further discussion of the employer-independent contractor relationship, see the Introduction to this Guide.

4. *See, e.g.,* Redinger v. Living, Inc., 689 S.W. 2d 415 (Tex. 1985).

5. *See, e.g.,* Miller v. Stouffer, 11 Cal. Rptr. 2d 454 (2d Dist. 1992).

6. *Cf.* Virginian Ry. Co. v. Early, 130 F.2d 548 (4th Cir. 1942) (going to and from place of employment within scope of employment) and Weiss v. Culpeper, 281 So.2d 372 (Fla. App. 1973) (going to and from work not within the scope of employment).

# § 1.6 Dissolution of the Employment Relationship

## [a] Breach of Contract

Claims for breach of contract in the employment context may be brought by either the employer or the employee, although litigation brought by an employee is more prevalent. Claims brought by an employee are usually styled as wrongful discharge claims based on a breach of either express or implied contracts.

*Breach by Employer.* The most common type of claim for wrongful discharge based on a breach of contract centers on an employee's claim that the employer promised not to terminate the relationship without good cause. Although the general rule in the employment context is that either party may terminate the relationship at will, this situation may be changed by actions or words of the employer. Even if the employment is not for a specified term, if the employer has promised not to terminate except for good cause, a discharge not for good cause may be considered a wrongful discharge based on an implied contract theory. (For a discussion of implied oral contracts, see § 1.3[a].) Such an implied right arises when the employer makes statements to the effect that as long as the employee's work is satisfactory, the employee has a future with the employer. These statements may be found in employee manuals but may also be upheld if merely spoken to the employee. (For a discussion of employee manuals, see § 1.3[c].)

Once a court determines that an employee may be fired only for cause, an inquiry into whether the cause was adequate will follow. Courts may consider such factors as how the employee is performing the job in question, whether the employee has breached any terms of the contract or is guilty of misconduct, and the employer's motivation for the discharge. The burden of proof will generally be on the employee as the plaintiff in a wrongful discharge action, but it may be placed on the employer if the employer pleads an affirmative defense, such as the statute of limitations. In any trial, the employer should be prepared to set forth the reasons for the termination. The majority of states have recognized claims for wrongful discharge based on a breach of contract. For treatment in individual states, see Table 4.2-1 (main volume).

*Breach by Employee.* Although less common, breach of contract actions are also brought by employers against employees. This type of claim can arise when there is a contract for a specified term of employment and the employee leaves the job before the end of the contract period. In this circumstance, because the employment was not at will, the employer may bring an action for breach of contract. Remedies for this type of action range from compensatory damages to injunctions preventing the employee from accepting other employment.

Of course, the employee may be able to raise a defense. For example, the employer may have breached the contract first, perhaps by failing to pay wages or by otherwise failing to satisfy its part of the contract.

Actions may also be brought against the employee for poor performance. Under common law in most states, and by statute in some, employees have implicitly promised that they possess and will use the requisite skill and knowledge to perform the employment. If the employee fails to perform at this level, the employer technically has a cause of action for breach of contract.

An action may also be brought against an employee for disloyalty or self-dealing. In all states, employees owe a fiduciary duty to their employers to serve the employer faithfully and not to monetarily damage the employer. This concept protects the employer from actions such as embezzlement and employees' acceptance of kickbacks.

An employee's fiduciary duty becomes an issue when the employee has somehow appropriated the employer's business. For example, an employee who decides to leave his employment to start a competing business and takes the employer's customer lists, current employees, or trade secrets with him may have violated his fiduciary duty to the employer.

Remedies for an employee's breach of contract include money damages and possible injunctions against use of the employer's assets in a competing business situation. On some occasions, profits from the competing business begun by an employee in violation of the fiduciary duty to the employer may be recovered as damages by the employer.[1]

### [b] Alternative Dispute Resolution in the Employment Context

Alternative dispute resolution (ADR) has become an increasingly popular means of resolving work-related disputes. General federal and state guidelines for ADR may be used to arbitrate, rather than litigate, claims under the federal civil rights laws pertaining to employment. Components of ADR include having an open-door policy, grievance procedures, mediation, arbitration, and minitrials.

ADR has many benefits, including reduction of complaints filed with agencies or courts, rapid dispute resolutions, decreased costs (compared with litigation), confidentiality, and potential for improved employer-employee relations. The United States Supreme Court has held that if an employee has signed an arbitration agreement, the employee may be compelled to arbitrate instead of bringing a lawsuit.[2] Thus, by requiring employees to sign arbitration agreements, an employer can limit its exposure to costly and time-consuming litigation.

The Federal Arbitration Act[3] and statutes in most states set standards for determining the enforceability of arbitration proceedings and the means by which arbitration awards may be enforced or vacated. State statutory law makes an important distinction between *arbitration,* which is frequently binding, and *mediation,* which is frequently nonbinding. Either of these options, however, is almost certainly less expensive than a trial in state or federal court. As the number of claims based on employment disputes continues to rise and the overall costs of litigation increase, employers may be more likely to obtain arbitration or mediation agreements from their prospective employees.

A binding arbitration agreement may be created by requiring employees to sign individual agreements calling for arbitration of employment claims.[4] In addition, an agreement to arbitrate may be created by specific provisions in an employee handbook.[5] Some of the most important considerations to be taken into account in developing an ADR policy include the following:

- What types of ADR will be utilized
- Which employees may be subject to ADR
- Which disputes will be resolved through ADR
- Which costs will be borne by the parties
- Whether the sides will have legal or other representation
- What rules of procedure will be followed
- What remedies will be available
- What recourse will be available for parties unsatisfied with the results of ADR

Although such an agreement may bar a judicial remedy, it should be noted that the EEOC apparently takes the position that an employee's right to file a charge, and the EEOC's right to investigate, are non-waivable. [EEOC Notice No 915.002, Enforcement Guidance on Non-waivable Employee Rights Under EEOC Enforced Statutes (Apr 10, 1997)]

### [c] Limiting Potential Postemployment Liability: Waivers and Releases

A waiver or release obtained at the time the employment relationship is terminated can be a valuable tool in

---

**§ 1.6**

1. Bakaly and Grossman, *The Modern Law of Employment Relationships,* §§ 7.1–7.8, 9.1–9.8 (Aspen 2d ed. 1989).

2. Gilmer v. Interstate/Johnson Lane Corp., 500 U.S. 20 (1991).

3. 9 U.S.C. § 1 *et seq.*

4. Mugnano-Bornstein v. Crowell, 42 Mass. App. Ct. 347, 677 N.E.2d 242, 1997 WL 126075 (Mass. App. 1997) (holding that former employee waived statutory right to jury trial of sexual harassment and gender discrimination claims, where she agreed in employment agreement to arbitrate "any controversy arising out of or in connection with [her] employment or termination of employment").

5. Nghien v. NEC Elecs, Inc., 25 F.3d 1437 (9th Cir. 1994), cert. denied, 115 S.Ct. 638 (1994).

preventing litigation or at least limiting liability. A waiver or release in this context is essentially an agreement under which the employee gives up the right to pursue claims against the employer arising from past events in exchange for something of value. Both state and federal courts have recognized the validity of waivers and releases in the employment context.[6]

Certain requirements must be met, however, for a waiver or release to be enforceable against a former employee. The touchstone of validity for such an agreement is that it be entered into knowingly and voluntarily. In addition, a release or waiver must usually provide a quid pro quo; that is, the employee must be given something to which he or she is not otherwise entitled in exchange for releasing or waiving his or her rights. Additional requirements may be set out by statute. For example, the federal Older Worker's Benefits Protection Act lists a number of specific requirements that must be met in order for a release of a claim under the federal Age Discrimination in Employment Act to be enforceable.

There follows a sample waiver or release. Although the sample is in keeping with federal and most state laws, care should be taken to make sure that any specific statutory requirements for a given state are followed.

### [d] Employer Liability for Blacklisting and Negative References

The majority of states have laws protecting employees from blacklists and at least some types of negative references. The degree of protection varies from state to state.

**Blacklisting.** Many states have specific statutes that protect employees from being placed on blacklists. Blacklists are often used by employers to coerce or intimidate employees by making it harder or impossible for them to find employment elsewhere. Blacklists are seldom put down in writing, but rather exist through oral, often implied understandings between employers. The motivation behind employer blacklisting can be a variety of reasons, such as the employee's exercise of the right to organize. This table does not, however, address situations in which the blacklisting activity is conducted in retaliation for "whistleblowing," or where the conduct is otherwise violative of antidiscrimination laws.

The most common blacklisting statute simply prohibits an employer from acting to prevent a former employee from obtaining employment. In some states, blacklisting activity has been made a criminal offense for which fines and/or jail sentences may be imposed. The laws of some states limit the prohibition against blacklisting to certain specific circumstances. For example, in Florida and Ohio, blacklisting statutes prohibit only the refusal to deal with someone based upon a foreign boycott or blacklist. New York and Rhode Island prohibit blacklisting only when it is done for the purpose of preventing blacklisted individuals from obtaining or retaining employment because of their exercise of rights provided under their states' respective labor laws. In other states, like Mississippi, the blacklisting statute is limited to specific industries, such as the telegraph and railroad industries.

Sometimes the manner in which the employer may prevent a former employee from obtaining employment is specifically prescribed. For example, in California, a statute provides only that a former employer may not use a misrepresentation to prevent a former employee from obtaining employment.

A number of states have enacted, as part of their prohibition against blacklisting, a specific statute addressing whether an employer may make a truthful statement about a former employee. In Kansas, an employer may furnish in writing, upon request, the cause of an employee's discharge. In most of the states with such a provision, the statute simply provides that the employer may make such truthful statements. The exact language of the statutes varies, however. Moreover, in some states, the employer may be required by statute to disclose to the employee the reasons for his dismissal. In Missouri, upon a proper request the employer must provide a written letter detailing the nature and character of the services performed and the true cause for the employee's discharge or voluntary dismissal. In Montana, the employer is required to provide a full, succinct, and complete statement of the reason for discharging the employee.

Although such an agreement may bar a judicial remedy, it should be noted that the EEOC apparently takes the position that an employee's right to file a charge, and the EEOC's right to investigate, are non-waivable. [EEOC Notice No 915.002, Enforcement Guidance on Non-waivable Employee Rights Under EEOC Enforced Statutes (Apr 10, 1997)]

---

6. *See, e.g.,* Alexander v. Gardner-Denver Co., 415 U.S. 36 (1974); Borman v. AT&T Communications, 875 F.2d 399 (2d Cir.), *cert. denied,* 493 U.S. 924 (1980); Cramer v. Newburgh Molded Products, 645 N.Y.S.2d 46 (App. Div. 2nd Dept. 1996) (employee's age discrimination claim was barred by his execution of employment termination agreement in which he expressly released employer from all claims including those arising under federal, state, or local laws prohibiting employment discrimination).

**References.** In addition, many states also provide protections for employers in the context of liability for statements made in employee references. Employees frequently are required by prospective employers to list prior jobs held. Often, the prospective employer will contact a former employer to obtain information on the employee's performance in the position held at the former place of employment. A negative reference from the former employer can decrease the likelihood that the employee will obtain the new job. When an employer provides an unfavorable reference, there is a possibility of exposure to a lawsuit instigated by the employee who has been harmed, usually under state libel or slander laws. Conversely, an employer may risk liability to third parties if the employer makes false "good" recommendations about a former employee's job performance.

The risk of liability has caused many companies to refuse to give references, or to simply disclose the dates worked and the salary earned by the employee. However, both the employee and the employer have an interest in making certain information available. The prospect of receiving a good recommendation provides a valuable incentive for employees to perform. The opposite is also true. The possibility of a negative reference may motivate some employees to perform better. Similarly, an employer has an interest in being able to provide references without undue exposure to liability.

The law has attempted to reach a balance between the interests of employers and employees in making certain information available and the interests of employees in preventing certain false or inappropriate information from being disclosed. In virtually all states, the case law with respect to defamation or libel provides a qualified, or conditional, privilege for the type of statements commonly made as part of a job reference. Typically, a statement is conditionally privileged if the publication is made in good faith in answer to one having a legitimate interest in the information sought. An employer whose statements are conditionally privileged is not subject to liability for the publication of those statements unless the privilege is lost or abused. A conditional privilege can be lost, for example, by publication of information with malice. The common-law definition of malice in this context is most often that the publication was made with knowledge of the statement's falsity, or with reckless disregard for the statement's truth or falsity. Minnesota law provides that malice may exist if there is such a gross disregard of the rights of the person injured as is equivalent to malice. Vermont law includes oppression and reckless disregard of the employee's rights as a basis for overcoming a qualified privilege.

Case law also indicates that the conditional privilege can be lost if the publication is excessive. Excessive publication can occur if: (1) the statement is made to more people than have a legitimate interest in the information; (2) the statements include nonprivileged material; or (3) the statements are made for a nonlegitimate purpose. As a Wisconsin Court has held, a conditional privilege can be abused by publication for some purpose other than that for which the privilege is given; publication to a person not reasonably deemed necessary for the accomplishment of the purpose of the privilege; inclusion of defamatory material not reasonably believed to be necessary; or inclusion of unprivileged as well as privileged material.

Under Pennsylvania case law, however, a letter from an employer articulating the reasons for the discharge is absolutely privileged and may not be the subject of a libel action, even if the allegations are false, and regardless of the actual motive behind the dismissal. This privilege may be lost only if the employer publishes the information to unauthorized persons.

Some states have codified the common-law rules with respect to conditional privilege. In Georgia, for example, a statute provides that a communication is qualifiedly privileged when made in good faith in answer to one having an interest in the information sought. These statutes apply generally and are not specifically directed to the employer-employee relationship.

A number of states have passed statutes that specifically limit the liability of employers for making certain statements. For example, an Arizona statute provides an employer immunity from civil liability unless the information is false and defamatory and is acted on to the harm of the employee, and the communicator knows the information is false or acts with reckless disregard of the information's truth or falsity. A New Mexico statute provides immunity unless the statement is knowingly false or deliberately misleading, was rendered with malicious purpose, or violated any civil right of the employee. A Texas statute provides a privilege for a written statement regarding an employee's cause of discharge.

A number of states, such as Colorado, Florida, Idaho, Indiana, and Oregon, have enacted statutes that provide that an employer who gives a reference, upon request, is presumed to be acting in good faith. This presumption can be rebutted only by a showing by the employee that the information was knowingly false, deliberately misleading, or disclosed for a malicious purpose. Under Ohio law, a plaintiff can rebut this presumption only by establishing by clear and convincing evidence that the communication was made with malice.

While most states do not attempt to prescribe exactly what information an employer may disclose, a Kansas statute provides absolute immunity for the disclosure of the following: (1) date of employment, (2) pay level, (3) job description and duties, and (4) wage history. An employer in Kansas is also immune from liability for the disclosure of (1) written employee evaluations that were conducted prior to the employee's separation from the employer and to which the employee shall be given a copy upon request and (2) whether the employee was voluntarily or involuntarily released from service and the reasons, in writing, in response to a written request.

Table 1.6-1 covers laws governing blacklisting and negative references. The table indicates whether the particular state has a statute that governs blacklisting, and sets forth whether the state more broadly prohibits an employer from acting to prevent a former employee from obtaining employment elsewhere. The table also shows whether a particular state has a statute that addresses the liability of employers for making truthful statements regarding former employees, as part of the state's prohibition against blacklisting, as well as any requirements that the employer must disclose the reasons for the employee's discharge.

Table 1.6-1 also indicates whether a particular state recognizes, by statute or case law, a conditional privilege for employee references. In most instances, the existence of such a privilege immunizes the employer from liability for false negative references, to the extent that the employer acted in good faith. The table sets forth what an employee must show to overcome the conditional privilege and thus to create liability on the part of the employer for false or defamatory statements.

# Table 1.6-1
## LAWS GOVERNING BLACKLISTING AND NEGATIVE REFERENCES

**NOTE:** Items presented under "Employer References" columns are based on case law of the state, except for the "Other" column, which may contain statutory law.

| | *Blacklisting Statutes* | | | | *Employee References* | | | |
|---|---|---|---|---|---|---|---|---|
| | *Does State Have Any Statutes Governing Blacklisting?* | *Does State Prohibit Preventing Former Employee From Obtaining Employment?* | *On Request, May Employer Make Truthful Statement About Former Employee?* | *Other* | *Does State Recognize Qualified Privilege for Employee References?* | *Standard Required to Overcome Presumption of Privilege* | *Other* | *Citations to Authority* |
| AL | Yes. | Yes. | State has no specific statutory authority. | Statue provides that any person who maintains a blacklist is guilty of a criminal misdemeanor. | Yes; publication made between previous employer and prospective employer is protected by conditional privilege if made in good faith. | Actual malice. | — | Ala. Code Ann. § 13A-11-123; *Gore v. Health-Tex, Inc.*, 567 So.2d 1307 (Ala. 1990). |
| AK | State has no specific statutory authority. | State has no specific statutory authority. | State has no specific statutory authority. | — | Yes, where publication is made in a reasonable manner for a proper purpose. | Privilege may be abused by knowledge or reckless disregard as to falsity, publication for a purpose other than purpose for which the privilege is given, publication to a person not reasonably believed to be necessary to the accomplishment of the particular privilege, or inclusion of defamatory material not reasonably believed necessary to accomplish the purpose for which the privilege was given. | — | *Schneider v. Pay'n Save Corp.*, 723 P.2d 619 (Alas. 1986). |

*(Table continues.)*

## Table 1.6-1 *(cont'd)*

## LAWS GOVERNING BLACKLISTING AND NEGATIVE REFERENCES

**NOTE:** Items presented under "Employer References" columns are based on case law of the state, except for the "Other" column, which may contain statutory law.

| | *Blacklisting Statutes* | | | | *Employee References* | | | |
|---|---|---|---|---|---|---|---|---|
| | *Does State Have Any Statutes Governing Blacklisting?* | *Does State Prohibit Preventing Former Employee From Obtaining Employment?* | *On Request, May Employer Make Truthful Statement About Former Employee?* | *Other* | *Does State Recognize Qualified Privilege for Employee References?* | *Standard Required to Overcome Presumption of Privilege* | *Other* | *Citations to Authority* |
| AZ | Yes. | Yes. | Yes. | — | See "Other" column. | See "Other" column. | Statute provides immunity from civil liability unless the information is false and defamatory and is acted on to the harm of the employee, and the communicator knows the information is false or acts with reckless disregard of the information's truth or falsity. | Ariz. Rev. Stat. Ann. § 23-1361. |
| AR | Yes. | Yes. | State has no specific statutory authority. | — | Yes, where exercised in a reasonable manner for a proper purpose. | Malice, defined as more than legal malice but possibly less than express malice or ill will. | — | Ark. Stat. Ann. § 11-3-202; *Navorro-Monzo v. Hughes*, 763 S.W.2d 635 (Ark. 1989); *Dillard Department Stores, Inc. v. Felton*, 634 S.W.2d 135 (Ark. 1982). |

| | | | | | | | | |
|---|---|---|---|---|---|---|---|---|
| CA | Yes. | Yes; statute prohibits a former employer from using a misrepresentation to prevent a former employee from obtaining employment. | Yes. | — | Yes, where speaker and recipient share common interest. | Malice. | — | Cal. Labor Code §§ 1050-1054; *Brown v. Kelly Broadcasting Co.*, 771 P.2d 406 (Cal. 1989); *Conkle v. Jeong*, 73 F.3d 909 (9th Cir. 1995). |
| CO | Yes. | Yes. | Yes; statute provides that banks, savings and loans, and other lending institutions are immune from civil liability for references and information regarding any employee's involvement in theft or embezzlement as long as the disclosure is made in good faith. | — | Yes. | Malice. | Statute provides that any employer who, upon request, provides fair and unbiased information about an employee is presumed to be acting in good faith and is immune from liability. The presumption of good faith can be rebutted by a showing that the information was knowingly false, deliberately misleading, or disclosed for a malicious purpose. | Colo. Rev. Stat. §§ 8-2-110-115, 8-3-108; *Thompson v. Public Service Co. of Colorado*, 800 P.2d 1299 (Colo. 1990). |
| CT | Yes. | Yes. | Yes. | — | Yes. | Malice. | — | Conn. Gen. Stat. Ann. §§ 31-51, 31-105, 31-134; *Torosyan v. Boehringer Ingleheim Pharmaceuticals, Inc.*, 662 A.2d 89 (Conn. 1995). |
| DE | State has no specific statutory authority. | State has no specific statutory authority. | State has no specific statutory authority. | — | Yes. | Qualified privilege must be exercised with good faith, without malice, and absent of any knowledge of falsity or desire to cause harm. | — | *Burr v. Atlantic Aviation Corp.*, 348 A.2d 179 (Del. Super. 1975). |

(Table continues.)

# Table 1.6-1 *(cont'd)*

## LAWS GOVERNING BLACKLISTING AND NEGATIVE REFERENCES

**NOTE:** Items presented under "Employer References" columns are based on case law of the state, except for the "Other" column, which may contain statutory law.

| | *Blacklisting Statutes* | | | | *Employee References* | | | |
|---|---|---|---|---|---|---|---|---|
| | *Does State Have Any Statutes Governing Blacklisting?* | *Does State Prohibit Preventing Former Employee From Obtaining Employment?* | *On Request, May Employer Make Truthful Statement About Former Employee?* | *Other* | *Does State Recognize Qualified Privilege for Employee References?* | *Standard Required to Overcome Presumption of Privilege* | *Other* | *Citations to Authority* |
| DC | State has no specific statutory authority. | State has no specific statutory authority. | State has no specific statutory authority. | — | Yes, where person making the statement believes he has a duty to a person with a corresponding interest. | Malice. | — | *Crowley v. North American Telecommunications,* 691 A.2d 1169 (D.C. App. 1997). |
| FL | Yes. | Yes. | Yes. | — | Yes. | Malice. | By statute, an employer who discloses information about a former employee's job performance to a prospective employer is presumed to act in good faith and, unless bad faith is shown, is immune from civil liability. The presumption of good faith is rebutted by showing the information was knowingly false or deliberately misleading, was rendered with malicious purpose, or violated any civil right of the former employee. | Fla. Stat. Ann. §§ 448.045, 542.34, 768.095; *John Hancock Mutual Life Insurance Co. v. Zalay,* 581 So.2d 178 (Fla. 2 DCA 1991). |

| | | | | | | | | |
|---|---|---|---|---|---|---|---|---|
| GA | State has no specific statutory authority. | State has no specific statutory authority. | State has no specific statutory authority. | — | Yes. | Malice. | By statute, communication is qualifiedly privileged when made in good faith in answer to one having an interest in the information sought. | Ga. Code Ann. § 51-5-7; *Cochran v. Sears, Roebuck, & Co.*, 34 S.E.2d 296 (Ga. App. 1945); *Rucker v. Gandy*, 279 S.E.2d 259 (Ga. App. 1981). |
| HI | Yes. | State has no specific statutory authority. | State has no specific statutory authority. | — | No specific case. General libel law may apply. | No specific case. General libel law may apply. | — | Haw. Rev. Stat. Ann. § 377-6(11). |
| ID | Yes. | Yes. | Yes. | — | Yes. | Bad faith, without belief in the truth of the matter communicated or with a reckless disregard of the truth or falsity of the matter. | By statute, an employer who in good faith provides information about the job performance of a former or current employee to a prospective employer may not be held liable for such disclosure. Statute creates presumption of good faith, rebuttable by evidence that the employer disclosed the information with actual malice or with deliberate intent to mislead. | Idaho Code § 44-201; *Arnold v. Diet Center, Inc.*, 746 P.2d 1040 (Idaho App. 1987). |
| IL | Yes. | State has no specific statutory authority. | State has no specific statutory authority. | — | Yes. | Actual malice. | — | 775 ILCS §§ 15/1 et seq.; *Krasinski v. United Parcel Service*, 530 N.E.2d 468 (Ill. 1988). |
| IN | Yes. | Yes. | Yes. | By statute, it is unlawful for any employment agency to circulate, publish, record, or issue any report or information to cause the discharge of any person employed in any legitimate service. | No specific case. See "Other" column. | No specific case. See "Other" column. | By statute, an employer that discloses information about a current or former employee is immune from civil liability for the disclosure and the consequences, unless it is proven that the information disclosed was known to be false at the time the disclosure was made. | Ind. Code Ann. §§ 22-5-3-1, 22-5-3-2. |

*(Table continues.)*

## Table 1.6-1 *(cont'd)*

## LAWS GOVERNING BLACKLISTING AND NEGATIVE REFERENCES

**NOTE:** Items presented under "Employer References" columns are based on case law of the state, except for the "Other" column, which may contain statutory law.

| | *Blacklisting Statutes* | | | | *Employee References* | | | |
|---|---|---|---|---|---|---|---|---|
| | *Does State Have Any Statutes Governing Blacklisting?* | *Does State Prohibit Preventing Former Employee From Obtaining Employment?* | *On Request, May Employer Make Truthful Statement About Former Employee?* | *Other* | *Does State Recognize Qualified Privilege for Employee References?* | *Standard Required to Overcome Presumption of Privilege* | *Other* | *Citations to Authority* |
| IA | Yes. | Yes. | Yes. | — | Yes. Elements to a qualified privilege defense to a defamation claim are (1) statements were made in good faith; (2) defendant has interest to be upheld; (3) statements were limited in scope to this purpose; (4) statements were made on a proper occasion; and (5) publication was in proper manner to proper parties only. | Actual malice. | — | Iowa Code Ann. §§ 730.1-730.3; *Taggert v. Drake University,* 549 N.W.2d 796 (Iowa 1996); *Jenkins v. Wal-Mart Stores, Inc.,* 910 F. Supp. 1399 (N.D. Iowa 1995). |
| KS | Yes. | Yes. | Yes. | By statute, an employer may furnish in writing, upon request, the cause of an employee's discharge. | Yes, where made in good faith between individuals with a corresponding interest in the matter. | Actual malice. | Statute provides absolute immunity for disclosure of the following: (1) date of employment; (2) pay level; (3) job description and duties; and (4) wage history. An employer is also immune from liability for the disclosure of: (1) written employee evaluations that were | Kan. Stat. Ann. §§ 44-117-44-119a; *Turner v. Halliburton Co.,* 722 P.2d 1106 (Kan. 1986). |

| | | | | | | | | |
|---|---|---|---|---|---|---|---|---|
| | | | | | | | conducted prior to the employee's separation from the employer and to which the employee shall be given a copy upon request; and (2) whether the employee was voluntarily or involuntarily released from service and the reasons, in writing, in response to a written request. | |
| KY | Yes. | Yes. | State has no specific statutory authority. | Statute is restricted to mine operators. | Yes. | Malice. | — | Ky. Rev. Stat. § 352.550; *Columbia Sussex Corp., Inc. v. Hay,* 627 S.W.2d 270 (Ky. 1981). |
| LA | Yes. | State has no specific statutory authority. | State has no specific statutory authority. | Statute is restricted to the purchase of merchandise from a particular seller. | Yes, where made in good faith between parties sharing an interest. | Malice. | — | La. Rev. Stat. § 23:963; *Martinez v. Soigneir,* 570 So.2d 23 (La. App. 3 Cir. 1990); *Baudoin v. Louisiana Power and Light Co.,* 540 So.2d 1283 (La. App. 5 Cir. 1989); *Verneuil v. Poirer,* 589 So.2d 1202 (La. App. 2 Cir. 1993). |
| ME | Yes. | Yes. | State has no specific statutory authority. | — | Yes. | Abuse of privilege—by making a statement outside the normal channels or with malicious intent. | — | Me. Rev. Stat. Ann. tit. 17, § 401; *Gautschi v. Maisel,* 565 A.2d 1009 (Me. 1989); *Staples v. Bangor Hydro-Electric Co.,* 629 A.2d 601 (Me. 1993). |
| MD | State has no specific statutory authority. | State has no specific statutory authority. | State has no specific statutory authority. | — | Yes. | Malice. | — | *Gay v. William Hill Manor, Inc.,* 536 A.2d 690 (Md. App. 1988). |

(Table continues.)

**Table 1.6-1** *(cont'd)*

LAWS GOVERNING BLACKLISTING AND NEGATIVE REFERENCES

**NOTE:** Items presented under "Employer References" columns are based on case law of the state, except for the "Other" column, which may contain statutory law.

| | *Blacklisting Statutes* | | | | *Employee References* | | | |
|---|---|---|---|---|---|---|---|---|
| | *Does State Have Any Statutes Governing Blacklisting?* | *Does State Prohibit Preventing Former Employee From Obtaining Employment?* | *On Request, May Employer Make Truthful Statement About Former Employee?* | *Other* | *Does State Recognize Qualified Privilege for Employee References?* | *Standard Required to Overcome Presumption of Privilege* | *Other* | *Citations to Authority* |
| MA | State has no specific statutory authority. | State has no specific statutory authority. | State has no specific statutory authority. | — | Yes. | If disclosure resulted from an expressly malicious motive, was recklessly disseminated, or involved a reckless disregard for the truth or falsity of the information. Privilege may also be lost in the case of unnecessary, unreasonable, or excessive publication on proof that the employer acted recklessly. | — | Mass. Gen. Laws ch. 231, § 91; *McCone v. New England Telephone and Telegraph Co.*, 471 N.E.2d 47 (Mass. 1984); *Bratt v. International Business Machines Corp.*, 467 N.E.2d 126 (Mass. 1984); *Humphrey v. National Semiconductor Corp.*, 463 N.E.2d 1197 (Mass. App. Ct. 1984). |
| MI | State has no specific statutory authority. | State has no specific statutory authority. | State has no specific statutory authority. | — | Yes. | Malice or reckless disregard for the truth. | — | *Dalton v. Herbruck Egg Sales Corp.*, 417 N.W.2d 496 (Mich. App. 1987); *Lawrence v. Syms Corp.*, 969 F. Supp. 1014 (E.D. Mich. 1997). |

| | | | | | | | | |
|---|---|---|---|---|---|---|---|---|
| MN | Yes. | Yes. | State has no specific statutory authority. | — | Yes, where statement is made in good faith and for a legitimate purpose. | Actual malice. | — | Minn. Stat. Ann. §§ 179.12(6), 179.60; *Lewis v. Equitable Life Assurance Society of the US,* 389 N.W.2d 876 (Minn. 1986); *Weissman v. Sri Lanka Curry House, Inc.,* 469 N.W.2d 471 (Minn. App. 1991); *Rosenbloom v. Senior Resource, Inc.,* 974 F. Supp. 738 (D. Minn. 1997). |
| MS | Yes. | Yes. | State has no specific statutory authority. | Statute applies only to telegraph, telephone, and railroad companies. | Yes. | Malice. | Statute also provides for qualified privilege. | Miss. Code Ann. §§ 77-9-725, 77-9-729, 95-1-1 et seq.; *Staheli v. Smith,* 548 So.2d 1299 (Miss. 1989). |
| MO | State has no specific statutory authority. | State has no specific statutory authority. | Yes. If a proper request is made by the employee under the statute, the employer must provide a written letter detailing the nature and character of the service performed and the true cause for the discharge or voluntary dismissal. | — | Yes. | Actual malice; defined as publication of false and defamatory statements either with the knowledge the statements were false or with reckless disregard for the truth or falsity of the statements. | — | Mo. Ann. Stat. § 290.140. *Wright v. Over-the-Road and City Transfer Drivers, Helpers, Dockmen and Warehousemen, Local No. 41, International Brotherhood of Teamsters, Chauffeurs, Warehousemen and Helpers of America,* 945 S.W.2d 481 (App. Ct. Mo. 1997). |

*(Table continues.)*

## Table 1.6-1 *(cont'd)*
## LAWS GOVERNING BLACKLISTING AND NEGATIVE REFERENCES

**NOTE:** Items presented under "Employer References" columns are based on case law of the state, except for the "Other" column, which may contain statutory law.

| | *Blacklisting Statutes* | | | | *Employee References* | | | |
|---|---|---|---|---|---|---|---|---|
| | *Does State Have Any Statutes Governing Blacklisting?* | *Does State Prohibit Preventing Former Employee From Obtaining Employment?* | *On Request, May Employer Make Truthful Statement About Former Employee?* | *Other* | *Does State Recognize Qualified Privilege for Employee References?* | *Standard Required to Overcome Presumption of Privilege* | *Other* | *Citations to Authority* |
| MT | Yes. | Yes. | Yes. On request, an employer must furnish a full, succinct, and complete statement of the reason for discharging the employee. | — | Yes. | Malice. | Statute also provides a qualified privilege. | Mont. Code Ann. §§ 39-2-801, 39-2-802, 39-2-803, 39-2-804; *Malquist v. Foley*, 714 P.2d 995 (Mont. 1986); *Rasmussen v. Bennett*, 741 P.2d 755 (Mont. 1987). |
| NE | State has no specific statutory authority. | State has no specific statutory authority. | State has no specific statutory authority. | — | Yes. | Malice (express or actual) or if there is such a gross disregard of the rights of the person injured as is equivalent to malice in fact. | — | *Bartels v. Retail Credit Co.*, 175 N.W.2d 292 (Neb. 1970); *Turner v. Welliver*, 411 N.W.2d 298 (Neb. 1987). |
| NV | Yes. | Yes. | Yes. | — | Yes. | Malice. | — | Nev. Rev. Stat. §§ 613.200, 613.210; *Ruth Simpson v. Mers, Inc.*, 1997 N.V. 6 (http://www.versuslaw.com) |

| | | | | | | | | |
|---|---|---|---|---|---|---|---|---|
| | | | | | | | | (Nevada, January 6, 1997). |
| NH | State has no specific statutory authority. | State has no specific statutory authority. | State has no specific statutory authority. | — | Yes, if statement is published on a lawful occasion, in good faith, for a lawful purpose, and with belief of truth. | If statement is published on an unlawful occasion, in bad faith, for an unjustifiable purpose, or without a reasonable belief in its truth. | — | *Pickering v. Frink & A.*, 461 A.2d 117 (N.H. 1983). |
| NJ | Yes. | Yes. | State has no specific statutory authority. | Statute prohibits blacklisting or preventing employment, based on sex, race, creed, and nationality. | Yes. | Malice or abuse on the part of the employer. | — | N.J. Stat. Ann. 10:5-12. *Erickson v. Marsh & McLennan Co., Inc.*, 569 A.2d 793 (N.J. 1990). |
| NM | Yes. | Yes. | Yes. | — | Yes, where the statement is made for a proper purpose to one having a legitimate interest in the statements. | Lack of belief or reasonable grounds for belief in the truth of the statement or publication for improper use. | Statute also provides immunity unless the statement is knowingly false or deliberately misleading, was rendered with malicious purpose, or violated any civil right of the employee. | N.M. Stat. Ann. §§ 30-13-3, 50-12-1; *Baker v. Bhajan*, 871 P.2d 374 (N.M. 1994). |
| NY | Yes. | Yes. | — | Statute prevents circulation of a blacklist for the purpose of preventing blacklisted individuals from obtaining or retaining employment because of their exercise of protected rights under state labor law. | Yes. | Malice. | — | N.Y. Labor Law § 704; *Kasachkoff v. City of New York*, 485 N.Y.S.2d 992; *aff'd*, 505 N.Y.S.2d 67 (A.D. 1985); *Weir v. Equifax Services, Inc.*, 620 N.Y.S.2d 675 (4 Dept. 1994); *McNaughton v. City of New York*, 650 N.Y.S.2d 772 (1 Dept. 1996); *Bolden v. Morgan Stanley & Co., Inc.*, 765 F. Supp. 830 (S.D. N.Y. 1991). |

*(Table continues.)*

# Table 1.6-1 *(cont'd)*
## LAWS GOVERNING BLACKLISTING AND NEGATIVE REFERENCES

**NOTE:** Items presented under "Employer References" columns are based on case law of the state, except for the "Other" column, which may contain statutory law.

| | *Blacklisting Statutes* | | | | *Employee References* | | | |
|---|---|---|---|---|---|---|---|---|
| | *Does State Have Any Statutes Governing Blacklisting?* | *Does State Prohibit Preventing Former Employee From Obtaining Employment?* | *On Request, May Employer Make Truthful Statement About Former Employee?* | *Other* | *Does State Recognize Qualified Privilege for Employee References?* | *Standard Required to Overcome Presumption of Privilege* | *Other* | *Citations to Authority* |
| NC | Yes. | Yes. | Yes. | — | Yes, where made in good faith. | Actual malice. | — | N.C. Gen. Stat. §§ 14-355, 14-356; *Harris v. NCNB National Bank of North Carolina*, 355 S.E.2d 838 (N.C. App. 1987). |
| ND | State has no specific statutory authority. | State has no specific statutory authority. | State has no specific statutory authority. | State constitution prevents exchange of blacklists between corporations. | Yes. | Abuse, defined as statements made with actual malice, without reasonable grounds for believing them to be true, or on a subject matter irrelevant to the common interest or duty. | — | N.D. Const. art. XII, §§ 17; *Soentgen v. Quain & Ramstad Clinic*, 467 N.W.2d 73 (N.D. 1991). |
| OH | State has no specific statutory authority. | State has no specific statutory authority. | State has no specific statutory authority. | Statute does prohibit refusal to deal with a person due to a foreign boycott or blacklist. | Yes. | Clear and convincing evidence that the communication was made with actual malice. Actual malice is defined as knowing that the statements are false or acting with reckless disregard for the statements' truth or falsity. | — | Ohio Rev. Code Ann. §§ 1331.02, 1331.99; *Jacobs v. Frank*, 573 N.E.2d 609 (1991); *Rinehart v. Mairano*, 602 N.E.2d 340 (Ohio App. 1991). |

| | | | | | | | | |
|---|---|---|---|---|---|---|---|---|
| OK | Yes. | Yes. | State has no specific statutory authority. | — | Yes; statement is a conditional or qualified privileged communication when made in good faith upon any subject matter in which the party communicating has an interest. | Malice. | — | Okla. Stat. Ann. tit. 40, §§ 172–173; *Hammett v. Hunter,* 117 P.2d 511 (Okla. 1941). |
| OR | Yes. | Yes. | State has no specific statutory authority. | — | No specific case. See “Other” column. | No specific case. See “Other” column. | By statute, an employer who discloses information about a former employee upon request by a prospective employer is presumed to be acting in good faith. Presumption may be overcome by a showing that the information disclosed was knowingly false or deliberately misleading, was rendered with malicious purpose, or violated any civil right of the employee protected by state labor laws. | Or. Rev. Stat. §§ 30.178, 659.230. |
| PA | State has no specific statutory authority. | State has no specific statutory authority. | State has no specific statutory authority. | — | Yes. | Knowledge of falsity or reckless disregard of the truth or falsity of the statement. | A letter from an employer to a discharged employee articulating the reasons for the discharge is absolutely privileged and may not be the subject of a libel action, even if the allegations are false, and regardless of the actual motive behind the dismissal. Privilege may be lost only if the employer publishes the information to unauthorized persons. | *DeLuca v. Reader,* 323 A.2d 309 (Pa. Super. 1974); *Goralski v. Pizzimenti,* 540 A.2d 595 (Pa. Cmwlth. 1980); *Yetter v. Ward Trucking Corp.,* 585 A.2d 1022 (Pa. Super. 1991); *Doe v. Kohn, Nast, & Graf, P.C.,* 862 F. Supp. 1310 (E.D. Pa. 1994). |

*(Table continues.)*

**Table 1.6-1** *(cont'd)*

LAWS GOVERNING BLACKLISTING AND NEGATIVE REFERENCES

**NOTE:** Items presented under "Employer References" columns are based on case law of the state, except for the "Other" column, which may contain statutory law.

| | *Blacklisting Statutes* | | | | *Employee References* | | | |
|---|---|---|---|---|---|---|---|---|
| | *Does State Have Any Statutes Governing Blacklisting?* | *Does State Prohibit Preventing Former Employee From Obtaining Employment?* | *On Request, May Employer Make Truthful Statement About Former Employee?* | *Other* | *Does State Recognize Qualified Privilege for Employee References?* | *Standard Required to Overcome Presumption of Privilege* | *Other* | *Citations to Authority* |
| RI | Yes. | Yes. | State has no specific statutory authority. | Statute is limited to blacklisting employees based on their exercise of their rights under state labor law. | No specific case. See "Other" column. | No specific case. See "Other" column. | By statute, an employer that, upon request by a prospective employer of a current or former employee, provides fair and unbiased information is presumed to be acting in good faith and is immune from civil liability for the disclosure. The presumption of good faith is rebuttable by a showing that the disclosure was knowingly false, deliberately misleading, disclosed for a malicious purpose, or violates the employee's civil rights. | R.I. Gen. Laws §§ 28-6.4-1, 28-7-13(2), 28-7-13(9). |
| SC | State has no specific statutory authority. | State has no specific statutory authority. | State has no specific statutory authority. | — | Yes. | Malice. | — | *Bell v. Bank of Abbeville*, 44 S.E.2d 328 (S.C. 1947). |

| | | | | | | | | |
|---|---|---|---|---|---|---|---|---|
| SD | State has no specific statutory authority. | State has no specific statutory authority. | State has no specific statutory authority. | — | Yes. | Malice. | Statute also recognized privilege. | S.D. Codified Laws §20-11-5; *Peterson v. City of Mitchell*, 499 N.W.2d 911 (S.D. 1993); *Keiser v. Southeast Properties*, 566 S.W.2d 833 (S.D. 1997). |
| TN | State has no specific statutory authority. | State has no specific statutory authority. | State has no specific statutory authority. | — | Yes. | Actual malice. | — | *Woods v. Helmi*, 758 S.W.2d 219 (Tenn. 1988). |
| TX | Yes. | Yes. | Yes. | — | Yes. | Malice or bad faith. | Statute also provides for a privilege for a written statement of cause of discharge. | Tex. Lab. Code Ann. § 52.031; Tex. Civil Stat. § 5206; *Schauer v. Memorial Care Systems*, 856 S.W.2d 437 (Tex. Civ. App. 1 Dist. 1993); *Procter & Gamble Manufacturing Co. v. Hagler*, 880 S.W.2d 123 (Tex. Civ. App. 6 Dist. 1994); *Burch v. Coca-Cola Co.*, 119 F.3d 305 (5th Cir. 1997). |
| UT | Yes. | Yes. | State has no specific statutory authority. | — | Yes. | Malice. | By statute, in a prosecution for criminal libel, a communication made by a person interested in the communication by one who is also interested, or who stands in such a position as to afford reasonable grounds for supposing his motive innocent, is presumed not to be malicious and is a privileged communication. | Utah Const. art. XII, § 19; Utah Code Ann. §§ 34-24-1, 34-24-2, 76-9-506; *Combes v. Montgomery Ward & Co.*, 228 P.2d 272 (Utah 1951). |

*(Table continues.)*

# **Table 1.6-1** *(cont'd)*

## LAWS GOVERNING BLACKLISTING AND NEGATIVE REFERENCES

**NOTE:** Items presented under "Employer References" columns are based on case law of the state, except for the "Other" column, which may contain statutory law.

| | *Blacklisting Statutes* | | | | *Employee References* | | | |
|---|---|---|---|---|---|---|---|---|
| | *Does State Have Any Statutes Governing Blacklisting?* | *Does State Prohibit Preventing Former Employee From Obtaining Employment?* | *On Request, May Employer Make Truthful Statement About Former Employee?* | *Other* | *Does State Recognize Qualified Privilege for Employee References?* | *Standard Required to Overcome Presumption of Privilege* | *Other* | *Citations to Authority* |
| VT | State has no specific statutory authority. | State has no specific statutory authority. | State has no specific statutory authority. | — | Yes. | Malice. | In a case involving internal communications of an employer, qualified privilege was established and could be overcome by knowledge of a statement's falsity or reckless disregard of the truth of the statement, conduct manifesting personal ill will, reckless disregard of the employee's rights, or oppression. | *Crump v. P & C Food Markets, Inc.*, 576 A.2d 441 (Vt. 1990); *Marcoux-Norton v. Kmart Corp.*, 907 F. Supp. 766 (D. Vt. 1993). |
| VA | Yes. | Yes. | Yes. | — | No specific case. See "Other" column. | No specific case. See "Other" column. | In a case dealing with a termination letter to an employee, privilege was recognized. The privilege may be overcome by malice. | Va. Code Ann. § 40.1-27; *Southeastern Tidewater Opportunity Project, Inc. v. Bade,* 435 S.E.2d 131 (Va. 1993). |

| | | | | | | | | |
|---|---|---|---|---|---|---|---|---|
| WA | Yes. | Yes. | State has no specific statutory authority. | — | Yes. | Malice, defined as knowledge or reckless disregard. | In a criminal prosecution for libel, a statute provides this definition of a privileged communication: a communication made by a person interested in the communication by one who is also interested, or who stands in such a position as to afford reasonable grounds for supposing his motive innocent, is presumed not to be malicious and is a privileged communication. | Wash. Rev. Code Ann. §§ 9.58.070, 49.44.010; *Turngren v. King County Department of Public Safety,* 686 P.2d 1110 (Wash. App.), *rev'd on other grounds* 705 P.2d 258 (Wash. 1984). |
| WV | State has no specific statutory authority. | State has no specific statutory authority. | State has no specific statutory authority. | — | Yes, where the communication is sent to one with an interest. | Abuse of privilege, generally equal to malice. | — | *Mauck v. City of Martinsburg,* 280 S.E.2d 216 (W.Va. 1981). |
| WI | Yes. | Yes. | Yes. | — | Yes. | Knowledge of falsity or reckless disregard. | Privilege can also be abused by publication for some purpose other than that for which a privilege is given, publication to a person not reasonably believed necessary for the accomplishment of the purpose of the privilege, inclusion of defamatory material not reasonably believed to be necessary, or inclusion of unprivileged as well as privileged material. | Wis. Stat. Ann. §§ 111.06(1)(k), 134.02; *State v. Giles,* 496 N.W.2d 133 (Wis. Ct. App. 1992). |
| WY | State has no specific statutory authority. | State has no specific statutory authority. | State has no specific statutory authority. | — | No specific case. General libel law may apply. | No specific case. General libel law may apply. | — | — |

# APPENDIX A

## AGREEMENT AND GENERAL RELEASE

This Agreement and General Release is entered into between __________, a resident of the State of __________ over the age of 18 years ("Employee") and __________, a corporation authorized to do business in the State of __________. Employer in consideration of the mutual promises and agreements made herein, agrees as follows:

1. In consideration of this Agreement and General Release, Employer shall pay to Employee the sum of __________ in severance pay to which the Employee is not otherwise entitled. This amount shall be paid as follows: ______________________________.

2. Employer shall also provide, in consideration for this Agreement and General Release, the following: ______________________________.

3. Employer shall not furnish any information about Employee to any third party that would adversely affect Employee's employment opportunities. All reference checks (both written and oral) will be answered in a neutral manner and will supply information concerning Employee's name, dates of employment, job title, job duties, and salary (if such information is requested).

4. In consideration of the foregoing, Employee shall not disclose to anyone any confidential information. For the purposes of this agreement, "confidential information" shall include any of Employer's confidential, proprietary, or trade secret information that is disclosed to Employee or Employee otherwise learns in the course of employment such as, but not limited to, business plans, customer lists, financial information or statements, accounting information or procedures, software diagrams, flow charts and product plans. Confidential information shall not include any information that (a) is or becomes publicly available through no act of Employee; (b) is rightfully received by Employee from a third party without restrictions; or (c) is independently developed by Employee.

5. Employee and Employer each release and fully discharge the other from all claims, demands, causes of action, claims for relief, and all liability for legal and equitable relief whatsoever arising out of or related to Employee's former employment up to the date of this agreement, including, but not limited to, any claim for personal injury, breach of contract, wrongful discharge, or any claim for discrimination because of race, sex, age, national origin, religion or disability, under Title VII of the Civil Rights Act of 1964, The Americans with Disabilities Act, The Age Discrimination in Employment Act, The Family and Medical Leave Act, and any other state or federal law or statute; except that this clause shall not apply to any benefits under unemployment or worker's compensation laws to which the employee may otherwise be entitled. Employee and Employer each covenant not to sue the other (and not to file any judicial or administrative charges against the other) with respect to any such liability.

6. The parties acknowledge that Employee has been given the opportunity to have twenty-one (21) days in which to review and consider this agreement before signing it, and has been advised to consult with an attorney in reviewing this agreement. Employee may revoke this agreement within seven days of signing, provided that the revocation is in writing and is received by Employer no later than the close of business on the seventh day after signing.

7. This agreement contains the entire understanding of the parties regarding its subject matter and may not be changed except by a written instrument signed by all parties. This agreement shall be governed by and construed in accordance with the laws of the State of __________. This agreement shall inure to the benefit of and be binding upon the parties and their respective heirs, successors, and assigns (including any successors by merger, sale of assets or other business transaction).

8. The parties acknowledge to each other that each of them has read the full contents of this agreement, understands that the agreement constitutes a contract, and represents that this agreement is entered into voluntarily.

9. The provisions of this Agreement and General Release shall be deemed severable, and the invalidity or unenforceability of any one or more of the provisions hereof shall not affect the validity and enforceability of the other provisions hereof.

IN WITNESS WHEREOF, the parties have executed, sealed and delivered this agreement this _____ day of __________, 19___.

______________________________
[SEAL]
Employee

[Corporate Seal]

EMPLOYER

By: ______________________________
[SEAL]
Authorized Officer

STATE of __________
__________ COUNTY

I, __________, a notary public for said County and State, do hereby certify that __________ personally appeared before me this day and acknowledged the due execution of the foregoing instrument.

Witness my hand and official seal, this _____ day of __________, 19___.

______________________________
Notary Public
My commission expires: ____________________

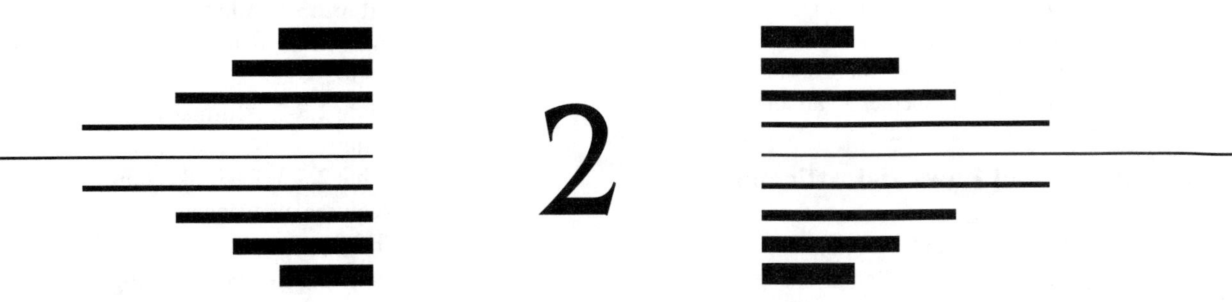

# Fair Employment Practices

*Tables in Part 2 cover protected classifications under fair employment practice (FEP) statutes, compliance with FEP statutes, exceptions to compliance, fair employment commission powers and procedures, appeal of commission rulings, remedies available for violations, additional FEP laws, and affirmative action requirements.*

# § 2.1 Overview: Increasing Importance of State Fair Employment Practice Laws

Over 30 years ago, Congress enacted the Civil Rights Act of 1964 containing Title VII, which prohibits discrimination in employment on the basis of race, color, national origin, religion, and sex. A year before, Congress had passed the Equal Pay Act of 1963, requiring employers to provide equal pay for equal work. Later, in 1967, Congress passed the Age Discrimination in Employment Act (ADEA), barring discrimination based on age in employment-related decisions. In the years following these landmark bills, Congress has adopted amendments offering protection to other groups historically deemed discrimination victims, including the handicapped.[1]

In the 1960s, a number of states also adopted similar fair employment practice (FEP) laws. In fact, some state laws even preceded the federal laws, which allowed for a degree of local control in discrimination issues. Today, most states have fair employment provisions analogous to Title VII and the ADEA. Most states also bar discrimination against persons with handicaps or disabilities, and many others have added to federal statutory provisions barring discrimination based on marital status or ancestry, for instance.

As a general rule, the states have followed federal precedent in interpreting their own fair employment laws; however, deference to federal precedent may be eroding.[2]

First, the remedies available under state laws are occasionally broader than those permitted under federal statutes. Title VII, the principal federal fair employment law, permits recovery of back pay and other lost benefits, and a prevailing plaintiff may recover compensatory and/or punitive damages up to a statutory "cap." Under the ADEA, a prevailing plaintiff may recover these same damages and, if the employer's conduct is willful, may recover an additional award of liquidated damages equal to the award for back pay and lost benefits. In contrast, many state laws permit unlimited compensatory or other damages.

Second, federal laws mandate very tight time frames (that is, statutes of limitations) for filing discrimination claims. Both Title VII and the ADEA require charges to be filed with the Equal Employment Opportunity Commission (EEOC) within 180 or 300 days, depending on the state. A number of states have laws that allow for longer periods, up to one year and beyond.

Third, although the federal courts were once widely viewed as the primary guardians of civil rights, that perception may be changing. The fear that state court judges might succumb to political or social pressures in deciding fair employment cases has dissipated to a large extent. In addition, state court judges have displayed an increasing understanding of fair employment issues.

**§ 2.1**

1. See Part 9, Summary of Federal Legislation, Guidelines, and Policy on Personnel Law.

2. See § 2.2[a] for a discussion of state court jurisdiction over Title VII employment discrimination claims.

# § 2.2 Current Issues in Fair Employment Practice Laws

## [a] State Court Jurisdiction over Title VII Claims

Although Title VII actions are typically brought in federal court, the proposition that state courts may exercise concurrent jurisdiction over Title VII claims has gained increasing acceptance. In *Donnelly,*[1] the Supreme Court held that none of the language in Title VII expressly confines jurisdiction to federal courts or ousts state courts of their presumptive jurisdiction.

Following the Supreme Court's lead in *Donnelly,* most state courts that have addressed the issue have decided to exercise their concurrent jurisdiction over Title VII claims. States that have done so include Arizona, Georgia, Maryland, Missouri, Massachusetts, New York, Ohio, Washington, and Wisconsin.[2] In *Kolodziej,*[3] the Massachusetts plaintiff was allowed to amend his state court complaint late in the proceedings to include a Title VII claim. In *Manning,*[4] the Ohio Supreme Court decided that Ohio courts could exercise jurisdiction over Title VII claims, but jurisdiction was limited to the Ohio Court of Claims.

Although the current trend in the state courts is to exercise jurisdiction over Title VII claims, the opinion in *Donnelly* does not seem to *mandate* that a state court do so. A state appellate court in Illinois declined to accept jurisdiction over a Title VII claim, even in light of the Supreme Court's opinion in *Donnelly.*[5] The court in *Wicks* held that a state court could not be compelled to accept a civil rights claim arising under federal law, since the Illinois legislature had provided that the exclusive remedy for an employment-based discrimination claim was provided for by the state Human Rights Act.

## [b] The Evolving Standard of Proof in Employment Discrimination Cases

Twenty years ago, the Supreme Court set out an analytical framework to be used in cases alleging employment discrimination.[6] Although the Court originally devised the framework in the context of a race discrimination case brought under Title VII of the Civil Rights Act of 1964, it has since been adapted to apply to cases involving discrimination based on age, sex, disability, and even bankruptcy. Moreover, this framework has

---

**§ 2.2**

1. Yellow Freight System, Inc. v. Donnelly, 494 U.S. 820 (1990).

2. Ford v. Revlon, Inc., 153 Ariz. 38, 734 P.2d 580 (1987); Collins v. Department of Transportation, 208 Ga. App. 53, 429 S.E.2d 707 (1993); Chappell v. Southern Maryland Hosp., Inc., 320 Md. 483, 578 A.2d 766 (1990); Kolodziej v. Smith, 412 Mass. 243, 588 N.E.2d 639 (1992); Woods v. Department of Corrections, 806 S.W.2d 761 (Mo. Ct. App. 1991); Walsh v. Goldman Sachs & Co., 185 A.D.2d 748, 586 N.Y.S.2d 608 (1st Dep't 1992); Manning v. Ohio State Library Bd., 62 Ohio St. 3d 24, 577 N.E.2d 650 (1992); Hiatt v. Walker Chevrolet Co., 120 Wash. 2d 57, 837 P.2d 618, 622 (1992); Lindas v. Cady, 150 Wis. 2d 421, 441 N.W.2d 705 (1989).

3. Kolodziej v. Smith, 412 Mass. 243, 588 N.E.2d 639 (1992).

4. Manning v. Ohio State Library Bd., 62 Ohio St. 3d 24, 577 N.E.2d 650 (1992).

5. Faulkner-King v. Wicks, 226 Ill. App. 3d 962, 590 N.E.2d 511, 517–18 (4th Dist. 1992).

6. McDonnell Douglas Corp. v. Green, 411 U.S. 792 (1973).

been borrowed by state courts in analyzing claims under state fair employment statutes.

The *McDonnell Douglas* formula, as it is often referred to, employs a series of shifting burdens of proof. Initially, the plaintiff has the burden of proving a prima facie case of discrimination. (For a discussion of the elements of a prima facie case, see main volume, § 9.2.) If the plaintiff succeeds in proving the prima facie case, the burden shifts to the defendant to articulate a legitimate, nondiscriminatory reason for the employment decision. Should the defendant carry this burden, the plaintiff must then have an opportunity to prove that the legitimate reasons offered by the defendant were not its true reasons but were a pretext for discrimination.[7]

The federal courts disagreed among themselves as to whether a plaintiff was entitled to judgment in his or her favor when a jury, or judge sitting as the trier of fact, rejected the employer's asserted reasons for its employment decision. In many jurisdictions, a plaintiff who proved that the employer's proffered reasons were false was, without any further inquiry, entitled to judgment. The Supreme Court resolved this controversy in *Hicks,*[8] holding that a plaintiff is not necessarily entitled to judgment in his or her favor upon a showing that the employer's proffered reasons are untrue.

As the Supreme Court noted, the plaintiff at all times bears the ultimate burden of persuasion to show intentional discrimination. Thus, in order to find in the plaintiff's favor, the jury must not only disbelieve the employer; it must also believe the plaintiff's explanation of intentional discrimination and must make a finding to that effect. This case, therefore, modifies the third stage of the *McDonnell Douglas* formula, clarifying what the plaintiff must do to prove pretext. In the wake of *Hicks,* for a plaintiff to prevail, the plaintiff must persuade the trier of fact both that the employer's asserted reasoning "was false, and that discrimination was the real reason" for its action.[9]

The Supreme Court stated, however, that the jury's disbelief of the reasons put forward by the employer (particularly if disbelief is accompanied by a suspicion of mendacity), together with the elements of the prima facie case, will permit the jury to infer the ultimate fact of intentional discrimination. Therefore, in many cases, if not most, a plaintiff who succeeds in discrediting the employer's proffered reasons will prevail because the jury will be permitted, although not required, to find in favor of the plaintiff upon presentation of such evidence.[10]

That *Hicks* did not portend a significantly increased burden for plaintiffs is illustrated by the interpretation placed on the *Hicks* ruling by the Third Circuit Court of Appeals. In *Fuentes v. Perskie,*[11] the Third Circuit held that to survive summary judgment on the pretext issue, the plaintiff "must point to some evidence, direct or circumstantial, from which a factfinder could reasonably either (1) disbelieve the employer's articulated legitimate reasons; or (2) believe that an invidious discriminatory reason was more likely than not a motivating or determinative cause of the employer's action."[12] The court further stated that the plaintiff's evidence "must allow a factfinder reasonably to infer that each of the employer's proffered non-discriminatory reasons . . . was either a post hoc fabrication or otherwise did not actually motivate the employment action."[13]

Demonstrating that the employer's decision was not prudent or wise is not sufficient. Rather, the plaintiff must "demonstrate such weaknesses, implausibilities, inconsistencies, incoherencies, or contradictions in the employer's proffered legitimate reasons for its action that a reasonable factfinder could rationally find them 'unworthy of credence'[.]"[14] As this case indicates, under the limiting instructions provided by the Supreme Court, a plaintiff will normally succeed on a discrimination claim if he or she is able to demonstrate that the employer's reasons for the challenged decision are false.

Despite the Supreme Court's limiting instructions, the modification of the *McDonnell Douglas* formula may present an additional obstacle to plaintiffs, at least in those jurisdictions that had held that a plaintiff was entitled to judgment as a matter of law upon a showing that the employer's reasons were false. It is now clear that a jury may, but is not compelled to, find in the plaintiff's favor upon a demonstration of the falsity of the employer's asserted justification.

7. McDonnell Douglas Corp. v. Green, supra, 411 U.S. at 802.

8. St. Mary's Honor Center v. Hicks, 113 S. Ct. 2742 (1993).

9. St. Mary's Honor Center v. Hicks, supra, 113 S. Ct. at 2752.

10. *See, e.g.,* Equal Employment Opportunity Commission v. Lilja Construction Corp., 62 FEP Cas. (BNA) 1192 (N.D. Cal. 1993) (holding that a showing that the only employee discharged for fighting was black, together with the court's rejection of the employer's explanation, warranted a finding for the discharged black employee).

11. Fuentes v. Perskie, 32 F.3d 759 (3d Cir. 1994).

12. Id. at 764.

13. Id.

14. Id.

The Supreme Court's holding affects the state courts as well as the federal courts. As discussed earlier, state courts have concurrent jurisdiction over Title VII employment discrimination claims. A court exercising jurisdiction over a Title VII claim must apply federal substantive law and is therefore bound by the Supreme Court's decision in *Hicks.* Furthermore, many state courts look to federal precedent under Title VII in construing similar provisions of state fair employment laws.

Several state courts have discussed the application of *Hicks* to claims under state fair employment laws. In *Harris,*[15] the court applied the *Hicks* analysis to a claim of employment discrimination under California law. As the court noted, under *Hicks,* "[t]he trier of fact *may* find intentional discrimination where it determines on the basis of substantial evidence that the employer's proffered reasons are pretextual, *but it is not required to do so.*" (Court's emphasis). Based on this reading of *Hicks,* the appellate court refused to overturn a jury verdict in the plaintiff's favor that was founded primarily on the fact that the jury did not believe the employer's proffered explanation.

The Supreme Court of Washington also followed *Hicks* in an employment discrimination claim brought under state law in *Kastanis.*[16] The court stated that the need to prove pretext drops from the case once the matter goes to the jury, and the plaintiff is therefore left with the ultimate burden to prove that the employer intentionally discriminated.

Several other courts have cited *Hicks,* indicating its potential future application in those states.[17]

It is significant to note, however, that the North Dakota Supreme Court has refused to apply *Hicks* in a sex discrimination claim under the North Dakota Human Rights Act.[18] The court explained that its rejection of *Hicks* is based on a crucial difference between the *North Dakota Rules of Evidence* and the *Federal Rules of Evidence.*

The court stated that under the *Federal Rules,* a presumption, such as that arising from a prima facie case of discrimination, shifts to the other party only the burden of production of evidence, not the ultimate burden of persuading the jury. By contrast, the *North Dakota Rules of Evidence* provides that once a presumption is established, the party against whom it is directed has the burden of proving that the nonexistence of the presumed fact is more probable than its existence.

Thus, North Dakota gives presumptions a stronger effect than they are given under the *Federal Rules of Evidence.* Consequently, under North Dakota law, if a plaintiff makes out a prima facie case, the burden of persuasion shifts to the defendant, and if the defendant fails to convince the jury that its action was motivated by nondiscriminatory reasons, judgment is in favor of the plaintiff.

As these cases indicate, the precise impact that *Hicks* will have on federal and state fair employment jurisprudence has yet to be defined. The case is certain to generate additional controversy and disagreement, however, and, as Justice Souter's dissent in *Hicks* portends, Congress may act to reverse what many perceive to be a civil rights setback.

### [c] The Use of After-Acquired Evidence in Defending Employment Decisions

A mixed-motive case is one in which both legitimate and discriminatory reasons are involved in the employer's making a certain employment decision. In such a case, if the employer is able to demonstrate that the same decision would have been made absent any discrimination, the plaintiff is entitled only to a declaration that the employer is guilty of discrimination, injunctive relief, and the portion of attorneys' fees directly attributable to the mixed-motive claim.[19] Where an employer makes an employment decision on the basis of a discriminatory motive, but later discovers a legitimate basis for the action, the issue in such a case revolves around the use and effect of after-acquired evidence.

The Tenth Circuit Court of Appeals has held that while evidence acquired by an employer during discovery regarding the plaintiff's 150 falsified claims during his employment as a field representative could not be said to constitute the actual "cause" of the plaintiff's discharge, it was relevant to his claim of "injury" and precluded the grant of any relief or remedy.[20] The court

15. Harris v. Hughes Aircraft Co., 19th Cal. App. 4th 129, 23 Cal. Rptr. 2d 343, 350 (2d Dist. 1993).

16. Kastanis v. Educational Employees Credit Union, 122 Wash. 2d 483, 859 P.2d 26 (1993).

17. *See, e.g.,* Dawson v. Allstate Insurance Co., 189 W. Va. 557, 433 S.E.2d 268 (1993); People v. Howard, 158 Misc. 2d 739, 601 N.Y.S.2d 548 (Nassau County Ct. 1993) (citing *Hicks* with approval in claim alleging racial discrimination in jury selection).

18. Schweigert v. Provident Life Insurance Co., 503 N.W.2d 225 (N.D. 1993).

19. 42 U.S.C. § 2000e-5(g)(2)(B).

20. Summers v. State Farm Mut. Auto Ins. Co., 864 F.2d 700, 708 (10th Cir. 1988).

stated that "[t]o argue . . . that this after-acquired evidence should be ignored is utterly unrealistic."[21]

In *Washington v. Lake County, Illinois,*[22] a jailer brought an action under Title VII alleging that he was discharged because he was black. The employer raised as a defense the fact that the plaintiff had lied on his job application by representing that he had not been convicted of any criminal offenses. Although the employer did not assert that this misrepresentation was the reason for the action—it was not discovered until after the employee had been discharged—the employer did contend that the same decision to discharge the jailer would have been made even in the absence of any discrimination, had the employer known of the misrepresentation. Thus, according to the employer's argument, the jailer was not injured by any alleged discrimination. The district court found this argument persuasive and granted summary judgment in favor of the defendant.

The plaintiff appealed the decision. The Seventh Circuit Court of Appeals followed *Summers, supra,* stating that "in situations involving 'after-acquired' evidence, the employer must show by a preponderance of evidence that, if acting in a race-neutral manner, it would have made the same employment decision had it known of the after-acquired evidence."[23] The court noted that this standard requires the court to look at the facts in each case and determine whether the particular employer would have made the same decision in the absence of a discriminatory motive.

This fact-specific inquiry, as another court noted, is necessary because "[t]here are many situations . . . in which an employer would not discharge an employee if it subsequently discovered resume fraud, although the employee would not have been hired absent that resume fraud."[24] In such a situation, "the employee indeed would suffer injury if discharged because of discrimination."[25] In addition, requiring the employer to demonstrate that it would have made the same decision with regard to that particular employee even in the absence of discrimination "weakens the incentive for an employer to engage in a fishing expedition for 'minor, trivial or technical infractions' on an employee's application or resume."[26]

In *Washington,* the court held that the employer met its burden of proof under the relevant standard. The seriousness of the misrepresentations and underlying criminal convictions and the employer's uncontradicted affidavits established that the criminal convictions, if known at the time, would have led to the jailer's immediate discharge.

The Sixth Circuit Court of Appeals had also followed the rule enunciated in *Summers.*[27] In *Millegan-Jensen,* the court held that the plaintiff was not entitled to a remedy under Title VII, even though she was found by the district court to have been the victim of sex discrimination and retaliation, because the employer presented evidence that the employee had lied on her job application about her previous conviction for driving while intoxicated. The court held that an employee who would not have been hired had the employer known the truth suffers no legal damage upon discharge.

The Eleventh Circuit Court of Appeals refused to follow *Summers,* stating that the Tenth Circuit's opinion in that case was based on an erroneous interpretation of a 1977 Supreme Court decision.[28] In that Supreme Court case,[29] the Court held that if a plaintiff established that the exercise of protected First Amendment rights was a substantial factor in an adverse employment decision, the defendant could avoid liability only if it satisfied the burden of proving "that it would have reached the same decision . . . even in the absence of the protected conduct."[30] According to the Eleventh Circuit, "[t]he *Summers* rule constitutes an unwarranted extension of *Mt. Healthy* in that the *Summers* rule ignores the lapse of time between the employment decision and the discovery of a legitimate motive for that decision."[31]

The Supreme Court has now resolved the after acquired evidence controversy. In *McKennon v. Nashville Banner Publishing Co.,*[32] an employee took personnel files and company records in anticipation of being fired and in support of her subsequent age discrimination claim. According to the complaint in *McKennon,* the plaintiff was fearful of being fired after 40 years with

21. Id.

22. 762 F. Supp. 199 (N.D. Ill. 1991), *aff'd* 969 F.2d 250 (7th Cir. 1992).

23. Id. at 255.

24. Bonger v. American Water Works, 789 F. Supp. 1102, 1106 (D. Colo. 1992).

25. Id.

26. Washington v. Lake County, Illinois, 969 F.2d at 256.

27. Johnson v. Honeywell Info. Sys., Inc., 955 F.2d 409 (6th Cir. 1992); Millegan-Jensen v. Michigan Technological University, 59 FEP Cases 1249, 975 F.2d 302 (6th Cir. 1992).

28. Wallace v. Dunn Const. Co., 968 F.2d 1174 (11th Cir. 1992).

29. Mt. Healthy City School Dist. Bd. of Educ. v. Doyle, 429 U.S. 274 (1977).

30. Id. at 287.

31. Wallace v. Dunn Const. Co., supra, 968 F.2d at 1179.

32. 63 U.S.L.W. 4089 (U.S. Jan. 23, 1995).

the same company as a secretary. Her fears were realized when her employer terminated her in 1990, pursuant to what the employer alleged was a reduction in force; however, the plaintiff had anticipated the termination of her employment and was skeptical of the employer's justification. Therefore, before she was terminated she had photocopied her own personnel file and other company records and taken them home with her. Her goal was to prove that the employer was not actually reducing its workforce, but rather was firing her in violation of the Age Discrimination in Employment Act.

When the employer learned in pretrial discovery that the plaintiff had taken records, it immediately moved for the case to be dismissed on the ground that, had it known of the plaintiff's unauthorized removal of the files, it would have fired her. The Sixth Circuit agreed with the employer and dismissed the plaintiff's suit.

The Supreme Court reversed the Sixth Circuit's decision, however, holding that the employer could not escape liability through the use of such after-acquired evidence. On the other hand, the Court held that the fact of the misconduct must be factored into the remedies available. Under the Court's ruling in *McKennon,* an employer can be held liable for back pay from the date of the discriminatory discharge to the date the employer discovered the misconduct. The Court further held, however, that an illegally discharged employee who would have eventually been terminated for misconduct cannot receive reinstatement or front pay.

Although most developments in the *after-acquired evidence doctrine* have occurred in cases involving alleged violations of *federal* employment discrimination laws, these developments seem highly likely to work their way into cases alleging violation of state fair employment practices (FEP) law. For example, an Oregon court held that while after-acquired evidence did not bar a discharged employee's discrimination suit under Oregon's fair employment statute, it could prevent an award of front pay, reinstatement, or injunctive relief.[33]

---

33. Furnish v. Merlo, No. 93-1052 D. Or. (June 8, 1994).

# § 2.3 Protected Classifications, Compliance, Prohibitions, and Exceptions

## [a] Protected Classifications

In Table 2.3-1, Parts A and B, the various protected classifications under state FEP statutes are noted. Of the 50 states and Washington, D.C., only a handful do not have comprehensive FEP laws applicable to both public and private employment. Mississippi has a "Discrimination in State Employment" law, which prohibits discrimination in state employment on the basis of race, color, religion, sex, national origin, age, and handicap. Similarly, Georgia has a fairly comprehensive FEP law, but it applies only to public employment. Alabama does not have any FEP statutes that are applicable to public or private employment.

Note that Table 2.3-1, Part A, classifies sexual harassment and discrimination against pregnancy separately. This is because some states expressly prohibit one or the other but not both. In most states, however, if the statute does not address one or the other issue, the general prohibition against discrimination based on sex would almost certainly encompass both. That is, an employer would not be permitted to discriminate against women based on pregnancy, even absent an express state statute. Similarly, courts are almost certain to recognize sex-based harassment as a violation of a ban on sex discrimination, even without an express state law.

Note also that this table lists only the provisions of the comprehensive FEP law. Additional, separate statutes addressing particular issues or augmenting or repeating provisions in the general law exist in some states, and they are listed in Table 2.5-1. Also, the provisions listed in the tables in Part 2 always apply to the comprehensive FEP law but may or may not apply to the separate FEP statutes listed in Table 2.5-1.

Tables 2.3-2 and 2.3-3 cover municipal sexual orientation ordinances.

**Are Testers Protected Under Fair Employment Practice Laws?** Traditionally, the plaintiff in an employment discrimination case is either an employee alleging that he or she was wrongfully terminated, transferred, or demoted, or an applicant for employment who alleges that he or she was denied employment on the basis of an impermissible decision-making factor.

In some recent cases, however, the plaintiff is not an actual employee or job applicant, but a "tester."

A typical tester is associated with an employee advocacy group and is a member of a class protected under the relevant FEP law, for example, a female, or a racial minority. The tester's job is to go through the motions of the application process with a certain employer, looking for evidence of discrimination. The issue is whether testers who have encountered employment discrimination have the right to sue the employers who discriminated against them.

The use of testers is not entirely new. The United States Supreme Court has held that testers have a cause of action for discrimination under the federal fair housing laws.[1] However, the Supreme Court has never decided and has never been presented with the issue of

---

**§ 2.3**

1. Havens Realty Corp. v. Coleman, 455 U.S. 363 (1982).

whether testers can sue for employment discrimination. Most state and federal fair employment laws prohibit discrimination against "any person" on the basis of a protected characteristic. However, they do not appear to require that such a person must actually intend to obtain employment. Therefore, in some instances testers have been successful in suits alleging employment discrimination.

In a recent case,[2] the District of Columbia Superior Court held that a tester was entitled to damages for sexual harassment. The facts of the case establish that the original plaintiff, a woman who was actually seeking a job, was sexually harassed by the defendant. The defendant ran a business that sold lists of employers, by category, to people seeking jobs. The plaintiff claimed that the defendant had offered to accept sexual favors instead of monetary payment for the employer lists that the defendant provided.

Instead of immediately suing, the original plaintiff told her story to a Washington, D.C. fair employment agency. The agency sent four testers—two women and two men—to pose as job-seekers in order to determine whether the defendant was acting in violation of the District of Columbia Human Rights Act, which prohibits employment discrimination based on sex. The two women testified that the defendant suggested that they might "pay" his fees with sexual favors instead of money, whereas the male testers testified that the defendant told them that they had to pay for the services in money.

Based on the reports of the original complainant and the two women testers, the Fair Employment Council of Greater Washington sued the defendant, alleging violation of the District of Columbia Human Rights Act. After hearing all of the evidence, the jury in the case returned a verdict finding the defendant liable and awarding $79,000 to the plaintiff in compensatory and punitive damages.

In an interesting twist to the case, the court allowed the testers to share the damage award with the original complainant. The testers argued, and successfully persuaded the jury, that, even though they were not actually seeking jobs, they were actually harassed and therefore entitled to damages. The defendant is appealing the verdict, arguing that his business falls outside the coverage of the District of Columbia Human Rights Act.

In another recent case,[3] the United States Circuit Court of Appeals for the District of Columbia reached the opposite result. In that case, the defendant was engaged in the business of referring job-seekers to potential employers. Two black testers and two similarly qualified white testers were sent by the Fair Employment Council (FEC) to check on the practices of the defendant. The complaint alleged that neither of the two black testers was referred to employers, while the two white testers were referred to employers.

The court held that the testers could not sue under Title VII, because they had sustained no injury. Noting that the testers presented false credentials in making application for jobs that they did not actually want, the court held that the defendant could not be said to have caused the testers any harm for which Title VII could provide a remedy. The court noted, however, that its decision was based on the remedies available under Title VII before the enactment of the Civil Rights Act of 1991, which amended Title VII. At the time of the discrimination against the testers, the court stated, Title VII would have allowed only an injunction as a remedy. The court left open the possibility that the testers could obtain damages under the amended version of Title VII.

In *Parr v. Woodmen of the World Life Insurance Society,*[4] the federal District Court for the Middle District of Georgia applied similar reasoning to deny standing to testers. The court held that a plaintiff whose primary purpose in interviewing for a job was to create the basis for an employment discrimination lawsuit was not a "bona fide applicant" for the job and, therefore, could not be damaged by the defendant's failure to hire him.

Employers should take note of these decisions, which indicate a solicitous attitude toward the use of testers. If employee advocacy groups, civil rights organizations, or lawyers begin using testers on a widespread basis, the likelihood of an employer facing a discrimination claim is greatly increased. Thus, the prevalence of the use of testers provides employers with an additional incentive to comply with fair employment laws and ensure that hiring officials follow appropriate policies and procedures.

---

2. Fair Employment Council of Greater Washington v. Molovinsky, (D.C. Superior Court, 1993).

3. Fair Employment Council of Greater Washington v. BMC Marketing Corp., (28 F.3d 1268 (D.C. Cir. 1994)).

4. 657 F. Supp. 1022 (M.D. Ga. 1987).

## [b] Who Must Comply

In general, state fair employment laws, like their federal counterparts, prohibit discrimination by employers, employment agencies, labor organizations, and other "persons." Table 2.3-4 lists states that have laws covering these categories and notes whether employers must have a minimum number of employees to be covered under their provisions. Under Title VII of the Civil Rights Act of 1964, only employers with 15 or more employees are covered, while the threshold under the ADEA is 20 employees. A number of state statutes have adopted these federal minimums, but others have either set a lower threshold or omitted any reference to a minimum. If a state sets no minimum, all employers in that state are covered.

## [c] What Is Prohibited

State FEP statutes generally cite specific prohibitions for employers, employment agencies, and labor organizations. Prohibitions are as follows:

- For Employer.
  —To refuse to hire or employ or to bar or to discharge from employment any individual or to discriminate against that individual in compensation or in terms, conditions, or privileges of employment on the basis of a protected characteristic.
- For Employment Agency.
  —To fail or refuse to classify properly or refer for employment or discriminate against any individual on the basis of a protected characteristic.
  —To participate in the printing or circulation of discriminatory statements, advertisements, or publications, in the use of discriminatory applications for employment, or in discriminatory preemployment inquiries.
- For Labor Organization.
  —To exclude from full membership rights or to expel from membership any individual or to discriminate against any member or employer on the basis of a protected characteristic.
- For Employer, Employment Agency, and Labor Organization.
  —To encourage or compel any person to engage in any action forbidden by the statutes.

**Sexual Harassment.** Like Title VII, most state fair employment statutes do not explicitly prohibit sexual harassment (see Table 2.3-1). Federal and state courts have recognized, however, that sexual harassment comes within the general prohibition against sex discrimination.

There are essentially two types of sexual harassment: (1) harassment in which tangible job benefits are granted or denied based on submission to or rejection of unwelcome sexual advances or conduct; and (2) harassment in which the conduct of others creates an intimidating, hostile, or offensive working environment. These two distinct types of harassment are referred to, respectively, as quid pro quo harassment and hostile environment harassment.

The federal Equal Employment Opportunity Commission has adopted guidelines specifically relating to sexual harassment.[5] These guidelines state that the principles of illegal harassment relate not only to sexual harassment but also to harassment based on race, color, religion, or national origin.[6] Some state courts apply similar principles to harassment based on race and other protected classifications.[7]

In construing their fair employment statutes, state courts often look to federal precedent in this area.[8] Although some states do apply different standards in analyzing harassment claims, the basic elements are usually the same. Therefore, although the law of each individual state should be consulted, both state and federal authorities are cited in the following general discussion.

---

5. 29 C.F.R. § 1604.11 (1994).

6. 29 C.F.R. § 1604.11 n.1.

7. *See, e.g.,* Village of Bellwood Board of Fire and Police Commissioners v. Human Rights Commission, 184 Ill. App. 3d 339, 541 N.E.2d 1248 (1989).

8. Board of Directors, Green Hills Country Club v. Illinois Human Rights Commission, 162 Ill. App. 3d 216, 514 N.E.2d 1227 (1987) (citing EEOC regulations and federal case law, and stating that while federal decisions are not controlling, they provide relevant and helpful precedents); Westmoreland Coal Company v. West Virginia Human Rights Commission, 181 W.Va. 368, 382 S.E.2d 562 (1989) (adopting federal definition of quid pro quo harassment). See also Mains v. II Morrow, Inc., 128 Or. App. 625, 877 P.2d 88 (1994); Lehmann v. Toys 'R' Us, Inc., 132 N.J. 587, 626 A.2d 445 (1993); Vainio v. Brookshire, 258 Mont. 273, 852 P.2d 596 (1993); Syndex Corporation v. Dean, 820 S.W.2d 869 (Tex. App. 1991); Kerans v. Porter Paint Company, 61 Ohio St.3d 486, 575 N.E.2d 428 (1991).

*Quid Pro Quo Sexual Harassment.* As a general rule, in order to show quid pro quo harassment, the following conditions must exist:[9]

1. The employee belongs to a protected group.
2. The employee was subject to unwelcome sexual harassment.
3. The harassment complained of was based upon sex.
4. The employee's reaction to the harassment complained of affected tangible aspects of the employee's compensation, terms, conditions, or privileges of employment.

In addition, the acceptance or rejection of the harassment by an employee must be an express or implied condition to the receipt of a job benefit or the cause of a tangible job detriment in order to create liability under this theory of sexual harassment. With quid pro quo harassment, the employee must also prove that he or she was deprived, or threatened with deprivation of a job benefit that he or she was otherwise qualified to receive, because of the employer's use of a prohibited criterion in making the employment decision.[10]

Although there had been some question regarding whether the mere threat of an adverse employment consequence could support a claim of quid pro quo harassment, the Supreme Court has now made it clear that a claim based solely on unfulfilled threats should be categorized as a hostile work environment claim which requires a showing of severe or pervasive conduct. To support a claim of quid pro quo harassment, an employee must show that a tangible employment action resulted from the employee's refusal to submit to a supervisor's sexual demands.[11]

*Hostile Environment Sexual Harassment.* Hostile environment sexual harassment was first recognized by the United States Supreme Court in *Meritor Savings Bank v. Vinson FSB.*[12] In *Meritor,* the Supreme Court recognized that a claim of "hostile environment" sexual harassment that causes noneconomic injury to the complainant is a form of sex discrimination actionable under Title VII.

The Supreme Court has since refined, to some extent, the nature of a plaintiff's burden in proving a claim of hostile environment sexual harassment.[13] The ultimate standard adopted by the Court is not so different from that already applied in most state and federal courts. Under the Supreme Court's standard, to be actionable as hostile environment sexual harassment, the conduct must be "severe or pervasive enough to create an objectively hostile or abusive work environment—an environment that a reasonable person would find hostile or abusive."[14] In addition, the victim must "subjectively perceive the environment to be abusive."[15]

Many state courts that have addressed the issue have adopted the "severe or pervasive" standard.[16] Although the term "pervasive" seems to imply multiple incidents of harassment, the Michigan Supreme Court has held that a single incident of harassment in a close working environment and perpetrated by the employer may suffice to state a claim of hostile work environment.[17]

The employee must show, however, that the harassment was sufficiently severe or pervasive so as to alter the conditions of employment and create an abusive work environment. An issue that has arisen in the context of applying this standard is whether the severity of the harassment should be judged from the perspective of a reasonable person or from the perspective of a reasonable woman.

In *Lehmann v. Toys 'R' Us, Inc.,*[18] the New Jersey Supreme Court adopted a test for analyzing sexual harassment claims that utilizes an objective gender-specific perspective. The court held that for a female to establish a claim of hostile environment sexual harassment, she must allege that the conduct occurred because

---

9. Lehmann v. Toys 'R' Us, Inc., 132 N.J. 587, 626 A.2d 445 (1993); Westmoreland Coal Company v. West Virginia Human Rights Commission, 181 W.Va. 368, 382 S.E.2d 562 (1989); Spencer v. General Electric Co., 894 F.2d 651 (4th Cir. 1990); Koster v. Chase Manhattan Bank, 687 F. Supp. 848, 861 (S.D.N.Y. 1988).

10. Spencer v. General Electric Co., 894 F.2d 651 (4th Cir. 1990); Koster v. Chase Manhattan Bank, 687 F. Supp. 848, 861 (S.D.N.Y. 1988).

11. Ellerth v. Burlington Industries, Inc., 118 S. Ct. 2275 (1998).

12. 477 US 57 (1986).

13. Harris v. Forklift Systems, Inc., 114 S. Ct. 367 (1993).

14. Id. at 370. See also Faragher v. City of Boca Raton, 118 S. Ct. 2275 (1998).

15. Id.

16. *See, e.g.,* Lehmann v. Toys 'R' Us, Inc., 132 N.J. 587, 626 A.2d 445 (1993); Radtke v. Everett, 442 Mich. 368, 501 N.W.2d 155 (1993); Bennett v. Corroon and Black Corp., 517 So.2d 1245 (La.App. 1988).

17. Radtke v. Everett, 442 Mich. 368, 501 N.W.2d 155 (1993).

18. 132 N.J. 587, 626 A.2d 445 (1993).

of her sex and that *a reasonable woman* would consider the conduct sufficiently severe or pervasive to alter the conditions of employment and create an intimidating, hostile, or offensive working environment. A few federal courts have applied a similar "reasonable woman" standard.[19]

This gender-specific standard is contrary to the standard proposed by the federal EEOC to sexual harassment cases brought under Title VII and applied by most federal courts. The Supreme Court has also indicated that it will apply a reasonable person standard. In *Harris v. Forklift Systems, Inc.,*[20] the court stated that to be actionable under Title VII, the harassment must be severe or pervasive enough to create an objectively hostile or abusive work environment—an environment that a reasonable person would find hostile or abusive. In a recent opinion,[21] the Michigan Supreme Court has also ruled that a reasonable person standard is to be applied in analyzing claims under Michigan's Civil Rights Act.

It appears, therefore, that in adopting a gender-specific test, the New Jersey Supreme Court is bucking the trend. In states where this issue has not yet been directly addressed, it is reasonable to assume that the courts will be more likely to follow the lead of the U.S. Supreme Court, the EEOC, and the majority of courts that have addressed the issue, and adopt a gender-neutral test for analyzing sexual harassment.

**Employer Liability for Sexual Harassment.** If an employee establishes that he or she was sexually harassed by a supervisor or other employee, the question remains whether the employer can be held liable. The appropriate analysis to be applied depends on the type of harassment involved. With respect to quid pro quo harassment, that is, harassment where a job benefit is conditioned upon submission to sexual advances or demands, the employer is held to be strictly or automatically liable.[22]

The Supreme Court has clarified the appropriate standard to be applied in determining employer liability for harassment by supervisory employees. Under the Supreme Court's recent pronouncement, in cases in which a tangible employment action results from a refusal to submit to a supervisor's sexual demands, the employer is automatically liable, and no defense is available to the employer. In cases in which no tangible employment action is taken, the employer will still be held liable unless it can prove as a matter of defense that:

1. The employer exercised reasonable care to prevent and correct promptly any sexually harassing behavior; and
2. The plaintiff employee unreasonably failed to take advantage of any preventive or corrective opportunities provided by the employer or to avoid harm otherwise.[23]

Like the federal courts, state courts generally follow common law agency principles in determining liability. Thus, in many cases the inquiry focuses on whether the harassing employee acted within the course and scope of his employment, whether the employer knew or should have known of the conduct, and whether the employer failed to take steps to correct the situation.[24]

The New Jersey Supreme Court has adopted a standard that holds an employer vicariously liable if the supervisor acted within the scope of his or her employment. In addition, even if the conduct was outside the scope of employment, an employer may be held liable if the employer contributed to the harm through its negligence, intent, or apparent authorization of the harassing conduct, or if the supervisor was aided in the commission of the harassment by the agency relationship. The court noted that the employer's failure to have an explicit policy that bans sexual harassment and that provides an effective procedure for the prompt investigation and remediation of harassment complaints could provide a basis for employer liability.[25] In *Board of Directors, Green Hills Country Club v. Illinois Human Rights Commission,*[26] the court held that under

19. Ellison v. Brady, 924 F.2d 872 (9th Cir. 1991); Jenson v. Eveleth Taconite Co., 824 F. Supp. 847 (D. Minn. 1993).

20. 114 S.Ct. 367 (1993).

21. Radtke v. Everett, 442 Mich. 368, 501 N.W.2d 155 (1993).

22. 29 C.F.R. § 1604.11(d).

23. Ellerth v. Burlington Industries, Inc., 118 S. Ct. 2257 (1998); Faragher v. City of Boca Raton, 118 S. Ct. 2275 (1998).

24. Alphonse v. Omni Hotels Management Corp., 643 So.2d 836 (La.App. 1994); Smith v. American Express Travel Related Services Company, Inc., 179 Ariz. 131, 876 P.2d 1166 (1994); Phelps v. Vassey, 113 N.C.App. 132, 437 S.E.2d 692 (1993); Vainio v. Brookshire, 258 Mont. 273, 852 P.2d 596 (1993); Kerans v. Porter Paint Company, 61 Ohio St.3d 486, 575 N.E.2d 428 (1991); Syndex Corporation v. Dean, 820 S.W.2d 869 (Tex.App. 1991) (expressly relying on federal case law).

25. Lehmann v. Toys 'R' Us, Inc., 132 N.J. 587, 626 A.2d 445 (1993).

26. 162 Ill.App.3d 216, 514 N.E.2d 1227 (1987).

Illinois law, an employer is strictly liable for sexual harassment of employees by supervisory personnel regardless of whether it is quid pro quo or hostile environment harassment.

**Employer Liability for Sexual Harassment by Nonemployees.** Employer liability for sexual harassment has traditionally been limited to acts of harassment committed by the employer's own employees; however, a trend is emerging in Title VII case law that expands employer liability to sexual harassment committed against workers by nonemployees. Because many states look to Title VII standards when interpreting their own FEPs (as discussed more fully in Part 9), state courts are likely to follow federal precedent on this issue.

The EEOC guidelines for Title VII make it clear that employers may be responsible for the acts of nonemployees when the employer "*knows* or *should have known* about the conduct and fails to take immediate and appropriate corrective action . . . [in light of] the extent of the employer's control and any other legal responsibility which the employer may have with respect to the conduct of such non-employees."[27] Although the Fifth Circuit has interpreted this regulation to mean that an employer may not be liable for an employee's sexual harassment by a nonemployee outside the workplace, an employer may be liable for an employee's sexual harassment by a nonemployee inside the workplace.[28] The Eleventh Circuit has also recognized that work environments can be made offensive by strangers.[29]

Under the EEOC regulation, the employer is liable only if it has actual or constructive knowledge of an employee's sexual harassment by a nonemployee. This standard parallels that of the employer's potential liability for acts of harassment committed by its own employees.[30] An employer may be found to have actual knowledge of sexual harassment if the employee has brought complaints to management, the employee has followed the complaint procedures for reporting sexual harassment, or if the employer has observed the sexually harassing conduct. Constructive knowledge can be imputed to the employer in cases where the employer reasonably should have known of the sexual harassment.

An employer will not be held liable for an employee's sexual harassment, however, if it takes prompt and appropriate corrective action to end the harassment upon learning of the offensive conduct. Thus, when an employee alleges that harassment has been committed by a nonemployee, the need for the employer to take prompt and effective remedial action cannot be overestimated.

There are steps that an employer can take to minimize or eliminate its potential liability for sexual harassment of an employee by nonemployees. One commentator has offered the following general recommendations: (1) recognize that sexual harassment pervades many work environments; (2) adopt and enforce an effective policy prohibiting and addressing sexual harassment; (3) conduct prompt and appropriate investigations into claims of harassment and institute an appropriate remedy; and (4) address any harassment, whether reported or not, upon finding out about it.[31]

### [d] Exceptions to Fair Employment Prohibitions

Table 2.3-5 identifies three common statutory exceptions to state fair employment laws:

1. Bona fide occupational qualifications;
2. Bona fide seniority or merit systems; and
3. Bona fide benefits programs.

**Bona Fide Occupational Qualifications.** A bona fide occupational qualification (BFOQ) generally applies to sex, religion, national origin, and age discrimination. Some classic BFOQs include hiring a woman as an attendant in a continuously used women's restroom, as a wet nurse, or as an actress.

Regarding age discrimination, BFOQs have generally been limited to safety-related matters, such as age limits for airline pilots and other jobs involving a great risk to the public. Attempted BFOQs based on customer preferences—hiring only women as airline attendants, for instance, or only men as waiters—have failed. A person's religion may also constitute a BFOQ for employment in nonsecular activities of religious institutions.

---

27. 29 C.F.R. § 1604.11(e) (1994).

28. Powell v. Las Vegas Hilton, 841 F. Supp. 1024 (D. Nev. 1992) (citing Whitaker v. Carney, 778 F.2d 216 (5th Cir. 1987).

29. *Powell* (citing Henson v. City of Dundee, 682 F.2d 897 (11th Cir. 1982).

30. *See* Meritor Savings Bank, FSB v. Vinson, 477 U.S. 57 (1986).

31. *See* J. Watson, "Employer Liability for the Sexually Harassing Actions of Its Customers," 19 *Employment Relations Law Journal* 146 (1994).

**Bona Fide Seniority or Merit Systems.** Many states allow employers to apply different compensation standards, employment terms, or privileges, as long as the intent of such differences is nondiscriminatory. In general, these bona fide seniority or merit systems immunize an employer or union from discriminatory claims. Considering the role played by labor unions in the enactment of Title VII (of the Civil Rights Act) and similar state laws, it is no surprise that such systems are protected not only by state laws but also by federal laws.

**Bona Fide Benefits Program.** Several states allow employers to use age-based benefits plans, as long as these plans were not adopted to avoid age discrimination laws; the terms of an employee benefits plan may *not* be used to excuse an employer's failure to hire an individual because of his or her age. The rationale underlying this exemption is that the cost differential allowed under many benefits plans between younger and older workers is not great enough to preclude hiring any person based on his or her age.

### [e] Employees Exempted from State Fair Employment Practice Laws

To be protected by the proscriptions contained in state FEP laws, a person must come within the particular statute's definition of "employee." Thus, the court may examine the relationship between the employer and the person alleging unlawful discrimination to determine whether the person is, in fact, an employee within the meaning of the statute. In addition, there are several common exemptions from the definition of "employee" under most state statutes.

**Specific Statutory Exemptions.** Many states specifically exclude members of the employer's family from the definition of "employee." The statutes in these states commonly exclude from coverage persons employed by their parents, spouse, or child, and, in some instances, their grandparents or grandchildren.

Another common exemption found in state fair employment statutes applies to domestic workers. The primary concern underlying this exemption is that private individuals not be subjected to liability under state FEP laws because of decisions regarding the employment of persons as workers in the private individual's home. Several states also exclude agricultural employees from FEP coverage. An interesting relic from the cold war can be found in three state fair employment statutes, which exclude from their coverage discrimination against individuals because of their association with communist organizations.

**Defining the Employment Relationship.** In addition to these specific exemptions, certain other persons may not be considered employees by virtue of their relationship to the employer. It has been held that individual partners of a partnership are not employees for purposes of counting employees,[32] and that shareholders in a professional corporation engaged in practice of law are not employees for purposes of Title VII.[33] Likewise, a general partner in an accounting firm has been held not to be an employee covered under Title VII.[34]

A member of the board of trustees of a corporation is generally not considered an employee protected by laws prohibiting employment discrimination.[35] However, in determining whether directors or board members of a corporation are employees protected by FEP statutes, the court will look beyond the title and consider whether the individual performs traditional employee duties. Thus, in one case, the sole officer of a corporation and her husband were deemed to be employees for determining the size of the corporation where they performed many of the day-to-day duties of the corporation.[36]

As noted in the introduction to this book, an independent contractor is outside the common-law concept of the employer-employee relationship. Nevertheless, an employer that denies employment to an individual who is an independent contractor may be liable under Title VII.[37] Thus, in one case, a nurse who was denied hospital privileges as a private duty nurse was permitted to bring an action against the hospital under Title VII, despite the fact that the hospital was not her employer.[38]

---

32. Burke v. Friedman, 556 F.2d 867 (7th Cir. 1977).

33. EEOC v. Dowd & Dowd, Ltd., 736 F.2d 1177 (7th Cir. 1984).

34. Wheeler v. Main Hurdman, 825 F.2d 257 (10th Cir. 1987).

35. *See* EEOC v. Pettegrove Truck Service, Inc., 716 F. Supp. 1430 (S.D. Fla. 1989); Schoenbaum v. Orange County Center for the Performing Arts, 677 F. Supp. 1036 (C.D. Cal. 1987).

36. EEOC v. Pettegrove Truck Service, Inc., supra.

37. Christopher v. Stouder Memorial Hospital, 936 F.2d 870, 56 F.E.P. Cas. (BNA) 345 (6th Cir. 1991).

38. *But see* Diggs v. Harris Hospital, 847 F.2d 270 (5th Cir. 1988) (physician whose hospital staff privileges were terminated could not maintain Title VII action against hospital, because she was an independent contractor rather than an employee).

One court has held that an employee of a food service company who worked as a cashier on the premises of an automaker could state a claim against the automaker based on obscene gestures and inappropriate touching of her body by an employee of the automaker. The court concluded that the plaintiff was not required to prove an employment relationship with the automaker in order to state a claim for a violation of Title VII.[39]

Unpaid volunteers are generally not considered *employees* within the meaning of Title VII, as they are not usually susceptible to the discriminatory practices that the Act was designed to eliminate.[40] Although students do not enjoy protection under Title VII, the EEOC has ruled that an intern in an orthopedic surgery program was both a student and an employee of the medical college and that therefore, her charge of sex discrimination was cognizable under Title VII.[41]

Although the cases cited above were decided under federal law, state courts will likely consider these federal rulings persuasive when construing state fair employment laws.

Exhibit 2.3-1 sets out the most common exemptions from the definition of "employees" under state fair employment laws.

### [f] Obesity as a Protected Classification Under Fair Employment Practice Laws

As a result of national studies showing that a significant percentage of Americans are overweight, the issue of whether discrimination based on obesity is prohibited by state or federal law has received increased attention. While the developing case law addresses the issue only of those who are greatly overweight (sometimes referred to as "morbidly obese"), the lack of a bright-line test for what is considered "overweight" could pose a problem for employers.

Many of the developments in this area have occurred and are occurring on the federal level under the Rehabilitation Act and the Americans with Disabilities Act. Because a majority of the state fair employment laws and disability laws are modeled on the federal statutes, these federal developments will very likely filter down to the state level in due time. There have also been several state cases on this issue, however, in what may be a trend toward increasing litigation of obesity discrimination claims.

When the case law on the issue of employment discrimination against obese people began to develop in the 1980s, the overwhelming trend of those cases was *not* to treat obesity as a "handicap" or a "disability" deserving of protection under the law. In a case often cited on this issue, the court reasoned that since obesity was not an "immutable" condition, such as blindness or lameness, obesity did not meet the definition of a "handicap" under the law.[42] Although this was a federal district court case, the holding of the case was that obesity was not a handicap under the Washington antidiscrimination statute.

Other courts followed this lead in declaring that obesity was not a handicap or disability. For example, a Pennsylvania court held that obesity was not, by itself, a handicap under the state's antidiscrimination statute.[43] Rather, the court stated that some other physical disability, such as diabetes, high blood pressure, or cardiovascular disease, must have been present in conjunction with the plaintiff's obesity. State courts in Missouri and North Dakota reached findings similar to those of the courts in Washington and Pennsylvania—namely, that obesity is not a protected class.

Starting in the 1980s, however, several courts began to recognize that obesity *could* be a handicap or disability subject to protection under the employment discrimination laws. For example, a New York court[44] held that New York's Human Rights law defined the term "disability" very broadly, and the court concluded that the plaintiff's obesity qualified as a disability. The court therefore determined that the defendant's refusal to hire the plaintiff based on her obesity was unlawful. Similarly, a court in New Jersey determined that under the New Jersey Law Against Discrimination, obesity fit the expansive statutory definition of "disability."[45]

The most recent decisions on the issue appear to be following the lead of the New York and New Jersey courts in holding that obesity *can* be a protected class under handicap discrimination laws. However,

---

39. King v. Chrysler Corp., 812 F. Supp. 151 (E.D. Mo. 1993).

40. Hall v. Delaware Council on Crime & Justice, 780 F. Supp. 241 (D. Del.), aff'd, 975 F.2d 1549 (3d Cir. 1992); Smith v. Berks Community Television, 657 F. Supp. 794, 43 F.E.P. Cas. (BNA) 814 (E.D. Pa. 1987).

41. EEOC Dec. 88-1, 47 F.E.P. Cas. (BNA) 1887 (June 27, 1988).

42. Greene v. Union Pac. R.R., 548 F. Supp. 3 (W.D. Wash. 1981).

43. Philadelphia Elec. Co. v. Pennsylvania Human Relations Dep't, 448 A.2d 701 (Pa. Cmwlth. Ct. 1982).

44. New York Div. of Human Rights v. Xerox, 480 N.E.2d 695 (1985).

45. Gimello v. Agency Rent-A-Car Syss., 594 A.2d 264 (App. Div. 1991).

these decisions differ on what the plaintiff is required to show in order to come under the antidiscrimination law's protection.

The California Supreme Court has decided that in order for the plaintiff to meet the definition of "physically disabled" under the California Fair Employment and Housing Act, the plaintiff must show medical evidence that her excessive weight was the result of a physiological condition.[46] The plaintiff in *Cassista* was unable to produce such evidence.

The California decision is in keeping with regulations issued by the EEOC relating to the determination of disability. The latest regulations observe that "it is important to distinguish between conditions that are impairments, and physical, psychological, environmental, cultural, and economic characteristics that are not impairments."[47] Examples of characteristics that the EEOC deems are not impairments, and are "not the result of a physiological disorder," include height, *weight,* and muscle tone.

According to the EEOC, obesity is a disability only if it is caused by a physiological disorder such as a hormone abnormality. This position reflects the sentiment that a person should not be entitled to protection under the disability laws unless some physical condition, largely beyond the person's control, is responsible for the disability.

Another line of authority suggests that whether or not obesity is caused by a physiological condition, an obese person may be considered disabled under fair employment laws. In *Cook,*[48] the court held that the defendant violated the federal Rehabilitation Act by refusing to hire the plaintiff because of her obesity. Significantly, in *Cook* there was no finding that the plaintiff's condition was the result of a physiological condition. The defendant in fact argued that since the plaintiff's obesity was caused, or at least exacerbated, by voluntary conduct, it could not qualify as a handicap or disability. The court specifically rejected this argument, however.

An interesting side note to this case is that the EEOC filed an amicus brief on behalf of the plaintiff, arguing that although obesity is not a "traditional" disability in the sense that an obese individual might be able to diet and lose weight, it is not necessary that a condition be immutable or involuntary to be covered. The EEOC's position is a signal that the EEOC, and some courts, may become increasingly sympathetic to persons who claim obesity discrimination, regardless of the cause of their obesity.

State legislatures may be addressing the obesity issue in the near future. Activists in some states have been lobbying to include weight along with race, sex, and other protected characteristics in state civil rights laws. Currently only two states, Michigan and Wisconsin, make weight an unlawful basis for employment discrimination. (See Table 2.3-1, Part B.) However, several states, including California, New York, and Texas, are considering proposals to prohibit discrimination on the basis of weight.

---

46. Cassista v. Community Foods Inc., 856 P.2d 1143 (Cal. Sept. 2, 1993).

47. 29 C.F.R. § 1630.2(h) (1994).

48. Cook v. State of Rhode Island, Department of Mental Health, Retardation, and Hospitals, 10 F.3d 17 (1st Cir. 1993).

# Table 2.3-1 Part A
## PROTECTED CLASSIFICATIONS UNDER STATE FAIR EMPLOYMENT PRACTICE LAWS

(See also text at § 2.3[a].)

**NOTE:** Although discrimination against pregnant employees and sexual harassment are often not explicitly prohibited in statutes, they are often barred in practice under a general prohibition against sex discrimination.

Some states do not explicitly prohibit discrimination on the basis of *both* national origin and ancestry. However, if a state statute specifically protects only one class, it is likely to be interpreted broadly and encompass members of both classes.

It should be noted that in some states an employee may bring a public policy wrongful discharge action based on a state's expressed policy against discrimination, even if no statute provides such a right, or if the state's statutes apply only to public employment. For states recognizing such a wrongful discharge action, see Table 4.4-2.

| | *Age* | *Race* | *Color* | *National Origin* | *Ancestry* | *Religion* | *Sex* | *Pregnancy* | *Sexual Harassment* | *Citations to Authority* |
|---|---|---|---|---|---|---|---|---|---|---|
| AL | No. | No. | No. | No. | No specific prohibitions, but see explanatory note above. | No. | No. | No specific prohibitions, but see explanatory note above. | No specific prohibitions, but see explanatory note above. | State has no comprehensive FEP act. |
| AK | Yes, see also Table 2.5-1. | Yes. | Yes. | Yes. | Yes. | Yes. | Yes. | Yes. | No specific prohibitions, but see explanatory note above. | Alaska Stat. §§ 18.80.200, 18.80.220, 18.80.300. |
| AZ | Yes, age 40 and over. | Yes. | Yes. | Yes. | No specific prohibitions, but see explanatory note above. | Yes. | Yes. | No specific prohibitions, but see explanatory note above. | No specific prohibitions, but see explanatory note above. | Ariz. Rev. Stat. Ann. §§ 41-1461, 41-1463, 41-1465. |
| AR | No, but see Table 2.5-1. | Yes. | No. | Yes. | Yes. | Yes. | Yes. | Yes. | No specific prohibitions, but see explanatory note above. | Ark. Code Ann. §§ 16-123-102, 16-123-107. |
| CA | Yes, older than 40. | Yes. | Yes. | Yes. | Yes. | Yes. | Yes. | Yes. | Yes. | Cal. Gov't Code §§ 12940, 12941, 12945. |
| CO | Yes. | Yes. | Yes. | Yes. | Yes. | Yes. | Yes. | No specific prohibitions, but see explanatory note above. | No specific statutory prohibitions, but see explanatory note above. | Colo. Rev. Stat. § 24-34-402. |

| | | | | | | | | | | |
|---|---|---|---|---|---|---|---|---|---|---|
| CT | Yes. | Yes. | Yes. | Yes. | Yes. | Yes. | Yes. | Yes. | Yes. Statute prohibits inquiry into childbearing age or plans, pregnancy, reproductive capability, use of birth control, and familial responsibilities. | Conn. Gen. Stat. Ann. §§ 46a-51, 46a-60. |
| DE | Yes, between 40 and 70. | Yes. | Yes. | Yes. | No specific prohibitions, but see explanatory note above. | Yes. | Yes. | No specific prohibitions, but see explanatory note above. | No specific prohibitions, but see explanatory note above. | Del. Code Ann. tit. 19, §§ 710, 711. |
| DC | Yes. | Yes. | Yes. | Yes. | No specific prohibitions, but see explanatory note above. | Yes. | Yes. | Yes. | No specific statutory prohibitions, but see explanatory note above. | D.C. Code Ann. §§ 1-2505, 1-2512. |
| FL | Yes. See also Table 2.5-1. | Yes. | Yes. | Yes. | Yes. | Yes. | Yes. | No specific prohibitions, but see explanatory note above. | No specific prohibitions, but see explanatory note above. | Fla. Stat. Ann. §§ 110.105, 760.02, 760.10. |
| GA | Yes, between 40 and 70. See also Table 2.5-1. | Yes. | Yes. | Yes. | No specific prohibitions, but see explanatory note above. | Yes. | Yes. | No specific prohibitions, but see explanatory note above. | No specific prohibitions, but see explanatory note above. | Ga. Code Ann. §§ 45-19-28, 45-19-29. (Apply to public employment only.) |
| HI | Yes. | Yes. | Yes. | Yes. | Yes. | Yes. | Yes. | Yes. | Yes. | Haw. Rev. Stat. §§ 378-2, 378-3. |
| ID | Yes. | Yes. | Yes. | Yes. | No specific statutory prohibitions, but see explanatory note above. | Yes. | Yes. | No specific prohibitions, but see explanatory note above. | No specific prohibitions, but see explanatory note above. | Idaho Code §§ 67-5901, 67-5902, 67-5909. |
| IL | Yes, age 40 and over. | Yes. | Yes. | Yes. | Yes. | Yes. | Yes. | No specific statutory prohibitions, but see explanatory note above. | Yes. | 775 ILCS §§ 5/1-101 *et seq.*, 5/2-101 *et seq.* |
| IN | Yes, between 40 and 70. | Yes. | Yes. | Yes. | Yes. | Yes. | Yes. | No specific prohibitions, but see explanatory note above. | No specific prohibitions, but see explanatory note above. | Ind. Code §§ 22-9-1-2, 22-9-1-3, 22-9-1-6, 22-9-1-13, 22-9-2-1, 22-9-2-2. |
| IA | Yes. | Yes. | Yes. | Yes. | No specific prohibitions, but see explanatory note above. | Yes. | Yes. | Yes. | Yes, for state employees. | Iowa Code Ann. §§ 19B.12, 216.2, 216.6. |

*(Table continues.)*

# Table 2.3-1 Part A *(cont'd)*

## PROTECTED CLASSIFICATIONS UNDER STATE FAIR EMPLOYMENT PRACTICE LAWS

(See also text at § 2.3[a].)

**NOTE:** Although discrimination against pregnant employees and sexual harassment are often not explicitly prohibited in statutes, they are often barred in practice under a general prohibition against sex discrimination.

Some states do not explicitly prohibit discrimination on the basis of *both* national origin and ancestry. However, if a state statute specifically protects only one class, it is likely to be interpreted broadly and encompass members of both classes.

It should be noted that in some states an employee may bring a public policy wrongful discharge action based on a state's expressed policy against discrimination, even if no statute provides such a right, or if the state's statutes apply only to public employment. For states recognizing such a wrongful discharge action, see Table 4.4-2.

| | *Age* | *Race* | *Color* | *National Origin* | *Ancestry* | *Religion* | *Sex* | *Pregnancy* | *Sexual Harassment* | *Citations to Authority* |
|---|---|---|---|---|---|---|---|---|---|---|
| KS | No, but see Table 2.5-1. | Yes. | Yes. | Yes. | Yes. | Yes. | Yes. | No specific prohibitions, but see explanatory note above. | No specific prohibitions, but see explanatory note above. | Kan. Stat. Ann. § 44-1009. |
| KY | Yes, age 40 and over. See also Table 2.5-1. | Yes. | Yes. | Yes. | No specific prohibitions, but see explanatory note above. | Yes. | Yes. | Yes. | No specific prohibitions, but see explanatory note above. | Ky. Rev. Stat. Ann. §§ 18A.140, 344.020–344.080. |
| LA | Yes, age 40 and over. See also Table 2.5-1. | Yes. | Yes. | Yes. | No specific prohibitions, but see explanatory note above. | Yes. | Yes. | Yes. | No specific prohibitions, but see explanatory note above. | La. Rev. Stat. Ann. §§ 23:301 *et seq.* |
| ME | Yes. | Yes. | Yes. | Yes. | Yes. | Yes. | Yes. | Yes. | Yes. | Me. Rev. Stat. Ann. tit. 5, §§ 4571, 4572, 4572-A, 4574, 4651 *et seq.* |
| MD | Yes. | Yes. | Yes. | Yes. | Yes. | Yes. | Yes. | Yes. | No specific prohibitions, but see explanatory note above. | Md. Ann. Code art. 49B, §§ 14, 16, 17. |
| MA | Yes, older than 40. See Table 2.5-1. | Yes. | Yes. | Yes. | Yes. | Yes. | Yes. | Yes. | Yes. | Mass. Gen. Laws ch. 151B, §§ 1, 4, ch. 272, § 98B. |
| MI | Yes. See also Table 2.5-1. | Yes. | Yes. | Yes. | No specific prohibitions, but see explanatory note above. | Yes. | Yes. | Yes. | Yes. | Mich. Stat. Ann. §§ 3.548(202), 3.548(203), 3.548(205). |

| | | | | | | | | | | |
|---|---|---|---|---|---|---|---|---|---|---|
| MN | Yes, older than 25. | Yes. | Yes. | Yes. | No specific prohibitions, but see explanatory note above. | Yes. | Yes. | Yes. | No specific prohibitions, but see explanatory note above. | Minn. Stat. Ann. § 363.03. |
| MS | Yes. | Yes. | Yes. | Yes. | No specific prohibitions, but see explanatory note above. | Yes. | Yes. | No specific prohibitions, but see explanatory note above. | No specific prohibitions, but see explanatory note above. | Miss. Code Ann. §§ 25-9-103, 25-9-149. (State has no comprehensive FEP act. Statute applies to public employment only.) |
| MO | Yes, between 40 and 70. | Yes. | Yes. | Yes. | Yes. | Yes. | Yes. | Yes. | Yes. | Mo. Rev. Stat. §§ 213.010, 213.055, 213.070, 213.125; Mo. Code Regs. tit. 4, § 180-3.050; Mo. Code Regs. tit. 8, §§ 60-3.040, 60-3.050, 60-3.070. |
| MT | Yes. | Yes. | Yes. | Yes. | No specific prohibitions, but see explanatory note above. | Yes. | Yes. | Yes. | Yes. Statute specifically mentions public employment only. | Mont. Code Ann. §§ 49-2-101, 49-2-102, 49-2-303, 49-2-308–49-2-311, Mont. Const. art. II, § 4. |
| NE | No, but see Table 2.5-1. | Yes. | Yes. | Yes. | Yes. | Yes. | Yes. | Yes. | Yes. | Neb. Rev. Stat. §§ 48-1101–48-1104; Neb. Admin. R. & Regs. § 1-8. |
| NV | Yes. | Yes. | Yes. | Yes. | No specific prohibitions, but see explanatory note above. | Yes. | Yes. | Yes. | No specific prohibitions, but see explanatory note above. | Nev. Rev. Stat. §§ 613.330, 613.335. |
| NH | Yes. | Yes. | Yes. | Yes. | Yes. | Yes. | Yes. | Yes. | Yes. | N.H. Rev. Stat. Ann. §§ 354-A:2, 354-A:6, 354-A:7, 354-A:8; N.H. Code Admin. R. Hum. §§ 401.01, 402.01–402.03, 403.01–403.03, 404.01–404.03. |
| NJ | Yes, age 40 and over. | Yes. | Yes. | Yes. | Yes. | Yes. | Yes. | Yes. | Yes. | N.J. Stat. Ann. §§ 10:3-1, 10:5-3, 10:5-4, 10:5-12; *Gilchrist v. Board of Educ.*, 155 N.J. Super. 358 (1978). |
| NM | Yes. | Yes. | Yes. | Yes. | Yes. | Yes. | Yes. | No specific prohibitions, but see explanatory note above. | No specific prohibitions, but see explanatory note above. | N.M. Stat. Ann. §§ 28-1-2, 28-1-7. |

*(Table continues.)*

## Table 2.3-1 Part A *(cont'd)*

## PROTECTED CLASSIFICATIONS UNDER STATE FAIR EMPLOYMENT PRACTICE LAWS

(See also text at § 2.3[a].)

**NOTE:** Although discrimination against pregnant employees and sexual harassment are often not explicitly prohibited in statutes, they are often barred in practice under a general prohibition against sex discrimination.

Some states do not explicitly prohibit discrimination on the basis of *both* national origin and ancestry. However, if a state statute specifically protects only one class, it is likely to be interpreted broadly and encompass members of both classes.

It should be noted that in some states an employee may bring a public policy wrongful discharge action based on a state's expressed policy against discrimination, even if no statute provides such a right, or if the state's statutes apply only to public employment. For states recognizing such a wrongful discharge action, see Table 4.4-2.

| | *Age* | *Race* | *Color* | *National Origin* | *Ancestry* | *Religion* | *Sex* | *Pregnancy* | *Sexual Harassment* | *Citations to Authority* |
|---|---|---|---|---|---|---|---|---|---|---|
| NY | Yes. See also Table 2.5-1. | Yes, subject to arbitration, as are other protected classes. | Yes. | Yes. | Yes. | Yes. | Yes. | Yes. | Yes. | N.Y. Exec. Law §§ 291, 292, 296; N.Y. Civ. Rights Law §§ 40-c, 42–44; N.Y. Ex. Or. 6; *Fletcher v. Kidder, Peabody & Co.*, 619 N.E.2d 998 (N.Y. 1993). |
| NC | Yes, age 40 and over. | Yes. | Yes. | Yes. | No specific prohibitions, but see explanatory note above. | Yes. | Yes. | No specific prohibitions, but see explanatory note above. | No specific prohibitions, but see explanatory note above. | N.C. Gen. Stat. §§ 126-16, 126-36, 168A-3 (statute applies to public employment only). |
| ND | Yes. See also Table 2.5-1. | Yes. | Yes. | Yes. | Yes. | Yes. | Yes. | Yes. | Yes. | N.D. Cent. Code §§ 14-02.4-01–14-02.4-06. |
| OH | Yes. See also Table 2.5-1. | Yes. | Yes. | Yes. | Yes. | Yes. | Yes. | Yes. | Yes. | Ohio Rev. Code Ann. §§ 4112.01, 4112.02; Ohio Admin. Code §§ 4112-5-02, 4112-5-05; *Collins v. Rizkana,* 652 N.E.2d 653 (Ohio 1995). |
| OK | Yes, age 40 and over. | Yes. | Yes. | Yes. | Yes. | Yes. | Yes. | No specific prohibitions, but see explanatory note above. | No specific prohibitions, but see explanatory note above. | Okla. Stat. tit. 25, §§ 1201, 1301–1306, 1311; tit. 74, §§ 840-2.9, 954. |

| | | | | | | | | | | |
|---|---|---|---|---|---|---|---|---|---|---|
| OR | Yes. | Yes. | Yes. | Yes. | Yes. | Yes. | Yes. | Yes. | Yes (by executive order). | Or. Rev. Stat. §§ 240.306, 659.010, 659.020, 659.029, 659.030. |
| PA | Yes, age 40 and over. | Yes. | Yes. | Yes. | Yes. | Yes. | Yes. | No specific prohibitions, but see explanatory note above. | No specific prohibitions, but see explanatory note above. | Pa. Const. art. I § 28; Pa. Stat. Ann. tit. 43, §§ 952–955. |
| RI | Yes, age 40 and over. | Yes. | Yes. | Yes. | Yes. | Yes. | Yes. | Yes. | Yes (by executive order). | R.I. Gen. Laws §§ 28-5-6, 28-5-7; R.I. Ex. Or. 85-13, §§ 1, 2. |
| SC | Yes, age 40 and over. | Yes. | Yes. | Yes. | No specific prohibitions, but see explanatory note above. | Yes. | Yes. | Yes. | No specific prohibitions, but see explanatory note above. | S.C. Code Ann. §§ 1-13-20, 1-13-30, 1-13-80. |
| SD | Yes, age 40 and over. Statute specifically mentions state employment only. | Yes. | Yes. | Yes. | Yes. | Yes. | Yes. | Yes. | Yes (by executive order). | S.D. Codified Laws §§ 3-6A-15, 20-13-1, 20-13-10; S.D. Ex. Or. 90-7. |
| TN | Yes. | Yes. | Yes. | Yes. | Yes. | Yes. | Yes. | No specific prohibitions, but see explanatory note above. | No specific prohibitions, but see explanatory note above. | Tenn. Code Ann. §§ 4-21-102, 4-21-301, 4-21-401, 4-21-407. |
| TX | Yes, age 40 and over. | Yes. | Yes. | Yes. | Yes. | Yes. | Yes. | Yes. | No specific prohibitions, but see explanatory note above. | Tex. Lab. Code Ann. §§ 21.051, 21.101, 21.106, 21.108, 21.110. |
| UT | Yes, older than 40. | Yes. | Yes. | Yes. | Yes. | Yes. | Yes. | Yes. | Yes. | Utah Code Ann. §§ 34-35-2, 34-35-6, 67-19-4. |
| VT | Yes, 18 or older. | Yes. | Yes. | Yes. | Yes. | Yes. | Yes. | No specific prohibitions, but see explanatory note above. | Yes. | Vt. Stat. Ann. tit. 21, §§ 495, 495d, 495h. |
| VA | Yes. | Yes. | Yes. | Yes. | No specific prohibitions, but see explanatory note above. | Yes. | Yes. | Yes. | No specific prohibitions, but see explanatory note above. | Va. Code Ann. §§ 2.1-116.10, 2.1-715, 2.1-716; Va. Const. art. I § 11. |
| WA | Yes, older than 40. See also Table 2.5-1. | Yes. | Yes. | Yes. | Yes. | Yes. | Yes. | No specific prohibitions, but see explanatory note above. | No specific prohibitions, but see explanatory note above. | Wash. Rev. Code §§ 49.12.200, 49.44.090, 49.60.010–49.60.040, 49.60.180, 49.60.205. |

*(Table continues.)*

# Table 2.3-1 Part A *(cont'd)*

## PROTECTED CLASSIFICATIONS UNDER STATE FAIR EMPLOYMENT PRACTICE LAWS

(See also text at § 2.3[a].)

**NOTE:** Although discrimination against pregnant employees and sexual harassment are often not explicitly prohibited in statutes, they are often barred in practice under a general prohibition against sex discrimination.

Some states do not explicitly prohibit discrimination on the basis of *both* national origin and ancestry. However, if a state statute specifically protects only one class, it is likely to be interpreted broadly and encompass members of both classes.

It should be noted that in some states an employee may bring a public policy wrongful discharge action based on a state's expressed policy against discrimination, even if no statute provides such a right, or if the state's statutes apply only to public employment. For states recognizing such a wrongful discharge action, see Table 4.4-2.

| | *Age* | *Race* | *Color* | *National Origin* | *Ancestry* | *Religion* | *Sex* | *Pregnancy* | *Sexual Harassment* | *Citations to Authority* |
|---|---|---|---|---|---|---|---|---|---|---|
| WV | Yes, older than 40. | Yes. | Yes. | Yes. | Yes. | Yes. | Yes. | Yes. | Yes. | W. Va. Code §§ 5-11-3, 5-11-9; *Frank's Shoe Store v. W. Va. Human Rights Comm'n,* 178 W. Va. 53, 365 S.E.2d 251 (1986). |
| WI | Yes, age 40 and over. | Yes. | Yes. | Yes. | Yes. | Yes. | Yes. | Yes. | Yes. | Wis. Stat. Ann. §§ 111.31, 111.32, 111.33, 111.36, 111.321, 111.322, 111.337. |
| WY | Yes, between 40 and 70. | Yes. | Yes. | Yes. | Yes. | Yes. | Yes. | No specific prohibitions, but see explanatory note above. | No specific prohibitions, but see explanatory note above. | Wyo. Stat. § 27-9-105. |

# Table 2.3-1 Part B
## PROTECTED CLASSIFICATIONS UNDER STATE FAIR EMPLOYMENT PRACTICE LAWS

(See also text at § 2.3[a].)

**KEY: Retaliation or Reprisal.** Discrimination based on an employee's making use of fair employment statute (for example, by alleging discrimination or by filing a claim).

| | *Sexual Orientation* | *Marital Status* | *Veteran Status* | *Handicap or Physical Disability* | *Mental Disorder* | *Political Orientation* | *Retaliation or Reprisal* | *Other Protected Classifications, Activities, or Conditions* | *Citations to Authority* |
|---|---|---|---|---|---|---|---|---|---|
| AL | No. | No. | No. | No, but see Table 2.5-1. | No. | No. | No. | None. | State has no comprehensive FEP act. |
| AK | No. | Yes. | No. | Yes. | Yes. See also Table 2.5-1. | No. | Yes. | Parenthood; changes in marital status. | Alaska Stat. §§ 18.80.200, 18.80.220. |
| AZ | No. | No. | No. | Yes. See also Table 2.5-1. | No. | No. | Yes. | None. Statute specifically exempts aliens and members of communist organizations. | Ariz. Rev. Stat. Ann. §§ 41-1462, 41-1463, 41-1464. |
| AR | No. | No. | No. | Yes. | Yes. | No. | Yes. | None. | Ark. Code Ann. §§ 16-123-107, 16-123-108. |
| CA | No, but see Table 2.5-1. | Yes. | No, although an employer is not prevented from giving preference to veterans. | Yes. | Yes (only for employers with 15 or more employees). | Yes. | Yes. | Medical condition; childbirth or related medical condition; family care leave; color blindness in state civil service. | Cal. Gov't Code §§ 12926, 12940, 12945.2, 19700-19703; Cal. Lab. Code § 1101. |
| CO | No. | No. | No. | Yes. | Yes. | No. | Yes. | Marriage to another employee. | Colo. Rev. Stat. §§ 24-34-301, 24-34-402. |
| CT | Yes. | Yes. | No. | Yes. See also Table 2.5-1. | Yes. | No. | Yes. | Status as parent or potential parent; history of mental illness; arrest records and erased conviction records. | Conn. Gen. Stat. Ann. §§ 46a-60, 46a-80, 46a-81c. |
| DE | No. | Yes. | No. | No, but see Table 2.5-1. | No, but see Table 2.5-1. | No. | No. | None. | Del. Code Ann. tit. 19, § 711. |

*(Table continues.)*

# Table 2.3-1 Part B *(cont'd)*

## PROTECTED CLASSIFICATIONS UNDER STATE FAIR EMPLOYMENT PRACTICE LAWS

(See also text at § 2.3[a].)

**KEY: Retaliation or Reprisal.** Discrimination based on an employee's making use of fair employment statute (for example, by alleging discrimination or by filing a claim).

| | *Sexual Orientation* | *Marital Status* | *Veteran Status* | *Handicap or Physical Disability* | *Mental Disorder* | *Political Orientation* | *Retaliation or Reprisal* | *Other Protected Classifications, Activities, or Conditions* | *Citations to Authority* |
|---|---|---|---|---|---|---|---|---|---|
| DC | Yes. | Yes. | No. | Yes. Reverse discrimination not prohibited; able-bodied worker not in protected class. See also Table 2.5-1. | Yes. | Yes. | Yes. | Personal appearance; family responsibilities; matriculation (status as student). No employer may refuse to reasonably accommodate an employee's religious observance. | D.C. Code Ann. §§ 1-2505, 1-2512, 1-2525. |
| FL | No, but see Table 2.5-1. | Yes, unless an antinepotism policy exists. | No. | Yes. See also Table 2.5-1. | No, unless "handicap" is defined to include mental disorders. | No. | Yes. | Persons who have or are perceived as having AIDS, ARC, or HIV. | Fla. Stat. Ann. §§ 760.10, 760.50. |
| GA | No. | No. | No. | Yes. See also Table 2.5-1. | Yes. See also Table 2.5-1. | No. | Yes. | Statute prohibits conspiracies. | Ga. Code Ann. §§ 45-19-1 *et seq.* (Applies to public employment only.) |
| HI | Yes. | Yes. | No. | Yes. | Yes. | No. | Yes. | Arrest and court records; assignment of income due to child support status; absence due to National Guard service. | Haw. Rev. Stat. §§ 378-1, 378-2. |
| ID | No. | No. | No. | Yes. See also Table 2.5-1. | Yes. See also Table 2.5-1. | No. | Yes. | None. | Idaho Code §§ 67-5901, 67-5902, 67-5909, 67-5911. |

| | | | | | | | | | |
|---|---|---|---|---|---|---|---|---|---|
| IL | No. | Yes. | No. (But see "Other Protected Classifications, Activities, or Conditions.") | Yes. See also Table 2.5-1. | Yes. See also Table 2.5-1. | No. | Yes. | Arrest records; citizenship status. | 775 ILCS §§ 5/1-101 *et seq.*; 5/2-101 *et seq.*; 5/6-101. |
| IN | No. | No. | No. | Yes. | Yes. | No. | Yes. | Rehabilitated drug users or those currently enrolled in rehabilitation programs. | Ind. Code §§ 22-9-1-2, 22-9-1-3, 22-9-1-6, 22-9-1-13, 22-9-5-6, 22-9-5-19. |
| IA | No. | No. | No. | Yes. See also Table 2.5-1. | Yes. See also Table 2.5-1. | No. | Yes. | Familial status; testing for AIDS. | Iowa Code Ann. §§ 216.2, 216.6, 216.11. |
| KS | No. | No. | No. | Yes. | Yes. | Yes. Applies to public employment only. | Yes. | None. | Kan. Stat. Ann. §§ 44-1002, 44-1009, 75-2941. |
| KY | No. | Yes. | No. | Yes. See also Table 2.5-1. | Yes. | Yes. Applies to public employment only. | Yes. | Smoking, as long as employee complies with workplace policy; AIDS diagnosis or HIV-positive persons. | Ky. Rev. Stat. Ann. §§ 18A.140, 207.135, 344.010, 344.020, 344.040 *et seq.* |
| LA | No. | No. | No. | Yes. See also Table 2.5-1. | Yes. See also Table 2.5-1. | Yes. | Yes. | Sickle cell trait; workers' compensation claimant; smoking, as long as employee complies with workplace policy; jurors. | La. Rev. Stat. Ann. §§ 23:301 *et seq.*, 23:961, 23:962, 23:964, 23:965, 23:966, 23:1361, 46:2253 *et seq.*, 51:2231 *et seq.* |
| ME | No. | No. | No. | Yes. See also Table 2.5-1. | Yes. | Yes. Applies to public employment only. | Yes. | None. | Me. Rev. Stat. Ann. tit. 5, § 4572. |
| MD | No. | Yes. | No. | Yes. | Yes. | Yes. Applies to public employment only. | Yes. | None. | Md. Ann. Code art 49B, §§ 14, 16. |
| MA | Yes, except for pedophiles. | Yes. | No. | Yes. See also Table 2.5-1. | Yes. See also Table 2.5-1. | No. | Yes. | Arrest or violation without conviction; first conviction for drunkenness, simple assault, speeding, minor traffic violation, affray, or disturbing the (*cont'd*) | Mass. Gen. Laws ch. 151B § 4. |

(*Table continues.*)

## Table 2.3-1 Part B *(cont'd)*

### PROTECTED CLASSIFICATIONS UNDER STATE FAIR EMPLOYMENT PRACTICE LAWS

(See also text at § 2.3[a].)

**KEY:** **Retaliation or Reprisal.** Discrimination based on an employee's making use of fair employment statute (for example, by alleging discrimination or by filing a claim).

| | *Sexual Orientation* | *Marital Status* | *Veteran Status* | *Handicap or Physical Disability* | *Mental Disorder* | *Political Orientation* | *Retaliation or Reprisal* | *Other Protected Classifications, Activities, or Conditions* | *Citations to Authority* |
|---|---|---|---|---|---|---|---|---|---|
| MA (*cont'd*) | | | | | | | | peace; conviction of a misdemeanor more than 5 years ago, unless applicant has been convicted for any offense within 5 years of application for employment. | |
| MI | No. | Yes. | No. | Yes. See also Table 2.5-1. | Yes. See also Table 2.5-1. | No. | Yes. | Height and weight; familial status; arrest or violation without conviction. | Mich. Stat. Ann. §§ 3.548(202), 3.548(203), 3.548(205), 3.548(205a), 3.548(701). |
| MN | Yes. | Yes. | No. | Yes. | Yes. | No. | Yes. | Status with regard to public assistance; membership or activity in a human rights commission; conviction of a crime. | Minn. Stat. Ann. §§ 363.03, 364.03, 364.04. |
| MS | No. | No. | No, but veterans are preferred in public employment. | Yes. See also Table 2.5-1. | No. | Yes. | Yes. | None. | Miss. Code Ann. §§ 25-9-149, 25-9-173, 25-9-303. State has no comprehensive FEP act. (Applies to public employment only.) |
| MO | No. | No. | No. | Yes. | Yes. | No. | Yes. | AIDS diagnosis; rehabilitated drug users. | Mo. Rev. Stat. §§ 191.665, 213.010, 213.055, 213.070; Mo. Code Regs. tit. 8, §§ 60-3.040, 60-3.050, 60-3.060. |

| | | | | | | | | | |
|---|---|---|---|---|---|---|---|---|---|
| MT | No. | Yes. | No, but veterans are preferred in public employment. | Yes. See also Table 2.5-1. | Yes. | Yes. | Yes. | None. | Mont. Code Ann. §§ 49-1-102, 49-2-301, 49-2-303, 49-2-308, 49-2-405, 49-3-201, 49-3-209; Mont. Const. art. II § 4; Mont. Ex. Or. 7-82; *Thompson v. Board of Trustees,* 627 P.2d 1229 (1981). |
| NE | No. | Yes. | No. | Yes. See also Table 2.5-1. | Yes. See also Table 2.5-1. | Yes, restricted to state and local government employees. | Yes. | Statute specifically excludes members of communist organizations; developmental disabilities; HIV testing. | Neb. Rev. Stat. §§ 20-160–20-162, 20-167, 48-1101–48-1104, 48-1109, 48-1114, 48-1115. |
| NV | No. | No. | No. | Yes. | Yes. | Yes. | Yes. | Lawful off-premises use of any products that do not adversely affect job performance or safety. See "Trends and Controversies in Human Resources Law," Exhibit i, for further discussion. | Nev. Rev. Stat. §§ 281.370, 613.040, 613.310, 613.330, 613.333, 613.340. |
| NH | Yes. | Yes. | No. | Yes. | Yes. | No. | Yes. | Familial status; tobacco use outside of employment. | N.H. Rev. Stat. Ann. §§ 155 *et seq.,* 275:37-a, 354-A:2, 354-A:6, 354-A:7, 354-A:19. |
| NJ | Yes. | Yes. | No. | Yes. | Yes. | No. | Yes. | Atypical hereditary cellular or blood trait; familial status; liability for service in the Armed Services. | N.J. Stat. Ann. §§ 10:5-3, 10:5-4, 10:5-4.1, 10:5-5, 10:5-12, 10:5-29; *Anderson v. Exxon Corp.,* 89 N.J. 483 (1983). |
| NM | Yes. | Yes. | No. | Yes. | Yes. | Yes, for state government employees. | Yes. | None. | N.M. Stat. Ann. §§ 10-9-21, 28-1-7; N.M. Ex. Or. 85-15. |
| NY | Yes. Applies to public employment only. | Yes. | No. | Yes. See also Table 2.5-1. | Yes. See also Table 2.5-1. | Yes, for civil service employees. | Yes. | Sickle cell trait; Tay-Sachs syndrome; carriers of Cooley's anemia; AIDS diagnosis; conviction; arrest record. | N.Y. Exec. Law §§ 292, 296; N.Y. Civ. Rights Law §§ 40-c, 47-b, 48; N.Y. Civ. Serv. Law § 107; N.Y. Ex. Or. 28; N.Y. Comp. Codes R. & Regs. tit. 12, §§ 600.1, 600.4; *State Div. of Human Rights ex rel. McDermott v. Xerox Corp.,* 480 N.E. 2d 695 (1985). |

*(Table continues.)*

## Table 2.3-1 Part B *(cont'd)*

## PROTECTED CLASSIFICATIONS UNDER STATE FAIR EMPLOYMENT PRACTICE LAWS

(See also text at § 2.3[a].)

**KEY: Retaliation or Reprisal.** Discrimination based on an employee's making use of fair employment statute (for example, by alleging discrimination or by filing a claim).

| | *Sexual Orientation* | *Marital Status* | *Veteran Status* | *Handicap or Physical Disability* | *Mental Disorder* | *Political Orientation* | *Retaliation or Reprisal* | *Other Protected Classifications, Activities, or Conditions* | *Citations to Authority* |
|---|---|---|---|---|---|---|---|---|---|
| NC | No. | No. | No, but veterans preferred in state employment. | Yes. See also Table 2.5-1. | Yes. See also Table 2.5-1. | Yes. | Yes. | None. | N.C. Gen. Stat. §§ 126-13, 126-16, 126-17, 126-36, 126-80, 126-85 (statute applies to public employment only). |
| ND | No. | Yes. | No. | Yes. | Yes. | Yes. | Yes. | Status with respect to public assistance; lawful activities off premises during nonworking hours. | N.D. Cent. Code §§ 14-02.5-01–14-02.5-06, 14-02.5-18, 54-44.3-22. |
| OH | No. | No. | No, but see Table 2.5-1. | Yes. | Yes. | No. | Yes. | Expunged arrest records; familial status. | Ohio Rev. Code Ann. §§ 4112.01, 4112.02; Ohio Admin. Code §§ 4112-5-02, 4112-5-08. |
| OK | No. | Yes. | No. | Yes. See also Table 2.5-1. | Yes. See also Table 2.5-1. | Yes. Applies to public employment only. | Yes. | None. | Okla. Stat. tit. 25, §§ 1302–1306; tit. 74, §§ 840-2.9, 954. |
| OR | No. | Yes. | No. | Yes. | Yes. | Yes. | Yes. | Expunged juvenile records; family relationships; workers' compensation; smoking; family leave; requiring breathalyzer, polygraph, or psychological tests; requiring genetic screening. | Or. Rev. Stat. §§ 236.380, 659.030, 659.035, 659.036, 659.165, 659.225, 659.227, 659.340, 659.380, 659.400–659.490. |

| | | | | | | | | | |
|---|---|---|---|---|---|---|---|---|---|
| PA | Yes. Applies to public employment only. | No. | No. | Yes. | Yes. | No. | Yes. | High school diploma and GED certificates must be given equal consideration; use of guide dogs or support animals; willingness or refusal to participate in abortions; familial status; association with handicapped persons. | Pa. Stat. Ann. tit. 43, §§ 953, 954, 955. |
| RI | Yes. | No. | No. | Yes. See also Table 2.5-1. | Yes. See also Table 2.5-1. | No. | Yes. | None. | R.I. Gen. Laws §§ 28-5-3, 28-5-5–28-5-7. |
| SC | No. | No. | No. | Yes. See Table 2.5-1. | Yes. See Table 2.5-1. | No. | Yes. | None. | S.C. Code Ann. §§ 1-13-20 *et seq.* |
| SD | No. | Yes. | No. | Yes. | Yes. | Yes. Applies to public employment only. | Yes. | None. | S.D. Codified Laws §§ 3-6A-15, 20-13-10, 20-13-10.1, 20-13-23.7, 20-13-26. |
| TN | No. | No. | No. | Yes. | Yes. | No. | Yes. | None. | Tenn. Code Ann. §§ 4-21-102, 4-21-301, 4-21-401. |
| TX | No. | No. | No. | Yes, excluding employees addicted to alcohol or controlled substances, and employees with AIDS or other communicable diseases. | Yes. | No. | Yes. | None. | Tex. Lab. Code Ann. §§ 21.002, 21.051, 21.105. |
| UT | No. | No. | No. | Yes. | Yes. | Yes. Applies to public employment only. | Yes. | None. | Utah Code Ann. §§ 34-35-2, 34-35-6, 67-19-4, 67-19-19; Utah Admin. R. §§ R468-1-1, R468-1-2, R468-16-3. |
| VT | Yes. | No. | No. | Yes. | Yes. | Yes. Applies to public employment only. | Yes. | AIDS diagnosis. | Vt. Stat. Ann. tit. 3, § 961; tit. 21, §§ 495, 497, 1726. |

*(Table continues.)*

## Table 2.3-1 Part B *(cont'd)*

## PROTECTED CLASSIFICATIONS UNDER STATE FAIR EMPLOYMENT PRACTICE LAWS

(See also text at § 2.3[a].)

**KEY:** **Retaliation or Reprisal.** Discrimination based on an employee's making use of fair employment statute (for example, by alleging discrimination or by filing a claim).

| | *Sexual Orientation* | *Marital Status* | *Veteran Status* | *Handicap or Physical Disability* | *Mental Disorder* | *Political Orientation* | *Retaliation or Reprisal* | *Other Protected Classifications, Activities, or Conditions* | *Citations to Authority* |
|---|---|---|---|---|---|---|---|---|---|
| VA | No. | Yes. | No. | Yes. See also Table 2.5-1. | Yes. See also Table 2.5-1. | Yes. Applies to public employment. | Yes. | None. | Va. Code Ann. §§ 2.1-116.10, 2.1-716, 51.5-41. (Law says classifications should be consistent with those outlined in federal statutes.) |
| WA | No. | Yes. | No. | Yes. See also Table 2.5-1. | Yes. | No. | Yes. | AIDS diagnosis; arrests and convictions; developmental disabilities. | Wash. Rev. Code §§ 49.60.172, 49.60.180, 49.60.210, 71A.10.040. |
| WV | No. | No. | No. | Yes. | Yes. | Yes, except for certain policy-making officials (exception determined by substance of position). | Yes. | Familial status; blindness. | W. Va. Code §§ 5-11-3, 5-11-9, 29-6-20. |
| WI | Yes. | Yes. | No. | Yes. | Yes. | Yes. Applies to public employment only. | Yes. | Arrest or conviction records; membership in any reserve component of armed forces; use or nonuse of lawful products off-premises and during nonworking hours; failure to take a lie detector test; height and weight, unless these are bona fide occupational | Wis. Stat. Ann. §§ 111.31, 111.32, 111.34, 111.36, 111.37, 111.321, 111.322, 111.335, 111.345, 111.372, 230.18–230.20. |

| | | | | | | | | | |
|---|---|---|---|---|---|---|---|---|---|
| | | | | | | | | qualifications; genetic testing. | |
| WY | No. | No. | No. | Yes. | Yes. | No. | Yes. | Tobacco use outside workplace and during nonworking hours. | Wyo. Stat. §§ 27-9-105–27-9-107. |

# Exhibit 2.3-1

## EMPLOYEES EXEMPTED FROM STATE FAIR EMPLOYMENT PRACTICE LAWS

**NOTE:** States not listed herein have no comprehensive FEP act.

### ALASKA

**Are Domestic Employees Exempted?** Yes.

**Are Members of the Employer's Family Exempted?** State has no statutory exemption.

**Are Agricultural Employees Exempted?** State has no statutory exemption.

**Other Exemptions.** Statute is not applicable to nonprofit, exclusively social, fraternal, charitable, or religious entities.

**Citations to Authority.** Alaska Stat. §§ 18.80.220, 18.80.300.

### ARIZONA

**Are Domestic Employees Exempted?** State has no statutory exemption.

**Are Members of the Employer's Family Exempted?** State has no statutory exemption.

**Are Agricultural Employees Exempted?** State has no statutory exemption.

**Other Exemptions.** Statute excludes from the definition of an unlawful employment practice any action or measure taken by an employer against an individual who is a member of a communist organization. Statute also excludes elected public officials and their immediate personal staffs.

**Citations to Authority.** Ariz. Rev. Stat. Ann. §§ 41-1461, 41-1463.

### ARKANSAS

**Are Domestic Employees Exempted?** State has no statutory exemption.

**Are Members of the Employer's Family Exempted?** Yes.

**Are Agricultural Employees Exempted?** State has no statutory exemption.

**Other Exemptions.** Statute excludes from coverage any individual employed outside of Arkansas; any individual employed under a special license in a nonprofit sheltered workshop or rehabilitation facility; statute is not applicable to nonprofit religious corporations, associations, societies, or other entities.

**Citations to Authority.** Ark. Code Ann. §§ 16-123-102, 16-123-103.

### CALIFORNIA

**Are Domestic Employees Exempted?** State has no statutory exemption.

**Are Members of the Employer's Family Exempted?** Yes.

**Are Agricultural Employees Exempted?** State has no statutory exemption.

**Other Exemptions.** Statute excludes from coverage any individual employed under a special license in a nonprofit sheltered workshop or rehabilitation facility. Nonprofit religious entities are also excluded.

**Citations to Authority.** Cal. Gov't Code §§ 12926, 12940, 12941, 12944, 12945.

### COLORADO

**Are Domestic Employees Exempted?** Yes.

**Are Members of the Employer's Family Exempted?** State has no statutory exemption.

**Are Agricultural Employees Exempted?** State has no statutory exemption.

**Other Exemptions.** Statute is not applicable to privately subsidized nonprofit religious entities.

**Citations to Authority.** Colo. Rev. Stat. §§ 24-34-401, 24-34-402.

### CONNECTICUT

**Are Domestic Employees Exempted?** Yes.

**Are Members of the Employer's Family Exempted?** Yes.

**Are Agricultural Employees Exempted?** State has no statutory exemption.

**Other Exemptions.** None.

**Citations to Authority.** Conn. Gen. Stat. Ann. §§ 46a-51, 46a-60.

### DELAWARE

**Are Domestic Employees Exempted?** Yes.

**Are Members of the Employer's Family Exempted?** Yes.

**Are Agricultural Employees Exempted?** Yes.

**Other Exemptions.** Statute is not applicable to privately subsidized nonprofit religious, fraternal, or charitable entities.

**Citations to Authority.** Del. Code Ann. tit. 19, §§ 710, 711.

### DISTRICT OF COLUMBIA

**Are Domestic Employees Exempted?** Yes.

**Are Members of the Employer's Family Exempted?** Yes

**Are Agricultural Employees Exempted?** State has no statutory exemption.

**Other Exemptions.** None.

**Citations to Authority.** D.C. Code Ann. §§ 1-2502, 1-2512.

### HAWAII

**Are Domestic Employees Exempted?** Yes.

**Are Members of the Employer's Family Exempted?** State has no statutory exemption.

**Are Agricultural Employees Exempted?** State has no statutory exemption.

**Other Exemptions.** Privately subsidized nonprofit religious entities may give hiring preference to individuals of the same religion or denomination.

**Citations to Authority.** Haw. Rev. Stat. §§ 378-1–378-3.

### IDAHO

**Are Domestic Employees Exempted?** Yes.

**Are Members of the Employer's Family Exempted?** State has no statutory exemption.

**Are Agricultural Employees Exempted?** State has no statutory exemption.

**Other Exemptions.** None.

**Citations to Authority.** Idaho Code §§ 67-5902, 67-5909.

### ILLINOIS

**Are Domestic Employees Exempted?** Yes.

**Are Members of the Employer's Family Exempted?** State has no statutory exemption.

**Are Agricultural Employees Exempted?** State has no statutory exemption.

**Other Exemptions.** Statute excludes elected public officials and their immediate personal staffs; principal administrative officers of the state or of any political subdivision, municipal corporation, or other governmental unit or agency; persons in vocational rehabilitation facilities certified under federal law who have been designated evaluees, trainees, or work activity clients. Statute is not applicable to privately subsidized nonprofit religious entities.

**Citations to Authority.** 775 Ill. Comp. Stat. Ann. § 5/2-101.

### INDIANA

**Are Domestic Employees Exempted?** Yes.

**Are Members of the Employer's Family Exempted?** Yes.

**Are Agricultural Employees Exempted?** State has no statutory exemption.

**Other Exemptions.** Statute excludes farm laborers under the age discrimination provision. Statute is not applicable to privately subsidized nonprofit religious, fraternal, educational, or charitable entities.

**Citations to Authority.** Ind. Code Ann. §§ 22-9-1-3, 22-9-2-10.

### IOWA

**Are Domestic Employees Exempted?** Yes.

**Are Members of the Employer's Family Exempted?** Yes.

**Are Agricultural Employees Exempted?** State has no statutory exemption.

**Other Exemptions.** None.

**Citations to Authority.** Iowa Code Ann. §§ 216.2, 216.6.

### KANSAS

**Are Domestic Employees Exempted?** Yes.

**Are Members of the Employer's Family Exempted?** Yes.

**Are Agricultural Employees Exempted?** State has no statutory exemption.

**Other Exemptions.** Statute is not applicable to nonprofit fraternal or social entities.

**Citations to Authority.** Kan. Stat. Ann. §§ 44-1002, 44-1009.

### KENTUCKY

**Are Domestic Employees Exempted?** Yes.

**Are Members of the Employer's Family Exempted?** Yes.

**Are Agricultural Employees Exempted?** State has no statutory exemption.

**Other Exemptions.** None.

**Citations to Authority.** Ky. Rev. Stat. Ann. §§ 344.030, 344.040, 344.050, 344.060, 344.070.

### LOUISIANA

**Are Domestic Employees Exempted?** Yes.

**Are Members of the Employer's Family Exempted?** Yes.

**Are Agricultural Employees Exempted?** State has no statutory exemption.

**Other Exemptions.** Statute does not apply to any employee of a school or other institution that is owned, supported, controlled, or managed by a particular religious corporation, association, or society, where the employment decision of said employer is related to the religious or moral beliefs, affiliations, or practices of the employee or applicant for employment.

**Citations to Authority.** La. Rev. Stat. Ann. § 23:301 *et seq.*

### MAINE

**Are Domestic Employees Exempted?** State has no statutory exemption.

**Are Members of the Employer's Family Exempted?** Yes.

**Are Agricultural Employees Exempted?** State has no statutory exemption.

**Other Exemptions.** Statute is not applicable to religious or fraternal entities not organized for profit and in fact not conducted for profit, with respect to employment of its members of the same religion or fraternity, except for purposes of disability-related discrimination.

**Citations to Authority.** Me. Rev. Stat. Ann. tit. 5, §§ 4553 4572.

### MARYLAND

**Are Domestic Employees Exempted?** State has no statutory exemption.

**Are Members of the Employer's Family Exempted?** State has no statutory exemption.

**Are Agricultural Employees Exempted?** State has no statutory exemption.

**Other Exemptions.** Statute excludes from coverage any elected public official or any person chosen by the official to be on the official's personal staff, any appointee at the policymaking level, and any immediate advisor with respect to the exercise of the constitutional or legal powers of the office.

**Citations to Authority.** Md. Ann. Code art. 49B, § 15(e).

### MASSACHUSETTS

**Are Domestic Employees Exempted?** Yes.

**Are Members of the Employer's Family Exempted?** Yes.

**Are Agricultural Employees Exempted?** State has no statutory exemption.

**Other Exemptions.** Statute is not applicable to nonprofit fraternal or social entities. Religious entities may give a preference in hiring to members of that religion.

**Citations to Authority.** Mass. Gen. Laws Ann. ch. 151B, §§ 1, 4.

### MICHIGAN

**Are Domestic Employees Exempted?** State has no statutory exemption.

**Are Members of the Employer's Family Exempted?** Yes.

**Are Agricultural Employees Exempted?** State has no statutory exemption.

**Other Exemptions.** None.

**Citations to Authority.** Mich. Comp. Laws Ann. §§ 37.2201–37.2205a.

### MINNESOTA

**Are Domestic Employees Exempted?** Yes.

**Are Members of the Employer's Family Exempted?** Yes.

**Are Agricultural Employees Exempted?** State has no statutory exemption.

**Other Exemptions.** Statute is not applicable to nonpublic service organizations whose primary function is providing occasional services to minors, with respect to qualifications of employees based on sexual orientation.

**Citations to Authority.** Minn. Stat. Ann. §§ 363.01–363.03.

### NEBRASKA

**Are Domestic Employees Exempted?** Yes.

**Are Members of the Employer's Family Exempted?** Yes.

**Are Agricultural Employees Exempted?** State has no statutory exemption.

**Other Exemptions.** Statute is not applicable to Native American tribes that employ; statute excludes from the definition of an unlawful employment practice any action or measure taken by an employer against an individual who is a member of a communist organization; statute is not applicable to privately subsidized nonprofit religious entities.

**Citations to Authority.** Neb. Rev. Stat. §§ 48-1102, 48-1103.

### NEVADA

**Are Domestic Employees Exempted?** State has no statutory exemption.

**Are Members of the Employer's Family Exempted?** State has no statutory exemption.

**Are Agricultural Employees Exempted?** State has no statutory exemption.

**Other Exemptions.** Statute excludes from the definition of an unlawful employment practice any action or measure taken by an employer against an individual who is a member of a communist organization; statute is not applicable to Native American tribes that employ or privately subsidized nonprofit religious entities.

**Citations to Authority.** Nev. Rev. Stat. §§ 613.310, 613.320, 613.330, 613.360.

### NEW HAMPSHIRE

**Are Domestic Employees Exempted?** Yes.

**Are Members of the Employer's Family Exempted?** Yes.

**Are Agricultural Employees Exempted?** Statute excludes agricultural services from coverage of prohibition against sex discrimination.

**Other Exemptions.** Statute excludes from coverage those employed seasonally. Statute is not applicable to nonprofit fraternal, charitable, educational, or religious entities.

**Citations to Authority.** N.H. Rev. Stat. Ann. §§ 275:36, 354-A:2, 354-A:7.

### NEW JERSEY

**Are Domestic Employees Exempted?** Yes.

**Are Members of the Employer's Family Exempted?** No.

**Are Agricultural Employees Exempted?** State has no statutory exemption.

**Other Exemptions.** Exclusively social or fraternal clubs may use club membership as a qualification for employment; religious entities may use religious affiliation as a qualification for employment.

**Citations to Authority.** N.J. Stat. Ann. §§ 10:5-5, 10:5-12.

### NEW YORK

**Are Domestic Employees Exempted?** Yes.

**Are Members of the Employer's Family Exempted?** Yes.

**Are Agricultural Employees Exempted?** State has no statutory exemption.

**Other Exemptions.** Religious entities may use religious affiliation as a qualification for employment.

**Citations to Authority.** N.Y. Exec. Law §§ 292, 296.

## NORTH DAKOTA

**Are Domestic Employees Exempted?** Yes.

**Are Members of the Employer's Family Exempted?** Yes.

**Are Agricultural Employees Exempted?** State has no statutory exemption.

**Other Exemptions.** The statute's definition of "employee" does not include a person elected to public office in the state or political subdivision and his or her immediate personal staff, yet it does include people subject to the civil service or merit system of a state government agency or political subdivision.

**Citations to Authority.** N.D. Cent. Code §§ 14-02.4-02, 14-02.4-10.

## OHIO

**Are Domestic Employees Exempted?** Yes.

**Are Members of the Employer's Family Exempted?** State has no statutory exemption.

**Are Agricultural Employees Exempted?** Yes.

**Other Exemptions.** Statute excludes any individual employed by the United States; newspaper delivery people; outside salespeople compensated by commissions or in a bona fide executive, administrative, or professional capacity; volunteers in health institutions; members of police or fire protection agencies; students employed part-time by political subdivisions of the state; individuals employed by a nonprofit camp or recreational area for children under age 18.

**Citations to Authority.** Ohio Rev. Code Ann. §§ 4112.01, 4112.02.

## OKLAHOMA

**Are Domestic Employees Exempted?** Yes.

**Are Members of the Employer's Family Exempted?** Yes.

**Are Agricultural Employees Exempted?** State has no statutory exemption.

**Other Exemptions.** Statute is not applicable to Native American tribes that employ nor to nonprofit bona fide membership clubs.

**Citations to Authority.** Okla. Stat. Ann. tit. 25, §§ 1201, 1301–1305, 1307; tit. 74, § 840-2.9.

## OREGON

**Are Domestic Employees Exempted?** Yes.

**Are Members of the Employer's Family Exempted?** Yes.

**Are Agricultural Employees Exempted?** State has no statutory exemption.

**Other Exemptions.** None

**Citations to Authority.** Or. Rev. Stat. §§ 659.010, 659.030.

## PENNSYLVANIA

**Are Domestic Employees Exempted?** Yes.

**Are Members of the Employer's Family Exempted?** Yes.

**Are Agricultural Employees Exempted?** Yes.

**Other Exemptions.** Statute recognizes exceptions based on applicable security regulations established by the United States or the Commonwealth of Pennsylvania. Religious entities may use religious affiliation as a qualification for employment.

**Citations to Authority.** Pa. Stat. Ann. tit. 43, §§ 954, 955; tit. 71, §§ 741.3, 741.905, 741.951.

## RHODE ISLAND

**Are Domestic Employees Exempted?** Yes.

**Are Members of the Employer's Family Exempted?** Yes.

**Are Agricultural Employees Exempted?** State has no statutory exemption.

**Other Exemptions.** Religious entities may use religious affiliation as a qualification for employment.

**Citations to Authority.** R.I. Gen. Laws §§ 28-5-6, 28-5-7.

## TENNESSEE

**Are Domestic Employees Exempted?** Yes.

**Are Members of the Employer's Family Exempted?** Yes.

**Are Agricultural Employees Exempted?** State has no statutory exemption.

**Other Exemptions.** Statute does not pertain to religious entities with respect to the employment of individuals of a particular religion to perform work connected with the administration by the entity of its religious activities.

**Citations to Authority.** Tenn. Code Ann. §§ 4-21-102, 4-21-401, 4-21-405.

**TEXAS**

**Are Domestic Employees Exempted?** State has no statutory exemption.

**Are Members of the Employer's Family Exempted?** Yes.

**Are Agricultural Employees Exempted?** State has no statutory exemption.

**Other Exemptions.** Statute excludes from coverage any elected public official.

**Citations to Authority.** Tex. Lab. Code Ann. §§ 21.002, 21.051, 21.054.

**UTAH**

**Are Domestic Employees Exempted?** State has no statutory exemption.

**Are Members of the Employer's Family Exempted?** Yes.

**Are Agricultural Employees Exempted?** State has no statutory exemption.

**Other Exemptions.** Statute permits an employer to give preference in employment to any person who has received more than one half of his or her total financial support from the employer during the preceding six months, regardless of whether or not the employer was or is legally obligated to furnish such support; and permits an employer to give preference in employment to any person whose education or training was substantially financed by the employer for a period of two or more years. Statute is not applicable to religious entities.

**Citations to Authority.** Utah Code Ann. §§ 34-35-2, 34-35-6.

**WASHINGTON**

**Are Domestic Employees Exempted?** Yes.

**Are Members of the Employer's Family Exempted?** Yes.

**Are Agricultural Employees Exempted?** State has no statutory exemption.

**Other Exemptions.** Statute is not applicable to nonprofit religious entities.

**Citations to Authority.** Wash. Rev. Code Ann. §§ 49.60.040, 49.60.190, 49.60.200.

**WEST VIRGINIA**

**Are Domestic Employees Exempted?** No.

**Are Members of the Employer's Family Exempted?** Yes.

**Are Agricultural Employees Exempted?** State has no statutory exemption.

**Other Exemptions.** None.

**Citations to Authority.** W. Va. Code §§ 5-11-3, 5-11-9; W. Va. Ex. Or. No. 16-78.

**WISCONSIN**

**Are Domestic Employees Exempted?** State has no statutory exemption.

**Are Members of the Employer's Family Exempted?** Yes.

**Are Agricultural Employees Exempted?** State has no statutory exemption.

**Other Exemptions.** Social or fraternal clubs may use club membership as a qualification for employment.

**Citations to Authority.** Wis. Stat. Ann. §§ 16.765, 111.32.

# Table 2.3-2
## MUNICIPAL SEXUAL ORIENTATION ORDINANCES

(Employees protected are male/female homosexuals, heterosexuals, and bisexuals. Definition of employers that must abide by the law includes employment agencies and labor organizations unless otherwise specified. See also text at § 2.3[a] and [e].)

**KEY: BFOQ.** Bona fide occupational qualification.

| *Municipality* | *Employers Exempted* | *Prohibited Activities* | *Exceptions to Statute* | *Enforcement* | *Statute of Limitations* | *Damages and Other Requirements* | *Citations to Authority* |
|---|---|---|---|---|---|---|---|
| Berkeley, CA | None. | Fail or refuse to hire or include in membership; discharge, limit, segregate, or classify. | BFOQ. | Civil action; injunction. | 1 year. | Costs and attorneys' fees; must award $200–$400; punitive damages available. | No. 5106-NS, §§ 1328 *et seq.* (effective as of 11/9/78). |
| Los Angeles, CA | None. | Fail or refuse to hire or include in membership; discharge, limit, segregate, or classify. | BFOQ. | Civil action; injunction. | 1 year. | Costs and attorneys' fees; must award $200–$400; punitive damages available. | Ord. No. 164516 (enacted 3/3/89). |
| Sacramento, CA | Fewer than 5 employees. | Fail or refuse to hire; discharge or discriminate; fail or refuse to refer for employment; exclude or expel from membership. | Bona fide benefit plans. | Court action. | 18 months. | Actual damages, costs, and attorneys' fees. Employers with 15 or more employees must post a notice. | Ord. No. 86-042 (enacted 5/1/86). |
| San Francisco, CA | None. | Fail or refuse to hire or include in membership; discharge, limit, segregate, or classify. | BFOQ; bona fide benefit plans. | File with Human Rights Commission; civil action; injunction; nonexclusivity of remedy. | 2 years. | 3 times damages; punitive damages; costs and attorneys' fees; must award $200–$400. | Police Code art. 33, §§ 3301 *et seq.* (enacted 11/20/85). |
| Denver, CO | Fewer than 20 employees. | Discharge, fail or refuse to hire, or otherwise discriminate, segregate, or classify. | BFOQ. | File with city agency. | 180 days. | Affirmative relief; compensatory damages; costs. | Ord. No. 623 (amended 10/15/90). |
| Washington, DC | None. | Fail or refuse to hire or include in membership; discharge, limit, segregate, or classify; harass because of sexual orientation. | Business necessity. | File with Human Rights Commission; civil action; injunction; nonexclusivity of remedy. | 1 year. | Hiring, reinstating, or upgrading of employee; costs and attorneys' fees; compensatory damages. | Human Rights Act of 1977, ch. 25, §§ 1-2501 *et seq.* |

| | | | | | | | |
|---|---|---|---|---|---|---|---|
| New York, NY | Fewer than 4 employees. | Fail or refuse to hire or include in membership; discharge, limit, segregate, or classify; harass because of sexual orientation. | BFOQ. | File with Human Rights Commission or civil action in state court. | 1 year (3 years in civil action). | Make whole remedies and front pay; civil penalty of up to $100,000. In court action, punitive damages are recoverable and fines may be imposed. | N.Y.C. Admin. Code, §§ 8–107 *et seq.* (enacted 1988; amended by Local Law No. 39, 9/16/91). |
| Pittsburgh, PA | Fewer than 4 employees. | Fail or refuse to hire; discharge, discriminate, segregate, or classify. | BFOQ. | File with city agency. | 1 year. | Make whole remedies. | Pittsburgh Code, tit. 6, art. 5, ch. 651 (enacted 3/20/90). |
| Alexandria, VA | Fewer than 4 employees. | Fail or refuse to hire or include in membership; discharge, limit, segregate, or classify; harass because of sexual orientation. | BFOQ. | File with Human Rights Commission. | 300 days. | Antiretaliatory provision. | Ord. No. 3498 (enacted 2/23/91). |

# Table 2.3-3

## OTHER MUNICIPAL/COUNTY ORDINANCES: SEXUAL ORIENTATION, PUBLIC/PRIVATE SECTOR

**KEY:** a (*) indicates that though no municipal ordinance prohibits discrimination on the basis of sexual orientation, such discrimination is prohibited by state statute.
a (**) indicates that though no municipal ordinance prohibits discrimination on the basis of sexual orientation, such discrimination is prohibited by state statute in public employment only.
a (***) indicates that though private employers are not generally prohibited from discriminating against homosexuals, such discrimination is prohibited for public contractors.

**Note.** The municipalities listed are those that have additional ordinances prohibiting discrimination on the basis of sexual orientation and that prohibit such discrimination in public and/or private employment. (See Table 2.3-2 for a more comprehensive treatment of municipal sexual orientation ordinances. See also state statutes in Table 2.3-1, Part B, to determine if sexual orientation is a protected classification.)

| | *Does ordinance prohibit discrimination in public employment?* | *Does ordinance prohibit discrimination in private employment?* |
|---|---|---|
| Phoenix, AZ | Yes. | No. |
| Tucson, AZ | No. | No. |
| Cathedral City, CA | Yes. | No. |
| Cupertino, CA | Yes. | No. |
| Daly City, CA | Yes. | Yes. |
| Laguna Beach, CA | Yes. | Yes. |
| Long Beach, CA | Yes. | No. |
| Mountain View, CA | Yes. | No. |
| Oakland, CA | Yes. | Yes. |
| Pacifica, CA | Yes. | No. |
| Pasadena, CA | Yes. | Yes. |
| San Diego, CA | Yes. | Yes. |
| San Jose, CA | Yes. | No.*** |
| San Mateo County, CA | Yes. | No. |
| Santa Barbara, CA | Yes. | No. |
| Santa Cruz County, CA | Yes. | No. |
| Yolo County, CA | Yes. | Yes. |
| Aspen, CO | Yes. | Yes. |
| Boulder, CO | Yes. | Yes. |
| Boulder County, CO | Yes. | No. |
| Telluride, CO | Yes. | Yes. |
| Hartford, CT | Yes. | No.* |
| New Haven, CT | Yes. | No.* |
| Stamford, CT | Yes. | No.* |
| Broward County, FL | Yes. | Yes. |
| Key West, FL | Yes. | Yes. |
| Miami Beach, FL | Yes. | Yes. |
| Tampa, FL | Yes. | Yes. |
| Atlanta, GA | Yes. | No. |
| Honolulu, HI | Yes. | No.* |

| | | |
|---|---|---|
| Champaign, IL | Yes. | Yes. |
| Chicago, IL | Yes. | Yes. |
| Cook County, IL | Yes. | Yes. |
| Evanston, IL | Yes. | No. |
| Oak Park, IL | Yes. | No. |
| Urbana, IL | Yes. | Yes. |
| Bloomington, IN | Yes. | Yes. |
| Lafayette, IN | Yes. | Yes. |
| West Lafayette, IN | Yes. | Yes. |
| Ames, IA | Yes. | Yes. |
| Iowa City, IA | Yes. | Yes. |
| New Orleans, LA | Yes. | Yes. |
| Portland, ME | Yes. | Yes. |
| Baltimore, MD | Yes. | Yes. |
| Howard County, MD | Yes. | Yes. |
| Montgomery County, MD | Yes. | Yes. |
| Rockville, MD | Yes. | Yes. |
| Takoma Park, MD | Yes. | No. |
| Amherst, MA | Yes. | Yes. |
| Boston, MA | Yes. | Yes. |
| Cambridge, MA | Yes. | Yes. |
| Malden, MA | Yes. | Yes. |
| Worcester, MA | Yes. | No.* |
| Ann Arbor, MI | Yes. | Yes. |
| Detroit, MI | Yes. | Yes. |
| East Lansing, MI | Yes. | No. |
| Flint, MI | Yes. | Yes. |
| Ingham County, MI | Yes. | No. |
| Minneapolis, MN | Yes. | Yes. |
| St. Paul, MN | Yes. | Yes. |
| Kansas City, MO | Yes. | Yes. |
| St. Louis, MO | Yes. | Yes. |
| Essex County, NJ | No.* | No.* |
| Albuquerque, NM | Yes. | No.* |
| Albany, NY | Yes. | Yes. |
| Alfred, NY | Yes. | Yes. |
| Brighton, NY | Yes. | No.** |
| Buffalo, NY | No.** | No.** |
| East Hampton, NY | Yes. | Yes. |
| Ithaca, NY | Yes. | Yes. |
| Rochester, NY | Yes. | No.** |
| Suffolk County, NY | Yes. | No. |
| Syracuse, NY | Yes. | Yes. |
| Tompkins County, NY | Yes. | Yes. |
| Troy, NY | No.** | No.** |
| Watertown, NY | No.** | No.** |
| Asheville, NC | Yes. | No. |
| Carboro, NC | Yes. | No. |
| Durham, NC | Yes. | No. |
| Cleveland, OH | Yes. | No. |
| Columbus, OH | Yes. | Yes. |
| Cuyahoga County, OH | Yes. | No. |
| Yellow Springs, OH | Yes. | Yes. |
| Portland, OR | Yes. | Yes. |
| Harrisburg, PA | Yes. | Yes. |
| Lancaster, PA | Yes. | Yes. |
| Northampton County, PA | Yes. | No.** |
| Philadelphia, PA | Yes. | Yes. |
| State College, PA | No.** | No.** |
| York, PA | Yes. | Yes. |
| Columbia, SC | Yes. | No. |
| Minnehaha County, SD | Yes. | No. |

*(Table continues.)*

## Table 2.3-3 *(cont'd)*

## OTHER MUNICIPAL/COUNTY ORDINANCES: SEXUAL ORIENTATION, PUBLIC/PRIVATE SECTOR

**KEY:** a (*) indicates that though no municipal ordinance prohibits discrimination on the basis of sexual orientation, such discrimination is prohibited by state statute.
a (**) indicates that though no municipal ordinance prohibits discrimination on the basis of sexual orientation, such discrimination is prohibited by state statute in public employment only.
a (***) indicates that though private employers are not generally prohibited from discriminating against homosexuals, such discrimination is prohibited for public contractors.

**Note.** The municipalities listed are those that have additional ordinances prohibiting discrimination on the basis of sexual orientation and that prohibit such discrimination in public and/or private employment. (See Table 2.3-2 for a more comprehensive treatment of municipal sexual orientation ordinances. See also state statutes in Table 2.3-1, Part B, to determine if sexual orientation is a protected classification.)

| | *Does ordinance prohibit discrimination in public employment?* | *Does ordinance prohibit discrimination in private employment?* |
|---|---|---|
| Austin, TX | Yes. | Yes. |
| Salt Lake County, UT | Yes. | No. |
| Burlington, VT | No.* | No.* |
| Arlington County, VA | Yes. | Yes. |
| Charlottesville, VA | Yes. | No. |
| Clallam County, WA | Yes. | No. |
| Seattle, WA | Yes. | Yes. |
| Vancouver, WA | Yes. | No. |
| Morgantown, WV | Yes. | No. |
| Dane County, WI | Yes. | No.* |
| Madison, WI | Yes. | Yes. |
| Milwaukee, WI | Yes. | No.* |

# Table 2.3-4
## WHO MUST COMPLY WITH STATE FAIR EMPLOYMENT PRACTICE LAWS

(See also text at § 2.3[b].)

**KEY:** **Apprenticeship program.** Indicates an employee training program. Age is not always a protected classification, because the idea behind apprenticeship programs is to train younger workers for a lifelong trade.
**Employer.** Indicates the number of employees a person, as that term is defined, must have to come within the application of the statute. Note, however, that in some states an employer with fewer than the statutory minimum numbers of employees may be held liable for discrimination based on a public policy wrongful discharge theory. See Part 4 for more information.
**Employment agency.** Any person procuring, with or without compensation, public or private employees or opportunities to work.
**Labor organization.** Any organization existing, in whole or in part, for the purpose of collective bargaining; dealing with employers concerning grievances, terms, or conditions of employment; or providing mutual aid or protection in connection with employment.
**Person.** One or more individuals, including, but not limited to, partnerships, associations, or corporations, legal representatives, trustees, receivers, or the state.

| | *Person* | *Employer* | *Employment Agency* | *Labor Organization* | *Apprenticeship Programs* | *Citations to Authority* |
|---|---|---|---|---|---|---|
| AL | — | — | — | — | — | State has no comprehensive FEP act. |
| AK | One or more individuals, labor unions, partnerships, associations, corporations, legal representatives, mutual companies, joint-stock companies, trusts, unincorporated organizations, trustees, trustees in bankruptcy, receivers, employees, employers, employment agencies, or labor organizations. | Yes, the state; person with 1 or more employees. | Yes. | Yes. | No statutory provision. | Alaska Stat. §§ 18.80.220, 18.80.300. |
| AZ | One or more individuals, governmental agencies, political subdivisions, labor unions, partnerships, associations, corporations, legal representatives, mutual companies, joint-stock companies, trusts, unincorporated organizations, trustees, trustees in bankruptcy or receivers. | Yes, person with 15 or more employees for each working day in 20 or more calendar weeks in current or preceding year. | Yes. | Yes. | Yes. | Ariz. Rev. Stat. Ann. §§ 41-1461, 41-1463. |
| AR | — | Yes, person with 9 or more employees in the state working 20 or more calendar weeks in current or preceding year. | State has no statutory requirements. | State has no statutory requirements. | No statutory provision. | Ark. Code Ann. §§ 16-123-102, 16-123-103. |
| CA | One or more individuals, limited liability companies, partnerships, associations, corporations, legal representatives, trustees, trustees in bankruptcy, and receivers or other fiduciaries. | Yes, the state and cities. Also, private employers with 5 or more employees; for allegations concerning harassment, person with 1 or more employees; for allegations concerning discriminating against mental disability, person with 15 or more employees. | Yes. | Yes. | Yes. | Cal. Gov't. Code §§ 12925, 12926, 12940, 12941, 12944, 12945; Op. Att'y Gen. No. 65-220 (1966). |

(Table continues.)

## Table 2.3-4 *(cont'd)*

## WHO MUST COMPLY WITH STATE FAIR EMPLOYMENT PRACTICE LAWS

(See also text at § 2.3[b].)

**KEY:** **Apprenticeship program.** Indicates an employee training program. Age is not always a protected classification, because the idea behind apprenticeship programs is to train younger workers for a lifelong trade.
**Employer.** Indicates the number of employees a person, as that term is defined, must have to come within the application of the statute. Note, however, that in some states an employer with fewer than the statutory minimum numbers of employees may be held liable for discrimination based on a public policy wrongful discharge theory. See Part 4 for more information.
**Employment agency.** Any person procuring, with or without compensation, public or private employees or opportunities to work.
**Labor organization.** Any organization existing, in whole or in part, for the purpose of collective bargaining; dealing with employers concerning grievances, terms, or conditions of employment; or providing mutual aid or protection in connection with employment.
**Person.** One or more individuals, including, but not limited to, partnerships, associations, or corporations, legal representatives, trustees, receivers, or the state.

| | *Person* | *Employer* | *Employment Agency* | *Labor Organization* | *Apprenticeship Programs* | *Citations to Authority* |
|---|---|---|---|---|---|---|
| CO | — | Yes, the state and every other person employing persons within the state. | Yes. | Yes. | Yes. | Colo. Rev. Stat. §§ 24-34-401, 24-34-402. |
| CT | One or more individuals, limited liability companies, partnerships, associations, corporations, legal representatives, trustees, trustees in bankruptcy, receivers, and the state and all political subdivisions and agencies thereof. | Yes, the state and any person with 3 or more employees. | Yes. | Yes. | Yes (state agencies only). | Conn. Gen. Stat. Ann. §§ 46a-51, 46a-59, 46a-60, 46a-75. |
| DE | One or more individuals, labor unions, partnerships, associations, corporations, legal representatives, mutual companies, joint-stock companies, trusts, unincorporated organizations, trustees, trustees in bankruptcy, or receivers. | Yes, the state and any person with 4 or more employees. | Yes. | Yes. | Yes. | Del. Code Ann. tit. 19, §§ 710, 711. |
| DC | Any individual, firm, partnership, mutual company, joint-stock company, corporation, association, organization, unincorporated organization, labor union, governmental agency, incorporated society, statutory or common-law trust, estate, executor, administrator, receiver, trustee, conservator, liquidator, trustee in bankruptcy, committee, assignee, officer, employee, principal or agent, legal or personal representative, real estate broker or salesman, or any agent or representative of any of the foregoing. | Yes, person with 1 or more employees. | Yes. | Yes. | Yes. | D.C. Code Ann. §§ 1-2502, 1-2512. |

| | | | | | | |
|---|---|---|---|---|---|---|
| FL | Includes an individual, association, corporation, joint apprenticeship committee, joint-stock company, labor union, legal representative, mutual company, partnership, receiver, trust, trustee in bankruptcy, or unincorporated organization; any other legal or commercial entity; the state; or any governmental entity or agency. | Yes, person with 15 or more employees for each working day in 20 or more calendar weeks in current or preceding year. | Yes. | Yes. | Yes. | Fla. Stat. Ann. §§ 760.02, 760.10. |
| GA | — | Any department, board, bureau, commission, authority, or other agency of the state that employs 15 or more employees within the state for each working day in each of 20 or more calander weeks in the current or preceding calendar year. | State has no statutory requirements. | State has no statutory requirements. | Yes. | Ga. Code Ann. §§ 45-19-22, 45-19-30. (Applies to public employment only.) |
| HI | One or more individuals including partnerships, associations, corporations, legal representatives, trustees, trustees in bankruptcy, receivers, or the state or any of its political subdivisions. | Yes, the state and any person with 1 or more employees. | Yes. | Yes. | Yes. | Haw. Rev. Stat. §§ 378-1, 378-2. |
| ID | An individual, association, corporation, joint apprenticeship committee, joint-stock company, labor union, legal representative, mutual company, partnership, any other legal or commerical entity, the state, or any governmental entity or agency. | Yes, person with 5 or more employees for each working day in 20 or more calendar weeks in current or preceding year, except for domestic servants hired to work in and about a person's household; any governmental agency within the state; any person who as a contractor or subcontractor furnishes material or performs work for the state. | Yes. | Yes. | No statutory provision. | Idaho Code §§ 67-5902, 67-5909. |
| IL | Includes one or more individuals, partnerships, associations or organizations, labor organizations, labor unions, joint apprenticeship committees, or union labor associations, corporations, the State of Illinois and its instrumentalities, political subdivisions, units of local government, legal representatives, trustees in bankruptcy or receivers. | Yes, person with 15 or more employees during 20 calendar weeks; for allegations concerning discrimination against physical or mental disability, person with 1 or more employees; the state and any of its political subdivisions, joint apprenticeship or training programs, and any party to a public contract, without regard to number of employees. | Yes. | Yes. | Yes. | 775 ILCS §§ 5/1-103, 5/2-101, 5/2-102. |
| IN | One or more individuals, partnerships, associations, limited liability companies, organizations, corporations, labor organizations, cooperatives, legal representatives, trustee, trustees in bankruptcy, receivers, and other organized groups of persons. | Yes, the state and any of its subdivisions; any person with 6 or more employees. | Yes. | Yes. | No statutory provision. | Ind. Code § 22-9-1-3. |
| IA | One or more individuals, partnerships, associations, corporations, legal representatives, trustees, receivers, and the State of Iowa. | Yes, the state and any of its political subdivisions; any person with 1 or more employees. | Yes. | Yes. | No statutory provision. | Iowa Code Ann. §§ 216.2, 216.6. |
| KS | One or more individuals, partnerships, associations, organizations, corporations, legal representatives, trustees, trustees in bankruptcy or receivers. | Yes, the state; persons with 4 or more employees. | Yes. | Yes. | Yes. | Kan. Stat. Ann. §§ 44-1002, 44-1009. |

*(Table continues.)*

## Table 2.3-4 *(cont'd)*

## WHO MUST COMPLY WITH STATE FAIR EMPLOYMENT PRACTICE LAWS

(See also text at § 2.3[b].)

**KEY:** **Apprenticeship program.** Indicates an employee training program. Age is not always a protected classification, because the idea behind apprenticeship programs is to train younger workers for a lifelong trade.
**Employer.** Indicates the number of employees a person, as that term is defined, must have to come within the application of the statute. Note, however, that in some states an employer with fewer than the statutory minimum numbers of employees may be held liable for discrimination based on a public policy wrongful discharge theory. See Part 4 for more information.
**Employment agency.** Any person procuring, with or without compensation, public or private employees or opportunities to work.
**Labor organization.** Any organization existing, in whole or in part, for the purpose of collective bargaining; dealing with employers concerning grievances, terms, or conditions of employment; or providing mutual aid or protection in connection with employment.
**Person.** One or more individuals, including, but not limited to, partnerships, associations, or corporations, legal representatives, trustees, receivers, or the state.

| | *Person* | *Employer* | *Employment Agency* | *Labor Organization* | *Apprenticeship Programs* | *Citations to Authority* |
|---|---|---|---|---|---|---|
| KY | Includes one or more individuals, labor organizations, joint apprenticeship committees, partnerships, associations, corporations, legal representatives, mutual companies, joint-stock companies, trusts, unincorporated organizations, trustees, trustees in bankruptcy, fiduciaries, receivers, or other legal or commercial entity; the state, any of its political or civil subdivisions or agencies. | Yes, person with 8 or more employees for each working day in 20 or more calendar weeks in current or preceding year; for allegations concerning discrimination against disability, person with 15 or more employees. | Yes. | Yes. | Yes. | Ky. Rev. Stat. Ann. §§ 344.010, 344.030, 344.040, 344.050, 344.060, 344.070. |
| LA | Includes one or more individuals, governments or governmental agencies, public authorities, labor organizations, corporations, legal representatives, partnerships, associations, trustees, trustees in bankruptcy, receivers, mutal companies, joint-stock companies, trusts, unincorporated organizations, or other organized groups of persons. | Yes, the state; employers of 15 or more for disability, race, color, religion, sex, and national origin; 20 or more for age and sickle-cell trait; 25 or more for pregnancy, childbirth, and related medical conditions. | Yes. | Yes. | Yes. | La. Rev. Stat. Ann. §§ 23:301 *et seq.* |
| ME | Includes one or more individuals, partnerships, associations, organizations, corporations, municipal corporations, legal representatives, trustees, trustees in bankruptcy, receivers and other legal representatives, and the state. | Yes, any person with 1 or more employees. | Yes. | Yes. | Yes. | Me. Rev. Stat. Ann. tit. 5, §§ 4553, 4572. |

| | | | | | | |
|---|---|---|---|---|---|---|
| MD | Includes one or more individuals, labor unions, partnerships, associations, corporations, legal representatives, mutual companies, joint-stock companies, trusts, unincorporated organizations, trustees, trustees in bankruptcy, or receivers. | Yes, the state; any person with 15 or more employees for each working day in 20 or more calendar weeks in current or preceding year. | Yes. | Yes. | Yes. | Md. Ann. Code art. 49B, §§ 15, 16. |
| MA | One or more individuals, partnerships, associations, corporations, legal representatives, trustees, trustees in bankruptcy, receivers, and the commonwealth and all political subdivisions, boards, and commissions thereof. | Yes, the commonwealth; person with 6 or more employees. | Yes. | Yes. | No statutory provision. | Mass. Gen. Laws ch. 151B, §§ 1, 4. |
| MI | An individual, agent, association, corporation, joint apprenticeship committee, joint-stock company, labor organization, legal representative, mutual company, partnership, receiver, trust, trustee in bankruptcy, unincorporated organization, the state or political subdivision of the state or an agency of the state, or any other legal or commercial entity. | Yes, person with 1 or more employees. | Yes. | Yes. | Yes. | Mich. Comp. Laws §§ 37.2103, 37.2201–37.2205. |
| MN | Includes partnerships, associations, corporations, legal representatives, trustees, trustees in bankruptcy, receivers, and the state. | Yes, person with 1 or more employees. | Yes. | Yes. | No statutory provision. | Minn. Stat. Ann. §§ 363.01–363.03. |
| MS | — | — | — | — | — | State has no comprehensive FEP act. |
| MO | Includes one or more individuals, corporations, partnerships, associations, organizations, labor organizations, legal representatives, mutual companies, joint-stock companies, trusts, trustees, trustees in bankruptcy, receivers, fiduciaries, or other organized groups of persons. | Yes, the state; person with 6 or more employees. | Yes. | Yes. | Yes. | Mo. Rev. Stat. §§ 213.010, 213.055, 213.070. |
| MT | One or more individuals, labor unions, partnerships, associations, corporations, legal representatives, mutual companies, joint-stock companies, trusts, unincorporated employees' associations, employers, employment agencies, or labor organizations. | Yes, person with 1 or more employees. | Yes. | Yes. | Yes. | Mont. Code Ann. §§ 49-1-102, 49-2-101, 49-2-303, 49-2-308, 49-4-101. |
| NE | One or more individuals, labor unions, partnerships, limited liability companies, associations, corporations, legal representatives, mutual companies, joint-stock companies, trusts, unincorporated organizations, trustees, trustees in bankruptcy or receivers. | Yes, the state; person with 15 or more employees for each working day in each of 20 or more calendar weeks in current or preceding year. | Yes. | Yes. | Yes. | Neb. Rev. Stat. §§ 48-214, 48-1102, 48-1104–48-1107. |
| NV | Includes the state and any of its political subdivisions. | Yes, person with 15 or more employees for each working day in each of 20 or more calendar weeks. | Yes. | Yes. | Yes. | Nev. Rev. Stat. §§ 613.310, 613.330. |

*(Table continues.)*

# Table 2.3-4 *(cont'd)*

## WHO MUST COMPLY WITH STATE FAIR EMPLOYMENT PRACTICE LAWS

(See also text at § 2.3[b].)

**KEY:** **Apprenticeship program.** Indicates an employee training program. Age is not always a protected classification, because the idea behind apprenticeship programs is to train younger workers for a lifelong trade.
**Employer.** Indicates the number of employees a person, as that term is defined, must have to come within the application of the statute. Note, however, that in some states an employer with fewer than the statutory minimum numbers of employees may be held liable for discrimination based on a public policy wrongful discharge theory. See Part 4 for more information.
**Employment agency.** Any person procuring, with or without compensation, public or private employees or opportunities to work.
**Labor organization.** Any organization existing, in whole or in part, for the purpose of collective bargaining; dealing with employers concerning grievances, terms, or conditions of employment; or providing mutual aid or protection in connection with employment.
**Person.** One or more individuals, including, but not limited to, partnerships, associations, or corporations, legal representatives, trustees, receivers, or the state.

| | *Person* | *Employer* | *Employment Agency* | *Labor Organization* | *Apprenticeship Programs* | *Citations to Authority* |
|---|---|---|---|---|---|---|
| NH | One or more individuals, partnerships, associations, corporations, legal representatives, mutual companies, joint-stock companies, trusts, trustees in bankruptcy, receivers, and the state and any of its political subdivisions. | Yes, person with 6 or more employees; the state and all political subdivisions thereof. | Yes. | Yes. | No statutory provisions. | N.H. Rev. Stat. Ann. §§ 354-A:2, 354-A:7. |
| NJ | Includes one or more individuals, partnerships, associations, organizations, labor organizations, corporations, legal representatives, trustees, trustees in bankruptcy, receivers, and fiduciaries. | Yes, all persons, including the state, any subdivision thereof, and all public officers, agencies, and boards. | Yes. | Yes. | Yes. | N.J. Stat. Ann. §§ 10:5-5, 10:5-12. |
| NM | One or more individuals, a partnership, association, organization, corporation, joint-venture, legal representative, trustees, receivers, or the state and all of its political subdivisions. | Yes, person with 4 or more employees. | Yes. | Yes. | Yes. | N.M. Stat. Ann. §§ 28-1-2, 28-1-7; N.M. Ex. Or. 85-15. |
| NY | Includes one or more individuals, partnerships, associations, corporations, legal representatives, trustees, trustees in bankruptcy, or receivers. | Yes, person with 4 or more employees. | Yes. | Yes. | Yes. | N.Y. Exec. Law §§ 292, 296, 310, 312. |
| NC | — | — | — | — | Yes (N.C. Admin. Code tit. 13, § 14.0800 *et seq.*) | State has no comprehensive FEP act. (Applies to public employment only.) |

| | | | | | | |
|---|---|---|---|---|---|---|
| ND | Individual, partnership, association, corporation, limited liability company, unincorporated organization, mutal company, joint-stock company, trust, agent, legal representative, trustee in bankruptcy, receiver, labor organization, public body, public corporation, and the state and all of its political subdivisions. | Yes, person within the state with 1 or more employees for more than a quarter of a year; person, wherever situated, who employs 1 or more employees whose services are performed in the state. | Yes. | Yes. | Yes. | N.D. Cent. Code §§ 14-02.4-02–14-02.4-05. |
| OH | One or more individuals, partnerships, associations, organizations, corporations, legal representatives, trustees, trustees in bankruptcy, receivers, and other organized groups of persons. Also includes any owner, lessor, assignor, builder, manager, broker, salesman, appraiser, agent, employee, lending institution, and the state and all political subdivisions, authorities, agencies, boards, and commissions of the state. | Yes, the state; any person with 4 or more employees. | Yes. | Yes. | Yes. | Ohio Rev. Code Ann. §§ 4112.01, 4112.02. |
| OK | Individual, association, corporation, joint apprenticeship committee, joint-stock company, labor union, legal representative, mutual company, partnership, receiver, trust, trustee, trustee in bankruptcy, unincorporated organization, any other legal or commercial entity, the state, or any governmental entity or agency. | Yes, person with 15 or more employees for each working day in each of 20 or more calendar weeks in current or preceding year; or any person who as a contractor or subcontractor performs work or provides services for the state. | Yes. | Yes. | Yes. | Okla. Stat. tit. 25, §§ 1201, 1301, 1303–1305; tit. 74, § 840-2.9. |
| OR | Includes one or more individuals, partnerships, associations, corporations, legal representatives, trustees, trustees in bankruptcy or receivers. | Yes, any person, including state agencies, political subdivisions, and municipalities, with 1 or more employees. | Yes. | Yes. | Yes. | Or. Rev. Stat. §§ 659.010, 659.030. |
| PA | Includes one or more individuals, partnerships, associations, organizations, corporations, legal representatives, trustees in bankruptcy or receivers. Also, any owner, lessor, assignor, builder, manager, broker, salesman, agent, employee, independent contractor, lending institution, and the commonwealth and all political subdivisions, authorities, boards, and commissions thereof. | Yes, the Commonwealth and any person with 4 or more employees. | Yes. | Yes. | No statutory provision. | Pa. Stat. Ann. tit. 43, §§ 954, 955; tit. 71, §§ 741.3, 741.905a. |
| RI | One or more individuals, partnerships, associations, organizations, corporations, legal representatives, trustees, trustees in bankruptcy, or receivers. | Yes, the state and any person with 4 or more employees. | Yes. | Yes. | No statutory provision. | R.I. Gen. Laws §§ 28-5-6, 28-5-7. |

*(Table continues.)*

# Table 2.3-4 *(cont'd)*
## WHO MUST COMPLY WITH STATE FAIR EMPLOYMENT PRACTICE LAWS

(See also text at § 2.3[b].)

**KEY:** **Apprenticeship program.** Indicates an employee training program. Age is not always a protected classification, because the idea behind apprenticeship programs is to train younger workers for a lifelong trade.
**Employer.** Indicates the number of employees a person, as that term is defined, must have to come within the application of the statute. Note, however, that in some states an employer with fewer than the statutory minimum numbers of employees may be held liable for discrimination based on a public policy wrongful discharge theory. See Part 4 for more information.
**Employment agency.** Any person procuring, with or without compensation, public or private employees or opportunities to work.
**Labor organization.** Any organization existing, in whole or in part, for the purpose of collective bargaining; dealing with employers concerning grievances, terms, or conditions of employment; or providing mutual aid or protection in connection with employment.
**Person.** One or more individuals, including, but not limited to, partnerships, associations, or corporations, legal representatives, trustees, receivers, or the state.

| | *Person* | *Employer* | *Employment Agency* | *Labor Organization* | *Apprenticeship Programs* | *Citations to Authority* |
|---|---|---|---|---|---|---|
| SC | Individuals, labor unions and organizations, joint apprenticeship committees, partnerships, associations, corporations, legal representatives, mutual companies, joint-stock companies, trusts, unincorporated organizations, trustees, trustees in bankruptcy, receivers, other legal or commercial entities, the state and any of its agencies or departments, and municipalities, counties, special purpose districts, school districts, and other local governments. | Yes, person with 15 or more employees for each working day in each of 20 or more calendar weeks in current or preceding year. | Yes. | Yes. | Yes. | S.C. Code Ann. §§ 1-13-30, 1-13-80. |
| SD | One or more individuals, partnerships, associations, limited liability companies, corporations, unincorporated organizations, mutual companies, joint-stock companies, trusts, agents, legal representatives, trustees, trustees in bankruptcy, receivers, labor organizations, public bodies, public corporations, and the state and any of its political subdivisions. | Yes, person with 1 or more employees. | Yes. | Yes. | No statutory provision. | S.D. Codified Laws §§ 20-13-1, 20-13-10, 20-13-11, 20-13-12; S.D. Admin. R. § 20.03:08:04. |
| TN | One or more individuals, governments, governmental agencies, public authorities, labor organizations, corporations, legal representatives, partnerships, associations, trustees, trustees in bankruptcy, receivers, mutual companies, joint-stock companies, trusts, unincorporated organizations, or other organized groups of persons. | Yes, the state and persons with 8 or more employees. | Yes. | Yes. | Yes. | Tenn. Code Ann. §§ 4-21-102, 4-21-402–4-21-404. |

| | | | | | | |
|---|---|---|---|---|---|---|
| TX | — | Yes, state, county, or municipality; person with 15 or more employees for each working day in each of 20 or more calendar weeks. | Yes. | Yes. | Yes. | Tex. Lab. Code Ann. §§ 21.002, 21.051–21.054. |
| UT | One or more individuals, partnerships, associations, corporations, legal representatives, trusts or trustees, receivers, and the state. | Yes, the state and every other person with 15 or more employees within the state for each working day in each of 20 or more calendar weeks in current or preceding calendar year. | Yes. | Yes. | Yes. | Utah Code Ann. §§ 34-35-2, 34-35-6. |
| VT | One or more individuals, employee organizations, labor organizations, partnerships, corporations, legal representatives, trustees, or any other natural or legal entity; the state, state colleges, and the University of Vermont. | Yes, person with 1 or more employees. | Yes. | Yes, but organization must represent at least 5 employees. | No statutory provision. | Vt. Stat. Ann. tit. 3, §§ 901, 902, 926, 961, 962, 1004; tit. 21, §§ 495, 495a, 495d. |
| VA | — | Yes, prohibition against discharge applies to employers employing more than 5 but fewer than 15 employees. | Yes. | Yes. | No statutory provision. | Va. Code Ann. §§ 2.1-716, 2.1-717, 51.5-41; Va. Ex. Or. 1-86. |
| WA | One or more individuals, partnerships, associations, organizations, corporations, cooperatives, legal representatives, trustees and receivers, or any other group of persons; it includes any owner, lessee, proprietor, manager, agent, or employee, whether one or more natural persons; and includes any political or civil subdivisions of the state and any agency or instrumentality of the state. | Yes, person with 8 or more employees. | Yes. | Yes. | Yes. | Wash. Rev. Code §§ 40.60.190, 49.04.100–49.04.130, 49.60.040, 49.60.180–49.60.200. |
| WV | One or more individuals, partnerships, associations, organizations, corporations, labor organizations, cooperatives, legal representatives, trustees, trustees in bankruptcy, receivers, and other organized groups of persons. | Yes, the state and any person with 12 or more employees. | Yes. | Yes. | Yes. | W. Va. Code §§ 5-11-3, 5-11-9. |
| WI | — | Yes, the state and any other person with 1 or more employees. | Yes. | Yes. | No statutory provision. | Wis. Stat. Ann. §§ 16.765, 111.32, 111.325. |
| WY | — | Yes, the state and any other person with 2 or more employees. | Yes. | Yes. | No statutory provision. | Wyo. Stat. §§ 27-9-102, 27-9-105. |

# Table 2.3-5
## EXCEPTIONS TO FAIR EMPLOYMENT PRACTICE PROHIBITIONS

(Some statutes contain specific exceptions to the FEP prohibitions, for example, age, in particular circumstances. Check state FEP statute for more details. See also text at § 2.3[d].)

| | *Bona Fide Occupational Qualification* | *Bona Fide Seniority System* | *Bona Fide Benefits Program* | *Citations to Authority* |
|---|---|---|---|---|
| AL | — | — | — | State has no comprehensive FEP act. |
| AK | Yes. | No. | No. | Alaska Stat. § 18.80.220. |
| AZ | Yes. | Yes. | Yes. | Ariz. Rev. Stat. Ann. § 41-1463. |
| AR | Yes. | Yes. | Yes. | Ark. Code Ann. § 16-123-103. |
| CA | Yes. | Yes. | Yes. | Cal. Gov't. Code §§ 12940, 12941, 12945. |
| CO | Yes. | Yes. | Yes. | Colo. Rev. Stat. § 24-34-402. |
| CT | Yes. | Yes. | Yes. | Conn. Gen. Stat. Ann. § 46a-60. |
| DE | Yes. | Yes. | Yes. | Del. Code Ann. tit. 19, § 711. |
| DC | Yes. | Yes. | Yes. | D.C. Code Ann. §§ 1-2512, 1-2513. |
| FL | Yes. | Yes. | Yes. | Fla. Stat. Ann. §§ 760.10, 760.50. |
| GA | Yes. | Yes. | Yes. | Ga. Code Ann. §§ 45-19-22, 45-19-31, 45-19-33–45-19-35. |
| HI | Yes. | Yes. | Yes. | Haw. Rev. Stat. § 378-3. |
| ID | Yes. | Yes. | Yes. | Idaho Code § 67-5910. |
| IL | Yes. | Yes. | Yes. | 775 ILCS § 5/2-104. |
| IN | Yes. | No. | Yes. | Ind. Code §§ 22-9-1-3, 22-9-2-10, 22-9-2-11. |
| IA | Yes. | No. | Yes. | Iowa Code Ann. §§ 216.6, 216.13. |
| KS | Yes. | Yes. | Yes. | Kan. Stat. Ann. §§ 44-1009, 44-1113. |
| KY | Yes, for religion and national origin. | Yes. | Yes. | Ky. Rev. Stat. Ann. §§ 344.045, 344.090, 344.100. |
| LA | Yes. | Yes. | Yes. | La. Rev. Stat. Ann. §§ 23:301 *et seq.* |
| ME | Yes. | Yes. | Yes. | Me. Rev. Stat. Ann. tit. 5, §§ 4572, 4572-A, 4573; *LeBlond v. Sentinel Service,* 635 A.2d 943 (Me. 1993). |
| MD | Yes. | Yes. | Yes. | Md. Ann. Code art. 49B, § 16. |

| | | | | |
|---|---|---|---|---|
| MA | Yes. | Yes. | Yes. | Mass. Gen. Laws ch. 151B, § 4. |
| MI | Yes. | Yes. | No. | Mich. Comp. Laws §§ 37.2208, 37.2211. |
| MN | Yes. | Yes. | No. | Minn. Stat. Ann. §§ 363.02, 363.03. |
| MS | — | — | — | State has no comprehensive FEP act. |
| MO | Yes. | Yes. | Yes. | Mo. Rev. Stat. § 213.055; Mo. Code Regs. tit. 8, § 60-3.040. |
| MT | Yes. | Yes. | Yes. | Mont. Code Ann. §§ 49-2-303, 49-2-402–49-2-405, 49-3-103. |
| NE | Yes. | No. | No. | Neb. Rev. Stat. § 48-1108. |
| NV | Yes. | Yes. | Yes. | Nev. Rev. Stat. §§ 613.350, 613.380. |
| NH | Yes. | No. | Yes. | N.H. Rev. Stat. Ann. § 354-A:7. |
| NJ | Yes. | Yes. | Yes. | N.J. Stat. Ann. § 10:5-12. |
| NM | Yes. | No. | Yes. | N.M. Stat. Ann. § 28-1-7. |
| NY | Yes. | No. | Yes. | N.Y. Exec. Law § 296. |
| NC | Yes. | No. | No. | N.C. Gen. Stat. §§ 126-16, 126-36. (Applies to public employment only.) |
| ND | Yes. | Yes. | Yes. | N.D. Cent. Code §§ 14-02.4-02, 14-02.4-05, 14-02.4-06, 14-02.4-08, 14-02.4-09. |
| OH | Yes. | Yes. | Yes. | Ohio Rev. Code Ann. § 4112.02; Ohio Admin. Code §§ 4112-3-15, 4112-5-05. |
| OK | Yes. | Yes. | Yes. | Okla. Stat. tit. 25, §§ 1302, 1306, 1308, 1309. |
| OR | Yes. | Yes. | Yes. | Or. Rev. Stat. §§ 659.028, 659.030. |
| PA | Yes. | Yes. | Yes. | Pa. Stat. Ann. tit. 43, § 953, 954, 955. |
| RI | Yes. | No. | No. | R.I. Gen. Laws § 28-5-7. |
| SC | Yes. | Yes. | Yes. | S.C. Code Ann. § 1-13-80. |
| SD | Yes. | Yes. | Yes. | S.D. Codified Laws §§ 20-13-10, 20-13-16–20-13-18. |
| TN | Yes. | Yes. | Yes. | Tenn. Code Ann. §§ 4-21-406, 4-21-407 (apply for religion, sex, and age). |
| TX | Yes. | Yes. | Yes. | Tex. Lab. Code Ann. §§ 21.102, 21.119. |
| UT | Yes. | Yes. | Yes. | Utah Code Ann. §§ 34-35-2, 34-35-6. |
| VT | Yes. | Yes. | Yes. | Vt. Stat. Ann. tit. 21, §§ 495a, 495d, 495f. |
| VA | Yes. | No. | No. | Va. Code Ann. § 51.1-154. (Exceptions for bona fide seniority system and bona fide benefits may be available; state statute must not be interpreted to repeal, supersede, or expand state or federal law relating to race, color, religion, national origin, sex, age, or disability.) |

(Table continues.)

**Table 2.3-5** *(cont'd)*

EXCEPTIONS TO FAIR
EMPLOYMENT PRACTICE PROHIBITIONS

(Some statutes contain specific exceptions to the FEP prohibitions, for example, age, in particular circumstances. Check state FEP statute for more details. See also text at § 2.3[d].)

| | *Bona Fide Occupational Qualification* | *Bona Fide Seniority System* | *Bona Fide Benefits Program* | *Citations to Authority* |
|---|---|---|---|---|
| WA | Yes. | No. | No. | Wash. Rev. Code § 49.60.180; Wash. Admin. Code §§ 162-12-130, 162-12-135, 162-16-020. |
| WV | Yes. | No. | Yes. | W. Va. Code § 5-11-9. |
| WI | Yes. | Yes. | Yes. | Wis. Stat. Ann. §§ 111.33, 111.34, 111.36, 111.37. |
| WY | Yes. | Yes. | Yes. | Wyo. Stat. § 27-9-105. |

# § 2.4 Disposition of FEP Violations

## [a] Commission Powers and Procedures

For the most part, state commissions have combined federal fair employment procedures with their own administrative law processes. Among other things, Table 2.4-1, Parts A and B, shows whether or not state fair employment commissions can hold public/nonpublic meetings, conciliate or resolve charges, seek court or injunctive relief, file other lawsuits, investigate charges, and propose remedies. The table also notes each state commission's statute of limitations—that is, the time limit for filing charges with these commissions.

In both Parts A and B of the table, the agency that administers state FEP law is referred to as the "state fair employment commission." The actual name of this agency may vary from state to state.

## [b] Appeal of Commission Rulings

In many states, a plaintiff alleging a violation of fair labor laws must first comply with state administrative procedures before filing an action in state court. After the state agency handling fair employment (referred to as the "state fair employment commission," although the name of the agency may vary from state to state) has ruled on the discrimination allegation, the aggrieved individual or employer may then "appeal" such decision to a state court.

In a number of states, the appeal is heard *de novo*—that is, the state court is free to issue its own opinion as though the commission ruling did not exist. In other states, however, the court must defer to the commission's factual findings, unless such findings go against the evidence or the commission seems to have acted arbitrarily or capriciously.

Table 2.4-2 shows which states require compliance with administrative procedures before plaintiffs can file unfair labor allegations in state courts. It also notes whether the complaint is examined by the court *de novo* and whether the aggrieved party will be represented by the state commission or may be represented by court-appointed counsel.

## [c] Remedies Available to Complainants

The Civil Rights Act of 1991 eliminated some of the incentives to pursue state FEP claims, by amending Title VII and the ADEA to provide for compensatory damages and punitive damages up to specified limits. In a few states, however, punitive damages are available without a statutory "cap." Consistent with federal law, state laws also provide for injunctive or equitable relief, including hiring, reinstatement, and promotion. Table 2.4-3 lists remedies available to complainants under state FEP laws.

**Alternative Remedies.** The remedies provided under state and federal FEP laws are not the only remedies available to employees who are subjected to discrimination. Private agreements and state common law may provide for alternative relief. In general, private agreements tend to limit the availability of relief under the FEP laws, whereas state common law fills in gaps that the FEP statutes do not cover.

For example, pursuant to a collective bargaining agreement or an employment contract, employment discrimination may be subject to arbitration, thus foreclosing resort to the FEP statutes. Under state common law, on the other hand, an employee action for wrongful discharge may be available against an employer who is too small to be covered by the FEP statutes.

# Table 2.4-1 Part A
## STATE FAIR EMPLOYMENT COMMISSION POWERS AND PROCEDURES

(See also text at § 2.4[a].)

**KEY:** **EEOC Deferral Agency.** An agency that can process charges for the EEOC. In a deferral state, the usual 180-day limit for filing charges under federal statutes is extended to 300 days.

| | *Time Limit for Filing Complaint with State Agency* | *Has EEOC-Certified Deferral Agency* | *Recommends that EEOC Start Title VII Action* | *Issues Rules, Regulations, or Guidelines* | *Holds Public Hearings* | *Holds Nonpublic Hearings* | *Monitors Compliance with State Fair Employment Laws* | *Monitors Compliance with Its Own Directives* | *Citations to Authority* |
|---|---|---|---|---|---|---|---|---|---|
| AL | — | — | — | — | — | — | — | — | State has no comprehensive FEP act. |
| AK | 300 days. | Yes. Anchorage agency also certified. | Yes. | Yes. | State has no statutory requirements. | Yes. | Yes. | Yes. | Alaska Stat. §§ 18.80.060, 18.80.120, 18.80.150; 29 C.F.R. § 1601.74. |
| AZ | 180 days. | Yes. | Yes. | Yes. | State has no statutory requirements. | Yes. | Yes. | Yes. | Ariz. Rev. Stat. Ann. §§ 41-1402, 41-1471, 41-1481; 29 C.F.R. § 1601.74. |
| AR | For filing in court, 1 year after occurrence of unlawful practice or 90 days after receipt of EEOC right-to-sue letter, whichever is later. | No. | State has no statutory requirements. | State has no statutory requirements. | State has no statutory requirements. | State has no statutory requirements. | State has no statutory requirements. | State has no statutory requirements. | Ark. Code Ann. §§ 16-123-101 *et seq.*; 29 C.F.R. § 1601.74. |
| CA | 1 year, except when knowledge of the unlawful practice was obtained af- | Yes. | Yes. | Yes. | Yes. | Yes. | Yes. | Yes. | Cal. Gov't Code §§ 12935, 12960, 12961, 12970, 12973; 29 C.F.R. § 1601.74. |

| | | | | | | | | |
|---|---|---|---|---|---|---|---|---|
| | ter 1 year, in which case the time limit may be extended up to 90 days from the end of the year. | | | | | | | |
| CO | 6 months. | Yes. | Yes. | Yes. | Can hold hearings, but statute does not specify if hearings are public or nonpublic. | Can hold hearings, but statute does not specify if hearings are public or nonpublic. | Yes. | Yes. | Colo. Rev. Stat. §§ 24-34-305, 24-34-306, 24-34-403; 29 C.F.R. § 1601.74. |
| CT | 180 days. | Yes. New Haven agency also certified. | Yes. | Yes. | Yes. | No. | Yes. | Yes. | Conn. Gen. Stat. Ann. §§ 46a-54, 46a-56, 46a-82, 46a-84; 29 C.F.R. § 1601.74. |
| DE | 90 days after occurrence of unlawful practice or 120 days after discovery. | Yes. | State has no statutory requirements. | Yes. | Yes. | No. | Yes. | Yes. | Del. Code Ann. tit. 19, §§ 712, 714; 29 C.F.R. § 1601.74. |
| DC | 1 year after discovery or occurrence of unlawful practice. | Yes. | State has no statutory requirements. | Yes. | Yes. | Yes. | Yes. | Yes. | D.C. Code Ann. §§ 1-1502, 1-2541, 1-2544, 1-2552; 29 C.F.R. § 1601.74. |
| FL | 365 days. | Yes. Also certified: Broward County, Clearwater, Dade County, Hillsborough County, Jacksonville, Lee County, Orlando, Pinellas County, St. Petersburg, and Tampa agencies. | Yes. | Yes. | Yes. | Yes. | Yes. | Yes. | Fla. Stat. Ann. §§ 760.06, 760.11; 29 C.F.R. § 1601.74. |

*(Table continues.)*

# Table 2.4-1 Part A *(cont'd)*

## STATE FAIR EMPLOYMENT COMMISSION POWERS AND PROCEDURES

(See also text at § 2.4[a].)

**KEY: EEOC Deferral Agency.** An agency that can process charges for the EEOC. In a deferral state, the usual 180-day limit for filing charges under federal statutes is extended to 300 days.

| | *Time Limit for Filing Complaint with State Agency* | *Has EEOC-Certified Deferral Agency* | *Recommends that EEOC Start Title VII Action* | *Issues Rules, Regulations, or Guidelines* | *Holds Public Hearings* | *Holds Nonpublic Hearings* | *Monitors Compliance with State Fair Employment Laws* | *Monitors Compliance with Its Own Directives* | *Citations to Authority* |
|---|---|---|---|---|---|---|---|---|---|
| GA | 180 days. | Yes. Richmond County agency also certified. | State has no statutory requirements. | Yes. | Yes. | Yes. | Yes. | Yes. | Ga. Code Ann. §§ 45-19-27, 45-19-36. (Applies to public employment only.); 29 C.F.R. § 1601.74. |
| HI | 180 days after the incident or the last incident in a pattern of discrimination. | Yes. | Yes. | Yes. | Yes. | State has no statutory requirements. | Yes. | Yes. | Haw. Rev. Stat. §§ 368-1 *et seq.*, 378-4; 29 C.F.R. § 1601.74. |
| ID | 1 year. | Yes. | State has no statutory requirements. | Yes. | State has no statutory requirements. | State has no statutory requirements. | Yes. | State has no statutory requirements. | Idaho Code §§ 67-5906–67-5908; 29 C.F.R. § 1601.74. |
| IL | 180 days. | Yes. Bloomington agency also certified. | State has no statutory requirements. | Yes. | Yes. | Yes. | Yes. | Yes. | 775 ILCS §§ 5/7-101, 5/7A-102; 29 C.F.R. § 1601.74. |
| IN | 180 days. | Yes. Also certified: Anderson, Bloomington, East Chicago, Evansville, Fort Wayne, Gary, Michigan City, and South Bend agencies. | State has no statutory requirements. | Yes. | Yes. | No. | Yes. | Yes. | Ind. Code §§ 22-9-1-3, 22-9-1-6, 22-9-1-11, 22-9-1-12.1; 29 C.F.R. § 1601.74. |

| | | | | | | | | | |
|---|---|---|---|---|---|---|---|---|---|
| IA | 180 days. | Yes. Fort Dodge–Webster County and Mason City agencies also certified. | State has no statutory requirements. | Yes. | Yes. | State has no statutory requirements. | Yes. | Yes. | Iowa Code Ann. §§ 216.5, 216.15; 29 C.F.R. § 1601.74. |
| KS | 6 months. | — | State has no statutory requirements. | Yes. | Yes. | State has no statutory requirements. | Yes. | Yes. | Kan. Stat. Ann. §§ 44-1004, 44-1005; 29 C.F.R. § 1601.74. |
| KY | 300 days. | Yes. Also certified: Lexington–Fayette Urban County, Louisville–Jefferson County, and Paducah agencies. | State has no statutory requirements. | Yes. | Yes. | Yes. | Yes. | Yes. | Ky. Rev. Stat. Ann. §§ 344.180, 344.190, 344.200, 344.210; *Jones v. AIRCO Carbide Chemical Co.*, 691 F.2d 1200 (6th Cir. 1982); 29 C.F.R. § 1601.74. |
| LA | 180 days. | Yes. | State has no statutory requirements. | Yes. | Yes. | Yes. | Yes. | Yes. | La. Rev. Stat. Ann. §§ 51:2235, 51:2257, 51:2259; 29 C.F.R. § 1601.74. |
| ME | 6 months. | Yes. | Yes. | Yes. | Can hold hearings, but statute does not specify if hearings are public or non-public. | Can hold hearings, but statute does not specify if hearings are public or non-public. | Yes. | State has no statutory requirements. | Me. Rev. Stat. Ann. tit. 5, §§ 4566, 4611, 4612; 29 C.F.R. § 1601.74. |
| MD | 6 months. | Yes. Baltimore, Howard County, Montgomery County, Prince George's County, and Rockville agencies also certified. | State has no statutory requirements. | Yes. | Yes. | No. | Yes. | State has no statutory requirements. | Md. Ann. Code art. 49B, §§ 3, 9A, 11, 14; 29 C.F.R. § 1601.74. |
| MA | 6 months. | Yes. | State has no statutory requirements. | Yes. | Yes. | No. | State has no statutory requirements. | State has no statutory requirements. | Mass. Gen. Laws ch. 151B, § 5; 29 C.F.R. § 1601.74. |

*(Table continues.)*

# Table 2.4-1 Part A *(cont'd)*

## STATE FAIR EMPLOYMENT COMMISSION POWERS AND PROCEDURES

(See also text at § 2.4[a].)

**KEY: EEOC Deferral Agency.** An agency that can process charges for the EEOC. In a deferral state, the usual 180-day limit for filing charges under federal statutes is extended to 300 days.

| | *Time Limit for Filing Complaint with State Agency* | *Has EEOC-Certified Deferral Agency* | *Recommends that EEOC Start Title VII Action* | *Issues Rules, Regulations, or Guidelines* | *Holds Public Hearings* | *Holds Nonpublic Hearings* | *Monitors Compliance with State Fair Employment Laws* | *Monitors Compliance with Its Own Directives* | *Citations to Authority* |
|---|---|---|---|---|---|---|---|---|---|
| MI | 180 days. | Yes. | State has no statutory requirements. | Yes. | Yes. | Yes. | State has no statutory requirements. | State has no statutory requirements. | Mich. Comp. Laws §§ 37.2601, 37.2602; 29 C.F.R. § 1601.74. |
| MN | 1 year. | Yes. Minneapolis and St. Paul agencies also certified. | State has no statutory requirements. | Yes. | Yes. | Yes. | Yes. | State has no statutory requirements. | Minn. Stat. Ann. §§ 363.05, 363.06, 363.071; 29 C.F.R. § 1601.74. |
| MS | — | — | — | — | — | — | — | — | State has no comprehensive FEP act. |
| MO | 180 days. | Yes. Kansas City and St. Louis agencies also certified. | State has no statutory requirements. | Yes. | Yes. | No. | Yes. | Yes. | Mo. Rev. Stat. §§ 213.030, 213.075; 29 C.F.R. § 1601.74. |
| MT | 180 days after occurrence of unlawful practice or 180 days after conclusion of qualified grievance procedure, but not to exceed 300 days after occurrence of unlawful practice. | Yes. | State has no statutory requirements. | Yes. | Can hold hearings, but statute does not specify if hearings are public or non-public. | Can hold hearings, but statute does not specify if hearings are public or non-public. | Yes. | Yes. | Mont. Code Ann. §§ 49-2-204, 49-2-501, 49-2-502, 49-2-505, 49-3-106, 49-3-304; 29 C.F.R. § 1601.74. |

| | | | | | | | | | |
|---|---|---|---|---|---|---|---|---|---|
| NE | 180 days. | Yes. Lincoln and Omaha agencies also certified. | State has no statutory requirements. | Yes. | Yes. | Yes. | State has no statutory requirements. | State has no statutory requirements. | Neb. Rev. Stat. §§ 48-1117–48-1124; 29 C.F.R. § 1601.74. |
| NV | 180 days. | Yes. | State has no statutory requirements. | Yes. | Yes. | Yes. | Yes. | Yes. | Nev. Rev. Stat. §§ 233.150, 233.160, 233.170, 613.405, 613.420, 613.430; 29 C.F.R. § 1601.74. |
| NH | 180 days. | Yes. | State has no statutory requirements. | Yes. | Yes. | Yes. | Yes. | Yes. | N.H. Rev. Stat. Ann. §§ 354-A:5, 354-A:7, 354-A:21; 29 C.F.R. § 1601.74. |
| NJ | 180 days. | Yes. | State has no statutory requirements. | Yes. | Yes. | Yes. | Yes. | Yes. | N.J. Stat. Ann. §§ 10:5-13, 10:5-14, 10:5-15, 10:5-18; 29 C.F.R. § 1601.74. |
| NM | 180 days. | Yes. | State has no statutory requirements. | Yes. | Yes. | Yes. | Yes. | Yes. | N.M. Stat. Ann. §§ 28-1-4, 28-1-10; 29 C.F.R. § 1601.74. |
| NY | 1 year. | Yes. New York City agency also certified. | State has no statutory requirements. | Yes. | Yes. | State has no statutory requirements. | Yes. | Yes. | N.Y. Exec. Law §§ 294, 295, 297; N.Y. Comp. Codes R. & Regs. tit. 9, §§ 465.2, 465.3, 466.9; 29 C.F.R. § 1601.74. |
| NC | 180 days. | Yes. Durham and New Hanover agencies also certified. | State has no statutory requirements. | State has no statutory requirements. | Yes. | State has no statutory requirements. | State has no statutory requirements. | State has no statutory requirements. | N.C. Gen. Stat. §§ 7A-759, 143-422.2, 143-422.3, 150B-23, 168A-11, 168A-12 (applies to public employment only); 29 C.F.R. § 1601.74. |
| ND | 300 days to file with labor department or 3 years to bring suit directly in district court. | Yes. | State has no statutory requirements. | State has no statutory requirements. | State has no statutory requirements. | State has no statutory requirements. | Yes. | Yes. | N.D. Cent. Code §§ 14-02.4-19, 14-02.4-21; 29 C.F.R. § 1601.74. |

*(Table continues.)*

## Table 2.4-1 Part A *(cont'd)*

## STATE FAIR EMPLOYMENT COMMISSION POWERS AND PROCEDURES

(See also text at § 2.4[a].)

**KEY:** **EEOC Deferral Agency.** An agency that can process charges for the EEOC. In a deferral state, the usual 180-day limit for filing charges under federal statutes is extended to 300 days.

| | *Time Limit for Filing Complaint with State Agency* | *Has EEOC-Certified Deferral Agency* | *Recommends that EEOC Start Title VII Action* | *Issues Rules, Regulations, or Guidelines* | *Holds Public Hearings* | *Holds Nonpublic Hearings* | *Monitors Compliance with State Fair Employment Laws* | *Monitors Compliance with Its Own Directives* | *Citations to Authority* |
|---|---|---|---|---|---|---|---|---|---|
| OH | 6 months. | Yes. Springfield and Youngstown agencies also certified. | Yes. | Yes. | Yes. | Yes, for good cause. | Yes. | Yes. | Ohio Rev. Code Ann. §§ 4112.03, 4112.04, 4112.05, 4112.06; 29 C.F.R. § 1601.74. |
| OK | 180 days. | Yes. | No. | No. | Can hold hearings, but statute does not specify if hearings are public or non-public. | Can hold hearings, but statute does not specify if hearings are public or non-public. | Yes. | Yes. | Okla. Stat. tit. 25, §§ 1501–1503; 29 C.F.R. § 1601.74. |
| OR | 1 year. | Yes. | State has no statutory requirements. | Yes. | Yes. | State has no statutory requirements. | State has no statutory requirements. | Yes. | Or. Rev. Stat. §§ 659.060, 659.103; Or. Civ. Rts. Proc. Rules 839-04-000 *et seq.*; 29 C.F.R. § 1601.74. |
| PA | 180 days. | Yes. Allentown, Philadelphia, Pittsburgh, and York agencies also certified. | State has no statutory requirements. | Yes. | Yes. | Yes. | State has no statutory requirements. | State has no statutory requirements. | Pa. Stat. Ann. tit. 43, §§ 952, 956, 957, 958.1, 959, 961.2; 29 C.F.R. § 1601.74. |

| | | | | | | | | | |
|---|---|---|---|---|---|---|---|---|---|
| RI | Not specified, but commission may issue complaint up to 1 year after alleged unfair practice. | Yes. | State has no statutory requirements. | Yes. | Yes. | Yes, for good cause. | Yes. | Yes. | R.I. Gen. Laws §§ 28-5-13, 28-5-16, 28-5-18; 29 C.F.R. § 1601.74. |
| SC | 180 days. | Yes. | State has no statutory requirements. | Yes. | Yes, unless good cause is shown. | Yes, if respondent is state agency. | Yes. | State has no statutory requirements. | S.C. Code Ann. §§ 1-13-70, 1-13-90; 29 C.F.R. § 1601.74. |
| SD | 180 days. | Yes. Sioux Falls agency also certified. | State has no statutory requirements. | Yes. | Can hold hearings, but statute does not specify if hearings are public or non-public. | Can hold hearings, but statute does not specify if hearings are public or non-public. | Yes. | Yes. | S.D. Codified Laws Ann. §§ 20-13-7, 20-13-27, 20-13-31, 20-13-35, 20-13-45; S.D. Admin. R. § 20:03:05:01; 29 C.F.R. § 1601.74. |
| TN | 180 days. | Yes. | State has no statutory requirements. | Yes. | Yes. | State has no statutory requirements. | Yes. | Yes. | Tenn. Code Ann. §§ 4-21-202, 4-21-303, 4-21-304; 29 C.F.R. § 1601.74. |
| TX | 180 days. | Yes. Austin, Corpus Christi, Fort Worth, and Wichita Falls agencies also certified. | State has no statutory requirements. | Yes. | State has no statutory requirements. | State has no statutory requirements. | Yes. | Yes. | Tex. Lab. Code Ann. §§ 21.003, 21.202; 29 C.F.R. § 1601.74. |
| UT | 180 days. | Yes. | State has no statutory requirements. | Yes. | Can hold hearings, but statute does not specify if hearings are public or non-public. | Can hold hearings, but statute does not specify if hearings are public or non-public. | Yes. | Yes. | Utah Code Ann. §§ 34-35-5, 34-35-7.1; Utah Admin. R. § R486-1-3; 29 C.F.R. § 1601.74. |
| VT | State has no statutory requirements. | Yes. | State has no statutory requirements. | Yes. | Can hold hearings, but statute does not specify if hearings are public or non-public. | Can hold hearings, but statute does not specify if hearings are public or non-public. | State has no statutory requirements. | Yes. | Vt. Stat. Ann. tit. 9, §§ 2458, 2459, 2460, 2462, 4552, 4553; tit. 21, §§ 495, 495b; 29 C.F.R. § 1601.74. |

*(Table continues.)*

# Table 2.4-1 Part A *(cont'd)*

## STATE FAIR EMPLOYMENT COMMISSION POWERS AND PROCEDURES

(See also text at § 2.4[a].)

**KEY:** **EEOC Deferral Agency.** An agency that can process charges for the EEOC. In a deferral state, the usual 180-day limit for filing charges under federal statutes is extended to 300 days.

| | *Time Limit for Filing Complaint with State Agency* | *Has EEOC-Certified Deferral Agency* | *Recommends that EEOC Start Title VII Action* | *Issues Rules, Regulations, or Guidelines* | *Holds Public Hearings* | *Holds Nonpublic Hearings* | *Monitors Compliance with State Fair Employment Laws* | *Monitors Compliance with Its Own Directives* | *Citations to Authority* |
|---|---|---|---|---|---|---|---|---|---|
| VA | 180 days. | Yes. Alexandria, Arlington County, Fairfax County, and Prince William County agencies also certified. | State has no statutory requirements. | Yes. | Yes. | Yes. | Yes. | State has no statutory requirements. | Va. Code Ann. §§ 2.1-717, 2.1-719, 2.1-720, 2.1-722; Va. Hum. Rts. Council Procs. §§ 1–13; 29 C.F.R. § 1601.74. |
| WA | 6 months. | Yes. Seattle and Tacoma agencies also certified. | State has no statutory requirements. | Yes. | Yes. | No. | Yes. | State has no statutory requirements. | Wash. Rev. Code §§ 49.60.110, 49.60.120, 49.60.140, 49.60.230, 49.60.250; Wash. Ex. Or. 83-12; Wash. Admin. Code §§ 162-04-020, 162-08-07, 162-08-211, 162-08-291; 29 C.F.R. § 1601.74. |
| WV | 365 days. | Yes. Charleston, Huntington, and Wheeling agencies also certified. | State has no statutory requirements. | Yes. | Yes. | Yes. | Yes. | Yes. | W. Va. Code §§ 5-11-8, 5-11-10; W. Va. Admin. Reg. §§ 77-2-3, 77-2-7, 77-2-15; 29 C.F.R. § 1601.74. |

| | | | | | | | | | |
|---|---|---|---|---|---|---|---|---|---|
| WI | 300 days. | Yes. Madison agency also certified. | State has no statutory requirements. | Yes. | Can hold hearings, but statute does not specify if hearings are public or non-public. | Can hold hearings, but statute does not specify if hearings are public or non-public. | Yes. | State has no statutory requirements. | Wis. Stat. Ann. §§ 111.375, 111.38, 111.39; 29 C.F.R. § 1601.74. |
| WY | 90 days. | Yes. | State has no statutory requirements. | Yes. | Yes. | No. | State has no statutory requirements. | State has no statutory requirements. | Wyo. Stat. §§ 27-9-104, 27-9-106; 29 C.F.R. § 1601.74. |

# Table 2.4-1 Part B

## STATE FAIR EMPLOYMENT COMMISSION POWERS AND PROCEDURES

(See also text at § 2.4[a].)

**KEY:** **EEOC Deferral Agency.** An agency that can process charges for the EEOC. In a deferral state, the usual 180-day limit for filing charges under federal statutes is extended to 300 days.

| | *Initiates Charges* | *Files Charges on Behalf of Individual or Class* | *Investigates Charges* | *Issues Findings or Determinations* | *Conciliates Charges (Attempts Settlement)* | *Proposes Remedies* | *Seeks Court Relief* | *Seeks Injunctive Relief (Nonmonetary Relief)* | *Citations to Authority* |
|---|---|---|---|---|---|---|---|---|---|
| AL | — | — | — | — | — | — | — | — | State has no comprehensive FEP act. |
| AK | Yes. | Yes. | Yes. | Yes. | Yes. | Yes. | Yes. | Yes. | Alaska Stat. §§ 18.80.100, 18.80.105, 18.80.110, 18.80.120, 18.80.130, 18.80.135, 18.80.145. |
| AZ | Yes. | Yes. | Yes. | Yes. | Yes. | Yes. | Yes. | Yes. | Ariz. Rev. Stat. Ann. § 41-1481. |
| AR | State has no statutory requirements. | State has no statutory requirements. | State has no statutory requirements. | State has no statutory requirements. | State has no statutory requirements. | State has no statutory requirements. | State has no statutory requirements. | State has no statutory requirements. | Ark. Code Ann. §§ 16-123-101 *et seq.* |
| CA | Yes. | Yes. | Yes. | Yes. | Yes. | Yes. | Yes. | Yes. | Cal. Gov't Code §§ 12960, 12961, 12963, 12963.7, 12964, 12965, 12970, 12973, 12974. |
| CO | Yes. | Yes. | Yes. | Yes. | Yes. | Yes. | Yes. | Yes. | Colo. Rev. Stat. §§ 24-34-306, 24-34-307. |

| | | | | | | | | | |
|---|---|---|---|---|---|---|---|---|---|
| CT | Yes. | Yes. | Yes. | Yes. | Yes. | Yes. | Yes. | Yes. | Conn. Gen. Stat. Ann. §§ 46a-54, 46a-56, 46a-82, 46a-83, 46a-86, 46a-89, 46a-89a, 46a-95. |
| DE | Yes. | Yes. | Yes. | Yes. | Yes. | Yes. | Yes. | Yes. | Del. Code Ann. tit. 19, §§ 712, 713. |
| DC | Yes. | Yes. | Yes. | Yes. | Yes. | Yes. | Yes. | Yes. | D.C. Code Ann. §§ 1-2544–2547, 1-2553, 1-2555. |
| FL | Yes. | Yes. | Yes. | Yes. | Yes. | Yes. | Yes. | Yes. | Fla. Stat. Ann. §§ 760.06, 760.11. |
| GA | Yes. | Yes. | Yes. | Yes. | Yes. | Yes. | Yes. | Yes. | Ga. Code Ann. §§ 45-19-27, 45-19-36, 45-19-43. (Applies to public employment only.) |
| HI | Yes. | Yes. | Yes. | Yes. | Yes. | No. | Yes. | Yes. | Haw. Rev. Stat. §§ 368-1 *et seq.*, 378-4. |
| ID | Yes. | Yes. | Yes. | Yes. | Yes. | No. | Yes. | Yes. | Idaho Code §§ 67-5906, 67-5907. |
| IL | Yes. | Yes. | Yes. | Yes. | Yes. | No. | Yes. | Yes. | 775 ILCS §§ 5/7-101, 5/7A-102. |
| IN | Yes. | Yes. | Yes. | Yes. | Yes. | No. | Yes, for enforcement of order. | Yes. | Ind. Code § 22-9-1-6. |
| IA | Yes. | Yes. | Yes. | Yes. | Yes. | Yes. | Yes. | Yes. | Iowa Code Ann. § 216.15. |
| KS | Yes. | Yes. | Yes. | Yes. | Yes. | Yes. | Yes, for enforcement of order. | Yes. | Kan. Stat. Ann. §§ 44-1004, 44-1005, 44-1011. |
| KY | Yes. | Yes. | Yes. | Yes. | Yes. | Yes. | Yes. | Yes. | Ky. Rev. Stat. Ann. §§ 344.200, 344.210, 344.230–344.260. |
| LA | Yes. | Yes. | Yes. | Yes. | Yes. | No. | Yes. | Yes. | La. Rev. Stat. Ann. §§ 51:2235, 51:2257, 51:2261, 51:2264. |
| ME | No. | Yes. | Yes. | Yes. | Yes. | Yes. | Yes. | Yes. | Me. Rev. Stat. Ann. tit. 5, § 4612. |

*(Table continues.)*

# Table 2.4-1 Part B *(cont'd)*

## STATE FAIR EMPLOYMENT COMMISSION POWERS AND PROCEDURES

(See also text at § 2.4[a].)

**KEY:** **EEOC Deferral Agency.** An agency that can process charges for the EEOC. In a deferral state, the usual 180-day limit for filing charges under federal statutes is extended to 300 days.

| | *Initiates Charges* | *Files Charges on Behalf of Individual or Class* | *Investigates Charges* | *Issues Findings or Determinations* | *Conciliates Charges (Attempts Settlement)* | *Proposes Remedies* | *Seeks Court Relief* | *Seeks Injunctive Relief (Nonmonetary Relief)* | *Citations to Authority* |
|---|---|---|---|---|---|---|---|---|---|
| MD | Yes. | Yes. | Yes. | Yes. | Yes. | No. | Yes. | Yes. | Md. Ann. Code art. 49B, §§ 7, 9A, 10, 12. |
| MA | Yes. | Yes. | Yes. | Yes. | Yes. | Yes. | Yes. | Yes. | Mass. Gen. Laws ch. 151B, § 5. |
| MI | Yes. | Yes. | Yes. | Yes. | Yes. | Yes. | Yes. | Yes. | Mich. Comp. Laws §§ 37.2602, 37.2603, 37.2604, 37.2605. |
| MN | Yes. | Yes. | Yes. | Yes. | Yes. | No. | Yes. | Yes. | Minn. Stat. Ann. §§ 363.06, 363.072. |
| MS | — | — | — | — | — | — | — | — | State has no comprehensive FEP act. |
| MO | Yes. | No. | Yes. | Yes. | Yes. | No. | Yes, for enforcement of order. | Yes. | Mo. Rev. Stat. §§ 213.030, 213.075. |
| MT | Yes. | Yes. | Yes. | Yes. | Yes. | No. | Yes. | Yes. | Mont. Code Ann. §§ 49-2-203, 49-2-501–49-2-504, 49-2-508, 49-3-106. |
| NE | No. | No. | Yes. | Yes. | Yes. | No. | No. | Yes. | Neb. Rev. Stat. §§ 48-1117, 48-1118, 48-1119. |
| NV | Yes. | Yes. | Yes. | Yes. | Yes. | No. | Yes. | Yes. | Nev. Rev. Stat. §§ 233.130, 233.160, 233.170. |

| | | | | | | | | | |
|---|---|---|---|---|---|---|---|---|---|
| NH | Yes. | Yes. | Yes. | Yes. | Yes. | No. | No. | Yes. | N.H. Rev. Stat. Ann. §§ 354-A:3, 354-A:4, 354-A:5, 354-A:21. |
| NJ | Yes. | Yes. | Yes. | Yes. | Yes. | Yes. | Yes. | Yes. | N.J. Stat. Ann. §§ 10:5-8, 10:5-13, 10:5-14, 10:5-17, 10:5-18. |
| NM | Yes. | Yes. | Yes. | Yes. | Yes. | No. | Yes. | Yes. | N.M. Stat. Ann. §§ 28-1-4, 28-1-5, 28-1-10, 28-1-12. |
| NY | Yes. | Yes. | Yes. | Yes. | Yes. | Yes. | Yes. | Yes. | N.Y. Exec. Law §§ 293–295, 297; N.Y. Comp. Codes R. & Regs. tit. 9, § 465.3. |
| NC | Yes. | No. | Yes. | Yes. | Yes. | No. | No. | No. | N.C. Gen. Stat. §§ 7A-759, 143-422.3, 150B-23; N.C. Admin. Code tit. 26, § 4.0001. |
| ND | Yes. | Yes. | Yes. | Yes. | Yes. | No. | No. | Yes. | N.D. Cent. Code §§ 14-02.4-19, 14-02.4-21. |
| OH | Yes. | No. | Yes. | Yes. | Yes. | No. | Yes. | Yes. | Ohio Rev. Code Ann. §§ 4112.03, 4112.05, 4112.06. |
| OK | Yes, for public employment. | No. | Yes. | Yes. | Yes. | No. | Yes. | Yes. | Okla. Stat. tit. 25 §§ 1501–1506; tit. 74, § 952. |
| OR | Yes. | Yes. | Yes. | Yes. | Yes. | Yes. | No. | Yes. | Or. Rev. Stat. §§ 240.379, 240.384, 240.391–240.394, 659.040, 659.050, 659.060, 659.121. |
| PA | Yes. | Yes. | Yes. | Yes. | Yes. | No. | Yes. | Yes. | Pa. Stat. Ann. tit. 43 §§ 957, 959, 959.2, 962. |
| RI | Yes. | No. | Yes. | Yes. | Yes. | No. | Yes, for enforcement of order. | Yes, for enforcement of order. | R.I. Gen. Laws §§ 28-5-13, 28-5-17, 28-5-18, 28-5-28, 28-5-36. |
| SC | No. | Yes. | Yes. | Yes. | Yes. | No. | Yes. | Yes. | S.C. Code Ann. §§ 1-13-70, 1-13-90, 43-33-550. |

*(Table continues.)*

## Table 2.4-1 Part B *(cont'd)*
## STATE FAIR EMPLOYMENT COMMISSION POWERS AND PROCEDURES

(See also text at § 2.4[a].)

**KEY: EEOC Deferral Agency.** An agency that can process charges for the EEOC. In a deferral state, the usual 180-day limit for filing charges under federal statutes is extended to 300 days.

| | *Initiates Charges* | *Files Charges on Behalf of Individual or Class* | *Investigates Charges* | *Issues Findings or Determinations* | *Conciliates Charges (Attempts Settlement)* | *Proposes Remedies* | *Seeks Court Relief* | *Seeks Injunctive Relief (Nonmonetary Relief)* | *Citations to Authority* |
|---|---|---|---|---|---|---|---|---|---|
| SD | Yes. | No. | Yes. | Yes. | Yes. | No. | Yes, for enforcement of order on conciliation agreement. | Yes. | S.D. Codified Laws Ann. §§ 20-13-28, 20-13-29, 20-13-32, 20-13-47; S.D. Admin. R. §§ 20:03:01:02, 20:03:02:01, 20:03:03:01, 20:03:04:03, 20:03:04:05. |
| TN | Yes. | No. | Yes. | Yes. | Yes. | Yes. | Yes. | Yes. | Tenn. Code Ann. §§ 4-21-202, 4-21-302, 4-21-303, 4-21-308. |
| TX | No. | Yes. | Yes. | Yes. | Yes. | Yes. | Yes. | Yes. | Tex. Lab. Code Ann. §§ 21.003, 21.204, 21.206, 21.210, 21.251. |
| UT | No. | No. | Yes. | Yes. | Yes. | Yes. | No. | No. | Utah Code Ann. § 34-35-7.1. |
| VT | No. | Yes. | Yes. | Yes. | Yes. | Yes. | Yes. | Yes. | Vt. Stat. Ann. tit. 9, §§ 2458, 2460, 2461, 4551–4553, tit. 21, § 495b. |
| VA | Yes. | Yes. | Yes. | Yes. | Yes. | Yes. | Yes, with approval of attorney general. | Yes, with approval of attorney general. | Va. Code Ann. §§ 2.1-719, 2.1-720. |

| | | | | | | | | | |
|---|---|---|---|---|---|---|---|---|---|
| WA | Yes. | Yes. | Yes. | Yes. | Yes. | Yes. | Yes, for enforcement of order. | Yes, for enforcement of order. | Wash. Rev. Code §§ 49.60.110, 49.60.120, 49.60.240, 49.60.260; Wash. Admin. Code §§ 162-04-020, 162-08-072, 162-08-094, 162-08-104, 162-08-305. |
| WV | Yes. | Yes. | Yes. | Yes. | Yes. | Yes. | Yes, for enforcement of order. | Yes, for enforcement of order. | W. Va. Code §§ 5-11-8, 5-11-10. |
| WI | No. | No. | Yes. | Yes. | Yes. | Yes. | No. | Yes, for enforcement of order. | Wis. Stat. Ann. §§ 111.39, 111.395. |
| WY | No. | Yes. | Yes. | Yes. | Yes. | Yes. | Yes, for enforcement of order. | Yes, for enforcement of order. | Wyo. Stat. §§ 27-9-104, 27-9-106. |

# Table 2.4-2
## APPEAL OF FAIR EMPLOYMENT COMMISSION RULINGS AND ACCESS TO STATE COURT

(See also text at § 2.4[b].)

**KEY:** ***De novo.*** Court may issue ruling based on its assessment of facts, disregarding prior ruling from other agency or commission.

| | *Prerequisites to Filing Lawsuit in State Court* | *Court Can Examine Complaint* De Novo | *Court Can Review Commission Ruling* | *Commission Representation Available* | *Individual Representation Allowed* | *Can Appeal State Court Decisions* | *Citations to Authority* |
|---|---|---|---|---|---|---|---|
| AL | — | — | — | — | — | — | State has no comprehensive FEP act. |
| AK | Complainant has 30 days after final action to appeal to superior court. | Yes. | Yes. | State has no statutory requirements. | Yes. | State has no statutory requirements. | Alaska Stat. §§ 18.80.135, 18.80.140, 44.62.560, 44.62.570. |
| AZ | If commission dismisses charge, complainant may bring civil action against respondent within 90 days of dismissal notification. Complainant may also bring civil action, if commission has not done so, within 90 days of filing charge; in any event, civil action is not allowed more than 1 year after charge was filed. | Yes. | Yes. | Yes. Commission may bring civil action against respondent if determination of reasonable cause to bring suit is made. | Yes. Court may appoint attorney for complainant upon application and in circumstances the court deems just. | State has no statutory requirements. | Ariz. Rev. Stat. Ann. §§ 41-1402, 41-1481. |
| AR | State has no statutory requirements. | State has no statutory requirements. | State has no statutory requirements. | State has no statutory requirements. | State has no statutory requirements. | State has no statutory requirements. | Ark. Code Ann. §§ 16-123-101 *et seq.* |
| CA | Complainant must file suit within 1 year after receiving notice of determination that no accusation will be issued or within 150 days after complaint was filed if there is a failure to issue the accusation. | State has no statutory requirements. | State has no statutory requirements. | State has no statutory requirements. | State has no statutory requirements. | State has no statutory requirements. | Cal. Gov't Code §§ 11523, 12965. |

| | | | | | | | |
|---|---|---|---|---|---|---|---|
| CO | Appeal of hearing officer's initial decision must be filed with Denver office within 90 days. Complainant may obtain court review of final commission order, including refusal to issue order, by bringing proceeding in court of appeals. Such proceeding is initiated by filing petition in district court within 30 days of commission's final order and serving copy to commission and all parties who appeared before commission. Thereafter, such proceeding will be processed under state appellate rules. Failure of written notice of hearing to be served within 270 days of filing of charge, or failure of hearing to be held within 120 days of filing terminates commission's jurisdiction over matter. Complainant can then file civil action in state court. | No, but objections not made before commission may be considered if extraordinary circumstances are present. | Yes. | State has no statutory requirements. | Yes. | Yes. Judgment and order of court final, subject to review as provided by law and court of appeals appellate rules. | Colo. Rev. Stat. §§ 24-34-306, 24-34-307. |
| CT | May appeal any judgment, injunctive relief, order of decree; appeal must be filed in judicial district where alleged discriminatory practice occurred or in judicial district in which appellant resides or transacts business. | No. | Yes. | State has no statutory requirements. | State has no statutory requirements. | Yes. | Conn. Gen. Stat. Ann. §§ 46a-94, 46a-94a, 46a-95; *Billings v. Comm'n on Human Rights and Opportunities,* 557 A.2d 147 (Conn. App. 1989). |
| DE | File petition in court of chancery within 30 days after order received from review board. Superior court of county where alleged violation occurred has jurisdiction to hear appeals of any review board decision. | No. Objection not urged at hearing will be considered by court only if good cause is shown. | Yes. Court may reverse or modify order, if substantial rights of petitioner have been prejudiced because commission's findings are clearly erroneous in view of the evidence. | State has no statutory requirements. | Yes. | State has no statutory requirements. | Del. Code Ann. tit. 19, § 712. |
| DC | Person aggrieved by commission's order or decision is entitled to court review under § 1-1510 of Administrative Procedure Act; must file written petition for such review in District of Columbia court of appeals. D.C. Code Ann. § 1-2556 allows private cause of action only if complainant (i) elected not to file complaint with commission; or (ii) had complaint dismissed because of administrative convenience; or (iii) withdrew complaint. | No, unless findings are unsupported by substantial evidence in the record. | Yes. | State has no statutory requirements. | Yes. | State has no statutory requirements. | D.C. Code Ann. §§ 1-1510, 1-2547, 1-2556. |

(Table continues.)

# **Table 2.4-2** *(cont'd)*

## APPEAL OF FAIR EMPLOYMENT COMMISSION RULINGS AND ACCESS TO STATE COURT

(See also text at § 2.4[b].)

**KEY:** ***De novo.*** Court may issue ruling based on its assessment of facts, disregarding prior ruling from other agency or commission.

| | *Prerequisites to Filing Lawsuit in State Court* | *Court Can Examine Complaint* De Novo | *Court Can Review Commission Ruling* | *Commission Representation Available* | *Individual Representation Allowed* | *Can Appeal State Court Decisions* | *Citations to Authority* |
|---|---|---|---|---|---|---|---|
| FL | Appeals of final commission action must be according to § 120.68, Florida Statutes, and Florida Rules of Appellate Procedure; appeal must be filed in district court of appeal. | If commission fails to conciliate or take final action on any complaint within 180 days of filing, aggrieved person may bring civil action in any court of competent jurisdiction. | Yes. | State has no statutory requirements. | State has no statutory requirements. | Yes. | Fla. Stat. Ann. § 760.11. |
| GA | Petition for review of any final order of special master must be filed for review in superior court in county in which alleged unlawful practice occurred or in superior court of respondent's residence within 30 days of final order. | No. | Yes. | No, except for action to secure judicial enforcement of preliminary order of special master. | Yes. Attorneys' fees may be awarded if complainant prevails. | Yes. All appeals must be in accordance with Chapter 13 of Title 50 of Georgia Administrative Procedure Act. | Ga. Code Ann. § 45-19-39. (Applies to public employment only.) |
| HI | Any person aggrieved by order of commission is entitled to judicial review. Additionally, complainant can bring civil action following proper filing of complaint by satisfying requirements for administrative release. | Yes. | Yes. | Yes. | State has no statutory requirements. | Yes. | Haw. Rev. Stat. §§ 368-12, 368-16, 378-5. |
| ID | None. Complainant has 2 years to pursue private cause of action. | State has no statutory requirements. | Yes. | Yes, for actions filed by the commission. | Yes. | State has no statutory requirements. | Idaho Code §§ 67-5908, 67-5908a. |
| IL | Complainant must file in appellate court within 35 days of commission's judgment. | No. | Yes. | State has no statutory requirements. | State has no statutory requirements. | State has no statutory requirements. | 775 ILCS §§ 5/7-101, 5/7A-102, 5/8-101 *et seq.* |

| | | | | | | | |
|---|---|---|---|---|---|---|---|
| IN | Judicial review is allowed after exhaustion of all administrative remedies. Right is waived unless petition is filed within 30 days of notice of final agency action. | No. | State has no statutory requirements. | Yes. | State has no statutory requirements. | State has no statutory requirements. | Ind. Code §§ 4-21.5-5-4, 4-21.5-5-5, 4-21.5-5-12, 22-9-1-6. |
| IA | Complainant must seek judicial review within 30 days after issuance of those final agency actions that are not of general applicability. Additionally, complainant can bring civil action following proper filing of complaint with commission by satisfying requirements of administrative release. | No. | Yes. | Yes. | State has no statutory requirements. | Yes. | Iowa Code Ann. §§ 17A.20, 216.15, 216.16. |
| KS | Any action of commission is subject to review in accordance with act for judicial review and civil enforcement of agency actions. | Yes. | Yes. | Yes. | Yes. | State has no statutory requirements. | Kan. Stat. Ann. § 44-1011. |
| KY | Complainant must file for review with circuit court within 30 days after receiving commission's order. | No, but objections not presented before commission may be raised for good cause. | Yes. | State has no statutory requirements. | Yes. | Yes. | Ky. Rev. Stat. Ann. § 344.240. |
| LA | Court review of commission action may be sought under Administrative Procedure Act. | State has no statutory requirements. | Yes. | State has no statutory requirements. | State has no statutory requirements. | Yes. | La. Rev. Stat. Ann. §§ 49:965, 51:2265. |
| ME | Appeal pursuant to Administrative Procedure Act. | No. | Yes. | Yes. | Yes. | Yes. | Me. Rev. Stat. Ann. tit. 5, §§ 4613, 4621, 4622, 11007, 11008. |
| MD | Court review of commission's final order may be sought in circuit court under Maryland Administrative Procedure Act. | State has no statutory requirements. | Yes. | State has no statutory requirements. | State has no statutory requirements. | State has no statutory requirements. | Md. Ann. Code art. 49B, §§ 10–12. |
| MA | Complainant must file petition for review in superior court within 30 days of commission's final order. | No, but objections not presented before commission may be raised in extraordinary circumstances. | Yes. | Yes. | State has no statutory requirements. | Yes. | Mass. Gen. Laws ch. 30A, § 14; ch. 151B, §§ 5, 6. |
| MI | Complainant must file petition in circuit court within 30 days of commission's final order. | Yes. | Yes. | State has no statutory requirements. | State has no statutory requirements. | Yes. | Mich. Comp. Laws § 37.2606. |
| MN | After final decision, court review may be sought in district court pursuant to state Administrative Procedure Act. | No. | Yes. | Yes. | State has no statutory requirements. | Yes. | Minn. Stat. Ann. §§ 14.63, 14.68, 14.69, 363.072. |

*(Table continues.)*

## Table 2.4-2 *(cont'd)*

## APPEAL OF FAIR EMPLOYMENT COMMISSION RULINGS AND ACCESS TO STATE COURT

(See also text at § 2.4[b].)

**KEY:** ***De novo.*** Court may issue ruling based on its assessment of facts, disregarding prior ruling from other agency or commission.

| | *Prerequisites to Filing Lawsuit in State Court* | *Court Can Examine Complaint* De Novo | *Court Can Review Commission Ruling* | *Commission Representation Available* | *Individual Representation Allowed* | *Can Appeal State Court Decisions* | *Citations to Authority* |
|---|---|---|---|---|---|---|---|
| MS | — | — | — | — | — | — | State has no comprehensive FEP act. |
| MO | Complainant must file petition in circuit court within 30 days of notice of commission's order. | No. | Yes. | State has no statutory requirements. | State has no statutory requirements. | Yes. | Mo. Rev. Stat. §§ 213.075, 213.077, 213.085, 213.111. |
| MT | Complainant must file petition within 30 days of notice of commission's decision. | No. | State has no statutory requirements. | State has no statutory requirements. | State has no statutory requirements. | Yes. | Mont. Code Ann. §§ 2-4-702–2-4-711, 49-2-505, 49-3-308; *European Health Spa v. Human Rights Comm'n*, 687 P.2d 1029 (1984); *Billings v. State Human Rights Comm'n*, 681 P.2d 33 (1984). |
| NE | Appeal must be made to district court within 30 days of decision and order in accordance with Administrative Procedure Act. | Yes. | Yes. | State has no statutory requirements. | State has no statutory requirements. | Yes. | Neb. Rev. Stat. §§ 48-1120, 84-917, 84-919. |
| NV | After final order, complainant must appeal to district court for review. | No. | Yes. | State has no statutory requirements. | State has no statutory requirements. | State has no statutory requirements. | Nev. Rev. Stat. §§ 233.170, 613.420. |

| | | | | | | | |
|---|---|---|---|---|---|---|---|
| NH | Within 30 days after commission's final order is served, complainant must file petition for review with superior court, together with written transcript of hearing before commission, and issue and serve an order of notice. | No, new evidence allowed only if reasonable grounds exist for failure to present it before commission. | Yes. | Yes. | State has no statutory requirements. | Yes, a superior court order affirming a decision of the commission is subject to review by the supreme court. | N.H. Rev. Stat. Ann. § 354-A:22; *Burns v. Town of Gorham*, 445 A.2d 1111 (N.H. 1982). |
| NJ | Any person aggrieved by final order may appeal to superior court or appellate division, as on appeal from any state agency. | State has no statutory requirements. | Yes. | State has no statutory requirements. | State has no statutory requirements. | State has no statutory requirements. | N.J. Stat. Ann. § 10:5-21. |
| NM | Complainant must file notice of appeal with district court within 30 days of commission's order. Individual defendants cannot be sued in district court unless and until the complainant exhausts his or her administrative remedies against those defendants. | Yes. | No. | State has no statutory requirements. | State has no statutory requirements. | State has no statutory requirements. | N.M. Stat. Ann. § 28-1-13; *Luboyeski v. Hill*, 872 P.2d 353 (N.M. 1994). |
| NY | Judicial review may be obtained by filing notice of petition and petition in the supreme court of the county wherein the unlawful discrimination occurred within 60 days after determination by commissioner. | No, but objections not presented before commission may be raised in extraordinary circumstances. | Yes. | Yes. | State has no statutory requirements. | Yes. | N.Y. Exec. Law § 298. |
| NC | Complainant must appeal to State Personnel Commission first. If still aggrieved, appeal may be made to state superior court. | No. | Yes. | State has no statutory requirements. | State has no statutory requirements. | State has no statutory requirements. | N.C. Gen. Stat. §§ 126-36, 126-37, 143.422.2, 143.422.3, 150A-1. |
| ND | Complainant must bring action directly to district court and follow state courts' judicial review procedure. | State has no statutory requirements. | State has no statutory requirements. | State has no statutory requirements. | State has no statutory requirements. | State has no statutory requirements. | N.D. Cent. Code §§ 14-02.4-19, 14-02.4-20, 14-02.4-21. |
| OH | Appeal may be filed in common pleas court within 30 days after final order is issued. | No, but objections not presented before commission may be raised in exceptional circumstances. | Yes. | Yes. | State has no statutory requirements. | Yes. | Ohio Rev. Code Ann. §§ 4112.06, 4112.061, 4112.210. |
| OK | After commission issues order, it must file enforcement petition with district court within 30 days if order is to have any legal effect. | Available when requested by a party. | Yes. | Yes. | Yes. | State has no statutory requirements. | Okla. Stat. Ann. tit. 25, §§ 1502 *et seq.* |
| OR | Complainant must file with court of appeals within 60 days of commission's final order. | No. | Yes. | State has no statutory requirements. | Yes. | Yes. | Or. Rev. Stat. §§ 183.310–183.550, 659.085, 659.095, 659.121. |

(*Table continues.*)

# **Table 2.4-2** *(cont'd)*

## APPEAL OF FAIR EMPLOYMENT COMMISSION RULINGS AND ACCESS TO STATE COURT

(See also text at § 2.4[b].)

**KEY:** ***De novo.*** Court may issue ruling based on its assessment of facts, disregarding prior ruling from other agency or commission.

| | *Prerequisites to Filing Lawsuit in State Court* | *Court Can Examine Complaint* De Novo | *Court Can Review Commission Ruling* | *Commission Representation Available* | *Individual Representation Allowed* | *Can Appeal State Court Decisions* | *Citations to Authority* |
|---|---|---|---|---|---|---|---|
| PA | Commission seeks enforcement of order by filing petition in court together with transcript of record; court review of order will then commence. | No. | Yes. | State has no statutory requirements. | State has no statutory requirements. | Yes. | Pa. Stat. Ann. tit. 43, §§ 336.5, 960, 962. |
| RI | Complainant must file petition in superior court in the county where alleged unlawful practice occurred or where respondent resides or transacts business. Complainant must also send transcript of record of commission hearings. Complainant must serve copy of petition to commission and all parties who appeared before commission. Additionally, following proper filing of complaint, complainant can bring civil action by satisfying requirements for administrative release and terminating commission proceedings. | No. | Yes. | Yes. | State has no statutory requirements. | Yes, to state supreme court. | R.I. Gen. Laws §§ 28-5-24.1, 28-5-29, 28-5-30, 28-5-31, 28-5-33, 28-5-35. |
| SC | Aggrieved parties must serve copy of petition to commission and all parties of record within 120 days of commission order in circuit court in county where either alleged unlawful practice occurred or hearing was conducted.<br>If commission unable to secure conciliation agreement, commission may bring suit in equity in circuit court within 30 days after issuing reasonable cause determination. Action must be brought within 1 year of alleged violation, except when respondent gives written consent. | No. | Yes. | State has no statutory requirements. | State has no statutory requirements. | Yes. | S.C. Code Ann. §§ 1-13-90, 1-23-380, 1-23-390, 43-33-50. |

| | | | | | | | |
|---|---|---|---|---|---|---|---|
| SD | Complainant or respondent aggrieved by final order or refusal to issue order may obtain review. Commission may obtain enforcement order in proceeding. | No. | Yes. | Yes. | State has no statutory requirements. | Yes. | S.D. Codified Laws Ann. §§ 1-26-1, *et seq.*, 20-13-47, 20-13-52. |
| TN | Complainant must file petition in chancery court where alleged discrimination occurred, or where respondent resides or transacts business, within 30 days after order is petitioned. Additionally, complainant can bring action in chancery court if commission has not held a hearing within 90 days or has not issued a final order within 180 days after complaint was filed. | No. | Yes. | State has no statutory requirements. | State has no statutory requirements. | Yes. | Tenn. Code Ann. §§ 4-21-304, 4-21-307. |
| TX | If commission conciliation fails after reasonable cause determination, commission may bring action if majority of commission agrees. Complainant may bring suit within 60 days after receiving notice of commission determination and within two years after filing complaint. | Yes. | No. | Yes. | Yes. | State has no statutory requirements. | Tex. Lab. Code Ann. §§ 21.251–21.256, 21.262. |
| UT | Parties may appeal only final orders of commission within 30 days pursuant to Utah Administrative Procedure Act. | No. | Yes. | State has no statutory requirements. | State has no statutory requirements. | Yes, as provided by Utah Administrative Procedure Act. | Utah Code Ann. §§ 34-35-7.1, 63-46b-12, 63-46b-16. |
| VT | Aggrieved person may bring action in superior court. | State has no statutory requirements. | State has no statutory requirements. | State has no statutory requirements. | State has no statutory requirements. | State has no statutory requirements. | Vt. Stat. Ann. tit. 21, §§ 495, 495b. |
| VA | Commission may seek court relief with approval of attorney general. No private cause of action available. | State has no statutory requirements. | Yes. | Yes. | State has no statutory requirements. | State has no statutory requirements. | Va. Code Ann. §§ 2.1-721, 2.1-725. |
| WA | Aggrieved party or commission may obtain court review of administrative law judge's order. | State has no statutory requirements. | Yes. | State has no statutory requirements. | State has no statutory requirements. | Yes. | Wash. Rev. Code §§ 34.05 *et seq.*, 49.60.270. |
| WV | Either party may appeal to supreme court of appeals within 30 days of receiving final commission order. Court may then determine whether or not to grant review. Additionally, provided that statute of limitations has not expired, complainant can bring civil action 90 days after filing complaint with commission by satisfying requirements for administrative release. | No. | Yes. | State has no statutory requirements. | Yes. | Yes. | W. Va. Code §§ 5-11-11, 5-11-13, 29A-5-4. |

*(Table continues.)*

## Table 2.4-2 *(cont'd)*

## APPEAL OF FAIR EMPLOYMENT COMMISSION RULINGS AND ACCESS TO STATE COURT

(See also text at § 2.4[b].)

**KEY:** ***De novo.*** Court may issue ruling based on its assessment of facts, disregarding prior ruling from other agency or commission.

| | *Prerequisites to Filing Lawsuit in State Court* | *Court Can Examine Complaint* De Novo | *Court Can Review Commission Ruling* | *Commission Representation Available* | *Individual Representation Allowed* | *Can Appeal State Court Decisions* | *Citations to Authority* |
|---|---|---|---|---|---|---|---|
| WI | Commission's findings and orders are subject to review in the appropriate district court. | No. | Yes. | Yes. | Yes. | State has no statutory requirements. | Wis. Stat. Ann. §§ 111.395, 227.52, 227.53, 227.57. |
| WY | Any aggrieved party may file petition in district court within 30 days after copy of final commission decision is served. Copies of petition must be served on all parties of record. | No, except for alleged irregularities in commission proceedings not shown in the record. | Yes. | State has no statutory requirements. | State has no statutory requirements. | Yes, to Supreme Court. | Wyo. Stat. §§ 27-9-107, 27-9-108. |

# Table 2.4-3

## REMEDIES AVAILABLE TO COMPLAINANTS

(See also text at § 2.4[c].)

| | *Monetary Relief* | | | *Injunctive/Equitable Relief* | | | | | |
|---|---|---|---|---|---|---|---|---|---|
| | *Back Pay* | *Compensatory Damages* | *Punitive Damages* | *Pre-hearing Injunction* | *Hiring* | *Reinstatement* | *Promotion* | *Attorneys' Fees/Costs* | *Citations to Authority* |
| AL | — | — | — | — | — | — | — | — | State has no comprehensive FEP act. |
| AK | Yes. | Not specifically mentioned, but available if appropriate. | Not specifically mentioned, but available if appropriate. | Yes, commission may seek temporary relief in superior court. Injunction not to exceed 10 days without consent of respondent or court finding of reasonable cause of unlawful practice. | Yes. | Yes. | Yes. | Yes. | Alaska Stat. §§ 18.80.105, 18.80.130. |
| AZ | Yes, excluding interim earnings and limited to 2 years prior to filing charge. | Not specifically mentioned, but available if appropriate. | Not specifically mentioned, but available if appropriate. | Yes, commission may seek temporary relief in state court. | Yes. | Yes. | Yes. | Yes. | Ariz. Rev. Stat. Ann. § 41-1481. |
| AR | Yes, plus interest; limited to 2 years prior to filing charge. | Yes, $15,000–$300,000 depending on number of employees. | Yes, $15,000–$300,000 depending on number of employees. | State has no statutory requirements. | Not specifically mentioned, but available if appropriate. | Not specifically mentioned, but available if appropriate. | Not specifically mentioned, but available if appropriate. | Yes. | Ark. Code Ann. § 16-123-107. |
| CA | Yes, but limited by 2-year statute of limitations. | Yes, not to exceed $50,000. | Yes, civil penalty payable to claimant up to $25,000. Administrative fines may also apply, but not to entities. | Yes. | Yes. | Yes. | Yes. | Yes. | Cal. Gov't Code § 12970. |

(Table continues.)

## Table 2.4-3 *(cont'd)*

## REMEDIES AVAILABLE TO COMPLAINANTS

(See also text at § 2.4[c].)

| | *Monetary Relief* | | | *Injunctive/Equitable Relief* | | | | | |
|---|---|---|---|---|---|---|---|---|---|
| | *Back Pay* | *Compensatory Damages* | *Punitive Damages* | *Pre-hearing Injunction* | *Hiring* | *Reinstatement* | *Promotion* | *Attorneys' Fees/Costs* | *Citations to Authority* |
| CO | Yes. | State has no statutory requirements. | State has no statutory requirements. | State has no statutory requirements. | Yes. | Yes. | Yes. | State has no statutory requirements. | Colo. Rev. Stat. § 24-34-405. |
| CT | Yes, limited to 2 years prior to filing charge, excluding interim earnings. (Interim earnings from unemployment compensation reimbursed to appropriate governmental agency.) | Yes. | State has no statutory requirements. | Yes. | Yes. | Yes. | Not specifically mentioned, but available if appropriate. | Yes. | Conn. Gen. Stat. Ann. §§ 46a-86, 46a-89, 46a-89c. |
| DE | Yes, excluding interim earnings. | State has no statutory requirements. | State has no statutory requirements. | Yes, between commission's final ruling and decision on appeal. | Yes. | Yes. | Not specifically mentioned, but available if appropriate. | Yes. | Del. Code Ann. tit. 19, § 712. |
| DC | Yes. | Yes. | Not specifically mentioned, but available if appropriate. Courts have interpreted statute as permitting recovery of such damages in private civil actions. | Yes. | Yes. | Yes. | Yes. | Yes. | D.C. Code Ann. §§ 1-2547, 1-2553. |

| | | | | | | | | | |
|---|---|---|---|---|---|---|---|---|---|
| FL | Yes, limited to 2 years prior to complaint. | Yes, including, but not limited to damages for mental anguish, loss of dignity, and other intangible injuries. | Yes, not to exceed $100,000 (the state and its agencies and subdivisions excluded). | State has no statutory requirements. | Not specifically mentioned, but available if appropriate. | Not specifically mentioned, but available if appropriate. | Not specifically mentioned, but available if appropriate. | Yes, computed consistently with Title VII. | Fla. Stat. Ann. § 760.07, 760.11. |
| GA | Yes, limited to 2 years prior to complaint, excluding interim earnings. | Not specifically mentioned, but available if appropriate. | No. | State has no statutory requirements. | Yes. | Yes. | Yes. | Not specifically mentioned, but available if appropriate. | Ga. Code Ann. § 45-19-38. (Applies to public employment only.) *Kilmark v. Board of Regents*, 334 S.E. 2d 890 (Ga. App. 1985). |
| HI | Yes, limited to 2 years prior to complaint. | Yes. | Yes. | Yes. | Yes. | Yes. | Yes. | Yes; expert witness fees also recoverable. | Haw. Rev. Stat. §§ 368-17, 378-5. |
| ID | Yes, limited to 2 years prior to complaint. | Yes. | Yes, limited to $1,000 for each willful violation. | State has no statutory requirements. | Yes. | Yes. | Yes. | State has no statutory requirements. | Idaho Code § 67-5908. |
| IL | Yes, plus fringe benefits lost. | Yes. | State has no statutory requirements. | Yes. | Yes. | Yes. | Yes. | Yes. | 775 ILCS §§ 5/7-101, 5/7A-102, 5/8A-102, 5/8A-104. |
| IN | Yes. | No. | No. | State has no statutory requirements. | Yes. | Yes. | Yes. | Yes. | Ind. Code §§ 22-9-1-6, 22-9-1-12.1. |
| IA | Yes, reduced by interim earnings and unemployment compensation. | Yes. | State has no statutory requirements. | Yes. | Yes. | Yes. | Yes. | Yes. | Iowa Code Ann. §§ 216.5, 216.15. |
| KS | Yes, reduced by interim earnings. | Damages for "pain, suffering, and humiliation" available but limited to $2,000. | State has no statutory requirements. | State has no statutory requirements. | Yes. | Yes. | Yes. | State has no statutory requirements. | Kan. Stat. Ann. §§ 44-1005, 44-1042. |
| KY | Yes, reduced by interim earnings. | Yes, including but not limited to humiliation and embarrassment damages. | State has no statutory requirements. | Yes. | Yes. | Yes. | Yes. | Yes. | Ky. Rev. Stat. Ann. §§ 344.200, 344.230, 344.450. |

*(Table continues.)*

## Table 2.4-3 *(cont'd)*

## REMEDIES AVAILABLE TO COMPLAINANTS

(See also text at § 2.4[c].)

| | *Monetary Relief* | | | *Injunctive/Equitable Relief* | | | | | |
|---|---|---|---|---|---|---|---|---|---|
| | *Back Pay* | *Compensatory Damages* | *Punitive Damages* | *Pre-hearing Injunction* | *Hiring* | *Reinstatement* | *Promotion* | *Attorneys' Fees/Costs* | *Citations to Authority* |
| LA | Yes, reduced by interim earnings and amounts earnable. | Yes, including but not limited to humiliation and embarrassment damages. | State has no statutory requirements. | Yes, commission may seek temporary relief in district court. | Yes. | Yes. | Yes. | Yes. | La. Rev. Stat. Ann. §§ 23:301 *et seq.*, 51:2261, 51:2264. |
| ME | Yes. | No. | Yes, civil penalty damages of $1,000 for 1st violation, $2,000 for 2nd violation, and $3,000 for 3rd and subsequent violations. | Yes, commission may seek temporary relief in superior court. | Yes. | Yes. | State has no statutory requirements. | Yes, but in limited circumstances. | Me. Rev. Stat. Ann. tit. 5, §§ 4612, 4614, 4622. |
| MD | Yes, reduced by interim earnings and limited to a 36-month period. | Yes, limited to a 36-month period. | State has no statutory requirements. | Yes, commission may seek temporary relief in district court to prevent irreparable harm. | Yes. | Yes. | Not specifically mentioned, but available if appropriate. | State has no statutory requirements. | Md. Ann. Code art. 49B, §§ 4, 11. |
| MA | Yes. | Yes. | No. Statute makes available to age discrimination claimants damages of up to 3 times actual damages, but not less than 2 times actual damages, for willful discrimination. | Yes, aggrieved party may seek prehearing injunction in superior court to prevent irreparable injury. | Yes. | Yes. | Yes. | Yes. | Mass. Gen. Laws ch. 151B, §§ 5, 9. |

| | | | | | | | | | |
|---|---|---|---|---|---|---|---|---|---|
| MI | Yes. | Yes. | No. | Yes. | Yes. | Yes. | Yes. | Yes. | Mich. Comp. Laws §§ 37.2603, 37.2605, 37.2802. |
| MN | Yes. | Yes. | Yes, not to exceed $8,500. | Yes. | Yes. | Yes. | Yes. | Yes. | Minn. Stat. Ann. §§ 363.06, 363.071. |
| MS | — | — | — | — | — | — | — | — | State has no comprehensive FEP act. |
| MO | Yes. | Yes. | Yes. | Yes, attorney general can seek temporary relief on authority of commission. | State has no statutory requirements. | Yes. | Yes. | Yes. | Mo. Rev. Stat. §§ 213.075, 213.111, 213.126. |
| MT | Yes. The court order may require any reasonable measure to correct the discriminatory practice. | Yes. The court order may require any reasonable measure to correct the discriminatory practice. | Not generally. (Willful violators may be fined $500 maximum or imprisoned up to 6 months and found guilty of a misdemeanor.) | Yes. | Yes. The court order may require any reasonable measure to correct the discriminatory practice. | Yes. The court order may require any reasonable measure to correct the discriminatory practice. | Yes. The court order may require any reasonable measure to correct the discriminatory practice. | Yes. | Mont. Code Ann. §§ 49-2-503, 49-2-505, 49-2-506, 49-2-601, 49-3-308, 49-3-309. |
| NE | Yes, limited to 2 years prior to complaint, reduced by interim earnings. | State has no statutory requirements. | State has no statutory requirements. | State has no statutory requirements. | Yes. | Yes. | Not specifically mentioned, but available if appropriate. | Yes. | Neb. Rev. Stat. §§ 48-1119, 48-1120. |
| NV | Yes, limited to 2 years from last unlawful act, plus fringe benefits. | Yes. | No. | Yes. | Not specifically mentioned, but available if appropriate. | Yes. | Not specifically mentioned, but available if appropriate. | Yes. | Nev. Rev. Stat. §§ 233.170, 233.180, 608.140. |
| NH | Yes, reduced by any unemployment compensation or interim earnings received. | Yes. | Administrative fines up to $50,000 for repeat offenders. | Yes, between commission's final ruling and decision on appeal. | Yes. | Yes. | Yes. | Yes. | N.H. Rev. Stat. Ann. § 354-A:21. |
| NJ | Yes. | Yes. | Yes. | Yes. | State has no statutory requirements. | Yes. | Yes. | Yes. | N.J. Stat. Ann. §§ 10:5-17, 10:5-27.1; *Levinson v. Prentice-Hall, Inc.*, 868 F.2d 558 (3d Cir. 1989). |

*(Table continues.)*

# Table 2.4-3 *(cont'd)*

## REMEDIES AVAILABLE TO COMPLAINANTS

(See also text at § 2.4[c].)

| | *Monetary Relief* | | | *Injunctive/Equitable Relief* | | | | | |
|---|---|---|---|---|---|---|---|---|---|
| | *Back Pay* | *Compensatory Damages* | *Punitive Damages* | *Pre-hearing Injunction* | *Hiring* | *Reinstatement* | *Promotion* | *Attorneys' Fees/Costs* | *Citations to Authority* |
| NM | State has no statutory requirements. | Yes. | State has no statutory requirements. | State has no statutory requirements. | State has no statutory requirements. | State has no statutory requirements. | State has no statutory requirements. | Yes. | N.M. Stat. Ann. § 28-1-13; *Behrmann v. Phototron Corp.*, 795 P.2d 1015 (N.M. 1990); *Lucero v. Aladdin Beauty Colleges, Inc.*, 871 P.2d 365 (N.M. 1994). |
| NY | Yes. | Yes. | No. | Yes. | Yes. | Yes. | Yes. | State has no statutory requirements. | N.Y. Exec. Law § 297; *Wantagh Union Free School Dist. v. N.Y.S. Human Rights*, 505 N.Y.S. 2d 713 (1986); *Thoreson v. Penthouse International, Ltd.*, 606 N.E.2d 1369 (N.Y. 1992). |
| NC | State has no statutory requirements. Law says that remedies should be consistent with those provided for in federal statutes and regulations. | State has no statutory requirements. Law says that remedies should be consistent with those provided for in federal statutes and regulations. | State has no statutory requirements. Law says that remedies should be consistent with those provided for in federal statutes and regulations. | State has no statutory requirements. | State has no statutory requirements. Law says that remedies should be consistent with those provided for in federal statutes and regulations. | State has no statutory requirements. Law says that remedies should be consistent with those provided for in federal statutes and regulations. | State has no statutory requirements. Law says that remedies should be consistent with those provided for in federal statutes and regulations. | State has no statutory requirements. Law says that remedies should be consistent with those provided for in federal statutes and regulations. | N.C. Gen. Stat. §§ 126-36; N.C.Admin. Code tit. 25, §§ 1B.0434, 1C.0203, 1I.0203. (Applies to public employment only.) |
| ND | Yes, reduced by interim earnings and | State has no statutory requirements. | State has no statutory requirements. | Yes. | State has no statutory requirements. | State has no statutory requirements. | State has no statutory requirements. | Yes. | N.D. Cent. Code §§ 14-02.4-20, 14-02.4-21. |

| | | | | | | | | | |
|---|---|---|---|---|---|---|---|---|---|
| | limited to 2 years prior to complaint. | | | | | | | | |
| OH | Yes, reduced by interim earnings. | State has no statutory requirements. | Civil penalties may be awarded. | No. | Yes. | Yes. | Yes. | State has no statutory requirements. | Ohio Rev. Code Ann. §§ 4112.05, 4112.06, 4112.99. |
| OK | Yes. | State has no statutory requirements. | State has no statutory requirements. | Yes. | Yes. | Yes. | Not specifically mentioned, but available if appropriate. | Yes. | Okla. Stat. tit. 25, §§ 1502.1, 1505, 1901. |
| OR | Yes, limited to 2 years prior to complaint. | Yes, or $200, whichever is greater. | Yes, not to exceed $2,500. | Yes. | Yes. | Yes. | Any equitable relief, as appropriate. | Yes. | Or. Rev. Stat. §§ 20.107, 240.560, 659.035, 659.050, 659.121. |
| PA | Yes. | Yes. | State has no statutory requirements. Courts have divided on availability of punitive damages under Pennsylvania law. | Yes, commission may seek temporary relief in state court. | Yes. | Yes. | Yes. | Yes. | Pa. Stat. Ann. tit. 43, §§ 959, 959.2, 961.2, 962. |
| RI | Yes. | Yes, for intentional discrimination. | Yes, by court order for malice, ill will, or reckless indifference. Punitive damages shall not be available against the state or its political subdivisions. | Yes, between commission's final ruling and decision on appeal. | Yes. | Yes. | Yes. | Yes. | R.I. Gen. Laws §§ 28-5-24, 28-5-29.1. |
| SC | Yes, reduced by interim earnings and amounts earnable; limited to 2 years prior to complaint. | State has no statutory requirements. | Civil penalties not in excess of $5,000 are available to handicapped persons aggrieved by discrimination. | State has no statutory requirements. | Yes. | Yes. | Yes. | State has no statutory requirements. Available to complainants filing under separate statute. | S.C. Code Ann. §§ 1-13-90, 43-33-540. |

*(Table continues.)*

# **Table 2.4-3** *(cont'd)*

## REMEDIES AVAILABLE TO COMPLAINANTS

(See also text at § 2.4[c].)

| | *Monetary Relief* | | | *Injunctive/Equitable Relief* | | | | | |
|---|---|---|---|---|---|---|---|---|---|
| | *Back Pay* | *Compensatory Damages* | *Punitive Damages* | *Pre-hearing Injunction* | *Hiring* | *Reinstatement* | *Promotion* | *Attorneys' Fees/Costs* | *Citations to Authority* |
| SD | Yes. | Yes, excluding damages for pain and suffering. | No. Repeat offenders and parties that fail to comply with the commission's orders may be assessed a civil penalty not to exceed $10,000. | State has no statutory requirements. | Yes. | Yes. | Yes. | Yes, only in a court action. | S.D. Codified Laws Ann. §§ 20-12-6, 20-13-35.1, 20-13-42, 20-13-47. |
| TN | Yes, excluding interim earnings or amounts earnable with due diligence. | Yes, including damages for humiliation and embarrassment. | State has no statutory requirements. While the statute does not specifically provide for such relief, remedies necessary and proper to eliminate discrimination are available. | State has no statutory requirements. | Yes. | Yes. | Yes. | Yes. | Tenn. Code Ann. §§ 4-21-306, 4-21-311. |
| TX | Yes, excluding interim earnings and limited to 2 years prior to complaint. | Yes, $50,000–$300,000, depending on number of employees. | Yes, $50,000–$300,000, depending on number of employees. Punitive damages shall not be available against a governmental entity. | Yes, provided that there is a substantial likelihood of success on the merits, and irreparable harm would befall complainant without such intervention. | Yes. | Yes. | Yes. | Yes. | Tex. Lab. Code Ann. §§ 21.210, 21.258, 21.259. |

| | | | | | | | | | |
|---|---|---|---|---|---|---|---|---|---|
| UT | Yes. | State has no statutory requirements. While the statute does not specifically provide for such relief, it says that the remedies are not necessarily limited to those named by law. | State has no statutory requirements. While the statute does not specifically provide for such relief, it says that the remedies are not necessarily limited to those named by law. | Yes, between commission's final ruling and decision on appeal. | State has no statutory requirements. While the statute does not specifically provide for such relief, it says that the remedies are not necessarily limited to those named by law. | Yes. | State has no statutory requirements. While the statute does not specifically provide for such relief, it says that the remedies are not necessarily limited to those named by law. | Yes. | Utah Code Ann. § 34-35-7.1. |
| VT | Yes. | Not specifically mentioned, but available if appropriate. | Yes. Civil penalties of not more than $10,000 may be imposed. | Yes, attorney general can seek temporary relief on authority of commission. | Not specifically mentioned, but available if appropriate. | Yes. | Not specifically mentioned, but available if appropriate. | Yes. | Vt. Stat. Ann. tit. 3, §§ 1002, 1003; tit. 9, §§ 2458–2460, 4552, 4553; tit. 21, §§ 495b, 495e. |
| VA | Yes, by court order only. | Yes. | Yes. | State has no statutory requirements. | Yes. | Yes. | Yes. | Yes. | Va. Code Ann. §§ 2.1-720.14, 2.1-725, 40.1-28.6, 51.5-40 *et seq.* |
| WA | Yes. | Yes. Maximum damages of $10,000 for humiliation and mental suffering. | State has no statutory requirements. | State has no statutory requirements. | Yes. | Yes. | Yes. | Yes. | Wash. Rev. Code §§ 49.60.030, 49.60.250; Wash. Admin. Code §§ 162-08-015, 162-08-062, 162-08-298. |
| WV | Yes. | State has no statutory requirements. Court has ruled that incidental damages for humiliation, embarrassment, emotional distress, and loss of dignity are available. | State has no statutory requirements. | State has no statutory requirements. | Yes. | Yes. | Yes. | Yes. | W. Va. Code § 5-11-10; W. Va. Admin. Reg. § 77-2-9; *State Human Rights Comm'n v. Pearlman Realty Agency*, 239 S.E.2d 145 (1977). |

*(Table continues.)*

**Table 2.4-3** *(cont'd)*

## REMEDIES AVAILABLE TO COMPLAINANTS

(See also text at § 2.4[c].)

| | *Monetary Relief* | | | *Injunctive/Equitable Relief* | | | | | |
|---|---|---|---|---|---|---|---|---|---|
| | *Back Pay* | *Compensatory Damages* | *Punitive Damages* | *Pre-hearing Injunction* | *Hiring* | *Reinstatement* | *Promotion* | *Attorneys' Fees/Costs* | *Citations to Authority* |
| WI | Yes, limited to 2 years prior to complaint. | State has no statutory requirements. Court has held compensatory and punitive damages not available under state law. | State has no statutory requirements. Court has held compensatory and punitive damages not available under state law. | State has no statutory requirements. | Yes, or compensation in lieu thereof for specific violations enumerated in state statute. | Yes, or compensation in lieu thereof, but not more than 1,000 times, or less than 500 times, former hourly wage. | State has no statutory requirements. While statute does not specifically provide for such relief, it says that remedies are not necessarily limited to those named by law. | State has no statutory requirements. Court has held reasonable attorneys' fees recoverable. | Wis. Stat. Ann. § 111.39; *Bachand v. Connecticut Gen. Life Ins. Co.*, 305 N.W.2d 149 (1981); *Watkins v. Labor & Industrial Review Comm'n*, 345 N.W. 2d 482 (1984). |
| WY | Yes. | State has no statutory requirements. | State has no statutory requirements. | State has no statutory requirements. | Yes. | Yes. | Yes. | State has no statutory requirements. | Wyo. Stat. §§ 24-4-303, 27-9-106, 27-9-107. |

# § 2.5 Additional Laws and Affirmative Action

## [a] Additional State Laws

The preceding tables in this Part generally reflect fair employment provisions contained under a single antidiscrimination statute in each state. In addition to these broad antidiscrimination statutes, a number of states have enacted separate statutory provisions that prohibit specific types of discrimination in employment practices. Table 2.5-1 shows states that have adopted additional, separate statutes applicable to employers and briefly outlines their provisions. A "No" entry in this table means that the state has not prohibited the specified type of discrimination by a *separate* statute; however, such a prohibition may be contained in the state's comprehensive FEP law. It is therefore important to consult Table 2.3-1, Parts A and B, to obtain complete information.

## [b] Affirmative Action Requirements

A number of states have adopted programs similar to the federal government's contracts program by requiring state contractors to develop affirmative action plans (AAPs). Generally, state programs are similar in scope to the federal programs and require the same types of plans, goals, and timetables. Therefore, compliance with the federal program may satisfy state requirements as well.

Table 2.5-2 shows states that have imposed affirmative action obligations on state contractors and on themselves. Because states often view themselves as "model" employers, they generally impose the same—or even more stringent—requirements on themselves as they impose on the business community.

## [c] Assessing the Validity of Affirmative Action Plans and Requirements

In the last decade, the United States Supreme Court and lower federal and state courts have gradually moved toward a more restrictive view of the kind and scope of affirmative action plans that can be upheld under the equal protection clause. Two recent decisions, *Adarand v. Pena*[1] and *Hopwood v. State of Texas,*[2] underscore this trend. In many cases, state and local legislatures have failed to keep up with Supreme Court jurisprudence on affirmative action plans, with the result that some state and local affirmative action plans that are in effect may no longer be constitutional. Government contract set-asides and mandated affirmative action plans are especially vulnerable to this gap between state and federal jurisprudence.

Because of the potential pitfalls presented by this situation, human resources professionals and corporate counsel must determine whether implementing or continuing a particular affirmative action plan may subject the employer to liability for reverse discrimination. The following discussion of recent decisions regarding affirmative action plans is designed to provide some guidance in making the determination.

**Government Mandated Affirmative Action Plans.** In 1989, the United States Supreme Court struck down a 30 percent minority subcontractor set-aside pro-

**§ 2.5**

1. 115 S. Ct. 2097 (1995).
2. 78 F.3d 932 (5th Cir. 1996).

vision enacted by the City Council of Richmond, Virginia. The Court found that the set-aside violated the Equal Protection Clause of the Fourteenth Amendment.[3] The Supreme Court's decision in *Croson* was significant in that it set out firm criteria for analyzing affirmative action plans, and, as a result of the Supreme Court's recent decision in *Adarand v. Pena,*[4] these criteria now apply to all affirmative action plans mandated by federal, state, or local government.

In *Croson,* the Court interpreted the Fourteenth Amendment to require "strict scrutiny" of the city's use of race-based classifications to award city contracts and rejected the argument that a remedial purpose excused the use of race as a deciding criterion in subcontractor selection. The Court then set out two general elements that must be met for state and local affirmative action plans to survive this strict scrutiny:

1. There must be a strong basis in evidence for the government's assertion that remedial action is necessary, and the interest served by the use of the preference must be "compelling."
2. The affirmative action plan must be "narrowly tailored" so that it remedies only the effects of past discrimination and goes no further.

More specifically, the Court stated that the compelling state interest requirement is not met by generalized findings of past societal discrimination against a protected class:

> While there is no doubt that the sorry history of both private and public discrimination in this country has contributed to a lack of opportunities for black entrepreneurs, this observation, standing alone, cannot justify a rigid racial quota in the awarding of public contracts . . . an amorphous claim that there has been past discrimination in a particular industry cannot justify the use of an unyielding racial quota.[5]

The Court found especially troubling Richmond's reliance on statistics that showed that minority-owned firms received a disproportionately small percentage of subcontracts in the construction industry compared to the minority population in Richmond as a whole. Noting that the construction industry is highly specialized, and further, that Richmond is in large part a minority city, the Court articulated its rather stringent compelling interest evidentiary requirement:

> In the employment context, we have recognized that for certain entry level positions or positions requiring minimal training, statistical comparisons of the racial composition of an employer's work force to the racial composition of the relevant population may be probative of a pattern of discrimination. [Citation omitted.] But where special qualifications are necessary, the relevant statistical pool for purposes of demonstrating discriminatory exclusion must be the number of minorities qualified to undertake the particular task.[6]

The Court also rejected Richmond's claim that its plan was narrowly tailored, because the means chosen (a 30 percent set-aside) did not consider less discriminatory measures.[7] The Supreme Court's decision in *Croson,* and the reiteration of the reasoning of that decision in *Adarand,* calls into question the constitutionality of set-aside affirmative action programs currently in effect in several states.[8]

Although controversial when handed down, *Croson* did not prove to be an anomaly; in 1995, the Court extended strict scrutiny to plans mandated by the federal government as well.[9] The clear message taken from these opinions is that affirmative action plans that set aside contracts for minority-owned firms in large measure no longer meet the requirements of the Fourteenth Amendment.

Likewise, the Supreme Court has indicated that strict scrutiny is to be applied to any state employment initiatives granting preference on the basis of race. In *Wygant,*[10] the Court held that a school board's interest in "providing minority role models for its minority students, as an attempt to alleviate the effects of societal discrimination" is not a compelling interest that could justify the use of racial preferences in layoff decisions.[11] In *United*

3. City of Richmond v. J.A. Croson Co., 488 U.S. 469 (1989).

4. 115 S. Ct. 2097 (1995).

5. Id. at 724.

6. Id. at 726.

7. Id. at 729.

8. It appears that certain affirmative action requirements involving state contract awards in California, Illinois, New Jersey, and Tennessee may not pass muster under the rigorous strict scrutiny demanded by the *Croson* Court. In addition, Adarand v. Pena, 115 S. Ct. 2097 (1995), extended to the federal government the requirements articulated in *Croson,* a move that brings the constitutionality of the District of Columbia's set-aside contracting directives into question. See Table 2.5-2.

9. Adarand v. Pena, 115 S. Ct. 2097 (1995).

10. Wygant v. Jackson Board of Education, 476 U.S. 267 (1986).

11. Id. at 274.

*States v. Paradise,*[12] however, the Court indicated that race-based government employment decisions were not *per se* unconstitutional. In *Paradise,* the Court held that a one-black-for-one-white promotion requirement implemented as an interim measure by the Alabama Department of Public Safety was permissible under the Fourteenth Amendment's Equal Protection Clause, even under strict scrutiny analysis. The Court found the plan narrowly tailored to serve its compelling purpose of eliminating the effects of long-term, open, and pervasive discrimination, which included the complete exclusion of blacks from upper levels of the department.

According to a recent decision from the Fifth Circuit Court of Appeals, *Croson* and *Adarand* dictate that a desire to effect racial balance no longer may serve as a justification for affirmative action plans.[13] *Hopwood* dealt with state-funded law school admission decisions rather than employment, but its reasoning is clearly applicable in the context of affirmative action plans implemented by employers. The decision is indicative of a growing judicial skepticism regarding the contention that racial diversity, in itself, is a sufficient justification for race-based affirmative action plans. The United States Supreme Court denied review of the *Hopwood* decision, and therefore the issue of the extent to which diversity may serve as a justification for affirmative action is not completely settled.

It is significant to note that *Hopwood* has been followed by other federal courts. A federal district court in Ohio applied the *Hopwood* rationale in striking down a minority set-aside provision applicable to city construction projects.[14]

Recent decisions from state courts, however, indicate that the debate over affirmative action will continue for some time. The Nevada Supreme Court recently upheld a state university's affirmative action policy, finding that because whites held 87 to 89 percent of full-time faculty positions and blacks only 1 percent, the university had demonstrated a compelling interest in fostering a culturally and ethnically diverse faculty. The court further held that the university's minority bonus policy, under which race was only one of several factors used in evaluating applicants, and which allowed a department to hire an additional faculty member following the initial placement of a minority candidate, was narrowly tailored to accelerate racial diversity.[15]

The Louisiana Supreme Court has held that the equal protection clause in Louisiana's state constitution was not intended to allow for race-conscious affirmative action programs.[16] Accordingly, the court struck down the minority set-aside provisions of the Louisiana Minority and Women's Business Enterprise Act, which permitted only certified minority business enterprises to bid on public contracts designated as minority set-aside projects.

**Voluntary Affirmative Action Plans.** In *United Steelworkers v. Weber,*[17] the Supreme Court held that, although Title VII protects members of a minority from discriminatory treatment, it also permits some voluntary race-conscious steps designed to rectify racial imbalances. In *Weber,* the employer and the union representing its employees agreed on a plan to rectify an almost total absence of minorities in the employer's skilled crafts. Under the plan, an on-the-job training program was set up that was to be 50 percent black, by its terms. The Supreme Court stated that to hold that Title VII forbids all voluntary race-conscious remedial schemes would "bring about an end completely at variance with the purpose of the statute." The Court held that, although some affirmative action plans might go too far in favoring minorities and thus violate Title VII, the one presented in *Weber* did not. The Court's decision in *Weber* thus left for further litigation the precise boundaries of permissible affirmative action.

Since *Weber,* the Supreme Court has defined more clearly the boundaries of permissible affirmative action plans. In *Johnson v. Transportation Agency,*[18] the Court upheld against a Title VII attack a voluntary affirmative action plan and articulated a two-part test to measure validity when an employer asserts a voluntary affirmative action plan as justification for a race- or gender-conscious employment decision as follows:

1. Consideration of race or gender must be justified by a manifest imbalance that reflects underrepresentation of women or minorities, and

12. 480 U.S. 149 (1987).

13. Hopwood v. State of Texas, 78 F.3d 932 (5th Cir. 1996).

14. Associated General Contractors v. City of Columbus, 936 F. Supp. 1363 (S.D. Ohio 1996).

15. University and Community College System of Nevada v. Farmer, 930 P.2d 730 (Nev. 1997).

16. Louisiana Associated General Contractors v. State, through Division of Admin., Office of State Purchasing, 669 So.2d 1185 (La. 1996).

17. 443 U.S. 193 (1979).

18. 480 U.S. 616 (1987).

2. The voluntary affirmative action plan must not unnecessarily trammel the rights of nonminority employees or create an absolute bar to their advancement.

Decisions in the circuit courts have further defined the point at which a voluntary affirmative action plan becomes prohibited reverse discrimination. Not surprisingly, litigation over voluntary affirmative action plans focuses on whether a manifest imbalance exists to justify the plan and on whether the plan unnecessarily trammels the rights of nonminority employees.

With respect to the requirement that a plan must be justified by a manifest imbalance, it has been held that an affirmative action plan based solely on a finding that a disparity existed between the percentage of minorities in a city's population as a whole and the percentage of minorities in the city's police and fire departments is not a sufficient basis to implement such a plan. Rather, the statistical comparison should focus on the relevant qualified labor pool, not the general population, to determine whether a manifest imbalance exists sufficient to justify affirmative action.[19]

With respect to the impact of the plan on nonminority employees, the Second Circuit Court of Appeals has held that layoffs of white teachers exclusively, in order to benefit minority group teachers, is an impermissible means of rectifying past injustices.[20]

**Conclusion.** As the foregoing discussion shows, it is in the employer's interest to review proposed or currently applied affirmative action plans, both government-mandated and voluntary, to ensure that they are within the acceptable parameters defined by the courts. If a government-mandated plan currently being implemented by the employer appears to be invalid, the agency charged with enforcing the affirmative action requirements should be consulted to determine whether any changes to agency interpretation or enforcement have been made.

### [d] California's Civil Rights Initiative and Other Legislative Efforts to End Affirmative Action

On November 5, 1996, the voters of California adopted Proposition 209, the California Civil Rights Initiative (CCRI), by a margin of 54–46 percent. The provision was designed to end government-sponsored or government-mandated affirmative action. As a result of the passage of the CCRI, Article I, Section 31 of the California Constitution was amended to provide as follows:

> The state shall not discriminate against, or grant preferential treatment to, any individual or group on the basis of race, sex, color, ethnicity, or national origin in the operation of public employment, public education, or public contracting.

This provision effectively invalidates state and local government affirmative action plans.

A federal district court had issued an injunction against enforcement of the provision, effectively delaying its implementation.[21] The Ninth Circuit Court of Appeals reversed the district court decision, however, and lifted the injunction.[22] A petition for discretionary review was filed with the United States Supreme Court. The Supreme Court denied the petition, allowing the ruling of the Court of Appeals to stand and clearing the way for the implementation of the CCRI.

The CCRI has inspired a number of similar efforts across the country. In Colorado, for example, a bill was introduced that would have barred the state, its agencies, universities, and community colleges from considering race, color, ethnicity, national origin, gender, or religion of any person as a factor in any decision pertaining to public employment, public education, or public contracting.[23] The bill was considered a likely target of a veto by the Governor, however, and was ultimately scuttled in committee and reduced to a study of affirmative action. A second bill has been introduced that would submit the issue to the voters.[24]

A bill that contains virtually the same language as the CCRI is also pending in the Alabama Senate, after passing the Alabama Senate Governmental Affairs Committee unanimously. Despite its unanimous approval at the committee level, even some supporters of the bill have predicted that it will fail. If the bill passes the legislature, it still must be approved by the voters in a statewide referendum before it would take effect.

---

19. Cygnar v. Chicago, 865 F.2d 827 (7th Cir. 1989); Janowiak v. South Bend, 836 F.2d 1034 (7th Cir. 1987); Hammon v. Barry, 826 F.2d 73 (D.C. Cir. 1987).

20. Crumpton v. Bridgeport Educ. Ass'n, 993 F.2d 1023 (2d Cir. 1993).

21. Coalition for Economic Equity v. Wilson, 946 F. Supp. 1480 (N.D. Cal. 1996).

22. Coalition for Economic Equity, et al. v. Wilson, 110 F.3d 1431, 1997 (9th Cir. 1997).

23. Colo. H.B. 1299.

24. Colo. H.B. 1336.

In Washington state, supporters of the Washington State Civil Rights Initiative have succeeded in placing the measure on the ballot for November 1998. Modeled on California's Proposition 209, the initiative would end race and sex preferences in state and local government hiring and contracting.

The American Civil Rights Coalition, a Sacramento organization formed by supporters of Proposition 209, has stated that similar efforts to roll back affirmative action are underway in Florida and Ohio. A measure that would have repealed a local affirmative action law was rejected by voters in the City of Houston. The Ninth Circuit decision upholding the validity of the CCRI will likely encourage efforts in other states. In light of these legislative initiatives and recent court decisions striking down affirmative action plans, human resources professionals should take care to keep abreast of the current status of affirmative action in all states in which their employers operate.

# Table 2.5-1
## ADDITIONAL PROHIBITIONS UNDER STATE FAIR EMPLOYMENT PRACTICE STATUTES

(See also text at § 2.5[a].)

**NOTE:** A "No" entry merely means that the specified type of discrimination is not prohibited by *separate* statutory provision, but such discrimination may be prohibited by the state's general fair employment statute. See Table 2.3-1 Part A and Table 2.3-1 Part B for further information.

| | *Age Discrimination* | *Handicap Discrimination* | *Veterans' Discrimination* | *Pay Discrimination* | *Discrimination by State Government Contractors* | *Other Requirements of Additional Laws* | *Citations to Authority* |
|---|---|---|---|---|---|---|---|
| AL | Yes, age 40 and over. Applies to employers of 20 or more. | Yes, state's policy is to employ physically handicapped in state service on same terms and conditions as the able-bodied. | No. | No. | No. | Prohibits discrimination in municipal positions on basis of race, sex, and political or religious affiliation. Any health care worker knowingly infected with HIV or Hepatitis B must notify the State Health Officer before performing invasive procedures. Information regarding any infected health care worker is deemed confidential. | Ala. Code §§ 11-43A-45, 21-7-8, 22-11A-60 *et seq.*, 25-1-20–25-1-29. |
| AK | No. | No. | No. | No. | No. | Discrimination against mental illness is prohibited; polygraph testing is prohibited; employees employed by the same employer for at least 35 hours a week for at least six consecutive months or for at least 17½ hours a week for at least 12 consecutive months may request family leave. | Alaska Stat. §§ 23.10.037, 23.10.500, 47.30.865. |
| AZ | Yes, age 40 and over. | Yes, prohibits discrimination against persons treated by government mental health agencies and persons with developmental disabilities; handicapped persons are given preference for civil service. | Yes, veterans are given preference for civil service. | Yes, prohibits sex-based wage discrimination. | Yes, employment discrimination is prohibited in state government contracts by government contractors and subcontractors. | State government employers may not discriminate on the basis of use or nonuse of tobacco products. | Ariz. Rev. Stat. Ann. §§ 23-341, 36-506, 36-551.01, 36-601-02, 38-492, 41-1465; Az. Ex. Or. 75-5 (4/28/75). |

| | | | | | | | |
|---|---|---|---|---|---|---|---|
| AR | Prohibited in public employment (age 40 and over). | Yes, state has policy of providing employment for physically handicapped persons on the same terms and conditions as the able-bodied. | Yes, veterans and their widows or widowers are given preference for civil service. | Yes, prohibits sex-based wage discrimination for comparable work. | Yes, discrimination based on race, color, creed, national origin, or ancestry in state contracts is prohibited. | None. | Ark. Code Ann. §§ 11-4-601, 11-4-610, 20-14-301, 21-3-202. |
| CA | No. | No. | Yes, veterans are given preference in retention for civil service layoffs. | Yes, prohibits sex-based wage discrimination. | Yes, discrimination in public works employment based on race, religion, color, national origin, ancestry, physical handicap, medical condition, marital status, or sex is prohibited. | Blood test for detecting AIDS cannot be used to determine insurability or suitability for employment. Discrimination based on sexual orientation and political activities or political affiliation is prohibited. Family leave law is applicable to employers of 50 or more employees, and it prohibits discrimination against employees requesting leave who have more than 12 months of service and at least 1250 hours of service within the previous 12-month period. Employers cannot seek information regarding an arrest that did not result in a conviction or a conviction that was sealed or expunged. It is unlawful for an employee to be denied an employment benefit based on height or weight unless pursuant to a permissible defense. Forbidding or preventing employee from participating in politics is prohibited. | Cal. Govt. Code §§ 12990, 19997.7; Cal. Lab. Code §§ 1101, 1102.1, 1197.5; Cal. Health & Safety Code § 121025. |
| CO | No. | No. | Yes, veterans are given preference for civil service hirings and protection from layoffs. | Yes, prohibits sex-based wage discrimination. | Yes, state residents are given preference in public works contracts. Discrimination based on race, color, creed, sex, age, or religion in employing persons for public works financed in whole or in part by the state is prohibited. | Employers are prohibited from requiring applicants to disclose sealed arrest records. | Colo. Rev. Stat. §§ 8-5-102, 8-17-101, 8-17-102, 24-72-308; Colo. Const. art. XII, § 15. |

*(Table continues.)*

# Table 2.5-1 *(cont'd)*

## ADDITIONAL PROHIBITIONS UNDER STATE FAIR EMPLOYMENT PRACTICE STATUTES

(See also text at § 2.5[a].)

**NOTE:** A "No" entry merely means that the specified type of discrimination is not prohibited by *separate* statutory provision, but such discrimination may be prohibited by the state's general fair employment statute. See Table 2.3-1 Part A and Table 2.3-1 Part B for further information.

| | *Age Discrimination* | *Handicap Discrimination* | *Veterans' Discrimination* | *Pay Discrimination* | *Discrimination by State Government Contractors* | *Other Requirements of Additional Laws* | *Citations to Authority* |
|---|---|---|---|---|---|---|---|
| CT | No. | Yes, prohibits discrimination based on mental retardation, learning disability, physical disability, or present or past history of mental disorder. | No. | Yes, prohibits sex-based wage discrimination. | Yes, discrimination by state contractors based on race, color, religion, age, marital status, national origin, ancestry, sex, sexual orientation, mental retardation, or physical disabilities is prohibited. | Family leave law prohibits discrimination against person requesting leave; employers with 20 or more employees may not reduce medical insurance coverage when employee or spouse reaches age 65. Discrimination on basis of tobacco use outside the workplace is prohibited. It is unlawful to disclose the results of HIV-related tests, except for specified safety purposes or when authorized or ordered by a court. Employers may not condition employment, transfer, or promotion on the sterilization of employee. | Conn. Gen. Stat. Ann. §§ 4a-60, 4a-60a, 5-248a, 19a-583, 31-40j, 31-40s, 31-40t, 31-75, 46a-60, 46a-61. |
| DE | No. | Yes, prohibits discrimination in employment based on handicap (physical or mental impairment) limiting 1 or more major life activities. | Yes, veterans are given preference in state employment. | Yes, prohibits sex-based wage discrimination. | Yes, discrimination by state contractors with regard to race, creed, color, sex, or national origin is prohibited. | Polygraph testing is prohibited. | Del. Code Ann. tit. 19 §§ 704, 717, 724, 1107A; tit. 29 §§ 6519A, 6920. |
| DC | No. | Yes, persons interfering with equal employment rights of physically handicapped may be fined up to $300 and imprisoned up to 90 days. | Yes, veterans are given preference in state employment. | No. | Yes, discrimination in employment by government contractors based on race, color, religion, national origin, sex, age, marital status, personal appearance, sexual orientation, family responsibilities, matriculation, political affilia- | Discrimination on basis of tobacco use is prohibited. No person shall be denied public or private employment because of receiving services for mental retardation. Employees are entitled to 16 workweeks of family or medical leave during any 24-month period. | D.C. Code Ann. §§ 1-607.3, 1-1185.8, 6-913.3, 6-1705, 6-1707, 6-1974, 36-1301, *et seq.* |

| | | | | | | | |
|---|---|---|---|---|---|---|---|
| | | | | | tion, or physical handicaps is prohibited. Discovery of willful noncompliance with antidiscrimination requirements may make government liable only for actual costs of services and materials for remainder of contract. | | |
| FL | Yes, for public employment. | Yes. (Persons with AIDS are protected as handicapped.) | Yes, veterans are given preference for employment in state agencies and in retention in the event of layoffs. | Yes, sex-based wage discrimination by employers with two or more employees is prohibited. Wage discrimination based on race or marital status is also prohibited. | No. | Employer may not use results of AIDS test to determine whether person is eligible for disability, health, or life insurance, or to screen or determine a person's suitability for or discharge from employment. Discrimination based on sickle cell trait is prohibited. Parental and family leave allowed for state career service employees. | Fla. Stat. Ann. §§ 110.221, 112.042–112.044, 295.07, 448.07, 448.075, 760.10, 760.50. |
| GA | Yes, prohibits employment discrimination against persons aged 40–70. | Yes, prohibits discrimination by employers with 15 or more employees against persons with physical or mental disabilities that substantially limit one or more major life activities. | Veterans given preference for civil service positions. | Yes, sex-based wage discrimination by employers with ten or more employees is prohibited. | No. | Results of AIDS test and related information are deemed confidential; state agencies cannot discriminate against wives of servicemen. | Ga. Code Ann. §§ 24-9-47, 34-1-2, 34-5-3, 34-6A-1 *et seq.*, 45-2-9, 45-2-21. |
| HI | No. | No. | No. | Yes, wage discrimination based on race, religion, or sex is prohibited. | No. | Employer may not condition employment on disclosure of AIDS test information. Employers with more than 100 employees for each working day during each of 20 or more calendar weeks must provide up to four weeks of family leave in any 12-month period. | Haw. Rev. Stat. §§ 325-101, 387-4, 398-1 *et seq.* |
| ID | No. | Yes, prohibits discrimination against disabled by any employer receiving state funds. | Yes, veterans are given preference for public employment. | Yes, requires equal pay for equal work, regardless of sex. | No. | Freedom from discrimination on basis of race, creed, color, sex, national origin, or ancestry is a civil right; violation is a misdemeanor. | Idaho Code §§ 44-1702, 56-707, 65-502. |

*(Table continues.)*

# **Table 2.5-1** *(cont'd)*

## ADDITIONAL PROHIBITIONS UNDER STATE FAIR EMPLOYMENT PRACTICE STATUTES

(See also text at § 2.5[a].)

**NOTE:** A "No" entry merely means that the specified type of discrimination is not prohibited by *separate* statutory provision, but such discrimination may be prohibited by the state's general fair employment statute. See Table 2.3-1 Part A and Table 2.3-1 Part B for further information.

| | *Age Discrimination* | *Handicap Discrimination* | *Veterans' Discrimination* | *Pay Discrimination* | *Discrimination by State Government Contractors* | *Other Requirements of Additional Laws* | *Citations to Authority* |
|---|---|---|---|---|---|---|---|
| IL | No. | No. | Yes, veterans are given preference for public works projects and civil service positions. | Yes, requires equal pay for equal work, regardless of sex. | Yes, discrimination in public works employment based on race, color, religion, sex, national origin, ancestry, age, marital status, physical or mental handicap, or unfavorable military discharge is prohibited. Contractors must have written sexual harassment policies and procedures; discrimination in employment under defense contract is prohibited under separate law. | Illinois Constitution prohibits employment discrimination based on race, color, creed, national ancestry, sex, or physical or mental handicap. Results of AIDS test and related information are deemed confidential. Discrimination based on lawful use of lawful products is prohibited. | 65 ILCS § 5/10-1-16; 410 ILCS §§ 305/9 *et seq.*; 775 ILCS § 5/2-105; 820 ILCS § 55/5; Const. art. I §§ 17–19. |
| IN | Yes, prohibits discrimination against persons between ages 40 and 69. | Yes, prohibits discrimination based on physical or mental impairment and against former users of illegal drugs who are enrolled in or have completed a drug rehabilitation program. | No. | Yes, provides for equal pay for equal work. | Yes, prohibits discrimination based on race, religion, color, sex, national origin or ancestry in public works contracts; violation may be deemed a material breach. Under separate statute, contractors violating antidiscrimination requirements may be fined $5 per person per day; subsequent violation could result in contract cancellation and forfeiture of money due. | Employment discrimination based on person's moral beliefs concerning abortion is prohibited. AIDS test results are deemed confidential. Discrimination based on use of tobacco products outside the workplace is prohibited. | Ind. Code §§ 5-16-6-1, 16-1-9.5-7, 16-34-1-6, 22-5-4-1, 22-9-1-10, 22-9-1-12.1, 22-9-2-1 *et seq.*, 22-9-5-1 *et seq.* |

| | | | | | | | |
|---|---|---|---|---|---|---|---|
| IA | No. | Yes, in state employment. | Yes, discrimination against employees on active military duty is prohibited. | Yes, requires equal pay for comparable work. | No. | Genetic testing as a condition of employment is prohibited. | Iowa Code Ann. §§ 29A.43, 70A.18, 216C.2, 729.6. |
| KS | Yes, prohibits discrimination against persons 18 years and older. | No. | Yes, veterans are given preference for civil service positions; veterans and their widows, widowers, or orphans are given preference in retention in the event of layoffs. | Yes, requires equal pay for equal work, regardless of sex. | Yes, prohibits discrimination based on race, religion, color, sex, disability, national origin, or ancestry in public works contracts. | Results of AIDS tests and related information are deemed confidential. Neither the state nor its agencies may enact any height requirements as a condition for employment. | Kan. Stat. Ann. §§ 44-1030, 44-1110 *et seq.,* 44-1205, 65-6002, 73-201, 75-2955. |
| KY | Yes, prohibits discrimination against individuals aged 40–70. | Yes, prohibits discrimination based on physical handicap, unless there is a bona fide occupational qualification. Physical handicap means a substantial disability that can be demonstrated by accepted medical technologies. Persons with AIDS are protected as handicapped. | Yes, veterans are given preference for classified civil service positions. | Yes, provides for equal pay for comparable work. | Yes, prohibits discrimination based on race, color, religion, sex, age, or national origin in public works contracts. | Employer cannot require as a condition of employment that employee work on the Sabbath, nor can employer discriminate in hiring or retraining employees on that basis. Specific protection required for individuals with HIV. Public employers are prohibited from discrimination based on employee's prior conviction. Employer cannot discriminate against smokers who comply with workplace regulations. | Ky. Rev. Stat. Ann. §§ 45.570, 207.130 *et seq.,* 337.420 *et seq.,* 344.010 *et seq.,* 436.160. |
| LA | Yes, prohibits discrimination based on age. | Yes, prohibits employment discrimination against otherwise qualified handicapped person when such handicap is unrelated to performance ability. | Yes, veterans preferred for state and local civil service. | No. | Yes, prohibits discrimination based on race, religion, national ancestry, age, sex, or physical condition. | Unlawful to intentionally discriminate in terms and conditions of employment based on race, color, religion, sex, disability, political affiliation, or national origin. Unlawful to discriminate in hiring, discharge, compensation, or terms and conditions of employment based on sickle cell trait. Unlawful to discriminate in terms and conditions of employment, compensation, promotion, or selection for training program based on pregnancy, childbirth, or related condition. Discrimination against smokers who comply with workplace smoking policy is prohibited. The results of AIDS tests are deemed confidential. Employers of 20 or more employees must provide paid leave for bone marrow donors. No employer may fire or otherwise discriminate against employee serving jury duty. | Const. art. 10 § 10; La. Rev. Stat. Ann. §§ 23:961, 23:962, 23:965, 23:966, 38:2315, 40:1299.31, 40:1299.124, 40:1299.190–40:1299.195, 46:2251 *et seq.* |

*(Table continues.)*

## **Table 2.5-1** *(cont'd)*

## ADDITIONAL PROHIBITIONS UNDER STATE FAIR EMPLOYMENT PRACTICE STATUTES

(See also text at § 2.5[a].)

**NOTE:** A "No" entry merely means that the specified type of discrimination is not prohibited by *separate* statutory provision, but such discrimination may be prohibited by the state's general fair employment statute. See Table 2.3-1 Part A and Table 2.3-1 Part B for further information.

| | *Age Discrimination* | *Handicap Discrimination* | *Veterans' Discrimination* | *Pay Discrimination* | *Discrimination by State Government Contractors* | *Other Requirements of Additional Laws* | *Citations to Authority* |
|---|---|---|---|---|---|---|---|
| ME | No. | Yes, prohibits discrimination against physically disabled in state employment. | No. | Yes, prohibits wage discrimination between employees performing comparable work in same establishment based on sex. | No. | Employers with 15 or more employees must comply with notification and training requirements to ensure a workplace free of sexual harassment. AIDS test results are deemed confidential; no health care facility may require that any employee or job applicant submit to an HIV test, except when based upon a bona fide occupational qualification. Unlawful to discriminate against members of state military forces. Employees other than managerial or part-time staff in retail or wholesale establishments may not be discriminated against for observing the Sabbath. Commission is required to promote gender equity in hiring of public school administrators. Employees who work for the same employer for 12 consecutive months are entitled to up to 10 consecutive work weeks of family medical leave. | Me. Rev. Stat. Ann. tit. 5, §§ 785, 4576, 19203 *et seq.*; tit. 17, § 1316; tit. 26, §§ 628, 806, 807, 844; tit. 37-B, § 342. |
| MD | No. | No. | No. | Yes, prohibits wage discrimination between sexes for comparable work. | Yes, prohibits discrimination based on sex, race, creed, color, or national origin in procurement contracts. | Employer cannot require polygraph test as condition of employment. | Md. Code Ann. Lab. §§ 3-304 *et seq.*, 3-702, 5-604. |

| | | | | | | | |
|---|---|---|---|---|---|---|---|
| MA | Yes, discrimination against individuals over age 40 subject to $500 maximum fine by labor commission. | Yes, prohibits employment discrimination against individual based solely on handicap if person has physical and mental capacity to perform job. | Yes, prohibits discrimination based on veteran status. Veterans are given preference for public works projects. | Yes, prohibits wage discrimination between sexes for comparable work. | Yes, prohibits discrimination based on race, color, religion, or nationality in public works employment. | Employer cannot require AIDS test or polygraph test as a condition of employment. Sexual harassment prohibited in state government employment. Citizens of the commonwealth given preference in public works projects. | Mass. Gen. Laws ch. 29 § 29F, ch. 111 § 70F, ch. 149 §§ 19B, 24A, 24B, 26, 105A, ch. 272 § 98B. |
| MI | Yes, prohibits discrimination based on age. | Yes, prohibits employment discrimination against individual with determinable physical or mental handicap if handicap is unrelated to job performance ability. (Michigan Handicappers' Civil Rights Act follows same procedures as state FEP.) | Yes, veterans shall be given preference for public employment. | Yes, it is illegal to discriminate based on sex in the payment of wages. | No. | Records pertaining to testing and treatment of AIDS or HIV infection must be kept confidential. | Mich. Stat. Ann. §§ 3.550(201) *et seq.*, 4.1221 *et seq.*, 14.15(5114a), 28.824. |
| MN | No. | No. | No. | Yes, requires equal pay for equal work, regardless of sex. | Yes, prohibits discrimination in public works contracts based on race, creed, or color. | Discrimination based on lawful use of lawful consumable products—including food, alcoholic or nonalcoholic beverages, and tobacco—during nonworking hours is prohibited. | Minn. Stat. Ann. §§ 181.59, 181.67, 181.938. |
| MS | No. | Yes, prohibits discrimination in state employment, and in any employment supported in whole or in part by public funds, against persons based on blindness or physical disabilities, unless disability affects work performance. | Yes, veterans are given preference in state hiring and layoffs. | No. | No. | None. | Miss. Code Ann. §§ 25-9-301, 25-9-303, 43-6-15, 57-67-37, 79-1-9. |
| MO | No. | No. | Yes, veterans are given preference in state hiring. | Yes, females must be paid at the same rate as males for comparable work. | No. | Employers may not discriminate against persons who refuse to participate in abortion procedures. Discrimination based on political beliefs or opinions is prohibited. | Mo. Rev. Stat. §§ 36.220, 130.028, 188.105, 188.120, 290.400 *et seq.* |

*(Table continues.)*

# **Table 2.5-1** *(cont'd)*

## ADDITIONAL PROHIBITIONS UNDER STATE FAIR EMPLOYMENT PRACTICE STATUTES

(See also text at § 2.5[a].)

**NOTE:** A "No" entry merely means that the specified type of discrimination is not prohibited by *separate* statutory provision, but such discrimination may be prohibited by the state's general fair employment statute. See Table 2.3-1 Part A and Table 2.3-1 Part B for further information.

| | *Age Discrimination* | *Handicap Discrimination* | *Veterans' Discrimination* | *Pay Discrimination* | *Discrimination by State Government Contractors* | *Other Requirements of Additional Laws* | *Citations to Authority* |
|---|---|---|---|---|---|---|---|
| MT | No. | Yes, discrimination based on physical handicap is prohibited; handicapped employees preferred in state employment. | Yes, veterans are given preference in state employment. | Yes, females must not be paid less than males for equivalent services. | Yes, all state and local government contracts must include provision prohibiting discrimination based on race, color, religion, political ideas, sex, age, marital status, disability, or national origin. | Discrimination based on lawful use of lawful products—including food, beverages, and tobacco—during nonworking hours is prohibited. Polygraph testing as a condition of employment is prohibited. Discrimination against members of organized militia is prohibited. | Mont. Code Ann. §§ 10-6-603, 39-2-304, 39-2-313, 39-3-104, 39-29-102–39-29-111, 39-30-101–39-30-207, 49-3-207, 49-4-101, 49-4-102. |
| NE | Yes, prohibits discrimination against persons over age 40. | Yes, state's policy is that disabled persons are to be employed in public service or employed by employers receiving state funding on the same terms and conditions as able-bodied persons. | Yes, veterans are given preference in state employment. | Yes, prohibits wage discrimination between sexes for comparable work. | Yes, prohibits discrimination based on race, color, creed, religion, or national origin by contractors. | Employer may not discriminate against individuals undergoing HIV testing or discriminate on the basis of an individual's HIV status or perceived status. | Neb. Rev. Stat. §§ 20-131, 20-168, 48-215, 48-225–48-231, 48-1004, 48-1122, 48-1219–48-1227. |
| NV | No. | No. | Yes, veterans are given preference for civil service positions and employment in public works contracts. | Yes, prohibits wage discrimination between employees based on sex. | Yes, prohibits discrimination based on race, color, creed, national origin, sex, or age in public works contracts. | AIDS test results are deemed confidential. | Nev. Rev. Stat. §§ 233.010 *et seq.*, 284.260, 338.125, 338.130, 441A.320, 608.017. |
| NH | No. | No. | Yes, veterans and their widows and widowers are given preference for employment in public works contracts. | Yes, requires equal pay for equal work, regardless of sex. | No. | Discrimination based on off-premises tobacco use during nonworking hours is prohibited. AIDS test results are deemed confidential. | N.H. Rev. Stat. Ann. §§ 141-F:7, 275:37, 275:37-a, 283:4. |

| | | | | | | | |
|---|---|---|---|---|---|---|---|
| NJ | Yes, prohibits discrimination in public employment against persons over age 40. | No. | Yes, provides for equal employment opportunities in public works contracts for Vietnam veterans. | Yes, prohibits discrimination in wage rate or payment method against any employee based on sex. | Yes, prohibits discrimination based on race, color, creed, national origin, ancestry, sex, sexual orientation, or marital status in public contracts. | Discrimination based on tobacco use is prohibited unless the employer has a rational basis for prohibiting tobacco use and that basis is reasonably related to employment. State employees shall be entitled to family leave of 12 weeks in any 24-month period. | N.J. Stat. Ann. §§ 2C:40A-1, 10:1-1 *et seq.*, 10:2-1, 10:3-1, 10:5-12, 10:5-31–10:5-33, 10:5-39, 10:5-40, 34:6B-1, 34:11-56.1, 34:11-56.2, 34:11B-1 *et seq.*; N.J. Exec. Or. 39. |
| NM | No. | No. | Yes. Veterans are given preference for civil service positions. | No. | Yes, prohibits discrimination based on sexual preference in public contracts. | Employer cannot require individual to disclose result of AIDS test as a condition of hiring, promotion, or continued employment, unless HIV status is related to a bona fide occupational qualification. Public employment of past criminal offenders is encouraged. Discrimination against smokers who comply with workplace policies is prohibited. | N.M. Stat. Ann. §§ 10-9-13.2, 28-2-1 *et seq.*, 28-10A-1, 28-15-1 *et seq.*, 50-11-3; N.M. Exec. Or. 85-15. |
| NY | Yes, prohibits age discrimination by public authorities, against building service employees, and in civil service recruitment. | Yes, prohibits discrimination against handicapped persons otherwise qualified for job; employers may not discriminate in the hiring or advancement of handicapped persons accompanied by a guide dog. | Yes, veterans are given preference in hiring and layoffs in state employment. | Yes, no employee will be paid at a rate less than the rate paid to employees of opposite sex in same establishment for equal work. | Yes, prohibits discrimination based on race, creed, color, disability, sex, or national origin in public works contracts. Violater will be fined $50 per person per day; violation may be considered a material breach, in which case all monies due may be forfeited. | Employers may not discriminate based on blindness or deafness. Employers also may not discriminate based on sickle cell trait or cancer or against carriers of Tay-Sachs disease or Cooley's anemia. Polygraph testing as a condition of employment is prohibited. Employers may not discriminate against a person seeking employment in a public school based on religion. Employers may not discriminate against employees for engaging in legal activities outside of work. | N.Y. Civ. Rights Law §§ 40-a, 40-c, 47-a, 48-a; N.Y. Pub. Auth. Law § 2851; N.Y. Exec. Law §§ 312, 313; N.Y. Labor Law §§ 190, 194, 220-e, 239; N.Y. Civ. Serv. Law §§ 50, 54, 55, 55-b, 55-c, 85. |
| NC | No. | Yes, prohibits discrimination based on physical or mental handicaps. | Yes, discrimination against members of the armed forces is prohibited. Veterans are given preference for civil service positions. | No. | No. | Employers may not deny employment or discharge an employee because of sickle cell trait, hemoglobin C trait, AIDS, or HIV infection. Discrimination based on race, age, sex, religion, color, handicap, or national origin is prohibited. Discrimination based on lawful use of lawful products during nonworking hours is prohibited. | N.C. Gen. Stat. §§ 95-28.1, 95-28.2, 126.80 *et seq.*, 127B-14, 128-15, 128-15.3, 130A-148, 143-422.1 *et seq.*, 168A-3–168A-11; N.C. Ex. Or. 18. |

*(Table continues.)*

# **Table 2.5-1** *(cont'd)*

## ADDITIONAL PROHIBITIONS UNDER STATE FAIR EMPLOYMENT PRACTICE STATUTES

(See also text at § 2.5[a].)

**NOTE:** A "No" entry merely means that the specified type of discrimination is not prohibited by *separate* statutory provision, but such discrimination may be prohibited by the state's general fair employment statute. See Table 2.3-1 Part A and Table 2.3-1 Part B for further information.

| | *Age Discrimination* | *Handicap Discrimination* | *Veterans' Discrimination* | *Pay Discrimination* | *Discrimination by State Government Contractors* | *Other Requirements of Additional Laws* | *Citations to Authority* |
|---|---|---|---|---|---|---|---|
| ND | Yes, prohibits discrimination against persons age 40 and over. | Yes. | Yes, veterans are given preference for state employment and certain state contracts. | Yes, prohibits wage discrimination based on sex and on other protected classifications. | No. | It is the policy of the state to prohibit discrimination on the basis of race, color, religion, sex, national origin, age, disability, familial status, public assistance status, or participation in lawful activities off employer's premises. Uncompensated family leave must be provided to state employees. AIDS or HIV-related test results are deemed confidential. | N.D. Cent. Code §§ 14-02.4-01, 23-07.5-05, 34-01-17, 34-06.1-01–34-06.1-09, 37-19.1-02, 39-3-04, 43-07-19, 54-44.3-01.1, 54-52.4-01–54-52.4-09. |
| OH | Yes, prohibits discrimination against applicants or employees over age 40. | No. | No. | Yes, prohibits wage disparity based on race, color, religion, sex, age, national origin, or ancestry. | Yes, prohibits discrimination in public works contracts based on race, color, religion, sex, handicap, national origin, or ancestry. | Employers may not question applicants about expunged arrest records or HIV infection. Discrimination against active members of armed forces is prohibited. | Ohio Rev. Code Ann. §§ 125.111, 153.59, 4101.17, 4111.01–4111.17, 4111.99, 4112.01 *et seq.* |
| OK | No. | Yes. | Yes, veterans are given preference for state employment; additional rights and protections afforded disabled veterans. | Yes, prohibits paying female employees at a rate less than that paid to male employees for comparable work. | Yes, prohibits discrimination in public works contracts based on race, creed, or color. | Discrimination based on use of tobacco products during nonworking hours is prohibited. Discrimination based on AIDS test results is prohibited; AIDS test results deemed confidential. State law authorizes family leave for state employees. | Okla. Stat. tit. 25, § 1901; tit. 40, §§ 195.1, 198.1, 500 *et seq.*, tit. 63, §§ 1-502.1, 1-502.2; tit. 72, §§ 402, 403; tit. 74, § 840-4.14. |

| | | | | | | | |
|---|---|---|---|---|---|---|---|
| OR | No. | No. | Yes, veterans are given preference for state employment. | Yes, prohibits discriminatory wage rates based on sex. | No. | Employer has duty to make reasonable accommodation for employee with AIDS if employee makes employer aware of condition; employer may not conduct HIV test without employee consent. Public and private employers must grant employee requests for up to 12 weeks of family medical leave within a 2-year period. | Or. Rev. Stat. §§ 408.230, 408.235, 433.045, 652.210–652.240, 659.015. |
| PA | No. | No. | No. | Yes, prohibits sex-based discrimination in wage rates for equal work. | Yes, prohibits discrimination in public works contracts based on race, color, creed, national origin, ancestry, sex, or age. | Polygraph testing as a condition of employment is prohibited. AIDS test results are deemed confidential. Employers allowed to consider applicants' prior convictions only to the extent that they are job-related. | Pa. Stat. Ann. tit. 18, §§ 7321, 9125; tit. 35, § 7606; tit. 43, §§ 153, 336.2–336.8. |
| RI | No. | Yes, prohibits discrimination against persons with real or perceived physical or mental impairments, persons with record of such impairments, persons or entities doing business in the state, and persons or entities regulated by state or receiving state financial assistance. Handicapped persons subject to the Human Rights Commission under the state's FEP law may act under this statute only if the fair employment commission has not acted on their complaints within 60 days or if the commission has taken final action. | Yes, veterans are given preference in public employment. | Yes, prohibits sex-based wage discrimination against any employee, excluding domestic servants and employees of social clubs or fraternal, charitable, educational, religious, scientific, or literary associations. | Yes, contractors failing to abide by equal opportunity statutes may be subject to forfeiture of money due and penalties. | Prohibits discrimination in employment based on positive AIDS test result. Prohibits discrimination against smokers; prohibits discrimination against union members; prohibits urine, blood, or genetic testing and lie detector tests as conditions for employment, advancement, or job retention. Family leave law covers employers with 50 or more employees. | R.I. Gen. Laws §§ 23-6-10 *et seq.*, 23-20.7.1-1, 28-5.1-10, 28-6-17–28-6-21, 28-6.1-1 *et seq.*, 28-6.5-1 *et seq.*, 28-6.6-1, 28-6.7-1 *et seq.*, 30-21-1 *et seq.*, 36-4-50, 42-87-1 *et seq.*, 42-112-1. |

*(Table continues.)*

# Table 2.5-1 *(cont'd)*

## ADDITIONAL PROHIBITIONS UNDER STATE FAIR EMPLOYMENT PRACTICE STATUTES

(See also text at § 2.5[a].)

**NOTE:** A "No" entry merely means that the specified type of discrimination is not prohibited by *separate* statutory provision, but such discrimination may be prohibited by the state's general fair employment statute. See Table 2.3-1 Part A and Table 2.3-1 Part B for further information.

| | *Age Discrimination* | *Handicap Discrimination* | *Veterans' Discrimination* | *Pay Discrimination* | *Discrimination by State Government Contractors* | *Other Requirements of Additional Laws* | *Citations to Authority* |
|---|---|---|---|---|---|---|---|
| SC | No. | Yes, prohibits discrimination against persons with handicap—meaning substantial physical or mental impairment verified by medical findings and reasonably certain to continue for life without substantial improvement; handicap must be unrelated to job performance ability. Statute excludes alcohol, drug, narcotics, or other substance abusers and persons regarded only as handicapped; mental impairment does not include mental illness. | Yes, honorably discharged veterans are given preference in public employment. | No. | No. | Discrimination based on tobacco use outside workplace is prohibited. State employees can use accrued sick leave for the purpose of caring for newly adopted child. | S.C. Code Ann. §§ 1-1-550, 8-11-155, 41-1-85, 43-33-510 *et seq.* |
| SD | Yes, prohibits discrimination against persons age 40 and over. | Yes, prohibits discrimination on the basis of physical disability. | Yes, veterans are given preference in state employment; disabled veterans given preference over nondisabled. | Yes, requires equal pay for equal work, regardless of sex. | No. | State cannot discriminate based on political affiliation. Municipalities and counties have authority to prohibit employment discrimination. Discrimination based on tobacco use off premises during nonworking hours is prohibited. | S.D. Codified Laws Ann. §§ 3-3-1 *et seq.*, 3-6A-15, 20-12-4, 60-12-15–60-12-21. |

| | | | | | | | |
|---|---|---|---|---|---|---|---|
| TN | No. | Yes, prohibits discrimination in employment based solely on physical, mental, or visual handicap. | No. | Yes, prohibits discrimination in wage rates based solely on sex. | No. | Family leave law applicable to employers of 100 or more employees. Civil action for malicious harassment available. Discrimination against smokers is prohibited. State agencies must post state's sexual harassment policy. State employees entitled to bereavement leave in the event of a family death. | Tenn. Code Ann. §§ 4-3-124, 8-50-103, 8-50-104, 8-50-113, 12-3-801 *et seq.*, 50-1-304, 50-2-201. |
| TX | No. | No. | No. | Yes, prohibits discrimination in wage rates in public service employment based solely on sex. | Yes. | Employer cannot require AIDS test unless HIV status relates to bona fide occupational qualification. | Tex. Gov't. Code Ann. § 659.001; Tex. Health & Safety Code Ann. § 81.102. |
| UT | No. | It is state policy that the visually handicapped and otherwise physically disabled shall be employed in state service on the same terms and conditions as the able-bodied, unless disability prevents work performance. | Veterans who are state residents and U.S. citizens are given preference for public works contracts. | No. | Yes, prohibits discrimination in employment by state contractors and subcontractors. Veterans who are state residents and U.S. citizens are given preference for public works contracts. | Polygraph testing is prohibited. | Utah Code Ann. §§ 26-30-3, 34-30-1, 34-35-6, 34-37-16, 71-10-2. |
| VT | No. | No. | No. | No. | Yes. | Employers may not require HIV tests as a condition of employment or discriminate based on AIDS infection unless negative HIV status is a bona fide occupational qualification. Employers may not discriminate on the basis of race, color, creed, sex, sexual orientation, or national origin. Discrimination against employee who makes worker's compensation claim is prohibited. Polygraph testing as a condition of employment is prohibited, except for law enforcement officers, persons working with precious metals or gems, and persons manufacturing regulated drugs. | Vt. Stat. Ann. tit. 3, § 961; tit. 21, §§ 494a, 494b, 495a, 710. |

*(Table continues.)*

# Table 2.5-1 *(cont'd)*

## ADDITIONAL PROHIBITIONS UNDER STATE FAIR EMPLOYMENT PRACTICE STATUTES

(See also text at § 2.5[a].)

**NOTE:** A "No" entry merely means that the specified type of discrimination is not prohibited by *separate* statutory provision, but such discrimination may be prohibited by the state's general fair employment statute. See Table 2.3-1 Part A and Table 2.3-1 Part B for further information.

| | *Age Discrimination* | *Handicap Discrimination* | *Veterans' Discrimination* | *Pay Discrimination* | *Discrimination by State Government Contractors* | *Other Requirements of Additional Laws* | *Citations to Authority* |
|---|---|---|---|---|---|---|---|
| VA | No. | Yes, unlawful to discriminate against persons whose physical and mental disabilities are unrelated to job performance. Separate statute allows persons with physical disabilities unrelated to job performance to seek a civil remedy in circuit court of chancery for equitable relief, compensatory damages, and attorney's fees. | No. | Yes, prohibits sex-based wage discrimination. | Yes, prohibits discrimination in employment under state contracts greater than $10,000. | Prohibits discrimination against smokers (government employees only). AIDS test results are deemed confidential. | Va. Code Ann. §§ 2.1-374–2.1-376, 32.1-36.1, 40.1-28.6, 51.5-3–51.5-46. |
| WA | Yes, prohibits discriminating against persons age 40 or older in public and private employment. | Yes, blind and physically disabled persons are to be employed in state service on same terms and conditions as able-bodied persons unless their disability interferes with job performance. Persons with developmental disabilities are protected under statutes prohibiting discrimination against the handicapped. | Yes, honorably discharged veterans preferred in certain public employment. | Yes, requires equal pay for equal work, regardless of sex. | No. | Polygraph testing as a condition of employment is prohibited. | Wash. Rev. Code §§ 41.06.150, 49.12.175, 49.44.090, 49.44.120, 70.84.080, 71A.10.040, 73.16.010; Wash. Admin. Code § 236-48-163; Wash. Ex. Or. 8-2-66, 70-01. |

| | | | | | | | |
|---|---|---|---|---|---|---|---|
| WV | No. | No. | No. | Yes, prohibits wage discrimination by any person, partnership, firm, or corporation with 1 or more employees. Statute excludes any state or municipal corporation with merit-based civil service system. | No. | AIDS test results are deemed confidential. Polygraph testing as a condition of employment is prohibited. Discrimination based on off-premises tobacco use is prohibited. | W. Va. Code §§ 16-3C-3, 21-3-19, 21-5-5a, 21-5B-1 *et seq.*, 29-6-4; W. Va. Admin. Reg. §§ 77-1-1–77-1-5. |
| WI | No. | No. | No. | Yes, it is the policy of the state to correct pay inequities based on gender, ethnicity, handicap, or race in the state civil service system. | Yes, prohibits discrimination in employment under public works contracts; requires state contractors to take affirmative action. | Employers cannot demand that current or prospective employees take test to determine if they have AIDS and cannot use test results to affect terms, conditions, or privileges of employment or termination of employees. Family leave law applicable to employers of 50 or more employees. | Wis. Stat. Ann. §§ 103.10, 103.15, 103.20, 230.01. |
| WY | No. | No. | Yes, veterans are given preference in some public employment. | Yes, prohibits wage discrimination. | Yes, executive order prohibits discrimination in employment under public works contracts in compliance with all state and federal antidiscrimination statutes. | AIDS test results are deemed confidential. | Wyo. Stat. §§ 19-6-102, 27-4-301–27-4-304, 35-4-132; Wyo. Ex. Or. 1976-6. |

# Table 2.5-2

## AFFIRMATIVE ACTION REQUIREMENTS

(See also text at § 2.5[b].)

**KEY:** **AAP.** Affirmative action program.
**EEOC.** Equal Employment Opportunity Commission.

| | *State Contracts* | *State Employment* | *Other Requirements* | *Citations to Authority* |
|---|---|---|---|---|
| AL | Cities and Class 2 municipalities must adopt ordinances that provide that reasonable efforts be made to ensure that all contractors with the municipality must have at least 15% participation by socially or economically disadvantaged individuals. | Yes, cities and municipalities shall adopt ordinances providing that all appointments made to positions in government fairly and adequately reflect the make-up of the community with due consideration to all demographic characteristics of the population. | Statute requires that the Alabama Compact for Leadership and Citizenship Education affirmatively include organizations representative of the racial, geographic, demographic, and urban/rural diversity of the state. | Ala. Code §§ 11-43C-92, 11-44C-93, 16-44A-18. |
| AK | No. | Yes, the governor must establish an equal opportunity program, must adopt annually an AAP for the executive branch, and must work with each agency to enhance equal employment opportunity, and each agency head must adopt an AAP to implement the state program in that agency. | None. | Alaska Stat. §§ 44.19.450 *et seq.* |
| AZ | Yes, executive order requires state contractors to take affirmative action to ensure that applicants and employees are treated without regard to their race, age, color, religion, sex, or national origin. | Yes, executive order requires state agencies to develop goals and timetables for underutilized minority, female, and handicapped workers. Governor's Affirmative Action Office coordinates AAPs in state government. | None. | Ex. Ors. 75-5, 93-20. |
| AR | No. | No. | All state supported colleges and universities shall prepare an AAP for the recruitment of minorities for faculty and staff positions. | Ark. Code Ann. § 6-63-103. |
| CA | Yes, state contracts must have statewide participation goals of not less than 15% for minority businesses, not less than 5% for businesses owned by women, and not less than 3% for disabled veterans. Goals apply to overall dollar amount awarded each year by department. Note: Although these requirements have not been formally repealed, they are invalidated by the CCRI. See introductory text at § 2.5[d]. | Yes, each state agency must adopt an AAP subject to approval and monitoring by state personnel board. Note: Although these requirements have not been formally repealed, they are invalidated by the CCRI. See introductory text at § 2.5[d]. | Law provides for AAP for women and minorities in apprenticeship programs. Law also provides for the implementation of AAPs in the hiring of employees, faculty, and administrative positions in California community colleges. Note: Although these requirements have not been formally repealed, they are invalidated by the CCRI. See introductory text at § 2.5[d]. | Cal. Pub. Cont. Code § 10115; Cal. Gov't Code §§ 19790 *et seq.*; Cal. Lab. Code § 3073; Cal. Educ. Code § 71028. Note, however, that the CCRI, which abolishes AAPs, has been enacted. See introductory text at § 2.5[d]. |

| | | | | |
|---|---|---|---|---|
| CO | Yes, executive order establishes a goal for minority participation in state procurement of 17 percent of total dollars spent. The director of each executive department is directed to make "significant and measurable" progress toward achieving the goal for minority participation in state procurement. | Yes, each department head must have an annual plan to take necessary action to recruit and hire members of protected groups, with the goal that the percentages of minorities and women within each department reflect at least the percentage of qualified persons from that group in the workforce in the state, and must annually report on the efforts made under the plan. | State Civil Rights Commission cannot require a quota system by rule or remedy. | Colo. Rev. Stat. § 24-50-141; Colo. Const. art. XII, § 13; Ex. Or. D0043 87 (12/10/87). |
| CT | Yes, state contractors must develop and file with the fair employment commission AAPs complying with regulations of the State Commission on Human Rights and Opportunities. Every contract with the state or any political subdivision of the state, other than a municipality, must contain provisions regarding nondiscrimination on basis of race, color, religion, sex, or sexual orientation. | Yes, each state agency, department, board, and commission must develop and implement an AAP for all aspects of personnel and administration and must file plans with the state human rights and opportunities commission. If the state commission disapproves of AAP in question, it may issue a certificate of noncompliance and institute a hiring freeze. | Each state department and agency must establish an upward mobility program as part of its AAP. Establishment of a Minority Business Enterprise Review Committee to conduct an ongoing study of contract awards, loans, or bonds made by the state. | Conn. Gen. Stat. Ann. §§ 4-61u, 4-61w, 4a-60, 4a-60a, 4a-61, 4a-62; *Romer v. Evans,* 116 S. Ct. 1620 (1996). |
| DE | No. | Each department and agency must develop an AAP with a statement of goals and objectives and methods to ensure equal employment opportunity and eliminate continuing patterns of discrimination. | The Governor's Council on Equal Opportunity will assist in the monitoring and evaluation of the agencies' implementation of and compliance with executive orders on affirmative action. The Director of the State Personnel Office must assist agencies in updating their AAPs, must develop professional recruiting efforts, and must employ other efforts to support and recruit a diverse workforce. | Del. Ex. Or. 28 (3/10/95). |
| DC | Yes, each District of Columbia agency must allocate its contracts to reach the goal of 35% of total dollars to local minority businesses. | Yes, every District of Columbia government agency will develop an AAP, including goals and actions the agency will take to secure equal employment opportunities. | Banks and savings and loans associations must submit AAPs for approval by the Office of Human Rights. To correct past discriminatory practices, employers can submit AAP plans giving preference to minorities for the commission's approval. | D.C. Code Ann. §§ 1-507, 1-508, 1-607.1 *et seq.,* 1-1141 *et seq.,* 1-2524. |
| FL | Yes, the legislature has enacted race and gender conscious remedial programs to ensure minority participation in the economic life of the state, in state contracts for the provision of commodities and services, and in construction contracts. | Yes, executive orders require state agencies to submit AAPs to the governor. Each state agency must develop and implement an AAP and report to the governor the results of its program. | Water management districts are authorized to implement regulations to achieve minority business enterprise procurement goals. | Fla. Stat. Ann. §§ 110.112, 287.09451, 373.607. |
| GA | No. | Quotas because of imbalances in employee ratios are prohibited; the governor may require each agency to develop its own AAP. | None. | Ga. Code Ann. § 45-19-35. |
| HI | No. | Yes, each department's affirmative action or equal employment opportunity officer must administer programs to promote equal employment opportunities and practices. | The Hawaii Strategic Development Corporation shall establish rules to ensure equal opportunity to minority-owned businesses and shall encourage the development of such businesses. | Haw. Ex. Or. 97-06; Admin. Dir. 4, 80-2, 82-2; Haw. R.S.A. § 211 F-7. |

*(Table continues.)*

# Table 2.5-2 *(cont'd)*

## AFFIRMATIVE ACTION REQUIREMENTS

(See also text at § 2.5[b].)

**KEY:** **AAP.** Affirmative action program.
**EEOC.** Equal Employment Opportunity Commission.

| | *State Contracts* | *State Employment* | *Other Requirements* | *Citations to Authority* |
|---|---|---|---|---|
| ID | No. | No, state employees are to be recruited, appointed, assigned, and promoted on the basis of merit only. | Each executive agency shall submit an annual AAP to the Governor setting forth all activities taken to effect the State Code of Fair Employment Practices. | Idaho Ex. Or. 95-8. |
| IL | Yes, state contractors must refrain from unlawful discrimination in employment and take affirmative action to ensure equal employment opportunity and to eliminate past discrimination. Not less than 12% of the total amount awarded in state contracts shall go to businesses owned by minorities, females, and the disabled. At least 10% of the total dollar amount awarded in state construction contracts shall go to minority and female owned businesses. Of those, 50% shall go to female owned businesses. | Yes, each state agency must comply with state affirmative action regulations, ensuring that all state departments, boards, commissions, and instrumentalities act to provide equal opportunity and to eliminate past discrimination. | Under the state's Minority Business Procurement Program, each agency must identify and monitor participation of minority businesses in the state government procurement process, increase set-aside categories, and establish goal of 12% participation by minority businesses in all nonbid discretionary procurement. | 30 ILCS §§ 575/1 *et seq.*; 775 ILCS §§ 5/2-105, 5/7-105, 5/7-106; Ill. Admin. Code tit. 44, §§ 750 *et seq.* |
| IN | No. | Yes, each state agency must establish an AAP annually; smaller agencies can establish only an AAP policy statement. | None. | Ind. Code § 4-15-12-5. |
| IA | Yes, the department of management must establish that contractors, vendors, and suppliers doing business with the state follow procedures to ensure that protected classes are afforded equal employment opportunities. | Yes, it is the policy of the state to apply AAPs to correct deficiencies in the state employment system; each state agency must prepare and submit an annual AAP. | The state shall apply AAPs to correct deficiencies in school district, area education agency, and community college employment systems. | Iowa Code Ann. §§ 19B.1 *et seq.* |
| KS | No. | No. | There are no AAP requirements, but it is not an unlawful employment practice for employers to fill vacancies in such a way as to eliminate or reduce imbalances in the workforce with respect to race, religion, color, sex, disability, national origin, or ancestry. Note: Such voluntary AAPs must meet criteria established under Title VII to be valid. See § 2.5[c]. | Kan. Stat. Ann. § 44-1009. |

| | | | | |
|---|---|---|---|---|
| KY | Yes, generally bidding contractor's minority workforce must reflect percentage of available minorities in bidding party's labor pool. For length of contract, contractor must satisfy, if possible, agreed-upon goals and timetables. Contractors are exempt if the contract is for $250,000 or less, fewer than 8 employees are used, only family members or relatives are hired, or only persons with a legitimate direct ownership in the business are hired. Failure to comply is a material breach of contract. | Yes, state government cabinets, departments, and agencies must develop programs to redress traditional and social discrimination that may have barred employment opportunities. | None. | Ky. Rev. Stat. Ann. §§ 18A.138, 45.570 *et seq.*; Ex. Or. 96-0612. |
| LA | No. | No. | Employers may voluntarily institute AAPs to eliminate or reduce imbalance with respect to race, creed, color, religion, sex, age, disability, or national origin. Note: Such voluntary AAPs must meet criteria established under Title VII to be valid. See § 2.5[c]. | La. Rev. Stat. § 51:2246. |
| ME | Yes, contractors with contracts exceeding $250,000 must pursue in good faith AAPs to increase number of minorities, women, and handicapped at all levels and in all segments of workforce where imbalances exist. | Yes, state agencies must pursue AAPs in good faith to increase number of minorities, women, and handicapped at all levels of the workforce where imbalances exist. There are no rigid quotas. | None. | Me. Rev. Stat. Ann. tit. 5, §§ 781 *et seq.*, tit. 23, § 1966. |
| MD | Yes, bid documents for state public works contracts and contracts themselves must contain clauses requiring bidder, contractor, and all subcontractors to develop and maintain AAPs to increase number of women and minorities. | Yes, each agency in executive branch of state government must submit an AAP with specific quantitative goals and timetables to correct inequality in workforce. | State Employer Selection Procedure Guidelines require all employers, unions, and employment agencies to take action in providing employment and training to members of protected classes. | Md. State Finance & Procurement Code Ann. §§ 14-301 *et seq.*; Md. State Personnel & Pensions Code §§ 5-201 *et seq.*; Md. Ex. Or. .01.01.19, 93.16. |
| MA | Yes, contractors must take affirmative action to eliminate discriminatory barriers. Contractors must, if possible, maintain on each project the targeted percentage of minority man-hours to total man-hours per job category. | Yes, each agency must institute an AAP to ensure that racial and sexual makeup of state workforce, at all levels, reflects racial and sexual makeup of population where job exists. | County commissioners must institute an AAP for each county. | Mass. Gen. Laws ch. 23A, § 44 (State Contracts), ch. 35, § 53A (State Employment). |
| MI | Yes, each agency awarding state public works contracts must institute programs to increase participation of blacks, Hispanics, Asians, Native Americans, and women. If the bidders for a state contract do not include a qualified minority or female owned and operated business, the contract shall be awarded to the lowest bidder otherwise qualified. | Yes, each agency, department, and commission must develop and implement plans to increase number of blacks, Hispanics, Asians, Native Americans, women, and handicapped persons at all levels of state government. | Employers may, subject to the State Civil Rights Commission's approval, adopt AAPs to eliminate the present effects of past discriminatory practices. An unapproved plan is invalid. | Mich. Comp. Laws §§ 37.2201 *et seq.*, 125.1221 *et seq.*, 450.771 *et seq.*, Mich. Ex. Or. 1994-16; *Victorson v. Dept. of Treasury,* 183 Mich. App. 318 (1990). |
| MN | Yes, contractors must agree to not discriminate in the hiring, promotion, or firing of employees on the basis of race, creed, or color. | Yes, each agency must implement a program to eliminate underutilization of qualified protected group members within state civil service through result-oriented procedures. | None. | Minn. Stat. Ann. §§ 43A.19, 43A.191, 181.59. |

*(Table continues.)*

# Table 2.5-2 *(cont'd)*

## AFFIRMATIVE ACTION REQUIREMENTS

(See also text at § 2.5[b].)

**KEY:** **AAP.** Affirmative action program.
**EEOC.** Equal Employment Opportunity Commission.

| | *State Contracts* | *State Employment* | *Other Requirements* | *Citations to Authority* |
|---|---|---|---|---|
| MS | Yes, agencies or governing authorities may set aside not more than 20% of their anticipated annual expenditures for the purchase of commodities from minority businesses. | No. | The Office of Minority Business Enterprises was created to develop, plan, and implement programs for qualified minority-owned businesses. | Miss. Code Ann. §§ 31-7-13, 57-69-3. |
| MO | Yes, state contractors must implement nondiscriminatory procedures for hiring, promotions, etc., and must give written notice of nondiscriminatory clauses to labor unions with which they have bargaining or other agreements. | Yes, state agencies must follow AAPs, comply with EEOC standards, practices, and procedures, and follow guidelines in determining whether their AAPs are discriminatory. Public employee retirement systems must use women and minority investment counselors and money managers. | State guidelines should be used in determining whether an AAP is discriminatory. Riverboat gamblers must file AAPs when applying for licenses. | Mo. Ann. Stat. §§ 33.750 *et seq.*, 37.020, 104.621; Mo. Code Regs. tit. 8, § 60-3.080. |
| MT | Yes, all state and local government contracts and subcontracts must contain provision that hiring will be nondiscriminatory. Preference may be given to state residents for certain contracts. Hiring preference may be given to resident Indians for construction contracts on Indian reservations. | Yes, hiring preference is given to qualified veterans and handicapped applicants. | Human rights commission follows affirmative action guidelines promulgated by the EEOC. | Mont. Code Ann. §§ 18-1-110, 18-2-403, 18-2-409, 39-29-102 *et seq.*, 39-30-101 *et seq.*, 49-3-207, 90-5-114. |
| NE | Yes, every contract to which the state or any of its political subdivisions is a party must contain provisions requiring the contractor and its subcontractors not to discriminate on the basis of race, color, religion, sex, disability, or national origin. | Yes, state government employers must work deliberately to eliminate barriers to employment and provide equal employment opportunities for all state citizens. | None. | Neb. Rev. Stat. §§ 48-1122, 81-1355 *et seq.* |
| NV | No. | Yes, agencies must report AAP progress to state personnel director. | State apprenticeship programs must have AAPs. | Nev. Rev. Stat. §§ 233.010 *et seq.*, 610.010–610.190, 613.400; Nev. Admin. Code § 284.114, §§ 610.510-610.615. |
| NH | No. | Yes, executive order affirms state's commitment to affirmative action in state employment. State personnel director must develop and implement an equal employment opportunity program. | Under Equal Employment Opportunity in Apprenticeship Programs, sponsor's plan must include procedures for identification, recruitment, and training of minority and female apprentices. | N.H. Ex. Or. 81-3. |

| | | | | |
|---|---|---|---|---|
| NJ | Yes, each contract bidder must have and file an AAP guaranteeing minorities employment in all job categories. State treasurer must approve plan based partially on percentage of minority groups in state from which workforce is drawn. No public works contract shall be awarded nor monies paid unless contractor has agreed to and guaranteed equal employment opportunities in accordance with an approved AAP (sexual orientation excepted). | Yes, state agencies must implement programs and establish goals to ensure that job applicant pool for state agency positions includes minorities, handicapped, and women, reflecting population in surrounding labor market. | All casino licensees shall establish a percentage of their contracts for goods and services with minority and women's business enterprises. | N.J. Stat. Ann. §§ 5:12-184 *et seq.*, 10:5-32, 11A:7-3 *et seq.* |
| NM | No. | Yes, all state departments, agencies, and universities must file AAPs establishing goals and timetables for correcting underutilization of protected groups in workforce. | None. | N.M. Ex. Or. 85-15. |
| NY | Yes, bidders and holders of state contracts must file AAPs with procedures to promote hiring and training of minorities on all contract work; all contracts to which the state is a party must contain nondiscrimination provisions. | Yes, each state agency must submit an AAP setting forth its goals and objectives for hiring minorities, women, disabled persons, and Vietnam veterans. | Under Apprenticeship Training Programs, each sponsor must submit an AAP, including procedures, methods, and programs to identify, recruit, and train minority apprentices. The commitments contained in the sponsor's AAP are not intended and shall not be used to discriminate against any qualified applicant or apprentice on the basis of age, race, color, religion, national origin, sex, disability, or marital status. | N.Y. Exec. Law §§ 310 *et seq.;* N.Y. Comp. Codes R. & Regs. tit. 5, § 142.1, tit. 9 §§ 1.43, 4.21, tit. 12, §§ 600.4, 600.5, 600.17; N.Y. Ex. Or. 6 §§ I.1–I.3. |
| NC | Yes, discrimination in awarding state contracts is prohibited. The state shall have a 10% goal for participation by minority businesses in the total value of work for each building contract. | Yes, state agencies must develop and implement plans to correct substantial disparities or other problems in the workforce, based partially on a comparison of percentages of minorities and women employed in job categories and percentages of qualified persons in those groups available in labor pool. | Under the Apprenticeship Program, sponsors must file and implement AAPs for minorities and women. | N.C. Gen. Stat. §§ 143-128; N.C. Admin. Code tit. 13, r. 14.0808. |
| ND | No. | No. | None. | State has no AAP provisions. |
| OH | Yes, contractors must submit and implement AAPs proposing methods to recruit minorities; state agencies must encourage minority contractors and suppliers to bid on state and state-assisted contracts. The Division of Human Resources must review agency employment actions and must take action against an agency not in compliance with its AAP. | Yes, state departments, agencies, commissions, and appointing authorities must initiate AAPs promoting equal opportunity in every aspect of personnel policy and practice. | Under the Apprenticeship Program, each sponsor must file and implement an AAP to provide equal opportunity in apprenticeships, allowing full utilization of minorities and women. | Ohio Rev. Code Ann. §§ 9.47, 125.11.1, 5525.03; Ohio Admin. Code §§ 123:1-49, 123:1-49-05, 123:1-49-06, 123:1-49-40—123:1-49-44, 123:2-3-01–123:2-14-01, 4101:1-5-01–4101:1-5-15, 4101:1-3-08; Ohio Ex. Ors. 1-27-72, 9-13-73, 84-9. |
| OK | Yes, all contracts to which the state is a party must contain a clause prohibiting discrimination on the basis of race, creed, or color. | Yes, state government agencies, boards, commissions, departments, and offices must submit and implement AAPs. Under state's optional hiring procedures, qualified females, blacks, Hispanics, Asian/Pacific Islanders, and Native American Indians/Alaskans may be hired in underutilized job class for which hiring goal has been set. | — | Okla. Stat. tit. 25, § 1310; tit. 40, § 195.1; tit. 74, §§ 840-2.1–840-2.3, 840-2.19, 840-4.12. |

*(Table continues.)*

# Table 2.5-2 *(cont'd)*

## AFFIRMATIVE ACTION REQUIREMENTS

(See also text at § 2.5[b].)

**KEY:** **AAP.** Affirmative action program.
**EEOC.** Equal Employment Opportunity Commission.

| | *State Contracts* | *State Employment* | *Other Requirements* | *Citations to Authority* |
|---|---|---|---|---|
| OR | Yes, same requirements as those for state employment. | Yes, all branches of state government, through AAPs, must provide fair and equal opportunities for employment and advancement in programs, services, and contract awards. | Under the Apprenticeship Program, each sponsor must file and implement an AAP providing for outreach and positive recruitment to increase minority and female participation.<br>Public Education: AAP sets forth procedures to follow in laying off minorities when staff reduction is required due to budgetary constraints or decreasing enrollments. | Or. Rev. Stat. §§ 182.100, 240.015, 240.306, 243.305, 279.055, 659.025, 659.027, 660 *et seq.*; Or. Ex. Or. 88-14, amended Or. Ex. Or. 96-38. |
| PA | Yes, state contractors must implement AAPs to ensure equal opportunity. Program must include analysis of areas where contractor may be discriminating, unintentionally or otherwise, against minorities and women; plan must be developed setting forth goals and timetables to correct such deficiencies. | Yes, AAPs must be developed for each agency to ensure fair employment at every level of government for blacks, Hispanics, Asians, American Indians, Alaskans, Pacific Islanders, handicapped and disabled persons, persons over age 40, and women. | Under Apprenticeship Programs, each sponsor must file and implement an AAP providing programs to increase minority and female participation. | Pa. Cons. Stat. Ann. tit. 43 §§ 1101.201 *et seq.*, tit. 73 §§ 390.1 *et seq.*; Pa. Ex. Or. 1996-9. |
| RI | Yes, division of purchases must require same commitment to equal employment opportunity and affirmative action in state contracts as exists in contracts controlled by federal Executive Orders 11246, 11375, and 11625. | Yes, each state department or agency must annually prepare an AAP according to criteria set forth by state equal opportunity office and submit it to the Governor's Executive Committee for Equal Opportunity. | None. | R.I. Gen. Laws §§ 28-5-40, 28-5.1-1–28-5.1-17; R.I. Ex. Or. 96-14. |
| SC | No. | Each state agency shall prepare an AAP to promote employment of racial minorities and women. These AAPs shall be submitted to the General Assembly each year for approval. | None. | S.C. Code Ann. § 1-13-110. |
| SD | No. | Yes, after each open, competitive exam, register of persons meeting minimum standards must be prepared; upon written request of appointing authority, some registers may be designated for jobs for which competition is limited to disadvantaged persons. Such request must document underrepresentation of protected class. | None. | S.D. Admin. R. §§ 55:01:02:04, 55:01:07:02.01. |
| TN | Yes, state contracts must be set aside for minority-owned businesses. | No. | None. | Tenn. Code Ann. §§ 12-3-801 *et seq.*; Ex. Or. No. 63. |

| | | | | |
|---|---|---|---|---|
| TX | Yes, each district shall establish an AAP to increase participation by disadvantaged businesses in public contract awards. | Yes, under executive order, governor's EEO office must establish a "Minority and Female Skills Bank," consisting of qualified minority and/or female applicants to be considered for state employment. | None. | Tex. Local Gov't Code Ann. §§ 375.221, 375.222; Tex. Ex. Or. MW-6. |
| UT | No. | Yes, fair employment review committee assists governor, director of division of personnel management, and fair employment practices coordinator in implementing state's AAP; state personnel management division must institute and implement state's equal employment opportunity program, while director must "act affirmatively" in administering personnel management system. | None. | Utah Code Ann. §§ 35A-5-106, 67-19-6.3; Utah Admin. R. § R468-5-7, R477-2-1-R477-2-10, R477-5-3. |
| VT | Yes, all state contracts must contain a provision that the contractor will comply with state FEP laws. | Yes, executive order declares state policy of equal employment and affirmative action, creates governor's council on affirmative action, and requires department of personnel to develop, implement, and monitor the state's AAP. | None. | Vt. Stat. Ann. tit. 21 § 495; Vt. Ex. Or. 13-93. |
| VA | Yes, for contracts over $10,000. | Yes, state appointing officials must take affirmative measures determined by director of department of personnel and training, emphasizing recruitment of qualified minorities, women, disabled persons, and older Virginians. | None. | Va. Code Ann. §§ 2.1-374 *et seq.*; Va. Ex. Or. 2(98); Va. State Per. Policy § 2.00. |
| WA | Yes, each state agency shall ensure that minority and women-owned businesses are afforded maximum practicable opportunity to participate in contracts for public works, goods, and services. | Yes, Human Rights Commission is responsible for monitoring compliance of state agencies with AAP goals to eliminate the underrepresentation of racial minorities, women, persons in protected age groups, persons with disabilities, Vietnam veterans, and disabled veterans in state government. | Joint apprenticeship programs receiving state assistance must include racial minorities and women, if available, in a ratio not less than the ratio of minorities and women to the actual population in the market concerned. | Wash. Rev. Code §§ 39.19.020 *et seq.*, 41.06.020–41.06.155, 43.43.340, 49.04.100–49.04.130, 49.74.005–49.74.050; Wash. Admin. Code §§ 251-01-015, 251-01-040, 251-01-285, 251-01-330, 251-23-010, 251-23-020–251-23-060, 296-04-300–296-04-390, 356-05-013–356-05-050; Wash. Ex. Or. 93-07. |
| WV | No. | Yes, executive order requires agency programs to propose positive, aggressive measures, including specific goals and timetables, for recruiting and training personnel, regardless of race, color, religion, national origin, political affiliation, handicap, sex, or age. Favoritism or discrimination because of political or religious opinions or race prohibited. | None. | W. Va. Code § 29-6-20; W. Va. Ex. Or. 16-78, art. Ic. |

*(Table continues.)*

## Table 2.5-2 *(cont'd)*

# AFFIRMATIVE ACTION REQUIREMENTS

(See also text at § 2.5[b].)

**KEY:** **AAP.** Affirmative action program.
**EEOC.** Equal Employment Opportunity Commission.

| | *State Contracts* | *State Employment* | *Other Requirements* | *Citations to Authority* |
|---|---|---|---|---|
| WI | Yes, state contracting agencies must include a nondiscrimination provision obligating contractors to take affirmative action to ensure equal employment opportunities, except with respect to sexual orientation. | Yes, all state government divisions must establish AAPs containing goals and timetables for recruitment, selection, hiring, training, promotion, transfer, layoff, compensation, and fringe benefits. | Affirmative action is required to provide equal opportunity in apprenticeship programs registered with state apprenticeship agency. | Wis. Stat. Ann. §§ 16.765, 230.01 *et seq.*; Wis. Admin. Code §§ 43.01–43.07, §§ Ind. 96.05, 96.06. |
| WY | No. | No. | None. | Wyo. Ex. Or. 1976-6. |

# Table 2.5-3
## RECORDKEEPING REQUIREMENTS UNDER STATE FEP LAWS

| | *Does State Have Statutory Recordkeeping Requirements?* | *Who Is Subject to the Requirements?* | *What FEP Records Must Be Kept?* | *Other* | *Citations to Authority* |
|---|---|---|---|---|---|
| AL | State has no specific statutory requirements. | State has no specific statutory requirements. | State has no specific statutory requirements. | State has no specific statutory requirements. | — |
| AK | Yes. | Employers, labor organizations, and employment agencies. | Records on age, sex, and race required to administer state civil rights laws. | State has no specific statutory requirements. | Alaska Stat. § 28.80.220. |
| AZ | Yes. | Employers with 15 or more employees, labor organizations with 15 or more members, and employment agencies. | Records as set forth by state regulations or records that would comply with U.S. EEOC guidelines. | An employer may apply for an exemption to the rule if compliance would create an undue hardship. | Ariz. Rev. Stat. Ann. § 41-1482. |
| AR | Yes. | All employers subject to wage discrimination laws. | Salaries, wage rates, job classifications, and terms and conditions for employment. | Records must be kept for three years. | Ark. Stat. § 11-4-612. |
| CA | Yes. | Employers with five or more employees, but not religious associations or nonprofit corporations; all labor organizations and employment agencies. | All applications, personnel/membership/employment reference records and files as provided under state FEP statutes. | Records must be kept for two years. If a complaint is filed, all records must be kept until the complaint is disposed of or the appeal is terminated. For purposes of state wage discrimination laws, all records of wage rates, wages, job classification, and terms and conditions of employment must be kept for two years. | Cal. Gov't Code § 12496; Cal. Labor Code § 1197.5. |
| CO | Yes. | Employers other than religious organizations. | Employers other than religious organizations must keep records on disability, age, sex, race, creed, color, and national origin of individuals as required by federal/state law. | State has no specific statutory requirements. | Colo. Rev. Stat. Ann. § 24-34-402. |
| CT | State has no specific statutory requirements. | State has no specific statutory requirements. | State has no specific statutory requirements. | State has no specific statutory requirements. | — |
| DE | Yes. | Employers with four or more employees (but not religious organizations or charitable associations); all employment agencies or labor organizations. | Such records as are specified under state FEP statutes. | An employer may receive an exemption for undue hardship. | Del. Code Ann. tit. 19 § 714. |

(Table continues.)

**Table 2.5-3** *(cont'd)*

RECORDKEEPING REQUIREMENTS UNDER STATE FEP LAWS

| | *Does State Have Statutory Recordkeeping Requirements?* | *Who Is Subject to the Requirements?* | *What FEP Records Must Be Kept?* | *Other* | *Citations to Authority* |
|---|---|---|---|---|---|
| DC | Yes. | All employers, employment agencies, and labor organizations. | Any regularly kept business records, including applications, credit/reference reports, personnel records, records pertaining to the status of an individual's enjoyment of rights protected by state FEP law. | Such records must be kept for six months. If a charge of discrimination is made, all records must be kept until final disposition of the charge. | D.C. Code Ann. § 1-2524. |
| FL | State has no specific statutory requirements. | State has no specific statutory requirements. | State has no specific statutory requirements. | State has no specific statutory requirements. | — |
| GA | State has no specific statutory requirements. | State has no specific statutory requirements. | State has no specific statutory requirements. | State has no specific statutory requirements. | — |
| HI | Yes. | All employers with one or more employees. | Any records relevant to discrimination. | State has no specific statutory requirements. | Haw. Rev. Stat. Ann. § 378-6. |
| ID | State has no specific statutory requirements. | State has no specific statutory requirements. | State has no specific statutory requirements. | State has no specific statutory requirements. | — |
| IL | State has no specific statutory requirements. | State has no specific statutory requirements. | State has no specific statutory requirements. | State has no specific statutory requirements. | — |
| IN | Yes. | Employers with six or more employees. Religious organizations and nonprofit corporations are exempt. | Records of employees' ages. | State has no specific statutory requirements. | Ind. Stat. Ann. § 22-9-2-6. |
| IA | State has no specific statutory requirements. | State has no specific statutory requirements. | State has no specific statutory requirements. | State has no specific statutory requirements. | — |
| KS | State has no specific statutory requirements. | State has no specific statutory requirements. | State has no specific statutory requirements. | State has no specific statutory requirements. | — |
| KY | Yes. | Employers with eight or more employees. Private membership clubs are exempt. | Any records relevant to the determination of whether a violation of state civil rights laws has occurred. | State has no specific statutory requirements. | Ky. Rev. Stat. § 344.250. |
| LA | Yes. | All employers subject to state human rights laws. | Any records relevant to the determination of whether a violation of the state human rights law has been committed. | An exemption may be granted if an employer can show that the recordkeeping requirement would create an undue hardship. | La. Rev. Stat. § 51:2262. |
| ME | State has no specific statutory requirements. | State has no specific statutory requirements. | State has no specific statutory requirements. | State has no specific statutory requirements. | — |

| | | | | | |
|---|---|---|---|---|---|
| MD | Yes. | All employers. | Wages, job classifications, and other conditions of employment as required by state law on wage discrimination based on sex. | State has no specific statutory requirements. | Md. Labor & Emp. Code Ann. § 3-305. |
| MA | Yes. | All employers, except religious, agricultural, or nonprofit organizations. | Records of the age of each employee. | A violation is punishable by a fine of $25–$100. | Mass. Gen. Laws Ann. tit. 149, § 24D. |
| MI | State has no specific statutory requirements. | State has no specific statutory requirements. | State has no specific statutory requirements. | State has no specific statutory requirements. | — |
| MN | State has no specific statutory requirements. | State has no specific statutory requirements. | State has no specific statutory requirements. | State has no specific statutory requirements. | — |
| MS | State has no specific statutory requirements. | State has no specific statutory requirements. | State has no specific statutory requirements. | State has no specific statutory requirements. | — |
| MO | State has no specific statutory requirements. | State has no specific statutory requirements. | State has no specific statutory requirements. | State has no specific statutory requirements. | — |
| MT | Yes. | All employers, labor organizations, and employment agencies. | Records on age, sex, and race. | State has no specific statutory requirements. | Mont. Code Ann. § 49-2-102. |
| NE | Yes. | Employers with 15 or more employees, employment agencies, and labor organizations. | All records relevant to the determination of whether an unlawful employment practice has been committed. | Employers with 25 or more employees are required to keep records of the wages, wage rates, job classifications, and other terms and conditions of employment for compliance with state laws against wage discrimination based on sex. | Neb. Rev. Stat. Ann. §§ 48-1117, 48-1225. |
| NV | State has no specific statutory requirements. | State has no specific statutory requirements. | State has no specific statutory requirements. | State has no specific statutory requirements. | — |
| NH | State has no specific statutory requirements. | State has no specific statutory requirements. | State has no specific statutory requirements. | State has no specific statutory requirements. | — |
| NJ | State has no specific statutory requirements. | State has no specific statutory requirements. | State has no specific statutory requirements. | State has no specific statutory requirements. | — |
| NM | State has no specific statutory requirements. | State has no specific statutory requirements. | State has no specific statutory requirements. | State has no specific statutory requirements. | — |
| NY | Yes. | All employers. | State has no specific statutory requirements. | There are no requirements under general FEP statutes as to what records must be kept, but employers are required to keep records of wage payment for all employees, pursuant to statute prohibiting wage discrimination based on sex. | N.Y. Lab. Law § 195. |
| NC | State has no specific statutory requirements. | State has no specific statutory requirements. | State has no specific statutory requirements. | State has no specific statutory requirements. | — |

*(Table continues.)*

**Table 2.5-3** *(cont'd)*

RECORDKEEPING REQUIREMENTS UNDER STATE FEP LAWS

| | *Does State Have Statutory Recordkeeping Requirements?* | *Who Is Subject to the Requirements?* | *What FEP Records Must Be Kept?* | *Other* | *Citations to Authority* |
|---|---|---|---|---|---|
| ND | Yes. | All employers. | Records of wages, wage rates, job classifications, and other terms and conditions of employment, as specified in the statutes prohibiting discrimination on the basis of sex. | State has no specific statutory requirements. | N.D. Cent. Code § 34-06.1-07. |
| OH | State has no specific statutory requirements. | State has no specific statutory requirements. | State has no specific statutory requirements. | State has no specific statutory requirements. | — |
| OK | Yes. | Employers with 15 or more employees, labor organizations, and employment agencies. | Employers with apprenticeship or training programs must keep such records as required by the state Human Rights Commission reasonably necessary to carry out the purposes of state laws prohibiting discrimination on the basis of race, color, religion, sex, national origin, age, or handicap. | State has no specific statutory requirements. | Okla. Stat. Ann. tit. 25, § 1507. |
| OR | State has no specific statutory requirements. | State has no specific statutory requirements. | State has no specific statutory requirements. | State has no specific statutory requirements. | — |
| PA | Yes. | All employers and labor organizations. | Records of wages, wage rates, job classifications, and terms and conditions of employment as required under state statute prohibiting discrimination on the basis of sex. | State has no specific statutory requirements. | Pa. Stat. Ann. tit. 43, § 336.6. |
| RI | State has no specific statutory requirements. | State has no specific statutory requirements. | State has no specific statutory requirements. | State has no specific statutory requirements. | — |
| SC | State has no specific statutory requirements. | State has no specific statutory requirements. | State has no specific statutory requirements. | State has no specific statutory requirements. | — |
| SD | Yes. | Employers with more than 25 employees. | Records of wages, wage rates, job classifications, and other terms and conditions as required by state law prohibiting wage discrimination based on sex. | State has no specific statutory requirements. | S.D. Codified Laws § 60-12-17. |

| | | | | | |
|---|---|---|---|---|---|
| TN | Yes. | Employers with eight or more employees, labor organizations, and employment agencies. | All records relevant to the determination of whether a violation of state law prohibiting discrimination on the basis of race, creed, color, religion, sex, age, or national origin has been committed. | State has no specific statutory requirements. | Tenn. Code Ann. § 4-21-308. |
| TX | Yes. | Employers with 15 or more employees, labor organizations, and employment agencies. | Employers under investigation for violations of state FEP laws must keep all records relevant to the determination of whether a violation has been committed. Employers with apprenticeship or training programs must keep all records reasonably necessary to carry out the purposes of state FEP laws, including lists of applicants and the chronological order in which applications were received. | All records must conform to standards required under 42 U.S.C. § 2000e-8(c). | Tex. Lab. Code Ann. §§ 21.301, 21.302, 21.303. |
| UT | State has no specific statutory requirements. | State has no specific statutory requirements. | State has no specific statutory requirements. | State has no specific statutory requirements. | — |
| VT | State has no specific statutory requirements. | State has no specific statutory requirements. | State has no specific statutory requirements. | State has no specific statutory requirements. | — |
| VA | State has no specific statutory requirements. | State has no specific statutory requirements. | State has no specific statutory requirements. | State has no specific statutory requirements. | — |
| WA | State has no specific statutory requirements. | State has no specific statutory requirements. | State has no specific statutory requirements. | State has no specific statutory requirements. | — |
| WV | State has no specific statutory requirements. | State has no specific statutory requirements. | State has no specific statutory requirements. | State has no specific statutory requirements. | — |
| WI | State has no specific statutory requirements. | State has no specific statutory requirements. | State has no specific statutory requirements. | State has no specific statutory requirements. | — |
| WY | State has no specific statutory requirements. | State has no specific statutory requirements. | State has no specific statutory requirements. | State has no specific statutory requirements. | — |

# Table 2.5-4
## NOTICE POSTING REQUIREMENTS UNDER STATE FEP LAWS

| | *Does State Have Statutory Notice Posting Requirements?* | *Who Is Subject to the Requirements?* | *Which FEP Notices Must Be Posted?* | *Other* | *Citations to Authority* |
|---|---|---|---|---|---|
| AL | State has no specific statutory requirements. | State has no specific statutory requirements. | State has no specific statutory requirements. | State has no specific statutory requirements. | — |
| AK | Yes. | Employers with 15 or more employees. | State-prepared notice on sexual harassment. | State has no specific statutory requirements. | Alaska Stat. §§ 18.80.220, 23.10.440. |
| AZ | Yes. | Employers or labor organizations with 15 or more employees or members, and employment agencies. | Notice prepared by the state civil rights division. | Intentional failure to post notices after the division delivers them is a petty offense. | Ariz. Rev. Stat. Ann. § 41-1483. |
| AR | State has no specific statutory requirements. | State has no specific statutory requirements. | State has no specific statutory requirements. | State has no specific statutory requirements. | — |
| CA | Yes. | Employers with five or more employees; religious organizations and nonprofit corporations are exempt. | Poster sent by the state. May be obtained through the Office of Documents and Publications of the Department of General Services. | Information sheet prepared by agency, or version prepared by employer, containing relevant information on sexual harassment shall be distributed. | Cal. Gov't Code § 12950. |
| CO | State has no specific statutory requirements. | State has no specific statutory requirements. | State has no specific statutory requirements. | State has no specific statutory requirements. | — |
| CT | Yes. | Employers, employment agencies, and labor organizations. | Any notices regarding statutory provisions distributed by the state Commission on Human Rights. Any employers with more than three employees must post information on the illegality of sexual harassment and the available remedies. | The failure to post a required notice may result in a fine up to $250. | Conn. Gen. Stat. Ann. § 46a-54, 46a-97. |
| DE | Yes. | Employers with four or more employees (but not religious or charitable associations), employment agencies, and labor organizations. | Notice prepared by the Department of Labor. | Willful failure to post the required notice is punishable by a fine up to $100. | Del. Code Ann. tit. 19, § 716. |
| DC | Yes. | All persons subject to discrimination laws, including employment agencies and labor organizations. | Notice prepared by DC Office of Human Rights. | State has no specific statutory requirements. | D.C. Code Ann § 1-2522. |
| FL | Yes. | Employers, employment agencies, and labor organizations. | Notice provided by the Commission on Human Rights. | State has no specific statutory requirements. | Fla. Stat. Ann. § 760.10. |

| | | | | | |
|---|---|---|---|---|---|
| GA | Yes. | Every employer with ten or more employees. | Notices regarding state prohibition of sexual discrimination. | State has no specific statutory requirements. | Ga. Code Ann. § 34-5-7. |
| HI | State has no specific statutory requirements. | State has no specific statutory requirements. | State has no specific statutory requirements. | State has no specific statutory requirements. | — |
| ID | State has no specific statutory requirements. | State has no specific statutory requirements. | State has no specific statutory requirements. | State has no specific statutory requirements. | — |
| IL | Yes. | Any entity covered by the state human rights law. | If a civil rights violation occurs, a state hearing officer may require the offender to post notices setting forth requirements for compliance with the state human rights act. | State has no specific statutory requirements. | 775 I.L.C.S. 5/8A-104. |
| IN | Yes. | Employers with at least 15 employees. Private membership clubs are exempt. | Notices as prescribed by 42 U.S.C. § 2000e-10 regarding disability discrimination. | State has no specific statutory requirements. | Ind. Stat. Ann. §§ 22-9-5-10, 22-9-5-25. |
| IA | Yes. | Any party found guilty of a violation of state civil rights laws. | As required by the state Civil Rights Commission, as a remedial action following a finding of a violation of state civil rights laws. | State has no specific statutory requirements. | Iowa Code Ann. § 216.15. |
| KS | Yes. | All employers with four or more employees, labor organizations, and employment agencies. | Notice prepared by state Human Rights Commission. Also, age discrimination notice prepared by state Human Rights Commission. | State has no specific statutory requirements. | Kan. Stat. Ann. §§ 44-1012, 44-1114. |
| KY | Yes. | Employers with two or more employees. | Notices containing abstracts or copies of state statutes regarding wage discrimination based on sex. | State Civil Rights Commission may require posting other notices. | Ky. Rev. Stat. §§ 337.433, 344.190. |
| LA | Yes. | Employers with 20 or more employees. | Notice prepared by the state Department of Labor setting forth information on age discrimination. | Employers are also required to post notices prepared by the state Department of Labor setting forth information on discrimination based on sickle-cell trait. Notice posting may also be required as a remedial action for offenders of the state civil rights laws. | La. Rev. Stat. §§ 23:311, 23:314, 23:351, 23:354, 51:2261. |
| ME | Yes. | Any employer subject to state human rights laws. | Any notice required by the state Human Rights Commission. | State has no specific statutory requirements. | Me. Rev. Stat. Ann. tit. 5, § 4566. |
| MD | Yes. | All employers. | Copies of state law on wage discrimination based on sex. | State has no specific statutory requirements. | Md. Lab. & Emp. Code Ann. § 3-306. |
| MA | Yes. | All employers with six or more employees (except nonprofit associations), employment agencies, and labor organizations. | Notice prepared by state Commission Against Discrimination. | A first violation carries a fine of \$10–\$100. Subsequent violations carry a fine of \$100–\$1000. | Mass. Gen. Laws. Ann. tit. 151B, § 7. |

*(Table continues.)*

## Table 2.5-4 *(cont'd)*
## NOTICE POSTING REQUIREMENTS UNDER STATE FEP LAWS

| | *Does State Have Statutory Notice Posting Requirements?* | *Who Is Subject to the Requirements?* | *Which FEP Notices Must Be Posted?* | *Other* | *Citations to Authority* |
|---|---|---|---|---|---|
| MI | Yes. | All employers, labor organizations, and employment agencies. | Notice containing information on the requirement of notification to an employer that an accommodation is needed for a handicapped employee. | State has no specific statutory requirements. | Mich. Comp. Laws Ann. § 37.1210. |
| MN | State has no specific statutory requirements. | State has no specific statutory requirements. | State has no specific statutory requirements. | State has no specific statutory requirements. | — |
| MS | State has no specific statutory requirements. | State has no specific statutory requirements. | State has no specific statutory requirements. | State has no specific statutory requirements. | — |
| MO | State has no specific statutory requirements. | State has no specific statutory requirements. | State has no specific statutory requirements. | State has no specific statutory requirements. | — |
| MT | Yes. | All employers, employment agencies, labor unions, educational institutions, and financial institutions. | Any notice as ordered by the state Commission for Human Rights. | Failure to comply with a Commission order to post a notice is a misdemeanor and carries a fine up to $50. | Mont. Code Ann. § 49-2-202. |
| NE | Yes. | Employers with 15 or more employees, employment agencies, and labor organizations. | Notice prepared by the state Fair Employment Commission setting forth provisions of the Fair Employment Practices Act. | Employers with 25 or more employees are required to post notices containing abstracts or copies of state laws prohibiting wage discrimination on the basis of sex. | Neb. Rev. Stat. Ann. §§ 48-1124, 48-1226. |
| NV | State has no specific statutory requirements. | State has no specific statutory requirements. | State has no specific statutory requirements. | State has no specific statutory requirements. | — |
| NH | Yes. | Employers with six or more employees, employment agencies, and labor unions; nonprofit associations are exempt. | Notice prepared by state Commission on Human Rights containing any relevant information necessary to explain state human rights laws. | State has no specific statutory requirements. | N.H. Rev. Stat. Ann. tit. 354-A, § 23. |
| NJ | Yes. | Contractors and subcontractors bidding on state, county, municipality, or other political subdivision public works contracts. | Notice stating that the contractor or subcontractor will not discriminate on the basis of age, race, creed, color, national origin, ancestry, marital status, affectional or sexual orientation, or sex. | State has no specific statutory requirements. | N.J. Stat. Ann. § 10:5-33. |

| | | | | | |
|---|---|---|---|---|---|
| NM | Yes. | Employers with four or more employees, labor organizations, and employment agencies. | Excerpts of the state Human Rights Act. | State has no specific statutory requirements. | N.M. Stat. Ann. § 28-1-14. |
| NY | State has no specific statutory requirements. | State has no specific statutory requirements. | State has no specific statutory requirements. | State has no specific statutory requirements. | — |
| NC | State has no specific statutory requirements. | State has no specific statutory requirements. | State has no specific statutory requirements. | State has no specific statutory requirements. | — |
| ND | State has no specific statutory requirements. | State has no specific statutory requirements. | State has no specific statutory requirements. | State has no specific statutory requirements. | — |
| OH | Yes. | Employers with four or more employees, labor organizations, and employment agencies. | Notice prepared or approved by the state Civil Rights Commission setting forth information on discrimination based on race, color, religion, sex, national origin, handicap, age, or ancestry. | State has no specific statutory requirements. | Ohio Rev. Code Ann. § 4112.07. |
| OK | State has no specific statutory requirements. | State has no specific statutory requirements. | State has no specific statutory requirements. | State has no specific statutory requirements. | — |
| OR | State has no specific statutory requirements. | State has no specific statutory requirements. | State has no specific statutory requirements. | State has no specific statutory requirements. | — |
| PA | Yes. | All employers and labor organizations. | Abstracts, as supplied by the state Department of Labor and Industry, of the state statute prohibiting discrimination on the basis of sex. | State has no specific statutory requirements. | Pa. Stat. Ann. tit. 43, § 336.7. |
| RI | Yes. | Employers with four or more employees, employment agencies, and labor unions. | Notice prepared or approved by state Commission Against Discrimination setting forth excerpts of state law prohibiting discrimination on the basis of race, color, religion, sex, disability, age, sexual orientation, or country of ancestral origin. | A violation carries a fine of $100–$500. | R.I. Gen. Laws § 28-5-37. |
| SC | State has no specific statutory requirements. | State has no specific statutory requirements. | State has no specific statutory requirements. | State has no specific statutory requirements. | — |
| SD | State has no specific statutory requirements. | State has no specific statutory requirements. | State has no specific statutory requirements. | State has no specific statutory requirements. | — |
| TN | Yes. | Employers with eight or more employees, labor organizations, and employment agencies. | Notices prepared or approved by the state Human Rights Commission dealing with state FEP laws. | State has no specific statutory requirements. | Tenn. Code Ann. § 4-21-202. |
| TX | State has no specific statutory requirements. | State has no specific statutory requirements. | State has no specific statutory requirements. | State has no specific statutory requirements. | — |
| UT | State has no specific statutory requirements. | State has no specific statutory requirements. | State has no specific statutory requirements. | State has no specific statutory requirements. | — |

*(Table continues.)*

## Table 2.5-4 *(cont'd)*
## NOTICE POSTING REQUIREMENTS UNDER STATE FEP LAWS

| | *Does State Have Statutory Notice Posting Requirements?* | *Who Is Subject to the Requirements?* | *Which FEP Notices Must Be Posted?* | *Other* | *Citations to Authority* |
|---|---|---|---|---|---|
| VT | Yes. | Employers, employment agencies, and labor organizations. | Notice containing elements of the employer's policy against sexual harassment. | Employers must also distribute the notice to their employees. | Vt. Stat. Ann. tit. 21, § 495h. |
| VA | State has no specific statutory requirements. | State has no specific statutory requirements. | State has no specific statutory requirements. | State has no specific statutory requirements. | — |
| WA | State has no specific statutory requirements. | State has no specific statutory requirements. | State has no specific statutory requirements. | State has no specific statutory requirements. | — |
| WV | Yes. | Employers with 12 or more employees, labor organizations, and employment agencies. | Notice prepared or approved by state Human Rights Commission setting forth excerpts of state statutes prohibiting discrimination on the basis of race, religion, color, national origin, ancestry, sex, blindness, handicap, or familial status. | State has no specific statutory requirements. | W. Va. Code § 5-11-17. |
| WI | State has no specific statutory requirements. | State has no specific statutory requirements. | State has no specific statutory requirements. | State has no specific statutory requirements. | — |
| WY | State has no specific statutory requirements. | State has no specific statutory requirements. | State has no specific statutory requirements. | State has no specific statutory requirements. | — |

# Wages, Hours, and Holidays

*Tables in Part 3 cover minimum wage requirements and exemptions, penalties for violating minimum wage laws and overtime provisions, recordkeeping requirements for adult employees and minors, penalties for violating recordkeeping requirements, penalties for violating child labor laws, and state holidays.*

# § 3.1 Overview: The Fair Labor Standards Act and State Regulation of Employment

Enacted in 1938, the federal Fair Labor Standards Act (FLSA) regulates minimum standards for wages and working hours for employees whose employers either engage in interstate commerce or produce goods for interstate commerce. Under the broad interpretation accorded interstate commerce, the FLSA protects most employees in the United States. The FLSA, however, does not preempt state legislation in areas of the FLSA's coverage; it merely sets minimum standards for wages and hours of employees. States are free to go further than the FLSA in enacting legislation to protect workers in these areas. Moreover, state legislation alone regulates the conduct of businesses that do not engage in interstate commerce or produce goods for interstate commerce, including businesses merely "affecting" interstate commerce.

As a result of the Small Business Job Protection Act, the federal minimum wage went up to $5.15 effective September 1, 1997.

Most states have enacted their own minimum wage acts that either supplement the FLSA or apply to businesses not covered under federal law. These state laws typically set

- Minimum wages and overtime provisions for most occupations
- Regulations for employment of minors
- Exemptions for some occupations
- Recordkeeping requirements
- Penalties for violations

Remember that many states have state commissions or labor departments that are authorized to promulgate regulations or wage orders implementing these state statutes. Therefore, in addition to reviewing statutory requirements, examine state administrative regulations as well.

## § 3.2 Ongoing Compensation Requirements and Penalties

Table 3.2-1 lists the statutory requirements relating to intervals of paying compensation. These laws require employers to pay all workers their regular wages at certain intervals, usually biweekly or semimonthly, although employers are almost always permitted to pay employees more frequently than required. A few states mandate that wages must be paid weekly or monthly. Certain types of workers, such as administrative, professional, or executive employees, are frequently exempt from the requirements. Several state legislatures have set compensation payment schedules for workers in particular occupations, such as agriculture, at intervals more frequent than other jobs. In a few states, the laws apply only to government or public service corporation employees.

Penalties for violations of the wage payment laws may be both civil and criminal. State laws often allow employees to recover costs and attorneys' fees in addition to other damages, and many states have provisions for extra fines or damages payable to either the state or the employee. These extra fines may be flat rates or a percentage of the total amounts owed to the employee or employees. Often each missed payment to each employee counts as a separate violation for purposes of penalties.

In the states that consider violation of the laws to be criminal, the act is usually classified as a misdemeanor, with the possibility of fines and imprisonment. Subsequent violations or violations by corporations may lead to stricter penalties.

# Table 3.2-1
## FREQUENCY OF PAYMENT OF COMPENSATION

| | *Wage Payment Requirements* | *Exceptions* | *Civil/Administrative Remedies* | *Criminal Penalties* | *Citations to Authority* |
|---|---|---|---|---|---|
| AL | Biweekly, or twice during each calendar month. Note: law applies only to public service corporations engaged in transportation and employing 50 or more workers. | — | — | Violation is a misdemeanor with a fine of $25–$250. | Ala. Code § 37-8-270. |
| AK | Semimonthly or monthly. | — | — | Fine of up to $1,000 and one year imprisonment. | Alaska Stat. §§ 23.05.140, 23.05.180, 23.05.280. |
| AZ | Semimonthly. | Compensation may be paid monthly to professional, administrative, or executive employees or outside salesmen, or employees employed in a supervisory capacity of out-of-state employers. | Employee may recover treble damages. | Violation is a petty offense with a maximum fine of $300. | Ariz. Rev. Stat. Ann. §§ 13-802, 23-351, 23-355, 23-356. |
| AR | Corporations must pay salesmen, mechanics, laborers, and certain other employees semimonthly. | Large businesses may pay qualified management and executive employees monthly. | — | Violation is a misdemeanor with a fine of $50–$500. | Ark. Code Ann. § 11-4-401. |
| CA | Semimonthly. Wages earned between the 1st and 15th of a month must be paid between the 16th and 26th of the month; wages earned between the 16th and end of the month must be paid between the 1st and 10th of the following month. Employer must post notice specifying regular paydays and the time and place of payment. | Qualified executive, administrative, or professional employees; employees of vehicle dealerships; public employees; and agricultural and domestic workers. | For initial violation, penalty of $50. For subsequent or willful violations, $100 or 25% of amounts owed. | Violation is a misdemeanor with a maximum penalty of a $1,000 fine and 6 months' imprisonment. | Cal. Lab. Code §§ 23, 204–205, 206, 207, 210, 215, 220. |
| CO | Monthly, unless otherwise mutually agreed. | — | $50 per day penalty payable to the state. Employee may recover costs and attorneys' fees in addition to damages. | — | Colo. Rev. Stat. §§ 8-4-105, 8-4-109, 8-4-110, 8-4-114. |
| CT | Weekly. | Labor commissioner may grant exceptions. | Civil penalty of double the amount owed; employee may recover costs and attorneys' fees in addition to damages. | Fine of $200–$5,000 and imprisonment of 3 months to 5 years, depending on the amount owed. | Conn. Gen. Stat. Ann. §§ 31-71b, 31-71d, 31-71g, 31-71i, 31-72. |

| | | | | | |
|---|---|---|---|---|---|
| DE | Monthly. | Governmental employees and railroad employees. | Civil penalty of $1,000–$5,000. Employee may recover costs and attorneys' fees in addition to liquidated damages of 10% of unpaid wages, per day. | — | Del. Code Ann. tit. 19 §§ 1102, 1103, 1112, 1113. |
| DC | Semimonthly. | Certain employers may continue to pay employees monthly, if that was their prior custom. | Employee may recover costs and attorneys' fees in addition to damages. | Violation is a misdemeanor with initial penalties of up to a $300 fine and 30 days' imprisonment. Subsequent violations carry penalties of up to a $1,000 fine and 90 days' imprisonment. | D.C. Code §§ 36-102, 36-107, 36-108. |
| FL | — | — | — | — | No state statutory provisions. |
| GA | Semimonthly. | Agricultural, sawmill, and turpentine workers; officials, heads, and subheads of departments. | — | — | Ga. Code Ann. § 34-7-2. |
| HI | Semimonthly. | Employers may receive exemptions from the director of labor. | Employee may recover costs and attorneys' fees in addition to unpaid wages and interest. | Fine of $100–$10,000 and 1 year imprisonment. | Haw. Rev. Stat. §§ 388-2, 388-10, 388-11. |
| ID | Monthly. | — | Maximum civil penalty of $500 per employer per pay period. Employee may recover costs and attorneys' fees in addition to treble damages. | — | Idaho Code §§ 45-608, 45-615. |
| IL | Semimonthly. | Executive, administrative, and professional employees may be paid once a month. State and federal governmental employees are exempt. Commissions may also be paid monthly. | — | Violation is a Class C misdemeanor with maximum penalties of a $1,500 fine and 30 days' imprisonment. | Ill. Comp. Stat. Ann. ch. 730 §§ 5/5-8-3, 5/5-9-1, ch. 820 §§ 115/1, 115/3, 115/14. |
| IN | Semimonthly or biweekly, at employee's request. | Agricultural, horticultural, and certain salaried employees are exempt. Specified types of employers may pay employees biweekly. | Employee may recover costs, attorneys' fees, and liquidated damages of up to double amounts owed. | — | Ind. Code Ann. §§ 22-2-4-1, 22-2-5-1, 22-2-5-1.1, 22-2-5-2, 22-2-5-3. |
| IA | Monthly, semimonthly, or biweekly. | Certain agricultural laborers are exempt. | Maximum civil penalty of $100. Employee may recover costs and attorneys' fees in addition to unpaid wages and liquidated damages. | — | Iowa Code §§ 91A.2, 91A.3, 91A.8, 91A.12. |
| KS | Monthly. | — | Administrative action for wages and damages. | — | Kan. Stat. Ann. §§ 44-314, 44-322a. |
| KY | Semimonthly. | Certain executives, administrators, supervisors, professionals, outside salesmen, and outside collectors are exempt. | Civil penalty of $100–$1,000, plus costs, attorneys' fees, and liquidated damages. | — | Ky. Rev. Stat. Ann. §§ 337.010, 337.020, 337.990. |

*(Table continues.)*

## Table 3.2-1 *(cont'd)*
## FREQUENCY OF PAYMENT OF COMPENSATION

| | *Wage Payment Requirements* | *Exceptions* | *Civil/Administrative Remedies* | *Criminal Penalties* | *Citations to Authority* |
|---|---|---|---|---|---|
| LA | Manufacturing, mining, and oil employees of businesses employing at least 10 workers and public service corporation employees must be paid biweekly or semimonthly. | Executive, administrative, professional, supervisory, or clerical employees, as well as salesmen, are exempt. Certain public service corporation employees are exempt. | — | Fine of $25–$250 and 10 days' imprisonment. | La. Rev. Stat. Ann. § 23.633. |
| ME | Weekly, for specified employers. Biweekly for municipalities unless employee agrees. | Municipalities may pay employees biweekly. | Civil penalty of $100–$500. Employee may recover costs, attorneys' fees, interest, and liquidated damages of double amount owed. | — | Me. Rev. Stat. Ann. tit. 26 §§ 621, 626-A. |
| MD | Semimonthly or biweekly. | Administrative, executive, and professional employees are exempt. | Employee may recover unpaid wages, costs, attorneys' fees, and damages of up to three times the amount owed. | Violation is a misdemeanor with a maximum fine of $1,000. | Md. Lab. Code Ann. Lab. & Empl. §§ 3-502, 3-507, 3-507.1, 3-508. |
| MA | Weekly or biweekly. | Qualified railroad and hospital employees; agricultural employees; and executive, administrative, and professional employees are exempt. | Employee may recover treble damages, costs, and attorneys' fees. | Fine of $500 to $3,000 and up to 2 months' imprisonment. | Mass. Gen. Laws Ann. ch. 149 §§ 148, 150. |
| MI | Wages earned during the first fifteen days of a month must be paid on or before the 1st day of the succeeding month. Wages earned from the 16th to the last day of a month must be paid by the 15th day of the succeeding month. | Certain agricultural employees are exempt. Employers may also set up weekly, biweekly, or monthly pay schedules and be in compliance if statutory guidelines are followed. | Civil penalties of 10% of wages due, and double wages due for repeated or flagrant violations. Employer may also owe a $1,000 penalty to the state. | Violation is a misdemeanor. If the employer intended to defraud the employee, punishment is a fine of up to $1,000 and one year of imprisonment. | Mich. Stat. Ann. §§ 17.277(2), 17.277(14), 17.277(15), 17.277(18). |
| MN | Every 30 days. | Public service corporation employees may be paid semimonthly. Transitory employees must be paid every 15 days. | Employee may recover reasonable costs, disbursements, witness fees, and attorneys' fees. | — | Minn. Stat. Ann. §§ 181.08, 181.10, 181.13, 181.17, 181.101 |
| MS | Public service corporations and employers engaged in manufacturing who employ 50 or more workers must pay employees semimonthly or biweekly. | Executive, administrative, and professional employees are exempt. | — | Violation is a misdemeanor with a fine of $25–$250. | Miss. Code Ann. §§ 71-1-35, 71-1-53. |

| | | | | | |
|---|---|---|---|---|---|
| MO | All corporations, factories, and railroad industry employers must pay employees semimonthly. | Executive, administrative, professional, and sales employees, and employees compensated on a commission basis are exempt. | Civil penalty of double wages owed. | Violation is a misdemeanor with a fine of $50–$500. | Mo. Rev. Stat. §§ 290.080, 290.090. |
| MT | Employees must be paid within 10 business days of the time wages become due and payable. | Professional, supervisory, and technical employees may be paid monthly. Agricultural employees are exempt. | Employee may recover costs and attorneys' fees in addition to damages. | Violation is a misdemeanor with a fine of $500 and 6 months' imprisonment. | Mont. Code Ann. §§ 39-3-204, 39-3-206, 39-3-207, 46-18-212. |
| NE | Employer must establish regular payday. | Certain independent employees are exempt. | Employee may recover costs and attorneys' fees in addition to damages. For willful violations, an additional penalty of double amount owed is payable to the state. | — | Neb. Rev. Stat. §§ 48-1229–48-1232. |
| NV | Semimonthly. For work done before the 1st day of a month, wages must be paid by 8:00 A.M. on the 15th of the month. For work done before the 16th day of the month, wages must be paid by 8:00 A.M. on the last day of the month. | Executive, administrative, and professional employees; supervisors; and outside salesmen may be paid monthly. | Employee may recover costs and attorneys' fees in addition to damages. | Violation is a misdemeanor with a maximum fine of $1,000 and 6 months' imprisonment. | Nev. Rev. Stat. §§ 193.150, 608.060, 608.140, 608.195. |
| NH | Weekly. | The labor commissioner may grant exemptions. | Employee may recover costs and attorneys' fees in addition to damages. | Willful violation is a misdemeanor with a $2,000 fine ($20,000 for corporations) and 1 year imprisonment. | N.H. Rev. Stat. Ann. §§ 275.42, 275.43, 275.45, 275.52, 275.53, 651.2. |
| NJ | Semimonthly. | Executive and supervisory employees may be paid monthly. | Administrative penalty of $250 for first offense and $500 for subsequent violations. | Knowing or willful violation is a disorderly persons offense with a fine of $100–$1,000. | N.J. Stat. Ann. §§ 34:11-4.2, 34:11-4.8, 34:11-4.10. |
| NM | Semimonthly. | Professional, administrative, and executive employees and outside salesmen may be paid monthly. | Employee may follow procedures for administrative remedy. | Violation is a misdemeanor with a fine of $25–$50 and 10–90 days' imprisonment. | N.M. Stat. Ann. §§ 50-4-2, 50-4-10, 50-4-11. |
| NY | Manual workers and railroad workers must be paid weekly. Salesmen working on a commission basis must be paid monthly. Clerical and other workers must be paid semimonthly. | Large employers may pay manual workers semimonthly. Certain executive, administrative, and professional employees are exempt. | Civil penalty of $50. Employee may recover costs and attorneys' fees and liquidated damages of 25% amount owed if violation was willful. | Violation is a misdemeanor with a fine of $100–$10,000 and 1 year imprisonment. | N.Y. Lab. Law §§ 190, 191, 197, 198, 198a. |
| NC | Employer must establish a regular payday that may be daily, weekly, biweekly, semimonthly, or monthly. | Bonuses and commissions may be paid as infrequently as annually if prescribed in advance. | Employee may recover costs, attorneys' fees, interest, and additional liquidated damages equal to amount owed unless employer was acting in good faith. | — | N.C. Gen. Stat. §§ 95-25.6, 95-25.7A, 95-25.22. |

(Table continues.)

## Table 3.2-1 *(cont'd)*
## FREQUENCY OF PAYMENT OF COMPENSATION

| | *Wage Payment Requirements* | *Exceptions* | *Civil/Administrative Remedies* | *Criminal Penalties* | *Citations to Authority* |
|---|---|---|---|---|---|
| ND | Monthly. | — | Employee may recover interest and double damages if employer has engaged in violations two times in prior year; treble damages if employer has three prior violations. | Willful violation is an infraction with a fine of $500. The second violation in one year is a Class B misdemeanor with a fine of $500 and 30 days' imprisonment. | N.D. Cent. Code §§ 12.1-32-01, 34-14-02, 34-14-07, 34-14-09.1. |
| OH | Semimonthly. | Exceptions for certain occupations where the custom is otherwise. | Employee may recover liquidated damages of the greater of $200 and 6% of the amount owed. | Violation is a first-degree misdemeanor with a fine of $1,000 and 6 months' imprisonment. | Ohio Rev. Code §§ 2929.21, 4113.15, 4113.99. |
| OK | Semimonthly. | Management-level employees are exempt. Government workers may be paid monthly. | Employee may recover costs and attorneys' fees in addition to unpaid wages and liquidated damages. | Violation is a misdemeanor with a maximum penalty of $500 and 1 year imprisonment. | Okla. Stat. tit. 21 § 10, tit. 40 §§ 165.2, 165.8, 165.9. |
| OR | At least every 35 days. | Certain piecework and forest product employees must be paid monthly. | Employee may recover costs and attorneys' fees in addition to damages. | — | Or. Rev. Stat. §§ 652.120, 652.130, 652.200. |
| PA | Semimonthly. | Railroad employees must be paid weekly. | Civil penalty of $50. Employee may recover costs, attorneys' fees, and additional liquidated damages of up to the greater of $500 or 25% of the amount due. | Violation is a summary offense with a maximum fine of $300 and up to 90 days' imprisonment. | Pa. Stat. Ann. tit. 43 §§ 251, 252, 255.1, 255.3, 260.3, 260.6, 260.8, 260.9a, 260.10, 260.112. |
| RI | Weekly. | Government employees and employees of religious, charitable, and literary institutions may be paid at other intervals. | Employee may bring civil action and recover penalty of up to 25% of amount owed. | Violation is a misdemeanor with a fine of $50–$100 and 10–90 days' imprisonment. | R.I. Gen. Laws §§ 28-14-2.2, 28-14-8, 28-14-17, 28-14-18.1. |
| SC | Employer must establish regular payday. | Employers with fewer than 5 employees and domestic employees. | Civil penalty. First offense is a warning; second and subsequent offenses subject to fine of $100. Employee may recover costs, attorneys' fees, and treble damages. | — | S.C. Code Ann. §§ 41-10-30, 41-10-60, 41-10-80. |
| SD | Monthly. | — | Employee may recover costs and attorneys' fees in addition to damages; double damages if violation was malicious. | Violation is a Class 2 misdemeanor with a fine of $200 and 30 days' imprisonment. | S.D. Codified Laws §§ 22-6-2, 60-11-7, 60-11-9, 60-11-13, 60-11-15, 60-11-24. |

| | | | | | |
|---|---|---|---|---|---|
| TN | All wages earned prior to the first day of the month must be paid by the 20th day of the month. Wages earned by the 16th of the month must be paid by the 5th day of the succeeding month. Regular paydays must be established and maintained. | Employers of fewer than 5 employees are exempt. | Civil penalty of $500–$1,000 for willful violations. Employer cannot be charged both civilly and criminally. | Violation is a Class B misdemeanor with a fine of $100–$500. Employer cannot be charged both civilly and criminally. | Tenn. Code Ann. § 50-2-103. |
| TX | Semimonthly. | Employees who are exempt under the overtime provisions of the FLSA may be paid monthly. | Employee may pursue administrative remedy, with penalty up to $1,000 for bad faith violations. | Violation is a 3rd degree felony if, at the time of hiring, employer intended to avoid wage payments. | Tex. Lab. Code Ann. §§ 61.011, 61.019, 61.051, 61.053. |
| UT | Semimonthly. | Government, agricultural, and domestic workers are exempt. | Administrative penalty of up to 5% daily of wages owed. 50% of that recovered goes to administrative funding; 50% goes to affected employee. | Violation is a misdemeanor. | Utah Code Ann. §§ 34-28-1, 34-28-3, 34-28-9. |
| VT | Weekly. | Wages may be paid biweekly or semimonthly if employer gives written notice. | Employee may recover costs, attorneys' fees, and double damages. | Fine of $500 and 1 year imprisonment. | Vt. Stat. Ann. tit. 21 §§ 342, 345, 347. |
| VA | Salaried employees must be paid monthly. Hourly employees must be paid biweekly or semimonthly. | Students and executive personnel are exempt. | Civil penalty of $1,000. Employee may recover costs and attorneys' fees in addition to damages and interest. | Willful violation is a Class 1 misdemeanor with a fine of $2,500 and 12 months' imprisonment. | Va. Code Ann. §§ 18.2-11, 18.2-12, 40.1-29. |
| WA | — | — | Employee may recover costs and attorneys' fees in addition to damages. | — | Wash. Rev. Code § 49.48.030. |
| WV | Biweekly. | Railroad employees may be paid semimonthly. | Employee may recover costs and attorneys' fees in addition to damages. | — | W. Va. Code §§ 21-5-2, 21-5-3, 21-5-12. |
| WI | Monthly. | Certain logging and agricultural employees may be paid quarterly. | Civil penalty of 50% of wages owed. | Fine of $500 and 90 days' imprisonment. | Wis. Stat. Ann. §§ 109.03, 109.11. |
| WY | Manufacturing, mining, and prospecting employees must be paid semimonthly. | Agricultural employees are exempt. Employer and employee may mutually agree to payments other than semimonthly. | — | Violation is a misdemeanor with a fine of $25–$100 and maximum 90 days' imprisonment. | Wyo. Stat. §§ 27-4-101, 27-4-103. |

# § 3.3 Minimum Wage Requirements and Exemptions

Table 3.3-1 lists the minimum hourly pay rates for employees both in nonexempt occupations and occupations most commonly exempted by law from minimum wage requirements. It is not an exhaustive list of the states' exemptions. The definitions of the exempted categories, while similar, vary from state to state, so carefully review relevant statutes to determine the exact parameters of those listed, exempted categories. Further, although exempt employees are not guaranteed the minimum hourly wage rate under state law, they may be entitled to a minimum hourly wage rate under the FLSA. As a result of the Small Business Job Protection Act, the federal minimum wage is $5.15 effective September 1, 1997.

Several states allow a training or opportunity wage to be paid to employees for the first 90 days of employment. These provisions usually apply only to employees under 20 years of age. In addition, most states that allow this lower wage prohibit the employer from displacing other employees in order to hire workers at the lower rate. One state, Nebraska, has specified that no more than 25 percent of the total hours paid by an employer may be at the training wage. See Table I in the "Trends and Controversies" section of this Guide for specific state provisions.

Some state legislatures do not set their minimum wage rates by statute but, instead, delegate this authority to a state commission or department of labor. These bodies set minimum wage rates by administrative regulations or wage orders and can also define exempt categories of employees as well as set penalties for violations. States that have set the minimum wage rate by statute also may have authorized commissions or labor departments to administer and enforce these laws.

# Table 3.3-1
## MINIMUM WAGE REQUIREMENTS AND EXEMPTIONS

(When state and federal minimum wages differ, the higher wage is to be paid. In some instances, state minimum wage covers particular employees not covered under federal law. In those instances, the state wage should be paid. See also text at § 3.3.)

**KEY:** **Lower.** Employees in this category may/shall receive wages lower than the prescribed minimum wage if provided for in regulation or order (generally to prevent curtailment of employment opportunities); they are subject to separate state minimum wage requirements.

*For further details on specific provisions of state subminimum wage laws, see Table I in the "Trends and Controversies" section of this Guide.

| | *Minimum Wage Rates for Nonexempt Employees* | *Bona Fide Executives, Administrators, or Professionals* | *Agriculture* | *Domestic Service* | *Outside Salesperson* | *Students* | *Learners or Apprentices* | *Handicapped Working in Special Environments* | *Citations to Authority* |
|---|---|---|---|---|---|---|---|---|---|
| AL | — | — | — | — | — | — | — | — | No state statutory provisions. |
| AK | $5.65 (50 cents more than the prevailing federal minimum wage). | Exempt from state minimum wage requirements if they meet exemption criteria. | Exempt from state minimum wage requirements if they meet exemption criteria. | Exempt from state minimum wage requirements if they meet exemption criteria. | Exempt from state minimum wage requirements if they meet exemption criteria. | Exempt from state minimum wage requirements; subminimum wage set by the Department of Labor. | Wages may be lowered by regulation or order of the commissioner. | Wages may be lowered by regulation or order of the commissioner. | Alaska Stat. §§ 23.10.055, 23.10.065, 23.10.070, 23.10.360. |
| AZ | — | — | — | — | — | — | Wages may be lower than wage for experienced minors by special application. | Wages may be lower than for non-handicapped minors by special application. | Ariz. Rev. Stat. Ann. §§ 23-313, 23-316, 23-317, 23-326. State has no comprehensive minimum wage law. Minimum wages set by wage board for any substantial number of minors who have been paid "oppressive and unreasonable wages." |

*(Table continues.)*

# Table 3.3-1 *(cont'd)*
## MINIMUM WAGE REQUIREMENTS AND EXEMPTIONS

(When state and federal minimum wages differ, the higher wage is to be paid. In some instances, state minimum wage covers particular employees not covered under federal law. In those instances, the state wage should be paid. See also text at § 3.3.)

**KEY:** **Lower.** Employees in this category may/shall receive wages lower than the prescribed minimum wage if provided for in regulation or order (generally to prevent curtailment of employment opportunities); they are subject to separate state minimum wage requirements.

*For further details on specific provisions of state subminimum wage laws, see Table I in the "Trends and Controversies" section of this Guide.

| | *Minimum Wage Rates for Nonexempt Employees* | *Bona Fide Executives, Administrators, or Professionals* | *Agriculture* | *Domestic Service* | *Outside Salesperson* | *Students* | *Learners or Apprentices* | *Handicapped Working in Special Environments* | *Citations to Authority* |
|---|---|---|---|---|---|---|---|---|---|
| AR | $5.15. | Exempt from state minimum wage requirements if they meet exemption criteria. | Exempt from state minimum wage requirements if they meet exemption criteria. | Not exempt. | Exempt from state minimum wage requirements if they meet exemption criteria. | Exempt from state minimum wage requirements if they meet exemption criteria; subminimum wage of 85%. | Wages may be lowered by special application. | Wages may be lowered by special application. | Ark. Code Ann. §§ 11-4-203, 11-4-210, 11-4-214, 11-4-215. |
| CA | $5.75 (set by regulation). | Exempt from state minimum wage requirements if they meet exemption criteria. | Not exempt (see CCR Article 14 for Minimum Wage Order § 11100). | Not exempt (see CCR Article 14 for Minimum Wage Order § 11100). | Exempt from state minimum wage requirements if they meet exemption criteria. | Exempt from state minimum wage requirements if they meet exemption criteria; subminimum wage of 85%. | May be exempt by special license. | May be exempt by special license. | Cal. Lab. Code §§ 1171, 1173, 1191, 1192; Cal. Const. art. XIV, § 1; Cal. Code of Regs. tit. 8, § 11100 (Order No. MW-88). Regulations are set by the Industrial Welfare Commission, see IWC wage orders. |
| CO | $5.15 (set by regulation). | Not exempt. | Not exempt. | Not exempt. | Exempt from state minimum wage requirements if they meet exemption criteria. | Students employed by sororities, fraternities, college clubs, or dormitories or employed in a work experience study | Not exempt. | Exempt from state minimum wage requirements if they meet exemption criteria; subminimum wage of 85%. | Colo. Rev. Stat. §§ 8-6-106, 8-6-108.5, 8-6-112; Colo. Code of Regs. (Order No. 21). |

| | | | | | | | | | |
|---|---|---|---|---|---|---|---|---|---|
| | | | | | | program are exempt. | | | |
| CT | $5.65; $6.15 effective 1/1/00 or the federal minimum wage set by the FLSA, plus .005%, rounded to the nearest whole cent, whichever is greater). | Exempt from state minimum wage requirements if they meet exemption criteria. | Not exempt. | Exempt from state minimum wage requirements if they meet exemption criteria. | Exempt from state minimum wage requirements if they meet exemption criteria. | Not exempt. | Exempt from state minimum wage requirements if they meet exemption criteria; subminimum wage at 85% for the first 200 hours. | May be exempt by special license. | Conn. Gen. Stat. Ann. §§ 31-58, 31-60–31-62, 31-67. |
| DE | $5.15 (if federal minimum wage is greater than $5.00, state minimum wage equals federal minimum wage). | Exempt from state minimum wage requirements if they meet exemption criteria. | Exempt from state minimum wage requirements if they meet exemption criteria. | Exempt from state minimum wage requirements if they meet exemption criteria. | Exempt from state minimum wage requirements if they meet exemption criteria. | Not exempt. | Wages may be set at rate lower than required state minimum wage. | Wages may be set at rate lower than required state minimum wage. | Del. Code Ann. tit. 19, §§ 901, 902, 905, 906. |
| DC | $6.15 (equals the federal minimum wage set by the FLSA, plus $1). | Exempt from state minimum wage requirements if they meet exemption criteria. | Not exempt. | Not exempt. | Exempt from state minimum wage requirements if they meet exemption criteria. | Students employed by institutions of higher learning may be paid the federal minimum wage. | Exempt from state minimum wage requirements if they meet exemption criteria. | Exempt from state minimum wage requirements if they meet exemption criteria. | D.C. Code §§ 36-220.1, 36-220.2, 36-220.3. |
| FL | — | — | — | — | — | — | — | — | No state statutory provisions. |
| GA | $3.25. | Not exempt. | Exempt from state minimum wage requirements if they meet exemption criteria. | Exempt from state minimum wage requirements if they meet exemption criteria. | Not exempt. | Exempt from state minimum wage requirements if they meet exemption criteria. | Not exempt. | May be exempt by authorization. | Ga. Code Ann. §§ 34-4-3, 34-4-4. |
| HI | $5.25. | Exempt from state minimum wage requirements if they meet exemption criteria. | Exempt from state minimum wage requirements if they meet exemption criteria. | Exempt from state minimum wage requirements if they meet exemption criteria. | Exempt from state minimum wage requirements if they meet exemption criteria. | May be exempt by special certificate. | May be exempt by special certificate. | May be exempt by special certificate. | Haw. Rev. Stat. §§ 387-1, 387-2, 387-9. |

*(Table continues.)*

## Table 3.3-1 *(cont'd)*
## MINIMUM WAGE REQUIREMENTS AND EXEMPTIONS

(When state and federal minimum wages differ, the higher wage is to be paid. In some instances, state minimum wage covers particular employees not covered under federal law. In those instances, the state wage should be paid. See also text at § 3.3.)

**KEY:** **Lower.** Employees in this category may/shall receive wages lower than the prescribed minimum wage if provided for in regulation or order (generally to prevent curtailment of employment opportunities); they are subject to separate state minimum wage requirements.

*For further details on specific provisions of state subminimum wage laws, see Table I in the "Trends and Controversies" section of this Guide.

| | *Minimum Wage Rates for Nonexempt Employees* | *Bona Fide Executives, Administrators, or Professionals* | *Agriculture* | *Domestic Service* | *Outside Salesperson* | *Students* | *Learners or Apprentices* | *Handicapped Working in Special Environments* | *Citations to Authority* |
|---|---|---|---|---|---|---|---|---|---|
| ID | $5.15. | Exempt from state minimum wage requirements if they meet exemption criteria. | Exempt from state minimum wage requirements if they meet exemption criteria. | Exempt from state minimum wage requirements if they meet exemption criteria. | Exempt from state minimum wage requirements if they meet exemption criteria. | May be exempt by special license. | May be exempt by special license. | May be exempt by special license. An employee under 20 years of age may be paid $4.25 for the first 90 days of employment. | Idaho Code §§ 44-1502, 44-1504–44-1506. |
| IL | $5.15 (state minimum wage must not be less than federal minimum wage). | Not exempt. | Exempt from state minimum wage requirements if they meet exemption criteria. | Exempt from state minimum wage requirements if they meet exemption criteria. | Exempt from state minimum wage requirements if they meet exemption criteria. | Exempt from state minimum wage requirements if they meet exemption criteria. | May be exempt by regulation; subminimum wage no less than 70% of minimum wage. | May be exempt by special license. | 820 Ill. Comp. Stat. Ann. §§ 105/2–105/6. |
| IN | $4.25 as of 10/1/98; $5.15 as of 3/1/99. | Exempt from state minimum wage requirements if they meet exemption criteria. | Exempt from state minimum wage requirements if they meet exemption criteria. | Not exempt. | Exempt from state minimum wage requirements if they meet exemption criteria. | Exempt from state minimum wage requirements if they meet exemption criteria. | Exempt from state minimum wage requirements if they meet exemption criteria (student nurses and apprentices for embalmer's and funeral director's licenses). An employee under 20 years | Exempt from state minimum wage requirements if they meet exemption criteria. | Ind. Code Ann. §§ 22-2-2-3, 22-2-2-4. |

| | | | | | | | | | |
|---|---|---|---|---|---|---|---|---|---|
| | | | | | | | of age may be paid $4.25 for the first 90 days of employment. | | |
| IA | $5.15 (state minimum wage cannot be lower than the federal minimum wage; state minimum wage for employees who have worked fewer than 90 days is $4.25). | Follows exemptions in FLSA, 29 USC § 213. | Follows exemptions in FLSA, 29 USC § 213. | Follows exemptions in FLSA, 29 USC § 213. | Follows exemptions in FLSA, 29 USC § 213. | Follows exemptions in FLSA, 29 USC § 213. | Follows exemptions in FLSA, 29 USC § 213. | Follows exemptions in FLSA, 29 USC § 213. | Iowa Code Ann. § 91D.1. |
| KS | $2.65. | Exempt from state minimum wage requirements if they meet exemption criteria. | Exempt from state minimum wage requirements if they meet exemption criteria. | Exempt from state minimum wage requirements if they meet exemption criteria. | Exempt from state minimum wage requirements if they meet exemption criteria. | Not exempt. | May be exempt by special permit. | May be exempt by special permit. | Kan. Stat. Ann. §§ 44-1202, 44-1203, 44-1207. |
| KY | $5.15. | Exempt from state minimum wage requirements if they meet exemption criteria. | Exempt from state minimum wage requirements if they meet exemption criteria. | Exempt from state minimum wage requirements if they meet exemption criteria. | Exempt from state minimum wage requirements if they meet exemption criteria. | May be exempt by special certificate. | May be exempt by special certificate. | May be exempt by special certificate. | Ky. Rev. Stat. Ann. §§ 337.010, 337.275. |
| LA | — | — | — | — | — | — | — | — | No state statutory provisions. |
| ME | $5.15 (state minimum wage equals federal minimum wage but may not exceed $5.15). May not exceed the average minimum wage of the 5 other New England states. | Exempt from state minimum wage requirements if they meet exemption criteria. | Exempt from state minimum wage requirements if they meet exemption criteria. | Exempt from state minimum wage requirements if they meet exemption criteria. | Exempt from state minimum wage requirements if they meet exemption criteria. | Not exempt. | May be exempt by special certificate. | May be exempt by special certificate. | Me. Rev. Stat. Ann. tit. 26, §§ 663, 664, 666, 667. |

*(Table continues.)*

# Table 3.3-1 *(cont'd)*

## MINIMUM WAGE REQUIREMENTS AND EXEMPTIONS

(When state and federal minimum wages differ, the higher wage is to be paid. In some instances, state minimum wage covers particular employees not covered under federal law. In those instances, the state wage should be paid. See also text at § 3.3.)

**KEY:** **Lower.** Employees in this category may/shall receive wages lower than the prescribed minimum wage if provided for in regulation or order (generally to prevent curtailment of employment opportunities); they are subject to separate state minimum wage requirements.

*For further details on specific provisions of state subminimum wage laws, see Table I in the "Trends and Controversies" section of this Guide.

| | *Minimum Wage Rates for Nonexempt Employees* | *Bona Fide Executives, Administrators, or Professionals* | *Agriculture* | *Domestic Service* | *Outside Salesperson* | *Students* | *Learners or Apprentices* | *Handicapped Working in Special Environments* | *Citations to Authority* |
|---|---|---|---|---|---|---|---|---|---|
| MD | $5.15 (statute states that state minimum wage must be at least the federal minimum wage). | Exempt from state minimum wage requirements if they meet exemption criteria. | Exempt from state minimum wage requirements if they meet exemption criteria. | Not exempt. | Exempt from state minimum wage requirements if they meet exemption criteria. | Not exempt. | Commissioner has power to set wage at 80% subminimum. | May be exempt by special certificate. | Md. Lab. Code [Lab. & Empl.] §§ 3-403, 3-410, 3-413, 3-414. |
| MA | $5.25. Minimum wage for agriculture is $1.60 except for children age 17 or younger. | Exempt from state minimum wage requirements if they meet exemption criteria. | Exempt from state requirements if they meet exemption criteria. | Exempt if under the age of 18. | Exempt from state minimum wage requirements if they meet exemption criteria. | Not exempt. | May be exempt by special certificate. | May be exempt by special certificate. | Mass. Gen. Laws Ann. ch. 151, §§ 1, 1a, 2, 2a, 7. |
| MI | $5.15. | Not exempt. | Not exempt generally, but workers of certain crop growers are exempt. | Not exempt. | Not exempt. | Not exempt. | May be exempt on motion. A training wage is allowed for the first 90 days of employment. | May be exempt on motion. | Mich. Stat. Ann. §§ 17.255(2)–17.255(4), 17.255(4b), 17.255(7) 17.255(14). |
| MN | $4.90 for small employer whose annual gross volume of sales made or business done is less than $500,000; | Exempt from state minimum wage requirements if they meet exemption criteria. | Exempt from state minimum wage requirements if they meet exemption criteria. | Not exempt. Only individual engaged in babysitting as a sole practitioner is exempt. | Exempt from state minimum wage requirements if they meet exemption criteria. | Not exempt. | May be exempt by permit. | May be exempt by permit. | Minn. Stat. Ann. §§ 177.23, 177.24, 177.28. |

| | | | | | | | | | |
|---|---|---|---|---|---|---|---|---|---|
| | $5.15 for large employer whose annual gross volume is $500,000 or more. | | | | | | | | |
| MS | — | — | — | — | — | — | — | — | No state statutory provisions. |
| MO | $5.15 (same as the federal minimum wage). | Exempt from state minimum wage requirements if they meet exemption criteria. | Exempt from state minimum wage requirements if they meet exemption criteria. | Exempt from state minimum wage requirements if they meet exemption criteria. | Exempt from state minimum wage requirements if they meet exemption criteria. | Not exempt. | May be lower, as provided by federal law. | May be lower, as provided by the director of the Department of Labor. | Mo. Rev. Stat. §§ 290.500, 290.502, 290.507, 290.515, 290.517. |
| MT | $5.15 for most employees (same as the FLSA); $4.00 for a business with annual gross sales of $110,000 or less. | Exempt from state minimum wage requirements if they meet exemption criteria. | In lieu of minimum wage, farmworkers may be paid a monthly wage of at least $635. | Exempt from state minimum wage requirements if they meet exemption criteria. | Exempt from state minimum wage requirements if they meet exemption criteria. | Exempt from state minimum wage requirements if they meet exemption criteria. | Exempt from state minimum wage requirements if they meet exemption criteria. | Exempt from state minimum wage requirements if they meet exemption criteria. | Mont. Code Ann. §§ 39-3-404, 39-3-406, 39-3-409. |
| NE | $5.15. | Exempt from state minimum wage requirements if they meet exemption criteria. | Exempt from state minimum wage requirements if they meet exemption criteria. | Babysitters are exempt from state minimum wage requirements. | Not exempt. | Not exempt. Student-learners paid at lower rate (75% of minimum wage). | Exempt from state minimum wage requirements if they meet exemption criteria. An employee under 20 years of age may be paid $4.25 for the first 90 days of employment. The lower wage may be continued for an additional 90 days of on-the-job training if the job requires technical or personal skills and the wage is approved by the commissioner of labor. | Exempt from state minimum wage requirements if they meet exemption criteria. | Neb. Rev. Stat. §§ 48-1202, 48-1203, 14-1203. |

(Table continues.)

# Table 3.3-1 *(cont'd)*
## MINIMUM WAGE REQUIREMENTS AND EXEMPTIONS

(When state and federal minimum wages differ, the higher wage is to be paid. In some instances, state minimum wage covers particular employees not covered under federal law. In those instances, the state wage should be paid. See also text at § 3.3.)

**KEY:** **Lower.** Employees in this category may/shall receive wages lower than the prescribed minimum wage if provided for in regulation or order (generally to prevent curtailment of employment opportunities); they are subject to separate state minimum wage requirements.

*For further details on specific provisions of state subminimum wage laws, see Table I in the "Trends and Controversies" section of this Guide.

| | *Minimum Wage Rates for Nonexempt Employees* | *Bona Fide Executives, Administrators, or Professionals* | *Agriculture* | *Domestic Service* | *Outside Salesperson* | *Students* | *Learners or Apprentices* | *Handicapped Working in Special Environments* | *Citations to Authority* |
|---|---|---|---|---|---|---|---|---|---|
| NV | $5.15 (state minimum wage must equal federal minimum wage unless the labor commissioner determines that the increase is contrary to the public interest). | Not exempt. | Exempt from state minimum wage requirements if they meet exemption criteria. | Exempt from state minimum wage requirements if they meet exemption criteria. | Exempt from state minimum wage requirements if they meet exemption criteria. | Not exempt; if under 18, subminimum wage at 85% of minimum wage. | Not exempt. | Exempt from state minimum wage requirements if they meet exemption criteria. | Nev. Rev. Stat. § 608.250. |
| NH | $5.15 (state minimum wage is $3.95 or the federal minimum wage, whichever is higher). | Not exempt. | Exempt from state minimum wage requirements if they meet exemption criteria. | Exempt from state minimum wage requirements if they meet exemption criteria. | Exempt from state minimum wage requirements if they meet exemption criteria. | Not exempt. | Not exempt; if under 16, subminimum wage at 75% and employer must keep evidence on file. | May be exempt by special authority. | N.H. Rev. Stat. Ann. §§ 279:21, 279:22, 279:22-aa. |
| NJ | $5.05. | Exempt from state minimum wage requirements if they meet exemption criteria. | Exempt from state minimum wage requirements if they meet exemption criteria. | Exempt from state minimum wage requirements if they meet exemption criteria; part-time child care in the home. | Exempt from state minimum wage requirements if they meet exemption criteria. | Not exempt, except full-time students employed by the college or university at which they are enrolled must be paid at least 85% of | May be exempt by special certificate. | May be exempt by special certificate. | N.J. Rev. Stat. Ann. §§ 34:11-56a4, 34:11-56a17. |

| | | | | | | | | |
|---|---|---|---|---|---|---|---|---|
| | | | | | current minimum wage. | | | |
| NM | $4.25. | Exempt from state minimum wage requirements if they meet exemption criteria. | Exempt from state minimum wage requirements if they meet exemption criteria. | Exempt from state minimum wage requirements if they meet exemption criteria. | Exempt from state minimum wage requirements if they meet exemption criteria. | Exempt from state minimum wage requirements if they meet exemption criteria. | Exempt from state minimum wage requirements if they meet exemption criteria. | May be exempt by special certificate. | N.M. Stat. Ann. §§ 50-4-21–50-4-23. |
| NY | $4.25. | Exempt from state minimum wage requirements if they meet exemption criteria. | Exempt from state minimum wage requirements if they meet exemption criteria. | Exempt from state minimum wage requirements if they meet exemption criteria. | Exempt from state minimum wage requirements if they meet exemption criteria. | Exempt from state minimum wage requirements if they meet exemption criteria. | Exempt from state minimum wage requirements if they meet exemption criteria. | Exempt from state minimum wage requirements if they meet exemption criteria. | N.Y. Lab. Law §§ 651, 652. |
| NC | $5.15. | Exempt from state minimum wage requirements if they meet exemption criteria. | Exempt from state minimum wage requirements if they meet exemption criteria. | Exempt from state minimum wage requirements if they meet exemption criteria. | Exempt from state minimum wage requirements if they meet exemption criteria. | Not exempt; subminimum wage at 90% rounded to the lowest nickel. | Not exempt; subminimum wage at 90% rounded to the lowest nickel. | May be exempt by regulation. | N.C. Gen. Stat. §§ 95-25.3, 95-25.14. |
| ND | $5.15 (set by Department of Labor). | Not exempt. | Not exempt. | Exempt from state minimum wage requirements if they meet exemption criteria. | May be exempt depending on employment requirements. | Exempt from state minimum wage requirements if they meet exemption criteria. | Wages may be lowered by special license. | Wages may be lowered by special license. | N.D. Cent. Code §§ 34-06-01, 34-06-03.1, 34-06-15; N.D. Admin. Code § 46.02. |
| OH | $5.15 if employer's gross annual sales over $500,000; $3.35 if gross annual sales between $150,000 and $500,000; $2.80 if gross annual sales below $150,000. | Exempt from state minimum wage requirements if they meet exemption criteria. | Exempt from state minimum wage requirements if they meet exemption criteria. | Exempt from state minimum wage requirements if they meet exemption criteria. Housekeepers not exempt. | Exempt from state minimum wage requirements if they meet exemption criteria. | Exempt from state minimum wage requirements if they meet exemption criteria; subminimum wage of 80% in some cases. | May be exempt by special license; subminimum wage of 85%. | Wages may be lowered by special license. | Ohio Rev. Code Ann. §§ 4111.01, 4111.02, 4111.06, 4111.07. |
| OK | $5.15 (same as federal minimum wage). | Exempt from state minimum wage requirements if they meet exemption criteria. | Exempt from state minimum wage requirements if they meet exemption criteria. | Exempt from state minimum wage requirements if they meet exemption criteria. | Exempt from state minimum wage requirements if they meet exemption criteria. | Wages may be lowered by special certificate. | Wages may be lowered by special certificate. | Wages may be lowered by special certificate. | Okla. Stat. tit. 40, §§ 197.2, 197.4, 197.11. |

*(Table continues.)*

## Table 3.3-1 *(cont'd)*

## MINIMUM WAGE REQUIREMENTS AND EXEMPTIONS

(When state and federal minimum wages differ, the higher wage is to be paid. In some instances, state minimum wage covers particular employees not covered under federal law. In those instances, the state wage should be paid. See also text at § 3.3.)

**KEY:** **Lower.** Employees in this category may/shall receive wages lower than the prescribed minimum wage if provided for in regulation or order (generally to prevent curtailment of employment opportunities); they are subject to separate state minimum wage requirements.

*For further details on specific provisions of state subminimum wage laws, see Table I in the "Trends and Controversies" section of this Guide.

| | *Minimum Wage Rates for Nonexempt Employees* | *Bona Fide Executives, Administrators, or Professionals* | *Agriculture* | *Domestic Service* | *Outside Salesperson* | *Students* | *Learners or Apprentices* | *Handicapped Working in Special Environments* | *Citations to Authority* |
|---|---|---|---|---|---|---|---|---|---|
| OR | $6.50. | Exempt from state minimum wage requirements if they meet exemption criteria. | Exempt from state minimum wage requirements if they meet exemption criteria. | Exempt from state minimum wage requirements if they meet exemption criteria. | Exempt from state minimum wage requirements if they meet exemption criteria. | Wages may be lowered by regulation; subminimum wage of 75%. | Wages may be lowered by regulation; subminimum wage of 75%. | Wages may be lowered by regulation; subminimum wage of 75%. | Or. Rev. Stat. §§ 653.020, 653.025, 653.030, 653.070. |
| PA | $5.15 (same as federal minimum wage). | Exempt from state minimum wage requirements if they meet exemption criteria. | Exempt from state minimum wage requirements if they meet exemption criteria. | Exempt from state minimum wage requirements if they meet exemption criteria. | Exempt from state minimum wage requirements if they meet exemption criteria. | May be exempt by special certificate; subminimum wage at 85%. | May be exempt by special certificate; subminimum wage at 85%. | May be exempt by certificate or license. | Pa. Code Ann. tit. 43, §§ 333.104, 333.105. |
| RI | $5.15. | Not exempt. | Not exempt. | Exempt from state minimum wage requirements if they meet exemption criteria. | Exempt from state minimum wage requirements if they meet exemption criteria. | Not exempt; students ages 14 and 15 working 24 hours or fewer per week may be paid 75% of minimum wage. Students working for religious, educational, librarial, or community nonprofit organizations may be paid 90% of minimum wage. | Wages may be lowered by special license. | Wages may be lowered by special license. | R.I. Gen. Laws §§ 28-12-2, 28-12-3, 28-12-5, 28-12-9, 28-12-10. |

| | | | | | | | | | |
|---|---|---|---|---|---|---|---|---|---|
| SC | — | — | — | — | — | — | — | — | No state statutory provisions. |
| SD | $5.15. | Not exempt. | Not exempt. | Exempt from state minimum wage requirements if they meet exemption criteria (babysitters). | Exempt from state minimum wage requirements if they meet exemption criteria. | Not exempt. | May be exempt by permit. Employee who is 18 or 19 years of age may be paid an opportunity wage as allowed under federal law. | May be exempt by permit. | S.D. Codified Laws §§ 60-11-3, 60-11-4.1, 60-11-5. |
| TN | — | — | — | — | — | — | — | — | No state statutory provisions. |
| TX | $3.35. | Exempt from state minimum wage requirements if they meet exemption criteria (doing farming and production of livestock). | Exempt from state minimum wage requirements if they meet exemption criteria. | Exempt from state minimum wage requirements if they meet exemption criteria. | Exempt from state minimum wage requirements if they meet exemption criteria. | Exempt from state minimum wage requirements if they meet exemption criteria. | Exempt from state minimum wage requirements if they meet exemption criteria. | Exempt from state minimum wage requirements if they meet exemption criteria. May require medical certificate, and may have subminimum wage of 60%. | Tex. Lab. Code Ann. §§ 62.051, 62.055, 62.057, 62.153, 62.154, 62.155, 62.160. |
| UT | $5.15 (or as established by the Labor Commission, but not to exceed federal minimum wage). | Not exempt. | Exempt from state minimum wage requirements if they meet exemption criteria. | Exempt from state minimum wage requirements if they meet exemption criteria. | Exempt from state minimum wage requirements if they meet exemption criteria. | Exempt from state minimum wage requirements if they meet exemption criteria. | Exempt from state minimum wage requirements if they meet exemption criteria. | Wages may be lower (set by Labor Commission). | Utah Code Ann. §§ 34-40-103, 34-40-104. |
| VT | $5.25. | Exempt from state minimum wage requirements if they meet exemption criteria. | Exempt from state minimum wage requirements if they meet exemption criteria. | Exempt from state minimum wage requirements if they meet exemption criteria. | Exempt from state minimum wage requirements if they meet exemption criteria. | Exempt from state minimum wage requirements if they meet exemption criteria. | Lower. | Lower. | Vt. Stat. Ann. tit. 21, §§ 383–385. |
| VA | $5.15 (state minimum wage must not be less than federal minimum wage). | Not exempt. | Exempt from state minimum wage requirements if they meet exemption criteria. | Exempt from state minimum wage requirements if they meet exemption criteria. | Exempt from state minimum wage requirements if they meet exemption criteria. | Exempt from state minimum wage requirements if they meet exemption criteria. | Exempt from state minimum wage requirements if they meet exemption criteria. | Exempt from state minimum wage requirements if they meet exemption criteria. | Va. Code Ann. §§ 40.1-28.9, 40.1-28.10. |

# **Table 3.3-1** *(cont'd)*

## MINIMUM WAGE REQUIREMENTS AND EXEMPTIONS

(When state and federal minimum wages differ, the higher wage is to be paid. In some instances, state minimum wage covers particular employees not covered under federal law. In those instances, the state wage should be paid. See also text at § 3.3.)

**KEY:** **Lower.** Employees in this category may/shall receive wages lower than the prescribed minimum wage if provided for in regulation or order (generally to prevent curtailment of employment opportunities); they are subject to separate state minimum wage requirements.

*For further details on specific provisions of state subminimum wage laws, see Table I in the "Trends and Controversies" section of this Guide.

| | *Minimum Wage Rates for Nonexempt Employees* | *Bona Fide Executives, Administrators, or Professionals* | *Agriculture* | *Domestic Service* | *Outside Salesperson* | *Students* | *Learners or Apprentices* | *Handicapped Working in Special Environments* | *Citations to Authority* |
|---|---|---|---|---|---|---|---|---|---|
| WA | $5.70; $6.50 as of 1/1/00 ($4.17 for minors under 16 in employment not covered by FLSA; $5.15 for minors under 16 in employment covered by FLSA). | Exempt from state minimum wage requirements if they meet exemption criteria. | Exempt from state minimum wage requirements if they meet exemption criteria. | Exempt from state minimum wage requirements if they meet exemption criteria. | Exempt from state minimum wage requirements if they meet exemption criteria. | Not exempt. | May be exempt by special certificate. | May be exempt by special certificate. | Wash. Rev. Code §§ 49.46.010, 49.46.020, 49.46.060. |
| WV | $5.15. | Exempt from state minimum wage requirements if they meet exemption criteria. | Exempt from state minimum wage requirements if they meet exemption criteria. | Not exempt. | Exempt from state minimum wage requirements if they meet exemption criteria. | Exempt from state minimum wage requirements if they meet exemption criteria. | Exempt from state minimum wage requirements if they meet exemption criteria. | Exempt from state minimum wage requirements if they meet exemption criteria. | W. Va. Code §§ 21-5C-1, 21-5C-2. |
| WI | $5.15 (set by regulation). $4.25 if under 20 years of age and employed fewer than 90 days. | Not exempt. | Exempt from state minimum wage requirements if they meet exemption criteria. | Exempt from state minimum wage requirements if they meet exemption criteria. | Not exempt. | Exempt from state minimum wage requirements if they meet exemption criteria. | May be lowered by regulation. | May be exempt by special license. | Wis. Stat. Ann. §§ 104.01, 104.02, 104.04, 104.07, 104.08. |

| | | | | | | | | |
|---|---|---|---|---|---|---|---|---|
| WY | $1.60. | Exempt from state minimum wage requirements if they meet exemption criteria. | Exempt from state minimum wage requirements if they meet exemption criteria. | Exempt from state minimum wage requirements if they meet exemption criteria. | Exempt from state minimum wage requirements if they meet exemption criteria. | Not exempt. | Exempt from state minimum wage requirements if they meet exemption criteria. | Not exempt. | Wyo. Stat. §§ 27-4-201, 27-4-202. |

# § 3.4 Overtime Compensation Requirements and Exemptions

Table 3.4-1 lists the number of hours per day or per week after which employees must be paid overtime compensation at the rate of one and a half times their regular pay rate. If there are no state requirements, the FLSA will be the only applicable law in that state. The table also shows those occupations most commonly exempted from these overtime compensation requirements. The listed exemptions do not constitute an exhaustive list of the states' exemptions. Further, the definitions of the exempted categories, while similar, vary from state to state, so carefully review relevant statutes to determine the exact parameters of these categories of exemption. Although exempt employees are not entitled to overtime compensation under state laws, they may be entitled to overtime compensation under the FLSA.

Some state legislatures do not set overtime compensation requirements by statute; instead, they delegate to a state commission or department of labor the authority to set overtime compensation by administrative regulations or wage orders, define exempt categories of employees, and set penalties for violations. States that do set overtime compensation requirements by statute may also have commissions or labor departments to administer and enforce their minimum wage acts. Therefore, human resources professionals should determine whether there are any applicable administrative regulations or wage orders before making any decision regarding overtime compensation.

# Table 3.4-1
## COVERAGE OF EMPLOYMENT CLASSIFICATIONS UNDER OVERTIME COMPENSATION STATUTES

(See also text at § 3.4.)

**KEY:** **Overtime Compensation.** The number of hours per week after which the employee must be paid overtime compensation at 1½ times the regular pay rate.

**NOTE:** Administrative regulations and wage orders may affect overtime requirements and exemptions. These regulations and orders are subject to change and should be consulted before making any decision regarding overtime compensation.

| | *Basic Overtime Compensation Requirements* | *Bona Fide Executives, Administrators, or Professionals* | *Agriculture* | *Domestic Service* | *Outside Salesperson* | *Students* | *Learners or Apprentices* | *Handicapped Employed Under Special Certificates* | *Citations to Authority* |
|---|---|---|---|---|---|---|---|---|---|
| AL | — | — | — | — | — | — | — | — | No state statutory provisions. |
| AK | 8 hours per day or 40 hours per week. Subject to DOL approval, an employer and employee may agree to a voluntary, flexible work hour plan of up to 10 hours per day, and 40 hours per week. | Excluded. | Excluded. | Excluded. | Excluded. | Covered. | Covered. | Covered. | Alaska Stat. §§ 23.10.055, 23.10.060; Alaska Admin. Code tit. 8 § 15.102. |
| AZ | No comprehensive law, but specified public employees may be compensated by receiving compensatory time off. | — | — | — | — | — | — | — | Ariz. Rev. Stat. Ann. §§ 23-391, 23-392. |
| AR | 40 hours. | Excluded. | Excluded. | Covered. | Excluded. | Covered. | Covered. | Covered. | Ark. Code Ann. §§ 11-4-203, 11-4-211. |

*(Table continues.)*

# Table 3.4-1 *(cont'd)*

## COVERAGE OF EMPLOYMENT CLASSIFICATIONS UNDER OVERTIME COMPENSATION STATUTES

(See also text at § 3.4.)

**KEY: Overtime Compensation.** The number of hours per week after which the employee must be paid overtime compensation at 1½ times the regular pay rate.

**NOTE:** Administrative regulations and wage orders may affect overtime requirements and exemptions. These regulations and orders are subject to change and should be consulted before making any decision regarding overtime compensation.

| | *Basic Overtime Compensation Requirements* | *Bona Fide Executives, Administrators, or Professionals* | *Agriculture* | *Domestic Service* | *Outside Salesperson* | *Students* | *Learners or Apprentices* | *Handicapped Employed Under Special Certificates* | *Citations to Authority* |
|---|---|---|---|---|---|---|---|---|---|
| CA | 40 hours per week (set by regulation). | — | — | — | — | — | — | — | Cal. Lab. Code § 1198; Cal Code of Regs. tit. 8 § 11040 (Order No. 4-98). |
| CO | 12 hours per day or 40 hours per week (set by regulation to apply equally to all employers in an industry or occupation). | Excluded. | Covered. | Covered. | Excluded. | Excluded if employed by sororities, fraternities, college clubs, or dormitories or employed in work experience study program. | Covered. | Covered. | Colo. Rev. Stat. § 8-6-111, Retail Trade, Food and Beverage, Health and Medical, Service Industries and Construction Industry Wage Order (Order No. 21, 10-1-97). |
| CT | 40 hours. | Excluded. | Excluded. | Excluded. | Excluded. | Covered. | Covered. | Excluded. | Conn. Gen. Stat. Ann. §§ 31-67, 31-76b, 31-76c, 31-76i. |
| DE | — | — | — | — | — | — | — | — | No state statutory provisions. |
| DC | 40 hours. | Excluded. | Covered. | Excluded. | Excluded. | Covered. | Covered. | Covered. | D.C. Code §§ 36-220.1, 36-220.2, 36-220.3. |
| FL | 10 hours per day is a legal day's work for manual laborers, unless a | — | — | — | — | — | — | — | Fla. Stat. Ann. § 448.01. |

| | | | | | | | | | |
|---|---|---|---|---|---|---|---|---|---|
| | contract states otherwise. | | | | | | | | |
| GA | — | — | — | — | — | — | — | — | No state statutory provisions. |
| HI | 40 hours (48 hours for agricultural employees). | Excluded. | Covered if employer employs 20 or more persons. | Excluded. | Excluded. | Covered. | Covered. | Covered. | Haw. Rev. Stat. §§ 387-1, 387-3. |
| ID | 40 hours. | Excluded. | Excluded. | Excluded. | Excluded. | Covered. | Covered. | Covered. | Idaho Code §§ 44-1502, 44-1504–44-1506. |
| IL | 40 hours. | Excluded. | Excluded. | Covered. | Exempt if they meet exemption criteria. | Covered. | Covered. | Covered. | Ill. Comp. Stat. Ann. ch. 820, § 105/4a. |
| IN | 40 hours. | Excluded. | Excluded. | Covered. | Excluded. | Excluded if they are employed by the institution they are attending. | Covered. | Excluded if employed by nonprofit organization providing services to the handicapped. | Ind. Code Ann. § 22-2-2-4. |
| IA | — | — | — | — | — | — | — | — | No state statutory provisions. |
| KS | 46 hours. | Excluded. | Excluded. | Excluded. | Excluded. | Covered. | Covered. | Covered. | Kan. Stat. Ann. §§ 44-1202, 44-1204, 44-1207. |
| KY | 40 hours. | Excluded. | Excluded. | Excluded. | Excluded. | Exempt if they meet exemption criteria. | Exempt if they meet exemption criteria. | Exempt if they meet exemption criteria. | Ky. Rev. Stat. Ann. §§ 337.010, 337.285. |
| LA | — | — | — | — | — | — | — | — | No state statutory provisions. |
| ME | 40 hours. | Excluded. | Excluded. | Excluded. | Excluded. | Covered. | Covered. | Covered. | Me. Rev. Stat. Ann. tit. 26, §§ 663, 664. |
| MD | 40 hours. | Excluded. | Covered for hours over 60 in workweek if exempt from FLSA requirements. | Covered. | Excluded. | Covered. | Covered. | Covered. | Md. Code Ann. [Lab. & Empl.] §§ 3-415, 3-420. |
| MA | 40 hours. | Excluded. | Excluded. | Covered. | Excluded. | Covered. | Excluded. | Excluded. | Mass. Gen. Laws Ann. ch. 151, § 1A. |

*(Table continues.)*

# **Table 3.4-1** *(cont'd)*
## COVERAGE OF EMPLOYMENT CLASSIFICATIONS UNDER OVERTIME COMPENSATION STATUTES

(See also text at § 3.4.)

**KEY:** **Overtime Compensation.** The number of hours per week after which the employee must be paid overtime compensation at 1½ times the regular pay rate.

**NOTE:** Administrative regulations and wage orders may affect overtime requirements and exemptions. These regulations and orders are subject to change and should be consulted before making any decision regarding overtime compensation.

| | *Basic Overtime Compensation Requirements* | *Bona Fide Executives, Administrators, or Professionals* | *Agriculture* | *Domestic Service* | *Outside Salesperson* | *Students* | *Learners or Apprentices* | *Handicapped Employed Under Special Certificates* | *Citations to Authority* |
|---|---|---|---|---|---|---|---|---|---|
| MI | 40 hours. | Excluded. | Excluded. | Covered. | Covered. | Covered. | Covered. | Covered. | Mich. Stat. Ann. § 17.255(4a). |
| MN | 48 hours. | Excluded. | Excluded. | Covered. | Excluded. | Covered. | Covered. | Covered. | Minn. Stat. Ann. §§ 177.23, 177.25, 177.28. |
| MS | — | — | — | — | — | — | — | — | No state statutory provisions. |
| MO | 40 hours. | Excluded. | Excluded. | Excluded. | Excluded. | Covered. | Covered. | Excluded. | Mo. Rev. Stat. §§ 290.500, 290.505, 290.507. |
| MT | 40 hours. | Excluded. | Excluded. | Excluded. | Excluded. | Excluded. | Excluded. | Excluded. | Mont. Code Ann. §§ 39-3-405, 39-3-406. |
| NE | — | — | — | — | — | — | — | — | No state statutory provisions. |
| NV | 8 hours per day or 40 hours per week. Employee may work 4 10-hour days by mutual agreement with employer without triggering overtime wage. | Excluded. | Excluded. | Excluded. | Excluded. | Covered. | Covered. | Excluded. | Nev. Rev. Stat. § 608.018. |
| NH | 40 hours. | Covered. | Excluded. | Excluded. | Excluded. | Covered. | Covered. | Covered. | N.H. Rev. Stat. Ann. § 279:21. |

| | | | | | | | | | |
|---|---|---|---|---|---|---|---|---|---|
| NJ | 40 hours. State employees in career, senior executive, and unclassified services are eligible for overtime compensation. | Excluded. | Excluded. | Covered. | Covered. | Covered. | Covered. | Covered. | N.J. Rev. Stat. Ann. § 11A:6-24, 34:11-56a4. |
| NM | 40 hours. | Excluded. | Excluded. | Excluded. | Excluded if they meet exclusion criteria. | Excluded. | Excluded. | Covered. | N.M. Stat. Ann. §§ 50-4-21, 50-4-22. |
| NY | 40 hours. | Excluded. | Excluded. | Non-residential, 40 hours; residential, 44 hours. | Excluded. | Excluded if they meet exclusion criteria. | Covered. | Covered. | New York Department of Labor Wage Orders, N.Y. Comp. Codes R. & Regs. tit. 12 § 142-2.2 (1990). |
| NC | 40 hours. | Excluded. | Excluded. | Excluded. | Excluded. | Covered. | Covered. | Covered. | N.C. Gen. Stat. §§ 95-25.4, 95-25.14. |
| ND | 40 hours (set by regulation). | Excluded. | Exempt if they meet exemption criteria. | Exempt if they meet exemption criteria. | May be exempt, depending on employment requirements. | Covered. | Covered. | Covered. | No state statutory provisions (overtime provisions are set out by Commissioner of Labor: N.D. Department of Labor Minimum Wage Order, N.D. Admin. Code § 46-02-07-02). |
| OH | 40 hours. | Excluded. | Excluded. | Excluded. | Excluded. | Covered. | Covered. | Covered. | Ohio Rev. Code Ann. § 4111.03. |
| OK | — | — | — | — | — | — | — | — | No state statutory provisions. |
| OR | 40 hours. | Covered. | Excluded. | Covered. | Covered. | Covered. | Covered. | Covered. | Or. Rev. Stat. § 653.261. |
| PA | 40 hours. | Excluded. | Excluded. | Excluded. | Excluded. | Covered. | Covered. | Covered. | Pa. Code Ann. tit. 43, §§ 333.104, 333.105. |
| RI | 40 hours. All work on Sunday and legal holidays must be compensated at a rate of 1½ times the normal wage per hour. | Excluded. | Excluded. | Excluded. | Excluded. | Covered. | Covered. | Covered. | R.I. Gen. Laws §§ 28-12-4.1, 28-12-4.3. |
| SC | — | — | — | — | — | — | — | — | No state statutory provisions. |

*(Table continues.)*

## Table 3.4-1 *(cont'd)*

## COVERAGE OF EMPLOYMENT CLASSIFICATIONS UNDER OVERTIME COMPENSATION STATUTES

(See also text at § 3.4.)

**KEY:** **Overtime Compensation.** The number of hours per week after which the employee must be paid overtime compensation at 1½ times the regular pay rate.

**NOTE:** Administrative regulations and wage orders may affect overtime requirements and exemptions. These regulations and orders are subject to change and should be consulted before making any decision regarding overtime compensation.

| | *Basic Overtime Compensation Requirements* | *Bona Fide Executives, Administrators, or Professionals* | *Agriculture* | *Domestic Service* | *Outside Salesperson* | *Students* | *Learners or Apprentices* | *Handicapped Employed Under Special Certificates* | *Citations to Authority* |
|---|---|---|---|---|---|---|---|---|---|
| SD | — | — | — | — | — | — | — | — | No state statutory provisions. |
| TN | — | — | — | — | — | — | — | — | No state statutory provisions. |
| TX | — | — | — | — | — | — | — | — | No state statutory provisions. |
| UT | 40 hours for public employees and for the workers of companies working on government contracts. | — | — | — | — | — | — | — | Utah Code Ann. § 34-30-8. |
| VT | 40 hours. | Excluded. | Excluded. | Excluded. | Excluded. | Excluded. | Covered. | Covered. | Vt. Stat. Ann. tit. 21, §§ 383, 384. |
| VA | — | — | — | — | — | — | — | — | No state statutory provisions. |
| WA | 40 hours. | Excluded. | Excluded. | Excluded. | Excluded. | Covered. | Covered. | Covered. | Wash. Rev. Code § 49.46.130. |
| WV | 40 hours. | Excluded. | Excluded. | Covered. | Excluded. | Excluded. | Excluded. | Excluded. | W. Va. Code § 21-5C-3. |
| WI | 40 hours per week (set by regulation). | Excluded if they meet exemption criteria. | Excluded if they meet exemption criteria. | Excluded if they meet exemption criteria. | Excluded if they meet exemption criteria. | Covered if working in industry regulated by wage order. | Excluded if they meet exemption criteria. | Covered if working in industry regulated by wage order. | Wis. Stat. Ann. § 103.02; Wis. Admin. Code §§ Ind. 74.03–74.04. |

| | | | | | | | | | |
|---|---|---|---|---|---|---|---|---|---|
| WY | 40 hours a week or 8 hours a day for state or county employees. | — | — | — | — | — | — | — | Wyo. Stat. § 27-5-101. |

## § 3.5 Penalties for Violating Minimum Wage Laws and Overtime Provisions

Tables 3.5-1 and 3.5-2 survey the statutory penalties for violating minimum wage laws and overtime compensation provisions, respectively. These tables list mandated fines and terms of imprisonment and note which states authorize both of these penalties for a single violation.

The "status" of the offense is also listed, but only if the state statute explicitly defines the nature of the offense. In states where a penalty is listed but the status of the offense is not defined, state court decisions interpreting the statutes must be reviewed in order to determine whether the offense is criminal or civil. Further, the "Civil Cause of Action" column indicates which states provide a private cause of action for an employee who has been injured by a violation of either the minimum wage or overtime provisions. This remedy frequently results in the recovery of unpaid wages and the award of a percentage of unpaid wages as liquidated damages and attorneys' fees. If a state lacks a civil cause of action, employees must apply to the state's commission or labor department in order to recover their unpaid wages.

# Table 3.5-1
## PENALTIES FOR VIOLATING MINIMUM WAGE LAWS

(See also text at § 3.5.)

**KEY:** **Status of Offense.** The status of the offense for employers violating overtime provisions is listed only if state labor statutes expressly classify the nature of the offense.
**Civil Cause of Action.** This indicates which states provide an employee with a private cause of action for a violation of minimum wage provisions.

| | | | | Civil Cause of Action | | | | |
|---|---|---|---|---|---|---|---|---|
| | *Status of Offense* | *Fines* | *Imprisonment* | *Unpaid Wages* | *Damages* | *Attorneys' Fees/Costs* | *Time Limit to File Civil Action* | *Citations to Authority* |
| AL | — | — | — | — | — | — | — | No state statutory provisions. |
| AK | — | $100–$2,000. | 10–90 days. | Yes. | Yes, liquidated damages equal to unpaid wages. | Yes. | 2 years. | Alaska Stat. §§ 23.10.110, 23.10.115, 23.10.140. (Enforcement is by injunction.) |
| AZ | — | No statutory requirements. | No statutory requirements. | Yes, treble wages due, minus wages actually paid. | No statutory requirements. | Yes. | No statutory requirements. | Ariz. Rev. Stat. Ann. § 23-327. (Statute applies to minors only.) |
| AR | — | $100 maximum (willful violations). | No. | Yes. | No statutory requirements. | Yes. | No statutory requirements. | Ark. Code Ann. §§ 11-4-206, 11-4-218. |
| CA | Civil penalty (in addition to other penalties). | $50 each employee, each pay period; $250 each employee, for each subsequent violation for the same offense, each pay period. | No. | Yes, plus interest. | Yes, liquidated damages equal to unpaid wages. | Yes. | No statutory requirements. | Cal. Lab. Code §§ 1193.6, 1194, 1194.2, 1194.5, 1197.1, 1199. (Enforcement may be by injunction.) |
| | Misdemeanor. | $100 minimum. | 30 days minimum. | | | | | |
| CO | Misdemeanor. | $100–$500 ($200–$1,000 for retaliation). | 30 days–1 year. | Yes. | No statutory requirements. | Yes. | No statutory requirements. | Colo. Rev. Stat. §§ 8-6-115, 8-6-116, 8-6-118. |

*(Table continues.)*

# Table 3.5-1 *(cont'd)*
## PENALTIES FOR VIOLATING MINIMUM WAGE LAWS

(See also text at § 3.5.)

**KEY:** **Status of Offense.** The status of the offense for employers violating overtime provisions is listed only if state labor statutes expressly classify the nature of the offense.
**Civil Cause of Action.** This indicates which states provide an employee with a private cause of action for a violation of minimum wage provisions.

| | | | | *Civil Cause of Action* | | | | |
|---|---|---|---|---|---|---|---|---|
| | *Status of Offense* | *Fines* | *Imprisonment* | *Unpaid Wages* | *Damages* | *Attorneys' Fees/Costs* | *Time Limit to File Civil Action* | *Citations to Authority* |
| CT | Civil penalty.<br>Criminal penalty. | $150 per offense.<br>$2,000–$5,000 (more than $2,000 unpaid wages).<br>$1,000–$2,000 ($1,000–$2,000 unpaid wages).<br>$500–$1,000 ($500–$1,000 unpaid wages).<br>$200–$500 (less than $500 unpaid wages). | No.<br>5 years maximum.<br>1 year maximum.<br>6 months maximum.<br>3 months maximum. | Yes, twice wage rate, minus wages actually paid. | No statutory requirements. | Yes. | No statutory requirements. | Conn. Gen. Stat. Ann. §§ 31-68, 31-69, 31-69a. |
| DE | Civil penalty. | $1,000–$5,000. | No. | Yes. | No statutory requirements. | Yes. | No statutory requirements. | Del. Code Ann. tit. 19, §§ 910, 911. |
| DC | — | $10,000 maximum. | 2nd offense: 6 months maximum. | Yes. | Yes, liquidated damages equal to unpaid wages. | Yes. | 3 years. | D.C. Code §§ 36-220.10, 36-220.11, 36-220.12. |
| FL | — | — | — | — | — | — | — | No state statutory provisions. |
| GA | — | No statutory requirements. | No statutory requirements. | Yes. | Yes, liquidated damages equal to unpaid wages. | Yes. | 3 years. | Ga. Code Ann. § 34-4-6. |
| HI | Misdemeanor. | $50–$500. | 1 year maximum. | Yes. | Yes, liquidated damages equal to unpaid wages for willful violations. | Yes. | No statutory requirements. | Haw. Rev. Stat. §§ 387-7, 387-12. (Enforcement may be by injunction.) |

| | | | | | | | | |
|---|---|---|---|---|---|---|---|---|
| ID | — | No statutory requirements. | No statutory requirements. | Yes. | Yes, both collection and liquidated damages. | Yes. | 6 months to 2 years, depending on action taken by employee. | Idaho Code §§ 44-1508, 45-614, 45-615. (Enforcement may be by injunction.) |
| IL | Class B misdemeanor. | $500 maximum. | 6 months maximum. | Yes. | Yes, punitive damages to employee if willful violation. Employer is also liable to the Department of Labor for 20% of the underpayment. | Yes. | 3 years. | 730 Ill. Comp. Stat. Ann. §§ 5/5-8-3, 5/5-9-1; 820 Ill. Comp. Stat. Ann. §§ 105/4, 105/12. |
| IN | Class C infraction.<br>Class A infraction (if knowingly violated). | $500 maximum.<br>$10,000 maximum. | No. | Yes. | Yes, liquidated damages equal to unpaid wages. | Yes. | 3 years. | Ind. Code Ann. §§ 22-2-2-3, 22-2-2-9, 22-2-2-11, 34-4-32-4. |
| IA | Civil penalty. | $100 maximum. | No. | Yes. | Yes, liquidated damages for intentional violations. | Yes. | No statutory requirements. | Iowa Code Ann. §§ 91A.8, 91A.12. |
| KS | — | $250–$1,000. | No. | Yes. | No statutory requirements. | Yes. | No statutory requirements. | Kan. Stat. Ann. §§ 44-1210, 44-1211. |
| KY | Civil penalty. | $100–$1,000. | No. | Yes. | Yes, liquidated damages equal to unpaid wages. Court need not award liquidated damages if employer acted in good faith. | Yes. | No statutory requirements. | Ky. Rev. Stat. Ann. §§ 337.385, 337.427, 337.990. |
| LA | — | — | — | — | — | — | — | No state statutory provisions. |
| ME | — | $50–$200. | No. | Yes. | Yes, liquidated damages equal to unpaid wages. | Yes. | No statutory requirements. | Me. Rev. Stat. Ann. tit. 26, §§ 670, 671. |
| MD | Misdemeanor. | $1,000 maximum. | No. | Yes. | No statutory requirements. | Yes. | No statutory requirements. | Md. Code Ann. [Lab. & Empl.] §§ 3-427, 3-428. |
| MA | — | $50–$200. | 10–90 days. | Yes, 3 times the wage differential. | No statutory requirements. | Yes. | No statutory requirements. | Mass. Gen. Laws Ann. ch. 151, §§ 19, 20. |
| MI | — | $1,000 maximum. | No. | Yes. | Yes, liquidated damages equal to unpaid wages. | Yes. | 3 years. | Mich. Stat. Ann. § 17.255(13). |
| MN | Misdemeanor. | $1,000 for each violation for each employee. ($700–$3,000 for retaliation). | 90 days maximum. | Yes. | Yes, liquidated damages equal to unpaid wages. | Yes. | No statutory requirements. | Minn. Stat. Ann. §§ 177.27, 177.32, 609.03. |

*(Table continues.)*

# Table 3.5-1 *(cont'd)*
## PENALTIES FOR VIOLATING MINIMUM WAGE LAWS

(See also text at § 3.5.)

**KEY:** **Status of Offense.** The status of the offense for employers violating overtime provisions is listed only if state labor statutes expressly classify the nature of the offense.
**Civil Cause of Action.** This indicates which states provide an employee with a private cause of action for a violation of minimum wage provisions.

| | | | | *Civil Cause of Action* | | | | |
|---|---|---|---|---|---|---|---|---|
| | *Status of Offense* | *Fines* | *Imprisonment* | *Unpaid Wages* | *Damages* | *Attorneys' Fees/Costs* | *Time Limit to File Civil Action* | *Citations to Authority* |
| MS | — | — | — | — | — | — | — | No state statutory provisions. |
| MO | Class C misdemeanor. | $300 maximum (individual); $1,000 maximum (corporation). | 15 days maximum. | Yes. | Yes, liquidated damages equal to full wage rate owed employee, less any amount actually paid by employer. | Yes. | 2 years. | Mo. Rev. Stat. §§ 290.525, 290.527, 516.140, 558.011, 560.016, 560.021. |
| MT | Misdemeanor. | $500 maximum. | 6 months maximum. | Yes. | Yes, up to 110% of unpaid wages. | Yes. | 18 months. | Mont. Code Ann. §§ 39-3-206, 39-3-207, 39-3-214, 39-3-407, 46-18-212. |
| NE | Class IV misdemeanor. | $100–$500. | No. | Yes. | No statutory requirements. | Yes. | No statutory requirements. | Neb. Rev. Stat. §§ 28-106, 48-1206. |
| NV | Misdemeanor. | $1,000 maximum. | 6 months maximum. | Yes. | No statutory requirements. | No statutory requirements. | 2 years. | Nev. Rev. Stat. §§ 193.150, 608.260, 608.290. |
| NH | Misdemeanor if committed by an individual; felony if committed by a corporation. Civil penalty. | $2,000 maximum (individual); $100,000 maximum (corporation). $1,000 maximum. | 1 year maximum. | Yes. | No statutory requirements. | Yes. | No statutory requirements. | N.H. Rev. Stat. Ann. §§ 273:11-a, 279:28, 279:29, 651:2. |

| | | | | | | | | |
|---|---|---|---|---|---|---|---|---|
| NJ | Disorderly persons offense. | $100–$1,000 for first offense; $500–$1,000 for subsequent offenses. Other administrative penalties may apply. $100–$1,000 for retaliation. | 10–90 days for first offense; 10–100 days for subsequent offenses. | Yes. | No statutory requirements. | Yes. | 2 years. | N.J. Rev. Stat. Ann. §§ 34:11-56a22, 34:11-56a24, 34:11-56a25. |
| NM | Misdemeanor. | $25–$300. | 10–90 days. | Yes. | Yes, unpaid wages, plus an equal amount as liquidated damages. | Yes. | No statutory requirements. | N.M. Stat. Ann. § 50-4-26. |
| NY | Class B misdemeanor. | $500 maximum (individual), $2,000 maximum (corporation); 2nd violation within 5 years: penalty, plus $10,000. | 3 months maximum. | Yes. | Yes, liquidated damages at 25% of unpaid wages for willful violations. | Yes. | 6 years. | N.Y. Lab. Law §§ 662, 663; N.Y. Penal Law §§ 70.15, 80.05, 80.10. |
| NC | — | No. | No. | Yes. | Yes, liquidated damages equal to unpaid wages. Court has discretion to deny damages if employer acted in good faith based on reasonable grounds. | Yes, plus interest. | 2 years. | N.C. Gen. Stat. § 95-25.22. |
| ND | Class B misdemeanor. | $500 maximum. | 30 days maximum. | Yes. | Yes, up to treble wages owed for employers with multiple past violations. | No statutory requirements. | No statutory requirements. | N.D. Cent. Code §§ 12.1-32-01, 34-06-19, 34-14-09.1. (The minimum wage provisions have been set by the Commissioner of Labor.) |
| OH | 3rd degree misdemeanor. | $500 maximum. | 60 days maximum. | Yes. | No statutory requirements. | Yes. | No statutory requirements. | Ohio Rev. Code Ann. §§ 2929.21, 4111.10, 4111.13, 4111.99. |
| OK | Misdemeanor. | $500 maximum. | 6 months maximum. | Yes, twice the amount of wages owed employee, minus actual wages paid. | No statutory requirements. | Yes, not less than $100. | No statutory requirements. | Okla. Stat. tit. 40, §§ 197.9, 197.13. |
| OR | — | No. | No. | Yes. | Yes, civil penalty. | Yes. | No statutory requirements. | Or. Rev. Stat. §§ 652.150, 653.055. |
| PA | — | $75–$300 ($500–$1,000 for retaliation). | 10–60 days (10–90 days for retaliation). | Yes. | No statutory requirements. | Yes. | No statutory requirements. | Pa. Code Ann. tit. 43, §§ 333.112, 333.113. |

*(Table continues.)*

# Table 3.5-1 *(cont'd)*

## PENALTIES FOR VIOLATING MINIMUM WAGE LAWS

(See also text at § 3.5.)

**KEY:** **Status of Offense.** The status of the offense for employers violating overtime provisions is listed only if state labor statutes expressly classify the nature of the offense.
**Civil Cause of Action.** This indicates which states provide an employee with a private cause of action for a violation of minimum wage provisions.

| | | | | *Civil Cause of Action* | | | | |
|---|---|---|---|---|---|---|---|---|
| | *Status of Offense* | *Fines* | *Imprisonment* | *Unpaid Wages* | *Damages* | *Attorneys' Fees/Costs* | *Time Limit to File Civil Action* | *Citations to Authority* |
| RI | — | $100–$500 ($100–$500 for retaliation). | 10–90 days. | Yes. | No statutory requirements. | Yes. | No statutory requirements. | R.I. Gen. Laws §§ 28-12-16, 28-12-17, 28-12-19. |
| SC | — | — | — | — | — | — | — | No state statutory provisions. |
| SD | Class 2 misdemeanor. | $200 per offense. | 30 days. | Yes. | No statutory requirements. | Yes. | No statutory requirements. | S.D. Codified Laws §§ 22-6-2, 60-11-3, 60-11-4. |
| TN | — | — | — | — | — | — | — | No state statutory provisions. |
| TX | — | No. | No. | Yes. | Yes, liquidated damages equal to unpaid wages. | Yes. | 2 years. | Tex. Lab. Code Ann. §§ 62.201, 62.202, 62.205. |
| UT | Class B misdemeanor (for repeated violations). Administrative fine. | $1,000 maximum (individual), $5,000 maximum (corporation, association); $500 maximum per violation. | 6 months maximum. No. | Yes, plus interest. | No statutory requirements. | Yes. | 2 years. | Utah Code Ann. §§ 34-40-202, 34-40-204, 34-40-205, 76-3-204, 76-3-301, 76-3-302. |
| VT | — | $100 maximum ($200 maximum for retaliation). | No. | Yes. | No statutory requirements. | Yes. | No statutory requirements. | Vt. Stat. Ann. tit. 21, §§ 394, 395. |
| VA | — | $10–$200 for knowing and intentional violations. | No. | Yes, plus 8% interest. | No statutory requirements. | Yes. | No statutory requirements. | Va. Code Ann. §§ 40.1-28.11, 40.1-28.12. |

| | | | | | | | | |
|---|---|---|---|---|---|---|---|---|
| WA | Gross misdemeanor. | $5,000 maximum. | 1 year maximum. | Yes. | No statutory requirements. | Yes. | No statutory requirements. | Wash. Rev. Code §§ 9A.20.021, 49.46.090, 49.46.100. |
| WV | Misdemeanor. (When resulting from retaliation or discrimination based on race, religion, color, origin, ancestry, age, or sex: misdemeanor.) | $100 maximum ($250–$1,000 for discrimination; $100–$500 for retaliation). | No. (1 year maximum for discrimination.) | Yes, up to 2 years. | No statutory requirements. | Yes. | No statutory requirements. | W. Va. Code §§ 21-5C-7, 21-5C-8. |
| WI | — | $10–$100. | No. | No statutory requirements. | No statutory requirements. | No statutory requirements. | No statutory requirements. | Wis. Stat. Ann. §§ 101.02, 104.04. |
| WY | — | No. | No. | Yes. | No statutory requirements. | Yes. | No statutory requirements. | Wyo. Stat. § 27-4-204. |

# Table 3.5-2
## PENALTIES FOR VIOLATING OVERTIME PROVISIONS

(See also text at § 3.5.)

**KEY:** **Status of Offense.** The status of the offense for employers violating overtime provisions is listed only if state labor statutes expressly classify the nature of the offense.
**Civil Cause of Action.** This indicates which states provide an employee with a private cause of action against the employer for a violation.

| | | | | *Civil Cause of Action* | | | | |
|---|---|---|---|---|---|---|---|---|
| | *Status of Offense* | *Fines* | *Imprisonment* | *Unpaid Wages* | *Damages* | *Attorneys' Fees/Costs* | *Time Limit to File Civil Action* | *Citations to Authority* |
| AL | — | — | — | — | — | — | — | No state statutory provisions. |
| AK | — | $100–$2,000. | 10–90 days. | Yes. | Yes, liquidated damages equal to unpaid wages. | Yes. | 2 years. | Alaska Stat. §§ 23.10.110, 23.10.115, 23.10.140. (Enforcement is by injunction.) |
| AZ | — | — | — | — | — | — | — | No state statutory provisions. |
| AR | — | $100 maximum (for willful violations). | No. | Yes. | No statutory requirements. | Yes. | No statutory requirements. | Ark. Code Ann. §§ 11-4-206, 11-4-218. |
| CA | Misdemeanor. | $100 maximum. | 30 days minimum. | Yes, plus interest. | No. | Yes. | No statutory requirements. | Cal. Lab. Code §§ 1193.6, 1194, 1194.5, 1198, 1199. (Enforcement is by injunction.) |
| CO | Misdemeanor. | $20–$100 (minors, 1st offense).<br>$100–$500 (minors, subsequent offense).<br>$250–$500 (dangerous jobs). | —<br>90 days maximum (minors, subsequent offense).<br>90 days–6 months. | No statutory requirements. | No statutory requirements. | No statutory requirements. | No statutory requirements. | Colo. Rev. Stat. §§ 8-12-104–8-13-103, 8-13-107–8-13-111. (For particular occupations and employees.) |

| | | | | | | | | |
|---|---|---|---|---|---|---|---|---|
| CT | Civil penalty. | $150 per offense.<br>$2,000–$5,000 (more than $2,000 unpaid wages).<br>$1,000–$2,000 ($1,000–$2,000 unpaid wages).<br>$500–$1,000 ($500–$1,000 unpaid wages).<br>$250–$500 (less than $500 unpaid wages). | No.<br>5 years maximum.<br>1 year maximum.<br>6 months maximum.<br>3 months maximum. | Yes, twice wage rate, minus wages actually paid. | No statutory requirements. | Yes. | No statutory requirements. | Conn. Gen. Stat. Ann. §§ 31-68, 31-69. |
| DE | — | — | — | — | — | — | — | No state statutory provisions. |
| DC | — | $10,000 maximum (for willful violations). | 6 months maximum. | Yes. | Yes, liquidated damages equal to unpaid wages. | Yes. | 3 years. | D.C. Code §§ 36-220.10, 36-220.11, 36-220.12. |
| FL | — | — | — | No statutory requirements. | No statutory requirements. | No statutory requirements. | 2 years. | Fla. Stat. Ann. § 95.11. |
| GA | — | — | — | — | — | — | — | No state statutory provisions. |
| HI | Misdemeanor. | $50–$500. | 1 year maximum. | Yes. | Yes, liquidated damages equal to unpaid wages for willful violations. | Yes. | No statutory requirements. | Haw. Rev. Stat. § 387-12. (Enforcement is by injunction.) |
| ID | — | No statutory requirements. | No statutory requirements. | Yes. | Yes, both collection and liquidated damages. | Yes. | 6 months to 2 years, depending on actions taken by employee. | Idaho Code §§ 44-1508, 45-614, 45-615. (Enforcement is by injunction.) |
| IL | Class B misdemeanor. | $500 maximum. | 6 months maximum. | Yes. | Yes, punitive damages to employee if willful violation. Employer is also liable to Department of Labor for 20% of underpayment. | Yes. | 3 years. | 730 Ill. Comp. Stat. Ann. §§ 5/5-8-3, 5/5-9-1; 820 Ill. Comp. Stat. Ann. §§ 105/11, 105/12. |
| IN | Class C infraction.<br>Class A infraction (if knowingly violated). | $500 maximum.<br>$10,000 maximum. | No. | Yes. | Liquidated damages equal to the amount of unpaid wages. | Yes. | 3 years. | Ind. Code Ann. §§ 22-2-2-4; 22-2-2-9; 22-2-2-11; 34-4-32-4. |
| IA | — | — | — | — | — | — | — | No state statutory provisions. |

*(Table continues.)*

## Table 3.5-2 *(cont'd)*

## PENALTIES FOR VIOLATING OVERTIME PROVISIONS

(See also text at § 3.5.)

**KEY:** **Status of Offense.** The status of the offense for employers violating overtime provisions is listed only if state labor statutes expressly classify the nature of the offense.
**Civil Cause of Action.** This indicates which states provide an employee with a private cause of action against the employer for a violation.

| | | | | *Civil Cause of Action* | | | | |
|---|---|---|---|---|---|---|---|---|
| | *Status of Offense* | *Fines* | *Imprisonment* | *Unpaid Wages* | *Damages* | *Attorneys' Fees/Costs* | *Time Limit to File Civil Action* | *Citations to Authority* |
| KS | — | $250–$1,000. | No. | Yes. | No statutory requirements. | Yes. | No statutory requirements. | Kan. Stat. Ann. §§ 44-1210, 44-1211. |
| KY | Civil penalty. | $100–$1,000. | No. | Yes. | Yes, liquidated damages equal to unpaid wages. Court need not award liquidated damages if employer acting in good faith. | Yes. | No statutory requirements. | Ky. Rev. Stat. Ann. §§ 337.385, 337.990. |
| LA | — | — | — | — | — | — | — | No state statutory provisions. |
| ME | — | $50–$200. | No. | Yes. | Yes, liquidated damages equal to unpaid wages. | Yes. | No statutory requirements. | Me. Rev. Stat. Ann. tit. 26, §§ 670, 671. |
| MD | Misdemeanor. | $1,000 maximum. | No. | Yes. | No statutory requirements. | Yes. | No statutory requirements. | Md. Code Ann. [Lab. & Empl.] §§ 3-427, 3-428. |
| MA | — | $50–$200. | 10–90 days. | Yes, 3 times the wage differential. | — | Yes. | — | Mass. Gen. Laws Ann. ch. 151, § 1B. |
| MI | — | No statutory requirements. | No. | Yes. | Yes, liquidated damages equal to unpaid wages. | Yes. | 3 years. | Mich. Stat. Ann. § 17.255(13). |
| MN | Misdemeanor. | $1,000 for each violation for each employee ($700–$3,000 for retaliation). | 90 days maximum. | Yes. | Yes, liquidated damages equal to unpaid wages. | Yes. | No statutory requirements. | Minn. Stat. Ann. §§ 177.27, 177.32, 609.03. |

| | | | | | | | | |
|---|---|---|---|---|---|---|---|---|
| MS | — | — | — | — | — | — | — | No state statutory provisions. |
| MO | Class C misdemeanor. | $300 maximum (individual); $1,000 maximum (corporation). | 15 days maximum. | Yes. | Yes, liquidated damages equal to full wage rate owed employee, less any amount actually paid by employer. | Yes. | 2 years. | Mo. Rev. Stat. §§ 290.525, 290.527, 558.011, 560.016, 560.021. |
| MT | Misdemeanor. | $500 maximum. | 6 months maximum. | Yes. | Yes, up to 110% of unpaid wages. | Yes. | 18 months. | Mont. Code Ann. §§ 39-3-206, 39-3-407, 46-18-212. |
| NE | — | — | — | — | — | — | — | No state statutory provisions. |
| NV | Misdemeanor. | $1,000 maximum. | 6 months maximum. | Yes. | No statutory requirements. | No statutory requirements. | 2 years. | Nev. Rev. Stat. §§ 193.150, 608.195. |
| NH | Misdemeanor if committed by an individual; felony if committed by a corporation. Civil penalty. | $2,000 maximum (individual); $100,000 maximum (corporation). $1,000 maximum. | 1 year maximum. | Yes. | No statutory requirements. | Yes. | No statutory requirements. | N.H. Rev. Stat. Ann. §§ 273:11-2, 279:28, 279:29, 651:2. |
| NJ | Disorderly persons offense. | $100–$1,000 for first offense; $500–$1,000 for subsequent offenses. Other administrative penalties may apply. $100–$1,000 for retaliation. | 10–90 days for first offense; 10–100 days for subsequent offenses. | Yes. | No statutory requirements. | Yes. | 2 years. | N.J. Rev. Stat. Ann. §§ 34:11-56a22, 34:11-56a24, 34:11-56a25. |
| NM | Misdemeanor. | $25–$300. | 10–90 days. | Yes. | Yes, liquidated damages equal to unpaid wages. | Yes. | No statutory requirements. | N.M. Stat. Ann. § 50-4-26. |
| NY | Discriminating against an employee who makes a wage-hour complaint is a Class B misdemeanor. | Up to $10,000. | — | Yes. | Yes, liquidated damages equal to 25% of unpaid wages if violation was willful. | Yes. | 6 years. | N.Y. Dept. of Labor Wage Ord.; N.Y. Lab. Law §§ 218, 219, 662–664. |

*(Table continues.)*

# **Table 3.5-2** *(cont'd)*
## PENALTIES FOR VIOLATING OVERTIME PROVISIONS

(See also text at § 3.5.)

**KEY:** **Status of Offense.** The status of the offense for employers violating overtime provisions is listed only if state labor statutes expressly classify the nature of the offense.
**Civil Cause of Action.** This indicates which states provide an employee with a private cause of action against the employer for a violation.

| | | | | *Civil Cause of Action* | | | | |
|---|---|---|---|---|---|---|---|---|
| | *Status of Offense* | *Fines* | *Imprisonment* | *Unpaid Wages* | *Damages* | *Attorneys' Fees/Costs* | *Time Limit to File Civil Action* | *Citations to Authority* |
| NC | — | No. | No. | Yes. | Yes, liquidated damages equal to unpaid wages. Court has discretion to deny damages if employer acting in good faith based on reasonable grounds. | Yes. | 2 years. | N.C. Gen. Stat. § 95-25.22. |
| ND | Class B misdemeanor. | $500 maximum. | 30 days maximum. | Yes. | Yes, up to treble wages owed for employers with multiple past violations. | No statutory requirements. | No statutory requirements. | N.D. Cent. Code §§ 12.1-32-01, 34-06-19. (Overtime provisions are set by Commissioner of Labor.) |
| OH | 3rd degree misdemeanor. | $500 maximum. | 60 days maximum. | Yes. | No statutory requirements. | Yes. | No statutory requirements. | Ohio Rev. Code Ann. §§ 2929.21, 4111.10, 4111.99. |
| OK | — | — | — | — | — | — | — | No state statutory provisions. |
| OR | — | No. | No. | Yes. | Yes, civil penalty. | Yes. | No statutory requirements. | Or. Rev. Stat. §§ 652.150, 653.055. |
| PA | — | $75–$300 ($500–$1,000 for retaliation). | 10–60 days (10–90 days for retaliation). | Yes. | No statutory requirements. | Yes. | No statutory requirements. | Pa. Code Ann. tit. 43, §§ 333.112, 333.113. |
| RI | — | $100–$500 ($100–$500 for retaliation). | 10–90 days. | Yes. | No statutory requirements. | Yes. | No statutory requirements. | R.I. Gen. Laws §§ 28-12-18, 28-12-19. |

| | | | | | | | | |
|---|---|---|---|---|---|---|---|---|
| SC | — | — | — | — | — | — | — | No state statutory provisions. |
| SD | — | — | — | — | — | — | — | No state statutory provisions. |
| TN | — | — | — | — | — | — | — | No state statutory provisions. |
| TX | — | — | — | — | — | — | — | No state statutory provisions. |
| UT | — | — | — | — | — | — | — | No state statutory provisions. |
| VT | — | $100 maximum ($200 maximum for retaliation). | No. | Yes. | No statutory requirements. | Yes. | No statutory requirements. | Vt. Stat. Ann. tit. 21, §§ 394, 395. |
| VA | — | — | — | — | — | — | — | No state statutory provisions. |
| WA | Gross misdemeanor. | $5,000 maximum. | 1 year maximum. | Yes. | No statutory requirements. | Yes. | No statutory requirements. | Wash. Rev. Code §§ 9A.20.021, 49.46.090, 49.46.100. |
| WV | Misdemeanor. (When resulting from retaliation or discrimination based on race, religion, color, origin, ancestry, age, or sex: misdemeanor.) | $100 maximum ($250–$1,000 for discrimination; $100–$500 for retaliation). | No. (1 year maximum for discrimination.) | Yes, up to 2 years. | No statutory requirements. | Yes. | No statutory requirements. | W. Va. Code §§ 21-5C-7, 21-5C-8. |
| WI | — | $10–$100. | No. | — | — | — | — | Wis. Stat. Ann. §§ 101.02, 104.04. |
| WY | — | — | — | — | — | — | — | — |

# § 3.6 State Laws on Employment of Minors

Generally, child labor laws are designed to protect the health, welfare, and safety of minors by prohibiting their employment in hazardous or overly strenuous occupations. Prohibited occupations include the manufacturing of explosives and dangerous chemicals, those requiring the use of dangerous power-driven machinery, and mining and construction. Often, these laws also prohibit minors from working in businesses that sell intoxicating beverages.

Common exemptions from these prohibitions include the employment of minors in any of the following circumstances:

- At home;
- Outside the home by parents or guardians;
- As apprentices;
- In vocational education positions;
- In agricultural jobs; and
- As delivery persons.

"Street trades," such as selling newspapers, shining shoes, and vending, are often covered under separate statutory provisions.

In addition, child labor laws often limit the number of hours a minor may be employed each day and each week; the number of hours per day generally depends on whether or not school is in session. Many states further require employers to obtain from minors age certificates or work permits, which are often issued by school superintendents.

Table 3.6-1 shows which states have child labor laws and indicates the age groups affected by these restrictions. Because states commonly set limits at ages 14, 16, and 18, these ages are listed separately. If states have provisions affecting other age groups, those statutes are reflected in the "Other Requirements" column. In practical terms, that means provisions affecting persons under age 21. Because of holdovers from previous statutes written when the age of majority was 21 and because of restrictions on the sale of alcohol to persons under age 21, a number of states have laws restricting the employment of persons under 21 which logically fall within the matter addressed in this table, though these persons are not legally minors. Some states also have specific restrictions on persons under the age of 11 or 9, for example, and these statutes are referred to by the category covering restrictions on persons under age 14.

# Table 3.6-1
## STATE LAWS ON EMPLOYMENT OF MINORS

(See also text at § 3.6.)

**KEY:** **Other Requirements.** These include requirements affecting age groups other than those listed in the table.
**Yes.** State has law limiting employment of all minors under that age unless otherwise exempt.
**No.** State has no law limiting employment of minors in that age group, although coverage of minors may be subsumed under a state law with a different age cap.

| | *Laws for Minors Under 14 Years* | *Laws for Minors Under 16 Years* | *Laws for Minors Under 18 Years* | *Other Requirements* | *Citations to Authority* |
|---|---|---|---|---|---|
| AL | Yes. | Yes. | Yes. | Yes. | Ala. Code §§ 25-8-32–25-8-44. |
| AK | Yes. | Yes. | Yes. | Yes. | Alaska Stat. §§ 23.10.335, 23.10.340, 23.10.350, 23.10.355. |
| AZ | Yes. | Yes. | Yes. | Yes. | Ariz. Rev. Stat. §§ 23-231–23-235; Ariz. Const. art. 18, § 2. |
| AR | Yes. | Yes. | Yes. | Yes. | Ark. Code Ann. §§ 11-6-104–11-6-110. |
| CA | Yes. | Yes. | Yes. | Yes. | Cal. Lab. Code §§ 1290, 1292–1298, 1308, 1308.1, 1308.5, 1309.5, 1310, 1391, 1391.1, 1391.2, 1394, 1394.1; West's Cal. Bus. & Prof. Code §§ 25663, 25663.5. |
| CO | Yes. | Yes. | Yes. | Yes. | Colo. Rev. Stat. §§ 8-12-104–8-12-114, 12-46-115. |
| CT | Yes. | Yes. | Yes. | Yes. | Conn. Gen. Stat. Ann. §§ 10-193, 30-81, 30-90a, 31-23–31-25. |
| DE | Yes. | Yes. | Yes. | No. | Del. Code Ann. tit. 19, §§ 501, 502, 504–508. |
| DC | Yes. | Yes. | Yes. | Yes. | D.C. Code §§ 25-125, 36-501–36-506, 36-514–36-516. |
| FL | No. | Yes. | Yes. | Yes. | Fla. Stat. Ann. §§ 450.021–450.161. |
| GA | Yes. | Yes. | Yes. | Yes. | Ga. Code Ann. §§ 39-2-1–39-2-21. |
| HI | Yes. | Yes. | Yes. | No. | Haw. Rev. Stat. §§ 390-1–390-7. |
| ID | Yes. | Yes. | No. | Yes. | Idaho Code §§ 44-1301–44-1308; Idaho Const. art. 13, § 4. |
| IL | Yes. | Yes. | Yes. | Yes. | 820 Ill. Comp. Stat. Ann. §§ 205/1–205/3, 205/7–205/16. |
| IN | Yes. | Yes. | Yes. | Yes. | Ind. Code Ann. §§ 20-8.1-4-1–20-8.1-4-32. |
| IA | Yes. | Yes. | Yes. | Yes. | Iowa Code Ann. §§ 92.1–92.21. |
| KS | Yes. | Yes. | Yes. | No. | Kan. Stat. Ann. §§ 38-601–38-604, 38-614. |
| KY | Yes. | Yes. | Yes. | Yes. | Ky. Rev. Stat. Ann. §§ 339.220–339.370. |

(Table continues.)

# Table 3.6-1 *(cont'd)*
## STATE LAWS ON EMPLOYMENT OF MINORS

(See also text at § 3.6.)

**KEY:** **Other Requirements.** These include requirements affecting age groups other than those listed in the table.
**Yes.** State has law limiting employment of all minors under that age unless otherwise exempt.
**No.** State has no law limiting employment of minors in that age group, although coverage of minors may be subsumed under a state law with a different age cap.

| | *Laws for Minors Under 14 Years* | *Laws for Minors Under 16 Years* | *Laws for Minors Under 18 Years* | *Other Requirements* | *Citations to Authority* |
|---|---|---|---|---|---|
| LA | Yes. | Yes. | Yes. | Yes. | La. Rev. Stat. §§ 23:161–23:171, 23:211–23:218, 23:251–23:258. |
| ME | Yes. | Yes. | Yes. | Yes. | Me. Rev. Stat. Ann. tit. 26, §§ 771–775. |
| MD | Yes. | Yes. | Yes. | No. | Md. Code Ann. [Lab. & Empl.] §§ 3-201–3-211, 3-213. |
| MA | Yes. | Yes. | Yes. | Yes. | Mass. Gen. Laws Ann. ch. 149, §§ 56–104. |
| MI | Yes. | Yes. | Yes. | Yes. | Mich. Stat. Ann. §§ 17.731(1)–17.731(12a), 17.731(14)–17.731(19). |
| MN | Yes. | Yes. | Yes. | No. | Minn. Stat. Ann. §§ 181A.01–181A.12. |
| MS | Yes. | Yes. | Yes. | No. | Miss. Code Ann. §§ 63-1-9, 71-1-17–71-1-21. |
| MO | Yes. | Yes. | Yes, persons under age 18 are not permitted to serve alcoholic beverages. | Yes, persons age 20 and under are not permitted to serve alcohol across a bar. | Mo. Rev. Stat. §§ 294.005–294.110, 311.300. |
| MT | Yes. | Yes. | Yes. | No. | Mont. Code Ann. §§ 41-2-103–41-2-118. |
| NE | Yes. | Yes. | Yes, minors may not sell or control alcohol. | Yes. | Neb. Rev. Stat. §§ 48-302–48-313, 53-180.02, 53-180.05. |
| NV | Yes. | Yes. | Yes. | No. | Nev. Rev. Stat. §§ 463.350, 609.185–609.270. |
| NH | Yes, minors under 12. | Yes. | Yes. | No. | N.H. Rev. Stat. Ann. §§ 276-A:1–276-A:22. |
| NJ | Yes. | Yes. | Yes. | Yes. | N.J. Rev. Stat. Ann. §§ 34:2-21.2–34:2-21.4, 34:2-21.6, 34:2-21.7, 34:2-21.17. |
| NM | Yes. | Yes. | Yes. | No. | N.M. Stat. Ann. §§ 50-6-1–50-6-16. |
| NY | Yes. | Yes. | Yes. | No. | N.Y. Lab. Law §§ 130–142. |
| NC | Yes. | Yes. | Yes. | Yes. | N.C. Gen. Stat. § 95-25.5. |

| | | | | | |
|---|---|---|---|---|---|
| ND | Yes. | Yes. | Yes. | No. | N.D. Cent. Code §§ 34-07-01–34-07-17.1. |
| OH | No. | Yes. | Yes. | Yes. | Ohio Rev. Code Ann. § 4109.07; 4301.22(A)(3). |
| OK | Yes. | Yes. | No. | No. | Okla. Stat. tit. 40, §§ 71–88. |
| OR | Yes. | Yes. | Yes. | No. | Or. Rev. Stat. §§ 653.315–653.370. |
| PA | Yes. | Yes. | Yes. | No. | Pa. Code Ann. tit. 43, §§ 41–71. |
| RI | Yes. | Yes. | Yes. | No. | R.I. Gen. Laws §§ 28-3-1, 28-3-11. |
| SC | No. | No. | Yes. | No. | S.C. Code Ann. §§ 16-15-385(A), 41-13-10–41-13-60, 53-1-120. (The State Director of Labor is responsible for issuing regulations governing the employment of minors.) |
| SD | Yes. | Yes. | Yes. | No. | S.D. Codified Laws §§ 35-4-79, 60-12-1–60-12-21. |
| TN | Yes. | Yes. | Yes. | No. | Tenn. Code Ann. §§ 50-5-101–50-5-114. |
| TX | Yes. | Yes. | No. | No. | Tex. Lab. Code Ann. §§ 51.002–51.014. |
| UT | Yes. | Yes. | Yes. | No. | Utah Code Ann. §§ 34-23-201–34-23-209. |
| VT | Yes. | Yes. | Yes. | No. | Vt. Stat. Ann. tit. 21, §§ 434, 436, 440. |
| VA | Yes. | Yes. | Yes. | No. | Va. Code Ann. §§ 40.1-78–40.1-100. |
| WA | Yes, domestic relations § 26.28.060 provides a penalty for employment of minors under 14 years old. | Yes. | Yes. | Yes. | Wash. Rev. Code §§ 26.28.060, 43.22.270, 49.12.121; Wash. Admin. Code §§ 29-125-010 *et seq.* (The State Commissioner or Director of Labor is responsible for issuing regulations governing employment of minors.) |
| WV | No. | Yes. | Yes. | No. | W. Va. Code §§ 21-6-1–21-6-7, 61-8-26. (The Commissioner of Labor may make rules and regulations to the extent necessary.) |
| WI | Yes. | Yes. | Yes. | No. | Wis. Stat. Ann. §§ 103.67, 103.78. |
| WY | No. | Yes. | No. | No. | Wyo. Stat. §§ 27-6-107–27-6-116. |

## § 3.7 Recordkeeping Requirements for Adult Employees and Minors

To monitor compliance with the minimum wage laws, state statutes often require employers to maintain employee records containing such information as personal data, wages, and work schedules. Table 3.7-1 surveys the statutory requirements regarding adult employees and notes the length of time employers must retain these records.

To police the employment of minors, many states have enacted statutes setting special recordkeeping requirements for minors in addition to standard records that must be kept for adults. Generally, two sets of records are kept, and the employee-minor will appear on both sets of records. All state recordkeeping requirements are in addition to federal recordkeeping requirements under the FLSA, to the extent applicable. Table 3.7-2 shows which states have such requirements for minors and also notes whether special age certificates or work permits are required to employ minors. Although these certificates and permits are generally issued under the authority of a school superintendent, the procedure for issuing them, as well as their content, varies from state to state.

# Table 3.7-1
## EMPLOYERS' RECORDKEEPING REQUIREMENTS FOR ADULT EMPLOYEES

(See also text at § 3.7.)

**KEY: Conditions of Employment.** Conditions of employment refer to temporary, seasonal, or part-time work, as well as situations requiring special authorization, such as maintaining a chauffeur's license.

| | *Name and Address* | *Occupation* | *Pay Rate* | *Wage per Week or Pay Period* | *Hours per Day or Week* | *Deductions per Pay Period* | *Conditions of Employment* | *Length of Time Records Must Be Preserved* | *Citations to Authority* |
|---|---|---|---|---|---|---|---|---|---|
| AL | — | — | — | — | — | — | — | — | No state statutory provisions. |
| AK | State law requires data to be kept. | State law requires data to be kept. | State law requires data to be kept. | State law requires data to be kept. | State law requires data to be kept. | State law does not specifically mandate data to be kept. | State law does not specifically mandate data to be kept. | 3 years. | Alaska Stat. § 23.10.100. (Additional data may be required by the Commissioner of Labor.) |
| AZ | — | — | — | — | — | — | — | — | No state statutory provisions. (Additional data may be required by the Commissioner of Labor.) |
| AR | State law requires data to be kept. | State law requires data to be kept. | State law requires data to be kept. | State law requires data to be kept. | State law does not specifically mandate data to be kept. | State law does not specifically mandate data to be kept. | State law does not specifically mandate data to be kept. | 3 years. | Ark. Code Ann. § 11-4-217. (Additional data may be required by the Commissioner of Labor.) |
| CA | State law requires data to be kept. | State law requires data to be kept. | State law requires data to be kept. | State law requires data to be kept. | State law requires data to be kept. | State law does not specifically mandate data to be kept. | State law does not specifically mandate data to be kept. | 3 years. | Cal. Lab. Code § 1174. |
| CO | State law requires data to be kept. | State law requires data to be kept. | State law requires data to be kept. | State law does not specifically mandate data to be kept. | State law requires data to be kept. | State law requires data to be kept. | State law does not specifically mandate data to be kept. | State regulation requires retention of records for 2 years. | Colo. Rev. Stat. § 8-6-107. |

(Table continues.)

# Table 3.7-1 *(cont'd)*
## EMPLOYERS' RECORDKEEPING REQUIREMENTS FOR ADULT EMPLOYEES

(See also text at § 3.7.)

**KEY:** **Conditions of Employment.** Conditions of employment refer to temporary, seasonal, or part-time work, as well as situations requiring special authorization, such as maintaining a chauffeur's license.

| | *Name and Address* | *Occupation* | *Pay Rate* | *Wage per Week or Pay Period* | *Hours per Day or Week* | *Deductions per Pay Period* | *Conditions of Employment* | *Length of Time Records Must Be Preserved* | *Citations to Authority* |
|---|---|---|---|---|---|---|---|---|---|
| CT | Statute does not require maintenance of data, but regulation does. | Statute does not require maintenance of data, but regulation does. | Statute does not require maintenance of data, but regulation does. | State law requires data to be kept. | State law requires data to be kept. | Statute does not require maintenance of data, but regulation does. | State law does not specifically mandate data to be kept. | 3 years. | Conn. Gen. Stat. Ann. § 31-66. (Additional data may be required by the Commissioner of Labor.) |
| DE | State law requires data to be kept. | State law requires data to be kept. | State law requires data to be kept. | State law requires data to be kept. | State law requires data to be kept. | State law does not specifically mandate data to be kept. | State law does not specifically mandate data to be kept. | 3 years. | Del. Code Ann. tit. 19, § 907. (Additional data may be required by the Commissioner of Labor.) |
| DC | State law requires data to be kept. | State law requires data to be kept. | State law requires data to be kept. | State law requires data to be kept. | State law requires data to be kept. | Statute does not require maintenance of data, but regulation does. | State law does not specifically mandate data to be kept. | 3 years. | D.C. Code § 36-220.7. (Additional data may be required by the Mayor.) |
| FL | — | — | — | — | — | — | — | — | No state statutory provisions. |
| GA | State law requires data to be kept. | State law requires data to be kept. | State law does not specifically mandate data to be kept. | State law requires data to be kept. | State law requires data to be kept. | State law does not specifically mandate data to be kept. | State law does not specifically mandate data to be kept. | 1 year. | Ga. Code Ann. §§ 34-2-11, 34-4-5. |
| HI | State law requires data to be kept. | State law requires data to be kept. | State law does not specifically mandate data to be kept. | State law requires data to be kept. | State law requires data to be kept. | State law does not specifically mandate data to be kept. | State law does not specifically mandate data to be kept. | State law does not specifically mandate data to be kept. | Haw. Rev. Stat. § 387-6. (Additional data may be required by the Commissioner of Labor.) |

| | | | | | | | | | |
|---|---|---|---|---|---|---|---|---|---|
| ID | State law does not specifically mandate data to be kept. | State law does not specifically mandate data to be kept. | State law does not specifically mandate data to be kept. | State law does not specifically mandate data to be kept. | State law does not specifically mandate data to be kept. | State law does not specifically mandate data to be kept. | State law does not specifically mandate data to be kept. | 2 years. | Idaho Code § 45-610. (At time of hiring, employer must inform employee of pay rate.) |
| IL | State law requires data to be kept. | State law requires data to be kept. | State law requires data to be kept. | State law requires data to be kept. | State law requires data to be kept. | Statute does not require maintenance of data, but regulation does. | State law does not specifically mandate data to be kept. | 3 years. | 820 Ill. Comp. Stat. Ann. §§ 105/7, 105/8. (Additional data may be required by the Commissioner of Labor.) |
| IN | State law does not specifically mandate data to be kept. | State law does not specifically mandate data to be kept. | State law does not specifically mandate data to be kept. | State law requires data to be kept. | State law requires data to be kept. | State law requires data to be kept. | State law does not specifically mandate data to be kept. | State law does not specifically mandate data to be kept. | Ind. Code Ann. § 22-2-2-8. |
| IA | Statute does not require maintenance of data, but regulation does. | State law does not specifically mandate data to be kept. | State law does not specifically mandate data to be kept. | State law requires data to be kept. | State law requires data to be kept. | State law requires data to be kept. | State law does not specifically mandate data to be kept. | 3 years. | Iowa Code § 91A.6. |
| KS | State law requires data to be kept. | State law requires data to be kept. | State law requires data to be kept. | State law requires data to be kept. | State law requires data to be kept. | State law does not specifically mandate data to be kept. | State law does not specifically mandate data to be kept. | 3 years. | Kan. Stat. Ann. § 44-1209. (Additional data may be required by the Commissioner of Labor.) |
| KY | Statute does not require maintenance of data, but regulation does. | Statute does not require maintenance of data, but regulation does. | Statute does not require maintenance of data, but regulation does. | State law requires data to be kept. | State law requires data to be kept. | State law does not specifically mandate data to be kept. | State law does not specifically mandate data to be kept. | 1 year. | Ky. Rev. Stat. Ann. § 337.320. (Additional data may be required by the Commissioner of Labor.) |
| LA | State law requires data to be kept. | State law requires data to be kept. | State law does not specifically mandate data to be kept. | State law requires data to be kept. | State law requires data to be kept. | State law does not specifically mandate data to be kept. | State law does not specifically mandate data to be kept. | 1 year. | La. Rev. Stat. Ann. § 23:14. (Additional data may be required by the Secretary of Labor.) |
| ME | State law does not specifically mandate data to be kept. | State law does not specifically mandate data to be kept. | State law does not specifically mandate data to be kept. | State law requires data to be kept. | State law requires data to be kept. | State law requires data to be kept. | State law does not specifically mandate data to be kept. | 3 years. | Me. Rev. Stat. Ann. tit. 26, § 665. |
| MD | State law requires data to be kept. | State law requires data to be kept. | State law requires data to be kept. | State law requires data to be kept. | State law requires data to be kept. | State law does not specifically mandate data to be kept. | State law does not specifically mandate data to be kept. | 3 years. | Md. Code Ann. [Lab. & Empl.] § 3-424. (Additional data may be required by the Commissioner of Labor.) |

*(Table continues.)*

# Table 3.7-1 *(cont'd)*
## EMPLOYERS' RECORDKEEPING REQUIREMENTS FOR ADULT EMPLOYEES

(See also text at § 3.7.)

**KEY: Conditions of Employment.** Conditions of employment refer to temporary, seasonal, or part-time work, as well as situations requiring special authorization, such as maintaining a chauffeur's license.

| | *Name and Address* | *Occupation* | *Pay Rate* | *Wage per Week or Pay Period* | *Hours per Day or Week* | *Deductions per Pay Period* | *Conditions of Employment* | *Length of Time Records Must Be Preserved* | *Citations to Authority* |
|---|---|---|---|---|---|---|---|---|---|
| MA | State law requires data to be kept. | State law requires data to be kept. | State law does not specifically mandate data to be kept. | State law requires data to be kept. | State law requires data to be kept. | State law does not specifically mandate data to be kept. | State law does not specifically mandate data to be kept. | 2 years. | Mass. Gen. Laws Ann. ch. 151, § 15. (Additional data may be required by the Commissioner of Labor.) |
| MI | State law does not specifically mandate data to be kept. | State law does not specifically mandate data to be kept. | State law does not specifically mandate data to be kept. | State law requires data to be kept. | State law requires data to be kept. | State law requires data to be kept. | State law does not specifically mandate data to be kept. | Statute does not require preservation, but state regulation requires preservation for 3 years. | Mich. Stat. Ann. § 17.255(11). (Statute requires that employer provide a statement to employee and maintain it in employer's records.) |
| MN | State law requires data to be kept. | State law requires data to be kept. | State law requires data to be kept. | State law requires data to be kept. | State law requires data to be kept. | State law does not specifically mandate data to be kept. | State law does not specifically mandate data to be kept. | 3 years. | Minn. Stat. Ann. § 177.30. (Additional data may be required by the Commissioner of Labor.) |
| MS | — | — | — | — | — | — | — | — | No state statutory provisions. |
| MO | State law requires data to be kept. | State law requires data to be kept. | State law requires data to be kept. | State law requires data to be kept. | State law requires data to be kept. | State law does not specifically mandate data to be kept. | State law does not specifically mandate data to be kept. | 3 years. | Mo. Rev. Stat. § 290.520. |
| MT | Statute does not specifically mandate data to be kept, but regulation does. | State law does not specifically mandate data to be kept. | Statute does not specifically mandate data to be kept, but regulation does. | State law does not specifically mandate data to be kept. | Statute does not specifically mandate data to be kept, but regulation does. | Statute does not specifically mandate data to be kept, but regulation does. | State law does not specifically mandate data to be kept. | State regulation requires retention of records for 3 years. | Mont. Admin. R. 24.16.6102. |

| | | | | | | | | | |
|---|---|---|---|---|---|---|---|---|---|
| NE | State law does not specifically mandate data to be kept. | State law requires data to be kept. | State law requires data to be kept. | State law requires data to be kept. | State law does not specifically mandate data to be kept. | State law does not specifically mandate data to be kept. | State law requires data to be kept. | State law does not specifically mandate data to be kept. | Neb. Rev. Stat. § 48-1225. (Provisions set under sex discrimination policy. Additional data may be required by the Commissioner of Labor.) |
| NV | State law does not specifically mandate data to be kept. | State law does not specifically mandate data to be kept. | State law does not specifically mandate data to be kept. | State law requires data to be kept. | State law requires data to be kept. | State law requires data to be kept. | State law does not specifically mandate data to be kept. | 2 years. | Nev. Rev. Stat. § 608.115. |
| NH | State law does not specifically mandate data to be kept. | State law requires data to be kept. | State law does not specifically mandate data to be kept. | State law requires data to be kept. | State law requires data to be kept. | State law does not specifically mandate data to be kept. | State law does not specifically mandate data to be kept. | State law does not specifically mandate data to be kept. | N.H. Rev. Stat. Ann. § 279:27. |
| NJ | State law does not specifically mandate data to be kept. | State law does not specifically mandate data to be kept. | State law requires data to be kept. | State law requires data to be kept. | State law requires data to be kept. | State law does not specifically mandate data to be kept. | State law does not specifically mandate data to be kept. | State law does not specifically mandate data to be kept. | N.J. Stat. Ann. § 34:11-56a20. (Additional data may be required by the Commissioner of Labor.) |
| NM | State law does not specifically mandate data to be kept. | State law does not specifically mandate data to be kept. | State law does not specifically mandate data to be kept. | State law requires data to be kept. | State law requires data to be kept. | State law does not specifically mandate data to be kept. | State law does not specifically mandate data to be kept. | 1 year. | N.M. Stat. Ann. § 50-4-9. |
| NY | State law requires data to be kept. | State law does not specifically mandate data to be kept. | State law requires data to be kept. | State law requires data to be kept. | State law requires data to be kept. | State law does not specifically mandate data to be kept. | State law does not specifically mandate data to be kept. | State law does not specifically mandate data to be kept. | N.Y. Lab. Law § 661. (Additional data may be required by the Commissioner of Labor.) |
| NC | Statute does not require maintenance of data, but regulation does. | Statute does not require maintenance of data, but regulation does. | Statute does not require maintenance of data, but regulation does. | State law requires data to be kept. | State law requires data to be kept. | Statute does not require maintenance of data, but regulation does. | State law requires data to be kept. | State regulation requires retention of records for 3 years. | N.C. Gen. Stat. § 95-25.15. (Additional data may be required by the Commissioner of Labor.) |
| ND | State law does not specifically mandate data to be kept, but employers must keep a register of names of employees. | State law does not specifically mandate data to be kept. | State law requires data to be kept. | State law does not specifically mandate data to be kept. | State law requires data to be kept. | State law does not specifically mandate data to be kept. | State law does not specifically mandate data to be kept. | State regulation requires retention of records for 6 years. | N.D. Cent. Code § 34-06-07. |

*(Table continues.)*

# Table 3.7-1 *(cont'd)*
## EMPLOYERS' RECORDKEEPING REQUIREMENTS FOR ADULT EMPLOYEES

(See also text at § 3.7.)

**KEY: Conditions of Employment.** Conditions of employment refer to temporary, seasonal, or part-time work, as well as situations requiring special authorization, such as maintaining a chauffeur's license.

| | *Name and Address* | *Occupation* | *Pay Rate* | *Wage per Week or Pay Period* | *Hours per Day or Week* | *Deductions per Pay Period* | *Conditions of Employment* | *Length of Time Records Must Be Preserved* | *Citations to Authority* |
|---|---|---|---|---|---|---|---|---|---|
| OH | State law requires data to be kept. | State law requires data to be kept. | State law requires data to be kept. | State law requires data to be kept. | State law requires data to be kept. | State law does not specifically mandate data to be kept. | State law does not specifically mandate data to be kept. | 3 years. | Ohio Rev. Code Ann. § 4111.08. (Additional data may be required by the Commissioner of Labor.) |
| OK | — | — | — | — | — | — | — | — | No state statutory provisions. |
| OR | State law requires data to be kept. | State law requires data to be kept. | State law does not specifically mandate data to be kept. | State law does not specifically mandate data to be kept. | State law requires data to be kept. | State law does not specifically mandate data to be kept. | State law does not specifically mandate data to be kept. | 2 years. | Or. Rev. Stat. § 653.045. (Additional data may be required by the Commissioner of Labor.) |
| PA | State law does not specifically mandate data to be kept. | State law does not specifically mandate data to be kept. | State law does not specifically mandate data to be kept. | State law requires data to be kept. | State law requires data to be kept. | State law does not specifically mandate data to be kept. | State law does not specifically mandate data to be kept. | 3 years. | Pa. Stat. Ann. tit. 43, § 333.108. |
| RI | State law requires data to be kept. | State law requires data to be kept. | State law requires data to be kept. | State law requires data to be kept. | State law requires data to be kept. | State law does not specifically mandate data to be kept. | State law does not specifically mandate data to be kept. | 3 years. | R.I. Gen. Laws § 28-12-12. (Additional data may be required by the Commissioner of Labor.) |
| SC | State law requires data to be kept. | State law does not specifically mandate data to be kept. | State law does not specifically mandate data to be kept, although employer must inform employee in | State law requires data to be kept. | State law does not specifically mandate data to be kept. | State law requires data to be kept. | State law does not specifically mandate data to be kept. | 3 years. | S.C. Code Ann. §§ 41-10-20, 41-10-30. (Statutes do not apply to employer of domestic labor in private homes or those employing fewer than 5 employees.) |

| | | | | | | | | | |
|---|---|---|---|---|---|---|---|---|---|
| | | | writing of normal hours agreed upon. | | | | | | |
| SD | State law does not specifically mandate data to be kept. | State law requires data to be kept (job classification). | State law requires data to be kept. | State law requires data to be kept. | State law does not specifically mandate data to be kept. | State law does not specifically mandate data to be kept. | State law requires data to be kept. | Reasonable period of time. | S.D. Codified Laws § 60-12-17. (Statute applies to employers with more than 25 employees.) |
| TN | — | — | — | — | — | — | — | — | No state statutory provisions. |
| TX | — | — | — | — | — | — | — | — | No state statutory provisions. |
| UT | State law requires data to be kept. Date of birth is also required. | State law does not specifically mandate data to be kept. | State law does not specifically mandate data to be kept. | State law requires data to be kept. | State law requires data to be kept. | State law does not specifically mandate data to be kept. | State law does not specifically mandate data to be kept. | 3 years. | Utah Code Ann. § 34-40-201. |
| VT | State law does not specifically mandate data to be kept. | State law does not specifically mandate data to be kept. | State law does not specifically mandate data to be kept. | State law requires data to be kept. | State law requires data to be kept. | State law does not specifically mandate data to be kept. | State law does not specifically mandate data to be kept. | State law does not specifically mandate data to be kept. | Vt. Stat. Ann. tit. 21, § 393. |
| VA | — | — | — | — | — | — | — | — | No state statutory provisions. |
| WA | State law requires data to be kept. | State law requires data to be kept. | State law requires data to be kept. | State law requires data to be kept. | State law requires data to be kept. | State law does not specifically mandate data to be kept. | State law does not specifically mandate data to be kept. | 3 years. | Wash. Rev. Code §§ 49.12.050, 49.46.070. (Additional data may be required by the Commissioner of Labor.) |
| WV | State law requires data to be kept. | Statute does not require maintenance of data, but regulation does. | State law requires data to be kept. | State law requires data to be kept. | State law requires data to be kept. | State law requires data to be kept. | State law does not specifically mandate data to be kept. | 2 years. | W. Va. Code § 21-5C-5. |
| WI | State law requires data to be kept. | State law does not specifically mandate data to be kept. | State law does not specifically mandate data to be kept. | State law requires data to be kept. | State law requires data to be kept. | State law does not specifically mandate data to be kept. | State law does not specifically mandate data to be kept. | 3 years. | Wis. Stat. Ann. § 104.09. (Additional data may be required by the Commissioner of Labor.) |
| WY | State law requires data to be kept. | State law requires data to be kept. | State law requires data to be kept. | State law requires data to be kept. | State law requires data to be kept. | State law does not specifically mandate data to be kept. | State law does not specifically mandate data to be kept. | 2 years. | Wyo. Stat. § 27-4-203. |

# Table 3.7-2
## SPECIAL RECORDKEEPING REQUIREMENTS FOR MINORS

(In addition to these special records, which employers must keep for minors, data on minors should still be kept with standard records. Thus, most employers will have 2 sets of records: 1 standard set—which contains data on all employees, including minors—and 1 set with data required for minors only. All state recordkeeping requirements are in addition to federal recordkeeping requirements under the FLSA, to the extent applicable. See also text at § 3.7.)

**KEY:** **Yes.** State law requires employers to keep these data on minors.
**No.** State law does not require employers to keep data specifically on minors, although general recordkeeping requirements may call for maintenance of such data.

| | *Address* | *Hours per Day or Week* | *Time Starting, Ending Work/Meals* | *Wages* | *Other Requirements* | *Work Permit or Age Certificate Required* | *Citations to Authority* |
|---|---|---|---|---|---|---|---|
| AL | No. | Yes. | Yes. | No. | List of employees under 16 years old. Post maximum hours, time starting–ending work/meal times. | Yes. | Ala. Code 1975 § 25-8-38(b). |
| AK | No. | No. | No. | No. | No. | Written authorization of Commissioner if minor is under 17 years old. | Alaska Stat. § 23.10.332. |
| AZ | No. | No. | No. | Industrial Commission may require employers to keep records of wages paid to minors, if deemed necessary. | No. | No. | Ariz. Rev. Stat. Ann. § 23-312. |
| AR | No. | No. | No. | No. | No. | Yes. | Ark. Code Ann. § 11-6-109. |
| CA | No. | Yes. | No. | Yes. | Names and ages. | Yes. | Cal. Lab. Code §§ 1174, 1299. |
| CO | No. | No. | No. | No. | Date of birth. | Yes. To obtain proof of age, employer may require minor to submit age certificate. Minors 14 or 15 years old have to obtain school release permit. | Colo. Rev. Stat. §§ 8-6-107, 8-12-111, 8-12-113. |
| CT | No. | No. | No. | No. | No. | Yes. | Conn. Gen. Stat. Ann. § 31-23. |
| DE | No. | No. | No. | No. | No. | Yes. | Del. Code Ann. tit. 19, §§ 501–510. |
| DC | No. | Yes. | Yes. | No. | Post rules and date of birth. | Yes. | D.C. Code §§ 36-220.7, 36-502, 36-507–36-512. |

| | | | | | | | |
|---|---|---|---|---|---|---|---|
| FL | No. | No. | No. | No. | Other proof of age if age certificate not required. Post child labor laws. | Yes. | Fla. Stat. Ann. §§ 232.08, 450.045. |
| GA | No. | No. | No. | No. | No. | Yes. | Ga. Code Ann. § 39-2-11. |
| HI | No. | No. | No. | No. | No. | Yes. | Haw. Rev. Stat. § 390-2. |
| ID | Yes. | No. | No. | No. | Ages. | No. | Idaho Code § 44-1303. |
| IL | Yes. | No. | No. | No. | Post abstract of Act 205, a list of those occupations for which employment of minors is prohibited, the hours when time is allowed for meals, and hours of labor. | Yes. | 820 Ill. Comp. Stat. Ann. §§ 205/5, 205/6, 205/10–205/12. |
| IN | No. | No. | Yes. | No. | Post rules and list of names and ages. | Yes. | Ind. Code Ann. §§ 20-8.1-4-1–20-8.1-4-32. |
| IA | No. | No. | No. | No. | Names and ages. | Yes. | Iowa Code § 92.10. |
| KS | No. | No. | No. | No. | Post rules. | Yes. | Kan. Stat. Ann. §§ 38-604, 38-605. |
| KY | Yes. | No. | Yes. | No. | Post rules and list of names and ages. | Yes. | Ky. Rev. Stat. Ann. §§ 339.360, 339.400. |
| LA | No. | No. | No. | No. | Post rules. | Yes. | La. Rev. Stat. Ann. §§ 23:181–23:191, 23-217. |
| ME | No. | Yes. | No. | No. | Post rules. | Yes. | Me. Rev. Stat. Ann. tit. 26, §§ 701, 702, 775. |
| MD | No. | No. | No. | No. | Post rules. | Yes. | Md. Code Ann. [Lab. & Empl.] §§ 3-205, 3-206, 3-214. |
| MA | No. | No. | No. | No. | Names and ages. | Yes. Minors age 14–16 must present permit granted by school superintendent. | Mass. Gen. Laws Ann. ch. 149, § 86. |
| MI | No. | Yes. | Yes. | No. | Post statutory sections. Keep records for at least 1 year. | Yes. | Mich. Stat. Ann. §§ 17.731(4), 17.731(13). (Additional data may be required by the Commissioner of Labor.) |
| MN | No. | No. | No. | No. | Date of birth as required by Department of Labor. | Yes. | Minn. Stat. Ann. §§ 181A.05–181A.12. |
| MS | No. | No. | No. | No. | Keep affidavit of parent or guardian and certificate issued by superintendent of school district stating: minor's place and date of birth, last school attended and grade pursued; name of school; and name of teacher in charge. | Yes. | Miss. Code Ann. § 71-1-19. |

*(Table continues.)*

# Table 3.7-2 *(cont'd)*

## SPECIAL RECORDKEEPING REQUIREMENTS FOR MINORS

(In addition to these special records, which employers must keep for minors, data on minors should still be kept with standard records. Thus, most employers will have 2 sets of records: 1 standard set—which contains data on all employees, including minors—and 1 set with data required for minors only. All state recordkeeping requirements are in addition to federal recordkeeping requirements under the FLSA, to the extent applicable. See also text at § 3.7.)

**KEY:** **Yes.** State law requires employers to keep these data on minors.
**No.** State law does not require employers to keep data specifically on minors, although general recordkeeping requirements may call for maintenance of such data.

| | *Address* | *Hours per Day or Week* | *Time Starting, Ending Work/Meals* | *Wages* | *Other Requirements* | *Work Permit or Age Certificate Required* | *Citations to Authority* |
|---|---|---|---|---|---|---|---|
| MO | No. | No. | No. | No. | Post list of employed minors under 16 years old. | Yes. | Mo. Rev. Stat. §§ 294.024, 294.045, 294.060. |
| MT | No. | No. | No. | No. | No. | No. | No state statutory provisions. |
| NE | No. | No. | No. | No. | Post list of employed minors, list of hours per day, start/stop hours, and time for meals. | Yes. | Neb. Rev. Stat. §§ 48-304, 48-310. |
| NV | No. | No. | No. | No. | No. | Yes. | Nev. Rev. Stat. § 392.110. |
| NH | No. | No. | No. | No. | Post hours of labor, time for meals, and maximum hours per day. | Yes. | N.H. Rev. Stat. Ann. §§ 276-A:4, 276-A:20. |
| NJ | Yes. | Yes. | Yes. | Yes. | Date of birth (keep 1 year). Post rules. | Yes. | N.J. Stat. Ann. §§ 34:2-21.5–34:2-21.9. |
| NM | No. | No. | No. | No. | Post list of employed minors who require labor permits. | Yes. | N.M. Stat. Ann. §§ 50-6-2, 50-6-7, 50-6-9. |
| NY | No. | Yes. | Yes. | No. | No. | Yes. | N.Y. Lab. Law §§ 131, 132, 135, 136, 144. |
| NC | No. | No. | No. | No. | No. | Yes. | N.C. Gen. Stat. § 95-25.5. |
| ND | No. | No. | No. | No. | Post names of employed minors, list of hours per day, start/stop times, and time for meals; complete and maintain Employment and Age Certificate of minors. | Yes. | N.D. Cent. Code § 34-07-02, 34-07-15. |

| | | | | | | | |
|---|---|---|---|---|---|---|---|
| OH | Yes. | Yes. | Yes. | Yes. | Keep (for 2 years) record of name, occupation, certificate or proof of age, and parent's or guardian's statement of consent. Post list of minors employed. | Yes. | Ohio Rev. Code Ann. §§ 4109.02, 4109.08, 4109.11. |
| OK | No. | Yes. | Yes. | No. | Keep on file list of names and ages of employed minors under 16 years old. | Yes. | Okla. Stat. tit. 40, §§ 77, 79. |
| OR | No. | No. | No. | No. | Post notice of maximum hours per week or day for minors employed. | Yes. | Or. Rev. Stat. §§ 653.310, 653.315. |
| PA | No. | No. | No. | No. | Keep list of minors and their permit numbers, name of school district issuing permit, date of issuance, date of birth, and occupation. Post statutory sections, hours of labor, maximum hours per day, and start/stop hours. | Yes. | Pa. Stat. Ann. tit. 43, §§ 49, 58.1, 63. |
| RI | No. | No. | No. | No. | Post minimum rate of pay, number of required work hours on each day of the week, and copy of §§ 28-3-1–28-3-20. | Yes. | R.I. Gen. Laws §§ 28-3-6, 28-3-12, 28-3-19. |
| SC | No. | No. | No. | No. | No. | No. | No state statutory provisions. (The Commissioner of Labor may pass regulations to prohibit oppressive child labor practices.) |
| SD | No. | No. | No. | No. | Keep list of minors employed. | Yes. | S.D. Codified Laws § 60-12-6. |
| TN | No. | No. | No. | No. | Keep evidence of age and other documentation. Post rules. | Yes. | Tenn. Code Ann. § 50-5-111. |
| TX | No. | No. | No. | No. | No. | Certification of age is not *required;* however, certificate of age may be obtained by any individual 14 years old or over to prove age. | Tex. Lab. Code Ann. § 51.022. |
| UT | No. | No. | No. | No. | No. | No. | No state statutory provisions. |
| VT | No. | No. | Yes. | No. | Yes. Post start/stop times, number of hours required each day, and the hours when time is allowed for meals for particular occupations. (Manufacturing and mechanical establishments *(cont'd)* | Yes. | Vt. Stat. Ann. tit. 21, §§ 431, 440, 441, 442. |

*(Table continues.)*

# **Table 3.7-2** *(cont'd)*
## SPECIAL RECORDKEEPING REQUIREMENTS FOR MINORS

(In addition to these special records, which employers must keep for minors, data on minors should still be kept with standard records. Thus, most employers will have 2 sets of records: 1 standard set—which contains data on all employees, including minors—and 1 set with data required for minors only. All state recordkeeping requirements are in addition to federal recordkeeping requirements under the FLSA, to the extent applicable. See also text at § 3.7.)

**KEY:** **Yes.** State law requires employers to keep these data on minors.
**No.** State law does not require employers to keep data specifically on minors, although general recordkeeping requirements may call for maintenance of such data.

| | *Address* | *Hours per Day or Week* | *Time Starting, Ending Work/Meals* | *Wages* | *Other Requirements* | *Work Permit or Age Certificate Required* | *Citations to Authority* |
|---|---|---|---|---|---|---|---|
| VT *(cont'd)* | | | | | facing unusual workloads because of seasonal or peak demand may, upon notice and approval by Commissioner of Labor, employ minors for more hours than otherwise specified; such employers must keep record of daily and weekly hours worked by minors.) | | |
| VA | No. | No. | Yes. | No. | Keep records for preceding 12 months for period of 36 months. | Yes. | Va. Code Ann. §§ 40.1-81.1, 40.1-84. |
| WA | No. | No. | No. | No. | Parent/School Authorization form, proof of age, home address, and telephone number. (Employer obtains minor work permit.) Although no recordkeeping requirement, the Department of Labor may inquire into wages, hours, and conditions of labor at any time. | Yes. | Wash. Rev. Code §§ 49.12.121, 49.12.123. |
| WV | No. | No. | No. | No. | Date of birth. | Yes. | W. Va. Code § 21-6-3. |
| WI | Yes. | Yes. | Yes (both). | No. | Date of birth. | Yes. | Wis. Stat. Ann. §§ 103.74, 103.75. |
| WY | No. | No. | No. | No. | No. | Yes. | Wyo. Stat. § 27-6-107. |

# § 3.8 Penalties for Violating Recordkeeping Requirements

Table 3.8-1 lists the statutory penalties—including fines and imprisonment—for employers that violate state recordkeeping requirements. The table also notes the status of the offense and indicates which states provide for a fine and imprisonment for a single violation.

The "status" of the offense is listed only if the state statute explicitly defines the nature of the offense. In some states, state court decisions interpreting the statute must be reviewed in order to determine whether the offense is criminal or civil.

Table 3.8-2 lists the statutory penalties for violating recordkeeping requirements for minors.

# Table 3.8-1
## PENALTIES FOR VIOLATING RECORDKEEPING REQUIREMENTS

(See also text at § 3.8.)

**KEY:** **Status of Offense.** The status of the offense is listed only if state labor statutes expressly define the nature of the offense.

| | *Status of Offense* | *Fines* | *Imprisonment* | *Citations to Authority* |
|---|---|---|---|---|
| AL | — | — | — | No state statutory provisions. |
| AK | — | $100–$2,000. | 10–90 days. | Alaska Stat. § 23.10.140. |
| AZ | — | — | — | No state statutory provisions. |
| AR | — | For willful violations $100 maximum. | State law does not provide a penalty. | Ark. Code Ann. § 11-4-206. |
| CA | Civil penalty (willful violation).<br>Misdemeanor. | $500.<br>$1,000 maximum. | State law does not provide a penalty.<br>6 months maximum. | Cal. Lab. Code §§ 1174.5, 1175; Cal. Penal Code § 19. |
| CO | — | — | — | No state statutory provisions. |
| CT | Civil penalty. | $25–$100. | State law does not provide a penalty. | Conn. Gen. Stat. Ann. §§ 31-69. |
| DE | Civil penalty. | $1,000–$5,000. | State law does not provide a penalty. | Del. Code Ann. tit. 19, § 910. |
| DC | — | $10,000 maximum. | 6 months maximum. | D.C. Code §§ 36-220.9, 36-220.10. |
| FL | — | — | — | No state statutory provisions. |
| GA | Misdemeanor. | $20–$200. | 6 months maximum. | Ga. Code Ann. § 34-2-13. |
| HI | — | $500 maximum. | 90 days maximum. | Haw. Rev. Stat. § 387-7. |
| ID | — | — | — | No state statutory provisions. |
| IL | Class B misdemeanor. | $500 maximum. | 6 months maximum. | 730 Ill. Comp. Stat. Ann. §§ 5/5-8-3, 5/5-9-1; 820 Ill. Comp. Stat. Ann. §§ 105/11. |
| IN | (General violation) Class C infraction.<br>(Second offense) Class B misdemeanor.<br>(Knowing or intentional) Class A infraction. | $500.<br>$1,000.<br>$10,000. | 60 days maximum.<br>180 days maximum.<br>1 year maximum. | Ind. Code Ann. §§ 22-2-2-11, 34-4-32-4, 35-50-3-2–35-50-3-4. |
| IA | Civil penalty. | $100 per violation. | State law does not provide a penalty. | Iowa Code § 91A.12. |
| KS | — | $250–$1,000. | State law does not provide a penalty. | Kan. Stat. Ann. § 44-1210. |
| KY | Civil penalty. | $100–$1,000. | State law does not provide a penalty. | Ky. Rev. Stat. Ann. § 337.990. |
| LA | — | $500 maximum. | State law does not provide a penalty. | La. Rev. Stat. Ann. § 23:16. |
| ME | — | $50–$200. | State law does not provide a penalty. | Me. Rev. Stat. Ann. tit. 26, § 671. |

| | | | | |
|---|---|---|---|---|
| MD | Misdemeanor. | $1,000 maximum. | State law does not provide a penalty. | Md. Code Ann. [Lab. & Empl.] § 3-428. |
| MA | — | $25–$100. | State law does not provide a penalty. | Mass. Gen. Laws Ann. ch. 151, § 19. |
| MI | — | — | — | No state statutory provisions. |
| MN | Misdemeanor. | $700 maximum ($200 maximum additional fine by commissioner). | 90 days maximum. | Minn. Stat. Ann. §§ 177.30, 177.32, 609.03. |
| MS | — | — | — | No state statutory provisions. |
| MO | Class C misdemeanor. | $300 maximum (individual); $1,000 maximum (corporation). | 15 days maximum. | Mo. Rev. Stat. §§ 290.525, 558.011, 560.016, 560.021. |
| MT | — | — | — | No state statutory provisions. |
| NE | Class V misdemeanor. | $100 maximum. | State law does not provide a penalty. | Neb. Rev. Stat. §§ 28-106, 48-1227. (Provisions are set under sex discrimination policy.) |
| NV | Misdemeanor. | $1,000 maximum. | 6 months maximum. | Nev. Rev. Stat. §§ 193.150, 608.195. |
| NH | Misdemeanor if committed by an individual.<br>Felony if committed by a corporation. | $1,000 maximum.<br>$20,000 maximum. | State law does not provide a penalty. | N.H. Rev. Stat. Ann. §§ 279:28, 651:2. |
| NJ | Disorderly persons offense. | 1st offense: $100–$1,000; subsequent offense: $500–$1,000. | 10–90 days; 10–100 days. | N.J. Stat. Ann. § 34:11-56a22. (Administrative penalties may also apply.) |
| NM | Misdemeanor. | $25–$50. | 10–90 days. | N.M. Stat. Ann. § 50-4-10. |
| NY | Class B misdemeanor. | 1st offense: $500 maximum (individual); $2,000 (corporation). 2nd offense within 5 years: penalty, plus $10,000 maximum. | 3 months maximum. | N.Y. Lab. Law § 662; N.Y. Penal Law §§ 70.15, 80.05, 80.10. |
| NC | Civil penalty. | $250 maximum per employee; $1,000 maximum per investigation. | State law does not provide a penalty. | N.C. Gen. Stat. §§ 95-25.21, 95-25.23A. |
| | Class 2 misdemeanor (knowingly keeping false records or knowingly making false statements). | $250 maximum. | 6 months maximum. | |
| ND | Class B misdemeanor. | $500 maximum. | 30 days maximum. | N.D. Cent. Code §§ 12.1-32-01, 34-06-19. |
| OH | 4th degree misdemeanor. | $250 maximum. | 30 days maximum. | Ohio Rev. Code Ann. §§ 2929.21, 4111.99. |
| OK | — | — | — | No state statutory provisions. |
| OR | — | — | — | No state statutory provisions. |
| PA | — | $100–$500. | State law does not provide a penalty. | Pa. Stat. Ann. tit. 43, § 333.112. |
| RI | Misdemeanor. | $100–$500 (violation of adult recordkeeping laws).<br>$10–$50 (violation of minor recordkeeping laws). | State law does not provide a penalty.<br>State law does not provide a penalty. | R.I. Gen. Laws § 28-3-6, 28-12-15. |
| SC | — | 1st offense: written warning; 2nd and subsequent offenses: $100 maximum. | State law does not provide a penalty. | S.C. Code Ann. § 41-10-80. |

*(Table continues.)*

## **Table 3.8-1** *(cont'd)*
## PENALTIES FOR VIOLATING RECORDKEEPING REQUIREMENTS

(See also text at § 3.8.)

**KEY: Status of Offense.** The status of the offense is listed only if state labor statutes expressly define the nature of the offense.

| | *Status of Offense* | *Fines* | *Imprisonment* | *Citations to Authority* |
|---|---|---|---|---|
| SD | — | — | — | No state statutory provisions. |
| TN | — | — | — | No state statutory requirements. |
| TX | — | — | — | No state statutory provisions. |
| UT | Administrative penalty. | $500 maximum per violation. | State law does not provide a penalty. | Utah Code Ann. § 34-40-202. |
| VT | — | $100 maximum. | State law does not provide a penalty. | Vt. Stat. Ann. tit. 21, § 394. |
| VA | — | — | — | State has no statutory provisions. (False statements in records generally required to be filed under Labor title carry penalties of $10,000 maximum, or maximum of 6 months imprisonment, or both. Va. Code Ann. § 40.1-51.4:2.) |
| WA | Gross misdemeanor. | $5,000 maximum. | 1 year maximum. | Wash. Rev. Code §§ 9.92.020, 49.46.100. |
| WV | Misdemeanor. | $100 maximum. | State law does not provide a penalty. | W. Va. Code § 21-5C-7. |
| WI | — | — | — | No state statutory provisions. |
| WY | — | — | — | No state statutory provisions. |

# Table 3.8-2
## PENALTIES FOR VIOLATING RECORDKEEPING REQUIREMENTS FOR MINORS

(See also text at § 3.8.)

**KEY: Status of Offense.** The status of the offense is listed only if state labor statutes expressly define the nature of the offense.

| | *Status of Offense* | *Fines* | *Imprisonment* | *Citations to Authority* |
|---|---|---|---|---|
| AL | Misdemeanor. | $100–$500; subsequent violations, $500–$1,000. | State law does not provide a penalty. | Ala. Code § 25-8-59. |
| AK | — | $100–$2,000. | 10–90 days. | Alaska Stat. § 23.10.140. |
| AZ | Petty offense. | $300 maximum (individual); $1,000 maximum (corporation). | State law does not provide a penalty. | Ariz. Rev. Stat. Ann. §§ 13-802, 13-803, 23-329. |
| AR | Civil penalty. | $50–$1,000. | State law does not provide a penalty. | Ark. Code Ann. § 11-6-103. |
| CA | Misdemeanor. | $1,000–$5,000; up to $10,000 for second or willful violation. | 6 months maximum. | Cal. Lab. Code § 1303. |
| CO | Misdemeanor. | $20–$100; for subsequent violations, $100–$500. | Subsequent offense: 90 days maximum. | Colo. Rev. Stat. § 8-12-116. |
| CT | (Violating certificate requirement for minors.) | $200 maximum. | State law does not provide a penalty. | Conn. Gen. Stat. Ann. § 31-23. |
| DE | (Violating certificate requirement for minors.) Civil penalty. | $10,000. | State law does not provide a penalty. | Del. Code Ann. tit. 19, § 509. |
| DC | — | $1,000–$3,000; subsequent violations, $3,000–$5,000. | 10–30 days; subsequent violations, 30–90 days. | D.C. Code § 36-513. |
| FL | 2nd degree misdemeanor. | $500 maximum ($2,500 maximum additional administrative fine may apply). | 60 days maximum. | Florida Stat. Ann. §§ 450.141, 775.082, 775.083. |
| GA | Misdemeanor. | $1,000 maximum. | 12 months maximum. | Ga. Code Ann. §§ 17-10-3, 39-2-20. |
| HI | — | $1,000 maximum. | 1 year maximum. | Haw. Rev. Stat. § 390-7. |
| ID | — | — | — | No state statutory requirements. |
| IL | Civil penalty.<br>Class A misdemeanor (willful violation). | $5,000 maximum.<br>$2,500 maximum. | State law does not provide a penalty.<br>364 days maximum. | Ill Comp. Stat. Ann. ch. 730, §§ 5/5-8-3, 5/5-9-1; ch. 820, §§ 205/17.3, 205/19. |
| IN | (Violating child labor posting requirements.) Civil penalty. | 1st offense: warning; subsequent offenses: $25. | State law does not provide a penalty. | Ind. Code Ann. § 20-8.1-4-31. |
| IA | Simple misdemeanor. | $100 maximum. | 30 days maximum. | Iowa Code §§ 92.20, 903.1. |
| KS | Misdemeanor. | $25–$100. | 30–90 days. | Kan. Stat. Ann. § 38-612. |

(*Table continues.*)

# Table 3.8-2 *(cont'd)*
## PENALTIES FOR VIOLATING RECORDKEEPING REQUIREMENTS FOR MINORS

(See also text at § 3.8.)

**KEY:** **Status of Offense.** The status of the offense is listed only if state labor statutes expressly define the nature of the offense.

| | *Status of Offense* | *Fines* | *Imprisonment* | *Citations to Authority* |
|---|---|---|---|---|
| KY | Civil penalty. | $100–$1,000. | State law does not provide a penalty. | Ky. Rev. Stat. Ann. § 339.990. |
| LA | —<br>Civil penalty (violating posting requirements). | $100–$500.<br>$500 maximum. | 30 days–6 months.<br>State law does not provide a penalty. | La. Rev. Stat. Ann. §§ 23:16, 23:231. |
| ME | Civil penalty. | 1st offense: $50–$250; 2nd offense within 3 years: $100–$1,000; subsequent offense within 3 years: $250–$2,500. | State law does not provide a penalty. | Me. Rev. Stat. Ann. tit. 26, § 704. |
| MD | Misdemeanor. | $10,000 maximum. | 1 year maximum. | Md. Code Ann. [Lab. & Empl.] § 3-216. |
| MA | (Penalties provided for in various provisions. Some are fines only, others allow for fines and imprisonment.) | — | — | Mass. Gen. Laws Ann. ch. 149, §§ 78, 79, 86, 97, 98. |
| MI | Misdemeanor. | $500 maximum. | 1 year maximum. | Mich. Stat. Ann. § 17.731, 22. |
| MN | Misdemeanor (employment of minor without proof of age).<br>Gross misdemeanor (repeated violations). | $25.<br>$3,000 maximum. | State law does not provide a penalty.<br>1 year maximum. | Minn. Stat. Ann. §§ 181A.12, 609.03. |
| MS | Misdemeanor. | $50–$100, plus state assessment of $48.50. | 10–60 days. | Miss. Code Ann. §§ 71-1-29, 99-19-73. |
| MO | Class C misdemeanor. | $300 maximum (individual); $1,000 maximum (corporation). | 15 days maximum. | Mo. Rev. Stat. Ann. §§ 294.110, 560.016, 560.021. |
| MT | — | — | — | No state statutory requirements. |
| NE | Class V misdemeanor. | $100 maximum. | State law does not provide a penalty. | Neb. Rev. Stat. §§ 28-106, 48-311. |
| NV | Misdemeanor. | $1,000 maximum. | 6 months maximum. | Nev. Rev. Stat. §§ 193.150, 609.270. |
| NH | Civil penalty (violating certificate requirements).<br>Civil penalty (additional administrative fine).<br>Misdemeanor. | $100 minimum.<br>$1,000 maximum.<br>$2,000 (individual); $20,000 (corporation). | State law does not provide a penalty.<br>State law does not provide a penalty.<br>State law does not provide a penalty. | N.H. Rev. Stat. Ann. §§ 276-A:5, 276-A:7, 276-A:7a, 651:2. |

| | | | | |
|---|---|---|---|---|
| NJ | Knowing: 4th degree offense<br>Unknowing: disorderly persons offense. | $10,000 maximum.<br>$100–$1,000. | 8 months maximum.<br>State law does not provide a penalty. | N.J. Stat. Ann. §§ 2C:43-1, 2C:43-3, 34:2-21.19. |
| NM | Misdemeanor. | $25–$300. | On default of fine payment: 5–15 days; 2nd offense: 30 days minimum; 3rd and subsequent offenses: 1–2 years. | N.M. Stat. Ann. § 50-6-12. |
| NY | Civil penalty. | 1st offense: $1,000 maximum;<br>2nd offense: $2,000 maximum;<br>3rd offense: $3,000 maximum. | State law does not provide a penalty. | N.Y. Lab. Law § 141. |
| NC | Civil penalty. | $250 maximum. | State law does not provide a penalty. | N.C. Gen. Stat. § 95-25.23. |
| ND | Infraction (but if 2nd offense within 1 year period, *may* treat as Class B misdemeanor). | $500 maximum. | 30 days maximum (for Class B misdemeanor). | N.D. Cent. Code §§ 12.1-32-01, 34-07-21. |
| OH | 3rd degree misdemeanor. | $500 maximum. | 60 days maximum. | Ohio Rev. Code Ann. §§ 2929.21, 4109.99. |
| OK | — | $500 maximum. | 10–30 days. | Okla. Stat. tit. 40, § 88. |
| OR | Civil penalty. | $1,000 maximum. | State law does not provide a penalty. | Or. Rev. Stat. § 653.370. |
| PA | —<br>— | 1st offense: $100–$300;<br>subsequent offense: $250–$1,000. | State law does not provide a penalty.<br>Subsequent offense: 10 days maximum. | Pa. Stat. Ann. tit. 43, § 65. |
| RI | Misdemeanor. | $5 maximum. | State law does not provide a penalty. | R.I. Gen. Laws § 28-3-6. |
| SC | — | — | — | No state statutory provisions. (The Commissioner of Labor may pass regulations to prohibit oppressive child labor practices.) |
| SD | Class 2 misdemeanor. | $200 per offense. | 30 days maximum. | S.D. Codified Laws §§ 60-12-6, 22-6-2. |
| TN | Class A misdemeanor.<br>Civil penalty (alternative to misdemeanor; Labor Commissioner cannot proceed both civilly and criminally). | $2,500 maximum.<br>$150–$1,000. | 11 months, 29 days maximum.<br>State law does not provide a penalty. | Tenn. Code Ann. §§ 40-35-111, 50-5-112. |
| TX | — | — | — | No state statutory requirements. |
| UT | — | — | — | No state statutory requirements. |
| VT | — | $5–$200. | Subsequent offense: 6 months maximum. | Vt. Stat. Ann. tit. 21, § 449. |
| VA | Civil penalty. | $1,000 maximum. | State law does not provide a penalty. | Va. Code Ann. § 40.1-113. (False statements in records required to be filed under the Labor title carry penalties of $10,000 maximum or maximum of 6 months' imprisonment, or both. Va. Code Ann. 40.1-51.4:2.) |
| WA | Misdemeanor. | $25–$1,000. | State law does not provide a penalty. | Wash. Rev. Code Ann. § 49.12.170. |

*(Table continues.)*

## **Table 3.8-2** *(cont'd)*
## PENALTIES FOR VIOLATING RECORDKEEPING REQUIREMENTS FOR MINORS

(See also text at § 3.8.)

**KEY: Status of Offense.** The status of the offense is listed only if state labor statutes expressly define the nature of the offense.

| | *Status of Offense* | *Fines* | *Imprisonment* | *Citations to Authority* |
|---|---|---|---|---|
| WV | Misdemeanor. | 1st offense: $20–$50;<br>2nd offense: $250–$5,000. | State law does not provide a penalty.<br>2nd offense: 30 days maximum. | W. Va. Code § 21-6-10. |
| WI | — | $25–$1,000; subsequent offense within 5 years: $250–$5,000. | Subsequent offense within 5 years: 30 days maximum. | Wis. Stat. Ann. § 103.82. |
| WY | Misdemeanor. | $750. | 100 days maximum. | Wyo. Stat. § 27-6-113. |

# § 3.9 Penalties for Violating Child Labor Laws

Table 3.9-1 describes the various statutory penalties for employers violating child labor laws. The "status" of the offense is also listed, but only if the state statute explicitly defines the nature of the offense. In cases in which a penalty is listed but the status of the offense is not defined, state court decisions interpreting these statutes must be reviewed to determine whether the penalty is criminal or civil.

# Table 3.9-1
## PENALTIES FOR VIOLATING CHILD LABOR LAWS

(See also text at § 3.9.)

**KEY:** **Status of Offense.** The status of the offense is listed if state labor statutes expressly classify the nature of the offense.
**No.** State law does not provide a penalty for violation.

| | *Status of Offense* | *Fines* | *Imprisonment* | *Citations to Authority* |
|---|---|---|---|---|
| AL | First offense: Class C misdemeanor. | 1st offense: $100–$500. | No. | Ala. Code § 25-8-59. |
| | Subsequent offense: Class B misdemeanor. | Subsequent offenses: $500–$1,000. | | |
| AK | Misdemeanor. | $500 maximum. | 90 days maximum. | Alaska Stat. § 23.10.370. |
| AZ | Class 2 misdemeanor. | $750 maximum (individual); $10,000 maximum (corporation). | 4 months maximum. | Ariz. Rev. Stat. Ann. §§ 13-707, 13-802, 13-803, 13-3621, 23-236–23-239. (Injunctive relief may also be available.) |
| | Civil penalty (cease and desist order). | $1,000 maximum. | | |
| AR | Civil penalty. | $50–$1,000. | No. | Ark. Code Ann. § 11-6-103. |
| CA | Misdemeanor. | $1,000–$5,000; $10,000 maximum if willful. | 6 months maximum. | Cal. Lab. Code §§ 1288, 1308, 1309, 1391. |
| | Civil penalty. | Class A: $5,000–$10,000; Class B: $500–$1,000. | | |
| CO | Misdemeanor. | 1st offense: $20–$100. | No. | Colo. Rev. Stat. § 8-12-116. |
| | | Subsequent offenses: $100–$500. | Subsequent offenses: 90 days maximum. | |
| CT | — | $100 maximum. | No. | Conn. Gen. Stat. Ann. §§ 10-194, 31-23, 31-24. |
| DE | Misdemeanor. | $10,000 maximum. | No. | Del. Code Ann. tit. 19, § 509. |
| | Civil penalty. | $10,000 maximum. | | |
| DC | — | 1st offense: $1,000–$3,000. | 1st offense: 10–30 days. | D.C. Code § 36-513. |
| | | 2nd or subsequent offense: $3,000–$5,000. | 2nd or subsequent offense: 30–90 days. | |
| FL | 2nd degree misdemeanor. | $2,500 maximum (in addition to imprisonment). | 60 days maximum. | Fla. Stat. Ann. §§ 450.141, 775.082, 775.083. |
| GA | Misdemeanor. | $1,000 maximum. | 12 months maximum. | Ga. Code Ann. §§ 17-10-3, 39-2-20, 39-2-21. (Injunctive relief may also be available.) |
| HI | — | $1,000 maximum for willful violation. | 1 year maximum for willful violation. | Haw. Rev. Stat. § 390-7. |

| | | | | |
|---|---|---|---|---|
| ID | — | $50 maximum; subsequent offenses: $5–$20 each day. | No. | Idaho Code §§ 44-1305–44-1307. |
| | Misdemeanor (employment of minors in dangerous or exhibition/theatrical occupations). | $50–$250. | 6 months maximum. | |
| | — | $50 minimum for employment in immoral surroundings. | 2 months minimum. | |
| IL | Civil penalty.<br>Class A misdemeanor (willful violation). | $5,000 maximum.<br>$5,000 maximum. | No.<br>Less than 1 year. | 730 Ill. Comp. Stat. Ann. §§ 5/5-5-1–5/5-5-14; 820 Ill. Comp. Stat. Ann. §§ 205/17.3, 205/19. |
| IN | Civil penalty. | 1st offense: warning letter.<br>Subsequent offense: $25–$100. | No. | Ind. Code Ann. § 20-8.1-4-31. |
| IA | Simple misdemeanor. | $100 maximum. | 30 days maximum. | Iowa Code §§ 92.20, 903.1. |
| KS | Misdemeanor. | $25–$100. | 30–90 days. | Kan. Stat. Ann. § 38-612. |
| KY | Civil penalty. | $100–$1,000; after notice, $100 per day. | No. | Ky. Rev. Stat. Ann. § 339.990. |
| LA | Civil penalty. | $100–$500. | 30 days–6 months. | La. Rev. Stat. Ann. §§ 23-231, 23-251. |
| | Contributing to the delinquency of minors (violating prohibition against employment of minors in exhibitions or endangering minor's health or morals). | $1,000 maximum, plus liability for civil penalty of $500 maximum. | 2 years maximum. | |
| ME | Forfeiture or civil penalty. | Strict liability:<br>1st offense: $250–$5,000.<br>2nd offense in 3 years: $500–$5,000.<br>3rd offense in 3 years: $2,000–$10,000.<br>Knowing violation:<br>1st offense: $500 minimum.<br>2nd within 3 years: $5,000–$20,000.<br>3rd within 3 years: $10,000–$50,000.<br>Recordkeeping violation:<br>1st offense: $50–$250.<br>2nd offense in 3 years: $100–$1,000.<br>3rd offense in 3 years: $250–$2,500. | No. | Me. Rev. Stat. Ann. tit. 26, §§ 704, 781. |
| MD | Misdemeanor. | $10,000 maximum. | 1 year maximum. | Md. Code Ann. [Lab. & Empl.] § 3-216. |
| MA | (Penalties provided for in various provisions. Some are fines only, others allow for both fine and imprisonment.) | — | — | Mass. Gen. Laws Ann. ch. 149, §§ 57, 78–83, 97–100, 104. |
| MI | Misdemeanor (generally under the statute). | $500 maximum. | 1 year maximum. | Mich. Stat. Ann. § 17.731(22).<br>(Note: Under § 17.731(12a), an employer may not employ an individual who is under 18 years of age in a job involving cash transactions in a fixed location after 8 P.M., unless supervised by someone older than 18. Under § 17.731(14a), a child may not perform in or be the subject of child abusive commercial activity.) |
| | 1st offense: misdemeanor. | $2,000 maximum. | 1 year maximum. | |
| | 2nd offense: misdemeanor. | $5,000 maximum. | 2 years maximum. | |
| | 3rd offense: felony. | $10,000 maximum. | 10 years maximum. | |
| | Felony (employment of a minor in child abusive commercial activity). | $20,000 maximum. | 20 years maximum. | |

*(Table continues.)*

# Table 3.9-1 *(cont'd)*
## PENALTIES FOR VIOLATING CHILD LABOR LAWS

(See also text at § 3.9.)

**KEY:** **Status of Offense.** The status of the offense is listed if state labor statutes expressly classify the nature of the offense.
**No.** State law does not provide a penalty for violation.

| | *Status of Offense* | *Fines* | *Imprisonment* | *Citations to Authority* |
|---|---|---|---|---|
| MN | Misdemeanor: any others violating or assisting in violation of provisions. | $500 maximum. | 90 days maximum. | Minn. Stat. Ann. §§ 181A.12, 609.03. |
| | Gross misdemeanor: repeated violations or if violation results in death or substantial bodily harm. | $3,000. | 1 year maximum. | |
| MS | Misdemeanor. | $50–$100, plus state assessment of $48.50. | 10–60 days. | Miss. Code Ann. §§ 71-1-29, 99-19-73. Note: Under § 71-3-107, compensation and death benefits shall be double the amount otherwise payable if the injured employee was under 18 at the time of the injury and his or her employment was in violation of Mississippi's labor laws. |
| MO | Class C misdemeanor. | $300 maximum (individual);<br>$1,000 maximum (corporation). | 15 days maximum. | Mo. Ann. Stat. §§ 294.110, 558.011, 560.016, 560.021. |
| MT | Misdemeanor. | $500 maximum. | 6 months maximum. | Mont. Code Ann. § 41-2-118, 46-18-212. |
| NE | Class V misdemeanor. | $100 maximum. | No. | Neb. Rev. Stat. §§ 28-106, 48-311. |
| NV | Misdemeanor. | $1,000 maximum. | 6 months maximum. | Nev. Rev. Stat. §§ 193.150, 609.270. |
| NH | Individual: misdemeanor. | $2,000 maximum. | 1 year maximum. | N.H. Rev. Stat. Ann. §§ 276-A:7, 276-A:7-a, 651:2. |
| | Corporation: felony. | $100,000 maximum. | | |
| | Civil penalty. | $1,000 maximum. | | |
| NJ | Knowing: 4th degree offense.<br>Unknowing: disorderly persons offense. | $10,000.<br>$1,000 maximum. | 18 months maximum.<br>No. | N.J. Stat. Ann. §§ 2C:43-3, 2C:43-6, 34:2-21.19. |
| | Administrative penalty (as alternative or in addition to other penalties). | 1st offense: $250 maximum; subsequent offense: $500 maximum. | No. | |
| NM | Misdemeanor. | $25–$300. | On default of fine payment: 5–15 days.<br>2nd offense: 30 days minimum.<br>3rd offense: 1–2 years. | N.M. Stat. Ann. § 50-6-12. |

| | | | | |
|---|---|---|---|---|
| NY | Civil penalty. | 1st offense: $1,000. | No. | N.Y. Lab. Law § 141. |
| | | 2nd offense: $2,000. | No. | |
| | | Subsequent offense: $3,000. (If violation results in serious injury or death, penalty is tripled.) | No. | |
| NC | Civil penalty. | $250 maximum. | No. | N.C. Gen. Stat. § 95-25.23. |
| ND | Infraction (but if 2nd offense within 1-year period, *may* treat as Class B misdemeanor). | $500 maximum, $10,000 maximum for Class B misdemeanor. | 30 days maximum (for Class B misdemeanor). | N.D. Cent. Code §§ 12.1-32-01, 34-07-21. |
| OH | Minor misdemeanor (1st offense). | $100 maximum. | No. | Ohio Rev. Code Ann. §§ 2929.21, 4109.99. |
| | 3rd degree misdemeanor (for subsequent offense). | $500 maximum. | 60 days maximum. | |
| OK | Misdemeanor. | $500 maximum. | 10–30 days. | Okla. Stat. tit. 40, § 88. |
| OR | Civil penalty. | $1,000 maximum per offense (per child employed). | No. | Or. Rev. Stat. § 653.370. |
| PA | — | 1st offense: $100–$300. | No. | Pa. Stat. Ann. tit. 43, § 65. |
| | — | Subsequent offense: $250–$1,000. | Subsequent offense: 10 days maximum. | |
| RI | Violation of overtime provisions: civil penalty. | $20 maximum. | No. | R.I. Gen. Laws §§ 28-3-15, 28-3-20. |
| | Violation of maximum continuous employment without meal time. | $50–$100. | No. | |
| | Other violations of hour provisions. | $20 maximum each offense. | No. | |
| | Other violations of child labor provisions: Misdemeanor. | $500 maximum. | No. | |
| | Violation where child is injured or killed in the course of such employment. | $5,000 maximum. | No. | |
| SC | — | 1st offense: written warning. | No. | S.C. Code Ann. § 41-13-25. |
| | — | 2nd and subsequent offenses: $10–$50. | No. | |
| SD | Class 2 misdemeanor. | $200 maximum per offense. | 30 days maximum. | S.D. Codified Laws §§ 22-6-2, 60-12-1–60-12-11. |
| TN | Class A misdemeanor. | $2,500 maximum. | 11 months, 29 days maximum. | Tenn. Code Ann. §§ 40-35-111, 50-5-112. |
| | Civil penalty (alternative to misdemeanor; Labor Commissioner cannot proceed both civilly and criminally). | $150–$1,000. | No. | |
| TX | Class B misdemeanor. | $10,000 maximum per violation (administrative).<br>$2,000 maximum per offense (criminal). | No. | Tex. Lab. Code Ann. §§ 51.011, 51.031; Tex. Penal Code Ann. § 12.23. |

*(Table continues.)*

## **Table 3.9-1** *(cont'd)*
## PENALTIES FOR VIOLATING CHILD LABOR LAWS

(See also text at § 3.9.)

**KEY:** **Status of Offense.** The status of the offense is listed if state labor statutes expressly classify the nature of the offense.
**No.** State law does not provide a penalty for violation.

| | *Status of Offense* | *Fines* | *Imprisonment* | *Citations to Authority* |
|---|---|---|---|---|
| UT | Administrative penalty. | $500 maximum. | No. | Utah Code Ann. §§ 34-23-401, 34-23-402, 76-3-204, 76-3-301, 76-3-302. |
| | Class B misdemeanor. | $1,000 maximum (individual); $5,000 maximum (corporation, association, partnership). | 6 months maximum. | |
| VT | — | $5–$200. | Subsequent offenses: 6 months maximum. | Vt. Stat. Ann. tit. 21, § 449. |
| VA | Civil penalty. | $1,000 maximum. | No. | Va. Code Ann. §§ 18.2-10, 40.1-103, 40.1-113. |
| | Class 6 felony (willful or negligent endangerment). | No. (At discretion of judge/jury, imprisonment not to exceed 12 months, or $2,500 maximum fine, or both.) | 1–5 years. (At discretion of judge/jury, imprisonment not to exceed 12 months, or $2,500 maximum fine, or both.) | |
| WA | Misdemeanor or gross misdemeanor. | Warning and then progressive fines up to $1,000 per day for continued violations. | Subsequent offenses: 1 year maximum; if death or permanent disability results: 10 years maximum. | Wash. Rev. Code §§ 49.12.170, 49.12.390, 49.12.410. |
| WV | Misdemeanor. | 1st offense: $20–$50. | No. | W. Va. Code § 21-6-10. |
| | | Subsequent offenses: $50–$200. | Subsequent offenses: 30 days maximum. | |
| WI | Civil forfeiture. | 1st offense: $25–$1,000. | | Wis. Stat. Ann. § 103.82. |
| | | Subsequent offense: $250–$5,000. | Subsequent offense: 30 days maximum. | |
| WY | Misdemeanor. | $750 maximum. | 100 days maximum. | Wyo. Stat. § 27-6-113. |

# § 3.10 State Holidays

Table 3.10-1 indicates designated holidays. These holidays are legal holidays. State government employees in a state recognizing a day as a legal holiday are generally entitled to that day off from work or other compensation or special arrangement. Private employers may elect to give their employees legal holidays off, but are not generally required by state law to do so, although many do so as a matter of local practice or custom. Those holidays listed in the "Other Days of Observance" column are days of observance other than legal holidays, and state government employees are not generally entitled to those days off from work.

# Table 3.10-1

## STATE HOLIDAYS

(January 1, Washington's Birthday (or 3rd Monday in February), Memorial Day (or last Monday in May), July 4, Labor Day (or 1st Monday in September), Veterans Day, and December 25 are state holidays in all 50 states and in the District of Columbia. See also text at § 3.10.)

| | *Martin Luther King, Jr.'s Birthday (or 3rd Monday in January)* | *Lincoln's Birthday* | *Columbus Day (or 2nd Monday in October)* | *Thanksgiving* | *Sunday* | *Other Days of Observance* | *Citations to Authority* |
|---|---|---|---|---|---|---|---|
| AL | A holiday under state law. | Not a holiday under state law. | A holiday under state law. | A holiday under state law. | A holiday under state law. | Robert E. Lee's birthday, 3rd Monday in January; Mardi Gras (in Mobile and Baldwin counties); Thomas Jefferson's birthday, 3rd Monday in February; Jefferson Davis's birthday, 1st Monday in June; Confederate Memorial Day, 4th Monday in April; personal leave day, state employees get one per year except in Baldwin and Mobile counties; days declared by governor to be state holidays in honor of a special event. If any holiday falls on Sunday, following Monday is holiday; if holiday falls on Saturday, preceding Friday is holiday. | Ala. Code § 1-3-8. |
| AK | A holiday under state law. | Not a holiday under state law. | Not a holiday under state law. | A holiday under state law. | A holiday under state law. | Ernest Greuning Day, February 6; Elizabeth Peratrovich Day, February 16; Seward's Day, last Monday in March; Bob Bartlett Day, April 20; Family Day, May 1; Alaska Day of Prayer, first Thursday in May; Dutch Harbor Remembrance Day, June 3; Alaska Flag Day, July 9; Wickersham Day, August 24; William A. Egan Day, October 8; Alaska Day, October 18; Anthony J. Dimond Day, November 30; Pearl Harbor Remembrance Day, December 7; any day appointed by governor or president. If holiday falls on Sunday, Sunday and Monday are both legal holidays; if holiday falls on Saturday, Saturday and preceding Friday are both legal holidays. | Alaska Stat. §§ 44.12.010–44.12.085. |
| AZ | A holiday under state law. | Not a holiday under state law. | A holiday under state law. | A holiday under state law. | A holiday under state law. | Prisoners of War Remembrance Day, April 9; Arbor Day, last Friday in April; Mother's Day, 2nd Sunday in May; Father's Day, 3rd Sunday in June; Korean War Veterans Day, July 27; American Family Day, 1st Sunday in August; Constitution Commemoration Day, September 17. If any holiday falls on Sunday, following Monday is holiday, except Mother's, Father's, Family, and Constitution Days and Sundays. If January 1, July 4, November 11, or December 25 falls on Saturday, | Ariz. Rev. Stat. Ann. §§ 1-301, 1-304, 1-306. |

| | | | | | | | |
|---|---|---|---|---|---|---|---|
| | | | | | | preceding Friday is holiday; if September 17 does not fall on Sunday, preceding Sunday is observed as Constitution Day. | |
| AR | A holiday under state law. | Not a legal holiday under state law (although recognized as a day of observance by state statute). | Not a legal holiday under state law (although recognized as a day of observance by state statute). | A holiday under state law. | Not a holiday under state law. | Robert E. Lee's birthday, 3rd Monday in January; General Douglas MacArthur Day, January 26; Arkansas Teacher's Day, first Tuesday in March; Arbor Day, 3rd Monday in March; Confederate Flag Day, Saturday preceding Easter Sunday; Prisoners of War Remembrance Day, April 9; Patriot's Day, April 19; Arkansas Bird Day, April 26; Good Friday, Friday before Easter; Jefferson Davis' birthday, June 3; White Cane Safety Day, October 15; Christmas Eve, December 24; employee's birthday; any holiday proclaimed by the governor. If any holiday falls on Sunday, following Monday is holiday; if holiday falls on Saturday, preceding Friday is holiday. | Ark. Code Ann. §§ 1-5-101, 1-5-103, 1-5-106, 1-5-107, 1-5-108, 1-5-109. |
| CA | A holiday under state law. | A holiday under state law. | A holiday under state law. | Not a holiday under state law. | A holiday under state law. | Japanese American Evacuation Day, February 19; Arbor Day, March 7; Cesar Chavez Day, March 31; Good Friday (noon to 3 P.M.); John Muir Day, April 21; Admission Day, September 9; California American Indian Day, 4th Friday in September; Cabrillo Day, September 28; Stepparent's Day, 1st Sunday in October; Pearl Harbor Day, December 7; Saturday (noon to midnight); any day appointed by governor or president for public fast, thanksgiving, or holiday. If January 1, February 12, July 4, September 9, November 11, or December 25 falls on Sunday, following Monday is holiday; if November 11 falls on Saturday, preceding Friday is holiday. | Cal. Gov't Code §§ 6700, 6701–6703, 6708–6717. |
| CO | A holiday under state law. | Not a holiday under state law. | A holiday under state law. | A holiday under state law. | Not a holiday under state law. | Susan B. Anthony Day, February 15; Arbor Day, 3rd Friday in April; Colorado Day, 1st Monday in August; Leif Erikson Day, October 9; any day appointed by governor or president as day of fasting, prayer, or thanksgiving. If any holiday falls on Sunday, following Monday is holiday. | Colo. Rev. Stat. §§ 24-11-101, 24-11-103–24-11-109, 24-11-111. |
| CT | A holiday under state law. | A holiday under state law. | A holiday under state law. | Not a holiday under state law. | Not a holiday under state law. | Greek-American Day, March 25; Austrian-American Day, May 14; Republic of China on Taiwan-American Day, October 10; Children's Day, 2nd Sunday in October; Hungarian Freedom Fighters' Day, October 23; Romanian-American Day, December 1; any day appointed or recommended by governor or president as day of fasting, thanksgiving, or religious observance. If any holiday falls on Sunday, following Monday is holiday; if holiday falls on Saturday, preceding Friday is holiday; if a December or January holiday falls on a school day, there will be no school that day. | Conn. Gen. Stat. Ann. §§ 1-4; 10-29a. |
| DE | A holiday under state law. | Not a holiday under state law. | A holiday under state law. | A holiday under state law. | Not a holiday under state law. | Saturday; Good Friday; Arbor Day, last Friday in April; General Election Day as it biennially occurs; in Sussex County, Return Day, 2nd day after general election (after 12 noon); Friday after Thanksgiving; Delaware Day, December 7. If any holiday falls on Sunday, following Monday is holiday; if holiday falls on Saturday, preceding Friday is holiday. | Del. Code Ann. tit. 1, §§ 501, 601, 602. |

(Table continues.)

## Table 3.10-1 *(cont'd)*

## STATE HOLIDAYS

(January 1, Washington's Birthday (or 3rd Monday in February), Memorial Day (or last Monday in May), July 4, Labor Day (or 1st Monday in September), Veterans Day, and December 25 are state holidays in all 50 states and in the District of Columbia. See also text at § 3.10.)

| | *Martin Luther King, Jr.'s Birthday (or 3rd Monday in January)* | *Lincoln's Birthday* | *Columbus Day (or 2nd Monday in October)* | *Thanksgiving* | *Sunday* | *Other Days of Observance* | *Citations to Authority* |
|---|---|---|---|---|---|---|---|
| DC | A holiday under state law. | Not a holiday under state law. | A holiday under state law. | A holiday under state law. | Not a holiday under state law. | Saturday afternoon; Presidential Inauguration Day; any public feast or thanksgiving day appointed by president. If any holiday falls on Sunday, following Monday is holiday; if holiday falls on Saturday, preceding Friday is holiday. | D.C. Code § 28-2701. |
| FL | A holiday under state law. | A holiday under state law. | A holiday under state law. | A holiday under state law. | A holiday under state law. | Robert E. Lee's birthday, January 19; Arbor Day, 3rd Friday in January; Susan B. Anthony's birthday, February 15; Save the Florida Panther Day, 3rd Saturday in March; Shrove Tuesday (Mardis Gras); Good Friday; Pascua Florida Day, April 2; Children's Day, 2nd Tuesday in April; Pan American Day, April 14; Patriot's Day, April 19; Confederate Memorial Day, April 26; Law Enforcement Memorial Day, May 15; Teacher's Day, 3rd Friday in May; Jefferson Davis's birthday, June 3; Flag Day, June 14; Juneteenth Day, June 19; Rosh Hashanah and Yom Kippur, designated as legal holidays by chief circuit judges; Grandmother's Day, 2nd Sunday in October; I Am an American Day, 3rd Sunday in October; General Election Day; Retired Teacher's Day, 3rd week in November. DeSoto Day (Manatee County), last day of DeSoto week; Parade Day and Gasparilla Day (Hillsborough County); If any holiday falls on Sunday, following Monday is holiday. | Fla. Stat. Ann. §§ 683.01–683.21. |
| GA | A holiday under state law. | Not a holiday under state law. | A holiday under state law. | A holiday under state law. | A holiday under state law. | Firefighter Appreciation Day, 1st Tuesday in February; Girls and Women in Sports Day, 1st Thursday in February; Law Enforcement Officer Appreciation Day, 2nd Monday in February; Former Prisoners of War Recognition Day, April 9; Peace Officer Memorial Day, May 15; Children's Day, 1st Sunday in October; Bird Day, 2nd Thursday in October; all days designated as of January 1, 1984, as public and legal holidays by the federal government; all other days designated by governor as public and legal holidays or as days of | Ga. Code Ann. §§ 1-4-1, 1-4-2, 1-4-5–1-4-10 (1990 revision). |

| | | | | | | | |
|---|---|---|---|---|---|---|---|
| | | | | | | fasting, prayer, or other religious observance. In such designation, governor will include as least 1 of the following: January 19, April 26, or June 3, or a suitable date in lieu thereof to commemorate the events observed by such dates. | |
| HI | A holiday under state law. | Not a holiday under state law. | Not a holiday under state law. | A holiday under state law. | Not a holiday under state law. | Baha'i New Year's Day, March 21; Prince Jonah Kuhio Kalanianaole Day, March 26; Good Friday; Buddha Day, April 8; Father Damien Deveuster Day, April 15; King Kamehameha I Day, June 11; Admission Day, 3rd Friday in August; Queen Lili'uokalani Day, September 2; Children's Day, 1st Sunday in October; Discoverers' Day, 2nd Monday in October; Respect for Our Elders Day, 3rd Sunday in October; Arbor Day, 1st Friday in November; Bodhi Day, December 8; all election days in the county where the election is held except primary and special election days; any holiday designated by the president or governor. If any holiday falls on Sunday, following Monday is holiday; if holiday falls on Saturday, preceding Friday is holiday. | Haw. Rev. Stat. §§ 8-1, 8-1.5, 8-2, 8-4, 8-4.5, 8-5.5, 8-7–8-11. |
| ID | A holiday under state law (celebrated as Martin Luther King, Jr.-Idaho Human Rights Day). | Not a holiday under state law. | A holiday under state law. | A holiday under state law. | A holiday under state law. | Decoration Day, last Monday in May. Any day appointed by president or governor. If any holiday falls on Sunday, following Monday is holiday; if holiday falls on Saturday, preceding Friday is holiday. | Idaho Code § 73-108. |
| IL | A holiday under state law. | A holiday under state law. | A holiday under state law. | A holiday under state law. | Not a holiday under state law. | Casimir Pulaski Holiday, 1st Monday in March; Vietnam War Veterans Day, March 29; Good Friday; Arbor and Bird Day, last Friday in April; Chaplain's Day, 1st Sunday in May; Mother's Day, 2nd Sunday in May; Citizenship Day, 3rd Sunday in May; Senior Citizens' Day, 3rd Sunday in May; Flag Day, June 14; Father's Day, 3rd Sunday in June; Gold Star Mother Day, 2nd Sunday in August; Grandmother's Day, 2nd Sunday in October; Coal Miner's Day, November 13; Pearl Harbor Remembrance Day, December 7; days on which general elections for members of the House of Representatives are held; days proclaimed by governor as legal holidays. | 5 Ill. Comp. Stat. Ann. §§ 490/10–490/95, 205 Ill. Comp. Stat. § 630/17. |
| IN | A holiday under state law. | A holiday under state law. | A holiday under state law. | A holiday under state law. | A holiday under state law. | George Rogers Clark Day, February 25; Casimir Pulaski Day, 1st Monday in March; Good Friday; Flag Day, June 14; Northwest Ordinance Day, July 13; Indiana Day, December 11; Election Day, the day of any general, municipal, or primary election. If holiday falls on Sunday, following Monday is holiday; if holiday falls on Saturday, preceding Friday is holiday. | Ind. Code Ann. §§ 1-1-9-1, 1-1-10-1, 1-1-11-1, 1-1-12.5-1–1-1-14-1. |

*(Table continues.)*

## Table 3.10-1 *(cont'd)*

## STATE HOLIDAYS

(January 1, Washington's Birthday (or 3rd Monday in February), Memorial Day (or last Monday in May), July 4, Labor Day (or 1st Monday in September), Veterans Day, and December 25 are state holidays in all 50 states and in the District of Columbia. See also text at § 3.10.)

| | *Martin Luther King, Jr.'s Birthday (or 3rd Monday in January)* | *Lincoln's Birthday* | *Columbus Day (or 2nd Monday in October)* | *Thanksgiving* | *Sunday* | *Other Days of Observance* | *Citations to Authority* |
|---|---|---|---|---|---|---|---|
| IA | A holiday under state law. | A holiday under state law. | Not a legal holiday under state law (celebrated as a day of observance). | A holiday under state law. | Not a holiday under state law. | Arbor Day, last Friday in April; Mother's Day, 2nd Sunday in May; Father's Day, 3rd Sunday in June; Independence Sunday, Sunday preceding July 4; Herbert Hoover Day, Sunday nearest August 10; Youth Honor Day, October 31; Friday after Thanksgiving is a paid holiday for state employees, but not a legal public holiday. If holiday listed above falls on Sunday, following Monday is holiday; if any holiday falls on Saturday, preceding Friday is holiday. | Iowa Code Ann. §§ 1C.1–1C.10. |
| KS | Not a holiday under state law, but has been designated a holiday by the governor. | A holiday under state law. | A holiday under state law. | A holiday under state law. | Not a holiday under state law. | Any day designated by the governor for observance of a holiday; Arbor Day, last Friday in March; Mothers' Day, 2nd Sunday in May; Flag Day, June 14; American Indian Day, 4th Saturday in September; General Pulaski's Memorial Day, October 11; Family Day, Sunday following Thanksgiving; Pearl Harbor Remembrance Day, December 7. | Kan. Stat. Ann. §§ 35-107, 35-201–35-206, 73-705; K.A.R. 1-9-2(b). |
| KY | A holiday under state law. | A holiday under state law. | A holiday under state law. | Not a holiday under state law. | Not a holiday under state law. | Robert E. Lee Day, January 19; Franklin D. Roosevelt Day, January 30; Barrier Awareness Day, May 7; Mother's Day, 2nd Sunday in May; Confederate Memorial Day and Jefferson Davis Day, June 3; Flag Day, June 14; Disability Day, August 2; General Pulaski's Day, October 11; Grandmother's Day, 2nd Sunday in October; Presidential Election Day, Tuesday after 1st Monday in November; days appointed by president or governor as days of thanksgiving. If holiday falls on Sunday, following Monday is holiday. | Ky. Rev. Stat. Ann. §§ 2.110, 2.120–2.140, 2.190. |
| LA | A holiday under state law. | Not a holiday under state law. | A holiday under state law. | A holiday under state law. | A holiday under state law. | Battle of New Orleans, January 8; Robert E. Lee Day, January 19; Arbor Day, 3rd Friday in January; Inauguration Day in the city of Baton Rouge; Doctors' Day, March 30; Good Friday; Confederate Memorial Day, June 3; Huey P. Long Day, August 30; All Saints Day, November 1; Acadian Day, Friday after Thanksgiving; My Nationality American Day, December 7; Christmas | La. Rev. Stat. Ann. §§ 1:55–1:58. |

| | | | | | | | |
|---|---|---|---|---|---|---|---|
| | | | | | | Eve, December 24; New Year's Eve, December 31. If January 1, July 4, or December 25 falls on Sunday, following Monday is holiday; if it falls on Saturday, preceding Friday is holiday. In the city courts of Hammond and Sulfur, Ward Four, Mardi Gras, and national observance of Martin Luther King Jr.'s birthday are legal holidays. Mardi Gras is a legal holiday for court clerks in the parishes of East and West Feliciana, East Baton Rouge, Iberville, Pointe Coupee, West Baton Rouge, St. John the Baptist, St. Charles, Lafourche, St. Mary, Assumption, Terrebonne, St. Martin, Ascension, St. James, St. Tammany, St. Bernard, Jefferson Davis, Livingston, Acadia, Vermillion, Calcasieu, Orleans, and Tangipativa. | |
| ME (Financial institutions:) | A holiday under state law. | Not a holiday under state law. | A holiday under state law. | Not a holiday under state law. | Not a holiday under state law. | Patriot's Day, 3rd Monday in April; any day proclaimed by governor or president. If January 1, July 4, November 11, or December 25 falls on Sunday, following Monday is holiday. | Me. Rev. Stat. Ann. tit. 9-B, § 141. |
| (Judiciary:) | A holiday under state law. | Not a holiday under state law. | A holiday under state law. | A holiday under state law. | A holiday under state law. | Patriot's Day, 3rd Monday in April. If any holiday listed in the statute falls on a Sunday, the following Monday shall be observed as a holiday. | Me. Rev. Stat. Ann. tit. 4, § 1051. |
| MD | A holiday under state law. | A holiday under state law. | A holiday under state law. | A holiday under state law. | Not a holiday under state law. | Maryland Day, March 25; Good Friday; Defenders' Day, September 12; each statewide general election day; any day appointed by governor or president. If holiday falls on Sunday, following Monday is holiday. | Md. Code of 1957, art. 1, § 27. |
| MA | A holiday under state law. | Not a legal holiday under state law (celebrated as a day of observance). | A holiday under state law. | A holiday under state law. | Not a holiday under state law. | 3rd Monday in April; March 17 and June 17, in Suffolk County only. If January 1, July 4, November 11, or December 25 falls on Sunday, following Monday is holiday. Note: approximately 90 days of observance enumerated by state statute are omitted from this list. | Mass. Gen. Laws Ann. ch. 4, § 7; ch. 6 §§ 12A-15RRR. |
| MI | A holiday under state law. | A holiday under state law. | A holiday under state law. | A holiday under state law. | Not a holiday under state law. | Grandparents' and Grandchildren Day, March 18; Arbor Day, March 26; John F. Kennedy Day, May 29; Log Cabin Day, last Sunday in June; American Family Day, 1st Sunday in August; Michigan Indian Day, 4th Friday in September; Casimir Pulaski Day, October 11; Saturday, noon to midnight. If January 1, February 12, July 4, November 11, or December 25 falls on Sunday, following Monday is holiday. | Mich. Stat. Ann. §§ 18.856, 18.861, 18.862, 18.881, 18.891. |
| MN | A holiday under state law. | Not a holiday under state law. | A holiday under state law. | A holiday under state law. | Not a holiday under state law. | Friday after Thanksgiving (executive branch only). If January 1, July 4, November 11, or December 25 falls on Sunday, following Monday is holiday; if it falls on Saturday, preceding Friday is holiday. | Minn. Stat. Ann. § 645.44. |
| MS | A holiday under state law. | Not a holiday under state law. | Not a holiday under state law. | A holiday under state law. | Not a holiday under state law. | Robert E. Lee's birthday, 3rd Monday in January; Confederate Memorial Day, last Monday in April; Hernando de Soto Day, May 8; Jefferson Davis's birthday; last Monday in May; Elvis Aron Presley Day, August 16. If any holiday falls on Sunday, following Monday is holiday. | Miss. Code Ann. § 3-3-7. |

*(Table continues.)*

# Table 3.10-1 *(cont'd)*

## STATE HOLIDAYS

(January 1, Washington's Birthday (or 3rd Monday in February), Memorial Day (or last Monday in May), July 4, Labor Day (or 1st Monday in September), Veterans Day, and December 25 are state holidays in all 50 states and in the District of Columbia. See also text at § 3.10.)

| | *Martin Luther King, Jr.'s Birthday (or 3rd Monday in January)* | *Lincoln's Birthday* | *Columbus Day (or 2nd Monday in October)* | *Thanksgiving* | *Sunday* | *Other Days of Observance* | *Citations to Authority* |
|---|---|---|---|---|---|---|---|
| MO | A holiday under state law. | A holiday under state law. | A holiday under state law. | A holiday under state law. | Not a holiday under state law. | Arbor Day, 1st Friday in April; Prisoners of War Remembrance Day, April 9; Jefferson Day, April 13; Law Day, May 1; Truman Day, May 8; Peace Officer's Memorial Day, May 15; Flag Day, June 14; Korean War Veterans' Day, July 27; Missouri Day, 3rd Wednesday in October; Pearl Harbor Remembrance Day, December 7; any general primary election day or general state election day. If holiday falls on Sunday, following Monday is holiday. | Mo. Rev. Stat. §§ 9.010–9.100. |
| MT | A holiday under state law. | Not a holiday under state law. | A holiday under state law. | A holiday under state law. | A holiday under state law. | Arbor Day, last Friday in April; state general election day. If any holiday (except Sunday) falls on Sunday, following Monday is holiday. | Mont. Code Ann. §§ 1-1-216, 1-1-225. |
| NE | A holiday under state law. | Not a holiday under state law. | A holiday under state law. | A holiday under state law. | Not a holiday under state law. | Arbor Day, last Friday in April; Friday after Thanksgiving. If holiday falls on Sunday, following Monday is holiday. If state holiday date differs from federal holiday schedule, federal schedule is observed, except for Veterans' Day. | Neb. Rev. Stat. § 62-301. |
| NV | A holiday under state law. | Not a legal holiday under state law (although recognized as a day of observance by state statute). | Not a holiday under state law (although recognized as a day of observance by state statute). | A holiday under state law. | Not a holiday under state law. | Arbor Day, last Friday in April; Law Day USA, May 1; Mother's Day, 2nd Sunday in May; Constitution Day, September 17; Nevada Indian Day, 4th Friday in September; Nevada Day, October 31; Family Day, Friday after 4th Thursday in November; Pearl Harbor Remembrance Day, December 7; days appointed by president. If January 1, July 4, October 31, November 11, or December 25 falls on Sunday, following Monday is holiday; if it falls on Saturday, preceding Friday is holiday. | Nev. Rev. Stat. §§ 236.015, 236.018–236.045. |
| NH | Not a holiday under state law (but Civil Rights Day is cele- | Not a holiday under state law. | A holiday under state law. | A holiday under state law. | Not a holiday under state law. | Fast Day, 4th Monday in April; day on which biennial election is held. If holiday falls on Sunday, following Monday is holiday. | N.H. Rev. Stat. Ann. §§ 288:1, 288:2. |

| | | | | | | | |
|---|---|---|---|---|---|---|---|
| | brated on third Monday in January). | | | | | | |
| NJ | A holiday under state law. | A holiday under state law. | A holiday under state law. | A holiday under state law. | Not a holiday under state law. | Volunteer Fireman's Day, 2nd Sunday in January; Volunteer First Aid and Rescue Squad Day, 3rd Sunday in January; Crispus Attucks Day, March 5; Good Friday; New Jersey Day, April 17; Take Our Daughters to Work Day, last Thursday in April; Law Day, May 1; Prayer Day, first Thursday in May; Vietnam Veterans' Remembrance Day, May 7; Mother's Day, 2nd Sunday in May; Senior Citizens' Day, May 15; Police, Fireman, and First Aid Recognition Day, 3rd Sunday in May; Grandparent's Day, last Sunday in May; New Jersey Shore Celebration Day, second Saturday preceding last Monday in May; Children's Memorial Day, May 25; Delaware Bay Day, 2nd Saturday in June; Lidice Memorial Day, June 10; Father's Day, 3rd Sunday in June; New Jersey POW/MIA Recognition Day, July 20; Korean War Veterans' Day, July 27; Native American Day, 4th Friday of September; New Jersey Retired Teachers' Day, 1st Sunday in November; Holocaust Remembrance Day, 27th day in month of Nissan in Hebrew calendar; Saturday; any day ordered or recommended by governor or president; any general election day in New Jersey. If holiday falls on Sunday, following Monday is holiday; if holiday falls on Saturday, preceding Friday is holiday for state employees. | N.J. Stat. Ann. §§ 36:1-1, 36:1-1.2, 36:1-8, 36:1-9, 36:2-3, 36:2-6, 36:2-7, 36:2-9, 36:2-10, 36:2-11, 36:2-16, 36:2-18–36:2-34, 36:2-37, 36:2-40, 36:2-42. |
| NM | A holiday under state law. | Not a holiday under state law. | A holiday under state law. | A holiday under state law. | Not a holiday under state law. | American Indian Day, 1st Tuesday in February; Guadalupe-Hildago Treaty Day, February 2; Arbor Day, 2nd Friday in March (holiday in all public schools); Bataan Day, April 9; Onate Day, day chosen in July; Ernie Pyle Day, August 3. If holiday falls on Sunday, following Monday is holiday. | N.M. Stat. Ann. §§ 12-5-1–12-5-5, 12-5-7, 12-5-9. |
| NY | A holiday under state law. | A holiday under state law. | A holiday under state law. | A holiday under state law. | Not a holiday under state law. | Haym Salomon Day, January 6; Lithuanian Independence Day, February 16; Pulaski Day, March 4; POW Recognition Day, April 9; Workers' Memorial Day, April 28; Women Veterans' Recognition Day, June 12; Flag Day, 2nd Sunday in June; Korean War Veterans' Day, June 25; John Barry Day & Uncle Sam Day in the State of New York, September 13; Friedrich Wilhelm von Steuben Memorial Day, September 17; New York State POW/MIA Recognition Day, 3rd Friday in September; Native-American Day, 4th Saturday in September; War of 1812 Day, last Saturday in September; General Election Day; Raoul Wallenberg Day, October 5; New Netherlands Day for the State of New York, October 11; Theodore Roosevelt Day, October 27; Pearl Harbor Day, December 7; half-holiday (Saturday, noon to midnight); days appointed by governor or president. If holiday falls on Sunday, following Monday is holiday (except Flag Day). | N.Y. Gen. Const. § 24. N.Y. Exec. § 168-a. |

(Table continues.)

# Table 3.10-1 *(cont'd)*

## STATE HOLIDAYS

(January 1, Washington's Birthday (or 3rd Monday in February), Memorial Day (or last Monday in May), July 4, Labor Day (or 1st Monday in September), Veterans Day, and December 25 are state holidays in all 50 states and in the District of Columbia. See also text at § 3.10.)

| | *Martin Luther King, Jr.'s Birthday (or 3rd Monday in January)* | *Lincoln's Birthday* | *Columbus Day (or 2nd Monday in October)* | *Thanksgiving* | *Sunday* | *Other Days of Observance* | *Citations to Authority* |
|---|---|---|---|---|---|---|---|
| NC | A holiday under state law. | Not a holiday under state law. | A holiday under state law. | A holiday under state law. | Not a holiday under state law. | Robert E. Lee's birthday, 3rd Monday of January; Greek Independence Day, March 25; Good Friday; Prisoner of War Recognition Day, April 9; Anniversary of Signing of Halifax Resolves, April 12; Confederate Memorial Day, May 10; Anniversary of Mecklenburg Declaration of Independence, May 20; American Family Day, 1st Sunday in August; Yom Kippur; general election days (1st Tuesday after 1st Monday in November); Pearl Harbor Remembrance Day, December 7. If holiday falls on Sunday, following Monday is holiday. | N.C. Gen. Stat. §§ 103-4, 103-7, 103-9, 103-10. |
| ND | A holiday under state law. | Not a holiday under state law. | Not a holiday under state law. | A holiday under state law. | A holiday under state law. | Good Friday; Bird Day, April 26; Worker's Memorial Day, April 28; Arbor Day, 1st Friday in May; Mother's Day, 2nd Sunday in May; Gold Star Mothers' Day, last Sunday in September; every day appointed by president or governor as public holiday. If January 1, July 4, November 11, or December 25 falls on Sunday, following Monday is holiday. If any holiday falls on Saturday, preceding Friday is holiday. | N.D. Cent. Code §§ 1-03-01–1-03-02.1, 1-03-06–1-03-09. |
| OH | A holiday under state law. | Not a holiday under state law. Celebrated as a holiday to be commemorated in schools. | A holiday under state law. | A holiday under state law. | Not a holiday under state law. | Ohio Statehood Day, March 1; World War I Day, April 6; Workers Memorial Day, April 28; Arbor Day, last Friday in April; Destroyer Escort Day, 3rd Saturday in June; Korean War Veterans' Day, July 27; Native American Indian Day, 4th Saturday in September; General Pulaski Memorial Day, October 11; Election Day from noon to 5:30 P.M. on 1st Tuesday after 1st Monday in November is a legal holiday; Saturday afternoon; any day appointed by president or governor as public holiday. If any holiday falls on Sunday, following Monday is holiday. | Ohio Rev. Code Ann. §§ 1.14, 5.20–5.30. |

| | | | | | | | |
|---|---|---|---|---|---|---|---|
| OK | A holiday under state law. | Not a holiday under state law. | Not a holiday under state law. | A holiday under state law. | A holiday under state law. | Youth Day, 3rd Sunday in March; Prisoners of War Remembrance Day, April 9; Jefferson Day, April 13; Oklahoma City Bombing Remembrance Day, April 19; Oklahoma Day, April 22; Bird Day, May 1; Mothers' Day, 2nd Sunday in May; Jim Thorpe Day, May 22; Shut-In Day, 1st Sunday in June; Senior Citizens' Day, Wednesday following 1st Sunday in May; Juneteenth National Freedom Day, 3rd Saturday in June; Indian Day, 1st Saturday after full moon in September; Cherokee Strip Day, September 16; Statehood Day, September 16; Oklahoma Historical Day, October 10; Will Rogers Day, November 4; State Election Days; Oklahoma Pearl Harbor Remembrance Day, December 7; Bill of Rights Day, December 15; Bill of Responsibilities Day, December 16; Saturdays; any day designated by president or governor. If any holiday (except Sunday) falls on Sunday, following Monday is holiday. | Okla. Stat. tit. 25, §§ 82.1, 82.2, 82.4, 84, 87, 90.3, 90.4, 90.5, 90.6, 90.8, 90.9, 9.10. |
| OR | A holiday under state law. | Not a holiday under state law. | Not a holiday under state law. | A holiday under state law. | A holiday under state law. | Every day appointed by governor; every day appointed by president as day of mourning, rejoicing, or other special observance, but only when governor also appoints that day as holiday. If any holiday (except Sunday) falls on Sunday, following Monday is holiday; if holiday falls on Saturday, preceding Friday is holiday. | Or. Rev. Stat. §§ 187.010–187.020. |
| PA | A holiday under state law. | Not a holiday under state law. | A holiday under state law. | A holiday under state law. | Not a holiday under state law. | Pennsylvanians with Disabilities Day, January 30; Lithuanian Independence Day, February 16; Charter Day, March 14; Bird Day, March 21; Good Friday; Local Government Day, April 15; Earth Day, April 22; Arbor Day, last Friday in April; American Loyalty Day, May 1; Commonwealth Day of Prayer and Celebration of Religious Freedom, 1st Thursday in May; Peace Officer's Memorial Day, May 15; Hubert H. Humphrey, Jr., Day, May 27; Rachel Carson Day, May 27; Flag Day, June 14; Pennsylvania German Day, June 28; Commodore John Barry Day, September 13; National Anthem Day, September 14; Pennsylvania POW/MIA Recognition Day, 3rd Friday in September; Birthday of William Penn, October 24; Shut-In Day, 3rd Sunday in October; Election Day, Tuesday after 1st Monday in November; half-holiday, Saturday, noon to midnight; any day appointed by governor or president. If January 1, February 12, June 14, July 4, November 11, or December 25 falls on Sunday, following Monday is holiday. | Pa. Stat. Ann. tit. 44, §§ 11, 16, 19.2, 22, 26–34, 36, 38, 40, 40.1, 40.2, 40.3, 40.4, 40.7, 40.8. |
| RI | A holiday under state law. | Not a holiday under state law. | A holiday under state law. | Not a holiday under state law but annually appointed and announced by the governor. | A holiday under state law. | Vietnam Veterans' Day, January 27; Founders' Day of Italian-American War Veterans, February 15; Lithuanian Independence Day, February 16; Retired Teachers' Day, 1st Wednesday in March; Peter Francisco Day, March 15; Social Workers' Day, 2nd Wednesday in March; Dauphine Day, April 21; Workers' Memorial Day, 4th Friday in April; Arbor Day, last Friday in April; Veterans of Foreign Wars Loyalty Day, May 1; Rhode Island Independence Day, May 4; Nurses' Day, 1st Monday in May; Friendship Day, 2nd Friday in May; National Police Memorial Day, May 15; *(cont'd)* | R.I. Gen. Laws §§ 25-1-2, 25-2-1, 25-2-4, 25-2-9–25-2-12, 25-2-14, 25-2-15, 25-2-17, 25-2-20, 25-2-24, 25-2-26–25-2-35, 25-2-37, 25-2-38. |

*(Table continues.)*

## Table 3.10-1 *(cont'd)*

### STATE HOLIDAYS

(January 1, Washington's Birthday (or 3rd Monday in February), Memorial Day (or last Monday in May), July 4, Labor Day (or 1st Monday in September), Veterans Day, and December 25 are state holidays in all 50 states and in the District of Columbia. See also text at § 3.10.)

| | *Martin Luther King, Jr.'s Birthday (or 3rd Monday in January)* | *Lincoln's Birthday* | *Columbus Day (or 2nd Monday in October)* | *Thanksgiving* | *Sunday* | *Other Days of Observance* | *Citations to Authority* |
|---|---|---|---|---|---|---|---|
| RI *(cont'd)* | | | | | | Itam-Vets Daisy Day, 1st Saturday in June; Gaspee Days, 2nd Saturday and the following Sunday in June; Destroyer Escort Day, 3rd Saturday in June; St. Jean-Baptiste Day, June 24; Disabled American Veterans' Day, July 31; Victory Day, 2nd Monday in August; Narragansett Indian Day, Saturday preceding 2nd Sunday in August; POW/MIAs Recognition Day, 3rd Friday in September; American Indian Heritage Day, September 24; General Casimir Pulaski Day, October 11; White Cane Safety Day, October 15; General Election Day, Tuesday after 1st Monday in November in election years; Disabled American Veteran's Day, December 7; other holidays appointed by governor, General Assembly, president, or Congress. If holiday falls on Sunday, following Monday is holiday. | |
| SC | A holiday under state law. | Not a holiday under state law. | Not a holiday under state law. | A holiday under state law. | Not a holiday under state law. | Robert E. Lee's birthday, January 19; South Carolina Day, March 18; Loyalty Day, May 1; Confederate Memorial Day, May 10; Mothers' Day, 2nd Sunday in May; Statehood Day, June 1; Jefferson Davis' birthday, June 3; Carolina Day, June 28; Family Day, last Sunday in August; General Pulaski Memorial Day, October 11; Grandmothers' Day, 2nd Sunday in October; Frances Willard Day, 4th Friday in October; Friday after Thanksgiving; Arbor Day, 1st Friday in December; December 26; general election days. If legal holiday falls on Sunday, following Monday is holiday; if holiday falls on Saturday, preceding Friday is holiday. | S.C. Code Ann. §§ 53-3-10–53-3-90, 53-3-140, 53-5-10–53-5-30. |

| | | | | | | | |
|---|---|---|---|---|---|---|---|
| SD | A holiday under state law. | Not a holiday under state law. | Not a holiday under state law (but 2nd Monday in October is celebrated as Native Americans' Day). | A holiday under state law. | A holiday under state law. | Arbor Day, last Friday in April; Little Big Horn Recognition Day, June 25; Bill of Rights Day, December 15; Wounded Knee Day, December 29. Every day appointed by president or governor for public fast, thanksgiving, or holiday. If January 1, July 4, November 11, or December 25 falls on Sunday, following Monday is holiday; if it falls on Saturday, preceding Friday is holiday. | S.D. Codified Laws §§ 1-5-1, 1-5-1.2, 1-5-8, 1-5-9. |
| TN | A holiday under state law. | Not a legal holiday under state law (although recognized as day of observance by state statute). | A holiday under state law. | A holiday under state law. | Not a holiday under state law. | Robert E. Lee Day, January 19; Franklin D. Roosevelt Day, January 30; Andrew Jackson Day, March 15; Good Friday; Mother's Day, 2nd Sunday in May; Statehood Day, June 1; Memorial or Confederate Decoration Day, June 3; Scottish, Scots-Irish Heritage Day, June 24; Nathan Bedford Forrest Day, July 13; Family Day, last Sunday in August; American Indian Day, 4th Monday in September; days of county, state, or national elections throughout the state; Saturday, noon to midnight; all days appointed by governor or president as fasting or thanksgiving. If any holiday falls on Sunday, following Monday is holiday; if holiday falls on Saturday, preceding Friday is holiday. | Tenn. Code Ann. §§ 15-1-101, 15-2-101–15-2-106, 15-2-108. |
| TX | A holiday under state law. | Not a legal holiday under state law. | Not a holiday under state law (although recognized as a day of observance by state statute). | A holiday under state law. | Not a holiday under state law. | Sam Rayburn Day, January 6; Confederate Heroes Day, January 19; Texas Independence Day, March 2; Former Prisoners of War Recognition Day, April 9; San Jacinto Day, April 21; Emancipation Day, June 19; Lyndon Baines Johnson Day, August 27; Father of Texas Day, November 3; election days throughout the state; Friday after Thanksgiving; Christmas Eve, December 24; December 26. State employees may take Rosh Hashanah, Yom Kippur, or Good Friday as a holiday in exchange for another state holiday (except for Friday after Thanksgiving and December 26). | Tex. Gov. Code Ann. §§ 662.003, 662.005, 662.006, 662.021, 662.041–662.045. |
| UT | A holiday under state law (also celebrated as Human Rights Day). | Not a holiday under state law. | A holiday under state law. | A holiday under state law. | A holiday under state law. | Pioneer Day, July 24; Personal Preference Day (selected by each employee); all days set apart by president or governor for fasting or thanksgiving. If any holiday falls on Sunday, following Monday is holiday; if holiday falls on Saturday, preceding Friday is holiday. | Utah Code Ann. § 63-13-2. |
| VT | A holiday under state law. | A holiday under state law. | A holiday under state law. | A holiday under state law. | Not a holiday under state law. | Town Meeting Day, 1st Tuesday in March; Arbor Day, 1st Friday in May; Bennington Battle Day, August 16. If any holiday falls on Sunday, following Monday is holiday; if holiday falls on Saturday, preceding Friday is holiday. | Vt. Stat. Ann. tit. 1, §§ 371, 372. |

*(Table continues.)*

# Table 3.10-1 *(cont'd)*

## STATE HOLIDAYS

(January 1, Washington's Birthday (or 3rd Monday in February), Memorial Day (or last Monday in May), July 4, Labor Day (or 1st Monday in September), Veterans Day, and December 25 are state holidays in all 50 states and in the District of Columbia. See also text at § 3.10.)

| | *Martin Luther King, Jr.'s Birthday (or 3rd Monday in January)* | *Lincoln's Birthday* | *Columbus Day (or 2nd Monday in October)* | *Thanksgiving* | *Sunday* | *Other Days of Observance* | *Citations to Authority* |
|---|---|---|---|---|---|---|---|
| VA | A holiday under state law (celebrated as Lee-Jackson-King Day). | Not a holiday under state law. | A holiday under state law. | A holiday under state law. | Not a holiday under state law. | Motherhood and Apple Pie Day, January 26; Day of Recognition for Bone Marrow Donor Programs, April 8; Arbor Day, 2nd Friday in April; Dogwood Day, 3rd Saturday in April; Commonwealth Day of Prayer, first Thursday in May; Mother's Day, 2nd Sunday in May; First Lady's Day in Virginia, June 2; Citizenship Day, September 17; Yorktown Day, October 19; Day of Recognition for Early Childhood and Day-care Providers and Professionals, October 22; Virginia Drug Free Day, last Saturday in October; Election Day; Veteran's Recognition Day, 2nd Saturday in November; Special Day of Appreciation for American Indians Residing in Virginia, Wednesday preceding Thanksgiving; Friday after Thanksgiving; Pearl Harbor Remembrance Day, December 7; any day appointed by governor or president. If any holiday falls on Sunday, following Monday is holiday; if holiday falls on Saturday, preceding Friday is holiday. | Va. Code Ann. §§ 2.1-21, 2.1-21.1, 2.1-21.2, 2.1-24, 2.1-24.1, 2.1-24.2, 2.1-25– 2.1-27, 2.1-27.2, 2.1-27.3, 2.1-27.6, 2.1-27.7, 2.1-27.8. |
| WA | A holiday under state law. | Not a legal holiday under state law (although recognized as a day of observance by state statute). | Not a holiday under state law (although recognized as a day of observance by legislative declaration). | A holiday under state law. | A holiday under state law. | Washington Army and Air National Guard Day, January 26; Former Prisoners of War Recognition Day, April 9; Purple Heart Recipient Recognition Day, August 7; Washington State Children's Day, 2nd Sunday in October; Friday after Thanksgiving. If any holiday (except Sunday) falls on Sunday, following Monday is holiday; if holiday falls on Saturday, preceding Friday is holiday. | Wash. Rev. Code § 1.16.050. |
| WV | A holiday under state law. | A holiday under state law. | A holiday under state law. | A holiday under state law. | Not a holiday under state law. | West Virginia Day, June 20; any national, state, or other election day throughout the district or municipality where the election is held; all days appointed or recommended by governor or president. If any holiday falls on Sunday, following Monday is holiday; if holiday falls on Saturday, preceding Friday is holiday. | W. Va. Code § 2-2-1. |

| | | | | | | | |
|---|---|---|---|---|---|---|---|
| WI | A holiday under state law. | Not a holiday under state law. | A holiday under state law. | A holiday under state law. | Not a holiday under state law. | Good Friday, 11 A.M. to 3 P.M.; Indian Rights Day, July 4; day of September primary elections; day of any municipal election in a first-class city; afternoons of primary elections are half holidays. If any holiday falls on Sunday, following Monday is holiday. | Wis. Stat. Ann. § 895.20. |
| WY | A holiday under state law (celebrated as Martin Luther King, Jr.-Wyoming Equality Day). | A holiday under state law. | Not a holiday under state law. | A holiday under state law. | Not a holiday under state law. | Arbor Day, last Monday in April; Native American Day, 3rd Friday in September; Nellie Tayloe Ross Day, November 29; Pearl Harbor Remembrance Day, December 7; Wyoming Day, December 10; upon declaration by governor, any day declared by president for national mourning, rejoicing, or emergency. If January 1, July 4, November 11, or December 25 falls on Sunday, following Monday is legal holiday. | Wyo. Stat. §§ 8-4-101–8-4-106. |

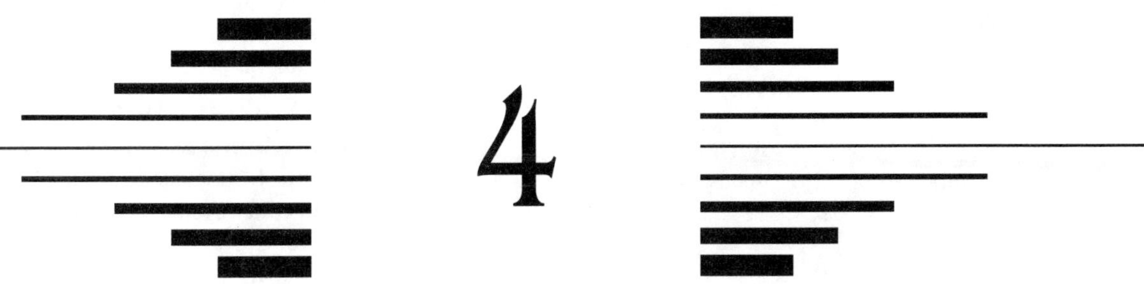

# Employment at Will

*Tables in Part 4 cover causes of action for wrongful discharge based on implied contracts, tort theories, and public policy violations; statutory restrictions on discharging employees; and remedies and defenses in wrongful discharge lawsuits.*

# § 4.1 Overview: Erosion of Traditional Employment-at-Will Doctrine

The traditional relationship between an employer and an employee hired for an indefinite term is called *employment at will.* In a pure at-will relationship, either party may terminate the relationship at any time, with or without cause or notice, absent a limiting statute or contractual agreement between the parties. As many as 75 million workers in this country are considered to be at-will employees, subject to discharge at any time and unprotected by specific laws or collective bargaining agreements; however, a dramatic change in the employer-employee relationship has occurred during the latter half of this century. More than two thirds of the states now recognize some exceptions to the employment-at-will rule, and the trend is clearly toward expanding employees' rights, through either legislation or court rulings.

## [a] Legislation Restricting At-Will Employment

The term *employment at will* is something of a misnomer. Few employers actually enjoy an unfettered right to terminate employees. Over half a century ago, both the federal and state governments began to enact laws limiting the employer's prerogative.

Following World War I, Congress enacted legislation designed to protect employees' rights to bargain collectively with employers through representatives of their own choosing, without fear of reprisal. The Railway Labor Act of 1926 secured collective bargaining rights for employees of the railroads—and later of the airlines—while the National Labor Relations Act of 1935 (NLRA) secured those rights for employees outside these two industries. Although the NLRA deals primarily with the rights of employees represented by labor unions, Section VII of the NLRA also deals with the rights of employees who are *not* represented by unions but who also engage in protected, concerted activities.

In addition to these labor laws, Congress has passed over a dozen laws restricting employers' at-will practices. (See Part 9, Summary of Federal Legislation, Guidelines, and Policies on Personnel Law.) Thus, although both the Federal Reserve Act and the Federal Home Loan Bank Act specifically allow covered banks to dismiss officers or employees "at pleasure," the trend since the 1960s has been to regulate employers' rights to discharge employees at will. A number of federal statutes also contain so-called whistle-blower provisions, which protect employees from retaliation for reporting employers for safety and environmental violations.

State legislatures have been no less prolific than Congress in restricting employers' rights to terminate employees at will. (See Part 2, Fair Employment Practices.) Almost every state has enacted fair employment practice (FEP) laws. A number of states, including California, Georgia, Louisiana, Montana, and South Dakota, have even codified the employment-at-will doctrine under common law.

## [b] Court Rulings on Wrongful Discharge

In areas where significant state or federal legislation is absent, the courts have recognized exceptions to the at-will rule based on these premises: implied contracts (including employer handbooks and manuals, oral representation, and promissory estoppel), covenants of good faith and fair dealing, and public policy. In addition to these new "causes of action," the courts sometimes refer to traditional tort theories to challenge the circumstances surrounding an employee's termination.

### [c] Remedies for Wrongful Discharge

Although the underlying principles in most unfair dismissal cases are usually the same, it is the *nature of the claim* that dictates the remedies available to a prevailing employee. For instance, if an employee bases a court claim on a *contractual* cause of action—that is, a cause of action based on a contract—the employee may be entitled to equitable relief, and, if appropriate, may recover back pay, front pay, and other compensatory damages. However, if an employee bases a court claim on a *tort* cause of action—a cause of action based on some wrong or injury—the employee may recover not only the damages available for contract claims but punitive damages for pain and suffering as well.

# § 4.2 Causes of Action for Wrongful Discharge Based on Implied Contracts

In deliberating discharge cases, some state courts have recognized implied-in-fact contracts and inferred from them a contractual obligation prohibiting employers from firing at-will employees. Implied contracts include the employer's written discharge procedures (in handbooks or manuals, for instance), oral representations of job security, the covenant of good faith and fair dealing, and promissory estoppel.

## [a] Employer Handbooks and Manuals

Some courts have taken the position that job security provisions in handbooks and manuals should be enforced as contracts. Those courts have held that an employer's written policies, communicated to employees in a handbook or manual, constitute a unilateral contract that is effective because each employee continues to perform job duties despite his or her freedom to quit. Using similar reasoning, other courts have ruled that handbooks create a bilateral contract. For information regarding how a disclaimer can be used to negate the creation of contractual rights, see Part 1 and Table 4.2-2.

## [b] Oral Representations

A number of courts have upheld discharged employees' claims that oral statements by an employer can create an enforceable contract, thereby restricting the employer's prerogative to fire employees at will. An example of an oral representation of job security might be a statement assuring that discharge will be "for good cause" only.

## [c] Covenant of Good Faith and Fair Dealing

Some courts maintain there is an implied covenant of good faith and fair dealing in employment that applies even to at-will employees. Essentially, this doctrine, which mixes public policy and contractual theories, states that a covenant, or contract, is implied in every employment relationship to prevent discharges made in bad faith. The trend, however, is toward rejecting an independent cause of action for breach of a covenant of good faith and fair dealing, absent an additional finding of an express or implied contract.

The remedies available to a prevailing plaintiff under this claim will depend on whether the court perceives the claim as a contractual cause of action or a tort cause of action. Punitive damages and damages for pain and suffering are available for tort claims, but not for contractual claims; compensatory damages, including back pay, front pay, and reinstatement, are available under both types of claims.

## [d] Promissory Estoppel

The doctrine of promissory estoppel, which has sometimes been applied to at-will employees, avoids injustice by permitting the enforcement of promises justifiably relied upon to a person's detriment. The classic example of promissory estoppel occurs when an individual quits a job in reliance on an offer of employment but is never given the opportunity to start work or is discharged shortly after beginning work.

States that recognize implied contracts are shown in Table 4.2-1. Table 4.2-1 shows which state courts have recognized that an at-will employment relationship can be modified by handbooks and manuals, oral representations of job security, or promissory estoppel. This table also shows which states recognize an implied covenant of good faith and fair dealing applicable to at-will employment.

Table 4.2-2 contains detailed information regarding state treatment of employee handbooks and manuals. For each state, the table covers the basic question of the circumstances under which provisions in a handbook or manual will be deemed to create a contract. The table also sets out the necessary requirements for an effective disclaimer that will operate to negate any contractual rights that might otherwise arise.

In some states, the employee must have been aware of the provisions in a manual at the time of the discharge to rely on those provisions in a later lawsuit. In addition, some courts have found that a handbook or manual may create not only a right not to be discharged except for cause, but it may also create a right to certain procedures that must be followed, even where an employee is discharged for cause. Finally, the employer's right to make changes to the handbook or manual is also covered in Table 4.2-2.

# Table 4.2-1
## CAUSES OF ACTION FOR WRONGFUL DISCHARGE BASED ON IMPLIED CONTRACTS

(See also text at § 4.2.)

**KEY:** **N/C.** No court case has been issued so far.
**N/R.** No ruling. The highest court of the state has not clearly expressed its position on this issue, and either the lower courts are divided or the federal courts, interpreting state law, are the only courts to have issued a decision.
**Promissory Estoppel.** Promise by employer that causes an employee or prospective employee to substantially alter his or her life circumstances.

| | *Handbooks and Manuals* | *Covenant of Good Faith and Fair Dealing* | *Oral Representations of Job Security* | *Promissory Estoppel* | *Citations to Authority* |
|---|---|---|---|---|---|
| AL | Yes. | Yes. | Yes. | Yes. | *Scott v. Lane,* 409 So. 2d 791 (Ala. 1982); *Chastain v. Kelly-Springfield Tire Co.,* 733 F.2d 1479 (11th Cir. 1984); *City of Huntsville v. Biles,* 489 So. 2d 509 (Ala. 1986); *Hoffman-LaRoche v. Campbell,* 512 So. 2d 725 (Ala. 1987); *Harrell v. Arrington,* 568 So. 2d 1356 (Ala. 1992); *Hanson v. New Technology, Inc.,* 594 So. 2d 96 (Ala. 1992); *Udcoff v. Freidman,* 614 So. 2d 436 (Ala. 1993); *Graham v. Community Action Agency of North Central Alabama, Inc.*, 702 So. 2d 1222 (Ala. 1997). |
| AK | Yes. | Yes. | Yes. | Yes. | *S.B. Mitford v. de Lasala,* 666 P.2d 1000 (Alaska 1983); *Eales v. Tanana Valley Medical-Surgical Group, Inc.,* 663 P.2d 958 (Alaska 1983); *Glover v. Sager,* 667 P.2d 1198 (Alaska 1983); *Jones v. Central Peninsula Gen. Hosp.,* 779 P.2d 783 (Alaska 1989); *French v. Jadon, Inc.,* 911 P.2d 20 (Alaska 1996); *Ramsey v. City of Sand Point,* 936 P.2d 126 (Alaska 1997); *Alaska Marine Pilots v. Hendsch,* 950 P.2d 98 (Alaska 1997). |
| AZ | Yes. | Yes. | Yes. | N/C. | *Wagenseller v. Scottsdale Memorial Hosp.,* 710 P.2d 1025 (Ariz. 1985); *Lindsey v. University of Arizona,* 754 P.2d 1152 (Ariz. Ct. App. 1987); *Gesina v. General Elec.,* 780 P.2d 1376 (Ariz. Ct. App. 1989); *Tingey v. Pixley-Richards West, Inc.,* 953 F.2d 1124 (9th Cir. 1992); *Huey v. Honeywell, Inc.,* 82 F.3d 327 (9th Cir. 1996). |
| AR | Yes. | Yes. | N/C. | Yes. | *Scholtes v. Signal Delivery Serv., Inc.,* 548 F. Supp. 487 (W.D. Ark. 1982); *Gladden v. Arkansas Children's Hosp.,* 728 S.W.2d 501 (Ark. 1987); *Smith v. American Greetings Corp.,* 804 S.W.2d 683 (Ark. 1991). |

*(Table continues.)*

# Table 4.2-1 *(cont'd)*

## CAUSES OF ACTION FOR WRONGFUL DISCHARGE BASED ON IMPLIED CONTRACTS

(See also text at § 4.2.)

**KEY:** **N/C.** No court case has been issued so far.
**N/R.** No ruling. The highest court of the state has not clearly expressed its position on this issue, and either the lower courts are divided or the federal courts, interpreting state law, are the only courts to have issued a decision.
**Promissory Estoppel.** Promise by employer that causes an employee or prospective employee to substantially alter his or her life circumstances.

| | *Handbooks and Manuals* | *Covenant of Good Faith and Fair Dealing* | *Oral Representations of Job Security* | *Promissory Estoppel* | *Citations to Authority* |
|---|---|---|---|---|---|
| CA | Yes. | Yes. | Yes. | Yes. | *Rabago-Alvarez v. Dart Indus.*, 127 Cal. Rptr. 222 (Cal. Ct. App. 1976); *Cleary v. American Airlines*, 168 Cal. Rptr. 722 (Cal. Ct. App. 1980); *Koehrer v. Superior Court*, 226 Cal. Rptr. 820 (Cal. Ct. App. 1986); *Foley v. Interactive Data Corp.*, 254 Cal. Rptr. 211 (1988); *Gantt v. Sentry Ins.*, 4 Cal. Rptr. 874 (Cal. 1992); *Walker v. Blue Cross of Cal.*, 6 Cal. Rptr. 2d 184 (Cal. Ct. App. 1992); *Milne Employees Assoc. v. Sun Carriers, Inc.*, 960 F.2d 1401 (9th Cir. 1992), *cert. denied*, 113 S.Ct. 292 (1993); *Rochlis v. Walt Disney Co.*, 23 Cal. Rptr. 2d 793 (Cal. Ct. App. 1993), *overruled*, 32 Cal. Rptr. 2d 230 (Cal. 1994); *Angell v. Peterson Tractor, Inc.*, 26 Cal. Rptr. 541 (Cal. Ct. App. 1994); *Haycock v. Hughes Aircraft Co.*, 28 Cal. Rptr. 2d 248 (Cal. Ct. App. 1994); *Kuhn v. Dept. of General Services*, 29 Cal. Rptr. 2d 191 (Cal. Ct. App. 1994); *Cooper v. Rykoff-Sexton, Inc.*, 29 Cal. Rptr. 2d 642 (Cal. Ct. App. 1994); *Davis v. Consolidated Freightways*, 34 Cal. Rptr. 2d 438 (Cal. Ct. App. 1994). |
| CO | Yes. | No. | N/R. | Yes. | *Rawson v. Sears, Roebuck & Co.*, 530 F. Supp. 776 (D. Colo. 1982); *Wing v. JMP Property Management Corp.*, 714 P.2d 916 (Colo. Ct. App. 1985); *Farmer v. Central Bancorporation*, 761 P.2d 220 (Colo. Ct. App. 1988); *Ferrera v. A.C. Nielsen*, 799 P.2d 458 (Colo. Ct. App. 1990); *Wilkerson v. Colorado*, 830 P.2d 1121 (Colo. Ct. App. 1992); *Decker v. Browning-Ferris Industries of Colorado, Inc.*, 931 P.2d 436 (Colo. 1997); *Soderlun v. Public Service Co. of Colorado*, 944 P.2d 616 (Colo. Ct. App. 1997); *George v. Ute Water Conservatory Dist.*, 950 P.2d 1195 (Colo. Ct. App. 1997). |
| CT | Yes. | Yes. | Yes. | Yes. | *Magnan v. Anaconda Indus., Inc.*, 479 A.2d 781 (Conn. 1984); *Cook v. Alexander & Alexander of Conn.*, 488 A.2d 1295 (Conn. Super. Ct. 1985); *Coelho v. Posi-Seal Int'l, Inc.*, 544 A.2d 170 (Conn. 1988); *Torosyan v. Bochringer Ingelheim Pharmaceuticals, Inc.*, 662 A.2d 89 (Conn. 1995); *Johnson v. Cheseborough-Pond's USA Co.*, 918 F. Supp. 543 (D. Conn. 1996). |
| DE | Yes. | Yes. | Yes. | N/C. | *Heideck v. Kent Gen. Hosp.*, 446 A.2d 1095 (Del. 1982); *Mann v. Cargill Poultry, Inc.*, (No. 88C-AU37) (WL 91102 1990 Del. Super. |

| | | | | | |
|---|---|---|---|---|---|
| | | | | | Ct. 1990); *Brandner v. Delaware State Hous. Auth.*, 605 A.2d 1 (Del. Ch. 1991); *Merrill v. Crothall-American, Inc.*, 606 A.2d 96 (Del. 1992); *Shearin v. E.F. Hutton Group, Inc.*, 652 A.2d 578 (Del. Ch. 1994); *Hitchens v. Yonker*, 943 F. Supp. 408 (D. Del. 1996). |
| DC | Yes. | N/R. | Yes. | N/R. | *Downey v. Firestone Tire & Rubber Co.*, 630 F. Supp. 676 (D.D.C. 1986); *Minihan v. American Pharmaceutical Ass'n*, 812 F.2d 726 (D.C. Cir. 1987); *Hodges v. Evans Fin. Corp.*, 823 F.2d 559 (D.C. Cir. 1987); *Nickeus v. Labor Agency of Metro Wash.*, 600 A.2d 813 (D.C. 1991); *Smith v. Union Labor Life Ins. Co.*, 620 A.2d 265 (D.C. 1993); *Simard v. Resolution Trust Corp.*, 639 A.2d 540 (D.C. 1994); *Perkins v. District Gov't Employees Fed. Credit Union*, 653 A.2d 842 (D.C. 1995); *Taylor v. Washington Metropolitan Area Trans. Auth.*, 922 F. Supp. 665 (D.D.C. 1996); *Willoughby v. Potomac Elec. Power Co.*, 100 F.3d 999 (D.C. Cir. 1996); *Sisco v. GSA Nat. Capital Federal Union*, 689 A.2d 52 (D.C. App. 1997). |
| FL | No. | N/C. | Yes. | Yes. | *Hope v. National Airlines, Inc.*, 99 So. 2d 244 (Fla. Dist. Ct. App. 1957); *Muller v. Stromberg Carlson Corp.*, 427 So. 2d 266 (Fla. Dist. Ct. App. 1983); *LaRocca v. Xerox Corp.*, 587 F. Supp. 1002 (S.D. Fla. 1984); *Kelly v. Gill*, 544 So. 2d 1162 (Fla. Dist. Ct. App. 1989). |
| GA | No. | No. | No. | No. | *Land v. Delta Air Lines*, 203 S.E.2d 316 (Ga. Ct. App. 1973); *Alterman Foods, Inc. v. Ingram*, 282 S.E.2d 186 (Ga. Ct. App. 1981); *Gunn v. Hawaiian Airlines, Inc.*, 291 S.E.2d 779 (Ga. Ct. App. 1982); *Alston v. Brown Transp. Corp.*, 356 S.E.2d 517 (Ga. Ct. App. 1987); *Lane v. K-Mart Corp.*, 378 S.E.2d 136 (Ga. Ct. App. 1989). |
| HI | Yes. | No. | Yes. | Yes. | *Parnar v. Americana Hotels, Inc.*, 652 P.2d 625 (Haw. 1982); *Ravelo v. County of Haw.*, 658 P.2d 883 (Haw. 1983); *Kinoshita v. Canadian Pac. Airlines*, 724 P.2d 110 (Haw. 1986); *Morishige v. Spencecliff Corp.*, 720 F. Supp. 829 (D. Haw. 1989); *Calleon v. Miyagi*, 876 P.2d 1278 (Haw. 1994). |
| ID | Yes. | Yes. | Yes. | Yes. | *C.K. Harkness v. City of Burley*, 715 P.2d 1283 (Idaho 1986); *Whitlock v. Haney Seed Co.*, 715 P.2d 1017 (Idaho Ct. App. 1986); *Metcalf v. Intermountain Gas Co.*, 778 P.2d 744 (Idaho 1989); *Sorensen v. Comm Tek, Inc.*, 799 P.2d 70 (Idaho 1990); *Ostrander v. Farm Bureau Mut. Ins. Co.*, 851 P.2d 946 (Idaho 1993); *Mitchell v. Zilog, Inc.*, 874 P.2d 520 (Idaho 1994); *Hummer v. Evans*, 923 P.2d 981 (Idaho 1996); *Jones v. Micron Technology, Inc.*, 923 P.2d 486 (Idaho App. 1996); *Hummer v. Evans*, 923 P.2d 981 (Idaho 1996). |
| IL | Yes. | Yes. | Yes. | Yes. | *Criscione v. Sears, Roebuck & Co.*, 384 N.E.2d 91 (Ill. App. Ct. 1978); *Scott v. Sears, Roebuck & Co.*, 798 F.2d 210 (7th Cir. 1986); *Duldulao v. St. Mary of Nazareth Hosp. Center*, 505 N.E.2d 314 (Ill. 1987); *Taylor v. Canteen Corp.*, 789 F. Supp. 279 (C.D. Ill. 1992); *Hicks v. Methodist Medical Center*, 593 N.E.2d 119 (Ill. 1992); *Johnson v. George J. Ball, Inc.*, 617 N.E.2d 1355 (Ill. App. Ct. 1993); *Vajda v. Arthur Andersen & Co.*, 624 N.E.2d 1343 (Ill. App. Ct. 1993); *Jacobs v. Mundelein College, Inc.*, 628 N.E.2d 201(Ill. App. Ct. 1993); *Frank v. South Suburban Hosp. Found.*, 628 N.E.2d 953 (Ill. App. Ct. 1993); *Kercher v. Forms Corp. of America, Inc.*, 630 N.E.2d 978 (Ill. App. Ct. 1994); *Corluka v. Bridgeford Foods of Illinois, Inc.*, 671 N.E. 2d 814 (Ill. App. 1996); *McInerney v. Charter Golf, Inc.*, 680 N.E.2d 1347 (Ill. 1997). |

*(Table continues.)*

## **Table 4.2-1** *(cont'd)*

## CAUSES OF ACTION FOR WRONGFUL DISCHARGE BASED ON IMPLIED CONTRACTS

(See also text at § 4.2.)

**KEY:** **N/C.** No court case has been issued so far.
**N/R.** No ruling. The highest court of the state has not clearly expressed its position on this issue, and either the lower courts are divided or the federal courts, interpreting state law, are the only courts to have issued a decision.
**Promissory Estoppel.** Promise by employer that causes an employee or prospective employee to substantially alter his or her life circumstances.

| | *Handbooks and Manuals* | *Covenant of Good Faith and Fair Dealing* | *Oral Representations of Job Security* | *Promissory Estoppel* | *Citations to Authority* |
|---|---|---|---|---|---|
| IN | Yes, but employee may have to provide additional independent consideration. | No. | Yes. | Yes. | *Hamblen v. Danners, Inc.*, 478 N.E.2d 926 (Ind. Ct. App. 1985); *Hostettler v. Pioneer Hi-Bred Int'l, Inc.*, 624 F. Supp. 169 (S.D. Ind. 1985); *Romack v. Public Serv. Co. of Ind.*, 511 N.E.2d 1024 (Ind. 1987); *Wior v. Anchor Industries, Inc.*, 669 N.E.2d 172 (Ind. 1996); *but see Weiser v. Godby Brothers, Inc.*, 659 N.E.2d 237 (Ind. Ct. App. 1996) (indicating circumstances in which there might exist a covenant of good faith and fair dealing); *Orr v. Westminister Village North, Inc.*, 689 N.E.2d 712 (Ind. 1997); *Dykes v. Depuy, Inc.*, 140 F.3d 31 (1st Cir. 1998). |
| IA | Yes. | No. | N/C. | Yes. | *High v. Sperry Corp.*, 581 F. Supp. 1246 (S.D. Iowa 1984); *McBride v. City of Sioux City*, 444 N.W.2d 85 (Iowa 1989); *Hunter v. Board of Trustees of Broadlawns Medical Ctr.*, 481 N.W.2d 510 (Iowa 1992); *French v. Foods, Inc.*, 495 N.W.2d 768 (Iowa 1993); *Borschel v. City of Perry*, 512 N.W.2d 565 (Iowa 1994); *Huegerich v. IBP, Inc.*, 547 N.W.2d 216 (Iowa 1996); *Butts v. University of Osteopathic Medicine & Health Services*, 561 N.W.2d 838 (Iowa App. 1997); *Jones v. Lake Park Care Center, Inc.*, 569 N.W.2d 369 (Iowa 1997). |
| KS | Yes. | No. | N/C. | Yes. | *Allegri v. Providence-St. Margaret Health Ctr.*, 684 P.2d 1031 (Kan. Ct. App. 1984); *Rouse v. Peoples Natural Gas Co.*, 605 F. Supp. 230 (D. Kan. 1985); *Greenlee v. Board of County Comm'r of Clay City*, 740 P.2d 606 (Kan. 1987); *Morris v. Coleman Co.*, 738 P.2d 841 (Kan. 1987); *Masterson v. Boliden-Allis, Inc.*, 865 P.2d 1031 (Kan. Ct. App. 1993); *Dickens v. Snodgrass, Dunlap, & Co.*, 872 P.2d 252 (Kan. 1994). |
| KY | Yes. | N/C. | Yes. | N/C. | *Shah v. American Synthetic Rubber Corp.*, 655 S.W.2d 489 (Ky. 983); *Nork v. Fetter Printing Co.*, 738 S.W.2d 824 (Ky. Ct. App. 1987). |
| LA | N/R. | N/R. | No. | N/R. | *Baynard v. Guardian Life Ins. Co.*, 399 So. 2d 1200 (La. Ct. App. 1981); *Frichter v. Nat'l Life & Accident Ins. Co.*, 620 F. Supp. 922 (E.D. La. 1985), *aff'd*, 790 F.2d 891 (5th Cir. 1986); *Gilbert v. Tulane Univ.*, 909 F.2d 124 (5th Cir. 1990); *Williams v. Touro Infirmary*, 578 So. 2d 1006 (La. Ct. App. 1991); *Finkle v. Majik Market*, 628 So. 2d 259 (La. Ct. App. 1993). |

| | | | | | |
|---|---|---|---|---|---|
| ME | Yes. | Yes | Yes. | Yes. | *Terrio v. Millenocket Community Hosp.*, 379 A.2d 135 (Me. 1977); *Larrabee v. Penobscott Frozen Foods, Inc.*, 486 A.2d 97 (Me. 1984); *Libby v. Calais Regional Hosp.*, 554 A.2d 1181 (Me. 1989); *Boivin v. Jones & Vining, Inc.*, 578 A.2d 187 (Me. 1990); *Stearns v. Emery-Waterhouse Co.*, 596 A.2d 72 (Me. 1991). |
| MD | Yes. | No. | Yes. | N/C. | *Paice v. Maryland Racing Comm'n*, 539 F. Supp. 458 (D. Md. 1982); *Page v. Carolina Coach Co.*, 667 F.2d 1156 (4th Cir. 1982); *Board of Trustees v. Fineran*, 541 A.2d 170 (Md. Ct. Spec. App. 1988); *Suburban Hosp. v. Dwiggins*, 596 A.2d 1069 (Md. 1991); *Haselrig v. Public Storage, Inc.*, 585 A.2d 294 (Md. Ct. Spec. App. 1991); *Yost v. Early*, 589 A.2d 1291 (Md. 1991). |
| MA | Yes. | Yes. | Yes. | No. | *Fortune v. National Cash Register Co.*, 364 N.E.2d 1251 (Mass. 1977); *Hobson v. McLean Hosp. Corp.*, 522 N.E.2d 975 (Mass. 1988); *Mullen v. Ludlow Hosp. Soc'y*, 592 N.E.2d 1342 (Mass. 1992); *Boothby v. Texon, Inc.*, 608 N.E.2d 1028 (Mass. 1993); *O'Brien v. Analog Devices, Inc.*, 606 N.E.2d 937 (Mass. App. Ct. 1993); *O'Brien v. New England Tel. & Tel. Co.*, 664 N.E.2d 843 (Mass. 1996); *Derrig v. Wal-Mart Stores, Inc.*, 942 F. Supp. 49 (D. Del. 1996). |
| MI | Yes. | N/R. | Yes. | Yes. | *Toussaint v. Blue Cross & Blue Shield*, 292 N.W.2d 880 (Mich. 1980); *Dzierwa v. Michigan Oil Co.*, 393 N.W.2d 610 (Mich. Ct. App. 1986); *Feaheny v. Caldwell*, 437 N.W.2d 358 (Mich. Ct. App. 1989), *leave appeal denied*, 434 Mich. 862 (1990); *Rowe v. Montgomery Ward & Co., Inc.*, 473 N.W.2d 268 (Mich. 1991); *Gonyea v. Motor Parts Fed. Credit Union*, 480 N.W.2d 297 (Mich. 1992); *Bradley v. Philip Morris, Inc.*, 501 N.W.2d 246 (Mich. Ct. App. 1993); *Rood v. General Dynamics Corp.*, 507 N.W.2d 591 (Mich. 1993); *Barber v. SMH, Inc.*, 509 N.W.2d 791 (Mich. Ct. App. 1993), *leave appeal denied*, 519 N.W.2d 891 (Mich. 1994); *Barnell v. Taubman Co.*, 512 N.W. 2d 13 (Mich. Ct. App. 1993); *Coleman-Nichols v. Tixon Corp.*, 513 N.W.2d 441 (Mich. Ct. App. 1994); *Rice v. ISI Mfg., Inc.*, 525 N.W.2d 533 (Mich. Ct. App. 1994); *Nieves v. Bell Indus., Inc.*, 517 N.W.2d 235 (Mich. Ct. App. 1994); *Lytle v. Malady*, 566 N.W.2d 582 (Mich. 1997); *Dolan v. Continental Airlines/Continental Exp.*, 563 N.W.2d 23 (Mich. 1997). |
| MN | Yes. | Yes. | Yes. | Yes. | *Pine River State Bank v. Hettille*, 333 N.W.2d 622 (Minn. 1983); *Eklund v. Vincent Brass & Aluminum Co.*, 351 N.W.2d 371 (Minn. Ct. App. 1984); *Dumas v. Kessler & Maguire Funeral Home, Inc.*, 380 N.W.2d 544 (Minn. Ct. App. 1986); *Knudsen v. Northwest Airlines*, 437 N.W.2d 733 (Minn. Ct. App. 1989), *rev'd*, 450 N.W.2d 131 (Minn. 1990); *Piekarski v. Home Owners Sav. Bank*, 956 F.2d 1484 (8th Cir. 1992), *cert. denied*, 113 S.Ct. 206 (1992); *Campbell v. Leaseway Customized Transp., Inc.*, 484 N.W.2d 41 (Minn. Ct. App. 1992); *Feges v. Perkins Restaurants, Inc.*, 483 N.W.2d 701 (Minn. 1992); *Spanier v. TCF Bank Sav.*, 495 N.W.2d 18 (Minn. Ct. App. 1993); *Larson v. Koch Ref. Co.*, 920 F. Supp. 1000 (D. Minn. 1996). |

*(Table continues.)*

# Table 4.2-1 *(cont'd)*

## CAUSES OF ACTION FOR WRONGFUL DISCHARGE BASED ON IMPLIED CONTRACTS

(See also text at § 4.2.)

**KEY:** **N/C.** No court case has been issued so far.
**N/R.** No ruling. The highest court of the state has not clearly expressed its position on this issue, and either the lower courts are divided or the federal courts, interpreting state law, are the only courts to have issued a decision.
**Promissory Estoppel.** Promise by employer that causes an employee or prospective employee to substantially alter his or her life circumstances.

| | *Handbooks and Manuals* | *Covenant of Good Faith and Fair Dealing* | *Oral Representations of Job Security* | *Promissory Estoppel* | *Citations to Authority* |
|---|---|---|---|---|---|
| MS | Yes. | No. | N/R. | N/R. | *Perry v. Sears, Roebuck & Co.*, 508 So. 2d 1086 (Miss. 1987); *Robinson v. Coastal Family Health Ctr., Inc.*, 756 F. Supp. 958 (S.D. Miss. 1990); *Empiregas, Inc. v. Bain*, 599 So. 2d 971 (Miss. 1992); *Bobbitt v. The Orchard, Ltd.*, 603 So. 2d 356, 361 (Miss. 1992); *Coleman v. Chevron Pascagoula Fed. Credit Union*, 616 So. 2d 310 (Miss. 1993); *Hartle v. Packard Elec.*, 626 So. 2d 106 (Miss. 1993); *Dandridge v. Chromcraft Corp.*, 914 F. Supp. 1396 (N.D. Miss. 1996); *Pegues v. Emerson Elec. Co.*, 913 F. Supp. 976 (N.D. Miss. 1996); *Cooper v. Drexel Chemical Co.*, 949 F. Supp. 1275 (N.D. Miss. 1996). |
| MO | Yes. | N/R. | No. | No. | *Neighbors v. Kirksville College of Osteopathic Medicine*, 694 S.W.2d 822 (Mo. Ct. App. 1985); *Johnson v. McDonnell Douglas Corp.*, 745 S.W.2d 661 (Mo. 1988); *Alfano v. AAIM Management Ass'n*, 770 S.W.2d 743 (Mo. Ct. App. 1989); *Remington v. Wal-Mart Stores, Inc.*, 817 S.W.2d 571 (Mo. Ct. App. 1991); *McCoy v. Spelman Memorial Hosp.*, 845 S.W.2d 727 (Mo. App. W.D. 1993); *Nichols v. American Nat. Ins. Co.*, 945 F. Supp. 1242 (E.D. Mo. 1996); *Patterson v. Tenet Healthcare, Inc.*, 113 F.3d 832 (8th Cir. 1997). |
| MT | In 1987 Montana passed a comprehensive law protecting at-will employees from discharge without cause; in retaliation for refusing to violate public policy or reporting public policy violations; and for a violation of handbook rules (for example, the employer did not follow a disciplinary procedure). The statute preempts all other causes of action arising from terminating at-will employees. | See "Handbooks and Manuals." | See "Handbooks and Manuals." | See "Handbooks and Manuals." | Mont. Code Ann. §§ 39-2-901 *et seq.*; *Gates v. Life of Mont. Ins. Co.*, 668 P.2d 213 (Mont. 1983); *Akhtar v. Van de Wetering*, 642 P.2d 149 (Mont. 1982); *Kittelson v. Archie Cochrane Motors, Inc.*, 813 P.2d 424 (Mont. 1991); *Buck v. Billings Montana Chevrolet, Inc.*, 811 P.2d 537 (Mont. 1991); *Mannix v. Butte Water Co.*, 854 P.2d 834 (Mont. 1993); *Beasley v. Semitool, Inc.*, 853 P.2d 84 (Mont. 1993); *Kearney v. KXLF Communications, Inc.*, 869 P.2d 772 (Mont. 1994). |

| | | | | | |
|---|---|---|---|---|---|
| NE | Yes. | N/C. | Yes. | Yes. | *Johnston v. Panhandle Coop. Ass'n,* 408 N.W.2d 261 (Neb. 1987); *Renner v. Wurdeman,* 434 N.W.2d 536 (Neb. 1989); *Blair v. Physicians Mut. Ins. Co.,* 496 N.W.2d 483 (Neb. 1993); *Overmier v. Parks,* 495 N.W.2d 620 (Neb. 1993); *Hillie v. Mutual of Omaha Ins. Co.,* 512 N.W.2d 358 (Neb. 1994); *Hamersky v. Nicholson Supply Co.,* 517 N.W.2d 382 (Neb. 1994); *Rains v. Becton, Dickinson and Co.,* 523 N.W.2d 506 (Neb. 1994). |
| NV | Yes. | Yes. | N/R. | N/C. | *Vancheri v. GNLV Corp.,* 777 P.2d 366 (Nev. 1989); *D'Angelo v. Gardner,* 819 P.2d 206 (Nev. 1991); *Brooks v. Hilton Casinos, Inc.,* 959 F.2d 757 (9th Cir. 1992), *cert. denied,* 113 S.Ct. 300 (1992); *Hirschhorn v. Sizzler Restaurants Int'l, Inc.,* 913 F. Supp. 1393 (D.Nev. 1995). |
| NH | Yes. | Yes. | Yes. | Yes. | *Panto v. Moore Business Forms, Inc.,* 574 A.2d 260 (N.H. 1988); *Butler v. Walker Power, Inc.,* 629 A.2d 91 (N.H. 1993); *Smith v. F.W. Morse & Co.,* 76 F.3d 413 (1st Cir. 1996). |
| NJ | Yes. | Yes. | Yes. | Yes. | *Shebar v. Sanyo Business Sys. Corp.,* 526 A.2d 1144 (N.J. 1987), *aff'd,* 544 A.2d 377 (N.J. 1988); *Linn v. Beneficial Commercial Corp.,* 543 A.2d 954 (N.J. 1988); *Preston v. Claridge Hotel & Casino, Ltd.,* 555 A.2d 12 (N.J. 1989); *Smith v. Squibb Corp.,* 603 A.2d 75 (N.J. Super. Ct. App. Div. 1992), *cert. denied,* 611 A.2d 649 (N.J. 1992); *Catalane v. Gilian Instrument Corp.,* 638 A.2d 1341 (N.J. Super. Ct. App. Div. 1994); *Witkowski v. Thomas J. Lipton, Inc.,* 643 A.2d 546 (N.J. 1994); *Lawrence v. National Westminister Bank New Jersey,* 98 F.3d 61 (3rd Cir. 1996); *Varello v. Hammond Inc.,* 94 F.3d 842 (3rd Cir. 1996); *McDermott v Chilton Co.,* 938 F. Supp. 240 (D.N.J. 1995); *Barone v. Gardner Asphalt Corp.,* 955 F. Supp. 337 (D. N.J. 1997); *Bonczek v. Carter Wallace, Inc.,* 701 A.2d 742 (N.J. Super. Ct. App. Div. 1997). |
| NM | Yes. | No. | Yes. | Yes. | *Kestenbaum v. Pennzoil Co.,* 766 P.2d 280 (N.M. 1988), *cert. denied,* 109 S.Ct. 3163 (1989); *Newberry v. Allied Stores, Inc.,* 773 P.2d 1231 (N.M. 1989); *Chavez v. Manville Prods. Corp.,* 777 P.2d 371 (N.M. 1989); *Paca v. K-Mart Corp.,* 775 P.2d 245 (N.M. 1989); *Bourgeous v. Horizon Healthcare Corp.,* 872 P.2d 852 (N.M. 1994); *Garcia v. Middle RioGrande Conservancy District,* 918 P.2d 7 (N.M. 1996); *Garrity v. Overland Sheepskin Co. of Taos,* 917 P.2d 1382 (N.M. 1996). |
| NY | Yes, if handbook or manual imposes an express limitation on employer's right to terminate. | No, except when the employee is a licensed attorney. | Yes. | N/R. | *Sabetay v. Sterling Drug, Inc.,* 514 N.Y.S.2d 209 (1987); *Dicocco v. Capital Area Community Health Plan, Inc.,* 525 N.Y.S.2d 417 (1988); *Lerman v. Medical Assocs. of Woodhull, P.C.,* 554 N.Y.S.2d 272 (1990); *Zolotar v. New York Life Ins. Co.,* 576 N.Y.S.2d 850 (1991); *Knudsen v. Quebecor Printing (U.S.A.), Inc.,* 792 F. Supp. 234 (S.D.N.Y. 1992); *Wieder v. Skala,* 593 N.Y.S.2d 752 (1992); *Brooks v. Key Pharmaceuticals, Inc.,* 583 N.Y.S.2d 673 (App. Div. 1992); *Nice v. Combustion Eng'g, Inc.,* 599 N.Y.S.2d 205 (App. Div. 1993); *Brooks v. Blue Cross,* 593 N.Y.S.2d 119 (App. Div. 1993); *Manning v. Norton Co.,* 592 N.Y.S.2d 154 (App. Div. 1993); *Stanton v. Highland Hosp. of Rochester,* 602 N.Y.S.2d 278 (App. Div. 1993); *O'Reilly v. Citibank,* 603 N.Y.S.2d 572 (App. Div. 1993); *Rich v. Coopervision, Inc.,* 604 N.Y.S.2d 429 (App. Div. 1993); *Doynow v. Nynex Pub. Co.,* 608 N.Y.S.2d 683 (App. Div. 1994); *Tramando v. Playboy* (*cont'd*) |

*(Table continues.)*

# Table 4.2-1 *(cont'd)*

## CAUSES OF ACTION FOR WRONGFUL DISCHARGE BASED ON IMPLIED CONTRACTS

(See also text at § 4.2.)

**KEY:** **N/C.** No court case has been issued so far.
**N/R.** No ruling. The highest court of the state has not clearly expressed its position on this issue, and either the lower courts are divided or the federal courts, interpreting state law, are the only courts to have issued a decision.
**Promissory Estoppel.** Promise by employer that causes an employee or prospective employee to substantially alter his or her life circumstances.

| | *Handbooks and Manuals* | *Covenant of Good Faith and Fair Dealing* | *Oral Representations of Job Security* | *Promissory Estoppel* | *Citations to Authority* |
|---|---|---|---|---|---|
| NY (*cont'd*) | | | | | *Enterprises, Inc.*, 609 N.Y.S.2d 124 (App. Div. 1994); *Mulder v. Donaldson, Lufkin & Jenrette*, 623 N.Y.S.2d 560 (App. Div. 1995); *Castro v. Local 1199*, 964 F. Supp. (S.D. N.Y. 1997); *Nunez v. A-T Financial Information Inc.*, 957 F. Supp. 438 (S.D. N.Y. 1997). |
| NC | No. | No. | No. | Yes. | *Salt v. Applied Analytical, Inc.*, 412 S.E.2d 97 (N.C. 1991); *Amos v. Oakdale Knitting Co.*, 416 S.E.2d 166 (N.C. 1992); *Boesche v. Raleigh-Durham Airport Auth.*, 432 S.E.2d 137 (N.C. Ct. App. 1993), *appeal dismissed*, 442 S.E.2d 320 (N.C. 1994), *but see Iturbe v. Wandel & Goltermann Technologies, Inc.*, 774 F. Supp. 959 (M.D.N.C. 1991), *aff'd* 23 F.3d 401 (4th Cir. 1994) (recognizing claim for bad faith discharge); *Lorbacher v. Housing Authority of City of Raleigh*, 493 S.E.2d 74 (N.C. Ct. App. 1997). |
| ND | Yes. | No. | N/C. | N/C. | *O'Connell v. Entertainment Enters., Inc.*, 317 N.W.2d 385 (N.D. 1982); *Bailey v. Perkins Restaurants, Inc.*, 398 N.W.2d 120 (N.D. 1986); *Hillesland v. Federal Land Bank Ass'n*, 407 N.W.2d 206 (N.D. 1987); *Rykowsky v. Dickinson Public School Dist. No. 1*, 508 N.W.2d 348 (N.D. 1993); *Aaland v. Lake Region Grain Co-op.*, 511 N.W.2d 244 (N.D. 1994); *Pratt v. Heartview Found.*, 512 N.W.2d 675 (N.D. 1994); *Osterman-Levitt v. MedQuest, Inc.*, 513 N.W.2d 70 (N.D. 1994). |
| OH | Yes. | No. | Yes. | Yes. | *Wallace v. Gray Drug, Inc.*, 1990 WL121500 (Ohio 1990); *Gargasz v. Nordson Corp.*, 587 N.E.2d 475 (Ohio 1991); *Sheppard v. Maumee Valley Girl Scout Council*, 1992 WL114607 (Ohio 1992); *Fodor v. First Nat'l Supermarkets, Inc.*, 589 N.E.2d 17 (Ohio 1992); *Allen v. Ethicon, Inc.*, 919 F. Supp. 1093 (S.D. Ohio 1996); *Weiper v. W.A. Hill & Assoc's*, 661 N.E.2d 796 (Ohio Ct. App. 1996); *Finsterwald-Maiden v. AAA S. Cent. Ohio*, 685 N.E.2d 786 (Ohio App. 1996). |
| OK | Yes. | No. | N/C. | N/C. | *Burk v. K-Mart Corp.*, 770 P.2d 24 (Okla. 1989); *Sargent v. Central Nat'l Bank & Trust Co.*, 809 P.2d 1298 (Okla. 1991); *Avey v. Hillcrest Medical Ctr.*, 815 P.2d 1215 (Okla. 1991); *Black v. Baker Oil Tools, Inc.*, 107 F.3d 1457 (10th Cir. 1997). |

| | | | | | |
|---|---|---|---|---|---|
| OR | Yes. | No. | Yes. | N/R. | *Potter v. Hatter Farms, Inc.,* 641 P.2d 628 (Or. 1982); *Sheets v. Knight,* 779 P.2d 1000 (Or. 1989); *Mobley v. Manheim Services Corp.,* 889 P.2d 1342 (Or. Ct. App. 1995). |
| PA | Yes. | No. | Yes. | No. | *DiBonaventura v. Consolidated Rail Corp.,* 539 A.2d 865 (Pa. 1988); *Arasi v. Neema Medical Servs., Inc.,* 595 A.2d 1205 (Pa. Super. Ct. 1991), *appeal denied,* 604 A.2d 247 (1991); *Jacques v. Akzo Int'l Salt, Inc.,* 619 A.2d 748 (Pa. Super. Ct. 1993); *Niehaus v. Delaware Valley Medical Center,* 631 A.2d 1314 (Pa. Super. Ct. 1993), *rev'd,* 649 A.2d 433 (Pa. 1994); *Steinberg v. 7-Up Bottling Co. of Philadelphia,* 636 A.2d 677 (Pa. Super. Ct. 1994); *Brozovich v. Dugo,* 651 A.2d 641 (Pa. Commw. Ct. 1994). |
| RI | No. | No. | No. | No. | *Pacheo v. Ratheon Co.,* 623 A.2d 464 (R.I. 1993). |
| SC | Yes. | N/R. | Yes. | N/R. | *Small v. Sprigs Indus., Inc.,* 357 S.E.2d 452 (S.C. 1987); *Hannah v. United Refrigerated Servs., Inc.,* 430 S.E.2d 539 (S.C. 1993); *Leahy v. Starflo Corp.,* 431 S.E.2d 567 (S.C. 1993); *Kumpf v. United Tel. Co.,* 429 S.E.2d 869 (S.C. Ct. App. 1993); *Bookman v. Shakespeare Co.,* 442 S.E.2d 183 (S.C. Ct. App. 1994); *King v. PYA/Monarch, Inc.,* 453 S.E.2d 885 (S.C. 1995); *Alston v. City of Camden,* 471 S.E.2d 174 (S.C. 1996); *Hindman v. Greenville Hospital Systems,* 947 F. Supp. 215 (D.S.C. 1996); *Hindman v. Greenville Hosp. Systems,* 947 F. Supp. 215 (D.S.C. 1996); *Dodgens v. Kent Mfg. Co.,* 955 F. Supp. 560 (D.S.C. 1997); *Prescott v. Farmers Telephone Co-op., Inc.,* 491 S.E.2d 698 (S.C. App. 1997). |
| SD | Yes. | No. | No. | No. | *Butterfield v. Citibank of S.D., N.A.,* 437 N.W.2d 857 (S.D. 1989); *Stedillie v. American Colloid Co.,* 967 F.2d 274 (8th Cir. 1992); *Niesent v. Homestake Min. Co. of California,* 505 N.W.2d 781 (S.D. 1993); *Bass v. Happy Rest, Inc.,* 507 N.W.2d 317 (S.D. 1993); *Nelson v. WEB Water Development Ass'n. Inc.,* 507 N.W.2d 691 (S.D. 1993); *Richardson v. East River Elec. Power Co-op., Inc.,* 531 N.W.2d 23 (S.D. 1995). |
| TN | Yes. | N/C. | N/R. | N/R. | *Richardson v. Goodall Rubber Co.,* 1986 WL9002 (Tenn. 1986); *D'Andrea v. Plough Sales Corp.,* 1987 WL15852 (Tenn. 1987); *Williams v. Maremont Corp.,* 776 S.W.2d 78 (Tenn. Ct. App. 1988); *Wilmer v. Tennessee Eastman Co.,* 919 F.2d 1160 (6th Cir. 1990); *Davis v. Connecticut Gen. Life Ins. Co.,* 743 F. Supp. 1273 (M.D. Tenn. 1990); *Randolph v. Dominion Bank of Middle Tenn.,* 826 S.W.2d 477 (Tenn. 1991); *Rose v. Tipton County Public Works Dept.,* 953 S.W.2d 690 (Tenn. App. 1997). |
| TX | N/R. | No. | No. | Yes. | *Johnson v. Ford Motor Co.,* 690 S.W.2d 90 (Tex. 1985); *Roberts v. Geosource Drilling Serv., Inc.,* 757 S.W.2d 48 (Tex. 1988); *Caton v. Leach Corp.,* 896 F.2d 939 (5th Cir. 1990); *Day & Zimmermann, Inc., v. Hatridge,* 1992 WL56700 (Tex. 1992); *Spuler v. Pickar,* 958 F.2d 103 (5th Cir. 1992); *Amador v. Tan,* 855 S.W.2d 131 (Tex. Ct. App. 1993); *Palmer v. Miller Brewing Co.,* 852 S.W.2d 57 (Tex. Ct. App. 1993); *Federal Express v. Dutschmann,* 846 S.W.2d 282 (Tex. 1993); *Jones v. Legal Copy, Inc.,* 846 S.W.2d 922 (Tex. Ct. App. 1993); *Farrington v. Sysco Food Servs., Inc.,* 865 S.W.2d 247 (Tex. Ct. App. 1993); *Collins v. Allied Pharmacy Mgmt., Inc.,* 871 S.W.2d 929 (Tex. Ct. App. 1994); *Vida v. El Paso Employees' Fed. Credit Union,* 885 *(cont'd)* |

*(Table continues.)*

## Table 4.2-1 *(cont'd)*

## CAUSES OF ACTION FOR WRONGFUL DISCHARGE BASED ON IMPLIED CONTRACTS

(See also text at § 4.2.)

**KEY:** **N/C.** No court case has been issued so far.
**N/R.** No ruling. The highest court of the state has not clearly expressed its position on this issue, and either the lower courts are divided or the federal courts, interpreting state law, are the only courts to have issued a decision.
**Promissory Estoppel.** Promise by employer that causes an employee or prospective employee to substantially alter his or her life circumstances.

| | *Handbooks and Manuals* | *Covenant of Good Faith and Fair Dealing* | *Oral Representations of Job Security* | *Promissory Estoppel* | *Citations to Authority* |
|---|---|---|---|---|---|
| TX *(cont'd)* | | | | | S.W.2d 177 (Tex. Ct. App. 1994); *Loftis v. Town of Highland Park*, 893 S.W.2d 154 (Tex. Ct. App. 1995); *Hockaday v. Texas Dep't of Criminal Justice, Pardons and Paroles Division*, 914 F. Supp. 1439 (S.D. Tex. 1996); *Mackey v. U.P. Enterprises, Inc.*, 935 S.W.2d 446 (Tex. App. 1996); *Wilson v. Sysco Food Service of Dallas, Inc.*, 940 F. Supp. 1003 (D. Tex. 1996); *McDonald v. City of Corinth, Tex.*, 102 F.3d 152 (5th Cir. 1996); *Montgomery County Hospital v. Brown*, 965 S.W.2d 501 (Tex. 1998). |
| UT | Yes. | No. | Yes. | N/C. | *Bruno v. Plateau Mining Co.*, 747 P.2d 1055 (Utah 1987); *Maxfield v. North Am. Phillips Consumer Elec. Corp.*, 724 F. Supp. 840 (D. Utah 1989); *Johnson v. Morton Thiokol, Inc.*, 818 P.2d 997 (Utah 1991); *Brehany v. Nordstrom, Inc.*, 812 P.2d 49 (Utah 1991); *Evans v. GTE Health Systems Inc.*, 857 P.2d 974 (Utah Ct. App. 1993), *aff'd*, 878 P.2d 1153 (Utah 1994); *Kirberg v. West One Bank*, 872 P.2d 39 (Utah Ct. App. 1994); *Dubois v. Grand Central*, 872 P.2d 1073 (Utah Ct. App. 1994); *Robertson v. Utah Fuel Co.*, 889 P.2d 1382 (Utah Ct. App. 1995). |
| VT | Yes. | No. | No. | Yes. | *Larose v. Agway, Inc.*, 508 A.2d 1364 (Vt. 1986); *Foote v. Simmonds Precision Products Co.*, 613 A.2d 1277 (Vt. 1992); *Baldwin v. Upper Valley Servs., Inc.*, 644 A.2d 316 (Vt. 1994); *Taylor v. National Life Ins. Co.*, 652 A.2d 466 (Vt. 1993); *Ross v. Times Mirror, Inc.*, 665 A.2d 580 (Vt. 1995); *Madden v. Omega Optical Inc.*, 683 A.2d 386 (Vt. 1996); *McKenney v. John V. Carr Son, Inc.*, 922 F. Supp. 967 (D. Vt. 1996). |
| VA | Yes. | N/R. | N/C. | Yes. | *Falls v. Virginia State Bar*, 397 S.E.2d 671 (Va. 1990); *Graham v. Central Fidelity Bank*, 428 S.E.2d 916 (Va. 1993); *Michael v. Sentara Health System*, 939 F. Supp. 1220 (E.D. Va. 1996). |
| WA | Yes. | No. | Yes. | N/C. | *Lawson v. Boeing Co.*, 792 P.2d 545 (Wash. 1990); *Gaglidari v. Denny's Restaurants, Inc.*, 815 P.2d 1362 (Wash. 1991); *Swanson v. Liquid Air Corp.*, 826 P.2d 664 (Wash. 1992); *Guild v. St. Martin's College*, 827 P.2d 286 (Wash. 1992); *Hill v. J.C. Penney, Inc.*, 852 P.2d 1111 (Wash. Ct. App. 1993), *petition for review denied*, 866 P.2d 39 (Wash. 1993); *Burnside v. Simpson Paper Co.*, |

| | | | | | |
|---|---|---|---|---|---|
| | | | | | 864 P.2d 937 (Wash. 1994); *Winspear v. Boeing Co.,* 880 P.2d 1010 (Wash. Ct. App. 1994); *Payne v. Sunnyside Community Hosp.,* 894 P.2d 1379 (Wash. Ct. App. 1995); *Nelson v. Soughland Corp.,* 894 P.2d 1385 (Wash. Ct. App. 1995); *Wlasiuk v. Whirlpool Corp.,* 914 P.2d 102 (Wash. Ct. App. 1996); *Bott v. Rockwell Int'l,* 908 P.2d 909 (Wash. Ct. App. 1996). |
| WV | Yes. | No. | Yes. | N/C. | *Freeman v. Poling,* 338 S.E.2d 415 (W. Va. 1985); *Collins v. Elkay Mining Co.,* 371 S.E.2d 46 (W. Va. 1988); *Shell v. Metropolitan Life Ins. Co.,* 396 S.E.2d 174 (W. Va. 1990); *Adkins v. Inco Alloys Int'l, Inc.,* 417 S.E. 2d 910 (W. Va. 1992); *Bowe v. Charleston Area Medical Center,* 428 S.E.2d 773 (W. Va. 1993); *Bailey v. Sewell Coal Co.,* 437 S.E.2d 448 (W. Va. 1993); *Dent v. Fruth,* 453 S.E.2d 340 (W. Va. 1994); *Miller v. Mutual Life Insurance Co.,* 455 S.E.2d 799 (W. Va. 1995). |
| WI | Yes. | No. | Yes. | No. | *Brockmeyer v. Dun & Bradstreet,* 335 N.W.2d 834 (Wis. 1983); *Ferraro v. Koelsch,* 368 N.W.2d 666 (Wis. 1985). |
| WY | Yes. | No. | Yes. | Yes. | *McDonald v. Mobil Coal Producing, Inc.,* 820 P.2d 986 (Wyo. 1991); *Durtsche v. American Colloid Co.,* 958 F.2d 1007 (10th Cir. 1992); *Sanchez v. Life Care Ctrs. of America, Inc.,* 855 P.2d 1256 (Wyo. 1993); *Wilder v. Cody Country Chamber of Commerce,* 868 P.2d 211 (Wyo. 1994); *Drake v. Cheyenne Newspapers, Inc.,* 891 P.2d 80 (Wyo. 1995); *Garcia v. UniWyo Federal Credit Union,* 920 P.2d 642 (Wyo. 1996); *Loghry v. Unicover Corp.,* 927 P.2d 706 (Wyo. 1996). |

# Table 4.2-2
## STATE COURT TREATMENT OF EMPLOYEE HANDBOOKS/MANUALS

(See also text at § 4.2.)

| | *Can a Handbook/Manual Create a Contract?* | *Must Employee Be Aware of Provisions?* | *Effect of Failure to Follow Procedures for Discipline Set Forth in Manual* | *Changes to Manual* | *Disclaimer* | *Other* | *Citations to Authority* |
|---|---|---|---|---|---|---|---|
| AL | May create a contract where the language is specific enough to constitute an offer, it is communicated to the employee, and the employee accepts it by continuing to work. To create an implied contract, the handbook must state that the listed causes are the only causes for discharge. | Yes. | — | — | No implied contract was created where handbook stated that employment was at-will and the employee signed an acknowledgment of the disclaimer. | — | *Hoffman-La Roche, Inc. v. Campbell,* 512 So.2d 725 (Ala. 1987); *Abney v. Baptist Medical Centers,* 597 So.2d 682 (Ala. 1992); *Mooney v. Harco Drug Co. Inc.,* 611 So.2d 235 (Ala. 1992); *Campisi v. Scoles Cadillac, Inc.,* 611 So.2d 296 (Ala. 1992); *Davis v. University of Montevallo,* 638 So.2d 754 (Ala. 1994); *Dykes v. Lane Trucking, Inc.,* 652 So.2d 248 (Ala. 1994). |
| AK | Employer may be bound by provisions in manual where manual creates reasonable expectation of rights. | — | — | — | Disclaimer must be unambiguous and conspicuous. | — | *Jones v. Central Peninsula General Hospital,* 779 P.2d 783 (Alaska 1989); *Parker v. Mat-Su Council on Prevention of Alcoholism and Drug Abuse,* 813 P.2d 665 (Alaska 1991). |
| AZ | Statement in manual may, by parties' conduct, become part of employment contract or create contract. | — | — | — | No contract was created where an unambiguous disclaimer stated that employees were terminable at-will and stated that the policies in the manual did not constitute a contract. | — | *Leikvold v. Valley View Community Hospital,* 688 P.2d 170 (Ariz. 1984); *Duke v. Arizona Board of Regents,* 721 P.2d 1159 (Ariz. App. 1986); *Duncan v. St. Joseph's Hospital and Medical Center,* 903 P.2d 1107 (Ariz. App. 1995). |
| AR | To create contractual obligations, the manual must specify that the listed grounds are the only grounds for discharge. | — | — | For change to be effective, employee must be notified. | Where employer changed handbook to include a disclaimer but failed to notify the employee, the disclaimer was ineffective. | It was a breach of contract where the manual set forth procedures to be followed for lay-offs and the employer failed to comply. | *Crain Industries, Inc. v. Cass,* 810 S.W.2d 910 (Ark. 1991); *Mertyris v. P.A.M. Transportation, Inc.,* 832 S.W.2d 823 (Ark. 1992). |

| | | | | | | | |
|---|---|---|---|---|---|---|---|
| CA | Handbook may become part of a contract. | — | — | Employer may alter unilaterally. | No contract based on the handbook where a disclaimer stated employment was terminable at-will and that progressive disciplinary provisions were not mandatory. | — | *Walker v. Northern San Diego County Hospital District,* 185 Cal. Rptr. 617 (Cal. App. 1982); *Burton v. Security Pacific National Bank,* 243 Cal. Rptr. 2d 277 (Cal. App. 1988); *Haggard v. Kimberly Quality Care, Inc.,* 46 Cal. Rptr. 2d 16 (Cal. App. 1995). |
| CO | Manual that contains statements limiting employer's right to fire employee may create a contract, where the intent to be bound is shown. For a contract to be established, manual procedures must constitute an offer, and the employee must accept and continue to work as consideration. | — | — | Employer may reserve right to unilaterally change manual; such right is also presumed. | Disclaimer may preclude contract, if clear and conspicuous, but disclaimer language is not by itself determinative of the question. Disclaimer was effective where employee signed a disclaimer and the manual also contained a disclaimer. Employee may not be bound by disclaimer, where manual states that just cause will be required for termination. | — | *Ferrara v. Nielson,* 799 P.2d 458 (Colo. App. 1990); *Evenson v. Colorado Farm Bureau Mutual Insurance Co.,* 879 P.2d 402 (Colo. App. 1993); *Schur v. Storage Technology Corp.,* 878 P.2d 51 (Colo. App. 1994); *Mariam v. Rocky Mountain Hospital and Medical Service,* 902 P.2d 429 (Colo. App. 1994); *Fair v. Red Lion Inn,* 920 P.2d 820 (Colo. App. 1995); *Silchia v. MCI Telecommunications Corp.,* 942 F. Supp. 1369 (D.Colo. 1996); *George v. Ute Water Conservatory Dist.,* 950 P.2d 1195 (Colo. Ct. App. 1997). |
| CT | Handbook may be one consideration as to whether a contract exists for firing only for cause. Requirements for formation of a unilateral contract must be met, including mutual assent. | Yes. | — | If change to manual gives employee greater rights, employee's continuation of work is acceptance of an offer of new rights. If the changes give the employee fewer rights, continued work is not conclusive evidence of acceptance. | — | — | *Finley v. Aetna Life & Casualty Co.,* 520 A.2d 208 (Conn. 1987); *Carbone v. Atlantic Richfield Co.,* 528 A.2d 1137 (Conn. 1987); *Barry v. Posi-Seal International, Inc.,* 647 A.2d 1031 (Conn. App. 1994), *rev'd in part on other grounds,* 672 A.2d 514 (Conn. 1995); *Torosyan v. Boehringer Ingelheim Pharmaceuticals, Inc.,* 662 A.2d 89 (Conn. 1995). |
| DE | To create contractual obligations, handbook must contain very clear and specific language limiting the employer's right to discharge. | — | — | — | — | — | *Peterson v. Beebe Medical Center,* 8 I.E.R. Cases (BNA) 10 (Del. Super. 1992). |

*(Table continues.)*

# **Table 4.2-2** *(cont'd)*
## STATE COURT TREATMENT OF EMPLOYEE HANDBOOKS/MANUALS

(See also text at § 4.2.)

| | *Can a Handbook/Manual Create a Contract?* | *Must Employee Be Aware of Provisions?* | *Effect of Failure to Follow Procedures for Discipline Set Forth in Manual* | *Changes to Manual* | *Disclaimer* | *Other* | *Citations to Authority* |
|---|---|---|---|---|---|---|---|
| DC | Creates contract only if the manual clearly establishes intent to create employment terminable only under specific conditions. | Not necessary that employees have read the manual to rely on manual provisions in a later lawsuit. | — | — | No implied contract created where manual contained disclaimers in three places and stated that employment was at-will. | — | *Nickens v. Labor Agency of Metropolitan Washington*, 600 A.2d 813 (D.C. App. 1991); *Perkins v. District Government Employees Federal Credit Union*, 653 A.2d 842 (D.C. App. 1995); *Atkins v. Industrial Telecommunications Association, Inc.*, 660 A.2d 885 (D.C. App. 1995); *Sisco v. GSA Nat. Capital Federal Union*, 689 A.2d 52 (D.C. App. 1997). |
| FL | No contractual obligations created where the manual merely expressed policy and did not exist at the time the employee was hired. | — | — | — | — | — | *Lurton v. Muldon Motor Co.*, 523 So. 2d 706 (Fla. App. 1988). |
| GA | Handbook will not create contractual obligations unless it states a specific length of employment. | — | Manual stating employee can be terminated only for cause and setting forth termination procedures is not a contract, and failure to follow the procedures is not actionable. | — | — | — | *Lane v. K-Mart Corp.*, 378 S.E.2d 136 (Ga. App. 1989); *Jones v. Chatham County*, 477 S.E.2d 889 (Ga. App. 1996). |
| HI | Handbook may create a contract where there is offer, acceptance, and consideration. Remaining on the job is considered sufficient | Yes. | Where manual provides that certain procedures will be followed to fire an employee, good cause for ter- | — | — | — | *Kinoshita v. Canadian Pacific Airlines, Inc.*, 724 P.2d 110 (Haw. 1986); *Calleon v. Miyagi*, 876 P.2d 1278 (Haw. 1994). |

| | | | | | | | |
|---|---|---|---|---|---|---|---|
| | consideration by the employee. | | mination is not required, but the procedures must be followed. | | | | |
| ID | Handbook may create unilateral employment contract where the employee continues to work after receipt of the manual. | Yes. | — | Revision of manual and signature of employee stating that he received the changes was effective to modify the manual. Employer may unilaterally alter the manual if reasonable notice of the change is given to the employee. | Disclaimer in manual prevents assertion of breach of contract claim. | — | *Watson v. Idaho Falls Consolidated Hospital, Inc.*, 720 P.2d 632 (Idaho 1986); *Spero v. Lockwood, Inc.*, 721 P.2d 174 (Idaho 1986); *Parker v. Boise Telco Federal Credit Union,* 129 Idaho 248, 923 P.2d 493 (1996); *Jones v. Micron Technology, Inc.*, 923 P.2d 486 (Idaho App. 1996); *Raedlin v. Boise Cascade Corp.*, 931 P.2d 621 (Idaho App. 1996). |
| IL | Handbook may create contract if the language clearly indicates an offer, it is distributed to the employee, and the employee continues to work after receiving it. General policy guidelines in a manual do not create a contract. | For handbook to create enforceable contract rights, the employee must be aware of its contents. | — | Employer may unilaterally change the handbook, superseding the old handbook. | Disclaimer may negate language otherwise indicating a contract, but disclaimer must be conspicuous. Disclaimer buried at the end of a manual and not in prominent type was ineffective to negate the promises in the manual. | — | *Hicks v. Methodist Medical Center,* 593 N.E.2d 119 (Ill. App. 1992); *Gaiser v. Village of Skokie,* 648 N.E.2d 205 (Ill. App. 1995); *Brown v. R.R. Donnelly & Sons Co.,* 650 N.E.2d 8 (Ill. App. 1995); *Wheeler v. Phoenix Co. of Chicago,* 658 N.E.2d 532 (Ill. App. 1995); *Hanna v. Marshall Field & Co.,* 665 N.E.2d 343 (Ill. App. 1996); *Corluka v. Bridgeford Foods of Illinois, Inc.,* 671 N.E.2d 814 (Ill. App. 1996). |
| IN | Handbook may alter at-will status where employee provides adequate independent consideration; giving up job prospects and relocating not found to be adequate independent consideration. Employee must have reasonably relied on the manual, believed an offer was made, and accepted it by continuing to work. | Yes. | — | — | Disclaimer was effective where it stated employer could terminate employee at will. | — | *Lavery v. Southlake Center,* 566 N.E.2d 1055 (Ind. App. 1991); *Wior v. Anchor Industries, Inc.,* 669 N.E.2d 172 (Ind. 1996); *Orr v. Westminister Village North, Inc.*, 689 N.E.2d 712 (Ind. 1997). |

*(Table continues.)*

**Table 4.2-2** *(cont'd)*

STATE COURT TREATMENT OF EMPLOYEE HANDBOOKS/MANUALS

(See also text at § 4.2.)

| | *Can a Handbook/Manual Create a Contract?* | *Must Employee Be Aware of Provisions?* | *Effect of Failure to Follow Procedures for Discipline Set Forth in Manual* | *Changes to Manual* | *Disclaimer* | *Other* | *Citations to Authority* |
|---|---|---|---|---|---|---|---|
| IA | Handbook is a unilateral contract when it is sufficiently definite in terms, it is communicated to and accepted by the employee, and the employee provides consideration by continuing to work. No contractual obligations created where the handbook contained no provisions limiting the grounds for discharge or stating that the employee could be discharged only for cause. | Generally required that employee be aware of the provisions, but employee is not necessarily required to have read the employment manual to rely on it in a later contract action. | Employer did not have an obligation to follow the procedures listed where the manual stated that the list of grounds for discharge was an example, not a limitation. | — | Disclaimer can prevent a handbook from creating a contract where the disclaimer is clear and coverage of the disclaimer is unambiguous. | — | *French v. Foods, Inc.*, 495 N.W.2d 768 (Iowa 1993); *Felczynski v. Amoco Oil Co.*, 533 N.W.2d 226 (Iowa 1995); *Vicks v. Heatilator, Inc.*, 537 N.W.2d 810 (Iowa App. 1995); *Anderson v. Douglas & Lomason Co.*, 540 N.W.2d 277 (Iowa 1995); *Phipps v. IASD Health Services Corp.*, 558 N.W.2d 198 (Iowa 1997); *Jones v. Lake Park Care Center, Inc.*, 569 N.W.2d 369 (Iowa 1997); *Phipps v. IASD Health Services Corp.*, 558 N.W.2d 198 (Iowa 1997); *Thompson v. City of Des Moines*, 564 N.W.2d 839 (Iowa 1997). |
| KS | Personnel policy in a manual can form the basis of an implied contract. A contract is created if the manual promises that the employee will be discharged only for cause. | Employee must be aware of the provisions, although the employee need not have actually read the handbook if aware of the provisions due to other communications from the employer. | — | — | Disclaimer may not prevent the creation of contractual obligations where the employee's claim is not based solely on the manual, but also on other policies of the employer. | — | *Masterson v. Boliden-Allis, Inc.*, 865 P.2d 1031 (Kan. App. 1993). |
| KY | Handbooks generally do not alter employee's contractual rights and are generally considered as mere statements of policy. | — | — | — | Disclaimer was effective where it stated that the manual created no contractual obligations. | — | *Nork v. Fetter Printing Co.*, 3 I.E.R. Cases (BNA) 667 (Ky. App. 1987). |

| | | | | | | | |
|---|---|---|---|---|---|---|---|
| LA | To create a contract, the handbook must specifically establish a fixed term (e.g. six months, one year, etc.) of employment. | — | — | — | Disclaimer was effective where it stated that the manual did not create an employment contract. | — | *Leger v. Tyson's Foods, Inc.*, 670 So. 2d 397 (La. App. 1996). |
| ME | No implied contract existed where the manual did not expressly state that discharge would occur only for cause. | — | — | — | — | — | *Libby v. Calais Regional Hospital*, 554 A.2d 1181 (Maine 1989). |
| MD | Policy statements limiting employer's right to discharge may create contractual rights. | — | Where a disclaimer existed, employee could not rely on the disciplinary procedures set forth in the manual. | Employer may reserve the right to change. | Disclaimer prevented contractual obligations where it stated that the handbook was not a contract, the employer reserved the right to alter it, and the employer reserved the right to discharge the employee at any time. Disclaimer must be unambiguous. | — | *Staggs v. Blue Cross of Maryland, Inc.*, 486 A.2d 798 (Md. Spec. App. 1985); *Haselrig v. Public Storage, Inc.*, 585 A.2d 294 (Md. Spec. App. 1991); *Bagwell v. Peninsula Regional Medical Center*, 665 A.2d 297 (Md. App. 1995). |
| MA | Personnel manual can create contract; manual that contained no disclaimer and provided more than just general guidance created a contract where the parties agreed that their obligations would include provisions found in the manual. | — | — | Employer may have to reserve the right to unilaterally modify the handbook. | No implied contract existed where the manual indicated it provided "guidance" as to policies. | — | *Jackson v. Action for Boston Community Development, Inc.*, 525 N.E.2d 411 (Mass. 1988); *O'Brien v. New England Telephone & Telegraph Co.*, 664 N.E.2d 843 (Mass. 1996). |
| MI | General statement about job security, without details regarding cause for termination was insufficient to create a contract. A manual with detailed disciplinary procedures did not create a contract. | — | — | For unilateral changes to be effective, reasonable notice must be given to the employee. | Provisions of handbook dealing with arbitration did not create contractual rights for employee where employer stated in handbook that no contract was created and employer did not intend to be bound by handbook provisions. For disclaimer to be effective, employee must be aware of it; where employer did not notify or distribute the disclaimer to the employee, the nature of *(cont'd)* | — | *Stopzynski v. Ford Motor Co.*, 503 N.W.2d 912 (Mich. App. 1993); *Coleman-Nichols v. Tixon Corp.*, 513 N.W.2d 441 (Mich. App. 1994); *Clement-Rose v. Michigan Health Care Corp.*, 538 N.W.2d 20 (Mich. App. 1995); *Foehr v. Republic Automotive Parts, Inc.*, 538 N.W.2d 420 (Mich. App. 1995); *Heurtebise v. Reliable Business Computers*, 550 N.W.2d 243 (Mich. 1996); *Lytle v. Malady*, 566 N.W.2d 582 (Mich. 1997). |

*(Table continues.)*

## Table 4.2-2 *(cont'd)*

## STATE COURT TREATMENT OF EMPLOYEE HANDBOOKS/MANUALS

(See also text at § 4.2.)

| | *Can a Handbook/Manual Create a Contract?* | *Must Employee Be Aware of Provisions?* | *Effect of Failure to Follow Procedures for Discipline Set Forth in Manual* | *Changes to Manual* | *Disclaimer* | *Other* | *Citations to Authority* |
|---|---|---|---|---|---|---|---|
| MI (*cont'd*) | | | | | the employment relationship created by the handbook was not changed. Where employee signed an at-will clause, no implied contract was created by the handbook. | | |
| MN | No contract was created where the manual did not contain detailed procedures for discharge for cause only. Definite policy language can create a contract. The handbook must indicate the employer's intent to create a contract. The employee may accept the contract by providing adequate consideration. | To enforce provisions of handbook, the handbook must have been communicated to the employee. | — | — | Disclaimer was effective where it clearly stated that no contractual rights were created. Disclaimer was considered prominent where it was located on the introductory page of the manual. | — | *Edwards v. County of Hennepinn,* 397 N.W.2d 584 (Minn. App. 1986); *Audette v. Northeast State Bank,* 436 N.W.2d 125 (Minn. App. 1989); *Michaelson v. Minnesota Mining & Manufacturing Co.,* 474 N.W.2d 174 (Minn. App. 1991); *Feges v. Perkins Restaurants, Inc.,* 483 N.W.2d 701 (Minn. 1992); *Ward v. Employee Development Corp.,* 516 N.W.2d 198 (Minn. App. 1994). |
| MS | To create a contract, manual must clearly state that the employer will follow the policies in the manual. | — | Where the manual set out disciplinary procedures, the employer was required to follow them for listed infractions, although the nature of the employment was not changed. | — | No implied contract was created where the handbook listed possible reasons for discharge but stated employee could be discharged for other reasons; a mere listing did not limit the employer. | — | *Robinson v. Board of Trustees of East Central Junior College,* 477 So. 2d 1352 (Miss. 1985); *Bobbitt v. Orchard, Ltd.,* 603 So. 2d 356 (Miss. 1992); *Hartle v. Packard Electric,* 626 So. 2d 106 (Miss. 1993). |
| MO | Where a manual was unilaterally adopted by the employer, no implied contract was formed. | — | — | — | — | — | *Enyeart v. Shelter Mutual Insurance Co.,* 784 S.W.2d 205 (Mo. App. 1989). |

| | | | | | | | |
|---|---|---|---|---|---|---|---|
| MT | Manual created no contract where it was distributed after the employee was hired; there was no contract because there was no bargaining or meeting of minds. | — | — | — | — | — | *Kittelson v. Archie Cochrane Motors, Inc.*, 813 P.2d 424 (Mont. 1991). Note: most wrongful discharge claims are preempted by the Montana Wrongful Discharge from Employment Act, Mont. Code Ann. § 39-2-901. |
| NE | Terms from manual may alter an employee's at-will status. To form a contract, the manual must be accepted, and consideration must be furnished. Continuing to work is sufficient consideration from the employee. | Yes. | — | — | No contract was created where the handbook stated the policies created no contractual obligations and reserved discretion in applying policies. | — | *Overmier v. Parks*, 495 N.W.2d 620 (Neb. 1993); *Hillie v. Mutual of Omaha Insurance Co.*, 512 N.W.2d 358 (Neb. 1994); *Hamersky v. Nicholson Supply Co.*, 517 N.W.2d 382 (Neb. 1994). |
| NV | No contract was created where the manual listed infractions but did not state that the listed reasons for discharge were exclusive or that the employee would not be discharged for other causes. | — | — | — | — | — | *Yeager v. Harrah's Club, Inc.*, 897 P.2d 1093 (Nev. 1995). |
| NH | — | — | No cause of action was created for an employee where, although the employer failed to follow the procedures in the manual, employee was at-will. | — | No implied contract was created where the handbook contained discharge procedures but the employee signed a statement indicating that the handbook created no contract but was merely a general guideline. | — | *Butler v. Walker Power, Inc.*, 629 A.2d 91 (N.H. 1993). |
| NJ | Handbook may create a contract where it contains job security and termination provisions that would reasonably indicate to an employee that contractual obligations existed, and if employee continued to work. | — | — | — | Implication that a manual creates a contract may be overcome where a disclaimer is clear, straightforward, prominent, unmistakably disclaims promises regarding terms of employment, and is expressed in language so clear that no employee could have reasonably thought the manual created a con- *(cont'd)* | Reference in manual to "maximum job security" caused court to be more inclined to find that the manual created a contract. Wide distribution of a manual tends to support the theory that a contract was created. | *Witkowski v. Thomas J. Lipton, Inc.*, 643 A.2d 546 (N.J. 1994); *Nicosia v. Wakefern Food Corp.*, 643 A.2d 554 (N.J. 1994); *Jackson v. Georgia-Pacific Corp.*, 685 A.2d 1329 (N.J. Super. Ct. App. Div. 1996); *Falco v. Community Medical Center*, 686 A.2d 1212 (N.J. Super. 1997). |

*(Table continues.)*

# Table 4.2-2 *(cont'd)*

## STATE COURT TREATMENT OF EMPLOYEE HANDBOOKS/MANUALS

(See also text at § 4.2.)

| | *Can a Handbook/Manual Create a Contract?* | *Must Employee Be Aware of Provisions?* | *Effect of Failure to Follow Procedures for Discipline Set Forth in Manual* | *Changes to Manual* | *Disclaimer* | *Other* | *Citations to Authority* |
|---|---|---|---|---|---|---|---|
| NJ *(cont'd)* | | | | | tract. Disclaimer was effective where, although not in bold type or set off, it was placed in the first paragraph of the section on termination. Disclaimer was not effective where it used confusing terms and was not placed in a prominent position and the text was not set off in any manner. | | |
| NM | Policy manual may create a contract where statements or language are explicit; general policy statements are ineffective. To create contract, manual must demonstrate employer's intent to limit its power to discharge. An employee's continuing to work is sufficient consideration for the employer's promise to limit the causes for discharge. | — | — | — | Express reservation of employer's right to fire employee for any reason prevented a personnel policy from creating a contract. A disclaimer may not prevent an implied contract where the employer's conduct indicates that firing may only occur for cause. | — | *Hartbarger v. Frank Paxton Co.*, 857 P.2d 776 (N.M. 1993); *Kiedrowski v. Citizens Bank*, 893 P.2d 468 (N.M. App. 1995); *Garrity v. Overland Sheepskin Co. of Taos*, 917 P.2d 1382 (N.M. 1996); *Garcia v. Middle Rio Grande Conservancy District*, 918 P.2d 7 (N.M. 1996). |
| NY | No contract created where employee did not detrimentally rely on the manual and the manual contained no provisions limiting the employer's right to discharge the employee | — | Employer may be required to comply with procedures for discipline or firing, but substantial compliance may be adequate. | Employer may reserve the right to unilaterally change the manual. | Where the disclaimer stated that the employee could be terminated immediately and that termination did not have to be for cause, no contract was created. | — | *Hanchard v. Facilities Development Corp.*, 628 N.Y.S.2d 4 (N.Y. 1995); *DePetris v. Union Settlement Association, Inc.*, 633 N.Y.S.2d 274 (N.Y. 1995); *Fieldhouse v. Stamford Hospital Society, Inc.*, 649 N.Y.S.2d 527 (N.Y. App. Div. 1996). |

| | | | | | | | |
|---|---|---|---|---|---|---|---|
| | or requiring the employer to follow specified personnel policies. | | | | | | |
| NC | Unilaterally promulgated handbook does not create contractual obligations. | — | — | — | — | In suit against employer, employee could not rely on manual distributed five years after employee began work. | *Rucker v. First Union National Bank*, 389 S.E.2d 622 (N.C. App. 1990); *Salt v. Applied Analytical, Inc.*, 412 S.E.2d 97 (N.C. App. 1991); *Lorbacher v. Housing Authority of City of Raleigh*, 493 S.E.2d 74 (N.C. Ct. App. 1997); *Paschal v. Myers*, 497 S.E.2d 311 (N.C. App. 1998). |
| ND | Handbook may create contractual obligations, but to do so, there must be a definite offer and acceptance. The entire manual will be considered to determine if the employer had the intent to limit the power to discharge. | Yes. | Employer was not required to follow disciplinary procedures where a disclaimer stated that no contractual obligations were created. | — | Handbook did not create a contract where the disclaimer stated that the handbook was not a contract and that the employee could be discharged for any reason. | — | *Bailey v. Perkins Restaurants, Inc.*, 398 N.W.2d 120 (N.D. 1986); *Rykowsky v. Dickinson Public School District No. 1*, 508 N.W.2d 348 (N.D. 1993); *Pratt v. Heartview Foundation*, 512 N.W.2d 675 (N.D. 1994); *Olson v. Souris River Telecommunications Co-op, Inc.*, 558 N.W.2d 333 (N.D. 1997). |
| OH | Handbook may create an implied contract if the employer and employee have agreed to create a contract. If there is no mutual assent, the handbook is merely a statement of general policy which creates no obligations. | — | Disciplinary procedure in manual indicated it was only a guide, and therefore the procedure need not be followed. | Employer may reserve the right to alter a manual. Issuance of a new manual was ineffective where the employee signed a statement acknowledging receipt but stated he did not agree with the claim on the form that employment was at-will. | Disclaimer was effective where it stated that the policies set forth were informational only and employer did not intend to be contractually bound by the provisions. Effective where it stated employment was at-will and the employer was free to terminate the employee. | — | *Hanly v. Riverside Methodist Hospital*, 603 N.E.2d 1126 (Ohio App. 1991); *Handler v. Merrill Lynch Life Agency, Inc.*, 635 N.E.2d 1271 (Ohio App. 1993); *McIntosh v. Roadway Express, Inc.*, 640 N.E.2d 570 (Ohio App. 1994); *Seta v. Reading Rock, Inc.*, 654 N.E.2d 1061 (Ohio App. 1995); *DeKoning v. Flower Mem. Hosp.*, 676 N.E.2d 614 (Ohio Com. Pl. 1996); *Finsterwald-Maiden v. AAA S. Cent. Ohio*, 685 N.E.2d 786 (Ohio App. 1996). |
| OK | Mere listings of some causes for discharge not enough to create a contractual obligation to discharge only for cause. | — | — | — | Handbook did not create contractual obligations where it contained a statement disclaiming any intent to form a contract. | — | *Hinson v. Cameron*, 742 P.2d 549 (Okla. 1987); *Avey v. Hillcrest Medical Center*, 815 P.2d 1215 (Okla. App. 1991). |

*(Table continues.)*

**Table 4.2-2** *(cont'd)*

STATE COURT TREATMENT OF EMPLOYEE HANDBOOKS/MANUALS

(See also text at § 4.2.)

| | *Can a Handbook/Manual Create a Contract?* | *Must Employee Be Aware of Provisions?* | *Effect of Failure to Follow Procedures for Discipline Set Forth in Manual* | *Changes to Manual* | *Disclaimer* | *Other* | *Citations to Authority* |
|---|---|---|---|---|---|---|---|
| OR | Handbook may create a contractual obligation where it lists grounds for discharge. Continued employment after distribution of handbook is consideration for any terms that are contractual. | — | — | — | Disclaimer was effective where it stated no contract was created and that the employee could be terminated at any time. Disclaimer must be unambiguous. | If handbook states it becomes binding upon the happening of an event, the event must occur for the parties to be bound. | *Frazier v. Minnesota Mining & Manufacturing Co.*, 728 P.2d 87 (Or. App. 1986); *Mobley v. Manheim Services Corp.*, 889 P.2d 1342 (Or. App. 1995); *Hreha v. Nemecek*, 849 P.2d 1131 (Or. App. 1993); *Lawson v. Umatilla County*, 139 F.3d 690 (9th Cir. 1998). |
| PA | For handbook to have contractual significance, it must in some way clearly state that it has such effect. An implied contract could be created if a reasonable person would interpret the manual as showing the employer's intent to alter the at-will rule. | — | List of reasons for discharge in manual was illustrative, not exclusive, where the handbook stated the reasons were illustrative only; the reasonable employee at-will would have understood. | Employer may retain the right to alter the handbook unilaterally. Extreme modifications require clear statement of intent to modify. | Disclaimer was effective where it provided that the manual was not intended to give rise to contractual obligations or alter the at-will rule. | — | *Ruzicki v. Catholic Cemeteries Association of Diocese of Pittsburgh*, 610 A.2d 495 (Pa. Super. 1992); *Luteran v. Loral Fairchild Corp.*, 688 A.2d 211 (Pa. Super. 1997); *Small v. Juanita College*, 682 A.2d 350 (Pa. Super. 1996). |
| RI | — | — | — | — | — | — | — |
| SC | Manual can create contractual obligations. | Yes, but employee need not have an actual copy of the manual in his possession. | If there is a procedure in the manual, the employer is generally required to follow it. | Any contractual rights created by a handbook may be unilaterally modified at any time by the employer, provided the employee receives notice of the modification. | Disclaimer in manual was waived by the employer's letter sent to a supervisor from which it could be inferred that the employer intended to waive the disclaimer. Disclaimer was ineffective where it was on the last page of the manual and was not set off with prominent type. Disclaimer was effective where it was conspicuous and stated | — | *Johnson v. First Carolina Financial Corp.*, 409 S.E.2d 804 (S.C. App. 1991); *Kumpf v. United Telephone Co. of Carolinas, Inc.*, 429 S.E.2d 869 (S.C. App. 1993); *Leahy v. Starflo Corp.*, 431 S.E.2d 567 (S.C. 1993); *Fleming v. Bordon, Inc.*, 450 S.E.2d 589 (S.C. 1994); *King v. PYA/Monarch, Inc.*, 453 S.E.2d 885 (S.C. 1995); *Alston v. City of Camden*, 471 S.E.2d 174 (S.C. 1996); *Prescott v. Farmers Tele-* |

| | | | | | | | |
|---|---|---|---|---|---|---|---|
| | | | | | the employee could be terminated at any time. | | *phone Co-op., Inc.*, 491 S.E.2d 698 (S.C. App. 1997). |
| SD | For contractual obligations to be formed, the language in the handbook must clearly indicate the employer's intention to change the at-will status of the employee. Handbook must expressly limit the right to dismiss the employee. Implied contract was found where the manual contained detailed list of exclusive grounds for discharge and specific procedures employer promised to follow. | — | Provisions setting forth guidelines for discharge did not create an implied contract to discharge only for cause where the provisions were not exclusive. | — | Disclaimer effective where it stated that no contract rights were created and the employee was at-will. | — | *Petersen v. Sioux Valley Hospital Association,* 486 N.W.2d 516 (S.D. 1992); *Niesent v. Homestake Mining Co. of California,* 505 N.W.2d 781 (S.D. 1993); *Nelson v. WEB Water Development Association, Inc.,* 507 N.W.2d 691 (S.D. 1993); *Richardson v. East River Electric Power Co-op, Inc.,* 531 N.W.2d 23 (S.D. 1995). |
| TN | To create a contract, a manual must clearly state that the employer is abandoning the at-will policy. | — | — | — | Effective where it stated that employer had the right to discharge the employee. | — | *Bringle v. Methodist Hospital,* 701 S.W.2d 622 (Tenn. App. 1985); *Godinet v. Thomas,* 7 I.E.R. Cases (BNA) 898 (Tenn. App. 1992); *Rose v. Tipton County Public Works Dept.*, 953 S.W.2d 690 (Tenn. App. 1997). |
| TX | Handbook may create contract, but it must use language clearly indicating an intent to do so. A manual that identified policies as "policies, practices, and guidelines" did not express the required intent. Manual must specifically and expressly curtail the right to terminate the employee. | Yes. | — | — | A specific disclaimer prevents an implied contract. Statement in handbook that policies did not create contractual rights prevented the formation of a contract. | — | *Goodyear Tire & Rubber Co. v. Portilla,* 836 S.W.2d 664 (Tex. App. 1992), *aff'd,* 879 S.W.2d 47 (Tex. 1994); *Federal Express Corp. v. Dutschmann,* 846 S.W.2d 282 (Tex. 1993); *Figueroa v. West,* 902 S.W.2d 701 (Tex. App. 1995); *Gamble v. Gregg County,* 932 S.W.2d 253 (Tex. App. 1996). |
| UT | Handbook may create contractual obligations where consistent with other actions of the employer. To create an implied contract, the employer must make an offer for discharge only for cause, with definite communication to the employee. | Yes. | — | Employer may unilaterally modify the manual and it will be effective if the employee has reasonable notice and continues in employment. | Disclaimer as to employee's status did not preclude action for contract violation based on employer's denial of sick leave. Disclaimer was effective where it was clear and conspicuous, based on prominence of text, placement, and language. Disclaimer may be modified by express or implied agreement. | — | *Hodgson v. Bunzl Utah, Inc.,* 844 P.2d 331 (Utah 1992); *Kirberg v. West One Bank,* 872 P.2d 39 (Utah App. 1994); *Trembly v. Mrs. Field's Cookies,* 884 P.2d 1306 (Utah App. 1994); *Hamilton v. Parkdale Care Center, Inc.,* 904 P.2d 1110 (Utah App. 1995); *Cook v. Zions First National Bank,* 919 P.2d 56 (Utah App. 1996). |

*(Table continues.)*

## Table 4.2-2 *(cont'd)*
## STATE COURT TREATMENT OF EMPLOYEE HANDBOOKS/MANUALS

(See also text at § 4.2.)

| | *Can a Handbook/Manual Create a Contract?* | *Must Employee Be Aware of Provisions?* | *Effect of Failure to Follow Procedures for Discipline Set Forth in Manual* | *Changes to Manual* | *Disclaimer* | *Other* | *Citations to Authority* |
|---|---|---|---|---|---|---|---|
| VT | Manual provisions may create a contract and may be used as evidence that the employee could be fired only for cause. | No. | Even if manual stating that employee could be fired after two bad reviews created a disciplinary procedure for bad performance, the employee could still be fired for reasons other than bad performance without following manual procedures. | Employer may unilaterally change the manual. | Disclaimers should be evaluated in the context of other portions of the manual and other circumstances of employment. | — | *Taylor v. National Life Insurance Co.*, 652 A.2d 466 (Vt. 1993); *Baldwin v. Upper Valley Services, Inc.*, 644 A.2d 316 (Vt. 1994); *Farnum v. Brattleboro Retreat, Inc.*, 671 A.2d 1249 (Vt. 1995); *Madden v. Omega Optical, Inc.*, 683 A.2d 386 (Vt. 1996). |
| VA | Manual may create contractual obligations where it specifically provides that discharge is only for cause. | — | — | Employer may alter manual; any alteration supersedes the previous manual. | Where the disclaimer stated that the employee could be terminated without cause, no implied contract was created. An acknowledgment form signed by the employee, stating that the employment was at-will, superseded a cause requirement in a manual. | — | *Progress Printing Co., Inc. v. Nichols,* 421 S.E.2d 428 (Va. 1992); *Graham v. Central Fidelity Bank,* 428 S.E.2d 916 (Va. 1993); *Michael v. Sentara Health System*, 939 F. Supp. 1220 (E.D.Va. 1996). |
| WA | Manual may create contract where it promises specific treatment in certain situations and where there is reliance by the employee. A statement of general policy was ineffective to create contractual rights. | — | Generally if an employer sets forth a procedure, it must be followed. | Employer may alter with reasonable notice to the employee. | Disclaimer precludes a contract if effectively communicated to the employee. It must state in a conspicuous manner that nothing in the manual creates contractual obligations and that the manual is simply a general state- | — | *Gaglidari v. Denny's Restaurants, Inc.*, 815 P.2d 1362 (Wash. 1991); *Burnside v. Simpson Paper Co.*, 864 P.2d 937 (Wash. 1994); *Payne v. Sunnyside Community Hospital,* 894 P.2d 1379 (Wash. App. 1995); *Magula v. Benton Franklin Title Insurance Co.*, 901 P.2d 313 (Wash. App. |

| | | | | | | | |
|---|---|---|---|---|---|---|---|
| | | | | | ment of company policy. Disclaimer should be considered in light of the surrounding circumstances; inconsistent practices may negate a disclaimer. | | 1995); *Bott v. Rockwell International,* 908 P.2d 909 (Wash. App. 1996); *Wlasiuk v. Whirlpool Corp.,* 914 P.2d 102 (Wash. App. 1996). |
| WV | Handbook may form a unilateral contract if it contains a definite promise not to discharge except for specified reasons and if the employee accepts by continuing to work. | Yes. | — | Employer may retain the right to alter, but the employee must be given notice of the changes. | Disclaimer effective where clear, conspicuous, and understandable by the employee. Employer was not bound by statements in handbook where the employer required each employee to sign a statement acknowledging that the employment was at-will and that the handbook provisions were not exclusive. | — | *Hogue v. Cecil I. Walker Machinery Co.,* 431 S.E.2d 687 (W. Va. 1993); *Dent v. Froth,* 453 S.E.2d 340 (W. Va. 1994); *Williams v. Precision Coil, Inc.,* 459 S.E.2d 329 (W. Va. 1995). |
| WI | Not all manuals will create a contract; to create a contract, the manual must contain express provisions that the employment is no longer at-will. Mere issuance of a handbook is not adequate to create a contract. | — | — | — | — | — | *Clay v. Horton Manufacturing Co., Inc.* 493 N.W.2d 379 (Wis. App. 1992); *Olson v. 3M Co.,* 523 N.W.2d 578 (Wis. App. 1994); *Wolf v. F & M Banks,* 534 N.W.2d 877 (Wis. App. 1995). |
| WY | Handbook may give rise to the implication that termination must be for cause. Court will look beyond specific terms to general tenor of handbook. To create a contract, the handbook must reasonably create the expectation that the employee will be discharged only for cause. | — | — | Employer may reserve the right to unilaterally alter the manual. | Conspicuous and unambiguous disclaimer may avoid the implication that the handbook requires cause for termination. Language of a disclaimer was sufficient where it was first in the handbook, in prominent type, and stated no contractual obligations were formed. Disclaimer was not effective where it was buried in the manual, not set off by prominent type, and was ambiguous in the context of other provisions in the manual implying cause was required for discharge. | — | *Sanchez v. Life Care Center of America, Inc.,* 855 P.2d 1256 (Wyo. 1993); *Lincoln v. Wackenhut Corp.,* 867 P.2d 701 (Wyo. 1994); *Garcia v. UniWyo Federal Credit Union,* 920 P.2d 642 (Wyo. 1996); *Loghny v. Unicover Corp.,* 927 P.2d 706 (Wyo. 1996); *Brodie v. General Chemical Corp.,* 934 P.2d 1263 (Wyo. 1997); *Davis v. Wyoming Medical Center, Inc.,* 934 P.2d 1246 (Wyo. 1997). |

# § 4.3 Causes of Action for Wrongful Discharge Based on Tort Theories

At-will employees who are discharged often use traditional tort theories to challenge their dismissals. Some theories commonly used in these cases are intentional infliction of emotional distress, interference with contractual relations, and defamation. Table 4.3-1 shows which states generally recognize these theories as well as which states allow for claims to be filed for violation of public policy.

## [a] Intentional Infliction of Emotional Distress

This tort was created to compensate persons who are victims of conduct deemed extreme and outrageous by society. Discharge alone, however, is not sufficient grounds to file a claim under this theory. In addition, the discharged employee must assert one of the following allegations: the employer harassed him or her, demanded illegal or improper conduct, or acted in some other extraordinary or outrageous manner.

## [b] Interference with Contractual Relations

An individual may have a cause of action for interference with an employment contract, even though the employment is at will. However, most states do not protect against the conduct of a party to the contract but, rather, against unlawful interference by third parties. That is, an employer cannot be liable for interference with its own contract.

## [c] Defamation

To establish a defamation claim, the discharged employee must allege that the employer published a defamatory or untrue statement about him or her to a third party. To contest the allegation, the employer, in turn, must prove that the statement is either true or protected by an "absolute or qualified privilege"—that is, the employer published the information with just cause (if the employee engaged in illegal activities, for example).

## [d] Public Policy

A growing number of states recognize an at-will discharge that violates public policy as a cause of action for wrongful, abusive, or retaliatory termination. In such a case, the employer may be liable in tort to the employee for damages resulting from discharge. Although the underlying principle in most public policy wrongful discharge cases is usually the same, it is the *nature of the claim* that dictates the damages available to prevailing employees. For example, punitive damages and damages for pain and suffering are available for tort but not for contractual claims.

The courts generally specify that a "public policy" sufficient to support such a cause of action must be based on a statute, regulation, constitutional provision, professional code of ethics, or other such tangible foundation rather than an individual employee's sensibilities. A growing number of states have enacted statutes, commonly referred to as "whistle-blower acts," to codify the public policy doctrine.

# Table 4.3-1
## CAUSES OF ACTION FOR WRONGFUL DISCHARGE BASED ON TORT THEORIES

(See also text at § 4.3.)

**KEY:** **Violation of Public Policy.** Although the courts generally construe discharge in violation of public policy to be a violation of an implied-in-law contract, they usually allow tort remedies, including punitive damages and a right to a jury trial.
**N/C.** No court case has been issued so far.
**N/R.** No ruling. The highest court of the state has not clearly expressed its position on this issue, and either the lower courts are divided or the federal courts, interpreting state law, are the only courts to have issued a decision.

| | *Intentional Infliction of Emotional Distress* | *Interference with Contractual Relations* | *Defamation* | *Violation of Public Policy* | *Citations to Authority* |
|---|---|---|---|---|---|
| AL | Yes. | Yes. | Yes. | No. | *Kemper & Co. Southeast, Inc. v. Cox & Associates,* 434 So. 2d 1380 (Ala. 1983); *McIssac v. W2EW-FM Corp.,* 495 So. 2d 649 (Ala. 1986); *Salter v. Alfa Ins. Co.,* 561 So. 2d 1050 (Ala. 1990); *Atkins Ford Sales, Inc. v. Royster,* 560 So. 2d 197 (Ala. 1990); *Forbus v. Sears Roebuck & Co.,* 958 F.2d 1036 (11th Cir. 1992); *Sparks v. Regional Medical Center,* 792 F. Supp. 735 (N.D. Ala. 1992); *Rowe v. Isbell,* 599 So. 2d 35 (Ala. 1992); *Goffer v. Marbury,* 956 F.2d 1045 (11th Cir. 1992); *Dykes v. Lane Trucking, Inc.,* 652 So. 2d 248 (Ala. 1994). |
| AK | Yes. | Yes. | Yes. | N/R. | *Long v. Newby,* 488 P.2d 719 (Alaska 1971); *Knight v. American Guard & Alert, Inc.,* 714 P.2d 788 (Alaska 1986); *Arco Alaska, Inc. v. Akers,* 753 P.2d 1150 (Alaska 1988); *Schneider v. Pay 'N Save Corp.,* 723 P.2d 619 (Alaska 1989); *French v. Jadon, Inc.,* 911 P.2d 20 (Alaska 1996). |
| AZ | Yes. | Yes. | Yes. | Yes. | *Wagenseller v. Scottsdale Memorial Hosp.,* 710 P.2d 1025 (Ariz. 1985); *Ford v. Revlon, Inc.,* 734 P.2d 580 (Ariz. 1987); *Loffa v. Intel Corp.,* 738 P.2d 1146 (Ariz. Ct. App. 1987); *Godbehere v. Phoenix Newspapers, Inc.,* 783 P.2d 781 (Ariz. 1989); *Tingey v. Pixley-Richards W., Inc.,* 953 F.2d 1124 (9th Cir. 1992); *Spratt v. Northern Automotive Corp.,* 958 F. Supp. 456 (D. Ariz. 1996). |
| AR | Yes. | Yes. | N/C. | Yes. | *M.B.M. Co. v. Counce,* 596 S.W.2d 681 (Ark. 1980); *Flynn v. McIlroy Bank & Trust Co.,* 697 S.W.2d 114 (Ark. 1985); *Sterling Drug, Inc. v. Oxford,* 743 S.W.2d 380 (Ark. 1988); *Ingram v. Pirelli Cable Corp.,* 747 S.W.2d 103 (Ark. 1988); *Smith v. American Greetings Corp.,* 804 S.W.2d 683 (Ark. 1991); *City of Green Forest v. Morse,* 873 S.W.2d 155 (Ark. 1994). |
| CA | Yes. | No. | Yes. | Yes. | *Agarwal v. Johnson,* 160 Cal. Rptr. 141 (Cal. 1979); *Tameny v. Atlantic Richfield Co.,* 164 Cal. Rptr. 839 (Cal. 1980); *Robinson v. Hewlett-Packard Corp.,* 228 Cal. Rptr. 591 (Cal. Ct. App. 1986); *Prevost v. First W. Bank,* 239 Cal. Rptr. 161 (Cal. Ct. App. 1987); *Hart v. National Mortgage & Land Co.,* 235 Cal. Rptr. 68 (Cal. Ct. App. 1987); *Lanouette v. Ciba-Geigy Corp.,* 832 P.2d 585 (Cal. 1992); *Gantt v. Sentry Ins.,* 4 Cal. Rptr. 2d 874 (Cal. 1992); *Livitsanos v. Superior Court* |

*(cont'd)*

*(Table continues.)*

# Table 4.3-1 *(cont'd)*
## CAUSES OF ACTION FOR WRONGFUL DISCHARGE BASED ON TORT THEORIES

(See also text at § 4.3.)

**KEY:** **Violation of Public Policy.** Although the courts generally construe discharge in violation of public policy to be a violation of an implied-in-law contract, they usually allow tort remedies, including punitive damages and a right to a jury trial.
**N/C.** No court case has been issued so far.
**N/R.** No ruling. The highest court of the state has not clearly expressed its position on this issue, and either the lower courts are divided or the federal courts, interpreting state law, are the only courts to have issued a decision.

| | *Intentional Infliction of Emotional Distress* | *Interference with Contractual Relations* | *Defamation* | *Violation of Public Policy* | *Citations to Authority* |
|---|---|---|---|---|---|
| CA *(cont'd)* | | | | | *of Los Angeles County,* 7 Cal. Rptr. 2d 808 (Cal. 1992); *Holmes v. General Dynamics Corp.,* 22 Cal. Rptr. 2d 172 (Cal. Ct. App. 1993); *Angell v. Peterson Tractor, Inc.,* 26 Cal. Rptr. 2d 541 (Cal. Ct. App. 1994); *Haycock v. Hughes Aircraft Co.,* 28 Cal. Rptr. 2d 248 (Cal. Ct. App. 1994); *Parada v. City of Colton,* 29 Cal. Rptr. 2d 309 (Cal. Ct. App. 1994); *Turner v. Anheuser-Busch, Inc.,* 32 Cal. Rptr. 2d 223 (Cal. 1994); *Barton v. New United Motor Mfg. Co.,* 51 Cal. Rptr. 2d 328 (Cal. Ct. App. 1996); *Stevenson v. Huntington Memorial Hosp.,* 941 P.2d 1157 (Cal. 1997); *White v. Ultramar, Inc.,* 73 Cal. Rptr. 2d 262 (Cal. Ct. App. 1998). |
| CO | Yes. | Yes. | Yes. | Yes. | *Trimble v. City & County of Denver,* 697 P.2d 716 (Colo. 1985); *Thompson v. Public Serv. of Colo.,* 800 P.2d 1299 (Colo. 1990); *Lorenz v. Martin Marietta Corp., Inc.,* 802 P.2d 1146 (Colo. Ct. App. 1991), *aff'd,* 823 P.2d 100 (Colo. 1992); *Allabashi v. Lincoln Nat'l Sales Corp.,* 824 P.2d 1 (Colo. Ct. App. 1991); *Martin Marietta Corp., Inc., v. Lorenz,* 823 P.2d 100 (Colo. 1992). |
| CT | Yes. | N/R. | Yes. | Yes. | *Sheets v. Teddy's Frosted Foods, Inc.,* 427 A.2d 385 (Conn. 1980); *Hart, Nininger & Campbell Assocs., Inc. v. Rogers,* 548 A.2d 758 (Conn. App. Ct. 1988); *Lockwood v. Professional Wheelchair Transp.,* 654 A.2d 1252 (Conn. App. Ct. 1995). |
| DE | N/C. | Yes. | Yes. | No. | *Battista v. Chrysler Corp.,* 454 A.2d 286 (Del. 1982); *Gaines v. Wilmington Trust Co.,* 608 A.2d 727 (Del. 1991); *Bobson v. Gulfstream Mktg., Ltd.,* 605 A.2d 583 (Del. Super. Ct. 1992). |
| DC | Yes. | Yes. | Yes. | Yes. Only covers employee's refusal to violate a statute. | *Howard Univ. v. Best,* 484 A.2d 958 (D.C. 1984); *Newman v. Legal Servs. Corp.,* 628 F. Supp. 535 (D.D.C. 1986); *Sorrells v. Garfinckel's,* 565 A.2d 285 (D.C. 1989); *Farrington v. Bureau of Nat'l Affairs, Inc.,* 596 A.2d 58 (D.C. 1991); *Adams v. George W. Cochran & Co.,* 597 A.2d 28 (D.C. 1991); *Smith v. Union Labor Life Ins. Co.,* 620 A.2d 265 (D.C. 1993); *Kerrigan v. Britches of Georgetowne, Inc.,* 705 A.2d 624 (D.C. 1997). |

| | | | | | |
|---|---|---|---|---|---|
| FL | Yes. | Yes. | Yes. | No. | *Metropolitan Life Ins. Co. v. McCarson,* 467 So. 2d 277 (Fla. 1985); *Hartley v. Ocean Reef Club, Inc.,* 476 So. 2d 1327 (Fla. Dist. Ct. App. 1985); *Florida Power & Light Co. v. Fleitas,* 488 So. 2d 148 (Fla. Dist. Ct. App. 1986); *O'Rear v. American Family Life Assurance Co.,* 784 F. Supp. 1561 (M.D. Fla. 1992); *Stockett v. Tolin,* 791 F. Supp. 1536 (S.D. Fla. 1992); *Ross v. Twenty-Four Collection, Inc.,* 617 So. 2d 428 (Fla. Dist. Ct. App. 1993); *Wiggens v. Southern Mgmt. Corp.,* 629 So. 2d 1022 (Fla. Dist. Ct. App. 1993). |
| GA | N/C. | Yes. | No. | No. | *Monahan v. Sims,* 294 S.E.2d 548 (Ga. Ct.. App. 1982); *Cummings v. Walsh Constr. Co.,* 561 F. Supp. 872 (S.D. Ga. 1983); *Borden v. Johnson,* 395 S.E.2d 628 (Ga. Ct. App. 1990); *Moore v. Barge,* 436 S.E.2d 746 (Ga. Ct. App. 1993); *Jellico v. Effingham County,* 471 S.E.2d 36 (Ga. Ct. App. 1996). |
| HI | Yes. | N/C. | N/C. | Yes. | *Parnar v. Americana Hotels, Inc.,* 652 P.2d 625 (Haw. 1982); *Leong v. Hilton Hotels Corp.,* 689 F. Supp. 1565 (D. Haw. 1988); *Smith v. Chaney Brooks Realty, Inc.,* 865 P.2d 170 (Haw. Ct. App. 1994). |
| ID | N/C. | Yes. | Yes. | Yes. Only contract damages are available. | *Barlow v. International Harvester Co.,* 522 P.2d 1102 (Idaho 1974); *Anderson v. Farm Bureau Mut. Ins. Co.,* 732 P.2d 699 (Idaho Ct. App. 1987); *Ostrander v. Farm Bureau Mut. Ins. Co.,* 851 P.2d 946 (Idaho 1993); *Hummer v. Evans,* 923 P.2d 981 (Idaho 1996). |
| IL | Yes. | Yes. | Yes. | Yes. | *Palmateer v. International Harvester Co.,* 421 N.E.2d 876 (Ill. 1981); *Powers v. Delnor Hosp.,* 481 N.E.2d 968 (Ill. App. Ct. 1985); *Milton v. Illinois Bell Tel. Co.,* 427 N.E.2d 829 (Ill. App. Ct. 1989); *Marczak v. Drexel Nat'l Bank,* 542 N.E.2d 787 (Ill. App. Ct. 1989); *Vajda v. Arthur Andersen & Co.,* 624 N.E.2d 1343 (Ill. App. Ct. 1993); *Jacobs v. Mundelein College, Inc.,* 628 N.E.2d 201 (Ill. App. Ct. 1993); *Selof v. Island Foods, Inc.,* 623 N.E.2d 386 (Ill. App. Ct. 1993); *Shearson Lehman Bros. v. Hedrich,* 639 N.E.2d 228 (Ill. App. Ct. 1994); *Buckner v. O'Brien,* 677 N.E.2d 1363 (Ill. App. 1997). |
| IN | Yes. | Yes. | Yes. | Yes. | *Frampton v. Central Ind. Gas Co.,* 297 N.E.2d 425 (Ind. 1973); *Moffett v. Gene B. Glick Co.,* 604 F. Supp. 229 (N.D. Ind. 1984); *McClanahan v. Remington Freight Lines, Inc.,* 517 N.E.2d 390 (Ind. 1988); *Bochnowski v. Peoples Fed. Sav. & Loan Ass'n,* 571 N.E.2d 282 (Ind. 1991); *Stivers v. Stevens,* 581 N.E.2d 1253 (Ind. Ct. App. 1992); *Tacket v. Delco Remy, A Div. of GMC,* 959 F.2d 650 (7th Cir. 1992). |
| IA | Yes. | Yes. | Yes. | Yes. | *Springer v. Weeks & Leo Co.,* 429 N.W.2d 558 (Iowa 1988); *Niblo v. Parr Mfg., Inc.,* 445 N.W.2d 351 (Iowa 1989); *Knudsen v. Chicago & N.W. Transp. Co.,* 464 N.W.2d 439 (Iowa 1990); *Lara v. Thomas,* 512 N.W.2d 777 (Iowa 1994); *Huegerich v. IBP, Inc.,* 547 N.W.2d 216 (Iowa 1996); *Phipps v. IASD Health Services Corp.,* 558 N.W.2d 198 (Iowa 1997). |
| KS | Yes. | Yes. | Yes. | Yes. | *Allegri v. Providence-St. Margaret Health Ctr.,* 684 P.2d 1031 (Kan. Ct. App. 1984); *Collins v. MBPXL Corp.,* 679 P.2d 746 (Kan. Ct. App. 1984); *Turner v. Halliburton Co.,* 722 P.2d 1106 (Kan. 1986); *Taiwo v. Vu,* 822 P.2d 1024 (Kan. 1991); *Rupp v. Purolator Courier Corp.,* 790 F. Supp. 1069 (D. Kan. 1992); *Laughinghouse v. Risser,* 786 F. Supp. 920 (D. Kan. 1992); *Source Direct, Inc. v. Mantell,* 870 P.2d 686 (Kan. Ct. App. 1994); *Dickens v. Snodgrass, Dunlap & Co.,* 872 P.2d 252 (Kan. 1994); *Ortega v. IBP, Inc.,* 874 P.2d 1188 (Kan. 1994). |
| KY | N/C. | N/C. | Yes. | Yes. | *Pari-Mutuel Clerks' Union of Ky. v. Kentucky Jockey Club,* 551 S.W.2d 801 (Ky. 1977); *Cullen v. South E. Coal Co.,* 685 S.W.2d 187 (Ky. Ct. App. 1984); *Wyant v. SCM Corp.,* 692 S.W.2d 814 (Ky. Ct. App. 1985). |

*(Table continues.)*

# Table 4.3-1 *(cont'd)*

## CAUSES OF ACTION FOR WRONGFUL DISCHARGE BASED ON TORT THEORIES

(See also text at § 4.3.)

**KEY:** **Violation of Public Policy.** Although the courts generally construe discharge in violation of public policy to be a violation of an implied-in-law contract, they usually allow tort remedies, including punitive damages and a right to a jury trial.
**N/C.** No court case has been issued so far.
**N/R.** No ruling. The highest court of the state has not clearly expressed its position on this issue, and either the lower courts are divided or the federal courts, interpreting state law, are the only courts to have issued a decision.

| | *Intentional Infliction of Emotional Distress* | *Interference with Contractual Relations* | *Defamation* | *Violation of Public Policy* | *Citations to Authority* |
|---|---|---|---|---|---|
| LA | Yes. | N/R. | Yes. | No. | *Steadman v. South Cent. Bell Tel. Co.,* 362 So. 2d 1144 (La. Ct. App. 1978); *Gil v. Metal Serv. Corp.,* 412 So. 2d 706 (La. Ct. App. 1982); *Martinez v. United States Fidelity & Guar.,* 412 So. 2d 109 (La. Ct. App. 1982), *aff'd,* 423 So. 2d 1088 (La. 1982); *Breaux v. South La. Elec. Coop. Ass'n,* 471 So. 2d 967 (La. Ct. App. 1985); *Baton Rouge Bldg. & Constr. Trades Council v. Jacobs Constructors, Inc.,* 804 F.2d 879 (5th Cir. 1986); *Juneau v. Avoyelles Parish Police Jury,* 482 So. 2d 1022 (La. Ct. App. 1986); *Rouly v. Enserch Corp.,* 835 F.2d 1127 (5th Cir. 1988); *Engrum v. Boise S. Co.,* 527 So. 2d 362 (La. Ct. App. 1988); *9 to 5 Fashions, Inc., v. Spurney,* 538 So. 2d 228 (La. 1989); *Herbert v. Placid Ref. Co.,* 564 So. 2d 371 (La. Ct. App. 1990); *Williams v. Touro Infirmary,* 578 So. 2d 1006 (La. Ct. App. 1990); *Martin v. Lincoln Gen. Hosp.,* 588 So. 2d 1329 (La. Ct. App. 1991); *Colbert v. B.F. Carvin Constr.,* 600 So. 2d 719 (La. Ct. App. 1992); *Prevost v. Eye Care and Surgery Ctr.,* 635 So. 2d 765 (La. Ct. App. 1994); *Stevenson v. Lavalco, Inc.,* 669 So. 2d 608 (La. 1996). |
| ME | N/C. | N/C. | Yes. | N/C. | *Heselton v. Wilder,* 496 A.2d 1063 (Me. 1985); *Pombriant v. Blue Cross/Blue Shield of Me.,* 562 A.2d 656 (Me. 1989); *Staples v. Bangor Hydro-Elec. Co.,* 561 A.2d 499 (Me. 1989). |
| MD | Yes. | N/C. | Yes. | Yes. | *Harris v. Jones,* 281 Md. 560, 380 A.2d 611 (Md. 1977); *Adler v. American Standard Corp.,* 596 A.2d 1069 (Md. 1981); *Adler v. American Standard Corp.,* 291 Md. 31, 432 A.2d 464 (Md. 1981); *Adler v. American Standard Corp.,* 538 F. Supp. 572 (D. Md. 1982); *Exxon Corp., USA v. Schoene,* 67 Md. 412, 508 A.2d 142 (Md. 1986); *Adler v. American Standard Corp.,* 830 F.2d 1303 (4th Cir. 1987); *Hanna v. Emergency Medicine Assocs., P.A.,* 551 A.2d 492 (Md. 1989); *Watson v. Peoples Sec. Life Ins. Co.,* 588 A.2d 760 (Md. 1991); *Batson v. Shiflett,* 602 A.2d 1191 (Md. 1992); *Caldor v. Bowden,* 625 A.2d 959 (Md. 1993); *Bleich v. Florence Crittenton Servs. of Baltimore, Inc.,* 632 A.2d 463 (Md. 1993); *Brandon v. Molesworth,* 672 A.2d 608 (Md. 1996). |

| | | | | | |
|---|---|---|---|---|---|
| MA | Yes. | Yes. | Yes. | Yes. | *Agis v. Howard Johnson Co.,* 371 Mass. 140, 355 N.E.2d 315 (Mass. 1976); *Madsen v. Erwin,* 395 Mass. 715, 481 N.E.2d 1160 (Mass. 1985); *DeRose v. Putnam Mgmt. Co.,* 496 N.E.2d 428 (Mass. 1986); *Mailhiot v. Liberty Bank & Trust Co.,* 24 Mass. 525, 510 N.E.2d 773 (Mass. 1987); *Mendez v. M.S. Walker, Inc.,* 26 Mass. 431, 528 N.E.2d 891 (Mass. 1988); *St. Clair v. Trustees of Boston Univ.,* 25 Mass. 662, 521 N.E.2d 1044 (Mass. 1988); *Hobson v. McLean Hosp. Corp.,* 422 Mass. 413, 522 N.E.2d 975 (Mass. 1988); *Norris v. Lumbermen's Mut. Casualty Co.,* 881 F.2d 1144 (1st Cir. 1989); *Flesner v. Technical Communications Corp.,* 575 N.E.2d 1107 (Mass. 1991); *Bergeson v. Franchi,* 783 F. Supp. 713 (D. Mass. 1992); *Wright v. Shriners Hosp. for Crippled Children,* 589 N.E.2d 1241 (Mass. 1992); *Mistishen v. Falcone Piano Co., Inc.,* 630 N.E.2d 294 (Mass. App. Ct. 1994); *Smith v. Mitre Corp.,* 949 F.Supp. 943 (D. Mass. 1997); *Upton v. JWP Businessland,* 682 N.E.2d 1357 (Mass. 1997); *Shea v. Emmanuel College,* 682 N.E.2d 1348 (Mass. 1997). |
| MI | N/R. | Yes. | Yes. | Yes. | *Sventko v. Kroger Co.,* 245 N.W.2d 151 (Mich. 1976); *Trombetta v. Detroit, Toledo & Ironton R.R.,* 265 N.W.2d 385 (Mich. Ct. App. 1978); *Suchodolski v. Michigan Consol. Gas Co.,* 316 N.W.2d 710 (Mich. 1982); *Watassek v. Michigan Dep't of Mental Health,* 372 N.W.2d 617 (Mich. 1985), *leave to appeal denied,* 424 Mich. 878 (1986); *Cockels v. International Business Expositions, Inc.,* 406 N.W.2d 465 (Mich. Ct. App. 1987); *Henry v. Hospital & Health Servs. Credit Union,* 416 N.W.2d 338 (Mich. Ct. App. 1987); *Sankar v. Detroit Bd. of Educ.,* 409 N.W.2d 213 (Mich. Ct. App. 1987); *Postell-Russell v. Inmont Corp.,* 691 F. Supp. 1 (E.D. Mich. 1988); *Pratt v. Brown Mach. Co.,* 855 F.2d 1225 (6th Cir. 1988); *Shannon v. Taylor AMC/Jeep, Inc.,* 245 N.W.2d 165 (Mich. Ct. App. 1988); *Smith v. Fergan,* 450 N.W.2d 3 (Mich. Ct. App. 1989); *Baughey v. Tecumseh Country Club, Inc.,* 778 F. Supp. 354 (E.D. Mich. 1991), *aff'd,* 1 F.3d 1240 (6th Cir. 1993); *Coleman-Nichols v. Tixon Corp.,* 513 N.W. 2d 441 (Mich. Ct. App. 1994); *Bradley v. Philip Morris Inc.,* 513 N.W.2d 797 (Mich. 1994); *Dolan v. Continental Airlines,* 526 N.W.2d 922 (Mich. Ct. App. 1995); *Phinney v. Perimutter,* 564 N.W.2d 532 (Mich. App. 1997). |
| MN | Yes. | Yes. | Yes. | Yes. | *Grouse v. Group Health Plan & Inc.,* 306 N.W.2d 114 (Minn. 1981); *Hubbard v. United Press Int'l, Inc.,* 330 N.W.2d 428 (Minn. 1983); *Brevik v. Kite Painting, Inc.,* 416 N.W.2d 714 (Minn. 1987); *Phipps v. Clark Oil & Ref. Corp.,* 408 N.W.2d 569 (Minn. 1987); *Vonch v. Carlson Cos.,* 439 N.W.2d 406 (Minn. 1989); *Knudsen v. Northwest Airlines, Inc.,* 437 N.W.2d 733 (Minn. Ct. App. 1989), *rev'd,* 450 N.W.2d 131 (Minn. 1990); *Nordling v. Northern States Power Co.,* 478 N.W.2d 498 (Minn. 1991); *Huyen v. Driscoll,* 479 N.W.2d 76 (Minn. Ct. App. 1991); *McGrath v. TCF Bank Sav.,* 509 N.W.2d 365 (Minn. 1993). |
| MS | Yes. | No. | Yes. | Yes. | *Vestal v. Oden,* 500 So. 2d 954 (Miss. 1986); *Laws v. Aetna Fin. Co.,* 667 F. Supp. 342 (N.D. Miss. 1987); *Soulsberry v. Atlantic Richfield Co.,* 673 F. Supp. 811 (Miss. 1987); *Garziano v. E.I. duPont de Nemours,* 818 F.2d 380 (5th Cir. 1987); *Perry v. Sears, Roebuck & Co.,* 508 So. 2d 1086 (Miss. 1987); *Staheli v. Smith,* 548 So. 2d 1299 (Miss. 1989); *McArn v. Allied Bruce-Terminix Co., Inc.,* 626 So. 2d 603 (Miss. 1993). |
| MO | No. | Yes. | N/C. | Yes. | *Boyle v. Vista Eyewear, Inc.,* 700 S.W.2d 859 (Mo. Ct. App. 1985); *Beasley v. Affiliated Hosp. Prods.,* 713 S.W.2d 557 (Mo. 1986); *Burger v. McGilley Memorial Chapels, Inc.,* 856 F.2d 1046 (8th Cir. 1988); *Yow v. Village of Eolia,* 859 S.W.2d 920 (Mo. Ct. App. 1993); *Lay v. St. Louis Helicopter Airways, Inc.,* 869 S.W.2d 173 (Mo. Ct. App. 1993); *Fields v. R.S.C.D.B., Inc.,* 865 S.W.2d 877 (Mo. Ct. App. 1993); *Clark v. Beverly Enters.-Missouri, Inc.,* 872 S.W.2d 522 (Mo. Ct. App. 1994); *Faust v. Ryder Commercial Leasing & Services,* 954 S.W.2d 383 (Mo. Ct. App. 1997). |

*(Table continues.)*

# Table 4.3-1 *(cont'd)*

## CAUSES OF ACTION FOR WRONGFUL DISCHARGE BASED ON TORT THEORIES

(See also text at § 4.3.)

**KEY:** **Violation of Public Policy.** Although the courts generally construe discharge in violation of public policy to be a violation of an implied-in-law contract, they usually allow tort remedies, including punitive damages and a right to a jury trial.
**N/C.** No court case has been issued so far.
**N/R.** No ruling. The highest court of the state has not clearly expressed its position on this issue, and either the lower courts are divided or the federal courts, interpreting state law, are the only courts to have issued a decision.

| | *Intentional Infliction of Emotional Distress* | *Interference with Contractual Relations* | *Defamation* | *Violation of Public Policy* | *Citations to Authority* |
|---|---|---|---|---|---|
| MT | Cause of action is preempted because a 1987 Montana statute protects at-will employees from discharge without cause; in retaliation for refusing to violate public policy or reporting a public policy violation; and for a violation of handbook rules (for example, the employer did not follow disciplinary procedure). | See "Intentional Infliction of Emotional Distress." | See "Intentional Infliction of Emotional Distress." | See "Intentional Infliction of Emotional Distress." | Mont. Code Ann. §§ 39-2-901 *et seq.*; *Harrison v. Chance,* 797 P.2d 200 (Mont. 1990); *Cummings v. Town of Plains,* 790 P.2d 486 (Mont. 1990); *Dagel v. City of Great Falls,* 819 P.2d 186 (Mont. 1991); *Lueck v. United Parcel Serv.,* 851 P.2d 1041 (Mont. 1993); *Kestell v. Heritage Health Care Corp.,* 858 P.2d 3 (Mont. 1993). |
| NE | N/C. | Yes. | N/C. | Yes. | *John R. Johnston v. Panhandle Coop. Ass'n,* 408 N.W.2d 261(Neb. 1987); *White v. Ardan, Inc.,* 430 N.W.2d 27 (Neb. 1988); *Hoschler v. Kozlik,* 529 N.W.2d 822 (Neb. Ct. App. 1995). |
| NV | Yes. | No. | N/R. | Yes. | *Moen v. Las Vegas Int'l Hotel, Inc.,* 521 P.2d 370 (Nev. 1974); *D'Angelo v. Gardner,* 819 P.2d 206 (Nev. 1991); *Falline v. GNLV Corp.,* 823 P.2d 888 (Nev. 1991); *Brooks v. Hilton Casinos, Inc.,* 959 F.2d 757 (9th Cir. 1992); *Blankenship v. O'Sullivan Plastics Corp.,* 866 P.2d 293 (Nev. 1993); *Shoen v. Amerco, Inc.,* 896 P.2d 469 (Nev. 1995). |
| NH | N/C. | Yes. | Yes. | Yes. | *Jespersen v. United States Fidelity & Guar. Co.,* 551 A.2d 530 (N.H. 1988); *Demetracopoulos v. Wilson,* 640 A.2d 279 (N.H. 1994). |
| NJ | Yes. | Yes. | Yes. | Yes. | *Noye v. Hoffmann-LaRoche Inc.,* 570 A.2d 12 (N.J. Super. Ct. App. Div. 1990), *cert. denied,* 584 A.2d 218 (N.J. 1990); *Fleming v. United Parcel Serv., Inc.,* 604 A.2d 657 (N.J. Super. Ct. Law Div. 1992), *aff'd,* 642 A.2d 1029 (N.J. Super. Ct. App. Div. 1994); *D'Agostino v. Johnson & Johnson, Inc.,* 628 A.2d 305 (N.J. 1993); *Haworth v. Deborah Heart and Lung Ctr.,* 638 A.2d 1354 (N.J. Super. Ct. App. Div. 1994); *Stehney v. Perry,* 101 F.3d 925 (3rd Cir. 1996); *Chelly v. Knoll Pharmaceuticals,* 685 A.2d 498 (N.J. Super. Ct. App. Div. 1996). |

| | | | | | |
|---|---|---|---|---|---|
| NM | N/R. | N/C. | N/C. | Yes. | *Melnick v. State Farm Mut. Auto. Ins. Co.*, 749 P.2d 1105 (N.M. 1988); *Newberry v. Allied Stores, Inc.*, 773 P.2d 1231 (N.M. 1989); *Bouie v. Autozone, Inc.*, 959 F.2d 875 (10th Cir. 1992); *Shovelin v. Central N.M. Elec. Coop.*, 850 P.2d 996 (N.M. 1993); *Lihosit v. I & W Inc.*, 913 P.2d 262 (N.M. Ct. App. 1996). |
| NY | No. | Yes. | Yes. | No. | *Fletcher v. Greiner,* 435 N.Y.S.2d 1005 (1980); *Murphy v. American Home Prods. Corp.*, 558 N.Y.S.2d 920 (1990); *Masten v. C.D.I. Travel, Inc.*, 577 N.Y.S.2d 59 (1991); *Petri v. Bank of N.Y.*, 582 N.Y.S.2d 608 (Sup. Ct. 1992); *Hurwitch v. Kercull,* 582 N.Y.S.2d 568 (App. Div. 1992); *Blatman v. Paribus North America, Inc.*, 604 N.Y.S.2d 70 (App. Div. 1993); *McDowell v. Dart,* 607 N.Y.S.2d 755 (App. Div. 1994); *Tramondo v. Playboy Enterprises, Inc.*, 609 N.Y.S.2d 124 (App. Div. 1994); *Kosson v. Algaze,* 610 N.Y.S.2d 227 (App. Div. 1994); *Ullman v. Norma Kamali, Inc.*, 616 N.Y.S.2d 583 (App. Div. 1994). |
| NC | Yes. | Yes. | Yes. | Yes. | *Sides v. Duke Univ.*, 328 S.E.2d 818 (N.C. Ct. App. 1985); *Hogan v. Forsyth Country Club Co.*, 340 S.E.2d 116 (N.C. 1986); *Shreve v. Duke Power Co.*, 354 S.E.2d 357 (N.C. 1987); *Williams v. Hillhaven Corp.*, 370 S.E.2d 423 (N.C. Ct. App. 1988); *Amos v. Oakdale Knitting Co.*, 416 S.E.2d 166 (N.C. 1992); *Daniel v. Carolina Sunrock Corp.*, 430 S.E.2d 306 (N.C. Ct. App. 1993), *rev'd* 436 S.E.2d 835 (N.C. 1993); *McMurry v. Cochrane Furniture Co.*, 425 S.E.2d 735 (N.C. Ct. App. 1993); *Boesche v. Raleigh-Durham Airport Auth.*, 432 S.E.2d 137 (N.C. Ct. App. 1993), *appeal dismissed,* 442 S.E.2d 320 (N.C. 1994); *Liggett Group, Inc. v. Sunas,* 437 S.E.2d 674 (N.C. Ct. App. 1993); *Wagoner v. Elkin City Schools' Board of Education,* 440 S.E.2d 119 (N.C. Ct. App. 1994); *Long v. Vertical Technologies, Inc.*, 439 S.E.2d 797 (N.C. Ct. App. 1994); *Vereen v. Holden,* 468 S.E.2d 471 (N.C. 1996); *Roberts v. First-Citizens Bank and Trust Co.*, 478 S.E.2d 809 (N.C. App. 1996). |
| ND | Yes. | N/C. | Yes. | Yes. | *Sadler v. Basin Elec. Power Coop.*, 431 N.W.2d 296 (N.D. 1988); *Soentgen v. Quain & Ramstad Clinic, P.C.*, 467 N.W.2d 73 (N.D. 1991); *Rykowsky v. Dickinson Public School Dist. No. 1,* 508 N.W.2d 348 (N.D. 1993); *Hummel v. Mid-Dakota Clinic, P.C.* 526 N.W.2d 704 (N.D. 1995). |
| OH | Yes. | N/C. | N/C. | Yes. | *Deoma v. City of Shaker Heights,* 587 N.E.2d 425 (Ohio 1990); *Tulloh v. Goodyear Atomic Corp.*, 584 N.E.2d 729 (Ohio 1992); *Stephenson v. Litton Sys., Inc.*, 646 N.E.2d 259 (Ohio Ct. App. 1994); *Juergens v. Strang, Klubnik & Assocs.*, 644 N.E.2d 1066 (Ohio Ct. App. 1994); *Delaney v. Skyline Lodge, Inc.*, 642 N.E.2d 395 (Ohio Ct. App. 1994); *Kramer v. Windsor Park Nursing Home, Inc.*, 943 F. Supp. 844 (D. Ohio 1996); *Moore v. Animal Fair Pet Ctr., Inc.*, 674 N.E.2d 1269 (Ohio Com. Pl. 1995); *Kulch v. Structural Fibers, Inc.*, 677 N.E.2d 308 (Ohio 1997). |
| OK | N/R. | N/C. | N/C. | Yes. | *Burk v. K-Mart Corp.*, 770 P.2d 24 (Okla. 1989); *Guinn v. Church of Christ,* 775 P.2d 766 (Okla. 1989); *Grace v. Foster,* 880 P.2d 902 (Okla. 1994); *Gilmore v. Enogex, Inc.*, 878 P.2d 360 (Okla. 1994); *Griffin v. Mullinix,* 947 P.2d 177 (Okla. 1997). |
| OR | Yes. | Yes. | N/R. | Yes. | *Sheets v. Knight,* 779 P.2d 1000 (Or. 1989); *Madani v. Kendall Ford, Inc.*, 818 P.2d 930 (Or. 1991); *Holien v. Sears, Roebuck & Co.*, 689 P.2d 1292 (Or. 1992); *McGanty v. Staudenraus,* 859 P.2d 1187 (Or. Ct. App. 1993); *Dalby v. Sisters of Providence In Or.*, 865 P.2d 391 (Or. Ct. App. 1993); *Anderson v. Evergreen Int'l Airlines,* 886 P.2d 1068 (Or. Ct. App. 1994); *Schram v. Albertson's Inc.*, 934 P.2d 483 (Or. App. 1997). |

*(Table continues.)*

# Table 4.3-1 *(cont'd)*
## CAUSES OF ACTION FOR WRONGFUL DISCHARGE BASED ON TORT THEORIES

(See also text at § 4.3.)

**KEY:** **Violation of Public Policy.** Although the courts generally construe discharge in violation of public policy to be a violation of an implied-in-law contract, they usually allow tort remedies, including punitive damages and a right to a jury trial.
**N/C.** No court case has been issued so far.
**N/R.** No ruling. The highest court of the state has not clearly expressed its position on this issue, and either the lower courts are divided or the federal courts, interpreting state law, are the only courts to have issued a decision.

| | *Intentional Infliction of Emotional Distress* | *Interference with Contractual Relations* | *Defamation* | *Violation of Public Policy* | *Citations to Authority* |
|---|---|---|---|---|---|
| PA | Yes. | Yes. | Yes. | Yes. | *Schweitzer v. Rockwell Int'l,* 586 A.2d 383 (Pa. 1990); *Paul v. Lankenau Hosp.,* 569 A.2d 346 (Pa. 1990); *Biborosch v. Transamerican Ins. Co.,* 603 A.2d 1050 (Pa. Super. Ct. 1992), *alloc. denied,* 615 A.2d 1310 (Pa. 1992); *Jacques v. Akzo Int'l Salt, Inc.,* 619 A.2d 748 (Pa. Super. Ct. 1993); *Kroen v. Bedway Sec. Agency, Inc.,* 633 A.2d 628 (Pa. Super. Ct. 1993); *Walker v. Grand Cent. Sanitation, Inc.,* 634 A.2d 237 (Pa. Super. Ct. 1993); *Holewinski v. Children's Hosp. of Pittsburgh,* 649 A.2d 712 (Pa. Super. Ct. 1994); *Perry v. Tioga County,* 649 A.2d 186 (Pa. Commw. Ct. 1994); *Rank v. Township of Annville,* 641 A.2d 667 (Pa. Commw. Ct. 1994). |
| RI | No. | No. | No. | No. | *Pacheo v. Raytheon Co.,* 623 A.2d 464 (R.I. 1993). |
| SC | N/R. | Yes. | N/C. | Yes. | *Moody v. McLellan,* 367 S.E.2d 449 (S.C. 1988). |
| SD | Yes. | N/C. | Yes. | Yes. | *Blote v. First Fed. Sav. & Loan Ass'n,* 422 N.W.2d 834 (S.D. 1988); *Finck v. City of Tea,* 443 N.W.2d 632 (S.D. 1989); *Niesent v. Homestake Min. Co. of California,* 505 N.W.2d 781 (S.D. 1993); *Bass v. Happy Rest, Inc.,* 507 N.W.2d 317 (S.D. 1993); *Nelson v. WEB Water Development Ass'n Inc.,* 507 N.W.2d 691 (S.D. 1993); *Richardson v. East River Elec. Power Co-op.,* 531 N.W.2d 23 (S.D. 1995). |
| TN | No. | No. | No. | Yes. | *Stewart v. Peterson,* 1988 WL 130313 (Tenn. 1988); *Watson v. Cleveland Chair Co.,* 789 S.W.2d 538 (Tenn. 1989); *Reynolds v. Ozark Motor Lines,* 887 S.W.2d 822 (Tenn. 1994); *Weber v. Moses,* 938 S.W.2d 387 (Tenn. 1996). |
| TX | Yes. | Yes, except at-will employee cannot bring this cause of action. | Yes. | Yes. Applies when employee is discharged for refusing to commit an illegal act and when employee is discharged primarily so that employer can avoid contributing to or paying benefits from a pension fund. | *Berry v. Doctor's Health Facilities,* 715 S.W.2d 60 (Tex. 1986); *Casas v. Wornick Co.,* 818 S.W. 2d 466 (Tex. Ct. App. 1991), *rev'd,* 856 S.W.2d 732 (Tex. 1993); *Exxon Corp. v. Allsup,* 808 S.W.2d 648 (Tex. Ct. App. 1991); *Einhorn v. LaChance,* 823 S.W.2d 405 (Tex. Ct. App. 1992); *Amador v. Tan,* 855 S.W.2d 131 (Tex. Ct. App. 1993); *Farrington v. Sysco Food Servs., Inc.,* 865 S.W.2d 247 (Tex. Ct. App. 1993); *Burgess v. El Paso Cancer Treatment Ctr.,* 881 S.W.2d 552 (Tex. Ct. App. 1994); *Vida v. El Paso Employees' Fed. Credit Union,* 885 S.W.2d 177 (Tex. Ct. App. 1994); *Higginbotham v. Allwaste, Inc.,* 889 S.W.2d 411 (Tex. Ct. App. 1994); *Hussong v. Schwan's Sales Enters.,* 896 S.W.2d 320 (Tex. Ct. App. 1995). |

| | | | | | |
|---|---|---|---|---|---|
| UT | Yes. | N/C. | N/C. | Yes. | *Brehany v. Nordstrom, Inc.*, 812 P.2d 47 (Utah 1991); *Winter v. Northwest Pipeline Corp.*, 820 P.2d 916 (Utah 1991); *Johnson v. Morton Thiokol, Inc.*, 818 P.2d 997 (Utah 1991); *Peterson v. Browning*, 832 P.2d 1280 (Utah 1992); *Dubois v. Grand Central*, 872 P.2d 1073 (Utah Ct. App. 1994). |
| VT | Yes. | Yes. | Yes. | Yes. | *Crump v. PC Food Mkts., Inc.*, 576 A.2d 441 (Vt. 1990); *Trepanier v. Getting Organized, Inc.*, 583 A.2d 583 (Vt. 1990); *Gallipo v. City of Rutland*, 656 A.2d 635 (Vt. 1994). |
| VA | Yes. | Yes. | Yes. | Yes. | *Federal Land Bank v. Birchfield*, 3 S.E.2d 405 (Va. 1939); *Chesapeake & Potomac Tel. Co. v. Dowdy*, 365 S.E.2d 751 (Va. 1988); *Elliott v. Shore Stop, Inc.*, 384 S.E.2d 752 (Va. 1989); *Snead v. Harbaugh*, 404 S.E.2d 53 (Va. 1991); *Lockhart v. Commonwealth Educ. Systems Corp.*, 439 S.E.2d 328 (Va. 1994); *Milton v. IIT Research Institute*, 138 F.3d 519 (4th Cir. 1998). |
| WA | N/C. | Yes. | Yes. | Yes. | *Messerly v. Asamera Minerals (U.S.) Inc.*, 780 P.2d 1327 (Wash. 1989); *Gaglidari v. Denny's Restaurants, Inc.*, 815 P.2d 1362 (Wash. 1991); *Lambert v. Morehouse*, 843 P.2d 1116 (Wash. Ct. App. 1993); *Bravo v. Dolsen Companies*, 888 P.2d 147 (Wash. 1995); *White v. State*, 929 P.2d 396 (Wash. 1997); *Reninger v. State Dept. of Corrections*, 951 P.2d 782 (Wash. 1998); *Wilson v. City of Monroe*, 490 S.E.2d 23 (Wash. Ct. App. 1997); *Anaya v. Graham*, 950 P.2d 16 (Wash. Ct. App. 1998). |
| WV | Yes. | Yes. | N/C. | Yes. | *Wiggins v. Eastern Associated Coal Corp.*, 357 S.E.2d 745 (W. Va. 1987); *Truman v. Farmers & Merchants Bank*, 375 S.E.2d 765 (W. Va. 1988); *Bowe v. Charleston Area Medical Ctr.*, 428 S.E.2d 773 (W. Va. 1993); *Hines v. Hills Dept. Stores*, 454 S.E.2d 385 (W. Va. 1994). |
| WI | Yes. | Yes. | Yes. | Yes. | *Bushko v. Miller Brewing Co.*, 396 N.W.2d 167 (Wis. 1986); *Garvey v. Buhler*, 430 N.W.2d 616 (Wis. 1988); *Zinda v. Louisiana Pac. Corp.*, 440 N.W.2d 548 (Wis. 1989); *Olson v. 3M Co.*, 523 N.W.2d 578 (Wis. Ct. App. 1994). |
| WY | Yes. | Yes. | N/C. | Yes. | *Town of Upton v. Whisler*, 824 P.2d 545 (Wyo. 1992); *Wilder v. Cody Country Chamber of Commerce*, 868 P.2d 211 (Wyo. 1994); *Hermreck v. United Postal Service*, 938 P.2d 863 (Wyo. 1997); *Townsend v. Living Centers Rocky Mountain, Inc.*, 947 P.2d 1297 (Wyo. 1997). |

# § 4.4 Causes of Action for Wrongful Discharge Based on Public Policy Violations

## [a] Public Policy

Underlying all public policy is the principle that no individual can lawfully engage in any activity that might be injurious to the public or detrimental to public welfare. Public policy, as established by federal and state laws and by court decisions, generally encompasses four broad categories of conduct:

1. Refusing to commit illegal or unethical acts;
2. Performing a legal duty (military service or jury duty);
3. Exercising legal rights (filing for workers' compensation, reporting unfair labor practices, or voting); and
4. Whistle-blowing (reporting employers for safety, health, or statutory violations).

Public policy exceptions to at-will employment are grounded in the belief that the law should not allow employees to be dismissed for engaging in activities beneficial to the public welfare—for instance, for opposing an employer's illegal activities. In determining whether a public policy overrides the employment-at-will rule, some courts have focused on the degree of interference with public concerns. Table 4.4-1 shows areas in which cases have been made for particular public policy violations in the various states.

## [b] Public Policy Against Discrimination

Many courts have considered the issue of whether the public policy expressed in a state fair employment practices (FEP) statute can support an exception to the at-will doctrine. (See Part 2 for specific information about state FEP laws.) There is presently, however, no consensus regarding whether such FEP laws give rise to a public policy cause of action. Moreover, there is some disagreement regarding what particular types of discrimination can be remedied by way of such a public policy cause of action. Table 4.4-2 sets out the current state of the law as revealed by reported court decisions.

*Discrimination Claims Against Small Employers.* The availability of a public policy cause of action based on discrimination presents a potential clash between the legislative and judicial branches of state governments. As indicated in Table 2.3-4, most state FEP laws apply only to employers with a certain minimum number of employees. By extending the coverage of these laws only to employers with a certain number of employees, state legislatures clearly intended to exempt employers with fewer employees. Recognizing a cause of action for wrongful discharge based on the public policy expressed in these statutes is essentially an "end run" around the number-of-employees requirement imposed by state legislatures. The result is that small employers, usually those with fewer than 15 employees, may face judicially created exposure to employment discrimination suits.

The Virginia Supreme Court, for example, has held that employment discrimination based on race is a sufficient breach of public policy to allow a claim of wrongful discharge.[1] The courts of Ohio[2] and Maryland have

**§ 4.4**

1. Lockhart v. Commonwealth Educ. Sys. Corp., 247 Va. 98, 439 S.E.2d 328 (1994).
2. Collins v. Rizkana, 652 N.E.2d 653 (Ohio 1995).

recognized the viability of similar claims.[3] In *Brandon v. Molesworth,* a discharged veterinarian brought a wrongful discharge action based on the public policy against sex discrimination in employment decisions articulated in the state's Fair Employment Practices Act (FEP Act). The employer argued that because he employed fewer than 15 people, which is a threshold requirement for the application of the Maryland FEP Act, he was exempt from the statute's enforcement provisions and its statement of policy. The court held that although the employee could not bring suit under the FEP Act itself because the employer did not have the requisite number of employees, the statute did not exempt small businesses from its policy against employment discrimination.[4] The employee could therefore use the FEP Act as a basis for the public policy exception even though the FEP Act's procedural requirements and enforcement mechanisms did not apply to the employer.[5]

Reversing the holding of the intermediate appellate court, the California Supreme Court held[6] that the public policy against discrimination was inseparable from the terms of the antidiscrimination statute and its definition of an employer; thus, the statute did not provide the basis for a fundamental public policy against discrimination by an employer with fewer than five employees.

As a recent decision from an intermediate appellate court reveals, however, a public policy discrimination claim is not foreclosed in California. In *Badih v. Myers,*[7] the court held that an employee could maintain an action for wrongful discharge in violation of public policy, based on her alleged discharge because of her pregnancy; although the employer was not subject to California's Fair Employment and Housing Act, because it employed fewer than five individuals, the necessary public policy could be found in the California constitution's prohibition against sex discrimination.

In some states, the public policy exception can be used only as a vehicle for discrimination claims if there is no other remedy available.[8]

In addition, if a state statute prohibiting the type of discrimination alleged states that it is the exclusive remedy, a public policy cause of action will be foreclosed. For example, in *Mannell v. American Tobacco Co.,*[9] the plaintiff alleged that she was wrongfully discharged in violation of the public policy against disability discrimination. The court dismissed the wrongful discharge claim on the basis that the Virginians with Disabilities Act (VDA) "is the statement of Virginia's public policy against disability discrimination" and that the VDA is "the exclusive state remedy for employment discrimination based on disability."[10] The court based its holding on the fact that the VDA, which constituted the statement of Virginia's public policy against disability discrimination, expressly stated that " 'the relief available for violations of this chapter shall be limited to the relief set forth in this section.' "[11]

The momentum in the courts seems to be toward expanding the public policy exception to the at-will rule. Thus, even for an employer in a state that does not provide a private remedy for employment discrimination, the state courts may recognize a public policy cause of action based on a state statute or constitutional provision.

---

3. Brandon v. Molesworth, 655 A.2d 1292 (Md. Ct. Spec. App. 1995), aff'd in pertinent part, 668 A.2d 1002 (Md. 1996).

4. Id. at 1301.

5. Id.

6. Jennings v. Marralle, 32 Cal. Rptr. 2d 275, 876 P.2d 1074 (1994).

7. 36 Cal. App. 4th 1289, 43 Cal. Rptr. 2d 229 (1995).

8. *See, e.g.,* Childers v. Chesapeake and Potomac Tel. Co. of Virginia, 881 F.2d 1259 (4th Cir. 1989). *See also* Kerrigan v. Magnum Entertainment, Inc., 804 F. Supp. 733 (D. Md. 1992) (stating that, although public policy claim could be brought in the absence of state remedy, where state provided private remedy for discrimination no wrongful discharge claim could be pursued).

9. 871 F. Supp. 854 (E.D. Va. 1994).

10. Id. at 862.

11. Id. (quoting Va. Code Ann. § 51.5-46).

# Table 4.4-1
## CAUSES OF ACTION FOR WRONGFUL DISCHARGE BASED ON PUBLIC POLICY VIOLATIONS

(This table excludes cause of action created by the statute itself. See also text at § 4.4.)

**KEY:** **N/C.** No court case has been issued so far.
**N/R.** No ruling. The highest court of the state has not clearly expressed its position on this issue, and either the lower courts are divided or the federal courts, interpreting state law, are the only courts to have issued a decision.

| | *For Jury Service, Military Service, and Voting* | *For Filing Workers' Compensation Claims* | *For Exercising Rights Under Federal or State Health and Safety Laws* | *For Whistle-Blowing* | *For Exercising Rights Under Federal or State Constitution* | *For Exercising Rights Under Fair Employment Laws* | *Citations to Authority* |
|---|---|---|---|---|---|---|---|
| AL | N/C. | N/C. | N/C. | N/C. | N/C. | N/C. | Statutory causes of action only. *See Twilley v. Daubert Coated Prods., Inc.*, 536 So. 2d 1364 (Ala. 1988); *Grant v. Butler,* 590 So. 2d 254 (Ala. 1991); *Lozier Corp. v. Gray,* 624 So. 2d 1034 (Ala. 1993); *Morgan v. Northeast Alabama Regional Medical Ctr.*, 624 So. 2d 560 (Ala. 1993); *Graham v. Shoals Distributing Inc.*, 630 So. 2d 417 (Ala. 1993); *White v. Midtown Restaurant Corp.*, 632 So. 2d 1330 (Ala. 1994); *S & D Griner, Inc., v. Colwell,* 671 So. 2d 690 (Ala. Cir. App. 1995); *Motion Industries, Inc. v. Pate*, 678 So. 2d 724 (Ala. 1996); *Golson v. Montgomery Coca-Cola Bottling Co., Ltd.*, 680 So. 2d 304 (Ala. Civ. App. 1996); *Rowe v. Wood Associates, Inc.*, 695 So. 2d 1210 (Ala. Cir. App. 1997). |
| AK | N/C. | N/C. | N/C. | Yes. | N/C. | N/C. | Alaska Stat. §§ 18.60.010–18.60.105; *Reed v. Municipality of Anchorage,* 782 P.2d 1155 (Alaska 1989). |
| AZ | N/C. | Yes. | No. | Yes. | No. | N/C. | *Wagner v. Globe,* 722 P.2d 250 (Ariz. 1986); *Douglas v. Wilson,* 774 P.2d 1356 (Ariz. Ct. App. 1989); *Olguin v. Inspiration Consol. Copper Co.,* 740 F.2d 1468 (9th Cir. 1984); *Thompson v. Better-Bilt Aluminum Products Co., Inc.*, 927 P.2d 781 (Ariz. Ct. App. 1996). |

| | | | | | | | |
|---|---|---|---|---|---|---|---|
| AR | N/C. | No. | N/C. | Yes. | Yes. | N/C. | *Sterling Drug, Inc. v. Oxford,* 294 Ark. 239, 743 S.W.2d 380 (1980); *MBM Co. v. Counce,* 268 Ark. 269, 596 S.W.2d 681 (1980); *Tackett v. Crain Automotive,* 899 S.W.2d 839 (Ark. 1995). |
| CA | N/C. | Yes. | Yes. | Yes. | Yes. | Yes. | *Hentzel v. Singer Co.,* 188 Cal. Rptr. 159 (Ct. App. 1982); *Portillo v. G.T. Price Prods., Inc.,* 182 Cal. Rptr. 291 (Ct. App. 1982); *Garcia v. Rockwell Int'l Corp.,* 232 Cal. Rptr. 490 (Ct. App. 1987); *Raley's, Inc. v. Workers' Compensation Appeals Bd.,* 271 Cal. Rptr. 230 (Ct. App. 1990); *Shoemaker v. Myers,* 4 Cal. Rptr. 2d 203 (Ct. App. 1992); *Platt v. Jack Cooper Transp. Co.,* 959 F.2d 91 (8th Cir. 1992); *Blom v. N.G.K. Spark Plugs (U.S.A.), Inc.,* 4 Cal. Rptr. 2d 139 (Ct. App. 1992); *Holmes v. General Dynamics Corp.,* 22 Cal. Rptr. 2d 172 (Ct. App. 1993); *Angell v. Peterson Tractor, Inc.,* 26 Cal. Rptr. 2d 541 (Ct. App. 1994); *Dyer v. W.C.A.B.,* 28 Cal. Rptr. 2d 30 (Ct. App. 1994); *Parada v. City of Colton,* 29 Cal. Rptr. 2d 309 (Ct. App. 1994); *Ely v. Wal-Mart, Inc.*, 875 F. Supp. 1422 (C.D. Cal. 1995); *Green v. Ralee Engineering Co.*, 61 Cal. Rptr.2d 352 (Cal. App. 1997); *Daly v. Exxon Corp.*, 63 Cal. Rptr.2d 727 (Cal. Ct. App. 1997). |
| CO | Jury Service: Yes;<br>Military Service: No;<br>Voting: No. | Yes. | Yes. | Yes. | Yes. | Yes. | *Corbin v. Sinclair Mktg., Inc.,* 684 P.2d 265 (Colo. Ct. App. 1984); *Lathrop v. Entenmann's, Inc.,* 770 P.2d 1367 (Colo. Ct. App. 1989), *cert. granted,* 778 P.2d 1370 (Colo. 1989); *Miedema v. Browning-Ferris Indus., Inc.,* 716 F. Supp. 1369 (D. Colo. 1989); *Martin Marietta Corp. v. Lorenz,* 823 P.2d 100 (Colo. 1992); *Rocky Mountain Hosp. and Medical Serv. v. Mariani,* 916 P.2d 519 (Colo. 1996); *Roe v. Cheyenne Mountain Conference Resort,* 920 F. Supp. 1153 (D. Colo. 1996). |
| CT | N/C. | Yes. | Yes. | Yes. | N/C. | N/C. | *Sheets v. Teddy's Frosted Foods,* 427 A.2d 385 (Conn. 1980); *Parsons v. United Technologies Corp.*, 700 A.2d 655 (Conn. 1997). |
| DE | Jury Service: No;<br>Military Service: Yes;<br>Voting: No. | No. | No. | No. | No. | No. | *Henry v. Anderson County,* 522 F. Supp. 1112 (E.D. Tenn. 1981); *Rizzo v. E.I. duPont de Nemours & Co.,* 1989 WL 135651 (Del. Super. 1991). |

*(Table continues.)*

# Table 4.4-1 *(cont'd)*

## CAUSES OF ACTION FOR WRONGFUL DISCHARGE BASED ON PUBLIC POLICY VIOLATIONS

(This table excludes cause of action created by the statute itself. See also text at § 4.4.)

**KEY:** **N/C.** No court case has been issued so far.
**N/R.** No ruling. The highest court of the state has not clearly expressed its position on this issue, and either the lower courts are divided or the federal courts, interpreting state law, are the only courts to have issued a decision.

| | *For Jury Service, Military Service, and Voting* | *For Filing Workers' Compensation Claims* | *For Exercising Rights Under Federal or State Health and Safety Laws* | *For Whistle-Blowing* | *For Exercising Rights Under Federal or State Constitution* | *For Exercising Rights Under Fair Employment Laws* | *Citations to Authority* |
|---|---|---|---|---|---|---|---|
| DC | N/C. | Yes. | Yes. | No. | N/C. | Yes. | *Adams v. George W. Cochran & Co.*, 597 A.2d 28 (D.C. 1991); *Abramson Assocs., Inc., v. District of Columbia Dep't of Employment Servs.*, 596 A.2d 549 (D.C. 1991); *Gray v. Citizens Bank*, 602 A.2d 1096 (D.C. 1992); *Nolting v. National Capital Group, Inc.*, 621 A.2d 1387 (D.C. 1993); *Arthur Young & Co. v. Sutherland*, 631 A.2d 354 (D.C. 1993); *Taylor v. Washington Metropolitan Area Transit Auth.*, 922 F. Supp. 665 (D.D.C. 1996). |
| FL | No. | No. | No. | Yes. | No. | No. | *DeMarco v. Publix Super Mkts., Inc.*, 360 So. 2d 134 (Fla. Dist. Ct. App. 1978), aff'd, 384 So. 2d 1253 (Fla. 1980); *Edenfield v. B&I Contractors, Inc.*, 624 So. 2d 389 (Fla. Dist. Ct. App. 1993); *Rehman v. ECC Intern. Corp.*, 698 So. 2d 921 (Fla. Dist. Ct. App. 1997). |
| GA | No. | No. | No. | No. | No. | No. | *A.R. Shelton v. Bowman Transp.*, 230 S.E.2d 762 (Ga. Ct. App. 1976); *West v. First Nat'l Bank*, 245 S.E.2d 46 (Ga. Ct. App. 1978); *Goodroe v. Georgia Power Co.* 251 S.E.2d 51 (Ga. Ct. App. 1978); *Jellico v. Effingham County*, 471 S.E.2d 36 (Ga. Ct. App. 1996). |

| | | | | | | | |
|---|---|---|---|---|---|---|---|
| HI | N/C. | Yes. | N/R. | Yes. | N/C. | Yes. | *Morishege v. Spencecliff Corp.*, 720 F. Supp. 829 (D. Haw. 1989); *Hummel v. Kamehameha Schools,* 749 F. Supp. 1023 (D. Haw. 1990); *Briggs v. Hotel Corp. of the Pac.,* 831 P.2d 1335 (Haw. 1992); *Smith v. Chaney Brooks Realty, Inc.*, 865 P.2d 170 (Haw. Ct. App. 1994). |
| ID | N/C. | N/C. | N/C. | Yes. | N/C. | N/C. | *Ray v. Nampay School District,* 814 P.2d 17 (Idaho 1991). |
| IL | Jury Service: Yes; Military Service: N/C; Voting: N/C. | Yes. | Yes. | Yes. | Yes. | N/C. | *Rozier v. St. Mary's Hosp.*, 411 N.E.2d 50 (Ill. App. Ct. 1980); *Palmateer v. International Harvester Co.,* 421 N.E.2d 876 (Ill. 1981); *Netzel v. United Parcel Serv.,* 537 N.E.2d 1348 (Ill. App. Ct. 1989); *Bilderback v. Admiral Co.,* 591 N.E.2d 36 (Ill. 1992); *Mitchell v. Deal,* 609 N.E.2d 378 (Ill. App. Ct. 1993), *cert. denied,* 616 N.E.2d 337 (Ill. 1993); *Selof v. Island Foods, Inc.,* 623 N.E.2d 386 (Ill. App. Ct. 1993); *Paskarnis v. Darien-Woodridge Fire Protection Dist.,* 623 N.E.2d 383 (Ill. App. Ct. 1993); *Bafia v. City Intern Trucks, Inc.,* 629 N.E.2d 666 (Ill. App. Ct. 1994); *Clark v. Owens-Brockway Glass Container, Inc.*, 1998 WL 111713 (Ill. App. 5 Dist). |
| IN | Yes. Cause of action for wrongful discharge when employee is discharged for exercising a statutorily conferred right or duty. | Yes. Cause of action for wrongful discharge when employee is discharged for exercising a statutorily conferred right or duty. | Yes. Claims against state, county, and local government entities limited by Indiana Tort Claims Act. | Yes. | N/C. | Yes. | *Moffett v. Gene B. Glick Co.,* 604 F. Supp. 229 (N.D. Ind. 1984); *Call v. Scott Brass, Inc.,* 553 N.E.2d 1225 (Ind. Ct. App. 1990); *Stivers v. Stevens,* 581 N.E.2d 1253 (Ind. Ct. App. 1992); *Steele v. McDonald's Corp.*, 686 N.E.2d 137 (Ind. Ct. App. 1997). |
| IA | N/C. | Yes. | Yes. | Yes. | Yes. | N/C. | *Springer v. Weeks & Leo Co.,* 475 N.W.2d 630 (Iowa 1991); *Clarey v. K-Products, Inc.,* 514 N.W.2d 900 (Iowa 1994); *Phipps v. IASD Health Services Corp.,* 558 N.W.2d 198 (Iowa 1997). |
| KS | N/C. | Yes. | Yes. | Yes. | Yes. | Yes. | *Murphy v. City of Topeka-Shawnee City Dep't of Labor Servs.,* 630 P.2d 186 (Kan. Ct. App. 1981); *Anco Constr. Co. v. Freeman,* 236 Kan. 626, 693 P.2d 1183 (1985); *Rowland v. Val-Ajax, Inc.,* 13 Kan. App.2d 149, 766 P.2d 819 (1988); *Palmer v. Brown,* 242 Kan. 893, 752 P.2d 685 (1988); *Coleman v. Safeway Stores,* 242 Kan. 804, 752 P.2d 645 (1988); *Pilcher v. Board of County Comm'rs,* 14 Kan. App.2d 206, 787 P.2d 1204 (1990); *White v. General Motors Corp.,* 908 F.2d 669 (10th Cir. 1990), *cert. denied,* 111 S.Ct. 788 (1991); *Stuart v. Beech Aircraft* *(cont'd)* |

*(Table continues.)*

# Table 4.4-1 *(cont'd)*

## CAUSES OF ACTION FOR WRONGFUL DISCHARGE BASED ON PUBLIC POLICY VIOLATIONS

(This table excludes cause of action created by the statute itself. See also text at § 4.4.)

**KEY:** **N/C.** No court case has been issued so far.
**N/R.** No ruling. The highest court of the state has not clearly expressed its position on this issue, and either the lower courts are divided or the federal courts, interpreting state law, are the only courts to have issued a decision.

| | *For Jury Service, Military Service, and Voting* | *For Filing Workers' Compensation Claims* | *For Exercising Rights Under Federal or State Health and Safety Laws* | *For Whistle-Blowing* | *For Exercising Rights Under Federal or State Constitution* | *For Exercising Rights Under Fair Employment Laws* | *Citations to Authority* |
|---|---|---|---|---|---|---|---|
| KS *(cont'd)* | | | | | | | *Corp.*, 753 F. Supp. 317 (D. Kan. 1990), *aff'd mem.*, 936 F.2d 584 (10th Cir. 1991); *Rupp v. Purolator Courier Corp.*, 790 F. Supp. 1069 (D. Kan. 1992); *Herman v. Western Fin. Corp.*, 869 P.2d 696 (Kan. 1994); *Sanjuan v. IBP, Inc.*, 919 F. Supp. 378 (D. Kan. 1996); *Ramirez v. IBP, Inc.*, 913 F. Supp. 1421 (D. Kan. 1995); *Sanjuan v. IBP, Inc.*, 941 F. Supp. 1000 (D. Kan. 1996); *Griffin v. Dodge City Co-op. Exchange*, 927 P.2d 958 (Kan. Ct. App. 1996); *Smith v. Midland Brake, Inc.*, 138 F.3d 1304 (10th Cir. 1998); *Lytle v. City of Haysville, Kan.*, 138 F.3d 857 (10th Cir. 1998). |
| KY | N/C. | Yes. | Yes. | Yes. | Yes. | N/C. | *Nork v. Fetter Printing Co.*, 738 S.W.2d 824 (Ky. Ct. App. 1987); *Overrite Transp. v. Gaddis*, 793 S.W.2d 129 (Ky. Ct. App. 1990); *Willoughby v. Gencorp, Inc.*, 809 S.W.2d 858 (Ky. Ct. App. 1990); *First Property Mgmt. Corp. v. Zarebidaki*, 867 S.W.2d 185 (Ky. 1993); *Stump v. Wal-Mart Stores, Inc.*, 942 F. Supp. 347 (E.D. Ky. 1996). |
| LA | No. | Yes. | Yes. | No. | No. | No. | *Gil v. Metal Serv. Corp.*, 412 So. 2d 706 (La. Ct. App. 1982); *Jones v. Friends of City Park*, 569 So. 2d 552 (La. Ct. App. 1990); *Lynn v. Berg Mechanical, Inc.*, 582 So. 2d 902 (La. Ct. App. 1991), *amended and aff'd as amended*, 649 So. 2d 139 (La. Ct. App. 1995); *Cahill v. Frank's Door* |

| | | | | | | | |
|---|---|---|---|---|---|---|---|
| | | | | | | | *& Bldg. Supply Co.*, 577 So. 2d 350 (La. Ct. App. 1991), *rev'd,* 590 So. 2d 53 (La. 1991); *Herbert v. Louisiana Dept. of Transp. and Dev.*, 630 So. 2d 318 (La. Ct. App. 1993); *Bruce v. Ampacet Corp.*, 634 So. 2d 1351 (La. Ct. App. 1994). |
| ME | N/C. | N/R. | N/C. | Yes. | N/C. | N/C. | *Bard v. Bath Iron Works Corp.*, 590 A.2d 152 (Me. 1991); *Devoid v. Clair Buick Cadillac, Inc.*, 669 A.2d 749 (Me. 1996). |
| MD | N/C. | Yes. | Yes. | Yes. | Yes. | Yes. | *Robinson v. Vitro Corp.*, 620 F. Supp. 1066 (D. Md. 1985); *Silkworth v. Ryder Truck Rental Inc.*, 70 Md. App. 264, 520 A.2d 1124, *cert. denied,* 310 Md. 2, 526 A.2d 954 (1987); *Ewing v. Koppers Co.*, 312 Md. 45, 537 A.2d 1173 (1988); *Finch v. Holladay-Tyler Printing, Inc.*, 322 Md. 197, 586 A.2d 1275 (1991); *Watson v. Peoples Sec. Life Ins. Co.*, 588 A.2d 760 (Md. 1991); *Miller v. Fairchild Inds., Inc.*, 629 A.2d 1293 (Md. 1993); *Bleich v. Florence Crittenton Servs. Inc.*, 632 A.2d 463 (Md. 1993); *Ayers v. ARA Health Servs., Inc.*, 918 F. Supp. 143 (D. Md. 1995). |
| MA | Jury Service: Yes; Military Service: N/C; Voting: N/C. | Yes. | N/C. | N/R. | N/C. | N/C. | *Mello v. Stop & Shop Cos.*, 524 N.E.2d 105 (Mass. 1988); *Smith-Pfeffer v. Superintendent of the Walter E. Fernald State School,* 533 N.E.2d 1368 (Mass. 1989); *Norris v. Lumberman's Mut. Cas. Co.*, 881 F.2d 1144 (1st Cir. 1989); *Smith v. Mitre Corp.*, 949 F. Supp. 943 (D. Mass. 1997); *Derrig v. Wal-Mart Stores Inc.*, 942 F. Supp. 49 (D. Mass. 1996); *Upton v. JWP Businessland*, 682 N.E.2d 1357 (Mass. 1997); *Flynn v. Menino*, 944 F. Supp. 81 (D. Mass. 1996). |
| MI | N/C. | Yes. | Yes. | Yes. | N/C. | Yes. | *Sventko v. Kroger Co.*, 245 N.W.2d 151 (Mich. Ct. App. 1976); *Trombetta v. Detroit, T & I R.R. Co.*, 265 N.W.2d 385 (Mich. Ct. App. 1978); *Dudewicz v. Norris-Schmid, Inc.*, 503 N.W.2d 645 (Mich. 1993); *Coleman-Nichols v. Tixon Corp.*, 513 N.W.2d 441 (Mich. Ct. App. 1994); *Dolan v. Continental Airlines/Continental Exp.*, 563 N.W.2d 23 (Mich. 1997); *Phinney v. Perlmutter*, 564 N.W.2d 532 (Mich. App. 1997). |
| MN | N/C. | N/C. | Yes. | Yes. | N/C. | N/C. | *McGrath v. TCF Bank Sav.*, 509 N.W.2d 365 (Minn. 1993). |

*(Table continues.)*

# **Table 4.4-1** *(cont'd)*
## CAUSES OF ACTION FOR WRONGFUL DISCHARGE BASED ON PUBLIC POLICY VIOLATIONS

(This table excludes cause of action created by the statute itself. See also text at § 4.4.)

**KEY:** **N/C.** No court case has been issued so far.
**N/R.** No ruling. The highest court of the state has not clearly expressed its position on this issue, and either the lower courts are divided or the federal courts, interpreting state law, are the only courts to have issued a decision.

| | *For Jury Service, Military Service, and Voting* | *For Filing Workers' Compensation Claims* | *For Exercising Rights Under Federal or State Health and Safety Laws* | *For Whistle-Blowing* | *For Exercising Rights Under Federal or State Constitution* | *For Exercising Rights Under Fair Employment Laws* | *Citations to Authority* |
|---|---|---|---|---|---|---|---|
| MS | N/C. | Yes. | N/C. | Yes. Discharge for reporting illegal acts violates public policy. | Yes. | N/C. | *Kelly v. Mississippi Valley Gas Co.*, 397 So. 2d 874 (1981); *Laws v. Aetna Fin. Co.*, 667 F. Supp. 342 (D. Miss. 1987); *McArn v. Allied Bruce-Terminix Co., Inc.*, 626 So. 2d 603 (Miss. 1993); *Boren v. Wolverine Tube, Inc.*, 966 F. Supp. 457 (N.D. Miss. 1997). |
| MO | Jury Service: Yes; Military Service; N/C, Voting: N/C. | Yes. | Yes. | Yes. | Yes. | Yes. | *Beasley v. Affiliated Hosp. Prods.*, 713 S.W.2d 557 (Mo. Ct. App. 1986); *Blair v. Steadley Co.*, 740 S.W.2d 329 (Mo. Ct. App. 1987); *Gannon v. Sherwood Medical Co.*, 749 F. Supp 979 (E.D. Mo. 1990); *Prewitt v. Factory Motor Parts, Inc.*, 747 F. Supp. 560 (W.D. Mo. 1990); *Hopkins v. Tip Top Plumbing & Heating Co.*, 805 S.W.2d 280 (Mo. Ct. App. 1991)—Note: *rehearing and/or transfer denied* March 5, 1991; *Kirk v. Mercy Hosp. Tri-County,* 851 S.W.2d 617 (Mo. Ct. App. 1993); *Graf v. Wire Rope Corp. of America,* 861 S.W.2d 588 (Mo. Ct. App. 1993); *Yow v. Village of Eolia,* 859 S.W.2d 920 (Mo. Ct. App. 1993); *Shawcross v. Pyro Prods., Inc.*, 916 S.W.2d 342 (Mo. Ct. App. 1995); *Adcock v. Newtec, Inc.*, 939 S.W.2d 426 (Mo. App. 1996); *Faust v. Ryder Commercial Leasing & Services*, 954 S.W.2d 383 (Mo. Ct. App. 1997); *Haley v. Retsinas*, 138 F.3d 1245 (9th Cir. 1998). |

| | | | | | | | |
|---|---|---|---|---|---|---|---|
| MT | In 1987 Montana enacted a comprehensive law protecting at-will employees from discharge without cause; in retaliation for refusing to violate public policy or for reporting public policy violations; and when handbook rules are violated (for example, employer did not follow disciplinary procedures). | See "For Jury Service, Military Service, and Voting." | See "For Jury Service, Military Service, and Voting." | See "For Jury Service, Military Service, and Voting." | See "For Jury Service, Military Service, and Voting." | See "For Jury Service, Military Service, and Voting." | Mont. Code Ann. §§ 39-2-901 *et seq.*; *Meech v. Hillhaven West, Inc.*, 776 P.2d 488 (Mont. 1989); *Motarie v. Northern Montana Joint Refuse Disposal District*, 907 P.2d 154 (Mt. 1995). |
| NE | N/C. | N/C. | Yes. | Yes. | N/C. | N/C. | See citations for Table 4.3-1. |
| NV | N/C. | Yes. | Yes. | N/C. | Yes. | N/C. | *Hansen v. Harrah's*, 675 P.2d 394 (Nev. 1984); *Sanders v. Ogden Allied Leisure Servs., Inc.*, 783 F. Supp. 531 (D. Nev. 1992); *Blackenship v. O'Sullivan Plastics Corp.*, 866 P.2d 293 (Nev. 1993); *Wayment v. Holmes*, 912 P.2d 816 (Nev. 1996). |
| NH | N/C. | N/C. | Yes. | Yes. | N/C. | N/C. | Appeal of *New Hampshire Department of Employment Security*, 672 A.2d 697 (N.H. 1996). |
| NJ | N/C. | Yes. | Yes. | Yes. | Yes. | Yes. | *Lally v. Copygraphics*, 428 A.2d 1317 (N.J. 1981); *Jackson v. Consol. Rail Corp.*, 538 A.2d 1310 (N.J. 1988); *Hennessey v. Coastal Eagle Point Oil Co.*, 609 A.2d 11 (N.J. 1992); *D'Agostino v. Johnson & Johnson, Inc.*, 628 A.2d 305 (N.J. 1993); *Abbamont v. Piscataway Tp. Bd. of Educ.*, 634 A.2d 538 (N.J. Super. Ct. App. Div. 1993), *cert. granted*, 641 A.2d 1039 (N.J. 1994); *Haworth v. Deborah Heart and Lung Ctr.*, 638 A.2d 1354 (N.J. Super. App. Div. 1994); *MacDougall v. Weichert*, 677 A.2d 162 (N.J. 1996); *Casciano v. Board of Review*, 693 A.2d 531 (N.J. Super. App. Div. 1997); *Mehlman v. Mobil Oil Corp.*, 707 A.2d 1000 (N.J. 1998); *Reames v. Dept. of Public Works, City of Paterson*, 707 A.2d 1377 (N.J. Super. App. Div. 1998). |
| NM | N/C. | Yes. | Yes. | Yes. | N/C. | Yes. | *Gutierrez v. Sundancer Indian Jewelry, Inc.*, 868 P.2d 1266 (N.M. Ct. App. 1993); *Gandy v. Wal-Mart Stores, Inc.*, 872 P.2d 859 (N.M. 1994); *Garrity v. Overland Sheepskin Co. of Taos*, 917 P.2d 1382 (N.M. 1996). |

*(Table continues.)*

## **Table 4.4-1** *(cont'd)*

## CAUSES OF ACTION FOR WRONGFUL DISCHARGE BASED ON PUBLIC POLICY VIOLATIONS

(This table excludes cause of action created by the statute itself. See also text at § 4.4.)

**KEY:** **N/C.** No court case has been issued so far.
**N/R.** No ruling. The highest court of the state has not clearly expressed its position on this issue, and either the lower courts are divided or the federal courts, interpreting state law, are the only courts to have issued a decision.

| | *For Jury Service, Military Service, and Voting* | *For Filing Workers' Compensation Claims* | *For Exercising Rights Under Federal or State Health and Safety Laws* | *For Whistle-Blowing* | *For Exercising Rights Under Federal or State Constitution* | *For Exercising Rights Under Fair Employment Laws* | *Citations to Authority* |
|---|---|---|---|---|---|---|---|
| NY | No. | Yes. | No. | Yes. | No. | Yes. | *Leibowitz v. Bank Leumi Trust Co.,* 152 A.D.2d 169, 548 N.Y.S.2d 513 (App. Div. 1989); *Graham v. New York State Div. of Human Rights,* 602 N.Y.S.2d 195 (App. Div. 1993); *Rompane v. Enzolabs, Inc.,* 608 N.Y.S.2d 989 (Sup. Ct. 1994); *Gleason v. Callanan Indus., Inc.,* 610 N.Y.S.2d 671 (App. Div. 1994); *Hogan v. 50 Sutton Place South Owners, Inc.,* 919 F. Supp. 738 (S.D.N.Y. 1996); *Gomanz v. Foote, Cone & Belding Communications, Inc.,* 644 N.Y.S.2d 224 (App. Div. 1996); *Bordell v. General Electric Co.,* 644 N.Y.S.2d 912 (N.Y. 1996); *Green v. Saratoga A.R.C.,* 650 N.Y.S.2d 441(App. Div. 1996); *Lawrence v. Consolidated Edison Co.,* 659 N.Y.S.2d 117 (App. Div. 1997). |
| NC | N/C. | Yes. | N/C. | Yes. | N/C. | N/C. | *Boesche v. Raleigh-Durham Airport Auth.,* 432 S.E.2d 137 (N.C. Ct. App. 1993), *appeal dismissed,* 442 S.E.2d 320 (N.C. 1994); *Daniel v. Carolina Sunrock Corp.,* 436 S.E.2d 835 (N.C. 1993); *Abels v. Renfro Corp.,* 436 S.E.2d 822 (N.C. 1993); *Conklin v. Carolina Narrow Fabrics Co.,* 439 S.E.2d 239 (N.C. Ct. App. 1994). |
| ND | N/C. | Yes. | N/C. | N/C. | N/C. | N/C. | — |

| | | | | | | | |
|---|---|---|---|---|---|---|---|
| OH | Jury Service: Yes; Military Service: N/C; Voting: N/C. | Yes. | Yes. | Yes. | N/C. | N/C. | *Shaffer v. Frontrunner, Inc.*, 566 N.E.2d 193 (Ohio 1990); *Wing v. Anchor Media, Ltd.*, 570 N.E.2d 1095 (Ohio 1991); *Yontz v. BMER Enters., Inc.*, 632 N.E.2d 527 (Ohio Ct. App. 1993); *Cooper v. Metal Sales Mfg. Corp.*, 660 N.E.2d 1245 (Ohio Ct. App. 1995); *Fox v. Bowling Green*, 668 N.E.2d 898 (Ohio 1996); *Moore v. Animal Farm Pet Ctr.*, Inc., 674 N.E.2d 1269 (Ohio Com. Pl. 1995); *DeKoning v. Flower Mem. Hosp.*, 676 N.E.2d 614 (Ohio Com. Pl. 1996). |
| OK | Jury Service: N/R; Military Service: N/C; Voting: N/C. | Yes. | N/C. | Yes. | N/C. | N/C. | *Vannerson v. Board of Regents*, 784 P.2d 1053 (Okla. 1990); *King v. Halliburton Co.*, 813 P.2d 1055 (Okla. 1991); *Tate v. Browning-Ferris, Inc.*, 833 P.2d 1218 (Okla. 1992); *Brown v. MFC Manufacturing Co. of Oklahoma*, 838 P.2d 524 (Okla. Ct. App. 1992); *Wallace v. Halliburton Co.*, 850 P.2d 1056 (Okla. 1993); *Wilson v. Hess-Sweitzer & Brant, Inc.*, 864 P.2d 1279 (Okla. 1993); *Hayes v. Eateries, Inc.*, 905 P.2d 778 (Okla. 1995); *Blackwell v. Shelter Mut. Ins. Co.*, 109 F.3d 1550 (10th Cir. 1997). |
| OR | Yes. | Yes. | Yes. | Yes. | Yes. | Yes. | *Nees v. Hocks*, 536 P.2d 512 (Or. 1975); *Brown v. Transcon Lines*, 588 P.2d 1087 (Or. 1978); *McCool v. Hillhaven Corp.*, 777 P.2d 1013 (Or. 1989); *McGanty v. Staudenraus*, 859 P.2d 1187 (Or. Ct. App. 1993); *Dalby v. Sisters of Providence In Or.*, 865 P.2d 391 (Or. Ct. App. 1993); *Archer v. Letica Corp.*, 868 P.2d 770 (Or. Ct. App. 1994). |
| PA | Jury Service: Yes; Military Service: No; Voting: No. | No. | No. | Yes, for government/ public employees only. | Yes. | No. | *Reuther v. Fowler & Williams, Inc.*, 386 A.2d 119 (Pa. 1978); *Field v. Philadelphia Elec. Co.*, 565 A.2d 1170 (Pa. Super. Ct. 1989); *Macken v. Lord Corp.*, 585 A.2d 1106 (Pa. 1991); *Krajsa v. Keypunch, Inc.*, 622 A.2d 355 (Pa. Super. Ct. 1993); *Smyth v. Pillsbury Co.*, 914 F. Supp. 97 (E.D.Pa. 1996); *Hunger v. Grand Central Sanitation*, 610 A.2d 173 (Pa. Super. Ct. 1996); *Shcik v. Shirley*, 691 A.2d 511 (Pa. Super. 1997); *McLaughlin v. Gastrointestinal Specialists, Inc.*, 696 A.2d 173 (Pa. Super. Ct. 1997). |
| RI | N/C. | N/C. | N/C. | No. | N/C. | N/C. | *Pacheo v. Ratheon Co.*, 623 A.2d 464 (R.I. 1993). |
| SC | Jury Service: Yes; Military Service: N/C; Voting: N/C. | Yes. | N/C. | Yes. | N/C. | N/C. | *Connelly v. Wometco Enter., Inc.*, 442 S.E.2d 204 (S.C. Ct. App. 1994); *Garner v. Morrison Knudsen Corp.*, 456 S.E.2d 907 (S.C. 1995). |

*(Table continues.)*

## Table 4.4-1 *(cont'd)*

## CAUSES OF ACTION FOR WRONGFUL DISCHARGE BASED ON PUBLIC POLICY VIOLATIONS

(This table excludes cause of action created by the statute itself. See also text at § 4.4.)

**KEY:** **N/C.** No court case has been issued so far.
**N/R.** No ruling. The highest court of the state has not clearly expressed its position on this issue, and either the lower courts are divided or the federal courts, interpreting state law, are the only courts to have issued a decision.

| | *For Jury Service, Military Service, and Voting* | *For Filing Workers' Compensation Claims* | *For Exercising Rights Under Federal or State Health and Safety Laws* | *For Whistle-Blowing* | *For Exercising Rights Under Federal or State Constitution* | *For Exercising Rights Under Fair Employment Laws* | *Citations to Authority* |
|---|---|---|---|---|---|---|---|
| SD | N/C. | Yes. | Yes. | N/C. | N/C. | N/C. | *Niesent v. Homestake Min. Co.,* 505 N.W.2d 781 (S.D. 1993). |
| TN | Jury Service: Yes; Military Service: N/C; Voting: N/C. | Yes. | N/C. | Yes. | Yes. | N/C. | *Jeffreys v. My Friend's Place, Inc.,* 719 F. Supp. 639 (M.D. Tenn. 1989); *Moskal v. First Tenn. Bank,* 815 S.W.2d 509 (Tenn. Ct. App. 1991); *Thomason v. Better Bilt Aluminum Prods., Inc.,* 831 S.W.2d 291 (Tenn. Ct. App. 1992); *Medley v. A.W. Chesterton Co.,* 912 S.W.2d 748 (Tenn. Ct. App. 1995); *Stein v. Davidson,* 945 S.W.2d 714 (Tenn. 1997). |
| TX (Recognizes public policy exception only if employee is fired for refusing to perform illegal act or for inquiring into the legality of an instruction from the employer.) | N/C. | Yes. | Yes. | Yes. | N/C. | Yes. | *Sabine Pilot Serv., Inc. v. Hauck,* 687 S.W.2d 733 (Tex. 1985); *Chemical Express Carriers, Inc. v. Pina,* 819 S.W.2d 585 (Tex. Ct. App. 1991); *Worsham Steel Co. v. Arias,* 831 S.W.2d 81 (Tex. Ct. App. 1992); *Stinnett v. Williamson County Sheriff's Dept.,* 858 S.W.2d 573 (Tex. Ct. App. 1993); *Tri-County Elec. Co-op., Inc. v. Tidwell,* 859 S.W.2d 109 (Tex. Ct. App. 1993); *Acme Boot Co. v. Montenegro,* 862 S.W.2d 806 (Tex. Ct. App. 1993); *Farrington v. Sysco Food Serv. Inc.,* 865 S.W.2d 247 (Tex. Ct. App. 1993); *Dubin v. Dal-Briar Corp.,* 871 S.W.2d 263 (Tex. Ct. App. 1994); *Johnston v. Del Mar Distrib. Co.,* 776 S.W.2d 768 (Tx. Ct. App. 1989) (*writ denied*); *Texas Department of Human Services v. Hinds,* 904 S.W.2d 629 (Tex. 1995); *Stroud v. VBFSB Holding Corp.,* 917 S.W.2d 75 (Tex. |

| | | | | | | | |
|---|---|---|---|---|---|---|---|
| | | | | | | | Ct. App. 1996); *Western Atlas Intern., Inc., v. Wilson*, 930 S.W.2d 782 (Tex. App. 1996). |
| UT | N/C. | N/C. | N/C. | N/C. | N/C. | N/C. | — |
| VT | N/C. | N/C. | N/C. | N/C. | N/C. | N/C. | — |
| VA | N/C. | N/C. | N/C. | N/C. | N/C. | Yes. | *Lockhart v. Commonwealth Educ. Sys. Corp.*, 439 S.E.2d 328 (Va. 1994); *Lawrence Chrysler Plymouth v. Brooks*, 465 S.E.2d 806 (Va. 1996). |
| WA | N/C. | Yes. | N/C. | Yes. | N/C. | Yes. | *Dicomes v. State*, 782 P.2d 1002 (Wash. 1989); *Bennett v. Hardy*, 784 P.2d 1258 (Wash. 1990); *Wilmot v. Kaiser Aluminum & Chem. Corp.*, 821 P.2d 18 (Wash. 1991); *Coville v. Cobrac Serv. Inc.*, 869 P.2d 1103 (Wash. Ct. App. 1994) See also, *Gardner v. Loomis Armored, Inc.*, 913 P.2d 377 (Wash. 1996) (recognizing public policy exception for employee who is fired for violating a company rule in order to assist a citizen held hostage at the scene of a crime); *Reninger v. State Dept. of Corrections*, 951 P.2d 782 (Wash. 1998). |
| WV | N/C. | Yes. | Yes. | N/C. | Yes. | Yes. | *Collins v. Elkay Mining Co.*, 371 S.E.2d 46 (W. Va. 1988); *Tritle v. Crown Airways Inc.*, 928 F.2d 81 (4th Cir. 1991); *West Virginia Dept. of Natural Resources v. Myers*, 443 S.E.2d 229 (W. Va. 1994); *Williamson v. Greene*, 490 S.E.2d 23 (W. Va. 1997); *Rollins v. Mason County Bd. of Educ.*, 489 S.E.2d 768. |
| WI | N/C. | N/C. | Yes. | No. | No. | N/C. | *Ward v. Frito-Lay, Inc.*, 290 N.W.2d 536 (Wis. 1980); *Hausman v. St. Croix Care Center, Inc.*, 558 N.W.2d 893 (Wis. App. 1996); *Kempfer v. Automated Fishing, Inc.*, 564 N.W.2d 692 (Wis. 1997); *Hausman v. St. Croix Care Center*, 571 N.W.2d 393 (Wis. 1997). |
| WY | N/C. | Yes. | N/C. | N/C. | N/C. | N/C. | *Griess v. Consolidated Freightways Corp.*, 776 P.2d 752 (Wyo. 1989); *Horne v. J.W. Gibson Well Serv. Co.*, 894 F.2d 1194 (10th Cir. 1990). |

# Table 4.4-2
## WRONGFUL DISCHARGE ACTIONS: STATE PUBLIC POLICY AGAINST DISCRIMINATION

**KEY:** An em-dash (—) indicates that there has been no court decision expressly recognizing cause of action.

**NOTE:** Although there may be no court decision expressly recognizing a cause of action based on a particular type of discrimination (e.g., age or sex), if state courts have recognized cause of action on behalf of one class of persons covered by statute, it is likely that future decisions will recognize causes of action on behalf of other classes of persons protected by statute.

| | *Age* | *Race* | *Sex* | *Disability* | *Other* | *Citations to Authority* |
|---|---|---|---|---|---|---|
| AL | — | — | — | — | No cause of action based on expressed public policy against discrimination is recognized in Alabama. | *Wright v. Dothan Chrysler Plymouth Dodge, Inc.*, 658 So. 2d 428 (Ala. 1995); *Howard v. Wolff Broadcasting Corp.*, 611 So. 2d 307 (Ala. 1992). |
| AK | — | — | — | — | — | — |
| AZ | — | — | Yes. | — | — | *Broomfield v. Lundell*, 767 P.2d 697 (Ariz. App. 1988). |
| AR | — | — | Yes. | — | — | *Lucas v. Brown & Root, Inc.*, 736 F.2d 1202 (8th Cir. 1984). |
| CA | No. | Yes. | Yes. | — | Yes, sexual orientation. Court recognized wrongful discharge claim where employer violated Family Rights Act. | *Stevenson v. Superior Court*, 60 Cal. Rptr. 2d 206 (Cal. App. 1996); *Jennings v. Marralle*, 876 P.2d 1074 (Cal. 1994); *Jackson v. Southern California Gas Co.*, 881 F.2d 638 (9th Cir. 1989); *Rojo v. Kliger*, 276 Cal. Rptr. 130, 801 P.2d 373 (1990); *Badih v. Myers*, 43 Cal. Rptr. 2d 229 (Cal. App. 1995); *Leibert v. Transworld Sys., Inc.*, 39 Cal. Rptr. 2d 65 (Cal. App. 1995); *Ely v. Wal-Mart, Inc.*, 875 F. Supp. 1422 (C.D. Cal. 1995). |
| CO | No. | — | — | — | No cause of action; statute provides only state remedy. | *Ferris v. Bakery, Confectionery & Tobacco Union, Local 26*, 867 P.2d 38 (Colo. App. 1993); *Brezinski v. F.W. Woolworth Co.*, 626 F. Supp. 240 (D. Colo. 1986). |
| CT | No. | No. | — | — | — | *Bennett v. Beirsdorf, Inc.*, 889 F. Supp. 46 (D. Conn. 1995). |
| DE | No. | — | — | — | — | *Finch v. Hercules, Inc.*, 809 F. Supp. 309 (D. Del. 1992). |
| DC | — | — | Yes. | — | — | *MacNabb v. MacCartee*, 804 F. Supp. 378 (D.D.C. 1992). |
| FL | — | — | No. | — | — | *Ponton v. Scarfone*, 468 So. 2d 1009 (Fla. 2 DCA 1985). |
| GA | Yes. | No. | No. | Yes. | No public policy cause of action based on pregnancy discrimination. | *Borden v. Johnson*, 395 S.E.2d 628 (Ga. App. 1990); *Green v. Sun Trust Banks, Inc.*, 399 S.E.2d 712 (Ga. App. 1990). |
| HI | — | — | — | — | No cause of action; statutory remedy is exclusive. | *Lui v. Intercontinental Hotels Corp. (Hawaii)*, 634 F. Supp. 684 (D. Haw. 1986). |
| ID | — | — | — | — | — | — |
| IL | — | — | — | — | — | — |

| | | | | | | |
|---|---|---|---|---|---|---|
| IN | — | No. | — | — | — | *Reeder-Baker v. Lincoln National Corp.*, 644 F. Supp. 983 (N.D. Ind. 1986). |
| IA | No. | — | — | — | — | *Grahek v. Voluntary Hosp. Coop. Assoc. of Iowa, Inc.*, 473 N.W.2d 31 (Iowa 1991). |
| KS | — | Yes. | — | — | Although one court has recognized public policy cause of action for race discrimination, courts in two decisions have refused to recognize public policy cause of action based on discrimination. | *Wynn v. Boeing Military Airplane Co.*, 595 F. Supp. 727 (D. Kan. 1984); *Tarr v. Riberglass, Inc.*, No. 83-4234 (D. Kan., unpublished, Feb. 6, 1984); *Robinson v. Colt Indus.*, No. 84-2472, slip op. at 9 (D. Kan., *unpublished*, Mar. 5, 1986). |
| KY | — | — | — | — | No cause of action recognized; statutory remedy is exclusive. | *Grzyb v. Evans*, 700 S.W.2d 399 (Ky. 1985). |
| LA | — | — | — | — | No cause of action recognized. | *Guillory v. St. Landry Parish Police Jury*, 802 F.2d 822 (5th Cir. 1986). |
| ME | — | — | — | — | — | — |
| MD | — | — | Yes. | — | — | *Brandon v. Molesworth*, 672 A.2d 608 (Md. 1996); *Kerrigan v. Magnum Entertainment Inc.*, 804 F. Supp. 733 (D. Md. 1992). |
| MA | No. | — | — | — | No cause of action recognized; statutory remedy is exclusive. | *Melley v. Gilette Corp.*, 475 N.E.2d 1227 (Mass. App. 1985); *Crews v. Memorex Corp.*, 588 F. Supp. 27 (D. Mass. 1984); *Borase v. M/A COM, Inc.*, 906 F. Supp. 65 (D. Mass. 1995). |
| MI | — | — | — | — | Cause of action recognized in general; statutory remedy is not exclusive. | *Pompey v. General Motors Corp.*, 189 N.W.2d 243 (Mich. 1971). |
| MN | No. | — | — | — | — | *Lilligren v. Midwest Communications*, 5 Ind. Empl. Rights Cases 124 (BNA) (D. Minn. 1989). |
| MS | — | — | — | — | — | — |
| MO | — | — | — | — | No cause of action recognized; statutory remedy is exclusive. | *Osborn v. Professional Serv. Indus., Inc.*, 872 F. Supp. 679 (W.D. Mo. 1994); *Wyrick v. TWA Credit Union*, 804 F. Supp. 1176 (W.D. Mo. 1992). |
| MT | — | — | Yes. | — | — | *Foster v. Albertsons, Inc.*, 835 P.2d 720 (Mont. 1992). |
| NE | — | — | — | — | — | — |
| NV | No. | — | — | — | — | *Sands Regent v. Valardson*, 777 P.2d 898 (Nev. 1989). |
| NH | No. | — | No. | No. | — | *Kopf v. Chloride Power Elec., Inc.*, 882 F. Supp. 1183 (D. N.H. 1995); *Smith v. F.W. Morse Co.*, 76 F.3d 413 (1st Cir. 1996); *but see Gardner v. Blue Mountain Forest Assoc.*, 902 F. Supp. 14 (D. N.H. 1995). |
| NJ | No. | — | — | — | Some court decisions have indicated that a cause of action may be recognized. | *Blum v. Witco Chem. Corp.*, 829 F.2d 367 (3d Cir. 1987); *Erickson v. Marsh & McLennon Co., Inc.*, 569 A.2d 793 (N.J. 1990); *Witkowski v. Thomas J. Lipton, Inc.*, 643 A.2d 546 (N.J. 1994); *Kapossy v. McGraw-Hill, Inc.*, 921 F. Supp. 234 (D. N.J. 1996). |
| NM | — | — | — | — | — | — |
| NY | — | — | — | — | No cause of action recognized. | *Murphy v. American Home Prods. Corp.*, 461 N.Y.S.2d 232 (Ct. App. 1983). |

*(Table continues.)*

## Table 4.4-2 *(cont'd)*
## WRONGFUL DISCHARGE ACTIONS: STATE PUBLIC POLICY AGAINST DISCRIMINATION

**KEY:** An em-dash (—) indicates that there has been no court decision expressly recognizing cause of action.

**NOTE:** Although there may be no court decision expressly recognizing a cause of action based on a particular type of discrimination (e.g., age or sex), if state courts have recognized cause of action on behalf of one class of persons covered by statute, it is likely that future decisions will recognize causes of action on behalf of other classes of persons protected by statute.

| | *Age* | *Race* | *Sex* | *Disability* | *Other* | *Citations to Authority* |
|---|---|---|---|---|---|---|
| NC | — | Yes. | Yes. | — | — | *Mumford v. CSX Transp.*, 878 F. Supp. 827 (M.D.N.C. 1994); *Phillips v. J.P. Stevens & Co., Inc.*, 827 F. Supp. 349 (M.D.N.C. 1993); *Hogan v. Forsyth Country Club Co.*, 340 S.E.2d 116 (N.C. App. 1986); *Percell v. International Business Machines, Inc.*, 765 F. Supp. 297 (E.D.N.C. 1991); *Harrison v. Edison Brothers Apparel Stores, Inc.*, 724 F. Supp. 1185 (M.D.N.C. 1989); *Mayse v. Protective Agency, Inc.*, 771 F. Supp. 267 (W.D.N.C. 1991). |
| ND | — | — | No. | — | — | *Bakken v. North American Coal Corp.*, 641 F. Supp. 1015 (D.N.D. 1986). |
| OH | — | — | Yes. | Yes. | No claim stated for discharge in violation of public policy against discrimination where employee claimed he was discharged in violation of a local ordinance prohibiting discrimination against homosexuals. | *Collins v. Rizkana*, 652 N.E.2d 653 (Ohio, 1995); *Clipson v. Schlessman*, 624 N.E.2d 220 (Ohio App. 1993); *White v. Federal Reserve Bank*, 660 N.E.2d 493 (Ohio App. 1995); *Greenwood v. Taft, Steltinius and Hollister*, 663 N.E.2d 1030 (Ohio Ct. App. 1995) *but see Wyckoff v. Forest City Auto Parts Co.*, 916 F. Supp. 683 (N.D. Ohio 1996); *DeKoning v. Flower Mem. Hosp.*, 676 N.E.2d 614 (Ohio Com. Pl. 1996). |
| OK | No. Preempted by statutory remedy. | Yes. | Yes, but employer must have 15 or more employees. | Yes. | Public policy exception does not extend to discriminatory failure to hire due to racial discrimination. | *Tate v. Browning-Ferris, Inc.*, 833 P.2d 1218 (Okla. 1992); *Katzer v. Baldor Elec. Co.*, 969 F.2d 935 (10th Cir. 1992); *but see Sarsycki v. United Parcel Serv.*, 862 F. Supp. 336 (W.D. Okla. 1994); *Williams v. Dub Ross Co.*, 895 P.2d 1344 (Okla. 1995); *Brown v. Ford*, 905 P.2d 223 (Okla. 1995); *List v. Anchor Paint Manufacturing Co.*, 910 P.2d 1101 (Okla. 1996). |
| OR | — | — | Yes. | — | No, for pregnancy. | *Holien v. Sears, Roebuck & Co.*, 689 P.2d 1292 (Or. 1994); *Cross v. Eastlund*, 796 P.2d 1214 (Or. App. 1990). |
| PA | — | — | No. | No. | No cause of action recognized. | *Kinnally v. Bell of Pennsylvania*, 748 F. Supp. 1136 (E.D. Pa. 1990); *Kelly v. National R.R. Passenger Corp.*, 731 F. Supp. 698 (E.D. Pa. 1990); *Mulgrew v. Sears Roebuck & Co.*, 868 F. Supp. 98 (E.D. Pa. 1994). |
| RI | — | — | — | — | No cause of action recognized for wrongful discharge. | *Pacheo v. Raytheon Co.*, 623 A.2d 464 (R.I. 1993). |
| SC | — | — | — | — | — | — |
| SD | — | — | — | — | — | — |
| TN | — | — | — | — | — | — |

| | | | | | | |
|---|---|---|---|---|---|---|
| TX | — | No. | Yes. | — | — | *Spiller v. Ella Smithers Geriatric Ctr.*, 919 F.2d 339 (5th Cir. 1990); *Roark v. Kidder, Peabody & Co., Inc.*, 959 F. Supp. 379 (N.D. Tex. 1997). |
| UT | — | — | — | — | No cause of action recognized. | *Amos v. Corporation of the Presiding Bishop of the Church of Jesus Christ of Latter-Day Saints*, 594 F. Supp. 791 (D. Utah 1984). |
| VT | Yes, if no statutory remedy. | — | No. | — | — | *Payne v. Rozendaal*, 520 A.2d 586 (Vt. 1986); *Fellows v. Earth Constr., Inc.*, 794 F. Supp. 531 (D.Vt. 1992). |
| VA | — | Yes. | Yes. | No, statutory remedy for disability discrimination exclusive. | — | *Lockhart v. Commonwealth Educ. Sys. Corp.*, 439 S.E.2d 328 (Va. 1994); *Ecklund v. Fuisz Technology, Ltd.*, 905 F. Supp. 335 (E.D. Va. 1995); *Mannell v. American Tobacco Co.*, 871 F. Supp. 854 (E.D. Va. 1994). |
| WA | No. | — | — | — | Yes, for marital status. | *Bennett v. Hardy*, 784 P.2d 1258 (Wash. 1990); *Magula v. Benton Franklin Title Insurance Co.*, 901 P.2d 313 (Wash. Ct. App. 1995) aff'd 930 P.2d 307 (Wash. 1997). |
| WV | — | — | Yes. | — | No, for national origin (preempted by statute). | *Williamson v. Greene*, 490 S.E.2d 23 (W.Va. 1997); *Guevara v. K-Mart Corp.*, 629 F. Supp. 1189 (D. W.Va. 1986). |
| WI | No. | — | No. | — | — | *Mursch v. Van Dorn Co.*, 627 F. Supp. 1310 (W.D. Wis. 1986); *Shanahan v. WITI-TV, Inc.*, 565 F. Supp. 219 (E.D. Wis. 1982); *Zywicki v. Moxness Products*, 31 FEP Cases 1348 (E.D. Wis. 1983). |
| WY | — | — | No. | — | — | *Ball v. City of Cheyenne, Wyoming*, 845 F. Supp. 803 (D. Wyo. 1993), *modified*, 54 F.3d 664 (10th Cir. 1995). |

# § 4.5 Statutory Restrictions on Discharging Employees

Over the years, the employment-at-will rule has been increasingly restricted by a wide range of federal statutes, state laws, and court rulings.

Table 4.5-1, Table 4.5-2, and Table 4.5-3 show which states have statutory restrictions on discharging employees for performing the legal duties of military service, jury service, and service as a witness in court, respectively. Table 4.5-4 indicates which states have statutes protecting the employee's right to vote according to his or her choice and which states have statutes requiring that employees not be penalized for taking time off to vote. Table 4.5-5 lists those states that have enacted statutes restricting employers from discharging employees because of wage garnishments and membership or nonmembership in labor organizations. Table 4.5-6 shows which states protect employees who file claims for workers' compensation or complaints with OSHA about retaliation. Table 4.5-7 covers individual state whistle-blower laws. Many of the statutes shown in the tables are civil service laws governing public employment.

Of course, employers are also restricted in their treatment of employees by both federal and state fair employment practices legislation. For information on antidiscrimination laws, see Part 2, Fair Employment Practices, and Part 9, Summary of Federal Legislation, Guidelines, and Policies on Human Resources Law. It should be noted that, to the extent that state law purports to provide less protection than that provided by federal law, the state law may be preempted.

# Table 4.5-1
## STATUTORY RESTRICTIONS ON DISCHARGING EMPLOYEES: MILITARY SERVICE LEAVE

(See also text at § 4.5.)

**NOTE:** An em-dash (—) means that no specific statutory authority exists; other authority, including case law, may apply.

| | *Are Employers Prohibited from Discharging Employees for Taking Military Leave?* | *Employers Covered by Statute* | | *How Many Days of Paid Leave per Year Is Employee Allowed?* | *Are Employers Required to Reemploy Persons Returning from Military Service?* | *Remedies and Penalties* | *Citations to Authority* |
|---|---|---|---|---|---|---|---|
| | | *Public* | *Private* | | | | |
| AL | Yes. | Yes. | Yes. | 168 working hours. | State has no statutory requirements. | State has no statutory requirements. | Ala. Code § 31-2-13. |
| AK | Yes. | Yes. | — | 16½ days for training duty; 5 days for governor-ordered active duty. | Yes. | Employer who deprives employee of employment because of employee's military membership is guilty of a misdemeanor, punishable by a fine of not more than $100. | Alaska Stat. §§ 26.05.340, 39.20.340, 39.20.350. |
| AZ | Yes. | Yes. | Yes. | 30 days in any 2 consecutive years. | Yes. | Employer who does not allow military leave is guilty of a Class 3 misdemeanor. Employer who discharges employee because of employee's military membership or absence from work to perform military duty is guilty of a Class 2 misdemeanor. | Ariz. Rev. Stat. Ann. §§ 26-167, 26-168. |
| AR | Yes. | Yes. | Yes. | 15 days for public employees. Any unused portion may be accumulated for use in the next calendar year to allow a maximum total of 30 leave days in any one calendar year. Public employees called to duty by governor or president in emergency situations are entitled to 30 days of paid leave, after which such employees will be granted leave without pay. | If returning from active duty, a public employee must apply for reemployment within 90 days of release from active duty. A public employee who enlists for a second consecutive tour of duty forfeits his reemployment rights. | Employer who does not reemploy is liable for costs and attorneys' fees. | Ark. Code Ann. §§ 12-62-413, 21-4-212. |

(Table continues.)

# Table 4.5-1 *(cont'd)*

## STATUTORY RESTRICTIONS ON DISCHARGING EMPLOYEES: MILITARY SERVICE LEAVE

(See also text at § 4.5.)

**NOTE:** An em-dash (—) means that no specific statutory authority exists; other authority, including case law, may apply.

| | *Are Employers Prohibited from Discharging Employees for Taking Military Leave?* | *Employers Covered by Statute* | | *How Many Days of Paid Leave per Year Is Employee Allowed?* | *Are Employers Required to Reemploy Persons Returning from Military Service?* | *Remedies and Penalties* | *Citations to Authority* |
|---|---|---|---|---|---|---|---|
| | | *Public* | *Private* | | | | |
| CA | Yes. | Yes. | Yes. | Public employee engaged in active duty for training, special exercises, or other activities is entitled to 180 days temporary leave per year, the first 30 of which will be paid. | Public employee returning from temporary duty has an absolute right to reemployment. If former position has ceased to exist during employee's absence, employee is entitled to position of like seniority, status, and pay. If another position does not exist, employee will have same rights he or she would have had if employee had occupied the position when it ceased to exist. Private employee who is member of California National Guard returning from active military duty ordered by the governor in time of emergency is entitled to reemployment if position was not temporary, employee receives certificate of satisfactory service, employee is still qualified to perform work duties, and employee applies for reemployment within 40 days after release from service, unless employer's changed circumstances make it unreasonable. Part-time employee must notify employer within 5 days after satisfactory service in the California National Guard. Employee so reinstated cannot be discharged without cause within 1 year of reinstatement. | Any employer who discriminates against employee because of employee's military membership or because employee is ordered to military duty is guilty of a misdemeanor and liable for employee's actual damages and reasonable attorneys' fees. Court may order private employer who does not comply with reemployment provision to comply and to compensate employee for lost wages and benefits. | Cal. Mil. & Vet. Code §§ 394 *et seq.* |
| CO | Yes. | Yes. | Yes. | 15 days for public employee training in the reserves; 15 unpaid days for private employees. | Yes. Public employee is entitled to reemployment if position still exists, employee is physically and mentally able to perform duties, employee submits evidence of satisfactory completion of military service, and | Employee may bring civil action for damages or equitable relief. | Colo. Rev. Stat. §§ 28-3-601 *et seq.*, 28-3-609 *et seq.* |

| | | | | | | | |
|---|---|---|---|---|---|---|---|
| | | | | | employee applies in writing for reemployment within 90 days of end of service or end of hospitalization that results from service, as long as that date falls within 1 year and 90 days of end of service. Employee so reinstated cannot be discharged without cause within 1 year of reinstatement. Elected or appointed public officer is entitled to reinstatement if officer files within 45 days of end of service a verified certificate stating that he or she has complied with above listed conditions for reemployment. Private employee who takes leave for military training, not exceeding 15 days, is entitled to reemployment if position was other than temporary, employee provides evidence of satisfactory completion of military duty, and employee is still qualified to perform work duties. | | |
| CT | Yes. Includes leave to attend drills, parades, and encampments. | Yes. | Yes, for military reserve or National Guard meetings or drills. | 30 days. | State employees have a right to reinstatement within 90 days after receiving a Certificate for Satisfactory Service. | — | Conn. Gen. Stat. Ann. §§ 5-255, 27-33, 27-33a. |
| DE | Yes. Leave must be allowed for reserve members on temporary active duty and for employees entering the armed forces or the National Guard. | Yes. | Yes. | 3 years unpaid leave for state employees. | Yes. | Employee may bring civil suit for damages and other appropriate relief. | Del. Code Ann. tit. 20, § 905; tit. 29, § 5105. |
| DC | — | — | — | — | — | — | State has no statutory provisions. |
| FL | Yes. | Yes. | Yes. | 17 days for state officers and employees engaged in reserve or guard training. 30 days for public employees engaged in active military service, including training and active duty. Employing authority also has discretion to pay public officials and employees after the first 30 days the amount necessary to bring (*cont'd*) | Yes. | Employee who has been employed for a period of at least 1 year prior to being ordered into active duty service may bring a civil suit for damages. Employer is also liable for attorneys' fees and court costs. | Fla. Stat. Ann. §§ 115.01 *et seq.*, 250.48, 250.482. |

(*Table continues.*)

## Table 4.5-1 *(cont'd)*

## STATUTORY RESTRICTIONS ON DISCHARGING EMPLOYEES: MILITARY SERVICE LEAVE

(See also text at § 4.5.)

**NOTE:** An em-dash (—) means that no specific statutory authority exists; other authority, including case law, may apply.

| | *Are Employers Prohibited from Discharging Employees for Taking Military Leave?* | *Employers Covered by Statute* | | *How Many Days of Paid Leave per Year Is Employee Allowed?* | *Are Employers Required to Reemploy Persons Returning from Military Service?* | *Remedies and Penalties* | *Citations to Authority* |
|---|---|---|---|---|---|---|---|
| | | *Public* | *Private* | | | | |
| FL *(cont'd)* | | | | total salary up to the level earned at the time employee was called to active military service. | | | |
| GA | Yes. | Yes. | Yes. | Public employees are entitled to salary for any time they are engaged in ordered military duty, up to 18 days per calendar year and not exceeding 18 days in any one continuous period of absence; if governor declares an emergency and orders public employees to active duty as National Guard members, the amount of compensable time is increased to 30 days per calendar year and not exceeding 30 days in any one continuous period of service. | Yes, employer must restore employee to the same or a similar position if employee receives certificate of completion of military service, employee is still qualified to perform duties, and employee applies for reemployment within 90 days after relief from military service, if the position is with a private employer, unless employer's changed circumstances make it unreasonable. Employee so reinstated shall not be discharged without cause within 1 year of reinstatement. Public employer must reemploy. National Guardsmen have 10 days to apply after end of service. | Private employer who does not reinstate employee can be required to comply by injunctive relief and may be ordered to compensate employee for any lost wages or benefits. | Ga. Code Ann. §§ 38-2-279, 38-2-280. |
| HI | Yes. | Yes. | Yes. | 15 days for public employees; none for private employees. If public employee is called to duty a second time in a calendar year, employee may elect to use the 15 paid days of leave for the next year in the current year. | Private employee who is a member of the National Guard is entitled to reinstatement to the same or a similar position, unless employee is no longer qualified because of disability sustained during military service or employer's changed circumstances make it unreasonable. If employee is no longer qualified for former position, he or she will be employed in a position for which he or she is qualified as will provide like seniority, status, and pay or the nearest approxima- | State has no statutory requirements. | Haw. Rev. Stat. §§ 79-20 *et seq.*, 121-43. |

| | | | | | | | |
|---|---|---|---|---|---|---|---|
| | | | | | tion thereof, unless employer's circumstances make it unreasonable to do so. Any person reinstated cannot be discharged without cause within 1 year of reinstatement. | | |
| ID | Yes. | Yes. | Yes. | 15 days for public employees. Private employees receive 15 days, but leave may be with or without pay at employer's discretion. | For training, yes, if position was not temporary, employee gives evidence of dates of departure and return 90 days before date of departure, employee gives evidence of satisfactory completion immediately after military duty, and employee is still qualified to perform work duties. Employee who is an Idaho National Guard member ordered to duty by governor is entitled to reemployment if U.S. government is not the employer, position was not temporary, release from duty occurred under honorable conditions, employee is physically qualified for employment, military duty did not exceed 1 year, and employee applies for reemployment within 30 days of release from duty. If employee is no longer qualified, employer must offer position for which employee is qualified that is most similar in seniority, status, and pay. Any employee reinstated cannot be discharged without cause for 1 year after reinstatement. | Employee may bring action for damages and equitable relief. | Idaho Code §§ 46-216, 46-224 *et seq.*, 46-407. |
| IL | Yes. Full-time employee other than an independent contractor shall be granted leave. | Yes. | — | Employee continues to receive regular compensation while in annual training. During basic training and for up to 60 days of advanced training, employee will receive regular compensation minus base military pay if military pay is less than employee's compensation. | State has no statutory requirements. | State has no statutory requirements. | Ill. Ann. Stat. ch. 5, ¶ 325/1. |
| IN | Yes. Employee must provide employer with evidence of dates of departure and return as soon as practicable before departure. Upon return, employee must furnish employer with evidence of satisfactory completion of training. | Yes. | Yes. | Public employee is entitled to 15 days of paid leave for training. Private employer has discretion to grant leave for training with or without pay. Public employee also is entitled to leave of absence for any time on active duty, but such leave is paid or unpaid at employer's discretion. Private employee is entitled to leave for active duty; pay at the discretion of the employer. | Yes. | Employer who denies leave of absence is subject to suit for damages. Employer who does not allow a state National Guard member to attend any assembly at which he or she has a duty to perform is guilty of a Class B misdemeanor. | Ind. Code Ann. §§ 10-2-4-2, 10-2-4-3, 10-2-4-3.5, 10-5-8-1, 10-5-9-1, 10-5-9-2. |

*(Table continues.)*

# Table 4.5-1 *(cont'd)*
## STATUTORY RESTRICTIONS ON DISCHARGING EMPLOYEES: MILITARY SERVICE LEAVE

(See also text at § 4.5.)

**NOTE:** An em-dash (—) means that no specific statutory authority exists; other authority, including case law, may apply.

| | *Are Employers Prohibited from Discharging Employees for Taking Military Leave?* | *Employers Covered by Statute* | | *How Many Days of Paid Leave per Year Is Employee Allowed?* | *Are Employers Required to Reemploy Persons Returning from Military Service?* | *Remedies and Penalties* | *Citations to Authority* |
|---|---|---|---|---|---|---|---|
| | | *Public* | *Private* | | | | |
| IA | Yes. | Yes. | Yes. | State has no statutory requirements. | Yes, if employment was not of a temporary nature, employee provides evidence of satisfactory completion of military duty, and employee is still qualified to perform work duties. | Violator is guilty of a simple misdemeanor. | Iowa Code Ann. § 29A.43. *Bewley v. Villisca Iowa Community Sch. Dist.*, 299 N.W.2d 904 (Iowa 1980). |
| KS | Yes, for the National Guard of Kansas. | Yes. | Yes. | State has no statutory requirements. | State has no statutory requirements. | Violator of military leave statute may be punished by a fine of $5–$50. | Kan. Stat. Ann. § 48-222. |
| KY | Yes. | Yes. | Yes. | 15 days for public employees. | Yes. | Violation of antidiscrimination statute carries a penalty of $100–$500 or at least 6 months' imprisonment. Failure to reemploy is a Class A misdemeanor. | Ky. Rev. Stat. Ann. §§ 36.140, 38.238, 38.250, 38.460, 38.990. |
| LA | Yes. | Yes. | Yes. | 15 days for public employee who is a member of the reserves. Public and private employers are not required to but are authorized to pay any employee who leaves for military service. | Yes, if employee is still qualified, absence does not exceed 5 years (except active duty in war or national emergency), employee timely reapplies, and employer's changed circumstances do not make it impossible. An employee absent 30 days or less must reapply on the first regular workday 8 hours after return; 31–180 days: must reapply not later than 14 days after return; 181 or more days: must reapply within 90 days of return. Two years is allowed if employee is injured. | Employee may bring action for compliance and lost wages and benefits. Employer may be held liable for costs and attorney fees. | La. Rev. Stat. Ann. §§ 29:401 *et seq.*, 42:394. |

| | | | | | | | |
|---|---|---|---|---|---|---|---|
| ME | Yes. | Yes. | Yes. | Public employees are entitled to paid leave for all annual training duties authorized by governor or federal law. | State has no statutory requirements. | Employer who does not allow leave is guilty of a Class E crime. | Me. Rev. Stat. Ann. tit. 37-B, § 342(5). |
| MD | Yes. | Yes. | Yes. | Public employees are entitled to 15 days paid leave. If called to active duty by the Governor, public employees are entitled to paid leave for period of active service. | Yes, public or private employee who is ordered to active duty or training is protected in civilian employment if position was other than temporary, employee applies for reemployment within 30 days after leaving military duty, and employee is still qualified to perform duties of position. If employee is no longer qualified to perform the duties of position because of disability sustained during military leave, employee is entitled to a position, the duties of which he or she is qualified to perform, as will provide like seniority, status, and pay or the nearest approximation thereof, unless employer's changed circumstances make it unreasonable. | Private employer who fails to reemploy may be required to reinstate employee and to compensate employee for lost wages and benefits. | Md. Ann. Code art. 65, § 32A, 42. |
| MA | Yes. | Yes. | Yes. | 17 days, but the leave may be with or without pay at employer's discretion. Public employees are entitled to paid leave if approved by vote of county commissioners or city council or of its inhabitants at a town meeting. State employees are entitled to paid leave when called into service by the governor. | Yes, if position was not temporary, employee gives employer notice of dates of departure and return, employee gives employer notice of satisfactory completion of military training, and employee is still qualified to perform duties of position. | Employee may bring civil action at law or equity for employer's failure to allow leave or failure to reemploy when reemployment is required. Employer who denies or deprives person of employment because of person's absence for military duty shall be subject to a fine of not more than $500, or imprisonment for not more than 6 months, or both. | Mass. Gen. Laws Ann. ch. 33, § 13, 59, 59A; ch. 149, § 52A; Op. Atty. Gen, Feb. 1, 1997, p. 122. |
| MI | Yes. | Yes. | Yes. | State has no statutory requirements. | Yes, if employee applies for reinstatement within 15 days of release from training duty. | Violator is guilty of a misdemeanor. | Mich. Stat. Ann. §§ 4.1487(1) *et seq.*, 28.630. |
| MN | Yes. | Yes. | Yes. | 15 days paid leave for public employees. Unpaid leave for service in time of war or emergency for private employees and for public employees in excess of 15 days. | Yes, a public employee ordered to an initial period of active duty for training for not less than 3 consecutive months is entitled to reemployment if employee applies for reinstatement within 31 days of release from duty after satisfactory service or discharge from hospitalization or if employee applies for reinstatement within 1 year after scheduled release, whichever is earlier. Employee so reinstated cannot be discharged without cause within 6 months of restoration. Public and private *(cont'd)* | Employer who discharges employee because of employee's military membership or who hinders employee from performing military service is guilty of a gross misdemeanor. | Minn. Stat. Ann. §§ 192.26, 192.34, 192.261. |

*(Table continues.)*

**Table 4.5-1** *(cont'd)*

## STATUTORY RESTRICTIONS ON DISCHARGING EMPLOYEES: MILITARY SERVICE LEAVE

(See also text at § 4.5.)

**NOTE:** An em-dash (—) means that no specific statutory authority exists; other authority, including case law, may apply.

| | *Are Employers Prohibited from Discharging Employees for Taking Military Leave?* | *Employers Covered by Statute* | | *How Many Days of Paid Leave per Year Is Employee Allowed?* | *Are Employers Required to Reemploy Persons Returning from Military Service?* | *Remedies and Penalties* | *Citations to Authority* |
|---|---|---|---|---|---|---|---|
| | | *Public* | *Private* | | | | |
| MN (*cont'd*) | | | | | employees are entitled to reemployment after time of war or emergency if position still exists, employee is able to perform duties, employee provides evidence of satisfactory completion of service, and employee applies for reinstatement within 90 days of end of service or discharge from hospitalization, as long as application is made within 1 year and 90 days of end of service. Employee so reinstated cannot be discharged without cause for 1 year after reinstatement. | | |
| MS | Yes. | Yes. | Yes. | 15 days for public employees. Leave for private employees may be without pay. | Private employees are entitled to reemployment if position was not temporary, employee gives evidence of satisfactory completion of service, duty, or training, and employee is qualified to perform duties of position. Public employees are entitled to reemployment if employee receives certificate noting satisfactory completion of service, employee is qualified to perform duties, and employee applies for reinstatement within 90 days of end of service or release from hospitalization lasting no more than 1 year. Public employee so reinstated cannot be discharged without cause for 1 year after reinstatement. | Employer who does not allow leave is guilty of a misdemeanor, punishable by a fine not to exceed $1,000, or imprisonment for not more than 6 months, or both. | Miss. Code Ann. §§ 33-1-15, 33-1-19, 33-1-21. |

| | | | | | | | |
|---|---|---|---|---|---|---|---|
| MO | Yes. | Yes. | Yes. | For public employees: 15 days for military service in the performance of duty or training under competent orders; unlimited leave for governor-ordered training or duty. | State has no statutory requirements. | Violator is guilty of a misdemeanor. State attorney general will enforce reemployment rights. | Mo. Ann. Stat. §§ 40.490, 41.730, 105.270. |
| MT | Yes. | Yes. | — | 15 days. Person must have been an employee for 6 months to be eligible for leave. | Yes, private employers are, if position was not temporary, employee receives certificate of completion, employee is still qualified to perform duties, and employee applies in writing for reemployment within 40 days of end of service. Public employers are, if position was not abolished. | If employer refuses to rehire, employee may bring action for reinstatement, lost wages, and benefits. | Mont. Code Ann. §§ 10-1-604, 10-2-211 *et seq.* |
| NE | Yes. | Yes. | — | 15 days. In times of emergency declared by governor, public employees are entitled to leave beyond 15 days. During such additional absence, employee shall receive such portion of his or her salary or compensation as will equal the loss he or she may suffer while in active service of the state. | Yes, private employee involuntarily ordered to active duty is entitled to reemployment if employee applies within 30 days of release from duty. Period of absence in such situations may be paid or unpaid at employer's discretion. Public employee is entitled to reemployment if employee applies within 30 days of release from duty and employee is still qualified to perform work duties. If employee is not qualified to perform duties, he or she is entitled to a position for which he or she is qualified as will provide the same seniority, status, and pay or the nearest approximation thereof. Employee so reinstated cannot be discharged without cause for 1 year after reinstatement. | Employee may bring civil action for damages and appropriate equitable relief. Violator is guilty of a Class IV misdemeanor. | Neb. Rev. Stat. §§ 55-160 *et seq.* |
| NV | Yes. | Yes. | Yes. | Leave is unpaid. | Yes, public employer must reinstate employee if employee applies for reinstatement within 90 days of end of service. | Employee may file complaint with labor commissioner within 60 days of termination. Employee is entitled to reinstatement, lost wages, and benefits. Violator is guilty of a misdemeanor. | Nev. Rev. Stat. Ann. §§ 284.365, 412.139, 412.1393, 412.1395. |
| NH | Yes. | Yes. | Yes. | State has no statutory requirements. | Yes. Applies to public employers. Employee must apply within 90 days of end of service. | For discriminating against employee because of military service or absence from work for military service, an employer who is a natural person (i.e., an individual rather than a corporation) is guilty of a misdemeanor; a corporate or any other employer is guilty of a felony. Employee may bring civil action for damages, injunctive relief, and reasonable costs and attorneys' fees. | N.H. Rev. Stat. Ann. §§ 97:1, 110-B:65. |

*(Table continues.)*

# Table 4.5-1 *(cont'd)*

## STATUTORY RESTRICTIONS ON DISCHARGING EMPLOYEES: MILITARY SERVICE LEAVE

(See also text at § 4.5.)

**NOTE:** An em-dash (—) means that no specific statutory authority exists; other authority, including case law, may apply.

| | *Are Employers Prohibited from Discharging Employees for Taking Military Leave?* | *Employers Covered by Statute* | | *How Many Days of Paid Leave per Year Is Employee Allowed?* | *Are Employers Required to Reemploy Persons Returning from Military Service?* | *Remedies and Penalties* | *Citations to Authority* |
|---|---|---|---|---|---|---|---|
| | | *Public* | *Private* | | | | |
| NJ | Yes. | Yes. | — | Public employee who is a U.S. reserve corps member is entitled to paid leave for all days that he or she will be engaged in field training. Public employee in an ad interim or temporary position who is a National Guard, Naval Militia, Air National Guard, or U.S. reserve corps member is entitled to 30 days of leave with pay if he or she has worked in the temporary position for 1 year or longer and without pay if he or she has worked in the temporary position for less than 1 year. Public employees entering military service in time of war or emergency are entitled to leave for the entire period of service and for 3 more months following discharge. If an employee is incapacitated as a result of service, leave shall extend 3 months after recovery or until the end of 2 years after discharge, whichever occurs first. Such leave may be with or without pay, except as otherwise provided by law. | Yes, if position was not temporary, employee receives certificate of completion of military service, employee is still qualified to perform duties of position, and employee applies for reemployment within 90 days of end of service, if position was with a private employer, unless employer's changed circumstances make it unreasonable to do so. Any person reinstated cannot be discharged without cause within 1 year of restoration. If leave occurs during war or emergency, public employee is entitled to resume position as long as he or she applies to do so before the end of leave of absence. | Court can order employer to comply and to restore lost wages and benefits. | N.J. Stat. Ann. §§ 38:23-1, 38:23-1.1, 38:23-3, 38:23-4, 38:23C-20. |

| | | | | | | | |
|---|---|---|---|---|---|---|---|
| NM | Yes. | Yes. | Yes. | 15 days for public employees. | Yes, if position was not temporary, employee is honorably discharged or entitled to a certificate of service, employee is still qualified to perform duties, and employee applies for reemployment within 90 days of end of service or end of hospitalization that extends not more than 1 year. | Violator is guilty of a misdemeanor. Public or private employers who do not reinstate employees are liable for lost wages and benefits. | N.M. Stat. Ann. §§ 20-4-6, 20-4-7, 28-15-1 *et seq.* |
| NY | Yes. | Yes. | Yes. | Public officers and employees are entitled to paid leave for a total of 30 days or 22 working days, whichever is greater, in one calendar year. | If leave is for active military duty: Yes, if position was not temporary, employee receives certificate of completion of military service, employee is still qualified to perform duties of position, and employee applies for reemployment within 90 days of end of service, if position was with private employer, unless employer's changed circumstances make it unreasonable. If leave is for drill, annual training, or instruction: Yes, if position is not temporary, employee is qualified to perform duties, and employee applies for reemployment within 10 days of end of such temporary service. If leave is for initial full-time training or initial active duty for training: Yes, if position is not temporary, employee is qualified to perform duties, and employee applies for reemployment within 60 days of end of such training. Public employees shall be reinstated to former position provided employee applies for reemployment within 90 days of end of service. | Court may order private employer to comply with provisions and to compensate employee for lost wages and benefits. | N.Y. Mil. Law §§ 242, 243, 317, 318. |
| NC | Yes. | Yes. | Yes. | Paid leave for public employees as provided by N.C. Governor. | Public or private employee who is a North Carolina National Guard member and who entered state duty under orders from the governor is entitled to reemployment if employee applies in writing for reemployment within 5 days of release from duty or hospitalization that resulted from duty and employee is still qualified to perform duties of position, unless employer's changed circumstances make it unreasonable. If employee is no longer qualified for previous position, he or she will be placed in another position for which he or she is qualified with like seniority, status, and pay, unless employer's changed circumstances make it unreasonable. | Public or private employer who discharges employee because of employee's performance of any emergency military duty is guilty of a Class 2 misdemeanor and shall be fined not more than $500 or imprisoned for more than 6 months. Public or private employer who does not reinstate employee is subject to injunctive order and compensation of employee for lost wages and benefits. | N.C. Gen. Stat. §§ 127A-116, 127A-201, 127A-202, 127A-203, 127B-11, 127B-12, 127B-14, 127B-15. |

*(Table continues.)*

## Table 4.5-1 *(cont'd)*
## STATUTORY RESTRICTIONS ON DISCHARGING EMPLOYEES: MILITARY SERVICE LEAVE

(See also text at § 4.5.)

**NOTE:** An em-dash (—) means that no specific statutory authority exists; other authority, including case law, may apply.

| | *Are Employers Prohibited from Discharging Employees for Taking Military Leave?* | *Employers Covered by Statute* | | *How Many Days of Paid Leave per Year Is Employee Allowed?* | *Are Employers Required to Reemploy Persons Returning from Military Service?* | *Remedies and Penalties* | *Citations to Authority* |
|---|---|---|---|---|---|---|---|
| | | *Public* | *Private* | | | | |
| ND | Yes. | Yes. | — | 20 days if employee has been in continuous employ of the state for 90 days immediately preceding leave of absence. Any leave of absence for a full or partial mobilization of the reserve and National Guard forces or emergency state active duty must be without loss of pay for the first 30 days, less any other paid leave granted during the calendar year. Employee must be given time off without pay or an opportunity to reschedule for weekend, daily, or hourly periods of training. | Yes, if employee applies within 90 days of discharge and is still qualified to perform duties. Reinstated employee cannot be discharged without cause for 1 year following reinstatement. | Person not rehired may appeal to department of veterans' affairs, which may order employer to comply with provision. Violator is guilty of an infraction. | N.D. Cent. Code §§ 37-01-25, 37-01-25.1, 52-09-26. |
| OH | Yes. | Yes. | — | Permanent public employees are entitled to paid leave for not more than 22 8-hour workdays or 176 hours per calendar year. Employee must provide employer with written authorization for military leave before being credited with such leave. If permanent public employee is called to duty in excess of the above time because of an executive order from the president or an act of Congress, employee is entitled to be paid during each month of | Yes, if employee applies for reemployment within 90 days of discharge or end of hospitalization lasting not more than 1 year and employee is still qualified to perform duties of position. If employee is not qualified because of a disability sustained during military service, he or she will be placed in another position for which he or she is qualified with like seniority, status, and pay. Reinstated employee cannot be discharged without cause for 1 year after reinstatement. | Employer who violates reinstatement provisions may be fined not more than $1,000, or imprisoned not more than 6 months, or both. The Veterans Service Commission also may order employer to comply with reinstatement provisions and to compensate employee for lost wages, less any amount received from other employment or from unemployment compensation. | Ohio Rev. Code Ann. §§ 5903.03, 5903.04, 5903.05, 5903.99, 5923.05. |

| | | | | | | | |
|---|---|---|---|---|---|---|---|
| | | | | the excess period the lesser of $500 or the difference between monthly civilian salary and monthly military pay. Employer, however, may elect to pay employee more than the required minimum amount. | | | |
| OK | Yes. | Yes. | Yes. | Public employees are allowed 20 days. After that period, employer may elect to pay employee's salary, less any military compensation. | Yes, if employee is still qualified and applies for reemployment within 90 days of discharge. If employee is no longer qualified because of disabilities sustained during service, employee is entitled to position for which he or she is qualified of most similar seniority, status, and pay. | Employer who takes adverse personnel action because of military leave is subject to fine of not more than $100, or imprisonment for not more than 30 days, or both. | Okla. Stat. Ann. tit. 44, §§ 208, 209; tit. 51 §§ 25.4 *et seq.* |
| OR | Yes. | Yes. | — | 15 days for employees who have worked for the state for at least 6 months before leave of absence. | Yes, if employee is qualified to perform duties, military service was less than 4 years (or less than 5 years if extended at the request of the federal government), and employee makes application within 90 days after employee is relieved from military duty or from hospitalization continuing after discharge for a period of not more than 1 year. If employee is no longer qualified to perform duties of previous position because of disabilities sustained during military duty, employer shall place employee in position for which he or she is qualified of like seniority, status, and pay. Reinstated employee cannot be discharged without cause for 1 year following reinstatement. | State has no statutory requirements. | Or. Rev. Stat. §§ 408.240, 408.270, 408.290. |
| PA | Yes. | Yes. | Yes. | Public employees are entitled to 15 days paid leave for training. Employer may elect to continue payments in excess of 15 days when employee is engaged in authorized training. Automatic unpaid leave for public employees ordered to active duty. Public or private employer must continue to provide health insurance and other benefits for the first 30 days of the employee's military duty. At end of that period, employer will give employee option of continuing health insurance and benefits at employee's expense. | At end of emergency or other duty, public or private employer shall restore employee to previous position unless employer's changed circumstances make it unreasonable to do so. If employee is no longer qualified to perform duties of previous position because of disability sustained during military duty, employer shall place employee in position for which he or she is qualified of like seniority, status, and pay, unless employer's changed circumstances make it unreasonable to do so. | State has no statutory requirements. | Pa. Cons. Stat. Ann. tit. 51, §§ 4102, 7301 *et seq.* |

*(Table continues.)*

# Table 4.5-1 *(cont'd)*

## STATUTORY RESTRICTIONS ON DISCHARGING EMPLOYEES: MILITARY SERVICE LEAVE

(See also text at § 4.5.)

**NOTE:** An em-dash (—) means that no specific statutory authority exists; other authority, including case law, may apply.

| | *Are Employers Prohibited from Discharging Employees for Taking Military Leave?* | *Employers Covered by Statute* | | *How Many Days of Paid Leave per Year Is Employee Allowed?* | *Are Employers Required to Reemploy Persons Returning from Military Service?* | *Remedies and Penalties* | *Citations to Authority* |
|---|---|---|---|---|---|---|---|
| | | *Public* | *Private* | | | | |
| RI | Yes. | Yes. | Yes. | Employee who is a member of the reserves receives leave for training, with or without pay, at the discretion of the employer. | National Guard members and reservists are entitled to reemployment if position was not temporary, employee gives evidence of satisfactory completion of duty, and employee is still qualified to perform duties. Employee who is a veteran is entitled to reemployment if employee applies for reinstatement within 40 days after honorable discharge, employee is still qualified to perform duties, and employer's changed circumstances do not make it unreasonable to do so. | Employer who discriminates against employee because of military membership is guilty of a misdemeanor, punishable by a fine of not more than $500, or imprisonment for not more than 1 year, or both. National Guard member or reservist who is discharged unlawfully or is not reinstated may bring civil action for damages and equitable relief. Employer who does not reinstate veteran is subject to a fine of $50–$500. | R.I. Gen. Laws §§ 30-11-1 *et seq.*, 30-21-1. |
| SC | Yes. | Yes. | — | 15 days. 30 additional days if leave is ordered for emergency situation. | Any South Carolina National Guard or South Carolina State Guard member ordered to duty by governor is entitled to reemployment if employee applies for reinstatement within 5 days of release from duty or hospitalization and employee is still qualified to perform duties of position, unless employer's changed circumstances make it unreasonable. If employee is no longer qualified for position, he or she will receive another position for which he or she is qualified of like seniority, status, and salary unless employer's changed circumstances make it unreasonable. | Employee may bring civil action for lost wages or benefits if employer fails to reinstate employee returning from military service. | S.C. Code Ann. §§ 8-7-90, 25-1-2310, 25-1-2320, 25-1-2330, 25-1-2340. |

| | | | | | | | |
|---|---|---|---|---|---|---|---|
| SD | Yes. | Yes. | — | 15 days with or without pay. | Yes, if position was not temporary, employee gives evidence of dates of departure and return to the extent reasonably possible, employee gives evidence of satisfactory completion of military duty, employee applies within 90 days of end of service, and employee is still qualified to perform duties. Veterans are entitled to reinstatement of professional or occupational licenses upon application within 6 months of end of service. | Employee may bring civil action for damages or equitable relief. | S.D. Codified Laws §§ 3-6-19, 3-6-22 *et seq.*, 3-12-86, 36-1-1 *et seq.* |
| TN | Yes. | Yes. | — | 15 days plus any additional days that result from a call to active state duty. | Yes, if employee applies for reemployment within 90 days of end of military duty or hospitalization continuing after military duty for not more than 1 year and employee is still qualified to perform work duties. If employee is not qualified to perform previous duties, the position no longer exists, or a person with greater seniority now holds the position, employee will be placed in another position of like seniority, status, and pay. Reinstated employee cannot be discharged within 1 year of reinstatement. | Commission of personnel may direct public employers to comply and compensate employee for lost wages. County chancery courts have jurisdiction and may issue orders requiring compliance and payment of lost wages. | Tenn. Code Ann. §§ 8-33-102, 8-33-104, 8-33-106, 8-33-107, 8-33-109. |
| TX | Yes. | Yes. | — | 15 days for public officers and employees; a member of the legislature is entitled to pay for all days that the member is absent from a session of the legislature and engaged in training. | Yes. Private employer must reinstate a permanent employee on return from active duty unless employer's changed circumstances make it unreasonable. Public employer must reinstate permanent employee on return from active military service if employee is released from duty under honorable conditions not later than the fifth anniversary of the date of induction, enlistment, or call to active military service and if employee is physically and mentally qualified to perform duties of position. If employee is no longer qualified to perform duties, he or she will be placed in a position for which he or she is qualified that has like seniority, status, and pay. Reinstated employee cannot be discharged without cause within 1 year of reinstatement. | Private employee who is not reinstated may bring civil action for damages not exceeding 6 months' compensation and reasonable attorneys' fees. For public employees, district court may require compliance. | Tex. Gov't Code Ann. §§ 431.005, 431.006, 613.001 *et seq.* |

*(Table continues.)*

# Table 4.5-1 *(cont'd)*
## STATUTORY RESTRICTIONS ON DISCHARGING EMPLOYEES: MILITARY SERVICE LEAVE

(See also text at § 4.5.)

**NOTE:** An em-dash (—) means that no specific statutory authority exists; other authority, including case law, may apply.

| | *Are Employers Prohibited from Discharging Employees for Taking Military Leave?* | *Employers Covered by Statute* | | *How Many Days of Paid Leave per Year Is Employee Allowed?* | *Are Employers Required to Reemploy Persons Returning from Military Service?* | *Remedies and Penalties* | *Citations to Authority* |
|---|---|---|---|---|---|---|---|
| | | *Public* | *Private* | | | | |
| UT | Yes. | Yes. | Yes. | State has no statutory requirements. | Yes, if public employee applies for reemployment within 40 days of discharge. Reinstated public employee cannot be discharged without cause for 1 year following reinstatement. | Employee may bring civil action for reinstatement, lost wages, benefits, costs, and attorneys' fees. Public or private employer who discriminates against employee because of employee's membership in a reserve component of the armed forces is guilty of a Class B misdemeanor. | Utah Code Ann. §§ 39-1-36, 39-3-1. |
| VT | Yes. | Yes. | Yes. | 15 days with or without pay. | Yes, if position is not temporary, employee gives evidence of dates of departure and return 30 days before departure, employee provides evidence of satisfactory completion of duty, and employee is still qualified to perform duties. | Employee may bring civil action for damages and equitable relief if employer takes adverse personnel action because of military leave. | Vt. Stat. Ann. tit. 21, §§ 491, 492, 493. |
| VA | Yes. | Yes. | — | 15 days for federally funded military duty, including training and active duty. | No public official or employee shall forfeit his title to office or position by reason of engaging in war service or being called forth by governor. Employer shall temporarily appoint someone to fulfill employees' responsibilities while employee is engaged in military service. | Employer who discharges or fails to employ person because that person is a member of the Virginia National Guard, Virginia State Defense Force, or naval militia is guilty of a misdemeanor, punishable by a fine of not more than $500, or imprisonment for not more than 30 days, or both. | Va. Code Ann. §§ 2.1-31, 44-93, 44-98. |

| | | | | | | | |
|---|---|---|---|---|---|---|---|
| WA | Yes. | Yes. | Yes. | 15 days for public employees. | Applies to public and private employees and employers: State organized militia member is entitled to reemployment if employee applies for reemployment at end of duty and tour of duty continues no longer than 3 months. Veteran is entitled to reemployment if position was not temporary and employer's changed circumstances do not make it unreasonable. Veteran seeking reinstatement must furnish proof of satisfactory completion of service, apply in writing within 90 days of end of service or end of hospitalization provided hospitalization does not extend more than 1 year, and return to former position within 3 months after serving 4 years or less, unless employee was ordered to additional service. If employee is no longer qualified to perform duties of former position, he or she is entitled to another position for which he or she is qualified that will provide similar seniority, status, and pay, or the nearest approximation thereof. | Any employer who discharges employee because of employee's membership in state organized militia or employee's absence from work for military duty with state organized militia is guilty of a gross misdemeanor, punishable by a fine of not more than $500, or imprisonment for not more than 6 months, or both. If veteran is not reinstated, the prosecuting attorney will bring action to require compliance with statute, and employer is liable for loss of wages and benefits. | Wash. Rev. Code Ann. §§ 38.24.060, 38.40.040 *et seq.*, 73.16.033, 73.16.035, 73.16.061. |
| WV | Yes. | Yes. | — | 30 days (usual compensation is in addition to military pay). Employee ordered to active duty by president is entitled to an additional 30 days' leave without loss of pay. | Yes. | Employer who takes adverse personnel action because of employee's military leave is guilty of a misdemeanor, punishable by a fine of not more than $500, or imprisonment for not more than 1 year, or both. | W. Va. Code §§ 15-1F-1, 15-1F-8, 15-1F-9. |
| WI | Yes. | Yes. | — | 30 days. State employees will receive normal civilian salary less any military pay. Leave will not be granted for fewer than 3 days. | Yes. Public employers of unclassified employees and private employers must reinstate employees called to military service or to national defense work as a civilian because of national emergency if position was not temporary, employee gives employer evidence of satisfactory completion of service, employee remains qualified to perform duties of position, employee applies for reemployment and resumes work within 90 days of end of service or within 6 months of release from hospitalization resulting from service, employer's changed circumstances do<br>(*cont'd*) | If employer refuses to reinstate, employee may bring civil action for reinstatement, lost wages, and benefits. | Wis. Stat. Ann. §§ 45.50, 45.51, 63.06, 230.32, 230.35(3)(a). |

(*Table continues.*)

## Table 4.5-1 *(cont'd)*

### STATUTORY RESTRICTIONS ON DISCHARGING EMPLOYEES: MILITARY SERVICE LEAVE

(See also text at § 4.5.)

**NOTE:** An em-dash (—) means that no specific statutory authority exists; other authority, including case law, may apply.

| | *Are Employers Prohibited from Discharging Employees for Taking Military Leave?* | *Employers Covered by Statute* | | *How Many Days of Paid Leave per Year Is Employee Allowed?* | *Are Employers Required to Reemploy Persons Returning from Military Service?* | *Remedies and Penalties* | *Citations to Authority* |
|---|---|---|---|---|---|---|---|
| | | *Public* | *Private* | | | | |
| WI *(cont'd)* | | | | | not make it unreasonable, and service was not for more than 4 years, unless it was extended by law. Any employee so reinstated cannot be discharged without cause for 1 year after restoration. Public employers of classified employees must reinstate employees called to military duty or to work for the federal government because of a national emergency if employment was not for a limited term, employee gives employer evidence of satisfactory completion of service, service was not more than 4 years unless employee was involuntarily retained for a longer period, employee remains qualified to perform duties of position, employee applies for reemployment within 180 days of release from service or release from hospitalization resulting from service, employer's changed circumstances do not make it unreasonable, and discharge is other than dishonorable. | | |
| WY | Yes. | Yes. | Yes. | 15 days for public employees. Public employee with more than 1 year of service may extend the military leave beyond 15 days but without pay. | Yes, public employers are required to reemploy if position still exists or term of position, if limited, has not expired, employee is physically and mentally capable of performing duties, employee gives evidence of sat- | District court has jurisdiction to require employer to comply with provisions and to compensate employee for lost wages and benefits. | Wyo. Stat. §§ 19-2-504, 19-2-505, 19-2-506. |

isfactory completion of service, military service does not exceed 4 years plus any additional period imposed by law, and employee applies in writing for reemployment within 30 days of release from military service or within 90 days of discharge from hospitalization resulting from service, but not later than 1 year and 90 days after end of service.

# Table 4.5-2
## STATUTORY RESTRICTIONS ON DISCHARGING EMPLOYEES: JURY SERVICE LEAVE

(See also text at § 4.5.)

**NOTE:** An em-dash (—) means that no specific statutory authority exists; other authority, including case law, may apply.

| | *Are Employers Restricted from Discharging Employees for Taking Leave for Jury Service?* | *Remedies and Penalties* | *Other Requirements* | *Citations to Authority* |
|---|---|---|---|---|
| AL | Yes. | Employee can bring civil action for actual and punitive damages. | Full-time employees are entitled to their usual compensation less any compensation received for service as a juror. | Ala. Code §§ 12-16-8, 12-16-8.1. |
| AK | Yes. | Employee can bring civil action for lost wages, other damages, and reinstatement. | Employer is not required to pay employee for time spent in jury service. | Alaska Stat. § 09.20.037. |
| AZ | Yes. | Violator is guilty of a Class 3 misdemeanor. | Employer is not required to pay employee for time spent in jury service. | Ariz. Rev. Stat. Ann. § 21-236. |
| AR | Yes. | Violator is guilty of a Class A misdemeanor. | Employee must give employer reasonable prior notice. Public employees serving as jurors shall be entitled to full compensation in addition to any fees paid for such services. | Ark. Code Ann. §§ 16-31-106, 21-4-213. |
| CA | Yes. | Employee can bring civil action for reinstatement and reimbursement for lost wages and work benefits. Employer who willfully refuses to rehire an eligible employee is guilty of a misdemeanor. | Employee must give employer reasonable prior notice. | Cal. Lab. Code § 230. |
| CO | Yes. | Discrimination against an employee for taking leave is a misdemeanor. Employee may bring civil action for failure to pay—court may award treble damages and attorneys' fees. | Employees are entitled to paid leave for first 3 days of service; pay is not to exceed $50 per day unless by mutual agreement. | Colo. Rev. Stat. §§ 13-71-126 *et seq.* |
| CT | Yes. | Violator is guilty of criminal contempt, punishable by a fine of not more than $500, or imprisonment for not more than 30 days, or both. Employee can bring civil action within 90 days of discharge for lost wages, reinstatement, and reasonable attorneys' fees. Lost wages cannot exceed 10 weeks. If employer still fails to compensate employee after employee has been awarded lost wages in a civil suit and if court has not excused employer from duty to compensate employee on a finding of extreme financial hardship to the employer, employer is liable to employee for damages. Court may award treble damages and reasonable attorneys' fees if employer acts willfully. | Full-time employees are entitled to paid leave for the first 5 days of jury service. | Conn. Gen. Stat. Ann. §§ 51-247, 51-247a. |

| | | | | |
|---|---|---|---|---|
| DE | Yes. | Violator is guilty of criminal contempt, punishable by a fine of not more than $500, or imprisonment for not more than 6 months, or both. Employee can bring civil action for lost wages, reinstatement, and reasonable attorneys' fees. | Employee must file civil action within 90 days of violation. | Del. Code Ann. tit. 10, § 4515. |
| DC | Yes. | Violator is guilty of criminal contempt. A first offense is punishable by a fine of not more than $300, or imprisonment for not more than 30 days, or both. Subsequent offenses are punishable by a fine of not more than $5,000, imprisonment for not more than 180 days, or both. Employee can bring civil action for lost wages, reinstatement, damages, and reasonable attorneys' fees. | Employee must bring civil action within 9 months of discharge. | D.C. Code Ann. § 11-1913. |
| FL | Yes. | Employer may be subject to contempt sanctions for threats of dismissal. A dismissed employee may recover compensatory and punitive damages and reasonable attorney's fees. | — | Fla. Stat. Ann. § 40.271. *Hill v. Winn-Dixie Stores, Inc.*, 699 F. Supp. 876 (M.D. Fla. 1988). |
| GA | Yes. | Violator is liable for actual damages and reasonable attorneys' fees. | Employee is entitled to salary while serving jury duty. 1989 Atty Gen. Op. No. 89-55. | Ga. Code Ann. § 34-1-3. |
| HI | Yes. | Violator is guilty of a petty misdemeanor. Employee may bring civil action for lost wages, reinstatement, and reasonable attorneys' fees. Damages recovered shall not exceed 6 weeks' lost wages. | Employee must bring civil action within 90 days of discharge. Public employees are entitled to paid leave. | Haw. Rev. Stat. §§ 79-14, 612-25. |
| ID | Yes. | Violator is guilty of criminal contempt punishable by a fine of not more than $300. Employee may bring a civil action for treble lost wages, reinstatement, and reasonable attorneys' fees. | Employee must bring civil action within 60 days of discharge. | Idaho Code § 2-218. |
| IL | Yes. | Violator may be charged with civil and criminal contempt of court and will be liable for damages, lost wages, benefits, reasonable attorneys' fees, and reinstatement. | Employee must give employer reasonable prior notice by delivering a copy of the summons to the employer within 10 days of the date it was issued. Employer is not obligated to pay employee for time spent in jury service. | Ill. Ann. Stat. ch. 705, ¶ 305/4.1. |
| IN | Yes. | Violator is guilty of a Class B misdemeanor. Employee may bring civil action for lost wages, reinstatement, and reasonable attorneys' fees. | Employee must bring civil action within 90 days of dismissal. | Ind. Code Ann. §§ 34-4-29.1, 35-44-3-10. |
| IA | Yes. | Violator is guilty of contempt. Employee may bring civil action for lost wages, reinstatement, and reasonable attorneys' fees. Damages shall not exceed 6 weeks' wages. | Employee must bring civil action within 60 days of discharge. | Iowa Code Ann. § 607A.45. |
| KS | Yes. Applies to permanent employees. | Violator may be liable for damages, including lost wages, actual damages, other benefits, reinstatement, attorneys' fees, and costs. | None. | Kan. Stat. Ann. § 43-173. |
| KY | Yes. | Violator employer is guilty of a Class B misdemeanor. Employee may bring a civil action for lost wages, reinstatement with full seniority and benefits, and attorneys' fees. Damages shall not exceed lost wages. | Employee must bring civil action within 90 days. | Ky. Rev. Stat. Ann. §§ 29A.160, 29A.990. |

*(Table continues.)*

# Table 4.5-2 *(cont'd)*

## STATUTORY RESTRICTIONS ON DISCHARGING EMPLOYEES: JURY SERVICE LEAVE

(See also text at § 4.5.)

**NOTE:** An em-dash (—) means that no specific statutory authority exists; other authority, including case law, may apply.

| | *Are Employers Restricted from Discharging Employees for Taking Leave for Jury Service?* | *Remedies and Penalties* | *Other Requirements* | *Citations to Authority* |
|---|---|---|---|---|
| LA | Yes. | Employer must reinstate employee in the same position, with the same wages and benefits, and will be fined $100–$1,000. | Public employer must pay employee for time spent in jury service up to 1 day. If employer does not pay, employer will be required to pay employee full wages for 1 day of the period taken for jury duty and will be fined $100–$500. | La. Rev. Stat. Ann. § 23:965. |
| ME | Yes. | Violator is guilty of a Class E crime. Employee can bring a civil action for lost wages, health insurance benefits, reinstatement, and reasonable attorneys' fees. Damages may not exceed 6 weeks' wages. | Employee must bring civil action within 90 days. | Me. Rev. Stat. Ann. tit. 14, § 1218. |
| MD | Yes. | Violators are subject to a fine not to exceed $1,000. | None. | Md. Code Ann. Cts. & Jud. Proc. §§ 8-105, 8-401. |
| MA | Yes. | Violator is guilty of contempt of court. An employer who fails to compensate a public employee while on jury duty is liable for treble damages and reasonable attorneys' fees. An employer who deprives a juror-employee of employment is liable for treble damages and reasonable attorneys' fees. | Public employees are entitled to their usual compensation less compensation for jury service. | Mass. Gen. Laws Ann. ch. 234 § 1B, 268 § 14A. |
| MI | Yes. | Violator is in contempt of court and guilty of a misdemeanor. | Employer cannot require extra hours of work beyond those normally worked by the employee when added to the hours spent in jury duty, unless employee voluntarily agrees. | Mich. Stat. Ann. § 27A.1348. |
| MN | Yes. | Violator is guilty of criminal contempt, punishable by a fine of not more than $700, or imprisonment for not more than 6 months, or both. Employee may bring civil action for lost wages, reinstatement, and reasonable attorneys' fees. Damages are not to exceed 6 weeks' wages. | Employee must bring civil action within 30 days. | Minn. Stat. Ann. § 593.50. |
| MS | Yes. | Violator is in contempt of court. | None. | Miss. Code Ann. § 13-5-23. |
| MO | Yes. | Employee may bring civil action for lost wages, other damages, reinstatement, and reasonable attorneys' fees. | Employee must bring civil action within 90 days of discharge. | Mo. Ann. Stat. § 494.460. |

| | | | | |
|---|---|---|---|---|
| MT | Yes. | State has no statutory requirements. | Applies only to public employees. Juror fees are to be applied against the amount due the employee from the employer unless employee elects to use annual leave for jury duty. Employer may request that the court excuse an employee who performs a needed function. | Mont. Code Ann. § 2-18-619. |
| NE | Yes. | Violator is guilty of a Class IV misdemeanor. | Employee must give employer reasonable prior notice. Employer may reduce employee's pay by the amount paid by the court. | Neb. Rev. Stat. § 25-1640. |
| NV | Yes. | Employee may bring civil action for damages equal to the amount of lost wages and benefits, reinstatement, reasonable attorneys' fees, and punitive or exemplary damages not to exceed $50,000. Violator is guilty of a gross misdemeanor. Dissuading a person from jury duty is a misdemeanor. | Employee must give employer prior notice at least 1 day before jury duty. | Nev. Rev. Stat. Ann. § 6.190. |
| NH | Yes. | Violator is in contempt of court. Employee may bring civil action for lost wages, reinstatement, and reasonable attorneys' fees. Damages cannot exceed lost wages. | Employee must bring civil action within 1 year of discharge. | N.H. Rev. Stat. Ann. § 500-A:14. |
| NJ | Yes. | Violator is guilty of a disorderly persons offense. Employee may bring civil action for economic damages, reinstatement, and reasonable attorneys' fees. | Full-time employees are entitled to their usual compensation less the amount of the per diem fee for each day of service. Employee must bring civil action within 90 days. | N.J. Stat. Ann. §§ 2B:20-16, 2B:20-17. |
| NM | Yes. | Violator is guilty of a petty misdemeanor. | None. | N.M. Stat. Ann. §§ 38-5-18, 38-5-19. |
| NY | Yes. | Violator is guilty of criminal contempt. | Employer may withhold wages of employee on jury service, except employer with more than 10 employees shall not withhold the first $40 of juror's daily wages during the first 3 days of jury service. Employee must notify employer before jury service begins. | N.Y. Jud. Law § 519. |
| NC | Yes. | Employer may be liable for reasonable damages and reinstatement of the discharged employee. | Employee must bring civil action within 1 year. | N.C. Gen. Stat. § 9-32. |
| ND | Yes. | Employee may bring civil action for lost wages, reinstatement, and reasonable attorneys' fees. Damages may not exceed 6 weeks' wages. Violator is guilty of a Class B misdemeanor. | Employee must bring civil action within 90 days. | N.D. Cent. Code § 27-09.1-17. |
| OH | Yes. Applies to permanent employees. | Violator is guilty of contempt of court. | Employee must give employer reasonable prior notice. Public employee is entitled to paid leave. | Ohio Rev. Code Ann. §§ 124.135, 2313.18. |
| OK | Yes. | Violator is guilty of a misdemeanor punishable by a fine not to exceed $5,000. Employee may bring civil action for actual damages, including past and future lost wages, mental anguish, all reasonable damages incurred in obtaining other suitable employment, and exemplary damages. | None. | Okla. Stat. Ann. tit. 38, §§ 34, 35. |

*(Table continues.)*

# Table 4.5-2 *(cont'd)*

## STATUTORY RESTRICTIONS ON DISCHARGING EMPLOYEES: JURY SERVICE LEAVE

(See also text at § 4.5.)

**NOTE:** An em-dash (—) means that no specific statutory authority exists; other authority, including case law, may apply.

| | *Are Employers Restricted from Discharging Employees for Taking Leave for Jury Service?* | *Remedies and Penalties* | *Other Requirements* | *Citations to Authority* |
|---|---|---|---|---|
| OR | Yes. | Court may order all appropriate relief, including reinstatement with back pay for discharged employee. Violator shall be subject to a civil penalty of not more than $500 for each violation. | This provision does not alter employer's policies or agreements with employee concerning employee's wages during times when employee serves as a juror. | Or. Rev. Stat. §§ 10.090, 10.992. |
| PA | Yes, but statute does not apply to an employer in a retail or service industry employing fewer than 15 persons or to a manufacturing employer with fewer than 40 employees. | Violator is guilty of a summary offense. Employee may bring civil action for lost wages, benefits, reinstatement, and reasonable attorneys' fees. Damages cannot exceed wages and benefits actually lost. | Employer is not required to compensate employee for employment time lost. | Pa. Stat. Ann. tit. 42, § 4563. |
| RI | Yes. | Violator is guilty of a misdemeanor. | Employer is not required to pay employee any compensation during jury service, absent contract or collective bargaining agreement to the contrary. | R.I. Gen. Laws § 9-9-28. |
| SC | Yes. | Dismissed employee may bring civil action for damages not to exceed 1 year's salary. Demoted employee may bring civil action for damages not to exceed the difference for 1 year between the original salary and the new, lower salary. | None. | S.C. Code Ann. § 41-1-70. |
| SD | Yes. | Violator is guilty of a Class 2 misdemeanor. | Jury service may be with or without pay at the discretion of the employer. | S.D. Codified Laws §§ 16-13-41.1, 16-13-41.2. |
| TN | Statute exempts an employer with fewer than 5 employees and any temporary employee who has worked for less than 6 months. Employee is excused from work if jury service exceeds 3 hours of the day. | Employee may bring action for reinstatement, lost wages, and benefits. Violator is guilty of a Class A misdemeanor. Employer who willfully refuses to reinstate employee is guilty of a Class A misdemeanor. | Employee must give employer prior notice the next working day after receiving a summons to report for jury duty. Employer may pay full compensation but is required to pay only usual compensation minus the compensation employee receives for jury service. Railroad employees who are paid based on mileage will receive the mileage pay they would have received if they had reported for work rather than for jury service. | Tenn. Code Ann. § 22-4-108. |

| | | | | |
|---|---|---|---|---|
| TX | Yes. Applies to private employers. | Employee may bring civil action for reinstatement, damages, and reasonable attorneys' fees. Damages may not exceed 6 months' wages. | Employee must give employer notice of intended return from jury service. Employee is entitled to reinstatement unless employer's changed circumstances make it impossible or unreasonable. | Tex. Civ. Prac. & Rem. Code Ann. §§ 122.001, 122.002, 122.003. |
| UT | Yes. | Violator is guilty of criminal contempt, punishable by a fine of not more than $500, or imprisonment for not more than 6 months, or both. Employee may bring civil action for lost wages, reinstatement, and reasonable attorneys' fees. Damages must not exceed 6 weeks' wages. | Employee must bring civil action within 30 days of violation. | Utah Code Ann. § 78-46-21. |
| VT | Yes. | Violator is fined not more than $200. | None. | Vt. Stat. Ann. tit. 21, § 499. |
| VA | Yes. | Violator is guilty of a Class 4 misdemeanor. | Employee must give employer reasonable notice. Employer cannot require employee to use sick leave or vacation time for jury duty. | Va. Code Ann. § 18.2-465.1. |
| WA | Yes. | Violator is guilty of a misdemeanor. Employee may bring civil action for damages, reinstatement, and reasonable attorneys' fees. | None. | Wash. Rev. Code Ann. § 2.36.165. |
| WV | Yes. | Violator is guilty of a misdemeanor, punishable by a fine of $100–$1,000, or imprisonment for not more than 60 days, or both. Employee can bring civil action for affirmative relief, including reinstatement, back pay, and reasonable attorneys' fees. | Employer is not required to pay employee for time spent in jury service. | W. Va. Code §§ 52-3-1, 61-5-25a. Op. Atty. Gen. No. 35, March 18, 1986. |
| WI | Yes. | Violator may be fined not more than $200 and may be required to make full restitution to the aggrieved employee, including back pay and reinstatement. | Public employees are entitled to paid leave. | Wis. Stat. Ann. §§ 230.35(3)(c), 756.255. |
| WY | Yes. | Employee can bring civil action for injunctive relief, including reinstatement, exemplary damages not to exceed $1,000, and reasonable costs and attorneys' fees. | Employee must bring civil action within 6 months of violation. | Wyo. Stat. § 1-11-401. |

# Table 4.5-3
## STATUTORY RESTRICTIONS ON DISCHARGING EMPLOYEES: LEAVE TO BE A WITNESS

| | *Are Employers Restricted from Discharging Employees for Taking Leave to Be a Witness?* | | | | |
|---|---|---|---|---|---|
| | *Civil Cases* | *Criminal Cases* | *Remedies and Penalties* | *Other Requirements* | *Citations to Authority* |
| AL | — | — | — | — | State has no statutory provisions. |
| AK | Yes. | Yes, if employee was the crime victim. | Employee may bring civil action for actual damages and may recover punitive damages of 3 times actual damages. | Leave does not have to be paid. | Alaska Stat. § 12.61.017. |
| AZ | — | — | — | — | State has no statutory provisions. |
| AR | — | — | — | — | State has no statutory provisions. |
| CA | Yes, unless employee is a litigant or is appearing by reason of his or her own misconduct. Applies to public employees.<br>A private employee cannot be discriminated against if reasonable notice is given. | Yes, unless employee is a litigant or is appearing by reason of his or her own misconduct. Applies to public employees.<br>A private employee cannot be discriminated against if reasonable notice is given. | —<br>A private employee is entitled to reinstatement, lost wages, and benefits. Failure to restore is a misdemeanor. | Public employee who is subpoenaed is entitled to paid leave less any amount received for his or her appearance, unless employee is a party or an expert witness. Public employer has discretion to grant paid leave, less any amount received, to other employee witnesses. Public or private employee who is victim or witness of crime is entitled to employer intercession services asking employer to minimize loss of pay and benefits because of employee's participation in criminal justice system. | Cal. Gov't Code §§ 1230, 1230.1; Cal. Labor Code 230; Cal. Penal Code § 13835.5. |
| CO | — | Yes, if employee is the crime victim or victim is a member of the employee's immediate family. | An employee may notify the victims' compensation and assistance coordinating committee. If the noncompliance cannot be resolved, the committee will refer employee's report to the governor, who will ask the attorney general to file suit to enforce compliance with this provision. | An employee who is a crime victim has the right to be provided with appropriate employer intercession services to encourage the victim's employer to cooperate with the criminal justice system to minimize the loss of employment, pay, or other benefits resulting from a victim's court appearances or other required meetings with criminal justice officials. | Colo. Rev. Stat. §§ 24-4.1-302.5(n), 24-4.1-303(8), (17). |

| | | | | | |
|---|---|---|---|---|---|
| CT | — | Yes, if in response to a legal subpoena. | Violator is guilty of criminal contempt, punishable by a fine of not more than $500, or imprisonment of not more than 30 days, or both. Within 90 days of violation, employee may bring civil action for damages, reinstatement, and reasonable attorneys' fees. | — | Conn. Gen. Stat. Ann. §§ 54-85b, 54-203(b)(7)(G). |
| DE | — | — | — | — | State has no statutory provisions. |
| DC | — | — | — | — | State has no statutory provisions. |
| FL | Yes, if employee is acting in response to a subpoena. | Yes, if employee is acting in response to a subpoena. | Employee may bring civil action for actual damages, punitive damages, and attorneys' fees. | — | Fla. Stat. Ann. § 92-57. |
| GA | Yes, if acting in response to a subpoena. | Yes, if acting in response to a subpoena, but not if employee is defendant. | Actual damages and attorneys' fees. | Employer may require reasonable notice of expected absence. | Ga. Code Ann. § 34-1-3. |
| HI | Yes. | Yes. | Violator is guilty of a petty misdemeanor. Employee may bring civil action for lost wages, reinstatement, and reasonable attorneys' fees. Damages for lost wages shall not exceed 6 weeks' wages. | Employee must bring civil action within 90 days of violation. Public employees are entitled to paid leave if the proceeding does not involve employee's outside employment or personal business affairs. | Haw. Rev. Stat. §§ 79-14, 621-10.5. |
| ID | — | — | — | — | State has no statutory provisions. |
| IL | — | Yes, if employee is acting in response to criminal subpoena. | Violator is in contempt of court. | Witnesses to violent crimes have right to be provided with appropriate employer intercession services to ensure that employers of witnesses will cooperate with the criminal justice system to minimize employee's loss of pay and other benefits as a result of court appearances. | Ill. Ann. Stat. ch. 725, ¶¶ 5/115-18, 120/5. |
| IN | — | Yes, if employee is acting in response to a subpoena. | Violator is guilty of a Class B misdemeanor. | — | Ind. Code Ann. § 35-44-3-11.1. |
| IA | — | Yes. | Violator is guilty of a simple misdemeanor. Employee may bring civil suit for reinstatement, actual damages, costs, and reasonable attorneys' fees. | — | Iowa Code Ann. § 910A.12. |
| KS | — | — | — | — | State has no statutory provisions. |
| KY | — | — | — | — | State has no statutory provisions. |
| LA | — | — | — | — | State has no statutory provisions. |

*(Table continues.)*

## Table 4.5-3 *(cont'd)*

## STATUTORY RESTRICTIONS ON DISCHARGING EMPLOYEES: LEAVE TO BE A WITNESS

| | *Are Employers Restricted from Discharging Employees for Taking Leave to Be a Witness?* | | | | |
|---|---|---|---|---|---|
| | *Civil Cases* | *Criminal Cases* | *Remedies and Penalties* | *Other Requirements* | *Citations to Authority* |
| ME | — | — | — | — | State has no statutory provisions. |
| MD | Yes, if employee is acting in response to a subpoena. | Yes, if employee is acting in response to a subpoena. | Violator may be fined not more than $1,000. | — | Md. Code Ann., Cts. & Jud. Proc. § 9-205. |
| MA | Yes. | Yes. | Violator is in contempt of court. In criminal cases, violator shall be fined not more than $200, or imprisoned not more than 1 month, or both. | Employee must notify employer of subpoena before the day of his or her attendance in court. | Mass. Gen. Laws Ann. ch. 258B § 3, ch. 268 §§ 14A, 14B. |
| MI | — | — | — | — | State has no statutory provisions. |
| MN | — | — | — | — | State has no statutory provisions. |
| MS | — | — | — | — | State has no statutory provisions. |
| MO | — | — | — | — | State has no statutory provisions. |
| MT | Yes. | Yes. | — | Applies only to public employees. Witness fees are to be applied against the amount due the employee from the employer, unless employee elects to use annual leave to comply with the subpoena. | Mont. Code Ann. § 2-18-619. |
| NE | — | — | — | — | State has no statutory provisions. |
| NV | Yes. | Yes. | Violator is guilty of a misdemeanor. Employee may bring action for reinstatement, lost wages, benefits, and reasonable attorneys' fees. | Victim or witness of crime may request prosecuting attorney, sheriff, or police chief to intercede on his or her behalf to minimize loss of pay and other benefits that would result from court appearances. | Nev. Rev. Stat. Ann. §§ 50.070, 178.5694. |
| NH | — | — | — | — | State has no statutory provisions. |
| NJ | — | — | — | — | State has no statutory provisions. |
| NM | — | — | — | — | State has no statutory provisions. |

| | | | | | |
|---|---|---|---|---|---|
| NY | — | Yes, if victim or pursuant to subpoena. | Violator is guilty of a Class B misdemeanor. | Upon employer's request, party seeking employee's testimony shall provide verification of employee's service as a witness. Leave may be with or without pay at employer's discretion. Employee must give employer notice. | N.Y. Penal Law § 215.14. |
| NC | — | No, but witness will be provided appropriate employer intercession services to seek employer's cooperation with criminal justice system and to minimize employee's loss of pay and other benefits resulting from services as a witness. | — | — | N.C. Gen. Stat. § 15A-825(4). |
| ND | Yes. | Yes. | Employee may bring civil action for lost wages, reinstatement, and reasonable attorneys' fees. Damages may not exceed 6 weeks' wages. Violator is guilty of Class B misdemeanor. | Employee must bring action within 90 days. | N.D. Cent. Code § 27-09.1-17. |
| OH | Yes. Applies to delinquency cases if employee is subpoenaed. | Yes, if pursuant to subpoena. | Employer who knowingly violates witness provisions is in contempt of court. | Public employee is entitled to paid leave if he or she is not a party to the action. Employer is not required to pay private employee for witness leave unless the proceeding concerns an offense against the employer or involves the employee in the course of employment. | Ohio Rev. Code Ann. §§ 124.135, 2151.211, 2945.451. |
| OK | — | — | — | — | State has no statutory provisions. |
| OR | — | — | — | — | State has no statutory provisions. |
| PA | — | Yes. | Violator commits a summary offense. Employee may bring civil action for reinstatement, lost wages, benefits, and reasonable attorneys' fees. Damages may not exceed wages and benefits actually lost. | Employer is not required to pay employee for time spent in court. | Pa. Cons. Stat. Ann. tit. 18, § 4957. |
| RI | — | — | — | — | State has no statutory provisions. |
| SC | Yes. | Yes. | Dismissed employee may bring civil action for damages not to exceed 1 year's salary. Demoted employee may bring civil action for damages not to exceed the difference for 1 year between original salary and the new lower salary. | Must be in response to a valid subpoena. | S.C. Code Ann. § 41-1-70. |

*(Table continues.)*

## Table 4.5-3 *(cont'd)*

## STATUTORY RESTRICTIONS ON DISCHARGING EMPLOYEES: LEAVE TO BE A WITNESS

| | *Are Employers Restricted from Discharging Employees for Taking Leave to Be a Witness?* | | | | |
|---|---|---|---|---|---|
| | *Civil Cases* | *Criminal Cases* | *Remedies and Penalties* | *Other Requirements* | *Citations to Authority* |
| SD | — | — | — | — | State has no statutory provisions. |
| TN | — | — | — | — | State has no statutory provisions. |
| TX | Yes. | Yes. | Violator may be found in contempt of court. Employee is entitled to reemployment if he or she gives employer notice as soon as practicable after release from subpoena of intent to return and if employer's changed circumstances do not make it unreasonable. Employee may recover damages not to exceed 6 months' compensation and reasonable attorneys' fees. | Must be in response to a valid subpoena. | Tex. Lab. Code Ann. § 52.051. |
| UT | — | — | — | — | State has no statutory provisions. |
| VT | Yes. | Yes. | Violator may be fined not more than $200. | — | Vt. Stat. Ann. tit. 21, § 499. |
| VA | Yes. | Yes, unless employee is the criminal defendant. | Violator is guilty of a Class 4 misdemeanor. | Employee must give employer reasonable notice. Employer cannot require employee to use sick leave or vacation time for time spent as a witness. | Va. Code Ann. § 18.2-465.1. |
| WA | — | — | — | — | State has no statutory provisions. |
| WV | — | — | — | — | State has no statutory provisions. |
| WI | Yes, for a proceeding pursuant to the Children's Code or Juvenile Justice Code. | Yes. | Violator may be fined not more than $200 and may be ordered to make full restitution to employee, including reinstatement and back pay. | Employee must give employer notice on or before first business day after receiving subpoena. If employee will testify in a proceeding as a result of a crime committed against employer or an incident that occurred in the course of employment, leave must be paid. | Wis. Stat. Ann. § 103.87. |

| | | | | | |
|---|---|---|---|---|---|
| WY | — | Yes. | Provision does not create a civil cause of action for damages. | Victim or witness, upon request, shall be assisted by law enforcement agencies, prosecuting attorney, or defense attorney in informing employer that the need for witness cooperation may necessitate the absence of the witness from work. | Wyo. Stat. Ann. §§ 1-40-209, 1-40-210. |

# Table 4.5-4
## STATUTORY RESTRICTIONS ON DISCHARGING EMPLOYEES: EXERCISING VOTING RIGHTS

(See also text at § 4.5.)

**NOTE:** An em dash (—) means that no specific statutory authority exists; other authority, including case law, may apply.

| | *Is There a Restriction on Using Employment Consequences to Influence Employee Vote?* | *Are Employers Required to Give Employees Time Off to Vote?* | *How Much Time Must the Employer Allow?* | *Remedies and Penalties* | *Other Requirements* | *Citations to Authority* |
|---|---|---|---|---|---|---|
| AL | Yes. | State has no statutory requirements. | State has no statutory requirements. | Employer who threatens to discharge employee or decrease employee's compensation to influence his vote is guilty of a misdemeanor and will be fined not less than $500. | None. | Ala. Code §§ 17-23-10, 17-23-11. |
| AK | — | Yes. | As much time as will enable voting if the employee does not have 2 consecutive hours off while the polls are open. Leave will be paid. | Refusal to allow employees time off to vote is a violation. Unlawful interference with voting is a Class C felony. | None. | Alaska Stat. §§ 15.15.100, 15.25.090, 15.56.030, 15.56.100. |
| AZ | Yes. | Yes. | If employee does not have 3 hours before the beginning or after the end of shift while the polls are open, employee may take as much time at beginning or end of workshift that, when added to time available outside working hours, will give employee 3 consecutive hours in which to vote. | Employer who does not allow time to vote or who reduces employee's pay for taking leave to vote is guilty of a Class 2 misdemeanor. Any person who intimidates another person to influence that person's vote is guilty of a Class 1 misdemeanor. Any person who offers employment to another person to influence that person's vote is guilty of a Class 2 misdemeanor. | Employee must notify employer before election day. Employer may specify the hours employee may take to vote. | Ariz. Rev. Stat. Ann. §§ 16-402, 16-1013, 16-1014. |
| AR | Yes. | Yes. | Employer must schedule work hours to give each employee an opportunity to vote. | Employer who fails to give sufficient time off to vote is fined $25–$250; any person who threatens or intimidates another person to influence that person's vote is guilty of a felony, punishable by a fine of not more than $5,000, or imprisonment for 1–5 years, or both, and is barred from holding public office or public employment. | None. | Ark. Code Ann. §§ 7-1-102 *et seq.* |

| | | | | | | |
|---|---|---|---|---|---|---|
| CA | Yes. | Yes. | Enough time that will enable employee to vote when added to the voting time available outside of working hours. Only 2 hours will be compensated. Time off will occur at end or beginning of employee's regular workshift. | State has no statutory requirements. | Employee must give employer at least 2 working days' notice if the employee, on the third working day before election, knows that time off will be needed. Employer must post information at least 10 days before election about the law that allows time off to vote. | Cal. Elec. Code §§ 14000, 14001, 14002; Cal. Lab. Code §§ 1101, 1102. |
| CO | Yes. | Yes. | 2 hours, unless employee has 3 consecutive hours outside working hours while the polls are open. | Employer who attempts to control employee's vote or does not allow time off to vote is guilty of a misdemeanor, punishable by a fine of not more than $1,000, or imprisonment for not more than 1 year, or both. A corporation that violates these provisions will forfeit its charter and its right to do business in the state. | Employee must give employer notice before election day. Employer decides which hours employee gets off to vote, but the hours will be at the beginning or end of the workshift if the employee so requests. Leave will be paid. | Colo. Rev. Stat. §§ 1-7-102, 1-13-719. |
| CT | Yes. | State has no statutory requirements. | State has no statutory requirements. | Violator may be fined $100–$500, or imprisoned 6–12 months, or both. | Employer cannot try to influence employee's vote at or within 60 days of an election by threat to withhold employment or by promise of employment. Employer cannot dismiss employee for any vote he or she has given. | Conn. Gen. Stat. Ann. § 9-365. |
| DE | Yes. | State has no statutory requirements. | State has no statutory requirements. | State has no statutory requirements. | None. | Del. Const. art. V, § 3. |
| DC | Yes. | — | — | Anyone who pays or offers any consideration to influence another person's vote may be fined not more than $10,000, or imprisoned not more than 1 year, or both. | — | D.C. Code Ann. § 1-1318. |
| FL | Yes. | State has no statutory requirements. | State has no statutory requirements. | Employer who attempts to influence employee's vote is guilty of a misdemeanor of the first degree. The penalty is a maximum fine of $1,000 and up to 1 year imprisonment. | None. | Fla. Stat. Ann. §§ 104.081, 775.082, 775.083. |
| GA | Yes. | Yes. | Employer must give sufficient time, not to exceed 2 hours, to vote to any employee who does not have 2 hours off before work after polls are open or after work before polls close. | Any person who uses or threatens to use force or violence or otherwise intimidates another person to influence the person's vote is guilty of a misdemeanor. | Employee must give employer reasonable notice of need to take time off to vote. Employer may specify the hours during which employee may leave to vote. | Ga. Code Ann. §§ 21-2-404, 21-2-567. |

*(Table continues.)*

## Table 4.5-4 *(cont'd)*

## STATUTORY RESTRICTIONS ON DISCHARGING EMPLOYEES: EXERCISING VOTING RIGHTS

(See also text at § 4.5.)

**NOTE:** An em dash (—) means that no specific statutory authority exists; other authority, including case law, may apply.

| | *Is There a Restriction on Using Employment Consequences to Influence Employee Vote?* | *Are Employers Required to Give Employees Time Off to Vote?* | *How Much Time Must the Employer Allow?* | *Remedies and Penalties* | *Other Requirements* | *Citations to Authority* |
|---|---|---|---|---|---|---|
| HI | Yes. | Yes. | 2 consecutive hours while the polls are open, unless employee already has 2 consecutive hours off duty while the polls are open. | Violator is subject to a fine of $50–$300. Persons found guilty of election fraud shall be subject to a fine of $100–$1,000, or up to 2 years imprisonment, or both. Persons found guilty shall also be disqualified from voting and holding elective office. | Employer may make appropriate deductions from salary or wages of an employee who does not vote during the 2 hours granted. | Haw. Rev. Stat. §§ 11-95, 19-3, 19-4, 19-8. |
| ID | Yes. | State has no statutory requirements. | State has no statutory requirements. | State has no statutory requirements. | None. | Idaho Code § 18-2319. |
| IL | Yes. | Yes. | 2 hours. | Anyone who pays or offers any valuable consideration to influence another person's vote shall be guilty of a Class 4 felony. | Employee must give employer notice before the day of election that he or she will be taking time to vote. Employer may set the hours. | Ill. Ann. Stat. ch. 10, ¶ 5/17-15, 5/29-1. |
| IN | Yes. | State has no statutory requirements. | State has no statutory requirements. | Anyone who uses financial inducement to influence another person's vote is guilty of a Class D felony. Employer who uses pay envelopes or posts signs containing threats intended to influence employee vote is guilty of a Class D felony. | None. | Ind. Code Ann. §§ 3-14-3-19, 3-14-3-21. |
| IA | Yes. | Yes. | If employee does not have 3 consecutive hours outside working hours while polls are open, employee will be given as much time as will in addition to his or her nonworking time total 3 consecutive hours while polls are open. | Employer who uses threat of discharge to influence employee vote or does not allow time off to vote is guilty of a simple misdemeanor. | Employer may designate hours for employee to vote. Employee must notify employer in writing before election day of need to take time off to vote. Leave will be paid. | Iowa Code Ann. §§ 49.109, 49.110. |

| | | | | | | |
|---|---|---|---|---|---|---|
| KS | Yes. | Yes. | 2 consecutive hours while the polls are open or amount of work time that, when added to time available before or after work, will total 2 consecutive hours while polls are open. | Employer who uses employment consequences to influence employee's vote or fails to provide time off is guilty of a Class A misdemeanor. | Employer may specify hours for employee to vote, but that time cannot include any part of the regular lunch period. Leave will be paid. | Kan. Stat. Ann. §§ 25-418, 25-2415. |
| KY | Yes. | Yes. | Employee can take sufficient time to vote without penalty if such time is not otherwise provided by employer. | Employer who tries to use employment consequences to influence employee's vote is guilty of a Class D felony. Any corporation that tries to influence employee vote by means including bribes, promises, or inducements shall be fined not more than $10,000 per offense and shall forfeit its charter or have its authority to do business revoked. | Employee must request leave to vote before the day of the election. Employee who takes time off to vote but does not actually vote under circumstances that do not prohibit him or her from voting may be subject to disciplinary action. | Ky. Rev. Stat. Ann. §§ 118.035, 121.310, 121.990. |
| LA | Yes. | State has no statutory requirements. | State has no statutory requirements. | Penalty for employer of 20 or more employees who seeks to control employee's vote: if an individual, a fine of $100–$1,000, or imprisonment for not more than 6 months, or both; if a firm, corporation, or association, a fine of $500–$2,000. Employer also is subject to paying employee damages. Any planter, manager, overseer, or other employer of laborers who tries to control employee vote will be fined $100–$500 and imprisoned for not more than 1 year. | None. | La. Rev. Stat. Ann. §§ 23:961, 23:962. |
| ME | Yes. | State has no statutory requirements. | State has no statutory requirements. | Anyone who influences another person's vote is guilty of a Class E crime. | None. | Me. Rev. Stat. Ann. tit. 21-A, § 674. |
| MD | Yes. | Yes. | 2 hours unless the employee already has 2 consecutive hours of off-duty time while the polls are open. | Employer who fails to provide adequate time off to vote is guilty of a misdemeanor, each offense being punishable by a fine not exceeding $500, or imprisonment for not more than 6 months, or both. Anyone who influences another person's vote will be punished by a fine of not more than $2,500, or imprisonment for not more than 5 years, or both. | Employee shall provide employer proof that he or she voted. Upon request, judges of election will give employee a receipt indicating proof of voting. | Md. Ann. Code art. 33, §§ 24-2, 24-26. |
| MA | Yes. | Yes. Statute applies to manufacturing, mechanical, and mercantile establishments. | 2 hours after the polls open, if employee applies for leave to vote. | Employer who influences or attempts to influence employee's vote is subject to a fine not in excess of $1,000, or imprisonment not in excess of 6 months, or both. | None. | Mass. Gen. Laws Ann. ch. 56, § 33; ch. 149, § 178. |
| MI | Yes. | State has no statutory requirements. | State has no statutory requirements. | Violator is guilty of a misdemeanor. | None. | Mich. Stat. Ann. § 6.1931(d). |

(Table continues.)

## Table 4.5-4 *(cont'd)*

## STATUTORY RESTRICTIONS ON DISCHARGING EMPLOYEES: EXERCISING VOTING RIGHTS

(See also text at § 4.5.)

**NOTE:** An em dash (—) means that no specific statutory authority exists; other authority, including case law, may apply.

| | *Is There a Restriction on Using Employment Consequences to Influence Employee Vote?* | *Are Employers Required to Give Employees Time Off to Vote?* | *How Much Time Must the Employer Allow?* | *Remedies and Penalties* | *Other Requirements* | *Citations to Authority* |
|---|---|---|---|---|---|---|
| MN | Yes. | Yes. | Sufficient time for voting on the morning of an election day. | Employer who fails to allow time to vote is guilty of a misdemeanor. Employer who uses employment consequences to influence employee's vote is guilty of a felony. | Time off to vote will be paid. | Minn. Stat. Ann. §§ 204C.04, 211B.13. |
| MS | Yes. | Yes. | Amount of time necessary to vote. | State has no statutory requirements. | None. | Miss. Code Ann. § 23-15-871. |
| MO | Yes. | Yes. | 3 hours, provided employee does not have 3 consecutive hours away from work while the polls are open. | Employer who uses employment consequences to influence employee's vote is guilty of a Class 3 election offense, a misdemeanor, punishable by imprisonment for not more than 1 year, or a fine of not more than $2,500, or both. Employer who fails to allow time off to vote is guilty of a Class 4 election offense. | Employee must notify employer of taking time to vote before the day of election. Employer may specify which workday hours employee may take off to vote. | Mo. Ann. Stat. §§ 115.635, 115.639. |
| MT | Yes. | State has no statutory requirements. | State has no statutory requirements. | Employer who uses employment consequences to influence employee's vote may be fined not more than $1,000, imprisoned for up to 6 months, or both. | None. | Mont. Code Ann. § 13-35-226. |
| NE | Yes. | Yes. | As much time as when added to available time outside working hours will give employee 2 consecutive hours while polls are open, if employee does not already have 2 consecutive hours away from work while polls are open. | Employer who uses employment consequences to influence employee's vote is guilty of a Class 4 felony. | Employee must notify employer before election day of taking time to vote. Employer may specify which workday hours employee may take off to vote. Employer may not deduct any amount from employee's usual compensation. | Neb. Rev. Stat. §§ 32-922, 32-1537. |

| | | | | | | |
|---|---|---|---|---|---|---|
| NV | Yes. | Yes. | Sufficient time to vote if it is impracticable for employee to vote before or after work. Sufficient time is defined as follows: 1 hour if distance between place of employment and polling place is 2 miles or less; 2 hours if distance is more than 2 but not more than 10 miles; and 3 hours if distance is more than 10 miles. | Employer who uses employment consequences to influence employee's vote is guilty of a gross misdemeanor. Employer who fails to allow time off to vote is guilty of a misdemeanor. | Employee must give employer notice before election day of taking time off to vote. Employer may designate hours employee will take to vote. Employer may not deduct any amount from employee's usual wages. | Nev. Rev. Stat. Ann. §§ 293.463, 293.710. |
| NH | Yes. | State has no statutory requirements. | State has no statutory requirements. | Anyone who uses threats of harm, including threats of pecuniary injury, to influence employee's vote is guilty of a Class B felony. | None. | N.H. Rev. Stat. Ann. §§ 640:2, 640:3. |
| NJ | Yes. | State has no statutory requirements. | State has no statutory requirements. | Employer who uses employment consequences to influence employee's vote is guilty of a misdemeanor, punishable by a fine of not more than $2,000, or imprisonment for not more than 5 years, or both. Corporation that uses employment consequences to influence employee vote will forfeit its charter. | None. | N.J. Stat. Ann. §§ 19:34-27, 19:34-30, 19:34-31. |
| NM | Yes. | Yes. | 2 hours, unless the workday begins more than 2 hours after polls open or ends more than 3 hours before polls close. | Employer who uses employment consequences to influence employee's vote is guilty of a fourth degree felony. Employer who fails to allow time off for voting is guilty of a misdemeanor, punishable by a fine of $50–$100. | Employer may specify hours during which employee may leave to vote. | N.M. Stat. Ann. §§ 1-12-42, 1-20-13. |
| NY | Yes. | Yes. | As much time so that, when added to the hours available to vote outside of work time, employee will be able to vote; unless employee has 4 consecutive hours outside of work time while the polls are open. Up to 2 hours of any leave taken will be with pay. | Employer who uses employment consequences to influence employee's vote is guilty of a felony. Employer who does not permit employee to attend election is guilty of a misdemeanor. Use of pay envelope to influence vote is a misdemeanor. Corporations that use pay envelopes to influence voting will forfeit corporate charter. | Employee must give employer notice not more than 10 and not less than 2 working days before the election. Employer must post signs informing employees of their right to leave for voting at least 10 days before every election. Notices must remain posted through the close of the polls. | N.Y. Elec. Law §§ 3-110, 17-118, 17-142, 17-144, 17-150. |
| NC | Yes. | State has no statutory requirements. | State has no statutory requirements. | Employer who uses employment consequences to influence employee's vote is guilty of a Class 2 misdemeanor. | None. | N.C. Gen. Stat. § 163–274(6). |
| ND | Yes. | No. Instead, employers are encouraged to give time off for voting. | Statute encourages employers to establish a program allowing employees time off from work for voting. | Any person who uses economic coercion to influence another person's vote is guilty of a Class A misdemeanor. | None. | N.D. Cent. Code §§ 12.1-14-02, 16.1-01-02.1. |

*(Table continues.)*

# Table 4.5-4 *(cont'd)*

## STATUTORY RESTRICTIONS ON DISCHARGING EMPLOYEES: EXERCISING VOTING RIGHTS

(See also text at § 4.5.)

**NOTE:** An em dash (—) means that no specific statutory authority exists; other authority, including case law, may apply.

| | *Is There a Restriction on Using Employment Consequences to Influence Employee Vote?* | *Are Employers Required to Give Employees Time Off to Vote?* | *How Much Time Must the Employer Allow?* | *Remedies and Penalties* | *Other Requirements* | *Citations to Authority* |
|---|---|---|---|---|---|---|
| OH | Yes. | Yes. | A reasonable amount of time to vote. | Employer who uses pay envelopes and posts signs containing threats to influence employee's vote is guilty of corrupt practices, punishable by a fine of $500–$1,000. Employer who does not allow employee a reasonable amount of time off to vote will be fined $50–$500. | None. | Ohio Rev. Code Ann. §§ 3599.05, 3599.06. |
| OK | Yes. | Yes. | 2 hours (more if employee lives far away), if employee does not have 3 consecutive hours while the polls are open. | Anyone who offers anything of value to influence another person's vote is guilty of a felony. Employer who fails to allow time off to vote is guilty of a misdemeanor, punishable by a fine of $50–$100. | Employee must give employer notice of taking time off to vote. Employer may specify which workday hours employee may take off to vote. If employee provides proof of voting, employee will not be subject to loss of compensation or other penalty because of taking time to vote. | Okla. Stat. Ann. tit. 26, §§ 7-101, 16-106. |
| OR | Yes. | State has no statutory requirements. | State has no statutory requirements. | Violator will be subject to a fine not to exceed $250. | None. | Or. Rev. Stat. § 260.665, 260.995. |
| PA | Yes. | State has no statutory requirements. | State has no statutory requirements. | Employer who uses pay envelopes or posts signs within 90 days of election imprinted with threats intended to influence employees' votes is guilty of a misdemeanor. Violator may be fined not more than $1,000, or imprisoned not more than 1 year, or both. | None. | Pa. Cons. Stat. Ann. tit. 18, § 4702; tit. 25, § 3547. |

| | | | | | | |
|---|---|---|---|---|---|---|
| RI | Yes. | State has no statutory requirements. | State has no statutory requirements. | Employer who, within 90 days of election, puts any printed material about any candidate in employee paychecks or who posts signs containing threats intended to influence employee vote is guilty of a felony. Individual employer shall forfeit the right to vote or hold public office; a corporate violator shall forfeit its charter. | None. | R.I. Gen. Laws § 17-23-6. |
| SC | Yes. | State has no statutory requirements. | State has no statutory requirements. | Any person who threatens a voter with the purpose of influencing his or her vote is guilty of a felony and may be fined at the discretion of the court, or imprisoned not more than 10 years, or both. | None. | S.C. Code Ann. § 7-25-80. |
| SD | Yes. | Yes. | 2 hours, if employee does not have 2 consecutive hours away from work while the polls are open. | Individual employer who places political statements in pay envelopes or, within 90 days of election, displays signs containing threats intended to influence employee's vote is guilty of a Class 2 misdemeanor; a corporate violator must forfeit its charter. Employer who fails to allow time off to vote is guilty of a Class 2 misdemeanor. | Employer may specify which workday hours employee may take off to vote. Employee's usual wages may not be reduced because of taking time to vote. | S.D. Codified Laws §§ 12-3-5, 12-26-13. |
| TN | Yes. | Yes. | Reasonable time not to exceed 3 hours as long as employee does not have 3 hours away from work while the polls are open. Employer may specify the hours during which employee may be absent. | Individual employer who uses employment consequences to influence employee's vote is guilty of a Class C misdemeanor. | Employer cannot display notices containing threats intended to influence employee vote within 90 days of an election. Employee must notify employer before noon of the day before the election about taking time off to vote. | Tenn. Code Ann. §§ 2-1-106, 2-19-134, 2-19-135. |
| TX | Yes. | Yes. | Sufficient time to vote, unless employee already has 2 consecutive hours outside working hours while the polls are open. | Corporation or labor organization that uses employment consequences to influence employee's vote is guilty of a third degree felony. Employer who fails to allow time off to vote is guilty of a Class C misdemeanor. | None. | Tex. Elec. Code Ann. §§ 253.102, 276.004. |
| UT | Yes. | Yes. | 2 hours, if employee does not have 3 hours away from work while the polls are open. | Employer who uses employment consequences to influence employee's vote is guilty of a Class B misdemeanor, punishable by a fine of not more than $1,000, or imprisonment for 5 years, or both. Violator cannot file a declaration of candidacy or take office during election cycle in which violation occurs or vote at any election unless his or her civil rights are restored. Employer who does not allow time off to vote is guilty of a Class B misdemeanor. | Employee must notify employer before election day about taking time off to vote. Employer may specify which workday hours employee may take off to vote. If employee requests leave at beginning or end of shift, employer will grant that request. Employer may not deduct any amount from employee's usual salary because of absence for voting. | Utah Code Ann. §§ 20A-1-601, 20A-3-103. |

*(Table continues.)*

## Table 4.5-4 *(cont'd)*

## STATUTORY RESTRICTIONS ON DISCHARGING EMPLOYEES: EXERCISING VOTING RIGHTS

(See also text at § 4.5.)

**NOTE:** An em dash (—) means that no specific statutory authority exists; other authority, including case law, may apply.

| | *Is There a Restriction on Using Employment Consequences to Influence Employee Vote?* | *Are Employers Required to Give Employees Time Off to Vote?* | *How Much Time Must the Employer Allow?* | *Remedies and Penalties* | *Other Requirements* | *Citations to Authority* |
|---|---|---|---|---|---|---|
| VT | Yes. | State has no statutory requirements. | State has no statutory requirements. | Anyone who uses threats or undue influence to sway employee's vote may be fined not more than $200. | None. | Vt. Stat. Ann. tit. 17, § 2017. |
| VA | Yes. | State has no statutory requirements. | State has no statutory requirements. | Any person who tries to influence another person's vote by threats or bribery is guilty of a Class 1 misdemeanor. | None. | Va. Code Ann. § 24.2-1005. |
| WA | Yes. | Yes. | Reasonable time, up to 2 hours while the polls are open, if employee does not already have 2 consecutive hours. Provision does not apply if employee has time to secure absentee ballot after employee learns work schedule for election day. | Anyone who uses threats, force, menace, or any unlawful means to influence employee's vote is guilty of either a Class C felony or a gross misdemeanor, depending on the circumstances. | Time off to vote will be paid. | Wash. Rev. Code Ann. §§ 29.85.060, 29.85.070, 49.28.120. |
| WV | Yes. | Yes. | 3 hours, if employee does not already have 3 consecutive hours while the polls are open. | Employer who uses employment consequences to influence employee's vote is guilty of corrupt practices, punishable by a fine of $1,000–$20,000, or imprisonment for not more than 1 year, or both. | Employee must give written 3-day notice to employer of intention to take time off to vote. For employees providing services in government, health care, hospitals, transportation, and communications, and for those working in production, manufacturing, and processing works requiring continuity in operation, the employer may specify which hours the employee may take off to vote. Employer may not deduct any amount from em- | W. Va. Code §§ 3-1-42, 3-9-15. |

| | | | | | | |
|---|---|---|---|---|---|---|
| | | | | | ployee's usual salary or wages because of absence for voting. | |
| WI | Yes. | Yes, but employer may take a deduction for time lost. | 3 hours. | Employer who does not allow time off or uses employment consequences to influence employee's vote is subject to a fine of not more than $1,000, or imprisonment for not more than 6 months, or both. | Employee must give employer notice before election day of intention to take time off to vote. Employer may specify which workday hours employee may take off to vote. | Wis. Stat. Ann. §§ 6.76, 12.07, 12.60, 103.18, 103.20. |
| WY | Yes. | Yes. | 1 hour, other than meal break, while the polls are open. | Anyone who knowingly and willfully offers a bribe or threatens economic retaliation to influence another person's vote may be guilty of a felony, punishable by a fine of not more than $10,000, imprisonment for not more than 5 years, or both. | Employer must not reduce employee's pay for time spent at the polls provided employee actually casts his or her legal vote. The hour to vote will be at the convenience of the employer. | Wyo. Stat. §§ 22-2-111, 22-26-101, 22-26-109, 22-26-111, 22-26-116. |

# Table 4.5-5
## STATUTORY RESTRICTIONS: WAGE GARNISHMENT, LABOR ORGANIZATION MEMBERSHIP

(See also text at § 4.5.)

**NOTE:** An em dash (—) means that no specific statutory authority exists; other authority, including case law, may apply. "Exception for more than one garnishment" means that either the statute explicitly states there is an exception, or the statute indicates the only restriction on adverse personnel actions is for an employee with only one garnishment.

| | *Wage Garnishment* | | | | *Labor Organization Membership* | | |
|---|---|---|---|---|---|---|---|
| | *Are Employers Restricted from Discharging Employees Whose Wages Are Subject to Garnishment?* | *Is There an Exception for More Than One Garnishment?* | *Remedies and Penalties* | *Citations to Authority* | *Are Employers Restricted from Making Labor Organization Membership or Nonmembership a Condition of Employment?* | *Remedies and Penalties* | *Citations to Authority* |
| AL | Yes. Applies to garnishments for child or spousal support. Applicants for employment are also protected. | — | Violator may be held in contempt of court. | Ala. Code § 30-3-70. | Yes. | Employee may bring civil suit to recover actual damages from the employer and any other person or group acting in concert with the employer. | Ala. Code §§ 25-7-30 *et seq.* |
| AK | Yes. | — | Court may order violator to pay civil penalty of not more than $1,000. Employee can bring action for reinstatement and restitution. | Alaska Stat. § 25.27.062(f). | Yes, if public employee objects to collective bargaining settlement based on religious convictions. Employee must pay amount equivalent to union dues, which will be distributed to charitable organization. | — | Alaska Stat. § 23.40.225. |
| AZ | Yes. Applies to garnishments for child support and spousal maintenance. Applicants for employment are also protected. | — | Violator is guilty of contempt and subject to fines at the court's discretion. Employee may bring civil action for actual damages, reinstatement, attorneys' fees, and costs. | Ariz. Rev. Stat. Ann. §§ 23-722.02, 25-323, 25-323.01, 25-503, 25-504. | Yes. | Employee is entitled to injunctive relief and damages. | Ariz. Rev. Stat. Ann. §§ 23-1305, 23-1306, 23-1307. |

| | | | | | | | |
|---|---|---|---|---|---|---|---|
| AR | — | — | — | State has no statutory provisions. | Yes. | Employer who enters contract with employee requiring or prohibiting labor organization membership as a condition of employment is guilty of a misdemeanor, punishable by a fine of $100–$5,000. Each day the unlawful contract is in effect or complied with constitutes a separate offense. | Ark. Code Ann. §§ 11-3-303, 11-3-304. |
| CA | Yes. | Yes. | Employer must pay wages of discharged employee until reinstatement, but not for more than 30 days and not in excess of the amount of wages earned during the 30 calendar days immediately preceding the date of the levy of execution on the employee's wages. | Cal. Lab. Code § 2929. | Yes. | Violator is guilty of a misdemeanor. | Cal. Lab. Code § 922. |
| CO | Yes. | No. | Violator may be liable for lost wages, reinstatement, costs, and reasonable attorneys' fees, if employee brings action within 90 days. Damages are not to exceed 6 weeks' wages. | Colo. Rev. Stat. § 13-54.5-110. | Yes. | Violator is guilty of a misdemeanor, punishable by a fine of $100–$500, or imprisonment for 6 months–1 year, or both. | Colo. Rev. Stat. §§ 8-2-102, 8-2-103. |
| CT | Yes. Applicants for employment are also protected. | Yes. Employer may take adverse personnel action when served with more than 7 wage garnishments against the employee in a calendar year. | Violator is liable for all lost earnings and benefits of employee. Violator also is subject to a fine of not more than $1,000. | Conn. Gen. Stat. Ann. §§ 52-361a(j), 52-362(j) and (k). | Yes. | The labor relations board may issue any orders to effectuate the policy of fair labor practices, including, but not limited to, orders for reinstatement and back pay. | Conn. Gen. Stat. Ann. §§ 31-105, 31-107. |
| DE | Yes. | — | — | Del. Code Ann. tit. 10, § 3509. | Yes. Applies to public employers and employees. | The Public Authority Relations Board has the ability to order appropriate relief, including reinstatement and damages. The board may petition the chancery court to enforce its orders. Any party adversely affected by the board's decision may appeal to the chancery court within 15 days of date board released its decision. | Del. Code Ann. tit. 19, §§ 1303, 1307, 1308, 1309. |

*(Table continues.)*

# Table 4.5-5 *(cont'd)*

## STATUTORY RESTRICTIONS: WAGE GARNISHMENT LABOR ORGANIZATION MEMBERSHIP

(See also text at § 4.5.)

**NOTE:** An em dash (—) means that no specific statutory authority exists; other authority, including case law, may apply.
"Exception for more than one garnishment" means that either the statute explicitly states there is an exception, or the statute indicates the only restriction on adverse personnel actions is for an employee with only one garnishment.

| | *Wage Garnishment* | | | | *Labor Organization Membership* | | |
|---|---|---|---|---|---|---|---|
| | *Are Employers Restricted from Discharging Employees Whose Wages Are Subject to Garnishment?* | *Is There an Exception for More Than One Garnishment?* | *Remedies and Penalties* | *Citations to Authority* | *Are Employers Restricted from Making Labor Organization Membership or Nonmembership a Condition of Employment?* | *Remedies and Penalties* | *Citations to Authority* |
| DC | Yes. | — | — | D.C. Code Ann. § 16-584. | Yes. | — | D.C. Code Ann. § 1-618.4. |
| FL | — | — | — | State has no statutory provision. | Yes. | Employee may bring civil action for damages. Punitive damages may be awarded if conduct was willful and with malice. | Fla. Stat. Ann. § 447.17. |
| GA | Yes. | Yes. | State has no statutory requirements. | Ga. Code Ann. § 18-4-7. | Yes. | — | Ga. Code Ann. §§ 34-6-6, 34-6-21, 34-6-22, 34-6-23, 34-6-24. |
| HI | Yes. | State has no statutory requirements. | Employee may file complaint with Department of Labor and Industrial Relations within 30 days of adverse action. The department may order reinstatement with or without back pay. Court has jurisdiction to enforce department's orders and review department's decisions. | Haw. Rev. Stat. § 378-32. | Yes, except employer may enter an all-union agreement with employees' bargaining representative unless a majority of employees have voted to revoke their bargaining representative's authority to enter such an agreement within 1 year before the agreement is made. | Employee may file complaint with the Labor Relations Board within 90 days of violation. Board may order appropriate relief, including reinstatement with or without back pay. Board's decisions are subject to judicial review. This provision does not preclude employee from pursuing relief in a civil action. | Haw. Rev. Stat. §§ 377-6, 377-9. |

| | | | | | | | |
|---|---|---|---|---|---|---|---|
| ID | Yes. Additional protection of garnishments for child support. | State has no statutory requirements. | For child support garnishment, employer may be liable for double lost wages, other damages, costs, and reasonable attorneys' fees. Civil penalty of not more than $300 for each violation. Court may order employer to reinstate the employee.<br>For other garnishments, employee must bring action within 90 days; damages may not exceed 6 weeks' wages. | Idaho Code §§ 28-45-105, 28-45-201(5), 32-1210. | Yes. | Violator is guilty of a misdemeanor punishable by a fine of not more than $1,000, or imprisonment of not more than 90 days, or both. Employee may bring civil action for injunction, damages, costs, and reasonable attorneys' fees. | Idaho Code §§ 44-2001 *et seq.* |
| IL | Yes. | Yes. | Violator is guilty of a Class A misdemeanor. | Ill. Ann. Stat. ch. 735, ¶ 5/12-818. | Yes. Applies to public employers and employees. | — | Ill. Ann. Stat. ch. 5, ¶¶ 315(6), 315/10(2). |
| IN | — | — | — | State has no statutory provisions. | Yes. | Violator is guilty of a Class B misdemeanor. | Ind. Code Ann. § 22-7-1-3. |
| IA | Yes. | State has no statutory requirements. | State has no statutory requirements. | Iowa Code Ann. § 642.21(2)(c). | Yes. | — | Iowa Code Ann. § 731.2. |
| KS | Yes. | State has no statutory requirements. | State has no statutory requirements. | Kan. Stat. Ann. § 60-2311. | Yes. | Injunctive relief is available; an action may be brought by the attorney general or a county attorney for suspension or revocation of business license. | Kan. Stat. Ann. §§ 44-809, 44-810, 44-814. |
| KY | Yes. | Yes. Atty Gen. Op. No. 78-433. | State has no statutory requirements. | Ky. Rev. Stat. Ann. § 427.140. | Yes. | — | Ky. Rev. Stat. Ann. § 336.130. |
| LA | Yes. Applicants for employment are also protected. | Yes. Employee may be discharged from employment if his or her earnings are subjected to 3 or more garnishments for unrelated debts in a 2-year period, but no garnishment resulting from an accident or illness causing a person to miss 10 or more consecutive days at work shall be considered for purpose of this provision. | Discharged employee has a right to reinstatement and back pay, but not damages. Person denied employment has a right to reasonable damages. | La. Rev. Stat. Ann. § 23:731. | Yes. | Violator is fined not less than $50 or imprisoned for not less than 30 days. | La. Rev. Stat. Ann. § 23:824. |

*(Table continues.)*

# Table 4.5-5 *(cont'd)*

## STATUTORY RESTRICTIONS: WAGE GARNISHMENT LABOR ORGANIZATION MEMBERSHIP

(See also text at § 4.5.)

**NOTE:** An em dash (—) means that no specific statutory authority exists; other authority, including case law, may apply.
"Exception for more than one garnishment" means that either the statute explicitly states there is an exception, or the statute indicates the only restriction on adverse personnel actions is for an employee with only one garnishment.

| | *Wage Garnishment* | | | | *Labor Organization Membership* | | |
|---|---|---|---|---|---|---|---|
| | *Are Employers Restricted from Discharging Employees Whose Wages Are Subject to Garnishment?* | *Is There an Exception for More Than One Garnishment?* | *Remedies and Penalties* | *Citations to Authority* | *Are Employers Restricted from Making Labor Organization Membership or Nonmembership a Condition of Employment?* | *Remedies and Penalties* | *Citations to Authority* |
| ME | Yes. | State has no statutory requirements. | State has no statutory requirements. | Me. Rev. Stat. Ann. tit. 9-A, § 5-106, tit. 14, § 3127-B(6). | No. | — | State has no statutory provisions. |
| MD | Yes. | Yes. | Violator is guilty of a misdemeanor, punishable by a fine of not more than $1,000, or imprisonment for not more than 1 year, or both. | Md. Code Ann. Comm. Law § 15-606. | — | — | State has no statutory provisions. |
| MA | Yes. Applies to garnishments for child support. | State has no statutory requirements. | Violator may be liable for lost wages, benefits, and reinstatement. | Mass. Gen. Laws Ann. ch. 119A, § 12(f)(2). | Yes. | — | Mass. Gen. Laws Ann. ch. 149, § 20. |
| MI | Yes. | No. | Violator may be liable for lost wages and reinstatement. | Mich. Stat. Ann. § 27A.4015. | Yes. | Violator is guilty of a misdemeanor. | Mich. Stat. Ann. § 423.17. |
| MN | Yes. | State has no statutory requirements. | Court may order violator to reinstate the employee, pay double lost wages, and provide any other relief. Employee must bring action within 90 days. | Minn. Stat. Ann. § 571.927. | Yes, except by means of provisions of collective bargaining agreements entered voluntarily by employer and employees or labor organization representing the employees. | — | Minn. Stat. Ann. § 179.12(3). |

| | | | | | | | |
|---|---|---|---|---|---|---|---|
| MS | Yes. Applies to garnishments for child support. | State has no statutory requirements. | Employer may be fined up to $50. | Miss. Code Ann. §§ 93-11-111(9), 93-11-117(2). | Yes, except this provision does not apply to employers and employees under the jurisdiction of the Federal Railway Labor Act. | — | Miss. Code Ann. § 71-1-47. |
| MO | Yes. | Yes. | Violator is guilty of a misdemeanor. | Mo. Ann. Stat. § 525.030(5) and (6). | State constitution gives employees right to organize collectively, but there exists no specific statutory authority prohibiting employers from making labor organization membership or nonmembership a condition of employment. | — | Mo. Const. art. 1, § 29. |
| MT | Yes. | State has no statutory requirements. | State has no statutory requirements. | Mont. Code Ann. § 39-2-302. | — | — | State has no statutory provision. |
| NE | Yes. | Yes. | State has no statutory requirements. | Neb. Rev. Stat. § 25-1558(6). | Yes. | — | Neb. Rev. Stat. § 48-217. |
| NV | Yes. | State has no statutory requirements. | State has no statutory requirements. | Nev. Rev. Stat. Ann. § 31.298. | Yes. | Violator is guilty of a misdemeanor. | Nev. Rev. Stat. Ann. § 613.130. |
| NH | — | — | — | State has no statutory provisions. | Yes. | Violator who is a natural person is guilty of a misdemeanor. Corporate violator is guilty of a felony. | N.H. Rev. Stat. Ann. §§ 275:1, 275.2. |
| NJ | Yes. | No. | State has no statutory requirements. | N.J. Stat. Ann. § 2A:170-90.4. | Yes. | Violator may be fined not more than $500, or imprisoned not more than 3 months, or both. Any contract making labor organization membership or nonmembership a condition of employment is void. | N.J. Stat. Ann. §§ 34:12-2 *et seq.* |
| NM | — | — | — | State has no statutory provisions. | Yes. | Violator is guilty of a misdemeanor. | N.M. Stat. Ann. § 50-2-4. |
| NY | Yes. | No. | Employee may bring civil action for reinstatement and lost wages. Such action must be brought within 90 days of violation. Damages cannot exceed 6 weeks' lost wages. *(cont'd)* | N.Y. Civ. Prac. L. & R. 5252. | Yes. | — | N.Y. Gen. Oblig. Law § 5-301. |

*(Table continues.)*

## Table 4.5-5 *(cont'd)*

## STATUTORY RESTRICTIONS: WAGE GARNISHMENT LABOR ORGANIZATION MEMBERSHIP

(See also text at § 4.5.)

**NOTE:** An em dash (—) means that no specific statutory authority exists; other authority, including case law, may apply. "Exception for more than one garnishment" means that either the statute explicitly states there is an exception, or the statute indicates the only restriction on adverse personnel actions is for an employee with only one garnishment.

| | *Wage Garnishment* | | | | *Labor Organization Membership* | | |
|---|---|---|---|---|---|---|---|
| | *Are Employers Restricted from Discharging Employees Whose Wages Are Subject to Garnishment?* | *Is There an Exception for More Than One Garnishment?* | *Remedies and Penalties* | *Citations to Authority* | *Are Employers Restricted from Making Labor Organization Membership or Nonmembership a Condition of Employment?* | *Remedies and Penalties* | *Citations to Authority* |
| NY (*cont'd*) | | | Violator also may be punished for contempt of court. Court may direct payment of fine up to $500 for first instance and up to $1,000 for subsequent instances. | | | | |
| NC | Yes. Applies only if 1 of any garnishments is for a debt owed to a public hospital. | State has no statutory requirements. | Employee may bring civil action for all appropriate relief, including injunction, back pay, damages, reinstatement, and reasonable costs and attorneys' fees. | N.C. Gen. Stat. §§ 131E-49, 131E-50. | Yes. | Employee may bring civil action for damages. | N.C. Gen. Stat. §§ 95-81, 95-82, 95-83. |
| ND | Yes. | State has no statutory requirements. | Employee may bring civil action within 90 days of discharge for double lost wages and order for reinstatement. | N.D. Cent. Code § 32-09.1-18. | Yes. | — | N.D. Cent. Code §§ 34-01-14, 34-09-01. |
| OH | Yes. Applies to garnishments that are for orders of support. | No. | Violator may be fined not more than $500. | Ohio Rev. Code Ann. §§ 2301.39, 3113.213(D). | Yes. | Contracts making labor organization membership or nonmembership a condition of employment are void. | Ohio Rev. Code Ann. § 4113.02. |

| | | | | | | | |
|---|---|---|---|---|---|---|---|
| OK | Yes. Applies to judgments arising from consumer credit sale, consumer lease, or consumer loan. | Yes, if the employer is served with 1 or more judgments against an employee on more than 2 occasions within 1 year. | State has no statutory requirements. | Okla. Stat. Ann. tit. 14A, § 5-106. | — | — | State has no statutory provisions. |
| OR | Yes. | State has no statutory requirements. | State has no statutory requirements. | Or. Rev. Stat. § 23.185(5). | Yes. Applies to public employees. | Employee may file written complaint with Employment Relations Board no later than 180 days after violation. Fee of $250 is imposed. | Or. Rev. Stat. § 243.672. |
| PA | Yes. Applies to garnishments that are orders of support. Employee must give employer notice of the garnishment. | No. | Violator may be in contempt of court and fined up to $1,000. Employee may bring action for damages. | Pa. Cons. Stat. Ann. tit. 23, § 4348(i) and (l). | Yes. | — | Pa. Stat. Ann. tit. 43, §§ 211.5, 211.6. |
| RI | Yes. Applies to garnishments for child support. | State has no statutory requirements. | State has no statutory requirements. | R.I. Gen. Laws § 15-5-24(e). | Yes. | Employee may bring civil action for damages, injunctive relief, and reasonable costs and attorneys' fees. | R.I. Gen. Laws § 28-6.6-1. |
| SC | Yes, if the garnishment is for the purpose of paying a judgment arising from a consumer credit sale, consumer lease, consumer loan, or a consumer-rental purchase agreement. | State has no statutory requirements. | State has no statutory requirements. | S.C. Code Ann. § 37-5-106. | Yes. | Violator is guilty of a misdemeanor, punishable by a fine of $10–$50 or imprisonment for 10–30 days. | S.C. Code Ann. § 41-1-20. |
| SD | — | — | — | State has no statutory provisions. | Yes. State attorney is responsible for enforcement. | Violator is guilty of a Class 2 misdemeanor. | S.D. Codified Laws §§ 60-8-3 *et seq.* |
| TN | — | — | — | State has no statutory provisions. | Yes. | Violator is guilty of a Class A misdemeanor. Each day employer is in violation constitutes a separate offense. | Tenn. Code Ann. §§ 50-1-203, 50-1-204. |
| TX | — | — | — | State has no statutory provisions. | Yes. | — | Tex. Lab. Code Ann. §§ 101.052, 101.053. |

*(Table continues.)*

## Table 4.5-5 *(cont'd)*

## STATUTORY RESTRICTIONS: WAGE GARNISHMENT LABOR ORGANIZATION MEMBERSHIP

(See also text at § 4.5.)

**NOTE:** An em dash (—) means that no specific statutory authority exists; other authority, including case law, may apply.
"Exception for more than one garnishment" means that either the statute explicitly states there is an exception, or the statute indicates the only restriction on adverse personnel actions is for an employee with only one garnishment.

| | *Wage Garnishment* | | | | *Labor Organization Membership* | | |
|---|---|---|---|---|---|---|---|
| | *Are Employers Restricted from Discharging Employees Whose Wages Are Subject to Garnishment?* | *Is There an Exception for More Than One Garnishment?* | *Remedies and Penalties* | *Citations to Authority* | *Are Employers Restricted from Making Labor Organization Membership or Nonmembership a Condition of Employment?* | *Remedies and Penalties* | *Citations to Authority* |
| UT | Yes. Additional protections for garnishments to pay child support. | Yes. | Employer who discharges employee because employee's wages are subject to garnishment for child support may be liable to employee for damages and to Office of Recovery Services for amount equal to debt, costs, interest, and attorneys' fees, up to $1,000. | Utah Code Ann. §§ 62A-11-316, 70C-7-104. | Yes. | Violator is guilty of a misdemeanor. Each day employer is in violation constitutes a separate offense. Employee may receive injunctive relief and damages. | Utah Code Ann. §§ 34-34-7 *et seq.* |
| VT | — | — | — | State has no statutory provisions. | Yes. | — | Vt. Stat. Ann. tit. 21, § 1344(a)(2)(E)(iii). |
| VA | Yes. | Yes. | State has no statutory requirements. | Va. Code Ann. § 34-29(f). | Yes. | — | Va. Code Ann. § 40.1-60. |
| WA | Yes. | Yes, if garnishments on 3 or more indebtednesses are served on the employer within 1 year. | If employer discharges or refuses to hire person because that person's wages are garnished because of debts owed for child support or spousal maintenance, that person may bring civil action for double damages, reinstatement, costs, and reasonable attorneys' fees. | Wash. Rev. Code Ann. §§ 6.27.170, 26.18.110. | Yes. | Contracts requiring or prohibiting labor organization membership as a condition of employment are void and unenforceable. | Wash. Rev. Code Ann. §§ 49.32.020, 49.32.030. |

| | | | | | | | |
|---|---|---|---|---|---|---|---|
| | | | Violator is subject to civil penalty of not more than $2,500. | | | | |
| WV | Yes. Applies to judgments arising from consumer credit sales or consumer loans. | No. | State has no statutory requirements. | W.Va. Code § 46A-2-131. | Yes. | Violator is fined not more than $5,000, or imprisoned not more than 10 years, or both. | W.Va. Code § 61-6-21(f). |
| WI | Yes. | No. | Employee may bring civil action for reinstatement, back wages, benefits, seniority rights, and reasonable attorneys' fees. | Wis. Stat. Ann. §§ 425.110, 812.43. | Yes, except employer may enter an all-union agreement with the voluntarily recognized representative of the employees in a collective bargaining unit if a majority of employees have voted by secret ballot in favor of such an agreement. Employers who are engaged in the building and construction industry or the motor freight industry or an employer who is an orchestra or band leader may enter into an all-union agreement without an employee vote. | Within 1 year of violation, employee may file a complaint with the employment relations commission for an injunction and reinstatement with or without back pay. This administrative remedy does not preclude employee from pursuing legal or equitable action in court. | Wis. Stat. Ann. §§ 111.04, 111.06, 111.07. |
| WY | Yes. | State has no statutory requirements. | Employee may bring civil action within 120 days for lost wages and order for reinstatement. Damages are not to exceed 30 days' lost wages, costs, and reasonable attorneys' fees. | Wyo. Stat. §§ 1-15-509, 40-14-506. | Yes. | Violator is guilty of a misdemeanor, punishable by a fine not to exceed $1,000, or imprisonment not to exceed 6 months, or both. Employee is entitled to damages and reinstatement. | Wyo. Stat. §§ 27-7-101, 27-7-109, 27-7-110, 27-7-113, 27-7-114, 27-7-115. |

# Table 4.5-6
## STATUTORY RESTRICTIONS ON RETALIATION: WORKERS' COMPENSATION AND OSHA

(See also text at § 4.5.)

**NOTE:** An em-dash (—) means that no specific statutory authority exists; other authority, including case law, may apply.

| | *Workers' Compensation Claim* | | | *OSHA Complaint* | | | |
|---|---|---|---|---|---|---|---|
| | *Employers Restricted from Discharging an Employee for Filing a Workers' Compensation Claim* | *Remedies and Penalties* | *Citations to Authority* | *Employers Restricted from Discharging an Employee for Filing an OSHA Complaint* | *Statute of Limitations for Filing* | *Remedies and Penalties* | *Citations to Authority* |
| AL | Yes. | — | Ala. Code § 25-5-11.1. | Yes. | — | — | Ala. Code § 25-5-11.1. |
| AK | Yes. | Employee may bring civil action for damages. | Alaska Stat. § 23.30.247. | Yes. | Employee has within 30 days of violation to file complaint with the Commissioner of Labor alleging discrimination. | Court has jurisdiction to grant injunction, reinstatement, and back pay. | Alaska Stat. § 18.60.089. |
| AZ | — | — | State has no statutory provision. | Yes. | Employee must file complaint with the Industrial Commission of Arizona within 30 days of violation. | Court has jurisdiction to grant injunction and all other appropriate relief, including reinstatement and back pay. | Ariz. Rev. Stat. Ann. § 23-425. |
| AR | Yes. | Violator may be guilty of a Class D felony and subject to a fine of up to $10,000. Prevailing party is entitled to recover costs and attorneys' fees. | Ark. Code Ann. § 11-9-107. | Yes. Applies to public employees' reports concerning hazardous substances. | — | Court may order all appropriate relief, including reinstatement, back wages, and reasonable costs and attorneys' fees. | Ark. Code Ann. §§ 8-7-1010, 8-7-1015. |
| CA | Yes. | Violator is guilty of a misdemeanor. Employee can bring administrative action before the Workers' Compensation Appeals Board for reinstatement and reimbursement of lost wages and benefits within 1 year of violation. | Cal. Lab. Code § 132a. | Yes. | — | Employee may bring civil action for reinstatement and reimbursement of lost wages and work benefits. Employer who willfully refuses to rehire is guilty of a misdemeanor. | Cal. Lab. Code § 6310. |

| | | | | | | | |
|---|---|---|---|---|---|---|---|
| | | Employee's compensation shall be increased by one half, but increase shall not exceed $10,000, together with costs and expenses not in excess of $250. | | | | | |
| CO | — | — | State has no statutory provision. | — | — | — | State has no statutory provision. |
| CT | Yes. | Employee may either bring civil action for reinstatement, back wages, benefits, other actual damages, punitive damages, reasonable attorneys' fees, and costs or file a complaint with the chairman of the Workers' Compensation Commission to receive a hearing under a commissioner, who also may award the above relief. Commissioner's decision is subject to judicial review. | Conn. Gen. Stat. Ann. § 31-290a. | Yes. | Employee may file complaint with labor commissioner within 30 days of violation. | If Labor Commissioner determines that discriminatory conduct took place, he or she shall bring an action against the violator in superior court, which has jurisdiction to restrain violations and to order all appropriate relief, including reinstatement and back pay. | Conn. Gen. Stat. Ann. § 31-379. |
| DE | Yes. | Violator is subject to a fine of $500–$3,000. Employee may bring civil action within 2 years of adverse action for lost wages, damages, costs, attorneys' fees, and reinstatement. Employee is not entitled to reinstatement and compensation if he or she is no longer qualified to perform duties of position. | Del. Code Ann. tit. 19, § 2365. | Yes. Applies to complaints concerning hazardous chemicals. | — | — | Del. Code Ann. tit. 19, § 726. |
| DC | Yes. | Violator may be fined $100–$1,000 as determined by the mayor. Employee may bring civil action for reinstatement and lost wages. Employee is not entitled to reinstatement and compensation if he or she is no longer qualified to perform duties of position. | D.C. Code Ann. § 36-342. | Yes. | Employee must file complaint within 60 days of violation with the District of Columbia Occupational Safety and Health Commission. | Commission has authority to order steps to end the violation, including reinstatement and back pay. Commission's decisions are subject to judicial review. | D.C. Code Ann. § 36-1217. |

*(Table continues.)*

# Table 4.5-6 *(cont'd)*

## STATUTORY RESTRICTIONS ON RETALIATION: WORKERS' COMPENSATION AND OSHA

(See also text at § 4.5.)

**NOTE:** An em-dash (—) means that no specific statutory authority exists; other authority, including case law, may apply.

| | *Workers' Compensation Claim* | | | *OSHA Complaint* | | | |
|---|---|---|---|---|---|---|---|
| | *Employers Restricted from Discharging an Employee for Filing a Workers' Compensation Claim* | *Remedies and Penalties* | *Citations to Authority* | *Employers Restricted from Discharging an Employee for Filing an OSHA Complaint* | *Statute of Limitations for Filing* | *Remedies and Penalties* | *Citations to Authority* |
| FL | Yes. | State has no statutory requirements. | Fla. Stat. Ann. § 440.205. | Yes. Applies to public employees only. | See Table 4.5-7. | Employee may elect civil action or administrative remedy after completion of investigation. Relief includes reinstatement, lost wages, and payment of legal costs and attorneys' fees. | Fla. Stat. Ann. § 112.3187. |
| GA | — | — | State has no statutory provision. | Applies to public employees' reports concerning hazardous chemicals. | — | — | Ga. Code Ann. §§ 45-22-7(l), 45-22-10. |
| HI | Yes, unless employee is no longer able to perform duties because of the work injury and employer has no other available work the employee is capable of performing. Applies to employers with 3 or more employees at the time of the work injury or employers who are not parties to collective bargaining agreements that prevent the continued employment of injured employees. | Employee may file complaint with Department of Labor and Industrial Relations within 30 days of adverse action or within 30 days of when injured employee is able to return to work. The department may order reinstatement with or without back pay. Court has jurisdiction to enforce department's orders and review department's decisions. | Haw. Rev. Stat. §§ 378-32(2), 378-33, 378-34, 378-35, 378-36. | Yes. | Employee must file complaint with the director of Labor and Industrial Relations within 60 days of violation. | Director can order all appropriate relief, including reinstatement and lost wages. This provision does not preclude employee from simultaneously bringing a cause of action for equitable or legal relief. | Haw. Rev. Stat. § 396-8. |

| | | | | | | | |
|---|---|---|---|---|---|---|---|
| ID | — | — | State has no statutory provision. | — | — | — | State has no statutory provision. |
| IL | Yes. | State has no statutory requirements. | Ill. Ann. Stat. ch. 820, ¶ 305/4(h). | — | — | — | State has no statutory provision. |
| IN | — | — | State has no statutory provision. | Yes. | 30 days. | Circuit courts have jurisdiction to restrain violations and order all appropriate relief, including reinstatement and back pay, after taking into account any interim earnings of the employee. | Ind. Code Ann. § 22-8-1.1-38.1. |
| IA | Yes. | — | Iowa Code Ann. § 85.18. | Yes. | Employee must file complaint with Labor Commissioner within 30 days of violation. | Employee may bring action for reinstatement and other appropriate relief. | Iowa Code Ann. § 88.9(3). |
| KS | — | — | State has no statutory provision. | Yes. | — | Violator is guilty of a misdemeanor, punishable by a fine of $25–$100. Each day violation exists constitutes a separate offense. | Kan. Stat. Ann. § 44-636(f), (g). |
| KY | Yes. | Employee may bring civil action to enjoin further violations and to recover actual damages, costs, and reasonable attorneys' fees. | Ky. Rev. Stat. Ann. § 342.197. | Yes. | Employee must file complaint with the Department of Workplace Standards Commissioner within a reasonable time after the adverse action. | Violator is subject to civil penalty of up to $10,000 for each violation. Employee may receive reinstatement and back pay. | Ky. Rev. Stat. Ann. §§ 338.121, 338.991(5). |
| LA | Yes. | Employee may recover a civil penalty equal to the amount of lost wages not to exceed 1 year's earnings, reasonable attorneys' fees, and costs. | La. Rev. Stat. Ann. § 23:1361. | — | — | — | State has no statutory provision. |
| ME | Yes. | Employee may bring action for reinstatement, lost wages, benefits, and reasonable attorneys' fees. | Me. Rev. Stat. Ann. tit. 39A, § 353. | Yes. | Employee must file complaint with Bureau of Labor Director within 30 days of violation. | Court has jurisdiction to order all appropriate relief, including reinstatement with back pay. Violator who refuses to comply within 60 days of notice of noncompliance is subject to civil penalties of not more than $500 for first violation and not more than $1,000 for each subsequent violation. | Me. Rev. Stat. Ann. tit. 26, §§ 570, 1723. |

*(Table continues.)*

## Table 4.5-6 *(cont'd)*

## STATUTORY RESTRICTIONS ON RETALIATION: WORKERS' COMPENSATION AND OSHA

(See also text at § 4.5.)

**NOTE:** An em-dash (—) means that no specific statutory authority exists; other authority, including case law, may apply.

| | *Workers' Compensation Claim* | | | *OSHA Complaint* | | | |
|---|---|---|---|---|---|---|---|
| | *Employers Restricted from Discharging an Employee for Filing a Workers' Compensation Claim* | *Remedies and Penalties* | *Citations to Authority* | *Employers Restricted from Discharging an Employee for Filing an OSHA Complaint* | *Statute of Limitations for Filing* | *Remedies and Penalties* | *Citations to Authority* |
| MD | Yes. | Violator is guilty of a misdemeanor, punishable by a fine of not more than $500, or imprisonment for not more than 1 year, or both. | Md. Ann. Code Lab. & Empl. § 9-1105. | Yes. | Employee must file written complaint with Commissioner of Labor and Industry within 30 days of adverse action. | Employee may receive injunctive relief, reinstatement, back pay, and any other appropriate relief. | Md. Code Ann., Lab. & Empl. § 5-604. |
| MA | Yes. | Violator is liable for lost wages, reinstatement, reasonable attorneys' fees, and other necessary relief. | Mass. Gen. Laws Ann. ch. 152, § 75B. | Yes. Applies to complaints concerning hazardous substances. | Employee must file complaint with Department of Labor and Industries Commissioner within 180 days of violation or date that employee obtained knowledge of violation. | Commissioner may take such remedial action as is appropriate, including the issuance of a cease or desist order or the ordering of any other affirmative steps to correct the violation and prevent its recurrence. Commissioner's decisions are subject to review in superior court. | Mass. Gen. Laws Ann. ch. 111F, § 13. |
| MI | Yes. | State has no statutory requirements. | Mich. Stat. Ann. §§ 17.237(125), 17.237(301)(11). | Yes. | Employee must file complaint with Department of Labor within 30 days. | Employee may bring administrative action for reinstatement and back pay. Administrative decision is subject to judicial review. | Mich. Stat. Ann. § 17.50(65). |
| MN | Yes. | Employee may bring civil action for costs, attorneys' fees, and punitive damages up to 3 times the amount of compensation to which employee is entitled. | Minn. Stat. Ann. § 176.82. | Yes. | 30 days. | Administrative law judge has jurisdiction to order, or employee may bring civil action in court for back pay, compensatory damages, reemployment, reinstatement of benefits, seniority rights, | Minn. Stat. Ann. §§ 182.654(9), 182.669. |

| | | | | | | | |
|---|---|---|---|---|---|---|---|
| | | | | | | costs, attorneys' and witness fees, and other equitable relief. | |
| MS | Yes. Applies to corporate employers. | Corporate employer may be liable for a $250 penalty for each violation. | Miss. Code Ann. § 79-1-9. | Yes. | — | Corporate employer may be liable for a $250 penalty for each violation. | Miss. Code Ann. § 79-1-9. |
| MO | Yes. | Employee may bring civil action for damages. | Mo. Ann. Stat. § 287.780. | — | — | — | State has no statutory provision. |
| MT | Yes. | State has no statutory requirements. | Mont. Code Ann. § 39-71-317. | — | — | — | State has no statutory provision. |
| NE | — | — | State has no statutory provisions. | Yes. | — | Employee is entitled to reinstatement, lost wages, and benefits. | Neb. Rev. Stat. § 48-443(4). |
| NV | — | — | State has no statutory provisions. | Yes. | Employee must file complaint with Division of Industrial Relations of the Department of Business and industry within 30 days of violation. Employee must first notify employer and Division of Industrial Relations of intent to file complaint. | Employee may bring action for reinstatement, lost wages, and benefits. | Nev. Rev. Stat. Ann. § 618.445. |
| NH | — | — | State has no statutory provisions. | Yes. | If employee's OSHA complaint concerned toxic substances in the workplace, employee must file complaint of retaliation with Commissioner of Labor within 30 days of violation or date employee first obtains knowledge of violation. | Employee may petition Commissioner of Labor to review employer's action. Commissioner may order reinstatement or such other relief deemed necessary. If employee's OSHA complaint concerned toxic substances in the workplace, Commissioner may refer matter to attorney general for appropriate action; violator also is subject to a civil penalty of not more than $2,500; each day employer is in violation constitutes a separate offense. | N.H. Rev. Stat. Ann. §§ 277:35-a, 277-A:7, 277-A:9. |

*(Table continues.)*

## Table 4.5-6 *(cont'd)*
## STATUTORY RESTRICTIONS ON RETALIATION: WORKERS' COMPENSATION AND OSHA

(See also text at § 4.5.)

**NOTE:** An em-dash (—) means that no specific statutory authority exists; other authority, including case law, may apply.

| | *Workers' Compensation Claim* | | | *OSHA Complaint* | | | |
|---|---|---|---|---|---|---|---|
| | *Employers Restricted from Discharging an Employee for Filing a Workers' Compensation Claim* | *Remedies and Penalties* | *Citations to Authority* | *Employers Restricted from Discharging an Employee for Filing an OSHA Complaint* | *Statute of Limitations for Filing* | *Remedies and Penalties* | *Citations to Authority* |
| NJ | Yes. | Violator may be fined $100–$1,000, or imprisoned for not more than 60 days, or both. Employee may bring action for reinstatement and back pay. If employee is no longer qualified to perform duties, he or she is not entitled to restoration and compensation. | N.J. Stat. Ann. § 34:15-39.1. | Yes. | Employee must bring civil action within 180 days of date he or she gains knowledge of violation. | Employee may file action with the Commissioner for all appropriate relief, including reinstatement, legal fees, and back pay. | N.J. Stat. Ann. § 34:6A-45. |
| NM | Yes. | Violator is subject to a civil penalty of up to $5,000, to be deposited in a workers' compensation fund. Employee is entitled to reinstatement. | N.M. Stat. Ann. § 52-1-28.2. | Yes. | Employee must file complaint with Secretary of Environment within 30 days of violation. | Court may order all appropriate relief, including an injunction and reinstatement with back pay. | N.M. Stat. Ann. § 50-9-25. |
| NY | Yes. | Employee may file a complaint within 2 years for reinstatement, lost compensation, attorneys' fees, and benefits. Violator is subject to a civil penalty of $100–$500, to be paid to the state treasury. | N.Y. Work. Comp. Law § 120. | Yes. | 1 year. | Violator is subject to a civil penalty of $200–$2,000. Court may grant injunctive relief within 2 years of the violation and all other appropriate relief, including reinstatement, restoration of seniority, lost compensation, damages, and reasonable attorneys' fees. | N.Y. Lab. Law §§ 215, 740. |

| | | | | | | | |
|---|---|---|---|---|---|---|---|
| NC | Yes. | Within 90 days of receiving a right-to-sue letter from the Commissioner of Labor, employee may bring civil action for injunctive relief, reinstatement, benefits, seniority rights, lost wages, and reasonable costs and attorneys' fees. If employer's violation was willful, employee is entitled to treble actual damages. | N.C. Gen. Stat. §§ 95-240 *et seq.* | Yes. | 180 days. | Within 90 days of receiving a right-to-sue letter from the Commissioner of Labor, employee may bring civil action for injunctive relief, reinstatement, benefits, seniority rights, lost wages, and reasonable costs and attorneys' fees. If employer's violation was willful, employee is entitled to treble actual damages. | N.C. Gen. Stat. §§ 95-130, 95-240 *et seq.* |
| ND | — | — | State has no statutory provisions. | — | — | — | State has no statutory provisions. |
| OH | Yes. | Employee may bring civil action within 180 days after discharge for reinstatement, back pay, and reasonable attorneys' fees. | Ohio Rev. Code Ann. § 4123.90. | Yes. | — | Employee may bring civil action for injunctive relief, reinstatement, back pay, benefits, seniority, costs, and attorneys' fees. | Ohio Rev. Code Ann. §§ 124.341, 4113.51 *et seq.* |
| OK | Yes. | Employer may be liable for damages and reinstatement, with punitive damages not to exceed $100,000. Employer does not have to rehire employee who is physically unable to perform duties. | Okla. Stat. Ann. tit. 85, §§ 5, 6. | Yes. Applies to public employees only. | — | — | Okla. Stat. Ann. tit. 40, § 403. |
| OR | Yes. | State has no statutory requirements. | Or. Rev. Stat. §§ 659.030(f), 659.410. | Yes. | Employee must file complaint with Commissioner of Bureau of Labor and Industries within 30 days after employee has reasonable cause to believe retaliatory action occurred. | In addition to pursuing administrative procedures, employee may bring civil action. Commissioner and court have jurisdiction to order all appropriate relief, including reinstatement with back pay. | Or. Rev. Stat. § 654.062. |
| PA | — | — | State has no statutory provisions. | — | — | — | State has no statutory provisions. |
| RI | — | — | State has no statutory provisions. | Yes. | Employee must file complaint with Director of Labor within 30 days of violation. | Court has jurisdiction to award all appropriate relief, including reinstatement, back pay, and other benefits. | R.I. Gen. Laws §§ 23-1.1-14, 28-20-21. |

*(Table continues.)*

# Table 4.5-6 *(cont'd)*

## STATUTORY RESTRICTIONS ON RETALIATION: WORKERS' COMPENSATION AND OSHA

(See also text at § 4.5.)

**NOTE:** An em-dash (—) means that no specific statutory authority exists; other authority, including case law, may apply.

| | *Workers' Compensation Claim* | | | *OSHA Complaint* | | | |
|---|---|---|---|---|---|---|---|
| | *Employers Restricted from Discharging an Employee for Filing a Workers' Compensation Claim* | *Remedies and Penalties* | *Citations to Authority* | *Employers Restricted from Discharging an Employee for Filing an OSHA Complaint* | *Statute of Limitations for Filing* | *Remedies and Penalties* | *Citations to Authority* |
| SC | Yes. | Employee may bring civil action within 1 year for lost wages and reinstatement. | S.C. Code Ann. § 41-1-80. | Yes. | Employee must file complaint with the Commissioner of Labor within 30 days of violation. | Court may order all appropriate relief, including reinstatement with back pay. | S.C. Code Ann. §§ 41-15-510, 41-15-520. |
| SD | — | — | State has no statutory provisions. | — | — | — | State has no statutory provisions. |
| TN | — | — | State has no statutory provisions. | Yes. | Employee must file complaint with Commissioner of Labor within 30 days of violation. | Court may order all appropriate relief, including an injunction, reinstatement, and back pay. | Tenn. Code Ann. §§ 50-3-106(7) and (8), 50-3-409. |
| TX | Yes. | Employee may bring civil action for reasonable damages, reinstatement, and injunctive relief. | Tex. Lab. Code Ann. §§ 451.001 *et seq.* | Yes. | Employee must bring action within 90 days of violation or date employee discovered violation or could have discovered it with reasonable diligence. | Employee may bring civil action for reinstatement, lost wages, benefits, seniority, costs, and reasonable attorneys' fees. | Tex. Lab. Code Ann. §§ 411.082 *et seq.* |
| UT | — | — | State has no statutory provision. | Yes. | Employee must file complaint with Occupational Safety and Health Division of Industrial Commission within 30 days of violation. | Division may order all appropriate relief, including reinstatement and back pay. | Utah Code Ann. § 34A-6-203. |

| | | | | | | | |
|---|---|---|---|---|---|---|---|
| VT | Yes. Also applies to applicants. | Attorney general or state's attorney may enforce provision by restraining prohibited acts and seeking civil penalties. | Vt. Stat. Ann. tit. 21, § 710. | Yes. | Employee must file complaint with Commissioner of Labor and Industry within 30 days of violation. | In addition to or in lieu of administrative remedy, employee may bring civil action for reinstatement, triple wages, damages, costs, and reasonable attorneys' fees. | Vt. Stat. Ann. tit. 21, §§ 231, 232. |
| VA | Yes. | Employee may bring civil action for actual damages, attorneys' fees, reinstatement, and back pay plus interest. | Va. Code Ann. § 65.2-308. | Yes. | Employee must file complaint with Safety and Health Codes Board within 30 days of violation. | Court has jurisdiction to award appropriate relief, including reinstatement and back pay with interest. | Va. Code Ann. §§ 40.1-51.1 *et seq.* |
| WA | Yes. | Employee may file complaint with Director of Labor and Industries within 90 days of violation. Court has jurisdiction to award all appropirate relief, including reinstatement with back pay. | Wash. Rev. Code Ann. § 51.48.025. | Yes. | Employee must file complaint with Director of Labor and Industries within 30 days of violation. | Court has jurisdiction to order all appropriate relief, including reinstatement with back pay. Employer who willfully or repeatedly violates provision may be fined not more than $70,000 per violation. Employer who receives citation for serious violation of provision may be fined not more than $7,000 per violation. Employer who receives citation for violation of provision may be fined not more than $7,000 per violation, unless violation is de minimis. | Wash. Rev. Code Ann. §§ 49.17.160, 49.17.180. |
| WV | Yes. | State has no statutory requirements. | W. Va. Code § 23-5A-1. | Yes. Applies to public employees only. | Employee must file complaint within 30 days of violation. | Employee may file complaint with Commissioner of Labor for back pay with interest and reinstatement. | W. Va. Code §§ 21-3A-4, 21-3A-13. |
| WI | Yes. | Violator is fined $50–$500 for each offense. Employee may bring action for up to 1 year's lost wages if employer refuses to rehire without reasonable cause. | Wis. Stat. Ann. § 102.35. | Yes. Applies to employee requests for information concerning toxic substances, infectious agents, and pesticides with which the employee works; applies to employee complaints and participation in proceedings concerning such substances. | Employee must file complaint with Department of Industry, Labor, and Human Relations within 30 days of violation or date employee first gained knowledge of violation. | Violator is assessed penalty of not more than $1,000 for each violation. For willful or repeated violations, each violator may be assessed a penalty of up to $10,000. Department may order appropriate relief, including reinstatement and back pay. | Wis. Stat. Ann. §§ 101.58 *et seq.*, 111.322(2m). |

*(Table continues.)*

# Table 4.5-6 *(cont'd)*

## STATUTORY RESTRICTIONS ON RETALIATION: WORKERS' COMPENSATION AND OSHA

(See also text at § 4.5.)

**NOTE:** An em-dash (—) means that no specific statutory authority exists; other authority, including case law, may apply.

| | *Workers' Compensation Claim* | | | *OSHA Complaint* | | | |
|---|---|---|---|---|---|---|---|
| | *Employers Restricted from Discharging an Employee for Filing a Workers' Compensation Claim* | *Remedies and Penalties* | *Citations to Authority* | *Employers Restricted from Discharging an Employee for Filing an OSHA Complaint* | *Statute of Limitations for Filing* | *Remedies and Penalties* | *Citations to Authority* |
| WY | No. | — | State has no statutory provisions. | Yes. | — | Violator is fined not more than $7,000 for each offense. Penalty for willful violations is $5,000–$70,000. | Wyo. Stat. §§ 27-11-107, 27-11-109(e). |

# Table 4.5-7
## STATUTORY RESTRICTIONS ON DISCHARGING EMPLOYEES: WHISTLE-BLOWING

(See also text at § 4.5.)

**NOTE:** An em-dash (—) means that no specific statutory authority exists; other authority, including case law, may apply.

| | *Are Employers Restricted from Discharging Employees for Whistle-blowing?* | *Are Public Employers Covered by the Statute?* | *Are Private Employers Covered by the Statute?* | *Action or Information Covered* | *Remedies and Penalties* | *Other Requirements* | *Citations to Authority* |
|---|---|---|---|---|---|---|---|
| AL | Yes. | Yes. | Yes. | State has no statutory requirements. | General tort remedies, including punitive and actual damages. | Employee must provide employer with written notice of a violation of a safety rule. | Ala. Code § 25-5-11.1. |
| AK | Yes. | Yes. | — | Employee's good faith report or participation in an investigation of a matter employee reasonably believes to be of public concern. | Employee may bring civil action for appropriate relief, including punitive damages. Violator is subject to a civil penalty of not more than $10,000. | Employer may require employee to make report to employer first. Employee does not have to submit such a report if he or she reasonably believes the employer will not act promptly to remedy the situation, one or more supervisors already know about the activity, an emergency is involved, or the employer will commit an act of reprisal against him or her. Municipality does not have to comply with these provisions if it has adopted an ordinance that provides substantially similar protection for its employees. Employer is required to post notices of this law. | Alaska Stat. §§ 39.90.100 *et seq.* |

(*Table continues.*)

## Table 4.5-7 *(cont'd)*
## STATUTORY RESTRICTIONS ON DISCHARGING EMPLOYEES: WHISTLE-BLOWING

(See also text at § 4.5.)

**NOTE:** An em-dash (—) means that no specific statutory authority exists; other authority, including case law, may apply.

| | *Are Employers Restricted from Discharging Employees for Whistle-blowing?* | *Are Public Employers Covered by the Statute?* | *Are Private Employers Covered by the Statute?* | *Action or Information Covered* | *Remedies and Penalties* | *Other Requirements* | *Citations to Authority* |
|---|---|---|---|---|---|---|---|
| AZ | Yes. | Yes. | — | Employee's written good faith disclosure to a public body of a matter of public concern that the employee reasonably believes to be a violation of law, mismanagement, waste, or abuse of authority. | Employee may bring civil action for back pay, general and special damages, reinstatement, costs, and attorneys' fees. Violator is subject to a civil penalty of up to $5,000. | A public employee must file a complaint with the State Personnel Board or other independent personnel board within 10 days of the retaliatory discharge. | Ariz. Rev. Stat. Ann. § 38-532. |
| AR | Yes, if employer employs 9 or more persons. | Yes. | Yes. | Employee who in good faith opposed any unlawful act or practice or because such individual in good faith made a charge, testified, assisted, or participated in any manner in an investigation, proceeding, or hearing. | Employee may bring civil action to enjoin further violations, to recover compensatory and punitive damages, and to recover costs of litigation and reasonable attorneys' fees. | — | Ark. Code Ann. § 16-23-108. |
| CA | Yes. | Yes. | Yes. | Public employee's written disclosure of information regarding gross mismanagement, significant waste of funds, abuse of authority, or a substantial and specific danger to public health or safety. Public or private employee's disclosure to a government or law enforcement agency of what the employee reasonably believes to be a violation of law. California State University employee's disclosure of improper governmental activities. | For public employer who discharges employee because of employee's disclosure of waste, abuse of authority, or danger to public safety: Employer who discharges employee with malicious intent may be fined not more than $10,000 and imprisoned up to 1 year. If the employee's manager or supervisor acted with malicious intent, he or she is individually liable for damages in a civil action brought by the employee and may also be liable for punitive damages | For public employer who discharges employee because of employee's disclosure of waste, abuse of authority, or danger to public safety: Employee must file the complaint within 60 days of the violation. This period shall be extended by the time spent exhausting administrative remedies. For California State University employees: Employee must file complaint within 1 year of retaliatory act with his or | Cal. Gov't Code §§ 8547.12, 53296 *et seq.;* Cal. Lab. Code §§ 1102.5, 1103. |

| | | | | | | | |
|---|---|---|---|---|---|---|---|
| | | | | | and reasonable attorneys' fees. For public or private employer who discharges employee for disclosing violation of law: Violator is guilty of a misdemeanor punishable by imprisonment not to exceed 1 year, or a fine not to exceed $1,000, or both for an individual, or a fine not to exceed $5,000 for a corporation. For California State University employer: Violator is subject to a fine of not more than $10,000, imprisonment for not more than 1 year, and university disciplinary action. Employee may bring civil action for actual damages, reasonable attorneys' fees, and, if violator's acts were malicious, punitive damages. | her supervisor or other university officer designated for that purpose. Action for damages is not available unless employee files such a complaint and the university fails to reach a decision regarding the complaint within time limits set by the trustees. This provision does not prohibit employee from seeking civil remedy if the university has not satisfactorily addressed the complaint within 18 months. | |
| CO | Yes. | Yes. | Yes, if under contract to a state agency. | Employee's disclosure of information regarding any action or policy, including waste, mismanagement, abuse of authority, any danger to the public's health, safety, or welfare, or other adverse effects to the interests of the state. | Employee may bring civil action for damages, costs, and other relief the court deems appropriate. | Employee is required to give the information to his or her supervisor before disclosure is made to another authority. | Colo. Rev. Stat. §§ 24-50.5-101, 24-50.5-103, 24-50.5-105, 24-114-102, 24-114-103. |
| CT | Yes. | Yes. | Yes. | Employee's verbal or written disclosure to a public body of a violation or suspected violation of law, rule, or regulation. | Employee may bring civil action for reinstatement, back wages, benefits, reasonable attorneys' fees, and costs. | Employee must exhaust all administrative remedies before bringing civil action. Employee must bring civil action within 90 days of violation or final administrative action, whichever is later. | Conn. Gen. Stat. Ann. §§ 16-8a, 31-51m. |
| DE | Yes. | Yes. | — | Employee's disclosure of a suspected violation of law. | Employee may bring civil action for injunctive relief and actual damages. | Employee must bring civil action within 90 days of violation. | Del. Code Ann. tit. 29, § 5115. |
| DC | No specific statutory prohibition exists, but statute provides that public employees are encouraged to report violations of law and misuse of government resources. | Yes. | — | Employee's disclosure of any violation of law or rule or any misuse of government resources. | State has no statutory requirements. | None. | D.C. Code Ann. § 1-619.1. |

*(Table continues.)*

## Table 4.5-7 *(cont'd)*

### STATUTORY RESTRICTIONS ON DISCHARGING EMPLOYEES: WHISTLE-BLOWING

(See also text at § 4.5.)

**NOTE:** An em-dash (—) means that no specific statutory authority exists; other authority, including case law, may apply.

| | *Are Employers Restricted from Discharging Employees for Whistle-blowing?* | *Are Public Employers Covered by the Statute?* | *Are Private Employers Covered by the Statute?* | *Action or Information Covered* | *Remedies and Penalties* | *Other Requirements* | *Citations to Authority* |
|---|---|---|---|---|---|---|---|
| FL | Yes. | Yes. | — | Employee's disclosure to an appropriate agency of any violation of law that creates a substantial and specific danger to the public's health, safety, or welfare or any improper use of governmental office, gross waste of funds, or any other abuse or gross neglect of duty. | Employee may be entitled to reinstatement, restoration of benefits and seniority rights, compensation for lost wages, benefits, and other lost remuneration, and reasonable costs and attorneys' fees. | For employee of state government agency: Employee may file a written complaint of retaliation with the Office of the Chief Inspector General or the office of the public counsel within 60 days of the adverse action. If the public counsel notifies employee that the investigation has been terminated, employee may bring a civil action within 180 days of receiving the notice or file a complaint against the employer with the Public Employees Relations Commission within 60 days of receiving the notice. For employee of a local government entity: If local government has an administrative procedure for handling such complaints, employee may file a complaint with the appropriate local government authority within 60 days of the retaliation. After the local government authority issues a final decision, employee | Fla. Stat. Ann. §§ 112.3187 *et seq.*, 112.31895. |

| | | | | | | | |
|---|---|---|---|---|---|---|---|
| | | | | | | may bring a civil action within 180 days. If the local government authority has no administrative procedure,employee may bring civil action within 180 days of the retaliation. | |
| GA | Yes. | Yes. | — | Employee's disclosure to employer of fraud, waste, or abuse in state programs under employer's jurisdiction. | Employee may bring civil suit for reinstatement. | Employee's identity must be kept confidential absent employee's consent. If disclosure of employee's identity becomes necessary and unavoidable during investigation, employee must be notified in writing at least 7 days before disclosure. | Ga. Code Ann. § 45-1-4. |
| HI | Yes. | Yes. | Yes. | Employee's disclosure to a public body of a violation or suspected violation of law or rule. | Employee may bring civil action for injunctive relief and actual damages, including reinstatement, back pay, benefits, seniority rights, costs, and reasonable attorneys' and witness fees. Violator is subject to a penalty of not more than $500 for each violation, with the money to be paid to the state's general fund. | Employee must bring action within 90 days of retaliatory discharge. Employer is required to post notices of this act. | Haw. Rev. Stat. §§ 378-61 *et seq.* |
| ID | Yes. | Yes. | — | Public employee's good faith report of a waste of public funds, property, or manpower or a violation or suspected violation of law. Report must be made at a time and in a manner that gives employer a reasonable opportunity to correct the waste or violation. In addition, any employer of farm workers may not discharge or otherwise discriminate against farm worker because he or she has instituted or participated in proceedings concerning sanitation facilities for farm workers. | For public employee provision: Violator is subject to a civil fine not to exceed $500. Employee may bring civil action for reinstatement, lost wages, benefits, seniority rights, and reasonable costs and attorneys' fees. For farm worker provision: Violator is guilty of a misdemeanor punishable by a fine of not more than $300. | Public employee must bring action within 180 days of violation. Public employer must use appropriate means to notify employees of their protections and obligations under this provision. | Idaho Code §§ 6-2101 *et seq.*, 44-1904, 44-1905. |

*(Table continues.)*

## Table 4.5-7 *(cont'd)*

## STATUTORY RESTRICTIONS ON DISCHARGING EMPLOYEES: WHISTLE-BLOWING

(See also text at § 4.5.)

**NOTE:** An em-dash (—) means that no specific statutory authority exists; other authority, including case law, may apply.

| | *Are Employers Restricted from Discharging Employees for Whistle-blowing?* | *Are Public Employers Covered by the Statute?* | *Are Private Employers Covered by the Statute?* | *Action or Information Covered* | *Remedies and Penalties* | *Other Requirements* | *Citations to Authority* |
|---|---|---|---|---|---|---|---|
| IL | Yes. | Yes. | Yes. | Employee's disclosure of mismanagement, waste, abuse of authority, a substantial and specific danger to public health or safety, or a violation of law, rule, or regulation. Employee's opposition to what he or she reasonably and in good faith believes to be unlawful discrimination, sexual harassment in employment, sexual harassment in higher education, discrimination based on citizenship status in employment or employee's act of filing a charge or participation in a proceeding under the Illinois Human Rights Act. | For employee discharged because of his or her opposition to discrimination or sexual harassment or his or her participation in a proceeding under the Illinois Human Rights Act: Employee must file complaint within 180 days of retaliation with the Illinois Department of Human Rights and is subject to administrative proceeding requirements under the Department and the Illinois Human Rights Commission, whose final orders are subject to judicial review in appellate court. Relief may include a cease and desist order, actual damages, reinstatement, and reasonable costs and attorneys' fees. | Identity of reporting employee must be kept confidential absent employee's consent. | Ill. Ann. Stat. ch. 5, ¶ 395/1, ch. 20, ¶ 415/19c.1, ch. 775, ¶¶ 5/6-101, 5/7A-102, 5/8-103, 5/8-111, 5/8A-102, 5/8A-103. |
| IN | Yes. | Yes. | Yes, if under public contract. | Employee's disclosure of misuse of public resources or of violations of laws, regulations, or rules. | Violator is guilty of a Class A infraction. | Employee of private employer must first report violation to employer, unless the employer is committing the violation, in which case employee may report the violation to employer or to any official or agency entitled to receive a report from the state Ethics Commis- | Ind. Code Ann. §§ 22-5-3-3, 36-1-8-8. |

| | | | | | | | |
|---|---|---|---|---|---|---|---|
| | | | | | | sion. If public or private employer fails to make a good faith effort at corrective action within a reasonable time, employee may report the violation to any person, agency, or organization. | |
| IA | Yes. | Yes. | — | Employee's disclosure to a public official or a law enforcement agency of mismanagement, abuse of funds or authority, a violation of law or rule, or a substantial and specific danger to public health or safety. | Violator is guilty of a simple misdemeanor. Employee may bring civil action for reinstatement with or without back pay, other equitable relief, attorneys' fees, and costs. | None. | Iowa Code Ann. §§ 70A.28, 70A.29. |
| KS | Yes. | Yes. | — | Employee's disclosure of a violation of law or regulation. | Employee working in classified service may file complaint with state Civil Service Board. Board may order all appropriate relief. Board's decisions are subject to judicial review. Violating supervisor in classified service may be suspended without pay for not more than 30 days. For willful or repeated violations, the supervisor may be required to forfeit his or her position with the state for a period of not more than 2 years. | Classified-service employee must file complaint within 30 days of retaliation. Employer must prominently display notices of this act. | Kan. Stat. Ann. § 75-2973. |
| KY | Yes. | Yes. | — | Employee's verbal or written disclosure to an appropriate body or authority of an actual or suspected violation of law, mismanagement, waste, fraud, abuse of authority, or a substantial and specific danger to public health or safety. | Employee may bring civil action for injunctive relief, punitive damages, or both, in addition to other administrative remedies. | Employer cannot require employee to give notice to employer before reporting a violation. Employee must bring civil action within 90 days of retaliation. | Ky. Rev. Stat. Ann. §§ 61.102, 61.103. |
| LA | Yes. | Yes. | Yes. | Employee's good faith disclosure of violations of environmental laws. | For public or private employee discharged because of his or her disclosure of environmental law violation: Employee may bring civil action for triple damages, costs, and attorneys' fees. Damages include lost wages, lost anticipated wages from a wage increase or promotion that would have resulted, any *(cont'd)* | None. | La. Rev. Stat. Ann. § 30:2027. |

*(Table continues.)*

## Table 4.5-7 *(cont'd)*

## STATUTORY RESTRICTIONS ON DISCHARGING EMPLOYEES: WHISTLE-BLOWING

(See also text at § 4.5.)

**NOTE:** An em-dash (—) means that no specific statutory authority exists; other authority, including case law, may apply.

| | *Are Employers Restricted from Discharging Employees for Whistle-blowing?* | *Are Public Employers Covered by the Statute?* | *Are Private Employers Covered by the Statute?* | *Action or Information Covered* | *Remedies and Penalties* | *Other Requirements* | *Citations to Authority* |
|---|---|---|---|---|---|---|---|
| LA *(cont'd)* | | | | | lost property resulting from lost wages, benefits, physical damages, and damages for emotional suffering. | | |
| ME | Yes. | Yes. | Yes, except employers of independent contractors engaged in lobster fishing. | Employee's good faith report to employer or a public body of what employee reasonably believes is a violation of law or a condition that risks any person's health or safety, employee's participation in an investigation or proceeding, or employee's good faith refusal to carry out an order that would expose any person to a condition that would result in serious injury or death. | Employee may file complaint with state Human Rights Commission. This section does not derogate any common-law rights of employee. | Employee is required to give initial report to employer, except if employee has specific reason to believe that the report will not result in prompt correction. Employer must post notice of the provisions of this law. | Me. Rev. Stat. Ann. tit. 26, §§ 831–840. |
| MD | Yes. | Yes. Applies to employees in the executive branch of state government. | — | Employee's disclosure of abuse of authority, gross mismanagement, gross waste of money, a substantial and specific danger to public health and safety, or a violation of law. If a disclosure is prohibited by law, the information is covered if the disclosure is made only to the attorney general. | Employee may bring administrative action for reinstatement, back pay, seniority rights, and removal of any adverse information from his or her employment record. Violator also may be subject to disciplinary action. | Employee must file complaint with Secretary of Personnel within 1 year of the day on which employee first knew or should have known of the violation. | Md. Code Ann., State Pers. §§ 3-301 *et seq.* |

| | | | | | | | |
|---|---|---|---|---|---|---|---|
| MA | Yes. | Yes. | — | Employee's disclosure or threatened disclosure to a supervisor or public body of what employee reasonably believes to be violations of law or risks to public health, safety, or the environment. | Employee may bring civil action within 2 years for injunctions, reinstatement, benefits, seniority rights, treble damages for lost wages and benefits, and reasonable costs and attorneys' fees, in addition to any other remedies available in common-law tort actions. | Employer must conspicuously display notices of this law. Before reporting to a public body, employee must inform a supervisor in writing and give employer a reasonable opportunity to correct the violation or practice unless employee is reasonably certain that the supervisor is aware of the violation and the situation constitutes an emergency, employee reasonably fears physical harm if he or she discloses to a supervisor, or employee discloses the violation to a law enforcement agency, prosecutorial office, or the judiciary evidence of what employee reasonably believes to be a crime. | Mass. Gen. Laws Ann. ch. 149, § 185. |
| MI | Yes. | Yes. | Yes. | Employee's disclosure to a public body of a violation or suspected violation of law or participation in a public hearing, investigation, inquiry, or court action. Also, employee's filing of a complaint or participation in a proceeding regarding state laws governing work hours and wages. | Employee may bring civil action for injunctive relief, actual damages, and reasonable attorneys' fees within 90 days of the violation. Court may order reinstatement, back pay, benefits, and seniority rights, and impose a civil fine of not more than $500. For disclosure of information regarding work hours and wage laws: Within 30 days of violation, employee may file complaint with the Department of Labor, which may order reinstatement with back pay. | None. | Mich. Stat. Ann. §§ 17.277(13), 17.428. |
| MN | Yes. | Yes. | Yes, except employers of independent contractors. | Employee's good faith disclosure of a violation or suspected violation of law, employee's participation in a hearing, or employee's refusal to perform an action that he or she believes to be a violation of the law. | Employee may bring civil action for damages, costs, reasonable attorneys' fees, and equitable relief. Employer who fails to notify employee of real reason for dismissal if employee requests that information is liable for a penalty of $25 per day per injured employee not to exceed $750 per employee. | Employee's identity must be kept confidential, absent employee's consent. If disclosure of employee's identity becomes necessary for prosecution, employee must be informed before disclosure. | Minn. Stat. Ann. §§ 181.931 *et seq.* |

*(Table continues.)*

# Table 4.5-7 *(cont'd)*
## STATUTORY RESTRICTIONS ON DISCHARGING EMPLOYEES: WHISTLE-BLOWING

(See also text at § 4.5.)

**NOTE:** An em-dash (—) means that no specific statutory authority exists; other authority, including case law, may apply.

| | *Are Employers Restricted from Discharging Employees for Whistle-blowing?* | *Are Public Employers Covered by the Statute?* | *Are Private Employers Covered by the Statute?* | *Action or Information Covered* | *Remedies and Penalties* | *Other Requirements* | *Citations to Authority* |
|---|---|---|---|---|---|---|---|
| MS | Yes. | Yes. | Yes. | Public employee's provision of information to an investigative body, regardless of whether the testimony is under oath. Any corporate employee's exercise of social, civil, or political rights. | Employee may bring action under the statute. A corporation may be fined $250 for each unlawful interference with the social, civil, or political rights of its employees. | None. | Miss. Code Ann. §§ 25-9-173, 79-1-9. |
| MO | Yes. | Yes. | — | Employee's disclosure of mismanagement, gross waste of funds, abuse of authority, a substantial and specific danger to public health or safety, or violation of law, rule, or regulation. | Employee may file administrative appeal within 30 days of disciplinary action with the state personnel advisory board. The board may order all appropriate relief, including reinstatement. Violator may be suspended without pay for up to 30 days. For willful or repeated violations, violator may be required to forfeit his or her position with the state and be disqualified from further state employment for not more than 2 years. | Employer must post a copy of this provision where it can reasonably be expected to come to the attention of all employees of the agency. | Mo. Ann. Stat. § 105.055. |
| MT | Yes. Statute also includes constructive discharge. | Yes. | Yes. | Employee's refusal to violate public policy or report of a violation of public policy. | Employee may bring civil action for up to 4 years' lost wages and benefits. Interim earnings must be deducted from damages awarded. Court may award punitive damages if employer acted with actual fraud or malice. | Employee must bring action within 1 year of discharge. Employee must exhaust internal procedures before filing suit. This statute precludes possible common-law remedies. | Mont. Code Ann. §§ 39-2-901 *et seq.* |

| | | | | | | | |
|---|---|---|---|---|---|---|---|
| NE | Yes. | Yes. | Yes. | Public or private employee's opposition to unlawful practice, participation in an investigation, or report of any violation of law or practice made unlawful by the Nebraska Fair Employment Act. Public employee's disclosure to public counsel or other official of what employee reasonably believes to be a violation of law, gross mismanagement, gross waste of funds, or a substantial and specific danger to public health or safety. | Public or private employee who is terminated because of reporting violation of Nebraska Fair Employment Act may file complaint with Equal Opportunity Commission within 300 days of adverse action. Commission's decisions are subject to judicial review. Employer who violates an order from Commission is guilty of a Class III misdemeanor. Public employee terminated because of report to public counsel or other official may file complaint with state Personnel Board. Board may order all appropriate relief, including back pay. Board decisions are appealable under the Administrative Procedures Act. | None. | Neb. Rev. Stat. §§ 48-1114, 48-1118, 48-1120, 48-1123. |
| NV | Yes. | Yes. | — | Employee's disclosure of information regarding improper governmental action. | If the disciplinary action was taken within 2 years after the disclosure of information, employee may file a complaint with Department of Personnel. | Employee must file complaint within 10 days of adverse action. Department's decisions are subject to judicial review. | Nev. Rev. Stat. Ann. § 281.641. |
| NH | Yes. | Yes. | Yes. | Employee's participation in an investigation, good faith report of a violation of law or rule, or refusal to carry out an illegal order. | After exhausting employer's internal grievance procedures, employee may obtain hearing with Commissioner of Labor, who may order reinstatement, back pay, restoration of benefits and seniority rights, or injunctive relief. Commissioner's decisions are subject to judicial review. | Employee must bring the violation to the attention of the supervisor first and offer the latter a reasonable opportunity to correct the violation before taking further action, unless employee has specific reason to believe employer will not promptly remedy the situation. Employer is required to post notice of this law. | N.H. Rev. Stat. Ann. §§ 275-E:1 *et seq.* |
| NJ | Yes. | Yes. | Yes. | Employee's disclosure to a supervisor or public body of activity of employer, or another employer with whom there is a business relationship, that employee reasonably believes is a violation of law, rule, or regulation, employee's participation in an investigation regarding the above, or employee's refusal (*cont'd*) | Employee may bring a civil action within 1 year of adverse action. All common law tort remedies are available in addition to any legal or equitable relief afforded by this provision or other statute. Court may order injunctive relief, reinstatement, restoration of full benefits and seniority rights, (*cont'd*) | Employee must bring the violation to the attention of a supervisor in writing and afford employer a reasonable chance to correct the violation before reporting to a public body. Initial disclosure to a supervisor is not required if the employee is reasonably certain that (*cont'd*) | N.J. Stat. Ann. §§ 34:19-3 *et seq.* |

*(Table continues.)*

## Table 4.5-7 *(cont'd)*
## STATUTORY RESTRICTIONS ON DISCHARGING EMPLOYEES: WHISTLE-BLOWING

(See also text at § 4.5.)

**NOTE:** An em-dash (—) means that no specific statutory authority exists; other authority, including case law, may apply.

| | *Are Employers Restricted from Discharging Employees for Whistle-blowing?* | *Are Public Employers Covered by the Statute?* | *Are Private Employers Covered by the Statute?* | *Action or Information Covered* | *Remedies and Penalties* | *Other Requirements* | *Citations to Authority* |
|---|---|---|---|---|---|---|---|
| NJ *(cont'd)* | | | | to participate in any activity employee reasonably believes is a violation of law, is fraudulent or criminal, or contravenes a clear mandate of public policy concerning public health, safety, or welfare or protection of the environment. | compensation for lost wages and benefits, reasonable costs and attorneys' fees, and punitive damages. Violator is subject to a civil fine not to exceed $1,000 for a first violation and not to exceed $5,000 for each subsequent violation. | the violation is known to one or more supervisors or if the employee reasonably fears physical harm as a result of the disclosure, provided that the situation is in the nature of an emergency. Employer must conspicuously post notices of employee's protections and obligations under this provision. | |
| NM | — | — | — | — | — | — | State has no statutory provisions. |
| NY | Yes. | Yes. | Yes. | Employee's disclosure to a supervisor or a public body of a violation of law, rule, or regulation that creates a substantial and specific danger to public health and safety, or employee's participation in an investigation or refusal to participate in an illegal activity. | Employee may bring civil action for injunction, reinstatement, benefits, seniority rights, lost wages, and reasonable costs and attorneys' fees. | Employee must bring action within 1 year of retaliation. Employee must report violation to supervisor first and allow reasonable time for a response before reporting the violation to a public body. Whistle-blower's status as an independent contractor is an employer defense. | N.Y. Lab. Law § 740. |

| | | | | | | | |
|---|---|---|---|---|---|---|---|
| NC | Yes. | Yes. | — | Employee's disclosure of fraud, misappropriation of state resources, activity of substantial and specific danger to public health and safety, or violation of law, rule, or regulation or employee's refusal to carry out an order that violates a law or poses a substantial and specific danger to public health and safety. | Employee may bring civil action for injunction, damages, reinstatement, seniority rights, costs, and reasonable attorneys' fees against the person or agency that is responsible for his or her discharge. If employer's violation is willful, the court shall award treble actual damages. | Employee must bring action within 1 year of violation. Employer must post notice or use other appropriate methods to keep employees informed of their protections and obligations. | N.C. Gen. Stat. §§ 95-241, 126-84 *et seq.* |
| ND | Yes. | Yes. | Yes. | Employee's good faith disclosure of a violation or suspected violation of law to employer, governmental body, or law enforcement official; participation in an investigation or hearing when requested by a public body; refusal to perform an action that the employee believes violates federal or state law. | Employee may bring civil action for injunction, damages, or both within 90 days after violation. Employee may seek assistance of the Commissioner of Labor to ensure compliance; an employer who willfully violates this section is guilty of an infraction. | — | N.D. Cent. Code § 34-01-20. |
| OH | Yes. | Yes. | Yes. | Public or private employee's disclosure of a violation of law by employer or fellow employee, provided that the violation is a criminal offense that is likely to cause an imminent risk of physical harm to persons or a hazard to public health or safety or is a felony. Public employee's report to supervisor of violation of law or misuse of public resources. Public employee may file report with prosecuting attorney or other legal officer instead of or in addition to report made to supervisor. | Employee may bring civil action within 180 days of retaliation for injunctive relief, reinstatement, back pay, benefits, seniority rights, costs, and reasonable attorneys' fees. Exclusive remedy for public employee terminated because of employee's report of violation of law or misuse of public resources is to file an appeal with the state Personnel Board of Review within 30 days of termination. Board may affirm or disaffirm employer's action and issue any order that is appropriate. | Employee must notify employer of the violation first. If employer has not made a reasonable, good faith effort to take corrective action within 24 hours of notification, employee may file written report with an appropriate public official or agency. If the violation is of air pollution control, solid and hazardous wastes, safe drinking water, or water pollution control statutes and the violation is a criminal offense, employee is not required to notify employer first and may report directly to an appropriate public official or agency either orally or in writing. | Ohio Rev. Code Ann. §§ 124.341, 4113.51 *et seq.* |
| OK | Yes. | Yes. | Yes. | Employee opposed discriminatory practice, filed a complaint, or testified in an investigation concerning discrimination. | State has no statutory requirements. | None. | Okla. Stat. Ann. tit. 25, § 1601. |

*(Table continues.)*

## Table 4.5-7 *(cont'd)*
## STATUTORY RESTRICTIONS ON DISCHARGING EMPLOYEES: WHISTLE-BLOWING

(See also text at § 4.5.)

**NOTE:** An em-dash (—) means that no specific statutory authority exists; other authority, including case law, may apply.

| | *Are Employers Restricted from Discharging Employees for Whistle-blowing?* | *Are Public Employers Covered by the Statute?* | *Are Private Employers Covered by the Statute?* | *Action or Information Covered* | *Remedies and Penalties* | *Other Requirements* | *Citations to Authority* |
|---|---|---|---|---|---|---|---|
| OR | Yes. | Yes. | Yes. | Public employee's disclosure of mismanagement, abuse of authority, gross waste of funds, substantial and specific danger to public health or safety, or violation of law, or employee's opposition to discrimination. Public or private employer's participation in a criminal proceeding. | In addition to filing administrative complaint with commissioner of Bureau of Labor and Industries, employee may bring civil action for injunctive relief and damages. If damages are awarded, the court shall award actual damages or $250, whichever is greater. | Employee's identity is to be kept confidential absent employee's written consent. Employee must bring action within 90 days of violation. | Or. Rev. Stat. §§ 659.030(f), 659.035, 659.510, 659.530, 659.535, 659.550. |
| PA | Yes. | Yes. | — | Employee's "good faith" reports to employer or appropriate authority of wrongdoing or waste. | Employee may bring civil action for reinstatement, back pay, benefits, seniority rights, actual damages, costs, and reasonable attorneys' and witness fees. Violator may be fined not more than $500. A violating employee of the state may be suspended from public service for not more than 6 months if employer committed the violation with intent to discourage disclosure of criminal activity. | Employee must bring action within 180 days of violation. Employer must post signs and use other appropriate means to keep employees informed of their protections and obligations. | Pa. Stat. Ann. tit. 43, §§ 1422 *et seq.* |
| RI | Yes. | Yes. | Yes. | Employee's disclosure of a violation of law, regulation, or rule, or employee's participation in an investigation. | Employee may bring civil action for injunctive relief, reinstatement, back pay, benefits, seniority rights, costs, and actual damages. | Employee must bring action within 1 year of retaliation if disclosure concerned a violation of law, regulation, or rule promulgated by Department of Labor. Employee must | R.I. Gen. Laws §§ 28-14-18 *et seq.*, 28-50-1 *et seq.* |

| | | | | | | | |
|---|---|---|---|---|---|---|---|
| | | | | | | bring action within 3 years of retaliation if disclosure concerned a violation of law, regulation, or rule promulgated under state or federal authority. | |
| SC | Yes. | Yes, except employers of the following employees: employees in Office of the Governor who work in governor's mansion or the State House; members of state boards and committees paid on a per day basis; inmate help in charitable, penal, or correctional institutions; students employed in institutes of learning; part-time professional personnel engaged in consulting work; chief administrative officers; employees of the Public Service Authority, State Ports Authority, or the Division of Public Railways of the Department of Commerce; teaching or research faculty members, professional librarians, academic administrators, or other people holding faculty appointments at postsecondary educational institutions; and athletic coaches and unclassified employees in athletic departments of postsecondary educational institutions. | — | Employee's good faith report of wrongdoing to an appropriate authority. Report must be in writing and be made within 60 days of when employee first learns of the wrongdoing. | Employee dismissed within 1 year of reporting wrongdoing may bring civil action for reinstatement, lost wages, actual damages not to exceed $15,000, and reasonable attorneys' fees not to exceed $10,000 for trial and $5,000 for appeal. | Employee must exhaust all administrative remedies before bringing action, and must start action within 1 year of adverse action or of exhausting administrative remedies. If the employee's report saves public money, 25% of net savings resulting from the first year of implementation of the report, but not more than $2,000, must be rewarded to the employee. | S.C. Code Ann. §§ 8-27-10 *et seq.* |

*(Table continues.)*

## Table 4.5-7 *(cont'd)*

## STATUTORY RESTRICTIONS ON DISCHARGING EMPLOYEES: WHISTLE-BLOWING

(See also text at § 4.5.)

**NOTE:** An em-dash (—) means that no specific statutory authority exists; other authority, including case law, may apply.

| | *Are Employers Restricted from Discharging Employees for Whistle-blowing?* | *Are Public Employers Covered by the Statute?* | *Are Private Employers Covered by the Statute?* | *Action or Information Covered* | *Remedies and Penalties* | *Other Requirements* | *Citations to Authority* |
|---|---|---|---|---|---|---|---|
| SD | Yes. | Yes. | Yes. | Employee's disclosure of a violation of state law through chain of command of employee's department or to attorney general. Also, employee's disclosure of wage violations. | Employee who believes he or she has been subject to retaliation for whistle-blowing may file grievance with the career service commission. | None. | S.D. Codified Laws §§ 3-6A-52, 60-11-17.1, 60-12-21. |
| TN | Yes. | Yes. | Yes. | Employee's refusal to participate in or remain silent about illegal activities. | Employee may file an action for the retaliatory discharge; however, if the action is intended to harass or cause needless increase in costs to the employer, the court may impose sanctions on the employee, including requiring employee to pay employer's reasonable expenses and attorneys' fees. | None. | Tenn. Code Ann. § 50-1-304. |
| TX | Yes. | Yes. | — | Employee's disclosure of a violation of law to appropriate law enforcement authority. | Employee may bring civil action for injunctive relief, actual damages, exemplary damages of $50,000 to $250,000, depending on size of employer, reinstatement, back pay, benefits, seniority rights, costs, and reasonable attorneys' fees. Violator is subject to a civil penalty not to exceed $1,000. | Employer who discharges whistle-blowing employee no later than 90 days after the employee's disclosure is presumed subject to rebuttal to be acting in retaliation. Otherwise employee has burden of proof. Employee must bring civil action within 90 days of the retaliatory discharge or date that employee discovered violation through reasonable diligence, but a local | Tex. Gov't Code Ann. §§ 554.001 *et seq.* |

| | | | | | | | |
|---|---|---|---|---|---|---|---|
| | | | | | | government employee must exhaust the locality's administrative procedures before bringing action. Local government employee must initiate the administrative procedures no later than 90 days after the violation or the date employee discovered the violation through reasonable diligence. Time spent exhausting administrative procedures does not count against the civil action statute of limitation period. If a final administrative decision is not rendered within 31 days of the beginning of administrative procedures, employee does not have to exhaust such procedures. | |
| UT | Yes. | Yes. | — | Employee's good faith disclosure of waste or violation or suspected violation of law, employee's participation in an investigation by a public body, or employee's refusal to carry out an order that employee reasonably believes violates a law. | Employee may bring civil action for reinstatement, back pay, benefits, seniority rights, actual damages, costs, and reasonable attorneys' and witness fees. Violator may be fined not more than $500 to be deposited in the state's general fund. | Employee must bring action against employer within 180 days of violation. Employer must post notices informing employees of this law. | Utah Code Ann. §§ 67-21-1 *et seq.* |
| VT | Yes. | Yes. | Yes. | Employee's complaint or participation in an investigation concerning discriminatory acts or practices. | Attorney general or state's attorney may enforce provision by restraining violations, seeking civil penalties, and conducting investigations. Employee may bring civil action for damages and equitable relief, including reinstatement, restitution of wages and benefits, costs, and reasonable attorneys' fees. | — | Vt. Stat. Ann. tit. 21, §§ 495(a)(5), 495(b). |
| VA | — | — | — | — | — | — | State has no statutory provisions. |

*(Table continues.)*

## Table 4.5-7 *(cont'd)*

## STATUTORY RESTRICTIONS ON DISCHARGING EMPLOYEES: WHISTLE-BLOWING

(See also text at § 4.5.)

**NOTE:** An em-dash (—) means that no specific statutory authority exists; other authority, including case law, may apply.

| | *Are Employers Restricted from Discharging Employees for Whistle-blowing?* | *Are Public Employers Covered by the Statute?* | *Are Private Employers Covered by the Statute?* | *Action or Information Covered* | *Remedies and Penalties* | *Other Requirements* | *Citations to Authority* |
|---|---|---|---|---|---|---|---|
| WA | Yes. | Yes. | — | Employee's good faith disclosure of improper governmental action. | Administrative law judge may order reinstatement of employee with or without back pay, injunctive relief, costs, and reasonable attorneys' fees. Administrative law judge may impose civil penalties of up to $3,000, payable by each person found to have retaliated against the employee, and may recommend that those persons either be suspended with or without pay or be dismissed. | For local government employee: Employee must provide written notice of the charge of retaliatory action within 30 days of the action. Employer has 30 days to respond. Employee may request administrative hearing within 15 days of receiving employer response or within 15 days of last day on which employer could have responded. Local and state government employers must post notices of the provisions of these laws. | Wash. Rev. Code Ann. §§ 42.40.010 *et seq.*, 42.41.010 *et seq.* |
| WV | Yes. | Yes. | — | Employee's good faith report to employer or appropriate authority of wrongdoing or waste or employee's participation in an investigation or proceeding. | Employee may bring civil action for reinstatement, benefits, back wages, seniority rights, actual damages, costs, and reasonable attorneys' and witness fees. Violator is subject to a civil penalty of not more than $500 to be deposited in the state's general fund. Court may order suspension of violating supervisor, except supervisor who is elected or appointed to public office for up to 6 months, if court finds | Employee must bring action within 180 days of violation. Employer is required to post notices informing employees of this law. | W. Va. Code §§ 6C-1-1 *et seq.*, 16-32-14. |

| | | | | | | | |
|---|---|---|---|---|---|---|---|
| | | | | | that employer acted with intent to discourage disclosure. | | |
| WI | — | — | — | — | — | — | State has no statutory provisions. |
| WY | Yes. Applies only to employers of health care facilities. | — | — | Employee's disclosure of a violation of law, rule, or regulation. | State has no statutory requirements. | None. | Wyo. Stat. § 35-2-910(b). |

# § 4.6 Remedies and Defenses in Wrongful Discharge Lawsuits

Table 4.6-1 shows the remedies that the states make available for discharges in violation of public policy, implied contracts, and the covenant of good faith and fair dealing. It excludes remedies for discharges in violation of fair employment statutes and for intentional torts such as intentional infliction of emotional distress and defamation.

Back pay and benefits are awardable for virtually all wrongful discharge claims and are usually calculated from the date of discharge or cessation of income to the date of judgment. Severance pay and/or other earned income may offset back pay.

Front pay and benefits are generally awardable if reinstatement is not a viable option or reinstatement will not make the employee "whole." In the latter circumstance, a partial front pay award may be made to account for any salary differential. Because at-will employment, by definition, may not be permanent, front pay is generally limited in duration.

In most states, damages for pain and suffering as well as punitive damages are available for intentional torts. However, there is a growing trend in a few states, notably California, to limit the tort remedies available in wrongful discharge actions. This is based upon the view that the employment relationship is essentially contractual in nature and, hence, that remedies for breach or termination of that relationship should be limited to contract remedies.

Employers can avoid forming implied-in-fact contracts in various ways. For example, an employer can include a written disclaimer of intent to form a contract in its handbook, orientation materials, or employment application. Table 4.6-2 shows which states recognize a disclaimer of intent as a defense and which states permit claims preempted by statutory remedies. The table also shows the time limits for filing various charges under the statute of limitations for each state.

# Table 4.6-1
## REMEDIES AVAILABLE FOR WRONGFUL DISCHARGE

(Remedies are for discharges in violation of public policy, implied contracts, and the covenant of good faith and fair dealing. See also text at § 4.6.)

**KEY:** **N/C.** No statute provides such a remedy, nor has any court case determined if such a remedy is available.

| | *Back Pay and Benefits* | *Front Pay and Benefits* | *Reinstatement* | *Damages for Pain and Suffering* | *Punitive Damages* | *Citations to Authority* |
|---|---|---|---|---|---|---|
| AL | Yes, employee can get remedy by claiming wrongful discharge in violation of public policy. | Yes, for discharge violating whistle-blower protection act. | N/C. | N/C. | Yes, by statute, for discharge violating a public obligation (jury service, wage garnishment, whistle-blowing) or a public right (seeking workers' compensation and voting). Also a court-created remedy for wrongful discharge. | Ala. Code §§ 12-16-8.1, 25-5-11.1, 36-26A-1–36-26A-7. *Grant v. Butler,* 590 So. 2d 254 (Ala. 1991); *Lozier Corp. v. Gray,* 624 So. 2d 1034 (Ala. 1993); *Motion Picture Industries, Inc. v. Pate,* 678 So. 2d 724 (Ala. 1996); *Leak Stop, Inc. v. Keenon,* 705 So. 2d 479 (Ala. Cir. App. 1997). |
| AK | Yes, by statute, for discharge violating a public obligation (jury service, witness service if employee was the crime victim, wage garnishment, whistle-blowing) or a public right (seeking workers' compensation and voting). Also a court-created remedy for wrongful discharge. | N/C. | Yes, for discharge violating a public obligation (jury service, wage garnishment, filing complaint with OSHA). | N/C. | Yes, for discharge violating a public obligation (whistle-blowing). No, for violation of good faith and fair dealing. Employee discharged because of taking leave to be a witness in a criminal case when employee was the crime victim may receive punitive damages of 3 times actual damages. | Alaska Stat. §§ 09.20.037, 12.61.017, 18.60.089, 25.27.062(f), 39.90.100 *et seq.*; *Walt v. State,* 751 P.2d 1345 (Alaska 1988); *Arco Alaska, Inc. v. Akers,* 753 P.2d 1150 (Alaska 1988); *Reed v. Municipality of Anchorage,* 782 P.2d 1155 (Alaska 1989); *Luedtke v. Nabors Alaska Drilling, Inc.,* 834 P.2d 1220 (Alaska 1992); *Alaska Marine Pilots v. Hendsch,* 950 P.2d 98 (Alaska 1997). |

*(Table continues.)*

# **Table 4.6-1** *(cont'd)*
## REMEDIES AVAILABLE FOR WRONGFUL DISCHARGE

(Remedies are for discharges in violation of public policy, implied contracts, and the covenant of good faith and fair dealing. See also text at § 4.6.)

**KEY: N/C.** No statute provides such a remedy, nor has any court case determined if such a remedy is available.

| | *Back Pay and Benefits* | *Front Pay and Benefits* | *Reinstatement* | *Damages for Pain and Suffering* | *Punitive Damages* | *Citations to Authority* |
|---|---|---|---|---|---|---|
| AZ | Yes, by statute, for discharge violating a public obligation (jury service, wage garnishment, whistle-blowing) or a public right (seeking workers' compensation and voting). Also a court-created remedy for wrongful discharge that violates public policy (damages in the form of lost medical insurance coverage). | N/C. | Yes, employee can get remedy by claiming wrongful discharge in violation of public policy. | N/C. | Yes, if harm to employee was intentional or disregarded by employer. | Ariz. Rev. Stat. Ann. §§ 12-541, 23-1501. *Fogelman v. Peruvian Assocs.*, 622 P.2d 63 (Ariz. Ct. App. 1980); *Fleming v. Pima County*, 685 P.2d 1301 (Ariz. 1984); *Thompson v. Better-Bilt Aluminum Prods. Co.*, 832 P.2d 203 (Ariz. 1992); *Spratt v. Northern Automotive Corp.*, 958 F. Supp. 456 (D. Ariz. 1996). |
| AR | Yes, by statute, for discharge violating a public obligation (jury service, wage garnishment, whistle-blowing) or a public right (seeking workers' compensation and voting). Also a court-created remedy for wrongful discharge. | N/C. | N/C. | N/C. | N/C. | Ark. Code Ann. § 11-9-107. *Proctor v. East Cent. Ark. EOC*, 291 Ark. 265, 724 S.W.2d 163 (1987); *Sterling Drug, Inc. v. Oxford*, 294 Ark. 239, 743 S.W.2d 380 (1988). |
| CA | Yes, by statute, for discharge violating a public obligation (jury service, wage garnishment, whistle-blowing) or a public right (seeking workers' compensation and voting). Also a court-created remedy for wrongful discharge. Court has discretion to withhold this remedy. | Yes, employee can get remedy by claiming wrongful discharge in violation of public policy. | Yes, by statute, for discharge violating a public obligation (jury service, wage garnishment, whistle-blowing) or a public right (seeking workers' compensation and voting). Also a court-created remedy for wrongful discharge. | Yes, employee can get remedy by claiming wrongful discharge in violation of public policy. Not available for claims based on breach of covenant of good faith and fair dealing except in insurance contracts. | Yes, for claims based upon violations of public policy. Tort damages can be awarded if the public policy violated affects the public, not only the individual. | Cal. Lab. Code §§ 132a, 230, 2929, 6310; Cal. Gov't Code §§ 53296 *et seq.*; *Tameny v. Atlantic Richfield*, 610 P.2d 1330 (Cal. 1980); *Comeaux v. Brown & Williamson Tobacco Co.*, 915 F.2d 1264 (9th Cir. 1990); *Lowe v. California Resources Agency*, 2 Cal. Rptr. 2d 558 (Cal. Ct. App. 1991); *Hunter v. Up-Right, Inc.*, 26 Cal. Rptr. 2d 8 (Cal. 1993); *Finch v. Brenda Raceway Corp.*, 27 Cal. Rptr. 2d 531 (Cal. Ct. App. 1994); *Dyer v. W.C.A.B.*, 28 Cal. Rptr. 2d 30 (Cal. Ct. App. 1994); *Lane v. Hughes Aircraft Co.*, 51 Cal. Rptr. 2d 882 (Cal. Ct. App. 1997). |

| | | | | | | |
|---|---|---|---|---|---|---|
| CO | Yes, by statute, for discharge violating a public obligation (jury service, wage garnishment, whistle-blowing) or a public right (seeking workers' compensation and voting). | N/C. | Yes, by statute, for discharge violating a public obligation (jury service, wage garnishment, whistle-blowing) or a public right (seeking workers' compensation and voting). Also a court-created remedy for wrongful discharge. | A court created remedy exists for wrongful discharge. | Yes. | Colo. Rev. Stat. §§ 24-50.5-105, 24-114-103; *Wing v. JMP Property Management Corp.*, 714 P.2d 916 (Colo. Ct. App. 1985); *Lanes v. O'Brien,* 746 P.2d 1366 (Colo. Ct. App. 1987). |
| CT | Yes, by statute, for discharge violating a public obligation (jury service, witness service in a criminal case, wage garnishment, whistle-blowing) or a public right (seeking workers' compensation and voting). Also a court-created remedy for wrongful discharge. | N/C. | Yes, by statute, for discharge violating a public obligation (jury service, witness service in a criminal case, wage garnishment, whistle-blowing) or a public right (seeking workers' compensation and voting). Also a court-created remedy for wrongful discharge. | N/C. | Yes, employee can get remedy by claiming wrongful discharge in violation of public policy. | Conn. Gen. Stat. Ann. §§ 54-85b, 54-203(b)(7)(G); *Ford v. Blue Cross & Blue Shield,* 578 A.2d 1054 (Conn. 1990); *Board of Educ. v. State Bd. of Labor Relations,* 584 A.2d 1172 (Conn. 1991). |
| DE | Yes, by statute, for discharge violating a public obligation (jury service, whistle-blowing) or a public right (seeking workers' compensation). | No. | Yes, for discharge violating a public obligation (jury service, whistle-blowing) or a public right (seeking workers' compensation). | No. | No. | Del. Code Ann. tit. 10, § 4515; tit. 19, § 2365; tit. 29, § 5115; *Knotts v. Bewick,* 467 F. Supp. 931 (D. Del. 1979); *Reiver v. Murdoch & Walsh, P.A.,* 625 F. Supp. 998 (D. Del. 1985). |
| DC | Yes, by statute, for discharge violating a public obligation (jury service, filing OSHA complaint) or a public right (seeking workers' compensation). | No. | Yes, for discharge violating a public obligation (jury service, filing OSHA complaint) or a public right (seeking workers' compensation). | No. | Yes, by statute (D.C. Human Rights Act). | D.C. Code Ann. §§ 11-1913, 36-342, 36-1217; *Wisconsin Ave. Nursing Home v. D.C. Comm'n on Human Rights,* 527 A.2d 282 (D.C. 1987); *Sorrells v. Garfinkel's*, 565 A.2d 285 (D.C. 1989); *Arthur Young & Co. v. Sutherland,* 631 A.2d 354 (D.C. 1993). |

*(Table continues.)*

# **Table 4.6-1** *(cont'd)*
## REMEDIES AVAILABLE FOR WRONGFUL DISCHARGE

(Remedies are for discharges in violation of public policy, implied contracts, and the covenant of good faith and fair dealing. See also text at § 4.6.)

**KEY: N/C.** No statute provides such a remedy, nor has any court case determined if such a remedy is available.

| | *Back Pay and Benefits* | *Front Pay and Benefits* | *Reinstatement* | *Damages for Pain and Suffering* | *Punitive Damages* | *Citations to Authority* |
|---|---|---|---|---|---|---|
| FL | Yes, by statute, for discharge violating a public obligation (witness service) or a public right (seeking workers' compensation). | Yes. | Yes, by statute, for discharge violating a public obligation (whistle-blowing). | Yes, by case law, for discharge violating a public right (seeking workers' compensation). | Yes, by case law, for discharge violating a public right (seeking workers' compensation). By statute for witness service. | Fla. Stat. Ann. §§ 92.57, 112.3187 *et seq.*, 448.101 *et seq.*; *Scott v. Otis Elevator Co.*, 572 So. 2d 902 (Fla. 1990); *McLaughlin v. Dep't of Natural Resources*, 581 So. 2d 968 (Fla. Dist. Ct. App. 1991). |
| GA | Yes, by statute, for discharge violating a public obligation (jury service, whistle-blowing) or a public right (voting). | No. | Yes, by statute, for discharge violating a public obligation (whistle-blowing). | No. | No. | Ga. Code Ann. §§ 34-1-3, 45-1-4; *Walters v. City of Atlanta*, 610 F. Supp. 715 (N.D. Ga. 1985), *stay denied*, 610 F. Supp. 734 (N.D. Ga. 1985), *aff'd in part, rev'd in part*, 803 F.2d 1135 (11th Cir. 1986); *Rogers v. Georgia Ports Auth.*, 183 Ga. App. 325, 358 S.E.2d 855 (1987); *Williams v. Roberts*, 904 F.2d 634 (11th Cir. 1990). |
| HI | Yes, by statute, for discharge violating a public obligation (jury service, witness service, wage garnishment, whistle-blowing) or a public right (seeking workers' compensation). Also a court-created remedy for wrongful discharge. | N/C. | Yes, by statute, for discharge violating a public obligation (jury service, witness service, wage garnishment, whistle-blowing) or a public right (seeking workers' compensation). Also a court-created remedy for wrongful discharge. | A court-created remedy exists for wrongful discharge. | A court-created remedy exists for wrongful discharge. | Haw. Rev. Stat. §§ 79-14, 377-9, 378-61 *et seq.*, 396-8, 612-23, 621-10.5. |

| | | | | | | |
|---|---|---|---|---|---|---|
| ID | Yes, by statute, for discharge violating a public obligation (jury service, wage garnishment, whistle-blowing). Also a court-created remedy for wrongful discharge. | Yes. | Yes, by statute, for discharge violating a public obligation (jury service, wage garnishment, whistle-blowing). Also a court-created remedy for wrongful discharge. | Yes, employee can get remedy by claiming wrongful discharge in violation of public policy. | Yes, employee can get remedy by claiming wrongful discharge in violation of public policy. | Idaho Code §§ 2-218, 6-2101, 45-606, 67-5309, 67-5908; *Jackson v. Minidoka Irrigation Dist.*, 98 Idaho 330, 563 P.2d 54 (1977); *O'Dell v. Basabe*, 810 P.2d 1082 (Idaho 1991). |
| IL | Yes, by statute, for discharge violating a public obligation (jury service, whistle-blowing). Also a court-created remedy for wrongful discharge. | N/C. | Yes, for discharge violating a public obligation (jury service, whistle-blowing). | N/C. | Employee cannot get remedy for breach of contract. Punitive damages are available for tort of retaliatory discharge in violation of public policy. Such damages are not available for claims under the Illinois Human Rights Act. | Ill. Ann. Stat. ch. 705, ¶ 305/4.1; ch. 775, ¶ 5/8-104; *Palmateer v. International Harvester Co.*, 421 N.E.2d 876 (Ill. 1981); *Johnson v. George J. Ball, Inc.*, 617 N.E.2d 1355 (Ill. App. Ct. 1993); *Heldenbrand v. Roadmaster Corp.*, 660 N.E.2d 1354 (Ill. App. 1996). |
| IN | Yes, by statute, for discharge violating a public obligation (jury service, wage garnishment, whistle-blowing) or a public right (seeking workers' compensation). Also a court-created remedy for wrongful discharge. | Yes, if action is in tort. | Yes, by statute, for discharge violating a public obligation (jury service, wage garnishment, whistle-blowing) or a public right (seeking workers' compensation). Also a court-created remedy for wrongful discharge. | Yes, employee can get remedy by claiming wrongful discharge in violation of public policy. | Yes, employee can get remedy by claiming wrongful discharge in violation of public policy. | Ind. Code Ann. §§ 22-5-3-3, 34-4-29-1, 36-1-8-8; *Call v. Scott Brass, Inc.*, 553 N.E.2d 1225 (Ind. Ct. App. 1990); *Remington Freight Lines, Inc. v. Larkey*, 644 N.E.2d 931 (Ind. Ct. App. 1994); *Williams v. Pharmacia Inc.*, 956 F. Supp.1457 (N.D. Ind. 1996). |
| IA | Yes, by statute, for discharge violating a public obligation (jury service, witness service, whistle-blowing) or a public right (seeking workers' compensation and voting). Also a court-created remedy for wrongful discharge in violation of public policy. | N/C. | Yes, for discharge violating a public obligation (jury service, witness service, filing complaint with OSHA, whistle-blowing). | N/C. | Employee cannot get remedy when a new cause of action for retaliatory discharge is recognized or when discharge occurred before cause of action was recognized. Employee can get remedy in misrepresentation claims. | Iowa Code Ann. §§ 70A.28, 88.9(3), 91A.4, 607A.45; *Lara v. Thomas*, 512 N.W.2d 777 (Iowa 1994); *Clarey v. K-Products, Inc.*, 514 N.W.2d 900 (Iowa 1994); *Hanson v. Hancock County Memorial Hosp.*, 938 F. Supp. 1419 (N.D. Iowa 1996). |

*(Table continues.)*

## Table 4.6-1 *(cont'd)*

## REMEDIES AVAILABLE FOR WRONGFUL DISCHARGE

(Remedies are for discharges in violation of public policy, implied contracts, and the covenant of good faith and fair dealing. See also text at § 4.6.)

**KEY: N/C.** No statute provides such a remedy, nor has any court case determined if such a remedy is available.

| | *Back Pay and Benefits* | *Front Pay and Benefits* | *Reinstatement* | *Damages for Pain and Suffering* | *Punitive Damages* | *Citations to Authority* |
|---|---|---|---|---|---|---|
| KS | Yes, by statute, for discharge violating a public obligation (jury service, whistle-blowing). Also a court-created remedy for wrongful discharge. | N/C. | Yes, for discharge violating a public obligation (jury service, whistle-blowing). | N/C. | Yes, when employer's conduct is willful or wanton violation of Worker's Compensation Act. | Kan. Stat. Ann. §§ 43-173, 44-315, 44-501 *et seq.* 75-2973; *Ramirez v. IBP, Inc.*, 950 F. Supp. 1074 (D. Kan. 1996); *Ramirez v. IBP, Inc.*, 950 F. Supp. 1074 (D. Kan. 1996); *Sanjuan v. IBP, Inc.*, 941 F. Supp. 1000 (D. Kan. 1996). |
| KY | Yes, by statute, for discharge violating a public obligation (jury service, whistle-blowing) or a public right (seeking workers' compensation). Also a court-created remedy for wrongful discharge. | N/C. | Yes, by statute, for discharge violating a public obligation (jury service, whistle-blowing) or a public right (seeking workers' compensation). Also a court-created remedy for wrongful discharge. | Yes, employee can get remedy by claiming wrongful discharge in violation of public policy. | Yes, by statute, for discharge violating a public obligation (jury service, whistle-blowing) or a public right (seeking workers' compensation). Also a court-created remedy for wrongful discharge. | Ky. Rev. Stat. Ann. §§ 29A.160, 29A.990, 61.102, 61.103, 337.055, 338.121; *Audiovox Corp. v. Moody,* 737 S.W.2d 468 (Ky. Ct. App. 1987); *Simpson County Steeplechase Association, Inc. v. Roberts,* 898 S.W.2d 523 (Ky. 1995). |
| LA | Yes, by statute, for discharge violating a public obligation (jury service, wage garnishment, whistle-blowing) or a public right (seeking workers' compensation). | No. | Yes. Reinstatement is a generally recognized remedy for wrongful discharge. | Yes, employee can get damages for emotional suffering under the act prohibiting reprisals against persons who report environmental violations. | No. | La. Rev. Stat. Ann. §§ 23:631, 23:632, 30:2027; *Cowart v. Lee,* 626 So. 2d 93 (La. Ct. App. 1993). |
| ME | Yes, by statute, for discharge violating a public obligation (jury service, whistle-blowing) or a public right (seeking workers' compensation). Also a court-created remedy for wrongful discharge. | N/C. | Yes, by statute, for discharge violating a public obligation (jury service, whistle-blowing) or a pub- | N/C. | Yes. | Me. Rev. Stat. Ann. tit. 14, § 1218; tit. 26, § 626; *Boivin v. Jones & Vining, Inc.,* 578 A.2d 187 (Me. 1990). |

| | | | | | | |
|---|---|---|---|---|---|---|
| | | | lic right (seeking workers' compensation). Also a court-created remedy for wrongful discharge. | | | |
| MD | Yes, by statute, for discharge violating a public obligation (reporting OSHA violation, whistle-blowing). Also a court-created remedy for wrongful discharge. | N/C. | Yes, for discharge violating a public obligation (reporting OSHA violation, whistle-blowing). | N/C. | Yes, employee can get remedy by claiming wrongful discharge in violation of public policy and showing malice. | Md. Code Ann. Lab. & Empl. Law §§ 3-305, 5-604; *Caldor v. Bowden,* 625 A.2d 959 (Md. 1993). |
| MA | Yes, by statute, for discharge violating a public obligation (wage garnishment, whistle-blowing) or a public right (seeking workers' compensation). Also a court-created remedy for wrongful discharge. | No. | Yes, for discharge violating a public obligation (wage garnishment, whistle-blowing) or a public right (seeking workers' compensation). | No. | Yes, by statute, for discharge violating a public obligation (whistle-blowing). | Mass. Gen. Laws Ann. ch. 119A, § 20; ch. 149, § 185, ch. 152, § 75B; *Kravetz v. Merchants Distribs., Inc.,* 387 Mass. 457, 440 N.E.2d 1278 (1982); *Olin v. Prudential Ins. Co. of Am.,* 798 F.2d 1 (1st Cir. 1986), *overruled by Gallagher v. Wilton Enterprises, Inc.,* 962 F.2d 120, 124 (1st Cir. 1992); *DeRose v. Putnam Management Co., Inc.,* 398 Mass. 205, 496 N.E.2d 428 (1986). |
| MI | Yes, by statute, for discharge violating a public obligation (wage garnishment, filing OSHA complaint, whistle-blowing). Also a court-created remedy for wrongful discharge. | Yes, employee can get remedy by claiming wrongful discharge in violation of public policy. | Yes, by statute, for discharge violating a public obligation (wage garnishment, filing OSHA complaint). Employee can also get remedy by claiming wrongful discharge in violation of public policy. | Yes, a court-created remedy exists for wrongful discharge. | No. | Mich. Comp. Laws §§ 408.475, 408.483, 600.4015, 600.8307; *Kocenda v. Archdiocese of Detroit,* 516 N.W.2d 132 (Mich. Ct. App. 1994); *Phillips v. Butterball Farms Co.,* 531 N.W.2d 144 (Mich. 1995). |
| MN | Yes, by statute, for discharge violating a public obligation (jury service, filing OSHA complaint, whistle-blowing) or a public right (seeking workers' compensation). Also a court-created remedy for wrongful discharge. Yes, by statute, for failure to offer continued employment following a workers' compensation claim, when employee is physically qualified. | N/C. | Yes, by statute, for discharge violating a public obligation (jury service, filing OSHA complaint, whistle-blowing) or a public right (seeking workers' compensation). Also a court-created remedy for wrongful discharge. | Yes, by case law for discharge for filing workers' compensation claim. | Yes, by statute, for filing workers' compensation claim. | Minn. Stat. Ann. §§ 176.82, 181.13, 181.14, 181.935, 182.669, 593.50; *Jensen v. Hercules, Inc.,* 524 N.W.2d 748 (Minn. Ct. App. 1994). |

*(Table continues.)*

## Table 4.6-1 *(cont'd)*
## REMEDIES AVAILABLE FOR WRONGFUL DISCHARGE

(Remedies are for discharges in violation of public policy, implied contracts, and the covenant of good faith and fair dealing. See also text at § 4.6.)

**KEY: N/C.** No statute provides such a remedy, nor has any court case determined if such a remedy is available.

| | *Back Pay and Benefits* | *Front Pay and Benefits* | *Reinstatement* | *Damages for Pain and Suffering* | *Punitive Damages* | *Citations to Authority* |
|---|---|---|---|---|---|---|
| MS | Yes, by statute, for discharge violating a public obligation (whistle-blowing). Also a court-created remedy for wrongful discharge. | N/C. | N/C. | N/C. | Yes. | Miss. Code Ann. §§ 25-9-145, 25-9-173; *Willard v. Paracelsus Health Care Corp.*, 681 So. 2d 539 (Miss. 1996). |
| MO | Yes, by statute, for discharge violating a public obligation (jury service, whistle-blowing) or a public right (seeking workers' compensation). Also a court-created remedy for wrongful discharge. | N/C. | Yes, for discharge violating a public obligation (jury service, whistle-blowing). | N/C. | Yes, employee can get remedy by claiming wrongful discharge in violation of public policy. | Mo. Ann. Stat. §§ 287.780, 290.110, 494.460; *Reed v. Sale Memorial Hosp. & Clinic*, 698 S.W.2d 931 (Mo. Ct. App. 1985), *appeal after remand*, 741 S.W.2d 819 (Mo. Ct. App. 1987); *Krasney v. Curators of Univ. of Mo.*, 765 S.W.2d 646 (Mo. Ct. App. 1989); *Self v. Lenertz Terminal, Inc.*, 854 S.W.2d 571 (Mo. Ct. App. E.D. 1993); *Clark v. Beverly Enterprises-Missouri, Inc.*, 872 S.W.2d 522 (Mo. Ct. App. 1994). |
| MT | In 1987 Montana enacted a comprehensive law protecting at-will employees from discharge without cause; in retaliation for refusing to violate public policy or for reporting a public policy violation; and when employers violate handbook rules. | See "Back Pay and Benefits." | See "Back Pay and Benefits." | See "Back Pay and Benefits." | See "Back Pay and Benefits." | Mont. Code Ann. §§ 39-2-302, 39-2-901 *et seq.*; *Gates v. Life of Mont. Ins. Co.*, 668 P.2d 213 (Mont. 1983); *In re Unfair Labor Practice*, 686 P.2d 185 (Mont. 1984); *Meech v. Hillhaven W., Inc.*, 776 P.2d 488 (Mont. 1989); *Heltborg v. Modern Mach.*, 795 P.2d 954 (Mont. 1990). |
| NE | Yes, by statute, for discharge violating a public obligation (filing OSHA complaint, whistle-blowing). Also a court-created remedy for wrongful discharge. | N/C. | Yes, by statute, for discharge violating a public obligation (filing OSHA complaint, whistle-blowing). | N/C. | N/C. | Neb. Rev. Stat. §§ 25-1558, 25-1640, 32-1537, 48-1114, 81-2701 *et seq.*; *Poppert v. Brotherhood of Railroad Trainmen*, 189 N.W.2d 469 (Neb. 1971); *Schuessler v. Benchmark Mktg.*, 500 N.W.2d 529 (Neb. 1993). |

| | | | | | | |
|---|---|---|---|---|---|---|
| NV | Yes, by statute, for discharge violating a public obligation (jury service, witness service, filing OSHA complaint). Also a court-created remedy for wrongful discharge. | N/C. | Yes, for discharge violating a public obligation (jury service, witness service, filing a complaint with OSHA). | N/C. | Yes, employee can get remedy by claiming wrongful discharge in violation of public policy. Punitive damages may not exceed $50,000 for discharge because of jury service. | Nev. Rev. Stat. Ann. §§ 6.190, 31.298, 50.070, 178.5694, 608.015, 613.330, 613.333, 618.445; *Hansen v. Harrah's,* 100 Nev. 60, 675 P.2d 394 (1984); *K-Mart Corp. v. Ponsock,* 732 P.2d 1364 (1987); *D'Angelo v. Gardner,* 819 P.2d 206 (1991). |
| NH | Yes, by statute, for discharge violating a public obligation (jury service, whistle-blowing). Also a court-created remedy for wrongful discharge. | N/C. | Yes, for discharge violating a public obligation (jury service, whistle-blowing). | N/C. | Yes, employee can get remedy by claiming wrongful discharge in violation of public policy. | N.H. Rev. Stat. Ann. §§ 275-E:1 *et seq.,* 500-A:14. |
| NJ | Yes, by statute, for discharge violating a public obligation (filing OSHA complaint, whistle-blowing) or a public right (seeking workers' compensation). Also a court-created remedy for wrongful discharge. | N/C. | Yes, for discharge violating a public obligation (filing a complaint with OSHA, whistle-blowing) or a public right (seeking workers' compensation). | Yes, employee can get remedy by claiming wrongful discharge in violation of public policy. | Yes, employee can get remedy by claiming wrongful discharge in violation of public policy. Also by statute for whistle-blowing. Not available for breach of covenant of good faith and fair dealing allegation. | N.J. Stat. Ann. §§ 2A:170-90.4, 10:5-12, 18A:17-47, 34:4A-13, 34:5A-17, 34:6A-45, 34:11-56a24, 34:19-1 *et seq.*; *Carlini v. Curtiss-Wright Corp.,* 176 A.2d 266 (N.J. 1961); *DeVries v. McNeil Consumer Prods. Co.,* 593 A.2d 819 (N.J. 1991); *Abbamont v. Piscataway Tp. Bd. of Educ.,* 634 A.2d 538 (N.J. Super. 1993), *cert. granted,* 641 A.2d 1039 (N.J. 1994); *Mehlman v. Mobil Oil Corp.,* 676 A.2d 1143 (N.J. Super. App. Div. 1996). |
| NM | Yes, by statute, for discharge violating a public obligation (filing OSHA complaint, whistle-blowing). Also a court-created remedy for wrongful discharge. | N/C. | Yes, for discharge violating a public obligation (filing a complaint with OSHA) or a public right (seeking workers' compensation). | Yes. | Yes, for discharge violating a public obligation or a public right (employee's right of association), or in suits with evidence of a culpable mental state. | N.M. Stat. Ann. §§ 1-12-42, 1-20-13, 38-5-18, 50-2-2, 50-9-25, 52-1-1 *et seq.,* 52-1-28.2, 74-3-16; *Vigil v. Arzola,* 699 P.2d 613 (1983), *modified,* 687 P.2d 1038 (N.M. 1984), *overruled in part,* 777 P.2d 371 (N.M. 1989); *Shovelin v. Central N.M. Elec. Co-Op.,* 850 P.2d 996 (N.M. 1993); *Bourgeous v. Horizon Healthcare Corp.,* 872 P.2d 852 (N.M. 1994); *Gandy v. Wal-Mart Stores, Inc.,* 872 P.2d 859 (N.M. 1994); *Rhein v. ADT Automotive, Inc.,* 930 P.2d 783 (N.M. 1996). |

*(Table continues.)*

**Table 4.6-1** *(cont'd)*
REMEDIES AVAILABLE
FOR WRONGFUL DISCHARGE

(Remedies are for discharges in violation of public policy, implied contracts, and the covenant of good faith and fair dealing. See also text at § 4.6.)

**KEY: N/C.** No statute provides such a remedy, nor has any court case determined if such a remedy is available.

| | *Back Pay and Benefits* | *Front Pay and Benefits* | *Reinstatement* | *Damages for Pain and Suffering* | *Punitive Damages* | *Citations to Authority* |
|---|---|---|---|---|---|---|
| NY | Yes, by statute, for discharge violating a public obligation (wage garnishment, filing OSHA complaint, jury service, whistle-blowing) or a public right (seeking workers' compensation). Also a court-created remedy for wrongful discharge. | Yes. | Yes, for discharge violating a public obligation (wage garnishment, jury service, filing OSHA complaint, whistle-blowing) or a public right (seeking workers' compensation). | Yes, for emotional distress. | No. | N.Y. Civ. Serv. Law § 107; N.Y. Lab. Law §§ 215, 740, 880; N.Y. Exec. Law § 296; N.Y. Jud. Law § 519; N.Y. Work. Comp. Law § 120; N.Y. Civ. Prac. L. & R. 5252; *Gross v. Board of Educ.,* 78 N.Y.2d 13, 571 N.Y.S.2d 200, 574 N.E.2d 438 (1991); *Scaduto v. Restaurant Assocs. Indus., Inc.,* 180 A.D.2d 458, 579 N.Y.S.2d 381 (App. Div. 1992); *Hoffman v. Altana, Inc.,* 603 N.Y.S.2d 499 (App. Div. 1993); *Herlihg v. Metropolitan Museum of Art,* 608 N.Y.S.2d 770 (Sup. Ct. 1994); *Bompane v. Enzolabs, Inc.,* 608 N.Y.S.2d 989 (Sup. Ct. 1994); *Gleason v. Callanan Industries, Inc.,* 610 N.Y.S.2d 671 (App. Div. 1994); *Sagendorf-Teal v. County of Rensselaer,* 100 F.3d 270 (N.Y. 1996). |
| NC | Yes, by statute, for discharge violating a public obligation (jury service, wage garnishment, filing OSHA complaint, whistle-blowing) or a public right (seeking workers' compensation). Also a court-created remedy for wrongful discharge. | N/C. | Yes, for discharge violating a public obligation (jury service, wage garnishment, filing a complaint with OSHA, whistle-blowing) or a public right (seeking workers' compensation). | Yes, for emotional distress. | Yes. | N.C. Gen. Stat. §§ 9-32, 95-25.20, 95-81, 95-83, 95-130, 95-240 *et seq.,* 96-15.1, 126-85, 131E-50; *Jones v. Department of Human Resources,* 268 S.E.2d 500 (N.C. 1980); *Privette v. University of N.C.,* 385 S.E.2d 185 (N.C. 1989); *Abels v. Renfro Corp.,* 436 S.E.2d 822 (N.C. 1993); *Wagoner v. Elkin City Schools' Bd. of Educ.,* 440 S.E.2d 119 (N.C. Ct. App. 1994), *cert. denied,* 447 S.E.2d 414 (N.C. 1994). |

| | | | | | | |
|---|---|---|---|---|---|---|
| ND | Yes, by statute, for discharge violating a public obligation (jury service, witness service, wage garnishment). Also a court-created remedy for wrongful discharge. | N/C. | Yes, for discharge violating a public obligation (jury service, witness service, wage garnishment). | N/C. | No, but employee is entitled, by statute, to double lost wages when discharge occurs because of wage garnishment. | N.D. Cent. Code §§ 14-02.4-03, 27-09.1-17, 32-03-07, 32-09.1-18, 34-01-14, 34-01-17, 34-01-20, 65-01-01; *Lee v. Walstad,* 368 N.W.2d 542 (N.D. 1985). |
| OH | Yes, by statute, for discharge violating a public obligation (filing OSHA complaint, whistle-blowing) or a public right (seeking workers' compensation). Also a court-created remedy for wrongful discharge. | Yes. | Yes, for discharge violating a public obligation (filing a complaint with OSHA, whistle-blowing) or a public right (seeking workers' compensation). | N/C. | N/C. | Ohio Rev. Code Ann. §§ 1513.39, 2313.18, 2716.05, 3113.21.3, 4112.02, 4113.52, 4123.90; *Willson v. Board of Trustees,* 1991 WL 274862 (Ohio 1991); *Zimmerman v. Eagle Mortgage Corp.,* 675 N.E.2d 480 (Ohio App. 1996). |
| OK | Yes, by statute, for discharge violating a public obligation (jury service) or a public right (seeking workers' compensation and voting). Also a court-created remedy for wrongful discharge. | Yes, by statute, for discharge violating a public obligation (jury service). | Yes, for discharge violating a public right (seeking workers' compensation). | N/C. | Yes. Punitive damages may not exceed $100,000 when discharge occurs because of seeking workers' compensation. | Okla. Stat. Ann. tit. 38, § 35; tit. 85, §§ 5, 6; *Burk v. K-Mart Corp.,* 770 P.2d 24 (Okla. 1989); *Wallace v. Halliburton Co.,* 850 P.2d 1056 (Okla. 1993); *Wilson v. Hess-Sweitzer & Brant, Inc.,* 864 P.2d 1279 (Okla. 1993); *Pettit v. Dolese Bros. Co.,* 943 P.2d 161 (Okla. App. 1997). |
| OR | Yes, by statute, for discharge violating a public obligation (jury service, filing OSHA complaint, whistle-blowing). Also a court-created remedy for wrongful discharge. | Yes. | Yes, for discharge violating a public obligation (jury service, filing a complaint with OSHA, whistle-blowing). | N/C. | N/C. | Or. Rev. Stat. §§ 10.090, 654.062, 658.452, 659.030, 659.035, 659.270; *Holien v. Sears, Roebuck & Co.,* 689 P.2d 1292 (Or. 1984); *Goldsborough v. Eagle Crest Partners, Ltd.,* 805 P.2d 723 (Or. Ct. App. 1991), *aff'd,* 838 P.2d 1069 (Or. 1992). *Tadsen v. Praegitzer Indus., Inc.,* 902 P.2d 586 (Or. Ct. App. 1995), *aff'd,* 928 P.2d. 980 (Or. 1996). |
| PA | Yes, by statute, for discharge violating a public obligation (jury service, service as a witness in a criminal trial, wage garnishment, whistle-blowing). Also a court-created remedy for wrongful discharge. | Yes. | Yes, for discharge violating a public obligation (jury service, service as a witness in a criminal trial, whistle-blowing). | N/C. | Yes, employee can get remedy by claiming wrongful discharge in violation of public policy. | Pa. Cons. Stat. Ann. tit. 18, § 4957; tit. 23, § 4348(i), (l); tit. 42, § 4565; Pa. Stat. Ann. tit. 43, §§ 1201.1, 1423, 1431; *Schweitzer v. Rockwell Int'l,* 586 A.2d 383 (Pa. Super. Ct. 1990); *Steinberg v. 7-Up Bottling Co. of Philadelphia,* 636 A.2d 677 (Pa. Super. Ct. 1994). |
| RI | Yes, by statute, for discharge violating a public obligation (filing OSHA complaint, whistle-blowing). | No. | Yes, for discharge violating a public obligation (filing a complaint with OSHA, whistle-blowing). | No. | No. | R.I. Gen. Laws §§ 28-14-18 *et seq.,* 28-20-21; *Pacheo v. Raytheon Co.,* 623 A.2d 464 (R.I. 1993). |

*(Table continues.)*

## Table 4.6-1 *(cont'd)*
## REMEDIES AVAILABLE FOR WRONGFUL DISCHARGE

(Remedies are for discharges in violation of public policy, implied contracts, and the covenant of good faith and fair dealing. See also text at § 4.6.)

**KEY: N/C.** No statute provides such a remedy, nor has any court case determined if such a remedy is available.

| | *Back Pay and Benefits* | *Front Pay and Benefits* | *Reinstatement* | *Damages for Pain and Suffering* | *Punitive Damages* | *Citations to Authority* |
|---|---|---|---|---|---|---|
| SC | Yes, by statute, for discharge violating a public obligation (jury service, witness service, filing OSHA complaint, whistle-blowing) or a public right (seeking workers' compensation). Also a court-created remedy for wrongful discharge. | Yes. | Yes, for discharge violating a public obligation (filing OSHA complaint, whistle-blowing) or a public right (seeking workers' compensation). | N/C. | N/C. | S.C. Code Ann. §§ 1-13-80, 8-27-20, 20-7-1315, 41-1-70, 41-1-80, 41-15-510, 41-15-520; *Campbell v. Bi-Lo, Inc.*, 392 S.E.2d 477 (S.C. 1990); *Chastain v. Owens Carolina, Inc.*, 426 S.E.2d 834 (S.C. Ct. App. 1993). |
| SD | A court-created remedy exists for wrongful discharge. | N/C. | N/C. | N/C. | Yes, employee can get remedy when authorized by statute and when employee claims intentional infliction of emotional distress. | S.D. Codified Laws §§ 16-13-41.1, 20-13-10 *et seq.*; *Bass v. Happy Rest, Inc.*, 507 N.W.2d 317 (S.D. 1993); *Nelson v. WEB Water Development Ass'n, Inc.*, 507 N.W.2d 691 (S.D. 1993). |
| TN | Yes, by statute, for discharge violating a public obligation (jury service, filing OSHA complaint, whistle-blowing). Also a court-created remedy for wrongful discharge. | N/C. | Yes, for discharge violating a public obligation (jury service, filing OSHA complaint). | N/C. | Yes, employee can get remedy by claiming wrongful discharge in violation of public policy. | Tenn. Code Ann. §§ 2-19-134, 4-21-401, 4-21-407, 22-4-108, 50-1-304, 50-3-106, 50-3-409; *Sasser v. Averitt Express, Inc.*, 839 S.W.2d 422 (Tenn. 1992); *Hodges v. S.C. Toof & Co.*, 833 S.W.2d 896 (Tenn. 1992); *Coffey v. Fayette Tubular Products*, 929 S.W.2d 326 (Tenn. 1996); *Cassidy v. Spectrum Rents*, 959 F. Supp. 823 (E.D. Tenn. 1997). |
| TX | Yes, by statute, for discharge violating a public obligation (jury service, filing OSHA complaint, whistle-blowing) or a public right (seeking workers' compensation). Also a court-created remedy for wrongful discharge. | Yes, employee can get remedy by claiming wrongful discharge in violation of public policy. | Yes, employee can get remedy by claiming wrongful discharge in violation of public policy. Also by | Yes, employee can get remedy by claiming wrongful discharge in violation of public policy. | Yes, employee can get remedy by claiming wrongful discharge in violation of public policy. Also by | Tex. Rev. Civ. Stat. Ann. arts. 101.052, 253.102; Tex. Civ. Prac. & Rem. Code Ann. §§ 122.001 *et seq.*; Tex. Gov't Code Ann. §§ 554.001 *et seq.*; Tex. Lab. Code Ann. §§ 411.082 *et seq.*, 451.001 *et seq.*; *Carna-* |

| | | | | | | |
|---|---|---|---|---|---|---|
| | | | statute for discharge violating a public obligation (jury service, filing OSHA complaint, whistle-blowing) or a public right (seeking workers' compensation). | | statute when discharge occurs because of whistle-blowing. | *tion Co. v. Borner,* 610 S.W.2d 450 (Tex. 1980); *Bonner v. Fleming Cos.,* 734 S.W.2d 764 (Tex. 1987); *Texas Dep't of Human Servs. v. Green,* 855 S.W.2d 136 (Tex. Ct. App. 1993); *City of La Porte v. Prince,* 851 S.W.2d 876 (Tex. Ct. App. 1993); *Martin v. Texas Dental Plans, Inc.*, 948 S.W.2d 799 (Tex. Ct. App. 1997), *Burlington Coat Factory Warehouse of El Paso, Inc. v. Flores,* 951 S.W.2d 542 (Tex. Ct. App. 1997); *Borg-Warner Protective Services Corp. v. Flores,* 955 S.W.2d 861 (Tex. Ct. App. 1997). |
| UT | Yes, by statute, for discharge violating a public obligation (jury service, wage garnishment, filing OSHA complaint, whistle-blowing). Also a court-created remedy for wrongful discharge. | N/C. | Yes, for discharge violating a public obligation (jury service, filing a complaint with OSHA, whistle-blowing). Also available for breach of implied contract, but only when damages are inadequate remedy. | N/C. | N/C. | Utah Code Ann. §§ 20A-3-103, 34-20-8, 35A-5-106, 35A-6-203, 62A-11-316, 67-21-1 *et seq.,* 70C-7-104, 78-46-21; *Thurston v. Box Elder County,* 892 P.2d 1034 (Utah 1995). |
| VT | Yes, by statute, for discharge violating a public obligation (filing OSHA complaint, whistle-blowing). Also a court-created remedy for wrongful discharge. | Yes. | Yes, for discharge violating a public obligation (filing a complaint with OSHA, whistle-blowing). | N/C. | N/C. Employee is entitled to treble lost wages when discharge occurs because of filing OSHA complaint. | Vt. Stat. Ann. tit. 21, §§ 231, 495, 710, 1621, 1726; *Haynes v. Golub Corp.*, 692 A.2d 377 (Vt. 1997). |
| VA | Yes, by statute, for discharge violating a public obligation (filing OSHA complaint) or a public right (seeking workers' compensation). Also a court-created remedy for wrongful discharge. | N/C. | Yes, for discharge violating a public obligation (filing OSHA complaint) or a public right (seeking workers' compensation). | N/C. | Yes, employee can get remedy by claiming wrongful discharge in violation of public policy. | Va. Code Ann. §§ 34-29, 40.1–51.1 *et seq.,* 65.2-308. |
| WA | Yes, by statute, for discharge violating a public obligation (jury service, wage garnishment, filing OSHA complaint, whistle-blowing) or a public right (seeking workers' compensation). Also a court-created remedy for wrongful discharge. | Yes, employee can get remedy by claiming wrongful discharge in violation of public policy. | Yes, for discharge violating a public obligation (jury service, wage garnishment, filing a complaint with OSHA, whistle-blowing) or a public right (seeking workers' compensation). | N/C. | N/C. Employee is entitled to double damages when discharge occurs because of wage garnishment. | Wash. Rev. Code Ann. §§ 2.36.165, 6.27.170, 19.30.190, 42.41.010 *et seq.,* 49.17.160, 49.60.172, 49.60.180, 51.48.025; *Wilmot v. Kaiser Aluminum & Chem. Corp.,* 821 P.2d 18 (Wash. 1991); *DeLahunty v. Cahoon,* 832 P.2d 1378 (Wash. Ct. App. 1992). |

*(Table continues.)*

**Table 4.6-1** *(cont'd)*

REMEDIES AVAILABLE
FOR WRONGFUL DISCHARGE

(Remedies are for discharges in violation of public policy, implied contracts, and the covenant of good faith and fair dealing. See also text at § 4.6.)

**KEY: N/C.** No statute provides such a remedy, nor has any court case determined if such a remedy is available.

| | *Back Pay and Benefits* | *Front Pay and Benefits* | *Reinstatement* | *Damages for Pain and Suffering* | *Punitive Damages* | *Citations to Authority* |
|---|---|---|---|---|---|---|
| WV | Yes, by statute, for discharge violating a public obligation (filing OSHA complaint, whistle-blowing). Also a court-created remedy for wrongful discharge. | N/C. | Yes, for discharge violating a public obligation (filing a complaint with OSHA, whistle-blowing). | Yes. | Yes. | W. Va. Code §§ 3-9-20, 6C-1-3, 16-32-14, 21-1A-4, 21-3-19, 21-3A-4, 21-3A-13, 21-5C-7, 46A-2-131; *Harless v. First National Bank in Fairmont,* 289 S.E.2d 692 (W. Va. 1982). *Wiggins v. Eastern Associated Coal Corp.,* 357 S.E.2d 745 (W. Va. 1987); *Brammer v. West Virginia Human Rights Comm'n,* 394 S.E.2d 340 (W. Va. 1990); *West Virginia Dept. of Natural Resources v. Myers,* 443 S.E.2d 229 (W. Va. 1994); *Vandevender v. Sheetz, Inc.,* 490 S.E.2d 678 (W. Va. 1997). |
| WI | Yes, by statute, for discharge violating a public obligation (jury service, witness service, wage garnishment, filing OSHA complaint, whistle-blowing) or a public right (seeking workers' compensation). Also a court-created remedy for wrongful discharge. | Yes. | Yes, for discharge violating a public obligation (jury service, witness service, wage garnishment, filing OSHA complaint). | N/C. | N/C. | Wis. Stat. Ann. §§ 101.58 *et seq.,* 102.35, 103.87, 111.06, 111.322, 425.110, 756.25, 812.43, 812.235; *Brockmeyer v. Dunn & Bradstreet,* 335 N.W.2d 834 (Wis. 1983); *Kempfer v. Automated Finishing, Inc.,* 564 N.W.2d 692 (Wis. 1997). |
| WY | Yes, by statute, for discharge violating a public obligation (jury service, wage garnishment). Also a court-created remedy for wrongful discharge. | N/C. | Yes, for discharge violating a public obligation (jury service, wage garnishment). | N/C. | N/C. | Wyo. Stat. §§ 1-11-401, 1-15-509, 15-5-116, 27-9-105, 40-14-506. |

# Table 4.6-2
## EMPLOYER DEFENSES TO WRONGFUL DISCHARGE LAWSUITS

(See also text at § 4.6.)

**KEY:** **Time Limit for Filing Claim Under Statute of Limitations:** In wrongful discharge cases, the time period during which a claim may be filed is triggered by the discharge; in defamation cases, the time period during which a claim may be filed is triggered by the first publication of defamatory remarks.

Time periods listed are based on general statute of limitation periods for torts in that state. Only in Texas has the state actually ruled on applicable statutes of limitation in cases of wrongful discharge in violation of public policy.

**Claim Preempted by Statutory Remedy:** Court will not allow a suit, because there is a federal or state statute covering the particular claim. This does not include defense of preemption under Federal Labor Law asserted by employers to wrongful discharge claims by union employees.

**N/C.** No court case has been issued so far.

**N/R.** No ruling. The highest court of the state has not clearly expressed its position on this issue, and either the lower courts are divided, or the federal courts, interpreting state law, are the only courts to have issued the decision.

**N/A.** Not applicable, because state does not recognize public policy and/or implied contract exceptions to the at-will rule or because no court case has definitively decided the issue.

| | *Time Limit for Filing Claim Under Statute of Limitations* | | | | | |
|---|---|---|---|---|---|---|
| | *Discharge in Violation of Public Policy (Tort)* | *Defamation* | *Discharge in Violation of Implied Contract* | *State Courts Permit Disclaimer as Defense to Implied Contract* | *Claim Preempted by Statutory Remedy* | *Citations to Authority* |
| AL | 2 years. | 2 years. | 2 years. | Yes. | N/C. | Ala. Code § 6-2-38. |
| AK | N/A. | 2 years. | 6 years. | N/C. | Yes. | Alaska Stat. §§ 09.10.050, 09.10.070; *Andrews v. Alaska Operating Engineers-Employers Training Trust Fund,* 871 P.2d 1142 (Alaska 1994), *cert. denied,* 115 S.Ct. 201 (1994). *But see Reed v. Anchorage,* 782 P.2d 1155 (Alaska 1989) (OSHA statute doesn't preempt claims of retaliatory discharge). |
| AZ | 1 year. | 1 year. | 1 year. | Yes. | Yes. | Ariz. Rev. Stat. Ann. §§ 12-541, 12-543, 12-550; *Southern Pacific Transp. Co. v. Superior Court in Pima County,* 739 P.2d 205 (Ariz. Ct. App. 1987); *Chambers v. Valley Nat'l Bank,* 721 F. Supp. 1128 (D. Ariz. 1988); *Duncan v. St. Joseph's Hospital and Medical Center,* 903 P.2d 1107 (Ariz. Ct. App. 1995). |

*(Table continues.)*

# Table 4.6-2 *(cont'd)*
## EMPLOYER DEFENSES TO WRONGFUL DISCHARGE LAWSUITS

(See also text at § 4.6.)

**KEY:** **Time Limit for Filing Claim Under Statute of Limitations:** In wrongful discharge cases, the time period during which a claim may be filed is triggered by the discharge; in defamation cases, the time period during which a claim may be filed is triggered by the first publication of defamatory remarks.

Time periods listed are based on general statute of limitation periods for torts in that state. Only in Texas has the state actually ruled on applicable statutes of limitation in cases of wrongful discharge in violation of public policy.

**Claim Preempted by Statutory Remedy:** Court will not allow a suit, because there is a federal or state statute covering the particular claim. This does not include defense of preemption under Federal Labor Law asserted by employers to wrongful discharge claims by union employees.

**N/C.** No court case has been issued so far.

**N/R.** No ruling. The highest court of the state has not clearly expressed its position on this issue, and either the lower courts are divided, or the federal courts, interpreting state law, are the only courts to have issued the decision.

**N/A.** Not applicable, because state does not recognize public policy and/or implied contract exceptions to the at-will rule or because no court case has definitively decided the issue.

| | *Time Limit for Filing Claim Under Statute of Limitations* | | | | | |
|---|---|---|---|---|---|---|
| | *Discharge in Violation of Public Policy (Tort)* | *Defamation* | *Discharge in Violation of Implied Contract* | *State Courts Permit Disclaimer as Defense to Implied Contract* | *Claim Preempted by Statutory Remedy* | *Citations to Authority* |
| AR | 5 years. | 3 years (libel); 1 year (slander). | 5 years. | Yes. | No. Yes, for claims dealing with workers' compensation. | Ark. Code Ann. §§ 16-56-104, 16-56-105, 16-56-115; *Bryant v. Southern Screw Mach. Prods. Co.,* 288 Ark. 602, 707 S.W.2d 321 (1986); *Mumphrey v. James River Paper Co.,* 777 F. Supp. 1458 (W.D. Ark. 1991); *Tackett v. Crain Automotive,* 899 S.W.2d 839 (Ark. 1995). |
| CA | 1 year. | 1 year. | 2 years. | Yes. | Yes, wrongful discharge claims preempted based on ERISA and workers' compensation laws. However, claims for wrongful discharge of bank officer under National Banking Act are not preempted. Claims for wrongful discharge in violation of public policy against discrimination also are not preempted. | Cal. Civ. Proc. Code §§ 339, 340; Cal. Lab. Code § 98.7(f); *Portillo v. G.T. Price Prods., Inc.,* 182 Cal. Rptr. 291 (Cal. Ct. App. 1982); *Baker v. Kaiser Aluminum & Chem. Corp.,* 608 F. Supp. 1315 (N.D. Cal. 1984); *Cole v. Fair Oaks Fire Protection Dist.,* 233 Cal. Rptr. 308 (Cal. 1987); *Potter v. Arizona S. Coach Lines, Inc.,* 248 Cal. Rptr. 284 (Cal. Ct. App. 1988); *Angell v. Peterson Tractor, Inc.,* 26 Cal. Rptr. 2d 541 (Cal. Ct. App. 1994); *AT&T Communications Inc. v. Superior Court,* 26 Cal. Rptr. 2d 802 (Cal. Ct. App. 1994); *Leibert v. Transworld Sys., Inc.,* 39 Cal. Rpt. 2d 65 (Cal. Ct. App. 1995). |

| | | | | | | |
|---|---|---|---|---|---|---|
| CO (The Colorado Supreme Court has held that resume fraud is a complete defense to a breach of implied contract or promissory estoppel claim.) | 2 years. | 1 year. | 2 years. | Yes. | No, state workers' compensation statute does not preempt claims of intentional infliction of emotional distress. State does not recognize the public policy exceptions to at-will employment. | Colo. Rev. Stat. §§ 13-80-102, 13-80-103; *Therrien v. United Air Lines,* 670 F. Supp. 1517 (D. Colo. 1987); *Martin Marietta Corp. v. Lorenz,* 823 P.2d 100 (Colo. 1992); *Crawford Rehabilitation Services, Inc., v. Weissman,* No. 95SC4S1 (Colo. June 9, 1997). |
| CT | 3 years. | 2 years. | 6 years. | N/C. | Yes, fair employment statute preempts a claim that discharge is in violation of public policy. Employee may bring civil action upon obtaining a release from Commission on Human Rights and Opportunities. | Conn. Gen. Stat. Ann. §§ 46a-100, 52-576, 52-577, 52-597. |
| DE | 2 years. | 2 years. | 3 years. | N/C. | N/C. | Del. Code Ann., tit. 10, §§ 8106, 8111, 8119. |
| DC | 3 years. | 1 year. | 3 years. | Yes. | N/A. | D.C. Code Ann. § 12-301; *Goos v. National Ass'n of Realtors,* 715 F. Supp. 2 (D.D.C. 1989). |
| FL | N/A. | 2 years. | 4 years. | N/A. | N/A. | Fla. Stat. Ann. § 95.11. |
| GA | N/A. | 1 year. | 4 years. | N/C. | N/A. | Ga. Code Ann. §§ 9-3-25, 9-3-33; *Loftin v. Brown,* 346 S.E.2d 114 (Ga. App. 1986). |
| HI | 2 years. | 2 years. | 6 years. | N/C. | Yes. | Haw. Rev. Stat. §§ 657-1, 657-4, 662-4; *Lapinad v. Pacific Oldsmobile,* 679 F. Supp. 991 (D. Haw. 1988); *Howard v. Daiichiya-Lore's Bakery, Inc.,* 714 F. Supp. 1108 (D. Haw. 1989); *Ross v. Stouffer Hotel Co. (Hawaii),* 879 P.2d 1037 (Hawaii 1994); *Ellison v. Northwest Airlines, Inc.,* 938 F. Supp. 1503 (D. Haw. 1996). |
| ID | 4 years. | 2 years. | 2 years. | Yes. | N/C. | Idaho Code §§ 5-217, 5-219, 5-224; *Sorenson v. Comm Tek, Inc.,* 118 Idaho 664, 799 P.2d 70 (1990); *Mitchell v. Zilog, Inc.,* 874 P.2d 520 (Idaho 1994). |
| IL | 2 years. | 1 year. | 5 years. | Yes. | Yes, fair employment statute and Illinois Human Rights Act preempt a claim that discharge is in violation of public policy. Federal OSHA provisions do not preempt claim that discharge is in violation of public policy. | Ill. Ann. Stat. ch. 735, ¶¶ 5/13-201, 5/13-202, 5/13-205; *Bahr v. Ellis & Robertson,* No. 85 C 956 (N.D. Ill. 1985) (1985 WL 3074); *Moore v. Illinois Bell Tel. Co.,* 508 N.E.2d 519 (Ill. App. Ct. 1987); *Hicks v. Resolution Trust Corp.,* 738 F. Supp. 279 (N.D. Ill. 1990); *Frank v. South Suburban Hosp. Found.,* 628 N.E.2d 953 (Ill. App. Ct. 1993); *Fragassi v. Neiburger,* 646 N.E.2d 315 (Ill. App. Ct. 1995). |

*(Table continues.)*

# Table 4.6-2 *(cont'd)*

## EMPLOYER DEFENSES TO WRONGFUL DISCHARGE LAWSUITS

(See also text at § 4.6.)

**KEY:** **Time Limit for Filing Claim Under Statute of Limitations:** In wrongful discharge cases, the time period during which a claim may be filed is triggered by the discharge; in defamation cases, the time period during which a claim may be filed is triggered by the first publication of defamatory remarks.

Time periods listed are based on general statute of limitation periods for torts in that state. Only in Texas has the state actually ruled on applicable statutes of limitation in cases of wrongful discharge in violation of public policy.

**Claim Preempted by Statutory Remedy:** Court will not allow a suit, because there is a federal or state statute covering the particular claim. This does not include defense of preemption under Federal Labor Law asserted by employers to wrongful discharge claims by union employees.

**N/C.** No court case has been issued so far.

**N/R.** No ruling. The highest court of the state has not clearly expressed its position on this issue, and either the lower courts are divided, or the federal courts, interpreting state law, are the only courts to have issued the decision.

**N/A.** Not applicable, because state does not recognize public policy and/or implied contract exceptions to the at-will rule or because no court case has definitively decided the issue.

| | *Time Limit for Filing Claim Under Statute of Limitations* | | | | | |
|---|---|---|---|---|---|---|
| | *Discharge in Violation of Public Policy (Tort)* | *Defamation* | *Discharge in Violation of Implied Contract* | *State Courts Permit Disclaimer as Defense to Implied Contract* | *Claim Preempted by Statutory Remedy* | *Citations to Authority* |
| IN | 2 years. | 2 years. | 2 years. | N/R. | Yes, fair employment statute preempts a claim that discharge is in violation of public policy. Indiana Tort Claims Act limits public policy claims against a state, county, or local government entity. | Ind. Code Ann. §§ 34-11-1-2, 34-11-2-7, 34-11-2-4. *Scott v. Union Tank Car Co.*, 402 N.E.2d 992 (Ind. Ct. App. 1980); *Lavery v. Southlake Center,* 566 N.E.2d 1055 (Ind. Ct. App. 1991). |
| IA | 2 years. | 2 years. | 5 years. | Yes. | Yes, state civil rights statute preempts a claim that discharge is in violation of public policy when claim is premised on discriminatory acts. | Iowa Code Ann. § 614.1; *Conaway v. Webster City Products Co.*, 431 N.W.2d 795 (Iowa 1988); *Borschel v. City of Perry,* 512 N.W.2d 565 (Iowa 1994); *Phipps v. IASD Health Services Corp.*, 558 N.W.2d 198 (Iowa 1997); *Vrban v. Deere & Co.*, 129 F.3d 1008 (8th Cir. 1997). |
| KS | 2 years. | 1 year. | 3 years. | Yes. | Yes, fair employment statute preempts a claim that discharge is in violation of public policy. | Kan. Stat. Ann. §§ 44-1010, 60-511–60-514; *ANCO Constr. Co. v. Freeman,* 236 Kan. 626, 693 P.2d 1183 (1985); *Masters v. Daniel Int'l Corp.*, 917 F.2d 455 (10th Cir. 1990); *Polson v. Davis,* 895 F.2d 705 (10th Cir. 1990); *Morris v. Coleman,* 783 P.2d 841 (Kan. 1987). |

| | | | | | | |
|---|---|---|---|---|---|---|
| KY | 5 years. | 1 year. | 5 years. | N/A. | N/C. | Ky. Rev. St. Ann. §§ 413.120, 413.140; *Brown v. Physicians Mut. Ins. Co.*, 679 S.W.2d 836 (Ky. Ct. App. 1984); *Pine v. Harold (Chubby) Baird Gate Co.*, 705 S.W.2d 947 (Ky. Ct. App. 1986). |
| LA | 1 year. | 1 year. | N/A. | Yes. | No. | La. Civ. Code Ann. art. 3492; *Jackson v. Ascension Parish School Bd.*, 573 So. 2d 501 (La. Ct. App.), *writ denied*, 569 So. 2d 989 (La. 1990); *Sampson v. Wendy's Management Inc.*, 593 So. 2d 336 (La. 1992); *Frost v. Metropolitan Life Ins. Co.*, 635 So. 2d 706 (La. Ct. App. 1994); *Leger v. Tyson Foods, Inc.*, 670 So. 2d 397 (La. Ct. App. 1996); *Smith v. Holloway Sportswear, Inc.*, 704 So. 2d 420 (La. Ct. App. 1997). |
| ME | N/A. | 2 years. | 6 years. | N/C. | N/A. | Me. Rev. Stat. Ann. tit. 14, §§ 752, 753; *MacDonald v. Eastern Fine Paper, Inc.*, 485 A.2d 228 (Me. 1984). |
| MD | 3 years. | 1 year. | 3 years. | Yes. | Yes, fair employment statute preempts a claim that discharge is in violation of public policy. Other statutory-based discharge allegations would be barred where statutes provide a remedy. | Md. Code Ann. Cts. & Jud. Proc. §§ 5-101, 5-105; *Castiglione v. Johns Hopkins Hosp.*, 69 Md. App. 325, 517 A.2d 786 (1986), *cert. denied*, 309 Md. 325, 523 A.2d 1013 (1986); *Chappell v. Southern Maryland Hosp., Inc.*, 320 Md. 483, 578 A.2d 766 (1990). |
| MA | 3 years. | 3 years. | 6 years. | Yes. | Yes, fair employment statute preempts a claim that discharge is in violation of public policy. ERISA preempts claim based on promissory estoppel and implied contract. | Mass. Gen. Laws Ann. ch. 260, §§ 2, 2A, 4; *Ourfalian v. Aro Mfg. Co.*, 577 N.E.2d 6 (Mass. App. Ct. 1991); *Fairney v. Savogran Co.*, 664 N.E.2d 5 (Mass. 1996). |
| MI | 3 years. | 1 year. | 6 years. | Yes. | Whistle-blowers' Protection Act preempts claim for wrongful discharge in violation of public policy. | Mich. Comp. Laws Ann. §§ 600.5805, 600.5807; *Schipani v. Ford Motor Co.*, 302 N.W.2d 307 (Mich. Ct. App. 1981); *Tyrna v. Odamo, Inc.*, 407 N.W.2d 47 (Mich. Ct. App. 1987); *Dalton v. Harbruck Egg Sales Corp.*, 417 N.W.2d 496 (Mich. Ct. App. 1987); *Wilson v. General Motors Corp.*, 454 N.W.2d 405 (Mich. Ct. App. 1990), *leave to appeal denied*, 437 Mich. 914 (1991); *Rome v. Montgomery Ward & Co.*, 473 N.W.2d 268 (Mich. 1991); *Dudewicz v. Norris Schmid, Inc.*, 503 N.W.2d 645 (Mich. 1993); *Vagts v. Perry Drug Stores*, 516 N.W.2d 102 (Mich. Ct. App. 1994); *Driver v. Hanley*, 523 N.W.2d 815 (Mich. Ct. App. 1994); *Dolan v. Continental Airlines*, 526 N.W.2d 922 (Mich. Ct. App. 1995); *Lytle v. Malady*, 530 N.W.2d 135 (Mich. Ct. App. 1995); *Heurtebise v. Reliable Business Computers*, 550 N.W.2d 243 (Mich. 1996). |

*(Table continues.)*

## Table 4.6-2 *(cont'd)*
## EMPLOYER DEFENSES TO WRONGFUL DISCHARGE LAWSUITS

(See also text at § 4.6.)

**KEY:** **Time Limit for Filing Claim Under Statute of Limitations:** In wrongful discharge cases, the time period during which a claim may be filed is triggered by the discharge; in defamation cases, the time period during which a claim may be filed is triggered by the first publication of defamatory remarks.

Time periods listed are based on general statute of limitation periods for torts in that state. Only in Texas has the state actually ruled on applicable statutes of limitation in cases of wrongful discharge in violation of public policy.

**Claim Preempted by Statutory Remedy:** Court will not allow a suit, because there is a federal or state statute covering the particular claim. This does not include defense of preemption under Federal Labor Law asserted by employers to wrongful discharge claims by union employees.

**N/C.** No court case has been issued so far.

**N/R.** No ruling. The highest court of the state has not clearly expressed its position on this issue, and either the lower courts are divided, or the federal courts, interpreting state law, are the only courts to have issued the decision.

**N/A.** Not applicable, because state does not recognize public policy and/or implied contract exceptions to the at-will rule or because no court case has definitively decided the issue.

| | *Time Limit for Filing Claim Under Statute of Limitations* | | | | | |
|---|---|---|---|---|---|---|
| | *Discharge in Violation of Public Policy (Tort)* | *Defamation* | *Discharge in Violation of Implied Contract* | *State Courts Permit Disclaimer as Defense to Implied Contract* | *Claim Preempted by Statutory Remedy* | *Citations to Authority* |
| MN | 2 years. | 2 years. | 2 years. | Yes. | Whistle-blower Act preempts common-law claim for wrongful discharge in violation of public policy. Claim under Minnesota Human Rights Act for wrongful discharge preempts claim under Whistle-blower Act. | Minn. Stat. Ann. § 541.07; *Lee v. Sperry Corp.*, 678 F. Supp. 1415 (D. Minn. 1987); *Harvet v. Unity Medical Ctr.*, 428 N.W.2d 574 (Minn. Ct. App. 1988); *Michaelson v. Minnesota Mining & Mfg. Co.*, 474 N.W.2d 174 (Minn. Ct. App. 1991); *Sandell v. Carlson Cos.*, 1992 WL213571 (Minn. Ct. App. 1992); *Williams v. St. Paul Ramsey Medical Ctr.*, 551 N.W.2d 483 (Minn. 1996). |
| MS | 3 years. | 1 year. | 1 year. | N/A. | No. | Miss. Code Ann. §§ 15-1-29, 15-1-35, 15-1-49; *Perry v. Sears Roebuck & Co.*, 508 So. 2d 1086 (1987); *Robinson v. Coastal Family Health Ctr.*, 756 F. Supp. 958 (S.D. Miss. 1990). |
| MO | 5 years. | 2 years. | 5 years. | Yes. | N/C. | Mo. Ann. Stat. §§ 516.120, 516.140; *Johnson v. Anheuser Busch, Inc.*, 876 F.2d 620 (8th Cir. 1989); *Prewitt v. Factory Motor Parts, Inc.*, 747 F. Supp. 560 (W.D. Mo. 1990); *Schweiss v. Chrysler Motors Corp.*, 922 F.2d 473 (8th Cir. 1990). |

| | | | | | | |
|---|---|---|---|---|---|---|
| MT | 1 year; comprehensive law protects at-will employees from discharge without cause; in retaliation for refusing to violate public policy or for reporting a public policy violation; and when employers violate handbook rules. | 1 year; comprehensive law protects at-will employees from discharge without cause; in retaliation for refusing to violate public policy or for reporting a public policy violation; and when employers violate handbook rules. | 1 year; comprehensive law protects at-will employees from discharge without cause; in retaliation for refusing to violate public policy or for reporting a public policy violation; and when employers violate handbook rules. | Comprehensive law protects at-will employees from discharge without cause; in retaliation for refusing to violate public policy or for reporting a public policy violation; and when employers violate handbook rules. | Comprehensive law protects at-will employees from discharge without cause; in retaliation for refusing to violate public policy or for reporting a public policy violation; and when employers violate handbook rules. | Mont. Code Ann. §§ 39-2-901 *et seq.*; *Malquist v. Foley,* 714 P.2d 995 (Mont. 1986); *Allmaras v. Yellowstone Basin Properties,* 812 P.2d 770 (Mont. 1991); *Fanrich v. Capitol Ford Lincoln Mercury,* 901 P.2d 112 (Mont. 1995). |
| NE | 4 years. | 1 year. | 4 years. | Yes. | N/C. | Neb. Rev. Stat. §§ 25-206, 25-207, 25-208, 25-212; *Cleasby v. Leo A. Daly Co.,* 376 N.W.2d 312 (Neb. 1985); *Hillie v. Mutual of Omaha Ins. Co.,* 512 N.W.2d 358 (Neb. 1994). |
| NV | 3 years. 2 years if the violation deals with workers' compensation. | 2 years. | 4 years. | N/A. | N/C. | Nev. Rev. Stat. Ann. § 11.190; *Torre v. J.C. Penney Co., Inc.,* 916 F. Supp. 1029 (D. Nev. 1996). |
| NH | 3 years. | 3 years. | 3 years. | Yes. | N/C. | N.H. Rev. Stat. Ann. § 508:4; *Butler v. Walker Power, Inc.,* 629 A.2d 91 (N.H. 1993). |
| NJ | 6 years. 2 years if the violation deals with workers' compensation. | 1 year. | 6 years. | Yes. | Yes, public policy claim preempted by Conscientious Employee Protection Act. | N.J. Stat. Ann. §§ 2A:14-1, 2A:14-2, 2A:14-3, 34:19-8; *Woolley v. Hoffmann-LaRoche, Inc.,* 491 A.2d 1257 (N.J. 1985), *modified,* 499 A.2d 515 (N.J. 1985); *Millison v. E.I. duPont de Nemours & Co.,* 501 A.2d 505 (N.J. 1985); *Catalane v. Gilian Instrument Corp.,* 638 A.2d 1341 (N.J. Super. Ct. App. Div. 1994), *cert. denied,* 642 A.2d 1006 (N.J. 1994); *Nicosia v. Wakefern Food Corp.,* 643 A.2d 554 (N.J. 1994); *Kapossy v. McGraw-Hill, Inc.,* 921 F. Supp. 234 (D.N.J. 1996); *Labree v. Mobil Oil Corp.,* 692 A.2d 540 (N.J. Super. App. Div. 1997). |
| NM | 4 years. | 4 years. | 4 years. | Yes. | No. | N.M. Stat. Ann. §§ 37-1-4, 37-1-8; *Michaels v. Anglo American Auto Auctions,* 869 P.2d 279 (N.M. 1994); *Gutierrez v. Sundancer Indian Jewelry, Inc.,* 868 P.2d 1266 (N.M. Ct. App. 1993); *Gandy v. Wal-Mart Stores,* 872 P.2d 859 (N.M. 1994); *Kiedrowski v. Citizens Bank,* 893 P.2d 468 (N.M. Ct. App. 1995). |

*(Table continues.)*

## **Table 4.6-2** *(cont'd)*
## EMPLOYER DEFENSES TO WRONGFUL DISCHARGE LAWSUITS

(See also text at § 4.6.)

**KEY:** **Time Limit for Filing Claim Under Statute of Limitations:** In wrongful discharge cases, the time period during which a claim may be filed is triggered by the discharge; in defamation cases, the time period during which a claim may be filed is triggered by the first publication of defamatory remarks.

Time periods listed are based on general statute of limitation periods for torts in that state. Only in Texas has the state actually ruled on applicable statutes of limitation in cases of wrongful discharge in violation of public policy.

**Claim Preempted by Statutory Remedy:** Court will not allow a suit, because there is a federal or state statute covering the particular claim. This does not include defense of preemption under Federal Labor Law asserted by employers to wrongful discharge claims by union employees.

**N/C.** No court case has been issued so far.

**N/R.** No ruling. The highest court of the state has not clearly expressed its position on this issue, and either the lower courts are divided, or the federal courts, interpreting state law, are the only courts to have issued the decision.

**N/A.** Not applicable, because state does not recognize public policy and/or implied contract exceptions to the at-will rule or because no court case has definitively decided the issue.

| | *Time Limit for Filing Claim Under Statute of Limitations* | | | | | |
|---|---|---|---|---|---|---|
| | *Discharge in Violation of Public Policy (Tort)* | *Defamation* | *Discharge in Violation of Implied Contract* | *State Courts Permit Disclaimer as Defense to Implied Contract* | *Claim Preempted by Statutory Remedy* | *Citations to Authority* |
| NY | N/A. | 1 year. | 6 years. | Yes. | N/A. | N.Y. Civ. Prac. L. & R. 213, 215; *Santulli v. Englert, Reilly & McHugh, P.C.*, 579 N.Y.S.2d 324, 586 N.E.2d 1014 (1992); *Stanton v. Highland Hosp. of Rochester*, 602 N.Y.S.2d 278 (App. Div. 1993); *Gomanz v. Foote, Cone & Belding Communications, Inc.*, 644 N.Y.S.2d 224 (App. Div. 1996). |
| NC | 3 years. | 1 year. | 3 years. | N/A. | N/C. | N.C. Gen. Stat. §§ 1-52, 1-54; *Walton v. Carolina Tel. & Tel. Co.*, 378 S.E.2d 427 (N.C. Ct. App. 1989), *cert. denied*, 381 S.E.2d 792 (N.C. 1989). |
| ND | 6 years. | 2 years. | 6 years. | Yes. | N/C. | N.D. Cent. Code §§ 28-01-16, 28-01-18; *Jilek v. Berger Elec., Inc.*, 441 N.W.2d 660 (N.D. 1989); *Pratt v. Heartview Found.*, 512 N.W.2d 675 (N.D.1994); *Osterman-Levitt v. MedQuest Inc.*, 513 N.W.2d 70 (N.D. 1994). |

| | | | | | | |
|---|---|---|---|---|---|---|
| OH | 4 years. | 1 year. | 6 years. | Yes. | N/C. | Ohio Rev. Code Ann. §§ 2305.07, 2305.09, 2305.11; *Gaumont v. Emery Air Freight Corp.*, 572 N.E.2d 747 (Ohio 1989); *Security Title & Guar. Co. v. Rukasin,* 1990 WL 9934 (Ohio 1990); *Aglinsky v. Cleveland Builders Supply Co.*, 589 N.E.2d 1365 (Ohio 1990); *Cardinal Fed. Sav. & Loan Ass'n v. Michaels Bldg. Co.*, 1991 WL 76870 (Ohio 1991). |
| OK | 2 years. | 1 year. | 3 years. | N/C. | Yes, for claim based on public policy against age discrimination. | Okla. Stat. Ann. tit. 12, § 95; *Central Nat'l Bank v. McDaniel,* 734 P.2d 1314 (Okla. 1986); *Ingram v. Oneok, Inc.*, 775 P.2d 810 (Okla. 1989); *Burk v. K-Mart Corp.*, 770 P.2d 24 (Okla. 1989); *List v. Anchor Paint Manufacturing Co.*, 910 P.2d 1101 (Okla. 1996). |
| OR | 2 years. | 2 years. | 6 years. | N/R. | N/C. | Or. Rev. Stat. §§ 12.080, 12.110; *Holien v. Sears, Roebuck & Co.*, 689 P.2d 1292 (Or. 1984); *Patton v. J.C. Penney Co.*, 719 P.2d 854 (Or. 1986); *Kofoid v. Woodard Hotels, Inc.*, 716 P.2d 771 (Or. 1986); *Georgetown Realty, Inc. v. Home Ins. Co.*, 1992 WL 82576 (Or. 1992); *Mobley v. Manheim Servs. Corp.*, 889 P.2d 1342 (Or. Ct. App. 1995). |
| PA | 2 years. | 1 year. | 4 years. | N/C. | Yes, fair employment statute preempts a claim that discharge is in violation of public policy but not a claim for intentional infliction of emotional distress. | Pa. Cons. Stat. Ann. tit. 42, §§ 5523, 5524, 5525; *Phillips v. Babcock & Wilcox,* 503 A.2d 36 (Pa. 1986); *Garcia v. Community Legal Servs. Corp.*, 524 A.2d 980 (Pa. 1987); *Schweitzer v. Rockwell Int'l,* 586 A.2d 383 (Pa. 1990). |
| RI | N/A. | 1 year (slander); 3 years (libel). | N/A. | N/A. | N/A. | R.I. Gen. Laws § 9-1-14; *O'Coin v. Woonsocket Institution Trust Co.*, 535 A.2d 1263 (R.I. 1988). |
| SC | 3 years. | 2 years. | 3 years. | Yes. | N/C. | S.C. Code Ann. §§ 15-3-530, 15-3-550; *Hannah v. United Refrigerator Services,* Inc., 430 S.E.2d 539 (S.C. Ct. App. 1993); *Leahy v. Starflo Corp.*, 431 S.E.2d 567 (S.C. 1993). |
| SD | 3 years. | 2 years. | 6 years. | N/C. | N/C. | S.D. Codified Laws §§ 15-2-13, 15-2-14, 15-2-15; *Daugaard v. Baltic Co-op. Bldg. Supply Ass'n,* 349 N.W.2d 419 (S.D. 1984). |
| TN | 1 year. | 6 months (slander); 1 year (libel). | 6 years. | Yes. | N/C. | Tenn. Code Ann. §§ 28-3-103, 28-3-104, 28-3-109; *Conley v. Jim Wright Constr. Co.*, 1991 WL 107871 (Tenn. 1991). |

*(Table continues.)*

# Table 4.6-2 *(cont'd)*

## EMPLOYER DEFENSES TO WRONGFUL DISCHARGE LAWSUITS

(See also text at § 4.6.)

**KEY:** **Time Limit for Filing Claim Under Statute of Limitations:** In wrongful discharge cases, the time period during which a claim may be filed is triggered by the discharge; in defamation cases, the time period during which a claim may be filed is triggered by the first publication of defamatory remarks.

Time periods listed are based on general statute of limitation periods for torts in that state. Only in Texas has the state actually ruled on applicable statutes of limitation in cases of wrongful discharge in violation of public policy.

**Claim Preempted by Statutory Remedy:** Court will not allow a suit, because there is a federal or state statute covering the particular claim. This does not include defense of preemption under Federal Labor Law asserted by employers to wrongful discharge claims by union employees.

**N/C.** No court case has been issued so far.

**N/R.** No ruling. The highest court of the state has not clearly expressed its position on this issue, and either the lower courts are divided, or the federal courts, interpreting state law, are the only courts to have issued the decision.

**N/A.** Not applicable, because state does not recognize public policy and/or implied contract exceptions to the at-will rule or because no court case has definitively decided the issue.

| | *Time Limit for Filing Claim Under Statute of Limitations* | | | *State Courts Permit Disclaimer as Defense to Implied Contract* | *Claim Preempted by Statutory Remedy* | *Citations to Authority* |
|---|---|---|---|---|---|---|
| | *Discharge in Violation of Public Policy (Tort)* | *Defamation* | *Discharge in Violation of Implied Contract* | | | |
| TX | 2 years. | 1 year. | 4 years. | Yes. | N/C. | Tex. Civ. Prac. & Rem. Code Ann. §§ 16.002, 16.003, 16.004; *American Medical Elecs., Inc. v. Korn,* 819 S.W.2d 573 (Tex. 1991); *Lane v. Port Terminal R.R. Ass'n,* 821 S.W.2d 623 (Tex. 1991); *Federal Express Corp. v. Dutschmann,* 846 S.W.2d 282 (Tex. 1993). |
| UT | 1 year. | 1 year. | 4 years. | Yes. | N/A. | Utah Code Ann. §§ 78-12-25, 78-12-29; *Pratt v. Board of Educ.,* 564 P.2d 294 (Utah 1979); *Davidson Lumber Sales, Inc. v. Bonneville Inv., Inc.,* 794 P.2d 11 (Utah 1990); *Dubois v. Grand Central,* 872 P.2d 1073 (Utah Ct. App. 1994); *Kirberg v. West One Bank,* 872 P.2d 39 (Utah Ct. App. 1994); *Hamilton v. Parkdale Care Ctr., Inc.,* 904 P.2d 1110 (Utah App. 1995). |
| VT | 3 years. | 3 years. | 6 years. | N/C. | N/C. | Vt. Stat. Ann. tit. 12, §§ 511, 512; *Aube v. O'Brien,* 433 A.2d 298 (Vt. 1981); *Robbins v. Harbour Indus., Inc.,* 556 A.2d 55 (Vt. 1988). |

| | | | | | | |
|---|---|---|---|---|---|---|
| VA | 2 years. | 2 years. | 3 years. | Yes. | N/C. | Va. Code Ann. §§ 8.01-243, 246, 248; *Federal Land Bank v. Birchfield,* 3 S.E.2d 405 (Va. 1939); *Prendergast v. Northern Va. Regional Park Auth.,* 313 S.E.2d 399 (Va. 1984); *Graham v. Central Fidelity Bank,* 428 S.E.2d 916 (Va. 1993); *Nguyen v. CNA Corp.,* 44 F.3d 234 (4th Cir. 1995). |
| WA | 3 years. | 2 years. | 3 years. | Yes. | Yes, for claim based on discharge due to opposition of sexual harassment. | Wash. Rev. Code Ann. §§ 4.16.080, 4.16.100; *Martin v. Patent Scaffolding,* 687 P.2d 362 (Wash. 1984); *Messerly v. Asamera Minerals (U.S.), Inc.,* 780 P.2d 1327 (Wash. 1989); *Birge v. Fred Meyer, Inc.,* 872 P.2d 49 (Wash. Ct. App. 1994), *petition for review denied,* 881 P.2d 253 (Wash. 1994); *Hume v. American Disposal Co.,* 880 P.2d 988 (Wash. 1994); *Payne v. Sunnyside Community Hosp.,* 894 P.2d 1379 (Wash. Ct. App. 1995); *Nelson v. Southland Corp.,* 894 P.2d 1385 (Wash. Ct. App. 1995); *Schonauer v. DCR Entertainment, Inc.,* 905 P.2d 392 (Wash. Ct. App. 1995); *Wlasiuk v. Whirlpool Corp.,* 914 P.2d 102 (Wash. Ct. App. 1996). |
| WV | 2 years. | 1 year. | 5 years. | Yes. | No, state Occupational Safety and Health Act does not preempt a claim that discharge is in violation of public policy. Yes, State Human Rights Act preempts cause of action based on public policy against discrimination. | W. Va. Code §§ 55-2-6, 55-2-12; *Guevara v. K-Mart Corp.,* 629 F. Supp. 1189 (D.W. Va. 1986); *Collins v. Elkay Mining Co.,* 371 S.E.2d 46 (W. Va. 1988); *Hall v. Nichols,* 400 S.E.2d 901 (W. Va. 1990); *Taylor v. Ford Motor Co.,* 408 S.E.2d 270 (W. Va. 1991). |
| WI | 2 years. | 2 years. | 6 years. | N/C. | Yes, fair employment statute preempts a claim that discharge is in violation of public policy. | Wis. Stat. Ann. §§ 893.43, 893.57; *McDonald v. Chicago, Milwaukee, St. Paul & Pac. R.R.,* 130 N.W.2d 794 (Wis. 1964). |
| WY | 4 years. | 1 year. | 8 years. | Yes, disclaimer must be sufficiently conspicuous. | N/A. | Wyo. Stat. § 1-3-105; *Ogle v. Caterpillar Tractor Co.,* 716 P.2d 334 (Wyo. 1986); *Richardson Assocs. v. Lincoln-Devore, Inc.,* 806 P.2d 790 (Wyo. 1991); *McDonald v. Mobil Coal Producing, Inc.,* 820 P.2d 986 (Wyo. 1991); *Sanchez v. Life Care Ctrs. of America, Inc.,* 855 P.2d 1256 (Wyo. 1993); *Lincoln v. Wackenhut Corp.,* 867 P.2d 701 (Wyo. 1994). |

# § 4.7 State Right-to-Work and Other Labor Laws

The field of organized labor—which involves the relationship between employees, unions, and employers—is largely regulated by the federal government through the National Labor Relations Act (NLRA). The NLRA contains requirements that govern various aspects of unionization, such as elections, picketing, striking, and unfair labor practices. Many states also have laws dealing with organized labor; these laws are frequently patterned after the NLRA. To the extent that the state laws regulate persons, industries, or issues not covered by the NLRA, state law applies. If the state law and the NLRA are in conflict, however, federal law preempts the state provisions.

Most states have a least some statutes dealing with employee rights in the area of organized labor. The provisions of a few states are applicable only to public employees; the provisions presented in Tables 4.7-1 and 4.7-2 are not restricted to public employers, but also deal with laws covering private employers. Table 4.7-1 covers right-to-work and other employee rights, while Table 4.7-2 sets out prohibited employer practices.

Many states have statutes known as right-to-work laws. These laws reflect the states' beliefs that employees should not be restricted in employment because of nonmembership in a union. In those states, a specific statute has been passed, stating that an employee has the right not to become a member of a union. These right-to-work laws would actually prevent union agreements that would otherwise be considered valid under the NLRA, because the NLRA itself provides that agreements for exclusive union representation are not permissible in a state that has outlawed such agreements.

Other common provisions dealing with employee rights are "yellow dog" and "closed shop" laws. A yellow dog law is essentially a law that provides that an employee cannot be required to agree not to become a member of a union in order to remain employed. A closed shop law provides that an employer cannot require all employees to become members of the union representing the workers of that employer. Some states do allow closed shops if statutory conditions are fulfilled. These conditions usually require that a certain number of employees vote on the option to become a closed shop.

Many states also specifically recognize employee rights in the areas of picketing and striking. Frequently, states do not have a specific statute authorizing picketing or striking, but those activities might be covered under a more general provision allowing employees to exercise lawful rights in the area of organized labor. Several states have placed restrictions on these activities. For example, some states prohibit picketing at a residence.

An emerging issue in the area of employee rights with respect to organized labor is whether unions should be required to obtain permission from union members in order to be able to use union dues for political purposes. Proposition 226 in California, referred to as a "paycheck protection" initiative by its supporters, would require organized labor to get permission from union members each year before using member dues for political purposes. The initiative will be on the June ballot in California. Two other states, Washington and Michigan, enacted somewhat similar provisions, and efforts are underway in 30 other states to place restrictions on the use of union dues for political purposes.

Table 4.7-2 covers state laws that prohibit certain labor practices by employers. One of the most common provisions is the prohibition of coercion or interference in any employee rights. These laws were designed to prevent such tactics as threats of violence against employees or even more subtle forms of coercion. In some states, both the employee and the family of the employee are protected against coercion, in order to prevent an employer from threatening the family of an employee and thereby coerce the employee into voting against having union representation. In many states, the law against coercion also applies to unions and employees in general.

Some states also provide that an employer may not discriminate against an employee with respect to terms and conditions of employment, based on the union status of the employee. In states where such a law applies, employers should take care not to make distinctions between union and nonunion employees. In addition, even if a state is not listed in Table 4.7-2 as having a provision prohibiting discrimination within employment, firing or refusing to hire employees based on their union status may be prohibited.

A few states also have statutory provisions requiring an employer to bargain with employees. These laws are designed to encourage a dialogue between the employer and union employees; frequently, penalties are provided for employers who refuse to bargain.

Finally, some states have enacted strikebreaker laws, which prohibit the use of strikebreakers. Usually, the law limits the prohibition to professional strikebreakers, as defined by the statute.

# Table 4.7-1
## STATE RIGHT-TO-WORK AND OTHER EMPLOYEE RIGHTS UNDER ORGANIZED LABOR LAWS

| | *Does State Have Right-to-Work Law?* | *Does State Have Yellow Dog Law?* | *Does State Have Closed Shop Law?* | *Does State Have Right-to-Strike Law?* | *Does State Have Right-to-Picket Law?* | *Other* | *Citations to Authority* |
|---|---|---|---|---|---|---|---|
| AL | Yes. | Yes. | Yes. | State has no specific statutory authority. | State has no specific statutory authority. | Union cannot require money as a condition for work, except for dues. | Ala. Code §§ 25-7-6, 25-7-12, 25-7-31, 25-7-33. |
| AK | State has no specific statutory authority. | State has no specific statutory authority. | State has no specific statutory authority. | State has no specific statutory authority. | State has no specific statutory authority. | State has no broad labor relations law for private employers. One statute states that the wage and hour laws do not limit the right of employees to bargain collectively. | Alaska Stat. § 23.10.125. |
| AZ | Yes. | Yes. | Yes. | State has no specific statutory authority. | Yes. Labor organization may picket if a bona fide dispute exists between employer and employees regarding wages or working conditions. | — | Ariz. Rev. Stat. §§ 23-1302, 23-1322, 23-1341. |
| AR | Yes. | State has no specific statutory authority. | Yes. | State has no specific statutory authority. | State has no specific statutory authority. | — | Ark. Code Ann. § 11-3-303. |
| CA | Yes. | Yes. | State has no specific statutory authority. | State has no specific statutory authority. | Yes. | Jurisdictional strikes are prohibited. Proposition 226, which will appear on the June ballot, would require organized labor to get permission from union members each year before using their dues for political purposes. | Cal. Civ. Proc. Code § 527.3; Cal. Lab. Code §§ 921, 1118. |
| CO | Yes. | Yes. | Yes, but employer may enter into an all-union agreement with employees if | Yes. | Yes. | Sit-down strikes are prohibited. Labor unions may not unjustly or unfairly | Colo. Rev. Stat. Ann. §§ 8-3-102, 8-3-103, 8-3-108, 8-3-109, 8-3-119. |

| | | | | | | | |
|---|---|---|---|---|---|---|---|
| | | | employees elect to do so. | | | discriminate with respect to membership. | |
| CT | State has no specific statutory authority. | Yes. | Law allows closed shops. | Yes. | Yes. | Picketing at a residence is prohibited. | Conn. Gen. Stat. Ann. §§ 31-105, 31-113, 31-120. |
| DE | State has no specific statutory authority. | State has no specific statutory authority. | State has no specific statutory authority. | State has no specific statutory authority. | State has no specific statutory authority. | — | — |
| DC | State has no specific statutory authority. | State has no specific statutory authority. | State has no specific statutory authority. | State has no specific statutory authority. | State has no specific statutory authority. | — | — |
| FL | Yes. | State has no specific statutory authority. | State has no specific statutory authority. | Yes. | Yes. | Jurisdictional strikes are prohibited. | Fla. Const. art. I, § 6; Fla. Stat. Ann. §§ 447.09, 447.13. |
| GA | Yes. | Yes. | Yes. | Yes. Employer must be given 30 days' notice. | State has no specific statutory authority. | — | Ga. Code Ann. §§ 34-6-1, 34-6-21, 34-6-23, 34-6-24. |
| HI | State has no specific statutory authority. | State has no specific statutory authority. | Closed shop may exist, but employees with bona fide religious objections to unions may be exempted. | Yes. Agricultural employers must be given 10 days' notice. | Yes. Picketing is allowed if employees have voted to strike. | Picketing of a residence is prohibited. | Haw. Rev. Stat. Ann. §§ 377-4, 377-4.5, 377-7, 377-12, 379A-1. |
| ID | Yes. | Yes. | Yes. | State has no specific statutory authority. | State has no specific statutory authority. | — | Idaho Code § 44-2001. |
| IL | State has no specific statutory authority. | Yes. | State has no specific statutory authority. | State has no specific statutory authority. | State has no specific statutory authority. | — | 820 Ill. Comp. Stat. Ann. 15/1. |
| IN | State has no specific statutory authority. | Yes. | State has no specific statutory authority. | State has no specific statutory authority. | State has no specific statutory authority. | — | Ind. Code Ann. § 22-6-1-3. |
| IA | Yes. | Yes. | Yes. | State has no specific statutory authority. | State has no specific statutory authority. | — | Iowa Code Ann. §§ 731.1, 731.2, 731.3, 731.4. |
| KS | Yes. | State has no specific statutory authority. | Closed shop may exist if statutory conditions are fulfilled. | State has no specific statutory authority. | Yes. | Picketing at a residence is prohibited. Jurisdictional strikes are prohibited. | Kan. Stat. Ann. 44 §§ 809, 809a. |
| KY | State has no specific statutory authority. | State has no specific statutory authority. | State has no specific statutory authority. | Yes. | Yes. | — | Ky. Rev. Stat. Ann. § 336.130. |
| LA | Yes. | Yes. | Yes. | State has no specific statutory authority. | State has no specific statutory authority. | — | La. Rev. Stat. Ann. §§ 23:823, 23:981, 23:983. |

*(Table continues.)*

## Table 4.7-1 *(cont'd)*

## STATE RIGHT-TO-WORK AND OTHER EMPLOYEE RIGHTS UNDER ORGANIZED LABOR LAWS

| | *Does State Have Right-to-Work Law?* | *Does State Have Yellow Dog Law?* | *Does State Have Closed Shop Law?* | *Does State Have Right-to-Strike Law?* | *Does State Have Right-to-Picket Law?* | *Other* | *Citations to Authority* |
|---|---|---|---|---|---|---|---|
| ME | State has no specific statutory authority. | State has no specific statutory authority. | State has no specific statutory authority. | State has no specific statutory authority. | State has no specific statutory authority. | — | — |
| MD | State has no specific statutory authority. | State has no specific statutory authority. | State has no specific statutory authority. | Yes. | Yes. | — | Md. Ann. Code art. 27, § 545. |
| MA | State has no specific statutory authority. | Yes. | State has no specific statutory authority. | State has no specific statutory authority. | State has no specific statutory authority. | — | Mass. Gen. Laws Ann. ch. 149, § 20A. |
| MI | Yes. | State has no specific statutory authority. | Closed shop may exist if statutory conditions are fulfilled. | Yes; employee may strike if statutory conditions are fulfilled. | Yes. | Jurisdictional strikes are prohibited. Certain restrictions are placed on use of union dues for political contributions. | Mich. Comp. Laws Ann. §§ 423.9, 423.9f, 423.14, 423.17. |
| MN | State has no specific statutory authority. | Yes. | State has no specific statutory authority. | State has no specific statutory authority. | State has no specific statutory authority. | Secondary strikes are prohibited. | Minn. Stat. Ann. §§ 179.40, 179.60, 185.09. |
| MS | Yes. | Yes. | Yes. | State has no specific statutory authority. | State has no specific statutory authority. | — | Miss. Const. art.7, § 198-A, Miss. Code Ann. § 71-7-47. |
| MO | State has no specific statutory authority. | State has no specific statutory authority. | State has no specific statutory authority. | State has no specific statutory authority. | State has no specific statutory authority. | — | — |
| MT | Yes; in certain small businesses. | State has no specific statutory authority. | State has no specific statutory authority. | State has no specific statutory authority. | State has no specific statutory authority. | — | Mont. Code Ann. tit. 39 § 33-101. |
| NE | Yes. | State has no specific statutory authority. | State has no specific statutory authority. | Yes. | State has no specific statutory authority. | Secondary strikes are prohibited. | Neb. Const. art. XV, § 13; Neb. Rev. Stat. Ann. §§ 48-903, 48-911. |
| NV | Yes. | Yes. | Yes. | State has no specific statutory authority. | Yes. | — | Nev. Rev. Stat. §§ 613.130, 613.220. |
| NH | State has no specific statutory authority. | State has no specific statutory authority. | State has no specific statutory authority. | Yes. | State has no specific statutory authority. | — | N.H. Rev. Stat. Ann. § 649.10. |

| | | | | | | | |
|---|---|---|---|---|---|---|---|
| NJ | State has no specific statutory authority. | Yes. | State has no specific statutory authority. | State has no specific statutory authority. | State has no specific statutory authority. | — | N.J. Stat. Ann. §§ 34:12-2, 34:12-3, 34:12-5. |
| NM | State has no specific statutory authority. | Yes. | State has no specific statutory authority. | State has no specific statutory authority. | State has no specific statutory authority. | — | N.M. Stat. Ann. § 50-2-4. |
| NY | State has no specific statutory authority. | Yes. | Closed shops may be allowed if statutory conditions are fulfilled. | Yes. | Yes. | — | N.Y. Lab. Law §§ 704, 713. |
| NC | Yes. | Yes. | Yes. | State has no specific statutory authority. | State has no specific statutory authority. | — | N.C. Gen. Stat. §§ 95-78, 95-79, 95-80, 95-81. |
| ND | Yes. | Yes. | State has no specific statutory authority. | State has no specific statutory authority. | State has no specific statutory authority. | Secondary picketing is prohibited. | N.D. Cent. Code §§ 34-08-02, 34-08-04, 34-09-01, 34-09-13, 34-12-02, 34-12-03. |
| OH | State has no specific statutory authority. | Yes. | State has no specific statutory authority. | State has no specific statutory authority. | State has no specific statutory authority. | — | Ohio Rev. Code Ann. § 4113.02. |
| OK | State has no specific statutory authority. | State has no specific statutory authority. | State has no specific statutory authority. | State has no specific statutory authority. | State has no specific statutory authority. | — | — |
| OR | Yes. | Yes. | Closed shops are allowed, but employees with bona fide religious objections must be exempted. | State has no specific statutory authority. | State has no specific statutory authority. | — | Or. Rev. Stat. Ann. §§ 661.020, 661.030, 661.110. |
| PA | State has no specific statutory authority. | Yes. | State has no specific statutory authority. | Yes. | State has no specific statutory authority. | Sitdown strikes and jurisdictional strikes are prohibited. | Pa. Stat. Ann. tit. 43, §§ 206e, 211.6, 211.37. |
| RI | State has no specific statutory authority. | State has no specific statutory authority. | Closed shops are not prohibited. | Yes. | State has no specific statutory authority. | — | R.I. Gen. Laws § 28-7-13. |
| SC | Yes. | Yes. | Yes. | State has no specific statutory authority. | State has no specific statutory authority. | — | S.C. Code Ann. §§ 41-7-10, 41-7-20, 41-7-30. |
| SD | Yes. | State has no specific statutory authority. | Yes. | Yes. | State has no specific statutory authority. | — | S.D. Codified Law §§ 60-8-3, 60-9A-14, 60-10-7. |
| TN | Yes. | State has no specific statutory authority. | State has no specific statutory authority. | State has no specific statutory authority. | State has no specific statutory authority. | — | Tenn. Code Ann. §§ 50-1-201, 50-1-202. |

*(Table continues.)*

**Table 4.7-1** *(cont'd)*

STATE RIGHT-TO-WORK AND OTHER EMPLOYEE RIGHTS UNDER ORGANIZED LABOR LAWS

| | *Does State Have Right-to-Work Law?* | *Does State Have Yellow Dog Law?* | *Does State Have Closed Shop Law?* | *Does State Have Right-to-Strike Law?* | *Does State Have Right-to-Picket Law?* | *Other* | *Citations to Authority* |
|---|---|---|---|---|---|---|---|
| TX | Yes. | Yes. | State has no specific statutory authority. | State has no specific statutory authority. | Statute prohibits picketing that results in losses to an employer. | Secondary picketing is prohibited. | Tex. Lab. Code Ann. §§ 101.052, 101.053, 101.252, 101.301. |
| UT | Yes. | Yes. | State has no specific statutory authority. | State has no specific statutory authority. | State has no specific statutory authority. | — | Utah Code Ann. §§ 34-19-13, 34-20-7. |
| VT | Yes. | State has no specific statutory authority. | Closed shops are not prohibited. | State has no specific statutory authority. | State has no specific statutory authority. | — | Vt. Stat. Ann. tit. 21, § 1503. |
| VA | Yes. | Yes. | Yes. | State has no specific statutory authority. | State has no specific statutory authority. | — | Va. Code Ann. §§ 40.1-58, 40.1-59, 40.1-60, 40.1-61. |
| WA | State has no specific statutory authority. | State has no specific statutory authority. | State has no specific statutory authority. | State has no specific statutory authority. | State has no specific statutory authority. | State has no broad labor law but does recognize the right to organize. Union must obtain permission from union members before using their dues for political purposes. | Wash. Rev. Code Ann. § 49.32.020. |
| WV | State has no specific statutory authority. | State has no specific statutory authority. | Closed shops may be allowed if statutory conditions are met. | State has no specific statutory authority. | State has no specific statutory authority. | Jurisdiction strikes are prohibited. | W. Va. Code Ann. §§ 21-1A-3, 21-1A-4. |
| WI | State has no specific statutory authority. | Yes. | State has no specific statutory authority. | Yes. | Yes. | — | Wis. Stat. Ann. §§ 103.46, 103.52, 103.53, 175.05. |
| WY | Yes. | Yes. | Yes. | State has no specific statutory authority. | State has no specific statutory authority. | — | Wyo. Stat. Ann. §§ 27-7-109, 27-7-110. |

## Table 4.7-2
## PROHIBITED EMPLOYER PRACTICES UNDER STATE ORGANIZED LABOR LAWS

| | *Does State Have Law Against Coercion/ Interference?* | *Does State Have Law Against Discrimination on the Basis of Union Status?* | *Does State Require Employer to Bargain?* | *Does State Have a Strikebreaker Law?* | *Other* | *Citations to Authority* |
|---|---|---|---|---|---|---|
| AL | Yes. Law protects employee and family of employee. | State has no specific statutory authority. | State has no specific statutory authority. | State has no specific statutory authority. | — | Ala. Code §§ 25-7-6, 25-7-11. |
| AK | State has no specific statutory authority. | State has no specific statutory authority. | State has no specific statutory authority. | State has no specific statutory authority. | — | — |
| AZ | Yes. Law protects employee and family of employee. | State has no specific statutory authority. | State has no specific statutory authority. | State has no specific statutory authority. | Law against coercion also applies to labor organizations. | Ariz. Rev. Stat. § 23-1304. |
| AR | State has no specific statutory authority. | Yes. | State has no specific statutory authority. | State has no specific statutory authority. | — | Const. Ark. Amd. 34 § 1 |
| CA | Yes. | State has no specific statutory authority. | State has no specific statutory authority. | Yes. Use of professional strikebreakers is prohibited. | — | Cal. Lab. Code §§ 922, 1134. |
| CO | Yes. | State has no specific statutory authority. | Yes. | State has no specific statutory authority. | Coercion law applies to all employees. | Colo. Rev. Stat. Ann. § 8-2-102, 8-2-108. |
| CT | Yes. | Yes. | Yes. | State has no specific statutory authority. | — | Conn. Gen. Stat. Ann. § 31-105. |
| DE | State has no specific statutory authority. | State has no specific statutory authority. | State has no specific statutory authority. | State has no specific statutory authority. | — | — |
| DC | State has no specific statutory authority. | State has no specific statutory authority. | State has no specific statutory authority. | State has no specific statutory authority. | — | — |
| FL | Yes. | State has no specific statutory authority. | State has no specific statutory authority. | State has no specific statutory authority. | — | Fla. Stat. Ann. § 447.09. |
| GA | Yes. | State has no specific statutory authority. | State has no specific statutory authority. | State has no specific statutory authority. | Coercion law applies to unions and other persons. | Ga. Code Ann. §§ 34-6-2, 34-6-6. |
| HI | Yes. | Yes. | Yes. | Yes; use of professional strikebreakers is prohibited. Employer may not offer permanent employment to an individual to encourage that individual to break the strike. | Law against coercion applies to employees. | Haw. Rev. Stat. Ann. §§ 377-6, 377-7, 379-2. |

*(Table continues.)*

## Table 4.7-2 *(cont'd)*
PROHIBITED EMPLOYER PRACTICES UNDER STATE ORGANIZED LABOR LAWS

| | *Does State Have Law Against Coercion/ Interference?* | *Does State Have Law Against Discrimination on the Basis of Union Status?* | *Does State Require Employer to Bargain?* | *Does State Have a Strikebreaker Law?* | *Other* | *Citations to Authority* |
|---|---|---|---|---|---|---|
| ID | Yes. | State has no specific statutory authority. | State has no specific statutory authority. | State has no specific statutory authority. | — | Idaho Code § 44-2006. |
| IL | State has no specific statutory authority. | State has no specific statutory authority. | State has no specific statutory authority. | Yes; use of professional strikebreakers is prohibited. | — | 820 Ill. Comp. Stat. Ann. 30/2. |
| IN | Yes. | State has no specific statutory authority. | State has no specific statutory authority. | State has no specific statutory authority. | — | Ind. Code Ann. § 22-7-1-3. |
| IA | State has no specific statutory authority. | Yes. | State has no specific statutory authority. | Yes, use of professional strikebreakers is prohibited. | — | Iowa Code Ann. §§ 731.2, 732.6. |
| KS | Yes. | Yes. | State has no specific statutory authority. | State has no specific statutory authority. | — | Kan. Stat. Ann. §§ 44-808, 44-809. |
| KY | Yes. | State has no specific statutory authority. | State has no specific statutory authority. | State has no specific statutory authority. | — | Ky. Rev. Stat. § 336.130. |
| LA | Yes. | State has no specific statutory authority. | State has no specific statutory authority. | Yes. Parties not directly involved in a strike cannot recruit replacement workers (professional strikebreakers prohibited). | — | La. Rev. Stat. Ann. §§ 23:824, 23:901. |
| ME | State has no specific statutory authority. | State has no specific statutory authority. | State has no specific statutory authority. | Yes; use of professional strikebreakers is prohibited. | — | Me. Rev. Stat. Ann. tit. 26, § 851. |
| MD | State has no specific statutory authority. | State has no specific statutory authority. | State has no specific statutory authority. | Yes, use of professional strikebreakers is prohibited. | — | Md. Lab. & Emp. Code Ann. § 4-403. |
| MA | Yes; general coercion law prohibits interference with employment or membership in a union. | State has no specific statutory authority. | State has no specific statutory authority. | Yes; use of professional strikebreakers is prohibited. | — | Mass. Gen. Laws ch. 149, §§ 19, 20, 22A. |
| MI | Yes. | Yes. | Yes. | State has no specific statutory authority. | — | Mich. Comp. Laws Ann. § 423.16. |

| | | | | | | |
|---|---|---|---|---|---|---|
| MN | Yes. | Yes. | State has no specific statutory authority. | Yes; use of professional strikebreakers is prohibited. | Coercion law also applies to unions. | Minn. Stat. Ann. §§ 179.11, 179.12, 179.60. |
| MS | State has no specific statutory authority. | State has no specific statutory authority. | State has no specific statutory authority. | State has no specific statutory authority. | — | — |
| MO | State has no specific statutory authority. | State has no specific statutory authority. | State has no specific statutory authority. | Yes; use of professional strikebreakers is prohibited. | — | Mont. Code Ann. § 39-33-202. |
| MT | State has no specific statutory authority. | State has no specific statutory authority. | State has no specific statutory authority. | State has no specific statutory authority. | — | — |
| NE | State has no specific statutory authority. | State has no specific statutory authority. | State has no specific statutory authority. | State has no specific statutory authority. | — | — |
| NV | State has no specific statutory authority. | State has no specific statutory authority. | State has no specific statutory authority. | State has no specific statutory authority. | Law against coercion applies to unions and specifies that unions may not coerce employees into joining a strike. | Nev. Rev. Stat. § 613.270. |
| NH | Yes. | State has no specific statutory authority. | State has no specific statutory authority. | State has no specific statutory authority. | — | N.H. Rev. Stat. Ann. § 275.1. |
| NJ | State has no specific statutory authority. | Law applies only to public employers. | State has no specific statutory authority. | State has no specific statutory authority. | — | N.J. Stat. Ann. § 34:13A-5.7. |
| NM | Yes. | State has no specific statutory authority. | State has no specific statutory authority. | State has no specific statutory authority. | — | N.M. Stat. Ann. § 50-2-1 *et seq.* |
| NY | Yes. | Yes. | Yes. | State has no specific statutory authority. | — | N.Y. Lab. Law §§ 703, 704. |
| NC | State has no specific statutory authority. | State has no specific statutory authority. | State has no specific statutory authority. | State has no specific statutory authority. | — | — |
| ND | Yes. | Yes. | Yes. | State has no specific statutory authority. | Law against coercion also applies to unions. | N.D. Cent. Code § 34-12-03. |
| OH | State has no specific statutory authority. | State has no specific statutory authority. | State has no specific statutory authority. | State has no specific statutory authority. | — | — |
| OK | State has no specific statutory authority. | State has no specific statutory authority. | State has no specific statutory authority. | State has no specific statutory authority. | — | — |
| OR | Yes. | Yes. | Yes. | Yes; use of professional strikebreakers is prohibited. | Coercion law also applies to unions. | Or. Rev. Stat. Ann. §§ 662.020, 662.215, 663.120. |
| PA | Yes. | Yes. | Yes. | State has no specific statutory authority. | Law against coercion applies to any individual and prohibits the hindering of persons desiring to work. | Pa. Stat. Ann. tit. 43, §§ 201, 211.6. |
| RI | Yes. | Yes. | Yes. | State has no specific statutory authority. | — | R.I. Gen. Laws §§ 28-6.6-1, 28-7-12. |

*(Table continues.)*

**Table 4.7-2** *(cont'd)*

PROHIBITED EMPLOYER PRACTICES UNDER STATE ORGANIZED LABOR LAWS

| | *Does State Have Law Against Coercion/ Interference?* | *Does State Have Law Against Discrimination on the Basis of Union Status?* | *Does State Require Employer to Bargain?* | *Does State Have a Strikebreaker Law?* | *Other* | *Citations to Authority* |
|---|---|---|---|---|---|---|
| SC | Yes. | State has no specific statutory authority. | State has no specific statutory authority. | State has no specific statutory authority. | — | S.C. Code Ann. § 41-7-70. |
| SD | Yes. | Yes. | Yes. | State has no specific statutory authority. | Coercion law applies to unions and protects employees and families of employees. | S.D. Codified Laws §§ 60-8-6, 60-9A-12, 60-9A-13. |
| TN | State has no specific statutory authority. | State has no specific statutory authority. | State has no specific statutory authority. | State has no specific statutory authority. | — | — |
| TX | State has no specific statutory authority. | State has no specific statutory authority. | State has no specific statutory authority. | State has no specific statutory authority. | Coercion statute prohibits its interference with an individual's right to work. | Tex. Lab. Code Ann. § 101.153. |
| UT | Yes. | Yes. | Yes. | State has no specific statutory authority. | Coercion law also applies to employees. | Utah Code Ann. § 34-20-8. |
| VT | Yes. | Yes. | Yes. | State has no specific statutory authority. | Coercion law also applies to unions. | Vt. Stat. Ann. tit. 21, § 1621. |
| VA | Yes. | State has no specific statutory authority. | State has no specific statutory authority. | State has no specific statutory authority. | — | Va. Code Ann. § 40.1-53. |
| WA | State has no specific statutory authority. | State has no specific statutory authority. | State has no specific statutory authority. | Replacing striking employees with out-of-state workers is prohibited. | — | Wash. Rev. Code Ann. § 49.44.100. |
| WV | Yes. | Yes. | Yes. | State has no specific statutory authority. | Law against coercion also applies to unions. | W. Va. Code Ann. § 21-1A-4. |
| WI | State has no specific statutory authority. | State has no specific statutory authority. | State has no specific statutory authority. | Yes; use of professional strikebreakers is prohibited. | — | Wis. Stat. Ann. § 103.545. |
| WY | State has no specific statutory authority. | State has no specific statutory authority. | State has no specific statutory authority. | State has no specific statutory authority. | — | — |

# 5

# Benefits

*Tables in Part 5 cover group health insurance (alcohol and drug abuse treatment, mental health treatment, maternity and dependent coverage, specified diseases or medical conditions, specified medical or surgical procedures, home care or specified facility, specified providers, prescriptions, prosthetic devices, medical supplies, and antidiscrimination provisions); health benefits continuation and conversion; group life insurance; wage payment laws; parental leave; legal expenses insurance; and dental insurance.*

# § 5.1 Overview: ERISA and State Regulation of Benefits

State-mandated employee benefits can be considered only within the context of the wide-reaching federal law, the Employee Retirement Income Security Act (ERISA), enacted in 1974. ERISA laid down comprehensive rules to protect the interests of employees in pension and welfare benefit plans. Congress expressly declared in ERISA its intention that all state and local laws that relate to employee benefit plans be preempted. This broad preemption provision in ERISA ensures that the administrative design and implementation of an employee benefit plan are governed by a single set of regulations, and it protects employee benefit plans from conflicting and inconsistent state and local regulation. Therefore, it is important to consider the applicability of ERISA's preemption provision to any state law that might otherwise govern the benefits provided by employers to their employees.

ERISA's preemption clause prevents a state from imposing any substantive requirements on employee benefit plans. This is true even where ERISA itself sets no minimum substantive requirements, such as in employee welfare benefits. Thus, states may not require employers to provide employees with comprehensive health coverage, day care services, or training programs. Because there are currently no federal requirements that employers provide these benefits, employers are generally free to establish whatever benefit plans they consider appropriate.

If a benefit appears to be regulated by a state or local law, regulation, or order, the employer may want to inquire whether ERISA and its preemption provision make it unnecessary to comply with the local regulation. Although the preemption provision in ERISA is broad, it is not without limitation. Courts have construed the preemption provision to apply only to state laws that regulate the terms and conditions of "employee benefit plans." In addition, state laws that affect employee benefit plans in too tenuous, remote, or peripheral a way have been held not to be preempted, because they do not "relate to" a plan.

**Determining ERISA Preemption.** Accordingly, a determination of whether a law is preempted is generally a three-step process:

1. Is an employee benefit plan subject to ERISA affected?
2. Does the law relate to the ERISA-covered plan?
3. Is there any exemption to ERISA's preemption provision that applies?

**Defining Employee Benefit Plans.** ERISA defines an employee benefit plan to include an *employee welfare benefit plan* and an *employee pension benefit plan.* A plan is an employee welfare benefit plan if it is a "plan, fund or program" established by an employer (or labor organization, or both) to provide "medical, surgical or hospital care benefits, benefits in the event of sickness, accident, disability, death or unemployment, or vacation benefits, apprenticeship or training programs, or day care centers, scholarship funds, or prepaid legal services." An employee pension benefit plan includes any "plan, fund or program" (again established by an employer, a labor organization, or both) providing retirement income or resulting in the deferral of income until some time after termination of employment. Based on these definitions, ERISA's term "employee benefit plan" has been held to apply to health plans, pension plans, and severance policies.

**Determining the Law's Relation to a Plan.** The next issue is whether the law relates to the employee benefit plan. A state law will be found to relate to a benefit plan if it has a connection with or reference to such a plan. The application of the preemption provision is so broad that it will displace even those state laws that may be consistent with ERISA's substantive requirements.

In addition to the statutory interpretations limiting the scope of preemption, ERISA expressly excludes from preemption a variety of state laws. For example, ERISA exempts from the general rule of preemption any "generally applicable state criminal law"; certain state insurance laws regulating multiple employer welfare arrangements; qualified domestic relations orders; and the Hawaii Prepaid Health Care Act. In addition, the "savings clause" in ERISA preserves any law of any state that regulates insurance, banking, or securities. This provision has been interpreted to protect any state law regulating the substantive terms of insurance contracts; however, such a state law cannot deem an employee benefit plan to be an insurance company in order to bring the plan within the scope of the state law. As a result, an employer's self-insured plan cannot be regulated under state insurance law through the guise of defining it as an insurance company subject to state regulation.

The United States Supreme Court has held that, as applied to patients with commercial insurance or HMO coverage under ERISA welfare plans, ERISA did not preempt New York State's system of hospital surcharges. The Supreme Court found that the New York State surcharge did not "relate to" employee benefit plans within the meaning of ERISA § 514(a) merely because it indirectly affects the cost of providing benefits by means of such plans. [New York State Conference of Blue Cross & Blue Shield Plans v. Travelers Ins. Co., 115 S. Ct. 1671 (1995)] The Supreme Court decision in *Travelers* left unresolved a number of issues, including the scope of the insurance law exception as applied to self-insured medical plans plainly governed by ERISA.

After the Supreme Court's decision in *Travelers,* the Second Circuit Court of Appeals held that ERISA preempted a New York State tax on gross receipts of medical centers, in the case of a medical center operated by a joint labor-management trust fund established under an employee welfare benefit plan. [NYSA-ILA Medical & Clinical Services Fund v. Axelrod, 27 F.3d 823 (2d Cir. 1994)] The Supreme Court reversed the Second Circuit Court of Appeals, however, holding that the tax was not preempted by ERISA. [De Buono v. NYSA-ILA Medical & Clinical Services Fund, No. 95-1594 (U.S. June 2, 1997)]

**Exemptions from ERISA's Preemption.** For purposes of determining whether a state law qualifies under the insurance law exception to ERISA's preemption provision, a court will consider whether the state law regulates the "business of insurance." The criteria relevant in determining whether a particular practice falls within the bounds of the business of insurance are as follows:

1. Whether the practice has the effect of transferring or spreading a policyholder's risk;
2. Whether the practice is an integral part of the policy relationship between insurer and insured; and
3. Whether the practice is limited to entities within the insurance industry.

If these three criteria are met, a state law regulating this practice will *not* be preempted by ERISA.

These principles should be kept in mind in determining whether any of the laws listed in the tables that follow are enforceable.

# § 5.2 Coverage Requirements for Group Health Insurance Plans

The primary focus of state-mandated employee benefits is on health care benefits. Virtually all states impose minimum requirements on group health insurance policies. Such laws are not preempted by ERISA when they regulate the business of insurance. Thus, to the extent that they affect benefit plans, they are generally not preempted by ERISA.

The tables in this chapter list applicable state laws involving group health insurance offered by insurers and other health care providers. The coverage requirements contained in these tables are directed at insurers, rather than employers, but the requirements obviously impact employers that are not self-insured. Although most states have general statutes that encompass all types of health care providers (e.g., insurers, nonprofit health service corporations, medical service corporations), some states have separate statutes for each type of health care provider. For ease of presentation, the tables refer only to general statutes and separate statutes pertaining to "insurers" of group health policies.

## [a] Federal Initiatives

In 1996, Congress enacted the Health Insurance Portability and Accountability Act (HIPAA). HIPAA allows for medical spending accounts and makes other changes in the administration of health care plans. Especially relevant to employers are the new portability requirements for health insurance. HIPAA limits the ability of insurers and employers to impose limitations on coverage of preexisting conditions and provides that preexisting conditions may be excluded only under the following circumstances:

1. The condition must be one for which the candidate for coverage has received medical advice, diagnosis, or care, or one for which treatment was recommended or received within the six months prior to the enrollment date;
2. The exclusion must be limited to a 12-month period (or 18 months in the case of a late enrollee) after the enrollment date; and
3. The period of a preexisting condition exclusion must be reduced by the length of the total of the periods of creditable coverage by the candidate, as of the enrollment date.

In addition, no preexisting condition restrictions may be placed on newborn or adopted children if covered within 30 days of birth or adoption. Creditable coverage includes coverage under group health plans, Medicare, health insurance coverage, and other similar types of coverage. When an individual ceases to be covered under a policy, the plan must provide written documentation of the periods of creditable coverage.

Under another HIPAA provision, employees and their dependents must be allowed to enroll in group coverage without waiting until an open enrollment period (although waiting period restrictions must be met) when specified events occur, such as the end of COBRA continuation coverage. Finally, HIPAA contains restrictions against discrimination based on health status, which includes, among other factors, genetic characteristics and a history of domestic abuse.

## [b] Small Employers

Although a few states with mandated benefit laws impose requirements on all group health insurance policies, 44 states (Alabama, Alaska, Arkansas, California,

Colorado, Connecticut, Delaware, Florida, Georgia, Idaho, Illinois, Indiana, Iowa, Kansas, Louisiana, Maine, Maryland, Massachusetts, Minnesota, Mississippi, Missouri, Montana, Nebraska, Nevada, New Hampshire, New Jersey, New Mexico, North Carolina, North Dakota, Ohio, Oklahoma, Oregon, Rhode Island, South Carolina, South Dakota, Tennessee, Texas, Utah, Vermont, Virginia, Washington, West Virginia, Wisconsin, and Wyoming) provide limited exemptions for group health insurance offered to employers with fewer than 25 employees, or fewer than 50 employees, depending on the state.

Small employer group policies are exempt from most of the mandates applicable to other employers, but they may nonetheless be required to include minimum coverage for specific types of health care.

Table 5.2-1 lists the states with small employer exemptions and the basic minimum coverage requirements.

Many states have recently enacted various types of health insurance reform. (For a discussion of recent federal health insurance reform, see [a] Federal Initiatives.) Some states have enacted comprehensive coverage based on employer mandates, and others have enacted minor legislation directed at insurance reform. Of the reforms attempted, only Hawaii's legislation (passed in 1974) has obtained the necessary ERISA waivers. Revisions to Hawaii's legislation and other states' reforms have been delayed until such time as they are able to receive ERISA exemptions. A description of the major portions of both the Hawaii Prepaid Health Care Act and other state reforms follows.

### [c] Hawaii Prepaid Health Care Act

The Hawaii Prepaid Health Care Act requires employers to provide their regular employees who work at least 20 hours a week with coverage under a qualified prepaid group health care plan. A qualified plan is required to provide a minimum level of benefits. The benefits include at least 120 days of inpatient hospital benefits; hospital outpatient care; surgical benefits, including anesthesiologist services and after-care visits; necessary home, office, and hospital visits by a physician; diagnostic laboratory services, X rays, and radiotherapeutic services; maternity benefits; substance abuse benefits at least comparable to benefits for any other illnesses; outpatient psychiatric benefits; and detoxification and acute care benefits. The detoxification benefits must include inpatient benefits of three visits of up to seven days per admission for alcohol abuse and three visits of up to 21 days per admission for other substance abuse.

Hawaii's law requires that the employer contribute at least one half of the premium cost for prepaid health care coverage, unless an applicable collective bargaining agreement specifies otherwise. In no case, however, can the employee be required to contribute more than 1.5 percent of his or her wages. Any employer that fails to provide coverage, as required under the Hawaii statute, is liable to pay the health care costs incurred by any eligible employees.

### [d] Other State Reforms

Oregon, Florida, and Washington all passed laws (in 1989, 1992, and 1993, respectively) requiring employers to provide health insurance for their employees. None of these plans has taken effect, because of state budgetary constraints and failure to obtain ERISA waivers. Massachusetts has, however, recently passed insurance reforms. All insurers with more than 5,000 subscribers in their small group plans will have to offer coverage to individuals as well. The state will also extend continuation coverage of group health insurance to groups with as few as two workers. A group of states (Arizona, California, Connecticut, Kentucky, Maine, Maryland, Missouri, New Jersey, New York, North Carolina, Oregon, Tennessee, Rhode Island, Utah, Vermont, and Washington) have begun the process of minor health care or health insurance reforms.

For example, Kentucky is experimenting with small-group insurance reforms. Currently, associations buying insurance for their members are exempted from certain rating restrictions if the association was formed before January 1, 1996. In addition, some local chambers of commerce have teamed up with insurers to offer group insurance at a lower rate.

New York has significantly changed the manner in which its hospital rates are set. In the past, the state set rates for hospital services. Starting on January 1, 1997, the New York Health Care Reform Act takes effect, and hospitals will negotiate directly with self-insured plans, commercial insurers, and other insurers in setting rates.

Oregon has renewed its commitment to universal coverage. In November of 1996, Oregon voters approved Measure 44, an initiative to increase the state cigarette tax. At the current time, the areas of expansion have not been determined, but some support does exist for expansion of coverage to those who have employer-based coverage but cannot afford premiums for individual or family coverage.

Vermont also increased its cigarette tax to fund additional health care reforms. Vermont's reforms are targeted to assist those who are at or below 150 percent of the federal poverty level.

### [e] Alcohol and/or Drug Abuse Treatment

One of the frequently mandated benefits under state law is group health insurance coverage for treatment of alcoholism. Mandated coverage of drug abuse is somewhat less widespread than treatment for alcoholism.

States typically use one of two methods to ensure coverage in this area. The most common method is to mandate that all group policies include the coverage specified in the state laws. The second method is to require that insurance companies offer policyholders (generally the employers) the option to have coverage for specified benefits in these areas included in the group policy. The employer can then choose whether this particular benefit will be available to employees under the group policy.

Most of the state statutory provisions specify a certain minimum level of coverage that all group policies must offer; however, a few states require that group policy insurers offer coverage for treatment of alcoholism and/or drug abuse without specifying any minimum levels. None of the state requirements in these areas is intended to prevent insurers from offering greater coverage. Rather, the statutory provisions set the minimum coverage that all insurers must make available to policyholders.

When states establish minimum requirements, they generally set limits for both outpatient visits and inpatient care and treatment. These requirements are typically stated in terms of minimum cost coverage, such as $500 per year, or a minimum number of days or visits that an insurer must cover, such as 30 visits per year. Sometimes the minimum outpatient or inpatient care requirements will be broken down into components, with minimum levels for specific types of treatments such as detoxification or rehabilitation. Often, inpatient care includes both inpatient hospitalization and partial hospitalization, and the regulations may set minimum levels for each. In this case, states often count two days of partial hospitalization as one day of inpatient care. Some states also allow insurers to set lifetime limits on the amount of coverage. Thus, for example, some states permit insurers to limit coverage of alcoholism and drug abuse to a maximum number of lifetime visits.

Table 5.2-2 shows which states require mandatory coverage of alcohol and drug abuse treatment and the minimum coverage requirements.

### [f] Mental Health Treatment

Group health insurance coverage for treatment of mental illness is frequently mandated under state law. The types of statutory provisions in this area are similar to those found in the area of treatment for alcoholism and drug abuse. Thus, many states with statutory provisions for coverage of mental health treatment mandate that insurers provide certain minimum coverage in all group policies. Other states require that the insurer issuing the group policy make the specified coverage available to each policyholder as an option.

As with the statutes that mandate coverage of treatment for alcoholism and drug abuse, regulatory provisions that require coverage of mental health benefits frequently set minimum coverage limits for outpatient visits and inpatient care and treatment. In setting inpatient coverage requirements, states sometimes specify minimum levels for both hospitalization and partial hospitalization under which two days of partial hospitalization are considered the equivalent of one day of inpatient hospitalization. Some states also allow group insurers to set a limit on total maximum benefits available over the lifetime of the policyholder.

Table 5.2-3 shows which states have mandatory coverage for mental health treatment and the minimum coverage for each state that has such requirements.

### [g] Maternity and Dependent Coverage

Many states have enacted statutes mandating that group health insurance provide coverage in the area of maternal health, pregnancy, and child care. State-mandated coverage in this general area includes

**Newborn Coverage.** Most states require group policies to cover newborns from the moment of birth, even if the insured individual's coverage does not specifically include dependents. Furthermore, many states require policies to cover adopted children from the date of custody. Generally, these provisions specifically require insurers to cover costs of premature birth, birth abnormalities, or congenital defects. The insurers are generally permitted to require that the insured individual notify them of a birth within a certain time period, and the insurers are also usually allowed to require a supplemental premium to cover the additional dependent.

**Continuation of Coverage for Dependents.** Most states require group health policies to cover mentally retarded or physically handicapped dependents of individual policyholders. Often, insurance policies specify that dependents are covered only until they attain a certain age, usually 18 or 21. State regulations, however, frequently provide that when a policy includes coverage for dependents, the insurer cannot terminate coverage of a handicapped child who is dependent on the policyholder for support, regardless of the age of that child.

**Pregnancy Benefits.** Some states require group health policies to cover pregnancy and maternity care under certain circumstances. In Virginia, for example, group accident insurance must cover pregnancy care in cases of rape or incest. In 1995 and 1996, many states passed statutes providing that if maternity is covered, a postdelivery hospital stay must be covered. In September 1996, Congress passed a bill with essentially the same provisions. The federal law mandates that a post-delivery stay of at least 48 hours be covered by the insurer.

**Fertility Treatment.** A few states specifically require group policies to cover the costs of fertility treatment, including in vitro fertilization.

**Preventive Health Care for Children.** Several states require group health policies to offer comprehensive care for children, such as routine examinations, lab tests, and immunizations.

The states' requirements are shown in Table 5.2-4.

### [h] Specified Diseases or Medical Conditions

Many states have enacted provisions requiring insurers to cover certain specified diseases or medical conditions, such as Alzheimer's disease or temporomandibular joint and craniomandibular disorders. (See Table 5.2-5.)

### [i] Specified Medical or Surgical Procedures

Some states specify the types of medical or surgical procedures or diagnostic tests that must be covered under any insurance policy. For example, states have required that group health policies include coverage for such diverse procedures as organ transplants and sterilization. (See Table 5.2-6.)

### [j] Coverage at Home or at a Specified Facility

A number of states have enacted legislation requiring that group health insurance policies include coverage for more generalized courses of treatment at certain locations. The most popular provision is coverage for home health care. However, some states also provide for coverage of nursing home care or care at an ambulatory surgical center. (See Table 5.2-7.)

### [k] Reimbursement of Specified Providers

Many states require that group health insurance policies provide for reimbursement of services of health care providers when the particular services provided are specifically covered under the policy. Thus, some states mandate that insurers reimburse individuals for services provided by such health care professionals as chiropractors, nurse-midwives, dentists, osteopaths, and social workers, when the services provided would be reimbursed under the insurance policy if performed by a physician. (See Table 5.2-8.)

### [l] Drugs and Prosthetic Devices

A few states require that group health insurance policies provide coverage for drugs and prosthetic devices. (See Table 5.2-9.)

### [m] Antidiscrimination Provisions and State Regulation of Utilization Review

Many states have provisions that prohibit insurers from denying or limiting coverage, or refusing to renew policies, to persons suffering from certain medical conditions. Most of these states prohibit insurers from discriminating against persons who are physically or mentally handicapped or blind. Several states also prohibit insurers from discriminating against persons who were exposed to diethylstilbestrol (DES) and persons who are diagnosed as having Acquired Immune Deficiency Syndrome (AIDS) or who have tested positive for the HIV virus. A few states have provisions limiting insurers' ability to deny coverage for a preexisting condition. Generally, these statutes mandate that, after a certain amount of time, coverage may not be denied because a condition existed prior to the insured's date of coverage. Recently, a few states have enacted laws prohibiting insurer discrimination against victims of domestic abuse. Bills on this issue have been introduced into several other state legislatures as well as both houses of Congress. (See Table 5.2-10.)

In addition, some states regulate the process of utilization review, a feature of managed care in which the insurer or utilization review firm determines the need for health care services. State regulation generally takes the form of mandating certain minimum procedures that must be followed by utilization review agents.

# Table 5.2-1
## COVERAGE REQUIREMENTS FOR INSURANCE PLANS OFFERED TO SMALL EMPLOYERS

(States listed in this table have separate statutory requirements for small employers who offer group health insurance.)

**KEY:** **Restrictions on premiums.** The statute provides some method to regulate or restrict the premium rates charged to small employers for a small employer health plan.
**Restrictions on cancellation.** The statute provides that the policy or plan shall be renewable at the option of the small employer, except for reasons such as nonpayment, noncompliance with the policy requirements, or fraud.

| | *Eligibility Criteria* | *Restrictions on* | | *Coverages* | | | | *Citations to Authority* |
|---|---|---|---|---|---|---|---|---|
| | | *Premiums* | *Cancellation* | *Preexisting Conditions* | *Minimum Inpatient* | *Minimum Outpatient* | *Additional* | |
| AL | Employer who during 50% of the preceding quarter employed at least 2 but not more than 50 employees, the majority of whom were employed within the state. | — | — | — | Requirements of small employer program as provided by regulation. | Requirements of small employer program as provided by regulation. | — | Ala. Code § 27-50-8. |
| AK | Employer who during 50% of the preceding 12 months employed at least 2 but not more than 50 employees, the majority within the state. | Yes. | Yes. | Plan may not deny benefits for a covered individual for losses incurred more than 12 months following the effective date of coverage for a preexisting condition. | State has no statutory requirements. | State has no statutory requirements. | Small employers must be offered a basic and standard health care plan. | Alaska Stat. §§ 21.56.110, 21.56.120, 21.56.140, 21.56.250. |
| AR | Employer who during 50% of the preceding year employed fewer than 25 employees. | Yes. | Yes. | — | — | — | — | Ark. Code Ann. §§ 23-86-101 *et seq.* |

*(Table continues.)*

# Table 5.2-1 *(cont'd)*

## COVERAGE REQUIREMENTS FOR INSURANCE PLANS OFFERED TO SMALL EMPLOYERS

(States listed in this table have separate statutory requirements for small employers who offer group health insurance.)

**KEY:** **Restrictions on premiums.** The statute provides some method to regulate or restrict the premium rates charged to small employers for a small employer health plan.
**Restrictions on cancellation.** The statute provides that the policy or plan shall be renewable at the option of the small employer, except for reasons such as nonpayment, noncompliance with the policy requirements, or fraud.

| | | *Restrictions on* | | *Coverages* | | | | |
|---|---|---|---|---|---|---|---|---|
| | *Eligibility Criteria* | *Premiums* | *Cancellation* | *Preexisting Conditions* | *Minimum Inpatient* | *Minimum Outpatient* | *Additional* | *Citations to Authority* |
| CA | Employer with at least 3, but no more than 50, employees on at least 50% of the preceding quarter's working days, the majority being employed in the state; any guaranteed association. | Yes. | Yes. | Preexisting condition provision shall not exclude coverage for a period beyond 6 months following the effective date of coverage with credit toward the 6 months for prior coverage if any break in coverage was less than 63 days. | State has no statutory requirements. | State has no statutory requirements. | Statute does not limit the application of other provisions in the insurance code. | Cal. Health & Safety Code Ann. § 1357.06 Cal. Ins. Code Ann. §§ 10700 *et seq.* |
| CO | Employer who during 50% of the preceding quarter employed no more than 50 employees, the majority within the state. | Yes. | Yes. | No provision relating specifically to small employer health plans. | State has no statutory requirements. | State has no statutory requirements. | Small employers are exempt from requirement of mandatory coverage of mental health benefits but insurer may offer coverage for mental health benefits. Children's preventive care must be covered. | Col. Rev. Stat. §§ 10-16-102, 10-16-104, 10-16-105. |
| CT | Employer must have employed no more than 50 employees, the majority being employed in the | Yes. | Yes. | Preexisting condition provision may not exclude coverage more than 12 months following the ef- | Form and level of coverage for small employer health care plans shall be established by the | None. | None. | Conn. Gen. Stat. Ann. §§ 38a-564, 38a-565, 38a-567, 38a-568. |

| | | | | | | | | |
|---|---|---|---|---|---|---|---|---|
| | state, on at least 50% of its working days in the preceding 12 months. | | | fective date of coverage. | board of directors of the small employer health insurance pool. | | | |
| DE | Employer who on 50% of its working days the preceding quarter employed no more than 50 employees, the majority being in the state. | Yes. | Yes. | Coverage must not be denied for losses incurred more than 12 months following the effective date of coverage due to a preexisting condition. | Basic coverage shall be offered according to guidelines created by the Health Benefit Plan Committee. | Basic coverage shall be offered according to guidelines created by the Health Benefit Plan Committee. | No other law mandating particular coverage shall apply to plans offered pursuant to this act. | Del. Code Ann. tit. 18 §§ 7201, 7205, 7206, 7207, 7211, 7213. |
| FL | Employer who on 50% of its work days in the preceding quarter employed not more than 50 employees, the majority being in the state. | Yes. | Yes. | Preexisting condition provisions must not exclude coverage more than 12 months following effective date of coverage. | Standard and basic health benefit plans must include inpatient coverage, subject to cost containment measures. | Standard and basic health benefit plans must include outpatient services, subject to cost containment measures. | Standard and basic health benefit plans must include coverage for newborn children, child care services, adopted children, mammograms, handicapped children, hospice, and emergency care out of geographic service area. Plans must also exclude coverage for services not medically necessary and must provide for preauthorization and continuation coverage. | Fla. Stat. Ann. §§ 627.6692, 627.6699. |
| GA | Employer must have 50 or fewer employees. | Yes. | No statutory requirements. | Coverage for named impairments may be waived. | No statutory requirements. | No statutory requirements. | No statutory requirements. | Ga. Code Ann. § 33-30-12. |
| ID | Employer who during 50% of its working days the previous quarter employed at least 2 but no more than 50 full-time employees, the majority within the state. | Yes. | Yes. | Benefits shall not be denied for covered expenses incurred over 12 months following the effective date of coverage due to a preexisting condition. | Basic coverage shall be offered according to guidelines created by the Health Benefit Plan Committee. | Basic coverage shall be offered according to guidelines created by the Health Benefit Plan Committee. | No law mandating coverage of specific benefits shall apply to plans offered pursuant to this act. | Id. Code §§ 41-4703, 41-4706, 41-4707, 41-4708. |

*(Table continues.)*

# Table 5.2-1 *(cont'd)*

## COVERAGE REQUIREMENTS FOR INSURANCE PLANS OFFERED TO SMALL EMPLOYERS

(States listed in this table have separate statutory requirements for small employers who offer group health insurance.)

**KEY:** **Restrictions on premiums.** The statute provides some method to regulate or restrict the premium rates charged to small employers for a small employer health plan.
**Restrictions on cancellation.** The statute provides that the policy or plan shall be renewable at the option of the small employer, except for reasons such as nonpayment, noncompliance with the policy requirements, or fraud.

| | *Eligibility Criteria* | *Restrictions on* | | *Coverages* | | | | *Citations to Authority* |
|---|---|---|---|---|---|---|---|---|
| | | *Premiums* | *Cancellation* | *Preexisting Conditions* | *Minimum Inpatient* | *Minimum Outpatient* | *Additional* | |
| IL | Employer must have no more than 25 employees. | No provision relating specifically to small employer health plans. | No provision relating specifically to small employer health plans. | No provision relating specifically to small employer health plans. | Basic coverage as provided under a group plan offered by any authorized insurer. | Basic coverage as provided under a group plan offered by any authorized insurer. | Small employers are exempt from most benefit requirements, but must offer coverage for newborns and adopted dependents and coverage for mammography. | Ill. Ann. Stat. ch. 215 ¶¶ 5/351B, 5/356. |
| IN | Employer who during 50% of its working days the previous year employed at least two but not more than 50 employees. | Yes. | Yes. | Benefits may not be excluded or limited for more than 9 months. | No statutory requirements. | No statutory requirements. | None. | Ind. Stat. Ann. §§ 27-8-15-1 *et seq.* |
| IA | Employer who during 50% of its working days the previous year employed no more than 50 employees. | Yes. | Yes. | No benefits shall be denied for losses incurred more than 12 months following the effective date of coverage due to a preexisting condition. The waiting period is waived if prior coverage existed within 63 days of the enrollment date. | Basic coverage shall be offered according to guidelines adopted by the insurance commissioner. | Basic coverage shall be offered according to guidelines adopted by the insurance commissioner. | No law mandating coverage of specific benefits shall apply to plans offered pursuant to this act. | Iowa Code Ann. §§ 513B.1, 513B.2, 513B.3, 513B.4, 513B.10, 513B.14. |

| | | | | | | | | |
|---|---|---|---|---|---|---|---|---|
| | | | | A genetic condition is not a preexisting condition. | | | | |
| KS | Employer must employ at least two but not more than 50 employees who do not otherwise have health insurance. | No provision relating specifically to small employer health plans. | No provision relating specifically to small employer health plans. | 90-day waiting period, otherwise no exclusion for preexisting condition. | All expenses for sickness or injury exceeding \$5,000 per year per individual or \$7,500 per year per family (inpatient and outpatient combined). | All expenses for sickness or injury exceeding \$5,000 per year per individual or \$7,500 per year per family (inpatient and outpatient combined). | Employees may be required to contribute part of the premium. | Kan. Stat. Ann. §§ 40-2209d, 40-2209f, 40-2240, 40-2241, 40-2243, 40-2244, 40-2245. |
| LA | Employer who during 50% of its working days the preceding year employed no more than three nor more than 35 employees. | Yes. | Yes. | No provision relating specifically to small employer health plans. | No statutory requirements. | No statutory requirements. | None. | La. Rev. Stat. Ann. §§ 22:228.1, 22:250.7. |
| ME | Employer who in the prior year employed fewer than 50 employees, the majority within the state. | Yes. | Yes. | No provision applying specifically to small employer health plans. Permitted to exclude coverage to late enrollees for preexisting conditions. | Basic coverage according to small group health plans defined by superintendent of the Bureau of Insurance. | Basic coverage according to small group health plans defined by superintendent of the Bureau of Insurance. | None. | Me. Rev. Stat. Ann. tit. 24-A, § 2808-B. |
| MD | Employer who during 50% of its working days the preceding year employed at least two but not more than 50 employees, the majority being within the state. | Yes. | Yes. | Coverage may not be limited due to preexisting conditions. | Insurance Commission shall adopt guidelines for a comprehensive standard health benefit plan, but minimum benefits shall be no less than the actuarial equivalent of the minimum benefits required to be offered by a federally qualified health maintenance organization. | Insurance Commission shall adopt guidelines for a comprehensive standard health benefit plan, but minimum benefits shall be no less than the actuarial equivalent of the minimum benefits required to be offered by a federally qualified health maintenance organization. | Subject to contingencies such as certain reports to the governor, the Maryland Health Insurance Reform Act has been amended to apply to all employers with a majority of employees located within the state for at least 50% of its working days the preceding year. | Md. Ins. Code §§ 15-1201 *et seq.* |

*(Table continues.)*

## Table 5.2-1 *(cont'd)*
## COVERAGE REQUIREMENTS FOR INSURANCE PLANS OFFERED TO SMALL EMPLOYERS

(States listed in this table have separate statutory requirements for small employers who offer group health insurance.)

**KEY:** **Restrictions on premiums.** The statute provides some method to regulate or restrict the premium rates charged to small employers for a small employer health plan.
**Restrictions on cancellation.** The statute provides that the policy or plan shall be renewable at the option of the small employer, except for reasons such as nonpayment, noncompliance with the policy requirements, or fraud.

| | | *Restrictions on* | | *Coverages* | | | | |
|---|---|---|---|---|---|---|---|---|
| | *Eligibility Criteria* | *Premiums* | *Cancellation* | *Preexisting Conditions* | *Minimum Inpatient* | *Minimum Outpatient* | *Additional* | *Citations to Authority* |
| MA | Employer who on 50% of its working days during the preceding year employed not more than 25 employees, the majority of whom worked in the commonwealth. A health carrier may choose to offer coverage to an employer with more than 25 employees. | Yes. | Yes. | Six-month waiting period, otherwise no exclusion for preexisting condition. | No statutory requirements. | No statutory requirements. | None. | Mass. Gen. Laws Ann. ch. 176J, § 1 *et seq.* |
| MI | Employer with 2 to 50 employees. | No statutory requirement. | No statutory requirement. | Coverage may be limited for 12 months due to a preexisting condition. | No statutory requirement. | No statutory requirement. | No statutory requirement. | Mich. Stat. Ann. § 24.13406(6). |
| MN | Employer who during 50% of its working days the preceding year employed no fewer than 2 nor more than 49 employees, the majority being within the state. | Yes. | Yes. | No provisions relating specifically to small employer health plans. | Under deductible-type plan, 80% of expenses after a $500 (individual) or $1,000 (family) deductible. Under copayment-type plan, 80% of expenses exceeding each $300 hospital admission. | Health care under deductible-type plan, 80% of expenses after a $500 (individual) or $1,000 (family) deductible. Under copayment-type plan, 80% of expenses exceeding $15 per visit to nonemergency facility and | Plan must also provide coverage for treatment of chemical dependency or mental illness, diagnostics, ambulance service, private nurse if medically necessary, child health, maternity, and medical equipment. | Minn. Stat. Ann. §§ 62L.02, 62L.03, 62L.05, 62L.08. |

| | | | | | | | | |
|---|---|---|---|---|---|---|---|---|
| | | | | | | $50 per visit to emergency facility. | Maximum out-of-pocket expenses shall be $3,000 (individual) or $6,000 (family) per year. Maximum lifetime benefit must be $500,000. | |
| MS | Employer who during 50% of the preceding year employed fewer than 25 employees. | Yes. | — | — | Insurance Commissioner shall approve plans submitted by insurers. | Insurance Commissioner shall approve plans submitted by insurers. | Expenses of hospital and physician must be covered. Small employer plans are not subject to other insurance coverage requirements. | Miss. Code Ann. § 83-9-303. |
| MO | Employer who on at least 50% of its working days the preceding quarter employed not less than 3 nor more than 25 employees, the majority of whom were employed in this state. | Yes. | Yes. | Plan shall not deny or limit benefits for a covered individual for losses incurred over 12 months following the effective date due to a preexisting condition. | Basic coverage to be designed and recommended by Health Benefit Plan Committee. | Basic coverage to be designed and recommended by Health Benefit Plan Committee. | Plan must cover maternity, mammography, newborns, and adopted dependents. | Mo. Rev. Stat. §§ 379.930 *et seq.* |
| MT | Employer with at least two but not more than 50 employees. | Yes. | Yes. | No claim shall be excluded more than 12 months following the effective date of coverage. | Basic or standard coverage as approved by the commissioner. | Basic or standard coverage as approved by the commissioner. | Plan must also cover mammograms, mental health treatment, and chemical dependency. | Mont. Code Ann. §§ 33-22-1202, 33-22-1203, 33-22-1803, 33-22-1809, 33-22-1810, 33-22-1811, 33-22-1827, 33-22-1828. |
| NE | Employer who during 50% of its working days the preceding quarter employed at least two but no more than 50 employees, the majority being within the state. | Yes. | Yes. | No claim shall be excluded more than 12 months following the effective date of coverage due to a preexisting condition. Genetic information is not considered to be a preexisting condition. | Basic coverage according to guidelines created by Health Benefit Plan Committee. | Basic coverage according to guidelines created by Health Benefit Plan Committee. | Coverage must include childhood immunizations. Other insurance coverage laws do not apply. | Neb. Rev. Stat. §§ 44-5229, 44-5230, 44-5246.02, 44-5253, 44-5258, 44-5259, 44-5264. |

(*Table continues.*)

## Table 5.2-1 *(cont'd)*

## COVERAGE REQUIREMENTS FOR INSURANCE PLANS OFFERED TO SMALL EMPLOYERS

(States listed in this table have separate statutory requirements for small employers who offer group health insurance.)

**KEY:** **Restrictions on premiums.** The statute provides some method to regulate or restrict the premium rates charged to small employers for a small employer health plan.
**Restrictions on cancellation.** The statute provides that the policy or plan shall be renewable at the option of the small employer, except for reasons such as nonpayment, noncompliance with the policy requirements, or fraud.

| | *Eligibility Criteria* | *Restrictions on* | | *Coverages* | | | | *Citations to Authority* |
|---|---|---|---|---|---|---|---|---|
| | | *Premiums* | *Cancellation* | *Preexisting Conditions* | *Minimum Inpatient* | *Minimum Outpatient* | *Additional* | |
| NV | Employer who during 50% of its working days in the prior year employed no fewer than 2 and no more than 25 employees. The employer must not have formed primarily for the purpose of purchasing insurance. Small employers may also form purchasing groups. | Yes. | Yes. | Coverage may not be excluded for more than 6 months if the employee enrolls through open enrollment, if the employee is a qualified late enrollee, or if the employee had prior coverage; 12 months if the employee is a late enrollee. | Basic medical and hospital care. | Basic medical and hospital care. | None. | Nev. Rev. Stat. §§ 689C.095, 689C.115, 689C.190, 689C.210, 689C.310, 689C.330, 689C.420. |
| NH | Employer with 1 to 100 employees. | Yes. | Yes. | Preexisting condition provisions shall not apply for any period in excess of 3 consecutive months ending while the plan is effective and in which the individual incurred no medical expenses in connection with the preexisting condition, nor for a period in excess of 9 months follow- | No statutory requirements. | No statutory requirements. | None. | N.H. Rev. Stat. Ann. §§ 420G:2, 420G:4, 420G:7. |

| | | | | | | | | |
|---|---|---|---|---|---|---|---|---|
| | | | | ing the effective date of coverage. | | | | |
| NJ | Employer who on at least 50% of its working days during the preceding quarter employed at least 2 but not more than 49 employees, the majority of whom worked within the state. | Yes. | Yes. | No plan shall contain preexisting condition provisions except as apply to late enrollees. For groups of two to six, prexisting conditions may be excluded for up to 180 days. | Basic coverage, including 21 days of hospitalization per year. | Basic coverage, including 12 physical exams for children under age 18; physical exams for adults (one every five years for ages 18–40, one every five years for ages 40–60, one every two years for ages 40–60, one every two years for ages 60 and older). | Plan must include preventive medicine, maternity benefits, including post-delivery stay of 48 to 96 hours; post-mastectomy stay of 48 to 72 hours; and coverage of metabolic disease formulas. | N.J. Rev. Stat. §§ 17B:27A-17, *et seq.* |
| NM | Employer who during 50% of the working days the preceding year employed no less than 2 nor more than 50 employees. | Yes. | Yes. | Coverage for losses shall not be excluded more than 6 months following effective date of coverage due to a preexisting condition. Individual must be given credit towards the 6 months for prior coverage if the prior coverage ended no more than 63 days before the current coverage began. | Hospitalization or combination of hospitalization and home care up to 25 days per year. | Basic coverage including 14 office visits for prenatal care per pregnancy plus diagnostic tests and counselling; 7 office visits per year for primary and preventive care. | Coverage must include well-baby, well-child care, immunizations, and mammography. | N.M. Stat. Ann. §§ 59A-23B-3, 59A-23C-3, 59A-23C-5, 59A-23C-5.1, 59A-23C-7.1. |
| NC | Employer who on at least 50% of its working days during the preceding quarter employed no more than 49 employees, the majority within the state. | Yes. | Yes. | Preexisting conditions provision may not limit coverage beyond 12 months following the initial effective date. | Basic coverage as approved by the insurance commissioner either in the form of insurance or in a form consistent with the basic method of operation of health maintenance organizations. | Basic coverage as approved by the insurance commissioner either in the form of insurance or in a form consistent with the basic method of operation of health maintenance organizations. | Plan must include coverage for mammograms, Pap smears, reconstructive breast surgery, and prostate-specific antigen tests. | N.C. Gen. Stat. Ann. §§ 58-50-110, 58-50-120, 58-50-125, 58-50-130, 58-50-155, 58-68-40, 58-68-45. |

*(Table continues.)*

# Table 5.2-1 *(cont'd)*

## COVERAGE REQUIREMENTS FOR INSURANCE PLANS OFFERED TO SMALL EMPLOYERS

(States listed in this table have separate statutory requirements for small employers who offer group health insurance.)

**KEY:** **Restrictions on premiums.** The statute provides some method to regulate or restrict the premium rates charged to small employers for a small employer health plan.
**Restrictions on cancellation.** The statute provides that the policy or plan shall be renewable at the option of the small employer, except for reasons such as nonpayment, noncompliance with the policy requirements, or fraud.

| | *Eligibility Criteria* | *Restrictions on* | | *Coverages* | | | | *Citations to Authority* |
|---|---|---|---|---|---|---|---|---|
| | | *Premiums* | *Cancellation* | *Preexisting Conditions* | *Minimum Inpatient* | *Minimum Outpatient* | *Additional* | |
| ND | Employer who during 50% of its workdays the previous quarter employed at least 3 but no more than 25 employees, the majority within the state. | Yes. | Yes. | Plan may not limit benefits for losses incurred more than 12 months following the effective date of coverage due to preexisting conditions. Individual must be given credit towards the 12 months for prior coverage, if the prior coverage ended no more than 63 days before the current coverage began. | Basic coverage as provided under a small group health plan approved by the insurance commissioner. | Basic coverage as provided under a small group health plan approved by the insurance commissioner. | Small employer plans are not required to cover substance abuse and mental health treatment, temporomandibular and craniomandibular joint treatment, mammography. These benefits must be offered to employees at employee expense. Other insurance coverage laws do not apply. | N.D. Cent. Code §§ 26.1-36.3-01, 26.1-36.3-04, 26.1-36.3-05, 26.1-36.3-06, 26.1-36.3-10. |
| OH | Employer who on at least 50% of its working days in the preceding year employed at least 2 but not more than 25 employees, the majority being in the state. | Yes. | Yes. | Preexisting condition provisions shall not exclude or limit coverage beyond 12 months following the individual's effective date of coverage. | Basic coverage as provided under a small employer health plan adopted by the board of directors of the small employer health reinsurance plan. | Basic coverage as provided under a small employer health plan adopted by the board of directors of the small employer health reinsurance plan. | None. | Oh. Rev. Code Ann. §§ 3924.01, 3924.02, 3924.03, 3924.04, 3924.10. |

| | | | | | | | | |
|---|---|---|---|---|---|---|---|---|
| OK | Employer who during 50% of its working days the preceding quarter employed no more than 50 employees, the majority within the state. | Yes. | Yes. | Preexisting condition provisions shall not exclude or limit coverage beyond 12 months following the individual's effective date of coverage. | Basic coverage as provided by any approved health benefit plan. | Basic coverage as provided by any approved health benefit plan. | None. | Ok. Stat. Ann. tit. 36 §§ 6512, 6515, 6516, 6519. |
| OR | Employer who during 50% of the working days in the preceding quarter employed no fewer than 3 and no more than 25 employees, the majority being within the state. | Yes. | Yes. | No exclusion of coverage more than 6 months following the effective date of coverage due to a preexisting condition. | Basic coverage as provided under a small group plan approved by the director of insurance. | Basic coverage as provided under a small group plan approved by the director of insurance. | Coverage must include treatment of substance abuse and mental and nervous conditions. | Or. Rev. Stat. §§ 743.730, 743.736, 743.737. |
| RI | Employer who during 50% of its working days the preceding quarter employed no more than 50 employees, the majority within the state. | Yes. | Yes. | Plan shall not limit benefits for losses incurred more than 12 months following the effective date of coverage due to a preexisting condition. | Under the economy plan, up to 20 days of inpatient care per year, including inpatient psychiatric and substance abuse care. | Under economy plan, outpatient care includes 4 office visits per year, 20 visits per year for psychiatric or substance abuse care, up to 20 visits per year of home nursing care. | Standard and economy plan are not subject to other mandated benefits. Economy plan must cover well-baby and well-child care, maternity care, screening for newborn metabolic and sickle-cell anemia, mammography, and Pap tests. | R.I. Gen. Laws §§ 27-50-3, 27-50-6, 27-50-7, 27-50-8, 27-50-12, 27-50-14. |
| SC | Employer who during 50% of the preceding year employed no more than 50 and no fewer than 2 employees. | Yes. | Yes. | Yes. Preexisting conditions must be covered within 12 months. | Coverage under a basic or standard plan as offered by any approved health benefit plan. | Coverage under a basic or standard plan as offered by any approved health benefit plan. | Insurers must offer a choice of at least two plans. Plans are not exempted from other insurance coverage laws. | S.C. Code Ann. §§ 38-71-1310 *et seq.* |
| SD | Employer who during 50% of its working days the preceding year employed no more than 50 and no fewer than 2 employees. | Yes. | No provision relating specifically to small employer health plans. | No provision relating specifically to small employer health plans. | Basic coverage as offered by any approved health benefit plan. | Basic coverage as offered by any approved health benefit plan. | Postdelivery stay of 48 to 96 hours. Plans may not be modified with respect to a particular person or disease. | S.D. Cod. Laws. Ann. §§ 58-18B-1, 58-18B-2, 58-18B-3. |

*(Table continues.)*

## Table 5.2-1 *(cont'd)*

## COVERAGE REQUIREMENTS FOR INSURANCE PLANS OFFERED TO SMALL EMPLOYERS

(States listed in this table have separate statutory requirements for small employers who offer group health insurance.)

**KEY:** **Restrictions on premiums.** The statute provides some method to regulate or restrict the premium rates charged to small employers for a small employer health plan.
**Restrictions on cancellation.** The statute provides that the policy or plan shall be renewable at the option of the small employer, except for reasons such as nonpayment, noncompliance with the policy requirements, or fraud.

| | *Eligibility Criteria* | *Restrictions on* | | *Coverages* | | | | *Citations to Authority* |
|---|---|---|---|---|---|---|---|---|
| | | *Premiums* | *Cancellation* | *Preexisting Conditions* | *Minimum Inpatient* | *Minimum Outpatient* | *Additional* | |
| TN | Employer who on at least 50% of its working days the preceding year employed not less than 3 and no more than 25 employees, the majority within the state. | Yes. | Yes. | Preexisting condition provision may not limit coverage beyond 12 months following the insured's effective date of coverage. | Basic coverage as approved by the insurance commissioner either in the form of insurance or in a form consistent with the basic method of operation of health maintenance organizations. | Basic coverage as approved by the insurance commissioner either in the form of insurance or in a form consistent with the basic method of operation of health maintenance organizations. | Mandated coverage in the basic plan is limited to that which is essential to the provision of basic primary care. | Tenn. Code Ann. §§ 56-7-2203, 56-7-2208, 56-7-2209. |
| TX | Employer who during 50% of the preceding year employed at least two but no more than 50 employees, the majority being in state. | Yes. | Yes. | Preexisting condition provision may not apply to expenses incurred after 12 months following the effective date of coverage. Individual must be given credit toward the 12 months for prior coverage, if the prior coverage ended no more than 63 days before the current coverage began. | Hospitalization of up to 5 days per policy per year required for basic plan. | State has no statutory requirements. | Small employers must be offered 3 types of plans. | Tex. Ins. Code arts. 26.02, 26.06(c), 26.21, 26.42, 26.49. |

| | | | | | | | | |
|---|---|---|---|---|---|---|---|---|
| UT | Employer who during 50% of its working days the previous quarter employed at least 1 and no more than 50 employees, the majority within the state. | Yes. | Yes. | Plan shall not exclude losses incurred more than 12 months following coverage due to preexisting conditions. | Basic coverage as provided by an approved health benefit plan. | Basic coverage as provided by an approved health benefit plan. | None. | Utah Code Ann. §§ 31A-30-103, 31A-30-106, 31A-30-107. |
| VT | Employer who during 50% of its working days the preceding quarter employed at least 1 but no more than 50 employees. | Yes. | No provision relating specifically to small employer health plans. | Plan may not deny coverage for losses incurred more than 12 months following the effective date of coverage due to preexisting conditions. Individual must be given credit towards the 12 months for prior coverage, if the prior coverage ended no more than 90 days before the current coverage began. | Basic coverage according to guidelines approved by the insurance commissioner. | Basic coverage according to guidelines approved by the insurance commissioner. | None. | Vt. Stat. Ann. tit. 8, § 4080a. |
| VA | Employer who during 50% of its working days the preceding year employed at least two unrelated employees, but not more than 25 employees. | Yes. | Yes. | Must be covered after 12 months. | Essential or standard plan as approved by insurance commissioner. | Essential or standard plan as approved by insurance commissioner. | Other insurance laws do not apply. | Va. Code Ann. § 38.2-3431. |
| WA | Employer must have fewer than 25 employees. | Yes. | No provision relating specifically to small employer health plans. | No provision relating specifically to small employer health plans. | Basic coverage as provided under a small group policy consistent with administrative regulations. | Basic coverage as provided under a small group policy consistent with administrative regulations. | Small employer insurance exempt from other mandated benefits. | Wash. Rev. Code Ann. § 48.21.045; Wash. Admin. Code R. 284-49-010. |
| WV | Employer who during 50% of the preceding year employed no more than 50 and no fewer than 2 employees. | Yes. | Yes. | Yes. Preexisting conditions must be covered within 12 months. | — | — | Child immunization services must be provided. | W.V. Code Ann. §§ 33-16D-1 *et seq.* |

*(Table continues.)*

## Table 5.2-1 *(cont'd)*

## COVERAGE REQUIREMENTS FOR INSURANCE PLANS OFFERED TO SMALL EMPLOYERS

(States listed in this table have separate statutory requirements for small employers who offer group health insurance.)

**KEY:** **Restrictions on premiums.** The statute provides some method to regulate or restrict the premium rates charged to small employers for a small employer health plan.
**Restrictions on cancellation.** The statute provides that the policy or plan shall be renewable at the option of the small employer, except for reasons such as nonpayment, noncompliance with the policy requirements, or fraud.

| | | *Restrictions on* | | *Coverages* | | | | |
|---|---|---|---|---|---|---|---|---|
| | *Eligibility Criteria* | *Premiums* | *Cancellation* | *Preexisting Conditions* | *Minimum Inpatient* | *Minimum Outpatient* | *Additional* | *Citations to Authority* |
| WI | Employer with not fewer than 2 nor more than 25 employees. | Yes. | Yes. | Plan may not deny coverage for losses incurred more than 12 months following the effective date of coverage due to a preexisting condition. | Basic coverage as provided by the plan formulated by the Small Employer Insurance Board. | Basic coverage as provided by the plan formulated by the Small Employer Insurance Board. | Health insurance mandates apply only to the extent determined by the board. | Wis. Stat. Ann. §§ 635.02, 635.05, 635.07, 635.17, 635.23, 635.29. |
| WY | Employer who during 50% of its working days the preceding quarter employed at least 2 but not more than 25 employees, the majority within the state. | Yes. | Yes. | Plan shall not exclude coverage for a period beyond 12 months following the individual's effective date of coverage due to a preexisting condition. | Basic coverage according to guidelines recommended by health benefit committee. | Basic coverage according to guidelines recommended by health benefit committee. | None. | Wyo. Stat. § 26-19-301. |

# Table 5.2-2
## MANDATORY COVERAGE FOR ALCOHOL AND/OR DRUG ABUSE TREATMENT

(See also text at § 5.2[e].)

**KEY:** **Mandatory coverage.** All group policies must include coverage for this benefit.
**Employer option.** Insurance companies must offer policyholders (employers) this benefit option, but employers may choose not to cover employees for this particular benefit.
**Intermediate care.** In Michigan, means the use of statutorily specified therapies such as chemotherapy, counseling, detoxification, and other ancillary services such as medical testing, diagnostic evaluation, and referral in a residential therapy setting.

| | *Type of Coverage* | *Minimum Yearly Inpatient Coverage* | *Minimum Yearly Outpatient Coverage* | *Minimum Lifetime Coverage* | *Citations to Authority* |
|---|---|---|---|---|---|
| AL | Employer option (alcoholism treatment only). | 30 days inpatient or equivalent (1 day inpatient equals 2 days at short-term residential facility or 3 days outpatient treatment). | 30 days inpatient or equivalent (1 day inpatient equals 2 days at short-term residential facility or 3 days outpatient treatment). | State has no statutory requirements. | Ala. Code § 27-20A-4. |
| AK | Mandatory coverage. | $9,600 over 24 months for inpatient and outpatient combined. | $7,000 over 24 months for inpatient and outpatient combined. | $19,200. | Alaska Stat. § 21.42.365. |
| AZ | — | — | — | — | State has no statutory provisions. |
| AR | Employer option. | $6,000 over 24 months for inpatient and outpatient combined. | $6,000 over 24 months for inpatient and outpatient combined. | $12,000. | Ark. Stat. Ann. § 23-79-139. |
| CA | Employer option (alcoholism treatment only). | State has no statutory requirements. | State has no statutory requirements. | State has no statutory requirements. | Cal. Ins. Code § 10123.6. |
| CO | Employer option (alcoholism treatment only). | 45 days. | $500. | State has no statutory requirements. | Colo. Rev. Stat. § 10-16-104(9). |
| CT | Mandatory coverage. | 45 days. | State has no statutory requirements. | State has no statutory requirements. | Conn. Gen. Stat. Ann. §§ 38a-533, 38a-539. |
| DE | — | — | — | — | State has no statutory provisions. |
| DC | Mandatory coverage. | 28 days, plus 12 days for detoxification. | 30 visits. | State has no statutory requirements. | D.C. Code Ann. §§ 35-2302, 35-2303. |
| FL | Employer option. | State has no statutory requirements. | State has no statutory requirements. | $2,000. | Fla. Stat. Ann. § 627.669. |
| GA | — | — | — | — | State has no statutory provisions. |

(*Table continues.*)

# Table 5.2-2 *(cont'd)*

## MANDATORY COVERAGE FOR ALCOHOL AND/OR DRUG ABUSE TREATMENT

(See also text at § 5.2[e].)

**KEY:** **Mandatory coverage.** All group policies must include coverage for this benefit.
**Employer option.** Insurance companies must offer policyholders (employers) this benefit option, but employers may choose not to cover employees for this particular benefit.
**Intermediate care.** In Michigan, means the use of statutorily specified therapies such as chemotherapy, counseling, detoxification, and other ancillary services such as medical testing, diagnostic evaluation, and referral in a residential therapy setting.

| | *Type of Coverage* | *Minimum Yearly Inpatient Coverage* | *Minimum Yearly Outpatient Coverage* | *Minimum Lifetime Coverage* | *Citations to Authority* |
|---|---|---|---|---|---|
| HI | Mandatory coverage. | 30 days inpatient or 60 days partial hospitalization (2 days partial equals 1 day inpatient; 2 days outpatient equals 1 day inpatient). | 12 visits and 30 physician or psychologist visits. | 2 treatment sessions. | Haw. Rev. Stat. §§ 431M-2, 431M-4. Note: Statutes are currently scheduled to be repealed as of 7/1/98. |
| ID | — | — | — | — | State has no statutory provisions. |
| IL | Mandatory coverage (alcoholism treatment only). | State has no statutory requirements. | State has no statutory requirements. | State has no statutory requirements. | Ill. Ann. Stat. ch. 215, ¶ 5/367(7). |
| IN | — | — | — | — | State has no statutory provisions. |
| IA | — | — | — | — | State has no statutory provisions. |
| KS | Mandatory coverage. | 30 days (applies to mental health coverage combined with alcoholism and drug abuse treatment). | 100% of first $100, 80% of next $100, 50% of next $1,640 (applies to mental health coverage combined with alcoholism and drug abuse treatment). | $7,500. | Kan. Stat. Ann. § 40-2,105. |
| KY | Employer option (alcoholism treatment only). | Emergency detoxification: 3 days at $40 per day; residential treatment: 10 days at $50 per day. | 10 visits at $10 per visit. | State has no statutory requirements. | Ky. Rev. Stat. Ann. §§ 304.18-130, 304.18-140. |
| LA | Employer option. | State has no statutory requirements. | State has no statutory requirements. | State has no statutory requirements. | La. Rev. Stat. Ann. § 22:215.5. |
| ME | Mandatory coverage. | State has no statutory requirements. | State has no statutory requirements. | State has no statutory requirements. | Me. Rev. Stat. Ann. 24-A § 2842. |
| MD | Mandatory coverage. | Same terms as for physical illness, with at least 60 days partial hospitalization. | 80% coverage for first 5 visits; 65% of 6 to 30 visits; 50% coverage for visits beyond 30. | Same as for physical illness. | Md. Ins. Code § 15-802. |

| | | | | | |
|---|---|---|---|---|---|
| MA | Mandatory coverage (alcoholism treatment only). | 30 days. | $500. | State has no statutory requirements. | Mass. Gen. Laws Ann. ch. 175, § 110(H). |
| MI | Mandatory coverage for intermediate and outpatient care; coverage for inpatient care is a required option. Policyholder may decline coverage if premium increases 3% or more. | State has no statutory requirements. | $1,500 for intermediate and outpatient combined. | State has no statutory requirements. | Mich. Stat. Ann. §§ 24.13425, 24.13609(1). |
| MN | Mandatory coverage. | 20% of total patient days allowed or 28 days. | 130 hours. | State has no statutory requirements. | Minn. Stat. Ann. § 62A.149. |
| MS | Mandatory coverage (alcoholism treatment only). | State has no statutory requirements. | State has no statutory requirements. | State has no statutory requirements. | Miss. Code Ann. §§ 83-9-27, 83-9-31. |
| MO | Employer option. | 21 days. | 26 days. | 10 episodes, not including detoxification in life-threatening situations. | Mo. Rev. Stat. §§ 376.779, 376.811. |
| MT | Mandatory coverage. | 30 days per year for mental health coverage and substance abuse treatment combined; and $4,000 per 24 months for substance abuse (alcoholism and drug abuse) treatment. | $1,000 for mental health coverage and substance abuse treatment combined. | $8,000 for substance abuse. | Mont. Code. Ann. § 33-22-703. |
| NE | Employer option (alcoholism treatment only). | 30 days. | State has no statutory requirements. | 2 inpatient treatments; 60 outpatient visits. | Neb. Rev. Stat. §§ 44-769, 44-778, 44-779, 44-780, 44-781. |
| NV | Mandatory coverage. | State has no statutory requirements. | State has no statutory requirements. | State has no statutory requirements. | Nev. Rev. Stat. §§ 689B.030, 689B.036. |
| NH | — | — | — | — | State has no statutory provisions. |
| NJ | Mandatory coverage (alcoholism treatment only). | State has no statutory requirements. | State has no statutory requirements. | No less than lifetime maximum for physical illness. | N.J. Rev. Stat. § 17B:27-46.1. |
| NM | Employer option (alcoholism treatment only). | 30 days. | 30 visits. | 2 benefit periods. | N.M. Stat. Ann. § 59A-23-6. |
| NY | Employer option. | Detoxification: 7 days; rehabilitation: 30 days. | 60 visits. | State has no statutory requirements. | N.Y. Ins. Law §§ 3221 (l)(6)(A), 3221 (l)(6)(B), 3221 (l)(7). |
| NC | Employer option. | $8,000 per 12 months for inpatient and outpatient combined. | $8,000 per 12 months for inpatient and outpatient combined. | $16,000. | N.C. Gen. Stat. § 58-51-50. |
| ND | Mandatory coverage. | Inpatient: 60 days; partial hospitalization: 120 days. | 20 visits. | State has no statutory requirements. | N.D. Cent. Code § 26.1-36-08. |
| OH | Mandatory coverage (alcoholism treatment only). | $550 for inpatient and outpatient combined. | $550 for inpatient and outpatient combined. | State has no statutory requirements. | Ohio Rev. Code Ann. § 3923.29. |
| OK | — | — | — | — | State has no statutory provisions. |

*(Table continues.)*

# Table 5.2-2 *(cont'd)*

## MANDATORY COVERAGE FOR ALCOHOL AND/OR DRUG ABUSE TREATMENT

(See also text at § 5.2[e].)

**KEY:** **Mandatory coverage.** All group policies must include coverage for this benefit.
**Employer option.** Insurance companies must offer policyholders (employers) this benefit option, but employers may choose not to cover employees for this particular benefit.
**Intermediate care.** In Michigan, means the use of statutorily specified therapies such as chemotherapy, counseling, detoxification, and other ancillary services such as medical testing, diagnostic evaluation, and referral in a residential therapy setting.

| | *Type of Coverage* | *Minimum Yearly Inpatient Coverage* | *Minimum Yearly Outpatient Coverage* | *Minimum Lifetime Coverage* | *Citations to Authority* |
|---|---|---|---|---|---|
| OR | Mandatory coverage. | State has no statutory requirements. | State has no statutory requirements. | Inpatient: $4,500 for adults, $4,000 for children (for hospitalization); $3,500 for adults, $3,000 for children (for residential programs); outpatient: $1,500 for adults, $2,000 for children; inpatient and outpatient combined: $8,500 for adults or children. | Or. Rev. Stat. § 743.556. |
| PA | Mandatory coverage. | 30 days. | 30 visits. | Inpatient: 90 days; outpatient: 120 days; 4 detoxification visits of up to 7 days. | Pa. Stat. Ann. tit. 40, §§ 908-2, 908-3, 908-4, 908-5. |
| RI | Mandatory coverage. | Detoxification: 3 occurrences or 21 days; rehabilitation: 30 days. | 30 hours per individual; 20 hours per family member. | 90 days intensive rehabilitation. | R.I. Gen. Laws § 27-38-1. |
| SC | Employer option of coverage for alcohol and drug abuse and mental illness; benefits of $2,000 per year for total coverage. | — | — | $10,000. | S.C. Code Ann. § 38-71-737. |
| SD | Employer option (alcoholism treatment only). | State has no statutory requirements. | State has no statutory requirements. | State has no statutory requirements. | S.D. Codified Laws Ann. §§ 58-18-7.1, 58-18-7.2. |
| TN | Employer option. | Policy must provide coverage that is no less than the coverage it provides for physical illness. | Policy must provide coverage that is no less than the coverage it provides for physical illness. | State has no statutory requirements. | Tenn. Code Ann. §§ 56-7-1009, 56-7-2601, 56-7-2602. |
| TX | Mandatory coverage. | Policy must provide coverage that is no less than the coverage it provides for physical illness. | Policy must provide coverage that is no less than the coverage it provides for physical illness. | 3 separate series of treatments for each covered individual. | Tex. Ins. Code Ann. art. 3.51-9. |

| | | | | | |
|---|---|---|---|---|---|
| UT | Employer option. | State has no statutory requirements. | State has no statutory requirements. | State has no statutory requirements. | Utah Code Ann. § 31A-22-715. |
| VT | Mandatory coverage (alcoholism treatment only). | Detoxification: 5 days per occurrence; inpatient and rehabilitation: 28 days per occurrence. | 90 hours per occurrence for patient and family. | Inpatient and rehabilitation: 56 days; outpatient: 180 hours for patient and family. | Vt. Stat. Ann. tit. 8, § 4098. |
| VA | Mandatory coverage. | 20 days for adults; 25 days for children. | 20 visits. | No less than lifetime maximum for physical illness, with 50% or more coinsurance for outpatient visits after the first 5 visits. | Va. Code Ann. § 38.2-3412.1. |
| WA | Mandatory coverage. | State has no statutory requirements. | State has no statutory requirements. | State has no statutory requirements. | Wash. Rev. Code § 48.21.180. |
| WV | Employer option (alcoholism treatment only). | 30 days. | $750. Outpatient coinsurance factor may not exceed 50% of coinsurance factor for physical illness generally. | $10,000 or 25% of the lifetime policy limit, whichever is less. | W. Va. Code § 33-16-3c. |
| WI | Mandatory coverage. | Lesser of 30 days or $7,000 (applies to nervous and mental disorders combined with alcoholism and drug treatment). | $2,000 (applies to nervous and mental disorders combined with alcoholism and drug treatment). | State has no statutory requirements. | Wis. Stat. Ann. § 632.89. |
| WY | — | — | — | — | State has no statutory provisions. |

# Table 5.2-3
## MANDATORY COVERAGE FOR MENTAL HEALTH TREATMENT

(See also text at § 5.2[f].)

**KEY:** **Mandatory coverage.** All group policies must include coverage for this benefit.
**Employer option.** Insurance companies must offer policyholders (employers) this benefit option, but employers may choose not to cover employees for this particular benefit.

| | *Type of Coverage* | *Minimum Yearly Inpatient Coverage* | *Minimum Yearly Outpatient Coverage* | *Minimum Lifetime Coverage* | *Citations to Authority* |
|---|---|---|---|---|---|
| AL | — | — | — | — | State has no statutory provisions. |
| AK | Employer option, for large employers. | — | — | No less than coverage for physical illness. | Alaska Stat. § 21.54.150. |
| AZ | — | — | — | — | State has no statutory provisions. |
| AR | Employer option; statute requires minimum coverage if conditions arising from mental illness are covered. | $7,500 for inpatient and outpatient combined. | $7,500 for inpatient and outpatient combined. | No less than lifetime maximum for physical illness. | Ark. Stat. Ann. § 23-86-113. |
| CA | Employer option, for specified disorders. | State has no statutory requirements. | State has no statutory requirements. | State has no statutory requirements. | Cal. Ins. Code §§ 10123.15, 10125. |
| CO | Mandatory coverage. | 45 days inpatient or 90 days partial hospitalization. | $1,000. | For biologically based mental illness, no less than coverage for physical illness. | Colo. Rev. Stat. §§ 10-16-104(5), 10-16-104(5.5). |
| CT | Mandatory coverage. | 60 days inpatient or 120 days partial hospitalization (2 days partial equals 1 day inpatient). | 50% coverage up to $2,000; additional coverage must be offered policyholder as option. | State has no statutory requirements. | Conn. Gen. Stat. Ann. § 38a-514. |
| DE | — | — | — | Insurers may comply with federal mental health parity laws. | Del. Code Ann. tit. 18, § 3564. |
| DC | Mandatory coverage. | 45 days. | 75% coverage for first 40 visits; 60% thereafter. | The greater of $80,000 or one third of the lifetime maximum for physical illness. | D.C. Code Ann. §§ 35-2302, 35-2304, 35-2305. |
| FL | Employer option. | 30 days. | $1,000. | State has no statutory requirements. | Fla. Stat. Ann. § 627.668. |
| GA | Employer option. | State has no statutory requirements. | State has no statutory requirements. | No less than lifetime maximum for physical illness. | Ga. Code Ann. § 33-24-28.1. |

| | | | | | |
|---|---|---|---|---|---|
| HI | Mandatory coverage. | 30 days inpatient or 60 days partial hospitalization (2 days partial equals 1 day inpatient; 2 days outpatient equals 1 day inpatient). | 12 visits and 30 physician or psychologist visits. | 2 treatment episodes. | Haw. Rev. Stat. §§ 431M-2, 431M-4. Note: Statutes are currently scheduled to be repealed as of 7/1/98. |
| ID | — | — | — | — | State has no statutory provisions. |
| IL | Employer option. | Lesser of $10,000 for inpatient and outpatient combined or 25% of lifetime policy limits. | Lesser of $10,000 for inpatient and outpatient combined or 25% of lifetime policy limits. | No less than lifetime maximum for physical illness. | Ill. Ann. Stat. ch. 215, ¶ 5/370C. |
| IN | — | — | — | If mental health benefits are provided, no less coverage than for physical illness. | Ind. Code Ann. § 27-8-5-15.6. |
| IA | — | — | — | — | State has no statutory provisions. |
| KS | Mandatory coverage. | 30 days; applies to combined mental health and substance abuse treatment. | 100% of first $100; 80% of next $100; 50% of next $1,640; applies to combined mental health and substance abuse treatment. | $7,500 or no less than coverage for physical illness. | Kan. Stat. Ann. §§ 40-2,105, 40-2258. |
| KY | Employer option. | Policy must provide coverage that is no less than the coverage it provides for physical illness. | Policy must provide coverage that is no less than the coverage it provides for physical illness. | No less than lifetime maximum for physical illness. | Ky. Rev. Stat. Ann. § 304.18-036. |
| LA | Employer option. | Policy must provide coverage that is no less than the coverage it provides for physical illness. | Policy must provide coverage that is no less than the coverage it provides for physical illness. | No less than lifetime maximum for physical illness. | La. Rev. Stat. Ann. §§ 22:250.5, 22:669. |
| ME | Mandatory coverage. | 60 days. | $2,000. | $100,000. | Me. Rev. Stat. Ann. tit. 24-A, § 2843. |
| MD | Mandatory coverage. | Same terms as for physical illness with at least 60 days partial hospitalization. | 80% coverage for first 5 visits; 65% of 6 to 30 visits; 50% coverage for visits beyond 30. | Same as for physical illness. | Md. Ins. Code § 15-802. |
| MA | Mandatory coverage. | 60 days. | $500. | State has no statutory requirements. | Mass. Gen. Laws Ann. ch. 175, § 47B. |
| MI | — | — | — | — | State has no statutory provisions. |
| MN | Mandatory coverage for outpatient treatment if inpatient treatment covered. | State has no statutory requirements. | 80% of first 10 hours; 75% of additional hours for serious and persistent mental illness. | State has no statutory requirements. | Minn. Stat. Ann. § 62A.152. |
| MS | Employer option. | Inpatient: 30 days; partial hospitalization: 60 days. | 25 visits at rate of 50% of covered expenses. | $50,000. | Miss. Code Ann. §§ 83-9-39, 83-9-41. |
| MO | Employer option. | Same coverage as for physical illness. | Same coverage as for physical illness. | No less than coverage for physical illness. | Mo. Rev. Stat. § 376.881. |
| MT | Mandatory coverage. | 21 days for mental health and substance abuse treatment combined. | $2,000 for mental health and substance abuse treatment combined. | No less than lifetime maximum for physical illness. | Mont. Code Ann. § 33-22-703. |

*(Table continues.)*

# Table 5.2-3 *(cont'd)*

## MANDATORY COVERAGE FOR MENTAL HEALTH TREATMENT

(See also text at § 5.2[f].)

**KEY:** **Mandatory coverage.** All group policies must include coverage for this benefit.
**Employer option.** Insurance companies must offer policyholders (employers) this benefit option, but employers may choose not to cover employees for this particular benefit.

| | *Type of Coverage* | *Minimum Yearly Inpatient Coverage* | *Minimum Yearly Outpatient Coverage* | *Minimum Lifetime Coverage* | *Citations to Authority* |
|---|---|---|---|---|---|
| NE | — | — | — | — | State has no statutory provisions. |
| NV | — | — | — | — | State has no statutory provisions. |
| NH | Mandatory coverage. | $3,000 per covered individual for inpatient and outpatient combined. | 15 hours (up to $3,000 per covered individual for inpatient and outpatient combined). | $10,000. Biologically-based mental illnesses must be covered to the same extent physical illness is covered. | N.H. Rev. Stat. Ann. §§ 415:18-a, 417-E:1. |
| NJ | — | — | — | — | State has no statutory provisions. |
| NM | — | — | — | If mental health benefits are provided, no less than coverage for physical illness. | N.M. Stat. Ann. § 59A-23E-18. |
| NY | Employer option. | 30 days. | $700. | State has no statutory requirements. | N.Y. Ins. Law § 3221 (l)(5)(A). |
| NC | — | — | — | If mental illness is covered, the cap may not be less than for physical illness. | N.C. Gen. Stat. § 58-51-55. |
| ND | Mandatory coverage. | Inpatient: 60 days; partial hospitalization: 120 days (2 days partial equals 1 day inpatient). | 30 hours. | State has no statutory requirements. | N.D. Cent. Code § 26.1-36-09. |
| OH | — | — | — | — | State has no statutory provisions. |
| OK | — | — | — | — | State has no statutory provisions. |
| OR | Mandatory coverage. | — | — | Inpatient: $4,000 for adults, $6,000 for children (for hospitalization); $1,000 for adults, $2,500 for children (for residential programs); inpatient and outpatient combined: $8,500 for adults, $10,500 for children. | Or. Rev. Stat. § 743.556. |
| PA | — | — | — | — | State has no statutory provisions. |

| | | | | | |
|---|---|---|---|---|---|
| RI | Mandatory coverage for serious mental illness under same conditions as other illnesses. | — | — | — | R.I. Gen. Laws § 27-38.2-1. |
| SC | Employer option of coverage for alcohol and drug abuse and mental illness; benefits of $2,000 per year for total coverage. | — | — | $10,000 or no less than for physical illness. | S.C. Code Ann. §§ 38-71-737, 38-71-880. |
| SD | — | — | — | Biologically-based mental illness must be covered on the same terms as physical illness. | S.D. Cod. Laws Ann. § 58-18-80. |
| TN | Mandatory coverage unless specifically excluded or rejected. | 20 days. | 25 visits. | No less than lifetime maximum for physical illness. | Tenn. Code Ann. §§ 56-7-1003, 56-7-2360, 56-7-2601. |
| TX | Employer option for serious mental illness only. | Policy must provide coverage that is no less than the coverage it provides for physical illness or 45 days. | Policy must provide coverage that is no less than the coverage it provides for physical illness or 60 days. | No limitation for serious mental illness; other mental illness must be covered on same terms as physical illness. | Tex. Ins. Code Ann. art. 3.51-14. |
| UT | — | — | — | — | State has no statutory provisions. |
| VT | Mandatory coverage. | Same as physical illness. | Same as physical illness. | Same as physical illness. | Vt. Stat. Ann. tit. 8, § 4089b. |
| VA | Mandatory coverage. | 20 days for adults; 25 days for children. | 20 visits. | No less than lifetime maximum for physical illness, with 50% or more coinsurance for outpatient visits after the first five visits. | Va. Code Ann. § 38.2-3412.1. |
| WA | Employer option. | State has no statutory requirements. | State has no statutory requirements. | State has no statutory requirements. | Wash. Rev. Code § 48.21.240. |
| WV | Employer option. | 45 days in mental hospital; same as for any other illness in general hospital. | Not to exceed 50 visits (50% coverage, up to $500). | Same as for physical illness. | W. Va. Code § 33-16-3a. |
| WI | Mandatory coverage. | Lesser of 30 days or $7,000 (limits apply to treatment for substance abuse and mental disorders). | $2,000 (limits apply to treatment for substance abuse and mental disorders). | State has no statutory requirements. | Wis. Stat. Ann. § 632.89. |
| WY | — | — | — | — | State has no statutory provisions. |

# Table 5.2-4
## MANDATORY MATERNITY AND DEPENDENT COVERAGE

(See also text at § 5.2[g].)

**KEY:** **Mandatory coverage.** All group policies must include coverage for this benefit. Unless otherwise noted, "Yes" indicates mandatory coverage.
**Employer option.** Insurance companies must offer policyholders (employers) this benefit option, but employers may choose not to cover employees for this particular benefit.

| | *Newborns* | *Extension to Certain Dependents* | *Fertility Treatment* | *Pregnancy* | *Preventive Care for Children* | *Citations to Authority* |
|---|---|---|---|---|---|---|
| AL | Yes. | No. | No. | No. | No. | Ala. Code § 27-19-38. |
| AK | Yes. Adopted children must also be covered. | No. | No. | No. | No. | Alaska Stat. § 21.42.345. |
| AZ | Yes. Coverage is mandatory also for birth of adopted children, if adopted within 1 year of birth, if insured is legally obligated to pay costs of birth, and if maternity benefits are covered. | Yes. | No. | No. If pregnancy is covered, post-delivery stay of 48 to 96 hours must be covered. | No. | Ariz. Rev. Stat. Ann. §§ 20-1402, 20-1407. |
| AR | Yes. Adopted children and nursery care for 5 days, or until mother is discharged, must also be covered. | Yes. | Yes, in vitro fertilization only. | No. | Yes, to age 18. | Ark. Stat. Ann. §§ 23-79-129, 23-79-137, 23-79-141, 23-86-108, 23-86-118, 23-98-102. |
| CA | Yes. Adopted children must also be covered. | Yes. | Employer option, except in vitro fertilization. | If policy covers pregnancy, it must also cover complications of pregnancy and prenatal diagnosis of genetic disorders for high-risk pregnancies. | Yes, to age 16, including screening for blood lead levels in children. Employer option to age 18. | Cal. Ins. Code §§ 10118, 10119, 10119.5, 10119.6, 10121.6, 10122, 10123.5, 10123.55, 10123.9. Cal. Health & Safety Code § 1374.55. |
| CO | Yes. Adopted children must also be covered. | No. | No. | Yes. Complications of pregnancy must also be covered. | No. | Colo. Rev. Stat. §§ 10-16-104(1), 10-16-104(1.5), 10-16-104(2), 10-16-104(3), 10-16-104(6.5). |
| CT | Yes. Adopted children must also be covered. | Yes. | Employer option. | No. If pregnancy is covered, postdelivery stay of 48 to 96 hours must be covered. | Yes, to age 6. | Conn. Gen. Stat. Ann. §§ 38a-515, 38a-516, 38a-530c, 38a-535, 38a-536, 38a-549. |

| | | | | | | |
|---|---|---|---|---|---|---|
| DE | Yes. | Yes. | No. | No. If pregnancy is covered, post-delivery stay must be covered to extent required by federal law. | If outpatient services are covered, mandatory coverage for lead screening tests for children at age 1, with additional tests to age 6 for children at high risk for lead poisoning. | Del. Code Ann. tit. 18, §§ 3511, 3550, 3554, 3556. |
| DC | Yes. | Yes. | No. | No. | Yes. Immunizations and blood tests (including test for sickle-cell anemia) for newborns. Unlimited visits to age 12; 3 visits per year between ages 12 and 18. | D.C. Code Ann. §§ 35-530, 35-1101, 35-1102. |
| FL | Yes. Adopted and foster children must also be covered. | Yes. | No. | No. If pregnancy is covered, postdelivery stay must be covered. | Yes, to age 16. | Fla. Stat. Ann. §§ 627.6406, 627.6562, 627.6574, 627.6575, 627.6578, 627.6579, 627.6615. |
| GA | Yes. Adopted children must also be covered. | Yes. | No. | If policy covers pregnancy, it must also cover complications of pregnancy and postdelivery stay to 48 to 96 hours. | Yes, to age 5. | Ga. Code Ann. §§ 33-24-22, 33-24-24, 33-24-28, 33-24-58 *et seq.*, 33-30-4.5 |
| HI | Yes. Adopted children must also be covered. | Yes. | Yes, one-time-only in vitro fertilization if pregnancy covered. | No. | Yes, to age 5. | Haw. Rev. Stat. §§ 431:10A-103, 431:10A-115, 431:10A-115.5, 431:10A-116.5, 431:10A-206, 431L-6. |
| ID | If policy covers newborns, it must do so from birth. Adopted children must also be covered. | Yes. | No. | If policy covers pregnancy, it must also cover complications of pregnancy. Policy may not restrict length of stay in hospital following delivery in any manner that would be in conflict with federal law. | No. | Idaho Code §§ 41-2203, 41-2210. |
| IL | If policy covers family members, it must cover newborn and adopted children. | Yes. | Yes, if pregnancy covered. | No. If pregnancy is covered, postdelivery stay of 48 to 96 hours must be covered. | No. | Ill. Ann. Stat. ch. 215, ¶¶ 5/356(c), 5/356(h), 5/356(m), 5/356r, 5/356s, 5/367.2, 5/367b, 5/367(5). |
| IN | Yes. Adopted children must also be covered. | Yes. | No. | No. If pregnancy is covered, postdelivery stay must be covered. | No. | Ind. Code §§ 27-8-5.6-2, 27-8-5-18, 27-8-5-19, 27-8-5-21, 27-8-24-1 *et seq.* |
| IA | Yes. Adopted children must also be covered. | No. | No. | No. If pregnancy is covered, postdelivery stay of 48 to 96 hours must be covered. | No. | Iowa Code Ann. §§ 514C.1, 514C.10, 514C.12. |

*(Table continues.)*

# Table 5.2-4 *(cont'd)*

## MANDATORY MATERNITY AND DEPENDENT COVERAGE

(See also text at § 5.2[g].)

**KEY:** **Mandatory coverage.** All group policies must include coverage for this benefit. Unless otherwise noted, "Yes" indicates mandatory coverage.
**Employer option.** Insurance companies must offer policyholders (employers) this benefit option, but employers may choose not to cover employees for this particular benefit.

| | *Newborns* | *Extension to Certain Dependents* | *Fertility Treatment* | *Pregnancy* | *Preventive Care for Children* | *Citations to Authority* |
|---|---|---|---|---|---|---|
| KS | Yes. Adopted children must also be covered. Coverage of expenses of birth of adopted child is an employer option. | No. | No. | No. | Yes, for immunizations to 72 months. | Kan. Stat. Ann. §§ 40-2, 102. |
| KY | Yes. Adopted children must also be covered. 5 days of hospital nursery care for well newborn is an employer option. | No. | No. | No. If pregnancy is covered, postdelivery stay of 48 to 96 hours must be covered. | No. | Ky. Rev. Stat. Ann. §§ 304.17A-140, 304.17A-145, 304.18-032, 304.18-033. |
| LA | Yes. Adopted children, unmarried grandchildren in the legal custody of a grandparent, and transportation of newborn to hospital or neonatal unit must also be covered. | Yes. | No. | No. Post-delivery stay and air or surface transport for premature birth and infant illness must be covered if pregnancy and family coverage are provided. | Yes, for immunizations to age 6. | La. Rev. Stat. Ann. §§ 22:215.1, 22:215.2, 22:215.4, 22:215.14, 22:227, 22:250.4. |
| ME | Yes. Adopted children must also be covered. | No. | No. | No. If pregnancy is covered, postdelivery stay must be covered. | No. | Me. Rev. Stat. Ann. tit. 24-A, §§ 2832, 2833, 2834, 2834-A, 2834-B. |
| MD | Yes. Adopted children and grandchildren must also be covered. | Yes. | Yes, in vitro fertilization only if policy covers pregnancy. | If policy covers pregnancy hospitalization, it must also cover hospitalization for childbirth and postdelivery stay of 48 to 96 hours; coverage for temporary disability due to pregnancy or childbirth is an employer option. | Yes. | Md. Ins. Code §§ 15-302, 15-401, 15-404, 15-408, 15-810, 15-812, 15-813, 15-817. |

| | | | | | | |
|---|---|---|---|---|---|---|
| MA | Yes. Adopted children must also be covered. | Yes. | Yes. | Yes. Postdelivery stay of 48 to 96 hours, prenatal and postnatal care must also be covered. | Yes, to age 6. | Mass. Gen. Laws Ann. ch. 175, §§ 47C, 47F, 47H, 110(E). |
| MI | Yes. | No. | No. | No. | No. | Mich. Stat. Ann. § 24.13611. |
| MN | Yes. Adopted children and grandchildren must also be covered. | Yes. | No. | Yes. Postdelivery stay of 48 to 96 hours must be covered. | Yes, to age 6 and immunizations to age 18. | Minn. Stat. Ann. §§ 62A.0411, 62A.042, 62A.047, 62A.14, 62A.27. |
| MS | Yes. Includes costs of transportation, up to $200. | Yes. | No. | No. | No. | Miss. Code Ann. §§ 83-9-33, 83-41-207. |
| MO | Yes. Adopted children must also be covered. | Yes. | No. | No. | Yes, employer option to age 12. Immunizations must be covered. | Mo. Rev. Stat. §§ 376.406, 376.426, 376.801, 376.816, 376.995. |
| MT | Yes. Adopted children must also be covered. | Yes. | No. | No. If pregnancy is covered, post-delivery stay of 48 to 96 hours must be covered. | Yes, through age 2. | Mont. Code. Ann. §§ 33-22-130, 33-22-133, 33-22-504, 33-22-506, 33-22-512. |
| NE | Yes. | Yes. | No. | No. | Yes, immunizations to age 6. | Neb. Rev. Stat. §§ 44-710.19, 44-761, 44-784. |
| NV | Yes. Adopted children and transportation to nearest treatment center must also be covered. | Yes. | No. | Mandatory coverage of complications of pregnancy. | No. | Nev. Rev. Stat. §§ 689B.033, 689B.035, 689B.260. |
| NH | Yes. Adopted children must also be covered. | Yes. | No. | Maternity benefits rider must be available at insured's request if policy does not cover maternity. If pregnancy is covered, postdelivery stay must be covered. | No. | N.H. Rev. Stat. Ann. §§ 415:18, 415:22, 415:22-a, 415-D:2-a. |
| NJ | Yes. | Yes. | No. | Employer option. If pregnancy is covered, postdelivery stay of 48 to 96 hours must be covered. | Yes, immunizations and lead screening. | N.J. Rev. Stat. §§ 17B:27-30, 17B:27-46.1 *et seq.* |
| NM | Yes. Transportation of newborn to nearest available facility must be covered. Adopted children must also be covered. | Yes. | No. | If policy covers pregnancy, it must also cover transportation of mother in a high-risk pregnancy. | Child immunizations must be covered. | N.M. Stat. Ann. §§ 59A-22-33, 59A-22-34, 59A-22-34.1, 59A-22-34.3, 59A-22-35. |
| NY | Yes. Adopted children must also be covered. | Yes. | No. | Yes. Postdelivery stay of 48 to 96 hours must be covered. | Mandatory coverage to age 19. | N.Y. Ins. Law §§ 3221(k)(5)(A), 3221(l)(8)(A), 3221(l)(8)(B), 4235(f)(1), 4235(f)(2); N.Y. Pub. Health Law § 2803-n. |

(Table continues.)

# Table 5.2-4 *(cont'd)*
## MANDATORY MATERNITY AND DEPENDENT COVERAGE

(See also text at § 5.2[g].)

**KEY:** **Mandatory coverage.** All group policies must include coverage for this benefit. Unless otherwise noted, "Yes" indicates mandatory coverage.
**Employer option.** Insurance companies must offer policyholders (employers) this benefit option, but employers may choose not to cover employees for this particular benefit.

| | *Newborns* | *Extension to Certain Dependents* | *Fertility Treatment* | *Pregnancy* | *Preventive Care for Children* | *Citations to Authority* |
|---|---|---|---|---|---|---|
| NC | Yes. Adopted and foster children must also be covered. | Yes. | No. | No. | No. | N.C. Gen. Stat. §§ 58-51-25, 58-51-30, 58-51-125. |
| ND | Yes. Adopted children must also be covered. | Yes. | No. | Yes. Policy may not exclude involuntary complications of pregnancy. If pregnancy is covered, postdelivery stay of 48 to 96 hours must be covered. | Yes, required in basic and standard small employer plans up to age 5. | N.D. Cent. Code §§ 26.1-36-07, 26.1-36-09.2, 26.1-36-09.4, 26.1-36-09.8, 26.1-36-22. |
| OH | Yes. Adopted children must also be covered. | Yes. | No. | No. If pregnancy is covered, postdelivery stay of 48 to 96 hours must be covered. | Yes, to age 9. | Ohio Rev. Code Ann. §§ 3923.24, 3923.26, 3923.40, 3923.55, 3923.63. |
| OK | Yes, including transportation of newborns. Adopted children must also be covered. | No. | No. | No. If pregnancy is covered, postdelivery stay of 48 to 96 hours must be covered. | Yes, immunizations to age 18. | Okla. Stat. tit. 36, §§ 6058, 6059, 6060.3, 6060.4. |
| OR | Yes. Adopted children must also be covered. | Yes. | No. | No. | No. | Or. Rev. Stat. §§ 743.707, 743.716. |
| PA | Yes. Adopted children must also be covered. | Yes. | No. | No. If pregnancy is covered, post-delivery stay of 48 to 96 hours must be covered. | Yes, for immunizations. | Pa. Stat. Ann. tit. 40, §§ 752, 771, 772, 775.1, 1583, 3503. |
| RI | Adopted children must be covered. | No. | Yes, if pregnancy is covered. | No. If pregnancy is covered, postdelivery stay of 48 to 96 hours must be covered. | Yes, to age 19; also, mandatory coverage for lead screening. | R.I. Gen. Laws §§ 23-24.6-9, 27-18-27, 27-18-30, 27-18-33.1, 27-38.1-1, 27-38.1-2, 27-38.1-3. |

| | | | | | | |
|---|---|---|---|---|---|---|
| SC | Yes. Adopted children must also be covered. | Yes. | No. | No. If pregnancy is covered, postdelivery stay of 48 to 96 hours must be covered. | No. | S.C. Code Ann. §§ 38-71-135, 38-71-140, 38-71-780. |
| SD | Yes. Adopted children must also be covered. | Yes. | No. | No. If pregnancy is covered, postdelivery stay of 48 to 96 hours must be covered. | No. | S.D. Codified Laws Ann. §§ 58-17-88, 58-18-31, 58-18-32, 58-18-76. |
| TN | Yes. Adopted children must also be covered. Pediatric nursery care is an employer option. | Yes. Age limit must be not lower than 24 for unmarried dependent children. | No. | No. If pregnancy is covered, postdelivery stay must be covered. | No. | Tenn. Code Ann. §§ 56-7-2301, 56-7-2302, 56-7-2350, 56-7-2604. |
| TX | Yes. Adopted children and grandchildren must also be covered. | Yes. | If policy covers pregnancy, coverage for in vitro fertilization is an employer option. | No. If pregnancy is covered, post-delivery stay of 48 to 96 hours must be covered. | Yes, immunizations to age 6. | Tex. Ins. Code Ann. art. 3.51-6, §§ 3A(a), 3B, 3D, 3E; art 3.70-2, art. 21.53F. |
| UT | Yes. Adopted children must also be covered. | Yes. | No. | No. | No. | Utah Code Ann. §§ 31A-22-610, 31A-22-610.5, 31A-22-611. |
| VT | Yes. Adopted children must also be covered. | Yes. | No. | No. | No. | Vt. Stat. Ann. tit. 8, §§ 4090, 4092, 4100C. |
| VA | Yes. Adopted children must also be covered. | Yes. | No. | Employer option. If policy covers accidents, it must cover pregnancy resulting from rape or incest. If pregnancy is covered, postdelivery stay must be covered. | Yes, to age 6. Coverage is required for medically necessary early intervention services, including speech and language therapy, occupational therapy, physical therapy, and assistive technology services from birth to age 3. | Va. Code Ann. §§ 38.2-3409, 38.2-3411, 38.2-3411.1, 38.2-3411.2, 38.2-3414, 38.2-3414.1, 38.2-3418, 38.2-3418.3. |
| WA | Yes. Adopted children must also be covered. | Yes. | No. | If policy covers pregnancy, coverage for prenatal diagnosis of congenital disorders is an employer option. | No. | Wash. Rev. Code §§ 48.21.150, 48.21.155, 48.21.244, 48.21.280. |
| WV | Yes. Adopted children must also be covered. | No. | No. | No. If pregnancy is covered, postdelivery stay of 48 to 96 hours must be covered. | Mandatory coverage for child immunizations, with no per-visit charge or co-payment. | W. Va. Code §§ 33-6-32, 33-16-3j, 33-16-12. |
| WI | Yes. Adopted children and newborns of insured's dependent child must also be covered. | Yes. | No. | No. | Mandatory coverage of blood lead tests for children under 6. | Wis. Stat. Ann. §§ 632.88, 632.895(5), 632.895(5m), 632.895(10), 632.896. |
| WY | Yes. Adopted children must also be covered. | Yes. | No. | No. | No. | Wyo. Stat. §§ 26-20-101, 26-22-401. |

# Table 5.2-5
## MANDATORY COVERAGE FOR SPECIFIED DISEASES OR MEDICAL CONDITIONS

(States not listed have no statutes governing mandatory coverage for specified illnesses and conditions. See also text at § 5.2[h].)

**KEY:** **Mandatory coverage.** All group policies must include coverage for this benefit. Unless otherwise noted, "Yes" indicates mandatory coverage.
**Employer option.** Insurance companies must offer policyholders (employers) this benefit option, but employers may choose not to cover employees for this particular benefit.
**DES.** Diethylstilbestrol. Exposure to this drug has been shown to cause a variety of reproductive and medical problems.

| | *Alzheimer's* | *Cleft Lip and Cleft Palate* | *Diabetes* | *DES* | *AIDS* | *Other Provisions* | *Citations to Authority* |
|---|---|---|---|---|---|---|---|
| AL | No. | No. | No. | No. | No. | Mandatory coverage for any valid claim dealing with sickle-cell anemia. | Ala. Code § 27-5-13. |
| AK | No. | No. | No. | No. | No. | Mandatory coverage for dental, hearing, and vision care. | Alaska Stat. § 21.42.385. |
| AZ | No. | Yes. | No. | No. | No. | None. | Ariz. Rev. Stat. § 20-1402. |
| AR | No. | No. | No. | No. | No. | Coverage for speech and hearing impairment is an employer option. | Ark. Stat. Ann. § 23-79-130. |
| CA | Yes, mandatory coverage required, except for preexisting condition, if long-term care facilities or home-based care is covered. | No. | Coverage for diabetic education programs is an employer option. | Yes. | Yes, except for certain policies contingent on medical review. | Mandatory coverage for osteoporosis and jawbone disorders. Coverage for footwear needed by persons suffering foot disfigurement and coverage for orthotic and prosthetic devices are employer options. | Cal. Ins. Code §§ 799.08, 10119.7, 10123.7, 10123.16, 10123.21, 10123.141, 10123.185, 10176.6. |
| CO | No. | Yes. | No. | No. | No. | None. | Colo. Rev. Stat. § 10-16-104(1). |
| CT | No. | No. | No. | No. | No. | Mandatory coverage for leukemia, if policy covers surgical removal of tumors, and for accidental ingestion of controlled drugs. | Conn. Gen. Stat. Ann. §§ 38a-518, 38a-542. |
| DC | No. | No. | No. | No. | Yes. | None. | D.C. Code Ann. § 35-223. |

| | | | | | | | |
|---|---|---|---|---|---|---|---|
| FL | No. | Yes. | Yes. | No. | Yes. Treatment can be limited only if there was a preexisting condition. | Treatment and diagnosis of osteoporosis for high-risk individuals must be covered. Mandatory coverage for treatments of bones and joints in the face or jaw. If treatment of breast cancer is covered, insurer may not limit inpatient care for breast cancer. | Fla. Stat. Ann. §§ 627.429, 627.6408, 627.6409, 627.65735, 627.65745, 627.66121, 627.6691, Fla. Law 98-66. |
| GA | No. | No. | No. | No. | No. | Mandatory coverage for temporomandibular joint disorders and jaw deformities. Coverage of bone marrow transplants for treatment of breast cancer and Hodgkin's disease is an employer option. | Ga. Code Ann. §§ 33-30-4.4, 33-30-14. |
| IL | No. | No. | No. | Yes. | No. | Coverage for temporomandibular joint and craniomandibular disorders is an employer option with maximum lifetime benefits of no less than $2,500. | Ill. Ann. Stat. ch. 215, ¶¶ 5/356f, 5/356q. |
| IN | No. | Yes, for newborns. | Yes. | No. | No. | None. | Ind. Code §§ 27-8-5.6-2, 27-8-14.5-6. |
| IA | No. | No. | Coverage for diabetic outpatient self-management education programs is an employer option. | No. | No. | None. | Iowa Code Ann. § 509.3. |
| KY | No. | No. | No. | No. | Yes. | Mandatory coverage for temporomandibular joint and craniomandibular disorders if treatment of skeletal disorders is covered. | Ky. Rev. Stat. Ann. §§ 304.12-013, 304.18-0365. |
| LA | No. | Yes, including coverage for secondary treatment. | Yes. | No. | No. | Mandatory coverage for treatment of attention deficit or hyperactivity disorders. | La. Rev. Stat. Ann. §§ 22:215.8, 22:215.15, 22:215.21. |
| ME | No. | No. | Yes. | No. | Yes. | None. | Me. Rev. Stat. Ann. tit. 24, § 2846. |
| MD | Employer option. Coverage of expenses for care of elderly for designated diseases is also an employer option. | Yes. | No. | No. | No. | Mandatory coverage for face, neck, and head bone and joint conditions if other skeletal bones and joints are covered. | Md. Ins. Code §§ 15-801, 15-818, 15-821. |
| MA | No. | No. | No. | Yes. | No. | Mandatory coverage for screening of lead poisoning in children. | Mass. Gen. Laws Ann. ch. 175, §§ 47C, 108C. |
| MI | No. | Yes. | No. | No. | No. | None. | Mich. Stat. Ann. § 24.13611. |

*(Table continues.)*

# Table 5.2-5 *(cont'd)*

## MANDATORY COVERAGE FOR SPECIFIED DISEASES OR MEDICAL CONDITIONS

(States not listed have no statutes governing mandatory coverage for specified illnesses and conditions. See also text at § 5.2[h].)

**KEY:** **Mandatory coverage.** All group policies must include coverage for this benefit. Unless otherwise noted, "Yes" indicates mandatory coverage.

**Employer option.** Insurance companies must offer policyholders (employers) this benefit option, but employers may choose not to cover employees for this particular benefit.

**DES.** Diethylstilbestrol. Exposure to this drug has been shown to cause a variety of reproductive and medical problems.

| | *Alzheimer's* | *Cleft Lip and Cleft Palate* | *Diabetes* | *DES* | *AIDS* | *Other Provisions* | *Citations to Authority* |
|---|---|---|---|---|---|---|---|
| MN | No. | Yes. | No. | Yes. Treatment can be limited only if there was a preexisting condition. | No. | Mandatory coverage for temporomandibular joint and craniomandibular disorders, phenylketonuria, port-wine stain treatment, lyme disease, and children's emotional handicaps. Coverage of treatment for conditions caused by breast implants may be limited only if condition was pre-existing. | Minn. Stat. Ann. §§ 62A.042, 62A.043, 62A.25, 62A.26, 62A.151, 62A.154, 62A.265, 62A.285, 62A.304. |
| MS | No. | No. | Yes. | No. | No. | Coverage for temporomandibular joint and craniomandibular disorders is an employer option. | Miss. Code Ann. § 83-9-45. Miss. 1998 Gen. Laws ch. 483, § 2. |
| MO | No. | Yes. | Yes. | No. | Yes. | Coverage for speech and hearing disorders is an employer option. | Mo. Rev. Stat. §§ 191.671, 376.385, 376.406, 376.781. |
| MT | No. | No. | No. | No. | No. | Mandatory coverage for phenylketonuria. | Mont. Code. Ann. § 33-22-131. |
| NE | No. | Yes. | No. | No. | No. | None. | Neb. Rev. Stat. § 44-710.19. |
| NV | No. | Yes. | No. | No. | No. | Mandatory coverage for temporomandibular disorders. | Nev. Rev. Stat. §§ 689B.033, 689B.0379. |
| NH | No. | No. | Yes. | No. | No. | None. | N.H. Rev. Stat. Ann. § 415:18-f. |
| NJ | No. | Yes. | Yes. | No. | No. | Mandatory coverage for Wilm's tumor and purchase of blood products, formulas for inherited metabolic disease, and infusion equipment for hemophilia home treatment. | N.J. Rev. Stat. §§ 17B:27-30, 17B:27-46.1c, 17B:27-46.1e. |

| | | | | | | | |
|---|---|---|---|---|---|---|---|
| NM | No. | No. | Yes. | No. | No. | Mandatory coverage for temporomandibular joint and craniomandibular disorders. | N.M. Stat. Ann. §§ 59A-16-13.1, 59A-22-41. |
| NY | No. | Yes. | Yes. | Yes. | No. | None. | N.Y. Ins. Law §§ 3225, 4235(f)(2). |
| NC | No. | Yes. | Yes. | No. | No. | None. | N.C. Gen. Stat. §§ 58-51-30, 58-51-61. |
| ND | No. | Yes. | No. | No. | No. | Mandatory coverage for temporomandibular joint and craniomandibular disorders. | N.D. Cent. Code §§ 26.1-36-07, 26.1-36-09.3. |
| OH | No. | Yes. | No. | No. | Yes, mandatory coverage unless there was a preexisting condition. | None. | Ohio Rev. Code Ann. §§ 3901.45, 3923.26. |
| OK | No. | No. | Yes. | No. | No. | None. | Okla. Stat. Ann. tit. 36, § 6060.2. |
| OR | No. | Yes. | Yes, mandatory coverage for diabetic outpatient self-management education programs only. | Yes. Coverage may not be denied or canceled because of exposure to DES. | No. | Mandatory coverage for Tourette syndrome. | Or. Rev. Stat. §§ 743.704, 743.707, 743.710, 743.717. |
| RI | No. | No. | Yes. | No. | No. | None. | R.I. Gen. Laws § 27-18-38. |
| SC | No. | Yes. | No. | No. | No. | None. | S.C. Code Ann. § 38-71-240. |
| SD | No. | Yes. | No. | No. | No. | Mandatory coverage for phenylketonuria. | S.D. Codified Laws §§ 58-18-33, 58-18-41. |
| TN | No. | No. | Yes. | No. | No. | Coverage for speech and hearing disorders is an employer option. Mandatory coverage of phenylketonuria. | Tenn. Code Ann. §§ 56-7-2505, 56-7-2603. |
| TX | No. | No. | Yes. | No. | Yes. | Temporomandibular joint disorders must be covered if skeletal joints covered. Coverage for speech and hearing impairments is an employer option. | Tex. Ins. Code Ann. art. 3.51-6, § 3C, art. 3.70-2(G), art. 3.78, art. 21.53A, art. 21.53D, art. 21.53G. |
| VT | No. | No. | Yes. | No. | No. | None. | Vt. Stat. Ann. tit. 8, § 4089c. |
| VA | No. | Yes. | No. | No. | No. | Yes, for hemophilia. | Va. Code Ann. §§ 38.2-3411, 38.2-4319. |

*(Table continues.)*

## Table 5.2-5 *(cont'd)*

## MANDATORY COVERAGE FOR SPECIFIED DISEASES OR MEDICAL CONDITIONS

(States not listed have no statutes governing mandatory coverage for specified illnesses and conditions. See also text at § 5.2[h].)

**KEY:** **Mandatory coverage.** All group policies must include coverage for this benefit. Unless otherwise noted, "Yes" indicates mandatory coverage.

**Employer option.** Insurance companies must offer policyholders (employers) this benefit option, but employers may choose not to cover employees for this particular benefit.

**DES.** Diethylstilbestrol. Exposure to this drug has been shown to cause a variety of reproductive and medical problems.

| | *Alzheimer's* | *Cleft Lip and Cleft Palate* | *Diabetes* | *DES* | *AIDS* | *Other Provisions* | *Citations to Authority* |
|---|---|---|---|---|---|---|---|
| WA | No. | No. | Yes. | No. | No. | Coverage for temporomandibular joint disorders is an employer option. Mandatory coverage for neurodevelopmental therapies for children age 6 and under. | Wash. Rev. Code §§ 48.21.143, 48.21.310, 48.21.320. |
| WV | No. | Yes. | Yes. | No. | No. | Coverage for temporomandibular joint and craniomandibular disorders is an employer option. | W. Va. Code §§ 33-6-32, 33-15C-1, 33-16-3f, 33-16-9, 33-16-16. |
| WI | No. | No. | If expenses for treatment are covered, supplies, equipment, and self-education programs must also be covered. | No. | Mandatory coverage for drug treatment if policy covers prescription drugs generally. Coverage for AIDS may not be excluded or limited unless same exclusions or limitations apply to other illnesses covered in the policy. | Mandatory coverage for kidney disease up to $30,000. | Wis. Stat. Ann. §§ 631.93, 632.895(4), 632.895(6), 632.895(9). |
| WY | No. | No. | Yes. | No. | No. | No. | Wyo. Stat. Ann. § 26-19-107. |

# Table 5.2-6 Part A
## MANDATORY COVERAGE FOR SPECIFIED MEDICAL PROCEDURES

(See also text at § 5.2[i].)

**KEY:** **Mandatory coverage.** All group policies must include coverage for this benefit. Unless otherwise noted, "Yes" indicates mandatory coverage.
**Employer option.** Insurance companies must offer policyholders (employers) this benefit option, but employers may choose not to cover employees for this particular benefit.

| | *Acupuncture* | *Mammograms* | *Cardiac Rehabilitation* | *Kidney Dialysis* | *Other Provisions* | *Citations to Authority* |
|---|---|---|---|---|---|---|
| AL | — | Yes, if mastectomy covered. | — | — | — | Ala. Code § 27-50-4. |
| AK | No. | Yes, if mastectomy covered. | No. | No. | Mandatory coverage for prostate cancer screening and cervical cancer screening. | Alaska Stat. §§ 21.42.353, 21.42.375, 21.42.395. |
| AZ | No. | Yes, if mastectomy covered. | No. | No. | None. | Ariz. Rev. Stat. Ann. § 20-1402. |
| AR | No. | Employer option. | No. | No. | Mandatory coverage for tests for hypothyroidism, sickle-cell disease, galactosemia, and phenylketonuria. | Ark. Stat. Ann. §§ 23-79-129, 23-79-140. |
| CA | Employer option. | Yes, if mastectomy covered. | No. | No. | Mandatory coverage for cytologic exams if cervical cancer treatment covered. May not exclude long-term or home care for Alzheimer's or other degenerative illnesses. | Cal. Ins. Code §§ 10123.8, 10123.16, 10123.18, 10123.81, 10127.3. |
| CO | No. | Yes. | No. | No. | Screening for prostate cancer is mandatory. | Colo. Rev. Stat. §§ 10-16-104(4), 10-16-104(10). |
| CT | No. | Yes. | No. | No. | Mandatory coverage for emergency ambulance services; occupational therapy if physical therapy covered; removal of breast implants and comprehensive rehabilitation. | Conn. Gen. Stat. Ann. §§ 38a-523, 38a-524, 38a-525, 38a-530, 38a-542. |
| DE | No. | Yes. | No. | No. | Mandatory coverage for Pap smears, prostate-specific antigen tests, and monitoring of ovarian cancer subsequent to treatment (if outpatient services are covered). | Del. Code Ann. tit. 18, §§ 3552, 3555. |
| DC | No. | Yes. | No. | No. | Mandatory coverage for Pap smears. | D.C. Code Ann. § 35-2402. |
| FL | No. | Yes. | No. | No. | If mastectomy is covered, post-surgery hospital stay must be covered. | Fla. Stat. Ann. §§ 627.64171, 627.6612, 627-6613, 627.66121. |
| GA | No. | Yes. | No. | No. | Mandatory coverage for Pap smears and prostate-specific antigen tests. | Ga. Code Ann. §§ 33-30-4.1, 33-30-4.2. |

*(Table continues.)*

# Table 5.2-6 Part A *(cont'd)*
## MANDATORY COVERAGE FOR SPECIFIED MEDICAL PROCEDURES

(See also text at § 5.2[i].)

**KEY:** **Mandatory coverage.** All group policies must include coverage for this benefit. Unless otherwise noted, "Yes" indicates mandatory coverage.
**Employer option.** Insurance companies must offer policyholders (employers) this benefit option, but employers may choose not to cover employees for this particular benefit.

| | *Acupuncture* | *Mammograms* | *Cardiac Rehabilitation* | *Kidney Dialysis* | *Other Provisions* | *Citations to Authority* |
|---|---|---|---|---|---|---|
| HI | — | Yes. | — | — | If pregnancy is covered, coverage of contraceptive services is an employer option. | Haw. Rev. Stat. §§ 431:10A-116, 431:10A-116.6, 431:10A-207. |
| ID | — | Yes, if mastectomy covered. | — | — | — | Idaho Code §§ 41-2210-A, 41-2218. |
| IL | No. | Yes. | No. | No. | Mandatory coverage for exam after criminal sexual assault and for blood processing and administration; for breast implant removal when medically necessary, except when implant was solely for cosmetic reasons and for Pap smears and prostate cancer testing. If mastectomy covered, post-surgery stay must be covered. | Ill. Ann. Stat. ch. 215, ¶¶ 5/356e, 5/356g, 5/356p, 5/356t, 5/356w, 5/367(8), 5/367(13). |
| IN | No. | Employer option. | No. | No. | None. | Ind. Code § 27-8-14-6. |
| IA | No. | Yes. | No. | No. | None. | Iowa Code Ann. § 514C.4. |
| KS | No. | Yes. | No. | No. | Mandatory coverage for Pap smears. | Kan. Stat. Ann. §§ 40-2229, 40-2230. |
| KY | No. | Yes, if mastectomy covered. | No. | No. | If treatment of breast cancer by chemotherapy is covered, treatment by bone marrow transplant must be covered. | Ky. Rev. Stat. Ann. §§ 304.17A-135, 304.18-098, 304.43-110. |
| LA | No. | Yes. | No. | No. | Coverage for rehabilitative therapy, speech and language pathology, occupational therapy is an employer option. Mandatory coverage for Pap smears and hearing-impaired interpreter expenses when used in connection with medical treatment. | La. Rev. Stat. Ann. §§ 22.215.10, 22.215.11, 22.230.1. |
| ME | No. | Yes, if radiological procedures are generally covered. | Employer option. | No. | Mandatory coverage for Pap smears. | Me. Rev. Stat. Ann. tit. 24, §§ 2837-A, 2837-C, 2837-E, 2845. |
| MD | No. | Yes. | No. | No. | None. | Md. Ins. Code §§ 15-814, 15-815, 15-819. |

| | | | | | | |
|---|---|---|---|---|---|---|
| MA | No. | Yes. | Yes. | No. | Mandatory coverage for cytologic screening exams and bone marrow transplants for treatment of breast cancer. | Mass. Gen. Laws Ann. ch. 175, §§ 47D, 47G, 47R. |
| MI | No. | Yes. | No. | No. | Mandatory coverage for breast cancer diagnostic services, including biopsy, breast cancer outpatient rehabilitation services, and breast cancer treatment services. | Mich. Stat. Ann. §§ 24.13613, 24.13616. |
| MN | No. | Yes. | No. | No. | Mandatory coverage for Pap smears and other cancer screening procedures. | Minn. Stat. Ann. §§ 62A.041, 62A.25, 62A.30. |
| MS | — | — | — | — | — | State has no statutory provisions. |
| MO | No. | Yes. | No. | No. | — | Mo. Rev. Stat. §§ 376.782, 376.805. |
| MT | No. | Yes. | No. | No. | If mastectomy is covered, post-surgery stay must be covered. | Mont. Code. Ann. §§ 33-22-132, 33-22-134, 33-22-135. |
| NE | — | Yes. | — | — | — | Neb. Rev. Stat. § 44-785. |
| NV | No. | Yes. | No. | No. | Mandatory coverage for cytologic screening exams. | Nev. Rev. Stat. §§ 689B.0374, 689B.0375. |
| NH | No. | Yes. | No. | No. | None. | N.H. Rev. Stat. Ann. §§ 415:18-c, 417-D:2. |
| NJ | No. | Yes. | No. | No. | Mandatory coverage for Pap smears, prostate cancer testing, autologous bone marrow transplants for treatment of Wilm's tumor and other cancer treatments. Coverage of health/wellness promotion programs is an employer option. Insurer must cover 72 hours of inpatient care following a mastectomy. | N.J. Rev. Stat. §§ 17B:27-46.1a, 17B:27-46.1e, 17B:27-46.1f, 17B:27-46.1h, 17B:27-46.1j, 17B:27-46.1n, 17B:27-46.1o, 17B:27-46.2, 17B:27-46.3, 17B:48-1 *et seq.*, 17B:48-6b. |
| NM | No. | Yes. | No. | No. | Mandatory coverage for cytologic screening (Pap smear exam). If mastectomy is covered, post-surgery stay must be covered. | N.M. Stat. Ann. §§ 59A-22-39, 59A-22-39.1, 59A-22-40. |
| NY | No. | Yes. | No. | No. | Mandatory coverage for preadmission tests and cytologic screening including Pap smears and pelvic exams. Mandatory coverage of emergency room treatment for conditions that a prudent layperson would consider an emergency. Mandatory coverage of inpatient treatment for breast cancer. | N.Y. Ins. Law §§ 3216, 3221(k)(2)(A), 3221(k)(3), 3221(k)(4), 3221(l)(11)(A), 3221(l)(14)(A). |
| NC | No. | Yes. | No. | No. | Mandatory coverage for Pap smears and prostate-specific antigen tests. | N.C. Gen. Stat. §§ 58-51-57, 58-51-58. |
| ND | No. | No. | No. | No. | Prostate cancer tests must be covered. | N.D. Cent. Code §§ 14-02.3-03, 26.1-36-09.1, 26.1-36-09.6. |
| OH | No. | Employer option. | No. | No. | Coverage of cytologic screening for cervical cancer is an employer option. | Ohio Rev. Code Ann. § 3923.52. |
| OK | No. | Yes. | No. | No. | Mandatory coverage of bone density testing for women age 45 or older. If mastectomy is covered, post-surgery stay of up to 48 hours must be covered. | Okla. Stat. tit. 36, §§ 6060, 6060.1, 6060.5. |

*(Table continues.)*

# Table 5.2-6 Part A *(cont'd)*
## MANDATORY COVERAGE FOR SPECIFIED MEDICAL PROCEDURES

(See also text at § 5.2[i].)

**KEY:** **Mandatory coverage.** All group policies must include coverage for this benefit. Unless otherwise noted, "Yes" indicates mandatory coverage.
**Employer option.** Insurance companies must offer policyholders (employers) this benefit option, but employers may choose not to cover employees for this particular benefit.

| | *Acupuncture* | *Mammograms* | *Cardiac Rehabilitation* | *Kidney Dialysis* | *Other Provisions* | *Citations to Authority* |
|---|---|---|---|---|---|---|
| OR | No. | Yes. | No. | No. | Mandatory coverage of pelvic exams and Pap smears. | Or. Rev. Stat. §§ 743.706, 743.727, 743.728. |
| PA | No. | Yes. | No. | No. | Mandatory coverage of emergency care when medically necessary and Pap smears. If mastectomy is covered, post-surgery stay must be covered. | Pa. Stat. Ann. tit. 18, §§ 3215, 3402; tit. 40, § 764c, 764d, 1574. |
| RI | No. | Yes. | No. | No. | Mandatory coverage for Pap smears, lead screening of children under age 6, newborn metabolic testing, and sickle-cell disease testing. Mandatory coverage of second and third opinions and specified new cancer therapies. If mastectomy is covered, post-surgery stay must be covered. | R.I. Gen. Laws §§ 23-13-14, 23-13-15, 23-24.6-9, 27-18-28, 27-18-36, 27-18-39, 27-18-40, 27-39-2, 27-39-3, 42-62-26. |
| SC | — | — | — | — | — | State has no statutory provisions. |
| SD | No. | Yes. | No. | No. | None. | S.D. Codified Laws Ann. § 58-18-36. |
| TN | No. | Yes, mandatory coverage if mastectomy is covered. | No. | No. | Coverage for bone density scans and chemotherapy, prostate cancer testing, and bone marrow transplants for cancer is required. | Tenn. Code Ann. §§ 56-7-2354, 56-7-2502, 56-7-2507, 58-7-2504, 58-7-2506. |
| TX | No. | Yes. | No. | No. | Mandatory coverage of bone density scanning and prostate cancer testing. If mastectomy is covered, post-surgery stay must be covered. | Tex. Ins. Code Ann. art. 3.70-2(H) art. 21.53C art. 21.53D, art. 21.53G, art. 21.53F. |
| UT | — | — | — | — | — | State has no statutory provisions. |
| VT | No. | Yes. | No. | No. | None. | Vt. Stat. Ann. tit. 8 § 4100a. |
| VA | No. | Employer option. | No. | No. | Pap smears, prostate cancer testing, and head/neck bone disorders must be covered. If mastectomy is covered, post-surgery stay must be covered. | Va. Code Ann. §§ 38.2-3418.1, 38.2-3418.1:1, 38.2-3418.1:2, 38.2-3418.2, 38.2-3418.3. |

| | | | | | | |
|---|---|---|---|---|---|---|
| WA | No. | Yes. | No. | No. | None. | Wash. Rev. Code §§ 48.21.225, 48.21.230. |
| WV | No. | Yes. | Yes. | No. | Mandatory coverage for Pap smears, emergency services, and rehabilitative services. | W. Va. Code §§ 33-16-3g, 33-16-3h, 33-16-3i. |
| WI | No. | Yes. | No. | Yes. | None. | Wis. Stat. Ann. §§ 632.895(4), 632.895(8). |
| WY | No. | No. | No. | No. | Testing for breast cancer, prostate cancer, and cervical cancer. | Wyo. Stat. Ann. § 26-19-107. |

# Table 5.2-6 Part B

## MANDATORY COVERAGE FOR SPECIFIED SURGICAL PROCEDURES

(See also text at § 5.2[i].)

**KEY:** **Mandatory coverage.** All group policies must include coverage for this benefit. Unless otherwise noted, "Yes" indicates mandatory coverage.
**Employer option.** Insurance companies must offer policyholders (employers) this benefit option, but employers may choose not to cover employees for this particular benefit.

| | *Reconstructive Surgery* | *Transplants* | *Second Opinion* | *Coverage of Abortion* | *Citations to Authority* |
|---|---|---|---|---|---|
| AL | — | — | — | — | State has no statutory provisions. |
| AK | No. | No. | No. | — | Alaska Stat. §§ 21.42.353, 21.42.375, 21.42.395. |
| AZ | Yes, mandatory coverage for breast surgery only, if mastectomy covered. | No. | No. | — | Ariz. Rev. Stat. Ann. § 20-1402. |
| AR | No. | No. | No. | — | Ark. Stat. Ann. §§ 23-79-129, 23-79-140. |
| CA | Yes, mandatory coverage for breast surgery only, if mastectomy covered. | No. | No. | — | Cal. Ins. Code §§ 10123.8, 10123.16, 10123.18, 10123.81, 10127.3. |
| CO | No. | No. | No. | — | Colo. Rev. Stat. §§ 10-16-104(4), 10-16-104(10). |
| CT | No. | No. | No. | — | Conn. Gen. Stat. Ann. §§ 38a-523, 38a-524, 38a-525, 38a-530, 38a-542. |
| DE | No. | No. | No. | — | Del. Code Ann. tit. 18, §§ 3552, 3555. |
| DC | No. | No. | No. | — | D.C. Code Ann. § 35-2402. |
| FL | Breast surgery is an employer option, if mastectomy covered. | No. | No. | — | Fla. Stat. Ann. §§ 627.64171, 627.6612, 627-6613, 627.66121. |
| GA | No. | Heart transplant is an employer option. | No. | — | Ga. Code Ann. §§ 33-30-4.1, 33-30-4.2. |
| HI | — | — | — | — | Haw. Rev. Stat. §§ 431:10A-116, 431:10A-116.6, 431:10A-207. |
| ID | — | — | — | Mandatory exclusion of coverage for elective abortion, waivable by an additional premium. | Idaho Code §§ 41-2210-A, 41-2218. |

| | | | | | |
|---|---|---|---|---|---|
| IL | Yes, mandatory coverage for breast surgery only, if mastectomy covered. | Yes. | No. | — | Ill. Ann. Stat. ch. 215, ¶¶ 5/356e, 5/356g, 5/356p, 5/367(8), 5/367(13). |
| IN | Yes, for breast reconstruction, if mastectomy covered. | No. | No. | — | Ind. Code §§ 27-8-5-26, 27-8-14-6. |
| IA | No. | No. | No. | — | Iowa Code Ann. § 514C.4. |
| KS | No. | No. | No. | — | Kan. Stat. Ann. §§ 40-2229, 40-2230. |
| KY | No. | No. | No. | No coverage for elective abortion, except by additional premium. | Ky. Rev. Stat. Ann. §§ 304.17A-135, 304.18-098, 304.43-110. |
| LA | Yes, for breast reconstruction, if mastectomy covered. | No. | No. | — | La. Rev. Stat. Ann. §§ 22.215.10, 22.215.11, 22:215.22, 22.230.1. |
| ME | Yes, for breast surgery, if mastectomy is covered. | No. | No. | — | Me. Rev. Stat. Ann. tit. 24, §§ 2837-A, 2837-C, 2837-E, 2845. |
| MD | Yes, for breast surgery. | No. | Yes. | — | Md. Ins. Code §§ 15-814, 15-815, 15-819. |
| MA | No. | No. | No. | — | Mass. Gen. Laws Ann. ch. 175, §§ 47D, 47G, 47R. |
| MI | Yes, mandatory coverage for breast surgery only. | No. | No. | — | Mich. Stat. Ann. §§ 24.13613, 24.13616. |
| MN | Yes. | No. | No. | Mandate for maternity benefits specifically excludes elective abortion. | Minn. Stat. Ann. §§ 62A.041, 62A.25, 62A.30. |
| MS | — | — | — | — | State has no statutory provisions. |
| MO | No. | No. | No. | Mandatory exclusion of coverage of elective abortion, except with additional premium. | Mo. Rev. Stat. §§ 376.782, 376.805. |
| MT | No. | No. | No. | — | Mont. Code. Ann. § 33-22-132. |
| NE | — | — | — | — | Neb. Rev. Stat. § 44-785. |
| NV | Yes, mandatory coverage for breast surgery only, if mastectomy covered. | No. | No. | — | Nev. Rev. Stat. §§ 689B.0374, 689B.0375. |
| NH | Yes, mandatory coverage for breast surgery, if mastectomy covered. | Yes, bone marrow transplants arising from the treatment of breast cancer. | No. | — | N.H. Rev. Stat. Ann. §§ 415:18-c, 417-D:2, 417-D:2-b. |
| NJ | Yes, mandatory coverage for breast surgery only. | No. | Employer option. | — | N.J. Rev. Stat. §§ 17B:27-46.1a, 17B:27-46.1e, 17B:27-46.1f, 17B:27-46.1h, 17B:27-46.1j, 17B:27-46.1n, 17B:27-46.1o, 17B:27-46.2, 17B:27-46.3, 17B:48-1 *et seq.*, 17B:48-6b. |
| NM | No. | No. | No. | — | N.M. Stat. Ann. §§ 59A-22-39, 59A-22-40. |

*(Table continues.)*

# Table 5.2-6 Part B *(cont'd)*

## MANDATORY COVERAGE FOR SPECIFIED SURGICAL PROCEDURES

(See also text at § 5.2[i].)

**KEY:** **Mandatory coverage.** All group policies must include coverage for this benefit. Unless otherwise noted, "Yes" indicates mandatory coverage.
**Employer option.** Insurance companies must offer policyholders (employers) this benefit option, but employers may choose not to cover employees for this particular benefit.

| | *Reconstructive Surgery* | *Transplants* | *Second Opinion* | *Coverage of Abortion* | *Citations to Authority* |
|---|---|---|---|---|---|
| NY | Yes, following breast surgery. | No. | Yes. | — | N.Y. Ins. Law §§ 3216, 3221(k)(2)(A), 3221(k)(3), 3221(k)(4), 3221(l)(11)(A), 3221(l)(14)(A). |
| NC | Yes, following breast surgery. | No. | No. | — | N.C. Gen. Stat. §§ 58-51-57, 58-51-58, 58-51-62. |
| ND | No. | No. | No. | Mandatory exclusion of coverage for abortion, except by additional premium. | N.D. Cent. Code §§ 14-02.3-03, 26.1-36-09.1, 26.1-36-09.6. |
| OH | No. | No. | No. | — | Ohio Rev. Code Ann. § 3923.52. |
| OK | No. | No. | No. | — | Okla. Stat. tit. 36, §§ 6060, 6060.1. |
| OR | Yes, mandatory coverage for maxillofacial (jaw) surgery only. | No. | No. | — | Or. Rev. Stat. §§ 743.706, 743.727, 743.728. |
| PA | Yes, following breast surgery. | No. | No. | Policies excluding coverage for abortions not necessary to avert the death of the mother or in cases of rape or incest are optional for the employer. Note: The statute containing this provision was ruled unconstitutional in *American College of Obstetricians & Gynecologists, Pennsylvania Section v. Thornburgh,* 737 F.2d 233 (3d Cir. 1984), *aff'd,* 106 S. Ct. 2169 (1986). | Pa. Stat. Ann. tit. 18, §§ 3215, 3402; tit. 40, § 764c, 764d, 1574. |
| RI | Yes, for breast reconstruction following a mastectomy. | No. | No. | Mandatory exclusion of elective abortion coverage except by optional rider with additional premium. | R.I. Gen. Laws §§ 23-13-14, 23-13-15, 23-24.6-9, 27-18-28, 27-18-36, 27-18-39, 27-18-40, 27-39-2, 27-39-3, 42-62-26. |
| SC | — | — | — | — | State has no statutory provisions. |
| SD | No. | No. | No. | — | S.D. Codified Laws Ann. § 58-18-36. |
| TN | Yes, for breast reconstruction, if mastectomy is covered. | No. | No. | — | Tenn. Code Ann. §§ 56-7-2354, 56-7-2502, 56-7-2507, 58-7-2504, 58-7-2506. |

| | | | | | |
|---|---|---|---|---|---|
| TX | Yes, for breast surgery. | No. | No. | — | Tex. Ins. Code Ann. art. 3.70-2(H) art. 21.53C art. 21.53D, art. 21.53G, art. 21.53F. |
| UT | — | — | — | — | State has no statutory provisions. |
| VT | No. | No. | No. | — | Vt. Stat. Ann. tit. 8 § 4100a. |
| VA | Yes, for breast surgery. | Employer option of coverage for bone marrow transplants for breast cancer. | No. | — | Va. Code Ann. §§ 38.2-3418.1, 38.2-3418.1:1, 38.2-3418.1:2, 38.2-3418.2, 38.2-3418.3. |
| WA | Yes, mandatory coverage for breast surgery only. | No. | No. | — | Wash. Rev. Code §§ 48.21.225, 48.21.230. |
| WV | No. | No. | No. | — | W. Va. Code §§ 33-16-3g, 33-16-3h, 33-16-3i. |
| WI | No. | No. | No. | — | Wis. Stat. Ann. §§ 632.895(4), 632.895(8). |
| WY | — | — | — | — | State has no statutory provisions. |

# Table 5.2-7
## MANDATORY COVERAGE FOR CARE AT HOME OR AT A SPECIFIED FACILITY

(See also text at § 5.2[j].)

**KEY:** **Mandatory coverage.** All group policies must include coverage for this benefit. Unless otherwise noted, "Yes" indicates mandatory coverage.
**Employer option.** Insurance companies must offer policyholders (employers) this benefit option, but employers may choose not to cover employees for this particular benefit.

| | *Home Health Care* | *Ambulatory Surgical Center* | *Hospice* | *Nursing Home* | *Outpatient Facility* | *Citations to Authority* |
|---|---|---|---|---|---|---|
| AL | — | — | — | — | — | State has no statutory provisions. |
| AK | — | — | — | — | — | State has no statutory provisions. |
| AZ | Yes. | No. | No. | No. | Yes. | Ariz. Rev. Stat. Ann. § 20-1402. |
| AR | — | — | — | — | — | State has no statutory provisions. |
| CA | Employer option, 100 visits per year. | No. | No. | No. | No. | Cal. Ins. Code § 10123.10. |
| CO | Employer option. | No. | Employer option. | No. | No. | Colo. Rev. Stat. § 10-16-104(8). |
| CT | Yes, mandatory coverage of up to 80 visits per year. | No. | No. | No. | No. | Conn. Gen. Stat. Ann. § 38a-520. |
| DE | — | — | — | — | — | State has no statutory provisions. |
| DC | — | — | — | — | — | State has no statutory provisions. |
| FL | Yes. | Yes. | No. | No. | No. | Fla. Stat. Ann. §§ 627.6616, 627.6617. |
| GA | No. | No. | No. | No. | Care in an outpatient facility is an employer option. | Ga. Code Ann. § 33-24-28.2. |
| HI | — | — | — | — | — | State has no statutory provisions. |
| ID | — | — | — | — | — | State has no statutory provisions. |
| IL | — | — | — | — | — | State has no statutory provisions. |
| IN | — | — | — | — | — | State has no statutory provisions. |
| IA | — | — | — | — | — | State has no statutory provisions. |
| KS | — | — | — | — | — | State has no statutory provisions. |

| | | | | | | |
|---|---|---|---|---|---|---|
| KY | Employer option. | Yes. | No. | No. | No. | Ky. Rev. Stat. Ann. §§ 304.18-035, 304.18-037. |
| LA | No. | Yes. | No. | No. | No. | La. Rev. Stat. Ann. § 22:223. |
| ME | Yes, employer option of not less than 90 visits per year. | No. | No. | No. | No. | Me. Rev. Stat. Ann. tit. 24, § 2837. |
| MD | Yes, mandatory coverage of up to 40 visits per year. | No. | Employer option. | Care of elderly for designated diseases is an employer option. | Yes. | Md. Ins. Code §§ 15-801, 15-808, 15-809, 15-819. |
| MA | Yes. | No. | Yes. | No. | No. | Mass. Gen. Laws Ann. ch. 175, §§ 47Q, 47S, 110(K). |
| MI | No. | No. | Employer option. | No. | No. | Mich. Stat. Ann. § 24.13615. |
| MN | No. | Yes. | No. | No. | No. | Minn. Stat. Ann. § 62A.153. |
| MS | — | — | — | — | — | State has no statutory provisions. |
| MO | — | Yes. | — | — | — | Mo. Rev. Stat. § 197.240. |
| MT | Employer option. | No. | Employer option. | No. | No. | Mont. Code Ann. § 33-22-1002. |
| NE | — | — | — | — | — | State has no statutory provisions. |
| NV | Yes. | No. | Yes. | No. | No. | Nev. Rev. Stat. § 689B.030. |
| NH | — | — | — | — | — | State has no statutory provisions. |
| NJ | Yes, mandatory coverage of up to 60 visits per year if inpatient hospitalization or nursing home care covered. | No. | No. | No. | No. | N.J. Rev. Stat. §§ 17B:27-51.4, 17B:27-51.5. |
| NM | Employer option, at least 100 visits per year. | No. | No. | No. | No. | N.M. Stat. Ann. § 59A-22-36. |
| NY | Yes, if inpatient care is covered, home health care must be covered. | No. | Employer option. | Employer option. | Ambulatory care in outpatient facility is an employer option. | N.Y. Ins. Law §§ 3221 (k)(1)(A), 3221 (k)(1)(E), 3221 (l)(2)(A), 3221 (l)(3)(A), 3221 (l)(10)(A). |
| NC | — | — | — | — | — | State has no statutory provisions. |
| ND | No. | Yes. | Yes. | Yes. | — | N.D. Cent. Code § 26.1-36.3. |
| OH | — | — | — | — | — | State has no statutory provisions. |
| OK | — | — | — | — | — | State has no statutory provisions. |
| OR | — | — | — | — | — | State has no statutory provisions. |
| PA | — | — | — | — | — | State has no statutory provisions. |
| RI | Yes, mandatory coverage. | — | — | — | — | R.I. Gen. Laws § 27-18-3. |
| SC | — | — | — | — | — | State has no statutory provisions. |
| SD | — | — | — | — | — | State has no statutory provisions. |

*(Table continues.)*

# Table 5.2-7 *(cont'd)*

## MANDATORY COVERAGE FOR CARE AT HOME OR AT A SPECIFIED FACILITY

(See also text at § 5.2[j].)

**KEY:** **Mandatory coverage.** All group policies must include coverage for this benefit. Unless otherwise noted, "Yes" indicates mandatory coverage.
**Employer option.** Insurance companies must offer policyholders (employers) this benefit option, but employers may choose not to cover employees for this particular benefit.

| | *Home Health Care* | *Ambulatory Surgical Center* | *Hospice* | *Nursing Home* | *Outpatient Facility* | *Citations to Authority* |
|---|---|---|---|---|---|---|
| TN | — | — | — | — | — | State has no statutory provisions. |
| TX | Yes, mandatory coverage of up to 60 visits per year. | No. | No. | No. | No. | Tex. Ins. Code Ann. art. 3.70-3B, § 3. |
| UT | — | — | — | — | — | State has no statutory provisions. |
| VT | Employer option, up to 40 visits per year. | No. | No. | No. | No. | Vt. Stat. Ann. tit. 8, § 4096. |
| VA | — | — | — | — | — | State has no statutory provisions. |
| WA | Employer option, at least 130 visits per year. | No. | Employer option. | No. | No. | Wash. Rev. Code § 48.21.220. |
| WV | Employer option, up to 100 visits per year. | No. | No. | No. | No. | W. Va. Code § 33-16-3b. |
| WI | Mandatory coverage. | No. | No. | Yes, up to 30 days. | No. | Wis. Stat. Ann. §§ 632.895(2), 632.895(3). |
| WY | — | — | — | — | — | State has no statutory provisions. |

# Table 5.2-8
## MANDATORY COVERAGE FOR SPECIFIED PROVIDERS

(Reimbursement for services provided is required only if the same services, provided by a physician, would be reimbursed. See also text at § 5.2[k].)

**KEY:** **Mandatory coverage.** All group policies must include coverage for this benefit. Unless otherwise noted, "Yes" indicates mandatory coverage.
**Employer option.** Insurance companies must offer policyholders (employers) this benefit option, but employers may choose not to cover employees for this particular benefit.

| | *Optometrists* | *Chiropractors* | *Dentists* | *Psychologists* | *Podiatrists* | *Social Workers* | *Nurse Practitioners or Nurse Midwives* | *Other Provisions* | *Citations to Authority* |
|---|---|---|---|---|---|---|---|---|---|
| AL | Yes. | Yes. | Yes. | Yes. | Yes. | No. | No. | Mandatory coverage for certified nurse anesthetists, home care providers, physician assistants, and any practitioner of the healing arts. Direct access to an obstetrician/gynecologist is mandatory. | Ala. Code §§ 27-1-10, 27-1-11, 27-1-15, 27-1-18, 27-1-19, 27-19-39, 27-19A-4, 27-46-1, 27-49-4, 27-51-2. But coverage for certified nurse anesthetists is preempted by ERISA for ERISA-governed plans. *Hayden v. Blue Cross and Blue Shield,* 843 F. Supp. 1427 (M.D. Ala. 1994). |
| AK | Yes. | Yes. | Yes. | Yes. | No. | Yes. | Yes, nurse midwives and nurse practitioners. | Mandatory coverage for osteopaths, naturopaths, physical therapists, and occupational therapists. | Alaska Stat. §§ 21.42.355, 21-42-385. |
| AZ | Yes. | Yes. | Yes. | Yes. | Yes. | No. | Yes, nurse practitioners. | None. | Ariz. Rev. Stat. Ann. §§ 20-1406, 20-1406.01, 20-1406.02, 20-1406.03, 32-801, 32-1201. |
| AR | Yes. | Yes. | Yes. | Yes. | Yes. | No. | No. | Coverage for psychological examiners, certified nurse anesthetists, and osteopaths is an employer option. | Ark. Stat. Ann. §§ 23-79-114, 23-79-142. |

*(Table continues.)*

# Table 5.2-8 *(cont'd)*

## MANDATORY COVERAGE FOR SPECIFIED PROVIDERS

(Reimbursement for services provided is required only if the same services, provided by a physician, would be reimbursed. See also text at § 5.2[k].)

**KEY:** **Mandatory coverage.** All group policies must include coverage for this benefit. Unless otherwise noted, "Yes" indicates mandatory coverage.
**Employer option.** Insurance companies must offer policyholders (employers) this benefit option, but employers may choose not to cover employees for this particular benefit.

| | *Optometrists* | *Chiropractors* | *Dentists* | *Psychologists* | *Podiatrists* | *Social Workers* | *Nurse Practitioners or Nurse Midwives* | *Other Provisions* | *Citations to Authority* |
|---|---|---|---|---|---|---|---|---|---|
| CA | Yes. | Yes. | Yes. | Yes. | Yes. | Yes. | Yes. | Mandatory coverage for marriage, family, and child counselors; speech pathologists; audiologists; acupuncturists; physical and occupational therapists; psychiatric mental health nurses, pharmacists, and opticians. | Cal. Ins. Code §§ 10125.1, 10176, 10179, 10353. |
| CO | Yes. | Yes. | Yes. | Yes. | Yes. | Yes. | No. | Mandatory coverage for osteopaths and registered professional nurses. | Colo. Rev. Stat. § 10-16-104(7). |
| CT | Yes. | Yes. | Yes. | Yes. | No. | Yes. | Yes. | Mandatory coverage for mental health clinical nurse specialists, marriage and family therapists, and audiologists. Direct access to an obstetrician/gynecologist is mandatory. | Conn. Gen. Stat. Ann. §§ 20-138d, 38a-514, 38a-517, 38a-526, 38a-530b, 38a-534. |
| DE | Yes. | Yes. | No. | No. | Yes. | No. | Yes, nurse midwives and nurse practitioners. | None. | Del. Code Ann. tit. 18, §§ 2318, 3553 tit. 24, §§ 511, 717, 2101. |
| DC | Yes. | No. | No. | Yes. | No. | No. | No. | None. | D.C. Code Ann. § 35-530. |

| | | | | | | | | | |
|---|---|---|---|---|---|---|---|---|---|
| FL | Yes. | Yes. | Yes. | No. | Yes. | No. | Yes, nurse midwives and advanced registered nurse practitioners. | Mandatory coverage for acupuncturists, nursing assistants, physician assistants, and massage therapists. | Fla. Stat. Ann. §§ 627.419, 627.6406, 627.6472, 627.6574, 627.6618, 627.6619. |
| GA | Yes. | Yes. | No. | Yes. | No. | No. | No. | None. | Ga. Code Ann. §§ 33-24-27, 33-24-27.1, 33-30-7. |
| HI | Yes. | No. | Yes. | Yes. | No. | No. | No. | None. | Haw. Rev. Stat. § 431:10A-116. |
| ID | — | — | — | — | — | — | — | — | State has no statutory provisions. |
| IL | Yes. | No. | No. | Yes. | Yes. | Yes. | No. | None. | Ill. Ann. Stat. ch. 215, ¶¶ 5/364.1, 5/370b, 5/370c. |
| IN | Yes. | Yes. | Yes. | Yes. | Yes. | No. | No. | Mandatory coverage for osteopaths and nurse anesthetists. | Ind. Code §§ 27-8-6-1, 27-8-6-5. |
| IA | Yes. | Yes. | Yes. | No. | No. | No. | No. | Mandatory coverage for registered nurses, physician assistants, nurse practitioners, and skilled nursing care. | Iowa Code Ann. §§ 509.3, 514C.11, 514C.2, 514C.3. |
| KS | Yes. | Yes. | Yes. | Yes. | Yes. | Yes. | Yes, nurse practitioners. | Mandatory coverage for osteopaths. | Kan. Stat. Ann. §§ 40-2, 100 *et seq.*, 40-2250, 65-2802. |
| KY | Yes. | Yes. | Yes. | Yes. | Yes. | Yes. | No. | Mandatory coverage for osteopaths. | Ky. Rev. Stat. Ann. §§ 304.18-0363, 304.18-095, 304.18-097. |
| LA | Yes. | Yes. | Yes. | Yes. | Yes. | Yes. | No. | Mandatory coverage for audiologists, speech pathologists, occupational therapists, and physical therapists. Direct access to an obstetrician/gynecologist is mandatory. | La. Rev. Stat. Ann. §§ 22.213.1, 22:215.17, 22:230.1, 22:662, 22:664, 22:665, 22:668, 22:669, 22:1513. |
| ME | Employer option. | Yes. | No. | Yes. | No. | Yes. | No. | Mandatory coverage for clinical nurse specialists and acupuncturists. | Me. Rev. Stat. Ann. tit. 24-A §§ 2744, 2835, 2837-B, 2840-A, 2841. |

*(Table continues.)*

# Table 5.2-8 *(cont'd)*
## MANDATORY COVERAGE FOR SPECIFIED PROVIDERS

(Reimbursement for services provided is required only if the same services, provided by a physician, would be reimbursed. See also text at § 5.2[k].)

**KEY:** **Mandatory coverage.** All group policies must include coverage for this benefit. Unless otherwise noted, "Yes" indicates mandatory coverage.
**Employer option.** Insurance companies must offer policyholders (employers) this benefit option, but employers may choose not to cover employees for this particular benefit.

| | *Optometrists* | *Chiropractors* | *Dentists* | *Psychologists* | *Podiatrists* | *Social Workers* | *Nurse Practitioners or Nurse Midwives* | *Other Provisions* | *Citations to Authority* |
|---|---|---|---|---|---|---|---|---|---|
| MD | Yes. | No. | No. | Yes. | Yes. | Yes. | Coverage for nurse practitioners and nurse midwives is an employer option. Mandatory coverage for nurse anesthetists. | Direct access to an obstetrician/gynecologist is mandatory. | Md. Ins. Code §§ 15-703, 15-707, 15-708, 15-709, 15-710, 15-713, 15-714, 15-816. |
| MA | Yes. | Yes. | Yes. | Yes. | Yes. | Yes. | Yes. | Mandatory coverage for certified nurse anesthetists. | Mass. Gen. Laws Ann. ch. 175, §§ 47B, 47E, 47Q, 108B, 108D, 110. |
| MI | Yes. | Yes. | Yes. | No. | Yes. | No. | No. | None. | Mich. Stat. Ann. §§ 24.12239, 24.12243, 24.13475. |
| MN | Yes. | Yes. | No. | Yes. | No. | No. | No. | Mandatory coverage for nursing services, including registered nurses and nurse practitioners. | Minn. Stat. Ann. §§ 62A.15, 62A.152, 62A.3091, 62A.3092. |
| MS | Yes. | Yes. | Yes. | Yes. | — | Yes. | Yes, nurse practitioners. | Direct access to an obstetrician/gynecologist is mandatory. | Miss. Code Ann. §§ 83-41-203, 83-41-209, 83-41-211, 83-41-213, 83-41-215, 83-41-217. |

| | | | | | | | | | |
|---|---|---|---|---|---|---|---|---|---|
| MO | — | — | — | — | — | — | — | — | State has no statutory provisions. |
| MT | Yes. | Yes. | Yes. | Yes. | Yes. | Yes. | Yes, nurse specialists. | Mandatory coverage for physician assistants, osteopaths, acupuncturists, licensed professional counselors, and denturists. | Mont. Code. Ann. §§ 33-22-111, 37-29-104. |
| NE | Yes. | Yes. | Yes. | Yes. | Yes. | No. | No. | Mandatory coverage for osteopaths. | Neb. Rev. Stat. § 44-513. |
| NV | No. | Yes. | No. | Yes. | No. | Yes. | No. | Mandatory coverage for marriage and family therapists, acupuncturists, and nursing services. | Nev. Rev. Stat. §§ 689B.038, 689B.039, 689B.0383, 689B.0385, 689B.045, 689B.049. |
| NH | Yes. | Yes. | No. | No. | Yes. | No. | Yes, nurse practitioners. | Mandatory coverage for osteopaths. | N.H. Rev. Stat. Ann. §§ 317-A, 415:5. |
| NJ | Yes. | Yes. | Yes. | Yes. | No. | No. | No. | Mandatory coverage for registered professional nurses. | N.J. Rev. Stat. §§ 17B:27-50, 17B:27-51, 17B:27-51.1, 17B:27-51.1a, 17B:27-51.8. |
| NM | Yes. | No. | No. | Yes. | Yes. | Yes. | Yes, nurse midwives. | Mandatory coverage for lay-midwives or registered nurses in expanded practice. | N.M. Stat. Ann. §§ 59A-22-32, 59A-22-32.1. |
| NY | Yes. | Yes. | Yes. | Yes. | Yes. | Yes. | No. | Mandatory coverage for physical therapists, speech pathologists, and audiologists. | N.Y. Ins. Law §§ 3221 (l)(4)(A), 3221 (l)(4)(D), 4235 (f)(4)(B), 4235 (f)(4)(C), 4235 (f)(4)(D), 4235 (f)(4)(E), 4235 (f)(4)(F), 4235(f)(4)(G), 4235(f)(4)(H). |
| NC | Yes. | Yes. | Yes. | Yes. | Yes. | Yes. | No. | Mandatory coverage for registered nurses and pharmacists. Direct access to an obstetrician/gynecologist is mandatory. | N.C. Gen. Stat. §§ 58-50-25, 58-50-30, 58-51-38. |

*(Table continues.)*

## **Table 5.2-8** *(cont'd)*
## MANDATORY COVERAGE FOR SPECIFIED PROVIDERS

(Reimbursement for services provided is required only if the same services, provided by a physician, would be reimbursed. See also text at § 5.2[k].)

**KEY:** **Mandatory coverage.** All group policies must include coverage for this benefit. Unless otherwise noted, "Yes" indicates mandatory coverage.
**Employer option.** Insurance companies must offer policyholders (employers) this benefit option, but employers may choose not to cover employees for this particular benefit.

| | *Optometrists* | *Chiropractors* | *Dentists* | *Psychologists* | *Podiatrists* | *Social Workers* | *Nurse Practitioners or Nurse Midwives* | *Other Provisions* | *Citations to Authority* |
|---|---|---|---|---|---|---|---|---|---|
| ND | Yes. | Yes. | No. | Yes. | No. | Yes. | Yes. | Mandatory coverage for registered nurses not working in a hospital or care facility and licensed addiction counselors. | N.D. Cent. Code §§ 26.1-36-04, 26.1-36-06, 26.1-36-08, 26.1-36-09, 26.1-36-09.5, 43-13-31. |
| OH | Yes. | Yes. | Yes. | Yes. | Yes. | No. | Yes, nurse midwives. | Mandatory coverage for osteopaths and mechanotherapists. | Ohio Rev. Code Ann. §§ 3923.23, 3923.23.1, 3923.23.2, 3923.23.3, 3923.23.4. |
| OK | Yes. | Yes. | Yes. | Yes. | Yes. | Yes. | No. | Mandatory coverage for osteopaths. | Okla. Stat. tit. 36, §§ 3634, 4404, 6051, 6054, 6055. |
| OR | Yes. | No. | Yes. | Yes. | No. | Yes. | Yes, nurse practitioners. | Mandatory coverage for denturists, acupuncturists, and physician assistants. | Or. Rev. Stat. §§ 743.703, 743.709, 743.712, 743.713, 743.714, 743.719, 743.722, 743.724. |
| PA | Yes. | Yes. | Yes. | Yes. | Yes. | No. | Yes. | Mandatory coverage for nursing services, osteopaths, and physical therapists. | Pa. Stat. Ann. tit. 40, §§ 768, 1502, 1511, 3001, 3002, 3024. |

| | | | | | | | | | |
|---|---|---|---|---|---|---|---|---|---|
| RI | No. | Yes. | No. | No. | Yes. | No. | Yes, nurse midwives and nurse practitioners. | Mandatory coverage for osteopaths; mandatory coverage for psychiatric and mental health nurse clinical specialists practicing in a private, nonprofit ambulatory care facility, mental health counselors, and family therapists. | R.I. Gen. Laws §§ 5-29-6, 5-30-11, 5-37-1, 27-18-25, 27-18-31, 27-18-34, 27-18-35. |
| SC | Yes. | Yes. | No. | Yes. | Yes. | No. | No. | Mandatory coverage for oral surgeons. | S.C. Code Ann. §§ 38-71-200, 38-71-210. |
| SD | Yes. | Yes. | Yes. | Yes. | Yes. | Yes. | No. | Mandatory coverage for osteopaths, nurse anesthetists, and mental health professionals. | S.D. Codified Laws Ann. §§ 58-17-53, 58-17-54, 58-17-56. |
| TN | Yes. | Yes. | Yes. | Yes. | Yes. | Yes. | Yes, nurse midwives. | Mandatory coverage for audiologists, nurse practitioners, nurse anesthetists, clinical nursing specialists, and speech pathologists. | Tenn. Code Ann. §§ 56-7-2401–56-7-2405, 56-7-2407, 56-7-2408, 56-7-2603. |
| TX | Yes. | Yes. | Yes. | Yes. | Yes. | Yes. | No. | Mandatory coverage for audiologists, speech pathologists, dieticians, osteopaths, telemedicine providers, and professional counselors. Direct access to an obstetrician/gynecologist is mandatory. | Tex. Ins. Code Ann. art. 3.70-1, art. 3.70-2(H), art. 21.52, art. 21.53D, art. 21.53F. |
| UT | Yes. | Yes. | Yes. | Yes. | Yes. | Yes. | Yes. | Mandatory coverage for all licensed health care providers. | Utah Code Ann. 31A-22-618. |
| VT | — | — | — | — | — | — | — | — | State has no statutory provisions. |
| VA | Yes. | Yes. | Yes. | Yes. | Yes. | Yes. | No. | Mandatory coverage for chiropodists, opticians, professional counselors, physical therapists, audiologists, speech pathologists, nurse midwives, and clinical mental health nurses. Direct access to an obstetrician/gynecologist is mandatory. | Va. Code Ann. §§ 38.2-3407.11, 38.2-3408, 38.2-3410. |

*(Table continues.)*

## Table 5.2-8 *(cont'd)*

## MANDATORY COVERAGE FOR SPECIFIED PROVIDERS

(Reimbursement for services provided is required only if the same services, provided by a physician, would be reimbursed. See also text at § 5.2[k].)

**KEY:** **Mandatory coverage.** All group policies must include coverage for this benefit. Unless otherwise noted, "Yes" indicates mandatory coverage.
**Employer option.** Insurance companies must offer policyholders (employers) this benefit option, but employers may choose not to cover employees for this particular benefit.

| | *Optometrists* | *Chiropractors* | *Dentists* | *Psychologists* | *Podiatrists* | *Social Workers* | *Nurse Practitioners or Nurse Midwives* | *Other Provisions* | *Citations to Authority* |
|---|---|---|---|---|---|---|---|---|---|
| WA | Yes. | Yes. | Yes. | Yes. | Yes. | No. | Yes. | Mandatory coverage for nursing services, denturists, and chiropodists. | Wash. Rev. Code §§ 48.20.390, 48.21.130, 48.21.140, 48.21.141, 48.21.142, 48.21.144, 48.21.146, 48.21.148. |
| WV | No. | Yes. | No. | No. | Yes. | No. | Yes. | Mandatory coverage for nursing services and osteopaths. | W. Va. Code §§ 33-16-3e, 33-16-10. |
| WI | Yes. | Yes. | Yes. | No. | No. | No. | Yes, nurse practitioners. | No. | Wis. Stat. Ann. § 632.87. |
| WY | No. | No. | Yes. | Yes. | No. | No. | No. | Mandatory coverage for registered dieti-tians. Statute also mandates coverage for any health care pro-vider licensed under state law. | Wyo. Stat. §§ 26-13-109, 26-22-101, 26-22-104. |

# Table 5.2-9
## MANDATORY COVERAGE FOR PRESCRIPTIONS, PROSTHETIC DEVICES, AND MEDICAL SUPPLIES

(States not listed have no statutes governing mandatory coverage for drugs and prosthetic devices. See also text at § 5.2[1].)

**KEY:** **Mandatory coverage.** All group policies must include coverage for this benefit. Unless otherwise noted, "Yes" indicates mandatory coverage.
**Employer option.** Insurance companies must offer policyholders (employers) this benefit option, but employers may choose not to cover employees for this particular benefit.

| | *Prosthetic Devices* | *Prescription Drugs* | *Nonprescription Formulas* | *Citations to Authority* |
|---|---|---|---|---|
| AK | No. | No. | Yes, formulas for phenylketonuria. | Alaska Stat. § 21.42.380. |
| AZ | Yes, following mastectomy, but only if mastectomy is covered. | No. | No. | Ariz. Rev. Stat. Ann., § 20-1402. |
| CA | Yes, following mastectomy, but only if mastectomy is covered; required option otherwise; and following laryngectomy. | No. | No. | Cal. Ins. Code §§ 10123.7, 10123.8, 10123.82. |
| CT | Yes, for devices following removal of tumors. | Yes, for hypodermic needles and syringes. | No. | Conn. Gen. Stat. Ann. §§ 38a-518a, 38a-542. |
| FL | Required option following mastectomy, but only if mastectomy is covered. | No. | No. | Fla. Stat. Ann. §§ 627.6408, 627.6612. |
| HI | No. | Yes, employer option for prescription contraceptive drugs and devices if prescription drugs and pregnancy are covered. | No. | Haw. Rev. Stat. § 431:10A-116.6. |
| IL | Yes, following mastectomy, but only if mastectomy is covered. | No. | No. | Ill. Ann. Stat. ch. 215, ¶ 5/356g. |
| IN | If mastectomy is covered, breast prosthetics must be covered. | Yes, supplies for treatment of diabetes. | — | Ind. Code Ann. §§ 27-8-5-26, 27-8-14.5-4. |
| LA | Yes, following cleft lip or palate correction, but only if such correction is covered. | No. | No. | La. Rev. Stat. Ann. § 22:215.8. |
| ME | No. | No. | Yes, coverage for medical foods for inborn errors of metabolism. | Me. Rev. Stat. Ann. tit. 24-A, §§ 2837-D, 2847-E. |
| MD | No. | No. | Mandatory coverage of blood products and low protein modified medical food products. | Md. Ins. Code §§ 15-803, 15-807. |

*(Table continues.)*

## Table 5.2-9 *(cont'd)*

## MANDATORY COVERAGE FOR PRESCRIPTIONS, PROSTHETIC DEVICES, AND MEDICAL SUPPLIES

(States not listed have no statutes governing mandatory coverage for drugs and prosthetic devices. See also text at § 5.2[k].)

**KEY:** **Mandatory coverage.** All group policies must include coverage for this benefit. Unless otherwise noted, "Yes" indicates mandatory coverage.
**Employer option.** Insurance companies must offer policyholders (employers) this benefit option, but employers may choose not to cover employees for this particular benefit.

| | *Prosthetic Devices* | *Prescription Drugs* | *Nonprescription Formulas* | *Citations to Authority* |
|---|---|---|---|---|
| MA | Yes, for scalp hair prosthesis for cancer patients. | No. | Yes, enteral formulas for Crohn's disease, ulcerative colitis, and other gastrointestinal problems, and formulas for phenylketonuria. | Mass. Gen. Laws Ann. ch. 32A, § 17E; ch. 175, §§ 47C, 47I, 47N. |
| MI | Yes, following mastectomy. | Yes, for antineoplastic drugs. | No. | Mich. Stat. Ann. §§ 24.13613, 24.13616(1). |
| MN | Yes, scalp hair prosthesis for loss suffered from alopecia areata. | No. | Yes, formulas for phenylketonuria. | Minn. Stat. Ann. §§ 62A.26, 62A.28. |
| NV | Yes, following mastectomy, but only if mastectomy is covered. | No. | No. | Nev. Rev. Stat. § 689B.0375. |
| NH | Yes, hair prosthesis is covered when other prostheses covered. | No. | Yes, for enteral formulas. | N.H. Rev. Stat. Ann. §§ 415:18-d, 415:18-e. |
| NJ | Yes, following mastectomy. | No. | No. | N.J. Rev. Stat. §§ 17B:27-46.1a, 17B:27-46.1m. |
| NY | No. | No. | Yes, formulas for phenylketonuria. | N.Y. Ins. Law §§ 3221-k(7), 3221-k(7)(A), 3221(k)(11). |
| ND | No. | Required option. | No. | N.D. Cent. Code § 26.1-36-06. |
| OR | Yes, maxillofacial devices. | No. | Yes, nonprescription enteral formulas. | Or. Rev. Stat. §§ 743.706, 743.729. |
| TX | No. | No. | Yes, formulas for phenylketonuria. | Tex. Ins. Code Ann. art. 3.79. |
| VA | — | If prescription drugs are covered, contraceptives must be covered. | — | Va. Code Ann § 38.2-3407.5:1. |
| WA | No. | No. | Yes, formulas for phenylketonuria. | Wash. Rev. Code § 48.21.300. |
| WV | — | Supplies and equipment for treatment of diabetes. | — | W. Va. Code Ann. § 33-16-16. |

# Table 5.2-10
## INSURER DISCRIMINATION PROHIBITIONS: SPECIFIED CONDITIONS

(States not listed here have no statutes governing insurer discrimination prohibitions covering persons with specified conditions. See also text at § 5.2[m].)

**KEY: DES.** Diethylstilbestrol. Exposure to this drug has been shown to cause a variety of reproductive and medical problems.

| | *AIDS* | *DES* | *Handicap or Blindness* | *Preexisting Conditions* | *State Regulation of Utilization Review* | *Other Provisions* | *Citations to Authority* |
|---|---|---|---|---|---|---|---|
| AL | No. | No. | No. | No. | Yes. | Insurer may not deny coverage because of sickle-cell anemia or discriminate on the basis of genetic testing. | Ala. Code §§ 27-3A-3 *et seq.*, 27-5-13, 27-51-2. |
| AK | No. | No. | Yes. | Yes. Insurer may not exclude coverage on the basis of a preexisting condition for longer than 12 months from the date of coverage. | No. | Insurer may not discriminate on the basis of genetic testing or domestic abuse. | Alaska Stat. §§ 21.54.100, 21.54.110. |
| AZ | No. | No. | Yes. | Yes. Insurer may not exclude coverage of a condition for which insured has previously tested negative. | Yes. | Insurer may not discriminate on basis of hemophilia, developmental delay or disability, or genetic conditions or against victims of domestic abuse. | Ariz. Rev. Stat. Ann. §§ 20-448, 20-2501 *et seq.* |
| CA | No. | Yes. | Yes. Insurer may not deny or limit coverage on basis of physical or mental impairment, or partial or total blindness. | Yes. Insurer may not exclude coverage for any individual on the basis of a preexisting condition for longer than 6 months from the date of coverage. Individual must be given credit toward the waiting period for coverage under a prior policy, if the prior coverage ended no later than 63 days before the current coverage began. | No. | Insurer may not discriminate against victims of domestic abuse or deny coverage on basis of sickle-cell, Tay-Sachs, thalassemia, x-linked hemophilia A traits, or other genetic traits. Self-insured employee plans may not discriminate on the basis of genetic characteristics. | Cal. Ins. Code §§ 10119.7, 10123.3, 10140, 10144.2; Cal. Health & Safety § 1357.51. |

*(Table continues.)*

# Table 5.2-10 *(cont'd)*

## INSURER DISCRIMINATION PROHIBITIONS: SPECIFIED CONDITIONS

(States not listed here have no statutes governing insurer discrimination prohibitions covering persons with specified conditions. See also text at § 5.2[m].)

**KEY: DES.** Diethylstilbestrol. Exposure to this drug has been shown to cause a variety of reproductive and medical problems.

| | *AIDS* | *DES* | *Handicap or Blindness* | *Preexisting Conditions* | *State Regulation of Utilization Review* | *Other Provisions* | *Citations to Authority* |
|---|---|---|---|---|---|---|---|
| CO | No. | No. | Yes. Insurer may not deny or limit coverage on basis of blindness or physical disability. | Yes. Insurer may not exclude coverage for any individual on the basis of a preexisting condition for longer than 6 months from the date of coverage. | Yes. | Insurer may not discriminate on the basis of genetic testing or domestic abuse. | Colo. Rev. Stat. §§ 10-3-1104, 10-3-1104.7, 10-16-102, 10-16-118, 10-16-214. |
| CT | No. | Yes. | Yes. Insurer may not deny or limit coverage on basis of blindness or physical or mental disability. | Yes. Comprehensive health care plans may not deny coverage of a preexisting condition for longer than 12 months from the date of coverage. | No. | Insurer may not discriminate against victims of domestic abuse. | Conn. Gen. Stat. Ann. §§ 38a-553, 38a-816. |
| DE | No. | No. | Yes. Insurer may not refuse to issue policy on the basis of blindness or deafness or other physical or mental condition. | Yes. Insurer may not apply preexisting condition clauses to losses incurred after 12 months from the date of coverage (and only if medical advice or treatment is sought in connection with the condition within 6 months from date of coverage). | No. | Insurer may not discriminate against victims of abuse. | De. Code Ann. tit. 18, §§ 2304, 2316, 3517, 3557, 3561. |
| DC | Yes. Insurer may not limit coverage or impose a deductible or co-insurance provision related to the care of AIDS, ARC, HIV, or diseases arising out of such conditions unless they apply generally to all benefits under the policy or contract. | No. | No. | No. | No. | None. | D.C. Code Ann. §§ 35-223, 35-1703, 35-1704. |

| | | | | | | | |
|---|---|---|---|---|---|---|---|
| FL | Yes. Insurer may exclude or limit coverage only as provided in preexisting condition clause. | No. | Yes. Insurer may not deny or charge unfairly discriminatory rates on basis of physical or mental impairment. | Yes. Preexisting conditions must be covered after 12 months, and insured must be given credit toward the 12 months for coverage under a prior policy, if the prior coverage ended no later than 63 days before the current coverage began. | No. | Insurer may not deny coverage or charge higher premium because of sickle-cell trait. Insurer may not discriminate based on health-status factors or genetic testing. | Fla. Stat. Ann. §§ 626.9707, 627.429, 627.4301, 627.607, 627.6045, 627.6561, 627.6576, 627.65625. |
| GA | No. | No. | No. | Yes. Insurer may not deny benefits for loss incurred more than 12 months after the date of coverage if loss is due to a preexisting condition. | No. | None. | Ga. Code Ann. § 33-24-26. |
| HI | Yes. Insurer may not discriminate on basis of HIV test. | No. | Yes. Insurer may not discriminate on basis of mental or physical impairment. | No. | No. | Insurer may not discriminate on the basis of genetic information. | Haw. Rev. Stat. §§ 431:10A-118, 431:13-103. |
| ID | No. | No. | No. | Yes. If employer has 50 or more employees, insurer cannot deny, exclude, or limit benefits for more than 12 months due to a preexisting condition. | No. | None. | Idaho Code § 41-2221. |
| IL | No. | Yes. | Yes. Insurer may not discriminate on basis of handicap, disability, or blindness. | No. | No. | Insurer may not deny coverage or exclude benefits because of fibrocystic breast condition unless biopsy indicates increased disposition to development of breast cancer. | Ill. Ann. Stat. ch. 215, ¶¶ 5/356f, 5/356n, 5/364. |
| IN | No. | No. | Yes. Insurer may not deny or limit coverage on basis of blindness or cancel policy based on mental or physical condition. | Yes. Benefits may not be excluded or limited for more than 12 months (as of 1/1/98) due to a preexisting condition, and credit against the waiting period must be given for time spent under preexisting condition clauses of other policies, if statutory conditions are met. (Note: prior to 1/1/98 statutes provided for 18-month exclusion period.) | Yes. | Insurer may not discriminate against victims of abuse or on the basis of genetic testing. | Ind. Code §§ 27-4-1-4, 27-8-5-2.5, 27-8-5-2.6, 27-8-5-19, 27-8-17 *et seq.*, 27-8-24.3-1 *et seq.*, 27-8-26-5 *et seq.* |
| IA | No. | No. | No. | No. | No. | Insurer may not discriminate because of a fibrocystic breast condition. | Iowa Code Ann. § 514C.7. |

*(Table continues.)*

# **Table 5.2-10** *(cont'd)*
## INSURER DISCRIMINATION PROHIBITIONS: SPECIFIED CONDITIONS

(States not listed here have no statutes governing insurer discrimination prohibitions covering persons with specified conditions. See also text at § 5.2[m].)

**KEY: DES.** Diethylstilbestrol. Exposure to this drug has been shown to cause a variety of reproductive and medical problems.

| | *AIDS* | *DES* | *Handicap or Blindness* | *Preexisting Conditions* | *State Regulation of Utilization Review* | *Other Provisions* | *Citations to Authority* |
|---|---|---|---|---|---|---|---|
| KS | No. | No. | Yes. Insurer may not discriminate on basis of mental or physical handicap. | Yes. After a 90 day waiting period, there may be no exclusions. | Yes. | Insurer may not discriminate on the basis of genetic testing. | Kan. Stat. Ann. §§ 40-22a03 *et seq.*, 40-2209, 40-2259. |
| KY | Yes. Insurer may not exclude coverage for HIV infection or deny coverage because of HIV diagnosis. | No. | Yes. Insurer may not discriminate on basis of blindness. | No. | Yes. | None. | Ky. Rev. Stat. Ann. §§ 304.12-013, 304.12-215, 311.131 *et seq.* |
| LA | No. | No. | Yes. Insurer may not discriminate on basis of disability. | Yes. Insurer may not deny or limit benefits for losses incurred more than 12 months following the date of coverage if losses are due to preexisting conditions. But insured may receive credit for time insured under a previous policy, if statutory conditions are met. | Yes. | Insurer may not discriminate on basis of sickle-cell trait, prenatal testing, genetic testing, or alcoholism (recovered). | La. Rev. Stat. Ann. §§ 22.215.12, 22:213.6, 22:213.7, 22:215.16, 22:229.2, 22:250.1 *et seq.*, 22.652.1, 22:2021 *et seq.*, 40:2721 *et seq.* |
| ME | Yes. Insurer may not discriminate on the basis of AIDS, ARC, or HIV, except for exclusions in certain cases for preexisting conditions. | No. | Yes. Insurer may not deny or limit coverage on basis of blindness and physical or mental handicap. | Yes. Insurer may not deny benefits for loss incurred more than 12 months after date of coverage if loss is due to a preexisting condition. | Yes. | Insurer may not discriminate against victims of domestic abuse. | Me. Rev. Stat. Ann. tit. 24-A, §§ 2159, 2159-A, 2159-B, 2629, 2749-B, 2711 *et seq.*, 2846, 2850. |
| MD | No. | Yes. | No. | No. | No. | Yes. Insurer may not discriminate on basis of mental illness or drug/alcohol abuse, or deny coverage because insured has breast implants. | Md. Ins. Code §§ 15-503, 15-504, 15-802. |

| | | | | | | | |
|---|---|---|---|---|---|---|---|
| MA | No. | Yes. | Yes. Insurer may not discriminate on basis of blindness, deafness, mental retardation, or physical impairment. | Yes. Insurer may not deny claim for loss incurred after 2 years from the date of coverage on basis that a condition not excluded by name existed prior to the date of coverage. | No. | Insurer may not discriminate against victims of abuse. | Mass. Gen. Laws Ann. ch. 175, §§ 108C, 108G, 193T. |
| MI | No. | No. | Yes. Insurer may not deny or limit coverage on basis of handicap. | Yes. Group policy may not limit coverage of an insured's preexisting condition if, during the period prior to the date of coverage, insured was enrolled in another group policy issued by the insurer. | No. | None. | Mich. Stat. Ann. §§ 24.12027, 24.13607. |
| MN | No. | Yes. | No. | No. | Yes. | Yes. Insurer may not discriminate on basis of fibrocystic breast condition. | Minn. Stat. Ann. §§ 62A.154, 62A.305, 62M.02 *et seq.* |
| MS | No. | No. | No. | Yes. Insurer may not deny benefits for loss incurred more than 6 months after the date of coverage if loss is due to a preexisting condition. | Yes. | None. | Miss. Code Ann. §§ 41-83-1 *et seq.*, 83-9-49. |
| MO | Yes. Insurer may not deny or limit coverage of AIDS on renewal of policy. | No. | No. | No. | Yes. | None. | Mo. Rev. Stat. §§ 191.671, 374.500 *et seq.* |
| MT | No. | No. | Yes. | Yes. Insurer may not deny benefits for loss incurred more than 12 months after the date of coverage if loss is due to a preexisting condition. | Yes. | Yes. Insurer may not refuse to consider an individual's application for disability insurance based solely on individual's genetic condition. | Mont. Code Ann. §§ 33-18-206, 33-22-110, 33-22-514, 33-22-526, 33-32-102 *et seq.* |
| NE | No. | No. | Yes. | Insurer may not deny benefits for loss incurred more than 12 months from date of coverage. Individual must be given credit toward the waiting period for coverage under a prior policy, if the prior coverage ended no later than 63 days before the current coverage began. | Yes. | Insurer may not discriminate on the basis of genetic testing or domestic abuse. | Neb. Rev. Stat. §§ 44-5401 *et seq.*, 44-6910, 44-6915, 44-6916. |

*(Table continues.)*

# Table 5.2-10 *(cont'd)*
## INSURER DISCRIMINATION PROHIBITIONS: SPECIFIED CONDITIONS

(States not listed here have no statutes governing insurer discrimination prohibitions covering persons with specified conditions. See also text at § 5.2[m].)

**KEY: DES.** Diethylstilbestrol. Exposure to this drug has been shown to cause a variety of reproductive and medical problems.

| | *AIDS* | *DES* | *Handicap or Blindness* | *Preexisting Conditions* | *State Regulation of Utilization Review* | *Other Provisions* | *Citations to Authority* |
|---|---|---|---|---|---|---|---|
| NH | No. | No. | Yes. | Yes. Insurer may not deny benefits for loss incurred more than 12 months after the date of coverage for loss due to preexisting condition. Individual must be given credit toward the waiting period for coverage under a prior policy, if the prior coverage ended no later than 63 days before the current coverage began. | No. | Insurer may not discriminate on the basis of health status, genetic testing, or domestic abuse. | N.H. Rev. Stat. Ann. §§ 420-G:4, 420-G:6, 420-G:7. |
| NJ | No. | No. | No. | Yes. Group policy may not limit coverage of an insured's preexisting condition for more than 12 months, and individual must be given credit toward the 12 months for prior coverage, if the prior coverage ended not more than 63 days before the current coverage began. | No. | Insurer may not discriminate based on genetic characteristics. | N.J. Rev. Stat. §§ 17B:27-46.1d, 17B:27-36.2, 17B:27-55, 17B:27-57, 17B:27-58, 17B:27A-17. |
| NM | No. | No. | Yes. | Insurer may not deny claim for loss incurred after 6 months from the date of coverage on basis that a condition not excluded by name existed prior to the date of coverage. Individual must be given credit toward the 6 months for coverage under a prior policy, if the prior coverage ended no | No. | Insurer may not discriminate on the basis of domestic abuse or genetic information. | N.M. Stat. Ann. §§ 59A-16-13.2, 59A-16B-4, 59A-23E-3, 59A-23E-5, 59A-23E-11. |

| | | | | | | | |
|---|---|---|---|---|---|---|---|
| | | | | more than 63 days before the current coverage began. | | | |
| NY | No. | Yes. | Yes. | Insurer may not exclude coverage of a preexisting condition for longer than 12 months following the date of coverage. Individual must be given credit toward the waiting period for coverage under a prior policy, if the prior coverage ended no later than 63 days before the current coverage began. | No. | Yes. Insurer may not refuse coverage because insured has been diagnosed with breast cancer if initial diagnosis was more than 3 years prior to the date of application. Insurer may not discriminate on the basis of genetic testing or domestic abuse. | N.Y. Ins. Law §§ 3221(q)(1), 3232, 3234, 3235. |
| NC | No. | No. | Yes. Insurer may not discriminate on basis of handicap, mental illness, or chemical dependency. | Insurer may not limit coverage of preexisting conditions for more than 12 months, and the individual must be given credit toward the 12 months for coverage under a prior policy, if the prior coverage ended not more than 63 days before the current coverage began. | Yes. | Yes. Insurer may not discriminate on basis of sickle-cell or hemoglobin C traits or health status factors, including genetic testing and domestic abuse. | N.C. Gen. Stat. §§ 58-50-60 *et seq.*, 58-51-45, 58-51-55, 58-68-30, 58-68-35. |
| ND | No. | No. | Yes. Insurer may not deny or limit coverage on basis of blindness or partial blindness, except for preexisting conditions. | Yes. Insurer may not deny claim for loss incurred after 12 months from the date of coverage on basis that a condition not excluded by name existed prior to the date of coverage. Insured must be given credit toward the 12 months for coverage under a prior policy, if the prior coverage ended no more than 63 days before the current coverage began. | Yes. | None. | N.D. Cent. Code §§ 26.1-04-03, 26.1-26.4-01, 26.1-36-05, 26.1-36.4-03. |
| OH | Yes. Insurer may not cancel coverage or refuse renewal because of AIDS, ARC, or HIV diagnosis. | No. | Yes. Insurer may not discriminate on basis of handicap or blindness. | No. | No. | Yes. Insurer cannot require genetic testing or discriminate on the basis of it. Insurer may not discriminate on the basis of domestic abuse. | Ohio Rev. Code Ann. §§ 3901.21(Q), 3901.21(T), 3901.45, 3901.49, 3999.16. |

*(Table continues.)*

# Table 5.2-10 *(cont'd)*
## INSURER DISCRIMINATION PROHIBITIONS: SPECIFIED CONDITIONS

(States not listed here have no statutes governing insurer discrimination prohibitions covering persons with specified conditions. See also text at § 5.2[m].)

**KEY: DES.** Diethylstilbestrol. Exposure to this drug has been shown to cause a variety of reproductive and medical problems.

| | *AIDS* | *DES* | *Handicap or Blindness* | *Preexisting Conditions* | *State Regulation of Utilization Review* | *Other Provisions* | *Citations to Authority* |
|---|---|---|---|---|---|---|---|
| OK | — | — | — | Insurer may impose limits on coverage of preexisting conditions. Individual must be given credit toward the waiting period for coverage under a prior policy, if the prior coverage ended no later than 63 days before the current coverage began. | Yes. | — | Okla. Stat. tit. 36, §§ 4509.2, 6552 *et seq.* |
| OR | No. | Yes. | No. | No. | No. | None. | Or. Rev. Stat. § 743.710. |
| PA | No. | No. | No. | Yes. Insurer may not deny claim for loss incurred after 3 years from the date of coverage on basis that a preexisting condition not excluded by name existed prior to the date of coverage. | Yes. | Insurer may not discriminate against victims of abuse. | Pa. Stat. Ann. tit. 40, § 753, Act. No. 1996-24 Act. No. 68, § 1. |
| RI | Yes. Insurer may not cancel or refuse renewal because of positive AIDS test result. | No. | No. | Yes. Insurer may not limit coverage for a preexisting condition or deny coverage based on a preexisting condition for individuals who were previously insured for 12 months prior to the date seeking coverage. | Yes. | None. | R.I. Gen Laws §§ 23-6-22, 23-6-24, 23-17.12-1 *et seq.*, 27-18-37. |

| | | | | | | | |
|---|---|---|---|---|---|---|---|
| SC | No. | No. | Yes. | Yes. Preexisting conditions must be covered no later than 12 months without medical care, treatment, or supplies ending after the date of coverage. Individual must be given credit toward the waiting period for coverage under a prior policy, if the prior coverage ended no later than 63 days before the current coverage began. | Yes. | Insurer may not discriminate on the basis of genetic testing or domestic abuse. | S.C. Code Ann. §§ 38-70-10 *et seq.*, 38-71-730, 38-71-850, 38-71-860. |
| SD | No. | No. | No. | Yes. Insurer may not exclude coverage of a preexisting condition for longer than 12 months following the date of coverage, and individual must be given credit toward the 12 months for coverage under a prior policy, if the prior coverage ended no more than 63 days before the current coverage began. | No. | Insurer may not exclude coverage for injuries sustained by an individual under the influence of drugs or alcohol, unless the injury was caused in the commission of a felony. | S.D. Codified Laws §§ 58-18-7.17, 58-18-45. |
| TN | No. | No. | No. | Insurer may not exclude coverage of a preexisting condition for longer than 12 months. Individual must be given credit toward the waiting period for coverage under a prior policy, if the prior coverage ended no later than 63 days before the current coverage began. | Yes. | Insurer may not discriminate based on genetic tests. | Tenn. Code Ann. §§ 56-6-701 *et seq.*, 56-7-2702 *et seq.*, 56-7-2803, 56-8-303. |
| TX | Yes. Insurer may not cancel coverage because of HIV or AIDS diagnosis. | No. | Yes. Insurer may not deny or limit coverage on basis of handicap. | Yes. Insurer may not deny benefits for loss incurred more than 12 months after the date of coverage if loss is due to a preexisting condition. | Yes. | Insurer may not discriminate based on fibrocystic breast condition or domestic abuse. | Tex. Ins. Code Ann. art. 3.51-6, art. 3.51-6D, art. 21.21-5, art. 21.21-6, art. 21.58A *et seq.* |
| UT | No. | No. | Yes. Insurer may not deny or limit coverage on the basis of a disability. | Yes. Insurer may not exclude coverage of a preexisting condition for longer than 12 months following the date of coverage. | No. | No. | Utah Code Ann. § 31A-22-605; Utah Admin. R. 540-80-3. |

*(Table continues.)*

# Table 5.2-10 *(cont'd)*
## INSURER DISCRIMINATION PROHIBITIONS: SPECIFIED CONDITIONS

(States not listed here have no statutes governing insurer discrimination prohibitions covering persons with specified conditions. See also text at § 5.2[m].)

**KEY: DES.** Diethylstilbestrol. Exposure to this drug has been shown to cause a variety of reproductive and medical problems.

| | *AIDS* | *DES* | *Handicap or Blindness* | *Preexisting Conditions* | *State Regulation of Utilization Review* | *Other Provisions* | *Citations to Authority* |
|---|---|---|---|---|---|---|---|
| VA | Yes. Insurer may not exclude or limit coverage for treatment of HIV infection or AIDS or complications or death arising therefrom. | No. | No. | Yes. Insurer may not exclude coverage of a preexisting condition for longer than 12 months following the date of coverage. Insurer must credit time under a prior policy toward the waiting period for coverage of preexisting conditions, if the prior coverage ended not more than 63 days before the current coverage began. | Yes. | None. | Va. Code Ann. §§ 32.1–137.7, 38.2-3401; 38.2-3514.1, 38.2-3531, 38.2-3432.3, 38.2-5300 *et seq.*; Va. Ins. Reg. 34 (May 1, 1990). |
| WA | No. | No. | Yes. Insurer may not deny or limit coverage on basis of sensory, mental, or physical handicap. | No. | No. | Yes. Insurer may not discriminate on basis of mastectomy or lumpectomy performed 5 or more years prior to date of coverage. | Wash. Rev. Code §§ 48.21.235, 48.30.300. |
| WV | Yes. Insurer may not cancel coverage or refuse renewal because of AIDS diagnosis. | No. | No. | Insurer may not exclude coverage of a preexisting condition for more than 12 months, and the individual must be given credit towards the 12 months for prior coverage, it the prior coverage ended not more than 63 days before the current coverage began. | No. | None. | W. Va. Code §§ 33-16-3k, 33-16-9. |

| | | | | | | | |
|---|---|---|---|---|---|---|---|
| WI | Yes. Insurer may not exclude or limit coverage or treatment of HIV infection or related condition unless exclusions or limitations apply generally to other illnesses. | No. | No. | Yes. Insurer may not exclude coverage of a preexisting condition for longer than 2 years following the date of coverage. | No. | Yes. Insurer may not require genetic testing or discriminate on the basis of it. | Wis. Stat. Ann. §§ 631.89, 631.93, 632.76. |
| WY | — | — | — | Yes. Insurer may not exclude coverage of a preexisting condition for longer than 12 months. | — | — | Wyo. Stat. § 26-19-107. |

# § 5.3 Health Benefits Continuation and Conversion

Many states have laws requiring that group health insurance policies provide certain employees and their dependents with the opportunity to continue their health benefits coverage under the employer's plan or convert to an individual policy if, because of certain events, they would otherwise lose coverage under their employer's health plan. Generally, state laws in this area list the specific occurrences that qualify a person or covered members of the person's family for continuation coverage or conversion rights, such as termination of employment, divorce, or death. The laws also list the events that can trigger the termination of coverage, such as failure to pay premiums or coverage under another plan.

Because most state laws regarding health benefits continuation and conversion are laws regulating the content of health insurance policies, they should satisfy ERISA's "savings" clause and, therefore, not be held to be preempted by ERISA. However, to the extent that states' continuation or conversion laws purport to apply to employee health benefit plans, rather than to the underlying health insurance policies, courts have held that those state laws are preempted.

## [a] COBRA Provisions

The Consolidated Omnibus Budget Reconciliation Act of 1985 (COBRA) contained provisions for extending group health care plans to qualified beneficiaries when those beneficiaries left the group covered by the health plan. Congress intended to provide some protection to employees and their families against the possibility of periods in which the employee or family member would have no health insurance available. Because of the difficulty and expense of joining a new plan and the possibility that preexisting conditions would not be covered, it was necessary to provide some assurance of coverage.

COBRA provides that group plans shall provide continuation coverage for qualified beneficiaries who lose coverage due to a qualified event. Not every insured person will qualify for continuation under these guidelines. First, the plan must be a group plan of the type subject to COBRA. COBRA applies to employee welfare benefit plans providing medical care to participants or beneficiaries directly or through insurance, reimbursement, or otherwise. Certain employers are exempt from COBRA; for example, those with fewer than 20 employees on a typical business day during the prior calendar year, church plans, and government plans.[1]

An individual must also be a qualified beneficiary to be eligible for COBRA continuation coverage. In general, COBRA provides coverage for employees covered under the plan and their spouses and dependents who were covered under the plan the day before the qualifying event.[2]

## [b] COBRA Qualifying Events

Qualifying events include the death of the covered employee, the termination or reduction of the employee's hours (other than for reasons involving gross misconduct), divorce or legal separation, entitlement to benefits under the Social Security Act, a dependent

**§ 5.3**

1. 29 U.S.C. § 1161.
2. 29 U.S.C. § 1167.

child's ceasing to be a dependent child, or the bankruptcy of the employer.[3]

When an employee or other qualified beneficiary elects COBRA coverage, the beneficiary is entitled to the same coverage as before the qualifying event. If the employer, however, makes changes in the plan with respect to beneficiaries still covered under the plan, the continuation coverage will also be subject to those changes.[4] The employee is required to pay the premiums under the continuation coverage, but the employer may not charge more than the employer's cost, plus a 2 percent administrative fee.[5] The length of the continuation coverage period varies, depending on the qualifying event, between 18 and 36 months, and the beneficiary must elect continuation coverage within 60 days of the qualifying event or the date of notice.

**State law.** Many states have laws requiring that group health insurance policies provide certain employees and their dependents with the opportunity to continue their health benefits coverage under the employer's plan or convert to an individual policy if, because of certain events, they would otherwise lose coverage under the employer's health plan. Generally, state laws in this area list the specific occurrences that would qualify an employee or covered member of the employee's family for continuation and/or conversion coverage, such as termination of employment, divorce, or death. The laws also the list the events that can trigger the termination of coverage, such as failure to pay premiums or coverage under another plan.

Because most state laws regarding health benefits continuation and conversion are laws that regulate the content of insurance policies, they should satisfy ERISA's savings clause and, therefore, should not be preempted by ERISA. Nevertheless, to the extent that some states' continuation or conversion laws purport to apply to employee health benefit plans, rather than the underlying insurance policies, courts have held those state laws to be preempted.

As discussed above, in 1986, Congress enacted the Consolidated Omnibus Budget Reconciliation Act (COBRA), which provided a federal right to continuation coverage. Although state laws would be preempted to the extent they provide a lesser level of rights to employees than provided by COBRA, states are generally free to provide greater protection to employees. Because a state's continuation coverage law may not be preempted and may impose requirements that differ from those imposed by COBRA, guidance on the interplay of state law with COBRA should be sought to ensure appropriate compliance with all applicable requirements.

**California Continuation Benefits Replacement Act (Cal-COBRA).** In 1997, the California legislature enacted Cal. Ins. Code § 10128.50 in order to extend continuation benefits to employees, and their dependents, of employers with 2 to 19 eligible employees who currently are not entitled to coverage under COBRA. Cal-COBRA provides those employees with rights similar to those guaranteed to employees covered by the federal provision.

### [c] Employer's Responsibilities Under COBRA

The employer has several responsibilities under COBRA. One of the most important is to provide *notice* to the qualified beneficiary of the right to COBRA coverage. Notice must be provided at the time of commencement of coverage and at the time a qualifying event occurs. The employee or other qualified beneficiary is responsible for informing the plan administrator of certain qualifying events, those of a dependent child's ceasing to have dependent status and a divorce or legal separation. For other qualifying events, however, the employer or plan administrator must determine that the event has occurred.[6]

Another employer responsibility is to continue coverage during the election period or when coverage is being retroactively reinstated. The qualified beneficiary has 60 days in which to choose continuation coverage. If the beneficiary decides not to continue coverage, the employer's responsibilities ended as of the qualifying event. If, however, the beneficiary elects continuation coverage, the coverage is retroactive from the date it would otherwise have ended. The employer may require that the beneficiary pay the charge for services incurred before the time that the beneficiary elects continuation coverage, but the beneficiary must be reimbursed.

The penalties for noncompliance with COBRA may be severe. If a plan fails to comply with COBRA, the employer is denied a tax deduction for any contributions or other expenses incurred in connection with the plan for any taxable year in which the plan did not comply for at least one day. In addition, certain highly compensated

3. 29 U.S.C. § 1163.
4. 29 U.S.C. § 1162.
5. 29 U.S.C. § 1162.
6. 29 U.S.C. § 1166.

employees may have to include the costs of the employer-provided coverage in their gross incomes.

### [d] The Health Insurance Portability and Accountability Act

In August 1996, the Health Insurance Portability and Accountability Act of 1996 (HIPAA) was passed. Rather than the sweeping health insurance reform discussed in 1994, the new legislation is targeted at a few specific areas. HIPAA provides for nondiscrimination, provisions to combat medical care fraud, and provisions to implement medical savings accounts. Of particular interest to employers are the eligibility, continuation coverage, and tax provisions of Titles I and III.

Title I contains the provisions for preexisting conditions and nondiscrimination. HIPAA provides that when an employee has been insured under an employer's health insurance plan, the employee may carry that insurability when moving to another group health plan. Group insurance plans may continue to exclude individuals with preexisting conditions for up to 12 months, but the new legislation changes how that 12 months is calculated. Under HIPAA, any "creditable prior coverage" may count toward the 12-month period. Creditable coverage means any coverage under any plan such as group insurance, COBRA, Medicare, and Medicaid. Any such coverage may be counted toward the 12-month period unless there is a break in coverage for longer than 63 days. Any waiting period imposed by the new employer does not count toward the 63-day limit.

The nondiscrimination provision prohibits insurers from imposing certain conditions on eligibility under group health plans. For example, a group health insurer may not base eligibility decisions on a certain health status, claims history, medical history, genetic information, or medical condition. Group insurers also may not discriminate on the basis of disability or evidence of insurability. The provision for evidence of insurability would apply, for example, to motorcyclists or victims of domestic violence. (A similar provision relating only to domestic abuse victims was passed by many state legislatures in the 1995–1996 sessions. These new laws prevented insurers from discriminating against an individual on the basis of that person's being a victim of domestic violence.)

In addition, Title I states that access must be given to individual coverage if an individual has at least 18 months of creditable coverage. This provision means that an insurer must offer an individual policy to a person who does not have alternate coverage if the insurer offers such policies in the state where the individual resides. No limitations on preexisting conditions may be imposed. The provisions contained in COBRA have also been amended to make the 11-month extension available to any qualified beneficiary (such as a dependent) who has a disability within the first 60 days of continuation coverage.

Title I of HIPAA also contains a provision that assists small employers in obtaining health insurance coverage for their employees. HIPAA states that health plan issuers must make any plan they offer to small employers (considered to be groups of 50 or fewer) available to all eligible small employers, despite health status or prior claims experience.

Title III of HIPAA contains tax provisions relevant to employers. HIPAA authorizes medical savings accounts for employees covered by employer-sponsored health insurance plans with high deductibles. The medical savings accounts would have a yearly maximum contribution of 65 percent of the deductible for individual coverage (at least $1,500 of deductible expenses) and 75 percent of the deductible for family coverage (at least $3,000 of deductible expenses). The medical savings accounts will be in a pilot program from 1997 until 2000. HIPAA also states that long-term care insurance premiums, when paid by an employer, are nontaxable to the employee, and it provides for withdrawals from IRAs for medical expenses exceeding 7.5 percent of an individual's adjusted gross income.

### [e] Table Legend

Tables 5.3-1 and 5.3-2 set forth the state statutory requirements for continuation coverage and conversion rights.

*Policyholder* refers to the employer.

*Beneficiary* refers to an employee's spouse or dependent covered by the policy.

*Mandatory* means all group policies must include conversion provisions.

*Optional* means insurance companies must offer policyholders this conversion option, but employers may choose not to purchase it (i.e., make conversion available to employees).

An em dash (—) indicates that the state has enacted no statutory requirements for that category.

# Table 5.3-1

## CONTINUATION OF BENEFITS COVERAGE

(See also text at § 5.3.)

| | *Events Triggering Continuation Coverage* | | | | | | *Events Triggering Premature Termination of Continuation Coverage* | *Citations to Authority* |
|---|---|---|---|---|---|---|---|---|
| | *Death* | *Job Termination* | *Reduction of Hours* | *Divorce or Legal Separation* | *Medicare Eligibility* | *Other Provisions* | | |
| AL | — | — | — | — | — | — | — | — |
| AK | — | — | — | — | — | — | — | — |
| AZ | — | — | — | — | — | — | — | — |
| AR | No. | Yes, if covered continuously for at least 3 months before termination, maximum of 120 days of continuation coverage. | No, unless reduction of hours operates to terminate membership in group. | Yes, maximum of 120 days of continuation coverage. | No. | Termination of employee's membership in the group policy will trigger continuation coverage. | Becoming eligible for Medicare; becoming eligible for similar benefits, including coverage for preexisting conditions, under another group policy; termination of group policy; failure to make timely payment. | Ark. Code Ann. § 23-86-114. |
| CA | Yes. For employers of 20 or more, 90 days must be added to the federal requirements. For employers of 2 to 19 employees, Cal-COBRA requires 36 months of continuation coverage. | Yes, for 90 additional days. Cal-COBRA requires 18 months continuation coverage for employers of 2 to 19 employees upon job termination, unless for gross misconduct. If employee is disabled upon termination, 29 months. | Yes, for 90 additional days. Cal-COBRA requires 18 months of continuation coverage for employers of 2 to 19 employees for reduction of hours. | Yes. For employers of 20 or more, 90 days must be added to the federal requirement. For employers of 2 to 19 employees, Cal-COBRA requires 36 months of continuation coverage. | Yes. For employers of 20 or more, 90 days must be added to the federal requirement. For employers of 2 to 19 employees, Cal-COBRA requires 36 months of continuation coverage. | Labor dispute, minimum of 6 months of continuation coverage; dependent child exceeding maximum age for dependent status, minimum of 90 days of continuation coverage; 5-year employees over age 60 when employment ends, until age 65 or other coverage applies, and for a spouse, 5 years beyond scheduled end of spouse's COBRA or Cal-COBRA; for a former spouse of a 5-year employee, un- *(cont'd)* | Becoming eligible for similar benefits; termination of group policy; failure to make timely payment; remarriage (of either spouse); fraud or misrepresentation in application for coverage; reemployed and eligible for benefits under new employer's group plan; insured establishes residence outside of state. | Cal. Ins. Code §§ 10116, 12692, 10116.5, 10128.50. |

*(Table continues.)*

# Table 5.3-1 *(cont'd)*

## CONTINUATION OF BENEFITS COVERAGE

(See also text at § 5.3.)

| | *Events Triggering Continuation Coverage* | | | | | | *Events Triggering Premature Termination of Continuation Coverage* | *Citations to Authority* |
|---|---|---|---|---|---|---|---|---|
| | *Death* | *Job Termination* | *Reduction of Hours* | *Divorce or Legal Separation* | *Medicare Eligibility* | *Other Provisions* | | |
| CA (*cont'd*) | | | | | | til age 65, when other coverage applies, or 5 years from scheduled end of covered former spouse's COBRA or Cal-COBRA benefits. | | |
| CO | Yes, 18 months. | Yes, if covered continuously for at least 6 months before termination, minimum of 18 months of continuation coverage. | No, unless reduction of hours operates to terminate membership in group. | Yes, 18 months. | No. | Employee's coverage terminated for any other reason except termination of group policy, minimum of 18 months of continuation coverage. | Becoming eligible for Medicare; termination of group policy; failure to make timely payment; becoming eligible for similar health coverage. | Colo. Rev. Stat. § 10-16-108. |
| CT | Yes, minimum of 156 weeks of continuation coverage. | Yes, minimum of 104 weeks of continuation coverage. | No, unless reduction of hours operates to terminate membership in group. | Yes, minimum of 156 weeks of continuation coverage. | No. | Employee's coverage terminated for any other reason, minimum of 104 weeks of continuation coverage. | Becoming eligible for similar benefits under another group policy; failure to make timely payment. | Conn. Gen. Stat. Ann. § 38a-538. Amendment changing terminated employee coverage from 78 to 104 weeks was preempted by ERISA. Op. Atty. Gen. No. 93-005. |
| DE | — | — | — | — | — | — | — | — |
| DC | — | — | — | — | — | — | — | — |
| FL | No. | No. | No. | No. | No. | For total disability, policy must have "reasonable" continuation provision upon discontinuance of the group policy. A discontinued policy must provide continuation of benefits in connec- | The end of the 90-day extended coverage period (for dental coverage only) or when insured becomes covered under a similar dental policy. | Fla. Stat. Ann. § 627.667. |

| | | | | | | | | |
|---|---|---|---|---|---|---|---|---|
| | | | | | | tion with treatment of an accident or illness incurred while the policy was in effect for at least 12 months major medical and 90 days other coverages. | | |
| GA | Yes, if surviving spouse is age 60 or older. | Yes, unless employee was terminated for cause, not continuously covered for at least 6 months before termination, or failed to pay premium; minimum of 3 months of continuation coverage. | No, unless reduction of hours operates to terminate membership in group. | Yes, if spouse is age 60 or older. | No. | Employee's coverage terminated for any other reason except nonpayment or discontinuance of group policy, minimum of 3 months of continuation coverage. Dependent child exceeding maximum age for dependent status is eligible for continuation coverage if in college or university, to age 25. | Becoming eligible for Medicare; coverage under another policy; termination of group policy; failure to make timely payment. | Ga. Code Ann. §§ 33-24-21.1, 33-24-21.2, 33-30-4. |
| HI | No. | No. | No. | No. | No. | If employee hospitalized or prevented from working due to sickness, 3 months of continuation coverage paid for by employer. | None. | Haw. Rev. Stat. § 393-15. |
| ID | — | — | — | — | — | — | — | — |
| IL | Yes. For spouse under 55, maximum of 2 years of continuation coverage; for spouse 55 or older, continuation coverage until spouse is eligible for Medicare. | Yes, unless employee is convicted of or admits to felony or theft in connection with work or was not continuously covered for at least 3 months before termination; maximum of 9 months of continuation coverage. | No, unless reduction of hours operates to terminate membership in group. | Yes. For spouse under 55, maximum of 2 years of continuation coverage; for spouse 55 or older, continuation coverage until spouse is eligible for Medicare. | No. | Termination of employee's membership in the group policy. | Becoming eligible for Medicare; coverage under another group policy; remarriage of former spouse; termination of group policy; failure to exercise conversion right; failure to make timely payment. | 215 Ill. Comp. Stat. Ann. 5/367, 5/367e, 5/367.2. |
| IN | — | — | — | — | — | — | — | — |

*(Table continues.)*

# Table 5.3-1 *(cont'd)*

## CONTINUATION OF BENEFITS COVERAGE

(See also text at § 5.3.)

| | *Events Triggering Continuation Coverage* | | | | | | *Events Triggering Premature Termination of Continuation Coverage* | *Citations to Authority* |
|---|---|---|---|---|---|---|---|---|
| | *Death* | *Job Termination* | *Reduction of Hours* | *Divorce or Legal Separation* | *Medicare Eligibility* | *Other Provisions* | | |
| IA | Yes, maximum of 9 months of continuation coverage. | Yes, if covered continuously for at least 3 months before termination, maximum of 9 months of continuation coverage. | No, unless reduction of hours operates to terminate membership in group. | Yes. Annulment also triggers continuation coverage; maximum of 9 months of continuation coverage. | No. | Termination of employee's membership in the group policy. | Becoming eligible for Medicare; failure to make timely payment; remarriage (former spouse); becoming eligible under another group policy; termination of group policy and employee becoming eligible for coverage under any replacement policy. | Iowa Code Ann. §§ 509B.2, 509B.3. |
| KS | Yes, 6 months. | Yes, if covered continuously for at least 3 months before termination; 6 months of continuation coverage. | No, unless reduction of hours operates to terminate membership in group. | Yes, 6 months. | No. | Any other event, including discontinuance of group policy, except nonpayment. | Becoming eligible for Medicare; becoming eligible for similar benefits; failure to make timely payment; discontinued policy replaced by another policy within 31 days. | Kan. Stat. Ann. § 40-2209. |
| KY | Yes, maximum of 18 months of continuation coverage. | Yes, if covered for at least 3 months before termination, maximum of 18 months of continuation coverage. | No. | Yes, maximum of 18 months of continuation coverage. | No. | Dependent child exceeding maximum age for dependent status, maximum of 18 months of continuation coverage. | Becoming eligible for Medicare; becoming eligible for other group coverage; termination of group policy with no replacement within 31 days; failure to make timely payment. | Ky. Rev. Stat. Ann. § 304.18-110. |
| LA | Yes, only for surviving spouses, age 50 and over. | Yes, if covered continuously for at least 3 months before termination; maximum of 12 months of | No, unless reduction of hours operates to terminate membership in group. | No. | No. | Termination of employee's membership in the group triggers continuation unless employee is eligible for coverage under | Becoming eligible for Medicare; termination of group policy; becoming eligible for benefits under another group plan; fail- | La. Rev. Stat. Ann. §§ 22:215.7, 22:215.13. |

| | | | | | | | | |
|---|---|---|---|---|---|---|---|---|
| | | continuation coverage. | | | | another group policy within 31 days, policy was terminated because of fraud or nonpayment of premium, or employee is eligible for continuation coverage under COBRA. | ure to make timely payment; remarriage (former spouse). | |
| ME | No. | Yes. Continuation coverage is required only if termination is due to temporary layoff or loss of employment caused by work-related injury or occupational disease and employee was covered for at least 6 months before termination; minimum of 6 months of continuation coverage. If total disability, minimum of 1 year of continuation coverage. | No. | No. | No. | Beneficiaries eligible for continuation coverage only if covered for at least 3 months before termination. | Becoming eligible for Medicare; becoming eligible for similar benefits; failure to make timely payment; if Workers' Compensation Board determines that the injury or disease entitling the employee to coverage is not compensable. | Me. Rev. Stat. Ann. tit. 24-A § 2809-A. |
| MD | Yes, if continuously covered for at least 30 days before termination; maximum of 18 months of continuation coverage. | Yes, unless employee is terminated for cause or was not covered for at least 3 months before termination; maximum of 18 months of continuation coverage. | No. | Yes, if continuously covered for at least 30 days before termination. | No. | None. | Becoming eligible for Medicare; becoming eligible for benefits under another group plan; covered under a nongroup policy; termination of group policy; failure to make timely payment; remarriage (former spouse); employee or beneficiary elected to drop coverage; dependent child attains limiting age. | Md. Ins. Code §§ 15-407, 15-408, 15-409. |
| MA | Yes, 39 weeks of continuation coverage. | Yes. Plant closing, 90 days of continuation coverage. Employee and his beneficiaries are eligible for continuation coverage when there is involuntary termination, 39 weeks. | No, unless reduction of hours operates to terminate membership in group. | Yes, spouse is eligible without additional premium; coverage continues as long as group member is covered, until such time as pro- *(cont'd)* | No. | Employee leaves group for any reason, 31 days of continuation coverage. Length of continuation coverage cannot exceed length of period during which the employee was recently covered under the group policy. | Becoming eligible for similar benefits; remarriage (either spouse); failure to make timely payment; if member spouse remarries, former spouse entitled to continuation *(cont'd)* | Mass. Gen. Laws Ann. ch. 175 §§ 110D, 110G, 110I. |

*(Table continues.)*

# **Table 5.3-1** *(cont'd)*

## CONTINUATION OF BENEFITS COVERAGE

(See also text at § 5.3.)

| | *Events Triggering Continuation Coverage* | | | | | | *Events Triggering Premature Termination of Continuation Coverage* | |
|---|---|---|---|---|---|---|---|---|
| | *Death* | *Job Termination* | *Reduction of Hours* | *Divorce or Legal Separation* | *Medicare Eligibility* | *Other Provisions* | | *Citations to Authority* |
| MA (*cont'd*) | | | | vided in divorce decree, or until either spouse remarries. | | | coverage through rider to family plan or conversion. | |
| MI | — | — | — | — | — | — | — | — |
| MN | Yes. | Yes, unless employee is terminated for gross misconduct; maximum of 18 months of continuation coverage. | Yes, maximum of 18 months of continuation coverage. | Yes. | Yes, maximum of 36 months of continuation coverage. | Dependent child exceeds maximum age for dependent status, maximum of 36 months of continuation coverage. | Covered under another group policy; failure to make timely payment. | Minn. Stat. Ann. §§ 62A.17, 62A.20, 62A.21, 62A.146. |
| MS | Yes, up to 12 months of continuation coverage. | Yes, up to 12 months of continuation coverage if employee was continuously covered for 3 months before termination. | Yes, up to 12 months of continuation coverage. | Yes, up to 12 months of continuation coverage. | Yes, up to 12 months of continuation coverage. | Termination of employee's membership in the group triggers continuation unless the policy was terminated because of fraud or failure to pay premiums, or if employee is eligible for continuation coverage under COBRA or for similar benefits within 31 days of termination. | Becoming eligible for Medicare; becoming eligible for similar benefits; termination of group policy; discontinuance of contributions; former spouse remarries and becomes covered by a group policy that does not exclude coverage of pre-existing conditions. | Miss. Code Ann. § 83-9-51. |
| MO | Yes, maximum of 9 months of continuation coverage. | Yes, if covered continuously for at least 3 months before termination, maximum of 9 months of continuation coverage. | No, unless reduction of hours operates to terminate membership in group. | Yes, maximum of 9 months of continuation coverage. | No. | Termination of employee's membership in the group policy, maximum of 9 months of continuation coverage. | Becoming eligible for Medicare; becoming eligible for similar benefits; termination of group policy; failure to make timely payment. | Mo. Rev. Stat. § 376.428. |

| | | | | | | | | |
|---|---|---|---|---|---|---|---|---|
| MT | Yes. | No. | Yes, continuation coverage is triggered with employer's consent; 1 year of continuation coverage. | No. | No. | — | — | Mont. Code Ann. §§ 33-22-503, 33-22-507. |
| NE | Yes, maximum of 1 year of continuation coverage. | Yes, unless employee is terminated for misconduct; maximum of 6 months of continuation coverage. | No. | No. | No. | — | Becoming eligible for Medicare; spouse covered by Medicaid; becoming eligible for benefits under another group policy; termination of group policy; exercise of conversion right; failure to make timely payment; remarriage (former spouse). | Neb. Rev. Stat. §§ 44-1640, 44-1643. |
| NV | Yes, 36 months of continuation coverage. | Yes, unless employee is terminated for gross misconduct or if employee voluntarily leaves employment; 18 months of continuation coverage for employee, 36 months of continuation coverage for spouse and dependent. | Yes; 18 months of continuation coverage for employee, 36 months of continuation coverage for spouse and dependent child. | Yes, 36 months of continuation coverage for spouse and dependent child. | Yes, 36 months of continuation coverage. | Employee and beneficiaries must be continuously covered for at least 12 months before termination; dependent child exceeds maximum age for dependent status, 36 months of continuation coverage. | Becoming eligible for Medicare; covered under another group policy; termination of group policy; failure to make timely payment; remarriage of former spouse who is eligible for coverage under new spouse's policy. | Nev. Rev. Stat. §§ 6898.240, 689B.245, 689B.249. Statutory requirements apply only to employers with fewer than 20 employees. |
| NH | Yes. If spouse is under 55, 36 months of continuation coverage. If spouse is 55 or older, coverage continues until spouse is eligible for coverage under another group policy or for Medicare, or until spouse remarries. | Yes, unless employee is dismissed for gross misconduct or has not been continuously covered for at least 6 months before termination; 18 months of continuation coverage, or 29 months if disabled at time of termination. | No, unless reduction of hours operates to terminate membership in group. | Yes. Former spouse may continue coverage until remarriage of member spouse, at which time former spouse may convert within 31 days. Under 55, 36 months of continuation coverage; 55 and over, coverage continues until former spouse is eligible for coverage under another group policy or for Medicare, or until former spouse remarries. | Yes, 36 months of continuation coverage. | Labor dispute, up to 6 months of continuation coverage; any other event, 18 months of continuation coverage, 24 months if disabled. Dependent child exceeds maximum age for dependent status, 36 months of continuation coverage. | Becoming eligible under another group policy; reemployment; failure to make timely payment; remarriage (former spouse). | N.H. Rev. Stat. Ann. § 415:18. |

*(Table continues.)*

## **Table 5.3-1** *(cont'd)*

## CONTINUATION OF BENEFITS COVERAGE

(See also text at § 5.3.)

| | *Events Triggering Continuation Coverage* | | | | | | *Events Triggering Premature Termination of Continuation Coverage* | |
|---|---|---|---|---|---|---|---|---|
| | *Death* | *Job Termination* | *Reduction of Hours* | *Divorce or Legal Separation* | *Medicare Eligibility* | *Other Provisions* | | *Citations to Authority* |
| NJ | No. | Yes, if covered continuously for at least 3 months before termination. | No. | No. | No. | Termination of employee's membership in the group due to disability; continuation available to person eligible for Medicare, subject to nonduplication of benefits. | Termination of group policy; failure to make timely payment; reemployed and eligible for benefits. | N.J. Rev. Stat. §§ 17B:27-51.11, 17B:27-51.12. |
| NM | No, but spouse may choose conversion. | Yes, 6 months of continuation coverage. | No, unless reduction of hours operates to terminate membership in group. | No, but former spouse may choose conversion. | No. | Termination of employee's membership in the group; continuation may be limited to coverage under a Medicare supplemental policy. | Becoming eligible for Medicare; coverage replaced by another insurer; termination of group policy; failure to make timely payment. | N.M. Stat. Ann. § 59A-18-16. |
| NY | Yes, maximum of 36 months of continuation coverage. | Yes, maximum of 18 months of continuation coverage; 29 months if disabled at time of termination and remains disabled throughout. | No, unless reduction of hours operates to terminate membership in group. | Yes, maximum of 36 months of continuation coverage. | Yes, maximum of 36 months of continuation coverage. | Termination of employee's membership in the group; dependent child exceeds maximum age for dependent status, 36 months of maximum continuation coverage. | Becoming eligible for Medicare; becoming eligible for coverage under another group plan; termination of group policy; failure to make timely payment. | N.Y. Ins. Law § 3221(m). |
| NC | No. | Yes, if covered continuously for 3 months before termination, maximum of 18 months of continuation coverage. | No, unless reduction of hours operates to terminate membership in group. | No. | No. | Termination of employee's membership in the group triggers continuation unless the policy was terminated because of failure to pay premiums or employee becomes eligible for similar benefits within 31 days. | Becoming eligible for similar benefits under another group arrangement; termination of group policy; failure to make timely payment. | N.C. Gen. Stat. §§ 58-53-5, 58-53-10, 58-53-15, 58-53-35. |

| | | | | | | | | |
|---|---|---|---|---|---|---|---|---|
| ND | No. | Yes, if covered continuously for at least 3 months before termination, maximum of 39 weeks of continuation coverage. | No, unless reduction of hours operates to terminate membership in group. | Yes, but only if divorce decree requires continuation coverage. Annulment may also trigger continuation coverage; maximum of 36 months of continuation coverage. | No. | Termination of employee's membership in the group, maximum of 39 weeks of continuation coverage. | Becoming eligible for Medicare; covered for similar benefits under another group policy; termination of group policy; failure to make timely payment; remarriage (former spouse). | N.D. Cent. Code §§ 26.1-36-23, 26.1-36-23.1. |
| OH | Yes, but insurer may offer conversion policy in lieu of continuation coverage. | Yes, if covered continuously for at least 3 months before termination, 6 months' maximum continuation coverage. | No, unless reduction of hours operates to terminate membership in group. | No, but insurer must offer conversion policy. | No. | Termination of employee's membership in the group. For reservists called to active duty, 18 months of continuation coverage; spouses and dependents may extend coverage for 36 months if the reservist dies, dependent no longer meets eligibility requirements, or there is a divorce. | Becoming eligible for Medicare; becoming eligible for benefits under another group policy; termination of group policy; failure to make timely payment. | Ohio Rev. Code Ann. §§ 3923.32, 3923.38, 3923.381. |
| OK | No. | Yes. If an employee has been covered for at least 6 months and the employment is terminated, there is continuation coverage for any loss that began when the insurance was in force. The extension of benefits shall last not less than 3 months for basic coverage and 6 months for major medical coverage. | No, unless reduction of hours operates to terminate membership in group. | No. | No. | Employee's coverage terminated for any other reason, minimum of 30 days of continuation coverage. | Becoming eligible for similar benefits. | Okla. Stat. tit. 36 § 4509. |
| OR | — | — | — | — | — | — | — | — |
| PA | — | — | — | — | — | — | — | — |
| RI | Yes, maximum of 18 months of continuation coverage. | Yes, if termination is involuntary, workplace ceases to exist, or size of workforce is permanently reduced; *(cont'd)* | No. | Yes, if right of continuation coverage included in divorce decree. Coverage con- *(cont'd)* | No. | Discontinuance of the total group contract; individual change in group; coverage may not exceed length of employment preceding termination. | Remarriage (former spouse); remarriage (member spouse); reemployed and eligible for benefits with new employer. | R.I. Gen. Laws §§ 27-19.1-1, 27-20.4-1, 27-20.4-4, 27-20.4-5. |

*(Table continues.)*

**Table 5.3-1** *(cont'd)*

## CONTINUATION OF BENEFITS COVERAGE

(See also text at § 5.3.)

| | *Events Triggering Continuation Coverage* | | | | | | *Events Triggering Premature Termination of Continuation Coverage* | *Citations to Authority* |
|---|---|---|---|---|---|---|---|---|
| | *Death* | *Job Termination* | *Reduction of Hours* | *Divorce or Legal Separation* | *Medicare Eligibility* | *Other Provisions* | | |
| RI (*cont'd*) | | maximum of 18 months of continuation coverage. | | tinues for as long as member spouse participates in the plan, until remarriage of either spouse, or until such time as provided in divorce decree. | | | | |
| SC | No. | Yes, if covered continuously for at least 6 months before termination, 6 months of continuation coverage. | No, unless reduction of hours operates to terminate membership in group. | Yes. Insurer cannot terminate coverage of former spouse unless so provided in divorce decree. | No. | Employee's coverage terminated for any reason other than nonpayment; 6 months of continuation coverage. | Failure to make timely payment; termination of group policy; becoming eligible for Medicare; becoming eligible for similar benefits under other group coverage. | S.C. Code Ann. §§ 38-71-170, 38-71-770. |
| SD | Yes, 36 months of continuation coverage. | Yes, if covered continuously for at least 6 months before termination, 18 months of continuation coverage. | No, unless reduction of hours operates to terminate membership in group. | Yes, 36 months of continuation coverage. | Yes, 36 months of continuation coverage. | Employee's coverage terminated for any reason other than discontinuance of group policy and replacement thereof, 18 months of continuation coverage. A qualified beneficiary who ceases to be qualified under the policy may continue for 36 months if employee remains covered under the policy. | Covered by similar benefits; failure to make timely payment. | S.D. Codified Laws Ann. §§ 58-18-7.5, 58-18-7.7, 58-18-7.12. |
| TN | Yes, minimum of 15 months of continuation coverage. | Yes, if covered continuously for at least 3 months before termination, | Yes, minimum of 3 months of continuation coverage. | Yes, minimum of 15 months of continuation coverage. Pre- | No. | Employee's coverage terminated for any reason other than discontinuance of group | Becoming eligible for Medicare; failure to make timely payment; termination of | Tenn. Code Ann. § 56-7-2312. |

| | | | | | | | | |
|---|---|---|---|---|---|---|---|---|
| | Premiums must be paid in 3-month increments. | minimum of 3 months of continuation coverage. | | miums must be paid in 3-month increments. | | policy or nonpayment; minimum of 3 months of continuation coverage. If coverage ends during pregnancy, continuation is required until 6 months after conclusion of pregnancy. | group policy; discontinued policy replaced by another policy within 31 days. | |
| TX | Yes, if covered continuously for at least 1 year before the death, minimum of 3 years of continuation coverage. | Yes, unless employee was terminated for cause or was not covered continuously for at least 3 months before termination, minimum of 6 months of continuation coverage. Insurer can offer conversion policy in lieu of continuation coverage. | No, unless reduction of hours operates to terminate membership in group. | Yes, if covered continuously for at least 1 year before the divorce or separation, minimum of 3 years of continuation coverage. | No. | Employee's coverage terminated for any reason other than nonpayment, minimum of 6 months of continuation coverage. Insurer can offer conversion policy in lieu of continuation coverage. | Becoming eligible for Medicare; becoming eligible for similar benefits; termination of group policy; failure to make timely payment. | Tex. Ins. Code Ann. art. 3.51-6 §§ 1(d)(3), 3B. |
| UT | Yes, 6 months of continuation coverage. | Yes, unless employee is terminated for gross misconduct; 6 months of continuation coverage. | No, unless reduction of hours operates to terminate membership in group. | Yes, 6 months of continuation coverage. | No. | Termination of coverage for any other reason; dependent ceases to be qualified family member, 6 months of continuation coverage. | Becoming eligible for similar benefits under another group policy; termination of group policy; failure to make timely payment; establishment of residence outside state; violation of a material condition of contract. | Utah Code Ann. §§ 31A-22-710, 31A-22-714. |
| VT | Yes, maximum of 6 months of continuation coverage. | Yes, unless employee is terminated for misconduct or was not covered continuously for at least 3 months before termination, maximum of 6 months of continuation coverage. | No. | No. | No. | — | Becoming eligible for Medicare; becoming eligible for benefits under another group policy; termination of group policy; failure to make timely payment. | Vt. Stat. Ann. tit. 8 §§ 4090a, 4090c. |
| VA | No. | Yes, if covered continuously for at least 3 months before termination, 90 days of continuation coverage. | No, unless reduction of hours operates to terminate membership in group. | No. | No. | Any other event except termination of group policy where employee is insurable under other replacement group coverage or health care plan, 90 days of continua- *(cont'd)* | Becoming eligible for Medicare. | Va. Code Ann. § 38.2-3541. |

*(Table continues.)*

**Table 5.3-1** *(cont'd)*

CONTINUATION OF BENEFITS COVERAGE

(See also text at § 5.3.)

| | *Events Triggering Continuation Coverage* | | | | | | *Events Triggering Premature Termination of Continuation Coverage* | *Citations to Authority* |
|---|---|---|---|---|---|---|---|---|
| | *Death* | *Job Termination* | *Reduction of Hours* | *Divorce or Legal Separation* | *Medicare Eligibility* | *Other Provisions* | | |
| VA (*cont'd*) | | | | | | tion coverage. (Policyholder must elect either continuation coverage or conversion). | | |
| WA | No. | Yes. Insurer must offer policyholder option to include continuation of coverage provision for any person becoming ineligible for coverage for any reason. | No. | No. | No. | Insurer must offer policyholder option to include continuation of coverage provision for any person becoming ineligible for coverage for any other reason. | — | Wash. Rev. Code § 48.21.250. |
| WV | No. | Yes, involuntary termination only; maximum of 18 months of continuation coverage. | No. | No. | No. | Policy must meet minimum policy coverage standards as promulgated by the insurance commissioner. | — | W. Va. Code § 33-16-3(e). |
| WI | Yes. | Yes, unless employee is terminated for misconduct in connection with employment or was not covered continuously for at least 3 months before termination. | No. | Yes. Annulment also triggers continuation coverage. Coverage continues until member spouse ceases to participate in plan. | No. | Insurer may require employee or beneficiary to elect conversion after 18 months of continuation coverage. | Becoming eligible for Medicare; becoming eligible for similar benefits under another group policy; failure to make timely payment; election to no longer be covered; establishment of residence outside of state. | Wis. Stat. Ann. § 632.897. |
| WY | — | — | — | — | — | — | — | — |

# Table 5.3-2
## TRIGGERING CONVERSION FROM GROUP TO INDIVIDUAL HEALTH INSURANCE POLICY

(See also text at § 5.3.)

**KEY:** **Mandatory.** All group policies must include conversion provisions.
**Optional.** Insurance companies must offer policyholders (employers) this conversion option, but employers may choose not to purchase it (i.e., make conversion option available to employees).

| | *Events that Trigger Conversion of Benefits* | | | | | | | |
|---|---|---|---|---|---|---|---|---|
| | *Death* | *Job Termination* | *Termination of Coverage* | *Divorce or Legal Separation* | *Dependent Child Ceasing to Be a Qualified Family Member* | *Scope of Statutory Requirement* | *Ineligibility Factors* | *Citations to Authority* |
| AL | — | — | — | — | — | — | — | — |
| AK | — | — | — | — | — | — | — | — |
| AZ | Yes. | No. | Yes, under any circumstances (other than the failure to pay premium) that are specifically stated in the policy whereby coverage terminates as to covered spouse or dependent child. | Yes. | Yes, if provided for in policy. | Mandatory. Conversion benefits available only to spouse and dependent children. | Becoming eligible for Medicare; eligibility or coverage for similar benefits that, together with converted policy, would constitute overinsurance; nonpayment of premium; fraud or misrepresentation in application for benefits. | Ariz. Rev. Stat. Ann. § 20-1408. |
| AR | Yes. | Yes. | Yes, under any circumstances other than failure to pay premium. Termination of continuation coverage also triggers conversion. | Yes. | Yes. | Mandatory. | Medicare; eligible for full benefits under another group policy, including coverage for preexisting conditions; terminated policy replaced by similar coverage within 31 days. | Ark. Code Ann. § 23-86-115. |
| CA | No. | Yes. | Yes, whenever coverage terminated by employer, unless there was a failure to pay premium. Insured must have been continuously covered for 3 months before termination. | No. | No. | Mandatory. | Medicare; nonpayment of premium; eligible or covered by similar benefits; terminated policy replaced by similar coverage within 60 days; failure *(cont'd)* | Cal. Ins. Code §§ 12672, 12673, 12677, 12679. |

*(Table continues.)*

## Table 5.3-2 *(cont'd)*

## TRIGGERING CONVERSION FROM GROUP TO INDIVIDUAL HEALTH INSURANCE POLICY

(See also text at § 5.3.)

**KEY:** **Mandatory.** All group policies must include conversion provisions.
**Optional.** Insurance companies must offer policyholders (employers) this conversion option, but employers may choose not to purchase it (i.e., make conversion option available to employees).

| | *Events that Trigger Conversion of Benefits* | | | | | | | |
|---|---|---|---|---|---|---|---|---|
| | *Death* | *Job Termination* | *Termination of Coverage* | *Divorce or Legal Separation* | *Dependent Child Ceasing to Be a Qualified Family Member* | *Scope of Statutory Requirement* | *Ineligibility Factors* | *Citations to Authority* |
| CA *(cont'd)* | | | | | | | to provide properly requested information; fraud or misrepresentation in application for benefits. | |
| CO | Yes. | Yes. Retirement also triggers conversion. | Yes, under any circumstances other than discontinuance of group policy or failure to pay premium. Insured must have been continuously covered for 3 months before termination. | Yes, as long as former spouse remains covered. | Yes. | Mandatory. | Medicare; eligible or covered for similar benefits that, together with converted policy, would constitute overinsurance; failure to provide properly requested information. | Colo. Rev. Stat. § 10-16-108. |
| CT | Yes. | Yes. | Yes, under any circumstances other than failure to pay premium. Termination of continuation coverage also triggers conversion. | Yes. | No. | Mandatory. | — | Conn. Gen. Stat. Ann. § 38a-538. |
| DE | — | — | — | — | — | — | — | — |
| DC | — | — | — | — | — | — | — | — |
| FL | Yes. | Yes. Retirement also triggers conversion. | Yes, under any circumstances other than failure to pay premium. Insured must have been continuously covered for | Yes. Annulment also triggers conversion. However, former spouse must be depen- | Yes. | Mandatory. | Medicare; eligible or covered for similar benefits that, with converted policy, constitute overinsurance; terminated policy re- | Fla. Stat. Ann. § 627.6675. |

| | | | | | | | | |
|---|---|---|---|---|---|---|---|---|
| | | | 3 months before termination. | dent for financial support. | | | placed by similar coverage within 31 days; failure to provide properly requested information; fraud or misrepresentation in application for benefits. | |
| GA | No. | Yes. | Yes, under any circumstances other than failure to pay premium. Insured must have been continuously covered for 6 months before termination. | No. | No. | Mandatory. | Medicare; failure to make timely premium payments; fraud or misrepresentation of material fact; immediate replacement of terminated policy by similar coverage. | Ga. Code Ann. § 33-24-21.1. |
| HI | — | — | — | — | — | — | — | — |
| ID | — | — | — | — | — | — | — | — |
| IL | Yes. | Yes. Retirement also triggers conversion. | Yes, under any circumstances other than failure to pay premium or discontinuance of group policy where there is a succeeding carrier. Insured must have been continuously covered for 3 months before termination. | Yes. | Yes. | Mandatory. | Medicare; eligible or covered for similar benefits that, with converted policy, constitute overinsurance; terminated policy replaced by similar coverage; failure to provide properly requested information. | 215 Ill. Comp. Stat. Ann. 5/367e. |
| IN | No. | Yes. | No. | Yes. | No, unless due to attainment of an age specified in the group policy. | Mandatory. | — | Ind. Code Ann. § 27-8-15-31. |
| IA | Yes. | Yes. Retirement also triggers conversion. | Yes, under any circumstances other than failure to pay premium. Insured must have been continuously covered for 3 months before termination. | Yes. Annulment also triggers conversion. Coverage continues while member spouse remains covered. | Yes. | Mandatory. | Medicare; eligible or covered by similar policy that, with converted policy, constitutes overinsurance; terminated policy replaced by similar coverage within 31 days; failure to provide properly requested information; fraud or misrepresentation in application for benefits. | Iowa Code Ann. §§ 509B.2, 509B.4. |

*(Table continues.)*

# Table 5.3-2 *(cont'd)*

## TRIGGERING CONVERSION FROM GROUP TO INDIVIDUAL HEALTH INSURANCE POLICY

(See also text at § 5.3.)

**KEY:** **Mandatory.** All group policies must include conversion provisions.
**Optional.** Insurance companies must offer policyholders (employers) this conversion option, but employers may choose not to purchase it (i.e., make conversion option available to employees).

| | *Events that Trigger Conversion of Benefits* | | | | | | | |
|---|---|---|---|---|---|---|---|---|
| | *Death* | *Job Termination* | *Termination of Coverage* | *Divorce or Legal Separation* | *Dependent Child Ceasing to Be a Qualified Family Member* | *Scope of Statutory Requirement* | *Ineligibility Factors* | *Citations to Authority* |
| KS | Yes. | Yes. Retirement also triggers conversion. | Yes, under any circumstances other than failure to pay premium. | Yes. | Yes. | Mandatory. | Medicare; eligible or covered for similar benefits that, with converted policy, constitute overinsurance; terminated policy replaced by similar coverage within 31 days; failure to provide properly requested information; fraud or misrepresentation in application for benefits. | Kan. Stat. Ann. § 40-2209. |
| KY | Yes. | Yes. | Yes, under any circumstances. Termination of continuation coverage also triggers conversion. Insured must have been covered for at least 3 months before termination. Dependent child has right to convert if he or she has reached upper age limit for coverage on original policy. | Yes. | Yes. | Mandatory. | Medicare; eligible or covered for similar benefits that, with converted policy, constitute overinsurance. | Ky. Rev. Stat. Ann. § 304.18-110. |

| | | | | | | | | |
|---|---|---|---|---|---|---|---|---|
| LA | Yes. | Yes. | Yes, under any circumstances unless termination of coverage was due to fraud. Insured must have been continuously covered for 3 months before termination. | Yes. | Yes. | Mandatory. | Medicare; eligible for or covered by similar benefits; terminated policy replaced by similar coverage within 31 days; failure to provide properly requested information; fraud or misrepresentation in application for benefits. | La. Rev. Stat. Ann. § 22:230.2. |
| ME | Yes. | Yes. Retirement also triggers conversion. | Yes, under any circumstances other than failure to pay premium. Insured must have been continuously covered for 3 months before termination. | Yes. | Yes. | Mandatory, for group policies issued before 1996. Optional for group policies issued on or after 1/1/96 and prohibited if insurer does not normally offer individual policies. | Medicare; eligible or covered for similar benefits that, with converted policy, constitute overinsurance; terminated policy replaced by similar coverage within 31 days. | Me. Rev. Stat. Ann. tit. 24-A § 2809-A. |
| MD | Yes. | Yes. | Yes, under any circumstances other than failure to pay premium. Insurer may limit conversion right to those who have been previously covered for at least 1 year. | Yes. | Yes. | Mandatory. | — | Md. Ins. Code §§ 15-412, 15-413, 15-414. |
| MA | — | — | — | — | — | — | — | — |
| MI | Yes. | Yes, unless terminated for gross misconduct. | Yes, under any circumstances other than failure to pay premium or fraud. | Yes. | Yes. | Required option. | Medicare; covered for similar benefits; terminated group coverage replaced by other group coverage. | Mich. Stat. Ann. § 24.13612. |
| MN | Yes. | Yes. | Yes, termination of continuation coverage. | Yes. | No. | Mandatory. | Covered under another qualified plan. | Minn. Stat. Ann. §§ 62A.17, 62A.21. |
| MS | — | — | — | — | — | — | — | — |

*(Table continues.)*

## Table 5.3-2 *(cont'd)*

## TRIGGERING CONVERSION FROM GROUP TO INDIVIDUAL HEALTH INSURANCE POLICY

(See also text at § 5.3.)

**KEY:** **Mandatory.** All group policies must include conversion provisions.
**Optional.** Insurance companies must offer policyholders (employers) this conversion option, but employers may choose not to purchase it (i.e., make conversion option available to employees).

| | *Events that Trigger Conversion of Benefits* | | | | | | | |
|---|---|---|---|---|---|---|---|---|
| | *Death* | *Job Termination* | *Termination of Coverage* | *Divorce or Legal Separation* | *Dependent Child Ceasing to Be a Qualified Family Member* | *Scope of Statutory Requirement* | *Ineligibility Factors* | *Citations to Authority* |
| MO | Yes. | Yes. Retirement also triggers conversion. | Yes, under any circumstances other than failure to pay premium. Insured must have been continuously covered for 3 months before termination. | Yes, if member spouse remains insured under the group policy. | Yes. | Mandatory. | Medicare; eligible for or covered by similar policy that, with converted policy, constitutes overinsurance; terminated policy replaced by similar coverage within 31 days; failure to provide properly requested information; fraud or misrepresentation in application for benefits. | Mo. Rev. Stat. §§ 376.397, 376.401. |
| MT | Yes. | Yes. | Yes. Insured must have been continuously covered for 3 months before termination. | Yes, if member spouse remains insured under the group policy. | Yes. | Mandatory. | Covered by another major medical plan. | Mont. Code Ann. §§ 33-22-508, 33-22-510. |
| NE | — | — | — | — | — | — | — | — |
| NV | Yes. | Yes. | Yes, under any circumstances except failure to pay premium or discontinuance of group policy. Insured must have been continuously covered for 3 months before termination. | Yes, if member spouse remains insured under the group policy. | Yes. | Mandatory. | Eligible for or covered by similar policy that, together with converted policy, would constitute overinsurance; failure to provide properly requested information; fraud or misrepresentation in application for benefits. | Nev. Rev. Stat. §§ 689B.120, 689B.130, 689B.140, 689B.190. |

| | | | | | | | | |
|---|---|---|---|---|---|---|---|---|
| NH | Yes. | Yes. | Yes, under any circumstances. Termination of continuation coverage also triggers conversion. Insured must have been covered for at least 60 days before termination. | Yes. Ex-spouse continues to be covered until remarriage of member spouse and then can convert. | Yes. | Mandatory. | Medicare; eligible or covered for similar benefits that, together with converted policy, would constitute overinsurance. | N.H. Rev. Stat. Ann. § 415:18. |
| NJ | — | — | — | — | — | — | — | — |
| NM | Yes. | Yes. | Yes, under any circumstances. | Yes. Annulment also triggers conversion. | No. | Mandatory. | Medicare; failure to pay premium; discontinuance of group policy. | N.M. Stat. Ann. § 59A-18-16. |
| NY | Yes. | Yes. | Yes, under any circumstances. Termination of continuation coverage also triggers conversion. Insured must have been continuously covered for 3 months before termination. | Yes. Annulment also triggers conversion. | Yes. | Mandatory. | Medicare (if so stipulated in converted policy); eligible or covered for similar benefits that, with converted policy, constitute overinsurance; terminated policy replaced by similar and continuous policy. | N.Y. Ins. Law § 3221(e). |
| NC | Yes. | Yes, if continuation coverage is completed. Retirement also triggers conversion. | Yes, under any circumstances except failure to pay premium or failure to elect continuation coverage. Insured must have been continuously covered for 3 months before termination. | Yes. | Yes. | Mandatory. | Medicare; eligible or covered for similar benefits that, with converted policy, constitute overinsurance; terminated policy replaced by similar coverage within 31 days; failure to provide properly requested information; fraud or misrepresentation in application for benefits. | N.C. Gen. Stat. §§ 58-53-45, 58-53-50, 58-53-70, 58-53-75, 58-53-110. |
| ND | No. | Yes, after continuation coverage ends. | Yes, after continuation coverage ends. | Yes. Annulment also triggers conversion. | No. | Mandatory. | Medicare; covered by another policy; former spouse reaches age 65. | N.D. Cent. Code § 26.1-36-23.1. |
| OH | Yes. | Yes. Retirement also triggers conversion. | Yes. Dependent child also has right to convert if he or she has reached upper age limit for coverage on original policy. Insured must have been covered for at least 1 year before termination. | Yes. Annulment also triggers conversion. | Yes. | Mandatory. | Medicare; eligible for or covered by policy that duplicates Medicare coverage; eligible for or covered by another group policy. | Ohio Rev. Code Ann. § 3923.122. |

*(Table continues.)*

## Table 5.3-2 *(cont'd)*
## TRIGGERING CONVERSION FROM GROUP TO INDIVIDUAL HEALTH INSURANCE POLICY

(See also text at § 5.3.)

**KEY:** **Mandatory.** All group policies must include conversion provisions.
**Optional.** Insurance companies must offer policyholders (employers) this conversion option, but employers may choose not to purchase it (i.e., make conversion option available to employees).

| | *Events that Trigger Conversion of Benefits* | | | | | | | |
|---|---|---|---|---|---|---|---|---|
| | *Death* | *Job Termination* | *Termination of Coverage* | *Divorce or Legal Separation* | *Dependent Child Ceasing to Be a Qualified Family Member* | *Scope of Statutory Requirement* | *Ineligibility Factors* | *Citations to Authority* |
| OK | Yes. | Yes. Retirement also triggers conversion. | Yes. | Yes. | No. | Optional, but if policy allows right to convert, it must extend that right to spouse if insured terminates employment or membership in the group, dies, or divorces. | — | Okla. Stat. tit. 36 § 4502.1. |
| OR | — | — | — | — | — | — | — | — |
| PA | Yes. | Yes. | Yes, under any circumstances other than failure to pay premium. Discontinuance of group policy also triggers conversion. Insured must have been continuously covered for 3 months before termination. | Yes. | Yes. | Mandatory. | Medicare; eligible or covered for similar benefits that, with converted policy, constitute overinsurance; terminated policy replaced by similar coverage within 31 days; failure to provide properly requested information; fraud or misrepresentation in application for benefits. | Pa. Stat. Ann. tit. 40 § 756.2. |
| RI | No. | No. | No. | Yes. Former spouse can convert at termination of continuation period. | No. | Mandatory. | — | R.I. Gen. Laws § 27-20.4-2. |

| | | | | | | | | |
|---|---|---|---|---|---|---|---|---|
| SC | No. | No. | No. | Yes. Only by entry of valid decree of divorce. | No. | — | No. | S.C. Code Ann. § 38-71-170. |
| SD | No. | Yes. | Yes. Insured must have been continuously covered for 6 months before termination. | No. | No. | Mandatory. | Medicare; covered for similar benefits that, with converted policy, constitute overinsurance; terminated policy replaced by similar coverage; failure to pay premium; fraud or misrepresentation in application for benefits. | S.D. Codified Laws Ann. §§ 58-18-7.6, 58-18-7.7, 58-18-7.11. |
| TN | Yes. | Yes. | Yes, under any circumstances other than failure to pay premium. Termination of continuation coverage also triggers conversion. | Yes. | No. | Mandatory. | Medicare; eligible or covered for similar benefits that, with converted policy, constitute overinsurance; terminated policy replaced by similar coverage within 31 days. | Tenn. Code Ann. §§ 56-7-2312, 56-7-2314. |
| TX | Yes, if coverage is otherwise terminated. | Yes, unless insured is involuntarily discharged for cause. | Yes, under any circumstances other than failure to pay premium or replacement of terminated policy by similar coverage within 31 days. | Yes, if coverage is otherwise terminated. | Yes, if coverage is otherwise terminated. | Mandatory. Insurer may offer continuation coverage in lieu of conversion coverage. | Medicare; eligible or covered for similar benefits under another policy. | Tex. Ins. Code Ann. art. 3.51-6 § 1(d)(3). |
| UT | Yes. | Yes. Retirement also triggers conversion. | Yes, any condition other than failure to pay premium. Insured must have been continuously covered for 6 months before termination. | Yes. | Yes. | Mandatory. | Medicare; terminated policy replaced by similar coverage including coverage of preexisting conditions; insurer may reduce benefits to extent coverage constitutes overinsurance; qualified for continuation coverage. | Utah Code Ann. §§ 31A-22-703, 31A-22-705, 31A-22-709, 31A-22-710. |
| VT | Yes. | Yes. | No. | No. | No. | Mandatory. | Medicare; eligible or covered for similar benefits that, with converted policy, constitute overinsurance; failure to elect continuation coverage or not eligible for continuation; failure to pay premium; failure to provide properly requested information. | Vt. Stat. Ann. tit. 8 §§ 4090d, 4090e, 4090f. |

*(Table continues.)*

# Table 5.3-2 *(cont'd)*

## TRIGGERING CONVERSION FROM GROUP TO INDIVIDUAL HEALTH INSURANCE POLICY

(See also text at § 5.3.)

**KEY:** **Mandatory.** All group policies must include conversion provisions.
**Optional.** Insurance companies must offer policyholders (employers) this conversion option, but employers may choose not to purchase it (i.e., make conversion option available to employees).

| | *Events that Trigger Conversion of Benefits* | | | | | | | |
|---|---|---|---|---|---|---|---|---|
| | *Death* | *Job Termination* | *Termination of Coverage* | *Divorce or Legal Separation* | *Dependent Child Ceasing to Be a Qualified Family Member* | *Scope of Statutory Requirement* | *Ineligibility Factors* | *Citations to Authority* |
| VA | No. | Yes, if job termination causes coverage to terminate. | Yes, any reason other than discontinuance of the group policy, where insured is insurable under another group policy. | No. | No. | Mandatory. Policyholder must have option to select either continuation coverage or conversion. | Medicare; eligible or covered for similar benefits that, with converted policy, constitute overinsurance. | Va. Code Ann. §§ 38.2-3416, 38.2-3541. |
| WA | No. | Yes, unless insured is terminated for misconduct. If terminated for misconduct, conversion must be offered to spouse and dependents. | Yes. | No. | No. | Mandatory. | Medicare; covered under another group policy. | Wash. Rev. Code § 48.21.260. |
| WV | Yes. | Yes. Retirement also triggers conversion. | Yes, any condition other than failure to pay premium. Discontinuance of group policy also triggers conversion. Insured must have been continuously covered for 3 months before termination. | Yes. | Yes. | Mandatory. | Medicare; eligible or covered for similar benefits that, with converted policy, constitute overinsurance; terminated policy is replaced by similar coverage within 31 days; failure to provide properly requested information; fraud or misrepresentation in application for benefits. | W. Va. Code §§ 33-16A-1, 33-16A-5, 33-16A-12, 33-16A-13. |

| | | | | | | | | |
|---|---|---|---|---|---|---|---|---|
| WI | Yes. | Yes, unless insured is discharged for misconduct in connection with employment. | Yes. Insured must have been continuously covered for 3 months before termination. | Yes. Annulment also triggers conversion. | No. | Mandatory. | Eligible or covered for similar benefits that, with converted policy, constitute overinsurance. | Wis. Stat. Ann. § 632.897. |
| WY | Yes. | Yes. | Yes, under any circumstances other than failure to pay premium. Insured must have been continuously covered for 3 months before termination. | Yes. | Yes. | Mandatory. | Medicare; eligible or covered for similar benefits that, with converted policy, constitute overinsurance; terminated policy is replaced by similar coverage within 31 days; failure to provide properly requested information; fraud or misrepresentation in application for benefits. | Wyo. Stat. §§ 26-22-201, 26-22-202. |

# § 5.4 State Regulation of Health Maintenance Organizations

Many employers have begun to use health maintenance organizations (HMOs) to provide health benefits to their employees. Nearly all states impose minimum requirements for HMO coverage, but HMO plans are generally not regulated to the extent that traditional individual or group health insurance plans are regulated.

The tables in this chapter list applicable state laws regarding coverage of persons who enroll in HMOs. In most instances, these laws do not apply directly to employers, but rather serve to regulate HMOs. Some states, however, require that employer-supported health benefit plans offer employees the option of enrollment in an HMO when a certain number of employees are covered.

## [a] Minimum Mandated Coverages

Most state-mandated minimum coverage requirements for HMOs represent the basic services HMOs must provide to those enrolled in their plans. A significant number of states require that HMO policies cover newborn or adopted children from the moment of birth or placement. Several of these states also provide that HMO policies must cover "certain dependents," usually handicapped persons who depend on the policyholder for support.

Some states mandate that HMOs cover pregnancy and treatment for infertility. Nearly half the states require that HMOs supply preventive care. Although preventive care is often listed as a basic health service, it may also be listed separately and broken down into subcategories such as health checkups for adults and well-child care.

Many states mandate HMO coverage of treatment for substance abuse and mental illness. Some, however, specifically exempt coverage of these services from HMO basic service requirements. Frequently, states also mandate that HMOs provide coverage for specific diseases or for procedures such as mammograms. In addition, the laws regulating HMOs may mandate coverage of certain facilities, providers, and pharmaceuticals. The basic coverages and services required by states are outlined in Table 5.4-1, Parts A and B.

## [b] Administration of HMOs

Many states provide that HMO policies must contain provisions for conversion or continuation coverage of policyholders or dependents. In addition, a few states limit HMOs' ability to discriminate on the basis of given health conditions.

Many states expressly exempt HMOs from other insurance laws, leaving them subject only to the statutory provisions that specifically regulate only HMOs. Table 5.4-2 displays the various requirements concerning HMO administration.

# Table 5.4-1 Part A
## REGULATION OF SERVICES PROVIDED BY HMOs: MANDATORY COVERAGES

(See also text at § 5.4[a].)

| | | *Mandatory Coverage* | | | | |
|---|---|---|---|---|---|---|
| | *Basic Health Services* | *Newborn/ Dependent Children* | *Pregnancy/Fertility Treatment* | *Preventive Care* | *Coverage of Emergency Services* | *Citations to Authority* |
| AL | Not specified. | No. | No. | No. | — | — |
| AK | Emergency care, inpatient hospital and physician care, and outpatient medical services. Specific exclusion of mental health and substance abuse services. | No. | No. | No. | — | Alaska Stat. §§ 21.86.020, 21.86.190, 21.86.900. |
| AZ | Emergency care, inpatient hospital and physician care, outpatient care (including laboratory/ radiological/diagnostic exams), and alternatives to hospital care, such as skilled nursing home care. | Mandatory coverage of newborn/adopted children. | No. | No. | — | Ariz. Rev. Stat. Ann. §§ 20-1051, 20-1057, 20-1065. |
| AR | Not specified. | Yes. Mandatory coverage extends to certain dependents. | No. | Yes, to age 18. | — | Ark. Code Ann. §§ 23-76-103, 23-79-141. |
| CA | Physician services, hospital inpatient and ambulatory care services, diagnostic laboratory and radiological services, home health and preventive health services, and emergency care (including ambulance and out-of-area coverage). | Mandatory coverage of dependents. | Mandatory coverage of infertility treatment. Coverage of prenatal diagnosis of genetic disorders of the fetus is a required option. | Yes. | HMO must cover emergency services until the enrollee is stabilized. HMO cannot require preapproval for emergency services and cannot require enrollee to pay for a nonemergency if a prudent layperson would have thought a condition existed causing the person's health to be in serious jeopardy, bodily functions to be seriously impaired, or a serious dysfunction of the body. | Cal. Health and Safety Code §§ 1345, 1367.3, 1367.35, 1367.7, 1371.1, 1371.4, 1374.55, 1374.57. |

*(Table continues.)*

## Table 5.4-1 Part A *(cont'd)*

## REGULATION OF SERVICES PROVIDED BY HMOs: MANDATORY COVERAGES

(See also text at § 5.4[a].)

| | | *Mandatory Coverage* | | | | |
|---|---|---|---|---|---|---|
| | *Basic Health Services* | *Newborn/ Dependent Children* | *Pregnancy/Fertility Treatment* | *Preventive Care* | *Coverage of Emergency Services* | *Citations to Authority* |
| CO | Emergency care, inpatient/outpatient hospital services, physician services, outpatient medical services, and laboratory and radiological services. | Mandatory coverage of newborns. | Mandatory coverage of pregnancy and complications of pregnancy. | Yes. | HMOs may not deny coverage for expenses incurred as a result of a life- or limb-threatening emergency, defined as any event the enrollee believes threatens life or limb in such a manner that a need for immediate medical care is required to prevent death or serious impairment of health. | Colo. Rev. Stat. §§ 10-16-102, 10-16-104, 10-16-407. |
| CT | Not specified. | No. | No. If pregnancy is covered, postdelivery stay of 48 to 96 hours must be covered. | No. | — | Conn. Gen. Stat. Ann. § 38a-530c. |
| DE | Usual physician services, hospitalization, laboratory/radiological services, emergency and preventive care, and out-of-area coverage. | Mandatory coverage of newborns. | No. | Yes, including lead screening. | — | Del. Code Ann. tit. 16, § 9102; tit. 18, §§ 3335, 3550, 3554. |
| DC | Not specified. | No. | No. | No. | — | — |
| FL | Emergency care. | If family is covered, newborns (injury, sickness, congenital birth defects, birth abnormalities, and transportation) and adopted children (with no exclusion for preexisting conditions) must be covered. | No. But if pregnancy is covered, postdelivery stay must be covered. | No. | HMO may not require preapproval of emergency services or use terms such as "life-threatening" to qualify emergency. HMO must cover emergency services up to the point where the provider can determine if an emergency exists. | Fla. Stat. Ann. §§ 641.513, 641.31, 641.513. |
| GA | Includes, at a minimum, preventive care, emergency care, inpatient hospital and physician care, and outpatient medical services. | No. | No. | Yes. | If enrollee seeks emergency services, provider may stabilize the enrollee without preapproval. | Ga. Code Ann. §§ 33-21-1, 33-21-5, 33-21-18.1. |

| | | | | | | |
|---|---|---|---|---|---|---|
| HI | Preventive care, emergency care, inpatient/outpatient physician and hospital care, diagnostic laboratory and radiological services. | Mandatory coverage of newborn/adopted children. | Contraceptive services are an employer option; if pregnancy is covered, in vitro fertilization must be covered. | Mandatory coverage of child health and supervision services. | — | Haw. Rev. Stat. §§ 431:10A-115.5, 431:10A-116, 431:10A-116.5, 431:10A-116.6, 432D-1. |
| ID | Physician and hospital services, laboratory/radiological services, emergency and preventive care, and out-of-area coverage. Mental health, alcohol/drug addiction, vision care, and long-term rehabilitation are excluded. | Mandatory coverage of newborn/adopted children. | Yes. If maternity is covered, HMO may not limit coverage of complications and may not restrict length of hospital stay. | Yes. | — | Idaho Code §§ 41-3903, 41-3923. |
| IL | Emergency care, inpatient hospital and physician care, outpatient medical services, mental health services, and care for drug and alcohol abuse. | Mandatory coverage of newborn/adopted children extends to certain dependents. | No. If pregnancy is covered, postdelivery stay of 48 to 96 hours must be covered. | No. | — | Ill. Rev. Stat. ch. 215, §§ 125/1-2, 125/4-8, 125/4-6.4, 125/4-9, 125/4-9.1. |
| IN | Preventive care, inpatient/outpatient hospital and physician care, diagnostic laboratory and radiological services, and emergency care. Specific exclusion of mental health services, services for drug and alcohol abuse, dental and vision care, and long-term rehabilitation services. | Mandatory coverage of adopted children. | No. | Yes. | — | Ind. Code §§ 27-8-5-21, 27-13-1-4. |
| IA | Emergency care, inpatient hospital and physician care, and outpatient medical services. | Mandatory coverage of newborns and adopted children. | No. If pregnancy is covered, postdelivery stay of 48 to 96 hours must be covered. | No. | — | Iowa Code §§ 514B.1, 514C.1, 514C.10, 514C.12. |
| KS | Physician and hospital services, laboratory and radiological services, emergency and preventive care, and out-of-area care. | No. | No. | Yes. | HMO may not base denial of payment solely on the failure of the enrollee to obtain preauthorization where the enrollee notifies the HMO of the receipt of emergency services within 24 hours or as soon as reasonably possible. | Kan. Stat. Ann. §§ 40-3202, 40-3229. |
| KY | Not specified. | Mandatory coverage of newborns if family coverage is provided. Coverage of nursery care for well newborns is a required option. | No. | No. | — | Ky. Rev. Stat. Ann. §§ 304.38-198, 304.38-199. |

*(Table continues.)*

# Table 5.4-1 Part A *(cont'd)*
## REGULATION OF SERVICES PROVIDED BY HMOs: MANDATORY COVERAGES

(See also text at § 5.4[a].)

| | | *Mandatory Coverage* | | | | |
|---|---|---|---|---|---|---|
| | *Basic Health Services* | *Newborn/ Dependent Children* | *Pregnancy/Fertility Treatment* | *Preventive Care* | *Coverage of Emergency Services* | *Citations to Authority* |
| LA | Emergency care, inpatient hospital and physician care, outpatient medical and chiropractic services, and laboratory and radiological services. Coverage of mental health services and services for substance abuse is a required option. | Transportation to hospital for birth/infant illness must be covered. | No. If pregnancy is covered, postdelivery stay must be covered. | No. | — | La. Rev. Stat. Ann. §§ 22:215.1, 22:250.4, 22-2002. |
| ME | Emergency and inpatient hospital care, inpatient/outpatient physician services, and laboratory and radiological services. | Mandatory coverage of newborn/adopted children extends to certain dependents. | No. | No. | — | Me. Rev. Stat. Ann. tit. 24-A, §§ 4202-A, 4234. |
| MD | Physician, hospitalization, laboratory, radiological, emergency, and preventive services; out-of-area coverage; and any other services mandated by the insurance commissioner. | Mandatory coverage of newborn/adopted children and grandchildren. | No. If pregnancy is covered, postdelivery stay of up to 4 days must be covered. | Yes. | HMO cannot require preapproval for emergency services and cannot require enrollee to pay for a nonemergency if a prudent layperson would have thought a condition existed causing the person's health to be in serious jeopardy, bodily functions to be seriously impaired, or a serious dysfunction of the body. | Md. Gen. Health Code Ann. §§ 19-701, 19-703, 19-706, 19-712.5; Md. Ins. Code §§ 15-401, 15-403. |
| MA | Reasonably comprehensive physician services, inpatient/outpatient services, and emergency health services. May include chiropractic, optometric, and podiatric services. | Mandatory coverage of infants and dependents. | Mandatory coverage of prenatal care/pregnancy, childbirth, postpartum care, including postdelivery stay of 48 to 96 hours, and infertility treatment. | Mandatory coverage for children. | — | Mass. Gen. Laws Ann. ch. 176G, §§ 1, 4, 4I. |
| MI | Physician, ambulatory, inpatient, emergency, and outpatient mental health services; care for substance abuse; diagnostic laboratory and radiological services; and home health and preventive services. | No. | No. | Yes. | — | Mich. Stat. Ann. § 14.15(21003). |

| | | | | | | |
|---|---|---|---|---|---|---|
| MN | Comprehensive services (including emergency care, ambulance services, inpatient hospital and physician care, and outpatient and preventive care). | No. | No. | Yes. | — | Minn. Stat. Ann. §§ 62D.02. |
| MS | Usual health care services; hospitalization; laboratory, radiological, preventive, and emergency services; and out-of-area coverage. | No. | No. | Yes. | — | Miss. Code Ann. § 83-41-303. |
| MO | Emergency care, inpatient hospital and physician care, and outpatient medical services. | No. | No. If pregnancy is covered, postdelivery stay of 48 to 96 hours must be covered. | Mandatory coverage of child health supervision services. | — | Mo. Rev. Stat. §§ 354.400, 376.801, 376.995. |
| MT | Consultative, diagnostic, therapeutic, and referral services by a provider; inpatient hospital and provider care; outpatient medical services; newborn coverage; treatment of alcohol/drug abuse and mental illness; laboratory and radiological services; preventive care (including immunizations, well-child care, health evaluations for adults, family planning, infertility treatment, mammograms, and treatment for phenylketonuria). | Mandatory coverage of newborn/adopted children. | Mandatory coverage of family planning and infertility treatment. | Mandatory coverage of health evaluations for adults, well-child care, and immunizations for children. | — | Mont. Code Ann. §§ 33-31-102, 33-31-114. |
| NE | Preventive and emergency care, inpatient/outpatient hospital and physician care, laboratory and radiological services, and out-of-area emergency coverage. | No. | No. | Yes. | — | Neb. Rev. Stat. § 44-3294. |
| NV | Not specified. | Mandatory coverage of newborn/adopted children. | HMO may not limit coverage of the complications of pregnancy. | No. | — | Nev. Rev. Stat. Ann. §§ 695C.172, 695C.173. |
| NH | Not specified. | Mandatory coverage of adopted children and extension to certain dependents. | HMO must make maternity benefits rider available. | No. | Yes, if there is onset of symptoms that could be expected to result in serious injury to health. | N.H. Rev. Stat. Ann. §§ 417-F:1, 420-B:8, 420-B:8-g, 420-B:8-j. |
| NJ | Emergency care, inpatient hospital and physician care, and outpatient medical services. | No. | Yes. Mandatory coverage of maternity services. | Yes. Preventive care for children including screening and treatment for lead poisoning. | — | N.J. Rev. Stat. §§ 26:2J-2, 26:2J-4.3, 26:2J-4.10. |

*(Table continues.)*

# Table 5.4-1 Part A *(cont'd)*

## REGULATION OF SERVICES PROVIDED BY HMOs: MANDATORY COVERAGES

(See also text at § 5.4[a].)

| | | *Mandatory Coverage* | | | | |
|---|---|---|---|---|---|---|
| | *Basic Health Services* | *Newborn/ Dependent Children* | *Pregnancy/Fertility Treatment* | *Preventive Care* | *Coverage of Emergency Services* | *Citations to Authority* |
| NM | Preventive, emergency, inpatient/outpatient hospital and physician care; and laboratory and radiological services. Specific exclusion of treatment for substance abuse, long-term rehabilitation, and vision and dental services. | Mandatory coverage of newborn/adopted children, including immunizations. | No. | Yes. | — | N.M. Stat. Ann. §§ 59A-46-2, 59A-46-37, 59A-46-38, 59A-46-38.2. |
| NY | Comprehensive health services (including physician services, inpatient/outpatient hospital services, diagnostic laboratory and radiological services, and emergency and preventive services). | No. | Yes. Postdelivery stay of 48 to 96 hours must also be covered. | Yes. | — | N.Y. Pub. Health Law § 4401; N.Y. Ins. Law §§ 3216, 3221. |
| NC | Not specified. | No. | No. | No. | — | — |
| ND | Preventive and emergency care, inpatient/outpatient hospital and physician care, and diagnostic laboratory and radiological services. | No. | Yes. HMO must cover complications of pregnancy. Post-delivery stay of 48 to 96 hours must be covered. | Yes. | — | N.D. Cent. Code §§ 26.1-18.1-01, 26.1-36-09.2, 26.1-36-09.8. |
| OH | Physician services, inpatient hospital and outpatient medical services, emergency, diagnostic laboratory and radiologic services, preventive care (including family planning, infertility services, physical exams, prenatal care and well-child care). | Mandatory coverage of newborn/adopted children extends to certain other dependents. | Mandatory coverage of infertility treatment, family planning, and prenatal care. If pregnancy is covered, post-delivery stay of 48 to 96 hours must be covered. | Yes. | — | Ohio Rev. Code Ann. §§ 1742.01, 1742.11, 1742.37, 1742.39, 1742.45. |
| OK | Comprehensive services (including allopathic, osteopathic, chiropractic, podiatric, optometric, and psychological services; outpatient diagnostic treatment; inpatient hospital care; short-term rehabilitation and physical therapy; emergency care; short-term outpatient mental health | No. | No. | Yes. | — | Okla. Stat. tit. 63, § 2503. |

| | | | | | | |
|---|---|---|---|---|---|---|
| | services; substance abuse; and home health and preventive care). | | | | | |
| OR | Usual physician services, hospitalization, laboratory and radiological services, emergency and preventive care, and out-of-area coverage. | No. | No. | Yes. | — | Or. Rev. Stat. § 442.015. |
| PA | Emergency care, inpatient hospital and physician care, ambulatory physician care, and outpatient and preventive medical services. | Mandatory coverage of newborns/adopted children. | No. If pregnancy is covered, postdelivery stay of 48 to 96 hours must be covered. | Yes. | — | Pa. Stat. Ann. tit. 40, §§ 771, 775.1, 1553, 1583. |
| RI | Usual physician services, hospitalization, laboratory and radiological services, emergency and preventive care, out-of-area coverage, and services of licensed midwives. | No. | If pregnancy is covered, treatment for infertility and post-delivery stay of 48 to 96 hours must be covered. | Yes. | — | R.I. Gen. Laws §§ 27-41-2, 27-41-30.1, 27-41-33. |
| SC | Emergency, inpatient hospital and physician care, and outpatient medical services. Specific exclusion of dental care and treatment for substance abuse and mental illness, although HMO may choose to cover these services. | No. | No. If pregnancy is covered, postdelivery stay of 48 to 96 hours must be covered. | No. | — | S.C. Code Ann. §§ 38-33-20, 38-71-135. |
| SD | Comprehensive health services (including emergency, inpatient hospital and physician care, outpatient medical services, and preventive care). | Mandatory coverage of newborn/adopted children. | No. If pregnancy is covered, postdelivery stay of 48 to 96 hours must be covered. | Yes. | — | S.D. Codified Laws Ann. §§ 58-41-1, 58-41-35.2, 58-41-112. |
| TN | Emergency care, inpatient hospital and physician care, ambulatory physician care, and outpatient and preventive medical services. | No. | No. | Yes. | Yes, if symptoms indicate an emergency could exist. | Tenn. Code Ann. §§ 56-32-202, 56-7-2355. |
| TX | Emergency care, inpatient hospital and medical services, and outpatient medical services. | Mandatory coverage of newborn/adopted children, including immunizations to age 6, extends to certain dependents. | Yes. Coverage of benefits for in vitro fertilization is a required option. Postdelivery staty of 48 to 96 hours must be covered. | No. | — | Tex. Ins. Code Ann. §§ 3.51-6, 3.70-2, 20A.02, 21.53F. |
| UT | Emergency, inpatient hospital and physician care, outpatient medical care, and out-of-area coverage. | No. | No. | No. | — | Utah Code Ann. § 31A-8-101. |

*(Table continues.)*

# Table 5.4-1 Part A *(cont'd)*

## REGULATION OF SERVICES PROVIDED BY HMOs: MANDATORY COVERAGES

(See also text at § 5.4[a].)

| | | *Mandatory Coverage* | | | | |
|---|---|---|---|---|---|---|
| | *Basic Health Services* | *Newborn/ Dependent Children* | *Pregnancy/Fertility Treatment* | *Preventive Care* | *Coverage of Emergency Services* | *Citations to Authority* |
| VT | Comprehensive services (including physician care, hospitalization, and laboratory and radiological services). | No. | No. | No. | — | Vt. Stat. Ann. tit. 8, § 5101. |
| VA | In-area and out-of-area emergency services, inpatient hospital and physician care, outpatient medical services, laboratory and radiological services, preventive health services, and limited treatment of mental illness and substance abuse. | Mandatory coverage of newborn/adopted children and certain dependents. | No. If pregnancy is covered, postdelivery stay must be covered. | Yes. Early intervention services must be covered to age 3. | HMO cannot require preapproval for emergency services and cannot require enrollee to pay for a nonemergency if a prudent layperson would have thought a condition existed causing the person's health to be in serious jeopardy, bodily functions to be seriously impaired, or a serious dysfunction of the body. HMO must reimburse enrollee for emergency care if the enrollee was referred by the HMO or the primary care physician or designee. | Va. Code Ann. §§ 38.2-3407.2, 38.2-3411, 38.2-3411.2, 38.2-3414.1, 38.2-3418.3, 38.2-4300, 38.2-4312.3. |
| WA | Comprehensive services (including basic consultative, diagnostic, and therapeutic services; emergency and preventive care; and inpatient hospital and outpatient physician care). | Mandatory coverage of newborn/adopted children extends to certain dependents. | If pregnancy is covered, prenatal testing must also be covered. | Yes. | — | Wash. Rev. Code §§ 48.46.020, 48.46.250, 48.46.320, 48.46.375, 48.46.490. |
| WV | Physician and hospital care; out-of-area coverage; pediatric, laboratory, and radiological services; emergency and short-term mental health services; immunizations; well-child care; periodic health evaluations for adults; voluntary family planning and infertility services; and childrens' eye and ear exams. | Mandatory coverage of adopted children extends to certain other dependents. | Mandatory coverage of family planning and infertility services. | Yes. Mandatory coverage for children and adults. | HMOs must cover emergency services. Preauthorization of emergency care shall not be required. | W. Va. Code Ann. §§ 33-16-11, 33-25A-2, 33-25A-8c, 33-25A-8d. |

| | | | | | | |
|---|---|---|---|---|---|---|
| WI | Not specified. | Mandatory coverage of adopted children and extension of certain services (mental health and substance abuse) to dependents. | No. | Yes, lead screening for children under 6. | — | Wis. Stat. Ann. §§ 609.75, 609.655, 609.85. |
| WY | Emergency and inpatient hospital and physician care and outpatient medical services. Specific exemption of mental health services and treatment for substance abuse. | No. | No. | No. | — | Wyo. Stat. § 26-34-102. |

# Table 5.4-1 Part B
## REGULATION OF SERVICES PROVIDED BY HMOs: MANDATORY COVERAGES

(See also text at § 5.4[a].)

| | *Mandatory Coverage* | | | | | |
|---|---|---|---|---|---|---|
| | *Alcohol or Substance Abuse and Mental Illness* | *Specific Diseases and Procedures* | *Specific Facilities* | *Specific Providers* | *Drugs and Prostheses* | *Citations to Authority* |
| AL | No. | If mastectomy is covered, mammograms must be covered. | No. | Yes, physician assistants. Direct access to an obstetrician/gynecologist is mandatory. | No. | Ala. Code §§ 27-1-19.1, 27-49-4, 27-50-4. |
| AK | No. State requirements for basic services specifically exclude coverage of substance abuse and mental health services. | No. | No. | No. | No. | Alaska Stat. § 21.86.900. |
| AZ | No. | Yes. If mastectomy is covered, mammograms and breast reconstruction must be covered. | Yes. If substance abuse or psychiatric services are covered, psychiatric hospitals must be covered. | No. | Yes. If mastectomy is covered, breast prostheses must be covered. | Ariz. Rev. Stat. Ann. § 20-1057. |
| AR | No. | Mandatory coverage for mammograms. | No. | Yes, optometrists, podiatrists, psychologists, dentists, and nurse anesthetists. | No. | Ark. Code Ann. §§ 23-79-114, 23-79-141. |
| CA | Yes. Coverage of alcoholism and chemical dependency is a required option. | Yes. If mastectomy is covered, mammograms and screening for cervical cancer must be covered. Mandatory coverage of osteoporosis. Coverage of diabetic self-education programs is a required option. | Yes. Coverage of home health care is a required option. | Yes, podiatrists. Direct access to an obstetrician/gynecologist is mandatory. | Yes. If mastectomy is covered, breast prostheses must be covered. Also, mandatory coverage of prosthetics following laryngectomy, other prosthetic and orthotic devices, jawbone disorders, and footwear for persons suffering foot disfigurement. | Cal. Health and Safety Code §§ 1367.2, 1367.5, 1367.6, 1367.18, 1367.19, 1367.61, 1367.65, 1367.66, 1367.67, 1367.68, 1367.69, 1373.11. |
| CO | Yes. Coverage of alcoholism and mental illness is a required option. | Yes. Mandatory coverage of mammograms and screening for prostate cancer. | Coverage of home health services and hospice care is a required option. | No. | No. | Colo. Rev. Stat. § 10-16-104. |

| | | | | | | |
|---|---|---|---|---|---|---|
| CT | No. | No. | No. | Direct access to an obstetrician/gynecologist is mandatory. | No. | Conn. Gen. Stat. Ann. §§ 38a-5306. |
| DE | No. | Yes. Mandatory coverage of Pap smears and prostate cancer screening tests. | No. | Yes, midwives. | No. | Del. Code Ann. tit. 18, §§ 3338, 3552, 3553. |
| DC | Yes. Mandatory coverage of substance abuse and mental illness. | Yes. Mandatory coverage of mammograms and cytologic screening. | No. | No. | No. | D.C. Code Ann. §§ 35-2302, 35-2402. |
| FL | No. | Yes, osteoporosis and cleft lip/cleft palate. If HMO covers bone/joint disorders, mandatory coverage of bones/joints of the face. If breast cancer is covered, HMO may not limit inpatient care for breast cancer and must cover reconstructive surgery. | No. | Yes, nurse midwives, optometrists, ophthalmologists, physician assistants, advanced registered nurse practitioners, and certified nurse anesthetists. HMO must provide direct access to dermatologists. | If breast cancer is covered, prosthetics must be covered. | Fla. Stat. Ann. §§ 627.419, 641.31, 641.31094. Fla. Law 98-66. |
| GA | No. | No. | No. | No. | No. | — |
| HI | Yes, for alcohol or substance abuse and mental illness. | Yes. Mandatory coverage of mammograms. | No. | Yes, optometrists, dentists, psychologists. | No. | Haw. Rev. Stat. §§ 431:10A-116, 431M:4. Note: statute mandating coverage for alcohol or substance abuse and mental illness is currently scheduled to be repealed as of 7/1/98. |
| ID | No. | Yes. If mastectomy is covered, mammograms must be covered. | No. | No. | No. | Idaho Code § 41-3926. |
| IL | Yes. Mandatory coverage for substance abuse. | Yes. Mandatory coverage of mammograms and examination and treatment of victims of sexual assault or abuse. Coverage for removal of noncosmetic breast implants is mandatory. | No. | No. | No. | Ill. Rev. Stat. ch. 215, §§ 125/1-2, 125/4-4, 125/4-6.1, 125/4-6.2. |
| IN | State requirements for basic services specifically exclude coverage of substance abuse. HMOs cannot impose limits on mental health coverage which are greater than limits imposed on other conditions. | If mastectomy covered, reconstructive breast surgery must be covered. | No. | No. | If mastectomy covered, breast prosthetics must be covered. HMO must cover drugs and supplies for diabetes. | Ind. Code §§ 27-8-14.5-4, 27-13-1-4, 27-13-7-14, 27-13-7-14.8. |

*(Table continues.)*

# Table 5.4-1 Part B *(cont'd)*
## REGULATION OF SERVICES PROVIDED BY HMOs: MANDATORY COVERAGES

(See also text at § 5.4[a].)

| | *Mandatory Coverage* | | | | | |
|---|---|---|---|---|---|---|
| | *Alcohol or Substance Abuse and Mental Illness* | *Specific Diseases and Procedures* | *Specific Facilities* | *Specific Providers* | *Drugs and Prostheses* | *Citations to Authority* |
| IA | No. | Yes. Mandatory coverage of mammograms. Coverage of diabetes self-management program is an employer option. | No. | Yes, optometrists and chiropractors; coverage of certified registered nurses, physician assistants, and advanced nurse practitioners is an employer option. | No. | Iowa Code §§ 514B.1, 514C.4, 514C.11. |
| KS | Yes. Mandatory coverage of substance abuse and mental illness treatment. | Yes. Mandatory coverage of mammograms and Pap smears. | No. | No. | No. | Kan. Stat. Ann. §§ 40-2229–40-2230. |
| KY | Yes. Mandatory coverage of mental illness treatment. | Yes. If mastectomy is covered, mammograms must be covered; if skeletal disorders are covered, temporomandibular joint and craniomandibular disorders must be covered. If treatment for breast cancer is covered, bone marrow transplants to treat breast cancer must be covered. | Yes. Coverage of home health care and long-term care benefits is a required option. | Yes, osteopaths, chiropractors, psychologists, clinical social workers, opthalmic dispensers, optometrists, podiatrists, and dentists. | No. | Ky. Rev. Stat. Ann. §§ 304.38-193, 304.38-195, 304.38-196, 304.38-210, 304.38-220, 304.38-1933, 304.38-1935, 304.38-1936, 304.38-1937, 304.38-1955. |
| LA | Yes. Coverage of substance abuse and mental illness treatment is a required option. HMO may not impose a cap on mental health coverage which is lower than the cap on physical illness. | Yes. Mandatory coverage for cleft lip/cleft palate surgery, reconstructive breast surgery, and treatment of diabetes. | No. | No. | No. | La. Rev. Stat. Ann. §§ 22:215.8, 22:215.21, 22:215-22, 22:150.5, 22-2002. |
| ME | Yes, mental health. | Yes. If mastectomy is covered, reconstructive surgery must be covered. Mandatory coverage of Pap tests. | No. | No. | Yes, mandatory coverage of medical foods for inborn metabolic errors and diabetes supplies. | Me. Rev. Stat. Ann. tit. 24-A, §§ 4234-A, 4236 (will be repealed on 3/1/98), 4237, 4238, 4240, 4242. |

| | | | | | | |
|---|---|---|---|---|---|---|
| MD | Yes. Mandatory coverage of mental illness treatments. | Yes, mandatory coverage of breast implant removal. | Yes, hospice care. | Direct access to an obstetrician/gynecologist is mandatory. | No. | Md. Gen. Health Code Ann. §§ 19-703, 19-706. |
| MA | Yes. Mandatory coverage of mental illness and alcoholism treatments. | Yes. Mandatory coverage of cardiac rehabilitation, cytologic screening, mammograms, and bone marrow transplants for treatment of breast cancer. | Yes. Mandatory coverage of home health care and hospice care. | Yes, podiatrists, certified nurse anesthetists, and nurse practitioners. | Yes. Mandatory coverage of scalp hair prosthesis for cancer patients, nonprescription enteral formulas, blood-glucose monitoring strips, and off-label drugs for cancer treatment. | Mass. Gen. Laws Ann. ch. 176G, §§ 4, 4B, 4C, 4D, 4E, 4F, 4H, 4J. |
| MI | Yes. Mandatory coverage of substance abuse and outpatient mental health services. | Yes. Mandatory coverage of mammograms. | Yes. Mandatory coverage of home health services and hospices. | Within three years from licensure, HMOs must cover chiropractors and specified optometrists. | Yes. Mandatory coverage for drugs used in antineoplastic surgery. | Mich. Stat. Ann. §§ 14.15(21003), 14.15(21054a), 14.15(21054b); Op. Atty. Gen. No. 5503, July 5, 1979. |
| MN | No. | No. | No. | No. | No. | — |
| MS | Yes. Coverage of treatment for mental illness and drug or alcohol abuse is a required option. | Yes. Mandatory coverage for temporomandibular joint and craniomandibular disorders. Coverage for diabetes treatment, up to $250, is mandatory. | No. | No. | No. | Miss. Code Ann. §§ 83-9-37, 83-9-45 1998 Gen. Laws ch. 483, § 1. |
| MO | HMO may not impose a cap on mental health coverage which is lower than the cap for physical illness. | Yes. Mandatory coverage of mammograms. | Yes, emergency services. | Direct access to an obstetrician/gynecologist is required. | No. | Mo. Rev. Stat. §§ 354.618, 376.381, 376.385, 376.782, 376.811. |
| MT | Yes. Mandatory coverage of substance abuse and mental illness treatments. | Yes. Mandatory coverage of mammograms and phenylketonuria. | No. | No. Direct access to an obstetrician/gynecologist is required. | Yes. Mandatory coverage of formulas for treatment of phenylketonuria. | Mont. Code Ann. §§ 33-22-1903, 33-31-102. |
| NE | No. | No. | No. | No. | No. | — |
| NV | Yes. Mandatory coverage of substance abuse treatment. | Yes. Mandatory coverage of mammograms, cytologic screening, and temporomandibular joint disorder. If mastectomy is covered, reconstructive surgery must be covered. | Yes. Mandatory coverage of hospice care. | Yes, acupuncturists, psychologists, family and marriage therapists, social workers, chiropractors, and registered nurses. | Yes. If mastectomy is covered, breast protheses must be covered. | Nev. Rev. Stat. Ann. §§ 695C.170, 695C.171, 695C.174, 695C.176, 695C.177, 695C.1735, 695C.1755, 695C.1773. |
| NH | Yes. Mandatory coverage of mental illness treatment. | Yes. Mandatory coverage of autologous bone marrow transplants and diabetes treatment. | No. | No. | Yes. Mandatory coverage of scalp hair prostheses and nonprescription enteral formulas. | N.H. Rev. Stat. Ann. §§ 420-B:8-b, 420-B:8-e, 420-B:8-f, 420-B:8-k, 420-B:8-ff. |

*(Table continues.)*

# Table 5.4-1 Part B *(cont'd)*
## REGULATION OF SERVICES PROVIDED BY HMOs: MANDATORY COVERAGES

(See also text at § 5.4[a].)

| | *Mandatory Coverage* | | | | | |
|---|---|---|---|---|---|---|
| | *Alcohol or Substance Abuse and Mental Illness* | *Specific Diseases and Procedures* | *Specific Facilities* | *Specific Providers* | *Drugs and Prostheses* | *Citations to Authority* |
| NJ | No. | Yes. Mandatory coverage of treatment for Wilm's tumor, pap smears, prostate cancer testing, reconstructive breast surgery and mammograms. If mastectomy is covered, inpatient stay of 48 to 72 hours must be covered. | No. | No. | Yes. Mandatory coverage for special diets for inherited metabolic disease. | N.J. Rev. Stat. §§ 26:2J-4.1, 26:2J-4.4, 26:2J-4.11, 26:2J-4.12, 26:2J-4.13, 26:2J-4.14, 26:2J-4.15, 26:2J-4.17. |
| NM | No. State requirements for basic services specifically exclude coverage of substance abuse treatment. | Yes. Mandatory coverage of diabetes, mammograms and cytologic screening for cervical cancer. If mastectomy is covered, inpatient stay of 48 to 72 hours must be covered. | Yes. Coverage of home health care is a required option. | Yes, doctors of oriental medicine. | No. | N.M. Stat. Ann. §§ 59A-46-2, 59A-46-36, 59A-46-40, 59A-46-41, 59A-46-41.1, 59A-46-42, 59A-46-43. |
| NY | No. | Yes. Mandatory coverage of immunizations and reconstruction and inpatient care for breast cancer. | Yes, home care. | Yes, chiropractors. Direct access to an obstetrician/gynecologist is mandatory. | Yes, enteral formulas. | N.Y. Pub. Health Law § 4405-a, 4406-b; N.Y. Ins. Law §§ 3221(k)(11)(A), 3216. |
| NC | Yes. HMO must offer benefits for treatment of chemical dependency. HMO may not impose a cap on treatment of mental illness which is lower than the cap on physical illness. | Yes. Mandatory coverage of mammograms, Pap smears, reconstructive breast surgery, diabetes, and prostate-specific antigen tests. | No. | No. | No. | N.C. Gen. Stat. §§ 58-67-70, 58-67-74, 58-67-75, 58-67-76, 58-67-77, 58-67-79. |

| | | | | | | |
|---|---|---|---|---|---|---|
| ND | Yes. Mandatory coverage of substance abuse and mental illness treatments, unless employer has fewer than 25 employees. | Yes. Mandatory coverage of mammograms, temporomandibular joint and craniomandibular disorders, unless employer has fewer than 25 employees. Mandatory coverage of prostate cancer tests. | No. | Yes, nurse practitioners. | Yes, mandatory coverage of foods for inherited metabolic disease. | N.D. Cent. Code §§ 26.1-36-08, 26.1-36-09, 26.1-36-09.1, 26.1-36-09.3, 26.1-36-09.6, 26.1-36-09.7, 26.1-36-12.3, 26.1-36-89.5. |
| OH | No. | Yes. Mandatory coverage of mammograms and cytologic screening for cervical cancer. | No. | No. | No. | Ohio Rev. Code Ann. § 1742.40. |
| OK | Yes. Mandatory coverage of substance abuse and mental health treatment. | Yes. Mandatory coverage of rehabilitation and physical therapy. | Yes. Mandatory coverage of home health care. | Yes, allopaths, osteopaths, chiropractors, podiatrists, optometrists, and psychologists. | No. | Okla. Stat. tit. 63, § 2503. |
| OR | No. | No. | No. | Yes, acupuncturists. | No. | Or. Rev. Stat. § 743.722. |
| PA | No. | Yes. Mandatory coverage of mammograms, gynecological care, and Pap smears. | Yes, emergency care. | Yes, certified nurse midwives. | No. | Pa. Stat. Ann. tit. 40, §§ 764c, 1574, 3001 Act 68, § 1. |
| RI | No. | Yes. Mandatory coverage of mammograms, diabetes, reconstructive breast surgery after mastectomy, and Pap smears. If mastectomy is covered, inpatient stay of 48 hours must be covered. | No. | Yes, midwives, nurse practitioners, and psychiatric and mental health nurse clinical specialists. | No. | R.I. Gen. Laws §§ 27-41-30, 27-41-36, 27-41-39, 27-41-43, 27-41-43.1, 27-41-44, 27-41-45. |
| SC | State requirements for basic services specifically exclude treatment for alcoholism/substance abuse and mental illness, although HMO may choose to cover. HMO may not impose a cap on mental illness which is lower than the cap for physical illness. | No. | No. | Yes, podiatrists, optometrists, and oral surgeons. | No. | S.C. Code Ann. §§ 38-33-20, 38-33-290, 38-71-880. |
| SD | Yes. Mandatory coverage of alcoholism treatment. Biologically based mental illness must be covered on the same terms as physical illness. | Yes. Mandatory coverage of mammograms and treatment of phenylketonuria. | No. | No. | Yes. Mandatory coverage of formulas for treatment of phenylketonuria. | S.D. Codified Laws Ann. §§ 58-41-35.1, 58-41-35.5, 58-41-98, 58-41-115. |

*(Table continues.)*

# Table 5.4-1 Part B *(cont'd)*
## REGULATION OF SERVICES PROVIDED BY HMOs: MANDATORY COVERAGES

(See also text at § 5.4[a].)

| | *Mandatory Coverage* | | | | | |
|---|---|---|---|---|---|---|
| | *Alcohol or Substance Abuse and Mental Illness* | *Specific Diseases and Procedures* | *Specific Facilities* | *Specific Providers* | *Drugs and Prostheses* | *Citations to Authority* |
| TN | Yes. Coverage of drug dependency treatment is a required option. HMO may not impose a cap on coverage of mental illness which is lower than the cap for physical illness. | Yes. Mandatory coverage of mammograms, diabetes, phenylketonuria, bone density testing, and prostate cancer testing. If the state TennCare program covers bone marrow transplants, HMOs must also cover bone marrow transplants. | No. | No. | No. | Tenn. Code Ann. §§ 56-7-2354, 56-7-2502, 56-7-2504, 56-7-2505, 56-7-2506, 56-7-2601, 56-7-2602, 56-7-2605. |
| TX | Yes. Mandatory coverage of benefits for chemical dependency treatment and treatment of certain serious mental illnesses. Required option of psychiatric day treatment if hospitalization for mental illness is covered. | Yes. Mandatory coverage for temporomandibular and craniomandibular joint disorders, bone mass measurement, diabetes, reconstructive breast surgery, and prostate cancer testing. Required option of coverage for speech and hearing treatment. If mastectomy is covered, inpatient stay of 48 hours must be covered. | No. | Direct access to an obstetrician/gynecologist is required. Access to telemedicine is required. | Yes. Mandatory coverage of formulas for treatment of phenylketonuria. | Tex. Ins. Code Ann. §§ 3.51-9, 3.51-14, 3.70-2, 3.79, 21.52G, 21.53A, 21.53C, 21.53D, 21.53F, 21.53G. |
| UT | No. | No. | No. | Direct access to an obstetrician/gynecologist is mandatory. | No. | Utah Stat. § 31A-8-105.5. |
| VT | No. | No. | No. | No. | No. | — |
| VA | Limited coverage of substance abuse and mental illness treatment. | Yes. Mandatory coverage for victims of rape or incest if "accidents" are covered. Coverage of mammograms, Pap smears, and coverage of bone marrow transplants are required | HMO must cover at least as much emergency care as any applicable federal law requires. | Yes, podiatrists and nurse midwives. Direct access to an obstetrician/gynecologist is mandatory. | If prescription drugs are covered, contraceptives must be covered. | Va. Code Ann. §§ 38.2-3407.5:1, 38.2-3407.6, 38.2-3407.10, 38.2-3407.11, 38.2-3408, 38.2-3418, 38.2-3418.1, 38.2-3418.1:1, 38.2-3418.1:2, 38.2-3418.3, 38.2-4300, 38.2-4312.3. |

| | | | | | | |
|---|---|---|---|---|---|---|
| | | options. Mandatory coverage for reconstructive breast surgery, hemophilia, and prostate cancer tests. If mastectomy is covered, inpatient stay of 48 hours must be covered. | | | | |
| WA | Yes. Mandatory coverage of chemical dependency treatment. Coverage of treatment for mental health is a required option. | Yes. Mandatory coverage of mammograms, diabetes, reconstructive breast surgery, and temporomandibular joint disorder. | No. | Yes, denturists and osteopaths. | Yes. Mandatory coverage of formulas for treatment of phenylketonuria. | Wash. Rev. Code §§ 48.46.272, 48.46.275, 48.46.280, 48.46.290, 48.46.350, 48.46.510, 48.46.530, 48.46.570, 48.46.575. |
| WV | No. | Yes. Mandatory coverage of mammograms, Pap smears, rehabilitation services, and treatment for temporomandibular joint and craniomandibular disorders. | No. | No. | No. | W. Va. Code §§ 33-16-3f, 33-25A-8a, 33-25A-8b. |
| WI | Yes. Mandatory coverage of court-ordered services for the mentally ill. | Yes. Mandatory coverage of mammograms. | No. | Yes, optometrists and chiropractors. | Yes. Mandatory coverage of drugs for treatment of HIV. | Wis. Stat. Ann. §§ 609.60, 609.65, 609.70, 609.80, 609.81. |
| WY | No. State requirements for basic services specifically exclude coverage of treatment for mental illness and substance abuse. | No. | No. | Yes, may not discriminate against any provider acting within the scope of his/her professional license, regardless of academic degree. | No. | Wyo. Stat. §§ 26-34-102, 26-34-134. |

# Table 5.4-2
## LEGISLATION REGULATING THE ADMINISTRATION OF HMOs

(See also text at § 5.4[b].)

| | *Continuation or Conversion Coverage* | *Prohibitions Against Discrimination* | *Exemption from Other Insurance Laws* | *Other Provisions* | *Citations to Authority* |
|---|---|---|---|---|---|
| AL | No. | HMO may not discriminate on the basis of genetic testing. | Yes. Provisions applicable to insurance and health care service plans do not apply to HMOs. | None. | Ala. Code §§ 27-21A-23, 27-51-2. |
| AK | No. | Yes. HMO may not discriminate on the basis of genetic information, domestic violence, or disability. Preexisting conditions must be covered after 12 months. | Yes. Other insurance laws do not apply to HMOs. | Employer-supported health benefit plans with 25 or more members must offer option of enrollment in an HMO. | Alaska Stat. §§ 21.54.100, 21.54.110, 21.86.310. |
| AZ | Yes, mandatory conversion coverage. | Yes. HMO may not cancel coverage on the basis of frequency of use and may not exclude coverage of a condition for which insured has tested negative. | No. | Preapproval procedures must be set forth in a disclosure form. | Ariz. Rev. Stat. Ann. §§ 20-1057, 20-1071, 20-1076. |
| AR | Yes, continuation coverage. | No. | Yes. Insurance laws do not apply to HMOs. | None. | Ark. Code Ann. §§ 23-76-104, 23-86-109. |
| CA | Yes, conversion coverage is mandatory; continuation coverage is a required option. | Yes. HMO may not deny or limit benefits on the basis of blindness, may not deny or limit coverage on the basis of physical or mental impairment (although it may opt out of this requirement), may not discriminate as to conditions attributable to DES exposure, may not deny coverage of Alzheimer's disease (unless the condition is preexisting), and may not refuse to enroll on the basis of genetic disability traits. | No. | None. | Cal. Health and Safety Code §§ 1367.4, 1367.8, 1367.9, 1373.14, 1374.7. |
| CO | Yes, mandatory continuation coverage. | No. | No. | No. | Colo. Rev. Stat. § 10-16-108. |
| CT | No. | No. | No. | None. | — |

| | | | | | |
|---|---|---|---|---|---|
| DE | No. | Yes. HMO may not cancel or refuse to renew a policy solely on the basis of the enrollee's health, unless there was a misrepresentation. Statutes also limit insurer's ability to exclude treatment for preexisting conditions. | No, specifically subject to other insurance laws. | None. | Del. Code Ann. tit. 18, §§ 3517, 6406. |
| DC | No. | Yes. HMO may not exclude coverage for HIV/AIDS unless exclusions apply to all benefits. | No. | None. | D.C. Code Ann. §§ 35-223, 35-2310. |
| FL | Yes, conversion coverage. | Yes. HMO may not discriminate against victims of domestic abuse. HMO may not exclude benefits for HIV/AIDS except as for any other condition, and may not cancel or refuse to renew coverage on the basis of either the enrollee's health status or needs or the prospective costs of health care services. Preexisting conditions must be covered after 12 months and insured must be given credit toward the 12 months for other coverage, if the past coverage was in effect within 63 days of the start of the present coverage. HMO cannot discriminate based on health status factors or genetic testing. | Yes. | Yes. HMO must provide emergency services without the prior approval of the insurer and within certain cost limitations. | Fla. Stat. Ann. §§ 627.4301, 641.201, 641.31, 641.3102, 641.31071, 641.31073, 641.3903, 641.3921, 641.3922, 641.6045. |
| GA | No. | Yes. HMO may not cancel or refuse to renew a policy except for enrollee's failure to pay premiums. | No. All other insurance laws not directly in conflict with HMO provisions apply. | None. | Ga. Code Ann. §§ 33-21-26, 33-21-28. |
| HI | No. | HMOs may not discriminate on the basis of genetic information. | Yes. | None. | Haw. Rev. Stat. §§ 432D-19, 432D-23, 432D-26. |
| ID | No. | Yes. Preexisting conditions must be covered after 12 months. | Yes. | HMO must exclude coverage of elective abortion unless additional premium is paid. | Idaho Code §§ 41-3921, 41-3924, 41-3940. |
| IL | Yes, continuation coverage. | Yes. HMO may not exclude benefits because enrollee has a fibrocystic breast condition, unless a biopsy indicates increased disposition to development of breast cancer; may not deny coverage for removal of breast implants when medically necessary unless implants were solely for cosmetic reasons; and may not deny coverage for certain organ transplants. | No. | None. | Ill. Rev. Stat. ch. 215, §§ 125/4-5, 125/4-6.2, 125/4-9.2, 125/4-16. |

*(Table continues.)*

**Table 5.4-2** *(cont'd)*

LEGISLATION REGULATING THE ADMINISTRATION OF HMOs

(See also text at § 5.4[b].)

| | *Continuation or Conversion Coverage* | *Prohibitions Against Discrimination* | *Exemption from Other Insurance Laws* | *Other Provisions* | *Citations to Authority* |
|---|---|---|---|---|---|
| IN | Yes, continuation coverage. | Yes. HMO may not discriminate based on genetic testing. | Yes. | None. | Ind. Code §§ 27-8-26-5 *et seq.*, 27-13-7-13, 27-13-29-1. |
| IA | No. | Yes. HMO may not exclude benefits or refuse to renew coverage because of a fibrocystic condition. | Yes. | None. | Iowa Code §§ 514B.32, 514C.7. |
| KS | No. | No. | No. | None. | — |
| KY | Yes, both continuation coverage and conversion coverage must be available. | No. | No. | None. | Ky. Rev. Stat. Ann. § 304.38-191. |
| LA | No. | Yes. HMO may not discriminate on the basis of domestic abuse, prenatal testing, genetic testing, or alcoholism (recovered). | Yes. | None. | La. Rev. Stat. Ann. §§ 22:213.6, 22:213.7, 22:229, 22:250.1 *et seq.*, 22:2016. |
| ME | Yes, continuation coverage. | Yes. HMO may not exclude coverage for AIDS except in a manner consistent with exclusions for all illness. | Yes. | None. | Me. Rev. Stat. Ann. tit. 24-A, §§ 2849, 4222, 4229. |
| MD | No. | Yes. HMO may not cancel a policy because of the enrollee's health status or discriminate on the basis of an enrollee's mental illness/ emotional disorder or drug/ alcohol abuse. | Yes. | None. | Md. Gen. Health Code Ann. §§ 19-706, 19-725. |
| MA | Yes, continuation coverage. | Yes, HMO may not discriminate against victims of domestic abuse. | Yes. | None. | Mass. Gen. Laws Ann. ch. 176G, §§ 4A, 5A, 19. |
| MI | Yes, continuation coverage. | HMO may not discriminate against victims of domestic abuse. | No. | None. | Mich. Stat. Ann. §§ 14.15(21072), 14.15(21087). |
| MN | Yes, both conversion coverage and continuation coverage. | Yes, based on receipt of workers' compensation. | No. | Elective abortion may not be a mandatory provision. | Minn. Stat. Ann. §§ 62D.101, 62D.12, 62E.16. |

| | | | | | |
|---|---|---|---|---|---|
| MS | Yes, continuation coverage. | No. | No. | None. | Miss. Code Ann. §§ 83-9-51, 83-41-303. |
| MO | No. | No. | Yes. | HMO may not cover elective abortion except with an additional premium. | Mo. Rev. Stat. §§ 354.505, 376.805. |
| MT | No. | Yes. HMO may not cancel a policy for reasons related to the enrollee's physical or mental condition. | Yes. | None. | Mont. Code Ann. §§ 33-31-102, 33-31-111, 33-31-312. |
| NE | No. | No. | Yes. | None. | Neb. Rev. Stat. § 44-32, 168. |
| NV | Yes, continuation coverage. | No. | Yes. | None. | Nev. Rev. Stat. Ann. §§ 695C.050, 695C.1707. |
| NH | No. | No. | No. | None. | — |
| NJ | Yes, continuation coverage. | Yes. HMO may not discriminate on the basis of genetic characteristics. HMO may not exclude coverage of a preexisting condition for more than 12 months, and the individual must be given credit toward the 12 months for prior coverage, if the prior coverage ended not more than 63 days before the current coverage began. | Yes. | None. | N.J. Rev. Stat. §§ 17B:27-55, 17B:27-57, 17B:27-58, 17B:27A-5, 17B:27A-27, 26:2J-4.3, 26:2J-4.13. |
| NM | Yes, both continuation coverage and conversion coverage. | No. | Yes. | None. | N.M. Stat. Ann. §§ 59A-46-30, 59A-46-32. |
| NY | No. | Insurer may not discriminate against victims of abuse, on the basis of genetic testing, or disability. HMO may not exclude coverage of a preexisting condition for more than 12 months, and the individual must be given credit toward the 12 months for prior coverage, if the prior coverage ended not more than 63 days before the current coverage began. | Yes. | Some employer-supported health benefits plans with more than 25 members must offer the option of enrollment in an HMO. | N.Y. Ins. Law §§ 2612, 3221(q)(1), 3232, N.Y. Pub. Health Law §§ 4407, 4411. |
| NC | No. | Yes. HMO may not refuse to enroll a person who is mentally ill or chemically dependent or charge a higher premium for a person with either condition, unless the condition was preexisting. HMO may not exclude coverage of a preexisting condition for more than 12 months, and the individual must be given *(cont'd)* | Yes. | None. | N.C. Gen. Stat. §§ 58-67-75, 58-67-170, 58-68-30. |

*(Table continues.)*

**Table 5.4-2** *(cont'd)*

LEGISLATION REGULATING THE ADMINISTRATION OF HMOs

(See also text at § 5.4[b].)

| | *Continuation or Conversion Coverage* | *Prohibitions Against Discrimination* | *Exemption from Other Insurance Laws* | *Other Provisions* | *Citations to Authority* |
|---|---|---|---|---|---|
| NC (*cont'd*) | | credit toward the 12 months for prior coverage, if the prior coverage ended not more than 63 days before the current coverage began. | | | |
| ND | Yes, continuation coverage. | HMO may not exclude coverage of a preexisting condition for more than 12 months, and the individual must be given credit toward the 12 months for prior coverage, if the prior coverage ended not more than 63 days before the current coverage began. | Yes. | None. | N.D. Cent. Code §§ 26.1-18.1 *et seq.*, 26.1-36.4-04. |
| OH | Yes, continuation coverage. | Yes. HMO may not discriminate on the basis of genetic screening tests or cancel or refuse to renew coverage on the basis of health status or requirements. | Yes. | Employer-supported health benefits plans with 25 or more members must offer employees the option of enrollment in an HMO. | Ohio Rev. Code Ann. §§ 1742.16, 1742.30, 1742.33, 1742.34, 1742.42. |
| OK | No. | No. | No. | None. | — |
| OR | No. | No. | No. | None. | — |
| PA | No. | Insurer may not discriminate against victims of abuse. | No. | None. | Act. No. 1996-24. |
| RI | No. | No. | Yes. | None. | R.I. Gen. Laws § 27-41-22. |
| SC | No. | Yes. HMO may not discriminate on the basis of genetic testing or domestic abuse. HMO may not exclude coverage of a preexisting condition for more than 12 months, and the individual must be given credit toward the 12 months for prior coverage, if the prior coverage ended not more than 63 days before the current coverage began. | Yes. | None. | S.C. Code Ann. §§ 38-33-240, 38-71-850, 38-71-860. |

| | | | | | |
|---|---|---|---|---|---|
| SD | Yes, both continuation coverage and conversion coverage. | Preexisting conditions may not be excluded for more than 12 months, and individual must be given credit toward the 12 months for coverage under a prior policy if the prior policy ended no more than 63 days before the current policy began. Insurer may not exclude coverage for injuries sustained while under the influence of drugs or alcohol, unless injury was sustained in the commission of a felony. | Yes. | None. | S.D. Codified Laws Ann. §§ 58-18-45, 58-41-26, 58-41-35.6, 58-41-51.2, 58-41-51.3. |
| TN | No. | HMO cannot discriminate based on genetic testing or domestic abuse. HMO may not exclude coverage of a preexisting condition for more than 12 months, and the individual must be given credit toward the 12 months for prior coverage, if the prior coverage ended not more than 63 days before the current coverage began. | No. | None. | Tenn. Code Ann. §§ 56-7-2702 *et seq.*, 56-7-2803, 58-8-303. |
| TX | No. | Yes. HMO may not exclude coverage for AIDS/HIV-related illnesses. HMO may not discriminate on the basis of domestic abuse. | No. | None. | Tex. Ins. Code Ann. §§ 3.51-6, 21.21-5. |
| UT | No. | No. | Yes, from selected provisions. | None. | Utah Code Ann. § 31A-8-103. |
| VT | No. | No. | Yes. | None. | Vt. Stat. Ann. tit 8, § 5112. |
| VA | No. | Yes. HMO must credit time under a prior policy toward the waiting period for coverage of preexisting conditions, subject to statutory criteria. | No. | None. | Va. Code Ann. § 38.2-3514.1. |
| WA | Yes, continuation and conversion coverage. | Yes. HMO may not cancel or reduce coverage on the basis of prenatal testing, may not cancel or refuse coverage on the basis of a mastectomy or lumpectomy performed more than 5 years ago, and may not deny coverage because of a handicap. | No. | None. | Wash. Rev. Code §§ 48.42.090, 48.46.285, 48.46.370, 48.46.440, 48.46.450, 48.46.460. |
| WV | No. | No. | Yes. | Employer-supported health benefit plans with at least 25 members must offer option of enrollment in an HMO. | W. Va. Code §§ 33-25A-24, 33-25A-28. |

*(Table continues.)*

**Table 5.4-2** *(cont'd)*

LEGISLATION REGULATING THE ADMINISTRATION OF HMOs

(See also text at § 5.4[b].)

| | *Continuation or Conversion Coverage* | *Prohibitions Against Discrimination* | *Exemption from Other Insurance Laws* | *Other Provisions* | *Citations to Authority* |
|---|---|---|---|---|---|
| WI | No. | Yes. HMO may not exclude or limit coverage for HIV/AIDS. | No. | None. | Wis. Stat. Ann. §§ 609.81, 631.93. |
| WY | No. | No. | Yes. | None. | Wyo. Stat. § 26-34-128. |

# § 5.5 State Administrative Requirements for Health Insurance

Section 5.5 contains certain state administrative requirements for group health insurance plans. Table 5.5-1 includes information on state-mandated grace periods for employer payments of health insurance premiums, incontestability provisions, and coverage requirements. Grace periods usually provide that an employer has a few days past the actual due date of the premium within which to make the payment without being subject to cancellation of the insurance. Incontestability provisions protect insurers from contesting the validity of the policy in general, and coverage requirements dictate the minimum number of employees or total group members who must be part of group insurance. Information on whether the state has any statute mandating coverage of spouses or dependents in group insurance is covered, and information on whether such persons as individual proprietors and partners are eligible under state definitions of employer-based group health insurance is also provided in Table 5.5-1.

Table 5.5-2 covers state coordination of benefits requirements. Coordination of benefits is a method of determining which insurance policy, when more than one may apply, is responsible for payment of benefits when a claim occurs. The general purpose of coordination of benefits is to prevent multiple payment for the same claim. Table 5.5-2 provides information on rules adopted by the states for three issues: (1) which plan covers a claim for dependent children who have applicable insurance through both parents and the parents are not separated or divorced, (2) which plan covers a claim for a person covered as an employee or dependent for one plan and as a laid-off or retired employee for another plan, and (3) whether the state allows insurance companies to provide for a limitation of liability when there is other valid insurance covering the same loss on an expense-incurred, provision-of-service, or any other basis.

# Table 5.5-1
## GRACE PERIOD FOR PREMIUM PAYMENTS, AND INCONTESTABILITY/COVERAGE REQUIREMENTS

(See also text at § 5.5.)

| | | | *Coverage Under Group Policy* | | | |
|---|---|---|---|---|---|---|
| | *Grace Period for Premium Payments* | *Incontestability Period* | *Minimum Number of Employees/Other Members* | *Coverage of Spouse/Dependents* | *Coverage of Individual Proprietors/Partners* | *Citations to Authority* |
| AL | State has no statutory requirements. | State has no statutory requirements. | State has no statutory requirements. | State has no statutory requirements. | Yes, individual proprietors and partners. | Ala. Code. § 27-20-1. |
| AK | State has no statutory requirements. | State has no statutory requirements. | State has no statutory requirements. | State has no statutory requirements. | Yes, individual proprietors and partners. | Alaska Stat. § 21.54.060. |
| AZ | State has no statutory requirements. | State has no statutory requirements. | 5 employees. | State has no statutory requirements. | Yes, individual proprietors and partners. | Ariz. Rev. Stat. Ann. § 20-1401. |
| AR | State has no statutory requirements. | State has no statutory requirements. | State has no statutory requirements. | State has no statutory requirements. | Yes, individual proprietors and partners. | Ark. Code Ann. § 23-86-106. |
| CA | State has no statutory requirements. | 2 years. | State has no statutory requirements. | State has no statutory requirements. | Yes, individual proprietors and partners if actively engaged in the business. | Cal. Ins. Code §§ 10270.55, 10291.5, 10350.2. |
| CO | 31 days. | 2 years. | 10 employees. | State has no statutory requirements. | Yes, individual proprietors and partners. | Colo. Rev. Stat. Ann. § 10-16-214. |
| CT | State has no statutory requirements. | State has no statutory requirements. | State has no statutory requirements. | State has no statutory requirements. | Individual proprietors and partners must be covered for injuries caused by work-related accidents. | Conn. Gen. Stat. Ann. § 38a-527. |
| DE | 31 days. | 2 years. | State has no statutory requirements. | If the employer pays the entire premium for dependent coverage, all dependents may be insured. | Yes, individual proprietors and partners. | Del. Code Ann. tit. 18, §§ 3502, 3511, 3513, 3514. |
| DC | State has no statutory requirements. | State has no statutory requirements. | State has no statutory requirements. | State has no statutory requirements. | State has no statutory requirements. | State has no statutory requirements. |
| FL | State has no statutory requirements. | State has no statutory requirements. | State has no statutory requirements. | State has no statutory requirements. | Yes, individual proprietors and partners. | Fla. Stat. Ann. § 627.653. |
| GA | State has no statutory requirements. | State has no statutory requirements. | 2 employees. | State has no statutory requirements. | Yes, individual proprietors and partners. | Ga. Code Ann. §§ 33-30-1, 33-30-4. |
| HI | State has no statutory requirements. | State has no statutory requirements. | State has no statutory requirements. | State has no statutory requirements. | Yes, individual proprietors and partners. | Haw. Rev. Stat. Ann. § 431:10A-201. |

| | | | | | | |
|---|---|---|---|---|---|---|
| ID | State has no statutory requirements. | State has no statutory requirements. | State has no statutory requirements. | State has no statutory requirements. | Yes, individual proprietors and partners. | Idaho Code § 41-2202. |
| IL | State has no statutory requirements. | State has no statutory requirements. | 10 employees. | State has no statutory requirements. | Yes, individual proprietors and partners. | 215 Ill. Comp. Stat. Ann. § 5/367. |
| IN | 31 days. | 2 years. | State has no statutory requirements. | State has no statutory requirements. | Yes, individual proprietors and partners. | Ind. Code Ann. §§ 27-8-5-16, 27-8-5-19. |
| IA | State has no statutory requirements. | State has no statutory requirements. | State has no statutory requirements. | State has no statutory requirements. | Yes, individual proprietors and partners. | Iowa Code Ann. § 509.1. |
| KS | State has no statutory requirements. | State has no statutory requirements. | 3 employees. | State has no statutory requirements. | Yes, individual proprietors and partners. | Kan. Stat. Ann. § 40-2209. |
| KY | State has no statutory requirements. | State has no statutory requirements. | State has no statutory requirements. | State has no statutory requirements. | Yes, individual proprietors and partners. | Ky. Rev. Stat. Ann. § 304.18-020. |
| LA | State has no statutory requirements. | State has no statutory requirements. | 1 employee. | State has no statutory requirements. | Yes, individual proprietors and partners. | La. Rev. Stat. Ann. §§ 20-2002, 20-2016. |
| ME | State has no statutory requirements. | State has no statutory requirements. | State has no statutory requirements. | State has no statutory requirements. | Yes, individual proprietors and partners. | Me. Rev. Stat. Ann. tit. 24-A, § 2804. |
| MD | State has no statutory requirements. | State has no statutory requirements. | State has no statutory requirements. | Insurer must allow continuous open enrollment for spouses/dependents who have lost coverage due to a spouse's involuntary termination of employment causing loss of group health insurance, but not where the termination was for cause. | Yes, individual proprietors and partners. | Md. Ins. Code §§ 15-302, 15-411. |
| MA | State has no statutory requirements. | State has no statutory requirements. | State has no statutory requirements. | State has no statutory requirements. | Yes, individual proprietors and partners. | Mass. Gen. Laws Ann. ch. 175, § 110. |
| MI | 7 days for premiums paid on a weekly basis, 10 days for premiums paid on a monthly basis, and 31 days for all other types of premiums. | 3 years. | 5 employees. | State has no statutory requirements. | Yes, individual proprietors and partners. | Mich. Stat. Ann. §§ 24.13408, 24.13410, 24.13601, 24.13610. |
| MN | State has no statutory requirements. | State has no statutory requirements. | Not fewer than 2 employees nor fewer than 10 members. | State has no statutory requirements. | Yes, individual proprietors and partners. | Minn. Stat. Ann. § 62A.10. |
| MS | 7 days for premiums paid on a weekly basis, 10 days for premiums paid on a monthly basis, and 31 days for all other types of premiums. | 2 years. | State has no statutory requirements. | State has no statutory requirements. | State has no statutory requirements. | Miss. Code Ann. § 83-9-5. |

*(Table continues.)*

## Table 5.5-1 *(cont'd)*

## GRACE PERIOD FOR PREMIUM PAYMENTS, AND INCONTESTABILITY/COVERAGE REQUIREMENTS

(See also text at § 5.5.)

| | *Grace Period for Premium Payments* | *Incontestability Period* | *Coverage Under Group Policy: Minimum Number of Employees/Other Members* | *Coverage of Spouse/Dependents* | *Coverage of Individual Proprietors/Partners* | *Citations to Authority* |
|---|---|---|---|---|---|---|
| MO | 31 days. | 2 years. | State has no statutory requirements. | State has no statutory requirements. | Yes, individual proprietors and partners. | Mo. Rev. Stat. §§ 376.421, 376.426. |
| MT | State has no statutory requirements. | State has no statutory requirements. | State has no statutory requirements. | State has no statutory requirements. | Yes, individual proprietors and partners. | Mont. Code Ann. § 33-22-501. |
| NE | State has no statutory requirements. | State has no statutory requirements. | 3 employees. | State has no statutory requirements. | Yes, individual proprietors and partners. | Neb. Rev. Stat. § 44-760. |
| NV | State has no statutory requirements. | State has no statutory requirements. | 2 employees. | State has no statutory requirements. | Eligible individuals for purposes of group insurance defined simply as "persons" in a group formed for a purpose other than obtaining insurance. | Nev. Rev. Stat. § 689B.020. |
| NH | 31 days. | 2 years. | State has no statutory requirements. | State has no statutory requirements. | State has no statutory requirements. | N.H. Rev. Stat. Ann. § 415:8. |
| NJ | 31 days. | 2 years. | 10 employees. | Yes, if the premiums are paid by the employer. | Yes, individual proprietors and partners. | N.J. Stat. Ann. §§ 17B:27-2, 17B:27-9, 17B:27-11, 17B:27-12. |
| NM | State has no statutory requirements. | State has no statutory requirements. | 1 employee. | State has no statutory requirements. | Yes, individual proprietors and partners. | N.M. Stat. Ann. § 59A-23-3. |
| NY | State has no statutory requirements. | State has no statutory requirements. | State has no statutory requirements. | State has no statutory requirements. | State has no statutory requirements. | State has no statutory requirements. |
| NC | 7 days for premiums paid on a weekly basis, 10 days for premiums paid on a monthly basis, and 31 days for all other types of premiums. | 2 years. | State has no statutory requirements. | State has no statutory requirements. | Yes, individual proprietors and partners. | N.C. Gen. Stat. §§ 58-51-15, 58-51-80. |
| ND | 31 days. | 2 years. | State has no statutory requirements. | State has no statutory requirements. | State has no statutory requirements. | N.D. Cent. Code § 26.1-36-05. |

| | | | | | | |
|---|---|---|---|---|---|---|
| OH | 7 days for premiums paid on a weekly basis, 10 days for premiums paid on a monthly basis, and 31 days for all other types of premiums. | 2 years. | 2 employees. | State has no statutory requirements. | Yes, individual proprietors and partners. | Ohio Rev. Code Ann. §§ 3923.04, 3923.12. |
| OK | State has no statutory requirements. | State has no statutory requirements. | 1 employee. | State has no statutory requirements. | Yes, individual proprietors and partners. | Okla. Stat. tit. 36, § 4501. |
| OR | State has no statutory requirements. | State has no statutory requirements. | State has no statutory requirements. | State has no statutory requirements. | Yes, individual proprietors and partners. | Or. Rev. Stat. § 743.522. |
| PA | 7 days for premiums paid on a weekly basis, 10 days for premiums paid on a monthly basis, and 31 days for all other types of premiums. | 3 years. | 10 employees. | State has no statutory requirements. | Yes, individual proprietors and partners. | Pa. Stat. Ann. tit. 40, §§ 753, 756.2. |
| RI | 7 days for premiums paid on a weekly basis, 10 days for premiums paid on a monthly basis, and 31 days for all other types of premiums. | 3 years. | State has no statutory requirements. | State has no statutory requirements. | State has no statutory requirements. | R.I. Gen. Laws § 27-18-3. |
| SC | 31 days. | 2 years. | 2 employees. | State has no statutory requirements. | Yes, individual proprietors and partners. | S.C. Code Ann. §§ 38-71-710, 38-71-730. |
| SD | State has no statutory requirements. | State has no statutory requirements. | State has no statutory requirements. | State has no statutory requirements. | Yes, individual proprietors and partners. | S.D. Codified Laws §§ 58-18-1–58-18-7. |
| TN | 7 days for premiums paid on a weekly basis, 10 days for premiums paid on a monthly basis, and 31 days for all other types of premiums. | 2 years. | State has no statutory requirements. | State has no statutory requirements. | Yes, individual proprietors and partners. | Tenn. Code Ann. §§ 56-26-108, 56-26-201. |
| TX | State has no statutory requirements. | 2 years. | State has no statutory requirements. | State has no statutory requirements. | Yes, individual proprietors and partners. | Tex. Ins. Code Ann. art. 3.51-6, § 1. |
| UT | State has no statutory requirements. | State has no statutory requirements. | State has no statutory requirements. | State has no statutory requirements. | Yes, individual proprietors and partners. | Utah Code Ann. §§ 31A-22-502, 31A-22-701. |
| VT | State has no statutory requirements. | State has no statutory requirements. | 1 employee. | State has no statutory requirements. | Yes, individual proprietors and partners. | Vt. Stat. Ann. tit. 8, § 4079. |
| VA | 31 days. | 2 years. | 2 employees. | State has no statutory requirements. | State has no statutory requirements. | Va. Code Ann. §§ 38.2-3523, 38.2-3527, 38.2-3528. |

*(Table continues.)*

## **Table 5.5-1** *(cont'd)*

## GRACE PERIOD FOR PREMIUM PAYMENTS, AND INCONTESTABILITY/COVERAGE REQUIREMENTS

(See also text at § 5.5.)

| | | | *Coverage Under Group Policy* | | | |
|---|---|---|---|---|---|---|
| | *Grace Period for Premium Payments* | *Incontestability Period* | *Minimum Number of Employees/Other Members* | *Coverage of Spouse/Dependents* | *Coverage of Individual Proprietors/Partners* | *Citations to Authority* |
| WA | State has no statutory requirements. | State has no statutory requirements. | State has no statutory requirements. | State has no statutory requirements. | Yes, individual proprietors and partners. | Wash. Rev. Code Ann. §§ 48.21.010, 48.21.020. |
| WV | State has no statutory requirements. | State has no statutory requirements. | 10 employees. | State has no statutory requirements. | Yes, individual proprietors and partners. | W. Va. Code Ann. § 33-16-2. |
| WI | 31 days. | 2 years. | State has no statutory requirements. | State has no statutory requirements. | Yes, individual proprietors and partners. | Wis. Stat. Ann. §§ 632.76, 632.78. |
| WY | 31 days. | 2 years. | State has no statutory requirements. | State has no statutory requirements. | Yes, individual proprietors and partners. | Wyo. Stat. §§ 26-19-102, 26-19-107. |

# Table 5.5-2

## COORDINATION OF BENEFITS

(See also text at § 5.5.)

**KEY:** **Birthday rule.** Means that the state has adopted the following rule to determine coordination of benefits when multiple plans may cover a given injury of a dependent child: The benefits of the parent whose birthday falls earlier in the year (month and day) are determined before those of the parent whose birthday falls later in the year.

| | *Order of Benefits for Dependent (Parents Not Separated or Divorced)* | *Benefits of Policy Covering Individual as an Employee Determined Before Policy Covering Same Individual as a Laid-Off or Retired Employee?* | *Does State Allow Limitation of Liability When There Is Other Valid Insurance Covering the Same Loss on a Provision-of-Service, Expense-Incurred, or Other Basis?* | *Citations to Authority* |
|---|---|---|---|---|
| AL | Birthday rule. | Yes. | Yes. | Ala. Code §§ 27-19-20, 27-19-21; Ala. Ins. Reg. 56. |
| AK | State suggests use of the birthday rule. | State has no statutory requirement. | Yes. | Alaska Stat. §§ 21.51.200, 21.51.210; Alaska Bulletin No. 80-8. |
| AZ | Birthday rule. | Yes. | Yes. | Ariz. Rev. Stat. Ann. §§ 20-1361, 20-1362; Ariz. Admin. Reg. R20-6-217. |
| AR | Birthday rule. | State has no statutory requirement. | No, unless aggregate benefits under all insurance exceed all covered incurred medical expenses. | Ark. Code Ann. § 23-86-111; Ark. Ins. Reg. 21, § 4. |
| CA | Birthday rule. | Yes. | Yes. | Cal. Ins. Code § 10369.5; Cal. Code Regs. tit. 10, §§ 2232.50–2232.58. |
| CO | Birthday rule. | Yes. | State has no statutory requirement. | Colo. Admin. Ins. Reg. 4-6-2. |
| CT | Birthday rule. | Yes. | State has no statutory requirement. | Conn. Agencies Regs. §§ 38a-480 *et seq.* |
| DE | Birthday rule. | State has no statutory requirement. | State has no statutory requirement. | Del. Ins. Reg. No. 61. |
| DC | State has no statutory requirement. | State has no statutory requirement. | State has no statutory requirement. | — |
| FL | Birthday rule. | Yes. | State has no statutory requirement. | Fla. Stat. Ann. § 627.4235. |
| GA | Birthday rule. | Yes. | State has no statutory requirement. | Ga. Ins. Reg. §§ 120-2-48 *et seq.* |
| HI | State has no statutory requirement. | State has no statutory requirement. | State has no statutory requirement. | — |
| ID | Birthday rule (state instructs director of department of insurance to follow National Association of Insurance Commissioner Rules). | Yes (state instructs director of department of insurance to follow National Association of Insurance Commissioner Rules). | Yes. | Idaho Code §§ 41-2121, 41-2122, 41-2216. |

*(Table continues.)*

# Table 5.5-2 *(cont'd)*

## COORDINATION OF BENEFITS

(See also text at § 5.5.)

**KEY:** **Birthday rule.** Means that the state has adopted the following rule to determine coordination of benefits when multiple plans may cover a given injury of a dependent child: The benefits of the parent whose birthday falls earlier in the year (month and day) are determined before those of the parent whose birthday falls later in the year.

| | *Order of Benefits for Dependent (Parents Not Separated or Divorced)* | *Benefits of Policy Covering Individual as an Employee Determined Before Policy Covering Same Individual as a Laid-Off or Retired Employee?* | *Does State Allow Limitation of Liability When There Is Other Valid Insurance Covering the Same Loss on a Provision-of-Service, Expense-Incurred, or Other Basis?* | *Citations to Authority* |
|---|---|---|---|---|
| IL | Birthday rule. | Yes. | Yes. | 215 Ill. Comp. Stat. Ann. §§ 5/357.18, 5/357.19, 5/367; Ill. Admin. Code tit. 50, §§ 2009.10 *et seq.* |
| IN | Birthday rule. | Yes. | Yes. | Ind. Code Ann. § 27-8-4-3; Ind. Admin. Code Reg. 760-1-38.1-13, 760-1-38.1-15. |
| IA | Birthday rule. | Yes. | State has no statutory requirement. | Iowa Admin. Code R. 191-38.1 *et seq.* |
| KS | Birthday rule. | Yes. | Yes. | Kan. Stat. Ann. § 40-2203; Kan. Admin. Regs. 40-4-34. |
| KY | Birthday rule. | Yes. | State has no statutory requirement. | 80 Ky. Admin. Regs. 18:030. |
| LA | Birthday rule. | Yes. | Yes. | La. Rev. Stat. Ann. § 22:315; La. Ins. Reg. 32 *et seq.* |
| ME | State has no statutory requirement. | State has no statutory requirement. | Yes. | Me. Rev. Stat. Ann. tit. 24-A, §§ 2722, 2723. |
| MD | State has no statutory requirement. | State has no statutory requirement. | Yes. | Md. Ins. Code §§ 15-222, 15-223. |
| MA | Birthday rule. | Yes. | State has no statutory requirement. | Mass. Regs. Code tit. 211, §§ 38.01 *et seq.* |
| MI | Birthday rule. | Yes. | Yes. | Mich. Comp. Laws Ann. §§ 500.3438–500.3440, 550.253. |
| MN | Birthday rule. | Yes. | State has no statutory requirement. | Minn. Ins. Reg. 2742.0100. |
| MS | State has no statutory requirement. | State has no statutory requirement. | State has no statutory requirement. | — |
| MO | Birthday rule. | No. | Yes. | Mo. Rev. Stat. § 376.777; 20 Mo. CSR 400-2.030. |
| MT | Birthday rule. | State has no statutory requirement. | Yes. | Mont. Code Ann. §§ 33-22-225, 33-22-226; Mont. Admin. Reg. 6.6.2401 *et seq.* |

| | | | | |
|---|---|---|---|---|
| NE | Birthday rule. | Yes. | Yes. | Neb. Rev. Stat. § 44-710.04; 210 Neb. Admin. Code ch 39. |
| NV | Birthday rule. | Yes. | State has no statutory requirement. | Nev. Rev. Stat. Ann. § 689B.064. |
| NH | Birthday rule. | Yes. | State has no statutory requirement. | N.H. Code Admin. R. Ann. Ins. 1904.05 *et seq.* |
| NJ | Birthday rule. | Yes. | State has no statutory requirement. | N.J. Admin. Code tit. 11, §§ 11:4-28.1 *et seq.* |
| NM | State has no statutory requirement. | State has no statutory requirement. | Yes. | N.M. Stat. Ann. §§ 59A-22-20, 59A-22-21. |
| NY | Birthday rule. | Yes. | State has no statutory requirement. | N.Y. Comp. Codes R. & Regs. tit. 11, § 52.23. |
| NC | Birthday rule. | Yes. | State has no statutory requirement. | N.C. Admin. Code tit. 11, r. 12.0514. |
| ND | Birthday rule. | Yes. | If other insurance from a policy issued by the insurer also covers the injury, resulting in aggregate indemnity in excess of the maximum limit, the excess insurance is void. | N.D. Cent. Code § 26.1-36-04; N.D. Admin. Code §§ 45-08-01.1 *et seq.* |
| OH | Birthday rule. | Yes. | Yes. | Ohio Rev. Code Ann. § 3902.13. |
| OK | Birthday rule. | Yes. | Yes. | Okla. Stat. Ann. tit. 36, § 4405; Okla. Ins. Reg. 365-10-11-1 *et seq.* |
| OR | Birthday rule. | Yes. | State has no statutory requirement. | Or. Admin. R. 836-20-765 *et seq.* |
| PA | State has no statutory requirement. | State has no statutory requirement. | Yes. | Pa. Stat. Ann. tit. 40, § 753. |
| RI | Birthday rule. | State has no statutory requirement. | Yes. | R.I. Gen. Laws § 27-18-4; R.I. Ins. Reg. XLVIII. |
| SC | Birthday rule. | Yes. | State has no statutory requirement. | 25A S.C. Code Ann. Regs. 69-43. |
| SD | Birthday rule. | Yes. | State has no statutory requirement. | S.D. Codified Laws § 58-18A-6. |
| TN | Birthday rule. | Yes. | State has no statutory requirement. | Tenn. Admin. Code 780-1-53. |
| TX | Birthday rule. | Yes. | State has no statutory requirement. | 28 Tex. Admin. Code § 3.3508. |
| UT | Birthday rule. | Yes. | State has no statutory requirement. | Utah Ins. Reg. R590-131. |
| VT | State has no statutory authority. | State has no statutory requirement. | Yes. | Vt. Stat. Ann. tit. 8, § 4066. |
| VA | State has no statutory requirement. | State has no statutory requirement. | State has no statutory requirement. | — |
| WA | Birthday rule. | Yes. | State has no statutory requirement. | Wash. Admin. Code §§ 284-51-010 *et seq.* |
| WV | Birthday rule. | Yes. | Yes. | W. Va. Code Ann. § 33-15-5; W. Va. Ins. Reg. 33-28-4. |
| WI | Birthday rule. | Yes. | Yes. | Wis. Admin. Code Ins. 3.40. |
| WY | Birthday rule. | Yes. | State has no statutory requirement. | Wyo. Ins. Reg. ch X. |

# § 5.6 Group Life Insurance

Almost all states regulate group life insurance policies offered to employees. As discussed in chapter 1, although a state law is preempted, if it purports to regulate an employee benefit plan covered by ERISA, any law that regulates the "business of insurance" would not be preempted.

The states do not require any minimum level of group life insurance coverage. However, the following provisions are common:

1. Most states provide that the insured individual can choose anyone to be the beneficiary. However, the employer is generally not permitted to be the beneficiary.
2. Many states set minimum limits on the number of employees (usually five to ten) that must be covered under a group policy.
3. Many state laws impose restrictions on who may pay premiums. Some states require employers to pay at least part of the premiums.
4. Virtually all states require insurance companies to allow a one-month grace period if a premium payment is late.
5. Virtually all states provide for mandatory conversion. That is, insurers must allow individuals who are covered under a group policy to convert to an individual policy if they terminate employment.

A few states prohibit insurers from excluding or reducing benefits when AIDS is a cause of death.

Tables 5.6-1 through 5.6-4 set out the states' requirements related to the provision of group life insurance.

Table 5.6-1 sets out basic requirements of group life insurance plans, as discussed above.

Table 5.6-2 sets out administrative requirements. In most states, following the death of an insured, an insurer may pay a sum of the proceeds from the insurance policy to a person who is "equitably entitled" to the money—usually because the individual paid for funeral and other expenses. In some cases, individuals other than those who might be covered under a strict definition of "employee" may be part of a group insurance plan. Directors, individual proprietors, and partners are, in many states, covered under the definition of "employee" for purposes of group life insurance offered to an employment group. Also, most states provide that after a certain period of time, often two years, the policy is incontestable. This means that after the period of time has run, the policy may not be contested by the insurer except for nonpayment of premiums. Many states also require that the insurer provide a certificate explaining coverage to *each* insured, not just to the policyholder/employer. These provisions are set forth in Table 5.6-2.

Table 5.6-3 sets out coverage requirements, which include the minimum coverage of employees and dependents. In many states, if part of the group insurance premium is to be paid by the employees, the policy may go into effect only if 75 percent of the eligible employees elect to participate. Many states also provide that if the employer is paying all of the premium, 100 percent of the eligible employees must be allowed to participate in the plan. In a few states, spouses and dependent children of all eligible employees must be covered if the plan is open to spouses and dependents and the employer pays 100 percent of the premiums for coverage of spouses and dependents. Finally, some states contain a limitation on the amount of insurance that may be purchased for spouses and dependents, often expressed as a percentage of the insurance on the life of the employee. These issues are covered in Table 5.6-3.

Table 5.6-4 contains state continuation and conversion requirements. In a few states, an employee must be allowed to continue group life insurance coverage during periods of total disability or labor disputes. Unless otherwise provided, for example in a collective bargaining agreement, the employee is responsible for paying the premiums during the continuation period. Continuation coverage usually ends when the employee gets coverage under a disability provision of the original policy or under another policy or when the group policy is discontinued. In most states, an employee must be allowed to convert to an individual policy, usually after termination of employment or termination of membership in the eligible class (often due to reduction of hours). A few states allow spouses and dependents the option to convert, usually following the death of the employee or a dependent's ceasing to be a qualified family member. Employees must usually elect continuation coverage within about 31 days, and the amount of coverage is almost always restricted to no more than the coverage that was lost due to the termination. States sometimes provide for very specific notification to the employee of conversion rights, so that the employee does not miss the time during which the policy may be converted. Many states also provide that if the group policy itself is terminated, some employees may have the right to convert. Continuation and conversion rights are covered in Table 5.6-4.

*(Table continues.)*

# Table 5.6-1
## GROUP LIFE INSURANCE BASIC REQUIREMENTS AND PROVISIONS

(See also text at § 5.6.)

| | *Employer Must Pay Part of the Premium* | *Minimum Number of Employees in Group Plan* | *Employer as Beneficiary Prohibited* | *Grace Period (Days)* | *Mandatory Conversion* | *Other Provisions* | *Citations to Authority* |
|---|---|---|---|---|---|---|---|
| AL | No. | State has no statutory requirements. | No. | 30. | Yes. | None. | Ala. Code §§ 27-18-3, 27-18-11. |
| AK | No. | 2. | No. | 31. | Yes. | None. | Alaska Stat. §§ 21.48.010, 21.48.110, 21.48.180. |
| AZ | Yes. | 10. | Yes. | 31. | Yes. | None. | Ariz. Rev. Stat. Ann. §§ 20-1252, 20-1259, 20-1266. |
| CA | Yes. | 10. | Yes. | State has no statutory requirements. | Yes. | None. | Cal. Ins. Code §§ 10202, 10209. |
| CO | No. | 3. | No. | 31. | Yes. | None. | Colo. Rev. Stat. §§ 10-7-201, 10-7-202. |
| CT | No. | State has no statutory requirements. | No. | State has no statutory requirements. | No. | None. | State has no statutory provisions. |
| DE | No. | State has no statutory requirements. | Yes. | 31. | Yes. | None. | Del. Code Ann. tit. 18, §§ 3102, 3112, 3113, 3120. |
| DC | Yes. | 10. | Yes. | 31. | Yes. | Insurer may not limit benefits based on fact that death was caused by AIDS, ARC, HIV, or diseases arising out of these conditions. | D.C. Code Ann. §§ 35-223, 35-514, 35-515, 35-516. |
| FL | No. | 2. | Yes. | 31. | Yes. | Insurer may not deny benefits based on fact that death was caused by exposure to HIV infection. | Fla. Stat. Ann. §§ 627.411, 627.552, 627.559, 627.566, 627.567. |
| GA | Yes. | 2. | Yes. | 31. | Yes. | None. | Ga. Code Ann. §§ 33-27-1, 33-27-3, 33-27-5. |
| HI | Yes. | 10. | Yes. | 30. | Yes. | None. | Haw. Rev. Stat. §§ 431:10D-202, 431:10D-213. |

| | | | | | | | |
|---|---|---|---|---|---|---|---|
| ID | Yes. | 5. | Yes. | 31. | Yes. | None. | Idaho Code §§ 41-2003, 41-2011, 41-2018. |
| IL | No. | State has no statutory requirements. | Yes. | 31. | Yes. | None. | Ill. Ann. Stat. ch.215, ¶¶ 5/230.1, 5/231.1. |
| IN | No. | State has no statutory requirements. | Yes. | 31. | Yes. | None. | Ind. Code §§ 27-1-12-37, 27-1-12-41. |
| IA | Yes. | 10. | Yes. | 31. | Yes. | None. | Iowa Code Ann. §§ 509.1, 509.2. |
| KS | Yes. | 3. | Yes. | 31. | Yes. | None. | Kan. Stat. Ann. §§ 40-433, 40-434. |
| KY | Yes, unless amount of insurance does not exceed $2,000 per life of any employee. | 10. | Yes. | 31. | Yes. | Benefits for HIV infection may not be different from those for any other health condition. | Ky. Rev. Stat. Ann. §§ 304.12-013, 304.16-030, 304.16-120, 304.16-190. |
| LA | No. | 1 at date of issue; for some plans, at least 10 new insureds must be added annually. | Yes. | 30. | Yes. | None. | La. Rev. Stat. Ann. §§ 22:175, 22:176. |
| ME | No. | State has no statutory requirements. | Yes. | 31. | Yes. | Insurer may not restrict or exclude coverage for death resulting from AIDS, ARC, or HIV. | Me. Rev. Stat. Ann. tit. 24-A, §§ 2603, 2614, 2621, 2622, 2629. |
| MD | Yes. | 10. | Yes. | 31. | Yes. | None. | Md. Ann. Code art. 48A, §§ 418, 427, 434. |
| MA | Yes. | 10. | Yes. | 31. | Yes. | None. | Mass. Gen. Laws Ann. ch. 175, §§ 133, 134, 134A. |
| MI | Yes. | 10. | Yes. | State has no statutory requirements. | Yes. | None. | Mich. Stat. Ann. §§ 24.12702, 24.14404, 24.14438. |
| MN | No. | State has no statutory requirements. | No. | Parties may agree to allow for a grace period. | Yes. | None. | Minn. Stat. Ann. §§ 61A.09, 61A.091, 61A.092, 61A.10, 62A.04. |
| MS | No. | State has no statutory requirements. | No. | State has no statutory requirements. | No. | None. | — |
| MO | No. | State has no statutory requirements. | Yes. | 31. | Yes. | None. | Mo. Rev. Stat. §§ 376.691, 376.697. |
| MT | Yes. | 10. | Yes. | 31. | Yes. | None. | Mont. Code Ann. §§ 33-20-1101, 33-20-1202, 33-20-1210. |
| NE | Yes. | 5. | Yes. | 31. | Yes. | None. | Neb. Rev. Stat. §§ 44-1602, 44-1607. |
| NV | No. | State has no statutory requirements. | No. | 31. | Yes. | None. | Nev. Rev. Stat. §§ 688B.030, 688B.050, 688B.120. |

*(Table continues.)*

## Table 5.6-1 *(cont'd)*
## GROUP LIFE INSURANCE REQUIREMENTS AND PROVISIONS

(See also text at § 5.6.)

| | *Employer Must Pay Part of the Premium* | *Minimum Number of Employees in Group Plan* | *Employer as Beneficiary Prohibited* | *Grace Period (Days)* | *Mandatory Conversion* | *Other Provisions* | *Citations to Authority* |
|---|---|---|---|---|---|---|---|
| NH | Yes. | 10. | Yes. | 31. | Yes. | None. | N.H. Rev. Stat. Ann. §§ 408:15, 408:16. |
| NJ | Yes. | 10. | Yes. | 31. | Yes. | None. | N.J. Rev. Stat. §§ 17B:27-2, 17B:27-11, 17B:27-19. |
| NM | No. | State has no statutory requirements. | Yes. | 31. | Yes. | None. | N.M. Stat. Ann. §§ 59A-21-4, 59A-21-12, 59A-21-20. |
| NY | No. | State has no statutory requirements. | Yes. | State has no statutory requirements. | No. | None. | N.Y. Ins. Law §§ 4216(b)(1), 4216(d). |
| NC | No. | 10. | Yes. | 31. | Yes. | None. | N.C. Gen. Stat. §§ 58-58-135, 58-58-140. |
| ND | No. | State has no statutory requirements. | No. | 31. | Yes. | None. | N.D. Cent. Code §§ 26.1-33-11, 26.1-33-12. |
| OH | Yes. | 10. | Yes. | 31. | Yes. | Insurer may not limit benefits if insured develops AIDS or tests HIV positive after effective date of policy. | Ohio Rev. Code Ann. §§ 3901.45, 3917.01, 3917.06. |
| OK | No. | 10. | Yes. | 31. | Yes. | None. | Okla. Stat. tit. 36, §§ 4101, 4103. |
| OR | No. | 75% of the eligible members of the group, or 10 employees, whichever is greater. | No. | 31. | Yes. | None. | Or. Rev. Stat. §§ 743.303, 743.312, 743.333. |
| PA | Yes. | 10. | Yes. | 31. | Yes. | None. | Pa. Stat. Ann. tit. 40, §§ 532.1, 532.2, 532.6. |
| RI | No. | State has no statutory requirements. | No. | State has no statutory requirements. | No. | None. | State has no statutory provisions. |
| SC | No. | 2. | No. | 31. | Yes. | None. | S.C. Code Ann. §§ 38-65-40, 38-65-210. |

| | | | | | | | |
|---|---|---|---|---|---|---|---|
| SD | Yes. | State has no statutory requirements. | Yes, unless employer is a nonprofit charitable organization and employee provides notarized statement of voluntariness. | 31. | Yes. | None. | S.D. Codified Laws Ann. §§ 58-16-2, 58-16-6, 58-16-36, 58-16-40. |
| TN | No. | State has no statutory requirements. | State has no statutory requirements. | 31. | Yes. | None. | Tenn. Code Ann. § 56-7-2305. |
| TX | Yes. | 10. | Yes. | 31. | Yes. | None. | Tex. Ins. Code Ann. art. 3.50, §§ 1(1)(b), 1(1)(c), 2(1), 2(8). |
| UT | No. | State has no statutory requirements. | Yes. | 30. | Yes. | None. | Utah Code Ann. §§ 31A-22-502, 31A-22-513, 31A-22-517, 31A-22-518. |
| VT | Yes. | 10. | Yes. | 31. | Yes. | None. | Vt. Stat. Ann. tit. 8, §§ 3803, 3813, 3820. |
| VA | No. | State has no statutory requirements. | Yes. | 31. | Yes. | Insurer may not deny or limit coverage based on death resulting from AIDS. | Va. Code Ann. §§ 38.2-3100.1, 38.2-3325, 38.2-3332; Va. Ins. Reg. 34 (May 1, 1990). |
| WA | Yes. | 10. | Yes. | 31. | Yes. | None. | Wash. Rev. Code §§ 48.24.020, 48.24.110, 48.24.180, 48.24.190. |
| WV | Yes, unless amount of insurance does not exceed $1,000 per life of any employee. | 10. | Yes. | 31. | Yes. | None. | W. Va. Code §§ 33-14-2, 33-14-9, 33-14-16. |
| WI | No. | State has no statutory requirements. | No. | 31. | Yes. | Insurer may not deny or limit benefits solely because death is caused by, or related to, HIV infection. | Wis. Stat. Ann. §§ 631.93, 632.56(5), 632.57. |
| WY | Yes. | State has no statutory requirements. | Yes. | 31. | Yes. | None. | Wyo. Stat. §§ 26-17-103, 26-17-111, 26-17-118, 26-17-119. |

# Table 5.6-2
## GROUP LIFE INSURANCE: ADMINISTRATIVE REQUIREMENTS

(See also text at § 5.6.)

**KEY:** A "—" indicates that the state has no statutory requirement.

| | *Portion of Proceeds Insurer May Pay as Equitable Entitlement* | *May Directors, Sole Proprietors, or Partners Be Covered?* | *Incontestability Provision* | *Does State Require Individual Life Insurance Certificate?* | *Citations to Authority* |
|---|---|---|---|---|---|
| AL | $500. | — | 2 years. | Yes. | Ala. Code §§ 27-18-4, 27-18-9, 27-18-10. |
| AK | $4,000. | — | 2 years. | Yes. | Alaska Stat. §§ 21.48.120, 21.48.160, 21.48.170. |
| AZ | $250. | Individual proprietors and partners may be covered if actively engaged in the business. Directors are not eligible unless otherwise qualified as bona fide employees. | 2 years. | Yes. | Ariz. Rev. Stat. Ann. §§ 20-1252, 20-1260, 20-1264, 20-1265. |
| AR | — | — | — | — | — |
| CA | — | Individual proprietors and partners may be covered if actively engaged in the business. | 2 years. | Yes. | Cal. Ins. Code §§ 10202.5, 10206, 10209. |
| CO | $5,000. | — | 2 years. | Yes. | Colo. Rev. Stat. § 10-7-202. |
| CT | — | — | — | — | — |
| DE | $2,000. | Individual proprietors and partners may be covered. | 2 years. | Yes. | Del. Code Ann. tit. 18, §§ 3102, 3114, 3118, 3119. |
| DC | $250. | Individual proprietors and partners may be covered if actively engaged in the business. Directors are not eligible unless otherwise qualified as bona fide employees. | 2 years. | Yes. | D.C. Code Ann. §§ 35-514, 35-515. |
| FL | $2,000. | Yes. | 2 years. | Yes. | Fla. Stat. Ann. §§ 627.552, 627.560, 627.564, 627.565. |
| GA | $500. | Individual proprietors and partners may be covered if actively engaged in the business. Directors are not eligible unless otherwise qualified as bona fide employees. | 2 years. | Yes. | Ga. Code Ann. §§ 33-27-1, 33-27-3; Op. Att'y. Gen. 1963–65, p. 663. |
| HI | $2,000. | Individual proprietors and partners may be covered if actively engaged in the business. Directors are not eligible unless otherwise qualified as bona fide employees. | 2 years. | Yes. | Haw. Rev. Stat. Ann. §§ 431:10D-202, 431:10D-213. |
| ID | $500. | Individual proprietors and partners may be covered if actively engaged in the business. Directors are not eligible unless otherwise qualified as bona fide employees. | 2 years. | Yes. | Idaho Code §§ 41-2003, 41-2012, 41-2016, 41-2017. |

| | | | | | |
|---|---|---|---|---|---|
| IL | $2,000. | Individual proprietors and partners may be covered. | 2 years. | Yes. | 215 Ill. Comp. Stat. Ann. §§ 5/230.1, 5/231.1. |
| IN | $2,000. | Individual proprietors and partners may be covered. | 2 years. | Yes. | Ind. Stat. Ann. §§ 27-1-12-37, 27-1-12-41. |
| IA | $500. | Yes. | 2 years. | Yes. | Iowa Code Ann. §§ 509.1, 509.2. |
| KS | $250. | Individual proprietors and partners may be covered if actively engaged in the business. Directors are not eligible unless otherwise qualified as bona fide employees. | 2 years. | Yes. | Kan. Stat. Ann. §§ 40-433, 40-434. |
| KY | $500. | Individual proprietors and partners may be covered if actively engaged in the business. Directors are not eligible unless otherwise qualified as bona fide employees. | 2 years. | — | Ky. Rev. Stat. §§ 304.16-030, 304.16-130, 304.16-170, 304.16-180. |
| LA | $250. | Individual proprietors and directors may be covered. Directors may not be covered unless they perform substantial duties for the employer in addition to those duties usually performed as directors. | 2 years. | Yes. | La. Rev. Stat. §§ 22:175, 22:176. |
| ME | $2,000. | Individual proprietors and partners may be covered. | 2 years. | Yes. | Me. Rev. Stat. Ann. tit. 24-A, §§ 2603, 2615, 2619, 2620. |
| MD | $2,500. | Individual proprietors and partners may be covered if actively engaged in the business. Directors are not eligible unless otherwise qualified as bona fide employees. | 2 years. | Yes. | Md. Ann. Code art. 48A, §§ 418, 428, 432, 433. |
| MA | $250. | Individual proprietors and partners may be covered if actively engaged in and devoting a substantial part of their time to the business. | 2 years. | Yes. | Mass. Gen. Laws Ann. ch. 175, § 134. |
| MI | — | — | 2 years. | Yes. | Mich. Stat. Ann. §§ 24.14432, 24.14438. |
| MN | — | — | 2 years. | — | Minn. Stat. Ann. § 61A.03. |
| MS | — | — | — | — | — |
| MO | $2,000. | Individual proprietors and partners may be covered. | 2 years. | Yes. | Mo. Ann. Stat. §§ 376.691, 376.697. |
| MT | $500. | Individual proprietors and partners may be covered if actively engaged in the business. Directors are not eligible unless otherwise qualified as bona fide employees. | 2 years. | Yes. | Mont. Code Ann. § 33-20-1101, 33-20-1203, 33-20-1207, 33-20-1208. |
| NE | $2,000. | Individual proprietors and partners may be covered if actively engaged in the business. Directors are not eligible unless otherwise qualified as bona fide employees. | 2 years. | Yes. | Neb. Rev. Stat. Ann. §§ 44-1602, 44-1607. |
| NV | $500. | Individual proprietors and partners may be covered. | 2 years. | Yes. | Nev. Rev. Stat. Ann. §§ 688B.020, 688B.060, 688B.100, 688B.110. |
| NH | $250. | Individual proprietors and partners may be covered. | 2 years. | Yes. | N.H. Rev. Stat. Ann. §§ 408:15, 408:16. |
| NJ | $500. | Individual proprietors and partners may be covered if actively engaged in the business. Directors are not eligible unless otherwise qualified as bona fide employees. | 2 years. | Yes. | N.J. Stat. Ann. §§ 17B:27-2, 17B:27-12, 17B:27-17, 17B:27-18. |

*(Table continues.)*

# Table 5.6-2 *(cont'd)*
## GROUP LIFE INSURANCE: ADMINISTRATIVE REQUIREMENTS

(See also text at § 5.6.)

**KEY:** A "—" indicates that the state has no statutory requirement.

| | *Portion of Proceeds Insurer May Pay as Equitable Entitlement* | *May Directors, Sole Proprietors, or Partners Be Covered?* | *Incontestability Provision* | *Does State Require Individual Life Insurance Certificate?* | *Citations to Authority* |
|---|---|---|---|---|---|
| NM | $2,000. | Yes. | 2 years. | Yes. | N.M. Stat. Ann. §§ 59A-21-4, 59A-21-13, 59A-21-17, 59A-21-18. |
| NY | $500. | Yes. | 2 years. | Yes. | N.Y. Ins. Law §§ 3220, 4216. |
| NC | — | Individual proprietors and partners may be covered. | 2 years. | Yes. | N.C. Gen. Stat. §§ 58-58-135, 58-58-140. |
| ND | $5,000. | — | 2 years. | Yes. | N.D. Cent. Code Ann. § 26.1-33-11. |
| OH | — | Individual proprietors and partners may be covered. | 2 years. | Yes. | Ohio Rev. Code Ann. §§ 3917.01, 3917.06. |
| OK | $500. | Individual proprietors and partners may be covered if actively engaged in the business. Directors are not eligible unless otherwise qualified as bona fide employees. | 2 years. | Yes. | Okla. Stat. Ann. tit. 36, §§ 4101, 4103. |
| OR | $500. | — | 2 years. | Yes. | Or. Rev. Stat. Ann. §§ 743.315, 743.327, 743.330. |
| PA | $250. | Individual proprietors and partners may be covered. | 2 years. | Yes. | Pa. Stat. Ann. tit. 40, §§ 532.1, 532.2, 532.6. |
| RI | — | — | — | — | — |
| SC | $2,000. | — | 2 years. | Yes. | S.C. Code § 38-65-210. |
| SD | — | Individual proprietors and partners may be covered if actively engaged in the business. Directors are not eligible unless otherwise qualified as bona fide employees. | 2 years. | Yes. | S.D. Codified Laws §§ 58-16-3, 58-16-35, 58-16-38. |
| TN | $500. | — | 2 years. | — | Tenn. Code Ann. § 56-7-2305. |
| TX | $250. | Individual proprietors and partners may be covered. | 2 years. | Yes. | Tex. Ins. Code Ann. art. 3.50, §§ 1, 2. |
| UT | $5,000. | Individual proprietors and partners may be covered. | 2 years. | — | Utah Code §§ 31A-22-502, 31A-22-514, 31A-22-516. |

| | | | | | |
|---|---|---|---|---|---|
| VT | $500. | Individual proprietors and partners may be covered if actively engaged in the business. Directors are not eligible unless otherwise qualified as bona fide employees. | 2 years. | Yes. | Vt. Stat. Ann. tit. 8, §§ 3803, 3814, 3818, 3819. |
| VA | $2,000. | Yes. Retired and former employees may also be covered. | 2 years. | Yes. | Va. Code Ann. §§ 38.2-3318.1, 38.2-3326, 38.2-3330, 38.2-3331. |
| WA | Greater of 10 percent or $1,000. | Individual proprietors and partners may be covered. | 2 years. | Yes. | Wash. Rev. Code Ann. §§ 48.24.020, 48.24.120, 48.24.160, 48.24.170. |
| WV | $500. | Individual proprietors and partners may be covered if actively engaged in the business. Directors are not eligible unless otherwise qualified as bona fide employees. | 2 years. | Yes. | W. Va. Code §§ 33-14-2, 33-14-10, 33-14-14, 33-14-15. |
| WI | $1,000. | — | — | — | Wis. Stat. Ann. § 632.56. |
| WY | $2,000. | Yes. | 2 years. | Yes. | Wyo. Stat. §§ 26-17-103, 26-17-112, 26-17-116, 26-17-117. |

# Table 5.6-3
## GROUP LIFE INSURANCE: COVERAGE REQUIREMENTS

(See also text at § 5.6.)

**KEY:** A "—" indicates that the state has no statutory requirements.

| | *Minimum Coverage When Employees Contribute Part of Premium* | *Must Spouses/ Dependents of All Eligible Employees Be Eligible for Coverage?* | *Limitation on Dependent Coverage* | *Minimum Coverage When Employer Pays All of Premium* | *Citations to Authority* |
|---|---|---|---|---|---|
| AL | — | — | — | — | — |
| AK | — | — | — | — | — |
| AZ | 75%. | — | 50% of insurance on employee, not to exceed $25,000 for a spouse or $5,000 for a child. | 100%. | Ariz. Rev. Stat. Ann. §§ 20-1252, 20-1257. |
| AR | — | — | — | — | — |
| CA | 75%. | — | 50% of amount for which employee is insured. | — | Cal. Ins. Code Ann. §§ 10202, 10203.4. |
| CO | — | — | — | — | — |
| CT | — | — | — | — | — |
| DE | — | Yes, if 100% of premium is paid by the employer. | Policyholder may request that dependent coverage be limited to a percentage of employee coverage. | 100%. | Del. Code Ann. tit. 18, §§ 3102, 3111. |
| DC | 75%. | — | — | 100%. | D.C. Code Ann. §§ 35-514. |
| FL | — | Yes, if 100% of premium is paid by the employer. | 50% of insurance on life of employee. | 100%. | Fla. Stat. Ann. §§ 627.552, 627.5575. |
| GA | — | Yes, if 100% of premium is paid by the employer. | — | 100%. | Ga. Code Ann. §§ 33-27-1, 33-27-2. |
| HI | 75%. | — | For a spouse, an amount equal to the amount for which the employee is insured. For a child, an amount that is the lesser of $5,000 or 50% of the employee's coverage, but for a child under 6 months of age at death, amount not in excess of $2,000. | 100%, except those who reject coverage in writing. | Haw. Rev. Stat. Ann. §§ 431:10D-202, 431:10D-212. |
| ID | 75%. | Yes, if 100% of premium is paid by employer. | — | 100%. | Idaho Code §§ 41-2003, 41-2009. |

| | | | | | |
|---|---|---|---|---|---|
| IL | — | Yes, if 100% of premium is paid by the employer. | 100% of amount for which employee is insured. | 100%. | 215 Ill. Comp. Stat. Ann. §§ 5/230.1, 5/230.3. |
| IN | — | Yes, if 100% of premium is paid by the employer. | 50% of amount for which employee is insured. | 100%, except those who reject coverage in writing. | Ind. Stat. Ann. §§ 27-1-12-37, 27-1-12-40. |
| IA | 75%. | — | — | 100%. | Iowa Code Ann. § 509.1. |
| KS | 75%. | Yes, if 100% of premium is paid by the employer. | 50% of amount for which employee is insured. | 100%. | Kan. Stat. Ann. § 40-433. |
| KY | 75%. | — | 50% of amount for which employee is insured. | 100%. | Ky. Rev. Stat. §§ 304.16-030, 304.16-085. |
| LA | 75%. | If 75% of insured employees elect to do so, insurance may be extended to all eligible spouses/ dependents. | 50% of amount for which employee is insured. | 100%. | La. Rev. Stat. § 22:175. |
| ME | — | Yes, if 100% of premium is paid by the employer. | — | — | Me. Rev. Stat. Ann. tit. 24-A, § 2611-A. |
| MD | 75%. | If 75% of insured employees elect, insurance may be extended to all eligible spouses/dependents. | 50% of amount for which employee is insured. | 100%. | Md. Ann. Code art. 48A, §§ 418, 422A. |
| MA | 75%, or 40% if each employee has been medically examined and found acceptable for ordinary insurance by an individual policy. | — | — | — | Mass. Gen. Laws Ann. ch. 175, § 133. |
| MI | 75%. | — | — | — | Mich. Stat. Ann. §§ 24.14404, 24.14426. |
| MN | — | — | — | — | — |
| MS | — | — | — | — | — |
| MO | — | Yes, if 100% of premium is paid by the employer. | — | 100%, except those who reject coverage in writing. | Mo. Ann. Stat. §§ 376.691, 376.695. |
| MT | 75%. | Yes, if 100% of premium is paid by the employer. | — | 100%. | Mont. Code Ann. §§ 33-20-1101, 33-20-1111. |
| NE | 75%. | — | — | 100%. | Neb. Rev. Stat. Ann. § 44-1602. |
| NV | — | — | — | — | — |
| NH | 75%. | — | — | 100%. | N.H. Rev. Stat. Ann. § 408:15. |
| NJ | 75%. | Yes, if 100% of premium is paid by the employer. | 50% of amount for which employee is insured or $5,000, whichever is less. Amount for child whose age at death is less than 6 months shall not exceed $100. | 100%. | N.J. Stat. Ann. §§ 17B:27-2, 17B:27-9. |

*(Table continues.)*

# Table 5.6-3 *(cont'd)*
## GROUP LIFE INSURANCE: COVERAGE REQUIREMENTS

(See also text at § 5.6.)

**KEY:** A "—" indicates that the state has no statutory requirements.

| | *Minimum Coverage When Employees Contribute Part of Premium* | *Must Spouses/ Dependents of All Eligible Employees Be Eligible for Coverage?* | *Limitation on Dependent Coverage* | *Minimum Coverage When Employer Pays All of Premium* | *Citations to Authority* |
|---|---|---|---|---|---|
| NM | — | — | — | 100%, except those who reject coverage in writing. | N.M. Stat. Ann. § 59A-21-4. |
| NY | Lesser of 50% or 50 employees. | — | For spouse, amount for which employee is insured; for dependent, $4,000. | — | N.Y. Ins. Law § 4216. |
| NC | — | — | — | 100%. | N.C. Gen. Stat. § 58-58-135. |
| ND | — | — | — | — | — |
| OH | 75%. | — | Lesser of $10,000 or 50% of amount for which employee is insured. | 100%. | Ohio Rev. Code Ann. § 3917.01. |
| OK | 75%. | — | 50% of amount for which employee is insured. | 100%. | Okla. Stat. Ann. tit. 36, §§ 4101, 4101.1. |
| OR | — | — | — | — | — |
| PA | — | — | — | 100%. | Pa. Stat. Ann. tit. 40, §§ 532.1, 532.2. |
| RI | — | — | — | — | — |
| SC | — | — | — | — | — |
| SD | 75%. | Yes, if 100% of premium is paid by the employer. | — | 100%. | S.D. Codified Laws §§ 58-16-6, 58-16-19. |
| TN | — | — | — | — | — |
| TX | 75%. | — | 50% of amount for which employee is insured. | 100%. | Tex. Ins. Code Ann. art. 3.50, §§ 1; art. 3.51-4A, § 1. |
| UT | — | Yes, if 100% of premium is paid by the employer. | — | 100%. | Utah Code §§ 31A-22-502, 31A-22-511. |
| VT | 75%. | Yes, if 100% of premium is paid by the employer. | Amount equal to amount for which employee is insured. | 100%. | Vt. Stat. Ann. tit. 8, §§ 3803, 3811. |

| | | | | | |
|---|---|---|---|---|---|
| VA | — | — | Amount equal to that for which employee is insured. | 100%. | Va. Code Ann. §§ 38.2-3818.1, 38.2-3323. |
| WA | 75%. | — | 50% of amount for which employee is insured. | 100%. | Wash. Rev. Code Ann. §§ 48.24.020, 48.24.030. |
| WV | 75%. | Yes, if 100% of premium is paid by the employer. | — | 100%. | W. Va. Code §§ 33-14-2, 33-14-7. |
| WI | — | — | — | — | — |
| WY | — | — | 50% of amount for which employee is insured. | — | Wyo. Stat. § 26-17-108. |

# Table 5.6-4
## GROUP LIFE INSURANCE: STATE CONTINUATION AND CONVERSION REQUIREMENTS

(See also text at § 5.6.)

**KEY:** A "—" indicates that the state has no statutory requirements.

| | *Continuation Requirements* | | | *Conversion Requirements* | | | | |
|---|---|---|---|---|---|---|---|---|
| | *Under What Circumstances May Employee Choose Continuation Coverage?* | *Maximum Length of Continuation Period* | *Disqualifying Events* | *Under What Circumstances May Employee or Dependent Choose Conversion Coverage?* | *When Must Employee or Dependent Elect Coverage?* | *What Amount of Coverage May Employee or Dependent Elect?* | *Other Conversion Rights* | *Citations to Authority* |
| AL | — | — | — | Termination of employment or membership in the class eligible for coverage. | Within 31 days from termination of coverage. | Amount of coverage that ceases due to termination of coverage minus any amount of life insurance the person becomes eligible for under a group policy within 31 days of the termination of coverage. | If group policy terminates, a person who has been insured for at least 5 years is entitled to a converted policy. An insured must be given notice of the right to a converted policy at least 15 days prior to the expiration of the period in which conversion coverage may be elected. | Ala. Code §§ 27-18-11, 27-18-12, 27-18-14. |
| AK | — | — | — | Termination of employment or termination of membership in the eligible class. | Within 31 days of termination of coverage. | Amount of coverage that ceases due to termination of coverage minus any amount of life insurance the person becomes eligible for under a group policy within 31 days of the termination of coverage. | If group policy terminates, a person who has been insured for at least 5 years is entitled to a converted policy. An insured must be given notice of the right to a converted policy at least 15 days prior to the expiration of the period in which conversion coverage may be elected. | Alaska Stat. §§ 21.48.180, 21.48.190, 21.48.210. |

| | | | | | | | | |
|---|---|---|---|---|---|---|---|---|
| AZ | — | — | — | Termination of employment or membership in the class eligible for coverage. | Within 31 days from termination of coverage. | Amount of coverage that ceases due to termination of coverage minus any amount of life insurance the person becomes eligible for under a group policy within 31 days of the termination of coverage. | If group policy terminates, a person who has been insured for at least 5 years is entitled to a converted policy. An insured must be given notice of the right to a converted policy at least 15 days prior to the expiration of the period in which conversion coverage may be elected. | Ariz. Rev. Stat. Ann. §§ 20-1266, 20-1267, 20-1269. |
| AR | — | — | — | — | — | — | — | — |
| CA | — | — | — | If employment terminates for any reason. | Within 31 days from termination of employment. | Amount for which employee was insured at the time of termination of employment. | Employee must be given notice of the right to a converted policy at least 15 days prior to the expiration of the period in which conversion coverage may be elected. | Cal. Ins. Code § 10209. |
| CO | — | — | — | Termination of employment or membership in the class eligible for coverage. | Within 31 days from termination of coverage. | Amount of coverage that ceases due to termination of coverage. | If group policy terminates, a person who has been insured for at least 5 years is entitled to a converted policy. An insured must be given notice of the right to a converted policy at least 15 days prior to the expiration of the period in which conversion coverage may be elected. | Colo. Rev. Stat. § 10-7-202. |
| CT | — | — | — | — | — | — | — | — |
| DE | If employee suffers total disability. | At least 6 months. | — | Termination of employment or membership in the class eligible for coverage. Conversion is also available to a dependent at the death of the employee or a dependent who ceases to be a qualified family member. | Within 31 days from termination of coverage. | Amount of coverage that ceases due to termination of coverage minus any amount of life insurance the person becomes eligible for under a group policy within 31 days of the termination of coverage. | If group policy terminates, a person who has been insured for at least 5 years is entitled to a converted policy. An insured must be given notice of the right to a converted policy at least 15 days prior to the expiration of the period in which conversion coverage may be elected. | Del. Code Ann. tit. 18, §§ 3120, 3121, 3123, 3125. |

*(Table continues.)*

# **Table 5.6-4** *(cont'd)*

## GROUP LIFE INSURANCE: STATE CONTINUATION AND CONVERSION REQUIREMENTS

(See also text at § 5.6.)

**KEY:** A "—" indicates that the state has no statutory requirements.

| | *Continuation Requirements* | | | *Conversion Requirements* | | | | |
|---|---|---|---|---|---|---|---|---|
| | *Under What Circumstances May Employee Choose Continuation Coverage?* | *Maximum Length of Continuation Period* | *Disqualifying Events* | *Under What Circumstances May Employee or Dependent Choose Conversion Coverage?* | *When Must Employee or Dependent Elect Coverage?* | *What Amount of Coverage May Employee or Dependent Elect?* | *Other Conversion Rights* | *Citations to Authority* |
| DC | — | — | — | Termination of employment or membership in the class eligible for coverage. | Within 31 days from termination of coverage. | Amount of coverage that ceases due to termination of coverage. | If group policy terminates, a person who has been insured for at least 5 years is entitled to a converted policy. An insured must be given notice of the right to a converted policy at least 15 days prior to the expiration of the period in which conversion coverage may be elected. | D.C. Code Ann. §§ 35-515, 35-516. |
| FL | If employee suffers total disability. | At least 6 months. | — | Termination of employment or of the employee's membership in the class, death of the employee, a dependent's ceasing to be a qualified family member. | Within 31 days from termination of coverage. | Amount of coverage that ceases due to termination of coverage minus any amount of life insurance the person becomes eligible for under a group policy within 31 days of the termination of the coverage. | If group policy terminates, a person who has been insured for at least 5 years is entitled to a converted policy. | Fla. Stat. Ann. §§ 627.566, 627.567, 627.5685. |

| | | | | | | | | |
|---|---|---|---|---|---|---|---|---|
| GA | — | — | — | Spouse may elect conversion coverage following employee's death, termination of employment, or termination in the eligible class. Employee may elect conversion coverage following termination of employment or termination in the eligible class. | Within 31 days from termination of coverage. | Amount of coverage that ceases due to termination of coverage minus any amount of life insurance the person becomes eligible for under a group policy within 31 days of the termination of coverage. | Spouse and/or employee insured for at least 5 years have conversion rights if group policy is terminated. | Ga. Code Ann. §§ 33-27-2, 33-27-3. |
| HI | — | — | — | Termination of employment or membership in the class eligible for coverage. | Within 30 days of the termination. | Amount that ceases due to the termination, but not less than $1,000 unless a smaller amount of coverage was provided, minus any amount of life insurance the person becomes eligible for under a group policy within 30 days of the termination of coverage. | If group policy terminates, a person who has been insured for at least 5 years is entitled to a converted policy. An insured must be given notice of the right to a converted policy at least 15 days prior to the expiration of the period in which conversion coverage may be elected. | Haw. Rev. Stat. Ann. §§ 431:10D-213, 431:10D-214. |
| ID | — | — | — | Termination of employment or membership in the class eligible for coverage; death of employee. | Within 31 days from termination of coverage. | Amount of coverage that ceases due to termination of coverage minus any amount of life insurance the person becomes eligible for under a group policy within 31 days of the termination of coverage. | If group policy terminates, a person who has been insured for at least 5 years is entitled to a converted policy. An insured must be given notice of the right to a converted policy at least 15 days prior to the expiration of the period in which conversion coverage may be elected. | Idaho Code §§ 41-2009, 41-2018, 41-2019, 41-2021. |
| IL | — | — | — | Termination of employment or of membership in the class, death of employee, or dependent's ceasing to be a qualified family member. | Within 31 days from termination of coverage. | Amount of coverage that ceases due to termination of coverage minus any amount of life insurance the person becomes eligible for under a group policy within 31 days of the termination of coverage. | If group policy terminates, a person who has been insured for at least 5 years is entitled to a converted policy. An insured must be given notice of the right to a converted policy at least 15 days prior to the expiration of the period in which conversion coverage may be elected. | 215 Ill. Comp. Stat. Ann. § 5/231.1. |

*(Table continues.)*

## **Table 5.6-4** *(cont'd)*
## GROUP LIFE INSURANCE: STATE CONTINUATION AND CONVERSION REQUIREMENTS

(See also text at § 5.6.)

**KEY:** A "—" indicates that the state has no statutory requirements.

| | *Continuation Requirements* | | | *Conversion Requirements* | | | | |
|---|---|---|---|---|---|---|---|---|
| | *Under What Circumstances May Employee Choose Continuation Coverage?* | *Maximum Length of Continuation Period* | *Disqualifying Events* | *Under What Circumstances May Employee or Dependent Choose Conversion Coverage?* | *When Must Employee or Dependent Elect Coverage?* | *What Amount of Coverage May Employee or Dependent Elect?* | *Other Conversion Rights* | *Citations to Authority* |
| IN | Total disability. | 6 months. | Discontinuance of group policy; coverage under disability provision of the group insurance. | Termination of employment or membership in the class eligible for coverage; death of employee, dependent's ceasing to be a qualified family member. | Within 31 days from termination of coverage. | Amount of coverage that ceases due to termination of coverage minus any amount of life insurance the person becomes eligible for under a group policy within 31 days of the termination of coverage. | If group policy terminates, a person who has been insured for at least 5 years is entitled to a converted policy. An insured must be given notice of the right to a converted policy at least 15 days prior to the expiration of the period in which conversion coverage may be elected. | Ind. Stat. Ann. §§ 27-1-12-41, 27-1-12-42. |
| IA | — | — | — | Termination of employment or membership in the class eligible for coverage. | Within 31 days from termination of coverage. | Amount not in excess of coverage that ceased due to termination. | If group policy terminates, person who has been insured for at least 5 years is entitled to a converted policy. | Iowa Code Ann. § 509.2. |
| KS | — | — | — | Termination of employment or membership in the class eligible for coverage; death of employee. | Within 31 days from termination of coverage. | Amount of coverage that ceases due to termination of coverage minus any amount of life insurance the person becomes eligible for under a group policy within 31 days of the termination of coverage. | If group policy terminates, a person who has been insured for at least 5 years is entitled to a converted policy. An insured must be given notice of the right to a converted policy at least 15 days prior to the expiration of the period in which conversion coverage may be elected. | Kan. Stat. Ann. §§ 40-434, 40-435. |

| | | | | | | | | |
|---|---|---|---|---|---|---|---|---|
| KY | — | — | — | Termination of employment or membership in the class eligible for coverage. | Within 31 days from termination of coverage. | Amount of coverage that ceases due to termination of coverage minus any amount of life insurance the person becomes eligible for under a group policy within 31 days of the termination of coverage. | If group policy terminates, person who has been insured for at least 5 years is entitled to a converted policy. | Ky. Rev. Stat. §§ 304.16-190, 304.16-200. |
| LA | — | — | — | Termination of employment or membership in the class eligible for coverage. | Within 31 days from termination of coverage. | Amount not in excess of amount that ceases due to termination nor less than $1,000, unless a smaller amount of coverage was provided under the policy. | If group policy terminates, a person who has been insured for at least 5 years is entitled to a converted policy. | La. Rev. Stat. § 22:176. |
| ME | Total disability. | 6 months. | Discontinuance of group policy, continuation coverage under disability provision of group policy. | Termination of employment or membership in the class eligible for coverage; death of employee; dependent's ceasing to be a qualified family member. | Within 31 days from termination of coverage. | Amount of coverage that ceases due to termination of coverage minus any amount of life insurance the person becomes eligible for under a group policy within 31 days of the termination of coverage. | If group policy terminates, a person who has been insured for at least 5 years is entitled to a converted policy. An insured must be given notice of the right to a converted policy at least 15 days prior to the expiration of the period in which conversion coverage may be elected. | Me. Rev. Stat. Ann. tit. 24-A, §§ 2621, 2622, 2625, 2628. |
| MD | — | — | — | Termination of employment or membership in the class eligible for coverage. | Within 31 days from termination of coverage. | Amount of coverage that ceases due to termination of coverage minus any amount of life insurance the person becomes eligible for under a group policy within 31 days of the termination of coverage. | If group policy terminates, a person who has been insured for at least 5 years is entitled to a converted policy. | Md. Ann. Code art. 48A, §§ 434, 435. |
| MA | — | — | — | Termination of employment or membership in the class eligible for coverage. | Within 31 days from termination of coverage. | Amount of coverage that ceases due to termination of coverage minus any amount of life insurance the person becomes eligible for under a group policy within 31 days (cont'd) | If group policy terminates, a person who has been insured for at least 5 years is entitled to a converted policy. An insured must be given notice of the right to a converted policy at least 15 days prior to (cont'd) | Mass. Gen. Laws Ann. ch. 175, §§ 134, 134A. |

*(Table continues.)*

# Table 5.6-4 *(cont'd)*

## GROUP LIFE INSURANCE: STATE CONTINUATION AND CONVERSION REQUIREMENTS

(See also text at § 5.6.)

**KEY:** A "—" indicates that the state has no statutory requirements.

| | *Continuation Requirements* | | | *Conversion Requirements* | | | | |
|---|---|---|---|---|---|---|---|---|
| | *Under What Circumstances May Employee Choose Continuation Coverage?* | *Maximum Length of Continuation Period* | *Disqualifying Events* | *Under What Circumstances May Employee or Dependent Choose Conversion Coverage?* | *When Must Employee or Dependent Elect Coverage?* | *What Amount of Coverage May Employee or Dependent Elect?* | *Other Conversion Rights* | *Citations to Authority* |
| MA *(cont'd)* | | | | | | of the termination of coverage, but not less than $2,000. | the expiration of the period in which conversion coverage may be elected. | |
| MI | — | — | — | Termination of employment. | Within 31 days from termination of coverage. | Amount equal to amount at time of termination. | — | Mich. Stat. Ann. § 24.14438. |
| MN | Voluntary or involuntary termination, layoff (but not termination for gross misconduct). | 18 months or until employee obtains coverage under another group policy, whichever is shorter. | — | Termination of employment or membership in the class eligible for coverage; expiration of continuation period. | Within 31 days from termination of coverage. | Amount equal to coverage ceasing due to termination. | — | Minn. Stat. Ann. §§ 61A.09, 61A.092. |
| MS | — | — | — | — | — | — | — | — |
| MO | Total disability. | 6 months. | Discontinuance of group policy, coverage under disability provision of group policy. | Termination of employment or membership in the class eligible for coverage; death of employee, dependent's ceasing to be a qualified family member. | Within 31 days from termination of coverage. | Amount of coverage that ceases due to termination of coverage minus any amount of life insurance the person becomes eligible for under a group policy within 31 days of the termination of coverage. | If group policy terminates, a person who has been insured for at least 5 years is entitled to a converted policy. An insured must be given notice of the right to a converted policy at least 15 days prior to the expiration of the period in which conversion coverage may be elected. | Mo. Ann. Stat. §§ 376.697, 376.699. |

| | | | | | | | | |
|---|---|---|---|---|---|---|---|---|
| MT | — | — | — | Termination of employment or membership in the class eligible for coverage; death of employee. | Within 31 days from termination of coverage. | Amount of coverage that ceases due to termination of coverage minus any amount of life insurance the person becomes eligible for under a group policy within 31 days of the termination of coverage. | If group policy terminates, a person who has been insured for at least 3 years is entitled to a converted policy. An insured must be given notice of the right to a converted policy at least 15 days prior to the expiration of the period in which conversion coverage may be elected. | Mont. Code Ann. §§ 33-20-1111, 33-20-1209, 33-20-1210, 33-20-1212. |
| NE | — | — | — | Termination of employment or membership in the class eligible for coverage; death of employee. | Within 31 days from termination of coverage. | Amount not in excess of coverage ceasing due to the termination. | If group policy terminates, a person who has been insured for at least 5 years is entitled to a converted policy. An insured must be given notice of the right to a converted policy at least 15 days prior to the expiration of the period in which conversion coverage may be elected. | Neb. Rev. Stat. Ann. §§ 44-1607, 44-1613, 44-1614. |
| NV | — | — | — | Termination of employment or membership in the class eligible for coverage. | Within 31 days from termination of coverage. | Amount of coverage that ceases due to termination of coverage minus any amount of life insurance the person becomes eligible for under a group policy within 31 days of the termination of coverage. | If group policy terminates, a person who has been insured for at least 5 years is entitled to a converted policy. An insured must be given notice of the right to a converted policy at least 15 days prior to the expiration of the period in which conversion coverage may be elected. | Nev. Rev. Stat. Ann. §§ 688B.120, 688B.130, 688B.160. |
| NH | Strike, lockout, or other labor dispute. | 6 months. | Full-time employment with another employer. | Termination of employment or membership in the class eligible for coverage. | Within 31 days from termination of coverage. | Amount not in excess of coverage ceasing due to termination. | — | N.H. Rev. Stat. Ann. §§ 408:16, 408:16-b. |
| NJ | — | — | — | Termination of employment or membership in the class eligible for coverage. | Within 31 days from termination of coverage. | Amount of coverage that ceases due to termination of coverage minus any amount of life insurance the person becomes eligible for under a group policy within *(cont'd)* | If group policy terminates, a person who has been insured for at least 5 years is entitled to a converted policy. An insured must be given notice of the right to a converted policy at least 15 days prior to *(cont'd)* | N.J. Stat. Ann. §§ 17B:27-19, 17B:27-20, 17B:27-24. |

*(Table continues.)*

## Table 5.6-4 *(cont'd)*

## GROUP LIFE INSURANCE: STATE CONTINUATION AND CONVERSION REQUIREMENTS

(See also text at § 5.6.)

**KEY:** A "—" indicates that the state has no statutory requirements.

| | *Continuation Requirements* | | | *Conversion Requirements* | | | | |
|---|---|---|---|---|---|---|---|---|
| | *Under What Circumstances May Employee Choose Continuation Coverage?* | *Maximum Length of Continuation Period* | *Disqualifying Events* | *Under What Circumstances May Employee or Dependent Choose Conversion Coverage?* | *When Must Employee or Dependent Elect Coverage?* | *What Amount of Coverage May Employee or Dependent Elect?* | *Other Conversion Rights* | *Citations to Authority* |
| NJ *(cont'd)* | | | | | | 31 days of the termination of coverage. | the expiration of the period in which conversion coverage may be elected. | |
| NM | Total disability. | 6 months. | Continuation coverage under disability provision of group policy, discontinuance of group policy. | Termination of employment or membership in the class eligible for coverage; death of employee. | Within 31 days from termination of coverage. | Amount of coverage that ceases due to termination of coverage minus any amount of life insurance the person becomes eligible for under a group policy within 31 days of the termination of coverage. | If group policy terminates, a person who has been insured for at least 5 years is entitled to a converted policy. An insured must be given notice of the right to a converted policy at least 15 days prior to the expiration of the period in which conversion coverage may be elected. | N.M. Stat. Ann. §§ 59A-21-19, 59A-21-20, 59A-21-22, 59A-21-23. |
| NY | — | — | — | Termination of employment or membership in the class eligible for coverage; employee's attainment of age 60 resulting in reduction of 20 percent or more of the coverage, death of employee, attainment of limiting age, divorce, annulment. If em- | Within 31 days from termination of coverage. | Amount of coverage that ceases due to termination of coverage minus any amount of life insurance the person becomes eligible for under a group policy within 31 days of the termination of coverage. | If group policy terminates, a person who has been insured for at least 5 years is entitled to a converted policy. An insured must be given notice of the right to a converted policy at least 15 days prior to the expiration of the period in which conversion coverage may be elected. | N.Y. Ins. Law §§ 3220, 4216. |

| | | | | | | | | |
|---|---|---|---|---|---|---|---|---|
| | | | | ployment is terminated due to disability, employee may receive a one-year conversion policy. | | | | |
| NC | — | — | — | Termination of employment or membership in the class eligible for coverage. | Within 31 days from termination of coverage. | Not in excess of amount that ceases due to the termination. | If group policy terminates, a person who has been insured for at least 5 years is entitled to a converted policy. | N.C. Gen. Stat. § 58-58-140. |
| ND | Total disability. | 6 months. | Discontinuance of group policy, continuation coverage under disability provision of group policy. | Termination of employment or membership in the class eligible for coverage; death of employee. | Within 31 days from termination of coverage. | Amount of coverage that ceases due to termination of coverage minus any amount of life insurance the person becomes eligible for under a group policy within 31 days of the termination of coverage. | If group policy terminates, a person who has been insured for at least 5 years is entitled to a converted policy. An insured must be given notice of the right to a converted policy at least 15 days prior to the expiration of the period in which conversion coverage may be elected. | N.D. Cent. Code Ann. §§ 26.1-33-11, 26.1-33-12. |
| OH | — | — | — | Termination of employment or membership in the class eligible for coverage; death of employee. | Within 31 days from termination of coverage. | Not in excess of amount of coverage at time of termination. | If group policy terminates, a person who has been insured for at least 5 years is entitled to a converted policy. | Ohio Rev. Code Ann. §§ 3917.01, 3917.06. |
| OK | — | — | — | Termination of employment or membership in the class eligible for coverage. | Within 31 days from termination of coverage. | Amount of coverage that ceases due to termination of coverage minus any amount of life insurance the person becomes eligible for under a group policy within 31 days of the termination of coverage. | If group policy terminates, person who has been insured for at least 5 years is entitled to a converted policy. | Okla. Stat. Ann. tit. 36, § 4103. |
| OR | — | — | — | Termination of employment or membership in the class eligible for coverage. | Within 31 days from termination of coverage. | Amount of coverage that ceases due to termination of coverage minus any amount of life insurance the person becomes eligible for under a group policy within 31 days of the termination of coverage. | If group policy terminates, a person who has been insured for at least 5 years is entitled to a converted policy. | Or. Rev. Stat. Ann. §§ 743.333, 743.336. |

*(Table continues.)*

**Table 5.6-4** *(cont'd)*

GROUP LIFE INSURANCE: STATE CONTINUATION AND CONVERSION REQUIREMENTS

(See also text at § 5.6.)

**KEY:** A "—" indicates that the state has no statutory requirements.

| | *Continuation Requirements* | | | *Conversion Requirements* | | | | |
|---|---|---|---|---|---|---|---|---|
| | *Under What Circumstances May Employee Choose Continuation Coverage?* | *Maximum Length of Continuation Period* | *Disqualifying Events* | *Under What Circumstances May Employee or Dependent Choose Conversion Coverage?* | *When Must Employee or Dependent Elect Coverage?* | *What Amount of Coverage May Employee or Dependent Elect?* | *Other Conversion Rights* | *Citations to Authority* |
| PA | — | — | — | Termination of employment or membership in the class eligible for coverage. | Within 31 days from termination of coverage. | Amount of coverage that ceases due to termination of coverage minus any amount of life insurance the person becomes eligible for under a group policy within 31 days of the termination of coverage. | If group policy terminates, a person who has been insured for at least 5 years is entitled to a converted policy. An insured must be given notice of the right to a converted policy at least 15 days prior to the expiration of the period in which conversion coverage may be elected. | Pa. Stat. Ann. tit. 40, §§ 532.6, 532.7. |
| RI | Labor dispute or involuntary layoff. Greater of 100 or 51% of eligible employees must elect continuation coverage. | Length of cessation of work. | Full-time employment with another employer. | — | — | — | — | R.I. Gen. Laws § 27-4-22.1. |
| SC | Total disability. | 6 months. | Discontinuance of group policy; coverage under disability provision of group policy. | Termination of employment or membership in the class eligible for coverage; death of employee. | Within 31 days from termination of coverage. | Amount of coverage that ceases due to termination of coverage minus any amount of life insurance the person becomes eligible for under a group policy within 31 days of the termination of coverage. | If group policy terminates, a person who has been insured for at least 5 years is entitled to a converted policy. An insured must be given notice of the right to a converted policy at least 15 days prior to the expiration of the period in which conver- | S.C. Code §§ 38-65-70, 38-65-110, 38-65-210. |

| | | | | | | | | |
|---|---|---|---|---|---|---|---|---|
| | | | | | | | sion coverage may be elected. | |
| SD | — | — | — | Termination of employment or membership in the class eligible for coverage; death of employee. | Within 31 days from termination of coverage. | Amount of coverage that ceases due to termination of coverage minus any amount of life insurance the person becomes eligible for under a group policy within 31 days of the termination of coverage. | If group policy terminates, a person who has been insured for at least 5 years is entitled to a converted policy. | S.D. Codified Laws §§ 58-16-21, 58-16-39, 58-16-40. |
| TN | — | — | — | Termination of employment or membership in the class eligible for coverage. | Within 31 days from termination of coverage. | Amount of coverage that ceases due to termination of coverage minus any amount of life insurance the person becomes eligible for under a group policy within 31 days of the termination of coverage. | If group policy terminates, a person who has been insured for at least 5 years is entitled to a converted policy. An insured must be given notice of the right to a converted policy at least 15 days prior to the expiration of the period in which conversion coverage may be elected. | Tenn. Code Ann. § 56-7-2305. |
| TX | — | — | — | Termination of employment or membership in the class eligible for coverage; death of employee. | Within 31 days from termination of coverage. | Not in excess of amount of coverage at time of termination. | If group policy terminates, a person who has been insured for at least 5 years is entitled to a converted policy. | Tex. Ins. Code Ann. art. 3.50, §§ 2, 6; art. 3.51-4A, § 3. |
| UT | Total disability. | 6 months. | Discontinuance of group policy, continuation coverage under disability provision of group policy. | Termination of employment or membership in the class eligible for coverage; death of employee; dependent's ceasing to be a qualified dependent. | Within 31 days from termination of coverage. | Amount of coverage that ceases due to termination of coverage minus any amount of life insurance the person becomes eligible for under a group policy within 30 days of the termination of coverage. | If group policy terminates, a person who has been insured for at least 5 years is entitled to a converted policy. | Utah Code §§ 31A-22-517, 31A-22-518, 31A-22-520. |
| VT | — | — | — | Termination of employment or membership in the class eligible for coverage; death of employee. | Within 31 days from termination of coverage. | Amount of coverage that ceases due to termination of coverage minus any amount of life insurance the person becomes eligible for under a group policy within 31 days of *(cont'd)* | If group policy terminates, a person who has been insured for at least 5 years is entitled to a converted policy. An insured must be given notice of the right to a converted policy at least 15 days prior to *(cont'd)* | Vt. Stat. Ann. tit. 8, §§ 3811, 3820, 3821, 3823. |

*(Table continues.)*

# Table 5.6-4 *(cont'd)*

## GROUP LIFE INSURANCE: STATE CONTINUATION AND CONVERSION REQUIREMENTS

(See also text at § 5.6.)

**KEY:** A "—" indicates that the state has no statutory requirements.

| | *Continuation Requirements* | | | *Conversion Requirements* | | | | |
|---|---|---|---|---|---|---|---|---|
| | *Under What Circumstances May Employee Choose Continuation Coverage?* | *Maximum Length of Continuation Period* | *Disqualifying Events* | *Under What Circumstances May Employee or Dependent Choose Conversion Coverage?* | *When Must Employee or Dependent Elect Coverage?* | *What Amount of Coverage May Employee or Dependent Elect?* | *Other Conversion Rights* | *Citations to Authority* |
| VT (*cont'd*) | | | | | | the termination of coverage. | the expiration of the period in which conversion coverage may be elected. | |
| VA | — | — | — | Termination of employment or membership in the class eligible for coverage; death of employee, dependent's ceasing to be a qualified family member. | Within 31 days from termination of coverage. | Amount of coverage that ceases due to termination of coverage minus any amount of life insurance the person becomes eligible for under a group policy within 31 days of the termination of coverage. | If group policy terminates, a person who has been insured for at least 5 years is entitled to a converted policy. | Va. Code Ann. §§ 38.2-3323, 38.2-3332, 38.2-3333. |
| WA | Strike, lockout, or other labor dispute. | 6 months. | — | Termination of employment or membership in the class eligible for coverage. | Within 31 days from termination of coverage. | Amount not in excess of amount ceasing due to termination nor less than $1,000, unless a smaller amount of coverage was provided under the policy. | If group policy terminates, a person who has been insured for at least 5 years is entitled to a converted policy. | Wash. Rev. Code Ann. §§ 48.24.025, 48.24.180, 48.24.190. |
| WV | — | — | — | Termination of employment or membership in the class eligible for coverage; death of employee. | Within 31 days from termination of coverage. | Amount equal to amount ceasing due to termination. | If group policy terminates, a person who has been insured for at least 5 years is entitled to a converted policy. An insured must be given notice of the right | W. Va. Code §§ 33-14-7, 33-14-16, 33-14-17, 33-14-20. |

| | | | | | | | | |
|---|---|---|---|---|---|---|---|---|
| | | | | | | | to a converted policy at least 15 days prior to the expiration of the period in which conversion coverage may be elected. | |
| WI | — | — | — | Termination of employment or membership in the class eligible for coverage. | Within 31 days from termination of coverage. | Amount equal to amount ceasing due to termination. | If group policy terminates, a person who has been insured for at least 5 years is entitled to a converted policy. | Wis. Stat. Ann. § 632.57. |
| WY | — | — | — | Termination of employment or membership in the class eligible for coverage; death of employee; dependent's ceasing to be qualified family member. | Within 31 days from termination of coverage. | Amount of coverage that ceases due to termination of coverage minus any amount of life insurance the person becomes eligible for under a group policy within 31 days of the termination of coverage. | If group policy terminates, a person who has been insured for at least 3 years is entitled to a converted policy. An insured must be given notice of the right to a converted policy at least 15 days prior to the expiration of the period in which conversion coverage may be elected. | Wyo. Stat. §§ 26-17-118, 26-17-119, 26-17-122. |

# § 5.7 Severance and Other Benefits Due Upon Termination

Most states have enacted "payment of wages" legislation, which requires an employer to pay terminating employees their full wages on their last date of work (or shortly thereafter). In some cases, these provisions require an employer to pay the employee for any unused vacation leave, holidays, and sick leave at the same time. Thus, in certain states, if an employee who has been terminated has not used all of the vacation or sick leave to which he or she was entitled, the employer may have to pay the employee for any such unused leave. Employers that fail to comply with state wage payment laws may have to pay liquidated damages to the employee and, in some cases, face criminal penalties. (Because case law is always in flux, guidance should be sought on recent judicial interpretations of wage payment statutes.)

With the exceptions of Maine, Massachusetts, Hawaii, Pennsylvania, and Rhode Island, which mandate certain severance benefits, these statutory provisions do not mandate that employers provide any particular fringe benefits. Rather, one of the purposes of this type of legislation, in addition to requiring the prompt payment of wages, is to establish a statutory mechanism to enforce the employer's contractual obligations to an employee when the employee terminates employment.

Maine, Massachusetts, Hawaii, Pennsylvania, and Rhode Island each require some form of severance payment to terminated employees under certain circumstances apparently beyond the employee's control. Hawaii's and Maine's statutes mandate severance payments to those employees who lose their jobs because their employers relocated or closed the local establishment. The Massachusetts, Pennsylvania, and Rhode Island statutes require severance payments to those employees terminated within two years following a change in control or buyout of the employer. However, these statutes protect only those employees who have the requisite number of years' service to the company before termination. In addition, Rhode Island's statute requires a severance payment to those employees terminated within one year preceding the transfer of control or buyout.

Several states, such as California, Colorado, and Kansas, require that terminated employees be paid for accrued vacation benefits on a pro rata basis. These state requirements are not always spelled out in the wage payment laws; they may be judicial interpretations that vacation benefits are actually a form of deferred compensation that accrues as the employee performs his or her services.

State wage payment statutes are preempted by ERISA to the extent that they purport to regulate employee benefit plans. However, regulations of the U.S. Department of Labor (DOL) provide that certain benefits paid out of the general assets of an employer constitute "payroll practices" rather than "employee benefit plans." These payroll practices include vacation pay, holiday and overtime premiums, and sick leave pay when paid out of the employer's general assets. The U.S. Supreme Court has upheld the validity of this DOL regulation, insofar as it relates to vacation benefits, in a case that specifically upheld a state statute that required employers to pay accrued vacation benefits upon an employee's termination. In addition, state wage payment statutes may be preempted by the National Labor Relations Act if a collective bargaining agreement covers the situation.

As Table 5.7-1 makes clear, wage payment statutes regarding when payment must be made generally differ, depending on whether the employee resigns or is discharged. If the employee resigns, the employer usually has to pay all wages due by the next payday. If the employee is discharged, however, payment must generally be made on the date of discharge or within a few days thereof.

### [a] Table Legend

With the exceptions of Maine, Massachusetts, Hawaii, Pennsylvania, and Rhode Island, these statutory provisions do not require employers to provide any particular fringe benefits, but they may establish a statutory mechanism to enforce an employer's contractual obligations to an employee or company policy when the employment is terminated.

An em dash (—) indicates that no state statute has been enacted for this category.

# Table 5.7-1
## SEVERANCE AND OTHER BENEFIT PAYMENTS REQUIRED UPON TERMINATION

(See also text at § 5.7.)

| | *Wages* | *Vacation* | *Holiday* | *Sick Leave* | *Severance* | *Date Due If Employee Discharged* | *Date Due If Employee Resigns* | *Citations to Authority* |
|---|---|---|---|---|---|---|---|---|
| AL | — | — | — | — | — | — | — | — |
| AK | Yes. Wages or other compensation. Department of Labor policy requires payment of unused vacation pay, holiday pay, severance pay, or other benefits agreed to by the employer. | Yes. | Yes. | No. | Yes. | Within 3 days. | Within 3 days. | Alaska Stat. § 23.05.140. |
| AZ | Yes. Wages defined to include severance, commissions, bonuses, sick pay, vacation pay, and other amounts promised when employer has practice of making these payments. | Yes. | No. | Yes. | Yes. Wages defined to include severance when employer has practice of making these payments. | Earlier of payday or within 3 days. | Payday. | Ariz. Rev. Stat. Ann. §§ 23-350, 23-353. |
| AR | Yes. | No. | No. | No. | No. | Within 7 days. | Not specified. | Ark. Stat. Ann. § 11-4-405. |
| CA | Yes. | Yes. If employer policy provides for paid vacations, employee entitled to vested vacation. | No. | No. | No. | Immediately. | Within 72 hours. If employee gives 72 hours' notice prior to resignation, then on date of resignation. | Cal. Labor Code §§ 201, 202, 227.3, 2926–2927. |

| | | | | | | | | |
|---|---|---|---|---|---|---|---|---|
| CO | Yes. | Yes. Case law appears to define wages as including vacation pay. | No. | No. | No. | Immediately. | Payday. | Colo. Rev. Stat. §§ 8-4-101, 8-4-104. *Harman v. Freedman,* 591 P.2d 1318 (Colo. S. Ct. 1979). See *Lee v. Great Empire Broadcasting, Inc.,* 794 P.2d 1032 (Colo. Ct. App. 1989); *Jet Courier Serv., Inc. v. Mulei,* 771 P.2d 486 (Colo. 1989). Not preempted by ERISA, *Massachusetts v. Morash,* 490 U.S. 107 (1989). |
| CT | Yes. Payment of accrued fringe benefits, including, but not limited to paid vacation, sick leave, and earned leave, due according to employer policy or collective bargaining agreement. | Yes. | No. | Yes. | No. | Next business day. | Payday. | Conn. Gen. Stat. Ann. §§ 31-71c, 31-76k. See *Gonchar v. City of Bridgeport,* No. 23-14-33, 1990. WL 269251 (Conn. Super. Ct. July 12, 1990); but see *Fulco v. Norwich Roman Catholic Diocese,* No. 51-40-40, 1991 WL 84035 (Conn. Super. Ct. May 3, 1991). |
| DE | Yes. Wages include commissions. | Yes. | No. | Yes. | No. Case law indicates wages do not include severance pay. | Immediately. Vacation pay is payable when due or within 30 days of becoming due. | Payday. Vacation pay is payable when due or within 30 days of becoming due. | Del. Code Ann. tit. 19, §§ 1101, 1103, 1109. *Dept. of Labor v. Green Giant,* 394 A. 2d 753 (Del. 1978). See *GMC v. Local 435 of the Int'l Union,* 546 A.2d 974 (Del. 1988). |
| DC | Yes. Wages include commissions. Department of Labor policy requires payment of unused vacation pay, holiday pay, or severance pay according to company policy. | Yes. Case law requires payment of vacation pay unless there is an agreement to the contrary. | Yes. | No. | Yes. | Next business day. | Earlier of next regular payday or within 7 days. | D.C. Code Ann. §§ 36-100, 36-103. See *Jones v. District of Columbia Parking Management Co.,* 268 A.2d 860 (D.C. 1970). |
| FL | — | — | — | — | — | — | — | — |
| GA | Yes. | No. | No. | No. | No. | Payday. | Payday. | Ga. Code Ann. § 34-7-5. |

*(Table continues.)*

# Table 5.7-1 *(cont'd)*

## SEVERANCE AND OTHER BENEFIT PAYMENTS REQUIRED UPON TERMINATION

(See also text at § 5.7.)

| | *Wages* | *Vacation* | *Holiday* | *Sick Leave* | *Severance* | *Date Due If Employee Discharged* | *Date Due If Employee Resigns* | *Citations to Authority* |
|---|---|---|---|---|---|---|---|---|
| HI | Yes. Wages include commissions. | No. | No. | No. | Yes. Any employer of 50 or more employees that relocates outside the state, closes, or partially closes, must pay eligible employees a dislocated worker allowance. An allowance equal to the difference between the employee's average weekly wage and unemployment compensation benefits must be paid for four weeks. | Immediately or next business day if time or conditions of discharge prevent immediate payment. | Payday. At time of resignation if employee gives one pay period notice. | Haw. Rev. Stat. Ann. §§ 388-1, 388-3, 394B-1. |
| ID | Yes. Wages include commissions. Department of Labor policy requires payment of unused vacation pay, holiday pay, and severance pay. | Yes. Case law indicates wages include earned vacation. | Yes. | No. | Yes. | Earlier of payday or 10 days, or 48 hours after written request. | Earlier of payday or 10 days, or 48 hours after written request. | Idaho Code §§ 45-601, 45-606. *Whitlock v. Haney Seed Co.*, 759 P.2d 919 (Idaho App. 1988). |
| IL | Yes. | Yes. | Yes. Department of Labor policy requires payment of earned holidays. | No. | No. | As soon as possible, but not later than next payday. | As soon as possible, but not later than next payday. | Ill. Ann. Stat. ch. 820, ¶ 115/5. |

| | | | | | | | | |
|---|---|---|---|---|---|---|---|---|
| IN | Yes. Case law indicates wages include commissions. | Yes. Case law requires payment of vacation pay on termination if that is employer's policy. | No. | No. | No. | Payday. | Payday. | Ind. Code §§ 22-2-5-1, 22-2-9-2. *Die & Mold, Inc. v. Western*, 448 N.E.2d 44 (Ind. App. 1983); *LiCocci v. Cardinal Assocs.*, 492 N.E.2d 48 (Ind. App. 1986). See *Olser Inst., Inc. v. Inglert*, 569 N.E. 2d 636 (Ind. 1991). |
| IA | Yes. Wages include commissions. Payment of vacation, holiday, sick leave, and severance due according to employer policy or agreement with employee. | Yes. | Yes. | Yes. | Yes. | Payday. | Payday. | Iowa Code Ann. §§ 91A.2, 91A.4; *Hengesteg v. Northern Engineering, Inc.*, 478 N.W. 2d 307 (Iowa App. 1991). |
| KS | Yes. | Yes. Case law appears to define wages as including vacation pay. | No. | No. | No. | Payday. | Payday. | Kan. Stat. Ann. § 44-315. See *Dollison v. Osborne County*, 737 P.2d 43 (Kan. 1987). |
| KY | Yes. Payment of vested vacation, severance, and earned bonuses due according to established employer policy or pursuant to agreement with employee. | Yes. | No. | No. | Yes. | Not later than next payday or 14 days. | Not later than next payday or 14 days. | Ky. Rev. Stat. Ann. §§ 337.010, 337.055; OAG 91-73. |
| LA | Yes. Wages include all fringes payable under a collective bargaining agreement and commissions. | Yes, if employee is eligible for and has accrued the right to take vacation with pay and the employee has not taken or been compensated for the vacation time as of the date of discharge. | No. | No. | No. | Within 3 days. | Earlier of next regular payday or 15 days from date of resignation. | La. Rev. Stat. Ann. § 23:631. See *Potvin v. Wright's Sound Gallery Inc.*, 568 So. 2d 623 (La. Ct. App. 1990); *Brown v. Navarre Chevrolet, Inc.*, 610 So. 2d 165 (App. 3d Cir. 1992); *Franklin v. Ram, Inc.*, 576 So. 2d 546 (App. 2d Cir. 1991). |
| ME | Yes. Case law indicates wages include commissions. | Yes. If terms of employment include paid vaca- *(cont'd)* | No. | No. | Yes. Any employer that relocates 100 miles distant from original location or *(cont'd)* | Earlier of payday or within 2 weeks after demand made. | Earlier of payday or within 2 weeks. | Me. Rev. Stat. Ann. tit. 26, §§ 625-B, 626, 629-A; *Community Telecommunications Corp. v.* *(cont'd)* |

*(Table continues.)*

## Table 5.7-1 *(cont'd)*

## SEVERANCE AND OTHER BENEFIT PAYMENTS REQUIRED UPON TERMINATION

(See also text at § 5.7.)

| | *Wages* | *Vacation* | *Holiday* | *Sick Leave* | *Severance* | *Date Due If Employee Discharged* | *Date Due If Employee Resigns* | *Citations to Authority* |
|---|---|---|---|---|---|---|---|---|
| ME *(cont'd)* | | tion, employee entitled to vacation pay. | | | terminates covered establishment must pay 1 week for each year worked to any employee of at least 3 years. | | | *Loughran,* 651 A.2d 373 (Me. 1994). See *Bellino v. Schlumberger Technologies, Inc.,* 753 F. Supp. 391 (D. Me. 1990). Severance not preempted by ERISA. *Ft. Halifax Packing v. Coyne,* 482 US.1 (1987). *Rowell v. Jones and Vining, Inc.,* 524 A.2d 1208 (Me. 1987). |
| MD | Yes. Wages include bonuses and commissions. | Yes. Wages include fringes, though fringes are not specifically defined. Department of Labor policy requires payment of vacation pay unless termination was for cause. | Yes. Wages include fringes, though fringes are not specifically defined. | Yes. Wages include fringes, though fringes are not specifically defined. | No. | Payday. | Payday. | Md. Code Ann., Labor and Employment, §§ 3-501, 3-505. *Rhoads v. F.D.I.C.,* 956 F. Supp. 1239 (D. Ind. 1997). |
| MA | Yes. Wages include commission. Payment of fringe benefits, sick leave due according to employer policy, or written contract with employee. | Yes. Payment due according to written or oral agreement with employee. | Yes. Payment due according to written or oral agreement with employee. | Yes. | Yes. Buyer of company must pay 2 weeks' pay for each year of service to employees with 3 or more years of service who are terminated within 2 years of the transfer of control. | Immediately. | Payday. | Mass. Gen. Laws Ann. ch. 149 §§ 148, 183. NOTE: The U.S. Court of Appeals, 1st Circuit, has held that Massachusetts' statute on severance pay is preempted by ERISA. *Simas v. Quaker Fabic Corp. of Fall River,* 6 F.3d. 849, (1st Cir. 1993). |

| | | | | | | | | |
|---|---|---|---|---|---|---|---|---|
| MI | Yes. Payment of vacation, holiday, and sick leave due according to written contract. | Yes. | Yes. | Yes. | No. | Immediately. Law allows modification of payment of fringes by written contract. | Immediately. Law allows modification of payment of fringes by written contract. | Mich. Stat. Ann. §§ 17.277(1), 17.277(4), 17.277(5). |
| MN | Yes. Payment of unused benefit (vacation, holiday, or severance) due according to company policy. | Yes. | Yes. | No. | Yes. | Within 24 hours. | By first scheduled payday. If first scheduled payday is within 5 days, payment may be delayed to the next payday, but may not be delayed more than 20 days. | Minn. Stat. Ann. §§ 181.11, 181.13, 181.14, 181.74, 181.145. |
| MS | Yes. Public employees are entitled to payments on termination of employment. | No. | No. | No. | No. | Rules to be developed by state agency and state auditor. | Rules to be developed by state agency and state auditor. | Miss. Code Ann. § 25-3-97. |
| MO | Yes. | Yes. Case law requires payment of vacation on termination, when that is employer's policy. | No. | No. | No. | Immediately. | Not specified. | Mo. Rev. Stat. § 290.110. See *Solter v. P.M. Place Stores Co.*, 748 S.W. 2d 919 (Mo. Ct. App. 1988). |
| MT | Yes. | Yes. Department of Labor policy requires payment of unused vacation pay. | No. | No. | No. | Earlier of the next regular payday or 15 days. If termination is for cause or employee is laid off, payment is due immediately unless otherwise specified in the personnel policy of the employer. | Earlier of the next regular payday or 15 days. | Mont. Code Ann. §§ 39-3-201, 39-3-205. |
| NE | Yes. Wages defined to include commissions even if employment agreement states otherwise. | Yes. Wages defined to include fringe benefits, including vacation. | No. | Yes. Wages defined to include fringe benefits, including sick leave. | No. | Earlier of payday or within 2 weeks. | Earlier of payday or within 2 weeks. | Neb. Rev. Stat. Ann. §§ 48-1229, 48-1230. *Moore v. Eggers Consulting Co.*, 562 N.W. 2d 534 (Neb. 1997). |
| NV | Yes. Wages defined to include commissions, but not bonuses or profit-sharing arrangements. | No. | No. | No. | No. | Immediately. | Earlier of payday or within 7 days. | Nev. Rev. Stat. §§ 608.012, 608.020, 608.030. |

*(Table continues.)*

# Table 5.7-1 *(cont'd)*

## SEVERANCE AND OTHER BENEFIT PAYMENTS REQUIRED UPON TERMINATION

(See also text at § 5.7.)

| | *Wages* | *Vacation* | *Holiday* | *Sick Leave* | *Severance* | *Date Due If Employee Discharged* | *Date Due If Employee Resigns* | *Citations to Authority* |
|---|---|---|---|---|---|---|---|---|
| NH | Yes. Wages defined as compensation, including hourly, health and welfare, and pension fund contributions pursuant to any agreement adopted for benefit of employee. For employees of governmental entities, wages include accrued, unused comp time. Payment of vacation, holiday, sick leave, or severance due according to employer's policy and practice. | Yes. | Yes. | Yes. | Yes. | Within 72 hours. | Payday. | N.H. Rev. Stat. Ann. §§ 275:42, 275:43, 275:44. Attorney General's Opinion 0-93-5 stating that severance is preempted by ERISA laws. |
| NJ | Yes. Wages include commissions, but not bonuses or profit-sharing arrangements. | No. | No. | No. | No. | Payday. | Payday. | N.J. Rev. Stat. §§ 34:11-4.1, 34:11-4.3. |
| NM | Yes. Wages or other compensation, including commissions. | No. | No. | No. | No. | Within 5 days. | Payday. | N.M. Stat. Ann. §§ 50-4-1, 50-4-4, 50-4-5. |
| NY | Yes. Wages defined to include commissions. | Yes, unless written policy excludes or limits entitlement to vacation. | Yes, unless written policy excludes or limits its entitlement to vacation. | Yes, only if sick during the pay period preceding termination. Otherwise, only by agreement. | No, unless due according to oral or written agreement. | Payday. | Payday. | N.Y. Labor Law §§ 190, 191, 191-c, 198-C. See *Ross v. Specialty Insulation Mfg. Co.*, 419 N.Y.S. 2d 311 (N.Y. App. Div. 1979); *Glenville Gage Co. v. Industrial Bd. of Appeals* 421 N.Y.S. 2d |

| | | | | | | | | |
|---|---|---|---|---|---|---|---|---|
| | | | | | | | | 408 (N.Y. App. Div. 1979), *aff'd,* 417 N.E. 2d 1009 (N.Y. 1980); *First Coinvestors, Inc. v. Carr,* 552 N.Y. S.2d 20 (1990, 1st Dept.). *Gilbert v. Burlington Industries, Inc.,* 765 F.2d 320 (2d Cir.), aff'd, 477 U.S. 901 (1985). Unfunded severance pay plan preempted by ERISA. |
| NC | Yes. Wages include severance, commissions, bonuses, and other amounts when employer has policy of making such payments. | Yes. | Yes. | Yes. | Yes. Wages include severance when employer has policy of making such payments. | Payday. | Payday. | N.C. Gen. Stat. §§ 95-25.2, 95-25.7 95-25-12. Note: The U.S. Court of Appeals, 4th Circuit, has ruled that North Carolina's statute on severance pay is preempted by ERISA. *Holland v. Burlington Industries, Inc.* 772 F.2d 1140 (4th Cir. 1985), *aff'd,* 477 U.S. 901 (1986). |
| ND | Yes. Wages or other compensation. | Yes. Case law and Administrative Code define wages as including vacation pay. | No. | No. | No. | By certified mail to the employee within 15 days or at the next regular pay period, whichever occurs first. | Payday. | N.D. Cent. Code § 34-14-03; N.D. Administrative Code tit. 46. See *Hopfauf v. Bismark Tire Ctr., Inc.,* 234 N.W. 2d 224 (1975). |
| OH | Yes. Includes commissions. | Yes. | Yes. | Yes. | Yes. | Under the general wage payment statute, the 1st of month, for wages earned up to 15th of preceding month; 15th of month, for wages earned in second half of preceding month. | Under the general wage payment statute, the 1st of month, for wages earned up to 15th of preceding month; 15th of month, for wages earned in second half of preceding month. | Ohio Rev. Code Ann. §§ 4111.01, 4113.15. |
| OK | Yes. Includes commissions. Payment of vacation, holiday, or severance due according to employer's established policy. | Yes. | Yes. | No. | Yes. | Payday. | Payday. | Okla. Stat. tit. 40, §§ 165.1, 165.3. See *Biggs v. Surrey Broadcasting Co.,* 811 P.2d 111 (Okla. App. 1991). |

*(Table continues.)*

# Table 5.7-1 *(cont'd)*
## SEVERANCE AND OTHER BENEFIT PAYMENTS REQUIRED UPON TERMINATION

(See also text at § 5.7.)

| | *Wages* | *Vacation* | *Holiday* | *Sick Leave* | *Severance* | *Date Due If Employee Discharged* | *Date Due If Employee Resigns* | *Citations to Authority* |
|---|---|---|---|---|---|---|---|---|
| OR | Yes. Case law appears to define wages as including all compensation contracted to be paid by employer. | Yes. Case law appears to define wages as including all compensation contracted to be paid by employer. | Yes. Case law appears to define wages as including all compensation contracted to be paid by employer. | Yes. Case law appears to define wages as including all compensation contracted to be paid by employer. | Yes. Case law appears to define wages as including all compensation contracted to be paid by employer. | Immediately. Not later than end of first business day after discharge. | Payment due immediately if employee gives more than 48 hours notice, excluding weekends and holidays. If employee fails to give 48 hours notice, payment is due on the earlier of payday or 5 days excluding weekends and holidays. | Or. Rev. Stat. § 652.140. See *State ex rel. Nilsen v. Oregon State Motor Ass'n,* 432 P. 2d 512 (Or. 1967); *Harryman v. Roseburg Rural Fire Protection Dist.,* 420 P. 2d 51 (Or. 1966). |
| PA | Yes. Wages include commissions. | Yes. | Yes. | Yes. | Yes. Buyer of company must pay 1 week severance pay for each year of service to each employee with 2 or more years of service who is terminated within 2 years of transfer of control of the company. | Payday. | Payday. | Pa. Stat. Ann. tit. 43, §§ 260.2a, 260.5; Pa. Stat. Ann. tit. 15, §§ 2581, 2582. |
| RI | Yes. Wages include accrued vacation for employees having completed at least one year of service. | Yes. | Yes. If employee is separated from payroll as a result of employer liquidating, merging, disposing of business, or moving the business out of state. | No. | Yes. Buyer of company must pay 2 weeks severance pay for each year of service to employees with 3 or more years of service who are terminated: within 2 years after transfer of control; within 1 year preceding transfer of | Payday; if employment terminated because of relocation, merger, or liquidation, payment must be made within 24 hours. | Not specified. | R.I. Gen. Laws §§ 28-7-19.2, 28-14-4. |

| | | | | | | | | |
|---|---|---|---|---|---|---|---|---|
| | | | | | control; during period when buyer increases ownership of voting securities from 5% to 50%. | | | |
| SC | Yes. Funds placed in pension or profit sharing plans are not wages. | Yes. | Yes. | Yes. | No. | Payday or within 48 hours. | Payday or within 48 hours. | S.C. Code Ann. §§ 41-10-10, 41-10-50. |
| SD | Yes. Wages or other compensation. | No. | No. | No. | No. | Next regular payday or as soon thereafter as employee returns any property of the employer in the employee's possession. | Payday. | S.D. Codified Laws Ann. §§ 60-11-10, 60-11-11. |
| TN | Yes. Wages or other compensation. | No. | No. | No. | No. | Under the general wage payment statute, on the 5th of month, for work prior to 16th of previous month, or 20th of month for work prior to 1st of month. | Under the general wage payment statute, on the 5th of month, for work prior to 16th of previous month, or 20th of month for work prior to 1st of month. | Tenn. Code Ann. § 50-2-103. |
| TX | Yes. Includes parental leave and other types of pay if there was a written agreement to provide the benefit. | Yes. | Yes. | Yes. | Yes. | Within 6 days. | Next regularly scheduled payday. | Tex. Lab. Code Ann. §§ 61.001, 61.014. |
| UT | Yes. | Yes. Department of Labor policy requires payment of vacation pay due under agreement between employer and employee or according to company policy. | No. | No. | No. | Within 24 hours. | Next regular payday. | Utah Code Ann. § 34-28-5. |

*(Table continues.)*

# Table 5.7-1 *(cont'd)*
## SEVERANCE AND OTHER BENEFIT PAYMENTS REQUIRED UPON TERMINATION

(See also text at § 5.7.)

| | *Wages* | *Vacation* | *Holiday* | *Sick Leave* | *Severance* | *Date Due If Employee Discharged* | *Date Due If Employee Resigns* | *Citations to Authority* |
|---|---|---|---|---|---|---|---|---|
| VT | Yes. Payment of unused vacation pay, holiday pay, severance pay, and other fringe benefits due according to employer's written policy. | Yes. | Yes. | No. | Yes. | Within 72 hours. | Last payday, or, if no regular payday, the following Friday. | Vt. Stat. Ann. tit. 21, § 342. |
| VA | Yes. | No. | No. | No. | No. | Payday. | Payday. | Va. Code Ann. § 40.1-29. |
| WA | Yes. | No. | No. | No. | No. | Payday. | Payday. | Wash. Rev. Code § 49.48.010. |
| WV | Yes. | Yes. | Yes. | Yes. | No. | Within 72 hours. | Payday. At time of resignation if employee gives one pay period notice. | W. Va. Code §§ 21-5-1, 21-5-4. |
| WI | Yes. Payment of fringe benefits due as agreed upon by the employer and employee. | This benefit is not regulated in Wisconsin; Wisconsin requires an employer to honor its commitments to employees, but there is no legal requirement to pay terminated employees for unused vacation leave. | This benefit is not regulated in Wisconsin; Wisconsin requires an employer to honor its commitments to employees, but there is no legal requirement to pay terminated employees for unused holiday pay. | No. | This benefit is not regulated in Wisconsin; Wisconsin requires an employer to honor its commitments to employees, but there is no legal requirement to pay terminated employees for unused holiday pay. | Regular payday or within a month (quarter for logging and farm employees), whichever is earlier. In the event of a plant closing, all wages must be paid within 24 hours. | Regular payday or within a month (quarter for logging and farm employees), whichever is earlier. | Wis. Stat. Ann. §§ 109.01, 109.03. |
| WY | Yes. | No. | No. | No. | No. | Within 5 days. | Within 5 days. | Wyo. Stat. Ann. § 27-4-104. |

# § 5.8 Family and Medical Leave

The Family and Medical Leave Act of 1993 (FMLA) governs all state and local laws and provides for family medical leave, pregnancy leave, parental leave, and other disability leave. It enables eligible employees to receive up to 12 weeks of unpaid leave per year when they are unable to work due to a serious health condition or need time off from work for the birth or adoption of a child or to care for a spouse or immediate family member who has a serious health condition.

The FMLA provides a minimum or basic package of rights and obligations, and state and local laws are permitted to exceed its minimum requirements. Thus, it does not supersede any state or local law that provides a greater level of rights or benefits than those afforded by federal law.

Basically, the FMLA prescribes the number of employees and employee distribution (i.e., employee geographic location in terms of radius around a worksite) in determining employer coverage. It also imposes a minimum yearly work hour requirement (1,250 hours per year) on every employee's entitlement to leave.

Further, under the FMLA, employees who return to work from leave generally are entitled to reinstatement in a "genuinely equivalent" job. However, the FMLA does not prohibit the denial of job reinstatement to certain highly paid, key personnel. The FMLA also permits denial of job reinstatement if an employer demonstrates that the employee returning from leave would not otherwise have been employed at the time of reinstatement (e.g., due to layoff, elimination of shift, or termination of work project).

The FMLA also sets forth various examples of serious health conditions that the act was designed to cover. The conditions range from heart attacks to back problems and include, for example, strokes, certain respiratory conditions, spinal injuries, and appendicitis.

Moreover, the FMLA broadly defines *health care providers* to include various professionals who are authorized under state law to practice medicine, as well as persons who are determined by the U.S. Secretary of Labor to be capable of providing health care services.

Finally, although the FMLA does not require a physician's certification of an employee's serious health condition, many state laws require some form of certification before leave is granted. The FMLA does, however, prescribe procedures for certification dispute resolution by requiring the employer, at its expense, to obtain a second or third opinion from an approved health care provider who has no prior or established relationship with the employer.

Thirty-nine states (Alabama, Alaska, Arkansas, California, Colorado, Connecticut, Delaware, Florida, Hawaii, Illinois, Idaho, Iowa, Kansas, Kentucky, Louisiana, Maine, Maryland, Massachusetts, Minnesota, Missouri, Montana, Nevada, New Jersey, New York, North Carolina, North Dakota, Ohio, Oklahoma, Oregon, Rhode Island, South Carolina, South Dakota, Tennessee, Texas, Utah, Vermont, Washington, West Virginia, and Wisconsin) and the District of Columbia presently have some form of family and/or medical leave laws. Exhibit 5.8-1 presents a state-by-state comparison of basic family and medical leave laws.

### [a] Who Is Covered Under the Family and Medical Leave Act?

Employers covered by the act include any employer engaged in commerce, or in an activity affecting commerce, who employed 50 or more employees for each working day during each of 20 or more calendar work weeks in the current or preceding year. Public agencies are also covered, without regard to number of employees, as are public and private elementary and secondary schools.

To be an eligible employee, an employee must have worked for the employer for at least 12 months and been employed for 1,250 hours during the 12-month period immediately preceding the start of the FMLA leave. The 12-month requirement need not be consecutive. The employee must also be employed at a work site where 50 or more employees are employed by the employer within 75 miles of the work site.

For the hourly requirement, *hours* has the same meaning as in the Fair Labor Standards Act (FLSA). Employers should therefore refer to their accounting under FLSA principles. If there is no record kept of actual hours worked (such as in the case of executives), the employer has the burden of showing that the employee has not worked the required number of hours.

The circumstances covered by FMLA include the following: birth of a child/care of a newborn; placement of a child with the employee for foster care or adoption; time needed to care for the employee's spouse, child, or parent with a serious health condition; time needed to care for the employee's own serious health condition that makes the employee unable to perform the functions of the employee's job.

The leave may begin before the birth of a child if medically necessary and before an adoption if the employee is required to be absent from work to complete the adoption process. Leave may be taken for treatment of an employee's substance abuse problem, but it is possible that the employee's job will not be protected. An employer may not terminate an employee for exercising rights under the FMLA, but in some circumstances it could fire an employee for substance abuse problems without violating the FMLA (although such a firing might violate other federal or state labor and/or employment laws). An employee may take FMLA time to care for an immediate family member with a substance abuse problem. If such leave is taken, no retaliation by the employer is allowed.

### [b] How Much Leave May an Employee Take, and How Is It Structured?

An employee is entitled to 12 work weeks of FMLA leave in a 12-month period. The *year* can be (at the employer's choice) a calendar year, fiscal year, a year based on the employee's starting dates, or 12 months from the date the employee's first FMLA leave began. The employer may choose how the year is to be defined, but the determination must be applied consistently to all employees. To change the formulation, an employer must provide employees with 60 days' notice. An employer may not implement a new method in order to avoid FMLA requirements. In certain cases, spouses employed by the same employer may be allowed a combined total of 12 weeks. The leave may be taken intermittently, but, if for purposes of birth, adoption, or placement for foster care of a child, the employer might have to agree. If the leave is taken for medical reasons, no employer agreement is necessary for the leave to be taken intermittently.

Leave under the FMLA generally may be unpaid. In some circumstances, an employee may choose, or an employer may require an employee to substitute, paid leave for FMLA leave. Paid vacation, personal, or family leave may be substituted for FMLA leave if the circumstances creating the need for FMLA leave are covered by the employer's leave policy regarding paid vacation, family, or personal leave. Paid medical or sick leave may be substituted for FMLA leave in situations where the employer's requirements for sick or medical leave are met. Usually, these alternate types of leaves may be elected by either the employee or the employer. However, an employer may not require compensatory time off (as covered by Section 7(o) of the Fair Labor Standards Act) to be substituted for FMLA leave, although the employee may elect to do so. The employer should make the decision as to whether paid leave will be used within two business days of the employee's request for leave. If an employer elects to have an employee use paid leave as FMLA leave, the employer should notify the employee promptly (generally within two business days) and confirm the decision in writing no later than the employee's next payday.

Generally, an employee's health benefits must continue during the employee's FMLA leave on the same conditions as if the employee had been continuously employed during the leave period. The same group health benefits must be maintained, and any changes made to the coverage of all the employees in the workforce will also apply to employees on FMLA leave. If an employee is usually responsible for a portion of the premiums, that responsibility will continue. Arrangements should be made for payments of premiums during the leave. Whether the employee is entitled to other benefits (such as holiday pay) will depend on the employer's established policy on providing such benefits when an employee is on paid leave.

Upon return from FMLA leave, an employee is entitled to reinstatement in the same position the employee held when the leave began, or in a position that is virtually identical with respect to pay, benefits, and working conditions. If the employee is no longer qualified due to the need to renew a license, take a class, or similar circumstance, the employee must be given a reasonable opportunity to fulfill the requirement after returning to work.

### [c] Posting and Recordkeeping Requirements Under the Act

Employers are required to post, in a conspicuous place, a notice explaining the act and providing information on filing complaints for violations of the act. If a significant portion of the workforce is not literate in English, the employer is responsible for providing the notice in a language in which the employees are literate. Willful violation of the posting requirement carries a penalty of up to $100, and failure to meet the posting requirement will prevent an employer from denying FMLA leave on the basis that the employee did not give advance notice. If an employer has an employee handbook or similar item, information about the FMLA must be provided in the handbook. Employers may use the FMLA fact sheet available from the wage and hour division to provide the information.

Employers must keep certain records to comply with the act. The records do not have to be in any particular format, but the necessary items must be kept for three years. The items required include the following: basic employee information, such as name, address, wages, and hours worked; dates the FMLA leave is taken (leave must be designated as FMLA leave); copies of employee notices of leave and communications from employers to employees regarding the leave; any documents regarding employer policies on the taking of paid and unpaid leave; premium payments of employee benefits; and records of any disputes between the employer and an eligible employee regarding terms of the leave. If an employer has any questions dealing with requirements under the FMLA, the nearest office of the wage and hour division should be contacted for assistance.

# Exhibit 5.8-1

## STATE FAMILY AND MEDICAL LEAVE LAWS

(States not listed have no statutory requirements. See also text at § 5.8.)

### ALABAMA

**Effective Date.** Currently effective.

**Employers Subject to Leave Laws.** State employers.

**Criteria for Eligibility.** State employees.

**Maximum Length of Leave.** Employees accrue leave at the rate of 4 hours per biweekly period worked, and may take up to 150 days for sick leave. For serious illness, employees may be advanced up to 24 additional days.

**Paid Leave.** Leave may be paid.

**Acceptable Reasons for Leave.** Serious illness of employee or of family member; leave may be used in lieu of maternity leave for days employee is actually disabled.

**Employment Guarantees After Leave.** State has no statutory requirements.

**Use of Vacation or Other Time-Off Benefits.** State has no statutory requirements.

**Certification Required.** Certification may be required.

**Effect of Leave on Other Benefits** (e.g., health, pension, retirement). State has no statutory requirements.

**Relationship of Family and Medical Leave Requirements to Pregnancy Disability Leave.** No separate provisions exist for pregnancy disability leave.

**Effect on Seniority Accrual During Leave.** State has no statutory requirements.

**Minimum Requirements for Notification to Employer.** State has no statutory requirements.

**Conditions for Denial of a Request for Leave.** State has no statutory requirements.

**Citations to Authority.** Ala. Admin. Code 670-X-14-.01, 670-X-14-.02, as cited in 4 Empl. Prac. Guide (CCH).

### ALASKA

**Effective Date.** Currently effective.

**Employers Subject to Leave Laws.** Employers with at least 21 employees.

**Criteria for Eligibility.** Employee must be employed for at least 35 hours per week or for at least 6 consecutive months or for at least 17.5 hours per week for at least 12 consecutive months.

**Maximum Length of Leave.** For health leave, 18 weeks in any 24-month period. For pregnancy or birth/adoption of child, 18 weeks in any 12-month period.

**Paid Leave.** State does not require paid leave.

**Acceptable Reasons for Leave.** Birth/adoption of child; serious health condition of employee, child, spouse, or parent.

**Employment Guarantees After Leave.** Employee is entitled to reinstatement in the same or equivalent position held prior to the leave.

**Use of Vacation or Other Time-Off Benefits.** Employee may use any accrued paid leave.

**Certification Required.** State has no statutory requirements.

**Effect of Leave on Other Benefits** (e.g., health, pension, retirement). Group health coverage continues, but employer may require employee to pay all or part of the cost of coverage during the leave.

**Relationship of Family and Medical Leave Requirements to Pregnancy Disability Leave.** No separate provisions exist for pregnancy disability leave.

**Effect on Seniority Accrual During Leave.** State has no statutory requirements.

**Minimum Requirements for Notification to Employer.** Reasonable notice is required where leave is foreseeable.

**Conditions for Denial of a Request for Leave.** If both spouses are employed at the same location and both request time off to care for a child or parent, employer may deny the request of one spouse.

**Citations to Authority.** Alaska Stat. §§ 23.10.500, 23.10.510, 23.10.550.

**ARKANSAS**

**Effective Date.** Currently effective.

**Employers Subject to Leave Laws.** Public employers.

**Criteria for Eligibility.** Employee must be a permanent or probationary employee of a state agency. Sick leave for employee illness accrues at the rate of 1 day per month employed, including the probationary period.

**Maximum Length of Leave.** 6 months.

**Paid Leave.** State does not require paid leave for illness of immediate family member; paid leave is given for employee illness.

**Acceptable Reasons for Leave.** Employee illness; care for immediate family member.

**Employment Guarantees After Leave.** Employee is entitled to reinstatement without loss of any rights unless the position is no longer available due to reduction of staff for budgetary reasons; whenever an employee is laid off because of budgetary reasons and is reinstated within 6 months, accumulated sick leave may be restored to the employee's credit.

**Use of Vacation or Other Time-Off Benefits.** Employee must first use all other accumulated leave.

**Certification Required.** Certification is required for more than 5 consecutive days of leave.

**Effect of Leave on Other Benefits** (e.g., health, pension, retirement). Employee must pay to participate in group insurance programs while on leave.

**Relationship of Family and Medical Leave Requirements to Pregnancy Disability Leave.** Employee may use leave without pay for pregnancy after sick leave and annual leave are used.

**Effect on Seniority Accrual During Leave.** State has no statutory provisions.

**Minimum Requirements for Notification to Employer.** Notification in advance, if possible, is required.

**Conditions for Denial of a Request for Leave.** State has no statutory provisions.

**Citations to Authority.** Ark. Code Ann. §§ 21-4-206–21-4-210.

**CALIFORNIA**

**Effective Date.** Currently effective.

**Employers Subject to Leave Laws.** For family and medical leave, public and private employers with 50 or more employees. For parental leave, employers with 25 or more employees.

**Criteria for Eligibility.** For family and medical leave, employee must be employed for at least 1 continuous year, for a minimum of 1,250 hours per year.

**Maximum Length of Leave.** 12 weeks in a 12-month period for family and medical leave; 40 hours per year for parental leave (not to exceed 8 hours per month).

**Paid Leave.** State does not require paid leave unless paid time-off benefits (e.g., vacation) are used.

**Acceptable Reasons for Leave.** For family and medical leave, birth/adoption of child or care of foster child; illness of employee, child, spouse, or parent. For parental leave, to visit a child's school or day care.

**Employment Guarantees After Leave.** Employee is entitled to reinstatement in the same or equivalent position and at the level of seniority held prior to the leave.

**Use of Vacation or Other Time-Off Benefits.** Employer may require employee to use vacation or other time-off benefits first before receiving the leave benefits; for example, using sick leave before requesting employee health leave.

**Certification Required.** Employer may require certification of illness if leave is taken to care for an ill child, spouse, or parent, as well as require a second or third opinion at employer's expense.

**Effect of Leave on Other Benefits** (e.g., health, pension, retirement). All benefits continue while on leave, the same as for other unpaid leave.

**Relationship of Family and Medical Leave Requirements to Pregnancy Disability Leave.** Pregnancy leave is stated separately; full pregnancy leave is 4 months.

**Effect on Seniority Accrual During Leave.** Seniority continues while on leave.

**Minimum Requirements for Notification to Employer.** Reasonable advance notice for planned leave is required; no notice for unforeseeable leave is required.

**Conditions for Denial of a Request for Leave.** Employer may deny request if leave exceeds 12 weeks in a 12-month period, if child's other parent is on leave or unemployed, if employee requesting leave is among the top 10 percent of highest paid employees, or if leave will create undue hardship for employer.

**Citations to Authority.** Cal. Gov't Code §§ 12945, 12945.2. Cal. Labor Code §§ 230.7, 230.8.

## COLORADO

**Effective Date.** Currently effective.

**Employers Subject to Leave Laws.** Employers with full- or part-time classified employees in the Colorado state personnel system.

**Criteria for Eligibility.** Employee must be employed for more than 1 year.

**Maximum Length of Leave.** 520 hours in a fiscal year.

**Paid Leave.** State requires paid sick leave; state does not require paid family leave unless paid time-off benefits (e.g., vacation) are used.

**Acceptable Reasons for Leave.** Birth/adoption of child; care for family member.

**Employment Guarantees After Leave.** Employee is entitled to reinstatement in position with the same classification held prior to the leave or equivalent classification.

**Use of Vacation or Other Time-Off Benefits.** Employer may require employee to use vacation and sick benefits before receiving leave benefits.

**Certification Required.** Employer may require certification of illness if leave is taken to care for an ill family member or for employee illness.

**Effect of Leave on Other Benefits** (e.g., health, pension, retirement). Employee pays for health benefits for any unpaid portion of leave.

**Relationship of Family and Medical Leave Requirements to Pregnancy Disability Leave.** No separate provisions exist for pregnancy disability leave.

**Effect on Seniority Accrual During Leave.** No effect on seniority for layoff; seniority for retirement stops accruing while on unpaid leave.

**Minimum Requirements for Notification to Employer.** Prior notice is required for more than 5 days of sick leave; 1 month's notice, if possible, is required for family leave.

**Conditions for Denial of a Request for Leave.** Sick leave may be denied for failure to notify or certify; family leave may be denied if the business will be harmed or if no certification is given.

**Citations to Authority.** Colo. Rev. Stat. § 19-5-211; 4 Colo. Code Regs. 801-2, ch. 7, P7-2-5, P7-4-12.

## CONNECTICUT

**Effective Date.** Currently effective.

**Employers Subject to Leave Laws.** All state agencies and private employers with 75 or more employees.

**Criteria for Eligibility.** Employee (public) must have permanent status; employee (private) must have at least 1 year of service and 1,000 hours of work.

**Maximum Length of Leave.** 24 weeks in a 2-year period for public employees; 16 weeks in a 2-year period for private employees.

**Paid Leave.** State does not require paid leave (for both public and private employees).

**Acceptable Reasons for Leave.** Birth/adoption of child; illness of employee, child, parent, or spouse.

**Employment Guarantees After Leave.** Employee is entitled to reinstatement in the position held prior to the leave or equivalent position (private employee), unless employee is disabled (public employee).

**Use of Vacation or Other Time-Off Benefits.** When other benefits exist that cover the same conditions as family leave, the length of family leave benefits is reduced (private employee).

**Certification Required.** Employer must require certification of illness if leave is taken to care for an ill child, parent, or spouse, or for employee illness.

**Effect of Leave on Other Benefits** (e.g., health, pension, retirement). Fringe benefits accrued prior to leave are restored at the end of leave.

**Relationship of Family and Medical Leave Requirements to Pregnancy Disability Leave.** Pregnancy leave is treated separately; employer must grant female employees a leave of reasonable length for pregnancy disability leave.

**Effect on Seniority Accrual During Leave.** Seniority benefits do not accrue while on leave.

**Minimum Requirements for Notification to Employer.** At least 2 weeks' notice is required for medical leave, if possible; reasonable notice of birth or adoption is required; 2 weeks' notice of expected date of return to work is required.

**Conditions for Denial of a Request for Leave.** When husband and wife are working for the same employer, leave may not exceed the total length of leave for a single eligible person in any 2-year period (except to care for sick child).

**Citations to Authority.** Conn. Gen. Stat. Ann. §§ 5-248a, 5-248b, 31-51kk–31-51-nn, 46a-60.

## DELAWARE

**Effective Date.** Currently effective.

**Employers Subject to Leave Laws.** State employers.

**Criteria for Eligibility.** Any employee who has been continuously employed on a full-time basis for at least 1 year.

**Maximum Length of Leave.** 6 weeks.

**Paid Leave.** State does not require paid leave.

**Acceptable Reasons for Leave.** Adoption of a child.

**Employment Guarantees After Leave.** Employee is entitled to reinstatement in position held at time of leave.

**Use of Vacation or Other Time-Off Benefits.** State has no statutory requirements.

**Certification Required.** State has no statutory requirements.

**Effect of Leave on Other Benefits** (e.g., health, pension, retirement). Vacation and sick leave do not accumulate.

**Relationship of Family and Medical Leave Requirements to Pregnancy Disability Leave.** No separate provisions exist for pregnancy disability leave.

**Effect on Seniority Accrual During Leave.** State has no statutory requirements.

**Minimum Requirements for Notification to Employer.** State has no statutory requirements.

**Conditions for Denial of a Request for Leave.** State has no statutory requirements.

**Citations to Authority.** Del. Code Ann. tit. 29, § 5116.

## DISTRICT OF COLUMBIA*

**Effective Date.** Currently effective.

**Employers Subject to Leave Laws.** All employers.

**Criteria for Eligibility.** Employee must have at least 1 year of continuous service and 1,000 hours of work in a 12-month period.

**Maximum Length of Leave.** For family and medical leave, 16 weeks in a 24-month period. For school-related leave, 24 hours per year.

**Paid Leave.** District does not require paid leave.

**Acceptable Reasons for Leave.** Birth/adoption of child or foster child; care for family member; employee illness. Visit to child's school.

**Employment Guarantees After Leave.** Employee is entitled to reinstatement in the position held prior to the leave or equivalent position.

**Use of Vacation or Other Time-Off Benefits.** Employee may elect to use paid sick, vacation, or personal benefits before receiving the leave benefits.

**Certification Required.** Employer may require certification of illness if leave is taken to care for a family member or for employee illness, as well as require a second or third opinion at employer's expense.

**Effect of Leave on Other Benefits** (e.g., health, pension, retirement). Health benefits continue while on leave; all other fringe benefits accrued prior to leave are restored at end of leave.

**Relationship of Family and Medical Leave Requirements to Pregnancy Disability Leave.** No separate provisions exist for pregnancy disability leave.

**Effect on Seniority Accrual During Leave.** Seniority benefits do not accrue while on leave.

**Minimum Requirements for Notification to Employer.** Reasonable notice, if possible, is required.

**Conditions for Denial of a Request for Leave.** When husband and wife are working for the same employer, leave may be limited to a combined total leave of 16 weeks in any 24-month period, and simultaneous leave may be restricted to a maximum of 4 weeks if harmful to employer.

**Citations to Authority.** D.C. Code Ann. §§ 36-1301, 36-1305, 36-1316, 36-1401, 36-1405, 36-1602; *Harrison v. Children's Nat'l Medical Ctr.,* 121 WLR 405 (Super. Ct. 1993).

*District government employees are permitted to register a domestic partner and receive leave for care for the partner or partner's child or leave for adoption of the partner's child. The leave is to be granted in a similar manner to that listed below.

## FLORIDA*

**Effective Date.** Currently effective for public employers.

**Employers Subject to Leave Laws.** All state agencies.

**Criteria for Eligibility.** Employee must have career service status.

**Maximum Length of Leave.** Up to 6 months (no other specification was given).

**Paid Leave.** State does not require paid leave.

**Acceptable Reasons for Leave.** Birth/adoption of child; serious family illness.

**Employment Guarantees After Leave.** Employee is entitled to reinstatement in the position held prior to the leave or equivalent position.

**Use of Vacation or Other Time-Off Benefits.** Employee may use accrued sick leave or annual leave to extend the leave benefits.

**Certification Required.** Employer may require certification of illness if leave is taken to care for ill family member or for employee illness.

**Effect of Leave on Other Benefits** (e.g., health, pension, retirement). All benefits continue while on paid leave; fringe benefits accrued prior to unpaid leave are restored at the end of the leave.

**Relationship of Family and Medical Leave Requirements to Pregnancy Disability Leave.** No separate provisions exist for pregnancy disability leave.

**Effect on Seniority Accrual During Leave.** Seniority benefits do not accrue while on leave.

**Minimum Requirements for Notification to Employer.** Notice is required.

**Conditions for Denial of a Request for Leave.** State has no statutory requirements.

**Citations to Authority.** Fla. Stat. Ann. § 110.221.

***Note:** Dade County has a family and medical leave ordinance that covers some private employees as well as public employees.

### HAWAII

**Effective Date.** Currently effective.

**Employers Subject to Leave Laws.** Public and private employers with 100 or more employees.

**Criteria for Eligibility.** Employee must be employed for 6 consecutive months.

**Maximum Length of Leave.** 4 weeks per calendar year.

**Paid Leave.** Employer has discretion.

**Acceptable Reasons for Leave.** Birth/adoption of child; care for child, spouse, or parent with serious health condition.

**Employment Guarantees After Leave.** Employee is entitled to reinstatement in the position held prior to the leave or equivalent position.

**Use of Vacation or Other Time-Off Benefits.** Employer may require employee to use any other paid leave before receiving the leave benefits, unless such paid leave is normally granted under the circumstances by employer's policy.

**Certification Required.** Employer may require certification of birth/adoption of a child.

**Effect of Leave on Other Benefits** (e.g., health, pension, retirement). All benefits continue to accrue while on leave and are restored at the end of leave.

**Relationship of Family and Medical Leave Requirements to Pregnancy Disability Leave.** Pregnancy leave is treated separately; employer must give a female employee who is disabled due to pregnancy and related conditions a leave of reasonable length.

**Effect on Seniority Accrual During Leave.** Seniority benefits accrue while on leave.

**Minimum Requirements for Notification to Employer.** Reasonable notice, if possible, is required.

**Conditions for Denial of a Request for Leave.** State has no conditions for denial of leave.

**Citations to Authority.** Haw. Rev. Stat. §§ 398-1–398-10.

### IDAHO

**Effective Date**. Currently effective.

**Employers Subject to Leave Laws.** State employers.

**Criteria for Eligibility.** State employees.

**Maximum Length of Leave.** 12 weeks per 12-month period.

**Paid Leave.** Paid leave is not required, but employees may choose to use available paid leave.

**Acceptable Reasons for Leave.** Birth/adoption of a child; illness of employee; illness of employee's child, spouse, or parent.

**Employment Guarantees After Leave.** Employee is entitled to reinstatement in the position held before the leave or in an equivalent position.

**Use of Vacation or Other Time-Off Benefits.** Accrued paid leave may be used by the employee or required by the employer.

**Certification Required.** Employer may require certification of a serious health condition and may require a second or third opinion (at employer's expense).

**Effect of Leave on Other Benefits.** Health benefits continue during leave on the same conditions as before leave, including any employee contributions to insurance.

**Relationship of Family and Medical Leave Requirements to Pregnancy Disability Leave.** Pregnancy disability leave is covered under sick leave.

**Effect on Seniority Accrual During Leave.** State has no statutory requirements.

**Minimum Requirements for Notification to Employer.** Reasonable notice may be required.

**Conditions for a Denial of a Request for Leave.** If spouses work for the same employer, they may be limited to a combined total of 12 weeks.

**Citations to Authority.** Idaho Admin. Code § 28:01:01:243.

### ILLINOIS

**Effective Date.** Currently effective.

**Employers Subject to Leave Laws.** Public and private employers with at least 50 employees.

**Criteria for Eligibility.** Employee must be employed for at least 6 months and work an average number of hours per week equal to at least one half of the full-time equivalent position.

**Maximum Length of Leave.** 8 hours during any school year (maximum of 4 hours on any given day).

**Paid Leave.** State does not require paid leave.

**Acceptable Reasons for Leave.** Child's school conferences and school activities.

**Employment Guarantees After Leave.** Not applicable.

**Use of Vacation or Other Time-Off Benefits.** Employee must first use other leave benefits (e.g., vacation, personal leave), except sick and disability leave benefits.

**Certification Required.** Employer may require documentation of school activity or conference.

**Effect of Leave on Other Benefits** (e.g., health, pension, retirement). Employee may not lose benefits for exercising right to take leave.

**Relationship of Family and Medical Leave Requirements to Pregnancy Disability Leave.** Not applicable.

**Effect on Seniority Accrual During Leave.** Not applicable.

**Minimum Requirements for Notification to Employer.** Written notification at least 7 days in advance is required, except for emergencies.

**Conditions for Denial of a Request for Leave.** Request may be denied if the leave would result in 75 percent of the employer's workforce or a shift taking leave at the same time.

**Citations to Authority.** ILCS ch. 820, §§ 147/10, 147/15, 147/30, 147/40.

## IOWA

**Effective Date.** Currently effective.

**Employers Subject to Leave Laws.** Employers with at least 4 employees.

**Criteria for Eligibility.** State has no minimum employment requirements.

**Maximum Length of Leave.** 8 weeks or the period of disability, whichever is less.

**Paid Leave.** State does not require paid leave.

**Acceptable Reasons for Leave.** Birth of child; disability related to pregnancy.

**Employment Guarantees After Leave.** State has no statutory requirements.

**Use of Vacation or Other Time-Off Benefits.** Employer may require employee first to use other disability benefits prior to leave.

**Certification Required.** Employer may require certification of condition of disability.

**Effect of Leave on Other Benefits** (e.g., health, pension, retirement). State has no statutory requirements.

**Relationship of Family and Medical Leave Requirements to Pregnancy Disability Leave.** No separate provisions exist for pregnancy disability leave.

**Effect on Seniority Accrual During Leave.** State has no statutory requirements.

**Minimum Requirements for Notification to Employer.** Timely notice is required.

**Conditions for Denial of a Request for Leave.** Leave may be denied for failure to provide notice and/or certification.

**Citations to Authority.** Iowa Code Ann. § 216.6.

## KANSAS

**Effective Date.** Currently effective.

**Employers Subject to Leave Laws.** All employers.

**Criteria for Eligibility.** State has no minimum employment requirements.

**Maximum Length of Leave.** Reasonable period of time.

**Paid Leave.** State does not require paid leave.

**Acceptable Reasons for Leave.** Birth of child.

**Employment Guarantees After Leave.** Employee is entitled to reinstatement in the position held prior to leave or equivalent position, if employee expresses an intention to return to work within a reasonable period of time after childbirth.

**Use of Vacation or Other Time-Off Benefits.** State has no statutory requirements.

**Certification Required.** State has no statutory requirements.

**Effect of Leave on Other Benefits** (e.g., health, pension, retirement). No loss of other benefits.

**Relationship of Family and Medical Leave Requirements to Pregnancy Disability Leave.** No separate provisions exist for pregnancy disability leave.

**Effect on Seniority Accrual During Leave.** State has no statutory requirements.

**Minimum Requirements for Notification to Employer.** State has no statutory requirements.

**Conditions for Denial of a Request for Leave.** State has no statutory requirements.

**Citations to Authority.** Kan. Stat. Ann. §§ 44-1009(a), 44-1030(a)(1) and accompanying regulations.

## KENTUCKY

**Effective Date.** Currently effective.

**Employers Subject to Leave Laws.** All employers.

**Criteria for Eligibility.** State has no minimum employment requirements.

**Maximum Length of Leave.** 6 weeks.

**Paid Leave.** State does not require paid leave.

**Acceptable Reasons for Leave.** Reception of an adopted child under age 7.

**Employment Guarantees After Leave.** State has no statutory requirements.

**Use of Vacation or Other Time-Off Benefits.** State has no statutory requirements.

**Certification Required.** State has no statutory requirements.

**Effect of Leave on Other Benefits** (e.g., health, pension, retirement). State has no statutory requirements.

**Relationship of Family and Medical Leave Requirements to Pregnancy Disability Leave.** Not applicable.

**Effect on Seniority Accrual During Leave.** State has no statutory requirements.

**Minimum Requirements for Notification to Employer.** Written notice is required.

**Conditions for Denial of a Request for Leave.** State has no statutory requirements.

**Citations to Authority.** Ky. Rev. Stat. Ann. § 337.015.

## LOUISIANA

**Effective Date.** Currently effective.

**Employers Subject to Leave Laws.** For pregnancy leave, employers with more than 25 employees; for bone marrow donor leave, employers with 20 employees.

**Criteria for Eligibility.** State has no minimum employment requirements.

**Maximum Length of Leave.** 6 weeks for disability arising from normal pregnancy or childbirth; pregnancy leave not to exceed 4 months; for bone marrow donor leave, up to 40 hours.

**Paid Leave.** For bone marrow donor leave, leave must be paid; for pregnancy leave, state does not require paid leave.

**Acceptable Reasons for Leave.** Birth of child or pregnancy and/or disability due to pregnancy, birth of child, or related medical condition. Any medical procedure required to donate bone marrow.

**Employment Guarantees After Leave.** For pregnancy leave, employee is entitled to the same benefits and privileges of other employees who are similarly situated in employment.

**Use of Vacation or Other Time-Off Benefits.** Employee may use any accrued vacation leave for pregnancy leave.

**Certification Required.** Employer may require verification for bone marrow donation.

**Effect of Leave on Other Benefits** (e.g., health, pension, retirement). State has no statutory requirements for pregnancy leave. For bone marrow donation leave, leave has no effect on other benefits.

**Relationship of Family and Medical Leave Requirements to Pregnancy Disability Leave.** No other provisions exist for pregnancy disability leave.

**Effect on Seniority Accrual During Leave.** State has no statutory requirements.

**Minimum Requirements for Notification to Employer.** Reasonable notice may be required by employer.

**Conditions for Denial of a Request for Leave.** State has no statutory requirements.

**Citations to Authority.** La. Rev. Stat. Ann. § 23:341, 23:342, 40:1299.124.

## MAINE

**Effective Date.** Currently effective.

**Employers Subject to Leave Laws.** Public and private employers with 15 or more employees.

**Criteria for Eligibility.** Employee must be employed for more than 1 consecutive year.

**Maximum Length of Leave.** 10 weeks in a 2-year period.

**Paid Leave.** Employer has discretion.

**Acceptable Reasons for Leave.** Birth/adoption or serious illness of child, parent, or spouse, or employee illness.

**Employment Guarantees After Leave.** Employee is entitled to reinstatement in the same or equivalent position held prior to the leave.

**Use of Vacation or Other Time-Off Benefits.** State has no statutory requirements.

**Certification Required.** Employer may require certification of illness if leave is taken to care for an ill child, parent, or spouse, or for employee illness.

**Effect of Leave on Other Benefits** (e.g., health, pension, retirement). Benefits may continue at employee expense.

**Relationship of Family and Medical Leave Requirements to Pregnancy Disability Leave.** No separate provisions exist for pregnancy disability leave.

**Effect on Seniority Accrual During Leave.** Seniority benefits do not accrue while on leave.

**Minimum Requirements for Notification to Employer.** 30 days' notice for nonemergencies is required.

**Conditions for Denial of a Request for Leave.** State has no conditions for denial of leave.

**Citations to Authority.** Me. Rev. Stat. Ann. tit. 26, §§ 844–845; 1997 Me. Laws C155.

## MARYLAND

**Effective Date.** Currently effective.

**Employers Subject to Leave Laws.** State employers.

**Criteria for Eligibility.** For sick leave, employee must be a service employee in the State Personnel Management System; for family leave, employee must be in the executive branch of state government.

**Maximum Length of Leave.** Varies. Sick leave accrues at the rate of 15 days per year, not to exceed 120 hours, and may be used any time. Up to 12 weeks in a 12-month period may be taken for family leave.

**Paid Leave.** Sick leave must be paid; family leave is without pay.

**Acceptable Reasons for Leave.** For sick leave, illness/disability of employee, death, illness, or disability of a member of employee's immediate family, and birth or placement of a child with employee for adoption. For family leave, birth/adoption of child, adoption of foster child, illness or disability in employee's immediate family, or care for employee's school-age child under 14 during school vacations.

**Employment Guarantees After Leave.** No statutory requirements for sick leave; guarantee of reinstatement in the same job for family leave.

**Use of Vacation or Other Time-Off Benefits.** No statutory requirements for sick leave; for family leave, employer may require employee to first use other leave benefits.

**Certification Required.** Certification is required for employee illness of more than 4 days in a 30-day period; for family leave, state has no statutory requirements.

**Effect of Leave on Other Benefits** (e.g., health, pension, retirement). For sick leave, state has no statutory requirements; for family leave, suspension of benefits except for health benefits.

**Relationship of Family and Medical Leave Requirements to Pregnancy Disability Leave.** No separate provisions exist for pregnancy disability leave.

**Effect on Seniority Accrual During Leave.** State has no statutory requirements.

**Minimum Requirements for Notification to Employer.** For sick leave, state has no statutory requirements; for family leave, prior approval is required.

**Condition for Denial of a Request for Leave.** For sick leave, no statutory requirements exist. A request for family leave may be denied, depending on the disruption to the work unit.

**Citations to Authority.** Md. State Pers. Code Ann. §§ 9-501–9-508, 9-1001 to 9-1005.

## MASSACHUSETTS

**Effective Date.** Currently effective.

**Employers Subject to Leave Laws.** Employers with at least 6 employees.

**Criteria for Eligibility.** Female employees who have been employed full-time for at least 3 consecutive months and have completed the probationary period.

**Maximum Length of Leave.** 8 weeks.

**Paid Leave.** Employer has discretion.

**Acceptable Reasons for Leave.** Birth/adoption of child.

**Employment Guarantees After Leave.** Employee is entitled to reinstatement in the same or equivalent position held prior to the leave, unless a layoff during the leave would have applied to the employee.

**Use of Vacation or Other Time-Off Benefits.** Employee may use accrued vacation and sick leave benefits to extend family leave.

**Certification Required.** State has no statutory requirements.

**Effect of Leave on Other Benefits** (e.g., health, pension, retirement). All benefits to which employee was entitled prior to the leave continue in effect; however, employer is not obligated to pay for the cost of benefits unless it does so for all employees on leave.

**Relationship of Family and Medical Leave Requirements to Pregnancy Disability Leave.** No separate provisions exist for pregnancy disability leave.

**Effect on Seniority Accrual During Leave.** Seniority benefits do not accrue during leave.

**Minimum Requirements for Notification to Employer.** At least 2 weeks' notice of anticipated absence is required.

**Conditions for Denial of a Request for Leave.** State has no statutory requirements.

**Citations to Authority.** Mass. Gen. Laws Ann. ch. 149, § 105D; ch. 151B, § 1(5).

## MINNESOTA

**Effective Date.** Currently effective.

**Employers Subject to Leave Laws.** For birth/adoption of child and illness, public and private employers with 21 or more employees; for school leave, employers with 1 employee; for bone marrow donor leave, employers with 20 or more employees.

**Criteria for Eligibility.** Employee must work an average number of hours per week equal to at least one half of the full-time equivalent position for at least 1 year. For bone marrow donor leave, an average of 20 hours per week.

**Maximum Length of Leave.** 6 weeks for birth/adoption of child or illness; an employer that has fewer than 21 employees and allows maternity leave must allow 4 weeks for the adoption of a child; 16 hours per year for school leave. For bone marrow donors, 40 hours.

**Paid Leave.** State does not require paid leave unless paid time-off benefits (e.g., vacation) are used. Bone marrow donor leave must be paid.

**Acceptable Reasons for Leave.** Birth/adoption or serious illness of child; child's school conferences and activities; bone marrow donation.

**Employment Guarantees After Leave.** Employee is entitled to reinstatement in the position held prior to the leave or equivalent position.

**Use of Vacation or Other Time-Off Benefits.** Employer may require that employee use sick leave to care for a sick child.

**Certification Required.** Employer may require verification of bone marrow donation.

**Effect of Leave on Other Benefits** (e.g., health, pension, retirement). All benefits are restored at the end of leave. Bone marrow donor leave has no effect on other benefits.

**Relationship of Family and Medical Leave Requirements to Pregnancy Disability Leave.** No separate provisions exist for pregnancy disability leave.

**Effect on Seniority Accrual During Leave.** Seniority benefits do not accrue while on leave.

**Minimum Requirements for Notification to Employer.** Prior notice may be required; notice of return date is required if leave is over 4 weeks.

**Conditions for Denial of a Request for Leave.** State has no conditions for denial of leave.

**Citations to Authority.** Minn. Stat. Ann. §§ 181.940–181.945.

## MISSOURI

**Effective Date.** Currently effective.

**Employers Subject to Leave Laws.** State employers.

**Criteria for Eligibility.** State employee adoptive parents who are primarily responsible for furnishing care of a child.

**Maximum Length of Leave.** Same length as that granted to biological parents by employer.

**Paid Leave.** Leave may be with or without pay.

**Acceptable Reasons for Leave.** Adoption of child.

**Employment Guarantees After Leave.** Employer may not penalize employee for exercising right to take leave.

**Use of Vacation or Other Time-Off Benefits.** Employee may first use sick leave, annual leave, and leave without pay.

**Certification Required.** State has no statutory requirements.

**Effect of Leave on Other Benefits** (e.g., health, pension, retirement). State has no statutory requirements.

**Relationship of Family and Medical Leave Requirements to Pregnancy Disability Leave.** No separate provisions exist for pregnancy disability leave.

**Effect on Seniority Accrual During Leave.** State has no statutory requirements.

**Minimum Requirements for Notification to Employer.** State has no statutory requirements.

**Condition for Denial of a Request for Leave.** State has no statutory requirements.

**Citations to Authority.** Mo. Rev. Stat. § 105.271.

## MONTANA

**Effective Date.** Currently effective.

**Employers Subject to Leave Laws.** All employers.

**Criteria for Eligibility.** Statute applies to all female employees.

**Maximum Length of Leave.** Reasonable leave.

**Paid Leave.** State does not require paid leave.

**Acceptable Reasons for Leave.** Pregnancy.

**Employment Guarantees After Leave.** Employee is entitled to reinstatement in the position held prior to the leave or equivalent position, unless a change in circumstances makes it impossible or unreasonable for employer to do so.

**Use of Vacation or Other Time-Off Benefits.** State has no statutory requirements.

**Certification Required.** Employer may require certification of disabling condition due to pregnancy.

**Effect of Leave on Other Benefits** (e.g., health, pension, retirement). Fringe benefits that employee had prior to the leave are restored when employee returns to work, unless a change in circumstances makes it impossible or unreasonable for employer to do so.

**Relationship of Family and Medical Leave Requirements to Pregnancy Disability Leave.** No separate provisions exist for pregnancy disability leave.

**Effect on Seniority Accrual During Leave.** Seniority benefits accrue during leave.

**Minimum Requirements for Notification to Employer.** State has no statutory requirements.

**Conditions for Denial of a Request for Leave.** State has no statutory requirements.

**Citations to Authority.** Mont. Code Ann. §§ 49-2-310, 49-2-311.

## NEVADA

**Effective Date.** Currently effective.

**Employers Subject to Leave Laws.** All employers.

**Criteria for Eligibility.** If employer offers leave benefits to employees for sickness or disability, it must offer leave benefits to female employees for pregnancy and related conditions; there are no minimum employment requirements.

**Maximum Length of Leave.** The state has no requirements except that if employers offer leave benefits for sickness and disability, they must also offer the same benefits for pregnancy and related conditions.

**Paid Leave.** The state has no requirements except that if employers offer leave benefits for sickness and disability, they must also offer the same benefits for pregnancy and related conditions.

**Acceptable Reasons for Leave.** Childbirth, miscarriage, or other natural resolution to pregnancy.

**Employment Guarantees After Leave.** State has no statutory requirements.

**Use of Vacation or Other Time-Off Benefits.** State has no statutory requirements.

**Certification Required.** State has no statutory requirements.

**Effect of Leave on Other Benefits** (e.g., health, pension, retirement). State has no statutory requirements.

**Relationship of Family and Medical Leave Requirements to Pregnancy Disability Leave.** No separate provisions exist for pregnancy disability leave.

**Effect on Seniority Accrual During Leave.** If employer offers protection against loss of seniority to employees for sickness or disability, it must offer the same protection to female employees for pregnancy and related conditions.

**Minimum Requirements for Notification to Employer.** State has no statutory requirements.

**Conditions for Denial of a Request for Leave.** State has no statutory requirements.

**Citations to Authority.** Nev. Rev. Stat. § 613.335.

## NEW JERSEY

**Effective Date.** Currently effective.

**Employers Subject to Leave Laws.** Employers with 50 or more employees.

**Criteria for Eligibility.** Employee must be employed for 1,000 hours for at least 1 year.

**Maximum Length of Leave.** 12 weeks in a 24-month period.

**Paid Leave.** Employer may provide paid, unpaid, or a combination of leave.

**Acceptable Reasons for Leave.** Birth/adoption of child and serious health condition of child, parent, or spouse.

**Employment Guarantees After Leave.** Employee is entitled to reinstatement in the position held prior to the leave or equivalent position, unless a layoff during the leave would have applied to the employee.

**Use of Vacation or Other Time-Off Benefits.** State has no statutory requirements.

**Certification Required.** Employer may require certification of illness if leave is taken to care for ill child, parent, or spouse; certification of birth or adoption may also be required. Employer may obtain second or third opinion at employer's expense.

**Effect of Leave on Other Benefits** (e.g., health, pension, retirement). All benefits continue in effect while on leave.

**Relationship of Family and Medical Leave Requirements to Pregnancy Disability Leave.** Family leave provisions supplement the state's temporary disability laws.

**Effect on Seniority Accrual During Leave.** Seniority benefits do not accrue while on leave.

**Minimum Requirements for Notification to Employer.** Prior notice, if possible, is required.

**Conditions for Denial of a Request for Leave.** Leave may be denied if employee is salaried and among the highest paid 5 percent of employees; leave may also be denied if it will cause substantial economic injury to employer.

**Citations to Authority.** N.J. Rev. Stat. §§ 34:11B-3–34:11B-13.

## NEW YORK

**Effective Date.** Currently effective.

**Employers Subject to Leave Laws.** All employers.

**Criteria for Eligibility.** If employer allows employees leave benefits for the birth of a child, it must offer the same leave benefits to adoptive parents; no minimum employment requirements.

**Maximum Length of Leave.** Leave benefits for adoptive parents must be the same as those extended to biological parents, except there is no entitlement to leave for adoption of a child after the child reaches the minimum age for attendance in public school, unless the child is handicapped or otherwise considered difficult to place for adoption.

**Paid Leave.** Leave benefits for adoptive parents must be the same as those extended to birth parents.

**Acceptable Reasons for Leave.** Birth/adoption of child.

**Employment Guarantees After Leave.** State has no statutory requirements.

**Use of Vacation or Other Time-Off Benefits.** State has no statutory requirements.

**Certification Required.** State has no statutory requirements.

**Effect of Leave on Other Benefits** (e.g., health, pension, retirement). State has no statutory requirements.

**Relationship of Family and Medical Leave Requirements to Pregnancy Disability Leave.** No separate provisions exist for pregnancy disability leave.

**Effect on Seniority Accrual During Leave.** State has no statutory requirements.

**Minimum Requirements for Notification to Employer.** State has no statutory requirements.

**Conditions for Denial of a Request for Leave.** State has no statutory requirements.

**Citations to Authority.** N.Y. Lab. Law § 201-c.

## NORTH CAROLINA

**Effective Date.** Currently effective.

**Employers Subject to Leave Laws.** All employers.

**Criteria for Eligibility.** Any employee who is a parent/guardian or standing in loco parentis to a school-age child.

**Maximum Length of Leave.** 4 hours per year.

**Paid Leave.** State does not require paid leave.

**Acceptable Reasons for Leave.** Involvement in child's school.

**Employment Guarantees After Leave.** Employer may not discharge, demote, or otherwise take any adverse action against an employee taking leave.

**Use of Vacation or Other Time-Off Benefits.** State has no statutory requirements.

**Certification Required.** Employer may require verification.

**Effect of Leave on Other Benefits** (e.g., health, pension, retirement). Not applicable.

**Relationship of Family and Medical Leave Requirements to Pregnancy Disability Leave.** No separate provisions exist for pregnancy disability leave.

**Effect on Seniority Accrual During Leave.** Not applicable.

**Minimum Requirements for Notification to Employer.** Leave is to be taken at a mutually agreed upon time; employer may request 48 hours' written notice.

**Conditions for Denial of a Request for Leave.** State has no statutory requirements.

**Citations to Authority.** N.C. Gen. Stat. § 95-28.3.

## NORTH DAKOTA

**Effective Date.** Currently effective.

**Employers Subject to Leave Laws.** State employers.

**Criteria for Eligibility.** Any employee who has been employed by the state for at least 1 year, working at least 20 hours per week.

**Maximum Length of Leave.** For part-time (20 hours per week) employee, 2 months. For full-time (40 hours per week) employee, 4 months.

**Paid Leave.** Leave is without pay, unless employer/employee policy specifies otherwise.

**Acceptable Reasons for Leave.** Newborn/adopted child, care for child/spouse/parent with serious health condition, or for employee illness/disability.

**Employment Guarantees After Leave.** Employee is entitled to reinstatement in the position held prior to the leave or equivalent position.

**Use of Vacation or Other Time-Off Benefits.** Employee may use up to 1 week of medical leave, if provided by employer, to care for a family member with a serious health condition. For leave due to pregnancy, employee may first use sick leave.

**Certification Required.** Employer may request certification of a serious health condition.

**Effect of Leave on Other Benefits** (e.g., health, pension, retirement). Health benefits continue, but employee may have to pay premiums.

**Relationship of Family and Medical Leave Requirements to Pregnancy Disability Leave.** No separate provisions exist for pregnancy disability leave.

**Effect on Seniority Accrual During Leave.** Seniority benefits do not accrue.

**Minimum Requirements for Notification to Employer.** Advance notice is required for birth/adoption of a child. Notice is required, if possible, for other leaves.

**Condition for Denial of a Request for Leave.** When husband and wife have the same employer, total leave for the couple may be limited to 4 months.

**Citations to Authority.** N.D. Cent. Code §§ 54-52.4-01–54-52.4-10.

## OHIO

**Effective Date.** Currently effective.

**Employers Subject to Leave Laws.** State employers.

**Criteria for Eligibility.** Employee must work at least 30 hours per week.

**Maximum Length of Leave.** 6 weeks.

**Paid Leave.** First 2 weeks unpaid, next 4 weeks paid at 70 percent of regular pay. Employee may opt to receive $2,000 for adoption expenses in lieu of paid leave.

**Acceptable Reasons for Leave.** Birth/adoption of child.

**Employment Guarantees After Leave.** No provision, but reinstatement implied.

**Use of Vacation or Other Time-Off Benefits.** Employee may use available sick, personal, or vacation leave for unpaid leave.

**Certification Required.** State has no statutory requirements.

**Effect of Leave on Other Benefits.** Employee will not receive holiday pay during leave.

**Relationship of Family and Medical Leave Requirements to Pregnancy Disability Leave.** No separate provisions for pregnancy disability leave.

**Effect on Seniority Accrual During Leave.** State has no statutory requirements.

**Minimum Requirements for Notification to Employer.** State has no statutory requirements.

**Conditions for a Denial of a Request for Leave.** State has no statutory requirements.

**Citations to Authority.** Ohio Rev. Code § 124.13.6.

## OKLAHOMA

**Effective Date.** Currently effective.

**Employers Subject to Leave Laws.** State employers. Employees participate in a shared leave program under which hours may be donated.

**Criteria for Eligibility.** Employee must be employed for at least 6 months.

**Maximum Length of Leave.** 12 weeks in any 12-month period.

**Paid Leave.** State does not require paid leave.

**Acceptable Reasons for Leave.** Birth/adoption of child or to care for family member.

**Employment Guarantees After Leave.** Employee is entitled to reinstatement in same position held prior to the leave.

**Use of Vacation or Other Time-Off Benefits.** Employee may first use any other benefits (e.g., sick leave, vacation leave without pay) before receiving the leave.

**Certification Required.** Employer may require certification of illness if leave is taken to care for ill family member.

**Effect of Leave on Other Benefits** (e.g., health, pension, retirement). Employee pays premium for continued health and life insurance benefits.

**Relationship of Family and Medical Leave Requirements to Pregnancy Disability Leave.** Family leave includes any pregnancy leave already taken by employee.

**Effect on Seniority Accrual During Leave.** State has no statutory requirements.

**Minimum Requirements for Notification to Employer.** Reasonable notice, if possible, is required.

**Conditions for Denial of a Request for Leave.** State has no conditions for denial of leave.

**Citations to Authority.** Okla. Stat. Ann. tit. 74, §§ 840-2.22–840-2.23 and accompanying regulations.

## OREGON

**Effective Date.** Currently effective.

**Employers Subject to Leave Laws.** Employers with 25 or more employees.

**Criteria for Eligibility.** Employee must be employed for 180 days for parental leave; employee must be employed for 180 days and average 25 hours of work per week for family leave.

**Maximum Length of Leave.** 12 weeks in a 12 month period. A woman who takes leave because of a pregnancy-related disability may take an additional 12 weeks for another purpose. An employee who takes 12 weeks of parental leave may take an additional 12 weeks of sick child leave.

**Paid Leave.** State does not require paid leave.

**Acceptable Reasons for Leave.** For family leave, care for serious condition of employee, spouse, child, parent, in-law for family leave; for parental leave, birth/adoption of child.

**Employment Guarantees After Leave.** Employee is entitled to reinstatement in the position held prior to the leave or equivalent position.

**Use of Vacation or Other Time-Off Benefits.** Employer may require employee to use accrued benefits (e.g., sick leave, vacation) during parental leave; employee may opt to use accrued benefits to extend family leave.

**Certification Required.** Employer may require certification of illness if leave is taken to care for ill child, spouse, parent, or in-law.

**Effect of Leave on Other Benefits** (e.g., health, pension, retirement). Benefits cease during leave unless employer is obligated to continue benefits under a separate contract.

**Relationship of Family and Medical Leave Requirements to Pregnancy Disability Leave.** Pregnancy leave is treated separately; the same reinstatement rights to employment under family leave and medical provisions are afforded for pregnancy leave.

**Effect on Seniority Accrual During Leave.** Seniority benefits do not accrue while on leave.

**Minimum Requirements for Notification to Employer.** 30 days' written notice is required. In emergency situations, verbal or written notice within 24 hours of commencement of leave is required.

**Conditions for Denial of a Request for Leave.** For family leave, when family member's health condition is not life threatening or terminal, request for leave may be denied if another family member is available to provide care; for parental leave, when husband and wife are working for same employer and their combined leave would exceed 12 weeks, employer may refuse request for both to take leave at the same time.

**Citations to Authority.** Or. Rev. Stat. §§ 659.389, 659.470–659.494.

## RHODE ISLAND

**Effective Date.** Currently effective.

**Employers Subject to Leave Laws.** Employers with at least 50 employees.

**Criteria for Eligibility.** Employee must be employed for at least 30 hours per week for at least 12 consecutive months with the same employer.

**Maximum Length of Leave.** 13 weeks in any 2 calendar years.

**Paid Leave.** If employer provides paid leave for less than the required 13 weeks, the balance of the required leave may be unpaid.

**Acceptable Reasons for Leave.** Birth/adoption of child; serious illness of child, parent, spouse, mother-in-law, father-in-law, or employee.

**Employment Guarantees After Leave.** Employee is entitled to reinstatement in the position held prior to the leave or an equivalent position.

**Use of Vacation or Other Time-Off Benefits.** State has no statutory requirements.

**Certification Required.** Employer may require certification of illness.

**Effect of Leave on Other Benefits** (e.g., health, pension, retirement). Health benefits continue in effect during leave; no loss of benefits accrued during leave.

**Relationship of Family and Medical Leave Requirements to Pregnancy Disability Leave.** No separate provisions exist for pregnancy disability leave.

**Effect on Seniority Accrual During Leave.** Seniority benefits accrue during leave.

**Minimum Requirements for Notification to Employer.** At least 30 days' notice is required, except for emergencies.

**Conditions for Denial of a Request for Leave.** State has no statutory requirements.

**Citations to Authority.** R.I. Gen. Laws §§ 28-48-1–28-48-4, 28-48-11.

## SOUTH CAROLINA

**Effective Date.** Currently effective.

**Employers Subject to Leave Laws.** State employers.

**Criteria for Eligibility.** Full-time state employees with accrued sick leave. Leave accrues at the rate of 15 days per year, and up to 180 days may be carried over to the next year.

**Maximum Length of Leave.** Statutory limits of 8 days to care for family member, 6 weeks for adoption of child.

**Paid Leave.** State requires paid leave.

**Acceptable Reasons for Leave.** Sickness of employee or family member; adoption of child where employee is person primarily responsible for child's care.

**Employment Guarantees After Leave.** State has no statutory requirements.

**Use of Vacation or Other Time-Off Benefits.** State has no statutory requirements.

**Certification Required.** State has no statutory requirements.

**Effect of Leave on Other Benefits** (e.g., health, pension, retirement). State has no statutory requirements.

**Relationship of Family and Medical Leave Requirements to Pregnancy Disability Leave.** No separate provisions exist for pregnancy disability leave.

**Effect on Seniority Accrual During Leave.** State has no statutory provisions.

**Minimum Requirements for Notification to Employer.** State has no statutory requirements.

**Conditions for Denial of a Request for Leave.** State has no statutory requirements.

**Citations to Authority.** S.C. Code Ann. §§ 8-11-40, 8-11-155.

**SOUTH DAKOTA**

**Effective Date.** Currently effective.

**Employers Subject to Leave Laws.** State employers.

**Criteria for Eligibility.** For personal leave, all state employees. For family and medical leave, employment with the state for 1 year and 1,250 hours.

**Maximum Length of Leave.** 40 hours per year for personal leave, 12 weeks per year for family and medical leave.

**Paid Leave.** For personal leave, employee must first use accrued sick leave. For family and medical leave, employee may use paid leave.

**Acceptable Reasons for Leave.** For personal leave, death or illness of immediate family member. For family and medical leave, birth, adoption or care of newborn, or serious health condition of employee, spouse, child, or parent.

**Employment Guarantees After Leave.** No provision, reinstatement implied.

**Use of Vacation or Other Time-Off Benefits.** Employee must use accrued sick leave for personal leave. For family and medical leave, employee may use sick leave, vacation leave, personal leave, or leave without pay.

**Certification Required.** State has no statutory requirements.

**Effect of Leave on Other Benefits.** State has no statutory requirements.

**Relationship of Family and Medical Leave Requirements to Pregnancy Disability Leave.** State has no statutory requirements.

**Effect on Seniority Accrual During Leave.** State has no statutory requirements.

**Minimum Requirements for Notification to Employer.** State has no statutory requirements.

**Conditions for a Denial of a Request for Leave.** State has no statutory requirements.

**Citations to Authority.** S.D. Reg. 55:01:22:02 *et seq.*

**TENNESSEE**

**Effective Date.** Currently effective.

**Employers Subject to Leave Laws.** Employers with 100 or more employees.

**Criteria for Eligibility.** Mothers of newborn or adopted children who have been employed full-time for 12 consecutive months.

**Maximum Length of Leave.** 4 months; can be extended with use of accrued paid time off.

**Paid Leave.** Employer may provide paid or unpaid leave, or a combination, at its discretion.

**Acceptable Reasons for Leave.** Birth/adoption of child; pregnancy.

**Employment Guarantees After Leave.** Employee is entitled to reinstatement in the position held prior to the leave or equivalent position if employee gives 3 months' notice unless a medical emergency prevents the employee from giving 3 months' notice. Failure to reinstate is acceptable if employee held a job position so unique that employer cannot fill the position temporarily after reasonable efforts.

**Use of Vacation or Other Time-Off Benefits.** State has no statutory requirements.

**Certification Required.** State has no statutory requirements.

**Effect of Leave on Other Benefits** (e.g., health, pension, retirement). Employer's obligation to pay for benefits ceases during leave, unless other on-leave employees receive benefits.

**Relationship of Family and Medical Leave Requirements to Pregnancy Disability Leave.** No separate provisions exist for pregnancy disability leave.

**Effect on Seniority Accrual During Leave.** Seniority benefits do not accrue during leave.

**Minimum Requirements for Notification to Employer.** Except in an emergency, 3 months' notice is required, plus declaration of intent to return to work.

**Conditions for Denial of a Request for Leave.** State has no conditions for denial of leave.

**Citations to Authority.** Tenn. Code Ann. § 4-21-408.

## TEXAS

**Effective Date.** Currently effective.

**Employers Subject to Leave Laws.** State employers.

**Criteria for Eligibility.** State employees.

**Maximum Length of Leave.** 6 weeks for parental leave; amount accrued for sick leave (sick leave accrues at the rate of 8 hours per month).

**Paid Leave.** Parental leave is unpaid; sick leave is paid.

**Acceptable Reasons for Leave.** Parental leave for birth/adoption of a child and for foster-child meetings; sick leave for illness of employee/family member and for disability due to pregnancy.

**Employment Guarantees After Leave.** State has no statutory requirements.

**Use of Vacation or Other Time-Off Benefits.** State has no statutory requirements.

**Certification Required.** State has no statutory requirements.

**Effect of Leave on Other Benefits** (e.g., health, pension, retirement). State has no statutory requirements.

**Relationship of Family and Medical Leave Requirements to Pregnancy Disability Leave.** No separate provisions exist for pregnancy disability leave.

**Effect on Seniority Accrual During Leave.** State has no statutory requirements.

**Minimum Requirements for Notification to Employer.** State has no statutory requirements.

**Condition for Denial of a Request for Leave.** State has no statutory requirements.

**Citations to Authority.** Tex. Gov. Code §§ 661.001 *et seq.*

**Note.** Public employees in Texas also have access to a aick leave pool. Employees who contribute to the pool may take time off for their own illness or injury or illness/injury of an immediate family member. A statement from the treating physician is required. Employees may withdraw up to one third of the time accrued in the pool or 90 days, whichever is less. Tex. Gov. Code § 661.006.

## UTAH

**Effective Date.** Currently effective.

**Employers Subject to Leave Laws.** All state agencies.

**Criteria for Eligibility.** Employee must be employed for at least 2 full pay periods (full-time employees) or for at least 40 hours per pay period (part-time employees).

**Maximum Length of Leave.** Half-time status up to 6 weeks; temporary disability up to 12 months.

**Paid Leave.** Paid leave is required for half-time leave; paid leave is not required for long-term leave.

**Acceptable Reasons for Leave.** Maternity/adoption of child or to care for spouse or dependents.

**Employment Guarantees After Leave.** Employee is entitled to reinstatement in a position with the same pay and seniority as the position held prior to the leave.

**Use of Vacation or Other Time-Off Benefits.** Employees may use sick leave or other annual benefits to offset or extend the leave benefits.

**Certification Required.** Employer may require certification of illness if leave is taken to care for children or spouse.

**Effect of Leave on Other Benefits** (e.g., health, pension, retirement). Sick leave accrues at 4 hours per pay period without limit; employee may pay premiums for continued health benefits.

**Relationship of Family and Medical Leave Requirements to Pregnancy Disability Leave.** Pregnancy leave is treated separately; length of maternity leave should be consistent with leave allowed for other temporary disability.

**Effect on Seniority Accrual During Leave.** Seniority benefits do not accrue during leave.

**Minimum Requirements for Notification to Employer.** Employee must apply for leave in writing.

**Conditions for Denial of a Request for Leave.** Employee must plan to return to work to get leave approved; also, leave must be beneficial to both the employee and the state.

**Citations to Authority.** Utah Admin. R. 468-8-5.3, 468-8-5.9.

## VERMONT

**Effective Date.** Currently effective.

**Employers Subject to Leave Laws.** For parental leave, employers with 10 or more employees; for family leave, employers with 15 or more employees.

**Criteria for Eligibility.** Employee must be employed an average of 30 hours per week for at least 12 months.

**Maximum Length of Leave.** 12 weeks of leave in any 12-month period.

**Paid Leave.** State does not require paid leave.

**Acceptable Reasons for Leave.** For family leave, illness of employee or to care for ill child, parent, parent-in-law, or spouse; for parental leave, birth/adoption of child.

**Employment Guarantees After Leave.** Employee is entitled to reinstatement in the position held prior to the leave or equivalent position, unless a layoff occurring during the leave would have affected the employee, or economic circumstances required hiring of permanent replacement because the job position was unique.

**Use of Vacation or Other Time-Off Benefits.** Employer may require employee to use up to 6 weeks of accrued sick leave or vacation time as part of the leave.

**Certification Required.** Employer may require certification if leave is taken for employee illness or to care for serious illness of family member.

**Effect of Leave on Other Benefits** (e.g., health, pension, retirement). All benefits continue while on leave, but employee may be required to pay premiums for benefits.

**Relationship of Family and Medical Leave Requirements to Pregnancy Disability Leave.** No separate provisions exist for pregnancy disability leave.

**Effect on Seniority Accrual During Leave.** Seniority benefits do not accrue during leave.

**Minimum Requirements for Notification to Employer.** Reasonable notice of departure and duration of leave is required.

**Conditions for Denial of a Request for Leave.** State has no conditions for denial of leave.

**Citations to Authority.** Vt. Stat. Ann. tit. 21 §§ 470–472a.

**Note.** Employees in Vermont may also take up to 24 hours of unpaid leave per year to attend school activities of a child or to take a child or parent to a medical appointment. Seven days' notice is required, except in the case of an emergency. An employee may use vacation or personal leave first. Vt. Stat. Ann. tit. 21, § 472a.

## WASHINGTON

**Effective Date.** Currently effective.

**Employers Subject to Leave Laws.** Private employers with 100 or more employees; all state agencies.

**Criteria for Eligibility.** Employee must be employed for at least 35 hours per week for prior 12 months.

**Maximum Length of Leave.** 12 weeks in a 24-month period.

**Paid Leave.** State does not require paid leave.

**Acceptable Reasons for Leave.** Birth/adoption of child; care for child under age 18 with terminal illness.

**Employment Guarantees After Leave.** Employee is entitled to reinstatement in the position held prior to the leave or equivalent position, unless employer's business conditions have changed significantly.

**Use of Vacation or Other Time-Off Benefits.** Employee may use sick leave for own illness and may use accrued vacation and sick benefits to extend the leave.

**Certification Required.** Employer may require certification of terminal illness or of premature birth or mother's illness.

**Effect of Leave on Other Benefits** (e.g., health, pension, retirement). All benefits continue while on leave, but employee may be required to pay for medical and dental benefits.

**Relationship of Family and Medical Leave Requirements to Pregnancy Disability Leave.** Family leave supplements any leave allowed for sickness or temporary disability due to pregnancy.

**Effect on Seniority Accrual During Leave.** Seniority benefits do not accrue during leave.

**Minimum Requirements for Notification to Employer.** 30 days' notice, if possible, prior to birth/adoption of child is required; 14 days' prior notice for child care is required.

**Conditions for Denial of a Request for Leave.** Leave may be denied or limited for up to 10 percent of the workforce or for key personnel. If both spouses work for the same employer, total leave time for the couple may be limited to 12 weeks in a 24-month period.

**Citations to Authority.** Wash. Rev. Code §§ 49.78.010–49.78.100, 49.78.110, 48.78.130, 49.78.140, 49.78.180–49.78.200.

**Note.** Recent amendment provides that this law will not be enforced while the federal act provides equal or greater leave, except § 49.78.070(1)(b), which requires reinstatement within 20 miles of former workplace. Wash. Rev. Code § 48.78.005.

## WEST VIRGINIA

**Effective Date.** Currently effective.

**Employers Subject to Leave Laws.** State agencies and county boards, divisions, and any units of the state and county boards of education.

**Criteria for Eligibility.** Employee must have permanent status working for pay at least 12 consecutive weeks.

**Citations to Authority.** 12 weeks in any 12-month period.

**Paid Leave.** State does not require paid leave.

**Acceptable Reasons for Leave.** Birth/adoption of child; illness of spouse, child, parent, or other dependent.

**Employment Guarantees After Leave.** Employee is entitled to reinstatement in the same position held prior to leave; employer may hire a temporary replacement during leave.

**Use of Vacation or Other Time-Off Benefits.** Employer may require that employee first use all other accrued annual and personal benefits prior to receiving the leave benefits. Employee may also choose to use other accrued leaves first.

**Certification Required.** Employer may require certification of illness if leave is taken to care for ill family member or dependent.

**Effect of Leave on Other Benefits** (e.g., health, pension, retirement). Health benefits continue during leave, but employee must pay premiums.

**Relationship of Family and Medical Leave Requirements to Pregnancy Disability Leave.** No separate provisions exist for pregnancy disability leave.

**Effect on Seniority Accrual During Leave.** Seniority does not accrue during leave.

**Minimum Requirements for Notification to Employer.** 2 weeks' written notice, if possible, is required.

**Conditions for Denial of a Request for Leave.** State has no conditions for denial of leave.

**Citations to Authority.** W. Va. Code Ann. §§ 21-5D-1 *et seq.*; *Hudok v. Board of Education of Randolph County,* 415 S.E.2d. 897 (W. Va. 1992).

## WISCONSIN

**Effective Date.** Currently effective.

**Employers Subject to Leave Laws.** Employers with 50 or more employees.

**Criteria for Eligibility.** Employee must be employed for more than 1 year and must have worked 1,000 hours in 52 weeks prior to leave.

**Maximum Length of Leave.** 8 weeks in a 12-month period; exact length depends on reason for leave. Up to 6 weeks for birth/adoption of child or care of foster child, 2 weeks for care of child/spouse/parent, and 2 weeks for employee illness.

**Paid Leave.** State does not require paid leave.

**Acceptable Reasons for Leave.** Birth/adoption of child or care of foster or treatment foster child; care for family member; employee's own illness.

**Employment Guarantees After Leave.** Employee is entitled to reinstatement in the position held prior to the leave or equivalent position.

**Use of Vacation or Other Time-Off Benefits.** Sick leave must be used first for employee illness; employee may substitute other benefits (e.g., vacation, sick leave) for the leave, but this will not extend the leave benefits.

**Certification Required.** Employer may require certification if leave is taken for employee illness or to care for ill family member.

**Effect of Leave on Other Benefits** (e.g., health, pension, retirement). Health care benefits continue during leave.

**Relationship of Family and Medical Leave Requirements to Pregnancy Disability Leave.** No separate provisions exist for pregnancy disability leave.

**Effect on Seniority Accrual During Leave.** Seniority does not accrue during leave.

**Minimum Requirements for Notification to Employer.** Prior notice, if possible, is required.

**Conditions for Denial of a Request for Leave.** Leave may be denied if employee fails to notify properly or to provide requested certification (except when leave involves emergency health care).

**Citations to Authority.** Wis. Stat. Ann. § 103.10.

# § 5.9 Legal Expenses Insurance

Thirty-two states have statutes authorizing the issuance of legal expenses insurance. These statutes address legal expenses insurance in a variety of ways. Many statutes provide for the establishment and operation of such insurance programs with a great deal of specificity, while other statutes reference state laws concerning life or casualty insurance as a guide to insurance regulation in general. Some states, such as Minnesota, merely list legal expenses insurance as a valid type of insurance coverage, with no accompanying regulation.

States define what constitutes legal expenses insurance differently. Several states require that the beneficiary of a legal expenses insurance policy be given an unqualified choice of attorney; however, many states grant insurers great latitude in selecting an attorney for the beneficiary. Illinois, Indiana, Michigan, New Hampshire, Oklahoma, and Rhode Island require that policies addressing group coverage must include a certain number of employees. Additionally, most statutes exempt legal services provided by unions or employee organizations from compliance with the statute; but some statutes state that union exemptions apply only if the services rendered concern simple legal matters discussed on an informal basis.

Though no state mandates any minimum level of benefits, several states limit the breadth of legal expenses insurance policy coverage. For example, sixteen states do not permit legal expenses insurance to include reimbursement for legal services incidental to other insurance coverages, and two states disallow such insurance to cover fines, judgments, penalties, or assessments. Also, in Mississippi, legal expenses insurance may not cover any service related to a tort action.

ERISA's definition of an employee welfare benefit plan includes any plan, fund, or program that is maintained for the purpose of providing "prepaid legal services." Accordingly, consideration should be given to the applicability of ERISA's preemption provision to state legal expenses insurance laws.

The state regulations concerning legal expenses insurance discussed above are set out in Table 5.9-1.

# Table 5.9-1

## LEGAL EXPENSES INSURANCE PROVISIONS

(See also text at § 5.9.)

**KEY:** A "—" indicates that the state has no statutory requirements.

| | *Statute Provides for the Authorization of Legal Expenses, Generally* | *Services Provided by Labor Unions or Other Voluntary Employee Organizations to Members Are Not Considered Legal Expenses Insurance* | *Is Group Coverage Specifically Authorized by Statute?* | *Must Legal Expenses Insurance Policies Address Coverage of Dependents?* | *Must Beneficiary Be Given Choice of Attorney?* | *Statute Prohibits Inclusion of Reimbursement for Legal Services Incidental to Other Insurance Coverage* | *Other Provisions* | *Citations to Authority* |
|---|---|---|---|---|---|---|---|---|
| AL | Yes. | Yes. | Yes. | — | Insurer may provide attorney, but policy must provide alternative to beneficiary if insurer's attorney cannot provide services. | Yes. | — | Ala. Code §§ 27-43-3, 27-43-4, 27-43-10. |
| AK | — | — | — | — | — | — | — | — |
| AZ | Yes. | Yes. | Yes. | — | Yes (at beneficiary's expense, unless policy provides otherwise). | — | — | Ariz. Rev. Stat. Ann. §§ 20-1097.01, 20-1097.04. |
| AR | Yes. | Yes. | Yes. | — | Yes (only to extent that costs are reasonably equivalent to those of attorney selected by insurer). | Yes. | — | Ark. Code Ann. §§ 23-91-203, 23-91-210. |
| CA | Yes. | — | Yes. | — | — | — | — | Cal. Ins. Code § 12121. |
| CO | — | — | — | — | — | — | — | — |

| | | | | | | | | |
|---|---|---|---|---|---|---|---|---|
| CT | Yes. | — | Yes (concerning certain nonprofit legal service companies). | Yes (concerning certain nonprofit legal service companies). | Yes, insurer may reasonably differentiate between the amount of services available from an attorney of beneficiary's choice as compared to an attorney of the insurer. | — | Legal expenses insurance is not limited to court costs or attorneys' fees. | Conn. Gen. Stat. Ann. §§ 38a-230, 38a-233, 38a-235, 38a-243. |
| DE | — | — | — | — | — | — | — | — |
| DC | — | — | — | — | — | — | — | — |
| FL | Yes. | Yes. | Yes. | — | Insurer may provide attorney, but policy must provide alternative to beneficiary if insurer's attorney cannot provide services. | Yes. | — | Fla. Stat. Ann. §§ 642.015, 642.017, 642.025. |
| GA | Yes. | — | Yes, but no member of the group is bound without written consent. | Yes. | Yes. | — | Legal expenses insurance shall not include fines, penalties, judgments, or assessments. | Ga. Code Ann. §§ 33-35-2, 33-35-8. |
| HI | Yes. | — | Yes. | Yes. | — | — | — | Haw. Rev. Stat. §§ 488-1, 488-3. |
| ID | — | — | — | — | — | — | — | — |
| IL | Yes. | — | Yes (minimum 10 employees). | — | Yes. | — | — | 215 Ill. Comp. Stat. Ann. 5/900. |
| IN | Yes. | — | Yes (minimum 10 employees). | — | — | — | — | Ind. Code § 27-7-8-3. |
| IA | Yes. | Yes, but only concerning simple matters discussed on an informal basis. | Yes. | — | — | Yes. | — | Iowa Code Ann. §§ 523F.2, 523F.5. |
| KS | Yes. | Yes. | — | — | — | — | — | Kan. Stat. Ann. § 40-4201. |
| KY | — | — | — | — | — | — | — | — |
| LA | Yes. | — | Yes. | — | — | — | Legal expenses insurance is not limited to court costs or attorneys' fees. | La. Rev. Stat. Ann. § 22:221. |

*(Table continues.)*

# Table 5.9-1 *(cont'd)*

## LEGAL EXPENSES INSURANCE PROVISIONS

(See also text at § 5.9.)

**KEY:** A "—" indicates that the state has no statutory requirements.

| | *Statute Provides for the Authorization of Legal Expenses, Generally* | *Services Provided by Labor Unions or Other Voluntary Employee Organizations to Members Are Not Considered Legal Expenses Insurance* | *Is Group Coverage Specifically Authorized by Statute?* | *Must Legal Expenses Insurance Policies Address Coverage of Dependents?* | *Must Beneficiary Be Given Choice of Attorney?* | *Statute Prohibits Inclusion of Reimbursement for Legal Services Incidental to Other Insurance Coverage* | *Other Provisions* | *Citations to Authority* |
|---|---|---|---|---|---|---|---|---|
| ME | Yes. | Yes. | Yes. | — | Yes. | Yes. | — | Me. Rev. Stat. Ann. tit. 24A, §§ 2881, 2884, 2886. |
| MD | — | — | — | — | — | — | — | — |
| MA | Yes. | — | Yes. | — | Yes, if beneficiary notifies insurer in writing. | — | — | Mass. Gen. Laws Ann. ch. 176H, §§ 2, 7. |
| MI | Yes. | — | Yes (minimum 5 employees). | — | — | — | — | Mich. Stat. Ann. § 24.12702. |
| MN | Yes. | — | — | — | — | — | — | Minn. Stat. Ann. § 60A.06. |
| MS | Yes. | — | Yes. | Yes. | Yes. | — | Legal expenses insurance shall not include fines, penalties, judgments, or assessments. Nor shall legal expenses insurance include the costs of any legal services concerning a tort action. | Miss. Code Ann. §§ 83-49-5, 83-49-13. |
| MO | Yes. | Yes. | — | — | — | — | — | Mo. Rev. Stat. § 379.901. |

| | | | | | | | | |
|---|---|---|---|---|---|---|---|---|
| MT | — | — | — | — | — | — | — | — |
| NE | Yes. | Yes. | Yes. | — | — | Yes. | — | Neb. Rev. Stat. §§ 44-3302, 44-3303, 44-3305. |
| NV | — | — | — | — | — | — | — | — |
| NH | Yes. | — | Yes (minimum 10 employees). | — | Yes. | Yes. | — | N.H. Rev. Stat. Ann. §§ 415-C:2, 415-C:3. |
| NJ | Yes. | Yes. | Yes. | — | — | Yes. | — | N.J. Rev. Stat. §§ 17:46C-3, 17:46C-6. |
| NM | — | — | — | — | — | — | — | — |
| NY | Yes, under experimental project. | — | — | — | Yes. | — | — | N.Y. Ins. Law § 1116. |
| NC | — | — | — | — | — | — | — | — |
| ND | Yes. | Yes, but only concerning simple matters discussed on an informal basis. | — | — | — | — | Statute prohibits inclusion of fines, penalties, judgments, or assessments. | N.D. Cent. Code §§ 26.1-19-02, 26.1-19-03. |
| OH | — | — | — | — | — | — | — | — |
| OK | Yes, for public employees (minimum 500 employees). | — | — | — | — | — | — | Okla. Stat. tit. 62, § 7.10. |
| OR | — | — | — | — | — | — | — | — |
| PA | — | — | — | — | — | — | — | — |
| RI | Yes. | — | Yes (minimum 10 employees). | — | Yes. | Yes. | — | R.I. Gen. Laws §§ 27-4.1-4, 27-4.1-5. |
| SC | Yes. | — | — | — | Yes. | — | — | S.C. Code Ann. §§ 38-75-510, 38-75-520. |
| SD | Yes. | Yes. | Yes. | — | Insurer may provide attorney, but policy must provide alternative to beneficiary if insurer's attorney cannot provide services. | Yes. | — | S.D. Codified Laws §§ 58-42-1, 58-42-2, 58-42-9. |
| TN | Yes. | Yes. | Yes. | — | — | Yes. | — | Tenn. Code Ann. §§ 56-43-103, 56-43-106. |

*(Table continues.)*

# Table 5.9-1 *(cont'd)*

## LEGAL EXPENSES INSURANCE PROVISIONS

(See also text at § 5.9.)

**KEY:** A "—" indicates that the state has no statutory requirements.

| | *Statute Provides for the Authorization of Legal Expenses, Generally* | *Services Provided by Labor Unions or Other Voluntary Employee Organizations to Members Are Not Considered Legal Expenses Insurance* | *Is Group Coverage Specifically Authorized by Statute?* | *Must Legal Expenses Insurance Policies Address Coverage of Dependents?* | *Must Beneficiary Be Given Choice of Attorney?* | *Statute Prohibits Inclusion of Reimbursement for Legal Services Incidental to Other Insurance Coverage* | *Other Provisions* | *Citations to Authority* |
|---|---|---|---|---|---|---|---|---|
| TX | Yes. | — | — | — | — | — | — | Tex. Ins. Code Ann. art. 3.95-4. |
| UT | Yes. | — | Yes. | — | Insurer may provide attorney, but policy must provide alternative to beneficiary if insurer's attorney cannot provide services. | — | — | Utah Code Ann. § 31A-22-1102. |
| VT | — | — | — | — | — | — | — | — |
| VA | Yes. | — | — | — | — | — | — | Va. Code Ann. § 38.2-127. |
| WA | — | — | — | — | — | — | — | — |
| WV | — | — | — | — | — | — | — | — |
| WI | — | — | — | — | — | — | — | — |
| WY | — | — | — | — | — | — | — | — |

## § 5.10 Dental Insurance

Some states regulate dental insurance, although generally not to the same degree that health insurance is regulated. For example, unlike state regulation of health insurance, states usually do not mandate that specific dental benefits be provided. Table 5.10-1 provides information on which states specifically regulate dental insurance and other types of dental care plans. In many cases, different types of dental insurance are subject to different regulations, much the same way as basic group health insurance is regulated separately from health maintenance organization health insurance. Even if a state does not specifically provide for separate regulation of dental insurance, however, insurers will be subject to general state insurance laws.

# Table 5.10-1
## STATE REGULATION OF DENTAL INSURANCE AND OTHER DENTAL COVERAGE PLANS

(See also text at § 5.10.)

**KEY:** A "—" indicates that the state has no statutory requirements.

| | *Regulation of Dental Benefits* | *Citations to Authority* |
|---|---|---|
| AL | State regulates dental insurance; however, the state statute was recently held to be preempted by ERISA in *Blue Cross & Blue Shield v. Nielson,* 917 F. Supp. 1532 (N.D. Ala. 1996). | Ala. Code §§ 27-19A-1–27-19A-11. |
| AK | State mandates that dental insurers must offer dental coverage at least equal to that provided under the public employees' retirement system. | Alaska Stat. § 21.42.385. |
| AZ | State regulates prepaid dental plans. | Ariz. Rev. Stat. Ann. §§ 20-1001–20-1019. A.A.C. R9-23-401 *et seq.* |
| AR | — | — |
| CA | State regulates dental insurance. | Cal. Ins. Code § 742.1. |
| CO | State regulates dental insurance and prepaid dental plans. | Colo. Rev. Stat. Ann. §§ 10-16-104, 10-16-501–10-16-512. |
| CT | State regulates dental insurance. | Conn. Gen. Stat. Ann. §§ 38a-577–38a-589. |
| DE | State regulates dental plans. | Del. Code Ann. tit. 18, §§ 3801–3823. |
| DC | — | — |
| FL | State regulates dental insurance. | Fla. Stat. Ann. § 625.6577. |
| GA | — | — |
| HI | State regulates prepaid dental insurance plans. | Haw. Rev. Stat. Ann. §§ 448D-1–448D-2. |
| ID | State regulates dental insurance. | Idaho Code § 54-3318. |
| IL | State regulates dental insurance and dental service plan corporations. | 215 Ill. Comp. Stat. Ann. § 110/15. |
| IN | — | — |
| IA | — | — |
| KS | State regulates prepaid dental plans. | Kan. Stat. Ann. §§ 40-4201–40-4211. |
| KY | State regulates prepaid dental plan organizations. | Ky. Rev. Stat. Ann. § 304.5-160. |
| LA | State regulates dental insurance. | La. Rev. Stat. Ann. §§ 22:213.5, 22:1510 *et seq.* |

| | | |
|---|---|---|
| ME | — | — |
| MD | State regulates dental plan organizations. | Md. Ins. Code § 14-401 *et seq.* |
| MA | State regulates dental service corporations and other dental insurance. | Mass. Gen. Laws Ann. ch. 175, § 110K, ch. 176E, §§ 1 *et seq.* |
| MI | State regulates dental care corporations. | Mich. Stat. Ann. §§ 24.650(9) *et seq.* |
| MN | State regulates dental insurance. | Minn. Stat. Ann. § 62A.136. |
| MS | State regulates dental care insurance and dental service corporations. | Miss. Code Ann. §§ 83-43-1, 83-51-1. |
| MO | State regulates prepaid dental plans and multiple employer self-insured plans. | Mo. Ann. Stat. §§ 354.700, 376.1000. |
| MT | — | — |
| NE | State regulates prepaid dental plans. | Neb. Rev. Stat. §§ 44-3801–44-3826. |
| NV | State regulates dental insurance plans. | Nev. Rev. Stat. §§ 679B.152, 695D.101–695D.310. |
| NH | — | — |
| NJ | State regulates dental plan organizations and dental service corporations. | N.J. Rev. Stat. §§ 17:48C-1, 17:48D-1. |
| NM | State regulates prepaid dental plans. | N.M. Stat. Ann. §§ 59A-48-1–59A-48-9. |
| NY | — | — |
| NC | — | — |
| ND | — | — |
| OH | State regulates dental service corporations. | Ohio Rev. Code Ann. § 1740.01. |
| OK | State regulates dental service corporations. | Okla. Stat. Ann. tit. 36, §§ 2671–2687. |
| OR | — | — |
| PA | — | — |
| RI | — | — |
| SC | State regulates HMO coverage of dental insurance. | S.C. Code Ann. § 38-33-20. |
| SD | — | — |
| TN | State regulates dental service plan corporations. | Tenn. Code Ann. § 56-30-101. |
| TX | — | — |
| UT | — | — |
| VT | — | — |
| VA | State regulates dental service plans. | Va. Code Ann. § 38.2-4500. |
| WA | State regulates dental insurance and mandates that employers of more than 25 employees who offer dental plans that limit providers must also offer a plan under which employees may choose providers and pay an equal portion of the premium for such coverage. | Wash. Rev. Code Ann. §§ 48.42.010, 49.64.040. |

*(Table continues.)*

## **Table 5.10-1** *(cont'd)*
## STATE REGULATION OF DENTAL INSURANCE AND OTHER DENTAL COVERAGE PLANS

(See also text at § 5.10.)

**KEY:** A "—" indicates that the state has no statutory requirements.

| | *Regulation of Dental Benefits* | *Citations to Authority* |
|---|---|---|
| WV | State regulates dental insurance provided by hospital or medical service corporations. | W. Va. Code Ann. § 33-24-1. |
| WI | — | — |
| WY | — | — |

# 6 Unemployment Compensation

*Tables in Part 6 cover employers subject to state unemployment compensation laws, unemployment disqualifications and exemptions, reestablishment of eligibility for unemployment insurance, benefits eligibility criteria and payouts, and employer contributions and recordkeeping requirements.*

## § 6.1 Overview: Federal-State Collaboration in Administering and Funding Unemployment Compensation

The state and federal governments participate in administering this country's unemployment insurance program, which covers about 97 percent of all wage and salary workers. The program is financed through taxes or "contributions" paid by employers to the federal government and the states. The federal government uses these monies to finance all federal and state administrative costs of the program; state-collected monies are used to pay weekly cash benefits, for limited periods, to workers who have become unemployed under certain conditions.

The Federal Unemployment Tax Act provides for a payroll tax, which every employer is required to pay and which represents an excise tax of 6.2 percent of the total wages paid to employees during the year. An employer is defined as any person or entity paying wages of $1,500 or more in any quarter in the current or preceding calendar year, or employing at least one person for a portion of a day in each of 20 different weeks during the current or preceding calendar year. The applicability of this Act to certain types of employers, such as agricultural and domestic service employers, is limited. Wages are defined as the total remuneration for employment, including employee benefits, less contributions to certain employee benefit plans, such as disability payments. The Federal Unemployment Tax Act also permits employers to offset the amount of the payroll tax by paying under an approved state unemployment compensation program.

Employers in each of the 50 states and the District of Columbia administer the state's self-contained unemployment program. The tax structure, qualifying requirements, benefits levels, and disqualification criteria are established by each state to conform with federal requirements.

The federal law further requires that:

- State-collected taxes be deposited immediately into the U.S. Treasury;
- Each state maintain an account in the Unemployment Trust Fund; and
- Each state allow employers reduced rates based on their unemployment experience.

Federal law also expressly requires state coverage of nonprofit organizations and governmental entities.

# § 6.2 Employers Subject to State Unemployment Compensation Laws

Table 6.2-1 lists the following five categories of employers subject to unemployment compensation laws:

**General.** Employers with quarterly payrolls of $1,500 or more in the current or preceding year or with at least one worker on at least one day in each of 20 weeks during the current or preceding calendar year.

**Agricultural.** Employers that paid wages in cash of $20,000 or more for agricultural labor in any quarter in the current or preceding calendar year or that employed 10 or more workers on at least one day in each of 20 different weeks in the current or preceding calendar year.

**Domestic.** Private home owners, local college clubs, or local chapters of a college fraternity or sorority paying wages in cash of $1,000 or more for domestic service during any quarter in the current or preceding calendar year.

**Nonprofit.** Tax-exempt nonprofit organizations that employed four or more persons for a portion of at least one day in each of 20 different weeks in the current or preceding calendar year. Churches and other religious organizations are normally exempt from unemployment compensation law.

**State Government.** Most state governmental entities including political subdivisions in many states.

# Table 6.2-1
## EMPLOYERS SUBJECT TO STATE UNEMPLOYMENT COMPENSATION LAWS

(See also text at § 6.2.)

| | *General* | *Agricultural* | *Domestic* | *Nonprofit* | *State Government* | *Citations to Authority* |
|---|---|---|---|---|---|---|
| AL | Yes. | Yes. | Yes. | Yes. | Yes. | Ala. Code §§ 25-4-8, 25-4-10. |
| AK | Any employer of 1 or more persons. | Yes. | Yes. | Yes. | Yes. | Alaska Stat. §§ 23.20.520, 23.20.525. |
| AZ | Yes. | Yes. | Yes. | Yes. | Yes. | Ariz. Rev. Stat. Ann. §§ 23-613, 23-615, 23-615.0. |
| AR | Any employer of 1 or more persons for at least 10 days in a calendar year, regardless of whether the days are consecutive. | Yes. | Yes. | Any employer of 1 or more persons for at least 10 days in a calendar year, regardless of whether the days are consecutive. | Yes. | Ark. Code Ann. §§ 11-10-208–11-10-210, 11-10-404, 11-10-713. |
| CA | Any employer of 1 or more persons if wages exceed $100 in any calendar quarter. | Any employer of 1 or more persons if wages exceed $100 in any calendar quarter. | Any employer who paid $1,000 or more in any calendar quarter. | Any employer of 1 or more persons. | Yes. | Cal. Unemp. Ins. Code §§ 605, 629, 634.5, 639, 675, 676. |
| CO | Any employer of 1 or more persons. | Yes. | Yes. | Yes. | Yes. | Colo. Rev. Stat. §§ 8-70-103, 8-70-109, 8-70-113, 8-70-114, 8-70-118, 8-70-120, 8-70-121. |
| CT | Yes. | Yes. | Yes. | Any employer of 1 or more persons in any 13 weeks of any calendar year. | Yes. | Conn. Gen. Stat. Ann. § 31-222. |
| DE | Yes. | Yes. | Yes. | Yes. | Yes. | Del. Code Ann. tit. 19, § 3302. |
| DC | Any employer of 1 or more persons. | Any employer of 1 or more persons. | Any employer who pays $500 in any calendar quarter. | Any employer of 1 or more persons. | Yes. | D.C. Code Ann. § 46-101. |
| FL | Yes. | Any employer of 5 or more employees on at least 1 day in each of 20 different weeks in the current or preceding calendar year or any employer who paid wages in cash of $10,000 or more in any quarter in the current or preceding calendar year. | Yes. | Yes. | Yes. | Fla. Stat. Ann. § 443.036. |

| | | | | | | |
|---|---|---|---|---|---|---|
| GA | Any employer of 1 or more persons. | Yes. | Yes. | Yes. | Yes. | Ga. Code Ann. §§ 34-8-33–34-8-35. |
| HI | Any employer of 1 or more persons in the current calendar year. | Yes. | Yes, if employer pays $225 to 1 employee in a calendar quarter and total wages of $1,000 in any calendar quarter. | Any employer of 1 or more persons in the current calendar year. | Yes. | Haw. Rev. Stat. §§ 383-1, 383-2, 383-7, 383-9. |
| ID | Yes. | Yes. | Yes. | Any employer of 1 or more persons. | Yes. | Idaho Code §§ 72-1304, 72-1315, 72-1322C. |
| IL | Yes. | Yes. | Yes. | Yes. | Yes. | Ill. Ann. Stat. ch. 820 ¶¶ 405/205, 405/211.1–405/211.5. |
| IN | Yes. | Yes. | Yes. | Yes. | Yes. | Ind. Code Ann. §§ 22-4-6-1, 22-4-7-1, 22-4-7-2, 22-4-8-2. |
| IA | Yes. | Yes. | Yes. | Any employer of 1 or more persons. | Yes. | Iowa Code Ann. §§ 96.4, 96.19. |
| KS | Yes. | Yes. | Yes. | Yes. | Yes. | Kan. Stat. Ann. § 44-703. |
| KY | Yes. | Yes. | Yes. | Yes. | Yes. | Ky. Rev. Stat. Ann. §§ 341.050, 341.055. |
| LA | Yes. | Yes. | Yes. | Yes. | Yes. | La. Rev. Stat. Ann. § 23:1472. |
| ME | Yes. | Yes. | Yes. | Yes. | Yes. | Me. Rev. Stat. Ann. tit. 26, § 1043. |
| MD | Any employer of 1 or more persons. | Yes. | Yes. | Yes. | Yes. | Md. Code Ann., Lab. & Empl. §§ 8-101, 8-207, 8-208, 8-211, 8-212. |
| MA | Any employer of 1 or more persons in each of 13 weeks or any employer paying wages of $1,500 in any calendar quarter. | Yes. | Yes. | Any employer of 1 or more persons. | Yes. | Mass. Gen. Laws Ann. ch. 151A, §§ 1, 4A, 6, 8–8B. |
| MI | Any employer of 1 or more persons in 20 different weeks or any employer paying wages of $1,000 in calendar year. | Yes. | Yes. | Yes. | Yes. | Mich. Comp. Laws Ann. §§ 421.41–421.43; Mich. Stat. Ann. §§ 17.543, 17.545. |
| MN | Any employer of 1 or more persons in current or preceding calendar year. | Any employer of 4 or more persons in 20 different weeks or any employer paying wages of $20,000 in any calendar quarter. | Yes. | Any employer of 1 or more persons in 20 different weeks. | Yes. | Minn. Stat. § 268.04. |
| MS | Yes. | Yes. | Yes. | Yes. | Yes. | Miss. Code Ann. §§ 71-5-11, 71-5-357. |

*(Table continues.)*

## Table 6.2-1 *(cont'd)*

## EMPLOYERS SUBJECT TO STATE UNEMPLOYMENT COMPENSATION LAWS

(See also text at § 6.2.)

| | *General* | *Agricultural* | *Domestic* | *Nonprofit* | *State Government* | *Citations to Authority* |
|---|---|---|---|---|---|---|
| MO | Yes. | Yes, if employer paid $20,000 or more during any calendar quarter or employed 10 or more persons in agricultural labor in 20 different weeks. | Yes. | Yes. | Yes. | Mo. Rev. Stat. §§ 288.032, 288.034. |
| MT | Any employer with annual payroll exceeding $1,000 in current or preceding calendar year. | Yes. | Yes. | Any employer of 1 or more persons. | Yes. | Mont. Code Ann. §§ 39-51-202–39-5-206. |
| NE | Yes. | Yes. | Yes. | Yes. | Yes. | Neb. Rev. Stat. §§ 48-602–48-604. |
| NV | Any employer of 1 or more persons during quarter for wages of $225 or more. | Yes. | Yes. | Yes. | Yes. | Nev. Rev. Stat. §§ 612.055, 612.090, 612.095, 612.110, 612.120, 612.121. |
| NH | Yes. | Yes. | Yes. | Any employer of 1 or more persons. | Yes. | N.H. Rev. Stat. Ann. §§ 282-A:8, 282-A:9, 282-A:19. |
| NJ | Any employer paying $1,000 or more in current or preceding calendar year. | Yes. | Yes. | Any employer paying $1,000 or more in current or preceding calendar year. | Yes. | N.J. Rev. Stat. §§ 43:21-4, 43:21-7.2, 43:21-8, 43:21-19. |
| NM | Any employer of 1 or more persons in each of 20 weeks or any employer paying wages of $450 in calendar quarter. | Yes. | Yes. | Any employer of 1 or more persons in each of 20 weeks or any employer paying wages of $450 in calendar quarter. | Yes. | N.M. Stat. Ann. §§ 51-1-42, 51-1-43. |
| NY | Any employer paying $300 or more in calendar quarter. | Yes. | Any employer paying wages of $500 or more in calendar quarter. | Yes. Also if wages of $1,000 or more are paid in any calendar quarter. | Yes. | N.Y. Lab. Law §§ 560–565. |
| NC | Yes. | Yes. | Yes. | Yes. | Yes. | N.C. Gen. Stat. § 96-8. |
| ND | Yes. | Yes. | Yes. | Yes. | Yes. | N.D. Cent. Code § 52-01-01. |
| OH | Yes. | Yes. | Yes. | Yes. | Yes. | Ohio Rev. Code Ann. § 4141.01. |

| | | | | | | |
|---|---|---|---|---|---|---|
| OK | Yes. | Yes. | Yes. | Yes. | Yes. | Okla. Stat. tit. 40, §§ 1-208, 1-210. |
| OR | Any employer of 1 or more persons in each of 18 weeks or any employer with total payroll of $225 or more in calendar quarter. | Yes. | Yes. | Any employer of 1 or more persons in each of 18 weeks or any employer with total payroll of $225 or more in calendar quarter. Certain exceptions apply. | Yes. | Or. Rev. Stat. §§ 657.025, 657.045, 657.050, 657.072, 657.092. |
| PA | Any employer of 1 or more persons. | Any employer who paid $20,000 or more during any calendar quarter, or who employed up to 10 persons during 20 different calendar weeks. | Any employer who paid $1,000 in any calendar quarter. | Any employer of 1 or more persons. | Yes. | Pa. Cons. Stat. Ann. tit. 43, §§ 753, 902. |
| RI | Any employer of 1 or more persons. | Any employer of 1 or more persons. | Yes. | Any employer of 1 or more persons. | Yes. | R.I. Gen. Laws §§ 28-42-3, 28-42-13. |
| SC | Yes. | Yes. | Yes. | Any employer of 4 or more in 20 different weeks. | Yes. | S.C. Code Ann. §§ 41-27-120, 41-27-210, 41-27-230. |
| SD | Yes. | Yes. | Yes. | Yes. | Yes. | S.D. Codified Laws Ann. §§ 61-1-4, 61-1-10.2, 61-1-10.3, 61-1-24, 61-1-25, 61-1-27. |
| TN | Yes. | Yes. | Yes. | Yes. | Yes. | Tenn. Code Ann. §§ 50-7-206, 50-7-207. |
| TX | Yes. | Any employer of 3 or more persons in each of 20 weeks for at least 1 day of each week during current or preceding year or any employer paying $6,250 cash remuneration in any calendar quarter. | Yes. | Yes. | Yes. | Tex. Lab. Code Ann. §§ 201.021, 201.023, 201.026, 201.027, 201.047. |
| UT | Any employer paying wages of $140 or more in any quarter. | Yes. | Yes. | Yes. | Yes. | Utah Code Ann. §§ 35-4-202–35-4-206. |
| VT | Yes. | Yes. | Yes. | Yes. | Yes. | Vt. Stat. Ann. tit. 21, § 1301. |
| VA | Yes. | Any employer who paid $20,000 or more in a quarter or who employed 10 or more individuals for some portion of 20 different weeks. | Yes. | Yes. | Yes. | Va. Code Ann. §§ 60.2-201, 60.2-210, 60.2-213, 60.2-214, 60.2-215. |

*(Table continues.)*

# Table 6.2-1 *(cont'd)*

## EMPLOYERS SUBJECT TO STATE UNEMPLOYMENT COMPENSATION LAWS

(See also text at § 6.2.)

| | *General* | *Agricultural* | *Domestic* | *Nonprofit* | *State Government* | *Citations to Authority* |
|---|---|---|---|---|---|---|
| WA | Any employer of 1 or more persons. | Yes. | Yes. | Any employer of 1 or more persons. | Yes. | Wash. Rev. Code §§ 50.04.090, 50.04.150, 50.04.155, 50.04.160, 50.44.010, 50.44.020, 50.44.030, 50.44.040, 50.44.060. |
| WV | Yes. | Yes. | Yes. | Yes. | Yes. | W. Va. Code § 21A-1A-15, 21A-1A-16.. |
| WI | Yes. | Yes. | Yes. | Yes. | Yes. | Wis. Stat. § 108.02. |
| WY | Any employer paying wages in excess of $500 in calendar year. | Yes. | Yes. | Yes. | Yes. | Wyo. Stat. §§ 27-3-103, 27-3-105, 27-3-107, 27-3-501, 27-3-502. |

# § 6.3 Unemployment Disqualifications and Exemptions

## [a] Disqualification

Table 6.3-1 surveys those events that will disqualify workers from collecting unemployment insurance benefits.

As the table shows, specific disqualification criteria vary from state to state, but the following conditions will generally disqualify workers in all 50 states and the District of Columbia from collecting unemployment benefits:

- Voluntarily leaving work without good cause;
- Misconduct connected with work;
- Refusal of suitable work without good cause;
- Labor disputes, such as strikes or lockouts;
- Illegal alien status; and
- Fraud.

## [b] Reestablishing Eligibility for Unemployment Insurance

Although all of the events described in this chapter and Table 6.3-1 disqualify workers from collecting unemployment insurance benefits, the duration of the disqualification varies from state to state. Table 6.3-4 sets out the requirements for reestablishing eligibility.

In many states, the disqualification period continues until the unemployed worker has been reemployed for a certain period of time or has earned a specified amount of money as wages. For example, in both California and New York, a worker who voluntarily leaves employment without good cause or who is discharged or suspended for misconduct is ineligible for benefits until he or she receives pay that is at least equal to 5 times the statutory benefit rate.[1] Ohio and Texas, which have similar provisions, require workers to be reemployed for 6 weeks or earn 6 times the statutory benefit rate to become reeligible.[2] Illinois, New Jersey, and Virginia have set slightly shorter time periods for reestablishing eligibility: 4 weeks (30 days for Virginia) of employment subsequent to quitting or being discharged or suspended for misconduct.[3]

Several states require longer periods of disqualification before a worker can become reeligible for unemployment insurance. For example, Connecticut requires a worker to earn 10 times the statutory benefit rate to become reeligible, and in Florida the required amount of earnings for reestablishing eligibility is 17 times the benefit rate.[4]

## [c] Eligibility

Table 6.3-2 (Parts A and B) shows which persons are not eligible for unemployment compensation under state law.

Many states have statutory provisions specifically dealing with the eligibility for unemployment compensation of persons classified as students. The effect of student status under these statutes is set out in Table 6.3-3.

---

**§ 6.3**

1. Cal. Unemp. Ins. Code § 1260 (West); N.Y. Lab. Law § 593 (McKinney).

2. Ohio Rev. Code Ann. § 4141.29(G) (Anderson); Tex. Lab. Code Ann. §§ 207.044, 207.045, 207.053 (Vernon).

3. 820 Ill. Comp. Stat. ch. 405, §§ 601, 602; N.J. Stat. Ann. § 43:21-5 (West); Va. Code Ann. § 60.2-618.

4. Conn. Gen. Stat. Ann. § 31-236 (West); Fla. Stat. Ann. § 443.101 (West).

# Table 6.3-1
## EVENTS THAT DISQUALIFY INDIVIDUALS FROM COLLECTING UNEMPLOYMENT COMPENSATION

(See also text at § 6.3.)

**KEY:** **Yes.** Specifically disqualified by state statute.
**No.** Not specifically disqualified by state statute.
**Pension disqualification.** Unemployment benefits are reduced by the amount an individual receives from a pension, retirement pay, or other annuity to the extent that such program is funded by an employer. May result in full benefit disqualification.
**Note.** In all states, professional athletes during off-season and employees of educational institutions between terms or during holidays and vacations are not eligible for unemployment compensation.

| | *Voluntarily Leaving Work to Attend School (i.e., enrolled 10 or more hours per week)* | *Voluntarily Leaving Work to Marry* | *Voluntarily Leaving Work to Move with Spouse* | *Voluntarily Leaving Work to Meet Domestic Obligations* | *Receipt of Unemployment Benefits Under Federal Law or Other State Law* | *Receipt of Pension, Retirement Pay, or Other Annuity* | *Other Disqualifying Events* | *Citations to Authority* |
|---|---|---|---|---|---|---|---|---|
| AL | No. | No. | No. | No. | Yes. | Yes. | Work on work-relief projects; discharge for misconduct including use of illegal drugs or refusal to submit to drug testing. | Ala. Code § 25-4-78. |
| AK | No. | No. | No. | No. | Yes. | Yes. | Aliens who are present unlawfully; discharge for misconduct; partial disqualification if employee is unemployed because of a labor dispute or if employee makes false statement or misrepresentation. | Alaska Stat. §§ 23.20.360, 23.20.362, 23.20.379, 23.20.381, 23.20.383, 23.20.387. |
| AZ | No. | No. | No. | No. | Yes. | Yes. | Customary suspension of all operations, except maintenance work, for not more than 4 weeks and not more than once per calendar year; discharge due to transportation difficulties, unless it can be shown that travel requirements exceed the normal practice in the business or that there were compelling personal circumstances that necessitated the termination. | Ariz. Rev. Stat. Ann. §§ 23-615, 23-617, 23-622, 23-775, 23-776. |

| | | | | | | | | |
|---|---|---|---|---|---|---|---|---|
| AR | No. | No. | No. | No. | Yes. | Yes. | Receipt of federal training or retraining allowance; making material false statement or misrepresentation. | Ark. Code Ann. §§ 11-10-507, 11-10-511, 11-10-513, 11-10-514, 11-10-515, 11-10-517, 11-10-518, 11-10-519. |
| CA | No. | No. | No. | No. | Yes. | Yes, only if he or she has not contributed to pension or retirement system. | Chronic absenteeism because of intoxication, reporting to job while intoxicated, or using intoxicants on the job; 24-hour absence from work because of incarceration; conviction for false statement or failure to disclose facts to obtain or increase benefits. | Cal. Unemp. Ins. Code §§ 642.1, 1255, 1255.3, 1256, 1256.5. |
| CO | No. | Yes. | Yes. | No. | Yes. | Yes. | Violation of statute or company memo that could potentially seriously damage employer's property or interests; insubordination; intoxication; incarceration; theft; actual or threatened assault; uncountenanced rudeness or offensive behavior; careless work; excessive tardiness or absenteeism; failure to meet established, defined standards. | Colo. Rev. Stat. §§ 8-70-131, 8-70-132, 8-73-108. |
| CT | Yes. | No. | No. | No. | Yes. | Yes. | Felonious conduct; larceny of more than $25 in property or services or any amount of cash; willful misconduct in course of employment; participation in illegal strike; receipt of severance or separation payments; discharge or suspension during period of imprisonment for 30 or more days. | Conn. Gen. Stat. Ann. §§ 31-222, 31-227, 31-236. |
| DE | No. | No. | No. | No. | Yes. | Yes. | Inability to work; receipt of sickness, disability, or workers' compensation; making false statement to obtain benefits; commitment to a penal institute. | Del. Code Ann. tit. 19, §§ 3313–3315. |
| DC | No. | No. | No. | No. | Yes. | Yes. | Failure to attend recommended training or retraining course. | D.C. Code Ann. §§ 46-108, 46-111. |

*(Table continues.)*

## Table 6.3-1 *(cont'd)*

## EVENTS THAT DISQUALIFY INDIVIDUALS FROM COLLECTING UNEMPLOYMENT COMPENSATION

(See also text at § 6.3.)

**KEY:** **Yes.** Specifically disqualified by state statute.
**No.** Not specifically disqualified by state statute.
**Pension disqualification.** Unemployment benefits are reduced by the amount an individual receives from a pension, retirement pay, or other annuity to the extent that such program is funded by an employer. May result in full benefit disqualification.
**Note.** In all states, professional athletes during off-season and employees of educational institutions between terms or during holidays and vacations are not eligible for unemployment compensation.

| | *Voluntarily Leaving Work to Attend School (i.e., enrolled 10 or more hours per week)* | *Voluntarily Leaving Work to Marry* | *Voluntarily Leaving Work to Move with Spouse* | *Voluntarily Leaving Work to Meet Domestic Obligations* | *Receipt of Unemployment Benefits Under Federal Law or Other State Law* | *Receipt of Pension, Retirement Pay, or Other Annuity* | *Other Disqualifying Events* | *Citations to Authority* |
|---|---|---|---|---|---|---|---|---|
| FL | No. | No. | No. Note, however, that there is case law stating that an employee who quits job to move with a spouse is not entitled to benefits. *Department of Air Force v. State Unemployment Appeals,* 486 So.2d 632 (Fla. App. 1 Dist. 1986). | No. Note that there is case law stating that leaving work to meet domestic obligations is voluntary, and therefore employee is not entitled to benefits. *Marguiles v. Pallott & Poppell,* 599 So.2d 195 (Fla. App. 3 Dist. 1992). | Yes. | Yes. | Receipt of wages in lieu of notice; temporary, partial, total, or permanent total disability payments under workers' compensation; misconduct; violation of criminal law punishable by imprisonment; false or fraudulent representation to obtain benefits. | Fla. Stat. Ann. §§ 443.036, 443.071, 443.091, 443.101. |
| GA | No. | No. | No. | No. | Yes. | Yes. | Physical assault; theft of property, goods, or money; failure to obey instructions or to discharge duties of employment; misrepresentation to obtain benefits; wages in lieu of notice. | Ga. Code Ann. §§ 34-8-193–34-8-195. |
| HI | No. | No. | No. | No. | Yes. | Yes. | Misconduct; misrepresentation to obtain benefits. | Haw. Rev. Stat. §§ 383-23.5, 383-29, |

| | | | | | | | | |
|---|---|---|---|---|---|---|---|---|
| | | | | | | | | 383-29.5, 383-30, 383-106. |
| ID | No. | Yes. | Yes. | Yes. | Yes. | Yes. | Misrepresentation to obtain benefits. | Idaho Code §§ 72-1312, 72-1366. |
| IL | No. | No. | No. | No. | Yes. | Yes. | Admission or conviction of work-related felony or theft; receipt of temporary disability benefits under workers' compensation; fraudulent misrepresentation to obtain benefits. | 820 Ill. Comp. Ann. 405/601, 405/602, 405/606, 405/611. |
| IN | No. | No. | No. | No. | Yes. | Yes. | Misrepresentation to obtain benefits; gross misconduct. | Ind. Code Ann. §§ 22-4-4-2, 22-4-15-1, 22-4-15-4, 22-4-15-5. |
| IA | No. | No. | No. | No. Employee may be absent from work for up to 10 days for personal reasons, and if employee is fired upon return to work, employee will still be eligible for benefits. | Yes. | Yes. | Receipt of vacation pay or pay in lieu of vacation; receipt of temporary disability compensation; separation or severance pay or dismissal pay; entitlement to wages in lieu of notice; false statement or misrepresentation to obtain benefits. | Iowa Code Ann. § 96.5. |
| KS | No. | No. | No. | No. | Yes. | Yes. | Receipt of workers' compensation; failure to apply for suitable work; misconduct or gross misconduct, except no disqualification for misconduct or gross misconduct if employer discharges employee after learning employee was seeking other work or when employee had given notice of future intent to quit. Additionally, disqualification does not result in the following situations: for discharge based on ineffective or unsatisfactory performance because of inability, incapacity, or lack of training provided employee is making a good faith effort to do his or her work; for isolated incidents of negligence; for good faith errors in judgment; for unsatisfactory work or conduct caused by cir- *(cont'd)* | Kan. Stat. Ann. §§ 44-703, 44-706. |

*(Table continues.)*

# Table 6.3-1 *(cont'd)*

## EVENTS THAT DISQUALIFY INDIVIDUALS FROM COLLECTING UNEMPLOYMENT COMPENSATION

(See also text at § 6.3.)

**KEY:** **Yes.** Specifically disqualified by state statute.
**No.** Not specifically disqualified by state statute.
**Pension disqualification.** Unemployment benefits are reduced by the amount an individual receives from a pension, retirement pay, or other annuity to the extent that such program is funded by an employer. May result in full benefit disqualification.
**Note.** In all states, professional athletes during off-season and employees of educational institutions between terms or during holidays and vacations are not eligible for unemployment compensation.

| | *Voluntarily Leaving Work to Attend School (i.e., enrolled 10 or more hours per week)* | *Voluntarily Leaving Work to Marry* | *Voluntarily Leaving Work to Move with Spouse* | *Voluntarily Leaving Work to Meet Domestic Obligations* | *Receipt of Unemployment Benefits Under Federal Law or Other State Law* | *Receipt of Pension, Retirement Pay, or Other Annuity* | *Other Disqualifying Events* | *Citations to Authority* |
|---|---|---|---|---|---|---|---|---|
| KS (*cont'd*) | | | | | | | cumstances beyond employee's control; or for employee's refusal to perform work in excess of contract for hire. | |
| KY | No. | No. | No. | No. | Yes. | Yes. | Failure to apply for suitable work. Disqualification does not result where employee left work that was at least 100 road miles, one way, from home in order to accept work closer to home, provided that there exists a bona fide job offer with a reasonable expectation of continued employment. | Ky. Rev. Stat. Ann. §§ 341.360, 341.370, 341.390. |
| LA | No. | No. | No. | No. | Yes. | Yes. | Discharge for use of illegal drugs; receipt of wages in lieu of notice; most workers' compensation payments. | La. Rev. Stat. Ann. §§ 23:1472, 23:1601. |
| ME | No. | No. | No. | No. | Yes. | Yes. | Discharge for conviction of work-related felony or misdemeanor or for absence greater than 2 work days due to incarceration for conviction of a criminal offense; receipt of dismissal wages, wages in lieu of notice, or | Me. Rev. Stat. Ann. tit. 26, §§ 1043, 1191–1193. |

| | | | | | | | | |
|---|---|---|---|---|---|---|---|---|
| | | | | | | | termination, vacation, or holiday pay. | |
| MD | Yes. | No. | Yes. | No. | Yes. | Yes. | Receipt of dismissal pay or wages in lieu of notice; receipt of vacation or holiday pay under certain circumstances; discharge or suspension for intentional conduct that results in bodily injury or property loss. | Md. Code Ann., Lab. & Empl. §§ 8-101, 8-220, 8-1001, 8-1006–8-1009. |
| MA | No. | No. | Yes. | No. | Yes. | Yes. | Absence caused by conviction of felony or misdemeanor; disciplinary suspension; receipt of certain workers' compensation payments. | Mass. Gen. Laws Ann. ch. 151A, §§ 1, 4A, 6, 25, 26, 47. |
| MI | No. | No. | No. | No. | Yes. | Yes. | Disciplinary layoff or suspension; failure without good cause to apply for suitable leave of absence due to incarceration; work-connected assault and battery or theft resulting in loss or damage of more than $25; participation in wildcat strikes or strikes in violation of collective bargaining agreements; discharge for intoxication while at work. | Mich. Comp. Laws Ann. §§ 421.42, 421.43; Mich. Stat. Ann. §§ 17.545, 17.547. |
| MN | No. | No. | No. | No. | Yes. | Yes. | Disciplinary suspension of 30 days or less; receipt of termination, severance, or dismissal pay or wages in lieu of notice; vacation allowance; workers' compensation payments for loss of wages. | Minn. Stat. §§ 268.04, 268.08, 268.09. |
| MS | No. | Yes. | Yes. | Yes. | Yes. | Yes. | Receipt of back pay or other compensation allocable to a week. | Miss. Code Ann. §§ 71-5-13, 71-5-513. |
| MO | No. | No. | No. | No. | Yes. | Yes. | Receipt of workers' compensation for temporary partial disability. | Mo. Rev. Stat. §§ 288.034, 288.040. |
| MT | No. | No. | No. | No. | Yes. | Yes. | Principal occupation is self-employment; failure to apply for suitable work; receipt of wages in lieu of notice, separation, or termination allowance; receipt of workers' compensation or Social Security disability payments. | Mont. Code Ann. §§ 39-51-504, 39-51-2203, 39-51-2302–39-51-2307. |

(*Table continues.*)

# Table 6.3-1 *(cont'd)*

## EVENTS THAT DISQUALIFY INDIVIDUALS FROM COLLECTING UNEMPLOYMENT COMPENSATION

(See also text at § 6.3.)

**KEY:** **Yes.** Specifically disqualified by state statute.
**No.** Not specifically disqualified by state statute.
**Pension disqualification.** Unemployment benefits are reduced by the amount an individual receives from a pension, retirement pay, or other annuity to the extent that such program is funded by an employer. May result in full benefit disqualification.
**Note.** In all states, professional athletes during off-season and employees of educational institutions between terms or during holidays and vacations are not eligible for unemployment compensation.

| | *Voluntarily Leaving Work to Attend School (i.e., enrolled 10 or more hours per week)* | *Voluntarily Leaving Work to Marry* | *Voluntarily Leaving Work to Move with Spouse* | *Voluntarily Leaving Work to Meet Domestic Obligations* | *Receipt of Unemployment Benefits Under Federal Law or Other State Law* | *Receipt of Pension, Retirement Pay, or Other Annuity* | *Other Disqualifying Events* | *Citations to Authority* |
|---|---|---|---|---|---|---|---|---|
| NE | No. | No. | No. | No. | Yes. | Yes. | Failure to apply for suitable work; receipt of wages in lieu of notice, dismissal, or separation allowance; temporary partial disability payments under workers' compensation law; Social Security benefits. | Neb. Rev. Stat. §§ 48-602, 48-604, 48-628. |
| NV | No. | No. | No. | No. | Yes. | Yes. | Receipt of wages in lieu of notice, severance pay, vacation pay, or back pay due to unlawful discharge; admission of or connection to work-connected assault, arson, sabotage, grand larceny, embezzlement, or wanton property destruction. | Nev. Rev. Stat. §§ 612.375, 612.380–612.448. |
| NH | No. | No. | No. | No. | Yes. | Yes. | Leaving self-employment or closing business; disciplinary layoff if for good cause. | N.H. Rev. Stat. Ann. §§ 282-A:9, 282-A:14, 282-A:15, 282-A:20, 282-A:28, 282-A:30–282-A:32, 282-A:38. |
| NJ | No. | No. | No. | No. | Yes. | Yes. | Receipt of payments in lieu of notice; disability benefits under temporary benefits law. | N.J. Rev. Stat. §§ 43:21-4–43:21-5a, 43:21-7. |

| | | | | | | | | |
|---|---|---|---|---|---|---|---|---|
| NM | No. | No. | No. | No. | Yes. | Yes. | Failure to apply for suitable work; discharge for misconduct connected with employment. | N.M. Stat. Ann. §§ 51-1-4, 51-1-7, 51-1-42. |
| NY | No. | Yes. | No. | No. | Yes. | Yes. | Receipt of benefits under another law; discharge for work-related felony. | N.Y. Lab. Law §§ 511, 592, 593, 600. |
| NC | No. | No. | No. | No. | Yes. | Yes. | Discharge for substantial fault connected with work but not rising to level of misconduct; receipt of back-pay awards. | N.C. Gen. Stat. §§ 96-4, 96-8, 96-12–96-14. |
| ND | No. | No. | No. | No. | Yes. | Yes. | Disciplinary suspension of 30 days or less caused by misconduct; fraud or omission of a material fact in application for benefits. | N.D. Cent. Code §§ 52-01-01, 52-06-02. |
| OH | No. | Yes. | Yes. | Yes. | Yes. | Yes. | Receipt of remuneration in lieu of notice; certain workers' compensation payments; separation or termination pay; vacation pay allocable to specific weeks; incarceration; dishonesty. | Ohio Rev. Code Ann. §§ 4141.01, 4141.29, 4141.31. |
| OK | No. | No. | No. | No. | Yes. | Yes. | Failure to apply for suitable work. | Okla. Stat. tit. 40, §§ 1-210, 2-411, 2-412. |
| OR | No. | No. | No. | No. | Yes. | Yes. | Receipt of vacation pay; work-connected felony or theft. | Or. Rev. Stat. §§ 657.030, 657.176, 657.205, 657.210, 657.221. |
| PA | No. | No. | No. | No. | Yes. | Yes. | Receipt of vacation pay; illegal receipt of benefits. | Pa. Cons. Stat. Ann. tit. 43, §§ 753, 792, 802, 804. |
| RI | No. | No. | No. | No. | Yes. | Yes. | Receipt of vacation pay. | R.I. Gen. Laws §§ 28-42-3, 28-42-8, 28-44-19, 28-44-19.1. |
| SC | No. | No. | No. | No. | Yes. | Yes. | Discharge for cause related to work; knowing acceptance of benefits to which not entitled. | S.C. Code Ann. §§ 41-27-260, 41-27-370, 41-35-120. |
| SD | No. | No. | No. | No. | Yes. | Yes. | Receipt of vacation pay; wages in lieu of notice; workers' compensation payments; disability payments; termination, severance, or dismissal pay; holiday pay. | S.D. Codified Laws Ann. §§ 61-6-20, 61-6-21. |

*(Table continues.)*

# Table 6.3-1 *(cont'd)*

## EVENTS THAT DISQUALIFY INDIVIDUALS FROM COLLECTING UNEMPLOYMENT COMPENSATION

(See also text at § 6.3.)

**KEY:** **Yes.** Specifically disqualified by state statute.
**No.** Not specifically disqualified by state statute.
**Pension disqualification.** Unemployment benefits are reduced by the amount an individual receives from a pension, retirement pay, or other annuity to the extent that such program is funded by an employer. May result in full benefit disqualification.
**Note.** In all states, professional athletes during off-season and employees of educational institutions between terms or during holidays and vacations are not eligible for unemployment compensation.

| | *Voluntarily Leaving Work to Attend School (i.e., enrolled 10 or more hours per week)* | *Voluntarily Leaving Work to Marry* | *Voluntarily Leaving Work to Move with Spouse* | *Voluntarily Leaving Work to Meet Domestic Obligations* | *Receipt of Unemployment Benefits Under Federal Law or Other State Law* | *Receipt of Pension, Retirement Pay, or Other Annuity* | *Other Disqualifying Events* | *Citations to Authority* |
|---|---|---|---|---|---|---|---|---|
| TN | No. | No. | No. | No. | Yes. | Yes. | Receipt of wages in lieu of notice; certain workers' compensation payments; fraud or omission of material fact in application for benefits causes a 4–52 week disqualification. | Tenn. Code Ann. §§ 50-7-207, 50-7-213, 50-7-303. |
| TX | Yes. | No. | No. | No. | Yes. | Yes. | Receipt of wages in lieu of notice; workers' compensation benefits; old-age Social Security benefits; misconduct. | Tex. Lab. Code Ann. §§ 201.061, 207.022, 207.023, 207.045, 207.049, 207.050. |
| UT | No. | No. | No. | No. | Yes. | Yes. | Discharge for work-related dishonesty constituting a crime; receipt of wages in lieu of notice, separation pay, or vacation pay. | Utah Code Ann. §§ 35-4-204, 35-4-404, 35-4-405. |
| VT | No. | No. | No. | No. | Yes. | Yes. | Conviction of felony or misdemeanor rendering claimant unable to perform all or essential part of duties; receipt of wages in lieu of notice, vacation pay, holiday pay, back-pay award, or settlement; certain workers' compensation payments. | Vt. Stat. Ann. tit. 21, §§ 1301, 1343, 1344. |

| | | | | | | | | |
|---|---|---|---|---|---|---|---|---|
| VA | No. | No. | No. | No. | Yes. | Yes. | Receipt of benefit to which not entitled; incarceration. | Va. Code Ann. §§ 60.2-219, 60.2-229, 60.2-604, 60.2-609, 60.2-612, 60.2-618. |
| WA | Yes. | No. | No. | No. | No. | Yes. | Admission of or connection to work-related felony or gross misconduct. | Wash. Rev. Code §§ 50.04.323, 50.04.330, 50.20.050, 50.20.060, 50.20.070, 50.20.080, 50.20.085, 50.20.090, 50.20.095, 50.20.118, 50.44.037, 50.44.040. |
| WV | Yes. | Yes. | Yes. | Yes. | Yes. | Yes. | Receipt of wages in lieu of notice; certain workers' compensation payments; unemployment due to vacation request that would require suspension of operations; false statements or failure to disclose a material fact to obtain or increase any unemployment benefit. | W. Va. Code § 21A-6-3. |
| WI | No. | No. | No. | No. | Yes. | Yes. | Self-employment; suspension, revocation, or nonrenewal of government license. | Wis. Stat. §§ 108.02, 108.04, 108.05. |
| WY | No. | No. | No. | No. | Yes. | Yes. | Certain self-employment; receipt of severance payments, termination allowances, or earned vacation pay; conviction of false statements or representations or failure to disclose material facts. | Wyo. Stat. §§ 27-3-102, 27-3-106, 27-3-307, 27-3-311, 27-3-313. |

# Table 6.3-2 Part A
## STATE UNEMPLOYMENT COMPENSATION LAW COVERAGE

(See also text at § 6.3.)

**KEY:** **Employee not covered.** Employee is not covered by provisions of state unemployment compensation law.
**Employee covered.** Employee is covered by provisions of state unemployment compensation law.
**Casual labor.** Service that is not in the course of an employer's trade or business unless the individual is paid more than $50 *and* the employer regularly retains the individual to perform such service.

| | | | *Relative* | | | | | | |
|---|---|---|---|---|---|---|---|---|---|
| | *Self-Employed* | *Railroad Employees* | *Employed by Child or Spouse* | *Minor Employed by Parent* | *Patients Employed by Hospital* | *Insurance Agents Wholly on Commission* | *Real Estate Agents Wholly on Commission* | *Casual Labor* | *Citations to Authority* |
| AL | Employee not covered. | Employee not covered. | Employee not covered. | Employee not covered. | Employee not covered. | Employee not covered. | Employee not covered. | Employee not covered. | Ala. Code §§ 25-4-10, 25-4-78. |
| AK | Employee not covered. | Employee not covered. | Employee not covered. | Employee not covered. | Employee not covered. | Employee not covered. | Employee not covered. | Employee not covered. | Alaska Stat. § 23.20.526. |
| AZ | Employee not covered. | Employee not covered. | Employee not covered. | Employee not covered. | Employee not covered. | Employee not covered. | Employee not covered. | Employee not covered. | Ariz. Rev. Stat. Ann. §§ 23-615, 23-617. |
| AR | Employee not covered. | Employee not covered. | Employee not covered. | Employee not covered. | Employee not covered. | Employee not covered. | Employee not covered. | Employee not covered. | Ark. Code Ann. § 11-10-210. |
| CA | Employee covered. | Employee not covered. | Employee not covered except to extent that employer and employee have elected to make contributions to unemployment compensation disability fund. | Employee not covered except to extent that employer and employee have elected to make contributions to unemployment compensation disability fund. | Employee not covered. | Employee covered. | Employee covered unless there is a written contract stating agent is not an employee for state tax purposes. | Employee not covered. | Cal. Unemp. Ins. Code §§ 601, 621, 631, 640, 647, 650 15 Ops. Atty. Cal. Gen. 311. |
| CO | Employee not covered. | Employee not covered. | Employee not covered. | Employee not covered. | Employee not covered. | Employee not covered. | Employee not covered. | Employee not covered. | Colo. Rev. Stat. §§ 8-70-103, 8-70-128, 8-70-129, 8-70-133, 8-70-136, 8-70-139. |
| CT | Employee not covered. | Employee not covered. | Employee not covered. | Employee not covered. | Employee not covered. | Employee not covered. | Employee not covered. | Employee not covered. | Conn. Gen. Stat. Ann. §§ 31-222, 31-235. |

| | | | | | | | | | |
|---|---|---|---|---|---|---|---|---|---|
| DE | Employee not covered. | Employee not covered. | Employee not covered. | Employee not covered. | Employee not covered. | Employee not covered. | Employee not covered. | Employee covered. | Del. Code Ann. tit. 19, § 3302. |
| DC | Employee not covered. | Employee not covered. | Employee not covered. | Employee not covered. | Employee covered. | Employee not covered. | Employee covered. | Employee not covered. | D.C. Code Ann. § 46-101. |
| FL | Employee not covered. | Employee not covered. | Employee not covered. | Employee not covered. | Employee not covered. | Employee not covered. | Employee not covered. | Employee not covered unless labor exceeds 200 man hours or it is performed on more than 10 days in any two consecutive months. | Fla. Stat. Ann. § 443.036. |
| GA | Employee not covered. | Employee not covered. | Employee not covered. | Employee not covered. | Employee not covered. | Employee not covered. | Employee not covered. | Employee not covered. | Ga. Code Ann. § 34-8-35. |
| HI | Employee not covered. | Employee not covered. | Employee not covered. | Employee not covered. | Employee covered. | Employee not covered. | Employee not covered. | Employee not covered unless wages are at least $50 in a quarter and employee works at least 24 days in any quarter. | Haw. Rev. Stat. § 383-7. |
| ID | Employee not covered. | Employee not covered. | Employee not covered. | Employee not covered. | Employee not covered. | Employee not covered. | Employee not covered. | Employee covered. | Idaho Code §§ 72-1316, 72-1316A. |
| IL | Employee not covered. | Employee not covered. | Employee not covered. | Employee not covered. | Employee not covered. | Employee not covered. | Employee not covered. | Employee covered. | 820 Ill. Comp. Stat. Ann. 405/217, 405/218, 405/222, 405/228, 405/230. |
| IN | Employee not covered. | Employee not covered. | Employee not covered. | Employee not covered. | Employee not covered. | Employee not covered. | Employee covered. | Employee not covered unless wages are at least $50 in a quarter and employee works at least 24 days in current or preceding quarter. | Ind. Code Ann. § 22-4-8-3. |
| IA | Employee not covered. | Employee not covered. | Employee not covered. | Employee not covered. | Employee not covered. | Employee covered. | Employee not covered. | Employee covered. | Iowa Code Ann. §§ 96.3, 96.19. |

*(Table continues.)*

# Table 6.3-2 Part A *(cont'd)*
## STATE UNEMPLOYMENT COMPENSATION LAW COVERAGE

(See also text at § 6.3.)

**KEY:** **Employee not covered.** Employee is not covered by provisions of state unemployment compensation law.
**Employee covered.** Employee is covered by provisions of state unemployment compensation law.
**Casual labor.** Service that is not in the course of an employer's trade or business unless the individual is paid more than $50 *and* the employer regularly retains the individual to perform such service.

| | | | Relative | | | | | | |
|---|---|---|---|---|---|---|---|---|---|
| | *Self-Employed* | *Railroad Employees* | *Employed by Child or Spouse* | *Minor Employed by Parent* | *Patients Employed by Hospital* | *Insurance Agents Wholly on Commission* | *Real Estate Agents Wholly on Commission* | *Casual Labor* | *Citations to Authority* |
| KS | Employee not covered. | Employee not covered. | Employee not covered. | Employee not covered. | Employee not covered. | Employee not covered. | Employee not covered. | Employee not covered unless wages are at least $200 in a quarter and employee works at least 24 days in current or preceding quarter. | Kan. Stat. Ann. § 44-703. |
| KY | Employee not covered. | Employee not covered. | Employee not covered. | Employee not covered. | Employee not covered. | Employee not covered. | Employee covered. | Employee not covered. | Ky. Rev. Stat. Ann. §§ 341.050, 341.055. |
| LA | Employee not covered. | Employee not covered. | Employee not covered. | Employee not covered. | Employee covered. | Employee not covered. | Employee not covered. | Employee not covered. | La. Rev. Stat. Ann. § 23:1472. |
| ME | Employee not covered. | Employee not covered. | Employee not covered. | Employee not covered. | Employee not covered. | Employee not covered. | Employee not covered. | Employee covered. | Me. Rev. Stat. Ann. tit. 26, § 1043. |
| MD | Employee not covered. | Employee not covered. | Employee not covered. | Employee not covered. | Employee not covered. | Employee not covered. | Employee not covered. | Employee not covered. | Md. Code Ann., Lab. & Empl. §§ 8-209, 8-213–8-215, 8-218, 8-1001. |
| MA | Employee not covered. | Employee not covered. | Employee not covered. | Employee not covered. | Employee not covered. | Employee not covered. | Employee not covered. | Employee not covered. | Mass. Gen. Laws Ann. ch. 151A, §§ 1, 2, 6. |
| MI | Employee not covered. | Employee not covered. | Employee not covered. | Employee not covered. | Employee not covered. | Employee not covered. | Employee not covered. | Employee covered. | Mich. Comp. Laws Ann. § 421.43; Mich. Stat. Ann. § 17.547. |
| MN | Employee not covered. | Employee not covered. | Employee not covered. | Employee not covered. | Employee not covered. | Employee not covered. | Employee not covered. | Employee not covered. | Minn. Stat. §§ 268.04, 268.09. |

| | | | | | | | | | |
|---|---|---|---|---|---|---|---|---|---|
| MS | Employee not covered. | Employee not covered. | Employee not covered. | Employee not covered. | Employee not covered. | Employee not covered. | Employee covered. Note: There is case law authority stating that real estate agents are not employees or real estate brokers. *MESC v. Clyde Scott, Realtor,* 242 Miss. 514, 137 So. 2d 164 (Miss. 1962). | Employee not covered. | Miss. Code Ann. §§ 71-5-11, 71-5-513. |
| MO | Employee not covered. | Employee not covered. | Employee not covered. | Employee not covered. | Employee covered, although patients employed by rehabilitation centers are exempt. | Employee not covered. | Employee not covered. | Employee covered. | Mo. Rev. Stat. §§ 288.030, 288.034. |
| MT | Employee not covered. | Employee not covered. | Employee not covered. | Employee not covered. | Employee not covered. | Employee not covered. | Employee not covered. | Employee not covered. | Mont. Code Ann. § 39-51-204. |
| NE | Employee not covered. | Employee not covered. | Employee not covered. | Employee not covered. | Employee not covered. | Employee not covered. | Employee not covered. | Employee not covered. | Neb. Rev. Stat. §§ 48-604, 48-628. |
| NV | Employee not covered. | Employee not covered. | Employee not covered. | Employee not covered. | Employee not covered. | Employee covered. | Employee not covered. | Employee covered. | Nev. Rev. Stat. §§ 612.105, 612.117, 612.125, 612.133. |
| NH | Employee not covered. | Employee not covered. | Employee not covered. | Employee not covered. | Employee not covered. | Employee not covered. | Employee not covered. | Employee not covered. | N.H. Rev. Stat. Ann. §§ 282-A:9, 282-A:14, 282-A:33. |
| NJ | Employee not covered. | Employee not covered. | Employee not covered. | Employee not covered. | Employee not covered. | Employee not covered. | Employee not covered. | Employee covered. | N.J. Rev. Stat. § 43:21-19. |
| NM | Employee not covered. | Employee not covered. | Employee not covered. | Employee not covered. | Employee not covered. | Employee not covered. | Employee not covered. | Employee covered. | N.M. Stat. Ann. §§ 51-1-7, 51-1-42. |
| NY | Employee not covered. | Employee not covered. | Employee not covered. | Employee not covered. | Employee covered, although patients employed by rehabilitation centers are exempt. | Employee covered. | Employee not covered. | Persons under 21 not covered. | N.Y. Lab. Law § 511; N.Y. Ment. Hyg. Law § 33.09. |
| NC | Employee not covered. | Employee not covered. | Employee not covered. | Employee not covered. | Employee not covered. | Employee not covered. | Employee not covered. | Employee not covered. | N.C. Gen. Stat. § 96-8. |

*(Table continues.)*

# Table 6.3-2 Part A *(cont'd)*

## STATE UNEMPLOYMENT COMPENSATION LAW COVERAGE

(See also text at § 6.3.)

**KEY:** **Employee not covered.** Employee is not covered by provisions of state unemployment compensation law.
**Employee covered.** Employee is covered by provisions of state unemployment compensation law.
**Casual labor.** Service that is not in the course of an employer's trade or business unless the individual is paid more than $50 *and* the employer regularly retains the individual to perform such service.

| | *Self-Employed* | *Railroad Employees* | *Relative* | | *Patients Employed by Hospital* | *Insurance Agents Wholly on Commission* | *Real Estate Agents Wholly on Commission* | *Casual Labor* | *Citations to Authority* |
|---|---|---|---|---|---|---|---|---|---|
| | | | *Employed by Child or Spouse* | *Minor Employed by Parent* | | | | | |
| ND | Employee not covered. | Employee not covered. | Employee not covered. | Employee not covered. | Employee not covered. | Employee not covered. | Employee not covered. | Employee not covered. | N.D. Cent. Code § 52-01-01. |
| OH | Employee not covered. | Employee not covered. | Employee not covered. | Employee not covered. | Employee not covered. | Employee not covered. | Employee covered. | Employee not covered. | Ohio Rev. Code Ann. §§ 4141.01, 4141.29, 4141.31. |
| OK | Employee not covered. | Employee not covered. | Employee not covered. | Employee not covered. | Employee not covered. | Employee not covered. | Employee not covered. | Employee covered. | Okla. Stat. tit. 40, § 1-210. |
| OR | Employee not covered. | Employee not covered. | Employee not covered. | Employee not covered. | Employee not covered. | Employee not covered. | Employee not covered. | Employee not covered if total payments less than $225 in any calendar quarter or performed in fewer than 18 weeks. | Or. Rev. Stat. §§ 657.025, 657.030, 657.050, 657.060, 657.075, 657.085. |
| PA | Employee not covered. | Employee not covered. | Employee not covered. | Employee not covered. | Employee not covered. | Employee not covered. | Employee not covered. | Employee not covered. | Pa. Cons. Stat. Ann. tit. 43, §§ 753, 801, 802, 802.4. |
| RI | Employee not covered. | Employee not covered. | Employee not covered. | Employee not covered. | Employee not covered. | Employee not covered. | Employee not covered. | Employee not covered. | R.I. Gen. Laws § 28-42-8. |
| SC | Employee not covered. | Employee not covered. | Employee not covered. | Employee not covered. | Employee not covered. | Employee not covered. | Employee not covered. | Employee not covered. | S.C. Code Ann. § 41-27-260. |
| SD | Employee not covered. | Employee not covered. | Employee not covered. | Employee not covered. | Employee not covered. | Employee not covered. | Employee covered. | Employee covered. | S.D. Codified Laws Ann. §§ 61-1-11, 61-1-18, 61-1-23, 61-1-28, 61-1-30. |
| TN | Employee not covered. | Employee not covered. | Employee not covered. | Employee not covered. | Employee not covered. | Employee not covered. | Employee not covered. | Employee covered. | Tenn. Code Ann. § 50-7-207. |

| | | | | | | | | | |
|---|---|---|---|---|---|---|---|---|---|
| TX | Employee not covered. | Employee not covered. | Employee not covered. | Employee not covered. | Employee not covered. | Employee not covered. | Employee not covered. | Employee covered. | Tex. Lab. Code Ann. §§ 201.065, 201.068, 201.071, 201.072. |
| UT | Employee not covered. | Employee not covered. | Employee not covered. | Employee not covered. | Employee not covered. | Employee not covered. | Employee not covered. | Employee not covered. | Utah Code Ann. §§ 35-4-204, 35-4-205. |
| VT | Employee not covered. | Employee not covered. | Employee not covered. | Employee not covered. | Employee not covered. | Employee not covered. | Employee not covered. | Employee not covered. | Vt. Stat. Ann. tit. 21, § 1301. |
| VA | Employee not covered. | Employee not covered. | Employee not covered. | Employee not covered. | Employee covered, although patients employed in rehabilitation centers are exempt. | Employee not covered. | Employee not covered. | Employee not covered. | Va. Code Ann. § 60.2-219. |
| WA | Employee not covered. | Employee not covered. | Employee not covered. | Employee not covered. | Employee not covered. | Employee not covered. | Employee not covered. | Employee not covered. | Wash. Rev. Code §§ 50.04.140, 50.04.180, 50.04.230, 50.04.270, 50.20.050, 50.44.040. |
| WV | Employee not covered. | Employee not covered. | Employee not covered. | Employee not covered. | Employee not covered. | Employee not covered. | Employee covered. | Employee covered. | W. Va. Code §§ 21A-1-3, 21A-6-3. |
| WI | Employee not covered. | Employee not covered. | Employee not covered. | Employee not covered. | Employee not covered. | Employee not covered. | Employee not covered. | Employee covered. | Wis. Stat. §§ 108.02, 108.04. |
| WY | Employee not covered. | Employee not covered. | Employee not covered. | Employee not covered. | Employee not covered. | Employee covered. | Employee not covered. | Employee covered. | Wyo. Stat. §§ 27-3-108, 27-3-313. |

# Table 6.3-2 Part B
## STATE UNEMPLOYMENT COMPENSATION LAW COVERAGE

(See also text at § 6.3.)

**KEY:** **Employee not covered.** Employee is not covered by provisions of state unemployment compensation law.
**Employee covered.** Employee is covered by provisions of state unemployment compensation law.
**Nonprofit organization.** Organization exempt from income tax pursuant to § 501(a) of the federal Internal Revenue Code (26 U.S.C. § 501(a) or 26 U.S.C. § 521) other than an organization described in 26 U.S.C. § 401(a), if the remuneration is less than $50 per quarter.
*Check specific state law for definition of "American vessel."

| | *Student Service for School, College, or University* | *Student at Nonprofit or Public Education Institution in Full-Time Work Study Program* | *Service by Spouse of Student for School, College, or University if under College Work Study Program* | *Minor Newspaper Carrier (under age 18)* | *Newspaper Distributor (not to consumer)* | *Commercial Fishing Vessel of Fewer than 10 Tons (except for salmon or halibut)* | *Student Nurses Employed in Hospital or Training School* | *Hospital Interns Who Completed 4 Years in Medical School* | *Part-Time Service for Nonprofit Organizations* | *Citations to Authority* |
|---|---|---|---|---|---|---|---|---|---|---|
| AL | Employee not covered. | Employee not covered. | Employee not covered. | Employee not covered. | Employee covered. | Employee not covered. | Employee not covered. | Employee not covered. | Employee not covered. | Ala. Code § 25-4-10. |
| AK | Employee not covered. | Employee not covered. | Employee covered. | Employee not covered. | Employee not covered. | Employee not covered if fewer than 10 workers or if pay is based on a share of the boat's catches. | Employee covered. | Employee covered. | Employee not covered. | Alaska Stat. § 23.20.526. |
| AZ | Employee not covered. | Employee not covered. | Employee not covered. | Employee not covered. | Employee not covered. | Employee covered. | Employee not covered. | Employee not covered. | Employee not covered. | Ariz. Rev. Stat. Ann. § 23-617. |
| AR | Employee not covered. | Employee not covered. | Employee covered. | Employee not covered. | Employee not covered. | Employee not covered. | Employee not covered. | Employee not covered. | Employee not covered. | Ark. Code Ann. § 11-10-210. |

| | | | | | | | | | | |
|---|---|---|---|---|---|---|---|---|---|---|
| CA | Employee not covered. | Statute exempts only students under the age of 22. | Employee not covered. | Employee not covered. | Employee not covered. | Employee covered. | Employee not covered. | Employee not covered. | Employee not covered. | Cal. Unemp. Ins. Code §§ 634.5, 641, 642, 642.1, 645, 646, 648, 649. |
| CO | Employee not covered. | Employee not covered. | Employee not covered. | Employee not covered. | Employee not covered. | Employee covered. | Employee covered. | Employee covered. | Employee not covered. | Colo. Rev. Stat. §§ 8-70-103, 8-70-118, 8-70-131, 8-70-132, 8-70-135, 8-70-140. |
| CT | Employee not covered. | Employee not covered. | Employee not covered. | Employee not covered. | Employee covered. | Employee covered. | Employee not covered. | Employee not covered. | Employee covered. | Conn. Gen. Stat. Ann. §§ 31-222, 31-235, 31-236. |
| DE | Employee not covered. | Employee not covered. | Employee covered. | Employee covered. | Employee covered. | Employee covered. | Employee covered. | Employee covered. | Employee covered. | Del. Code Ann. tit. 19, § 3302. |
| DC | Employee not covered. | Employee covered. | Employee covered. | Employee not covered. | Employee covered. | Employee not covered. | Employee not covered. | Employee not covered. | Employee not covered. | D.C. Code Ann. § 46-101. |
| FL | Employee not covered. | Employee not covered. | Employee covered. | Employee not covered. | Employee covered. | Employee covered. | Employee not covered. | Employee not covered. | Employee not covered. | Fla. Stat. Ann. § 443.036. |
| GA | Employee not covered. | Employee not covered. | Employee not covered. | Employee not covered. | Employee covered. | Employee not covered. | Employee not covered. | Employee not covered. | Employee not covered. | Ga. Code Ann. § 34-8-35. |
| HI | Employee not covered. | Employee covered. | Employee covered. | Employee not covered. | Employee covered. | Employee not covered unless employer employed at least 1 person on any day in 20 different calendar weeks. | Employee not covered. | Employee not covered. | Employee not covered. | Haw. Rev. Stat. §§ 383-7, 383-29. |
| ID | Employee not covered. | Employee not covered. | Employee covered. | Employee not covered. | Employee covered. | Employee covered. | Employee not covered. | Employee not covered. | Employee covered. | Idaho Code § 72-1316A. |
| IL | Employee not covered. | Employee not covered. | Employee not covered. | Employee not covered. | Employee covered. | Employee covered if working on an American vessel* whose operating office is located in Illinois. | Employee not covered. | Employee not covered. | Employee not covered. | Ill. Comp. Stat. Ann. ch. 820 ¶¶ 405/211, 405/216, 405/223–405/225, 405/227, 405/230. |

*(Table continues.)*

# Table 6.3-2 Part B *(cont'd)*
## STATE UNEMPLOYMENT COMPENSATION LAW COVERAGE

(See also text at § 6.3.)

**KEY:** **Employee not covered.** Employee is not covered by provisions of state unemployment compensation law.
**Employee covered.** Employee is covered by provisions of state unemployment compensation law.
**Nonprofit organization.** Organization exempt from income tax pursuant to § 501(a) of the federal Internal Revenue Code (26 U.S.C. § 501(a) or 26 U.S.C. § 521) other than an organization described in 26 U.S.C. § 401(a), if the remuneration is less than $50 per quarter.
*Check specific state law for definition of "American vessel."

| | *Student Service for School, College, or University* | *Student at Nonprofit or Public Education Institution in Full-Time Work Study Program* | *Service by Spouse of Student for School, College, or University if under College Work Study Program* | *Minor Newspaper Carrier (under age 18)* | *Newspaper Distributor (not to consumer)* | *Commercial Fishing Vessel of Fewer than 10 Tons (except for salmon or halibut)* | *Student Nurses Employed in Hospital or Training School* | *Hospital Interns Who Completed 4 Years in Medical School* | *Part-Time Service for Nonprofit Organizations* | *Citations to Authority* |
|---|---|---|---|---|---|---|---|---|---|---|
| IN | Employee not covered. | Employee not covered. | Employee not covered. | Employee not covered. | Employee not covered. | Employee covered if working on an American vessel* or aircraft whose operating office is located in Indiana. | Employee not covered. | Employee not covered. | Employee not covered. | Ind. Code Ann. §§ 22-4-7-1, 22-4-8-2, 22-4-8-3. |
| IA | Employee not covered. | Employee not covered. | Employee not covered. | Employee covered. | Employee covered. | Employee covered if working on an American vessel* whose operating office is located in Iowa. | Employee covered. | Employee covered. | Employee covered. | Iowa Code Ann. § 96.19. |

| | | | | | | | | | | |
|---|---|---|---|---|---|---|---|---|---|---|
| KS | Employee not covered. | Employee not covered. | Employee covered. | Employee not covered. | Employee covered. | Employee covered if working on an American vessel* or aircraft whose operating office is located in Kansas. | Employee covered. | Employee covered. | Employee not covered. | Kan. Stat. Ann. § 44-703. |
| KY | Employee not covered. | Employee not covered. | Employee not covered. | Employee not covered. | Employee covered. | Employee covered if working on an American vessel* or aircraft whose operating office is located in Kentucky. | Employee not covered. | Employee not covered. | Employee not covered. | Ky. Rev. Stat. Ann. §§ 341.050, 341.055. |
| LA | Employee not covered. | Employee not covered. | Employee covered. | Employee not covered. | Employee covered. | Employee covered if working on an American vessel* whose operating office is located in Louisiana. | Employee not covered. | Employee not covered. | Employee not covered. | La. Rev. Stat. Ann. § 23:1472. |
| ME | Employee not covered. | Employee not covered. | Employee covered. | Employee not covered. | Employee covered. | Employee not covered. | Employee not covered. | Employee not covered. | Employee not covered if pay is less than $150. | Me. Rev. Stat. Ann. tit. 26, § 1043. |
| MD | Employee not covered. | Employee not covered. | Employee not covered. | Employee not covered. | Employee covered. | Employee not covered. | Employee not covered. | Employee not covered. | Employee not covered. | Md. Code Ann., Lab. & Empl. §§ 8-208, 8-210, 8-218–8-220. |
| MA | Employee not covered. | Employee not covered. | Employee not covered. | Employee not covered. | Employee covered. | Employee not covered. | Employee not covered. | Employee not covered. | Employee not covered. | Mass. Gen. Laws Ann. ch. 151A, §§ 4A, 6. |
| MI | Employee not covered. | Employee not covered. | Employee not covered. | Employee not covered. | Employee covered. | Employee not covered. | Employee covered. | Employee covered. | Employee not covered. | Mich. Comp. Laws Ann. §§ 421.42, 421.43; Mich. Stat. Ann. §§ 17.545, 17.547. |
| MN | Employee not covered. | Employee not covered. | Employee covered. | Employee not covered. | Employee covered. | Employee covered. | Employee not covered. | Employee not covered. | Employee not covered. | Minn. Stat. §§ 268.04, 268.06. |

*(Table continues.)*

# Table 6.3-2 Part B *(cont'd)*

## STATE UNEMPLOYMENT COMPENSATION LAW COVERAGE

(See also text at § 6.3.)

**KEY:** **Employee not covered.** Employee is not covered by provisions of state unemployment compensation law.
**Employee covered.** Employee is covered by provisions of state unemployment compensation law.
**Nonprofit organization.** Organization exempt from income tax pursuant to § 501(a) of the federal Internal Revenue Code (26 U.S.C. § 501(a) or 26 U.S.C. § 521) other than an organization described in 26 U.S.C. § 401(a), if the remuneration is less than $50 per quarter.
*Check specific state law for definition of "American vessel."

| | *Student Service for School, College, or University* | *Student at Nonprofit or Public Education Institution in Full-Time Work Study Program* | *Service by Spouse of Student for School, College, or University if under College Work Study Program* | *Minor Newspaper Carrier (under age 18)* | *Newspaper Distributor (not to consumer)* | *Commercial Fishing Vessel of Fewer than 10 Tons (except for salmon or halibut)* | *Student Nurses Employed in Hospital or Training School* | *Hospital Interns Who Completed 4 Years in Medical School* | *Part-Time Service for Nonprofit Organizations* | *Citations to Authority* |
|---|---|---|---|---|---|---|---|---|---|---|
| MS | Employee not covered. | Statute exempts only students under the age of 22. | Employee not covered. | Employee not covered. | Newspaper distributor who owns his or her own truck, hires or discharges his or her own employees, distributes newspapers or magazines in his or her own territory, and receives no salary, wages, or other remuneration from the publisher is not an employee of the publisher. | Employee covered if working on an American vessel* whose operating office is located in Mississippi. | Employee not covered. | Employee not covered. | Employee not covered. | Miss. Code Ann. § 71-5-11; MESC Reg. Tr-28. |

| | | | | | | | | | | |
|---|---|---|---|---|---|---|---|---|---|---|
| MO | Employee not covered. | Employee not covered. | Employee not covered. | Employee not covered. | Employee covered. | Employee covered. | Employee covered. | Employee covered. | Employee covered. | Mo. Rev. Stat. §§ 288.030, 288.034. |
| MT | Employee not covered. | Employee not covered. | Employee not covered. | Employee not covered. | Employee covered. | Employee covered. | Employee covered. | Employee covered. | Employee covered. | Mont. Code Ann. §§ 39-51-203–39-51-205. |
| NE | Employee not covered. | Employee not covered. | Employee not covered. | Employee not covered. | Employee not covered. | Employee covered. | Employee not covered. | Employee not covered. | Employee not covered. | Neb. Rev. Stat. §§ 48-602, 48-604. |
| NV | Employee not covered. | Employee not covered. | Employee not covered. | Employee not covered. | Employee covered. | Employee covered. | Employee covered. | Employee covered. | Employee not covered. | Nev. Rev. Stat. §§ 612.070, 612.118–612.121, 612.130. |
| NH | Employee not covered. | Employee not covered. | Employee not covered. | Employee not covered. | Employee covered. | Employee not covered. | Employee not covered. | Employee not covered. | Employee not covered. | N.H. Rev. Stat. Ann. § 282-A:9. |
| NJ | Employee not covered. | Employee not covered. | Employee not covered. | Employee covered. | Employee covered. | Employee covered. | Employee not covered. | Employee not covered. | Employee covered. | N.J. Rev. Stat. § 43:21-19. |
| NM | Employee not covered. | Employee not covered. | Employee covered. | Employee not covered. | Employee covered. | Employee covered. | Employee covered. | Employee covered. | Employee covered. | N.M. Stat. Ann. § 51-1-42. |
| NY | Employee not covered. | Employee not covered. | Employee not covered. | Employee covered. | Employee covered. | Employee covered. | Employee covered. | Employee covered. | Employee covered. | N.Y. Lab. Law § 511. |
| NC | Employee not covered. | Employee not covered. | Employee not covered. | Employee not covered. | Employee not covered. | Employee not covered. | Employee covered. | Employee covered. | Employee not covered. | N.C. Gen. Stat. § 96-8. |
| ND | Employee not covered. | Employee not covered. | Employee not covered. | Employee not covered. | Employee covered. | Employee covered. | Employee not covered. | Employee not covered. | Employee not covered. | N.D. Cent. Code § 52-01-01. |
| OH | Employee not covered. | Employee not covered. | Employee covered. | Employee not covered. | Employee covered. | Employee covered. | Employee not covered. | Employee not covered. | Employee not covered. | Ohio Rev. Code Ann. § 4141.01. |
| OK | Employee not covered. | Employee not covered. | Employee not covered. | Employee not covered. | Employee covered. | Employee covered. | Employee not covered. | Employee not covered. | Employee covered. | Okla. Stat. tit. 40, § 1-210. |
| OR | Employee not covered. | Employee not covered. | Employee not covered. | Employee not covered. | Employee covered. | Employee covered. | Employee not covered. | Employee covered. | Employee covered. | Or. Rev. Stat. §§ 657.030, 657.056, 657.080, 657.085. |
| PA | Employee not covered. | Employee not covered. | Employee not covered. | Employee not covered. | Employee covered. | Employee covered. | Employee not covered. | Employee not covered. | Employee not covered. | Pa. Cons. Stat. Ann. tit. 43, §§ 753, 892. |

*(Table continues.)*

## Table 6.3-2 Part B *(cont'd)*
## STATE UNEMPLOYMENT COMPENSATION LAW COVERAGE

(See also text at § 6.3.)

**KEY:** **Employee not covered.** Employee is not covered by provisions of state unemployment compensation law.
**Employee covered.** Employee is covered by provisions of state unemployment compensation law.
**Nonprofit organization.** Organization exempt from income tax pursuant to § 501(a) of the federal Internal Revenue Code (26 U.S.C. § 501(a) or 26 U.S.C. § 521) other than an organization described in 26 U.S.C. § 401(a), if the remuneration is less than $50 per quarter.
*Check specific state law for definition of "American vessel."

| | *Student Service for School, College, or University* | *Student at Nonprofit or Public Education Institution in Full-Time Work Study Program* | *Service by Spouse of Student for School, College, or University if under College Work Study Program* | *Minor Newspaper Carrier (under age 18)* | *Newspaper Distributor (not to consumer)* | *Commercial Fishing Vessel of Fewer than 10 Tons (except for salmon or halibut)* | *Student Nurses Employed in Hospital or Training School* | *Hospital Interns Who Completed 4 Years in Medical School* | *Part-Time Service for Nonprofit Organizations* | *Citations to Authority* |
|---|---|---|---|---|---|---|---|---|---|---|
| RI | Employee not covered. | Employee not covered. | Employee covered. | Employee covered. | Employee covered. | Employee not covered. | Employee covered. | Employee covered. | Employee not covered. | R.I. Gen. Laws §§ 28-42-3, 28-42-8, 28-42-10. |
| SC | Employee not covered. | Statute exempts only students under the age of 22. | Employee not covered. | Employee not covered. | Employee covered. | Employee not covered. | Employee not covered. | Employee not covered. | Employee not covered. | S.C. Code Ann. §§ 41-27-120, 41-27-260. |
| SD | Employee not covered. | Employee not covered. | Employee not covered. | Employee not covered. | Employee covered. | Employee covered. | Employee not covered. | Employee not covered. | Employee not covered. | S.D. Codified Laws Ann. §§ 61-1-10.9, 61-1-22, 61-1-23, 61-1-26. |
| TN | Employee not covered. | Employee not covered. | Employee not covered. | Employee covered. | Employee covered. | Employee not covered if fewer than 10 workers. | Employee covered. | Employee covered. | Employee not covered. | Tenn. Code Ann. § 50-7-207. |

| | | | | | | | | | | |
|---|---|---|---|---|---|---|---|---|---|---|
| TX | Employee not covered. | Employee not covered. | Employee covered. | Employee not covered. | Employee covered. | Employee not covered, if 10 workers or less and crew members' pay is share of catch. | Employee not covered. | Employee not covered. | Employee covered. | Tex. Lab. Code Ann. §§ 201.068, 201.069, 201.073, 201.075. |
| UT | Employee not covered. | Employee not covered. | Employee not covered. | Employee not covered. | Employee covered. | Employee covered. | Employee covered. | Employee covered. | Employee not covered. | Utah Code Ann. §§ 35-4-204, 35-4-205. |
| VT | Employee not covered. | Statute exempts only students under the age of 22. | Employee not covered. | Employee covered. | Employee covered. | Employee not covered. | Employee covered. | Employee covered. | Employee not covered. | Vt. Stat. Ann. tit. 21, § 1301. |
| VA | Employee not covered. | Employee not covered. | Employee covered. | Employee not covered. | Employee covered. | Employee not covered. | Employee not covered. | Employee not covered. | Employee not covered. | Va. Code Ann. § 60.2-219. |
| WA | Employee not covered. | Statute exempts only students under the age of 22. | Employee not covered. | Employee not covered. | Employee covered. | Employee covered. | Employee covered. | Employee covered. | Employee covered. | Wash. Rev. Code §§ 50.04.100, 50.04.240, 50.44.037, 50.44.040. |
| WV | Employee not covered. | Employee not covered. | Employee not covered. | Employee covered. | Employee covered. | Employee covered. | Employee covered. | Employee covered. | Employee covered. | W. Va. Code § 21A-1-3. |
| WI | Employee not covered. | Employee not covered. | Employee not covered. | Employee not covered. | Employee covered. | Employee covered. | Employee not covered. | Employee not covered. | Employee not covered. | Wis. Stat. § 108.02. |
| WY | Employee not covered. | Employee not covered. | Employee not covered. | Employee not covered. | Employee covered. | Employee covered. | Employee covered. | Employee covered. | Employee covered. | Wyo. Stat. §§ 27-3-102, 27-3-107, 27-3-108. |

# Table 6.3-3
## EFFECT OF STUDENT STATUS ON UNEMPLOYMENT INSURANCE ELIGIBILITY

(See also text at § 6.3.)

**KEY:** **Employee not covered.** Employee is not covered by provisions of state unemployment compensation law.
**Employee covered.** Employee is covered by provisions of state unemployment compensation law.

| | *Full-Time Student Employed by Organized Summer Camp* | *Student Service for School, College, or University* | *Student at Nonprofit or Public Education Institution in Full-Time Work Study Program* | *Service by Spouse of Student for School, College, or University if under College Work Study Program* | *Citations to Authority* |
|---|---|---|---|---|---|
| AL | Not specifically excluded. | Employee not covered. | Employee not covered. | Employee not covered. | Ala. Code § 25-4-10. |
| AK | Not specifically excluded. | Employee not covered. | Employee not covered. | Employee covered. | Alaska Stat. § 23.20.526. |
| AZ | Not specifically excluded. | Employee not covered. | Employee not covered. | Employee not covered. | Ariz. Rev. Stat. Ann. § 23-617. |
| AR | Not specifically excluded. | Employee not covered. | Employee not covered. | Employee covered. | Ark. Code Ann. § 11-10-210. |
| CA | Employee not covered. | Employee not covered. | Employee not covered. | Employee not covered. | Cal. Unemp. Ins. Code §§ 642, 642.1, 646. |
| CO | Not specifically excluded. | Employee not covered. | Employee not covered. | Employee not covered. | Colo. Rev. Stat. §§ 8-70-103, 8-70-131, 8-70-132. |
| CT | Not specifically excluded. | Employee not covered. | Employee not covered. | Employee not covered. | Conn. Gen. Stat. Ann. §§ 31-222, 31-235, 31-236. |
| DE | Not specifically excluded. | Employee not covered. | Employee not covered. | Employee covered. | Del. Code Ann. tit. 19, § 3302. |
| DC | Not specifically excluded. | Employee not covered. | Employee covered. | Employee covered. | D.C. Code Ann. § 46-101. |
| FL | Not specifically excluded. | Employee not covered. | Employee not covered. | Employee covered. | Fla. Stat. Ann. § 443.036. |
| GA | Not specifically excluded. | Employee not covered. | Employee not covered. | Employee not covered. | Ga. Code Ann. § 34-8-35, 34-8-196. |
| HI | Not specifically excluded. | Employee not covered. | Employee not covered. | Employee covered. | Haw. Rev. Stat. §§ 383-7, 383-29. |
| ID | Not specifically excluded. | Employee not covered. | Employee not covered. | Employee covered. | Idaho Code § 72-1316A. |
| IL | Not specifically excluded. | Employee not covered. | Employee not covered. | Employee not covered. | 820 Ill. Comp. Stat. Ann. 405/211, 405/216, 405/223–405/225, 405/227, 405/230. |
| IN | Not specifically excluded. | Employee not covered. | Employee not covered. | Employee not covered. | Ind. Code Ann. §§ 22-4-7-1, 22-4-8-2, 22-4-8-3. |
| IA | Not specifically excluded. | Employee not covered. | Employee not covered. | Employee not covered. | Iowa Code Ann. § 96.19. |
| KS | Not specifically excluded. | Employee not covered. | Employee not covered. | Employee covered. | Kan. Stat. Ann. § 44-703. |
| KY | Not specifically excluded. | Employee not covered. | Employee not covered. | Employee not covered. | Ky. Rev. Stat. Ann. §§ 341.050, 341.055. |

| | | | | | |
|---|---|---|---|---|---|
| LA | Not specifically excluded. | Employee not covered. | Employee not covered. | Employee covered. | La. Rev. Stat. Ann. § 23:1472. |
| ME | Employee not covered. | Employee not covered. | Employee not covered. | Employee covered. | Me. Rev. Stat. Ann. tit. 26, § 1043. |
| MD | Employee not covered. | Employee not covered. | Employee not covered. | Employee not covered. | Md. Code Ann., Lab. & Empl. §§ 8-208, 8-210, 8-218–8-220. |
| MA | Employee not covered. | Employee not covered. | Employee not covered. | Employee not covered. | Mass. Gen. Laws Ann. ch. 151A, §§ 4A, 6. |
| MI | Not specifically excluded. | Employee not covered. | Employee not covered. | Employee not covered. | Mich. Comp. Laws Ann. § 421.43; Mich. Stat. Ann. § 17.547. |
| MN | Not specifically excluded. | Employee not covered. | Employee not covered. | Employee covered. | Minn. Stat. §§ 268.04, 268.06. |
| MS | Not specifically excluded. | Employee not covered. | Employee not covered. | Employee not covered. | Miss. Code Ann. § 71-5-11. |
| MO | Employee not covered. | Employee not covered. | Employee not covered. | Employee not covered. | Mo. Rev. Stat. §§ 288.030, 288.034. |
| MT | Not specifically excluded. | Employee not covered. | Employee not covered. | Employee not covered. | Mont. Code Ann. §§ 39-51-204, 39-51-205, 39-51-2203. |
| NE | Not specifically excluded. | Employee not covered. | Employee not covered. | Employee not covered. | Neb. Rev. Stat. §§ 48-602, 48-604. |
| NV | Not specifically excluded. | Employee not covered. | Employee not covered. | Employee not covered. | Nev. Rev. Stat. §§ 612.070, 612.118–612.121, 612.130. |
| NH | Employee not covered, but student not disqualified if camp is run by a nonprofit organization. | Employee not covered. | Employee not covered. | Employee not covered. | N.H. Rev. Stat. Ann. § 282-A:9. |
| NJ | Not specifically excluded. | Employee not covered. | Employee not covered. | Employee not covered. | N.J. Rev. Stat. § 43:21-19. |
| NM | Not specifically excluded. | Employee not covered. | Employee not covered. | Employee covered. | N.M. Stat. Ann. § 51-1-42. |
| NY | Employee not covered. | Employee not covered. | Employee not covered. | Employee not covered. | N.Y. Lab. Law § 511. |
| NC | Employee not covered. | Employee not covered. | Employee not covered. | Employee not covered. | N.C. Gen. Stat. § 96-8. |
| ND | Not specifically excluded. | Employee not covered. | Employee not covered. | Employee not covered. | N.D. Cent. Code § 52-01-01. |
| OH | Employee not covered if working for day camp open for fewer than 12 weeks a year. | Employee not covered. | Employee not covered. | Employee covered. | Ohio Rev. Code Ann. § 4141.01. |
| OK | Not specifically excluded. | Employee not covered. | Employee not covered. | Employee not covered. | Okla. Stat. tit. 40, § 1-210. |
| OR | Employee not covered. | Employee not covered. | Employee not covered. | Employee not covered. | Or. Rev. Stat. §§ 657.030, 657.056, 657.080, 657.085. |
| PA | Not specifically excluded. | Employee not covered. | Employee not covered. | Employee not covered. | Pa. Cons. Stat. Ann. tit. 43, §§ 753, 892. |
| RI | Not specifically excluded. | Employee not covered. | Employee not covered. | Employee covered. | R.I. Gen. Laws §§ 28-42-3, 28-42-8, 28-42-10. |
| SC | Not specifically excluded. | Employee not covered. | Employee not covered. | Employee not covered. | S.C. Code Ann. §§ 41-27-120, 41-27-260. |
| SD | Not specifically excluded. | Employee not covered. | Employee not covered. | Employee not covered. | S.D. Codified Laws Ann. § 61-1-22. |
| TN | Employee not covered. | Employee not covered. | Employee not covered. | Employee not covered. | Tenn. Code Ann. § 50-7-207. |
| TX | Employee not covered. | Employee not covered. | Employee not covered. | Employee covered. | Tex. Lab. Code Ann. § 201.069. |

*(Table continues.)*

## Table 6.3-3 *(cont'd)*

## EFFECT OF STUDENT STATUS ON UNEMPLOYMENT INSURANCE ELIGIBILITY

(See also text at § 6.3.)

**KEY:** **Employee not covered.** Employee is not covered by provisions of state unemployment compensation law.
**Employee covered.** Employee is covered by provisions of state unemployment compensation law.

| | *Full-Time Student Employed by Organized Summer Camp* | *Student Service for School, College, or University* | *Student at Nonprofit or Public Education Institution in Full-Time Work Study Program* | *Service by Spouse of Student for School, College, or University if under College Work Study Program* | *Citations to Authority* |
|---|---|---|---|---|---|
| UT | Not specifically excluded. | Employee not covered. | Employee not covered. | Employee not covered. | Utah Code Ann. §§ 35-4-203, 35-4-204. |
| VT | Employee not covered. | Employee not covered. | Employee not covered. | Employee not covered. | Vt. Stat. Ann. tit. 21, § 1301. |
| VA | Employee not covered. | Employee not covered. | Employee not covered. | Employee covered. | Va. Code Ann. § 60.2-219. |
| WA | Not specifically excluded. | Employee not covered. | Employee not covered. | Employee not covered. | Wash. Rev. Code §§ 50.04.100, 50.04.240, 50.44.037, 50.44.040. |
| WV | Not specifically excluded. | Employee not covered. | Employee not covered. | Employee not covered. | W. Va. Code § 21A-1-3. |
| WI | Not specifically excluded. | Employee not covered. | Employee not covered. | Employee not covered. | Wis. Stat. § 108.02. |
| WY | Not specifically excluded. | Employee not covered. | Employee not covered. | Employee not covered. | Wyo. Stat. §§ 27-3-102, 27-3-107, 27-3-108. |

# Table 6.3-4
## REESTABLISHING ELIGIBILITY FOR UNEMPLOYMENT INSURANCE

(See also text at § 6.3.)

| | *Voluntarily Leaving Work Without Good Cause* | *Discharged Because of Misconduct/for Good Cause* | *Failing to Apply for Work When So Directed by the State/Failing to Accept Available Suitable Work When Offered* | *Other Provisions* | *Citations to Authority* |
|---|---|---|---|---|---|
| AL | Employee must return to insured employment and earn 10 times the weekly benefit amount. | For a dishonest or criminal act employee must return to insured employment and earn 10 times the weekly benefit amount. For other misconduct employee is disqualified for 4–7 weeks depending on severity of misconduct. | No requalification required, but automatically disqualified for 1–10 weeks. | If employee is discharged because of revocation of required license, employee must regain license. | Ala. Code § 25-4-78. |
| AK | Employee is automatically disqualified for 5 weeks, but may reestablish eligibility by earning 8 times the weekly benefit amount. | Employee is automatically disqualified for 5 weeks, but may reestablish eligibility by earning 8 times the weekly benefit amount. | Employee is automatically disqualified for 5 weeks, but may reestablish eligibility by earning 8 times the weekly benefit amount. If the misconduct is a felony in connection with work, the employee is disqualified for 51 weeks or until he or she earns 20 times the weekly benefit amount. | If employee is discharged because of felony or theft in connection with work, employee must return to work and earn 20 times the weekly benefit amount. | Alaska Stat. § 23.20.379. |
| AZ | Employee must return to work and earn 5 times the weekly benefit amount. | Employee must return to work and earn 5 times the weekly benefit amount. | Employee must return to work and earn 8 times the weekly benefit amount. | None. | Ariz. Rev. Stat. Ann. §§ 23-775, 23-776. |
| AR | Employee must have 30 days of employment covered by an unemployment compensation law. | If employee is discharged for misconduct in connection with work on account of dishonesty, working under the influence of intoxicants, or willful violation of safety rules, employee must return to work for 10 weeks, earning the weekly benefit amount in each of the weeks. Otherwise the employee is disqualified for 8 weeks with no requalification required. | Employee is disqualified for 8 weeks; no requalification required. | If employee is discharged due to refusal to report back to work within 1 week after notice of recall from strike: employee must return to work for 30 days. | Ark. Code Ann. §§ 11-10-512, 11-10-513, 11-10-514, 11-10-515. |

*(Table continues.)*

# Table 6.3-4 *(cont'd)*
## REESTABLISHING ELIGIBILITY FOR UNEMPLOYMENT INSURANCE

(See also text at § 6.3.)

| | *Voluntarily Leaving Work Without Good Cause* | *Discharged Because of Misconduct/for Good Cause* | *Failing to Apply for Work When So Directed by the State/Failing to Accept Available Suitable Work When Offered* | *Other Provisions* | *Citations to Authority* |
|---|---|---|---|---|---|
| CA | Employee must return to work and earn 5 times the weekly benefit amount. | Employee must return to work and earn 5 times the weekly benefit amount. | No requalification required, but automatically disqualified for 2 weeks. | If employee is discharged because of chronic absenteeism because of the use of intoxicants: employee must return to work and earn 5 times the weekly benefit or doctor must certify that employee has entered or completed treatment program and is able to return to work. | Cal. Unemp. Ins. Code §§ 1256.5, 1260. |
| CO | No requalification required. | No requalification required. | No requalification required. | None. | No statutory provision. |
| CT | Employee must return to work and earn 10 times the weekly benefit amount. | Employee must return to work and earn 10 times the weekly benefit amount. | Employee must return to work and earn 6 times the weekly benefit amount. | If employee is sentenced to prison for 30 days+: employee must return to work and earn 10 times the weekly benefit amount. | Conn. Gen. Stat. Ann. § 31-236. |
| DE | Employee must return to work for 4 weeks and earn 4 times the weekly benefit amount. | Employee must return to work for 4 weeks and earn 4 times the weekly benefit amount. | Employee must return to work and earn 4 times the weekly benefit amount. | None. | Del. Code Ann. tit. 19, § 3315. |
| DC | Employee must return to work for 10 weeks and earn 10 times the weekly benefit amount. | Employee must return to work for 8 weeks and earn 8 times the weekly benefit amount. For gross misconduct, employee must return to work for 10 weeks and earn 10 times the weekly benefit amount. | Employee must return to work and earn 10 times the weekly benefit amount. | None. | D.C. Code Ann. § 46-111. |
| FL | Employee must return to work and earn 17 times the weekly benefit amount. | Employee must return to work and earn 17 times the weekly benefit amount, but disqualification may not exceed 52 weeks after week of discharge. | Employee must return to work and earn 17 times the weekly benefit amount. | If employee is sentenced to prison for a criminal act connected with employment or discharged because of dishonest act connected with work, employee must return to work and earn 17 times the weekly benefit amount. | Fla. Stat. Ann. § 443.101. |

| | | | | | |
|---|---|---|---|---|---|
| GA | Employee must return to work and earn 10 times the weekly benefit amount. | Employee must return to work and earn 10 times the weekly benefit amount. | Employee must return to work and earn 10 times the weekly benefit amount. | If employee is discharged because of intentional conduct resulting in a physical assault or bodily injury or because of theft of goods worth $100 or less, employee must return to work and earn 12 times the weekly benefit amount.<br><br>If employee is discharged due to intentional conduct resulting in property loss in excess of $2,000 or theft in excess of $100: employee must return to work and earn 16 times the weekly benefit amount. | Ga. Code Ann. § 34-8-194. |
| HI | Employee must return to work and earn 5 times the weekly benefit amount. | Employee must return to work and earn 5 times the weekly benefit amount. | Employee must return to work and earn 5 times the weekly benefit amount. | Employee is disqualified for duration of unemployment that results from a labor dispute; employee is disqualified for week in which misrepresentation to obtain benefits is determined and for the following 24 calendar months. | Haw. Rev. Stat. § 383-30. |
| ID | Employee must return to work and earn 12 times the weekly benefit amount. | Employee must return to work and earn 12 times the weekly benefit amount. | Employee must return to work and earn 12 times the weekly benefit amount. | Employee is disqualified for duration of unemployment that results from a labor dispute; employee is disqualified for 52 weeks for making a misrepresentation to obtain benefits and must repay all benefits received as a result of the misrepresentation. | Idaho Code § 72-1366. |
| IL | Employee must return to work for 4 weeks and earn 4 times the weekly benefit amount. | Employee must return to work for 4 weeks and earn 4 times the weekly benefit amount. | Employee must return to work for 4 weeks and earn 4 times the weekly benefit amount. | Employee has no benefits rights upon admission or conviction of felony or theft in connection with work. | 820 Ill. Comp. Stat. Ann. 405/601–405/603. |
| IN | Employee must return to work for 8 weeks and earn 8 times the weekly benefit amount. | Employee must return to work for 8 weeks and earn 8 times the weekly benefit amount. | Employee must return to work for 8 weeks and earn 8 times the weekly benefit amount. | Employee is disqualified for duration of labor dispute. | Ind. Code Ann. §§ 22-4-15-1, 22-4-15-2, 22-4-15-3. |
| IA | Employee must return to work and earn 10 times the weekly benefit amount. | Employee must return to work and earn 10 times the weekly benefit amount. | Employee must return to work and earn 10 times the weekly benefit amount. | Employee is disqualified for duration of labor dispute; discharge for gross misconduct results in cancellation of all wage credits. | Iowa Code Ann. § 96.5. |
| KS | Employee must return to work and earn 3 times the weekly benefit amount. | Employee must return to work and earn 3 times the weekly benefit amount.<br><br>Gross misconduct: Employee must return to work and earn 8 times the weekly benefit amount. | Employee must return to work and earn 3 times the weekly benefit amount. | Employee is disqualified for duration of labor dispute; employee is disqualified for 1 year for false or fraudulent representation. | Kan. Stat. Ann. § 44-706. |

*(Table continues.)*

# Table 6.3-4 *(cont'd)*
## REESTABLISHING ELIGIBILITY FOR UNEMPLOYMENT INSURANCE

(See also text at § 6.3.)

| | *Voluntarily Leaving Work Without Good Cause* | *Discharged Because of Misconduct/for Good Cause* | *Failing to Apply for Work When So Directed by the State/Failing to Accept Available Suitable Work When Offered* | *Other Provisions* | *Citations to Authority* |
|---|---|---|---|---|---|
| KY | Employee must return to work for 10 weeks and earn 10 times the weekly benefit amount. | Employee must return to work for 10 weeks and earn 10 times the weekly benefit amount. | Employee must return to work for 10 weeks and earn 10 times the weekly benefit amount. | None. | Ky. Rev. Stat. Ann. § 341-370. |
| LA | Employee must return to work and earn 10 times the weekly benefit amount. | Employee must return to work and earn 10 times the weekly benefit amount. | Employee must return to work and earn 10 times the weekly benefit amount. | None. | La. Rev. Stat. Ann. § 23:1601. |
| ME | Employee must return to work and earn 4 times the weekly benefit amount. | Employee must return to work and earn 4 times the weekly benefit amount. | Employee must return to work and earn 8 times the weekly benefit amount. | If employee is discharged for a criminal act connected with work, employee must return to work and earn 8 times the weekly benefit amount or $600, whichever is greater. | Me. Rev. Stat. Ann. tit. 26, § 1193. |
| MD | Employee must return to work and earn 15 times the weekly benefit amount. | For gross misconduct, an employee must return to work and earn 20 times the weekly benefit amount. For aggravated misconduct, he or she must return to work and earn 30 times the weekly benefit amount. | Employee must return to work and earn 10 times the weekly benefit amount. | None. | Md. Code Ann., Lab. & Empl. §§ 8-1001, 8-1002, 8-1002.1, 8-1003, 8-1005. |
| MA | Employee must return to work and earn 8 times the weekly benefit amount. | Employee must return to work and earn 8 times the weekly benefit amount. | Employee must return to work for 8 weeks. | None. | Mass. Gen. Laws Ann. ch. 151A, § 25. |
| MI | Employee must return to work and earn 7 times the weekly benefit amount or earn 40 times the state minimum wage, whichever is less. | Employee must return to work and earn 7 times the weekly benefit amount or earn 40 times the state minimum wage, whichever is less. | Employee must return to work for 6 weeks. | If employee is incarcerated, or participates in a strike contrary to the provisions of an applicable collective bargaining agreement, employee must return to work for 6 weeks.<br>If employee is discharged because of assault, battery, or theft or destruction of property in excess of $25, employee must return to work for 13 weeks. | Mich. Comp. Laws § 421.29; Mich. Stat. Ann. § 17.531. |

| | | | | | |
|---|---|---|---|---|---|
| MN | Employee must return to work for 4 weeks and earn 8 times the weekly benefit amount. | Employee must return to work for 4 weeks and earn 8 times the weekly benefit amount. For gross misconduct, an employee must return to work and earn 12 times the weekly benefit amount. | Employee must return to work for 4 weeks and earn 8 times the weekly benefit amount. | None. | Minn. Stat. § 268.09. |
| MS | Employee must return to work and earn 8 times the weekly benefit amount. | Employee must return to work and earn 8 times the weekly benefit amount. | Disqualification may continue for up to 12 weeks; no requalification required. | None. | Miss. Code Ann. § 71-5-513. |
| MO | Employee must return to work and earn 10 times the weekly benefit amount. | Employee must return to work and earn 10 times the weekly benefit amount. | Employee must return to work and earn 10 times the weekly benefit amount. | None. | Mo. Rev. Stat. § 288.050. |
| MT | Employee must return to work and earn 6 times the weekly benefit amount. | Employee must return to work and earn 8 times the weekly benefit amount. For gross misconduct, an employee is totally disqualified for one year. | Employee must return to work and earn 6 times the weekly benefit amount. | None. | Mont. Code Ann. §§ 39-51-2302, 39-51-2303, 39-51-2304. |
| NE | Employee loses benefits for 7–10 weeks; no requalification required. | Employee loses benefits for 7–10 weeks; no requalification required. | Employee loses benefits for 7–10 weeks and must return to work and earn 4 times the weekly benefit amount (extended benefits only). | None. | Neb. Rev. Stat. § 48-628.03. |
| NV | Employee must return to work for 10 weeks and earn 10 times the weekly benefit amount. | Employee must return to work for 15 weeks and earn 15 times the weekly benefit amount. | Employee must return to work and earn 15 times the weekly benefit amount. | None. | Nev. Rev. Stat. §§ 612.380, 612.385, 612.390. |
| NH | Employee must return to work for 5 consecutive weeks and earn at least 20% more than the weekly benefit amount in each week. | Employee must return to work for 5 consecutive weeks and earn at least 20% more than the weekly benefit amount in each week. | Employee must return to work for 5 consecutive weeks and earn at least 20% more than the weekly benefit amount. | None. | N.H. Rev. Stat. § 282-A:32. |
| NJ | Employee must return to work for 4 weeks and earn 6 times the weekly benefit amount. | Employee is disqualified for 5 weeks. For gross misconduct the employee must return to work for 4 weeks and earn 6 times the weekly benefit amount to be requalified. | Employee loses benefits for 3 weeks. | None. | N.J. Rev. Stat. § 43:21-5. |
| NM | Employee must return to work and earn 5 times the weekly benefit amount. | Employee must return to work and earn 5 times the weekly benefit amount. | Employee must return to work and earn 5 times the weekly benefit amount. | None. | N.M. Stat. Ann. § 51-1-7. |
| NY | Employee must return to work and earn 5 times the weekly benefit amount, working at least 3 days in each week. | Employee must return to work and earn 5 times the weekly benefit amount, working at least 3 days in each week. If the employee is discharged due to the commission of a felony in connection with work, he or she is disqualified for one year. | Employee must return to work and earn 5 times the weekly benefit amount, working at least 3 days in each week. | None. | N.Y. Lab. Law § 593. |

*(Table continues.)*

## Table 6.3-4 *(cont'd)*

## REESTABLISHING ELIGIBILITY FOR UNEMPLOYMENT INSURANCE

(See also text at § 6.3.)

| | *Voluntarily Leaving Work Without Good Cause* | *Discharged Because of Misconduct/for Good Cause* | *Failing to Apply for Work When So Directed by the State/Failing to Accept Available Suitable Work When Offered* | *Other Provisions* | *Citations to Authority* |
|---|---|---|---|---|---|
| NC | Employee must return to work for 5 weeks and earn 10 times the weekly benefit amount. | Employee must return to work for 5 weeks and earn 10 times the weekly benefit amount. | Employee must return to work for 5 weeks and earn 10 times the weekly benefit amount. | If employee is discharged due to failure to attend a vocational school when so directed by the state or due to the sale of an employee-owned business: employee must return to work and earn 10 times the weekly benefit amount. | N.C. Gen. Stat. § 96-14. |
| ND | Employee must return to work and earn 8 times the weekly benefit amount. | Employee must return to work and earn 10 times the weekly benefit amount. | Employee must return to work and earn 10 times the weekly benefit amount. | None. | N.D. Cent. Code § 52-06-02. |
| OH | Employee must return to work for 6 weeks earning 6 times the weekly benefit amount in each week, and not less than 27.5% of the statewide average weekly wage. | Employee must return to work for 6 weeks earning 6 times the weekly benefit amount in each week, and not less than 27.5% of the statewide average weekly wage. | Employee must return to work for 6 weeks earning 6 times the weekly benefit amount in each week, and not less than 27.5% of the statewide average weekly wage. | If employee quits to marry: employee must return to work for 6 weeks earning one-half the weekly benefit amount in each week or $60, whichever is less. | Ohio Rev. Code Ann. § 4141.29. |
| OK | Employee must return to work and earn 10 times the weekly benefit amount. | Employee must return to work and earn 10 times the weekly benefit amount. | Employee must return to work and earn 10 times the weekly benefit amount. | None. | Okla. Stat. tit. 40, §§ 2-404, 2-406, 2-418. |
| OR | Employee must return to work and earn 4 times the weekly benefit amount. | Employee must return to work and earn 4 times the weekly benefit amount. | Employee must return to work and earn 4 times the weekly benefit amount. | None. | Or. Rev. Stat. § 657.176. |
| PA | No requalification required. | No requalification required. | No requalification required. | None. | — |
| RI | Employee must return to work for 4 weeks, earning 20 times the state minimum wage in each week. | Employee must return to work for 4 weeks, earning 20 times the state minimum wage in each week. | Employee must return to work for 4 weeks, earning 20 times the state minimum wage in each week. | None. | R.I. Gen. Laws §§ 28-44-17, 28-44-18, 28-44-20. |
| SC | Employee must return to work and earn 8 times the weekly benefit amount. | Ineligibility will continue for 5–26 weeks; no requalification required. | Employee must return to work and earn 8 times the weekly benefit amount. | None. | S.C. Code Ann. § 41-35-120. |

| | | | | | |
|---|---|---|---|---|---|
| SD | Employee must return to work for 6 weeks earning the weekly benefit amount in each week. | Employee must return to work for 6 weeks earning the weekly benefit amount in each week. | Employee must return to work for 6 weeks earning the weekly benefit amount in each week. | None. | S.D. Codified Laws Ann. §§ 61-6-13– 61-6-15. |
| TN | Employee must return to work and earn 10 times the weekly benefit amount. | Employee must return to work and earn 10 times the weekly benefit amount. | Employee must return to work and earn 10 times the weekly benefit amount. | None. | Tenn. Code Ann. § 50-7-303. |
| TX | Employee must return to work and either work 6 weeks or earn 6 times the weekly benefit amount. | Employee must return to work and either work 6 weeks or earn 6 times the weekly benefit amount. | Employee must return to work and either work 6 weeks or earn 6 times the weekly benefit amount. | None. | Tex. Lab. Code Ann. §§ 207.044, 207.045, 207.047. |
| UT | Employee must return to work and earn 6 times the weekly benefit amount. | For misconduct not amounting to a criminal act, employee must return to work and earn 6 times the weekly benefit amount. For a felony or other criminal act in connection with work, the employee is disqualified for one year. | Employee must return to work and earn 6 times the weekly benefit amount. | None. | Utah Code § 35-4-405. |
| VT | Employee must return to work and earn 6 times the weekly benefit amount. | Employee must return to work and earn 6 times the weekly benefit amount (gross misconduct only). | Employee must return to work and earn 6 times the weekly benefit amount. | None. | Vt. Stat. Ann., tit. 21, § 1344. |
| VA | Employee must return to work for 30 days, whether consecutive or not. | Employee must return to work for 30 days, whether consecutive or not. | Employee must return to work for 30 days, whether consecutive or not. | If employee is incarcerated following conviction for an unlawful act: after release, employee must return to work for 30 days, whether consecutive or not. If an employee receives benefits by misrepresentation, he or she shall be ineligible to receive further benefits until he or she pays back the sum he or she received. | Va. Code Ann. § 60.2-618. |
| WA | Employee must return to work for 5 weeks and earn 5 times the weekly benefit amount. | Employee must return to work for 5 weeks and earn 5 times the weekly benefit amount. | Employee must return to work for 5 weeks and earn 5 times the weekly benefit amount. | None. | Wash. Rev. Code §§ 50.20.050, 50.20.060, 50.20.080. |
| WV | Employee must return to work for 30 days. | Employee must return to work for 30 days for certain specified misconduct. | No requalification required. | None. | W. Va. Code § 21A-6-3. |
| WI | Employee must return to work and earn 4 times the weekly benefit amount. | Employee must return to work and earn 4 times the weekly benefit amount. | Employee must return to work and earn 4 times the weekly benefit amount. | None. | Wis. Stat. § 108.04. |
| WY | Employee must return to work and earn 12 times the weekly benefit amount. | Employee must return to work and earn 12 times the weekly benefit amount. | Employee must return to work and earn 12 times the weekly benefit amount. | None. | Wyo. Stat. § 27-3-311. |

## § 6.4 Benefits Eligibility Criteria and Payouts

Table 6.4-1 shows the criteria used to determine whether an individual is eligible for unemployment compensation benefits. The *base period* refers to the one-year period that determines wages to be used to calculate benefits. *Benefits year* is the 52-week period beginning after a claim is filed. To qualify for unemployment compensation, the employee-claimant must have earned "minimum qualifying wages." The formula used to determine if the claimant has done so is listed in the last column in Table 6.4-1.

Table 6.4-2 shows the benefits payouts in the various states. Again, a formula is used, this time to calculate the weekly benefit amount (WBA). However, the WBA is further defined by each state's maximum and minimum payouts. The waiting period—the period of unemployment during which a claimant does not receive compensation but must satisfy unemployment requirements to eventually qualify for compensation—is listed in column one.

Column two in Table 6.4-2 shows the maximum number of weeks for which an unemployed person can recover benefits in each state. In November 1991, Congress enacted a federally funded emergency unemployment benefits program that temporarily extended the maximum benefit weeks in each state by 13 or 20 weeks. In early 1992, Congress extended the emergency program with an additional 13 weeks of benefits. The emergency program expired on July 4, 1992.

# Table 6.4-1
## CRITERIA USED TO DETERMINE BENEFITS ELIGIBILITY

(See also text at § 6.4.)

**KEY:** **Average weekly wage.** Employee's average weekly wage.
**State average weekly wage.** Fixed amount determined by the state.
**Base period.** One-year period that determines wages to be used to calculate benefits.
**High quarter.** Quarter in base period when claimant earns highest wages.
**Weekly benefit amount.** Weekly unemployment benefit amount as determined by the state.

| | *Base Period (First 4 of last 5 completed calendar quarters immediately preceding filing of claim and establishment of benefit year.)* | *Benefit Year (One-year or 52-week period beginning week a valid claim is filed.)* | *Qualifying Formula (Claimant must earn minimum qualifying wages in base period.)* | *Citations to Authority* |
|---|---|---|---|---|
| AL | Yes. | Yes. | $1\frac{1}{2} \times$ high quarter. | Ala. Code §§ 25-4-1, 25-4-3, 25-4-77; 1C Unempl. Ins. Rep. (CCH), Ala., ¶¶ 3001, 3011. |
| AK | Yes. | Yes. | $1,000, with wages in 2 quarters. | Alaska Stat. §§ 23.20.350, 23.20.375, 23.20.520; 1C Unempl. Ins. Rep. (CCH), Alaska, ¶¶ 3001, 3012. |
| AZ | Yes. | Yes. | $1\frac{1}{2} \times$ high quarter and $1,000 in high quarter. | Ariz. Rev. Stat. Ann. §§ 23-605, 23-609, 23-771; 1C Unempl. Ins. Rep. (CCH), Ariz., ¶ 3013. |
| AR | Yes. | Yes. | 27 × weekly benefit amount with wages in 2 quarters. | Ark. Code Ann. §§ 11-10-201, 11-10-203, 11-10-210, 11-10-507, 11-10-522; 1C Unempl. Ins. Rep. (CCH), Ark., ¶¶ 3001, 3014. |
| CA | 4 quarters ending 4–7 calendar months before benefit year. | Yes. | (1) $1,300 in high quarter or (2) $900 in high quarter and $1\frac{1}{4} \times$ high quarter in base period. | Cal. Unemp. Ins. Code §§ 1275, 1276, 1281; 1C Unempl. Ins. Rep. (CCH), Cal., ¶¶ 3001, 3015. |
| CO | Yes. | Yes. | 40 × weekly benefit amount. | Colo. Rev. Stat. §§ 8-70-103, 8-70-111, 8-73-107; 1C Unempl. Ins. Rep. (CCH), Colo., ¶¶ 3001, 3016. |
| CT | Yes. | Yes. | 40 × weekly benefit amount and $1\frac{1}{2} \times$ high quarter; or wages in 20 different weeks. | Conn. Gen. Stat. Ann. §§ 31-232d, 31-230, 31-235; 1C Unempl. Ins. Rep. (CCH), Conn., ¶¶ 3001, 3017. |
| DE | Yes. | Yes. | 36 × weekly benefit amount, but not less than $720. | Del. Code Ann. tit. 19, §§ 3302, 3313, 3314; 1C Unempl. Ins. Rep. (CCH), Del., ¶¶ 3001, 3018. |

(Table continues.)

## **Table 6.4-1** *(cont'd)*
## CRITERIA USED TO DETERMINE BENEFITS ELIGIBILITY

(See also text at § 6.4.)

**KEY:** **Average weekly wage.** Employee's average weekly wage.
**State average weekly wage.** Fixed amount determined by the state.
**Base period.** One-year period that determines wages to be used to calculate benefits.
**High quarter.** Quarter in base period when claimant earns highest wages.
**Weekly benefit amount.** Weekly unemployment benefit amount as determined by the state.

| | *Base Period (First 4 of last 5 completed calendar quarters immediately preceding filing of claim and establishment of benefit year.)* | *Benefit Year (One-year or 52-week period beginning week a valid claim is filed.)* | *Qualifying Formula (Claimant must earn minimum qualifying wages in base period.)* | *Citations to Authority* |
|---|---|---|---|---|
| DC | Yes. | Yes. | $1\frac{1}{2} \times$ high quarter but not less than $1,950 with $1,300 in 1 quarter. | D.C. Code Ann. §§ 46-101, 46-108; 1C Unempl. Ins. Rep. (CCH), D.C., ¶¶ 3001, 3019. |
| FL | Yes. | Yes. | $1\frac{1}{2} \times$ high quarter; at least $3,400 wages in high quarter. | Fla. Stat. Ann. §§ 443.036, 443.091;1C Unempl. Ins. Rep. (CCH), Fla., ¶¶ 3001, 3020. |
| GA | Yes. | Yes. | $1\frac{1}{2} \times$ high quarter; wages in 2 quarters or $40 \times$ weekly benefit amount. | Ga. Code Ann. §§ 34-8-21, 34-8-23, 34-8-25, 34-8-193; 1C Unempl. Ins. Rep. (CCH), Ga., ¶¶ 3001, 3021. |
| HI | Yes. | Yes. | $26 \times$ weekly benefit amount; earnings in 2 quarters. | Haw. Rev. Stat. §§ 383-1, 383-29; 1C Unempl. Ins. Rep. (CCH), Haw., ¶¶ 3001, 3022. |
| ID | Yes. | Yes. | $1\frac{1}{4} \times$ high quarter; at least $1,144 wages in highest quarter; wages in 2 quarters. | Idaho Code §§ 72-1306, 72-1308, 72-1367; 1C Unempl. Ins. Rep. (CCH), Idaho, ¶¶ 3001, 3023. |
| IL | Yes. | Yes. | $1,600 wages; $440 in non–high quarter. | 820 Ill. Comp. Stat. Ann. 405/237, 405/242, 405/500; 1C Unempl. Ins. Rep. (CCH), Ill., ¶¶ 3001, 3024. |
| IN | Yes. | Yes. | $1\frac{1}{4} \times$ high quarter; $1,650 in last 2 quarters; $2,750 in base period. If a worker received benefits in the preceding year, he or she must have earned wages in employment this year in an amount greater than his or her previous benefit amount in each of 8 weeks. | Ind. Code Ann. §§ 22-4-2-12, 22-4-2-12.5, 22-4-2-21, 22-4-14-5; 1C Unempl. Ins. Rep. (CCH), Ind., ¶¶ 3001, 3025. |

| | | | | |
|---|---|---|---|---|
| IA | Yes. | Yes. | $1\frac{1}{4} \times$ high quarter; high quarter wages must be at least 3.5% of state average weekly wage; non–high quarter must be at least 1.75% of state average weekly wage. | Iowa Code Ann. §§ 96.4, 96.19; 1C Unempl. Ins. Rep. (CCH), Iowa, ¶¶ 3001, 3026. |
| KS | Yes. | Yes. | $30 \times$ weekly benefit amount; wages in 2 quarters. | Kan. Stat. Ann. §§ 44-703, 44-705; 1C Unempl. Ins. Rep. (CCH), Kan., ¶¶ 3001, 3027. |
| KY | Yes. | Yes. | $1\frac{1}{2} \times$ high quarter; $8 \times$ weekly benefit amount in last two quarters; at least $750 in high quarter; at least $750 outside high quarter. | Ky. Rev. Stat. Ann. §§ 341.090, 341.350; 1C Unempl. Ins. Rep. (CCH), Ky., ¶¶ 3001, 3028. |
| LA | Yes. | Yes. | $1\frac{1}{2} \times$ high quarter. | La. Rev. Stat. Ann. §§ 23:1472, 23:1600; 1C Unempl. Ins. Rep. (CCH), La., ¶¶ 3001, 3029. |
| ME | Yes. | Yes. | $2 \times$ annual worker's average weekly wage in each of 2 quarters; $6 \times$ worker's average weekly wage in base period. | Me. Rev. Stat. Ann. tit. 26, §§ 1043, 1192; 1C Unempl. Ins. Rep. (CCH), Me., ¶¶ 3001, 3030. |
| MD | Yes. | Yes. | $1\frac{1}{2} \times$ high quarter; wages in 2 quarters, with $576.01 in 1 quarter. | Md. Code Ann., Lab. & Empl. §§ 8-101, 8-802; 1C Unempl. Ins. Rep. (CCH), Md. ¶¶ 3001, 3031. |
| MA | 52 weeks preceding benefit year. | Yes. | $30 \times$ weekly benefit amount; not less than $2,400. | Mass. Gen. Laws Ann. ch. 151A, §§ 1, 4A, 24; 1C Unempl. Ins. Rep. (CCH), Mass., ¶¶ 3001, 3032. |
| MI | 52 weeks preceding benefit year. | Yes. | • 20 weeks where earning is greater than or equal to $20 \times$ state minimum hourly wage, or<br>• 14 weeks work with wages of $20 \times$ state average weekly wage. | Mich. Comp. Laws §§ 421.45–421.46a, 421.50; Mich. Stat. Ann. §§ 17.549–17.550(1), 17.554; 1C Unempl. Ins. Rep. (CCH), Mich., ¶¶ 3001, 3033. |
| MN | Yes. | Yes. For claims effective January 1, April 1, July 1, or October 1, the 53-week period beginning with the first week a valid claim is filed. | $1\frac{1}{4} \times$ high quarter; at least $1,000 in high quarter; wages in 2 quarters. | Minn. Stat. Ann. §§ 268.04, 268.06, 268.07; 1C Unempl. Ins. Rep. (CCH), Minn., ¶¶ 3001, 3034. |
| MS | Yes. | Yes. | $40 \times$ weekly benefit amount with $780 in 1 quarter and wages in 2 quarters. | Miss. Code Ann. §§ 71-5-11, 71-5-511, 71-5-513; 1C Unempl. Ins. Rep. (CCH), Miss., ¶¶ 3001, 3035. |
| MO | Yes. | Yes. | $1,000 or more in at least 1 quarter and either (1) $1\frac{1}{2} \times$ high quarter or (2) wages in 2 quarters and base period wages of $1\frac{1}{2} \times$ minimum taxable wage base. | Mo. Rev. Stat. §§ 288.030, 288.060; 1C Unempl. Ins. Rep. (CCH), Mo., ¶¶ 3001, 3036. |
| MT | Yes. | Yes. | $1\frac{1}{2} \times$ high quarter; must be at least 7% of average annual wage or 50% of average annual wage. | Mont. Code Ann. §§ 39-51-201, 39-51-2105, 39-51-2201; 1C Unempl. Ins. Rep. (CCH), Mont., ¶¶ 3001, 3037. |
| NE | Yes. | Yes. | $1,200 wages, $400 in each of 2 quarters. | Neb. Rev. Stat. §§ 48-602, 48-627; 1C Unempl. Ins. Rep. (CCH), Neb., ¶¶ 3001, 3038. |

*(Table continues.)*

# Table 6.4-1 *(cont'd)*
## CRITERIA USED TO DETERMINE BENEFITS ELIGIBILITY

(See also text at § 6.4.)

**KEY:** **Average weekly wage.** Employee's average weekly wage.
**State average weekly wage.** Fixed amount determined by the state.
**Base period.** One-year period that determines wages to be used to calculate benefits.
**High quarter.** Quarter in base period when claimant earns highest wages.
**Weekly benefit amount.** Weekly unemployment benefit amount as determined by the state.

| | *Base Period (First 4 of last 5 completed calendar quarters immediately preceding filing of claim and establishment of benefit year.)* | *Benefit Year (One-year or 52-week period beginning week a valid claim is filed.)* | *Qualifying Formula (Claimant must earn minimum qualifying wages in base period.)* | *Citations to Authority* |
|---|---|---|---|---|
| NV | Yes. | Yes. | $1\frac{1}{2}$ × high quarter or wages in at least 3 of 4 base period quarters. | Nev. Rev. Stat. Ann. §§ 612.025, 612.030, 612.375; 1C Unempl. Ins. Rep. (CCH), Nev., ¶¶ 3001, 3039. |
| NH | Calendar year preceding benefit year. | April 1 to March 31. | $2,800 wages, $1,200 in each of 2 quarters. | N.H. Rev. Stat. Ann. §§ 282-A:2, 282-A:4, 282-A:25; 1C Unempl. Ins. Rep. (CCH), N.H., ¶¶ 3001, 3040. |
| NJ | Yes. | 364 days beginning with the day on which valid claim filed. | (1) 20 weeks work and weekly wages of 20% of state average weekly wage or (2) 12 × state average weekly wage in base period or (3) 770 hours of farm labor. | N.J. Stat. Ann. §§ 43:21-4, 43:21-19; 1C Unempl. Ins. Rep. (CCH), N.J., ¶¶ 3001, 3041. |
| NM | Yes. | Yes. | $1\frac{1}{4}$ × high quarter. | N.M. Stat. Ann. §§ 51-1-5, 51-1-42; 1C Unempl. Ins. Rep. (CCH), N.M., ¶¶ 3001, 3042. |
| NY | 52 weeks ending on Sunday preceding filing of valid original claim. | Begins Monday after valid claim is filed. | (1) 20 weeks with wage equal to minimum worker's average weekly wage of $81 or (2) 15 weeks in last 52 weeks with wage equal to minimum of $81 worker's average weekly wage and 40 weeks in last 104 weeks with at least $3,240 during 40 weeks. | N.Y. Lab. Law §§ 520, 521, 527, 590; 1C Unempl. Ins. Rep. (CCH), N.Y., ¶¶ 3001, 3043. |
| NC | Yes. | Yes. | $1\frac{1}{2}$ × high quarter not less than 6 × state average weekly wage. | N.C. Gen. Stat. § 96-8; 1C Unempl. Ins. Rep. (CCH), N.C., ¶¶ 3001, 3044. |
| ND | Yes. | Yes. | 1.3 × high quarter; wages in 2 quarters. | N.D. Cent. Code §§ 52-01-01, 52-06-04; 1C Unempl. Ins. Rep. (CCH), N.D., ¶¶ 3001, 3045. |

| | | | | |
|---|---|---|---|---|
| OH | Yes. | Yes. | 20 qualifying weeks in base period; wages of 27½ percent of state average weekly wage. | Ohio Rev. Code Ann. § 4141.01; 1C Unempl. Ins. Rep. (CCH), Ohio, ¶¶ 3001, 3046. |
| OK | Yes. | Yes. | 1½ × high quarter with not less than $1,500 total wages. | Okla Stat. tit. 40, §§ 1-202, 1-204, 2-207; 1C Unempl. Ins. Rep. (CCH), Okla., ¶¶ 3001, 3047. |
| OR | Yes. | Yes. | $1,000 earnings in base period and 6 × weekly benefit amount. | Or. Rev. Stat. §§ 657.010, 657.150; 1C Unempl. Ins. Rep. (CCH), Or., ¶¶ 3001, 3048. |
| PA | Yes. | Yes. | $800 or more in high quarter; $1,320 or more in base year; at least 20% of base period wages outside high quarter. | Pa. Cons. Stat. Ann. tit. 43, §§ 753, 801, 804; 1C Unempl. Ins. Rep. (CCH), Pa., ¶¶ 3001, 3049. |
| RI | Yes. | Yes. | 200 × minimum hourly wage in one quarter and base period wages of 1½ × high quarter, but base period wages must be at least 400 × minimum hourly wage. | R.I. Gen. Laws §§ 28-42-3, 28-44-11; 1C Unempl. Ins. Rep. (CCH), R.I., ¶¶ 3001, 3051. |
| SC | Yes. | Yes. | 1½ × high quarter, but not less than $900 with $540 in 1 quarter. | S.C. Code Ann. §§ 41-27-150, 41-27-160, 41-27-310; 1C Unempl. Ins. Rep. (CCH), S.C., ¶¶ 3001, 3052. |
| SD | Yes. | Yes. | $728 or more in high quarter; 20 × weekly benefit amount in non–high quarter wages. | S.D. Codified Laws Ann. §§ 61-1-1, 61-6-7; 1C Unempl. Ins. Rep. (CCH), S.D., ¶¶ 3001, 3053. |
| TN | Yes. | Yes. | 40 × weekly benefit amount; lesser of 6 × weekly benefit amount or $900 outside high quarter. | Tenn. Code Ann. §§ 50-7-217, 50-7-218, 50-7-301, 50-7-302; 1C Unempl. Ins. Rep. (CCH), Tenn., ¶¶ 3001, 3054. |
| TX | Yes. | Yes. | 37 × weekly benefit amount; wages in 2 quarters. | Tex. Lab. Code Ann. §§ 201.011, 207.021; 1C Unempl. Ins. Rep. (CCH), Tex., ¶¶ 3001, 3055. |
| UT | Yes. | Yes. | (1) 1½ × high quarter or<br>(2) 20 weeks with wages each week of at least 5% of monetary base period wage requirement and 8% of insured average annual fiscal year wage. | Utah Code Ann. §§ 35-4-201, 35-4-403; 1C Unempl. Ins. Rep. (CCH), Utah, ¶¶ 3001, 3056. |
| VT | Yes. | Yes. | $1,299 in quarter; additional base period wages of at least 40% of high quarter; additional base period wages at least 4 × weekly benefit amount. | Vt. Stat. Ann. tit. 21, §§ 1301, 1338; 1C Unempl. Ins. Rep. (CCH), Vt., ¶¶ 3001, 3057. |
| VA | Yes. | Yes. | Earnings of at least $2,750 in highest 2 quarters. | Va. Code Ann. §§ 60.2-204, 60.2-206, 60.2-602, 60.2-607, 60.2-611, 60.2-612; 1C Unempl. Ins. Rep. (CCH), Va., ¶¶ 3001, 3058. |
| WA | Yes. | Yes. | 680 hours of wage-earning work. | Wash. Rev. Code Ann. §§ 50.04.020, 50.04.030; 1C Unempl. Ins. Rep. (CCH), Wash., ¶¶ 3001, 3059. |

*(Table continues.)*

# **Table 6.4-1** *(cont'd)*
## CRITERIA USED TO DETERMINE BENEFITS ELIGIBILITY

(See also text at § 6.4.)

**KEY:** **Average weekly wage.** Employee's average weekly wage.
**State average weekly wage.** Fixed amount determined by the state.
**Base period.** One-year period that determines wages to be used to calculate benefits.
**High quarter.** Quarter in base period when claimant earns highest wages.
**Weekly benefit amount.** Weekly unemployment benefit amount as determined by the state.

| | *Base Period (First 4 of last 5 completed calendar quarters immediately preceding filing of claim and establishment of benefit year.)* | *Benefit Year (One-year or 52-week period beginning week a valid claim is filed.)* | *Qualifying Formula (Claimant must earn minimum qualifying wages in base period.)* | *Citations to Authority* |
|---|---|---|---|---|
| WV | Yes. | Yes, or 53 weeks if claim is effective first day of a quarter. | $2,200; wages in 2 quarters. | W. Va. Code §§ 21A-1-3, 21A-6-1; 1C Unempl. Ins. Rep. (CCH), W. Va., ¶¶ 3001, 3060. |
| WI | Yes. | Yes. | 30 × weekly benefit amount; wages in non–high quarter of 8 × weekly benefit amount. | Wis. Stat. Ann. §§ 108.02, 108.04, 108.05; 1C Unempl. Ins. Rep. (CCH), Wis., ¶¶ 3001, 3061. |
| WY | Yes. | Yes. | 1.4 × high quarter; 8% of state average annual wage in base period; 5% state average annual wage in high quarter; 8 × weekly benefit amount of current claim. | Wyo. Stat. §§ 27-3-102, 27-3-301, 27-3-306; 1C Unempl. Ins. Rep. (CCH), Wyo., ¶¶ 3001, 3062. |

# Table 6.4-2
## UNEMPLOYMENT COMPENSATION BENEFITS PAYOUTS

(See also text at § 6.4.)

**KEY:** **Average weekly wage.** Employee's average weekly wage.
**State average weekly wage.** Fixed amount determined by the state.
**Base period.** One-year period that determines wages to be used to calculate benefits.
**High quarter.** Quarter in base period in which claimant earns highest wages.
**Daily average.** Average daily wage the state calculates for various categories of workers.

| | | | Weekly Benefit Amount | | | |
|---|---|---|---|---|---|---|
| | *Waiting Period* | *Maximum Benefit Weeks* | *Formula* | *Minimum ($) (Range indicates that employee may receive additional income for a dependent.)* | *Maximum ($) (Range indicates that employee may receive additional income for a dependent.)* | *Citations to Authority* |
| AL | None. | 26. | $^{1}/_{24}$ of average of 2 high quarters. | 45. | 190 or amount required under federal Unemployment Tax Act. | Ala. Code §§ 25-4-72, 25-4-74, 25-4-75; 1C Unempl. Ins. Rep. (CCH), Ala. ¶¶ 3001, 3011. |
| AK | 1 week. | 26. | If more than 90% earnings are in high quarter, base period – other 3 quarters × 10. If less than 90% earnings in high quarter, total wages in base period. | 44-116. | 248-320. | Alaska Stat. §§ 23.20.350, 23.20.375; 1C Unempl. Ins. Rep. (CCH), Alaska, ¶¶ 3001, 3012. |
| AZ | 1 week. | 26. | $^{1}/_{25}$ of high quarter. | 40. | 185. | Ariz. Rev. Stat. Ann. §§ 23-771, 23-779, 23-780; 1C Unempl. Ins. Rep. (CCH), Ariz., ¶¶ 3001, 3013. |
| AR | 1 week. | 26. | $^{1}/_{26}$ of high quarter up to $66^{2}/_{3}$% of state average weekly wage. | 53. | 294. | Ark. Code Ann. §§ 11-10-502, 11-10-504, 11-10-507; 1C Unempl. Ins. Rep. (CCH), Ark., ¶¶ 3001, 3014. |
| CA | 1 week. | 26. | $^{1}/_{23}$–$^{1}/_{33}$ of high quarter; if high quarter wages exceed $4,966.99, the maximum weekly benefit amount will be 39% of those wages divided by 13. | 40. | 230. | Cal. Unemp. Ins. Code §§ 1280, 1281; 1C Unempl. Ins. Rep. (CCH), Cal., ¶¶ 3001, 3015. |
| CO | 1 week. | 26. | 60% of $^{1}/_{26}$ of 2 high quarters, up to 50% of $^{1}/_{52}$ of base period earnings. | 25. | 314. | Colo. Rev. Stat. §§ 8-73-101, 8-73-104; 1C Unempl. Ins. Rep. (CCH), Colo., ¶¶ 3001, 3016. |
| CT | None. | 26. | $^{1}/_{26}$ of highest 2 quarters up to 60% of state average weekly wage plus $10 for each dependent up to 50% of weekly benefit amount or 5 dependents. | 15-65. | 362-412. | Conn. Gen. Stat. Ann. §§ 31-231a, 31-235; 1C Unempl. Ins. Rep. (CCH), Conn., ¶¶ 3001, 3017. |

(Table continues.)

# Table 6.4-2 *(cont'd)*
## UNEMPLOYMENT COMPENSATION BENEFITS PAYOUTS

(See also text at § 6.4.)

**KEY:** **Average weekly wage.** Employee's average weekly wage.
**State average weekly wage.** Fixed amount determined by the state.
**Base period.** One-year period that determines wages to be used to calculate benefits.
**High quarter.** Quarter in base period in which claimant earns highest wages.
**Daily average.** Average daily wage the state calculates for various categories of workers.

| | | | | *Weekly Benefit Amount* | | |
|---|---|---|---|---|---|---|
| | *Waiting Period* | *Maximum Benefit Weeks* | *Formula* | *Minimum ($) (Range indicates that employee may receive additional income for a dependent.)* | *Maximum ($) (Range indicates that employee may receive additional income for a dependent.)* | *Citations to Authority* |
| DE | None. | 26. | $1/46$ of 2 high quarters if fund is greater than or equal to $90 million, $1/52$ if less. | 20. | 300 if trust fund balance is at least 200 million; 265 if trust fund is less than 200 million but equal to or greater than 165 million; 245 if trust fund balance is less than 165 million but greater than 150 million; 225 if trust fund balance is less than 150 million but greater than 90 million; 205 if trust fund is less than 90 million. | Del. Code Ann. tit. 19, § 3313; 1C Unempl. Ins. Rep. (CCH), Del., ¶¶ 3001, 3018. |
| DC | 1 week. | 26. | $1/26$ of high quarter up to $66\frac{2}{3}$% of state average weekly wage plus $5 per dependent up to $20. | 50. | 309–329. | D.C. Code Ann. §§ 46-101, 46-108, 46-110; 1C Unempl. Ins. Rep. (CCH), D.C., ¶¶ 3001, 3019. |
| FL | 1 week. | 26. | $1/26$ of high quarter. | 32. | 288. | Fla. Stat. Ann. §§ 443.091, 443.111; 1C Unempl. Ins. Rep. (CCH), Fla., ¶¶ 3001, 3020. |
| GA | None. | 26. | $1/50$ of 2 high quarters or $1/25$ of highest quarter, if alternative qualifying wages are used. | 37. | 224. | Ga. Code Ann. §§ 34-8-191, 34-8-193, 34-8-195; 1C Unempl. Ins. Rep. (CCH), Ga., ¶¶ 3001, 3021. |
| HI | 1 week. | 26. | $1/21$ of high quarter up to 75% of state average weekly wage. | 5. | 356. | Haw. Rev. Stat. §§ 383-22, 383-24, 383-29; 1C Unempl. Ins. Rep. (CCH), Haw., ¶¶ 3001, 3022. |

| | | | | | | |
|---|---|---|---|---|---|---|
| ID | 1 week. | 26. | $1/26$ of high quarter. | 44. | 265. | Idaho Code §§ 72-1329, 72-1366, 72-1367; 1C Unempl. Ins. Rep. (CCH), Idaho, ¶¶ 3001, 3023. |
| IL | 1 week. | 26. | 49.5% of average weekly wage in 2 highest quarters, up to 49.5% of state average weekly wage; 58.5% of average weekly wage in two highest quarters; up to 58.5% of state average weekly wage if claimant has nonworking spouse; 65.5% of average weekly wage in two highest quarters; up to 65.5% of state average weekly wage if claimant has dependent child. | 51. | 251–332. | 820 Ill. Comp. Stat. Ann. 405/401, 405/403; 1C Unempl. Ins. Rep. (CCH), Ill., ¶¶ 3001, 3024. |
| IN | 1 week. | 26. | 5% of first $2,000 in high quarter plus 4% of remainder of high quarter wages. | 50. | 236. | Ind. Code Ann. §§ 22-4-11-1, 22-4-12-2, 22-4-12-4, 22-4-14-4; 1C Unempl. Ins. Rep. (CCH), Ind., ¶¶ 3001, 3025. |
| IA | None. | 26. | $1/19$–$1/23$ of high quarter. | 35–43. | 251–307. | Iowa Code Ann. §§ 96.3, 96.4; 1C Unempl. Ins. Rep. (CCH), Iowa, ¶¶ 3001, 3026. |
| KS | 1 week. | 26. | 4.25% of high quarter up to 60% of state average weekly wage. | 73. | 292. | Kan. Stat. Ann. §§ 44-704, 44-704a; 1C Unempl. Ins. Rep. (CCH), Kan., ¶¶ 3001, 3027. |
| KY | None. | 26. | 1.185% of total base period wages up to 55% of state average weekly wage. | 39. | 268. | Ky. Rev. Stat. Ann. §§ 341.350, 341.380; 1C Unempl. Ins. Rep. (CCH), Ky., ¶¶ 3001, 3028. |
| LA | 1 week. | 26. | Maximum weekly benefit amount is $66\frac{2}{3}$ of state's average weekly wage. | 10. | 215. | La. Rev. Stat. Ann. §§ 23:1472, 23:1592, 23:1595, 23:1600; 1C Unempl. Ins. Rep. (CCH), La., ¶¶ 3001, 3029. |
| ME | 1 week. | 26. | $1/22$ of high quarter up to 52% of state average weekly wage plus $10 for each dependent up to $1/2$ of weekly benefit amount. | 37. | 227. | Me. Rev. Stat. Ann., tit. 26, §§ 1043, 1191, 1192; 1C Unempl. Ins. Rep. (CCH), Me., ¶¶ 3001, 3030. |
| MD | None. | 26. | $1/24$ of high quarter plus $8 for each dependent up to $40 per week. | 25. | 250. | Md. Code Ann., Lab. & Empl. §§ 8-803, 8-804, 8-808; 1C Unempl. Ins. Rep. (CCH), Md., ¶¶ 3001, 3031. |
| MA | 1 week. | 30. | 50% of average weekly wage in the base period but not more than 57.5% of state average weekly wage. | 24–36. | 382–573. | Mass. Gen. Laws Ann. ch. 151A, §§ 23, 29, 30; 1C Unempl. Ins. Rep. (CCH), Mass., ¶¶ 3001, 3032. |
| MI | None. | 26. | 67% of after-tax average weekly wage. | 43. | 300. | Mich. Comp. Laws §§ 421.8, 421.27, 421.28; Mich. Stat. Ann. §§ 17.508, 17.529, 17.530; 1C Unempl. Ins. Rep. (CCH), Mich., ¶¶ 3001, 3033. |
| MN | 1 week. | 26. | $1/26$ of high quarter. | 38. | 331. | Minn. Stat. Ann. §§ 268.04, 268.07, 268.073, 268.08; 1C Unempl. Ins. Rep. (CCH), Minn., ¶¶ 3001, 3034. |

*(Table continues.)*

# Table 6.4-2 *(cont'd)*
## UNEMPLOYMENT COMPENSATION BENEFITS PAYOUTS

(See also text at § 6.4.)

**KEY:** **Average weekly wage.** Employee's average weekly wage.
**State average weekly wage.** Fixed amount determined by the state.
**Base period.** One-year period that determines wages to be used to calculate benefits.
**High quarter.** Quarter in base period in which claimant earns highest wages.
**Daily average.** Average daily wage the state calculates for various categories of workers.

| | *Waiting Period* | *Maximum Benefit Weeks* | *Weekly Benefit Amount* — *Formula* | *Weekly Benefit Amount* — *Minimum ($) (Range indicates that employee may receive additional income for a dependent.)* | *Weekly Benefit Amount* — *Maximum ($) (Range indicates that employee may receive additional income for a dependent.)* | *Citations to Authority* |
|---|---|---|---|---|---|---|
| MS | 1 week. | 26. | $^1/_{26}$ of high quarter. | 30. | 190. | Miss. Code Ann. §§ 71-5-503, 71-5-507, 71-5-511; 1C Unempl. Ins. Rep. (CCH), Miss., ¶¶ 3001, 3035. |
| MO | 1 week, may be compen- sable. | 26. | 4.5% of high quarter. | 45. | 205. | Mo. Rev. Stat. §§ 288.030, 288.038, 288.060; 1C Unempl. Ins. Rep. (CCH), Mo., ¶¶ 3001, 3036. |
| MT | 1 week. | 26. | (1) 1% annual wage or (2) 1.9% of 2 highest quarters, up to 60% of state average weekly wage. | 61. | 246. | Mont. Code Ann. §§ 39-51-2104, 39-51-2201, 39-51-2204; 1C Unempl. Ins. Rep. (CCH), Mont., ¶¶ 3001, 3037. |
| NE | 1 week. | 26. | $^1/_{20}$–$^1/_{24}$ of high quarter. | 36. | 206; 214 as of 1/1/00. | Neb. Rev. Stat. §§ 48-624–48-628; 1C Unempl. Ins. Rep. (CCH), Neb., ¶ 3038. |
| NV | None. | 26. | $^1/_{25}$ of high quarter. | 16. | 258. | Nev. Rev. Stat. Ann. §§ 612.340, 612.355; 1C Unempl. Ins. Rep. (CCH), Nev., ¶¶ 3001, 3039. |
| NH | None. | 26. | .8–1.1% of annual wages. | 32. | 275. | N.H. Rev. Stat. Ann. §§ 282-A:14, 282-A:25, 282-A:30, 282-A:31; 1C Unempl. Ins. Rep. (CCH), N.H., ¶¶ 3001, 3040. |
| NJ | 1 week. | 26. | 60% of average weekly wage + dependent's allowance of up to $56^2/_3$% of state average weekly wage. | 69. | 390. | N.J. Stat. Ann. §§ 43:21-3, 43:21-4, 43:21-27; 1C Unempl. Ins. Rep. (CCH), N.J., ¶¶ 3001, 3041. |
| NM | 1 week. | 26. | $^1/_{26}$ of high quarter; not less than 10% nor more than 50% of state average weekly wage. | 44. | 224. | N.M. Stat. Ann. §§ 51-1-4, 51-1-5; 1C Unempl. Ins. Rep. (CCH), N.M., ¶¶ 3001, 3042. |

| | | | | | | |
|---|---|---|---|---|---|---|
| NY | 1 week. | 26. | 50% of average weekly wage. | 40. | 300. | N.Y. Lab. Law § 590; 1C Unempl. Ins. Rep. (CCH), N.Y., ¶¶ 3001, 3043. |
| NC | 1 week. | 26. | $\frac{1}{26}$ of high quarter up to $66\frac{2}{3}$% of state average weekly wage. | 15. | 322. | N.C. Gen. Stat. §§ 96-12, 96-13; 1C Unempl. Ins. Rep. (CCH), N.C., ¶¶ 3001, 3044. |
| ND | 1 week. | 26. | $\frac{1}{65}$ of the sum of 2 high quarters + $\frac{1}{2}$ of wages in 3rd highest quarter, up to 65% of state average weekly wage. | 43. | 271. | N.D. Cent. Code §§ 52-06-01, 52-06-04, 52-06-05; 1C Unempl. Ins. Rep. (CCH), N.D., ¶¶ 3001, 3045. |
| OH | 1 week. | 26. | 50% of average weekly wage. | 68. | 267–358. | Ohio Rev. Code Ann. §§ 4141.01, 4141.29, 4141.30; 1C Unempl. Ins. Rep. (CCH), Ohio, ¶¶ 3001, 3046. |
| OK | 1 week. | 26. | $\frac{1}{25}$ of high quarter. | 16. | 266. | Okla. Stat. Ann. tit. 40, §§ 2-104, 2-106, 2-206; 1C Unempl. Ins. Rep. (CCH), Okla., ¶¶ 3001, 3047. |
| OR | 1 week. | 26. | 1.25% of base period wages up to 64% of state average weekly wage. | 81. | 346. | Or. Rev. Stat. §§ 657.150, 657.155; 1C Unempl. Ins. Rep. (CCH), Or., ¶¶ 3001, 3048. |
| PA | 1 week. | 26. | $\frac{1}{23}$–$\frac{1}{25}$ high quarter wage up to $66\frac{2}{3}$% of state average weekly wage plus $5 for one dependent and $3 for second dependent. | 35–43. | 375–383. | Pa. Cons. Stat. Ann. tit. 43, §§ 801, 804; 1C Unempl. Ins. Rep. (CCH), Pa., ¶¶ 3001, 3049. |
| RI | 1 week. | 26. | 4.62% of high quarter up to 85% of state average weekly wage plus greater of $10 or 5% of benefit rate per dependent, up to 5 dependents. | 42. | 364. | R.I. Gen. Laws §§ 28-44-6, 28-44-9, 28-44-14; 1C Unempl. Ins. Rep. (CCH), R.I., ¶¶ 3001, 3051. |
| SC | 1 week. | 26. | 50% of average weekly wage up to $66\frac{2}{3}$% of state average weekly wage. | 20. | 229. | S.C. Code Ann. §§ 41-35-40, 41-35-50, 41-35-110; 1C Unempl. Ins. Rep. (CCH), S.C., ¶¶ 3001, 3052. |
| SD | 1 week. | 26. | $\frac{1}{26}$ of high quarter up to 62% of state average weekly wage. | 28. | 203. | S.D. Codified Laws Ann. §§ 61-6-2, 61-6-6, 61-6-8; 1C Unempl. Ins. Rep. (CCH), S.D., ¶¶ 3001, 3053. |
| TN | 1 week. | 26. | $\frac{1}{26}$ of average of 2 high quarters. | 30. | 255. | Tenn. Code Ann. §§ 50-7-301, 50-7-302; 1C Unempl. Ins. Rep. (CCH), Tenn., ¶¶ 3001, 3054. |
| TX | 1 week, may be compensable. | 26. | $\frac{1}{25}$ of high quarter. | 44. | 280. | Tex. Lab. Code Ann. §§ 207.002, 207.005, 207.021; 1C Unempl. Ins. Rep. (CCH), Tex., ¶¶ 3001, 3055. |
| UT | 1 week. | 26. | $\frac{1}{26}$ of high quarter up to 60% of state insured average fiscal year weekly wage. | 1. | 272. | Utah Code Ann. §§ 35-4-401, 35-4-403; 1C Unempl. Ins. Rep. (CCH), Utah, ¶¶ 3001, 3056. |
| VT | 1 week. | 26. | $\frac{1}{45}$ of 2 high quarters. | 31. | 225. | Vt. Stat. Ann. tit. 21, §§ 1338, 1340, 1343; 1C Unempl. Ins. Rep. (CCH), Vt., ¶¶ 3001, 3057. |

(Table continues.)

# Table 6.4-2 *(cont'd)*
## UNEMPLOYMENT COMPENSATION BENEFITS PAYOUTS

(See also text at § 6.4.)

**KEY:** **Average weekly wage.** Employee's average weekly wage.
**State average weekly wage.** Fixed amount determined by the state.
**Base period.** One-year period that determines wages to be used to calculate benefits.
**High quarter.** Quarter in base period in which claimant earns highest wages.
**Daily average.** Average daily wage the state calculates for various categories of workers.

| | | | Weekly Benefit Amount | | | |
|---|---|---|---|---|---|---|
| | *Waiting Period* | *Maximum Benefit Weeks* | *Formula* | *Minimum ($) (Range indicates that employee may receive additional income for a dependent.)* | *Maximum ($) (Range indicates that employee may receive additional income for a dependent.)* | *Citations to Authority* |
| VA | 1 week. | 26. | $\frac{1}{50}$ of 2 high quarters. | 55. | 228. | Va. Code Ann. §§ 60.2-602, 60.2-607, 60.2-612; 1C Unempl. Ins. Rep. (CCH), Va., ¶¶ 3001, 3058. |
| WA | 1 week. | 30. | $\frac{1}{25}$ of average of 2 high quarters; wages up to 70% of state average weekly wage. | 78. | 410. | Wash. Rev. Code Ann. §§ 50.20.010, 50.20.120; 1C Unempl. Ins. Rep. (CCH), Wash., ¶¶ 3001, 3059. |
| WV | 1 week. | 26. | 1.0% of annual wages up to $66\frac{2}{3}$% of state average weekly wage. | 24. | 311. | W. Va. Code §§ 21A-6-1, 21A-6-10; 1C Unempl. Ins. Rep. (CCH), W. Va., ¶¶ 3001, 3060. |
| WI | None. | 26. | 4% of high quarter wages. | 43. | 290. | Wis. Stat. Ann. §§ 108.05, 108.151; 1C Unempl. Ins. Rep. (CCH), Wis., ¶¶ 3001, 3061. |
| WY | 1 week. | 26. | 4% of high quarter up to 55% of state average weekly wage. | 17. | 241. | Wyo. Stat. §§ 27-3-303, 27-3-304, 27-3-306, 27-3-316; 1C Unempl. Ins. Rep. (CCH), Wyo., ¶¶ 3001, 3062. |

## § 6.5 Employer Contributions and Recordkeeping Requirements

Table 6.5-1 shows employers' contribution obligations to the state unemployment insurance fund and lists the returns and reports that must be filed on contributions, employees' wages, and, for terminated employees, filing for unemployment compensation.

Tax rates are listed in the first three columns of Table 6.5-1. Most state unemployment laws list standard contribution rates. However, experience or "merit" ratings permit states to vary their employer contribution rates on the basis of an individual employer's employment experience. States may also adopt lower rates for new employers. Additionally, companies with records of fewer unemployment claims will pay lower tax rates. The fourth column lists voluntary contribution provisions by state. Voluntary payments may allow an employer to obtain reduced rates on its normal tax payments in those states having reserve-ratio or benefit-ratio systems. Those payments are credited to the employer's account.

The eighth column in Table 6.5-1 lists the record-retention period specified by state law. Note that the federal recordkeeping requirement is four years.

# Table 6.5-1
## EMPLOYER CONTRIBUTIONS AND RECORDKEEPING REQUIREMENTS

(See also text at § 6.5.)

**KEY:** **Voluntary contribution provision.** Some states allow voluntary contributions to the state unemployment compensation fund. This reduces payments under an employer's regular tax rate.

| | *Tax Rates (%)* | | | | *Returns and Reports* | | | | |
|---|---|---|---|---|---|---|---|---|---|
| | *Standard* | *Maximum* | *Minimum* | *Voluntary Contribution Provision* | *Employer's Contributions Report (due on or before last day of month following end of each quarter unless noted.)* | *Employees' Wages Report (due on or before last day of month following end of each quarter unless noted.)* | *Terminated Employee's Return Form (submitted when employee files for unemployment compensation.)* | *Record-Retention Period* | *Citations to Authority* |
| AL | 2.7. | 5.4. | .35 if benefit ratio = 0; .75 if benefit ratio > 0. | No. | Form UC-CR-4. | Form UC-CR-1. | Return Form Ben-241 within 4 business days. | Must retain for 5 years. | Ala. Code §§ 25-4-16, 25-4-40.1, 25-4-51, 25-4-54, 25-4-116.; 1C Unempl. Ins. Rep. (CCH), Ala., ¶¶ 3002, 3011. |
| AK | IATR. | 5.4. | 1.0. | No. | Form 1004. | Form 1004 A. | Furnish information of anything that might render claimant ineligible within 10 days of mailing notice of claim. | Must retain for 5 years. | Alaska Stat. §§ 23.05.080, 23.20.170, 23.20.290, 23.20.310; 1C Unempl. Ins. Rep. (CCH), Alaska, ¶¶ 3002, 3012. |
| AZ | 5.4. | 5.4. | 0.1. | Yes. Payment made on or before January 31 is credited to account as of most recent computation date of employer's liability. | Form UC-018. | Form UC-018. | Upon request, send separation notice within 24 hours. | Must retain for 4 years. | Ariz. Rev. Stat. Ann. §§ 23-726–23-730; 1C Unempl. Ins. Rep. (CCH), Ariz., ¶¶ 3002, 3013. |

| | | | | | | | | | |
|---|---|---|---|---|---|---|---|---|---|
| AR | 3.3. | 6.4. | 0.5. | Yes. Within 30 days of mailing rate notice. No later than March 12. | Form ESD-Ark-209B. | Form ESD-Ark-209C. | Furnish information within 7 days of mailing notice of claim. | Must retain for 5 years. | Ark. Code Ann. §§ 11-10-303, 11-10-318, 11-10-702–11-10-708, 11-10-717; 1C Unempl. Ins. Rep. (CCH), Ark., ¶¶ 3002, 3014. |
| CA | 5.4. | 5.4. | 1.1. | Yes. | Form DE-6. | Form DE-6. | Furnish information within 10 days of mailing notice of claim or within 15 days of mailing notice of computation. | Must retain for 4 years. | Cal. Unemp. Ins. Code §§ 977, 982; 1C Unempl. Ins. Rep. (CCH), Cal., ¶¶ 3002, 3015. |
| CO | 1.7. | 5.4. | 0.0. | Yes. Before March 15 of rate year. | Form UITR-1. | Form UITR-1(a). | Return Form B-290 within 9 days of date indicated on form. | Must retain for 5 years. | Colo. Rev. Stat. §§ 8-72-107, 8-76-102, 8-76-103, 8-76-104; 1C Unempl. Ins. Rep. (CCH), Colo., ¶¶ 3002, 3016. |
| CT | 5.4. | 6.9. | 2.0. | No. | Form UC-2. | Form Conn. UC-5A. | Immediately after separation give worker copy of Form UC-61. | Must retain for 4 years. | Conn. Gen. Stat. Ann. §§ 31-222, 31-225, 31-225a, 31-254; 1C Unempl. Ins. Rep. (CCH), Conn., ¶¶ 3002, 3017. |
| DE | 5.4. | 8.5. | 0.6. | No. | Forms UC-8 and UC-8A. | Form UC-8A. | Give worker Form UC-100A within 24 hours of separation. Return Form UC-119 within 3 days of claim notice. | Must retain for 4 years. | Del. Code Ann. tit. 19, §§ 3348, 3350; 1C Unempl. Ins. Rep. (CCH), Del., ¶¶ 3002, 3018. |
| DC | 3.1. | 7.0. | 1.6. | No. | Form DC DOES-UC-30. | Form DC DOES-UC-30. | Send Form DC DOES-10a to board and worker within 48 hours. | Must retain for 5 years. | D.C. Code Ann. §§ 46-103, 46-114; 1C Unempl. Ins. Rep. (CCH), D.C., ¶¶ 3002, 3019. |
| FL | 5.4. | 5.4. | 0.0 | No. | Form UCT-6. | Form UCT-6W. | Furnish information within 10 days of mailing notice of initial determination of claim. | Must retain for 5 years. | Fla. Stat. Ann. §§ 443.131, 443.141; 1C Unempl. Ins. Rep. (CCH), Fla., ¶¶ 3002, 3020. |

*(Table continues.)*

# Table 6.5-1 *(cont'd)*
## EMPLOYER CONTRIBUTIONS AND RECORDKEEPING REQUIREMENTS

(See also text at § 6.5.)

**KEY: Voluntary contribution provision.** Some states allow voluntary contributions to the state unemployment compensation fund. This reduces payments under an employer's regular tax rate.

| | *Tax Rates (%)* | | | | *Returns and Reports* | | | | |
|---|---|---|---|---|---|---|---|---|---|
| | *Standard* | *Maximum* | *Minimum* | *Voluntary Contribution Provision* | *Employer's Contributions Report (due on or before last day of month following end of each quarter unless noted.)* | *Employees' Wages Report (due on or before last day of month following end of each quarter unless noted.)* | *Terminated Employee's Return Form (submitted when employee files for unemployment compensation.)* | *Record-Retention Period* | *Citations to Authority* |
| GA | 5.4. | 5.4. | 0.04. | Yes. | Form DOL 4. | Form DOL 4. | Employer furnishes Form DOL-800 to terminated worker. | Must retain for 7 years. | Ga. Code Ann. §§ 34-8-152, 34-8-155, 34-8-156; 1C Unempl. Ins. Rep. (CCH), ¶¶ 3002, 3021. |
| HI | 5.4. | 5.4. | 0.2. | No. | Form UC-B6. | Form UC-B6A. | Employer returns Form UC-BP-4 within 5 calendar days of mailing date. | Must retain for 5 years. | Haw. Rev. Stat. §§ 383-66, 383-68; 1C Unempl. Ins. Rep. (CCH), Haw., ¶¶ 3002, 3022. |
| ID | 1.5. | 5.4. | 0.2. | No. | Form I-71-20. | Form I-71-26. | Within 2 days of receipt of claim notice, employer returns Form I-77-501. Employer gives Form I-77-514 to terminated worker. | Must retain for 3 years. | Idaho Code §§ 72-1347A, 72-1350; 1C Unempl. Ins. Rep. (CCH), Idaho, ¶¶ 3002, 3023. |
| IL | 2.7. | 6.8. | 0.6. | No. | Forms UI-3. | Form UI-40. | Within 7 days of date of claim notice, employer sends Form Ben-22, Notice of Possibility of | Must retain for 5 years. | 820 Ill. Comp. Stat. Ann. 405/1505, 405/1506.1, 405/1801; 1C Unempl. Ins. Rep. |

| | | | | | | | | | |
|---|---|---|---|---|---|---|---|---|---|
| | | | | | | | Ineligibility to Director. Employer gives terminated worker Form Ben-39 within 5 days of layoff. | | (CCH), Ill., ¶¶ 3002, 3024. |
| IN | 5.4. | 5.4. | 0.2. | Yes. Within 30 days of mailing of notice but within 120 days of beginning of year. | Form UC-1. | Form UC-5A-S. | Within 10 days of mailing of claim notice, employer submits Form 501. | Must retain for 5 years. | Ind. Code Ann. §§ 22-4-10-5, 22-4-11-2, 22-4-11-3; 1C Unempl. Ins. Rep. (CCH), Ind., ¶¶ 3002, 3025. |
| IA | For construction industry, 7.05; for nonconstruction employers, 1.05. | 7.05. | 0.05. | No. | Form 60-0103. | Form 60-0103. | Within 10 days of termination under disqualifying conditions, employer notifies commission and sends Form 60-0154. | Must retain for 5 years. | Iowa Code Ann. §§ 96.7, 96.11, 96.14; 1C Unempl. Ins. Rep. (CCH), Iowa, ¶¶ 3002, 3026. |
| KS | Varies by industry. | 6.0. | 0 for employers with a positive account balance; 1.1 for employers with a negative account balance. | Yes. Within 30 days of mailing notice but within 120 days of beginning of year. | Form K-CNS 100 due quarterly on or before 25th day of following month (5-day grace period). | Form K-CNS 100. | Employer furnishes Form K-Ben-451 within 48 hours of request. | Must retain for 5 years. | Kan. Stat. Ann. §§ 44-703, 44-710, 44-710a, 44-714; 1C Unempl. Ins. Rep. (CCH), Kan., ¶¶ 3002, 3027. |
| KY | 3.0. | 9.0. | 0.3; .27 as of 1/1/99. | Yes. Within 20 days of mailing notice but within 120 days of beginning of year. | Form UI 3. | Form UI 3. | Form UI 412-A or UI 412-B to employee and commission. | Must retain for 6 years. | Ky. Rev. Stat. Ann. § 341.270; 1C Unempl. Ins. Rep. (CCH), Ky., ¶¶ 3002, 3028. |
| LA | 2.7. | 6.47. | .22. | Yes. Within 30 days of mailing of notice or within 25 days of receipt of notice. | Form LDOLES-4. | Form LDOLES-4. | Within 72 hours of termination under disqualification, employer sends Form LDOLES-77 to commission and worker. | Must retain for 5 years. | La. Rev. Stat. Ann. §§ 23:1534–23:1536, 23:1541, 23:1660; 1C Unempl. Ins. Rep. (CCH), La., ¶¶ 3002, 3029. |
| ME | 5.4. | 7.9. | 2.8. | Yes. Within 30 days of mailing notice. 10-day extension for good cause. | Form Me. C-1. | Form Me. C-1. | Employer furnishes Form Me. B-1.1 at time of termination. | Must retain for 4 years. | Me. Rev. Stat. Ann. tit. 26, § 1221; 1C Unempl. Ins. Rep. (CCH), Me., ¶¶ 3002, 3030. |

*(Table continues.)*

# Table 6.5-1 *(cont'd)*
## EMPLOYER CONTRIBUTIONS AND RECORDKEEPING REQUIREMENTS

(See also text at § 6.5.)

**KEY:** **Voluntary contribution provision.** Some states allow voluntary contributions to the state unemployment compensation fund. This reduces payments under an employer's regular tax rate.

| | *Tax Rates (%)* | | | | *Returns and Reports* | | | | |
|---|---|---|---|---|---|---|---|---|---|
| | *Standard* | *Maximum* | *Minimum* | *Voluntary Contribution Provision* | *Employer's Contributions Report (due on or before last day of month following end of each quarter unless noted.)* | *Employees' Wages Report (due on or before last day of month following end of each quarter unless noted.)* | *Terminated Employee's Return Form (submitted when employee files for unemployment compensation.)* | *Record-Retention Period* | *Citations to Authority* |
| MD | 7.5. | 7.5. | 0.3. | No. | Form DEED-OUI-15. | Form DEED-OUI-16. | Employer returns Form DEED-OUI-207 within date shown on notice. | Must retain for 5 years. | Md. Code Ann., Lab. & Empl. §§ 8-607–8-612; 1C Unempl. Ins. Rep. (CCH), Md., ¶¶ 3002, 3031. |
| MA | 5.4. | 7.7. | 1.8. | No. | Form 0001. | Form WR-1. | Employer furnishes Form 0590-A upon termination. | Must retain for 4 years. | Mass. Gen. Laws Ann. ch. 151A, §§ 14, 14C, 38, 39; 1C Unempl. Ins. Rep. (CCH), Mass., ¶¶ 3002, 3032. |
| MI | 5.4. | 10.0 | 0.1. | Yes. Within 30 days of mailing notice but within 120 days of beginning of year. | Form MESC 1022 or MESC 1020. | Each employer must file quarterly Form MESC 1017. | Employer furnishes worker with Form MESC 1711 at time of termination. | Must retain for 6 years. | Mich. Comp. Laws §§ 421.13, 421.19, 421.19a; Mich. Stat. Ann. §§ 17.513, 17.520, 17.520(1); 1C Unempl. Ins. Rep. (CCH), Mich., ¶¶ 3002, 3033. |

| | | | | | | | | | |
|---|---|---|---|---|---|---|---|---|---|
| MN | 5.4. | 9.1. | 0.2. | Yes. Allowable if payment is made in 30-day period following notice of contribution rate. Commissioner may allow up to 120 days for good cause. | Form MDES-1. | Form MDES-1D. | Employer furnishes Form MES-1528 within 7 days of state's request. | Must retain for 8 years. | Minn. Stat. Ann. §§ 268.06, 268.10, 268.12; 1C Unempl. Ins. Rep. (CCH), Minn., ¶¶ 3002, 3034. |
| MS | 5.4. | 5.4. | 0.5. | No. | Form UI-2. | Form UI-3. | Employer furnishes information upon request by commission. | Must retain for 5 years. | Miss. Code Ann. §§ 13-1-151, 71-5-351, 71-5-353, 71-5-355, 71-5-361, 71-5-365; 1C Unempl. Ins. Rep. (CCH), Miss., ¶¶ 3002, 3035. |
| MO | 2.7. | 7.2. | 0.0. | Yes. On or before January 15 of rate year. | Forms MODES-4 and MODES-10A. | Forms MODES-10A-R44. | Employer furnishes worker with copy of MODES-2351. Within 7 days of the last payroll week, employer must give MODES-B-15 to worker every week for up to 5 weeks. | Must retain for 3 years. | Mo. Rev. Stat. §§ 288.120, 288.125, 288.126, 288.130; 1C Unempl. Ins. Rep. (CCH), Mo., ¶¶ 3002, 3036. |
| MT | 6.4. | 6.4. | 0.1. | No. | Form UI-5. | Form UI-5. | Upon receipt of Form UI-202-A, employer should return notice if employer questions claimant's eligibility. | Must retain for 5 years. | Mont. Code Ann. §§ 39-51-301, 39-51-603, 39-51-1218; 1C Unempl. Ins. Rep. (CCH), Mont., ¶¶ 3002, 3037. |
| NE | 5.4. | 5.4. | 0.05. | Yes. If received on or before March 10, considered paid as of beginning of year. | Form UI-11. | Form UI-11. | Employer furnishes worker with a termination card, Form UI-411, when separated from employment permanently, indefinitely, or for an expected duration of 7 days or more. | Must retain for 4 years. | Neb. Rev. Stat. §§ 48-649, 48-652; 1C Unempl. Ins. Rep. (CCH), Neb., ¶¶ 3002, 3038. |
| NV | 5.4. | 5.4. | 0.25. | No. | Form NUCS-4072. | Form NUCS-4072. | Immediately after termination, employer furnishes worker with Form NUCS-209. | Must retain for 4 years. | Nev. Rev. Stat. Ann. §§ 612.260, 612.540, 612.550; 1C Unempl. Ins. Rep. (CCH), Nev., ¶¶ 3002, 3039. |

*(Table continues.)*

# Table 6.5-1 *(cont'd)*

## EMPLOYER CONTRIBUTIONS AND RECORDKEEPING REQUIREMENTS

(See also text at § 6.5.)

**KEY:** **Voluntary contribution provision.** Some states allow voluntary contributions to the state unemployment compensation fund. This reduces payments under an employer's regular tax rate.

| | *Tax Rates (%)* | | | | *Returns and Reports* | | | | |
|---|---|---|---|---|---|---|---|---|---|
| | *Standard* | *Maximum* | *Minimum* | *Voluntary Contribution Provision* | *Employer's Contributions Report (due on or before last day of month following end of each quarter unless noted.)* | *Employees' Wages Report (due on or before last day of month following end of each quarter unless noted.)* | *Terminated Employee's Return Form (submitted when employee files for unemployment compensation.)* | *Record-Retention Period* | *Citations to Authority* |
| NH | 5.4. | 6.5. | 0.05. | No. | Form C-2. | Form C-2. | Within 7 days after Employer Report Card is filed, Form NH-25 is mailed to certifying officer. | Must retain for 6 years. | N.H. Rev. Stat. Ann. §§ 282-A:82, 282-A:85, 282-A:87, 282-A:117, 282-A:118, 282-A:145; 1C Unempl. Ins. Rep. (CCH), N.H., ¶¶ 3002, 3040. |
| NJ | 5.4. | 5.4. | 0.4. | Yes. Within 30 days of mailing notice, extended to 60 days for good cause, but not exceeding 120 days after start of contribution year. | Form UC-27. | Form WR-30. | Employer furnishes worker with copy of Form BC 10. | Must retain for 5 years. | N.J. Stat. Ann. §§ 43:21-7, 43:21-14, 43:21-16, 43:21-52; 1C Unempl. Ins. Rep. (CCH), N.J., ¶¶ 3002, 3041. |
| NM | 5.4. | 5.4. | 0.3. | Yes. Credited as of computation date if paid on or before March 1. | Form ES-903A. | Form ES-903A. | Employer furnishes Form ES-442 within 5 working days after receipt of form. | Must retain for 4 years. | N.M. Stat. Ann. §§ 51-1-11, 51-1-27; 1C Unempl. Ins. Rep. (CCH), N.M., ¶¶ 3002, 3042. |

| | | | | | | | | | |
|---|---|---|---|---|---|---|---|---|---|
| NY | 5.4. | 6.4. | 1.5. | Yes. Credited as of December 31 if made by April 1. | Form IA 5. | Form IA 5. | Employer furnishes worker with Form IA 12.3. | Must retain for 3 years. | N.Y. Lab. Law §§ 570, 575–577, 581; 1C Unempl. Ins. Rep. (CCH), N.Y., ¶¶ 3002, 3043. |
| NC | 1.2. | 5.7. | 0.0. | Yes. Within 30 days of mailing notice. Credited as of previous July 31. | Form NCUI 101. | Form NCUI-101-X-625. | Employee must fill out Form NCUI 500. | Must retain for 5 years. | N.C. Gen. Stat. § 96-9; 1C Unempl. Ins. Rep. (CCH), N.C., ¶¶ 3002, 3044. |
| ND | Maximum rate. | 8.5, for highway construction employers. | 0.1. | Yes. By April 30. | Form NDUC 303. | Form NDUC 303. | Employer returns Form NDUC-211(a) within 7 days of notice. | Must retain for 5 years. | N.D. Cent. Code § 52-04-05; 1C Unempl. Ins. Rep. (CCH), N.D., ¶¶ 3002, 3045. |
| OH | 2.7; construction employers' rate is 5.2. | 6.5. | 0.1. | Yes. By December 31. | Form UCO-2e. | Form UCO-2QR. | Employer furnishes Form BUC-400 to worker. Employer must return Form BUC-425-R within 10 days of date of mailing of form from state. | Must retain for 5 years. | Ohio Rev. Code Ann. §§ 4141.01, 4141.18, 4141.24, 4141.25; 1C Unempl. Ins. Rep. (CCH), Ohio, ¶¶ 3002, 3046. |
| OK | 1.1. | 5.5. | 0.1. | No. | Form OES 3. | Form OES 3. | Employer furnishes each worker with copy of folder, "Information for Workers." | Must retain for 4 years. | Okla. Stat. Ann. tit. 40, §§ 3-103, 3-109, 3-113, 3-301, 4-502; 1C Unempl. Ins. Rep. (CCH), Okla., ¶¶ 3002, 3047. |
| OR | .64–5.4. | 5.4. | 1.0. | No. | Form OQL or Form OQS. | Form OQL or Form OQS. | Employer furnishes information on Form 220, 220-A, 220-B, or 220-X within 10 days. | Must retain for 5 years. | Or. Rev. Stat. §§ 657.430, 657.435, 657.457, 657.458, 657.462, 657.475, 657.660; 1C Unempl. Ins. Rep. (CCH), Or., ¶¶ 3002, 3048. |
| PA | 5.4–9.2. | 9.2. | 1.5. | Yes. Within 30 days of mailing notice but within 120 days of start of year. Extension for good cause. | Forms UC-2 and UC-2A. | Forms UC-2 and UC-2A. | Employer furnishes information on Form UC-45 or UC-45A within 4 days of receipt of form. | Must retain for 4 years. | Pa. Cons. Stat. tit. 43, §§ 766, 781.1, 781.8, 782, 784; 1C Unempl. Ins. Rep. (CCH), Pa., ¶¶ 3002, 3049. |

*(Table continues.)*

# Table 6.5-1 *(cont'd)*
## EMPLOYER CONTRIBUTIONS AND RECORDKEEPING REQUIREMENTS

(See also text at § 6.5.)

**KEY: Voluntary contribution provision.** Some states allow voluntary contributions to the state unemployment compensation fund. This reduces payments under an employer's regular tax rate.

| | *Tax Rates (%)* | | | | *Returns and Reports* | | | | |
|---|---|---|---|---|---|---|---|---|---|
| | *Standard* | *Maximum* | *Minimum* | *Voluntary Contribution Provision* | *Employer's Contributions Report (due on or before last day of month following end of each quarter unless noted.)* | *Employees' Wages Report (due on or before last day of month following end of each quarter unless noted.)* | *Terminated Employee's Return Form (submitted when employee files for unemployment compensation.)* | *Record-Retention Period* | *Citations to Authority* |
| RI | 2.35. | 8.4. | 2.3. | No. | Form DES-TX-17. | Form DES-TX-17. | Employer furnishes Form DES-550 to worker prior to or at time of termination. | Must retain for 4 years. | R.I. Gen. Laws §§ 28-42-38, 28-42-38.1, 28-43-8, 28-43-8.1, 28-43-8.3; 1C Unempl. Ins. Rep. (CCH), R.I., ¶¶ 3002, 3051. |
| SC | 5.4. | 5.4. | 0.54. | Yes. As of January 1, 1986, not permitted to obtain lower rate. | Form UCE-101. | Form UCE-120. | Employer furnishes Form UCB-214-A within 7 days from when date claim was filed. | Must retain for 5 years. | S.C. Code Ann. §§ 41-29-150, 41-31-10, 41-31-50; 1C Unempl. Ins. Rep. (CCH), S.C., ¶¶ 3002, 3052. |
| SD | 1.9 nonconstruction; construction employers pay 6.7. | 7.7. | 0.0. | Yes. Must be before February 1 to affect rates for current year. | Form DOL-UID-21. | Form DOL-UID-21. | Separation notices no longer required. Determination allowing benefits becomes final unless employer files protest within 9 days after date of notice of termination. | Must retain for 4 years. | S.D. Codified Laws §§ 61-3-2, 61-5-18.14, 61-5-20.2, 61-5-24, 61-5-24.1; 1C Unempl. Ins. Rep. (CCH), S.D., ¶¶ 3002, 3053. |

| | | | | | | | | | |
|---|---|---|---|---|---|---|---|---|---|
| TN | 5.5. | 10.0. | 0.0. | No. | Form DES-220.5. | Form DES-220.5. | Employer furnishes worker with termination notice within 24 hours. | Must retain for 7 years. | Tenn. Code Ann. §§ 50-7-402, 50-7-403, 50-7-701, 50-7-707; 1C Unempl. Ins. Rep. (CCH), Tenn., ¶¶ 3002, 3054. |
| TX | 2.7. | 6.27. | .27. | No. | Form C-3. | Form C-4. | Employer furnishes information within 10 days after commission mails Form B-3. | Must retain for 4 years. | Tex. Lab. Code Ann. §§ 204.006, 204.042, 204.043, 204.048; 1C Unempl. Ins. Rep. (CCH), Tex., ¶¶ 3002, 3055. |
| UT | 5.4. | 9.0. | 0.2. | No. | Form 3. | Form 3. | Employer furnishes worker with Form 637 A at time of termination. | Must retain for 3 years. | Utah Code Ann. §§ 35-4-303, 35-4-502, 35-4-506; 1C Unempl. Ins. Rep. (CCH), Utah, ¶¶ 3002, 3056. |
| VT | 5.4. | 5.9. | 0.6. | No. | Form C101. | Form C101. | Employer delivers or mails worker a copy of Rule 13 within 24 hours after worker is terminated. | Must retain for 6 years. | Vt. Stat. Ann. tit. 21, §§ 1314, 1314a, 1324, 1326, 1365, 1370; 1C Unempl. Ins. Rep. (CCH), Vt., ¶¶ 3002, 3057. |
| VA | 5.4. | 6.2. | 0.0 | No. | Form VEC-FC-20. | Form VEC-FC-20. | Employer furnishes Form VEC-B-10(c) to commission within 5 days after receipt of form. | Must retain for 4 years. | Va. Code Ann. §§ 60.2-114, 60.2-512, 60.2-515, 60.2-526, 60.2-528, 60.2-530, 60.2-531; 1C Unempl. Ins. Rep. (CCH), Va., ¶¶ 3002, 3058. |
| WA | 2.5. | 5.4. | 0.5. | Yes. Due February 15. | Form EMS 5208. | Form 5208. | Employer notifies department if claimant should be disqualified within 10 days upon receipt of notice that worker has filed claim. | Must retain for 4 years. | Wash. Rev. Code Ann. §§ 50.12.070, 50.12.080, 50.12.140, 50.16.070, 50.29.025; 1C Unempl. Ins. Rep. (CCH), Wash., ¶¶ 3002, 3059. |

*(Table continues.)*

# Table 6.5-1 *(cont'd)*
## EMPLOYER CONTRIBUTIONS AND RECORDKEEPING REQUIREMENTS

(See also text at § 6.5.)

**KEY:** **Voluntary contribution provision.** Some states allow voluntary contributions to the state unemployment compensation fund. This reduces payments under an employer's regular tax rate.

| | *Tax Rates (%)* | | | | *Returns and Reports* | | | | |
|---|---|---|---|---|---|---|---|---|---|
| | *Standard* | *Maximum* | *Minimum* | *Voluntary Contribution Provision* | *Employer's Contributions Report (due on or before last day of month following end of each quarter unless noted.)* | *Employees' Wages Report (due on or before last day of month following end of each quarter unless noted.)* | *Terminated Employee's Return Form (submitted when employee files for unemployment compensation.)* | *Record-Retention Period* | *Citations to Authority* |
| WV | 2.7. | 8.5. | 1.5. | Yes. Within 30 days of mailing of rate notice. | Form WVUC-A-154A. | Form WVUC-A-154. | Employer furnishes Forms WVUC-B-6A and WVUC-B-175 within 4 days of receipt of form. | Must retain for 5 years. | W. Va. Code §§ 21A-5-5, 21A-10-4, 21A-5-10, 21A-5-10b, 21A-10-11, 21A-5-17a; 1C Unempl. Ins. Rep. (CCH), W. Va., ¶¶ 3002, 3060. |
| WI | Combined rate closest to but not less than 5.4%. | 9.75. | 0.02. | Yes. During November. After November under certain circumstances, but not later than 120 days after start of year. | Form UC-101. | Form UC-7823 or UC-7827. | Employer returns Form UC-203 or UC-23 within 7 days of receipt of form. | State has no statutory requirements. | Wis. Stat. Ann. §§ 108.04, 108.18; 1C Unempl. Ins. Rep. (CCH), Wis., ¶¶ 3002, 3061. |
| WY | 8.5. | 8.8. | 0.3. | No. | Form WYO-47. | Form WYO-47. | Employer gives each worker notice of benefit rights; employer furnishes Form WYO-147 at time of termination; employer furnishes WYO-11 within 5 days of receipt. | Must retain for 4 years. | Wyo. Stat. §§ 27-3-502, 27-3-503, 27-3-510; 1C Unempl. Ins. Rep. (CCH), Wyo., ¶¶ 3002, 3062. |

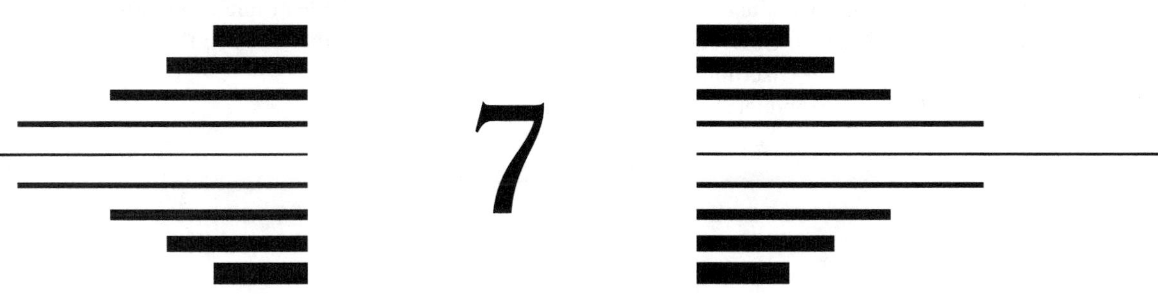

# 7

# Workplace Privacy

*Tables in Part 7 cover workplace testing (polygraph, drug, and AIDS testing); use of conviction and arrest records in hiring decisions; use of consumer credit reports; prohibitions against blacklisting; and employee access to personnel files.*

## § 7.1 Overview: Expansion of Privacy Rights in the Workplace

Privacy encompasses many different issues, but, at the common-law—or nonstatutory—level, it generally encompasses four discrete subjects:

1. Prohibition against commercial appropriation of another person's name or likeness;
2. Protection against the public disclosure of private information;
3. Protection against an invasion of another's seclusion; and
4. A bar on placing another in a false light in the public eye.

A clear trend of increasing recognition and protection of employee privacy rights is emerging. For example, the federal Employee Polygraph Protection Act of 1988 has, for the most part, given employees the right to reject employer demands for submission to polygraph testing. (See Part 9 for more on the wide protections offered by this Act.) Some state legislatures have passed laws that afford additional protection against mandatory polygraph testing. Because of the increasing legislative recognition of employees' rights to refuse polygraph tests, some employers have begun using pencil and paper honesty tests and personality tests to replace polygraph tests. In response to employers' use of these other tests, some states are amending their polygraph statutes so that they include prohibitions against employers' use of honesty tests and personality tests in addition to polygraph and stress analysis tests.

Some states have passed legislation that limits the parameters of drug testing. Early attention was given to passing legislation that encouraged a "drug-free workplace," but more recently state legislators appear to be focusing their efforts on protecting individual privacy. An emerging technology that may have workplace implications is DNA or genetic testing, which raises serious social and moral issues and may well affect employees in the areas of benefits and privacy.

Clearly, privacy in the workplace is an issue that will continue to be hotly debated, as legislators, judges, and employers try to balance the needs of business with the rights of employees.

# § 7.2 Regulation of Workplace Testing

## [a] Employers' Use of Polygraph Tests

A "lie detector" may be a polygraph, deceptograph, voice stress analyzer, psychological stress evaluator, or other similar device, the results of which are used to render an opinion regarding the honesty or dishonesty of an individual.

The federal Employee Polygraph Protection Act of 1988 prohibits private employers from directly or indirectly requiring or requesting a lie detector test as part of the job application procedure or as a term or condition of employment or continued employment. An employer is also prohibited from inquiring about the results of lie detector tests involving employees. Exceptions to this rule are made for drug companies and general security companies.

This federal law, however, permits employers to *request* an employee to take a polygraph as part of an ongoing investigation of economic loss, *if* the employee had access to the lost property *and* the employer has a reasonable suspicion that the employee was involved in such loss. An employer giving such a voluntary polygraph examination is subject to various procedural requirements.

Generally, federal law preempts any state laws in the field, although states are permitted to enact *more stringent* laws. Most state statutes omit either some or all of the federal exceptions noted above and/or require a greater degree of procedural safeguards for such polygraph examinations.

Table 7.2-1 shows states' regulation of polygraph tests.

## [b] Drug Testing Legislation

Various government and private sources estimate that employee substance abuse currently costs businesses between $50 billion and $100 billion annually. It is no surprise, then, to find that many employers are considering—or have already implemented—employee drug testing programs to curb this serious problem in the workplace.

In response, several states have enacted statutes governing how employers may use employee drug tests. Some state laws make it difficult to test applicants and employees by requiring employers who wish to conduct drug testing to pay the extra costs of sponsoring required employee assistance programs (EAPs). To avoid these extra costs, some employers choose not to test for drugs. Other states require employers to use only certified laboratories that apply appropriate methodologies to conduct the tests.

Exhibit 7.2-1 shows those states that, to date, have enacted drug testing laws, and it highlights the most important provisions, including who is covered, testing procedures, enforcement, and violation penalties.

## [c] Regulation of AIDS Testing and Local AIDS Ordinances

Several states now have statutes or local laws restricting an employer's ability to require an AIDS test as a condition of employment. In some states, mandatory AIDS testing is prohibited; other states prohibit using a positive test result as a basis for discrimination. Many states have determined that AIDS is a handicap and apply existing state laws preventing handicap discrimination in employment.[1] Other states have held that persons infected with the HIV virus are not handicapped.[2]

The Americans With Disabilities Act (ADA), which prohibits employers from discriminating against qualified individuals with disabilities, protects people infected or perceived to be infected with the HIV virus or AIDS from many discriminatory practices.[3] The ADA defines individuals with disabilities as persons who (1) have a physical or mental impairment that substantially limits one or more major life activities; (2) have a record of such an impairment; and/or (3) are regarded as having such an impairment. As the United States Supreme Court has held, persons with AIDS qualify as individuals with disabilities under the ADA's definition.[4]

Although AIDS is now clearly a disability under the ADA, the states, under similar state acts, must determine whether a person with AIDS has the characteristics of a disability as defined by the state statute.

Table 7.2-2 shows which states have enacted laws on AIDS testing as well as their significant provisions. In addition, Table 7.2-3 lists selected local and municipal ordinances regulating AIDS testing and prohibiting discrimination.

---

**§ 7.2**

1. *See, e.g.,* Benjamin R. v. Orkin Exterminating Co., 182 W. Va. 615, 390 S.E.2d 814 (1990).

2. *See, e.g.,* Burgess v. Your House of Raleigh, Inc., 326 N.C. 205, 388 S.E.2d 134 (1990).

3. 42 U.S.C. § 12112.

4. Bragdon v. Abott, 118 S. Ct. 2196 (1998).

# Table 7.2-1
## REGULATION OF EMPLOYERS' USE OF POLYGRAPH TESTS

(See also text at § 7.2[a].)

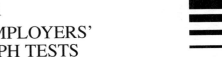

| | *State Statute More Stringent Than Federal Statute* | *Use or Administration of Test as a Condition of Employment Specifically Prohibited* | *Employers' Right to Request, Under Limited Circumstances, That Employees Undergo Testing* | *Penalties for Violation of Statute* | *Other Requirements* | *Citations to Authority* |
|---|---|---|---|---|---|---|
| AL | No. | Not specifically prohibited by state statute, but see federal prohibitions discussed in introductory text. | Employer may request under limited circumstances. | State has no statutory requirements. | None. | *Hood v. Alabama State Personnel Bd.*, 516 So. 2d 680 (Ala. Civ. App. 1987) (where the rules of continuing employment specifically require an employee to submit to a polygraph test, the results can be used to terminate the employee). |
| AK | Yes. | Specifically prohibited. | Employer may not request. | Violator is guilty of a misdemeanor punishable by a fine of not more than $1,000, or by imprisonment for not more than one year, or both. | Police officers and those seeking employment as police officers may be tested by state or its political subdivisions. | Alaska Stat. § 23.10.037. |
| AZ | No. | State has no specific statutory provision, but see federal prohibitions discussed in introductory text. | Employer may request under limited circumstances as specified by federal law. | State has no statutory requirements. | None. | — |
| AR | No. | Not specifically prohibited by state statute, but see federal prohibitions discussed in introductory text. | Employer may request. | State has no statutory requirements. | None. | *Jackson v. Kinark Corp.*, 282 Ark. 548, 669 S.W.2d, 898 (1984). |
| CA | No. | Specifically prohibited, except in government employment. Public safety officers can refuse the test. | Employer may request, but must inform the person in writing that a polygraph test cannot be required. | State has no statutory requirements. | Additional procedural rules apply. | Cal. Lab. Code § 432.2; Cal. Gov't Code § 3307; *Long Beach City Employees Ass'n v. City of Long Beach,* 41 Cal. 3d 937, 227 Cal. Rptr. 90, 719 P.2d 660 (1986). |

| | | | | | | |
|---|---|---|---|---|---|---|
| CO | No. | State has no specific statutory provision, but see federal prohibitions discussed in introductory text. | Employer may request under limited circumstances as specified by federal law. | State has no statutory requirements. | None. | — |
| CT | Yes. | Specifically prohibited. | Employer may not request. | Violator is fined $250–$1,000 for each violation. | Noncivilian employees in police department are exempt. Violators of statute are to be fined. | Conn. Gen. Stat. Ann. § 31-51g. |
| DE | Yes. | Specifically prohibited. | Employer may not request. | Violator is fined not less than $1,000 nor more than $5,000. | Law enforcement officers are exempt when they are carrying out their official duties. Violators of statute are to be fined or imprisoned. | Del. Code Ann. tit. 19, § 704. |
| DC | Yes. | Specifically prohibited. | Employer may not request. | Violator is guilty of a misdemeanor punishable by a fine of $500, or 30 days in jail, or both. | Does not apply to criminal, internal, or pre-employment investigations conducted by Fire, Police, or Corrections Department. However, no person may be denied employment based solely on the results of a preemployment lie detector test. | D.C. Code Ann. § 36-802. |
| FL | No. | Not specifically prohibited by state statute, but see federal prohibitions discussed in introductory text. | Employer may request. | State has no statutory requirements. | None. | *Farmer v. City of Ft. Lauderdale,* 427 So. 2d 187 (Fla.), *cert. denied,* 464 U.S. 816, 104 S. Ct. 74 (1983); *contra, State Dep't of Highway Safety v. Zimmer,* 398 So. 2d 463 (Fla. Dist. Ct. App. 1981). |
| GA | No. | Not specifically prohibited by state statute, but see federal prohibitions discussed in introductory text. | Public employees can be dismissed from employment upon refusal to take a polygraph test if informed that (1) questions will relate specifically and narrowly to the performance of official duties; (2) answers cannot be used against employees in subsequent criminal prosecutions; and (3) the penalty for refusal is dismissal. | Any person who suffers damages as a result of a polygraph examination is entitled to actual damages sustained, together with reasonable attorneys' fees, filing fees, and costs of the action. Damages may include back pay for the period in which person did not work or was denied a job. | None. | Ga. Code Ann. § 51-1-37; *Moss v. Central State Hosp.,* 179 Ga. App. 359, 346 S.E.2d 580 (1986). |
| HI | Yes. | Specifically prohibited. | Employer may request. | Violator is fined $100–$1,000 for each violation. | Law enforcement agencies and law enforcement applicants are exempt. | Haw. Rev. Stat. §§ 378-26 *et seq.* |
| ID | Yes. | Specifically prohibited. | Employer may request. | Violator is guilty of a misdemeanor. | State or federal law enforcement agency or a political subdivision or governmental entity of the state may require employee to take a polygraph test. | Idaho Code §§ 44-903–44-904. |

*(Table continues.)*

## Table 7.2-1 *(cont'd)*

REGULATION OF EMPLOYERS' USE OF POLYGRAPH TESTS

(See also text at § 7.2[a].)

| | *State Statute More Stringent Than Federal Statute* | *Use or Administration of Test as a Condition of Employment Specifically Prohibited* | *Employers' Right to Request, Under Limited Circumstances, That Employees Undergo Testing* | *Penalties for Violation of Statute* | *Other Requirements* | *Citations to Authority* |
|---|---|---|---|---|---|---|
| IL | No. | Not specifically prohibited by state statute, but see federal prohibitions discussed in introductory text. | Employer may request preemployment or periodic employment tests. | State has no statutory requirements. | Additional procedural rules apply. Examiner is restricted from questioning in certain areas unless directly related to the employment. | 225 Ill. Comp. Stat. Ann. § 430/14.1. |
| IN | No. | State has no specific statutory provision, but see federal prohibitions discussed in introductory text. | Employer may request under limited circumstances as specified by federal law. | State has no statutory requirements. | None. | — |
| IA | Yes. | Specifically prohibited. | Employer may not request. | Violator is guilty of a serious misdemeanor. Enforced by private civil action. Hiring, reinstatement, or other equitable relief are available to prevailing employee or applicant. | State or any political subdivision can require the test of law enforcement and corrections officers. | Iowa Code Ann. § 730.4. |
| KS | No. | State has no specific statutory provision, but see federal prohibitions discussed in introductory text. | Employer may request under limited circumstances as specified by federal law. | State has no statutory requirements. | None. | — |
| KY | Yes. | Not specifically prohibited by state statute, but see federal prohibitions discussed in introductory text. | Employer may request. | State has no statutory requirements. | None. | *Douthitt v. Kentucky Unemployment Ins. Comm'n,* 676 S.W.2d 472 (Ky. Ct. App. 1984) (holding that it is unreasonable to require employees to submit to a test for unemployment compensation benefits purposes). |

| | | | | | | |
|---|---|---|---|---|---|---|
| LA | No. | Not specifically prohibited by state statute, but see federal prohibitions discussed in introductory text. | Employer may request. | State has no statutory requirements. | None. | *Ballaron v. Equitable Shipyards, Inc.*, 521 So. 2d 481 (La. App. 4 Cir. 1988), writ denied, 522 So. 2d 571 (La. 1988) (holding that employer could dismiss at-will employees for refusing to consent to polygraph examinations that were part of a personnel investigation). |
| ME | Yes. | Specifically prohibited. | Employer may not request. Employee may request, but the results cannot be used against the employee. | Violator is guilty of a Class D crime. | Employees of and applicants for employment with law enforcement agencies may be tested. Additional procedural rules apply. | Me. Rev. Stat. Ann. tit. 32, §§ 7166, 7167. |
| MD | Yes. | Specifically prohibited. | Employer may request. | Violator is guilty of a misdemeanor and subject to a fine not exceeding $100. | Employment application forms must state that employers cannot require submission to a lie detector test. Statute does not apply to the federal government, employees of the Division of Corrections, law enforcement officers, and other specified correctional officers. | Md. Lab. and Emp. Code Ann. § 3-702. |
| MA | Yes. | Specifically prohibited. | Employer may not request. | Violator is subject to a fine of $300–$1,000. Subsequent violations are punishable by fines of not more than $1,500 or by imprisonment for not more than 90 days, or both. Employee may bring action within 3 years of the violation for injunctive relief, actual damages, and treble damages for any loss of wages or other benefits. These damages shall equal or exceed $500 for each violation. Employee may also be awarded attorneys' fees and costs. | Employment application forms must bear information on polygraph law. | Mass. Gen. Laws Ann. ch. 149, § 19B. |
| MI | Yes. | Specifically prohibited. | Employer may not request. | An examiner who administers a polygraph test to an employee or applicant in violation of statutory restrictions is guilty of a misdemeanor, and may be subject to a fine of not more than $1,000, or imprisonment of up to 90 days, or both. | Employee may request testing. Additional procedural rules apply. A member of the police department may be requested to submit to a polygraph test (Op. Att'y Gen. No. 6542 (1988)). | Mich. Comp. Laws Ann. § 37.203. |

*(Table continues.)*

## **Table 7.2-1** *(cont'd)*
## REGULATION OF EMPLOYERS' USE OF POLYGRAPH TESTS

(See also text at § 7.2[a].)

| | *State Statute More Stringent Than Federal Statute* | *Use or Administration of Test as a Condition of Employment Specifically Prohibited* | *Employers' Right to Request, Under Limited Circumstances, That Employees Undergo Testing* | *Penalties for Violation of Statute* | *Other Requirements* | *Citations to Authority* |
|---|---|---|---|---|---|---|
| MN | Yes. | Specifically prohibited. | Employer may not request. | Employee may bring civil action for damages, costs, attorneys' fees, and other equitable relief. Injunctive relief is available. | Employee may request testing. Additional procedural rules apply. | Minn. Stat. Ann. §§ 181.75, 181.76. |
| MS | No. | State has no specific statutory provision, but see federal prohibitions discussed in introductory text. | Employer may request under limited circumstances as specified by federal law. | State has no statutory requirements. | None. | — |
| MO | No. | Not specifically prohibited by state statute, but see federal prohibitions discussed in introductory text. | Employer may request. | State has no statutory requirements. | None. | *Gibson v. Hummel*, 688 S.W. 2d 4 (Mo. App. Ct. 1985) (holding that at-will employee may be required to submit to polygraph testing as condition of future employment). |
| MT | Yes. | Specifically prohibited. | Employer may not request. | State has no statutory requirements. | None. | Mont. Code Ann. § 39-2-304. |
| NE | Yes. | Specifically prohibited. Provision does not apply to employment in public law enforcement. | Employer may request. | Violator is guilty of a Class II misdemeanor. | If employee consents to the test, the employer must not ask questions concerning the employee's sexual practices, labor union, political, or religious affiliations, or marital relationships. Additional procedural rules apply. Provision does not apply to employment in public law enforcement. | Neb. Rev. Stat. § 81-1932; *White v. State*, 248 Neb. 977, 540 N.W.2d 354 (1995). |

| | | | | | | |
|---|---|---|---|---|---|---|
| NV | Yes. | Specifically prohibited. | Employer may not request. For each violation, civil penalty of not more than $9,000. Injunctive relief is also available. | Violator is liable for civil penalty of not more than $9,000 for each violation. Employer is liable for reinstatement, promotion, or hiring of employee, costs, and attorneys' fees. Action by employee must be brought within 3 years of the alleged violation. | Exceptions: Provisions do not apply to state or political subdivisions of the state. Employer may request employee to take a lie detector test during an ongoing investigation involving economic loss or physical injury. Applicants may be asked to take test if position involves protecting commodities. Employers authorized to manufacture, distribute, or dispense controlled substances may require polygraph tests of certain employees and prospective employees. | Nev. Rev. Stat. §§ 613.440–613.510. |
| NH | No. | Not specifically prohibited by state statute, but see federal prohibitions discussed in introductory text. | Employer may request. | State has no statutory requirements. | None. | *O'Brien v. Papa Gino's of America, Inc.*, 780 F.2d 1067 (1st Cir. 1986). |
| NJ | Yes. | Specifically prohibited. | Employer may not request. | Violator commits a disorderly persons offense. | Exception for employers that manufacture, distribute, or dispense controlled substances. | N.J. Stat. Ann. § 2C:40A-1. |
| NM | No. | State has no specific statutory provision, but see federal prohibitions discussed in introductory text. | Employer may request under limited circumstances as specified by federal law. | State has no statutory requirements. | None. | — |
| NY | Yes. | Specifically prohibited. | Employer may not request. | Violator is guilty of a Class B misdemeanor for the first conviction and a Class A misdemeanor for each subsequent violation. | None. | N.Y. Lab. Law § 735. |
| NC | No. | State has no specific statutory provision, but see federal prohibitions discussed in introductory text. | Employer may request under limited circumstances as specified by federal law. | State has no statutory requirements. | None. | — |
| ND | No. | State has no specific statutory provision, but see federal prohibitions discussed in introductory text. | Employer may request under limited circumstances as specified by federal law. | State has no statutory requirements. | None. | — |

*(Table continues.)*

## **Table 7.2-1** *(cont'd)*
## REGULATION OF EMPLOYERS' USE OF POLYGRAPH TESTS

(See also text at § 7.2[a].)

| | *State Statute More Stringent Than Federal Statute* | *Use or Administration of Test as a Condition of Employment Specifically Prohibited* | *Employers' Right to Request, Under Limited Circumstances, That Employees Undergo Testing* | *Penalties for Violation of Statute* | *Other Requirements* | *Citations to Authority* |
|---|---|---|---|---|---|---|
| OH | No. | State has no specific statutory provision, but see federal prohibitions discussed in introductory text. | Employer may request under limited circumstances as specified by federal law. | State has no statutory requirements. | None. | — |
| OK | No. | State has no specific statutory provision, but see federal prohibitions discussed in introductory text. | Employer may request under limited circumstances as specified by federal law. | State has no statutory requirements. | None. | — |
| OR | Yes. | Specifically prohibited. | Employer may request. | Enforced by the Commissioner of the Bureau of Labor and Industries. Employee has 2 years to file civil action for injunctive relief and other equitable relief. | Examinations during civil or criminal judicial proceedings and during criminal investigations are exempt, if the individual consents to the examination. | Or. Rev. Stat. §§ 659.225, 659.227. |
| PA | Yes. | Specifically prohibited. | Employer may request. | Violator is guilty of a misdemeanor in the second degree. | Those in law enforcement or those who dispense or have access to narcotics or dangerous drugs may be required to take a polygraph test as a condition for obtaining or continuing employment. | 18 Pa. Cons. Stat. Ann. § 7321. |

| | | | | | | |
|---|---|---|---|---|---|---|
| RI | Yes. | Specifically prohibited. | Employer may not request. | Violator is guilty of a misdemeanor punishable by a fine of not more than $1,000. Employee can bring civil action for punitive damages, actual damages, attorneys' fees, and costs. | Exception for law enforcement agencies in performance of official duties. | R.I. Gen. Laws §§ 28-6.1-1–28-6.1-4. |
| SC | No. | State has no specific statutory provision, but see federal prohibitions discussed in introductory text. | Employer may request under limited circumstances as specified by federal law. | State has no statutory requirements. | None. | — |
| SD | No. | State has no specific statutory provision, but see federal prohibitions discussed in introductory text. | Employer may request under limited circumstances as specified by federal law. | State has no statutory requirements. | None. | — |
| TN | Yes. | Specifically prohibited. | Employer may request. | Violator is guilty of a Class C misdemeanor. | Employer cannot take any personnel action based solely on test results. It is unlawful for any person to include any question concerning a subject's sexual behavior or orientation, unless relevant to the exam. Additional procedural rules apply. | Tenn. Code Ann. §§ 62-27-123–62-27-128. |
| TX | No. | Not specifically prohibited by state statute, but see federal prohibitions discussed in introductory text. | Employer may request. | State has no statutory requirements. | An officer of the Department of Public Safety cannot be disciplined because of refusal to take a polygraph test. | Tex. Gov't Code Ann. § 411.007. |
| UT | No. | State has no specific statutory provision, but see federal prohibitions discussed in introductory text. | Employer may request under limited circumstances as specified by federal law. | State has no statutory requirements. | None. | — |
| VT | Yes. | Specifically prohibited. | Employer may not request. | Violator is fined $500–$1,000, or imprisoned not more than 6 months, or both. Employee can also receive amount of wage loss and reinstatement to previous position. | Exceptions for employers that retail or manufacture precious metals or gems; manufacture or sell controlled substances; are a police agency; or are otherwise permitted under federal law. | Vt. Stat. Ann. tit. 21, §§ 494a, 494b. |

*(Table continues.)*

## **Table 7.2-1** *(cont'd)*
## REGULATION OF EMPLOYERS' USE OF POLYGRAPH TESTS

(See also text at § 7.2[a].)

| | *State Statute More Stringent Than Federal Statute* | *Use or Administration of Test as a Condition of Employment Specifically Prohibited* | *Employers' Right to Request, Under Limited Circumstances, That Employees Undergo Testing* | *Penalties for Violation of Statute* | *Other Requirements* | *Citations to Authority* |
|---|---|---|---|---|---|---|
| VA | No. | Not specifically prohibited by state statute, but see federal prohibitions discussed in introductory text. | Employer may request. | Violator is guilty of a Class 1 misdemeanor. | Additional procedural rules apply. Employer cannot ask prospective employee questions about sexual activities, unless such sexual activity resulted in a criminal conviction. The chief executive officer of a law-enforcement agency may require polygraph testing of employees pursuant to an internal administrative investigation. | Va. Code Ann. §§ 40.1-51.4:3, 40.1-51.4:4. |
| WA | Yes. | Specifically prohibited. | Employer may request. | Violator is guilty of a misdemeanor. In a civil action, the court may award punitive damages in the amount of $500 to prevailing employee, in addition to actual damages, attorneys' fees, and costs. | Tests may be required for applicants for employment with a law enforcement agency, or for applicants or employees of employers that manufacture, distribute, or dispense controlled substances, or for persons in sensitive positions directly involving national security. | Wash. Rev. Code Ann. §§ 49.44.120, 49.44.130, 49.44.135. |
| WV | Yes. | Specifically prohibited. | Employer may not request. Case law deems an employer demand that employee take polygraph or similar test as a condition of employment constitutes a violation of public policy. | Violator is guilty of a misdemeanor punishable by a fine of not more than $500. | Exceptions: Provisions do not apply to applicants or employees of employers that manufacture, distribute, or dispense drugs, to law enforcement agencies, or to military forces of the state. | W. Va. Code §§ 21-5-5a, 21-5-5b, 21-5-5d; *Cordle v. General Hugh Mercer Corp.*, 325 S.E. 2d 111 (S. Ct. W. Va. 1984). |

| | | | | | | |
|---|---|---|---|---|---|---|
| WI | Yes. | Specifically prohibited. | Employer may request under certain circumstances. | Violator is guilty of a Class B misdemeanor. | Employers whose facilities, materials, or operations may have an impact on the safety or welfare of the public or the national security of the United States may test employees. Employers whose primary business involves currency, negotiable securities, precious commodities or instruments, and proprietary information may test prospective employees. Testing is also permitted for employers whose primary business involves controlled substances. | Wis. Stat. Ann. §§ 111.37, 942.06. |
| WY | No. | State has no specific statutory provision, but see federal prohibitions discussed in introductory text. | Employer may request under limited circumstances as specified by federal law. | State has no statutory requirements. | None. | — |

## Exhibit 7.2-1
## DRUG TESTING LEGISLATION

(States not listed here have no statutes governing drug testing in the workplace. See also text at § 7.2[b].)

KEY:
**EAP.** Employee assistance program.
**DOL.** Department of Labor.
**GC/MS.** Gas chromatography/mass spectrometry test.
**Reasonable suspicion/probable cause.** States may vary on what would be required to prove either reasonable suspicion or probable cause. The law is not specific in defining these terms.
**NIDA.** National Institute for Drug Abuse.

### ALABAMA

**Who Is Covered by Statute.** Employers subject to Alabama's Workers' Compensation law.

**Applicant Testing.** Applicant testing is required to qualify for workers' compensation insurance premium discounts.

**Employee Testing.** Employee testing is allowed.

**Conditions for Conducting Tests.** Tests must be conducted by qualified testing laboratories.

**Testing Process Requirements.** Testers must follow quality control and information dissemination procedures.

**How Test Results Are Used.** Employers may establish reasonable work rules related to employee possession, use, sale, or solicitation of drugs and may take action based upon a violation of those rules.

**Enforcement of Statute.** State has no statutory requirements.

**Employee Remedies.** State has no statutory requirements.

**Employer Penalties.** State has no statutory requirements.

**Who Pays for Testing.** Employer shall pay the costs of all drug tests that the employer requires of employees. Employee or applicant shall pay the cost of any additional tests not required by the employer.

**Employee Assistance Benefits.** Employer must advise employees of EAP, if employer offers program, or advise employees of employer's resource file of assistance programs.

**Other Requirements.** One time only, prior to testing, all employees and job applicants shall be given a notice of testing.

**Citations to Authority.** Ala. Code §§ 25-5-330–25-5-340.

### ALASKA

**Who Is Covered by Statute.** Employers with one or more employees.

**Applicant Testing.** Applicant testing is allowed.

**Employee Testing.** Employee testing is allowed.

**Conditions for Conducting Tests.** Tests must be conducted by qualified testing laboratories.

**Testing Process Requirements.** Testers must follow quality control and information dissemination procedures.

**How Test Results Are Used.** An employer may take adverse employment action based on positive drug test or refusal of employee to provide a drug testing sample.

**Enforcement of Statute.** State has no statutory requirements.

**Employee Remedies.** Employee may bring action for defamation of character, libel, or slander if results were disclosed to a person other than employer, authorized agent, tested employee, or tested applicant.

**Employer Penalties.** Employer is not liable for monetary damages if employer's reliance on a false positive test was reasonable and in good faith.

**Who Pays for Testing?** Employer shall pay the cost of drug testing.

**Employee Assistance Benefits.** State has no statutory requirements.

**Other Requirements.** None.

**Citations to Authority.** Alaska Stat. §§ 23.10.600 *et seq.*

## ARIZONA

**Who Is Covered by Statute.** All private employers.

**Applicant Testing.** Applicant testing is allowed.

**Employee Testing.** Employer may require the collection and testing of samples for any job-related purposes consistent with business necessity.

**Conditions for Conducting Tests.** Drug testing shall be conducted by a certified laboratory.

**Testing Process Requirements.** Confirmation of positive drug test results for employers shall be by use of a different chemical process than was used in the initial drug screen.

**How Test Results Are Used.** Test results may be used by employer to take adverse employment action against employee or applicant.

**Enforcement of Statute.** State has no statutory requirements.

**Employee Remedies.** Causes of action for defamation of character, libel, slander, and damage to reputation are available if information disclosed was a false positive result, the false positive result was disclosed negligently, and all other elements of causes of action are satisfied.

**Employer Penalties.** State has no statutory requirements.

**Who Pays for Testing?** Employer shall pay all actual costs for drug and alcohol impairment testing. Employer may, at its discretion, pay the costs for drug testing of prospective employees.

**Employee Assistance Benefits.** State has no statutory requirements.

**Other Requirements.** Testing for the presence of drugs shall be carried out within the terms of a written policy that has been distributed to every employee.

**Citations to Authority.** Ariz. Rev. Stat. Ann. §§ 23-493 *et seq.*

## CALIFORNIA

**Who Is Covered by Statute.** All private employers with 25 or more employees.

**Applicant Testing.** State has no statutory requirements.

**Employee Testing.** Employee testing is allowed.

**Conditions for Conducting Tests.** State has no statutory requirements.

**Testing Process Requirements.** State has no statutory requirements.

**How Test Results Are Used.** Employer may refuse to hire, and may discharge, an employee who, because of his/her current use of alcohol or drugs, is either unable to perform his/her duties or cannot perform them in a manner that would not endanger his/her health or safety or the health or safety of others.

**Enforcement of Statute.** State has no statutory requirements.

**Employee Remedies.** State has no statutory requirements.

**Employer Penalties.** State has no statutory requirements.

**Who Pays for Testing?** State has no statutory requirements.

**Employee Assistance Benefits.** State has no statutory requirements.

**Other Requirements.** Employer must make reasonable efforts to keep confidential the fact that an employee was enrolled in a rehabilitation program.

**Citations to Authority.** Cal. Lab. Code §§ 1025, 1026.

## CONNECTICUT

**Who Is Covered by Statute.** All employers, current and former employees, and applicants, but not the state or its political subdivisions.

**Applicant Testing.** Applicant testing is allowed only if (1) prospective employee is informed in writing, (2) test is conducted in accordance with stated methodology, and (3) prospective employee is given a copy of any positive test result.

**Employee Testing.** Employee testing is allowed if reasonable suspicion exists. Random testing of persons in safety-sensitive positions, as defined by DOL, is allowed. Testing must be done in conjunction with employee participation in EAP.

**Conditions for Conducting Tests.** Use of witnesses is prohibited.

**Testing Process Requirements.** Two tests are required, one by screening method and the other by GC/MS. Positive test results must be disclosed.

**How Test Results Are Used.** Test results may be used to screen out drug-using applicants or to discharge or discipline employees.

**Enforcement of Statute.** Enforcement is by private civil action and state action.

**Employee Remedies.** Employees may seek attorneys' fees and court costs, damages, and injunctive relief.

**Employer Penalties.** None.

**Who Pays for Testing?** State has no statutory requirements.

**Employee Assistance Benefits.** State has no statutory requirements.

**Other Requirements.** Statute addresses urinalysis only; it does not include other drug-testing methods. Drug test results must be filed with medical records, subject to disclosure under separate statute. Preemployment drug test is required of all school bus operators.

**Citations to Authority.** Conn. Gen. Stat. Ann. §§ 31-51t–31-51z, 14-276a(d).

## DELAWARE

**Who Is Covered by Statute.** School bus drivers.

**Applicant Testing.** State has no statutory requirements.

**Employee Testing.** State has no statutory requirements.

**Conditions for Conducting Tests.** State has no statutory requirements.

**Testing Process Requirements.** State has no statutory requirements.

**How Test Results Are Used.** Positive test results are grounds for termination.

**Enforcement of Statute.** State has no statutory requirements.

**Employee Remedies.** State has no statutory requirements.

**Employer Penalties.** State has no statutory requirements.

**Who Pays for Testing?** Employer pays for initial test. Subsequent test costs are paid by employee.

**Employee Assistance Benefits.** State has no statutory requirements.

**Other Requirements.** State has no statutory requirements.

**Citations to Authority.** Del. Code Ann. tit. 14 § 2910.

## FLORIDA

**Who Is Covered by Statute.** Any agency within the state government.

**Applicant Testing.** Applicant testing is allowed. All positive tests must be confirmed by GC/MS.

**Employee Testing.** Employee testing is allowed where a reasonable suspicion of drug use exists, or where test is conducted pursuant to routine fitness testing or follow-up testing.

**Conditions for Conducting Tests.** Tests must be conducted by certified laboratories.

**Testing Process Requirements.** Person must be informed of positive results. Within 5 working days of receipt of results, applicants and employees have the right to explain or rebut positive results. All information is confidential.

**How Test Results Are Used.** Test results may be used as grounds for termination or disqualification of employment if a confirmation test is performed and if employee did not complete rehabilitation program. Test results may also be used as a basis for refusal to hire applicant.

**Enforcement of Statute.** Enforcement is by civil suit.

**Employee Remedies.** Employees may seek back pay and benefits, attorneys' fees, and injunctive relief.

**Employer Penalties.** None.

**Who Pays for Testing?** State has no statutory requirements.

**Employee Assistance Benefits.** State has no statutory requirements.

**Other Requirements.** State has no other statutory requirements.

**Citations to Authority.** Fla. Stat. Ann. § 112.0455; *City of Palm Bay v. Bauman,* 475 So. 2d 1322 (Fla. Dist. Ct. App. 1985). (Provisions are part of amendment to state workers' compensation statute. Regulations establish standards for conducting tests that, if followed, provide employers with certain presumptions and benefits under the law.)

## GEORGIA

**Who Is Covered by Statute.** Employees working for the state or contract workers who provide personal services for the state in high-risk jobs. Any applicant for state or public school employment.

**Applicant Testing.** Applicant testing is allowed for state or public school employment.

**Employee Testing.** Employee testing is allowed, but only an employee working in a high-risk job may be tested at random.

**Conditions for Conducting Tests.** Tests must be conducted by qualified testing laboratories.

**Testing Process Requirements.** Testers must follow quality control and information dissemination procedures.

**How Test Results Are Used.** Test results may be used as grounds for termination of employment or disqualification from employment.

**Enforcement of Statute.** State has no statutory requirements.

**Employee Remedies.** State has no statutory requirements.

**Employer Penalties.** State has no statutory requirements.

**Who Pays for Testing?** State has no statutory requirements.

**Employee Assistance Benefits.** State has no statutory requirements.

**Other Requirements.** State has no other statutory requirements.

**Citations to Authority.** Ga. Code Ann. §§ 45-20-90 *et seq.*

### HAWAII

**Who Is Covered by Statute.** Any person, agency, employer, or other entity requesting an individual to submit to a drug test.

**Applicant Testing.** State has no statutory requirements.

**Employee Testing.** State has no statutory requirements.

**Conditions for Conducting Tests.** Test must be conducted by certified laboratories only.

**Testing Process Requirements.** Persons must be informed of test and of which drugs are subject to detection in writing.

**How Test Results Are Used.** State has no statutory requirements.

**Enforcement of Statute.** Enforcement is by private civil suit; state also may pursue action for injunctive relief.

**Employee Remedies.** Employees may recover actual damages.

**Employer Penalties.** Violators are subject to civil fines of $1,000–$10,000 per violation, plus costs and attorneys' fees.

**Who Pays for Testing?** All costs including confirmation testing shall be paid by employer.

**Employee Assistance Benefits.** State has no statutory requirements.

**Other Requirements.** State has no other statutory requirements.

**Citations to Authority.** Haw. Rev. Stat. § 329B.

### ILLINOIS

**Who Is Covered by Statute.** Any individual performing services for an employer. An employer is any person employing 15 or more employees; any person employing one or more employees, when a complainant alleges civil rights violations due to discrimination; the state or any political subdivision; or any party to a public contract.

**Applicant Testing.** Applicant testing is allowed but not encouraged, prohibited, or restricted.

**Employee Testing.** Employee testing is allowed but not encouraged, prohibited, or restricted.

**Conditions for Conducting Tests.** State has no statutory requirements.

**Testing Process Requirements.** State has no statutory requirements.

**How Test Results Are Used.** Results can be used to remove persons from safety-sensitive duties.

**Enforcement of Statute.** State has no statutory requirements.

**Employee Remedies.** State has no statutory requirements.

**Employer Penalties.** State has no statutory requirements.

**Who Pays for Testing?** State has no statutory requirements.

**Employee Assistance Benefits.** State has no statutory requirements.

**Other Requirements.** State has no other statutory requirements.

**Citations to Authority.** Ill. Comp. Stat. Ann. ch. 775 §§ 5/2-101, 5/2-104.

### INDIANA

**Who Is Covered by Statute.** Any individual performing services for an employer. An employer is any person engaged in an industry affecting commerce that has at least 15 employees for each working day in the last 20 calendar weeks. Corporations wholly owned by the government are exempt.

**Applicant Testing.** Applicant testing is allowed but not encouraged, prohibited, or restricted.

**Employee Testing.** Employee testing is allowed but not encouraged, prohibited, or restricted.

**Conditions for Conducting Tests.** State has no statutory requirements.

**Testing Process Requirements.** State has no statutory requirements.

**How Test Results Are Used.** Results can be used to remove persons from safety-sensitive duties.

**Enforcement of Statute.** State has no statutory requirements.

**Employee Remedies.** State has no statutory requirements.

**Employer Penalties.** State has no statutory requirements.

**Who Pays for Testing?** State has no statutory requirements.

**Employee Assistance Benefits.** State has no statutory requirements.

**Other Requirements.** State has no other statutory requirements.

**Citations to Authority.** Ind. Code Ann. §§ 22-9-5-9, 22-9-5-10, 22-9-5-24.

## IOWA

**Who Is Covered by Statute.** All employers, employees, and applicants.

**Applicant Testing.** An employer shall not require or request applicants to submit to a drug test as a condition of employment unless employer includes notice that a drug test will be part of pre-employment physical in any job advertisement soliciting applicants. (See **Other Requirements** for exceptions.)

**Employee Testing.** Employee testing is allowed for probable cause. Employees must be in jobs where impairment would pose a danger to other employees, the public, or employer's property. Random testing is prohibited.

**Conditions for Conducting Tests.** Tests must be conducted by certified laboratories only.

**Testing Process Requirements.** Positive test results must be disclosed. Retest must be administered at testee's request. Applicants and employees have the right to explain or rebut positive results.

**How Test Results Are Used.** Test results may be used to screen out drug-using applicants or to discharge or discipline employees. An employee's first offense results in referral to an EAP at employer's expense or according to plan.

**Enforcement of Statute.** Enforcement is by private civil action; state pursues violation of statute.

**Employee Remedies.** Employees may seek back pay, attorneys' fees and court costs, reinstatement, and injunctive relief.

**Employer Penalties.** Employer violations are simple misdemeanors.

**Who Pays for Testing?** State has no statutory requirements.

**Employee Assistance Benefits.** Employer shall provide substance abuse evaluation.

**Other Requirements.** Drug test is allowed during annual employee physical on 30-days' notice. Statute does not apply to persons covered under federal statutes or regulations unless such statutes or regulations are deemed unenforceable by federal court order. Exceptions: This statute does not apply to preemployment drug tests for peace or corrections officers, drug tests for employees of nuclear regulatory facilities, or to drug tests required for workers' compensation.

**Citations to Authority.** Iowa Code Ann. § 730.5.

## KANSAS

**Who Is Covered by Statute.** Persons taking office as Governor, Lieutenant Governor, or Attorney General, or for safety-sensitive positions in state government (state police officers who carry firearms, state correction officers, appointed heads of state agencies, and Governor's staff). Also, employees of mental health institutions.

**Applicant Testing.** Applicant testing is allowed for applicants for safety-sensitive positions in state government, but applicants must first be given conditional offer of employment.

**Employee Testing.** Employee testing is allowed, based on reasonable suspicion of illegal drug use.

**Conditions for Conducting Tests.** State has no statutory requirements.

**Testing Process Requirements.** The results of any test administered as part of a program authorized by this law/section are confidential and must not be disclosed publicly.

**How Test Results Are Used.** No person may be terminated solely due to positive results of a drug test administered as part of a program authorized by this law/section if (1) the employee has not previously had a valid positive test result and (2) the employee undergoes drug evaluation and successfully completes any education or treatment program recommended as a result of the evaluation.

**Enforcement of Statute.** State has no statutory requirements.

**Employee Remedies.** State has no statutory requirements.

**Employer Penalties.** State has no statutory requirements.

**Who Pays for Testing?** State has no statutory requirements.

**Employee Assistance Benefits.** State has no statutory requirements.

**Other Requirements.** Any public announcement or advertisement soliciting applications for certain positions must give notice of the drug screening program.

**Citations to Authority.** Kan. Gen. Stat. Ann. §§ 75-4362–75-4363.

## LOUISIANA

**Who Is Covered by Statute.** Employers who are not subject to a federally mandated drug testing program.

**Applicant Testing.** There are no restrictions to testing.

**Employee Testing.** There are no restrictions to testing; rehabilitation (EAP) is permitted but not required.

**Conditions for Conducting Tests.** Tests must be conducted by certified laboratories only. Tests must meet NIDA guidelines. Use of witnesses is limited.

**Testing Process Requirements.** Dual confirmation is required; results go to medical review officer.

**How Test Results Are Used.** State has no statutory requirements.

**Enforcement of Statute.** State has no statutory requirements.

**Employee Remedies.** State has no statutory requirements.

**Employer Penalties.** State has no statutory requirements.

**Who Pays for Testing?** State has no statutory requirements.

**Employee Assistance Benefits.** State has no statutory requirements.

**Other Requirements.** Testing law is subject to state unemployment compensation law and sets forth employee testing requirements in order to support a misconduct discharge and, thus, deny benefits.

**Citations to Authority.** La. Rev. Stat. Ann. §§ 49:1001 *et seq.*, 23:1601.

### MAINE

**Who Is Covered by Statute.** All employers, employees, and applicants. (Employees at nuclear power plants are exempt.) Written policy is required. Employers with 20 or more full-time employees must establish an EAP as a condition for employee drug testing.

**Applicant Testing.** Applicant testing is allowed, but only after conditional offer of employment has been made.

**Employee Testing.** Employee testing is allowed for probable cause. Random testing is permitted with union-management agreement and for safety-sensitive positions. EAP-related testing is permitted, but only for rehabilitation purposes; results are *not* disclosable to employer.

**Conditions for Conducting Tests.** Use of witnesses is prohibited. Tampering constitutes a refusal to be tested. Tests must be supervised by physicians or nurses and conducted in medical facilities. (First-aid stations are medical facilities.) Chain-of-custody record (who handled sample and when) is required. Qualified testing laboratories are required.

**Testing Process Requirements.** Positive test results must be disclosed. Dual confirmation is required: first step is screen; confirming test method is GC/MS. Marijuana metabolite cut-off is 20 mg/ml on confirming test. Retest must be administered at testee's request. Sample must be preserved for 1 year.

**How Test Results Are Used.** Test results may be used as a factor to screen out drug-using applicants or to discharge or discipline employees; an employee's first offense results in referral to an EAP. Discharge is permitted for refusal to take test or for failure to comply with or complete a rehabilitation program within a 6-month period. Applicants and employees have 3 days after positive test to produce evidence explaining or contesting result.

**Enforcement of Statute.** Enforcement is by private civil action; state pursues violation of statute.

**Employee Remedies.** Employees may seek back pay (3 times lost wages), attorneys' fees and court costs, reinstatement, civil damages, and injunctive relief.

**Employer Penalties.** None.

**Who Pays for Testing?** Employees and applicants shall pay all the costs of subsequent tests and samples taken.

**Employee Assistance Benefits.** Employer with more than 20 employees must have in existence an EAP before establishing any substance abuse testing program.

**Other Requirements.** Policy must be approved by state DOL. Employees affected by new policy must be given 30-days' notice; changes to existing policy are effective 60 days after notice. Employers must consult with employees before implementing employee part of program. Employers do not have to consult with present employees about applicant part of program. Probable-cause finding must be written. Employee returning to workforce after drug-related absence may be tested between 90 days and 1 year following first confirmed test.

**Citations to Authority.** Me. Rev. Stat. Ann. tit. 26, §§ 681–690.

### MARYLAND

**Who Is Covered by Statute.** All employers, employees, applicants, and contractors.

**Applicant Testing.** There are no restrictions to testing.

**Employee Testing.** Employees and applicants may be tested without limitation, provided a certified laboratory is used.

**Conditions for Conducting Tests.** Tests must be conducted by certified laboratories only.

**Testing Process Requirements.** Positive test results must be disclosed.

**How Test Results Are Used.** State has no statutory requirements.

**Enforcement of Statute.** State pursues violation of statute.

**Employee Remedies.** State has no statutory requirements.

**Employer Penalties.** State has no statutory requirements.

**Who Pays for Testing?** State has no statutory requirements.

**Employee Assistance Benefits.** State has no statutory requirements.

**Other Requirements.** Principal purpose of statute is to ensure use of certified laboratories.

**Citations to Authority.** Md. Health-Gen. Code Ann. § 17-214.

## MINNESOTA

**Who Is Covered by Statute.** All employees, independent contractors, persons working for independent contractors who perform services for compensation for an employer, and applicants for employment in such capacity. Written policy is required.

**Applicant Testing.** Applicant testing is allowed, but only after conditional offer of employment has been made and is pursuant to a written policy. In addition, this test must be requested or required of all applicants. Notice of drug test during preemployment process is required.

**Employee Testing.** Employee testing is allowed if reasonable suspicion of drug use exists. Postaccident and EAP-related testing is also allowed. Random testing of employees in safety-sensitive positions is permitted. Testing during routine physical examination is allowed if at least 2-week notice is given.

**Conditions for Conducting Tests.** Tests must be conducted by certified laboratories only; chain-of-custody record (who handled sample and when) is required.

**Testing Process Requirements.** Positive test results must be disclosed. Dual confirmation is required: first step is screen; confirming test method is GC/MS. Retest must be administered at testee's request. Samples must be preserved for 6 months.

**How Test Results Are Used.** Test results may be used to screen out drug-using applicants or to discharge or discipline employees. An employee's first offense results in referral to an EAP.

**Enforcement of Statute.** Enforcement is by private civil action.

**Employee Remedies.** Employees may seek back pay, reinstatement, and damages.

**Employer Penalties.** None.

**Who Pays for Testing?** State has no statutory requirements.

**Employee Assistance Benefits.** State has no statutory requirements.

**Other Requirements.** Nothing in section shall be construed to interfere with or diminish any employee protections relating to drug and alcohol testing already provided under collective bargaining agreement that exceeds the minimum standards for employee protection provided in sections.

**Citations to Authority.** Minn. Stat. Ann. §§ 181.950 *et seq.*

## MISSISSIPPI

**Who Is Covered by Statute.** All employees and applicants.

**Applicant Testing.** Applicant testing is allowed. Notice of test must be in writing on the application.

**Employee Testing.** Employee testing by private employers is allowed where there is reasonable suspicion. Random testing of government employees is allowed in law enforcement, public health, high security, or drug interdiction positions.

**Conditions for Conducting Tests.** Tests must be conducted by certified laboratories and must satisfy chain-of-custody requirement.

**Testing Process Requirements.** Positive test results must be disclosed in writing. Employees have the right to explain or rebut positive test results.

**How Test Results Are Used.** Test results may be used to discipline or discharge employees or as grounds for refusing employment to applicants, but only after test results are verified by confirming tests.

**Enforcement of Statute.** Enforcement is by private civil action; injunctive relief is available for violation of the chapter.

**Employee Remedies.** Employees may seek damages, including attorneys' fees.

**Employer Penalties.** None.

**Who Pays for Testing?** Employer shall pay the costs of all drug and alcohol tests requested or required of employee or job applicant.

**Employee Assistance Benefits.** State has no statutory requirements.

**Other Requirements.** State has no other statutory requirements.

**Citations to Authority.** Miss. Code Ann. §§ 71-7-1 *et seq.*

## MONTANA

**Who Is Covered by Statute.** All employers, employees, and applicants. Written policy is required.

**Applicant Testing.** Applicant testing is prohibited except for jobs in hazardous environments or those involving security, public safety, or fiduciary responsibility. Applicants for jobs involving intrastate commercial transportation are subject to testing.

**Employee Testing.** Employee testing is allowed if reasonable suspicion exists. Employees may also be tested if they are involved in an accident causing damage in excess of $1,500 or causing personal injury.

**Conditions for Conducting Tests.** Chain-of-custody record (who handled sample and when) is required.

**Testing Process Requirements.** Test results must be disclosed. Retest must be administered at testee's request.

**How Test Results Are Used.** Test results may be used to screen out drug-using applicants or to discharge or discipline employees. Adverse action may not be taken against a testee who presents a reasonable explanation for or a medical opinion on the test results.

**Enforcement of Statute.** State pursues violation of statute.

**Employee Remedies.** State has no statutory requirements.

**Employer Penalties.** Employer violations are misdemeanors.

**Who Pays for Testing?** Testing is at employer's expense, and all employees must be compensated at their regular rate for time attributable to the testing program.

**Employee Assistance Benefits.** State has no statutory requirements.

**Other Requirements.** Drug testing for continuing employees in jobs involving intrastate commercial motor carrier transportation is permitted during biennial physical.

**Citations to Authority.** Mont. Code Ann. § 39-2-205 *et seq.*

### NEBRASKA

**Who Is Covered by Statute.** Employees, applicants, and employers with 6 or more employees and all government entities.

**Applicant Testing.** State has no statutory requirements.

**Employee Testing.** State has no statutory requirements.

**Conditions for Conducting Tests.** Tests must be conducted by certified laboratories only; chain-of-custody record (who handled sample and when) is required.

**Testing Process Requirements.** Positive test results must be disclosed. Dual confirmation is required: first step is screen; confirming test method is GC/MS. Samples must be preserved for 180 days.

**How Test Results Are Used.** Tests may be used to discharge or discipline employees.

**Enforcement of Statute.** State has no statutory requirements.

**Employee Remedies.** State has no statutory requirements.

**Employer Penalties.** Violations of the statute are misdemeanors.

**Who Pays for Testing?** State has no statutory requirements.

**Employee Assistance Benefits.** State has no statutory requirements.

**Other Requirements.** Employee may request a blood test. Employee refusal to submit to a test may result in denial of continued employment.

**Citations to Authority.** Neb. Rev. Stat. Ann. §§ 48-1901 *et seq.*

### NORTH CAROLINA

**Who Is Covered by Statute.** Individuals who are employees of examining employer or applicants for employment with examiner and who are requested or required by examiner to submit to controlled substance examination.

**Applicant Testing.** Applicant testing is allowed.

**Employee Testing.** Employee testing is allowed.

**Conditions for Conducting Tests.** Tests must be conducted by approved laboratories. Examiner shall use only laboratories that have demonstrated satisfactory performance in the proficiency testing programs of the NIDA or the College of American Pathology. Chain-of-custody record (who handled, labeled, and identified examination samples and when) is required.

**Testing Process Requirements.** Approved laboratory must confirm any sample that produces a positive result by a second examination of the sample utilizing GC/MS or an equivalent scientifically accepted method.

**How Test Results Are Used.** State has no statutory requirements.

**Enforcement of Statute.** State pursues violation of statute.

**Employee Remedies.** None.

**Employer Penalties.** Any examiner who violates the provisions of this Article shall be subject to a civil penalty of up to $250 per examinee, with the maximum not to exceed $1,000 per investigation by the Commissioner of Labor or the Commissioner's authorized representative.

**Who Pays for Testing?** State has no statutory requirements.

**Employee Assistance Benefits.** State has no statutory requirements.

**Other Requirements.** None.

**Citations to Authority.** N.C. Gen. Stat. §§ 95-230 *et seq.*

### OKLAHOMA

**Who Is Covered by Statute.** All employers, employees, and applicants. Written policy is required.

**Applicant Testing.** Applicants may be requested or required to undergo testing upon conditional offer of employment, provided that testing is required of all applicants who receive a conditional offer for a particular employment classification.

**Employee Testing.** Employee testing is allowed when the employer has a reasonable suspicion of an employee violation, for post-accident inquiries, for post-rehabilitation testing up to 2 years commencing with the employee's return to work, and as part of a routinely scheduled employee fitness-for-duty medical examination. Random testing is allowed for employees who are police officers, have drug interdiction responsibilities, are authorized to carry firearms, are involved in activities directly affecting the safety of others, or work in direct contact with inmates, juvenile delinquents, or children in state custody.

**Conditions for Conducting Tests.** Testing must be done by qualified testing facilities. Chain-of-custody record (who handled sample and when) is required. Use of witnesses is prohibited.

**Testing Process Requirements.** Dual confirmation is required: first step is screen; confirming test is GC, GC/MS, or an equivalent, scientifically accepted method.

**How Test Results Are Used.** Applicant refusal to undergo test or a confirmed positive test result may be used as a basis for refusal to hire. Employee may be discharged for refusal to undergo test or for a confirmed positive test. Employer cannot request or require test if an EAP is not provided.

**Enforcement of Statute.** Enforcement is by civil action within 2 years of the person's discovery of the alleged willful violation or of the exhaustion of any internal administrative remedies.

**Employee Remedies.** Employee or applicant may seek injunctive relief; compensatory damages, including employment, reinstatement, promotion, payment of lost wages, and reinstatement to full benefits and seniority rights; court costs; and attorneys' fees.

**Employer Penalties.** Willful and knowing violation of this act is a misdemeanor punishable by a fine of $100—$5,000 or imprisonment for not more than 1 year, or both.

**Who Pays for Testing?** Employer shall pay all costs of drug testing, and employees shall be compensated at their regular rate for time involved in drug testing.

**Employee Assistance Benefits.** Drug or alcohol testing shall not be requested or required of employee unless employer provides an employee assistance program.

**Other Requirements.** Test results are to remain confidential and kept separate from other personnel records.

**Citations to Authority.** Okla. Stat. Ann. tit. 40, §§ 552 *et seq.*

## OREGON

**Who Is Covered by Statute.** All employees and applicants (breathalyzer test only).

**Applicant Testing.** Applicant testing is allowed, but breathalyzer test may be administered only if applicant consents or if employer has reasonable grounds to believe applicant is under the influence of alcohol.

**Employee Testing.** Employee testing is allowed, but breathalyzer test may be administered only if employee consents or if employer has reasonable grounds to believe employee is under the influence of alcohol.

**Conditions for Conducting Tests.** Testing by third party is required.

**Testing Process Requirements.** State has no statutory requirements.

**How Test Results Are Used.** Test results may be used to screen out applicants or to discharge or discipline employees.

**Enforcement of Statute.** Statute is enforced by Commissioner of the Bureau of Labor and Industries.

**Employee Remedies.** None.

**Employer Penalties.** Violation is treated as unlawful employment practice.

**Who Pays for Testing?** State has no statutory requirements.

**Employee Assistance Benefits.** State has no statutory requirements.

**Other Requirements.** None.

**Citations to Authority.** Or. Rev. Stat. §§ 659.225–659.227.

## RHODE ISLAND

**Who Is Covered by Statute.** All employers and employees, except those covered by federal Department of Transportation regulations or other federal requirements.

**Applicant Testing.** Employer can require job applicant to submit to drug testing if (1) the given offer is conditioned on a negative drug test, (2) the applicant provides the test sample in private, and (3) positive test results are confirmed by means of gas chromatography/mass spectrometry or technology recognized as being at least as scientifically accurate.

**Employee Testing.** Testing is allowed where a reasonable suspicion of drug use exists.

**Conditions for Conducting Tests.** Use of witnesses is prohibited.

**Testing Process Requirements.** Positive test results must be disclosed. Dual confirmation is required: first step is screen; confirming test method is GC/MS. Retest must be administered at testee's request at employer's cost. Employee has the right to rebut or explain test result. Employees testing positive are not terminated but are referred to a substance abuse professional (EAP professional, for example).

**How Test Results Are Used.** Employees testing positive shall not be terminated on that basis but shall be referred to a substance abuse professional.

**Enforcement of Statute.** Enforcement is by private civil action; injunctive relief, punitive damages, and attorneys' fees are available to prevailing employee. Criminal sanction; violations are misdemeanors; penalty as noted by statute.

**Employee Remedies.** Employees may obtain attorneys' fees and court costs, damages (including punitive damages), and injunctive relief.

**Employer Penalties.** Employer penalties include criminal sanction (with a fine of up to $1,000, imprisonment for 1 year, or both).

**Who Pays for Testing?** Subsequent tests are at employee's expense.

**Employee Assistance Benefits.** State has no statutory requirements.

**Other Requirements.** Testing must be conducted in conjunction with a bona fide rehabilitation program.

**Citations to Authority.** R.I. Gen. Laws §§ 28-6.5-1, 28-6.5-2.

## SOUTH DAKOTA

**Who Is Covered by Statute.** State government employees in safety-sensitive positions.

**Applicant Testing.** Applicant testing is allowed. Any printed public announcement or advertisement soliciting applications for employment in a safety-sensitive position in state government shall include a statement of the requirements of the drug screening program established under this chapter for applicants and employees holding such positions.

**Employee Testing.** Employee testing is allowed if there is reasonable suspicion of illegal drug use by any such person.

**Conditions for Conducting Tests.** State has no statutory requirements.

**Testing Process Requirements.** Test results must be confidential and made available to applicants and employees who make written requests for them.

**How Test Results Are Used.** State has no statutory requirements.

**Enforcement of Statute.** State has no statutory requirements.

**Employee Remedies.** None.

**Employer Penalties.** Any person responsible for recording, reporting, or maintaining medical information required pursuant to the provisions of this chapter, who knowingly or intentionally discloses or fails to protect medical information declared to be confidential or who compels another person to disclose such medical information is guilty of a Class 2 misdemeanor.

**Other Requirements.** State has no other statutory requirements.

**Citations to Authority.** S.D. Codified Laws Ann. §§ 23-3-64–23-3-69.

## TENNESSEE

**Who Is Covered by Statute.** All employers.

**Applicant Testing.** Applicant testing is allowed.

**Employee Testing.** Employee testing is allowed if there is a reasonable suspicion of drug or alcohol abuse by such employee. Employees may also be tested after an accident and as part of a routine fitness-for-duty physical.

**Conditions for Conducting Tests.** Chain of custody procedures established by governmental authority must be followed. Testing must be conducted at licensed laboratory.

**Testing Process Requirements.** Confidentiality must be ensured. Commission of Labor may adopt rules regarding retention and storage procedures and minimum cut-off detection levels.

**How Test Results Are Used.** Test results may be used for disciplinary action including termination. Employer may not discipline, discharge, or refuse to hire on the basis of a positive test result that has not been verified.

**Enforcement of Statute.** State has no statutory requirements.

**Employee Remedies.** State has no statutory requirements.

**Employer Penalties.** State has no statutory requirements.

**Who Pays for Testing?** Employer shall pay the cost of all drug tests that the employer requires of the employee.

**Employee Assistance Benefits.** Employer's Drug Policy Statement must include names and telephone numbers of EAP and drug and alcohol rehabilitation programs. Employer is not required to provide these programs.

**Other Requirements.** Prior to testing, employer shall give all employees and job applicants a written policy statement on alcohol and drug testing.

**Citations to Authority.** Tenn. Code Ann. §§ 50-9-101 *et seq.*

## UTAH

**Who Is Covered by Statute.** All employers, employees, and applicants. Employer does not include the federal or state government or any local political subdivision. Written policy is required.

**Applicant Testing.** There are no restrictions to applicant testing.

**Employee Testing.** Employee testing is allowed for the following purposes: potential impairment of individual employee, investigations of workplace accidents or theft, maintenance of safety, or maintenance of productivity.

**Conditions for Conducting Tests.** Chain-of-custody record (who handled sample and when) is required. Privacy of the individual being tested must be considered.

**Testing Process Requirements.** Dual confirmation is required: first step is screen; confirming test method is GC/MS.

**How Test Results Are Used.** Test results may be used to screen out drug-using applicants or to discharge or discipline employees. Employee referrals to an EAP are at sole discretion of employer.

**Enforcement of Statute.** Enforcement is by private civil action. Cause of action available only if test result is false positive; employers enjoy rebuttable presumption that test result is accurate if employer complied with statute; law bars damages if employer acted in good faith.

**Employee Remedies.** Employees may seek damages.

**Employer Penalties.** None.

**Who Pays for Testing?** Drug and alcohol testing shall be deemed work time for purposes of compensation and benefits for current employees. Employer shall pay all the costs of testing required by employer.

**Employee Assistance Benefits.** State has no statutory requirements.

**Other Requirements.** In order to be able to test employees, employers and management must submit to testing on a periodic basis.

**Citations to Authority.** Utah Code Ann. §§ 34-38-1 *et seq.*

## VERMONT

**Who Is Covered by Statute.** All employers, employees, and applicants. Written policy is required.

**Applicant Testing.** Applicant testing is allowed, but only after conditional offer of employment has been made. Applicants residing over 200 air miles from test site need not be given conditional offer (and thus may be tested first). Ten-day notice must be given before testing. The test must be given in conjunction with a physical exam.

**Employee Testing.** An employee may be tested if probable cause exists and employer has an EAP available. Random testing is prohibited.

**Conditions for Conducting Tests.** Tests must be conducted by certified laboratories only; chain-of-custody record (who handled sample and when) is required.

**Testing Process Requirements.** Positive test results must be disclosed. Dual confirmation is required. Retest must be administered at testee's request. Samples must be preserved for 90 days. Tests showing therapeutic levels of tested drug must be reported as negative. Employer cannot require or request a blood sample for a drug test.

**How Test Results Are Used.** Test results may be used to screen out drug-using applicants or to discharge or discipline employees. An employee's first offense results in referral to an EAP. The employee may be terminated if, after completion of an EAP, the employee receives another positive drug test result.

**Enforcement of Statute.** Enforcement is by private civil action; state pursues violation of statute.

**Employee Remedies.** Employees may seek attorneys' fees and court costs, damages, and injunctive relief.

**Employer Penalties.** Employer penalties include civil penalty (civil fine of $500–$2,000) and criminal sanction (criminal fine of $500–$1,000, imprisonment for not more than 6 months, or both).

**Who Pays for Testing?** Employee can retest sample at a laboratory at employee's expense.

**Employee Assistance Benefits.** To require, request, or conduct drug testing, employer must have available an EAP provided by employer or benefits are available to the extent provided by a policy of health insurance or under contract by a nonprofit hospital service corporation.

**Other Requirements.** If urinalysis is positive, testee may request, at own expense, a blood test. Results must be kept confidential.

**Citations to Authority.** Vt. Stat. Ann. tit. 21, §§ 511–520.

## WASHINGTON

**Who Is Covered by Statute.** All employers. Employer does not include any governmental entity.

**Applicant Testing.** Applicants may be required to submit to drug test after offer of employment is extended.

**Employee Testing.** Employee testing is allowed on a random basis, based on reasonable suspicions, or after workplace accident.

**Conditions for Conducting Tests.** Chain of custody procedures must be followed. Employer must inform employee within 5 working days after receipt of positive test result. Testing must be conducted at a certified laboratory.

**Testing Process Requirements.** Confidentiality must be ensured. Initial test having a positive result must be verified by a confirmation test.

**How Test Results Are Used.** Employer may terminate employee for refusing to submit to a drug or alcohol test, failure to comply with last-chance agreement, and upon second verified positive drug or alcohol test result.

**Enforcement of Statute.** State has no statutory requirements.

**Employee Remedies.** State has no statutory requirements.

**Employer Penalties.** State has no statutory requirements.

**Who Pays for Testing?** Employer shall pay the cost of all drug and alcohol tests, initial and confirmation, that the employer requires of the employee. Employee or applicant shall pay the costs of additional tests not required by employer.

**Employee Assistance Benefits.** EAP is required by statute. The EAP shall provide the employer with a system for dealing with employees whose job performances are declining due to unresolved problems, including alcohol and other drug-related problems, marital problems, legal, and financial problems.

**Other Requirements.** State has no statutory requirements.

**Citations to Authority.** Wash. Rev. Code §§ 49.82.020 *et seq.*

## WEST VIRGINIA

Note: The West Virginia Supreme Court has held that it is contrary to the state's public policy for a private employer to require employees to submit to drug testing since such testing portends an invasion of the individual's right to privacy.

**Citations to Authority.** *Twigg v. Hercules Corp.,* 185 W. Va. 155, 406 S.E.2d 52 (1990).

# Table 7.2-2
## AIDS TESTING IN THE WORKPLACE: STATUTES AND POLICIES

(States not listed have passed no legislation governing AIDS testing in the workplace. The following states have enacted statutes that protect the confidentiality of HIV test results: AL, AZ, CO, CT, DE, GA, HI, ID, IL, IN, IA, KS, LA, ME, MD, MI, MO, MT, NV, NH, NJ, NY, ND, OH, OK, OR, PA, TX, VA, WV, and WI. See also text at § 7.2[c].)

**KEY:** **Bona fide occupational qualification.** A limited defense to charge of discrimination. (See Glossary.)
**Person with AIDS.** Encompasses both persons with AIDS and persons who have tested positive for the human immunodeficiency virus (HIV) that causes AIDS. Although state statute may not specifically classify AIDS as a handicap or disability, state courts may follow federal law under which person with AIDS may be considered to be a person with a disability.

*With respect to whether AIDS is classified as a handicap, the Supreme Court in *Bragdon v. Abott,* 118 S. Ct. 2196 (1998), held that the ability to reproduce and to bear children constitutes a major life activity within the meaning of the American With Disabilities Act (ADA). The court found that HIV status is a physical impairment that interferes with the ability to have children and that individuals infected with HIV are covered by the ADA. The court stated that HIV infection satisfies the statutory and regulatory definition of physical impairment. Most state courts are likely to follow the Supreme Court's ruling in construing state fair employment practices statutes.

| | *AIDS Classified as a Handicap** | *Mandatory Testing Prohibited* | *Prohibition Against Use of Positive AIDS Test to Discriminate* | *Other Requirements* | *Citations to Authority* |
|---|---|---|---|---|---|
| AL | State has no statutory requirements. | Yes. Must obtain informed consent of person to be tested. | State has no statutory requirements. | Testing facility shall maintain confidentiality regarding HIV test results. | Ala. Code §§ 22-11A-50–22-11A-54. |
| AZ | Yes. Attorney General's Opinion Number R86-005 (1987). | Yes. Must obtain written informed consent of person to be tested. Consent may be withdrawn at any time before drawing the sample. | State has no statutory requirements. | Civil Rights Act governs whether employment decision can be made based on AIDS test result (1987 Attorney General Opinion). State law protects confidentiality of HIV/AIDS test results. | Ariz. Rev. Stat. Ann. § 36-663. |
| AR | State has no statutory requirements. | Informed consent not required for HIV test for health care provider or employee of health care facility who has direct skin or mucous membrane contact with blood of patient. | State has no statutory requirements. | None. | Ark. Code Ann. § 20-15-905. |
| CA | Yes. Fair Employment and Housing Act. | Must obtain written informed consent of person to be tested. | Yes. | None. | Cal. Gov't Code § 12940; Cal. Health & Safety Code §§ 121132, 121135; *Chalk v. United States District Court,* 840 F.2d 701 (9th Cir. 1988); *Raytheon Co. v. California Fair Employment and Housing Comm'n,* 261 Cal. Rptr. 197 (Cal. App. 2 Dist. 1989). |

| | | | | | |
|---|---|---|---|---|---|
| CO | Yes. Colorado Civil Rights Commission ruling. | Must obtain written informed consent of person to be tested. | State has no statutory requirements. | State law protects confidentiality of HIV/AIDS test results. | Colo. Rev. Stat. § 10-3-1104.5. |
| CT | Yes. Connecticut Commission on Human Rights and Opportunities. | Yes. No employer shall order HIV-related test without first receiving written informed consent or oral informed consent. Whenever practical, written consent shall be obtained. Informed consent shall be obtained without undue inducement or any element of compulsion, fraud, deceit, duress, or other form of constraint or coercion. | State has no statutory requirements. | No person who obtains HIV-related information may disclose or be compelled to disclose such information except to the classes of persons to whom disclosure of such information may be required, authorized, or permitted by law. Explanation of confidentiality protections afforded confidential HIV-related information including the circumstances under which it is given must also be provided. When communicating the test result, the person ordering the test must provide counseling or referrals for counseling. | Conn. Gen. Stat. Ann. §§ 19a-581 *et seq.*; Regs. Conn. State Agencies §§ 46a-54-41 *et seq.* |
| DE | Yes. Delaware Attorney General. | Must obtain consent of person to be tested. Exception to consent exists if the health of a health care worker has been threatened during the course of duties as a result of exposure to blood or other bodily fluids. | State has no statutory requirements. | State law protects confidentiality of HIV/AIDS test results. Infected teachers and school employees may continue working (State Board of Education and Department of Public Instruction Guidelines). | Del. Code Ann. tit. 16, §§ 1201–1205. |
| DC | Yes. D.C. Office of Human Rights. | State has no statutory requirements. | Yes. Statute incorporates business necessity test. | None. | D.C. Code Ann. §§ 1-2502, 1-2503. |
| FL | Yes. By statute. | Yes. Must obtain informed consent of person to be tested, unless absence of HIV is a bona fide occupational qualification. | Yes. State law authorizes state to administer voluntary tests to identify persons with AIDS, but test results may not be used to discriminate against prospective or current employees. | Violation of nondiscrimination law permits recovery of larger of $1,000 or actual damages; if violation is willfull, recovery is larger of $5,000 or actual damages, plus attorneys' fees and other costs. | Fla. Stat. Ann. §§ 381.004, 760.50; FCHR No. 85-0624, 2 Empl. Prac. Guide (CCH) ¶ 5014 (1985). |
| GA | State has no statutory requirements. | State has no statutory requirements. | State has no statutory requirements. | State law protects confidentiality of HIV/AIDS test results. A person can be ordered to submit to an HIV test if the state has evidence that the person is reasonably likely to be infected. | Ga. Code Ann. §§ 24-9-40.1, 24-9-47, 31-17A-3. |
| HI | State has no statutory requirements. | Employer may test employee with consent, but may not compel test. | State has no statutory requirements. | State law protects confidentiality of HIV/AIDS test results. Results may be released to schools, preschools, and day care centers. | Haw. Rev. Stat. §§ 325-101(a), 325-101(c). |
| ID | State has no statutory requirements. | State has no statutory requirements. | State has no statutory requirements. | State law protects confidentiality of test results. | Idaho Code § 39-610. |

*(Table continues.)*

# Table 7.2-2 *(cont'd)*

## AIDS TESTING IN THE WORKPLACE: STATUTES AND POLICIES

(States not listed have passed no legislation governing AIDS testing in the workplace. The following states have enacted statutes that protect the confidentiality of HIV test results: AL, AZ, CO, CT, DE, GA, HI, ID, IL, IN, IA, KS, LA, ME, MD, MI, MO, MT, NV, NH, NJ, NY, ND, OH, OK, OR, PA, TX, VA, WV, and WI. See also text at § 7.2[c].)

**KEY:** **Bona fide occupational qualification.** A limited defense to charge of discrimination. (See Glossary.)
**Person with AIDS.** Encompasses both persons with AIDS and persons who have tested positive for the human immunodeficiency virus (HIV) that causes AIDS. Although state statute may not specifically classify AIDS as a handicap or disability, state courts may follow federal law under which person with AIDS may be considered to be a person with a disability.

*With respect to whether AIDS is classified as a handicap, the Supreme Court in *Bragdon v. Abott,* 118 S. Ct. 2196 (1998), held that the ability to reproduce and to bear children constitutes a major life activity within the meaning of the American With Disabilities Act (ADA). The court found that HIV status is a physical impairment that interferes with the ability to have children and that individuals infected with HIV are covered by the ADA. The court stated that HIV infection satisfies the statutory and regulatory definition of physical impairment. Most state courts are likely to follow the Supreme Court's ruling in construing state fair employment practices statutes.

| | *AIDS Classified as a Handicap** | *Mandatory Testing Prohibited* | *Prohibition Against Use of Positive AIDS Test to Discriminate* | *Other Requirements* | *Citations to Authority* |
|---|---|---|---|---|---|
| IL | Yes. Illinois Human Rights Commission. | Yes, except for emergency medical workers, firefighters, and law enforcement officers exposed to HIV. | State has no statutory requirements. | State law protects confidentiality of test results and patient identity. | 410 Ill. Comp. Stat. Ann. §§ 305/1 *et seq.* |
| IN | State has no statutory requirements. | Yes, except for certain medical diagnoses and emergencies. Can test with informed consent. Consent may be withdrawn at any time. | State has no statutory requirements. | State law protects confidentiality of medical information, including AIDS tests. | Ind. Code Ann. §§ 16-41-6-1 *et seq.* |
| IA | Yes. Iowa Civil Rights Act. | Yes, but may test only with consent. | Yes. | State law protects confidentiality of HIV/AIDS test results. | Iowa Code Ann. §§ 141.1 *et seq.* |
| KS | Yes. | Yes. Must obtain consent of person to be tested. | Yes. | State law protects confidentiality of test results. | Kan. Stat. Ann. §§ 65-6001 *et seq.* |
| KY | Yes. | Yes, unless absence of HIV is bona fide occupational qualification. | Yes, unless absence of HIV is bona fide occupational qualification; burden of proof on employer. | Duty of accommodation applies. Nothing prevents the employer from making pre-employment inquiries as to the handicap. | Ky. Rev. Stat. Ann. §§ 207.130 *et seq.* |
| LA | Yes. Louisiana Civil Rights for the Handicapped. | Yes. Informed consent required of person to be tested. | State has no statutory requirements. | State protects confidentiality of test results. | La. Rev. Stat. Ann. §§ 40:1300.11 *et seq.* |

| | | | | | |
|---|---|---|---|---|---|
| ME | Yes. Maine Human Rights Commission Ruling. | Yes. Must obtain informed consent of person to be tested. Exception: employee of health care facility may be tested if it is bona fide occupational qualification. | State has no statutory requirements. | State law protects confidentiality of test results and patient identity. Violation of law permits recovery of actual damages, civil penalty of $1,000 (up to $5,000, if violation deemed willful), plus attorneys' fees and costs. | Me. Rev. Stat. Ann. tit. 5, §§ 19203, 19204. |
| MD | Yes. Maryland Handicap Guidelines. | Yes. Informed consent required of person to be tested. | State has no statutory requirements. | State protects confidentiality of test results and patient identity. | Md. Health-General Code Ann. § 18-336. |
| MA | Yes. Massachusetts Commission Against Discrimination ruling. | Yes. Must obtain written informed consent of person to be tested. | Yes. | Employees with AIDS may remain on the job; employer must protect confidentiality of employees with AIDS; AIDS testing will not be routinely conducted among state workers (state policy). | Mass. Gen. Laws Ann. ch. 111, § 70F; *Estate of McKinley v. Boston Harbor Hotel,* Mass. Comm'n Against Discrimination, No. 90-B-EM-1263 (Aug. 10, 1992). |
| MI | Yes. Civil Rights Commission and Michigan Civil Rights Act. | Yes. Must obtain informed consent of person to be tested. Ann Arbor city regulation covering present and prospective city employees prohibits mandatory testing. | Yes. Detroit law covers all employers; Ann Arbor city regulation covers present and prospective city employees. | State law protects confidentiality of HIV test results and patient identity. | Mich. Comp. Laws Ann. §§ 37.1103, 333.5131, 333.5133; *Sanchez v. Lagoudakis,* 486 N.W.2d 657 (Mich. 1992). |
| MN | Yes. Minnesota Human Rights Commission. | Yes. St. Paul city policy covering present and prospective city employees prohibits mandatory testing. | Yes. State court ruling applies to all employers; State Department of Employee Relations policy covers state employees; governor's executive order covers present and prospective state employees. | State law requires reasonable accommodation. | Minn. Stat. Ann. §§ 363.01 *et seq.* |
| MO | Yes. | State has no statutory requirements. | Yes. State fair employment law prohibits discrimination against persons with AIDS unless such persons present a danger to co-workers or others. | State law protects confidentiality of HIV test results. Routine screening for positive antibody test not recommended under employment guidelines. Employment policies applicable on same basis as for persons with other conditions affecting job performance (State Department of Health 1986 Guidelines). | Mo. Rev. Stat. §§ 191.650–191.695; *Rose City Oil Co. v. Missouri Comm'n on Human Rights,* 832 S.W.2d 314 (Mo. Ct. App. 1992). |
| MT | Yes. Montana Commission for Human Rights. | Yes. Must obtain written, informed consent of person to be tested. | State has no statutory requirements. | State law prohibits disclosure of identity of subjects of AIDS tests. | Mont. Code Ann. §§ 50-16-1007, 50-16-1009. |
| NE | Yes. | No. | Yes, unless person with AIDS cannot perform requirements of job or poses threat to health and safety of others. | No specific statutory provision dealing with AIDS. Topic is covered under fair employment practice laws for physical disabilities. | Neb. Rev. Stat. §§ 48-1101–48-1125. |

*(Table continues.)*

## Table 7.2-2 *(cont'd)*

## AIDS TESTING IN THE WORKPLACE: STATUTES AND POLICIES

(States not listed have passed no legislation governing AIDS testing in the workplace. The following states have enacted statutes that protect the confidentiality of HIV test results: AL, AZ, CO, CT, DE, GA, HI, ID, IL, IN, IA, KS, LA, ME, MD, MI, MO, MT, NV, NH, NJ, NY, ND, OH, OK, OR, PA, TX, VA, WV, and WI. See also text at § 7.2[c].)

**KEY:** **Bona fide occupational qualification.** A limited defense to charge of discrimination. (See Glossary.)
**Person with AIDS.** Encompasses both persons with AIDS and persons who have tested positive for the human immunodeficiency virus (HIV) that causes AIDS. Although state statute may not specifically classify AIDS as a handicap or disability, state courts may follow federal law under which person with AIDS may be considered to be a person with a disability.

*With respect to whether AIDS is classified as a handicap, the Supreme Court in *Bragdon v. Abott,* 118 S. Ct. 2196 (1998), held that the ability to reproduce and to bear children constitutes a major life activity within the meaning of the American With Disabilities Act (ADA). The court found that HIV status is a physical impairment that interferes with the ability to have children and that individuals infected with HIV are covered by the ADA. The court stated that HIV infection satisfies the statutory and regulatory definition of physical impairment. Most state courts are likely to follow the Supreme Court's ruling in construing state fair employment practices statutes.

| | *AIDS Classified as a Handicap** | *Mandatory Testing Prohibited* | *Prohibition Against Use of Positive AIDS Test to Discriminate* | *Other Requirements* | *Citations to Authority* |
|---|---|---|---|---|---|
| NH | State has no statutory requirements. | Yes. Must obtain informed consent of person to be tested, with certain exceptions. | State has no statutory requirements. | State law protects confidentiality of test results and identity of patient. | N.H. Rev. Stat. Ann. § 141-F. |
| NJ | Yes. | Yes. | Yes. | State law protects confidentiality of HIV test information. | N.J. Stat. Ann. §§ 10:5-1, 26:5C *et seq.* |
| NM | Yes. State Attorney General's Office. | No. | Yes, bar to requiring disclosure of HIV test results as condition of employment unless bona fide occupational qualification; burden of proof on employer. | None. | N.M. Stat. Ann. § 28-10A-1. |
| NY | Yes. | Yes. Must obtain informed, written consent of person to be tested. Consent may be withdrawn at any time. | Yes. | State law protects confidentiality of test results. | N.Y. Pub. Health Laws §§ 2780–2787; N.Y. Comp. Codes R. & Regs, tit. 8, §§ 108, 109; *Barton v. N.Y. City Commission on Human Rights,* 140 Misc. 2d 554, 531, N.Y.S.2d 979 (1988). |
| NC | State has no statutory requirements. Under judicial interpretation, person who tests positive for HIV, but who is otherwise asymptomatic, is not a "handicapped person" within | Yes, for employees, except as part of annual medical examination. | Yes, unless continued employment poses risks to person with AIDS or others. Job applicants can be denied employment solely on the basis of a confirmed positive test for the AIDS virus. | Statute may be enforced by civil action; back pay and attorneys' fees available. | N.C. Gen. Stat. § 130A-148; *Burgess v. Your House of Raleigh, Inc.,* 326 N.C. 205, 388 S.E.2d 134 (1990). |

| | | | | | |
|---|---|---|---|---|---|
| | meaning of North Carolina Handicapped Persons Protection Act. | | | | |
| ND | Yes. ND state agency ruling. | Yes. Must obtain written consent of person to be tested. | State has no statutory requirements. | State law protects confidentiality of test results. | N.D. Cent. Code §§ 23-07.5-01, 23-07.5-02, 23-07.5-05. |
| OH | Yes. Ohio Civil Rights Commission. | Yes. Must obtain informed consent of person to be tested. Cincinnati Board of Health regulation covering private and government employees prohibits mandatory testing. | Yes. Cincinnati Board of Health regulation covers private and government employees. | State law protects confidentiality of HIV test results. Employers immune from liability to employees for workplace transmission of HIV unless they act recklessly. | Ohio Stat. tit. 37, §§ 3701.24.2, 3701.24.3, 3701.24.9. |
| OK | State has no statutory requirements. | Yes. Must obtain written consent from person to be tested. | State has no statutory requirements. | State protects confidentiality of test results. | Okla. Stat. Ann. tit. 63 §§ 1-502.2, 1-502.3. |
| OR | Yes. Oregon Attorney General ruling. | In general, yes; informed consent or court order must be obtained to mandate testing. | State has no statutory requirements. | State law protects confidentiality of HIV/AIDS test results. | Or. Rev. Stat. § 433.045. |
| PA | Yes. Pennsylvania Human Relations Act. | Yes. Must obtain informed, written consent from person to be tested. State executive order applies to state employees; Philadelphia mayoral executive order covers city employees and clients. | Yes. Federal court ruling; state executive order applies to state employees; Philadelphia mayoral executive order covers city employees and clients. | State law protects confidentiality of test results. | Pa. Stat. tit. 35 §§ 7601 *et seq.* |
| RI | Yes. Rhode Island Human Rights Commission. | Yes. Must obtain informed consent of person to be tested. | Yes, unless the person with AIDS poses clear and present danger to others. | State law protects confidentiality of HIV test results. | R.I. Gen. Laws §§ 23-6-13, 23-6-17, 23-6-22. |
| SC | Yes. South Carolina Human Affairs Commission. | Yes. State Department of Health and Environmental Control policy prohibits testing of present and prospective state employees without prior consent. | Yes. State Department of Health and Environmental Control policy covers present and prospective state employees. | Testing of a person without consent is allowed if health care worker is exposed to blood during treatment and reasonable medical judgment indicates significant risk of HIV exposure. | S.C. Code Ann. § 44-29-230; see Dep't of Health & Environmental Control, chs. 61, 65. |
| TX | Yes. State Attorney General's Opinion. | Yes. State statute prohibits testing by employers unless bona fide occupational qualification can be shown; employer has burden of proof. | Yes. State court ruling. Austin city ordinance covers employers with 16 or more workers, employment agencies, and labor unions. | State law protects confidentiality of HIV test results. Violation of law permits recovery of actual damages, civil penalty of $1,000 (up to $5,000, if violation deemed willful), plus attorneys' fees and costs. | Tex. Health & Safety Code Ann. §§ 81.102–81.104. |
| VT | Yes. Fair Employment Practices Act. | Yes. | Yes. Requiring HIV test as condition of job is unlawful employment practice, as is discriminating against persons with AIDS. | None. | Vt. Stat. Ann. tit. 21, § 495. |
| VA | State has no statutory requirements. | Yes. Informed consent required except in specified cases involving health care employees. | State has no statutory requirement. | State law protects confidentiality of test results. Unauthorized disclosure is punishable by a civil penalty up to $5,000. | Va. Code Ann. §§ 32.1-36.1, 32.1-37.2, 32.1-45.1. |

*(Table continues.)*

## Table 7.2-2 *(cont'd)*
## AIDS TESTING IN THE WORKPLACE: STATUTES AND POLICIES

(States not listed have passed no legislation governing AIDS testing in the workplace. The following states have enacted statutes that protect the confidentiality of HIV test results: AL, AZ, CO, CT, DE, GA, HI, ID, IL, IN, IA, KS, LA, ME, MD, MI, MO, MT, NV, NH, NJ, NY, ND, OH, OK, OR, PA, TX, VA, WV, and WI. See also text at § 7.2[c].)

**KEY:** **Bona fide occupational qualification.** A limited defense to charge of discrimination. (See Glossary.)
**Person with AIDS.** Encompasses both persons with AIDS and persons who have tested positive for the human immunodeficiency virus (HIV) that causes AIDS. Although state statute may not specifically classify AIDS as a handicap or disability, state courts may follow federal law under which person with AIDS may be considered to be a person with a disability.

*With respect to whether AIDS is classified as a handicap, the Supreme Court in *Bragdon v. Abott,* 118 S. Ct. 2196 (1998), held that the ability to reproduce and to bear children constitutes a major life activity within the meaning of the American With Disabilities Act (ADA). The court found that HIV status is a physical impairment that interferes with the ability to have children and that individuals infected with HIV are covered by the ADA. The court stated that HIV infection satisfies the statutory and regulatory definition of physical impairment. Most state courts are likely to follow the Supreme Court's ruling in construing state fair employment practices statutes.

| | *AIDS Classified as a Handicap** | *Mandatory Testing Prohibited* | *Prohibition Against Use of Positive AIDS Test to Discriminate* | *Other Requirements* | *Citations to Authority* |
|---|---|---|---|---|---|
| WA | Yes. Washington State Human Rights Commission. | Yes, absent bona fide occupational qualification. | Yes. Discrimination barred absent bona fide occupational qualification; burden of proof on employer. | Employers immune from liability for HIV transmission in workplace unless grossly negligent. | Wash. Rev. Code § 49.60.172. |
| WV | Yes. West Virginia Human Rights Act. | Yes. Must obtain consent from person to be tested. Certain exceptions apply. Testing can be required by the courts for persons convicted of prostitution, sexual abuse, sexual assault, incest, or sexual molestation. | No. | State law protects confidentiality of HIV test results. | W. Va. Code §§ 5-11-3(m), 16-3C1 to 16-3C-9; *Benjamin R. v. Orkin Exterminating Co.,* 182 W. Va. 615, 390 S.E.2d 814 (1990). |
| WI | Yes. State Attorney General's Ruling. | Yes. State Attorney General's Ruling. | Yes. State law prohibits use of test results by employers to discriminate unless state health officials find substantial risk of transmission through employment. | State law protects confidentiality of HIV test results. | Wis. Stat. Ann. § 103.15; *Racine Unified School Dist. v. Labor and Ind. Review Comm'n,* 476 N.W.2d 707 (1991). |

# Table 7.2-3
## MUNICIPAL AIDS ORDINANCES: TESTING AND DISCRIMINATION PROVISIONS

(See also text at § 7.2[c].)

| | *Employers Covered by Statute* | *Employers Exempted by Statute* | *Prohibited Activities* | *Exceptions to Statute* | *How Statute Is Enforced* | *Statute of Limitations* | *Damages and Miscellaneous Regulations* | *Citations to Authority* |
|---|---|---|---|---|---|---|---|---|
| Berkeley, CA | Employers, employment agencies, and labor organizations. | Under 15 employees. | Failure or refusal to hire; limitation, segregation, or classification; exclusion from membership. No AIDS testing. | If there is bona fide occupational qualification or employee benefit system. | Civil action; injunction; nonexclusivity of remedy. | 1 year. | Costs; attorneys' fees; up to 3 times damages, but not less than $1,000. Antiretaliatory clause. | Ord. No. 5712-NS, 1986 §§ 13.30 *et seq.* |
| Los Angeles, CA | Employers, employment agencies, and labor organizations. | None. | Failure or refusal to hire; limitation, segregation, or classification; exclusion from membership. | If there is bona fide occupational qualification; also, compliance with Center for Disease Control (CDC) workplace guidelines is an affirmative defense to an action under the ordinance. | Civil action; injunction; nonexclusivity of remedy. | 1 year. | Actual damages; costs; attorneys' fees; punitive damages. | Ord. No. 160289 (amended 7/17/86). |
| Sacramento, CA | Employers, employment agencies, and labor organizations. | None. | Failure or refusal to hire; limitation, segregation, or classification; exclusion from membership. | If there is bona fide occupational qualification. | Civil action. | 1 year. | Actual damages; costs; attorneys' fees. | Ord. No. 87-045, ch. 74 (enacted 5/12/87). |
| San Francisco, CA | Employers, employment agencies, and labor organizations. | None. | Failure or refusal to hire; limitation, segregation, or classification; exclusion from membership. Testing and retaliation are prohibited. | If there is bona fide occupational qualification. | Civil action; mediation by Human Rights Commission. | 2 years. | Up to 3 times actual damages, but at least $1,000. Costs; attorneys' fees; punitive damages. | Ord. No. 499-85 §§ 3801 *et seq.* (enacted 12/20/85). |

*(Table continues.)*

## **Table 7.2-3** *(cont'd)*
## MUNICIPAL AIDS ORDINANCES: TESTING AND DISCRIMINATION PROVISIONS

(See also text at § 7.2[c].)

| | *Employers Covered by Statute* | *Employers Exempted by Statute* | *Prohibited Activities* | *Exceptions to Statute* | *How Statute Is Enforced* | *Statute of Limitations* | *Damages and Miscellaneous Regulations* | *Citations to Authority* |
|---|---|---|---|---|---|---|---|---|
| San Jose, CA | Employers, employment agencies, and labor organizations and agents thereof. | None. | Discharge; failure or refusal to hire; discrimination, limitation, segregation, or classification; exclusion from membership; failure or refusal to refer for employment. | If there is bona fide occupational qualification. | Civil action; injunctive relief, non-exclusivity of remedy. | 2 years. | Actual damages up to 3 times such damages, but not less than $1,000; costs, attorneys' fees, punitive damages. | Ord. No. 22878 (enacted 2/5/85). |
| Santa Clara County, CA | Employers, employment agencies, and labor organizations. | None. | Failure or refusal to hire; limitation, segregation, or classification; exclusion from membership. No AIDS testing. | If there is bona fide occupational qualification or employee benefit system. | Civil action; injunction; nonexclusivity of remedy. | 2 years. | Nonwaiverability clause; retaliation is unlawful. | Ord. No. NS-300.423 (enacted 12/8/87). |
| West Hollywood, CA | Employers, employment agencies, and labor organizations. | None. | Failure or refusal to hire; limitation, segregation, or classification; exclusion from membership. No AIDS testing. | If there is bona fide occupational qualification or employee benefit system. | Civil action; injunction; nonexclusivity of remedy. | 1 year. | Actual damages; costs; attorneys' fees. Not less than $250, nor more than $10,000; punitive damages where indicated. | Ord. No. 77 (enacted 9/5/85). |
| Washington, DC | Employers, employment agencies, and labor organizations. | None. | Failure or refusal to hire; limitation, segregation, or classification; exclusion from membership. No AIDS testing. | Business necessity. | Civil action; injunction; nonexclusivity of remedy. File with Human Rights Commission. | 1 year. | AIDS defined as disability covered under Act. | Human Rights Act of 1977, ch. 25 §§ 1-2501 *et seq.* |

| | | | | | | | | |
|---|---|---|---|---|---|---|---|---|
| Detroit, MI | Employers, employment agencies, and labor organizations and agents thereof. | None. | Discharge; failure or refusal to hire; discrimination, limitation, segregation, or classification; exclusion from membership, failure or refusal to refer for employment. | If there is bona fide occupational qualification or employee benefit system. | Civil action; injunctive relief, nonexclusivity of remedy. No criminal penalties for violation of ordinance. | 180 days. | Actual damages; costs; attorneys' fees; exemplary damages (court option). | Ord. No. 33-88, ch. 27, art. 7 (enacted 7/14/88). |
| Toledo, OH | Employers, employment agencies, and labor organizations and agents thereof. | None. | Discharge; failure or refusal to hire; discrimination, limitation, segregation, or classification; exclusion from membership; failure or refusal to refer for employment. | If there is bona fide occupational qualification. | Civil action; injunctive relief, nonexclusivity of remedy. | None. | Actual damages; attorneys' fees; costs. | Ord. No. 390-89, Mun. Code ch. 158 (passed 5/2/89). |
| Philadelphia, PA | Municipal employers and providers of municipal services. | None. | Failure or refusal to hire; limitation, segregation, or classification; exclusion from membership. No AIDS testing. | If there is bona fide occupational qualification. | Civil action; injunction; nonexclusivity of remedy. File with Human Rights Commission. | 90 days. | Possible disciplinary action taken against offending employee; employers must educate employees about AIDS. | Exec. Order No. 4-86, ch. 9-1700 (Philadelphia Code) (enacted 7/26/90). |
| Austin, TX | Employers, employment agencies, and labor organizations. | Under 16 employees. | Failure or refusal to hire; limitation, segregation, or classification; exclusion from membership. No AIDS testing. | If there is bona fide occupational qualification. | Civil action; injunction; nonexclusivity of remedy. File with Human Rights Commission. | 180 days. | Up to $200 per offense per day; retaliation is prohibited. | Ord. No. 86-1211-V (passed 12/86). |

# § 7.3 Use of Conviction and Arrest Records in Hiring Decisions

Several states have enacted statutes restricting an employer's ability to request and use an individual's arrest or conviction record as a condition of employment. Generally, these laws allow inquiries into prior convictions when they are job-related but prohibit inquiries into prior arrests. States not restricting inquiries into arrest or conviction records generally prohibit discrimination based on those records. In addition, many states have laws that provide for expunging or sealing conviction or arrest records; expunged or sealed records are generally deemed not to exist. States allowing this procedure usually do not permit an employer to inquire about records that have been expunged or sealed. Although this procedure may or may not entitle an individual to say he or she has never been convicted, it does not entitle the individual to say he or she has never been arrested.

Several states do not have statutory restrictions on an employer's ability to request and use an individual's arrest and conviction records; instead, they provide guidelines suggesting certain behavior in this area. These guidelines generally prohibit inquiries into arrest records but allow inquiries into prior convictions that are job-related. Table 7.3-1 shows which states have laws or guidelines in this area as well as some specific provisions. Note that the Equal Employment Opportunity Commission (EEOC) has ruled that the use of conviction and arrest records in employment practices may have a disproportionately large discriminatory effect on some races and, therefore, may be forbidden under federal law.

# Table 7.3-1
## EMPLOYERS' USE OF CONVICTION AND ARREST RECORDS IN HIRING DECISIONS

(See also text at § 7.3.)

**KEY:** **Sealed record.** A sealed or expunged criminal or juvenile record is one that has been closed by court order or operation of law and one to which an employer would not have access when conducting an applicant or employee investigation.

| | *Are Employers Restricted from Requesting or Using Arrest Records?* | *Are Employers Restricted from Requesting or Using Conviction Records?* | *May Arrest or Conviction Records Be Sealed?* | *Guidelines in Addition to State Statute* | *Citations to Authority* |
|---|---|---|---|---|---|
| AL | State has no statutory requirements. | Certain employers must check applicants who will supervise minors. | Yes. Certain juvenile arrest and conviction records. | None. | Ala. Code §§ 26-20-1, 26-20-2, 41-9-601, 41-9-642. |
| AK | State has no statutory requirements. | Current offender information may be provided for any purpose, except if its release would unreasonably compromise the privacy of a minor or vulnerable adult. Past conviction information can be provided for any purpose if less than 10 years has elapsed since discharge. Past conviction information of serious offenses may be provided if used to determine whether or not to grant supervisory powers over minors. | Yes. Certain juvenile arrest and conviction records. Information that is sealed may be provided for criminal justice employment purposes. | None. | Alaska Stat. §§ 12.62.160, 12.62.180. |
| AZ | No. | No. State is required to obtain criminal history information for school bus drivers. | Yes. Conviction may be set aside but not erased. | Inquiries into arrest are inappropriate, unless there is a compelling need (AZ Preemployment Inquiry Guide). | Ariz. Rev. Stat. §§ 28-3228, 41-1750. |
| AR | State has no statutory requirements. | State has no statutory requirements. | Yes. Certain juvenile arrest and conviction records; certain other conviction records. | No statute specifically provides for the exemption of names of juveniles arrested for felonies but not charged as delinquent juveniles; thus detention faculty logs are not exempt from the Freedom of Information Act. *Troutt Bros. v. Emison,* 841 S.W.2d 604 (1992). | Ark. Code Ann. §§ 9-27-309, 16-93-301–16-93-302. |

*(Table continues.)*

# Table 7.3-1 *(cont'd)*

## EMPLOYERS' USE OF CONVICTION AND ARREST RECORDS IN HIRING DECISIONS

(See also text at § 7.3.)

**KEY:** **Sealed record.** A sealed or expunged criminal or juvenile record is one that has been closed by court order or operation of law and one to which an employer would not have access when conducting an applicant or employee investigation.

| | *Are Employers Restricted from Requesting or Using Arrest Records?* | *Are Employers Restricted from Requesting or Using Conviction Records?* | *May Arrest or Conviction Records Be Sealed?* | *Guidelines in Addition to State Statute* | *Citations to Authority* |
|---|---|---|---|---|---|
| CA | Yes. No public or private employer may request information regarding (1) any arrest not resulting in conviction or (2) pre- or posttrial diversion, except for persons seeking employment as peace officers, in criminal justice agencies, or as health workers with access to drugs or patients. Employers may inquire about arrests for which applicant is awaiting trial. | No. | Yes. Arrest records of persons who are determined to be factually innocent and who establish facts that lead no reasonable person to entertain a strong suspicion that the arrestee is guilty of the crimes charged. | Question concerning convictions permitted as long as employer notes that conviction does not constitute an absolute bar to employment (CA Preemployment Inquiry Guidelines). | Cal. Lab. Code §§ 432.7, 432.8; Cal. Penal Code §§ 851.8, 11105.3; *People v. Matthews,* 9 Cal. Rptr. 2d 348, 7 Cal. App. 4H.1052 (1992). |
| CO | Yes. Employers may not request sealed records. | Yes. Employers may not request sealed records. | Yes. Records of arrests not resulting in conviction. Arrest record pertaining to a sexual conviction may not be sealed under certain conditions. | Questions concerning arrest not permitted and conviction inquiry limited to those that are job-related (CO Preemployment Inquiry Guideline). | Colo. Rev. Stat. § 24-72-308. |
| CT | Yes. Information may be disclosed to personnel department or hiring chief only. | Yes. | Yes. Records of arrests not resulting in conviction (except if person found not guilty by reason of insanity); conviction records of persons absolutely pardoned. | State policy is to encourage hiring all persons, including those with criminal convictions. | Conn. Gen. Stat. Ann. §§ 31-51i, 54-142a. |
| DE | Yes. Employers may not inquire into expunged records. An exception exists for applicants with law enforcement agencies. | Yes. Employers may not inquire into expunged records. An exception exists for applicants with law enforcement agencies. | Yes. Records of certain arrests not resulting in conviction and certain juvenile arrests. | None. | Del. Code Ann. tit. 10, § 1001; tit. 11, §§ 4371–4375. |
| DC | State has no statutory requirements. | State has no statutory requirements. | Yes. Records of arrests may be sealed if prosecution was terminated without conviction and before trial and motion to seal is brought within 120 days after charges are dismissed, or motion may be brought within 3 years after prosecution if for | None. | D.C. S.C.R.-Criminal 118. |

| | | | | | |
|---|---|---|---|---|---|
| | | | good cause and to prevent manifest injustice, or any time thereafter if government does not object. | | |
| FL | Yes. Discrimination is not permitted in public hiring. | Yes. Discrimination is not permitted in public hiring. | Court may in its discretion seal arrest records, except those for certain violations where the person was found or pled guilty. | Persons shall not be disqualified from employment by the state solely because of prior conviction, unless crime was a felony or first degree misdemeanor and directly related to position of employment sought. This does not apply to law enforcement agencies or the fire department. | Fla. Stat. Ann. §§ 112.011, 943.059. |
| GA | No. Employer may obtain criminal records from the Georgia Crime Information Center. In the event an adverse employment decision is made based on record obtained, applicant must be informed of decision, fact that record was obtained, and the effect of the content of the record on the employment decision. | No. Employer may obtain criminal records from the Georgia Crime Information Center. In the event an adverse employment decision is made based on record obtained, applicant must be informed of decision, fact that record was obtained, and the effect of the content of the record on the employment decision. | Yes. Arrest and conviction records may be sealed at court's discretion under certain circumstances. | Failure to inform applicant of use of record and impact on decision is a misdemeanor. | Ga. Code Ann. §§ 17-4-27, 35-3-34, 35-3-35, 42-8-63. |
| HI | Yes. Employers may not inquire into arrests not resulting in conviction. | No. Employer may consider convictions that are job-related. State may not disqualify anyone from employment solely because of a prior conviction; however, a person convicted of a felony may be denied a liquor license. | Yes. Certain arrests not resulting in conviction and certain convictions. | Inquiries into conviction not permitted unless conviction is substantially related to applicant's ability to perform job duties (HI Preemployment Inquiry Guide). | Haw. Rev. Stat. §§ 378-1, 831-3.1, 831-3.2. |
| ID | State has no statutory requirements. | State has no statutory requirements. | Yes. Certain juvenile arrest and conviction records. | Inquiries concerning arrest records deemed "high risk" question (ID Preemployment Inquiry Guide). | Id. Code § 20-525A. |
| IL | Yes. Employers may not inquire into sealed or expunged arrest records; exception is for information obtained from Department of State Police. | Yes. Employers may not inquire into sealed or expunged conviction records; exception is for information obtained from Department of State Police. | Yes. Certain arrests not resulting in conviction. | None. | 775 Ill. Comp. Stat. Ann. 5/2-103. |
| IN | Employers may obtain limited criminal history if person is applicant for employment with a noncriminal justice organization or individual, or has volunteered to work with children. | Employers may obtain limited criminal history if person is applicant for employment with a noncriminal justice organization or individual, or has volunteered to work with children. | Yes. Certain arrests not resulting in conviction. | Inquiries concerning arrest, record of convictions, or summary offenses may be discriminatory (IN Preemployment Inquiry Guide). | Ind. Code Ann. §§ 5-2-5-5, 35-38-5-1. |
| IA | No. | No. | Yes. Arrest record when court defers judgment of guilt and discharges defendant at its discretion. | None. | Iowa Code Ann. § 22.7. |

*(Table continues.)*

# Table 7.3-1 *(cont'd)*
## EMPLOYERS' USE OF CONVICTION AND ARREST RECORDS IN HIRING DECISIONS

(See also text at § 7.3.)

**KEY:** **Sealed record.** A sealed or expunged criminal or juvenile record is one that has been closed by court order or operation of law and one to which an employer would not have access when conducting an applicant or employee investigation.

| | *Are Employers Restricted from Requesting or Using Arrest Records?* | *Are Employers Restricted from Requesting or Using Conviction Records?* | *May Arrest or Conviction Records Be Sealed?* | *Guidelines in Addition to State Statute* | *Citations to Authority* |
|---|---|---|---|---|---|
| KS | Employers may require a job applicant to sign a release allowing employer access to the applicant's criminal history for the purpose of determining the applicant's fitness for employment. Employers may also request information concerning pending investigations and proceedings from a criminal justice agency. | Employers may require a job applicant to sign a release allowing the employer access to the applicant's criminal history for the purpose of determining the applicant's fitness for employment. Employers may also request information concerning pending investigations and proceedings from a criminal justice agency. | Yes. Certain arrest and conviction records. | None. | Kan. Stat. Ann. §§ 22-4707, 22-4708, 22-4710. |
| KY | State has no statutory requirements. | Employers may request sex crime and violent offense information if applicant or employee will have supervisory or disciplinary power over minors. | Yes. Nonfelony juvenile arrest and conviction records. | Discrimination in public employment or in the obtaining of a license based on prior conviction of crime is not permitted unless conviction was a felony, high misdemeanor, or misdemeanor for which a jail sentence may be imposed, or conviction otherwise directly relates to position of employment sought. | Ky. Rev. Stat. Ann. §§ 17.160, 17.165, 335B.010 *et seq.*, 610.320 *et seq.* |
| LA | State has no statutory requirements. | Yes. Discrimination not permitted unless conviction was a felony and conviction directly relates to position of employment sought. | Yes. Certain arrests not resulting in conviction. | Applicants cannot be ineligible for employment solely because of prior criminal record, except if applicant is convicted of a felony and such conviction directly relates to position of employment sought. | La. Rev. Stat. Ann. §§ 37:2950, 44:9. |
| ME | No. | No. | Yes. Records of juvenile detention. | None. | Me. Rev. Stat. Ann. tit. 16, § 612-A. |

| | | | | | |
|---|---|---|---|---|---|
| MD | Yes. Employers may not request information in sealed records or inquire about arrests not resulting in conviction. | Yes. Employers may not request information in sealed records. | Yes. Certain arrest and conviction records. | Any paper-and-pencil or performance measure used as a basis for any employment decision, including specific qualifying or disqualifying personal history or background requirements, must be relevant to the performance of the job in question (Guidelines on Employee Selection Procedure). | Md. Ann. Code art. 27, §§ 735–741. |
| MA | Yes. Employers may not inquire about arrests not resulting in conviction. | Yes. Employers may not inquire about convictions for certain misdemeanors. Special requirements about arrests or convictions must be printed on employment application form. | Yes. Certain conviction records. | Employers may ask applicants if they have been imprisoned, convicted of a sexual or drug offense, or arrested or convicted for a felony (MA Commission Against Discrimination Guidelines). | Mass. Gen. Laws Ann. ch. 276, § 100A; ch. 151B, § 4. |
| MI | Yes. Employers may not request arrest records of prospective employees, except for those regarding pending felony charges. | No. | State has no statutory requirements. | Inquiries concerning prior convictions or pending felony charges permitted; arrest inquiries prohibited (MI Preemployment Inquiry Guidelines). | Mich. Comp. Laws Ann. § 37.2205a. |
| MN | Yes. Public employers may not discriminate based on records. Public employers may not request information of arrests not followed by a valid conviction. | Yes. Public employers may not discriminate based on records. Public employers may not request information about convictions that have been annulled or expunged or about misdemeanor convictions for which no jail sentence can be imposed. | State has no statutory requirements. | State policy encourages employment of ex-offenders; criminal inquiries should be made through state agency; criminal record should not be automatic bar to employment (MN Guidelines for Preventing Discrimination). Applicant denied public employment as a result of prior conviction is entitled to written notice of the grounds and reason for denial. | Minn. Stat. Ann. §§ 364.03 *et seq.* |
| MS | Yes. Authorized employers may request sex offense criminal history records of employees who will supervise children. | Yes. Authorized employers may request sex offense criminal history records of employees who will supervise children. | Certain arrest and conviction records may be expunged. | None. | Miss. Code Ann. §§ 45-31-1, 99-15-57, 99-19-71. |
| MO | Yes. | Yes. Discrimination not permitted, unless reasonable relationship exists between conviction and job qualifications. | State has no statutory requirements. | No inquiries into arrest records are acceptable; inquiries about the number and kinds of arrests are inadvisable; inquiries about prior convictions are permitted (MO Commission on Human Rights). | Mo. Ann. Stat. §§ 561.016, 561.021. |
| MT | Yes. | Yes. Employers may not inquire about misdemeanor convictions or deferred prosecutions. | State has no statutory requirements. | None. | Mont. Code Ann. §§ 44-5-301 *et seq.* |
| NE | Employer cannot access arrest records in which, after 1-year interval, active prosecution is neither completed nor pending. | No. | State has no statutory requirements. | None. | Neb. Rev. Stat. § 29-3523. |

*(Table continues.)*

## Table 7.3-1 *(cont'd)*

## EMPLOYERS' USE OF CONVICTION AND ARREST RECORDS IN HIRING DECISIONS

(See also text at § 7.3.)

**KEY: Sealed record.** A sealed or expunged criminal or juvenile record is one that has been closed by court order or operation of law and one to which an employer would not have access when conducting an applicant or employee investigation.

| | *Are Employers Restricted from Requesting or Using Arrest Records?* | *Are Employers Restricted from Requesting or Using Conviction Records?* | *May Arrest or Conviction Records Be Sealed?* | *Guidelines in Addition to State Statute* | *Citations to Authority* |
|---|---|---|---|---|---|
| NV | Yes. | No. | Yes. Certain arrest and conviction records. | Employers may not inquire about arrest records but may inquire about prior convictions; conviction inquiries must be accompanied by statement that conviction will not necessarily disqualify applicant from the position. Special restrictions apply to information relating to sexual offenses. (Guide to Pre-Employment Inquiries Issued by NV Equal Rights Commission). | Nev. Rev. Stat. §§ 179A.100, 179A.240. |
| NH | No. | No. | Yes. Conviction records if sentence includes probation or conditional discharge. | Employers may not inquire about arrest records but may inquire about prior convictions within previous 5 years (N.H. Preemployment Inquiry Guidelines). | N.H. Rev. Stat. Ann. § 651:5. |
| NJ | No. | No. | Yes. Certain conviction records. | Employers may not inquire about arrest records but may inquire about prior convictions if reasonably related to job (Division of Civil Rights Guide to Preemployment Inquiries). | N.J. Rev. Stat. Ann. §§ 2C:51-2, 2C:52-1 *et seq.* |
| NM | Yes. Arrest record must be a valid conviction in order to be used in connection with an application for public employment. | Yes. Misdemeanor convictions not involving moral turpitude may not be used in connection with application for any public employment. | State has no statutory requirements. | None. | N.M. Stat. Ann. § 28-2-3. |
| NY | Yes. Request and use of arrest record is prohibited, unless action is pending. | Yes. Employers may not discriminate based on convictions, unless (1) conviction is reasonably related to job or (2) granting employment would involve unreasonable risk to property, safety, or welfare of individuals or general public. If | State has no statutory requirements. | Conviction inquiries should be limited to job-related matters (N.Y. Job Interviewing Guide, pt. VII). | N.Y. Exec. Law § 296. |

| | | | | | |
|---|---|---|---|---|---|
| | | applicant is refused employment due to criminal record, applicant may request and receive from employer within 30 days a written statement of reasons employment was denied. | | | |
| NC | State has no statutory requirements. | State has no statutory requirements. | Yes. Records of arrests not resulting in conviction and juvenile records. | None. | N.C. Gen. Stat. § 15A-146. |
| ND | Yes. | No. | State has no statutory requirements. | None. | N.D. Cent. Code § 12-60-16.6. |
| OH | Unlawful to question applicant for employment about any arrest under the juvenile code for which records have been expunged. | Yes. Employers may not question applicant about conviction records sealed under first-offenders law, unless question is substantially related to employment position. | Yes. Records of certain misdemeanor arrests and certain convictions under first-offenders law. | Employer inquiries into arrests are unlawful; conviction inquiries are permitted if reasonably related to job qualifications (OH Civil Rights Commission Guide). | Ohio Rev. Code Ann. §§ 2151.358, 2953.32 *et seq.* |
| OK | Yes. Employers may not request information in sealed records. | Yes. Employers may not request information in sealed records. | Yes. Certain arrest and conviction records. | None. | Okla. Stat. Ann. tit. 22, § 19. |
| OR | No. Employers may request arrest record if the arrest is less than a year old and there has been no acquittal or dismissal. | Yes. Employers may request conviction records but must notify applicant of such request. | Yes. Certain juvenile arrest and conviction records and certain conviction records. | None. | Or. Rev. Stat. § 181.560. |
| PA | No. | Yes. Employers may request felony and misdemeanor conviction records only if reasonably related to job qualifications; applicant must be informed if decision *not* to hire is based on record. | Yes. Certain juvenile conviction records. | None. | Pa. Stat. Ann. tit. 18, §§ 9123, 9124, 9125. |
| RI | Yes, except for applications for law enforcement or agency positions. | No. | State has no statutory requirements. | Arrest inquiries prohibited; conviction inquiries are permissible under some circumstances (R.I. Preemployment Inquiry Guide). | R.I. Gen. Laws § 28-5-7. |
| SC | Yes. Employers may not obtain records of arrests not resulting in conviction. | State has no statutory requirements. | Yes. Records of arrests not resulting in conviction are destroyed. | Day care facilities may not hire anyone convicted of certain moral crimes. | S.C. Code Ann. §§ 17-1-40, 20-7-2730. |
| SD | State has no statutory requirements. | State has no statutory requirements. | State has no statutory requirements. | Preemployment inquiries into arrest or conviction records are suspect, unless substantially related to employment (Division of Human Rights Preemployment Inquiries). | State has no statutory provisions. |
| TN | State has no statutory requirements. | State has no statutory requirements. | Yes. Certain juvenile records and arrest records where the charge has been dismissed or the person acquitted. | None. | Tenn. Code Ann. §§ 37-1-155, 40-32-101. |

*(Table continues.)*

## **Table 7.3-1** *(cont'd)*
## EMPLOYERS' USE OF CONVICTION AND ARREST RECORDS IN HIRING DECISIONS

(See also text at § 7.3.)

**KEY:** **Sealed record.** A sealed or expunged criminal or juvenile record is one that has been closed by court order or operation of law and one to which an employer would not have access when conducting an applicant or employee investigation.

| | *Are Employers Restricted from Requesting or Using Arrest Records?* | *Are Employers Restricted from Requesting or Using Conviction Records?* | *May Arrest or Conviction Records Be Sealed?* | *Guidelines in Addition to State Statute* | *Citations to Authority* |
|---|---|---|---|---|---|
| TX | Yes, except criminal history records of applicants for security-sensitive positions in institutions of higher education and of applicants to certain state commissions and other institutions. | Yes, except criminal history records of applicants for security-sensitive positions in institutions of higher education and of applicants to certain state commissions and other institutions. | Felony or misdemeanor arrest records may be expunged if charges were dismissed, person was acquitted, or person was pardoned. | None. | Tex. Gov't Code Ann. §§ 411.081 *et seq.*; Tex. Code Crim. Proc. Ann. art. 55.01 *et seq.* |
| UT | No. Employers may request arrest records except those that have been expunged. | State has no statutory requirements. | Yes. Certain arrest and conviction records. Record of conviction for a capital felony, first degree felony, second degree forcible felony, or a sexual act against a minor cannot be expunged. | Preemployment inquiries into arrest records are improper; preemployment inquiries into prior felony convictions are permitted; recommended that requests for conviction records be related to the job (Industrial Commission of UT Preemployment Inquiry Guide). | Utah Code Ann. §§ 77-18-10, 77-18-11. |
| VT | State has no statutory requirements. | State has no statutory requirements. | Conviction records of minors may be sealed by order of court. | None. | Vt. Stat. Ann. tit. 33, § 5538. |
| VA | Yes. Employers may not inquire regarding sealed records, but may obtain criminal history record information about continuing employees or applicants for positions in criminal justice agencies. Public service agencies may obtain criminal history record information about employees or applicants when employment involves personal contact with the public or when past conduct is inappropriate to the considered employment. | Yes. Employers may not inquire regarding sealed records but may request information concerning criminal convictions if employee or applicant will work with children or adults at day care facility or nursing home. | Records of arrests not resulting in convictions. | None. | Va. Code Ann. §§ 19.2-389, 19.2-392.2, 19.2-392.4. |

| | | | | | |
|---|---|---|---|---|---|
| WA | State has no statutory requirements. | Employers may make written request for conviction record check if employee or applicant needs bond for employment, will work with trade or national secrets, or will have unsupervised access to children or vulnerable adults. | State has no statutory requirements. | All inquiries into arrests are unfair; unfair to discriminate based on arrest record. Inquiries into convictions occurring in past 7 years are permissible if reasonably related to job qualifications; such inquiries must be accompanied by disclaimer that conviction record will not necessarily bar employment (WA State Human Rights Employment Practices). | Wash. Rev. Code Ann. §§ 43.43.815, 43.43.830–43.43.832. |
| WV | Yes. Use of arrest and conviction records is prohibited unless employer first obtains applicant's consent. | State has no statutory requirements. | Fingerprints and other information may be returned to persons acquitted of charges. | Preemployment inquiries into arrest records are prohibited; inquiries into prior convictions are permissible if reasonably related to job qualifications (WV Human Rights Commission Preemployment Inquiry Guide). | W. Va. Code § 15-2-24. |
| WI | Yes. Use of arrest records is prohibited, unless (1) relevant to employee's bondability or (2) charges pending are job-related. | Yes. Use of conviction records is prohibited unless job-related or relevant to employee's bondability. | State has no statutory requirements. | Arrest inquiries barred, except concerning pending charges; employer permitted to decline hiring person with pending charge that is job-related; use of conviction information permitted when job-related (WI Preemployment Inquiry Guidelines). | Wis. Stat. Ann. § 111.335. |
| WY | — | — | Conviction records of minors and violations of municipal ordinances may be sealed by order of the court. | — | Wyo. Stat. Ann. § 14-6-241. |

## § 7.4 Use of Consumer Credit Reports

Many states have statutes permitting a consumer credit reporting agency to furnish a consumer credit report to a person who it has reason to believe will use the information for employment purposes. Generally, a consumer credit report is defined as a written, oral, or other communication of information by a consumer credit reporting agency bearing on a consumer's creditworthiness, credit standing, credit capacity, character, general reputation, personal characteristics, or mode of living. Employment purposes are generally defined as the evaluation of an individual for employment, promotion, reassignment, or retention as an employee. Many statutes require an employer to notify the individual of a request for the consumer credit report.

The federal Fair Credit Reporting Act (FCRA) also regulates employers in this area. The FCRA permits an employer to request a consumer report in generally the same manner as is provided in state statutes. It also permits an employer to procure or cause to be prepared an investigative consumer credit report on an individual when the report is to be used for purposes of employment for which the individual has not specifically applied. The FCRA defines an investigative consumer credit report as one that contains information obtained through personal interviews with neighbors, friends, or associates of the consumer regarding that person's character, general reputation, personal characteristics, or mode of living. The FCRA does not annul, alter, affect, or exempt any person subject to the provisions of the Act from complying with the laws of any state in this area, except to the extent that the state law is inconsistent with any provisions of the Act and, then, only to the extent of the inconsistency. Table 7.4-1 illustrates the applicable state provisions in this area. (See also § 9.5[d] for more on the FCRA.)

# Table 7.4-1
## EMPLOYERS' USE OF CONSUMER CREDIT REPORTS

(States not listed have no statutes governing employer use of consumer credit reports. See also text at § 7.4.)

**KEY: Employment purposes.** The evaluation of an individual for employment, promotion, reassignment, or retention as an employee.

| | *Can Employer Obtain Report for Employment Purposes?* | *Notification Requirements* | *Citations to Authority* |
|---|---|---|---|
| AZ | Yes. | If employer makes adverse employment decision based on consumer credit report, employer, upon request, must supply individual with name and address of reporting agency. | Ariz. Rev. Stat. Ann. §§ 44-1691–44-1693. |
| CA | Yes. | No later than 3 days after employer requests investigative consumer credit report, employer must inform the individual of such request, unless the report is sought for purposes of promotion, reassignment, retention of employment, or to determine whether employee is engaged in criminal activity likely to result in loss to employer. If employment is denied based on consumer credit report, employer must give applicant name and address of reporting agency. | Cal. Civ. Code § 1786.16. |
| KS | Yes. | Employer must notify individual in writing of employer's request for individual's consumer credit report no later than 3 days after requesting the report. Employer cannot request such report unless it is to be used for purposes of employment for which the individual has not specifically applied. Strict procedures also apply when public record information, such as arrests, tax liens, and the like, are likely to have an adverse effect on individual's ability to obtain employment. | Kan. Stat. Ann. §§ 50-703 *et seq.* |
| LA | Yes. | Any person denied employment based on a credit report is entitled to a free copy of his or her credit report provided that he or she requests it within 60 days of the denial. | La. Rev. Stat. § 9:3571.1. |
| ME | Yes. | Employer must give notice to individual if employer obtains consumer credit report for use in determining employment eligibility, promotion, reassignment, or retention as an employee. Denial of any benefit based on the report must be disclosed in writing to individual. Reporting agency must supply individual with name and address of requesting employer and information provided. | Me. Rev. Stat. Ann. tit. 10, §§ 1311 *et seq.* |
| MD | Yes. | Consumer agency must notify individual of each report furnished to employer. If employment is denied based on such report, employer must notify individual and supply name and address of reporting agency. | Md. Comm. Law Code Ann. §§ 14-1201, 14-1212. |
| MA | Yes. | If employer requests *investigative* consumer credit report, it must make clear and accurate disclosure to individual of nature and scope of investigation. Employer must also disclose if employment is denied or terminated wholly or partly based on any consumer credit report. Upon request, individual may obtain a copy of any report furnished by consumer credit agency for employment purposes within 2 years preceding individual's request for disclosure. Reporting agency must supply individual with name and address of requesting employer. | Mass. Gen. Laws Ann. ch. 93, §§ 50 *et seq.* |
| MN | Yes. | Employer must make disclosure to individual that a consumer credit report may be obtained or prepared for employment purposes. This notice must inform individual of the right to request additional information on the nature of the report. For an investigative consumer credit report, the notice must inform individual about the report's possible content. If adverse employment action is taken against individual based on information in the report, employer shall notify individual and inform individual of his/her right to receive a copy of the report. | Minn. Stat. Ann. §§ 13C.001 *et seq.* |

*(Table continues.)*

## Table 7.4-1 *(cont'd)*
## EMPLOYERS' USE OF CONSUMER CREDIT REPORTS

(States not listed have no statutes governing employer use of consumer credit reports. See also text at § 7.4.)

**KEY: Employment purposes.** The evaluation of an individual for employment, promotion, reassignment, or retention as an employee.

| | *Can Employer Obtain Report for Employment Purposes?* | *Notification Requirements* | *Citations to Authority* |
|---|---|---|---|
| MT | Yes. | Employer must notify individual within 3 days after requesting *investigative* consumer credit report, unless report is for purposes of employment for which individual has applied. Since this exception is inconsistent with federal law, employers should notify individuals whenever requesting investigative consumer reports. If any consumer credit report contributes wholly or partly to denial of employment, employer must supply individual with name and address of reporting agency. | Mont. Rev. Codes Ann. §§ 31-3-101–31-3-153. |
| NE | Yes. | Consumer credit agencies must inform individuals of any request for credit report. Statute contains no specific employment provisions. | Neb. Rev. Stat. § 20-149. |
| NH | Yes. | If employer requests *investigative* consumer credit report, employer must make clear and accurate disclosure to individual of nature and scope of investigation. Employer must also disclose when employment is denied wholly or partly based on any consumer credit report. Upon request, consumer credit agencies must disclose to individuals all recipients of consumer credit reports furnished for employment purposes within 2 years preceding individual's request for disclosure. The reporting agency must supply individual with name and address of requesting party. | N.H. Rev. Stat. Ann. §§ 359B *et seq.* |
| NJ | Yes. | Employer may not obtain credit report unless consumer is notified in writing before report is procured that consumer report may be obtained for employment purposes. Before taking adverse employee action, employer shall provide consumer with copy of credit report and description in writing of consumer's legal rights. | N.J. Stat. Ann. § 56:11-31. |
| NM | Yes. | None. | N.M. Stat. Ann. §§ 56-3-1–56-3-5. |
| NY | Yes. | Consumer credit agencies must disclose to individual, upon request, all recipients of consumer credit reports furnished for employment purposes within 2 years preceding individual's request for disclosure. Employer may not request report unless employer informs applicant that report may be requested; employer also must inform applicant that report has been requested. No employer may disseminate consumer credit report or investigative consumer credit report to any other person unless such person has legitimate business need for the information in connection with a business transaction involving individual concerned in the report. | N.Y. Gen. Bus. Law §§ 380 *et seq.* |
| OK | Yes. | Upon request of individual, consumer reporting agency must disclose the names and addresses of those parties to whom it has furnished individual's consumer credit report for employment purposes within 2-year period preceding request. | Ok. Stat. Ann. tit. 24 § 147. |

# § 7.5 Blacklisting, References, and Personnel Records

Table 7.5-1 lists those states having (1) antiblacklisting statutes, which generally prohibit employers from preparing, using, or circulating a list of persons designated for special avoidance, antagonism, or enmity and (2) laws that specifically address individual employee references. This table does not address the blacklisting of employees for union activities, which is commonly proscribed as an unfair labor practice under state and federal laws.

Table 7.5-2 lists those states that have passed laws regulating employee access to personnel files. Some of these laws apply to the public sector only.

# Table 7.5-1
## LAWS GOVERNING BLACKLISTING AND REFERENCES

(See also text at § 7.5.)

| | *Does State Have Any Statutes Governing Blacklisting?* | *Prohibition Against Employer Acting to Prevent Former Employee from Obtaining Employment?* | *On Request, May Employer Make Truthful Statements about Former Employee?* | *On Request, Must Employer Furnish Former Employee with Written Reasons for Discharge?* | *Penalties for Violation of Statute* | *Citations to Authority* |
|---|---|---|---|---|---|---|
| AL | Yes. | Yes. | State has no statutory requirements. | State has no statutory requirements. | Violator is guilty of a misdemeanor. | Ala. Code § 13A-11-123. |
| AK | — | — | — | — | — | State has no statutory provisions. |
| AZ | Yes. | Yes. | Yes. | State has no statutory requirements. | Violator is guilty of a Class 2 misdemeanor. | Ariz. Rev. Stat. Ann. §§ 23-1361, 23-1362. |
| AR | Yes. | Yes. | Yes. | State has no statutory requirements. | Violator may incur a fine of $100–$500, or be imprisoned for 1 year, or both. | Ark. Stat. Ann. § 11-3-202. |
| CA | Yes. | Yes. | Yes. | State has no statutory requirements. | Violator is guilty of a misdemeanor. | Cal. Lab. Code § 1050; *Newberry v. Pacific Racing Ass'n*, 854 F.2d 1142 (9th Cir. 1988) (holding that former employer can make truthful statements about former employee, as long as no misrepresentation is involved). |
| CO | Yes. | Yes. | Yes. | State has no statutory requirements. | Violator is guilty of a misdemeanor, punishable by a fine of $10–$250, or imprisonment for not more than 60 days, or both. | Colo. Rev. Stat. §§ 8-2-111.5, 8-2-114, 8-2-115. |
| CT | Yes. | Yes. | Yes. | State has no statutory requirements. | Violator may incur a fine of $50–$200. | Conn. Gen. Stat. Ann. § 31-51. |
| DE | — | — | — | — | — | State has no statutory provisions. |
| DC | — | — | — | — | — | State has no statutory provisions. |

| | | | | | | |
|---|---|---|---|---|---|---|
| FL | Yes. | Yes. | Yes, upon request of prospective employer or former employee. Employer is presumed to be acting in good faith, and unless lack of good faith is shown by clear and convincing evidence, employer is immune from civil liability for such disclosure or its consequences. | State has no statutory requirements. | Violator is guilty of a misdemeanor of the first degree. | Fla. Stat. Ann. §§ 448.045, 768.095. |
| GA | — | — | — | — | — | State has no statutory provisions. |
| HI | Yes. | State has no statutory requirements. | State has no statutory requirements. | State has no statutory requirements. | State has no statutory requirements. | Haw. Rev. Stat. § 377-6. |
| ID | Yes. | — | Yes. | — | — | Idaho Code § 44-201. |
| IL | Yes. | Yes. Statute covers financial institutions, shipping companies, and governmental agencies. | State has no statutory requirements. | State has no statutory requirements. | State has no statutory requirements. | 775 Ill. Comp. Stat. Ann. §§ 15/1 *et seq.* |
| IN | Yes. | Yes. | Yes. | Yes. | Violator is guilty of a Class C infraction and, in a civil action, is liable for penal damages to the discharged employee. | Ind. Code Ann. §§ 22-5-3-1, 22-5-3-2. |
| IA | Yes. | Yes. | Yes. | State has no statutory requirements. | Violator is liable for treble damages. | Iowa Code Ann. §§ 730.1–730.3. |
| KS | Yes. | Yes. | Yes. | State has no statutory requirements. | Violator may incur a fine of $100 and may be imprisoned 30 days for each offense. Violator is also liable for treble damages, attorneys' fees, and costs. | Kan. Stat. Ann. §§ 44-117–44-119. |
| KY | Yes, but statute is restricted to mining industry. | Yes, but statute is restricted to mining industry. | State has no statutory requirements. | State has no statutory requirements. | Violator may incur a fine of $100–$1,000 for each violation. | Ky. Rev. Stat. Ann. § 352.550. |
| LA | Yes. | Yes, but statute is restricted to the purchase of merchandise from a particular seller. | State has no statutory requirements. | State has no statutory requirements. | Violator may incur a fine of $50–$100, or may be imprisoned for 30–90 days, or both. | La. Rev. Stat. Ann. § 23:963. |
| ME | Yes. | Yes. | State has no statutory requirements. | State has no statutory requirements. | Violator may incur a fine of not more than $500 or may be imprisoned for not more than 2 years. | Me. Rev. Stat. Ann. tit. 17, § 401. |
| MD | — | — | — | — | — | State has no statutory provisions. |

*(Table continues.)*

**Table 7.5-1** *(cont'd)*

LAWS GOVERNING
BLACKLISTING AND REFERENCES

(See also text at § 7.5.)

| | *Does State Have Any Statutes Governing Blacklisting?* | *Prohibition Against Employer Acting to Prevent Former Employee from Obtaining Employment?* | *On Request, May Employer Make Truthful Statements about Former Employee?* | *On Request, Must Employer Furnish Former Employee with Written Reasons for Discharge?* | *Penalties for Violation of Statute* | *Citations to Authority* |
|---|---|---|---|---|---|---|
| MA | — | — | — | — | — | State has no statutory provisions. |
| MI | — | — | — | — | — | State has no statutory provisions. |
| MN | Yes. | Yes. | State has no statutory requirements. | State has no statutory requirements. | Violator is guilty of a misdemeanor. | Minn. Stat. Ann. § 179.60. |
| MS | Statute only covers telephone, telegraph, and railroad companies. | Statute covers only telephone, telegraph, and railroad companies. | State has no statutory requirements. | State has no statutory requirements. | Violator is liable for actual and exemplary damages. | Miss. Code Ann. §§ 77-9-725, 77-9-727, 77-9-729. |
| MO | State has no statutory requirements. | State has no statutory requirements. | State has no statutory requirements. | Yes. | A violator is liable for compensatory damages based on the content of the letter. If the violator refuses to issue a letter outright, he may be liable for punitive damages. | Mo. Ann. Stat. § 290.140. |
| MT | Yes. | Yes. | Yes. | Yes. | Violator is liable for punitive damages and is guilty of a misdemeanor. | Mont. Code Ann. §§ 39-2-801–39-2-804. |
| NE | — | — | — | — | — | State has no statutory provisions. |
| NV | Yes. | Yes. | Yes, but employer may make such statements only at the time the employee leaves or is discharged. | Yes. | Violator may incur a fine of not more than $5,000. | Nev. Rev. Stat. §§ 613.200, 613.210. |
| NH | — | — | — | — | — | State has no statutory provisions. |
| NJ | Yes. | Yes. | State has no statutory requirements. | State has no statutory requirements. | State has no statutory requirements. | N.J. Stat. Ann. § 10:5-12. |

| | | | | | | |
|---|---|---|---|---|---|---|
| NM | Yes. | Yes. | Yes. | State has no statutory requirements. | Violator is guilty of a misdemeanor. | N.M. Stat. Ann. § 30-13-3. |
| NY | Yes. | Yes. | State has no statutory requirements. | State has no statutory requirements. | State has no statutory requirements. | N.Y. Exec. Law § 296(13); N.Y. Lab. Law § 704. |
| NC | Yes. | Yes. | Yes. | State has no statutory requirements. | Violator is guilty of a class 3 misdemeanor and may be fined an amount not exceeding $500. | N.C. Gen. Stat. §§ 14-355, 14-356. |
| ND | — | — | — | — | — | N.D. Const. art. XII § 17. (No statutory provisions; state constitution prohibits exchange of blacklists between corporations.) |
| OH | — | — | — | — | — | State has no statutory provisions. |
| OK | Yes. | Yes. | State has no statutory requirements. | State has no statutory requirements. | Violator shall be fined a sum not less than $100 and not greater than $500. Any victim of blacklisting shall have a cause of action to recover damages. | Okla. Stat. Ann. tit. 40, §§ 172, 173. |
| OR | Yes. | Yes. | State has no statutory requirements. | State has no statutory requirements. | State has no statutory requirements. | Ore. Rev. Stat. § 659.230. |
| PA | — | — | — | — | — | State has no statutory provisions. |
| RI | Yes. | Yes. | State has no statutory requirements. | State has no statutory requirements. | State has no statutory requirements. | R.I. Gen. Laws § 28-7-13. |
| SC | — | — | — | — | — | State has no statutory provisions. |
| SD | — | — | — | — | — | State has no statutory provisions. |
| TN | — | — | — | — | — | State has no statutory provisions. |
| TX | Yes. | Yes. | Yes. | Yes. Although still technically required by statute, this provision was declared unconstitutional by the Texas Supreme Court in 1914. A recent Opinion of the Texas Attorney General indicates that, while still on the books, the statute is presently unenforceable. [Op. Atty. Gen., No. JM-1116 (1989)] | Violator may be fined $50–$250, or may be imprisoned for 30–90 days, or incur both fine and imprisonment. | Tex. Lab. Code Ann. § 52.031. |

*(Table continues.)*

## **Table 7.5-1** *(cont'd)*

## LAWS GOVERNING BLACKLISTING AND REFERENCES

(See also text at § 7.5.)

| | *Does State Have Any Statutes Governing Blacklisting?* | *Prohibition Against Employer Acting to Prevent Former Employee from Obtaining Employment?* | *On Request, May Employer Make Truthful Statements about Former Employee?* | *On Request, Must Employer Furnish Former Employee with Written Reasons for Discharge?* | *Penalties for Violation of Statute* | *Citations to Authority* |
|---|---|---|---|---|---|---|
| UT | Yes. | Yes. | State has no statutory requirements. | State has no statutory requirements. | Violator is guilty of a felony punishable by a fine of $55–$1,000 and imprisonment for 60 days–1 year. | Utah Code Ann. §§ 34-24-1, 34-24-2. |
| VT | — | — | — | — | — | State has no statutory provisions. |
| VA | Yes. | Yes. | Yes. | State has no statutory requirements. | Violator is guilty of a misdemeanor punishable by a fine of $100–$500. | Va. Code Ann. § 40.1-27. |
| WA | Yes. | Yes. | State has no statutory requirements. | State has no statutory requirements. | Violator is guilty of a misdemeanor punishable by a fine of $100–$1,000, or imprisonment for 90 days to 1 year, or both fine and imprisonment. | Wash. Rev. Code Ann. § 49.44.010. |
| WV | — | — | — | — | — | State has no statutory provisions. |
| WI | Yes. | Yes. | Yes, regarding discharge. | State has no statutory requirements. | Violator may incur a fine of $100–$500. | Wis. Stat. Ann. §§ 111.06, 134.02. |
| WY | — | — | — | — | — | State has no statutory provisions. |

# Table 7.5-2 Part A
## EMPLOYEES' ACCESS TO PERSONNEL RECORDS

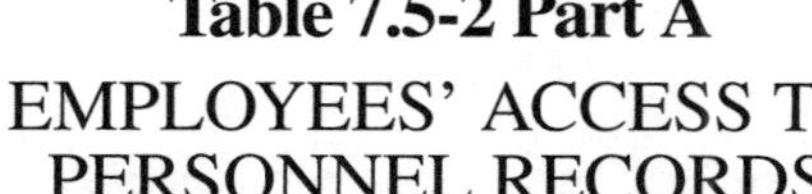

(See also text at § 7.5.)

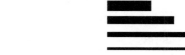

| | *Employers Covered by Statute* | | *May Records Be Reviewed?* | *Are There Penalties for Employer Violations?* | *Citations to Authority* |
|---|---|---|---|---|---|
| | *Public* | *Private* | | | |
| AL | — | — | — | — | State has no statutory provisions. |
| AK | Yes. | Yes. | Yes. | State has no statutory requirements. | Alaska Stat. § 23.10.430. |
| AZ | — | — | — | — | State has no statutory provisions. |
| AR | Yes. | No. | Yes. | Yes, if negligent. Violator shall be guilty of a misdemeanor, punishable by a fine of not more than $200, or by imprisonment of 30 days, or both, or a sentence of appropriate public service or education. | Ark. Code Ann. §§ 25-19-104, 25-19-105. |
| CA | No. | Yes. | Yes. At reasonable times and intervals. | Employer who violates any provision of this chapter shall be guilty of a misdemeanor, punishable by a fine of not less than $100, or by imprisonment of not less than 30 days, or both. | Cal. Lab. Code §§ 1198.5, 1199. |
| CO | Yes. | No. | Yes. | State has no statutory requirements. | Colo. Rev. Stat. § 24-72-204. |
| CT | No. | Yes. | Yes. Twice per year. | No. | Conn. Gen. Stat. Ann. §§ 31-128a–31-128h. |
| DE | Yes. | Yes. | Yes. Except for reasonable cause, employer may limit inspection to once per year. Employer may require requesting employee to inspect records on employee's free time. | Yes, not less than $1,000 and not more than $5,000 for each violation. | Del. Code Ann. tit. 19, §§ 730–735. |
| DC | Yes. | No. | Yes. | State has no statutory requirements. | D.C. Code Ann. §§ 1-632.1 *et seq.* |
| FL | Statutory requirements apply to employees of public educational institutions only. | No. | Yes. | No. | Fla. Stat. Ann. § 231.291. |

*(Table continues.)*

# Table 7.5-2 Part A *(cont'd)*
## EMPLOYEES' ACCESS TO PERSONNEL RECORDS

(See also text at § 7.5.)

| | *Employers Covered by Statute* | | *May Records Be Reviewed?* | *Are There Penalties for Employer Violations?* | *Citations to Authority* |
|---|---|---|---|---|---|
| | *Public* | *Private* | | | |
| GA | — | — | — | — | State has no statutory provisions. |
| HI | — | — | — | — | State has no statutory provisions. |
| ID | Statutory requirements apply to employees of public educational institutions only. | No. | Yes. | No. | Idaho Code § 33-518. |
| IL | Yes. Statutory requirements apply to employers with 5 or more employees. | Yes. | Yes. Twice per year at reasonable intervals. | Yes. Actual damages plus costs. $200 penalty plus costs, reasonable attorneys' fees, and actual damages if violation is willful. | 820 Ill. Comp. Stat. Ann. §§ 40/1 *et seq.* |
| IN | — | — | — | — | State has no statutory provisions. |
| IA | Yes. | Yes. | Yes. | Employer is immune from civil liability unless employer acted unreasonably in providing information. | Iowa Code Ann. §§ 91B.1, 91B.2. |
| KS | — | — | — | — | State has no statutory provisions. |
| KY | Yes. | No. | Yes. Upon written request. | No. | Ky. Rev. Stat. Ann. § 18A.020. |
| LA | — | — | — | Yes. Reasonable attorneys' fees and costs in addition to access to the records requested. | La. Rev. Stat. Ann. § 23:1016. |
| ME | Yes. | Yes. | Yes. | Yes. $25 per day up to $500. | Me. Rev. Stat. Ann. tit. 26, § 631. |
| MD | — | — | — | — | State has no statutory provisions. |
| MA | Yes. | Yes. Upon written request by employee. | Yes. | Yes. $500–$2,500. | Mass. Gen. Laws Ann. ch. 149, § 52C. |
| MI | Yes. | Yes. Statutory requirements apply to employers with 4 or more employees. | Yes. Twice per year. | Yes. Actual damages plus costs. If violation is willful, $200 penalty plus costs, reasonable attorneys' fees, and actual damages. | Mich. Comp. Laws Ann. §§ 423.501–423.511. |
| MN | Yes. | Yes. Statutory requirements apply to employers with 1 or more employees. | Yes. Once per 6 months. | Yes, up to a $5,000 fine, together with costs and attorneys' fees. | Minn. Stat. Ann. §§ 181.960–181.966. |

| | | | | | |
|---|---|---|---|---|---|
| MS | — | — | — | — | State has no statutory provisions. |
| MO | — | — | — | — | State has no statutory provisions. |
| MT | — | — | — | — | State has no statutory provisions. |
| NE | — | — | — | — | State has no statutory provisions. |
| NV | Yes. Employee must have been employed for 60 days to receive a copy of records. | Yes. Employee must have been employed for 60 days to receive a copy of records. | Yes. | No. | Nev. Rev. Stat. § 613.075. |
| NH | Yes. | Yes. | Yes. | No. | N.H. Rev. Stat. Ann. § 275.56. |
| NJ | — | — | — | — | State has no statutory provisions. |
| NM | — | — | — | — | State has no statutory provisions. |
| NY | — | — | — | — | State has no statutory provisions. However, *Bigelow v. Board of Trustees,* 472 N.E.2d 1001 (1984) appears to create in certain situations the right for public employees to have access to their personnel files and an opportunity to submit a written response. |
| NC | Yes. | No. | Yes. | Yes. Any public official or employee who shall knowingly and willfully permit an unauthorized person access to a confidential file shall be guilty of a Class 3 misdemeanor and upon conviction shall only be fined in the discretion of the court but not in excess of $500. | N.C. Gen. Stat. §§ 126-23–126.28. |
| ND | Yes. | No. | Yes. | No. | N.D. Cent. Code § 54-06-21. |
| OH | — | — | — | — | State has no statutory provisions. |
| OK | Yes. | No. | Yes. | — | Okla. Stat. Ann. tit. 51 § 24A.7. |
| OR | Yes. | Yes. | Yes. | No. | Or. Rev. Stat. § 652.750. |
| PA | Yes. | Yes. | Yes. Employer may require requesting employee to inspect records on employee's free time. Except for reasonable cause, employer may limit inspection to once per year. | No. | Pa. Stat. tit. 43, §§ 1321 *et seq.* |
| RI | Yes. | Yes. | Yes. Three times per year. | Yes. $100 or less. | R.I. Gen. Laws §§ 28-6.4-1, 28-6.4-2. |
| SC | — | — | — | — | State has no statutory provisions. |
| SD | Yes. | No. | Yes. | No. | S.D. Codified Laws Ann. § 3-6A-31. |
| TN | Yes. | No. | Yes. | No. | Tenn. Code Ann. § 8-50-108. |

*(Table continues.)*

## Table 7.5-2 Part A *(cont'd)*

### EMPLOYEES' ACCESS TO PERSONNEL RECORDS

(See also text at § 7.5.)

| | *Employers Covered by Statute* | | *May Records Be Reviewed?* | *Are There Penalties for Employer Violations?* | *Citations to Authority* |
|---|---|---|---|---|---|
| | *Public* | *Private* | | | |
| TX | Yes (employees of certain sheriffs' departments). | No. | Yes. | No. | Tex. Local Gov't Code Ann. § 157.904. |
| UT | Yes. | No. | Yes. | No. | Utah Code Ann. §§ 67-18-1, 67-18-5. |
| VT | Yes. | No. | Yes. | Yes. Reasonable attorneys' fees and costs in addition to access to the records requested. | Vt. Stat. Ann. tit. 1, §§ 316, 317, 319. |
| VA | — | — | — | — | State has no statutory provisions. |
| WA | Yes. | Yes. | Yes. Once per year. | No. | Wash. Rev. Code Ann. §§ 49.12.240, 49.12.250, 49.12.260. |
| WV | — | — | — | — | State has no statutory provisions. |
| WI | Yes. | Yes. | Yes. Twice per year. | Yes. $10–$100 per violation. Each day of refusal or failure to comply is a separate violation. | Wis. Stat. Ann. § 103.13. |
| WY | — | — | — | — | State has no statutory provisions. |

# Table 7.5-2 Part B

## EMPLOYEES' SPECIFIC RIGHTS

(See also text at § 7.5.)

| | *Which Employees May Inspect Records?* | *May Employees Obtain a Copy of the Records?* | *May Records Be Corrected?* | *Records That May Be Reviewed by Employee* | *Records That May Not Be Reviewed by Employee* | *Citations to Authority* |
|---|---|---|---|---|---|---|
| AL | — | — | — | — | — | State has no statutory provisions. |
| AK | Current employees; former employees. | Yes. Employer may recover copy costs from employee. | State has no statutory requirements. | Personnel file and other information maintained by employer concerning employee. | State has no statutory requirements. | Alaska Stat. § 23.10.430. |
| AZ | — | — | — | — | — | State has no statutory provisions. |
| AR | Current employees; former employees; appointed agents. | Yes. | State has no statutory requirements. | Personnel and evaluation records. | — | Ark. Code Ann. §§ 25-19-104, 25-19-105. |
| CA | Current employees. | State has no statutory requirements. | State has no statutory requirements. | Employment, promotion, compensation, disciplinary, and termination records. | Investigation of possible criminal offense; letter of reference. | Cal. Lab. Code §§ 1198.5, 1199. |
| CO | — | — | State has no statutory requirements. | Personnel file and other information maintained by employer concerning employee. | State has no statutory requirements. | Colo. Rev. Stat. § 24-72-204. |
| CT | Current employees; former employees. | Yes. Employer may recover copy costs from employee. | Yes, if employer agrees or if employee includes written explanation about any conflicting information. | Employment, promotion, compensation, transfer, termination, and disciplinary records and evaluations. | Stock option; bonus; references; plans for future operations; contents of separately maintained security file; test information that would invalidate test; documents for use in civil, criminal, or grievance procedures. | Conn. Gen. Stat. Ann. §§ 31-128a–31-128h. |
| DE | Current employees; laid-off employees with reemployment rights; employees on leave of absence. | No. Employees are permitted only to make notes of the records. | Yes. | Employment, wages, commendations, disciplinary actions, fringe benefit information, employment history, leave, retirement, evaluations, and medical records. | Records relating to criminal investigation; civil, criminal, or grievance procedures; references; information available under Fair Credit Reporting Act; plans for future operations. | Del. Code Ann. tit. 19, §§ 730–735. |

*(Table continues.)*

# Table 7.5-2 Part B *(cont'd)*

## EMPLOYEES' SPECIFIC RIGHTS

(See also text at § 7.5.)

| | *Which Employees May Inspect Records?* | *May Employees Obtain a Copy of the Records?* | *May Records Be Corrected?* | *Records That May Be Reviewed by Employee* | *Records That May Not Be Reviewed by Employee* | *Citations to Authority* |
|---|---|---|---|---|---|---|
| DC | Current employees; appointed agents. | State has no statutory requirements. | Yes. | All records except those designated as nonreviewable. | Information received from confidential source; medical and mental health records if physician would hesitate to inform patient of its exact nature and outcome; testing information; investigatory records; references; information available under the Fair Credit Reporting Act. | D.C. Code Ann. §§ 1-632.1 *et seq.* |
| FL | Current employees; appointed agents. | Yes. Employer may recover copy costs from employee. | Yes, employee can request a formal inquiry into matters believed to be false. | Employee performance evaluations. | State has no statutory requirements. | Fla. Stat. Ann. § 231.291. |
| GA | — | — | — | — | — | State has no statutory provisions. |
| HI | — | — | — | — | — | State has no statutory provisions. |
| ID | Current employees; appointed agents. | State has no statutory requirements. | Yes, employee shall be provided timely notice of all material placed in the file and shall be afforded the opportunity to attach a rebuttal. | All records may be reviewed except those designated as nonreviewable. | Recommendation letters may not be reviewed by employee. | Idaho Code § 33-518. |
| IL | Current employees, laid-off employees with reemployment rights; employees on leave of absence; grievance representatives. | Yes. Employer may recover copy costs from employee. | Yes. | Employment, promotion, transfer, and compensation records, discharge or other disciplinary records, and test scores. | References; test documents; materials used by management for planning purposes; personal information about another employee if disclosure would constitute a clearly unwarranted invasion of privacy; investigatory or security records. | 820 Ill. Comp. Stat. Ann. §§ 40/1 *et seq.* |
| IN | — | — | — | — | — | State has no statutory provisions. |

| | | | | | | |
|---|---|---|---|---|---|---|
| IA | Current employees. | Yes. Employer may recover copy costs from employee, as long as cost does not exceed $5. | No. | Performance evaluations; disciplinary records; other information concerning employer-employee relations. | Employment references written for employee. | Iowa Code Ann. § 91B.1. |
| KS | — | — | — | — | — | State has no statutory provisions. |
| KY | Current employees. | Yes. | Yes. Employee may attach a written response to the file. | Rates of compensation, evaluations, changes in status records, and disciplinary records. | Any examination materials. | Ky. Rev. Stat. Ann. § 18A.020. |
| LA | Current employees; former employees; appointed agents. | State has no statutory requirements. | — | Employee exposed to toxic substances may obtain information on the substances and adverse health effects from employer's records of other employee exposures. | — | La. Rev. Stat. Ann. § 23:1016. |
| ME | Current employees; former employees. | Yes. Employer may recover copy costs from employees. | State has no statutory provisions. | Evaluations; reports regarding employee's character, credit, work habits, compensation, and nonprivileged medical records. | State has no statutory requirements. | Me. Rev. Stat. Ann. tit. 26, § 631. |
| MD | — | — | — | — | — | State has no statutory provisions. |
| MA | Current employees; former employees. Employees in positions that may lead to tenure or are tenured at private institutions of higher learning are not covered by the statute. | Yes. Employer may recover copy costs from employee. | Yes. | Employment, promotion, transfer, compensation, and disciplinary records. | Information of a personal nature about person other than employee if disclosure would constitute a clearly unwarranted invasion of privacy. | Mass. Gen. Laws Ann. ch. 149, § 52C. |
| MI | Current employees; former employees. | Yes. Employer may recover copy costs from employee. | Yes. | Employment, promotion, transfer, compensation, and disciplinary records. | Employee references if identity of person making reference would be disclosed; employer's staff planning; medical records made or obtained by employer if records available to employee from doctor or medical facility involved; personal information regarding another employee if it would constitute a clearly unwarranted invasion of privacy; criminal investigation; grievance investigations separately kept; records maintained by educational institution; records kept by, and in sole possession of, executive, administrative, or professional employee. | Mich. Comp. Laws Ann. §§ 423.501–423.511. |

*(Table continues.)*

# Table 7.5-2 Part B *(cont'd)*

## EMPLOYEES' SPECIFIC RIGHTS

(See also text at § 7.5.)

| | *Which Employees May Inspect Records?* | *May Employees Obtain a Copy of the Records?* | *May Records Be Corrected?* | *Records That May Be Reviewed by Employee* | *Records That May Not Be Reviewed by Employee* | *Citations to Authority* |
|---|---|---|---|---|---|---|
| MN | Current employees; former employees who assert inspection right within one year of termination. | Yes. Employer may not recover copy costs from employee. | Yes. | Employment, retirement compensation, commendation, disciplinary, and benefits records. | Investigative, educational, and test information; salary system and staff planning; comments kept only by administrative, executive, supervisor, or professional employee; medical records available from health care provider; written references. | Minn. Stat. Ann. §§ 181.960–181.966. |
| MS | — | — | — | — | — | State has no statutory provisions. |
| MO | — | — | — | — | — | State has no statutory provisions. |
| MT | — | — | — | — | — | State has no statutory provisions. |
| NE | — | — | — | — | — | State has no statutory provisions. |
| NV | Current employees; former employees who assert inspection right within 60 days of termination. | Yes. Employer may recover copy costs from employee. | Yes. If employer determines that employee's personnel file is inaccurate, employer must correct. | Employment and disciplinary records. | Confidential reports from previous employers or investigative agencies; investigation regarding arrest or conviction for any legal violation. | Nev. Rev. Stat. § 613.075. |
| NH | Current employees. | Yes. Employer may recover copy costs from employee. | Yes. | State has no statutory requirements. | Law enforcement or government security investigation records. | N.H. Rev. Stat. Ann. § 275.56. |
| NJ | — | — | — | — | — | State has no statutory provisions. |
| NM | — | — | — | — | — | State has no statutory provisions. |

| | | | | | | |
|---|---|---|---|---|---|---|
| NY | — | — | — | — | — | State has no statutory provisions. However, *Bigelow v. Board of Trustees,* 472 N.E.2d 1001 (1984) appears to create in certain situations the right for public employees to have access to their personnel files and an opportunity to submit a written response. |
| NC | Applicants; current employees; former employees; appointed agents. | Yes. | Yes, employee may follow grievance procedures to have the inaccurate information removed. | Promotion, demotion, compensation, transfer, leave, evaluations, disciplinary action, and termination records. | References; medical information at discretion of physician. | N.C. Gen. Stat. §§ 126-23–126.28. |
| ND | Current employees; appointed agents. | Yes. Employer may recover copy costs from employee. | Yes. | Employee's character and performance. | Employer may maintain separate notes or records of employee's performance to be used in preparing evaluations or when taking disciplinary action. | N.D. Cent. Code § 54-06-21. |
| OH | — | — | — | — | — | State has no statutory provisions. |
| OK | Current employee. | Yes. | — | Personnel file. | — | Okla. Stat. Ann. tit. 51 § 24A.7. |
| OR | Current employees; former employees who assert inspection right within 60 days of termination. | Yes. Employer may recover copy costs from employee. | State has no statutory requirements. | Employment, promotion, compensation, termination, or other disciplinary records. | Conviction, arrest, or investigation of criminal acts; confidential reports from previous employers. | Or. Rev. Stat. § 652.750. |
| PA | Current employees; laid-off employees with reemployment rights; employees on leave of absence; appointed agents. | No. Employees are permitted only to make notes of the records. | Yes. Pennsylvania Act entrusts Bureau of Labor Standards with authority to enforce statute; therefore, any corrections employees want made to their personnel files will be made only after notice and hearing with the Bureau. | Employment application, promotion, compensation, commendations, discipline, benefits, leave, and evaluations records. | Records relating to an investigation of criminal offense; references; civil, criminal, or grievance procedures; medical records; materials used by employer to plan future operations; information available to employee under Fair Credit Reporting Act. | Pa. Stat. tit. 43, §§ 1321 *et seq.* |
| RI | Current employees; former employees; appointed agents. | Yes. Employer may recover copy costs from employee. | State has no statutory requirements. | Employment, disciplinary, promotion, termination, and compensation records. | Criminal offense records; grievances; references; medical records; recommendations; managerial records kept or used only by employer; confidential reports from previous employers; managerial planning records. | R.I. Gen. Laws §§ 28-6.4-1, 28-6.4-2. |

*(Table continues.)*

# Table 7.5-2 Part B *(cont'd)*

## EMPLOYEES' SPECIFIC RIGHTS

(See also text at § 7.5.)

| | *Which Employees May Inspect Records?* | *May Employees Obtain a Copy of the Records?* | *May Records Be Corrected?* | *Records That May Be Reviewed by Employee* | *Records That May Not Be Reviewed by Employee* | *Citations to Authority* |
|---|---|---|---|---|---|---|
| SC | — | — | — | — | — | State has no statutory provisions. |
| SD | Current employees. | State has no statutory requirements. | State has no statutory requirements. | Records maintained by the Bureau of Personnel, including personnel appraisals. | State has no statutory requirements. | S.D. Codified Laws Ann. § 3-6A-31. |
| TN | Current employees. | Yes. Employer may recover copy costs from employee. | State has no statutory requirements. | Contents of personnel file. | State has no statutory requirements. | Tenn. Code Ann. § 8-50-108. |
| TX | — | — | Yes. | Contents of personnel file, including commendations, disciplinary records, and evaluations. | State has no statutory requirements. | Tex. Local Gov't Code Ann. § 157.904. |
| UT | Current employees. | Yes. Employer may recover copy costs from employee. | State has no statutory requirements. | Contents of personnel file. | Documents subject to access provisions in Title 63, Chapter 2, Government Records Access and Management Act. | Utah Code Ann. §§ 67-18-1, 67-18-5. |
| VT | Current employees; appointed agents. | Yes. Employer may recover copy costs from employee. | State has no statutory requirements. | Hiring, evaluation, promotion, disciplinary, and personal finance records; medical or psychological facts. | State has no statutory requirements. | Vt. Stat. Ann. tit. 1, §§ 316, 317, 319. |
| VA | — | — | — | — | — | State has no statutory provisions. |
| WA | Current employees; former employees who assert inspection right within 2 years of termination. | State has no statutory requirements. | Yes. Employee retains this right for a period not to exceed 2 years. | All contents except records designated as unreviewable. | Investigation of possible criminal offense; records compiled in anticipation of lawsuit that would not be available to another party under rules of pretrial discovery for causes pending in the superior courts. | Wash. Rev. Code Ann. §§ 49.12.240, 49.12.250, 49.12.260. |
| WV | — | — | — | — | — | State has no statutory provisions. |

| | | | | | | |
|---|---|---|---|---|---|---|
| WI | Current employees; former employees; grievance representatives. | Yes. Employer may recover copy costs from employees. | Yes. | Employment, promotion, transfer, compensation, disciplinary action, and medical records, if employer determines that release will not have detrimental effect on employee; if employer determines that release will have a detrimental effect, employer may release records to employee's doctor. | Investigation of possible criminal offense; references; test documents; materials used by employer for management planning; personal information about another person if it would constitute a clearly unwarranted invasion of privacy; records relating to a pending claim between employee and employer. | Wis. Stat. Ann. § 103.13. |
| WY | — | — | — | — | — | State has no statutory provisions. |

# § 7.6 Employee Privacy Rights in Workplace Computer Systems and Electronic Mail

As employers expand the use of computers in the office, and more employees perform a significant portion of their work on a computer, the computer may become the employee's desk, workspace, and file drawer, all in one. If an employee has some recognized limited privacy interest in his or her workspace, a logical conclusion may be that the employee has a similar privacy interest in his or her computer.

An employer may have compelling reasons to examine the information contained within an employee's computer. There may be a concern that the employee is using the computer for outside projects or personal uses, or even for illegal purposes. The employer may want to check the status of work-related projects by examining the files kept by the employee. The employer may also want to keep track of the employee's productivity. All these traditional employer concerns are easier to monitor when the employee performs his/her job with the help of a computer. If all the computers in an office are networked to a central unit, then an employer can examine an employee's work without ever entering the employee's "physical" workspace, and the employee's privacy interest may be more tenuous.

Employers may also have access to employees' electronic mail, or E-mail. E-mail may consist of messages sent from one computer station to another, messages sent via a local or national network, or messages sent to other employees through an office or companywide network. An employee may have a privacy interest in personal E-mail that would restrict the employer's right to view these messages, or limit the employer's use and disclosure of the information obtained from the employee's E-mail.

The scope of any potential employee privacy interest related to computer technology in the workplace is beginning to receive attention. Several recent California cases addressed an employer's right to read employee E-mail. In addition, bills have been proposed in the United States Congress and in several state legislatures that would limit an employer's freedom to electronically monitor employees. Indeed, many state statutes already on the book, although not directly dealing with employee privacy, could possibly be used by employees hoping to carve out a new privacy right. The future may hold increased notice requirements and other restrictions on employers, expanding the areas of the workplace where employees have established privacy interests.

## [a] Existing Federal Law and Computer Privacy

Federal law does not appear to directly regulate an employer's access to employee files and electronic messages contained in or transmitted via an employer-owned computer system. However, the Electronic Communications Privacy Act of 1986, an amendment to Title III of the Omnibus Crime Control and Safe Streets Act, included electronically stored and transmitted information within the federal wiretap laws.[1] This amendment does protect an individual's privacy interest in E-mail and other electronically stored information. However, this protection may not be applicable in the workplace, because of the business-extension exception.

---

**§ 7.6**

1. 18 U.S.C. §§ 2510, 2701 (1993).

Several commentators have written about this amendment and its potential effect in the workplace.[2] Despite Congress' apparent concern for limiting access to private information stored in computer systems and local or nationwide networks, there are several exceptions that appear to insulate employers from liability. First, the act exempts providers of communications services from any limitations on access or disclosure of information stored by their systems.[3] Second, the interception of electronic communications is exempted from regulation if done by an employer or employee engaged in an activity necessary to the service provided during the normal course of business or if the interception is necessary to protect the employer's property rights.[4]

Further, the regulation exempts access of information when done with the consent of the employee (or other person).[5] Because implied consent is good enough under this Act, simply giving notice to the employee that the employer may monitor or access the employee's computer files or E-mail may be sufficient to avoid application of this statute.

### [b] The Future of Computer Privacy in the Workplace

Concern about the potential for invasion of employee privacy rights is growing as the workplace becomes more computerized and employee monitoring devices become more sophisticated. Evidence of this concern can be found at the highest levels of the federal government. During the 103d Congress, Senator Paul Simon (D-Ill) introduced a bill to increase the workplace privacy rights of employees. The Privacy for Consumers and Workers Act[6] was written to prevent abuses of electronic monitoring in the workplace and in other areas. Although the bill was not acted upon by the 103d Congress and Senator Simon had no plans to reintroduce it, the bill provides an excellent example of where the future of workplace privacy may be heading.

"Electronic monitoring" is defined broadly enough in the bill to include most computer-based methods of collecting or retrieving information about another person. Retrieval of employee E-mail is included in this definition, as is the viewing of information stored on an employee's hard disk drive, and electronic monitoring of an employee's work (e.g., monitoring the number of keystrokes an employee makes during a given period). The definition of collectible data is similarly broad, encompassing any personal data that by some distinctive mark can be identified as the employee's—including any written analyses or evaluations.

Senator Simon's bill would mandate that employers meet the following requirements before conducting electronic monitoring and before using the information collected:

1. Employers must provide specific notice that monitoring will be conducted; and
2. Employers must notify employees of
   - **a.** the forms of monitoring that will be used,
   - **b.** the type of information to be collected,
   - **c.** the use to be made of the data, and
   - **d.** any performance expectations against which the employee may be measured.

The coverage of the bill extends beyond the established employment relationship. The monitoring used by the employer must also be discussed with potential employees if the methods would impact them if hired. Also, if the employer engages in monitoring that may affect customers or the general public, then they, too, must be given notice.

Other than the regular monitoring described above, the bill would also limit the employer's use of periodic or random monitoring. New employees with fewer than 60 days' experience may be randomly monitored; employees with five or more years of experience may not be randomly monitored. Work groups are subject to this type of monitoring if it is limited to two hours per calendar week and if the employees in the group are given the notice required not less than 24 hours nor more than 72 hours prior to monitoring. An exception to the prior notice requirement is provided if the employer has a reasonable suspicion that an employee is or is about to be engaged in criminal conduct, willful gross misconduct, or conduct that has a significant adverse economic impact on the employer.

The bill would limit the way an employer can use the information collected by electronic monitoring. If the employer collects data related to the amount of work performed, this data cannot be used as the sole basis for employee performance evaluations or setting production quotas. In most instances, the employer must allow the employee access to the data collected.

---

2. See, e.g., Baumhart, *The Employer's Right to Read Employee E-mail: Protecting Property or Personal Prying,* 8 The Labor Lawyer 849, 923 (1992).
3. 18 U.S.C. §§ 2701(c), 2702(b).
4. 18 U.S.C. § 2511(2)(a)(i).
5. 18 U.S.C. § 2511(2)(d).
6. S.B. 984, 103d Congress, 1st Sess. (1993).

The bill would provide the employer access to data maintained by an employee if an immediate business need exists, the employee is not available, and the data is alphanumeric in nature. Additionally, the data so accessed may not be used for disciplinary purposes, and the employee must be notified that the data was accessed.

Employee privacy rights are detailed in the bill. Any data intentionally collected must be confined to the employee's work. The employer must not conduct electronic monitoring of an employee who is exercising first amendment rights. Disclosure of personal data is limited to the employee to whom the data pertains, unless disclosure is to officers or employees of the employer who have a legitimate need for the information in the performance of their duties, or to law enforcement officials with proper warrant. If the data affects public health and safety or involves illegal conduct by a public official, the data may also be disclosed to the public.

Despite the failure of this bill to gain approval, the potential for abuse of new computer technology continues to be an important issue. In August 1995, a bill was introduced in the House of Representatives that would ensure that the prohibitions of the Communications Act of 1934[7]—penalizing those convicted of making obscene or harassing telephone calls—apply equally to faxes and electronic mail transmitted over telephone lines.[8]

### [c] State Efforts to Address Computer Privacy

The states, too, have begun to address workplace privacy in connection with computer-based communications. In some cases, bills introduced to address this concern have failed to gain legislative approval. In other states, only the criminal statutes relating to wiretapping and eavesdropping have addressed the potential for abuses in computer-based communications. A few states, however, have taken the first steps toward recognizing computer-based workplace privacy interests. Moreover, it is possible that some state courts might recognize a claim based on state constitutional privacy rights or a tort claim for invasion of privacy.

Legislators in Arkansas rejected a bill that would have provided significant new protection for employees' privacy in the workplace. A bill introduced in 1995 would have required employers to notify employees of all personal surveillance that might occur in the workplace, including camera surveillance and reviewing computer E-mail.[9] In Maryland, a bill was reported unfavorably out of committee that would have prohibited the use of electronic mail for the purpose of annoying, abusing, tormenting, harassing, or embarrassing other persons.[10]

Virginia provides an example of how some states have addressed the issue of computer information privacy. Both Georgia and West Virginia have statutes substantially similar to the Virginia statute.[11] The Virginia statute makes illegal the use of a computer or computer network to intentionally examine, without authority, "any employment, salary, credit or any other financial or personal information relating to any other person."[12] Under this provision, intentional examination occurs when the offender reviews the information relating to another person after the offender knows or should know that he or she lacks the authority to review the information.[13] A person without authority is one who either has no right or permission from the owner of the computer or exceeds the scope of the right or permission.[14]

The Virginia statute does not make clear whether an employer may freely examine the computer system used by an employee and the information stored therein. Of course, if an employee provides his/her own computer at work, then the employer must gain permission from the owner before examining the information it contains. If the employer owns the computer and makes it available to the employee for work-related tasks, then, as the owner, the employer would presumably be able to retrieve and examine information contained in the computer at will.

With respect to public employees, a provision in the Colorado public records law[15] requires any state or agency, institution, or political subdivision that maintains an electronic mail system to adopt a written policy on the monitoring of electronic mail communications and the circumstances under which it will be conducted. The policy must include a statement that correspondence

7. 47 U.S.C.S. § 223 (1995).
8. H.B. 2213, 104th Cong., Reg. Sess. (1995).
9. Arkansas H.B. No. 2017, 80th Regular Session (1995).
10. Maryland H.B. No. 441, 1995 Legislative Session.
11. Ga. Code Ann. § 16-9-93; W. Va. Code § 61-3C-12.
12. Va. Code § 18.2-152.5 (1988).
13. Id.
14. Va. Code § 18.2-152.2 (1988).
15. Colo. Rev. Stat. §§ 27-72-201 *et seq.* (1997).

of the employee in the form of electronic mail may be a public record under the public records law and, therefore, may be subject to public inspection.[16] However, the Colorado public records law evinces a concern for the privacy interests of public employees by expressly excluding from its definition of "records" electronic mail messages, regardless of whether the messages are produced or stored using state-owned equipment or software. Electronic mail, however, may be considered a public record if the recipient has previously segregated and stored such messages as evidence of the organization, functions, policies, decisions, procedures, operations, or other activities of the government, or because of the value of official governmental data in such messages.[17]

Michigan law recognizes the privacy concerns of private-sector employees through a statute regarding the employment of prisoners in private companies. Under this statute, inmates may be placed in private companies only where they do not have access to, among other kinds of information, any employee information that includes electronic mail addresses.[18]

California has enacted more extensive provisions regarding computer information and privacy, including a section on computer-based crimes. Identified in this section as a crime is the unauthorized use of data that is either internal or external to a computer, computer system, or computer network.[19]

Delaware also has similar statutes proscribing unauthorized access to a computer system and misuse of computer system information.[20] To come within the protection of these statutes, an employee faces the same hurdle of overcoming an employer's ownership of the computer and authorization to use the data contained therein. Further, the section is not intended to apply to any employee labor relations activities otherwise within the scope and protection of state and federal labor laws. Another California statute provides some protection for employees who have suffered a threat of violence through a workplace communication, including electronic mail.[21]

Some states have revised their wiretapping and eavesdropping statutes to include computer surveillance or have otherwise specifically provided that unauthorized examination of computer records is prohibited.[22] A number of states, however, have not revised older wiretap statutes, which deal only with general interception of wire and oral communications. These statutes prohibited only wiretapping and other secretive methods of recording or hearing private information. A typical example of this type of statute can be found in Massachusetts.[23] Although an employee may argue that electronically stored and transmitted data is covered by this type of statute, such an argument may be weakened by the fact that, unlike the federal and other state statutes that have been revised to include new computer technologies, these older state statutes specifically cover only wire and oral communications.

Despite the absence of clear state regulation on the issue, employers may still face exposure to state judicial remedies for privacy violations. Typically, such claims are based on the degree of privacy interest an employee has in the workplace. California has recognized the privacy interests of private-sector employees under its state constitution.[24] Several other states also recognize more limited privacy rights for private individuals.

An employee may also assert a tort claim in state court, either for unreasonable intrusion into an employee's private matters or for unauthorized disclosure of personal facts. Both of these theories have been accepted by courts in other areas of workplace privacy, but they have apparently not been used to vindicate computer and E-mail privacy rights. Several cases involving employer monitoring of employee E-mail, however, have been brought in California; no reported decisions have as yet been issued in these cases.[25]

---

16. Colo. Rev. Stat. § 24-72-204.5 (1997).

17. Colo. Rev. Stat. § 24-80-101(1)(f) (1997).

18. Mich. Comp. Laws § 800.327a (1997); Mich. Stat. Ann. § 28.1540(7a) (Lawyers Cooperative Publishing, 1997).

19. Cal. Penal Code § 502 (West 1988).

20. Del. Code Ann. title 11 §§ 932, 935 (1995).

21. Cal. Code Civ. Proc. § 527.8 (West 1995).

22. See, e.g., N.C. Gen. Stat. § 15A–28b (1996); N.J.S.A. § 2A:156A-2 (1995); N.Y. Penal Law § 250.05 (McKinney 1989); 18 P.A.C.S. § 5725 (1995).

23. Mass. Gen. Laws Ann. ch. 272, § 99 (West 1990).

24. Soroka v. Dayton Hudson Corp., 1 Cal. Rptr. 2d 77 (Cal. App. 1 Dist. 1991).

25. Bourke v. Nissan Motor Co., No. YC 003979 (Cal. Sup. Ct., Los Angeles) (two employees were placed on a "final warning" after a supervisor viewed their E-mail and found personal messages); Flannagan v. Epson America, Inc., No. BC 007036 (Cal. Sup. Ct., Los Angeles); Shoars v. Epson America, Inc., No. SWC 112749 (Cal. Sup. Ct., Los Angeles) (employee allegedly saw employer viewing another employee's E-mail; employee was fired shortly thereafter); Cameron v. Mentor Graphics, No. 716361 (Cal. Sup. Ct., Santa Clara Cty) (employer monitored employees' messages transmitted over Internet, not an employer-owned system). These cases were cited in Baumhart, *supra*.

A recently reported case from a federal court in Pennsylvania refused to recognize a privacy interest on the part of an employee where an employer intercepted the worker's electronic mail and consequently terminated the employee based on the content of the messages.[26] In *Smyth v. Pillsbury Co.,* 914 F. Supp. 97 (E.D. Pa. 1996), the employer maintained an internal e-mail system. The employer had repeatedly assured its employees that all E-mail communications would remain confidential and privileged and that it would not intercept employees' E-mail communications or use such communications against employees. The plaintiff in the case sent an E-mail message from his home computer to his supervisor via the system and, relying on management's assurances of confidentiality, made critical remarks about the employer. The worker was later informed that he was to be terminated for transmitting inappropriate and unprofessional comments over the E-mail system. The federal court sitting in diversity found that the employee failed to establish a claim for wrongful termination under Pennsylvania law. The only exception to at-will employment in Pennsylvania is where the termination violates clearly defined public policy, such as a policy stated in statute, regulation, or rule, and the court found that the employer's actions violated no such policy. The court also rejected the theory that the employer had committed the tort of intrusion upon seclusion, finding that the employee had no reasonable expectation of privacy in his communications through the company E-mail system, regardless of the employer's assurances of privacy. Furthermore, even if the employee did have a reasonable expectation of privacy in the E-mail messages, the court held that there was no substantial invasion highly offensive to a reasonable person. Distinguishing the E-mail case from those involving a required urinalysis or search of personal property, the court noted that the employer had not forced the employee to reveal personal information; rather, the employee voluntarily placed his personal comments upon the employer's system. Finally, the court noted, the employer's interest in preventing inappropriate and unprofessional comments was greater than the employee's privacy interest in his comments.

A federal court in Nevada also refused to recognize a privacy interest on the part of employees in an internal paging system similar to an E-mail system. In *Bohach v. City of Reno,* 932 F. Supp. 1232 (D. Nev. 1996), two police officers brought claims under the Fourth Amendment and the Electronic Communications Privacy Act when their employer, the Reno Police Department, initiated an internal affairs investigation based upon the contents of messages sent between them by means of the police department's paging system. The department's paging system allowed the display of brief alphanumeric messages on pagers given to police officers and members of the press. The court held that the police officers had no reasonable expectation of privacy in messages sent via the system, since the officers had been notified that all messages through the system were logged on to the network, and because of those characteristics of the system which distinguished it from use of the public telephone system, such as the limited audience to whom messages could be communicated. Since they could establish no reasonable expectation of privacy, the officers could not state a claim under the Fourth Amendment, the court held. The court also rejected the officers' claims that the department had violated the Electronic Communications Privacy Act, because the department, as the provider of the service, was permitted under the statute to access communications in electronic storage.[27]

The viability of claims in the area of computer privacy may rest on the degree to which the employee has an expectation of privacy in the computer workstation. If the computer, and E-mail or other messages sent through an employer computer network, are considered part of the employee's desk or workspace, or the E-mail is used as a private messaging system, then the employee may have a reasonable expectation of privacy in the system, the files, and the messages sent through the network. Generally a court will look to the surrounding facts to determine if an employee has a reasonable expectation of privacy in a particular area. These factors include whether an employee took precautions to ensure privacy in an area, the way the employee used the area, and the extent to which the employee can or has in the past excluded others from this area.[28]

In the computer setting, these factors may translate into whether the employee accessed the computer system with a private password. Another factor may be whether employees share a computer, or if all computers are networked into a central system. Employer examina-

26. *Smyth v. Pillsbury Co.,* 914 F. Supp. 97 (E.D. Pa. 1996).

27. Conversely, employees may be subject to suit for violating the Electronic Communications Privacy Act by accessing electronically stored messages. *See* Wesley College v. Pitts, 974 F. Supp. 375 (D. Del. 1997).

28. People v. Holland 591 N.Y.S.2d 744, 746 (N.Y. City Crim. Ct. 1992) (citing People v. Rodriguez, 513 N.Y.S.2d 75 (1987)).

tion of E-mail might be particularly troublesome if the correspondence can be labeled as private in some way or is sent to a specific person who may need a password to access the message. Note, however, that electronic messages sent to specific employees or posted on an employer's computer bulletin board have been ruled admissable evidence in an employee's discrimination case against the employer.[29]

### [d] Conclusion

The federal and state statutes, as well as state common law, may be viewed and interpreted broadly enough that an employer could conceivably face exposure to liability for intercepting or accessing employees' computerized personal information or messages. An employer who monitors information stored in or transmitted from employees' computers should take the following steps to avoid litigation based on asserted privacy rights:

1. Put employees on notice that their E-mail or computer workstations are subject to review and access by the employer.
2. Promulgate guidelines regarding access to employee computers and messages and the circumstances under which messages may be viewed or the information in computer files retrieved or disseminated.
3. Take steps to prevent employees from developing any expectation of privacy in their computer files and messages. For example, the use of secret passwords, known only to the employee, for accessing files and sending information may support an expectation of privacy. Thus, such passwords should be used only if they are justified by security considerations.

---

29. See, e.g., Plymouth Police Brotherhood v. Labor Relations Commission, 630 N.E.2d 599 (Mass. 1994); Strauss v. Microsoft Corp., 1995 WL 326492 (S.D.N.Y. 1995).

## § 7.7 Employment Decisions Based on Off-Duty Conduct

Several states have recently enacted statutes dealing with discrimination against employees for off-duty conduct. The majority of these statutes prohibit employers from discriminating against an employee for engaging in certain types of lawful conduct both outside the workplace and during nonworking hours.

These statutes provide some exceptions, however, where discrimination on the basis of employees' off-duty conduct is permitted. For example, most states do not prohibit discrimination on the basis of off-duty activity if the activity adversely affects the employee's job performance. Finally, the statutes generally provide a procedure for aggrieved employees to follow when subjected to employer discrimination and allow for remedies to an employee who prevails.

Of all the states that have such statutes, the New York statute is the most comprehensive. This statute makes it unlawful for any employer or employment agency to refuse to hire, employ, or license, or to discharge or otherwise discriminate against any individual in a term or condition of employment because of the following:

- An individual's lawful political activities (including running or campaigning for office or attending fundraising events) that occur off the employer's premises and during nonworking hours.
- An individual's legal use of consumable products off the premises and during nonworking hours.
- An individual's legal recreational activities (including leisure activities such as sports, games, hobbies, exercise, reading, and watching television or movies) that occur while the employee is off-duty and off the employer's premises.
- An individual's membership in a union.[1]

The precise scope of the New York statute is currently the subject of some debate in the courts. For example, one court has held that cohabitation is a protected outside recreational activity under the New York law.[2] Another court has held, however, that dating is not within the statute's purview.[3]

Two other states have broad statutes limiting employer discrimination on the basis of employee off-duty conduct. Both Colorado and North Dakota have statutes that prohibit an employer from discriminating against employees who participate in *lawful activities* while off-duty and off the employer's premises. Although these statutes are not as specific as the New York statute, the term *lawful activity* may be interpreted to protect activities at least as diverse as those enumerated above.

The majority of states that have addressed the issue of employee conduct outside of work have limited their statutes to cover an employee's lawful use of *lawful products* while the employee is off-duty and off the employer's premises. These statutes are typically concerned with the lawful, off-duty use of alcohol and tobacco, although food is occasionally included. (For laws relating to the use of tobacco in the workplace, see Part 8.) Because of the negative health effects of the use

**§ 7.7**

1. N.Y. Lab. Law § 201-d.
2. Pasch v. Katz Media Corp., 10 IER Cas. 1574 (S.D.N.Y. 1995).
3. New York v. Wal-Mart Stores, 207 A.D.2d 150, 621 N.Y.S.2d 158 (3d Dept. 1995).

or misuse of alcohol and tobacco, many of these statutes allow employers to discriminate in the provision of health or other insurance; however, they also provide an aggrieved employee with procedures and remedies for violations. States that have such statutes include Illinois, Minnesota, Missouri, Nevada, North Carolina, Wisconsin, and Wyoming.

These statutes are by their terms narrower than the state statutes that address an employee's lawful *activities* while outside work. For example, a state statute that prohibits discrimination against employees for *lawful use of lawful products* cannot prevent discrimination on account of employee off-duty political campaigning; however, such activity is expressly protected in New York and could be protected under the statutes of Colorado and North Dakota.

The characteristics of all of the state statutes that address employee off-duty conduct are set out in Table 7.7-1. Exhibit 7.7-1 provides more detailed information on the statutes.

# Table 7.7-1
## SUMMARY OF LAWS PROTECTING OFF-DUTY CONDUCT

**NOTE:** This table provides, in quick reference form, the information set out in more detail in Exhibit 7.7-1. Under the "Protected Conduct" column, a "yes" indicates that the statute in question specifically refers to the activity; (—) indicates that the activity is not specifically mentioned by the statute. Nevertheless, some activities that are not specifically mentioned may in fact be covered. For example, a statute stating that the use of lawful products is protected also protects the use of tobacco products, although not specifically stated. The "Exceptions to Law" column lists the instances in which an employer is allowed to discriminate on the basis of the use of the product or the activity. Some of the most common exceptions include the following: if the employee has violated a workplace policy, such as a no smoking at work policy; if the use of the product would create a conflict of interest; if use or nonuse of the product is a bona fide occupational qualification; or if the employer is a nonprofit organization whose primary purpose is to discourage the use of the product.

| | *Protected Conduct* | *Exceptions to Law* | *Insurance Requirements* | *Procedures and Remedies* | *Citation to Authority* |
|---|---|---|---|---|---|
| AZ | Use of tobacco products: yes, state employees.<br>Use of alcohol: —<br>Use of "lawful products": —<br>Other: — | — | — | Criminal action: violation is a petty offense.<br>Civil action: statute provides for administrative action. See Exhibit i.<br>Damages: —<br>Costs and attorneys' fees: —<br>Prerequisites to civil action: — | Ariz. Rev. Stat. Ann. § 36-602. |
| CO | Use of tobacco products: —<br>Use of Alcohol: —<br>Use of "lawful products": —<br>Other: lawful activities (including marriage and plans to marry) that are off-duty and off employer's premises. | Bona fide occupational qualifications; conflicts of interest. | — | Criminal Action: —<br>Civil action: yes.<br>Damages: wages and benefits.<br>Costs and attorneys' fees: yes.<br>Prerequisites to civil action: employee must mitigate damages. | Colo. Rev. Stat. Ann. §§ 24-34-401 *et seq.* |
| CT | Use of tobacco products: yes.<br>Use of alcohol: —<br>Use of "lawful products": —<br>Other: — | Statute does not apply to nonprofit employers whose objective is to discourage use of tobacco products, or to municipal hiring practices involving paid firefighters and police officers. | — | Criminal action: violation is an infraction.<br>Civil action: —<br>Damages: —<br>Costs and attorneys' fees: —<br>Prerequisites to civil action: — | Conn. Gen. Stat. Ann. § 41-40s. |
| DC | Use of tobacco products: yes.<br>Use of alcohol: —<br>Use of "lawful products": —<br>Other: — | Workplace smoking restrictions and bona fide occupational qualifications. | — | Criminal action: —<br>Civil action: yes.<br>Damages: all damages, including lost or back wages.<br>Costs and attorneys' fees: yes, at court's discretion.<br>Prerequisites to civil action: exhaustion of grievance procedures. | D.C. Code Ann. § 6-913.3. |

| | | | | | |
|---|---|---|---|---|---|
| IL | Use of tobacco products: —<br>Use of alcohol: —<br>Use of "lawful products": yes.<br>Other: — | • If use of the product interferes with an employee's job performance.<br>• Statute does not apply to employers whose primary purpose is to discourage use of a lawful product. | Differentiation between employees based on use or nonuse of lawful products during nonworking hours is permitted if the rates reflect actual price differences and the employees are given notice of the rates. | Criminal action: —<br>Civil action: yes.<br>Damages: actual damages.<br>Costs and attorneys' fees: yes, costs.<br>Prerequisites to civil action: filing complaint with an administrative department. | 820 ILCS 55/1 *et seq.* |
| IN | Use of tobacco products: yes.<br>Use of alcohol: —<br>Use of "lawful products": —<br>Other: — | Statute does not apply to churches and religious organizations. | — | Criminal action: —<br>Civil action: yes.<br>Damages: lost wages and benefits.<br>Costs and attorneys' fees: yes.<br>Prerequisites to civil action: — | Ind. Code Ann. §§ 22-5-4-1 *et seq.* |
| KY | Use of tobacco products: yes.<br>Use of alcohol: —<br>Use of "lawful products": —<br>Other: — | Employees who fail to comply with workplace smoking policies may be dismissed. | — | Criminal action: —<br>Civil action: general remedies for employment discrimination. See Exhibit 7.7-1.<br>Damages: see Exhibit 7.7-1.<br>Costs and attorneys' fees: see Exhibit 7.7-1.<br>Prerequisites to civil action: see Exhibit 7.7-1. | Ky. Rev. Stat. Ann. § 344.040. |
| LA | Use of tobacco products: yes.<br>Use of alcohol: —<br>Use of "lawful products": —<br>Other: — | Employees who fail to comply with workplace smoking policies may be dismissed. | — | Criminal action: yes, employer may be fined $250 for a first offense, $500 for a subsequent offense.<br>Civil action: —<br>Damages: —<br>Costs and attorneys' fees: —<br>Prerequisites to civil action: — | La. Rev. Stat. Ann. § 23:996. |
| ME | Use of tobacco products: yes.<br>Use of alcohol: —<br>Use of "lawful products": —<br>Other: — | • If nonuse is bona fide occupational qualification.<br>• Conflicts of interest.<br>• Employees who fail to comply with workplace smoking policies may be dismissed. | Employers may have a health or life insurance policy which makes distinctions based on the use or nonuse of tobacco if the different rates charged to the employee reflect actual price differences charged to the employer. | Criminal action: —<br>Civil action: yes.<br>Damages: all wages and benefits due through the date of judgment.<br>Costs and attorneys' fees: —<br>Prerequisites to civil action: — | Me. Rev. Stat. Ann. tit. 26, § 597. |
| MN | Use of tobacco products: —<br>Use of alcohol: —<br>Use of "lawful products": —<br>Other: use of "lawful consumable products." | • If nonuse is bona fide occupational qualification.<br>• If employee's job performance is affected.<br>• If conflict of interest.<br>• If use constitutes failure to comply with a program to end chemical dependency. | Insurance that makes distinctions based on the use or nonuse of lawful products during nonworking hours is permitted if the different rates charged to the employee reflect actual price differences. | Criminal action: —<br>Civil action: yes.<br>Damages: wages and benefits.<br>Costs and attorneys' fees: yes.<br>Prerequisites to civil action: — | Minn. Stat. Ann. § 181.938. |
| MS | Use of tobacco products: yes.<br>Use of alcohol: —<br>Use of "lawful products": —<br>Other: — | Failure to comply during working hours with a workplace smoking policy. | — | Criminal action: —<br>Civil action: yes, must be brought within 1 year of violation.<br>Damages: yes, wages, benefits, reinstatement.<br>Costs and attorneys' fees: yes.<br>Prerequisites to civil action: — | Miss. Code Ann. §§ 71-7-23, 71-7-25, 71-7-33. |

*(Table continues.)*

# Table 7.7-1 *(cont'd)*
## SUMMARY OF LAWS PROTECTING OFF-DUTY CONDUCT

**NOTE:** This table provides, in quick reference form, the information set out in more detail in Exhibit 7.7-1. Under the "Protected Conduct" column, a "yes" indicates that the statute in question specifically refers to the activity; (—) indicates that the activity is not specifically mentioned by the statute. Nevertheless, some activities that are not specifically mentioned may in fact be covered. For example, a statute stating that the use of lawful products is protected also protects the use of tobacco products, although not specifically stated. The "Exceptions to Law" column lists the instances in which an employer is allowed to discriminate on the basis of the use of the product or the activity. Some of the most common exceptions include the following: if the employee has violated a workplace policy, such as a no smoking at work policy; if the use of the product would create a conflict of interest; if use or nonuse of the product is a bona fide occupational qualification; or if the employer is a nonprofit organization whose primary purpose is to discourage the use of the product.

| | *Protected Conduct* | *Exceptions to Law* | *Insurance Requirements* | *Procedures and Remedies* | *Citation to Authority* |
|---|---|---|---|---|---|
| MO | Use of tobacco products: yes.<br>Use of alcohol: yes.<br>Use of "lawful products": —<br>Other: — | • If the employee's job performance if affected.<br>• If the employer's principal business is health care promotion. | — | Criminal action: —<br>Civil action: —<br>Damages: —<br>Costs and attorneys' fees: —<br>Prerequisites to civil action: — | Mo. Ann. Stat. § 290.145. |
| MT | Use of tobacco products: —<br>Use of alcohol: —<br>Use of "lawful products": yes.<br>Other: — | • If nonuse is bona fide occupational qualification.<br>• If employee's job performance is affected.<br>• If employer is nonprofit organization whose primary objective is to discourage use of a lawful product.<br>• If employer takes action based on belief that action is permitted under substance abuse program, professional contract, or collective bargaining agreement. | Insurance that makes distinctions based on the use or nonuse of lawful products during nonworking hours is permitted if the different rates charged to the employee reflect actuarial differences. | Criminal action: —<br>Civil action: yes, must be brought within one year of violation.<br>Damages: yes, money damages; other measures may be taken by court.<br>Costs and attorneys' fees: yes.<br>Prerequisites to civil action: within 120 days of the alleged violation, employee must initiate any available internal grievance procedure. | Mont. Code Ann. §§ 39-2-313, 39-2-314. |
| NV | Use of tobacco products: —<br>Use of alcohol: —<br>Use of "lawful products": —<br>Other: "Lawful use of any products." | If employee's job performance is affected or safety of other employees is affected. | — | Criminal action: —<br>Civil action: yes.<br>Damages: wages, benefits, order of reinstatement.<br>Costs and attorneys' fees: yes.<br>Prerequisites to civil action: — | Nev. Rev. Stat. Ann. § 613.333. |
| NH | Use of tobacco products: yes.<br>Use of alcohol: —<br>Use of "lawful products": —<br>Other: — | Failure to comply with workplace smoking policy. | State has no statutory requirements. | Criminal action: —<br>Civil action: —<br>Damages: —<br>Costs and attorneys' fees: —<br>Prerequisites to civil action: — | N.H. Rev. Stat. Ann. § 275:37-a. |

| | | | | | |
|---|---|---|---|---|---|
| NJ | Use of tobacco products: yes.<br>Use of alcohol: —<br>Use of "lawful products": —<br>Other: — | If employer has a rational basis for opposing tobacco use that is reasonably related to the employment. | Statute has no impact on the terms and conditions of any employer-sponsored health or life insurance plans. | Criminal action: —<br>Civil action: yes.<br>Damages: yes, injunctive relief and compensatory and consequential damages. There are also civil penalties of up to $5000.<br>Costs and attorneys' fees: yes.<br>Prerequisites to civil action: action must be brought within one year. | N.J. Rev. Stat. Ann. §§ 34:6B-1 *et seq.* |
| NM | Use of tobacco products: yes.<br>Use of alcohol: —<br>Use of "lawful products": —<br>Other: — | • Failure to comply with workplace smoking policy.<br>• If smoking threatens an employer's legitimate conflict of interest policy designed to protect trade secrets, proprietary information, or other proprietary interests.<br>• If nonuse is bona fide occupational qualification. | State has no statutory requirements. | Criminal action: —<br>Civil action: yes.<br>Damages: all wages due up to the date of judgment.<br>Costs and attorneys' fees: yes.<br>Prerequisites to civil action: — | N.M. Stat. Ann. §§ 50-11-1 *et seq.* |
| NY | Use of tobacco products: —<br>Use of alcohol: —<br>Use of "lawful products": —<br>Other: lawful political activities, legal use of consumable products, recreational activities occurring off the employer's premises, and membership in a union. See Exhibit 7.7-1 for coverage of dating and cohabitation. | • If nonuse is bona fide occupational qualification.<br>• If use constitutes conflict of interest.<br>• If violation of a substance or alcohol abuse policy, violation of a collective bargaining agreement.<br>• If use results in habitually poor performance. | Differentiation between employees based on legal use of consumable products or recreational activities is permitted if the rates reflect actual price differences and the employees are given notice of the rates. | Criminal action: —<br>Civil action: yes, by employee or attorney general.<br>Damages: equitable relief and other damages in a suit by employee; $500 in civil fine in suit by attorney general.<br>Costs and attorneys' fees: —<br>Prerequisites to civil action: — | N.Y. Lab. Law § 201-d. |
| NC | Use of tobacco products: —<br>Use of alcohol: —<br>Use of "lawful products": covers only lawful use.<br>Other: — | • If employee's job performance is affected.<br>• If nonuse is bona fide occupational qualification and fundamental objectives of organization. If failure to comply with workplace substance abuse program. | Differentiation between employees based on lawful use of lawful products is permitted if the rates reflect actual price differences, the employees are given notice of the rates, and the employer contributes an equal amount on behalf of each employee. | Criminal action: —<br>Civil action: yes, must be brought within 1 year of violation.<br>Damages: wages, benefits, reinstatement.<br>Costs and attorneys' fees: yes.<br>Prerequisites to civil action: — | N.C. Gen. Stat. § 95-28.2. |
| ND | Use of tobacco products: —<br>Use of alcohol: —<br>Use of "lawful products": —<br>Other: lawful activity. | • Bona fide occupational qualifications.<br>• National security interests. | State has no statutory requirements. | Criminal action: —<br>Civil action: yes, employee may also file complaint with department of labor.<br>Damages: injunctive relief, back pay.<br>Costs and attorneys' fees: yes, attorney's fees.<br>Prerequisites to civil action: — | N.D. Cent. Code §§ 14-02.4-03 *et seq.* |
| OK | Use of tobacco products: yes.<br>Use of alcohol: —<br>Use of "lawful products": —<br>Other: — | • Failure to comply with a workplace smoking policy.<br>• If nonuse is bona fide occupational qualification.<br>• If use constitutes conflict of interest. | Differentiation between employees based on tobacco use is permitted if the rates reflect actual price differences. | Criminal action: —<br>Civil action: yes.<br>Damages: all lost wages and benefits.<br>Costs and attorneys' fees: —<br>Prerequisites to civil action: — | Okla. Stat. Ann. tit. 40, §§ 500 *et seq.* |

*(Table continues.)*

## Table 7.7-1 *(cont'd)*

## SUMMARY OF LAWS PROTECTING OFF-DUTY CONDUCT

**NOTE:** This table provides, in quick reference form, the information set out in more detail in Exhibit 7.7-1. Under the "Protected Conduct" column, a "yes" indicates that the statute in question specifically refers to the activity; (—) indicates that the activity is not specifically mentioned by the statute. Nevertheless, some activities that are not specifically mentioned may in fact be covered. For example, a statute stating that the use of lawful products is protected also protects the use of tobacco products, although not specifically stated. The "Exceptions to Law" column lists the instances in which an employer is allowed to discriminate on the basis of the use of the product or the activity. Some of the most common exceptions include the following: if the employee has violated a workplace policy, such as a no smoking at work policy; if the use of the product would create a conflict of interest; if use or nonuse of the product is a bona fide occupational qualification; or if the employer is a nonprofit organization whose primary purpose is to discourage the use of the product.

| | *Protected Conduct* | *Exceptions to Law* | *Insurance Requirements* | *Procedures and Remedies* | *Citation to Authority* |
|---|---|---|---|---|---|
| OR | Use of tobacco products: —<br>Use of alcohol: —<br>Use of "lawful products": yes.<br>Other: — | • If nonuse is bona fide occupational qualification.<br>• If use constitutes conflict of interest.<br>• If use violates collective bargaining agreements. | Differentiation between employees based on tobacco use is permitted if the rates reflect actual price differences. | Criminal action: yes.<br>Civil action: yes, Bureau of Labor handles enforcement.<br>Damages: yes.<br>Costs and attorneys' fees: —<br>Prerequisites to civil action: — | Or. Rev. Stat. § 659.380. |
| RI | Use of tobacco products: yes.<br>Use of alcohol: —<br>Use of "lawful products": —<br>Other: — | If employer is a nonprofit organization with a primary purpose of discouraging the use of tobacco products by the general public. | State has no statutory requirements. | Criminal action: —<br>Civil action: yes.<br>Damages: treble damages, injunctive relief.<br>Costs and attorneys' fees: yes.<br>Prerequisites to civil action: — | R.I. Gen. Laws §§ 23-20.7-1–23-20.7-7. |
| SC | Use of tobacco products: yes.<br>Use of alcohol: —<br>Use of "lawful products": —<br>Other: — | State has no statutory requirements. | State has no statutory requirements. | Criminal action: —<br>Civil action: —<br>Damages: —<br>Costs and attorneys' fees: —<br>Prerequisites to civil action: — | S.C. Code Ann. § 41-1-85. |
| SD | Use of tobacco products: yes.<br>Use of alcohol: —<br>Use of "lawful products": —<br>Other: — | • If nonuse is a bona fide occupational qualification.<br>• If use constitutes a conflict of interest.<br>• If employee is full-time firefighter. | Differentiation in health or life insurance policies between employees based on tobacco use is permitted. | Criminal action: —<br>Civil action: yes.<br>Damages: all wages and benefits due up to the date of judgment.<br>Costs and attorneys' fees: —<br>Prerequisites to civil action: — | S.D. Codified Laws § 60-4-11. |
| TN | Use of tobacco products: —<br>Use of alcohol: —<br>Use of "lawful products": —<br>Other: "Use of an agricultural product not regulated by the Alcoholic Beverage Commission and not otherwise proscribed by law." | Failure to comply with workplace policy. | State has no statutory requirements. | Criminal action: —<br>Civil action: not specifically authorized, but see Exhibit 7.7-1.<br>Damages: —<br>Costs and attorneys' fees: —<br>Prerequisites to civil action: — | Tenn. Code Ann. § 50-1-304. |

| | | | | | |
|---|---|---|---|---|---|
| VA | Use of tobacco products: yes.<br>Use of alcohol: —<br>Use of "lawful products": —<br>Other: — | State has no statutory requirements. | State has no statutory requirements. | Criminal action: —<br>Civil action: —<br>Damages: —<br>Costs and attorneys' fees: —<br>Prerequisites to civil action: — | Va. Code Ann. § 15.2-1504. |
| WV | Use of tobacco products: yes.<br>Use of alcohol: —<br>Use of "lawful products": —<br>Other: — | Nonprofit employers who have a primary objective of discouraging use of tobacco products by the general public. | Differentiation in health or life insurance policies between employees based on tobacco use is permitted and different premium rates charged to employees reflect actual differential costs to employer. | Criminal action: —<br>Civil action: —<br>Damages: —<br>Costs and attorneys' fees: —<br>Prerequisites to civil action: — | W. Va. Code § 21-3-19. |
| WI | Use of tobacco products: —<br>Use of alcohol: —<br>Use of "lawful products": yes.<br>Other: — | • If nonuse is bona fide occupational qualification.<br>• If use constitutes conflict of interest.<br>• If employee's job performance is affected.<br>• If employer is a nonprofit organization whose primary purpose is to discourage use.<br>• If employee is firefighter who smokes off-duty. | Differentiation in insurance policies between employees based on use of a lawful product is permitted. Different premium rates charged to employees reflect actual differential costs to the employer; employees are given notice of the rates. | Criminal action: —<br>Civil action: yes, by labor department.<br>Damages: reinstatement and compensation.<br>Costs and attorneys' fees: —<br>Prerequisites to civil action: Employee must file administrative action with labor department; labor department will bring the action. | Wis. Stat. Ann. §§ 111.321, 111.35. |
| WY | Use of tobacco products: yes.<br>Use of alcohol: —<br>Use of "lawful products": —<br>Other: — | Bona fide occupational qualifications. | Differentiation in insurance policies between employees based on tobacco use is permitted and different premium rates charged to employees reflect actual differential costs to employer and employees are given notice of the rates. | Criminal action: —<br>Civil action: yes, employee may bring action under fair employment statute.<br>Damages: back pay and injunctive relief.<br>Costs and attorneys' fees: —<br>Prerequisites to civil action: — | Wyo. Stat. Ann. § 27-9-105. |

## Exhibit 7.7-1

## DETAILED COVERAGE OF STATUTES THAT PROHIBIT DISCRIMINATION BASED ON OFF-DUTY CONDUCT

### ARIZONA

**Acts Prohibited.** State employers may not discriminate against employees or other persons on the basis of use or nonuse of tobacco products.

**When Discrimination Is Permitted.** State has no statutory requirements.

**Insurance Requirements.** State has no statutory requirements.

**Procedures and Remedies.** Employee has the right to be represented by an employee association with respect to a grievance related to smoking. A violation of the law is a petty offense.

**Citations to Authority.** Ariz. Rev. Stat. Ann. § 36-601.02.

### COLORADO

**Acts Prohibited.** An employer may not terminate an employee based on the employee's lawful activities (including marriage and plans to marry) that are off-duty and off the employer's premises.

**When Discrimination Is Permitted.** If the activity affects a bona fide occupational qualification of the employee's job or creates a conflict of interest related to the employer's business.

**Insurance Requirements.** State has no statutory requirements.

**Procedures and Remedies.** An employee may institute an individual civil suit to recover wages and benefits and may also be awarded costs and attorneys' fees. An employee must mitigate his or her damages.

**Citations to Authority.** Colo. Rev. Stat. §§ 24-34-401 *et seq.*

### CONNECTICUT

**Acts Prohibited.** An employer may not fail or refuse to hire, or discharge or otherwise discriminate against any person with respect to compensation, terms, conditions, or privileges of employment because the person uses or does not use tobacco outside the course of employment. It is also unlawful to require as a condition of employment that any employee or applicant abstain from smoking or using tobacco products outside the course of employment.

**When Discrimination Is Permitted.** The statute does not apply to a nonprofit employer that has as one of its primary objectives discouraging the use of tobacco products by the general public, or to municipal hiring practices involving paid firefighters and police officers.

**Insurance Requirements.** State has no statutory requirements.

**Procedures and Remedies.** Employers who violate the workplace smoking statutes are guilty of an (unspecified) infraction. No private cause of action is specifically set out in the statute.

**Citations to Authority.** Conn. Gen. Stat. Ann. § 31-40s.

### DISTRICT OF COLUMBIA

**Acts Prohibited.** No employer may discharge, refuse to hire or otherwise discriminate against any employee with respect to any condition of employment on the basis of use of tobacco or tobacco products.

**When Discrimination Is Permitted.** An employer may establish workplace smoking restrictions that are required or permitted by law and may establish tobacco use restrictions that constitute bona fide occupational qualifications.

**Insurance Requirements.** State has no statutory requirements.

**Procedures and Remedies.** Employees and applicants for employment have a private cause of action and may recover all damages, including lost or back wages. At the court's discretion, the prevailing party in such an action may recover attorneys' fees as part of costs. Prior to commencing a civil action, an employee or applicant for employment must exhaust all grievance procedures or other remedies.

**Citations to Authority.** D.C. Code. Ann. § 6-913.3.

### ILLINOIS

**Acts Prohibited.** An employer may not discriminate against an employee based on the employee's lawful use of lawful products during nonworking hours and off the premises of the employer.

**When Discrimination Is Permitted.** If the employer is an organization with the primary purpose of discouraging the use of a lawful product, or if the use of the product interferes with the employee's job performance.

**Insurance Requirements.** For insurance purposes, differentiation between employees based on use or nonuse of lawful products during nonworking hours is permitted if the different rates charged employees reflect actual price differences and the employer gives the employees notice of the rates.

**Procedures and Remedies.** An aggrieved employee may file a complaint with an administrative department and may institute an individual action if no resolution is reached. A prevailing employee is entitled to actual damages and costs.

**Citations to Authority.** 820 ILCS 55/1 *et seq.*

### INDIANA

**Acts Prohibited.** An employer may not fail or refuse to hire, or discharge or otherwise discriminate against any person with respect to compensation, terms, conditions, or privileges of employment because the person uses tobacco products outside the course of employment. It is also unlawful to require as a condition of employment that any employee or applicant abstain from smoking or using tobacco products outside the course of employment.

**When Discrimination Is Permitted.** Statute does not apply to churches or religious organizations.

**Insurance Requirements.** State has no statutory requirements.

**Procedures and Remedies.** An aggrieved employee or prospective employee may bring a civil action against the employer to enforce the statute. Available damages include lost wages and benefits, costs, and reasonable attorneys' fees.

**Citations to Authority.** Ind. Code Ann. §§ 22-5-4-1 *et seq.*

### KENTUCKY

**Acts Prohibited.** An employer may not fail or refuse to hire, or discharge or otherwise discriminate against any person with respect to compensation, terms, conditions, or privileges of employment because the person is a smoker or a nonsmoker. It is also unlawful to require as a condition of employment that any employee or applicant abstain from smoking or using tobacco products outside the course of employment.

**When Discrimination Is Permitted.** If an employee fails to comply with any workplace policy concerning smoking, an employer may discipline or discharge that employee.

**Insurance Requirements.** State has no statutory requirements.

**Procedures and Remedies.** An aggrieved employee has recourse to the same procedures and remedies available to any victim of employment discrimination in the state. (See Table 2.3-1 Part A and Part B for Kentucky employment discrimination procedures and remedies.)

**Citations to Authority.** Ky. Rev. Stat. Ann. § 344.040.

### LOUISIANA

**Acts Prohibited.** An employer may not fail or refuse to hire, or discharge or otherwise discriminate against any person with respect to compensation, terms, conditions, or privileges of employment because the person is a smoker or a nonsmoker. It is also unlawful to require as a condition of employment that any employee or applicant abstain from smoking or using tobacco products outside the course of employment.

**When Discrimination Is Permitted.** If an employee fails to comply with any workplace policy concerning smoking, an employer may discipline or discharge that employee.

**Insurance Requirements.** State has no statutory requirements.

**Procedures and Remedies.** An employer who violates the provisions of this law shall be fined up to $250 for the first offense and up to $500 for any subsequent offense. No private right of action is specifically provided for in the statute.

**Citations to Authority.** La. Rev. Stat. Ann. § 23:966.

### MAINE

**Acts Prohibited.** An employer may not fail or refuse to hire, or discharge or otherwise discriminate against any person with respect to compensation, terms, conditions, or privileges of employment because the person uses tobacco products outside the course of employment. It is also unlawful to require as a condition of employment that any employee or applicant abstain from smoking or using tobacco products outside the course of employment.

**When Discrimination Is Permitted.** If an employee fails to comply with any workplace policy concerning smoking, an employer may discipline or discharge that employee. Discrimination is also permitted if smoking affects a bona fide occupational qualification or creates a conflict of interest for the employer.

**Insurance Requirements.** It is not discriminatory for an employer to have in effect a health or life insurance policy that makes distinctions concerning the type or cost of coverage based on whether the employee uses tobacco if the different rates charged to the employee reflect actual price differences to the employer.

**Procedures and Remedies.** An aggrieved employee may bring a civil suit for damages in circuit court and may be awarded all wages and benefits that have been due up to and including the date of judgment.

**Citations to Authority.** Me. Rev. Stat. Ann. tit. 26, § 597.

## MINNESOTA

**Acts Prohibited.** A private employer may not discriminate against an employee based on the employee's off-duty and off-premises use of "lawful consumable products."

**When Discrimination Is Permitted.** If the use of the products affects a bona fide occupational qualification of the employee's job, affects the employee's job performance, creates a conflict of interest related to the employer's business, or if the employee fails to comply with a program to end chemical dependency.

**Insurance Requirements.** For insurance purposes, differentiation between employees based on use or nonuse of lawful products during nonworking hours is permitted if the different rates charged employees reflect actual price differences.

**Procedures and Remedies.** An aggrieved employee may bring a civil action for wages and benefits, and may also be awarded court costs and attorneys' fees.

**Citations to Authority.** Minn. Stat. Ann. § 181.938.

## MISSISSIPPI

**Acts Prohibited.** It is unlawful for an employer to require as a condition of employment that any employee or applicant abstain from smoking or using tobacco products during nonworking hours.

**When Discrimination Is Permitted.** If an employee fails to comply during working hours with any workplace policy concerning smoking, an employer may discipline or discharge that employee.

**Insurance Requirements.** State has no statutory requirements.

**Procedures and Remedies.** An employee must bring a civil action against the employer within one year of the alleged violation. Employee may bring a civil action for wages and benefits, may seek reinstatement, and may also be awarded court costs and attorneys' fees.

**Citations to Authority.** Miss. Code Ann. §§ 71-7-23, 71-7-25, 71-7-33.

## MISSOURI

**Acts Prohibited.** An employer may not discriminate against an employee based on the employee's use of lawful alcohol or tobacco products during nonworking hours and off the premises of the employer.

**When Discrimination Is Permitted.** If the use of the lawful product interferes with the employee's job performance or the employer is an organization whose principal business is health care promotion.

**Insurance Requirements.** State has no statutory requirements.

**Procedures and Remedies.** The statute does not create a cause of action for injunctive relief, damages, or other relief.

**Citations to Authority.** Mo. Ann. Stat. § 290.145.

## MONTANA

**Acts Prohibited.** An employer may not discriminate against an employee based on the employee's legal use of a lawful product off the employer's premises during nonworking hours.

**When Discrimination Is Permitted.** If the use of a lawful product conflicts with a bona fide occupational qualification reasonably related to the employee's job, affects the employee's performance of job-related responsibilities, if the employer is a nonprofit organization whose primary objective is to discourage the use of one or more lawful products by the general public, or if the employer takes action based on the belief that its actions are permissible under a substance abuse program, professional contract, or collective bargaining agreement.

**Insurance Requirements.** For health or other insurance purposes, differentiation between employees may be made, based on their use or nonuse of a lawful product, if the distinctions reflect actuarial differences in providing employee benefits.

**Procedures and Remedies.** An employee may bring a civil action against an employer within one year of the alleged violation, and the court may require any reasonable measure to correct the discriminatory practice, including pecuniary damages and attorneys' fees. Prior to filing an action, the employee shall, within 120 days of the alleged violation, initiate any internal grievance procedure available.

**Citations to Authority.** Mont. Code Ann. §§ 39-2-313, 39-2-314.

## NEVADA

**Acts Prohibited.** An employer may not discriminate against an employee based on the employee's lawful use of any products during nonworking hours and off the premises of the employer.

**When Discrimination Is Permitted.** If the use of any product adversely affects the employee's job performance or the safety of other employees.

**Insurance Requirements.** State has no statutory requirements.

**Procedures and Remedies.** An employee may bring a civil action for wages and benefits and an order of reinstatement, and a prevailing employee may be awarded court costs and attorneys' fees.

**Citations to Authority.** Nev. Rev. Stat. Ann. § 613.333.

## NEW HAMPSHIRE

**Acts Prohibited.** It is unlawful for an employer to require as a condition of employment that any employee or applicant abstain from smoking or using tobacco products outside the course of employment.

**When Discrimination Is Permitted.** If an employee fails to comply with any workplace policy concerning smoking, an employer may discipline or discharge that employee.

**Insurance Requirements.** State has no statutory requirements.

**Procedures and Remedies.** The statute does not specifically provide for a private right of action by an aggrieved employee.

**Citations to Authority.** N.H. Rev. Stat. Ann. § 275:37-a.

## NEW JERSEY

**Acts Prohibited.** An employer shall not refuse to hire any person or take any adverse action against an employee with respect to compensation, terms, conditions, or other privileges because that person does or does not smoke or use other tobacco products.

**When Discrimination Is Permitted.** If the employer has a rational basis for opposing tobacco use that is reasonably related to the employment. Nothing in the act is to be construed to affect other laws, rules, or workplace policies concerning tobacco use on premises.

**Insurance Requirements.** Statute has no impact on the terms and conditions of any employer-sponsored health or life insurance plans, including the right of such plans to differentiate between smokers and nonsmokers with regard to the amount of any employee contributions or copayments.

**Procedures and Remedies.** Any aggrieved person may institute a civil action within one year asking for injunctive relief and compensatory and consequential damages, and the court may award attorneys' fees and costs. Also, a civil penalty may be assessed in the amount of $2,000 for the first offense and $5,000 for each subsequent offense.

**Citations to Authority.** N.J. Rev. Stat. Ann. §§ 34:6B-1 *et seq.*

## NEW MEXICO

**Acts Prohibited.** An employer may not fail or refuse to hire, or discharge or otherwise discriminate against any person with respect to compensation, terms, conditions, or privileges of employment because the person is a smoker or a nonsmoker. It is also unlawful to require as a condition of employment that any employee or applicant abstain from smoking or using tobacco products outside the course of employment.

**When Discrimination Is Permitted.** If an employee fails to comply with any workplace policy concerning smoking, an employer may discipline or discharge that employee. Also, the protection of the statute does not apply when employee smoking materially threatens an employer's legitimate conflict of interest policy reasonably designed to protect trade secrets, proprietary information, or other proprietary interests or when employee smoking relates to a bona fide occupational requirement.

**Insurance Requirements.** State has no statutory requirements.

**Procedures and Remedies.** An aggrieved employee may bring a civil suit for damages and may be awarded all wages due up to and including the date of judgment, and all court costs and reasonable attorneys' fees. Employee is required to mitigate damages.

**Citations to Authority.** N.M. Stat. Ann. §§ 50-11-1 *et seq.*

## NEW YORK

**Acts Prohibited.** An employer or employment agency may not discriminate against an employee on account of lawful political activities, legal use of consumable products, or recreational activities that occur off the employer's premises and off-duty, or an employee's membership in a union. **Note.** There is some disagreement regarding the scope of activities encompassed by this provision. *Compare State v. Wal-Mart Stores, Inc.* 207 A.D.2d 150, 621 N.Y.S.2d 158 (3d Dept. 1995) (holding that protected legal recreational activities pursued outside of work do not include a dating relationship; therefore, employer's no-dating policy did not violate the statute), *with Pasch v. Katz Media Corp.*, 1995 U.S. Dist. LEXIS (S.D.N.Y. 1995) (holding that cohabitation is protected outside recreational activity under the New York law).

**When Discrimination Is Permitted.** If the activity affects a bona fide occupational qualification of the employee's job or creates a conflict of interest related to the employer's business; if the employee violates a substance or alcohol abuse policy or collective bargaining agreement; or if the employee's actions lead to habitually poor performance. An employer may escape liability if it believed that its actions were required by law.

**Insurance Requirements.** In the provision of health or other insurance based on legal use of consumable products or recreational activities, an employer may differentiate between employees if the difference in rates reflects an actual price difference and the employer gives the employees notice of the rate differences.

**Procedures and Remedies.** An aggrieved employee may institute an action for equitable relief and damages, or the attorney general may bring an action seeking injunctive relief and civil penalties of up to $500.

**Citations to Authority.** N.Y. Lab. Law § 201-d.

### NORTH CAROLINA

**Acts Prohibited.** An employer may not discriminate against an employee based on the employee's lawful use of lawful products during nonworking hours and off the premises of the employer.

**When Discrimination Is Permitted.** If the use of a lawful product adversely affects the employee's job performance, or affects a bona fide occupational qualification of the employee's job, or relates to the fundamental objectives of the employer's organization. An employer may take adverse action if an employee fails to comply with the employer's substance abuse prevention program.

**Insurance Requirements.** For insurance purposes, differentiation between employees based on use or nonuse of lawful products during nonworking hours is permitted if the different rates charged employees reflect actual price differences, the employer gives the employee notice of the rates, and the employer contributes an equal amount on behalf of each employee.

**Procedures and Remedies.** An employee may bring a civil action within 1 year of violation for wages and benefits and an order of reinstatement; a prevailing employee may be awarded court costs and attorneys' fees.

**Citations to Authority.** N.C. Gen. Stat. § 95-28.2.

### NORTH DAKOTA

**Acts Prohibited.** An employer may not discriminate against an employee for participation in a lawful activity that is off the employer's premises and off-duty.

**When Discrimination Is Permitted.** If the activity affects a bona fide occupational qualification of the employee's job or affects a national security interest.

**Insurance Requirements.** State has no statutory provisions.

**Procedures and Remedies.** An employee may bring an individual court action or may file a complaint with the department of labor. A prevailing employee is entitled to injunctive relief, backpay (minus mitigated damages), and reasonable attorneys' fees.

**Citations to Authority.** N.D. Cent. Code §§ 14-02.4-03 *et seq.*

### OKLAHOMA

**Acts Prohibited.** An employer may not discharge or otherwise discriminate against any person with respect to compensation, terms, conditions, or privileges of employment because the person is a nonsmoker or smokes or uses tobacco products outside the course of employment. It is also unlawful to require as a condition of employment that any employee or applicant abstain from smoking or using tobacco products during nonworking hours.

**When Discrimination Is Permitted.** If an employee fails to comply with any workplace policy concerning smoking, an employer may discipline or discharge that employee. Discrimination is also permitted if smoking affects a bona fide occupational qualification or creates a conflict of interest for the employer.

**Insurance Requirements.** It is not discriminatory for an employer to have in effect a health or life insurance policy that makes distinctions for the type or cost of coverage based on whether the employee uses tobacco if the different rates charged to the employee reflect actual price differences to the employer.

**Procedures and Remedies.** The sole remedy for an aggrieved employee is a civil suit for damages including all wages and benefits of which the employee has been deprived by reason of the violation.

**Citations to Authority.** Okla. Stat. Ann. tit. 40, §§ 500 *et seq.*

### OREGON

**Acts Prohibited.** It is a discriminatory employment practice for any employer to require as a condition of employment that any employee or prospective employee refrain from using "lawful products" off the premises of the employer during nonworking hours.

**When Discrimination Is Permitted.** If discrimination on the basis of smoking relates to a bona fide occupational requirement or is necessary to avoid a conflict of interest or the appearance of a conflict of interest. The statute also is inapplicable when a collective bargaining agreement prohibits the off-duty use of any lawful product.

**Insurance Requirements.** It is not discriminatory for an employer to have in effect a health or life insurance policy that makes distinctions for the type or cost of coverage based on whether the employee uses tobacco, as long as the differences in charges to employees reflect actual price differences to employers.

**Procedures and Remedies.** The statute is enforced by the Commissioner of the Bureau of Labor. Violators are subject to civil and criminal remedies and penalties.

**Citations to Authority.** Or. Rev. Stat. § 659.380.

### RHODE ISLAND

**Acts Prohibited.** An employer or its agent shall not require as a condition of employment that any employee or prospective employee refrain from smoking or using tobacco products outside the course of his or her employment, or otherwise discriminate against any individual with respect to the terms of his or her employment for smoking or using tobacco products.

**When Discrimination Is Permitted.** Any employer that is a nonprofit organization that, as one of its primary purposes or objectives, discourages the use of tobacco products by the general public is exempt from the nondiscrimination requirement.

**Insurance Requirements.** State has no statutory requirements.

**Procedures and Remedies.** Person discriminated against can bring civil action, where court can award three times actual damages to employee, provide injunctive relief, and award fees and costs to the prevailing plaintiff.

**Citations to Authority.** R.I. Gen. Laws § 23-20.7-1–23-20.7-7.

### SOUTH CAROLINA

**Acts Prohibited.** The use of tobacco products outside the workplace must not be the basis of personnel action, including but not limited to, employment, termination, demotion, or promotion of an employee.

**When Discrimination Is Permitted.** State has no statutory requirements.

**Insurance Requirements.** State has no statutory requirements.

**Procedures and Remedies.** No private cause of action is specifically set out in the statute.

**Citations to Authority.** S.C. Code Ann. § 41-1-85.

### SOUTH DAKOTA

**Acts Prohibited.** It is a discriminatory employment practice for an employer to discharge an employee due to that employee's engaging in any use of tobacco products off the premises of the employer during nonworking hours.

**When Discrimination Is Permitted.** If discrimination on the basis of smoking relates to a bona fide occupational requirement or is necessary to avoid a conflict of interest or the appearance of a conflict of interest. Statute does not apply to full-time firefighters.

**Insurance Requirements.** It is not discriminatory for an employer to have in effect a health or life insurance policy that makes distinctions for the type or cost of coverage based on whether the employee uses tobacco.

**Procedures and Remedies.** An aggrieved employee may bring a civil suit for damages in circuit court and may be awarded all wages and benefits that have been due up to and including the date of judgment.

**Citations to Authority.** S.D. Codified Laws Ann. § 60-4-11.

### TENNESSEE

**Acts Prohibited.** No employee shall be discharged or terminated solely for participating or engaging in the use of an agricultural product not regulated by the Alcoholic Beverage Commission that is not otherwise proscribed by law if such employee participates or engages in such activity during the times when the employee is off-duty.

**When Discrimination Is Permitted.** While at work, the employee must use such products in compliance with employer policies or may face discharge.

**Insurance Requirements.** State has no statutory requirements.

**Procedures and Remedies.** Although an employee suit for discharge under the statute is not specifically authorized, a provision of the statute warns that employees who file frivolous lawsuits claiming that they were discharged in retaliation for off-duty activity shall be charged with the other parties' costs, including reasonable attorneys' fees.

**Citations to Authority.** Tenn. Code Ann. § 50-1-304.

### VIRGINIA

**Acts Prohibited.** No employee or applicant for employment with the Commonwealth or any of its political subdivisions shall be required to smoke or use tobacco products on the job, or to abstain from smoking or using tobacco products outside the course of employment.

**When Discrimination Is Permitted.** State has no statutory requirements.

**Insurance Requirements.** State has no statutory requirements.

**Procedures and Remedies.** State has no statutory requirements.

**Citations to Authority.** Va. Code Ann. § 15.2-1504.

## WEST VIRGINIA

**Acts Prohibited.** It is unlawful for an employer to discriminate against a person solely because that person uses tobacco products off the premises of the employer during nonworking hours.

**When Discrimination Is Permitted.** The statute does not apply to a nonprofit employer that has as one of its primary objectives discouraging the use of tobacco products by the general public.

**Insurance Requirements.** It is not discriminatory for an employer to have in effect a health, disability, or life insurance policy that makes distinctions between employees for type or price of coverage based on the employee's use of tobacco. Any differential premium rates charged to employees must reflect actual differential costs to the employer.

**Procedures and Remedies.** State has no statutory requirements.

**Citations to Authority.** W.Va. Code § 21-3-19.

## WISCONSIN

**Acts Prohibited.** An employer may not discriminate against an employee based on the employee's use or nonuse of lawful products during nonworking hours and off the premises of the employer.

**When Discrimination Is Permitted.** If the use of lawful products affects a bona fide occupational qualification of the employee's job, creates a conflict of interest, affects the employee's job performance, or if the employer is an organization whose primary purpose is to encourage or discourage the use of a lawful product. It is not discrimination to refuse to hire a firefighter who smokes tobacco off-duty and off-premises.

**Insurance Requirements.** For insurance purposes, differentiation between employees based on use or nonuse of lawful products during nonworking hours is permitted if the different rates charged employees reflect actual price differences and the employer gives the employee notice of the rates.

**Procedures and Remedies.** No private right of action is created by the statute. An employee files an administrative complaint and, if no conciliation can be reached with the employer, the labor department brings an action for reinstatement or compensation on the employee's behalf.

**Citations to Authority.** Wis. Stat. Ann. §§ 111.321, 111.35.

## WYOMING

**Acts Prohibited.** An employer may not discriminate on the basis of an employee's or prospective employee's use or nonuse of tobacco products outside the course of employment.

**When Discrimination Is Permitted.** If nonuse of tobacco is a bona fide occupational qualification of the job.

**Insurance Requirements.** For insurance purposes, differentiation between employees based on use or nonuse of tobacco is permitted if the different rates charged to employees reflect actual price differences and the employer gives the employees notice of the rates.

**Procedures and Remedies.** An aggrieved employee may bring action under the state fair employment statute, and may recover appropriate relief, including backpay and injunctive relief.

**Citations to Authority.** Wyo. Stat. § 27-9-105.

# § 7.8 Policy Guidance for Workplace Privacy Issues

## [a] Drug Testing

According to the American Management Association, 81 percent of all major corporations now test employees or new hires for drug use. That figure is almost 4 times the rate of testing 10 years ago. Moreover, periodic or random drug testing of employees has increased by over 1,200 percent in the same time period. The following text provides an employer who is considering implementing a drug testing program with guidelines concerning the issues that should be addressed before any program is begun. Employers who currently have drug testing programs in place may use these guidelines to review and possibly improve existing programs.

As an initial step, before any testing measures are considered, an employer must first implement a substance abuse policy. It may be a good idea to make the substance abuse policy part of an overall employee health policy addressing areas such as physical fitness, diet, stress management, preventive medicine, and any other physical or mental health concerns.

Before implementing a substance abuse policy, the employer should consult internally. Management, labor, and medical staff should be consulted in implementing a policy. Various goals are achieved by internal consultation, including employee awareness and cooperation and early identification of employee needs and concerns.

If the employer's workforce is unionized, the employer should consult with the union in implementing a substance abuse policy. The National Labor Relations Board (NLRB) has ruled that with respect to current employees, compulsory drug testing amounts to a substantial change in the terms and conditions of employment and is therefore subject to mandatory bargaining under the National Labor Relations Act. Accordingly, an employer may not implement new rules or change prior policies regarding drug testing that affect current employees without first submitting the matter to collective bargaining. The NLRB has also ruled that a union's waiver of its right to bargain over such testing must be clear and unmistakable, and thus the right is not waived merely because, for instance, the union has acquiesced in the employer's unilateral implementation of a requirement that new employees undergo testing at the time of hire. In contrast, in a separate decision, the NLRB ruled that an employer is not required to enter into collective bargaining before implementing a testing requirement for job applicants. It was determined that because preemployment drug testing does not vitally affect the interests of current employees, it is not within the scope of required bargaining under the National Labor Relations Act.

The employer should also be sure to check any state or local laws regulating drug testing. Some states have regulations that cover who may be tested, when testing can occur, and what procedures are to be utilized.

If the employer needs further assistance in developing a substance abuse policy, the National Institute on Drug Abuse (NIDA) is a helpful source.[1] Finally, the

**§ 7.8**

1. The NIDA may be contacted at the following address: The National Institute on Drug Abuse, 5600 Fishers Lane, Rockville, MD 20857.

employer should consult an attorney before implementing the policy.

A substance abuse policy should address the following issues:

- What is prohibited?
- When and where do the prohibitions apply?
- How will the policy be enforced?
- What discipline is appropriate?
- What rehabilitation will be provided?

These issues are more fully discussed in subsequent sections. Suggested provisions of substance abuse policies, including drug testing provisions, are also provided.

It is important for employers to provide their employees and supervisors with *adequate notice* of the provisions of the substance abuse policy and of any enforcement procedures and discipline that may result from implementation of the policy. Such notice is crucial in order to protect employee morale, as well as to forewarn employees about what level of privacy they might expect at work. Notice may be provided in one or more of the following ways:

- Publish provisions of policy in employee handbook.
- Post provisions of policy on bulletin board.
- Send employees personal letters explaining policy.
- Include a copy of policy with employee paychecks.
- Conduct employee meetings and/or training sessions to familiarize employees with policy and answer employee questions concerning the policy.

### What should the substance abuse policy prohibit, and when and where should its provisions apply?

Employers should formulate a substance abuse policy to reflect their needs and the needs of their employees. It is important to set out the purposes of such a policy. For example, the policy might state that its purposes are as follows:

- ☐ To establish and maintain a safe and healthy work environment for all employees;
- ☐ To reduce absenteeism and tardiness and to improve employee productivity;
- ☐ To improve the reputation of the company and its employees within the community and the industry in general;
- ☐ To reduce the number of accidental injuries to employees or employer property; and
- ☐ To provide rehabilitation for any employee who desires or needs it.

Once the purposes of the policy are set out, the employer must decide what is to be prohibited and when and where the prohibitions will apply. A typical policy should include the following provisions:

- ☐ Prohibit all employees from being under the influence of alcohol or illegal drugs during working hours;
- ☐ Provide that no alcoholic beverage will be brought or consumed on company premises, except in connection with company-authorized events;
- ☐ Provide that no prescription drug will be brought on company premises by any person other than the one for whom it is prescribed;
- ☐ Prohibit the use, sale, possession, transfer, or purchase of illegal drugs on company property or while performing company business;
- ☐ Provide that any employee whose off-duty abuse of alcohol or illegal or prescription drugs results in excessive absenteeism or tardiness or is the cause of accidents or poor work performance will be referred for rehabilitation and will face termination if he or she refuses; and
- ☐ Provide that any employee who commits an unlawful act on or off company premises or whose conduct discredits the employer in any way will be subject to discipline, including termination.

It is always advisable to define the terms that are used in a substance abuse policy. For example, the policy may:

- ☐ Define an alcoholic beverage as any beverage that may be legally sold and consumed and has an alcoholic content in excess of 3 percent by volume;
- ☐ Define a drug as any substance other than alcohol capable of altering an individual's mood, perception, pain level, or judgment;
- ☐ Define a prescription drug as any substance prescribed for individual consumption by a licensed medical practitioner; and
- ☐ Define an illegal drug as any drug or controlled substance the use, possession, or sale of which is prohibited by law.

As noted below, the employer will have to formulate provisions relating to enforcement, punishment, and rehabilitation.

## How should the substance abuse policy be enforced?

Of course, a primary method of enforcement of a substance abuse policy is drug testing. In implementing a drug testing policy, the employer should keep the following considerations in mind:

1. *Testing of employees should not be random or without notice.* As a general rule, drug testing of employees should be required only when the employer has cause to believe that it is necessary. The following are situations where drug and alcohol testing is generally viewed as appropriate:

   - Preemployment screening of all job applicants;
   - After work-related employee accidents;
   - When employee is seen using illegal substance on the job; and
   - When poor performance indicates substance abuse.

Random testing of employees should generally be avoided, since it is viewed by employees, and sometimes by arbitrators or the courts, as an unnecessary and illegal invasion of privacy. An exception to this general rule exists for employers involved in particularly sensitive areas or those involved in activities that could potentially endanger the public.

Retesting should be considered for employees and job applicants who initially test positive in order to confirm the results of the initial test. Retesting should also be considered for employees who have tested positive in the past.

2. *Procedures for testing should be established.* In implementing a drug testing policy, employers should establish procedures for carrying out the tests themselves. Some considerations include:

   - Procedures for taking samples of blood or urine
   - Having the employee present at all possible times
   - Sealing sample containers in the employee's presence
   - Establishing a "chain of custody" in order to prevent tampering

3. *A testing laboratory should be contacted.* In order to actually complete the testing, the employer must:

   - Chose a laboratory on the basis of its experience, reputation, accuracy, and price;
   - Determine the drugs for which employees will be tested—employers most commonly test for cocaine, marijuana, quaaludes, amphetamines, barbiturates, opiates, PCP, methadone, librium, valium, and alcohol; and
   - Determine which types of tests to conduct—common tests include thin-layer chromatography, enzyme immunoassay, radio-immunoassay, and gas chromatography.

4. *A documentation system should be established.* An employer should develop an "incident report form" for supervisors, and this form should be used to record any substance abuse on the job. Further, documentation should be retained for all testing done on applicants or employees. This documentation should be kept separate from the personnel file for privacy reasons.

## What discipline is appropriate?

Discipline of employees is important in order to enforce the substance abuse policy properly. Discipline is a sensitive matter, and the employer should carefully consider appropriate disciplinary actions for violations of the policy and fully inform employees (via the employee handbook and methods discussed above) in advance as to what such disciplinary actions will be. The employer should consider whether and to what extent to discipline employees for (1) testing positive for drug or alcohol use; (2) refusing to take a drug test; or (3) refusing to use rehabilitation options.

The employer should also consider whether (1) to punish illegal drug use more severely than alcohol use; (2) to punish on-premises users more severely; (3) the employee's past record of abuse will be relevant; (4) the employee's length of service will be relevant; and (5) the employee's willingness to undergo rehabilitation will be relevant. The employer should make it clear that the employee is being disciplined for work-related problems that occur as a result of substance abuse (e.g., increased absenteeism, lack of concentration, and the like). The employer should avoid taking disciplinary action based on a chemical dependency alone.

## What rehabilitation should be provided?

Employee rehabilitation is an important objective of any substance abuse policy. Most employers agree that in the long run, treatment is less costly than discharge when an employee's drug or alcohol problem is discovered. By encouraging treatment, the employer can work with the employee to solve the problem and continue the employment relationship, rather than terminating the employee and hiring someone new and untrained.

Employee rehabilitation can occur either through an employer-sponsored program or through an outside rehabilitation service. Rehabilitation should be combined with progressive disciplinary action to ensure that employees take seriously the need to seek and complete rehabilitation.

**Developing an Employee Assistance Plan.** An employee assistance program (EAP) is a job-based program designed to assist employees whose performance level at work is being adversely affected by drug abuse or other personal problems. An EAP provides for assessment of employee problems or concerns and referral to appropriate services/resources for resolution. Many employers are turning to EAPs to help combat substance abuse problems and other emotional problems. EAPs can help save money in terms of less absenteeism, fewer accidents, lower turnover of workforce, savings in workers' compensation claims, decreased use of medical and insurance benefits, and lower employee replacement costs. Employee problems may be related to alcohol or other drug abuse, marital difficulties, financial crises, or legal problems, among others. EAPs help identify and resolve employees' problems by providing various forms of confidential short-term counseling, referral, and follow-up services.

Almost any company, regardless of size, can provide its employees the services of an EAP. Employers can provide EAP services in-house or contract with outside providers. Smaller companies may join with other companies in a cooperative arrangement to start an EAP for its employees. EAP consortiums allow smaller companies to enjoy the benefits and services of an EAP at prices typically available only to larger companies.

A key factor in the success of an EAP is training supervisors and educating employees about the objectives of the program. Supervisors need to understand the company's drug policy and supervisors' role in implementing and enforcing the plan. Supervisors need to understand the effects of substance abuse in the workplace and how to refer those suspected of having a substance abuse problem to those who are qualified to make a diagnosis and offer assistance. Although the role of supervisors in making EAP referrals is important, it should be noted that EAPs are more effective at reducing costs when employees refer themselves to counseling rather than being referred by a supervisor. Therefore, employees need to understand how the EAP works and how they can get help for substance abuse problems.

For an EAP to be effective, the availability of services must be continually communicated to employees and supervisors. An EAP will be more effective if the services it provides to employees are confidential. Employees are more likely to use the plan if they feel they can freely communicate without fear that information will be disclosed to the employer. The plan will be most effective in achieving the desired results if employees are referred to the EAP as soon as the problem is detected.

An EAP can be implemented in a number of ways. An employer can, for example, simply insert language similar to the following in an employee handbook or other document explaining employee benefits:

**Employee Assistance Program**

The company offers an employee assistance program (EAP) benefit for employees and their dependents. The EAP provides confidential assessment, referral, and short-term counseling for employees who need or request it. If an EAP referral to a treatment provider outside the EAP is necessary, costs may be covered by the employee's medical insurance, but the costs of such outside services are the employee's responsibility.

For employers who contract with outside vendors to administer the EAP, a policy similar to the following can be used:

**Employee Assistance Program**

Policy Statement

The goals of the company's employee assistance program (EAP) are to motivate employees to seek help with personal problems, and to improve, maintain, or restore employee productivity through early identification and assistance with these problems.

The Company has contracted with EAP Vendor to provide comprehensive employee assistance services to employees and their immediate family members. EAP Vendor provides a confidential evaluation, short-term counseling, and referral services providing assistance to those experiencing problems that may affect job performance or family life.

Use of Employee Assistance Plan

1. Employees and dependents are eligible to make use of the EAP.

2. Employees may contact the EAP directly at 999-9999 for assistance. Employees with problems are especially encouraged to seek help before health or job performance is seriously affected. In addition to self-referrals, an employee may utilize the program through a management referral.

3. All contacts with the EAP are confidential. No information specific to any employee will be released without the employee's written consent.

4. When an employee's job performance or attendance becomes unsatisfactory, and the employee has been unable to correct the job problems with normal supervisory assistance, the supervisor, in consultation with the Personnel Department, may formally recommend that the employee utilize the EAP.

5. Use of the EAP is voluntary. Acceptable job performance and attendance remain the employee's responsibility whether or not he or she chooses to seek assistance from the EAP.

6. Leave procedures will apply to treatment for psychological or alcohol and drug problems on the same basis as they apply to other illnesses and health problems.

7. If an EAP referral to a treatment provider outside the EAP is necessary, costs may be covered by the employee's medical insurance, but the costs of such outside services are the employee's responsibility.

## What potential problems are posed by employer drug testing?

Employers should remember that drug testing is not a foolproof method of enforcement of a substance abuse policy. There are some inherent technical problems in testing, including the possibility of false positives or certain drug or chemical interactions that may skew results. Further, testing can lead to higher employment costs related to test implementations, employee morale problems, and increased employee civil rights and tort litigation. All of these possibilities should be considered prior to implementation of any testing.

The potential application of the Americans With Disabilities Act (ADA) should also be kept in mind. The ADA applies to all employers with 15 or more employees. It requires employers to attempt to accommodate persons with disabilities, unless accommodation would result in an undue hardship.

The ADA expressly permits an employer to deny employment opportunities to an individual because he or she is currently engaging in the use of illegal drugs; however, the Act prohibits discrimination against a person who has successfully completed drug rehabilitation or who is participating in a supervised or professionally recognized self-help drug rehabilitation program and who is no longer engaging in the illegal use of drugs. The Act also protects from discrimination a person who is erroneously regarded as being a current drug user but who is in fact not using drugs. The ADA permits employers to administer tests for illegal drug use to applicants and employees, and it allows employers to take adverse action based on drug test results. It is conceivable, however, that a person who tests positive for drug use may try to challenge the accuracy of the results in an effort to show that he or she was erroneously regarded as a current user of illegal drugs.

Most states have enacted laws that prohibit disability discrimination in employment by both private and public employers. Although the scope of coverage varies from state to state, many of these laws apply to alcoholics and drug users, and they may prohibit adverse employment decisions based solely on positive drug test results. It is therefore always advisable to consult the laws of each state, and to consult with an attorney, before implementing any drug testing policy.

Another potential problem that employers should consider is that the implementation of a drug testing policy may alter the general rule that the employment relationship is "at will." It has been held that an employer's implementation of a drug testing policy and procedures relating to the policy created a limited exception to the employment-at-will rule.[2]

In *Qualls,* the employer terminated an employee who allegedly interfered with the administration of a drug test. However, the rules and procedures that the employer established pertaining to the drug testing policy were not followed in terminating the employee. The employer argued that because the employment relationship was at-will, the employee could be terminated whether or not she had actually interfered with the test. The court disagreed, holding that the creation of the policy and procedures for drug testing, and the publication of the same in the employee handbook, mandated that an employee be terminated for alleged violation of the drug policy *only in accordance with such policy.*

Employers should be aware that drug testing policies and procedures must be followed not only by employees but also by employers.

2. Qualls v. Hickory Springs Manufacturing Co., 8 BNA IER Cas. 834 (8th Cir. 1993).

### Are there alternative methods of employee substance abuse control?

Employers might wish to consider methods other than (or in addition to) drug testing to enforce a substance abuse policy. These methods include:

1. On-premises searches of employees or employee spaces;
2. Video surveillance;
3. Polygraph testing (see Table 7.2-1); or
4. Undercover operatives.

Care should always be taken before employing any of these methods in order to avoid intruding on employee privacy or creating employee morale problems. At the very least, employees should be informed via the employee handbook before searches or polygraph tests are undertaken.

## [b] Electronic Monitoring

As the discussion in § 7.6 shows, communications transmitted over companywide computer networks, such as E-mail and voice mail, raise some new concerns for employers and human resources professionals. While employers find it useful to engage in electronic monitoring of computer data and computerized communications for the purposes of checking on the status of projects, assessing employee productivity for performance evaluations, and investigating problems in the workplace, they realize that such monitoring is not without potential problems. Surreptitious monitoring can create stress and low morale among employees, which can result in higher health care costs and increased turnover. In addition, there is the risk of litigation and potential exposure to damages if employees should bring civil actions, claiming that their employers violated their right to privacy by monitoring their electronic communications. (See § 7.6[b] for discussion of a number of recent cases.)

At present, federal law does not appear to prohibit electronic monitoring in the workplace. Although the Electronic Communications Privacy Act of 1986 includes electronically transmitted information within the prohibitions of federal wiretap laws, the business-extension and prior-consent exceptions allow workplace monitoring by employers under certain conditions.[3]

In 1993, a bill was proposed by Senator Paul Simon (D.-Ill.) that would explicitly extend the federal law to regulate electronic monitoring in the workplace by employers. Briefly summarized, the bill would require an employer to provide general notice to current and prospective employees that the employer engages in workplace monitoring and specific written notice to those employees who would be subjected to monitoring. In addition, random monitoring would be significantly restricted. For further discussion of the proposed legislation, see § 7.6[b].

As a result of the uncertainty and fluidity of the law in this area, electronic monitoring can become a trap for the unwary employer. Conflict between employees and employers may develop because the parties have different expectations. Employees may believe that E-mail, with its password requirements, is beyond the reach of unintended recipients and use workplace E-mail to communicate personal details to fellow employees. Employers, on the other hand, may consider all E-mail and other communications transmitted over workplace computers as business-related resources and, therefore, feel it is appropriate to monitor and review such communications.

To avoid potential problems concerning employee privacy, an employer should develop and implement a well-defined policy on electronic monitoring. Ideally, such a policy should balance the needs of the employer with the privacy interests of the employees. The following guidelines will help an employer that is considering the implementation of an electronic monitoring program. An employer that has already implemented electronic monitoring in the workplace can also use these guidelines to review its existing policy.

### Determine the Applicable Federal and State Laws

In addition to the federal law, there are certain state constitutional, statutory, and common-law prohibitions that may restrict electronic monitoring in the workplace. The applicability of such restrictions may depend on whether the employer is a public entity or a private enterprise.

### Ensure that Supervisors and Managers Understand the Applicable Legal Restrictions

To implement a lawful electronic monitoring program, management must thoroughly understand the applicable legal restrictions on electronic monitoring. Otherwise, managers and supervisors cannot effectively

---

3. Passed as an amendment to Title III of the Omnibus Crime Control and Safe Streets Act, the Electronic Communications Privacy Act of 1986 is codified as amended at 18 U.S.C. §§ 2510, 2701 (1993).

implement the company's policy and may expose the company to legal penalties.

### Provide Employees with Written Notice of the Policy

The employer should advise its employees that they are subject to specified monitoring practices. Forewarning employees that they are being monitored precludes the development of a "reasonable expectation of privacy." Notice does not have to be given specifically when the employee is being monitored. The employer can secure additional protection by asking employees to sign a document giving the employer the right to monitor computer data and workplace communications electronically. Notice may be provided in the following ways:

1. Publish provisions of policy in employee handbook.
2. Post provisions of policy on bulletin board.
3. Send employees personal letters explaining policy.
4. Include a copy of policy with employee paychecks.
5. Conduct employee meetings to familiarize employees with policy and answer any questions concerning policy.

### Support Restrictions on Some Types of Monitoring

Employers should respect employee privacy by not monitoring highly private areas such as restrooms and lounges. An electronic monitoring program should stay within the scope of its purpose. In general, monitoring should be confined to the workspace and should be as unobtrusive as possible.

### Be Able to Justify Monitoring from Its Inception

Electronic monitoring should be implemented only to serve a legitimate business interest, such as evaluating productivity or investigating workplace theft. Investigation of a specific employee is justified if the employer has "individualized suspicion" that the employee's conduct is adverse to its legal interests.

### Limit Electronic Surveillance as Necessary to Protect the "Business Use" Exception

Monitoring should take place in the "ordinary course of business." When the policy serves the employer's legitimate business needs and when the subject matter monitored is one in which the employer has a legal interest, monitoring is likely to be considered to be undertaken in the ordinary course of business.

### Use Reasonable Procedures to Govern the Use and Disclosure of Information Gathered Through Monitoring

When the information gathered is to be used as the basis for disciplinary action, the employee should have access to the information gathered. In addition, the employee should be given the opportunity to rebut the information or the employer's interpretation of it. Disclosure of the information gathered through monitoring should be limited to those with a "need to know."

These general guidelines are intended to help employers and human resources professionals in the development and implementation of a lawful electronic monitoring program. Of course, it is always advisable to consult with corporate or outside counsel before any sensitive employment policy is implemented.

## [c] Internet Use Policy

Business use of the Internet has experienced extraordinary growth in this decade. It is now commonplace for employees to have access to the Internet, and as the United States moves ever closer to an information worker/service type of economy, even more workers will need access to the Internet to perform their jobs effectively. Although the business uses of the Internet are many, much of the information available to employees on the Internet is not related to performance of the worker's job. Thus, many employers have recognized that unrestricted use of the Internet by employees has the potential to drain, rather than to enhance, productivity. The solution may be to implement a policy outlining the permissible parameters of employee Internet use, or an Internet Acceptable Use Policy (IAUP).

An IAUP is a written agreement, signed by employees, that sets out the permissible workplace uses of the Internet. In addition to describing permissible uses, an IAUP should specifically set out prohibited uses, rules of on-line behavior, and access privileges. Penalties for violations of the policy, including security violations and vandalism of the system, should also be covered. Anyone using a company's Internet connection should be required to sign an IAUP and to know that it will be kept on file as a legal, binding document.

There are many reasons an employer may want to institute an IAUP. The Internet can be a magnificent source of detailed, current information that can enhance employee productivity. The Internet also allows access to a vast amount of purely entertainment-related features. Thus, in a very real sense, providing access to the Internet carries with it the same potential for productivity drain as placing a television on every employee's desk. It is not surprising then, that loss of productivity is the number one reason for drafting an Internet Acceptable Use Policy.

Another reason to institute an IAUP is to shield the employer from possible sexual harassment suits. As in most communications media, some of the pictures, video, sound, and text on the Internet is sexually oriented. If such material is brought into the workplace, it has the potential to create a hostile work environment, thereby exposing the employer to liability under federal or state prohibitions against sex discrimination.

Technological reasons for supporting the implementation of an IAUP include restricting use of the Internet to work-related matters to prevent a drain on limited computer resources. Access to the Internet costs a business money, either in fees to Internet service providers, or in hardware costs necessary to accommodate increased network traffic and data storage. An employee's inappropriate use may negatively affect other employees' speed of access or storage space for work products. An IAUP can inform employees about the use of storage space and bandwidth on the system in order to maximize utility to all employees. Restrictions that serve this interest include directives against downloading games or other nonwork-related files; directives against downloading large files that can be obtained off-line; and instructions to move old or seldom used files, programs, or E-mail to alternative storage.

Employers who have sensitive data on their computer systems, be it company plans, customer demographic data, or product designs, may need a clause in their IAUPs concerning trade secrets. It should be made clear to employees that under no circumstances should proprietary company information be passed through the Internet, or that such material be encrypted if transmitted over the Internet.

Employers should institute guidelines that prohibit illegal use of the Internet in general. A directive that employees take care not to violate copyright laws should be included in every IAUP. Gambling via the Internet may also be a concern, and an IAUP should contain a prohibition against such activity not only because of its potentially adverse effect on productivity but also because the activity may be illegal.

An example of an Internet Acceptable Use Policy follows. The restrictiveness of an IAUP should vary depending on the type of business an employer conducts and how much autonomy each worker is given. Penalties may include warnings, suspension or revocation of Internet access, and outright termination.

It should also be noted that, in enforcing any IAUP, an employer must take care to respect worker's privacy rights. For discussion of employee privacy rights in computer use and electronic mail, see § 7.6.

### Sample Internet Acceptable Use Policy

#### The XYZ Corporation<br>Internet Acceptable Use Policy

As a condition of providing Internet access to its employees, the XYZ Corporation places certain restrictions on workplace use of the Internet. XYZ Corporation encourages employee use of the Internet:

- To communicate with fellow employees and clients regarding matters within an employee's assigned duties;
- To acquire information related to, or designed to facilitate the performance of, regular assigned duties; and
- To facilitate performance of any task or project in a manner approved by an employee's supervisor.

Please be advised that your use of the Internet access provided by XYZ Corporation expressly prohibits the following:

- Dissemination or printing of copyrighted materials (including articles and software) in violation of copyright laws.
- Sending, receiving, printing, or otherwise disseminating proprietary data, trade secrets, or other confidential information of XYZ Corporation in violation of company policy or proprietary agreements.
- Offensive or harassing statements or language including disparagement of others based on their race, national origin, sex, sexual orientation, age, disability, religious, or political beliefs.
- Sending or soliciting sexually oriented messages or images.
- Operating a business, usurping business opportunities, or soliciting money for personal gain, or searching for jobs outside XYZ Corporation.

- Sending chain letters, gambling, or engaging in any other activity in violation of local, state, or federal law.

Disciplinary action for violation of XYZ Corporation's Internet Acceptable Use Policy may include, but is not limited to, termination, suspension, or transfer of the offending employee. In cases involving less serious violations, disciplinary action may consist of a warning or reprimand. Remedial action may also include counseling, changes in work assignments, or other measures designed to prevent future misconduct. The measure of discipline will correspond to the potential effect of the offense on the company and fellow employees.

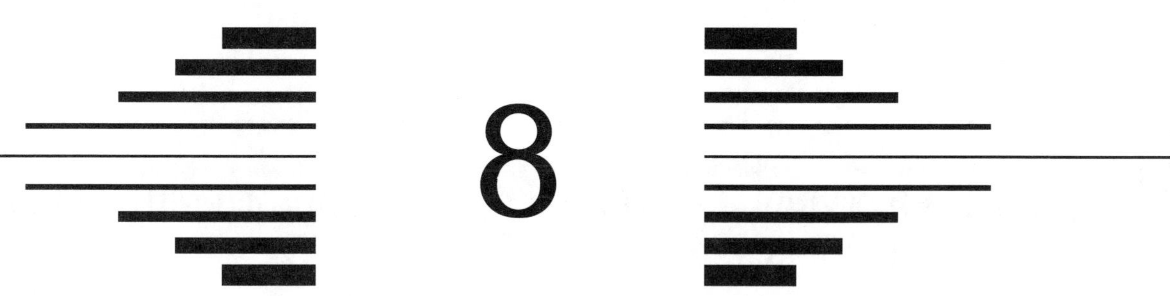

# Health and Safety

*Part 8.1 covers state occupational safety and health requirements and the relationship between the federal and state regulatory scheme. The exhibit and table in Part 8.2 list jurisdictions that have passed ordinances governing smoking in the workplace. Exhibit 8.2-1 lists states that have passed statutes regulating smoking. Table 8.2-1, dealing with municipal smoking ordinances, is meant to be illustrative rather than comprehensive; literally hundreds of municipalities have approved such statutes.*

# § 8.1 Overview: Occupational Safety and Health Act and State Analogues

## [a] Federal Regulation

The basic statutory scheme governing occupational health and safety is the Occupational Safety and Health Act (OSHA),[1] which regulates private employers. OSHA applies to all jurisdictions, including most U.S. territories and Indian reservations.[2] OSHA does not, however, apply to workplaces regulated by other federal schemes, such as the statutes promulgated to regulate the atomic energy, aviation, maritime, mining, and railroad industries, to the extent that those provisions are inconsistent with OSHA requirements.[3]

All entities considered to be "employers" are subject to OSHA regulations. An employer is any person, including an individual, partnership, corporation, etc., with at least one employee, who is engaged in a business affecting interstate commerce.[4] A business includes any commercial or noncommercial activity, and the test of whether it affects commerce is a broad one. Any activity in preparation for or winding up a business engaged in interstate commerce "affects" interstate commerce. Any business using materials or services performed in other states, maintaining its business on navigable waters, or using the United States mail is entirely covered by the definition of employer.[5] It is highly unlikely that a business could be excluded from OSHA coverage by failing to meet the definition of employer. Small employers, defined as those with 10 or fewer employees are, however, exempt from certain portions of OSHA, such as some of the recordkeeping provisions and penalties for nonserious violations.[6] Although the federal government is not covered by OSHA, individual agencies must promulgate their own health and safety standards.[7] States and political subdivisions are exempt from OSHA.[8]

An employer for the purposes of OSHA must also have "employees."[9] The test of whether a particular worker is an employee is quite similar to the tests used in other contexts relating to independent contractor status. Considerations include how payments are made, who may direct the worker, whether the employer may fire the worker or change the conditions of employment, and what status the worker reasonably believes he or she has.

Under OSHA, two types of standards apply to each employer. The first is the general duty for each employer to provide employees with a workplace free of hazards that might cause death or serious harm.[10] Because of the general duty clause, lack of a specific standard will not protect an employer if a serious hazard exists. The hazard must be likely to cause death or serious physical harm, even if the chance of an accident actually occurring is small.

**§ 8.1**

1. 29 U.S.C.A. §§ 651 *et seq.*
2. 29 U.S.C.A. § 653.
3. 29 U.S.C.A. §§ 653 *et seq.*
4. 29 U.S.C.A. § 652.
5. *See, e.g.,* Brennan v. Occupational Safety and Health Review Commission, 492 F.2d 1027 (2d Cir. 1974).
6. 29 C.F.R. §§ 1975 *et seq.*
7. 29 U.S.C.A. § 668.
8. 29 U.S.C.A. § 652.
9. Id.
10. 29 U.S.C.A. § 654.

The second type of standard is the specific standard, also called the general industry standards.[11] The general industry standards consist of elaborate regulations for hazards in the workplace, from stairs to noise exposure to hazardous waste. Some of these standards are applicable to many industries, others are quite specific. There is a procedure by which employers may apply for variances from the general industry standards.[12]

### [b] Relationship Between State and Federal Regulations

Only about half of the jurisdictions in the United States have extensive regulation of workplaces within their borders. States may, under OSHA, formulate plans by which the states assert jurisdiction over areas not regulated by the federal standards.[13] States may also create a comprehensive plan under which federal occupational safety and health enforcement is replaced by state enforcement, at least with respect to issues covered by the state plan.[14] States without plans are subject to federal laws. To receive approval of a plan, a state submits it to the Secretary of Labor. The approval process takes several years, and certain requirements must be met. For example, state plans must provide for a right of entry for inspectors, develop standards that will be as effective as federal standards, and staff and fund the applicable agency appropriately.[15] The state plan must contain reporting requirements that meet the federal standards for reporting and recordkeeping.[16]

### [c] State Requirements and Penalties for Noncompliance

Tables 8.1-1 through 8.1-4 contain some of the basic requirements under the state plans, as well as the penalties for failure to comply with the requirements.

Most states define an "employer" as any entity employing one or more individuals. Public employers are usually included, as required by federal law. Some types of employers, such as domestic service employers, are excluded from the definition of an employer in some states. In general, an "employee" is any person working for an employer; there are some exclusions for self-employed persons, domestic laborers, etc.

11. 29 U.S.C.A. § 8654.
12. *See* 29 U.S.C.A. § 655.
13. 29 U.S.C.A. § 667.
14. Id.
15. 29 C.F.R. § 1902; 29 U.S.C.A. § 667.
16. Id.

Table 8.1-1 covers primary occupational safety and health requirements, including key definitions and requirements for reporting of serious accidents. The definition of "serious accident" differs from state to state, but it frequently means that one or more employees were hospitalized. Some states require notice to the appropriate state agency within hours of such an accident, others not for days. A few states simply mandate that the federal reporting and recordkeeping requirements will apply.

Table 8.1-1 also covers antidiscrimination provisions. State plans usually prohibit discrimination against employees on the basis that the employee submitted a complaint regarding safety standards, testified at a hearing, or in any way exercised rights provided under the statutes. The state antidiscrimination statutes provide for a reporting procedure to the state agency responsible for OSHA compliance. Usually the report must be made within 30 to 180 days of the alleged violation of employee rights. After a violation is reported in a timely fashion, the state agency will conduct an investigation and make a report to the employee as to its decision on whether discrimination has occurred. The agency will usually have the authority to request the state attorney general to bring an action against the employer if a violation is found; remedies may include reinstatement, back pay, and other appropriate relief.

Safety and health statutes frequently require employers to furnish some protective equipment and to pay for certain medical exams (usually after exposure to hazardous substances). Education and training programs, provided at the employer's expense, may also be required. Finally, many states provide that an employee testifying as a witness at a state commission hearing dealing with a violation of safety or health requirements in a workplace may be reimbursed for travel and other expenses and may receive monetary compensation in the form of a witness fee. Benefits mandated by state occupational safety and health statutes appear in Table 8.1-2.

There are also, in most states, employee rights with respect to state safety and health inspections of the employer's facility. Usually, employees have the right to request inspections if an imminent danger exists, and an employee representative may accompany the state inspector through the facility. Most states require that names of employees requesting inspections or otherwise communicating with the state inspector remain confidential (i.e., not released to the employer). In many states, an employee who has requested a hearing has the right to receive an explanation of a state determination that no safety or health violation exists, or to request review of such a decision. State inspections are covered in Table 8.1-3.

Table 8.1-4 provides information regarding penalties for violating state occupational safety and health provisions. There are both civil and criminal penalties for violations of state OSHA statutes. Civil penalties generally consist of several levels of fines. Less serious violations, such as failure to post required notices and other serious and nonserious violations usually carry a penalty of about $7,000, although it is much lower in a few states. Willful or repeated violations are treated in a much harsher manner, with fines of $70,000 or more.

Criminal penalties are usually severe. Some of the most harshly punished crimes under state OSHA laws are making a false statement in any report or other document maintained under the statute and willfully or repeatedly violating a statute and thereby causing death or serious injury to an employee. The criminal penalties generally consist of fines of at least $10,000 and imprisonment ranging from 6 months to 2 years. Subsequent violations are almost always treated more strictly than first offenses; fines and jail time are often doubled. A few states provide for harsh penalties for violations of the antidiscrimination statutes.

### [d] Proposed OSHA Rule Regarding Workplace Smoking

As the *1999 State by State Guide to Human Resources Law* goes to press, there is no OSHA regulation in effect regarding workplace smoking. However, OSHA has come under increased pressure to promulgate regulations in this area as the result of a 1993 decision by the District of Columbia Circuit Court of Appeals denying the DOL's motion to dismiss a suit brought to compel OSHA to regulate tobacco smoking in the workplace.[17] In addition, the controversial report issued by the Environmental Protection Agency (EPA) in 1993 designating environmental tobacco smoke a Class A carcinogen, more dangerous than radon or benzene, has heightened public awareness of the problem.

On April 5, 1994, OSHA announced a proposed regulation dealing with indoor air quality and workplace smoking. In a press release, OSHA characterized the rule as part of "an effort to secure a safe and healthful work environment for America's workforce."

17. Action on Smoking and Health v. Department of Labor, No. 92-1037 (D.C. Cir. May 20, 1993).

In a statement issued with the proposed rule, Secretary of Labor Robert B. Reich stated:

> Every day in this country more than 20 million working men and women face unnecessary health threats because of poor indoor air quality and environmental tobacco smoke. The proposed rule is designed to tackle these problems. We are confident that compliance with the rule will reduce the suffering and disease associated with poor indoor air quality and environmental tobacco smoke. OSHA has taken this action to prevent thousands of heart disease deaths, hundreds of lung cancer deaths, and the respiratory diseases and other ailments linked to these hazards.

According to Reich, "the proposed rule is an investment in prevention. Lives will be saved, health care costs reduced, and productivity increased."

Assistant Secretary of Labor Joseph A. Dear, head of OSHA, added that "the rule is one of the most extensive ever proposed by OSHA. The environmental tobacco smoke provisions in the proposal apply to more than 6 million workplaces under OSHA jurisdiction, while the indoor air provisions apply to more than 4.5 million non-industrial worksites."

The proposal on indoor air quality evoked the largest response in the agency's history, with more than 100,000 comments received when the comment period closed in August 1995. Hearings on the proposed regulation began on September 10, 1994, and ran until March 13, 1995. The post-hearing comment period ended January 16, 1996. Currently, OSHA is reviewing comments and testimony and has not established a target date for a final determination on the issue.

Under the proposed rule, non-industrial workplaces include offices, schools and training centers, commercial establishments, health care facilities, cafeterias, and factory break rooms. The proposal would require affected employers to write and implement indoor air quality compliance plans, including plans for inspection and maintenance of current building ventilation systems, to ensure that the systems are functioning as designed. The proposal would not require all building owners and employers to install new ventilation systems. However, in buildings where smoking is not prohibited by employers or local requirements, the proposal would require employers to designate smoking areas that are separate, enclosed rooms exhausted directly to the outside. Other proposed provisions would require employers to maintain healthy air quality during renovation, remodeling, and similar activities.

Following are pertinent facts about the health effects of poor indoor air quality and environmental tobacco smoke, the scope of the proposal, and the proposed compliance requirements:

- Poor indoor air quality has been shown to result in headaches, respiratory infections, wheezing, nausea, dizziness, respiratory allergies, Legionnaire's disease, influenza, colds, measles, pulmonary tract infections, and other ailments.
- Exposure to environmental tobacco smoke has been linked to heart disease, lung cancer, decreases in pulmonary function, low birthweight babies, miscarriages, a number of birth defects, and other illnesses and diseases.
- Of more than 70 million employees working indoors, OSHA estimates that 21 million are exposed to poor indoor air and millions of others are exposed to environmental tobacco smoke.

The scope of the OSHA proposal includes:

- Provisions for indoor air quality that will apply to 70 million workers and more than 4.5 million non-industrial indoor work environments, including offices, schools, commercial establishments, health care facilities, cafeterias, and break rooms.
- Environmental tobacco smoke provisions that will apply to industrial and non-industrial work environments—all of the over 6 million work environments under OSHA jurisdiction.

Some of the requirements that will be placed on employers under the proposed rule are as follows:

- Employers must develop and implement indoor air quality compliance plans.
- Employers are required to ensure proper functioning of building ventilation systems that affect indoor air quality.
- Employers who do not prohibit smoking must designate non-working smoking areas that are enclosed and exhausted directly to the outside.
- Employers who do not control their building's ventilation systems must demonstrate a good-faith effort to comply.
- Full implementation of the standard must go into effect one year from the effective date.

The full text of the proposed OSHA rule is reprinted below. It should be noted, however, that the proposed rule is subject to change as it makes its way through the rule-making process.

TEXT OF PROPOSED RULE

§ 1910.1033 Indoor Air Quality

**(a) Scope and application**

(1) The provisions set forth in this section apply to all nonindustrial work environments.

(2) The provisions set forth in paragraph (e)(1) of this section, which address employee exposure to tobacco smoke, apply to all indoor or enclosed workplaces under OSHA jurisdiction.

**(b) Definitions**

*Air contaminants* refers to substances contained in the vapors from paint, cleaning chemicals, pesticides, and solvents, particulates, outdoor air pollutants, and other airborne substances which together may cause material impairment to employees working within the nonindustrial environment.

*Assistant Secretary* means the Assistant Secretary of Labor for Occupational Safety and Health, U.S. Department of Labor, or designee.

*Building-Related Illness* describes specific medical conditions of known etiology which can be documented by physical signs and laboratory findings. Such illnesses include sensory irritation when caused by known agents, respiratory allergies, asthma, nosocomial infections, humidifier fever, hypersensitivity pneumonitis, Legionnaires' disease, and the signs and symptoms characteristic of exposure to chemical or biologic substances such as carbon monoxide, formaldehyde, pesticides, endotoxins, or mycotoxins.

*Building systems* include but are not limited to the heating, ventilation and air-conditioning (HVAC) system, the potable water systems, the energy management system, and all other systems in a facility which may impact indoor air quality.

*Designated person* means a person who has been given the responsibility by the employer to take necessary measures to assure compliance with this section, and who is knowledgeable in the requirements of this standard and the specific building systems servicing the affected building or office.

*Designated smoking area* means a room, in a nonwork area, in which smoking of tobacco products is permitted.

*Director* means the Director, National Institute for Occupational Safety and Health (NIOSH), U.S. Department of Health and Human Services, or designee.

*Employer* means all persons defined as employers by Sec. 3(5) of the Occupational Safety and Health Act of 1970 including employers (such as building owners or lessees) who control the ventilation or maintenance of premises where employees of other employers work.

*HVAC system* means the collective components of the heating, ventilation and air conditioning system including, but not limited to, filters and frames, cooling coil condensate drip pans and drainage piping, outside air dampers and actuators, humidifiers, air distribution ductwork, automatic temperature controls, and cooling towers.

*Nonindustrial work environment* means an indoor or enclosed work space such as, but not limited to, offices, educational facilities, commercial establishments, and healthcare facilities; and office areas, cafeterias, and break rooms located in manufacturing or production facilities used by employees. Nonindustrial work environments do not include manufacturing and production facilities, residences, vehicles, and agricultural operations.

*Renovation and remodeling* means building modification involving activities that include but are not limited to: removal or replacement of walls, ceilings, floors, carpet, and components such as moldings, cabinets, doors, and windows; painting, decorating, demolition, surface refinishing, and removal or cleaning of ventilation ducts.

**(c) Indoor air quality (IAQ) compliance program**

(1) All employers with workplaces covered by paragraph (a)(1) of this section shall establish a written IAQ compliance program.

(2) The employer shall identify a designated person who is given the responsibility to assure implementation of the IAQ compliance program.

(3) Written plans for compliance programs shall include at least the following:

(i) A written narrative description of the facility building systems;

(ii) Single-line schematics or as-built construction documents which locate major building system equipment and the areas that they serve;

(iii) Information for the daily operation and management of the building systems, which shall include at least a description of normal operating procedures, special procedures such as seasonal start-ups and shutdowns, and a list of operating performance criteria including, but not limited to, minimum outside air ventilation rates, potable hot water storage and delivery temperatures, range of space relative humidities, and any space pressurization requirements;

(iv) A general description of the building and its function including, but not limited to, work activity, number of employees and visitors, hours of operation, weekend use, tenant requirements, and known air contaminants released in the space;

(v) A written maintenance program for the maintenance of building systems which shall be preventive in scope and reflect equipment manufacturer's recommendations and recommended-good-practice as determined by the building systems maintenance industry. At a minimum, the maintenance program shall describe the equipment to be maintained, and recommend maintenance procedures and frequency of performance; and

(vi) A checklist for the visual inspection of building systems.

(4) The following additional information, if available, shall be retained by the employer to assist in potential indoor air quality evaluations:

(i) As-built construction documents;

(ii) HVAC system commissioning reports;

(iii) HVAC systems testing, adjusting and balancing reports;

(iv) Operations and maintenance manuals;

(v) Water treatment logs; and

(vi) Operator training materials.

(5) The employer shall establish a written record of employee complaints of signs or symptoms that may be related to building-related illness to include at least information on the nature of the illness reported, number of employees affected, date of employee complaint, and remedial action, if any, taken to correct the source of the problem.

**(d) Compliance program implementation.** Employers shall assure compliance with this section by implementing at least the following actions:

(1) Maintain and operate the HVAC system to assure that it operates up to original design specifications and continues to provide at least the minimum outside air ventilation rate, based on actual occupancy, required by the building code, mechanical code, or ventilation code applicable at the time the facility was constructed, renovated, or remodeled, whichever is most recent;

(2) Conduct building systems inspection and maintenance in accordance with paragraph (c);

(3) Assure that the HVAC system is operating during all work shifts, except during emergency HVAC repairs and during scheduled HVAC maintenance;

(4) Implement the use of general or local exhaust ventilation where housekeeping and maintenance activities involve use of equipment or products that could reasonably be expected to result in hazardous chemical or

particulate exposures to employees working in other areas of the building or facility;

(5) Maintain relative humidity below 60% in buildings with mechanical cooling systems;

(6) The employer shall monitor carbon dioxide levels when routine maintenance under paragraph (d)(1) is done. When the carbon dioxide level exceeds 800 ppm, the employer shall check to make sure the HVAC system is operating as it should. If it is not, the employer shall take necessary steps to correct deficiencies if they exist;

(7) Assure that buildings without mechanical ventilation are maintained so that windows, doors, vents, stacks, and other portals designed or used for natural ventilation are in operable condition;

(8) Assure that mechanical equipment rooms and any nonducted air plenums or chases that transport air are maintained in a clean condition, hazardous substances are properly stored to prevent spillage, and asbestos, if friable, is encapsulated or removed so that it does not enter the air distribution system;

(9) Assure that inspections and maintenance of building systems are performed by or under the supervision of the designated person;

(10) Establish a written record of building system inspections and maintenance required to be performed under this section;

(11) Assure that employees performing work on building systems are provided with and use appropriate personal protective equipment as prescribed in 29 *C.F.R.* 1926, subpart E, Personal Protective and Life Saving Equipment; 29 *C.F.R.* 1926.52, Occupational Noise Exposure; 29 *C.F.R.* 1910, subpart I, Personal Protective Equipment; and 29 *C.F.R.* 1910.95 Occupational Noise Exposure;

(12) Evaluate the need to perform alterations of the building systems to meet the minimum requirements specified in paragraph (d) of this section in response to employee complaints of building-related illnesses; and

(13) Take such remedial measures as the evaluation shows to be necessary.

**(e) Controls for specific contaminant sources**

(1) Tobacco smoke

(i) In workplaces where the smoking of tobacco products is not prohibited, the employer shall establish designated smoking areas and permit smoking only in such areas;

(ii) The employer shall assure that designated smoking areas are enclosed and exhausted directly to the outside, and are maintained under negative pressure (with respect to surrounding spaces) sufficient to contain tobacco smoke within the designated area;

(iii) The employer shall assure that cleaning and maintenance work in designated smoking areas is conducted only when no smoking is taking place;

(iv) The employer shall assure that employees are not required to enter designated smoking areas in the performance of normal work activities;

(v) The employer shall post signs clearly indicating areas that are designated smoking areas;

(vi) The employer shall post signs that will clearly inform anyone entering the workplace that smoking is restricted to designated areas; and

(vii) The employer shall prohibit smoking within designated smoking areas during any period that the exhaust ventilation system servicing that area is not properly operating.

(2) Other indoor air contaminants

(i) The employer shall implement measures such as the relocation of air intakes and other pathways of building entry, where necessary, to restrict the entry of outdoor air contaminants such as vehicle exhaust fumes, into the building; and

(ii) When general ventilation is inadequate to control air contaminants emitted from point sources within workspaces, the employer shall implement other control measures such as local-source-capture exhaust ventilation or substitution.

(3) Microbial contamination

(i) The employer shall control microbial contamination in the building by routinely inspecting for, and promptly repairing, water leaks that can promote growth of biologic agents;

(ii) The employer shall control microbial contamination in the building by promptly drying, replacing, removing, or cleaning damp or wet materials; and

(iii) The employer shall take measures to remove visible microbial contamination in ductwork, humidifiers, other HVAC and building system components, or on building surfaces when found during regular or emergency maintenance activities or during visual inspection.

(4) Use of cleaning and maintenance chemicals, pesticides, and other hazardous chemicals in the workplace

(i) The employer shall assure that these chemicals are used and applied according to manufacturers' recommendations; and

(ii) The employer shall inform employees working in areas to be treated with potentially hazardous chemicals, at least within 24 hours prior to application, of the type of chemicals intended to be applied.

**(f) Air quality during renovation and remodeling**

(1) General. During renovation or remodeling, the employer shall assure that work procedures and appropriate controls are utilized to minimize degradation of the indoor air quality of employees performing such activities and employees in other areas of the building.

(2) Work plan development

(i) Before remodeling, renovation, or similar activities are begun the employer shall meet with the contractor or individual(s) performing the work and shall develop and implement a work plan designed to minimize entry of air contaminants to other areas of the building during and after performance of the work; and

(ii) The work plan shall consider all of the following where appropriate:

(a) Requirements of this standard;

(b) Implementation of means to assure that HVAC systems continue to function effectively during remodeling and renovation activities;

(c) Isolation or containment of work areas and appropriate negative pressure containment;

(d) Air contaminant suppression controls or auxiliary air filtration/cleaning; and

(e) Controls to prevent air contaminant entry into the HVAC air distribution system.

(3) Prior notification of employees who work in the building

(i) The employer shall notify employees at least 24 hours in advance, or promptly in emergency situations, of work to be performed on the building that may introduce air contaminants into their work area; and

(ii) Notification shall include anticipated adverse impacts on indoor air quality or workplace conditions.

**(g) Employee information and training**

(1) The employer shall provide training for maintenance workers and workers involved in building system operation and maintenance which shall include at least the following:

(i) Training in the use of personal protective equipment (PPE) needed in operating and maintaining building systems;

(ii) Training on how to maintain adequate ventilation of air contaminants generated during building cleaning and maintenance; and

(iii) Training of maintenance personnel on how to minimize adverse effects on indoor air quality during the use and disposal of chemicals and other agents.

(2) All employees shall be informed of:

(i) The contents of this standard and its appendices; and

(ii) Signs and symptoms associated with building-related illness and the requirement under subparagraphs (d)(12) and (d)(13) of this section directing the employer to evaluate the effectiveness of the HVAC system and to take remedial measures to the HVAC system if necessary, upon receipt of complaints from employees of building-related illness.

(3) Availability of training material. The employer shall make training materials developed in response to paragraph (g), including this standard and its appendices, available for inspection and copying by employees, designated employee representatives, the Director, and the Assistant Secretary.

**(h) Recordkeeping**

(1) Maintenance records. The employer shall maintain inspection and maintenance records required to be established under paragraph (d), which shall include the specific remedial or maintenance actions taken, the name and affiliation of the individual performing the work, and the date of the inspection or maintenance activity.

(2) Written IAQ compliance program. The employer shall maintain the written compliance program and plan required to be established under paragraph (c) of this section.

(3) Employee complaints. The employer shall maintain a record of employee complaints of signs or symptoms that may be associated with building-related illness required to be established under paragraph (c)(5) of this section. These complaints shall be promptly transmitted to the designated person for resolution.

(4) Retention of records. The employer shall retain records required to be maintained under this section for at least the previous three years, except that records required to be maintained under paragraphs (h)(1) and (h)(2) of this section need not be retained for three years if rendered obsolete by the establishment and replacement of more recent records, or rendered irrelevant due to HVAC system replacement or redesign.

(5) Availability. The records required to be maintained by this paragraph shall be available on request to employees and their designated representative and the Assistant Secretary for examination and copying.

(6) Transfer of records. Whenever the employer ceases to do business, records that are required to be maintained by paragraph (h) of this section shall be provided to and retained by the successor employer.

Dates—

(1) Effective date. This section shall become effective [INSERT DATE 60 DAYS FROM PUBLICATION].

(2) Start-up dates. Employers shall have implemented all provisions of this standard no later than one year from the effective date.

### [e] Other Proposed Federal Legislation

In addition to the proposed OSHA regulation, a bill introduced by Rep. Henry A. Waxman (D-Calif.) in the House of Representatives on November 3, 1993, would ban smoking in most public buildings nationwide. If passed, the bill[18] would restrict or ban smoking in any "public facility," defined as any building entered regularly by 10 or more individuals at least one day per week. The full text of the bill was reprinted in the 1995 edition of the *State by State Guide to Human Resources Law.*

After the November 1994 elections, the bill was killed in committee. The committee is now chaired by Representative Tom Bliley (R-Va).

At press time, it does not appear that any further legislative restrictions on tobacco will pass the Republican-controlled Congress, and anti-smoking activists have concentrated their efforts on the executive branch and its agencies. One of the regulatory efforts of the anti-smoking lobby has been to pressure OSHA to issue workplace smoking regulations. The OSHA regulations that are printed in this edition of the *State by State Guide to Human Resources Law* (see § 8.1[d]) are still proceeding through the rule-making process and may result in wide-ranging restrictions on workplace smoking if and when they become final agency rules; however, OSHA is not the only executive agency that has considered regulating smoking.

The Food and Drug Administration (FDA) proposed to regulate tobacco products on August 10, 1995. The proposed rule was published in the Federal Register on August 11, 1995, and the FDA received more than 700,000 comments on the regulation, the most in the history of federal rule-making. The FDA asserted jurisdiction over cigarettes and smokeless tobacco by concluding that cigarettes and smokeless tobacco are combination products having both a drug component (nicotine) and a device component (processed tobacco, filters, ventilation systems, and/or porous pouches). In August 1996, the FDA published the final rule in the Federal Register.

A summary of the FDA regulations is set out below:[19]

—*Sales and Distribution.* The rule makes the sale of cigarettes and tobacco products to individuals younger than the age of 18 a violation of federal law. The rule also requires retailers to check the identification of any person 26 years of age or younger who wishes to buy cigarettes or smokeless tobacco products, prohibits free samples, and eliminates most "impersonal" methods of sale that do not allow age verification, such as self-service displays and vending machines. Vending machines are permitted only in facilities where the retailer or operator ensures that no person younger than 18 is present or permitted to enter. Manufacturers, distributors, and retailers are legally responsible for complying with the regulations.

—*Labeling and Advertising.* Advertising that reaches children would be in a black-and-white, text-only format. Outdoor advertising of tobacco products located within 1,000 feet of schools and playgrounds would be banned. The sale and distribution of non-tobacco items by tobacco companies, such as hats and T-shirts that carry cigarette logos, are prohibited, and sponsorship of sporting and other events is limited to the corporate name only.

Tobacco companies, advertising agencies, and retail stores challenged the regulation in court. The suits argued that any step by the FDA to regulate tobacco as a drug would eventually lead to a mandatory ban on the use of all tobacco products and that the advertising regulations are a violation of the First Amendment. On April 26, 1997, a Federal District Court in Greensboro, North Carolina, ruled that the FDA has jurisdiction under the Federal Food, Drug, and Cosmetic Act to regulate nicotine-containing cigarettes and smokeless tobacco.[20] With respect to the tobacco rule, the Court upheld all restrictions involving youth access and labeling, including the prohibition on sales of cigarettes and smokeless tobacco products to persons under 18 years of age, the identification check requirements, and the ban on self-service displays and vending machines. The Court invalidated the FDA's restrictions on advertising,

18. 1993 House Resolution 3434.

19. 61 Fed. Reg. 44395 (8/28/96).

20. *Coyne Beaham v. U.S. Food and Drug Administration,* No. 95-00591 (M.D.N.C., April 25, 1997).

however. Both the tobacco industry and the government are appealing the portions of the ruling unfavorable to their respective positions. (See § 8.1[f] for further discussion of litigation that affects smoking in the workplace, either directly or indirectly).

### [f] The Tobacco Settlement

In June 1997, as a result of the increasing number of tobacco-related lawsuits, the tobacco industry and 40 state attorneys general reached a $368.5 billion settlement designed to defray medical and other costs related to smoking currently borne by the states. Under the proposed settlement, smoking would be banned in public places, workplaces, and fast-food restaurants. The following is a summary of the major provisions that would go into effect should the settlement be approved:

**Punitive Damages.** The tobacco companies would pay $50 billion, and in return, future punitive damage awards would be barred. Individuals would still be able to sue companies for compensatory damages, but class-action lawsuits for past tobacco company actions would be banned.

**Annual Payments.** Tobacco companies would pay on average $15 billion a year until the year 2022. The payments would be available to smokers suing for illness and death, to cover medical costs for the states who brought the action, to fund state and federal anti-smoking campaigns and research, and for smoking cessation programs.

**Advertising and Marketing.** Tobacco companies would agree to significant restrictions on advertising cigarettes.

**Regulation.** The settlement would give the FDA regulatory authority over tobacco products. The FDA could reduce the amount of nicotine in cigarettes and completely ban it in 2009 if the FDA could show that the reduction would bring about significant health benefits and would not cause a significant demand for black market cigarettes. Cigarettes would also be required to come with warnings such as "Smoking can kill you" and "Smoking causes cancer." Smoking in public places, workplaces, and fast-food restaurants would be banned.

**Reduction of Youth Smoking.** Tobacco companies would be required to make efforts to reduce smoking among young people, and the companies would be fined if targeted decreases in youth smoking are not met.

In order for the settlement to go into effect, it must be approved by Congress and the President. President Clinton has stated that the agreement's restriction on the FDA is unreasonable because it hampers FDA attempts to regulate nicotine in cigarettes. President Clinton said that any settlement agreement should include an increased tax on cigarettes if smoking among children does not decline.

The settlement proposal was changed and modified as it worked its way through the approval process. Several senators drafted settlement bills imposing higher taxes on cigarettes. Senator John McCain drafted a bill that sets a target of a 60 percent reduction of youth smoking within ten years and bars the use of animals, cartoons, and humans from tobacco advertisements. The $506 billion tobacco settlement bill introduced by McCain caps the amount that tobacco companies could lose in lawsuits at $6.5 billion a year but does not offer the other protections demanded by the tobacco industry. The Senate Commerce Committee passed McCain's bill by a 19 to 1 vote.

In April of 1998 the tobacco companies rejected McCain's settlement bill and abandoned the possibility of national settlement, stating that the settlement process was broken beyond repair. Several state representatives have recently met with tobacco officials to see if there is a way to salvage a national settlement. President Clinton and some members of Congress have said that legislation to protect children from smoking will go on with or without the industry's approval.

### [g] Increased Litigation of Claims Involving Exposure to Second-Hand Smoke

Based in large part on the findings of the EPA report on the effects of second-hand tobacco smoke, or environmental tobacco smoke (ETS) prepared in 1992, there has been a flurry of litigation involving smokers, employers, and tobacco companies. Much of this litigation deals with issues related to smoking in the workplace.

In *Broin,*[21] nonsmoking flight attendants who alleged that they were forced to breathe second-hand smoke on the job were allowed to pursue their class-action lawsuit against the tobacco company defendants. The nonsmoking flight attendants contend that the smoke from passengers' cigarettes caused the class-members to become ill. The alleged injuries occurred before Congress banned in-flight smoking in 1989.

The tobacco agreement had put in jeopardy this class action suit on behalf of 60,000 flight attendants. The case was in the middle of jury selection when the settlement was announced. A motion filed by the flight attendants' lawyers to issue an order that the trial would continue despite the settlement was denied, although the judge indicated that a verdict in the case would eventually be reached.[22] The class action suit was settled in

21. Broin v. Philip Morris, 92-1405 (Fla. App. 3d Dist. Mar. 1994).

22. Van Voris, "Trial's on Despite Smoke Deal," *The National Law Journal,* at A1, July 7, 1997.

October 1997, with tobacco companies agreeing to pay $300 million to establish a research foundation for diseases attributed to cigarette smoking.

Although *Broin* is an example of employees' seeking to hold the tobacco industry liable, many of the cases spawned by the 1993 EPA report on second-hand smoke attempt to hold employers liable for allowing smoking in the workplace. Other cases of note include:

1. A suit brought by Melvin Belli and a class of plaintiffs against the tobacco industry, seeking damages on behalf of smokers (employees and non-employees) who were injured as a result of smoking.
2. A suit brought by restaurant patrons against several fastfood restaurants, including McDonald's and Burger King, alleging that the restaurants' failure to totally ban smoking was an indication that they were not "reasonably accommodating" patrons or employees with respiratory problems. The court held that the ADA does not require the fast-food restaurants to ban smoking in the entire restaurant in order to reasonably accommodate customers with respiratory problems.[23]
3. Suits brought by Mississippi, Florida, Minnesota, West Virginia, and other state attorneys general against 13 of the largest tobacco companies to recover health-care costs that the state claims were directly caused by smoking. Texas, Minnesota, Mississippi, and Florida have settled their lawsuits against the tobacco industry. Thirty-seven other state attorneys general are proceeding in their lawsuits against the tobacco industry.[24]

Not surprisingly, smokers, some employers, and the tobacco companies are seeking judicial relief from certain anti-smoking measures. For example, the Philip Morris Company has filed suit against the City of San Francisco, attempting to overturn the strict anti-smoking ordinance that the city passed in 1993. Philip Morris joined with local bar and hotel owners and employers in contending that the city ordinance is preempted by state workplace safety regulations. The suit seeking to overturn the city smoking ordinance is the first of its kind and is a change from the tobacco companies' usual strategy of addressing smoking regulations at the federal or state level; however, as noted in § 8.2, local governments are becoming increasingly stringent in regulating smoking in public places and the workplace.

In another suit, the American Tobacco Company obtained a subpoena for the membership list of an anti-smoking computer network after the network was mentioned in a deposition in a wrongful-death lawsuit filed by a smoker's widow against R.J. Reynolds Tobacco Company and American Tobacco. American Tobacco is seeking a list of the people or organizations funding the network and a copy of all strategy sessions that are posted by computer, as well as the network's membership lists.

### [h] The Controversy over Second-Hand Smoke

Most of the increased litigation, legislation, and regulation in the area of smoking control has been driven, at least in part, by the widely publicized 1993 EPA report on the dangers of second-hand smoke.

In perhaps the most significant tobacco-related litigation, tobacco companies have brought suit challenging the findings in the EPA's report. The companies maintain that there are significant flaws in the scientific data that the agency used to reach the conclusions in the report and that, therefore, the report should not be used as the basis for making policy decisions about smoking in public places or in the workplace. In addition to relying on the findings of industry-funded research projects, the tobacco companies are relying on a Congressional study that provides some support for their position.

In March 1994, the Congressional Research Service (CRS)[25] provided Congress with an economic analysis (CRS Report 94-214E) of the Clinton Administration's proposal to raise the federal excise tax on cigarettes to help pay for the Administration's health care plan, the rationales for such an increase, as well as the effects and concerns about the tax. The CRS investigated various costs associated with smoking, including those that might be associated with second-hand smoke.

---

23. Staron v. McDonald's, No. 3:93CV00665 (D.Conn. Mar. 1994).

24. Susan Hadden, "Another State, Another Loss for Big Tobacco," *US News & World Report,* May 18, 1998.

25. The Congressional Research Service works exclusively for the U.S. Congress, conducting research, analyzing legislation, and providing information at the request of committees, members, and their staffs. The CRS makes such research available, without partisan bias, in many forms, including studies, reports, compilations, digests, and background briefings. Upon request, the CRS assists committees in analyzing legislative proposals and issues and in assessing the possible effects of these proposals and their alternatives. The service's senior specialists and subject analysts also provide personal consultations in their respective fields of expertise.

In the report, and in written testimony submitted to Congress on May 11, 1994, by the authors of the report, the CRS characterized as "weak" and "uncertain" the epidemiological evidence that the EPA and others have used to support claims concerning the health effects of second-hand smoke. The CRS stated, "[O]ur evaluation was that the statistical evidence does not appear to support a conclusion that there are substantial health effects of passive smoking."

Regarding the EPA study, the CRS made the following specific comments:

> The EPA study analyzed and summarized 30 studies of passive smoking lung cancer effects. Critics have questioned how a passive smoking effect can be discerned from a group of 30 studies of which six found a statistically significant (but small) effect, 24 found no statistically significant effect, and six of the 24 found a passive smoking effect opposite to the expected relationship.
>
> • • • •
>
> EPA attempted to standardize this diverse group of studies to account for statistically important differences in their methodologies. In this process, EPA reduced the standard for statistical significance from the usual standard, and the one generally used in the original studies. It is unusual to return to a study after the fact, lower the required significance level, and declare its results to be supportive rather than unsupportive of the effect one's theory suggests should be present, but our conclusion about the "uncertainty" of the EPA results is not dependent upon this change in significance levels. However, the issue raised by the change in the statistical significance standard should not be ignored.
>
> • • • •
>
> Two epidemiological studies that each covered a large number of observations were published in 1992 after the cutoff date for inclusion in the EPA report. The one with the largest number of observations found no overall increased risk of lung cancer among nonsmoking spouses of smokers, the other found an increased, but not statistically significant, lung cancer risk.
>
> • • • •
>
> The existence of an exposure threshold for disease onset below which many passive smokers fall is not implausible. Most organisms have the capacity to cleanse themselves of some level of contaminants. It is for this reason that public policy usually does not insist that every unit of air or water pollution be removed from the environment; the damage of low-level pollutants is sufficiently small (through the self-cleansing process) that removal is not cost-effective.
>
> • • • •
>
> These studies do not have (and indeed cannot have) very precise estimates of exposure from environmental tobacco smoke. The data are based on interviews of the subjects or their relatives. If errors in measurement occur in a systematic way that is correlated with development of a disease, the effect would be to bias the results. An example would be if those individuals who developed lung cancer (or relatives of those individuals) remembered or perceived their exposure differently from those who did not develop the disease.
>
> • • • •
>
> In sum, this analysis suggests . . . that the absence of controls or the inability to control for other factors may be a major problem in relying on epidemiological estimates of the health effects of passive smoking. To restate this criticism, if wives or children of smokers share in poor health habits or other factors that could contribute to illness, statistical associations found between disease and passive smoking could be incidental or misleading.

These comments on the EPA's conclusions about second-hand smoke have caused some to doubt the EPA's claim that second-hand smoke is a Class A, or known, human carcinogen that is responsible for 3,000 lung cancer deaths annually and numerous other health problems nationwide. These perceived scientific difficulties in the EPA's study of second-hand smoke are fueling debate about whether national policy should be based on the study's conclusions.

Aside from the controversy over the EPA's report, there is growing controversy and concern among smokers, the tobacco companies, and some employers about the practical effects of the proposed OSHA regulation.

The proposed OSHA standard would regulate smoking in *all* indoor workplaces under the agency's jurisdiction. There are no proposed exceptions or exclusions to this coverage, in contrast to most state and local laws, which allow for various exceptions. (See Exhibit 8.2-1 and Table 8.2-1.) Some of the practical difficulties of covering *all* indoor workplaces include:

- Restricting or prohibiting smoking in private residences. Under the fairly broad definition of "employee" in the Occupational Safety and Health Act, a maid, nanny, nurse, repair person, delivery person, or any other individual who is paid to perform work in a house could be an employee protected by the regulations.
- Restricting or prohibiting smoking in hotels and motels. The regulation would not only affect meeting or conference rooms, but also sleeping rooms if a maid or other employee were working there. It is unclear whether smoking would be

prohibited only while such an employee is present, or at all times.

- Restricting or prohibiting smoking in private offices. Although the OSHA proposal allows designated smoking areas if separately ventilated, such areas are required to be "non-working areas." By definition, this would prohibit smoking in private offices, because a private office is presumably a working area for its occupant.
- Restricting or prohibiting smoking in restaurants and bars. If a designated smoking area must not be a normal work area, it is difficult to imagine how a restaurant or bar could permit smoking, because waiters and bartenders normally work throughout the establishment. Even if a restaurant or bar designated a separately ventilated smoking area, conceivably the regulation could require that no employee may be ordered to enter the area to provide service.
- Restricting or prohibiting smoking in vehicles. The no-smoking restriction might extend to a company car or truck, or even the employee's personal vehicle if used for company business. This restriction may apply even when the employee is in the vehicle alone, if the vehicle is considered a normal work area.

Although OSHA may adopt certain exceptions and administrative interpretation or changes to the rule, ameliorating some of these potential effects, employers should be aware that the proposed rule will have a significant impact on the workplace and should keep abreast of any developments in the regulatory process.

# Table 8.1-1
## STATE OCCUPATIONAL SAFETY REQUIREMENTS

**KEY:** SAF indicates that the state requirement is the same as the federal requirement.

| | *Who Is an Employer?* | *Reporting Requirements for Serious Accidents?* | *Who Is an Employee?* | *Employee's Remedy for Discrimination?* | *Citations to Authority* |
|---|---|---|---|---|---|
| AK | Any person, including the state, with one or more employees. With respect to toxic and hazardous substance requirements, a person operating a workplace that is used primarily as a personal residence is not an employer. | Report to nearest division immediately but in no event later than 8 hours after receipt of notice that accident has occurred, if fatality or serious injury. | Any person who works for an employer. Domestic laborers are not employees under toxic and hazardous substance laws. | File complaint with department of labor within 30 days. | Alaska Stat. §§ 18.60.010 *et seq.* |
| AZ | Any individual, including the state, employing one or more persons. Self-employed persons are included, domestic labor employers are excluded. | Employer must make periodic reports on work-related deaths and injuries. | Any person except as domestic laborer. | File complaint within 30 days of violation with Industrial Commission. | Ariz. Rev. Stat. Ann. §§ 23-401 *et seq.* |
| CA | The state and state agencies; counties, cities, districts, all public and quasi-public corporations and public agencies therein; every person, including any public service corporation, that has any natural person in service; and the legal representative of any deceased employer. | For death of an employee, report must be filed within 5 days. | Any person who is required or directed by an employer to engage in any employment, or to go to work or be at any time in any place of employment. | File complaint with Commissioner within 30 days of the violation. | Cal. Lab. Code Ann. §§ 6300 *et seq.*; Cal Health & Safety Code Ann. § 25910. |
| CT | The state and any political subdivision. | SAF. | Any person engaged in service to an employer in a business of the employer. | File a complaint with the labor commissioner within 30 days. | Conn. Gen. Stat. Ann. §§ 31-367 *et seq.* |
| DC | Any entity employing at least one person, includes district government. | Fatalities or serious injuries must be reported to the mayor within 24 hours. | Individual working for compensation, other than a domestic servant. | File complaint with Commissioner within 60 days of the violation. | D.C. Code Ann. §§ 36-1200 *et seq.* |
| FL | Any entity carrying on employment, including the state and political subdivisions. | — | Every person engaged in employment under any appointment or contract for hire or apprenticeship. | — | Fla. Stat. Ann. §§ 442 *et seq.* |
| HI | All private and state/county persons or entities with one or more employees, except domestic service employers. | SAF. | Any person working for an employer, other than a domestic laborer. | File complaint with department of labor and industrial relations within 60 days of violation. | Haw. Rev. Stat. §§ 396-1 *et seq.* |
| IL | Any entity engaged in any business, including the state and political subdivisions. | As prescribed by the director of labor; must include all reporting provisions of the Illinois Workers Compensation Act. | Any person employed by an employer, including the state and political subdivisions. | SAF. | 820 ILCS 225/.01 *et seq.* |

| | | | | | |
|---|---|---|---|---|---|
| IN | Any individual or organization, including the state, employing one or more persons. | Deaths or serious injuries of 5 or more employees must be reported to the commissioner within 48 hours. | Any person employed by an employer. | File complaint with division of labor within 30 days of the violation. | Ind. Code Ann. §§ 22-8-1.1 *et seq.* |
| IA | Any person, including the state, agencies, and political subdivisions, with one or more employees. | SAF. | Any person employed for pay by an employer. | File a complaint with the division of labor within 30 days of the violation. | Iowa Code §§ 88.1 *et seq.* |
| KY | Any person or entity employing one or more persons, but not if a federal agency other than the U.S. Department of Labor exercises statutory authority over occupational safety and health of the employer. | For fatalities or serious accidents, reports must be made to the department of labor within 48 hours. | Any person employed by an employer. | File complaint with department of labor within 120 days of the violation. | Ky. Rev. Stat. Ann. §§ 338.011 *et seq.* |
| MD | Any person or entity, including the state and all agencies employing one or more persons. Persons who employ individuals and lease their services to others are included. | Report must be made within 8 hours of a fatal or serious accident. | Any person employed by an employer. | File complaint with the division of labor and industry within 30 days of the violation. | Md. Ann. Code L. & Emp. §§ 5-101 *et seq.* |
| MI | Any person or organization, including the state, employing one or more persons. Domestic employers and mines are excluded. | Fatal or serious accidents must be reported to the department of labor within 8 hours. | A person committed to work by an employer. | — | Mich. Comp. Laws Ann. §§ 408.1001 *et seq.* |
| MN | Any person or entity, with one or more employees, including the state and its political subdivisions. | SAF. | Any person employed by an employer. | File complaint with department of labor and industry within 30 days of the violation. | Minn. Stat. Ann. §§ 182.65 *et seq.* |
| NV | Any person or entity employing persons, including the state and political subdivisions. | Fatalities and serious accidents must be reported to the division within 8 hours. | Any person in a place of employment. | File complaint with division of industrial relations within 30 days of the violation. | Nev. Rev. Stat. §§ 618.005 *et seq.* |
| NM | Any person or entity employing one or more employees, unless regulated by a federal agency other than OSHA or under certain radioactive materials regulations. | SAF. | Any person employed by an employer except a domestic worker or a volunteer firefighter. | File a complaint with the secretary of the department of labor within 30 days of the violation. | N.M. Stat. Ann. §§ 50-9-1 *et seq.* |
| NJ | State, agencies, or political subdivisions. | Fatalities should be reported to the Department of Labor and Industry in the quickest possible manner. | Any public employee. | File complaint with commissioner within 180 days of knowledge of violation. | N.J. Stat. Ann. §§ 34:6A-25 *et seq.* |
| NY | A person employing a mechanic, workingman or laborer, whether the owner, proprietor, agent, superintendent, foreman, or any other subordinate. The state and any political subdivision or agency. | SAF. | Any person working for an employer. | File a complaint with the commissioner of labor within 30 days of the violation. | N.Y. Lab. Law § 227-a. |
| NC | A person engaged in business and having employees, including the state and political subdivisions. Domestic labor employers are not included. | SAF. | Any person working for an employer except specified miners, railroad workers, and workers subject to the Atomic Energy Act. | File complaint with division of workplace retaliatory discrimination within 180 days of the violation. | N.C. Gen. Stat. §§ 95-126 *et seq.* |
| OR | Any person with one or more employees, including state and political subdivisions. | Fatalities or serious accidents must be reported within 24 hours. | Any person working for an employer for compensation. | File complaint with department of labor within 30 days of the violation. | Or. Rev. Stat. Ann. §§ 654.001 *et seq.* |

*(Table continues.)*

## Table 8.1-1 *(cont'd)*
## STATE OCCUPATIONAL SAFETY REQUIREMENTS

**KEY:** SAF indicates that the state requirement is the same as the federal requirement.

| | *Who Is an Employer?* | *Reporting Requirements for Serious Accidents?* | *Who Is an Employee?* | *Employee's Remedy for Discrimination?* | *Citations to Authority* |
|---|---|---|---|---|---|
| RI | Any entity employing one or more persons, includes the state, agencies, and political subdivisions. | — | Any person working for an employer. | An employee believing he or she was discriminated against or discharged in violation of § 28-20-1, *et seq.*, may file a written complaint with the director within 30 days. | R.I. Gen. Laws §§ 28-20-1 *et seq.* |
| SC | All employers as defined by state employment laws are covered. | SAF. | All employees as defined by state employment laws. | File complaint with division of labor within 30 days of the violation. | S.C. Code Ann. §§ 41-15-10 *et seq.* |
| TN | Any private person engaged in a business with one or more employees, and county, metropolitan, and municipal governments. | Fatalities and serious accidents must be reported to the division of workers compensation within 14 days. | Any person performing services for another, including lawfully or unlawfully employed minors. | File complaint with department of labor within 30 days of the violation. | Tenn. Code Ann. §§ 50-3-101 *et seq.* |
| TX | Person who has control or custody of any employment, place of employment, or employee. | Commission may require employers to report accidents, personal injuries, or fatalities. | Individual who works for an employer for compensation. | File complaint within 90 days of violation. | Tex. Labor Code Ann. §§ 411.001 *et seq.* |
| UT | All entities with one or more persons working except those covered by the Atomic Energy Act or otherwise not subject to federal OSHA jurisdiction. | Fatalities must be reported to the division within 1 hour; serious injuries within 8 hours. | Any person working for an employer. | File complaint with industrial commission within 30 days of the violation. | Utah Code Ann. §§ 34A-6-101 *et seq.* |
| VT | Any person who employs one or more persons, including state, agencies, and political subdivisions. | SAF. | Any person working for compensation except independent contractors. | File complaint with department of labor within 30 days of violation. | Vt. Stat. Ann. tit. 21, §§ 201 *et seq.* |
| VA | Employer is defined by general labor and employment laws. | Fatal or serious injuries must be reported to the department of labor and industry within 8 hours. | Any person employed by an employer. | File complaint with department of labor and industry within 30 days of the violation. | Va. Code Ann. §§ 40.1-51.1 *et seq.* |
| WA | Any person with one or more persons employed, includes state and political subdivisions, and charitable organizations. | Periodic reports of fatalities and serious injuries must be made. | Any person employed by an employer or working under an independent contract for personal labor. | File complaint with department of labor and industries within 30 days of the violation. | Wash. Rev. Code Ann. §§ 49.17.010 *et seq.* |

| | | | | | |
|---|---|---|---|---|---|
| WV | The state and all subdivisions, except for the department of corrections, the department of health, and the legislature. | SAF. | Any public employee of the state or state agency. | File a complaint with the commissioner of labor within 30 days of the violation. | W.Va. Code Ann. §§ 21-3A-1 *et seq.* |
| WI | The state, any agency or political subdivision of the state. | — | Any employee of the state, of any agency or of any political subdivision of the state. | File complaint with department of labor within 30 days of the violation. | Wis. Stat. Ann. § 101.055. |
| WY | All persons employing one or more persons for hire. State OSHA commission may exempt a trade or business if it determines federal requirements are adequate. | SAF. | Any person employed by an employer for pay, except persons self-employed in agriculture. | File complaint with occupational safety and health department within 30 days of the violation. | Wyo. Stat. §§ 27-11-101 *et seq.* |

# Table 8.1-2
## STATE OCCUPATIONAL SAFETY REQUIREMENTS: MANDATED BENEFITS

**KEY:** "Yes" means that the employer must provide the benefit.
SAF means that the state has adopted federal OSHA rules on the topic.
The term "general mandate" means that the state does not have a specific statute requiring that the employer provide the benefit, but the employer is subject to the state's general mandate that the employer provide a safe workplace.

| | *Must Employer Furnish Protective Equipment?* | *Must Employer Provide Education for Employees?* | *Is Employee Entitled to Compensation for Serving as Witness in OSHA Proceeding?* | *Must Employer Pay for Safety-Related Medical Examinations?* | *Other Benefit Mandates* | *Citations to Authority* |
|---|---|---|---|---|---|---|
| AK | Yes. | Yes, employer must conduct safety education programs. | Yes. If employee appears at the request of the employer, compensation must equal any wages lost by the employee in order to testify; if the employee appears at the request of the state, the employee shall be compensated $30 per day plus transportation costs. | — | — | Alaska Stat. §§ 18.60.066, 18.60.075, 18.60.098. |
| AZ | No specific provision, but employer is subject to general mandate. | No specific provision, but employer is subject to general mandate. | Yes, employee may receive a witness fee and compensation for travel expenses. | — | — | Ariz. Rev. Stat. Ann. §§ 23-403, 23-432. |
| CA | Yes. | Yes. | — | — | — | Cal. Lab. Code Ann. §§ 6401, 6401.7, 6403. |
| CT | State regulations must make provisions for required protective equipment. | SAF. | — | Yes, state may require for employee who has been exposed to hazardous materials. | — | Conn. Gen. Stat. Ann. §§ 31-370, 31-372. |
| DC | State regulations must make provisions for required protective equipment. | No specific provision, but employer is subject to general mandate. | — | Yes, state may require. | — | D.C. Code Ann. §§ 36-1203, 36-1208. |
| HI | Yes. | No specific provision, but employer is subject to general mandate. | Yes, employee may receive a witness fee and compensation for travel expenses. | Yes, state may require for employee who has been exposed to hazardous materials. | — | Haw. Rev. Stat. §§ 396-4, 396-6, 396-7. |

| | | | | | | |
|---|---|---|---|---|---|---|
| IL | State regulations must make provisions for required protective equipment. | Yes, as to toxic substances in the workplace. | — | Yes, for employee who has been exposed to hazardous materials. | — | 820 ILCS §§ 225/4, 255/16. |
| IN | State standards may require employer to furnish protective equipment. | SAF. | — | Yes, for employee who has been exposed to hazards in the workplace. | — | Ind. Code Ann. §§ 22-8-1.1-16.2, 22-8-1.1-17.1. |
| IA | No specific provision, but employer is subject to general mandate. | No specific provision, but employer is subject to general mandate. | Yes. Employee may receive a witness fee and compensation for travel expenses. | Yes, state may require for employee who has been exposed to hazardous materials. | — | Iowa Code §§ 88.1, 88.5, 88.6. |
| KY | No specific provision, but employer is subject to general mandate. | No specific provision, but employer is subject to general mandate. | — | — | — | Ky. Rev. Stat. Ann. § 338.031. |
| MD | State standards may require employer to furnish protective equipment. | No specific provision, but employer is subject to general mandate. | — | — | — | Md. Lab. & Emp. Code Ann. §§ 5-104, 5-309. |
| MI | Yes, when required by specific standard promulgated by Commission. Factors include whether equipment is transferable between employees, whether it is maintained by the employer, whether it remains at the worksite, the amount of personal use of the equipment, and any other relevant factors. | Yes, with respect to exposure to hazardous materials. | — | — | — | Mich. Comp. Laws Ann. §§ 408.1011, 408.1014a, 408.1046. |
| MN | No specific provision, but employer is subject to general mandate. | Yes, before exposure to hazardous material. Training must be updated at periods no greater than one year. | — | — | — | Minn. Stat. Ann. § 182.653. |
| NV | Yes. | Yes, unless employer has 10 or fewer employees. | Yes, employee may receive a witness fee and compensation for travel expenses. | State may require employer to pay for a medical exam for an employee who has been exposed to hazardous materials. | An employee working on a safety committee must be paid regular wages for the time spent working on committee business. | Nev. Rev. Stat. §§ 618.295, 618.375, 618.383, 618.385, 618.505. |
| NM | No specific provision, but employer is subject to general mandate. | No specific provision, but employer is subject to general mandate. | Yes, employee may receive a witness fee and compensation for travel expenses. | Yes, for employee who has been exposed to hazardous materials. | — | N.M. Stat. Ann. §§ 50-9-5, 50-9-5.1, 50-9-7, 50-9-18. |
| NY | SAF. | Yes, for toxic substance exposure. For other types of employment, SAF. | SAF. | SAF. | SAF. | N.Y. Lab. Law §§ 27-a *et seq.*, 878. |

*(Table continues.)*

# Table 8.1-2 *(cont'd)*

## STATE OCCUPATIONAL SAFETY REQUIREMENTS: MANDATED BENEFITS

**KEY:** "Yes" means that the employer must provide the benefit.
SAF means that the state has adopted federal OSHA rules on the topic.
The term "general mandate" means that the state does not have a specific statute requiring that the employer provide the benefit, but the employer is subject to the state's general mandate that the employer provide a safe workplace.

| | *Must Employer Furnish Protective Equipment?* | *Must Employer Provide Education for Employees?* | *Is Employee Entitled to Compensation for Serving as Witness in OSHA Proceeding?* | *Must Employer Pay for Safety-Related Medical Examinations?* | *Other Benefit Mandates* | *Citations to Authority* |
|---|---|---|---|---|---|---|
| NC | No specific provision, but employer is subject to general mandate. | No specific provision, but employer is subject to general mandate. | Yes, employee may receive a witness fee and compensation for travel expenses. | — | — | N.C. Gen. Stat. §§ 95-129, 95-136. |
| OR | Yes. | No specific provision, but employer is subject to general mandate. | Yes, employee may receive a witness fee and compensation for travel expenses. | — | — | Or. Rev. Stat. Ann. §§ 654.010, 654.025. |
| RI | No specific provision, but employer is subject to general mandate. | No specific provision, but employer is subject to general mandate. | — | — | — | R.I. Gen. Laws § 28-20-8. |
| SC | No specific provision, but employer is subject to general mandate. | No specific provision, but employer is subject to general mandate. | — | Yes, for employee who has been exposed to hazardous materials. | — | S.C. Code Ann. §§ 41-15-80, 41-15-400. |
| TN | No specific provision, but employer is subject to general mandate. | SAF. | Yes, employee may receive a witness fee and compensation for travel expenses. | Yes, for employee who has been exposed to hazardous materials. | — | Tenn. Code Ann. §§ 50-3-105, 50-3-202, 50-3-203, 50-3-2010. |
| UT | No specific provision, but employer is subject to general mandate. | No specific provision, but employer is subject to general mandate. | Yes, employee may receive a witness fee and compensation for travel expenses. | Yes, for employee who has been exposed to hazardous materials. | — | Utah Code Ann. §§ 35A-6-201, 35A-6-202, 35A-6-301. |
| VT | State safety commission must promulgate standards requiring suitable protective equipment to be provided by the employer. | No specific provision, but employer is subject to general mandate. | — | State may require employer to pay for a medical exam for an employee who has been exposed to hazardous materials. | — | Vt. Stat. Ann. tit. 21, §§ 201, 223, 224. |
| VA | No specific provision, but employer is subject to general mandate. | No specific provision, but employer is subject to general mandate. | — | — | — | Va. Code Ann. § 40.1-51.1. |

| | | | | | | |
|---|---|---|---|---|---|---|
| WA | No specific provision, but employer is subject to general mandate. | No specific provision, but employer is subject to general mandate. | — | Yes, for employee who has been exposed to hazardous materials. | — | Wash. Rev. Code Ann. §§ 49.17.060, 49.17.240. |
| WV | No specific provision, but employer is subject to general mandate. | No specific provision, but employer is subject to general mandate. | — | State may require employer to pay for a medical exam for an employee who has been exposed to hazardous materials. | — | W.Va. Code Ann. §§ 21-3A-5, 21-3A-7. |
| WY | No specific provision, but employer is subject to general mandate. | No specific provision, but employer is subject to general mandate. | — | Yes, for employee who has been exposed to hazards or environmental conditions that may be detrimental to the employee's health. | — | Wyo. Stat. §§ 27-11-105, 27-11-113. |

# Table 8.1-3
## STATE OCCUPATIONAL SAFETY REQUIREMENTS: INSPECTIONS

**KEY:** SAF means that the state has adopted federal OSHA rules on the topic.
"—" means that the state does not have specific statutory authority on the subject.

| | *Employee Has the Right to Participate in State Inspection* | *Employee Entitled to Wages While Participating in State Inspection* | *Communications Between Employee and State Inspector Are Confidential* | *Employee Has the Right to Request a State Inspection* | *Identity of Employee Requesting Inspection Is Confidential* | *Employee Rights if Inspection Does Not Result in a Citation* | *Citations to Authority* |
|---|---|---|---|---|---|---|---|
| AK | Yes. | Yes. | Yes. | Yes. | Yes. | Employee receives written explanation of why a citation was not issued and may request a review of that decision. | Alaska Stat. §§ 18.60.087, 18.60.088. |
| AZ | Yes. | — | Yes. | Yes. | Yes. | Employee or employee representative shall be notified in writing of the determination. | Ariz. Rev. Stat. Ann. § 23-408. |
| CA | — | — | — | Yes. | Yes. | Employee will be notified of any decision and the reasons for the decision. The state will conduct an informal review of any decision not to issue a citation and will inform the employee in writing of the result of the review. | Cal. Lab. Code Ann. § 6309. |
| CT | Yes. | Yes. | Yes. | Yes. | Yes. | Employee will receive written notification of the determination. | Conn. Gen. Stat. Ann. § 31-374. |
| DC | Yes. | Yes, employees are paid for a reasonable amount of time. | Yes. | Yes. | Yes. | Employee will receive a written statement of the final disposition of the case and the reasons. | D.C. Code Ann. § 36-1212. |
| HI | Yes. | — | Yes. | Yes. | Yes. | Employee will be given notice stating the decision not to take compliance action and the reasons therefor, and the procedures for review of the decision. | Haw. Rev. Stat. Ann. § 396-8. |
| IL | SAF. | — | SAF. | SAF. | SAF. | SAF. | 820 ILCS 225/4. |
| IN | Yes. | — | Yes. | Yes. | Yes. | Employee shall be notified of the decision and may request review. | Ind. Code Ann. §§ 22-8-1.1-24.1, 22-8-1.1-24.3. |
| IA | Yes. | — | Yes. | Yes. | Yes. | Employee will receive written notification of the determination. | Iowa Code Ann. § 88.6 |
| KY | Yes. | — | Yes. | Yes. | Yes. | Employee shall receive written notification of the determination. | Ky. Rev. Stat. Ann. §§ 338.111, 338.121. |

| | | | | | | | |
|---|---|---|---|---|---|---|---|
| MD | Yes. | — | Yes. | Yes. | — | Employee may ask for a review of any refusal to issue a citation and will receive a written statement of the reasons for the final disposition. | Md. Lab. & Emp. Code Ann. §§ 5-208, 5-209. |
| MI | Yes. | Yes. | Yes. | Yes. | Yes. | Employee will receive written notification of the determination and may request a review. Employee will be given a written statement of the final disposition of the complaint and the reasons for the disposition. | Mich. Comp. Laws Ann. §§ 408.1028, 408.1029. |
| MN | Yes. | — | Yes. | Yes. | Yes. | Employee shall receive written notification of the determination and may request review. | Minn. Stat. Ann. § 182.659. |
| NV | Yes. | Yes, if employee would have otherwise been compensated for working during time of inspection. | Yes. | Yes. | Yes. | Employee may request review of the decision and shall receive a written statement of the reasons for the final disposition of the case. | Nev. Rev. Stat. Ann. §§ 618.425, 618.435. |
| NJ | Yes. | Yes. | Yes. | Yes. | Yes. | — | N.J. Stat. Ann. § 34:6A-26. |
| NM | Yes. | — | Yes. | Yes. | Yes. | Employee shall receive written notification of the determination and may request review. | N.M. Stat. Ann. § 50-9-10. |
| NY | Yes. | — | — | Yes. | Yes. | — | N.Y. Lab. Law § 27-a. |
| NC | Yes. | — | Yes. | Yes. | Yes. | Employee shall receive written notification of the determination and may request review. Employee will receive written statement of the reasons for the final disposition of the case. | N.C. Gen. Stat. § 95-136. |
| OR | Yes. | — | Yes. | Yes. | Yes. | — | Or. Rev. Stat. Ann. §§ 654.062, 654.067. |
| RI | Yes. | — | Yes. | Yes. | Yes. | Employee shall receive written notification of the determination and may seek review. | R.I. Gen. Laws §§ 28-20-12, 28-20-13. |
| SC | Yes. | Yes. | Yes. | Yes. | Yes. | Employee shall receive written notification of the determination and may seek review. | S.C. Regs. 71-505, 71-506, 71-507, 71-508, 71-509. |
| TN | Yes. | — | Yes. | Yes. | Yes. | Employee shall receive written notification of the determination and may request review. | Tenn. Code Ann. §§ 50-3-106, 50-3-301, 50-3-303, 50-3-304. |
| UT | Yes. | — | Yes. | Yes. | Yes. | Employee shall receive written notification of the determination and may seek review. | Utah Code Ann. § 34A-6-301. |

*(Table continues.)*

# **Table 8.1-3** *(cont'd)*
## STATE OCCUPATIONAL SAFETY REQUIREMENTS: INSPECTIONS

**KEY:** SAF means that the state has adopted federal OSHA rules on the topic.
"—" means that the state does not have specific statutory authority on the subject.

| | *Employee Has the Right to Participate in State Inspection* | *Employee Entitled to Wages While Participating in State Inspection* | *Communications Between Employee and State Inspector Are Confidential* | *Employee Has the Right to Request a State Inspection* | *Identity of Employee Requesting Inspection Is Confidential* | *Employee Rights if Inspection Does Not Result in a Citation* | *Citations to Authority* |
|---|---|---|---|---|---|---|---|
| VT | Yes. | — | — | Yes. | Yes. | Employee shall receive written notification of the determination and request review. | Vt. Stat. Ann. tit. 21, § 206. |
| VA | Yes. | — | Yes. | Yes. | Yes. | Employee shall receive written notification of the determination. | Va. Code Ann. §§ 40.1-49.8, 40.1-51.1, 40.1-51.2. |
| WA | Yes. | — | Yes. | Yes. | Yes. | Employee shall receive written notification of the determination and may request review. | Wash. Rev. Code Ann. §§ 49.17.070, 49.17.100, 49.17.110. |
| WV | Yes. | — | Yes. | Yes. | Yes. | Employee shall receive written notification of the determination. | W.Va. Code § 21-3A-8. |
| WI | Yes. | Yes. | — | Yes. | Yes. | Employee will receive written notification of the determination. Employee may request a hearing to review the decision. | Wis. Stat. Ann. § 101.055. |
| WY | Yes. | — | — | Yes. | Yes. | Employee shall receive written notification of the determination and may request review. | Wyo. Stat. Ann. 27-11-108, Wyoming OHSC Rules of Procedure. |

# Table 8.1-4
## STATE OCCUPATIONAL SAFETY PENALTIES

| | *Civil Penalties* | *Criminal Penalties for False Statements and Fatalities* | *Citations to Authority* |
|---|---|---|---|
| AK | For most violations, $7,000. For repeated or willful violations, up to $70,000. | For false statements or willful violations, a fine of up to $10,000, imprisonment for up to 6 months, or both. For a second willful violation, a fine of up to $20,000, imprisonment for up to 1 year, or both. | Alaska Stat. §§ 18.60.010 *et seq.* |
| AZ | For most violations, $7,000. For willful or repeated violations, $70,000, plus an additional penalty of $25,000 for each employee disability or death (payable to employee or dependents). | Knowing violation causing a death is a class 6 felony, with a fine of $1,000,000 for an enterprise or $150,000 for an individual and 1½ years imprisonment. A second such violation is a class 5 felony with the same fines but 2 years imprisonment. Making a false statement is a class 2 misdemeanor, with a fine of up to $10,000 for an enterprise, $750 for an individual, and up to 4 months imprisonment. | Ariz. Rev. Stat. Ann. §§ 23-401 *et seq.* |
| CA | Most violations carry a penalty of $7,000; willful or repeated violations are $10,000. | Most violations are misdemeanors, with a maximum fine of $5,000 and up to 6 months imprisonment, or both. Violation of an order carries a fine of up to $70,000 and up to 6 months imprisonment, or both, if death or serious injury results. Making a false statement carries a fine of up to $70,000 and up to 6 months imprisonment, or both. | Cal. Lab. Code Ann. §§ 6300 *et seq.*; Cal. Health & Safety Code Ann. § 25910. |
| CT | Most violations carry a penalty of up to $1,000. Willful or repeated violations carry a penalty of up to $20,000. | For willful violations causing a death, a maximum fine of $10,000 ($20,000 for a subsequent offense) and up to 6 months (1 year for a subsequent offense) imprisonment. For false statements, a maximum fine of $10,000 and up to 6 months imprisonment. | Conn. Gen. Stat. Ann. §§ 31-367 *et seq.* |
| DC | Most violations carry a penalty of $1,000; $10,000 for willful violations. | Willful violations and false statements carry a maximum fine of $10,000, up to 6 months imprisonment, or both. Subsequent violations carry a maximum fine of $20,000, up to 1 year imprisonment, or both. | D.C. Code Ann. §§ 36-1200 *et seq.* |
| FL | Violations carry a penalty of not less than $100 nor more than $5,000 for each day violation continues. Total penalty for each violation may not exceed $50,000. | Knowingly making a false statement is a misdemeanor of the second degree, which carries a fine up to $500, imprisonment for up to 60 days, or both. | Fla. Stat. Ann. §§ 442 *et seq.* |
| HI | Most violations carry a penalty of $7,000. Repeated or willful, $70,000; violations of prohibition against discrimination, $1,000. | Making a false statement carries a penalty of $10,000, imprisonment for up to 6 months, or both. Willful violation causing death carries a fine of up to $70,000 and imprisonment of up to 6 months (1 year for subsequent violations), or both. | Haw. Rev. Stat. §§ 396-1 *et seq.* |
| IL | SAF. | SAF. | 820 ILCS 225/4. |
| IN | Most violations carry a penalty of $7,000; willful or repeated violations, $70,000. | — | Ind. Code Ann. §§ 22-8-1.1 *et seq.* |
| IA | Most violations carry a penalty of $1,000; $10,000 for willful or repeated violations. | Making a false statement is a serious misdemeanor. A willful violation causing a death is a serious misdemeanor with a fine of up to $1,000, imprisonment for up to 1 year, or both. A second such violation is an aggravated misdemeanor with a maximum fine of $5,000, imprisonment for up to 2 years, or both. | Iowa Code §§ 88.1 *et seq.* |
| KY | Most violations carry a fine of $7,000; $70,000 for willful or repeated violations; $10,000 for violations of the antidiscrimination statute. | Knowingly making a false statement carries a maximum fine of $10,000, imprisonment for up to 6 months, or both. | Ky. Rev. Stat. §§ 338.011 *et seq.* |

*(Table continues.)*

## Table 8.1-4 *(cont'd)*
## STATE OCCUPATIONAL SAFETY PENALTIES

| | *Civil Penalties* | *Criminal Penalties for False Statements and Fatalities* | *Citations to Authority* |
|---|---|---|---|
| MD | Most violations carry a penalty of $7,000; $70,000 for repeated serious violations. | Knowingly making a false statement carries a fine of up to $5,000, imprisonment for up to 6 months, or both. A willful violation causing a death carries a maximum fine of $10,000 and up to 6 months imprisonment, or both. A second such violation carries a maximum fine of $20,000 and up to 1 year imprisonment, or both. | Md. Ann. Code L. & Emp. §§ 5-101 *et seq.* |
| MI | Most violations carry a penalty of $7,000; $70,000 for willful or repeated violations. | Making a false statement carries a maximum fine of $10,000, imprisonment for 6 months, or both. Violation causing the death of an employee carries a maximum fine of $10,000, imprisonment for up to one year, or both. A second such violation carries a maximum fine of $20,000 and imprisonment for up to 3 years, or both. | Mich. Comp. Laws Ann. §§ 408.1001 *et seq.* |
| MN | Most violations carry a penalty of $7,000; $70,000 for willful or repeated violations; $25,000 for violations resulting in a fatality. | Knowingly making a false statement or willfully violating a standard carries a maximum fine of $20,000 and up to 6 months imprisonment, or both. Subsequent willful violations carry a maximum fine of $35,000 and up to 1 year imprisonment, or both. | Minn. Stat. Ann. §§ 182.65 *et seq.* |
| NV | Most violations carry a penalty of $2,000; $10,000 for willful or repeated violations. | Knowingly making a false statement or a willful violation causing a death carries a maximum fine of $20,000 and up to 6 months imprisonment, or both. A subsequent violation causing a death carries a maximum fine of $40,000, 1 year imprisonment, or both. | Nev. Rev. Stat. §§ 618.005 *et seq.* |
| NM | Most violations carry a penalty of $7,000; $70,000 for willful or repeated violations. | Knowingly making a false statement or willfully violating a standard causing a death of an employee carries a maximum fine of $10,000, up to 6 months imprisonment, or both. Subsequent violations causing fatalities carry a maximum fine of $20,000, up to 1 year imprisonment, or both. | N.M. Stat. Ann. §§ 50-9-1 *et seq.* |
| NJ | Violation of act is punishable by a penalty not to exceed $1,000. | — | N.J. Stat. Ann. § 34:6A-41. |
| NY | For most violations, $50 per day. For serious violations, $200 per day. | — | N.Y. Lab. Law § 27-a. |
| NC | Most violations carry a penalty of $7,000; $70,000 for willful violations. | Knowingly making a false statement or violating a standard causing the death of an employee carries a maximum fine of $10,000, imprisonment of up to 6 months, or both. Subsequent violations causing fatalities carry a maximum fine of $20,000, imprisonment for up to 6 months, or both. | N.C. Gen. Stat. §§ 95-126 *et seq.* |
| OR | Most violations carry a penalty of $7,000; state regulations also provide for penalties of $300 or more; $70,000 for willful or repeated violations. | Willful violation causing a fatality carries a penalty of up to $10,000, imprisonment for not more than 6 months, or both. A subsequent violation carries a maximum penalty of $20,000, imprisonment for up to 1 year, or both. | Or. Rev. Stat. Ann. §§ 654.001 *et seq.* |
| RI | Most violations carry a penalty of $1,000; $10,000 for repeated or willful violations. | Knowingly making a false statement carries a maximum fine of $10,000, up to 1 year imprisonment, or both. A violation causing a fatality carries a maximum fine of $10,000, up to 6 months imprisonment, or both. A subsequent such violation carries a maximum fine of $20,000, up to 2 years imprisonment, or both. | R.I. Gen. Laws §§ 28-20-1 *et seq.* |

| | | | |
|---|---|---|---|
| SC | Most violations carry a penalty of $7,000; $70,000 for willful or repeated violations. | Knowingly making a false statement or willfully violating a rule thereby causing a fatality carries a penalty of up to $10,000, imprisonment for up to 6 months, or both. A subsequent violation causing a fatality carries a maximum fine of $20,000, imprisonment up to 1 year, or both. | S.C. Code Ann. §§ 41-15-10 *et seq.* |
| TN | Most violations carry a penalty of $7,000; $70,000 for willful or repeated violations. | Knowingly making a false statement is a misdemeanor with a maximum fine of $50, imprisonment for up to 30 days, or both. Violation causing a fatality carries a maximum fine of $10,000, imprisonment for up to 6 months, or both. A second such violation carries a maximum fine of $20,000, imprisonment up to 1 year, or both. | Tenn. Code Ann. §§ 50-3-101 *et seq.* |
| TX | Violation is a Class B misdemeanor. | — | Tex. Labor Code Ann. § 411.046. |
| UT | Most violations carry a penalty of $7,000; $70,000 for willful or repeated violations. | Knowingly making a false statement carries a fine of up to $70,000, up to 6 months imprisonment, or both. Willful violation causing a fatality carries a maximum fine of $10,000, up to 6 months imprisonment, or both. A subsequent such violation carries a maximum fine of $20,000, up to 1 year imprisonment, or both. | Utah Code Ann. §§ 35-9-1 *et seq.* |
| VT | Most violations carry a penalty of $7,000; $70,000 for willful or repeated violations. | Knowingly making a false statement carries a maximum fine of $10,000, up to 6 months imprisonment, or both. Violation resulting in a fatality carries a maximum fine of $20,000, up to 1 year imprisonment, or both. | Vt. Stat. Ann. tit. 21, §§ 201 *et seq.* |
| VA | Most violations carry a penalty of $7,000; $70,000 for willful or repeated violations. | Knowingly making a false statement carries a maximum fine of $10,000, up to 6 months imprisonment, or both. A violation causing a fatality carries a maximum fine of $10,000, up to 6 months imprisonment, or both. A subsequent such violation carries a maximum fine of $140,000, 1 year imprisonment, or both. | Va. Code Ann. §§ 40.1-40 *et seq.* |
| WA | Most violations carry a penalty of $7,000; $70,000 for willful or repeated violations. | Knowingly making a false statement is a gross misdemeanor with a maximum fine of $10,000, up to 6 months imprisonment, or both.<br>A violation causing a fatality is a gross misdemeanor with a maximum fine of $100,000, up to 6 months imprisonment, or both. A subsequent such violation carries a maximum fine of $200,000, up to 1 year imprisonment, or both. | Wash. Rev. Code Ann. §§ 49.17.010 *et seq.* |
| WV | Employer in violation receives a citation from the Department of Labor. | — | W.Va. Code Ann. §§ 21-3A-1 *et seq.* |
| WY | Most violations carry a penalty of $7,000; $70,000 for willful or knowing violations. | Making a false representation carries a maximum penalty of $10,000, up to 6 months imprisonment, or both. A violation causing a fatality carries a maximum fine of $10,000, up to 6 months imprisonment, or both. A subsequent such violation carries a maximum fine of $20,000, up to 6 months imprisonment, or both. | Wyo. Stat. §§ 27-11-101 *et seq.* |

## § 8.2 State and Local Smoking Laws

Few issues have provoked more contention in the workplace than smoking. Studies outlining the deleterious effect of second-hand smoke on nonsmokers have caused the controversy to intensify.[1] Although OSHA does not currently govern smoking in the workplace (see § 8.1 for proposed OSHA regulations), federal or state laws prohibiting discrimination against employees on the basis of handicap or disability may be applicable to smoking or nonsmoking employees. For example, an employee who is highly allergic to tobacco smoke may qualify as "handicapped" under the Rehabilitation Act of 1973, or as a "qualified individual with a disability" under the Americans with Disabilities Act (ADA). If an employee so qualifies, an employer may be required to reasonably accommodate the employee, perhaps by altering the work area, installing ventilation systems, or offering employment in a separate location. On the other hand, an employee who is addicted to tobacco may similarly argue that he or she qualifies as handicapped or as a disabled individual entitled to reasonable accommodation that includes requiring the designation of a smoking area accessible to the employee.

Employees who leave their jobs because of adverse reactions to second-hand smoke may argue that they are entitled to disability payments or unemployment compensation; however, an employee hoping to recover such payments must demonstrate a severe reaction to smoke such that he or she was required to leave work involuntarily. An employee who can show that his or her injury was caused by inhalation of second-hand smoke, and was "job-related," may be entitled to workers' compensation.

Smoking in the workplace may also be subject to collective bargaining. If smoking in the workplace is considered a term or condition of employment, an employer may be required to negotiate with a union or its employees concerning the characteristics of any smoking rules or regulations that are adopted.

Because OSHA has not yet preempted the field of workplace smoking regulation, state common law is still in full force in this area. Some state courts have begun to recognize a common-law right of action by a nonsmoking employee against his or her employer. The cases tend to rely on negligence principles and involve allegations that the employer breached its duty to use all reasonable care to provide a reasonably safe workplace for its employees. If irreparable harm can be shown, a plaintiff might also be entitled to an injunction.

Following are a number of recent decisions involving workplace smoking. A Georgia appeals court recently refused to dismiss an employee's claim that her extreme sensitivity to pipe smoke was a "disability" under the Georgia handicap law, thus leaving open the question whether such sensitivity may be protected.[2] However, other courts have rejected claims that sensitivity to smoke is a disability or handicap that requires reasonable accommodation.

In one case,[3] the federal district court held that the

**§ 8.2**

1. See Surgeon General's Report on the Health Consequences of Involuntary Smoking (1986); see also the Environmental Protection Agency's risk assessment on environmental tobacco smoke (ETS) (1992).

2. Richardson v. Hennly, Ga. App. Ct. (1993).

3. Harmer v. Virginia Electric and Power Co., E.D. Va. 1993.

ADA does not require an employer to declare an entire building smoke-free in order to reasonably accommodate an asthmatic employee. The Fourth Circuit Court of Appeals also recently held that to be considered an employee with a disability under the federal Rehabilitation Act, the employee must show that her allergy to tobacco smoke generally prevents her from obtaining jobs in her field, rather than preventing her from continuing in her current position.[4]

Aside from the reactions of individual employers and employees, states and local governments have promulgated smoking regulations to address a wide variety of issues. Some smoking laws are concerned primarily with regulating smoking in "public places" and generally have only an incidental effect on employment. Other laws specifically address smoking in the workplace and attempt to balance the interests of smoking and nonsmoking employees. Different jurisdictions have approached the issue of accommodating smoking or nonsmoking employees from entirely different perspectives. Some states require certain employers to set aside designated smoking areas and have passed specific legislation that protects the rights of employees who smoke. For example, Kentucky has recently passed a statute that regulates governmental smoking policies in order to protect government employees who smoke. Under the statute, any smoking policy that applies to a government workplace must *require* accessible indoor smoking areas and must favor allowing smoking in open public areas of such workplaces. The statute is similar to a measure recently passed in North Carolina, which protects certain employees who wish to smoke in the workplace.

In contrast to these "pro-smoker" rules are the extensive prohibitions on workplace smoking embodied in the laws of other jurisdictions. In 1994, the city of Los Angeles followed the lead of San Francisco in passing what has been termed one of the most restrictive anti-smoking measures ever. (See Table 8.2-1 for the recent Los Angeles and San Francisco ordinances.) Several states—California, Delaware, Utah, Washington, Maryland, Tennessee, and Vermont—also passed stringent new laws restricting smoking in public places, including the workplace.

Maryland enacted legislation (effective March 27, 1995) that modified the workplace smoking regulations that were administratively enacted in 1994. The new legislative provisions ease smoking restrictions somewhat from the restrictions promulgated by the Commissioner of Labor and Industry. Smoking is now allowed in any generally recognized bar or tavern, including those located in restaurants. Smoking is allowed in a separate, enclosed room of a restaurant, as long as the room does not exceed 40 percent of the total area of the restaurant. Smoking is also now allowed in 40 percent of the sleeping rooms of a hotel or motel.

Tennessee and Vermont have also recently enacted smoking prohibitions that restrict or prohibit smoking on or near school grounds or other areas where children are likely to be, including youth group-care homes, day-care centers, children's residential treatment facilities, museums, and zoos. The restrictions in both states became effective on July 1, 1995, and affect employees who work in such places as well as the children who visit them.

The California measure, which was signed by Gov. Pete Wilson on July 21, 1994, bans smoking in most indoor workplaces. The law provides, however, that for purposes of the prohibition on smoking, the term "place of employment" does not apply to (1) certain portions of a hotel, motel, or other lodging establishment; (2) meeting rooms or banquet rooms, subject to certain exceptions; (3) retail or wholesale tobacco shops; (4) private smokers' lounges; (5) cabs of trucks or truck tractors as specified; (6) bars, taverns, and gaming clubs, subject to certain prescribed conditions; (7) warehouse facilities; (8) theatrical sites; (9) medical research or treatment sites; (10) employee breakrooms under prescribed conditions; (11) smoking areas for patients in long-term health care facilities, as defined; and (12) specified smoking areas designated by employers with fewer than five employees. The act generally provides for misdemeanor penalties for violations, and it specifies certain applicable fines.

Significantly, the act states that its smoking prohibition "shall constitute a uniform statewide standard for regulating the smoking of tobacco products in enclosed places of employment and shall supersede and render unnecessary the local enactment or enforcement of local ordinances regulating the smoking of tobacco products in enclosed places of employment." This language clearly indicates the state legislature's intent to preempt local legislation.

For the characteristics of various state and local smoking laws, see Exhibit 8.2-1, State Smoking Laws, and Table 8.2-1, Municipal Smoking Ordinances. For rules relating to employees' use of tobacco while off duty, see § 7.7.

---

4. Gupton v. Virginia, 62 U.S.L.W. 2441 (4th Cir. 1993).

## Exhibit 8.2-1
STATE SMOKING LAWS

**Note:** The "Nonretaliation" entry discusses statutory provisions that bar discrimination against employees who exercise their rights under the smoking statute (e.g., their right to complain about smoke, or their right to smoke at work, as allowed by the state statute). A distinct set of state statutes that bars discrimination against employees who choose to smoke while off-duty is compiled at Exhibit 7.7-1.

### ALABAMA

**Coverage/Focus of the Statutes.** No state statute regulates smoking in public places or the workplace.

**Places Where Smoking Is Prohibited.** State has no statutory requirements.

**Exceptions/Places Where Smoking Is Permitted.** State has no statutory requirements.

**Notice Requirements.** State has no statutory requirements.

**Cost-Benefit/Waiver Requirements.** State has no statutory requirements.

**Nonretaliation.** State has no statutory requirements.

**Enforcement.** State has no statutory requirements.

**Local Laws/Preemption.** State has no statutory requirements.

**Other Requirements.** None.

**Citations to Authority.** None.

### ALASKA

**Coverage/Focus of the Statutes.** State statutes focus on regulating smoking in public places; however, there are specific provisions regulating smoking in places of employment.

**Places Where Smoking Is Prohibited.** Smoking is prohibited in schools, public assemblies, and health care facilities. Except in designated areas, smoking is prohibited in most other public areas, including public office buildings.

**Exemptions/Places Where Smoking Is Permitted.** Smoking is permitted in places of business that designate smoking sections and make reasonable accommodations to protect the health of nonsmokers by utilizing physical barriers and ventilation. In schools, smoking is allowed in well-ventilated areas off limits to minors.

**Notice Requirements.** Employers must conspicuously display signs indicating where smoking is prohibited or permitted. Signs for nonsmoking areas read "Smoking Prohibited By Law—Maximum Fine $50" and include the international symbol for no smoking. The Department of Environmental Conservation will provide signs upon request.

**Cost-Benefit/Waiver Requirements.** State has no statutory requirements.

**Nonretaliation.** State has no statutory requirements.

**Enforcement.** The Commissioner of Environmental Conservation enforces the statutes and may levy fines. Any officer of the peace may issue a citation. Multiple fines are prohibited, but any party may institute an action to enjoin repeated violations. Civil fines for smoking in a prohibited area range from $10 to $50. Civil fines for failing to post signs range from $20 to $300.

**Local Laws/Preemption.** State has no statutory requirements.

**Other Requirements.** The Commissioner of Environmental Conservation must take measures to inform the public of the statutes' requirements.

**Citations to Authority.** Alaska Stat. §§ 18.35.300 *et seq.*

**ARIZONA**

**Coverage/Focus of the Statutes.** State statutes focus on regulating smoking in certain public places and in state buildings; the statutes' effect on employment is largely incidental.

**Places Where Smoking Is Prohibited.** Smoking is prohibited in indoor public areas, including state-owned buildings, theaters, libraries, museums, school buildings, and waiting rooms of health care facilities and doctors' offices.

**Exemptions/Places Where Smoking Is Permitted.** Smoking is permitted in designated areas where physical barriers and ventilation prevent the drift of smoke to nonsmoking areas.

**Notice Requirements.** Employers must post signs designating a smoking area as such.

**Cost-Benefit/Waiver Requirements.** In state-owned buildings, if smoke drifts into a nonsmoking area, the state must physically modify the building, install new ventilation systems, or prohibit smoking entirely.

**Nonretaliation.** No state employer may discriminate on the basis of employee use or nonuse of tobacco.

**Enforcement.** Anonymous complaints may be made to the relevant state department. A violator is guilty of a petty offense.

**Local Laws/Preemption.** State has no statutory requirements.

**Other Requirements.** Persons using tobacco for religious or ceremonial reasons and prison inmates are exempt from the provisions of the statute. School boards decide whether smoking is prohibited in schools. Nothing in this section shall require the establishment of a smoking area in any state building that has been previously a nonsmoking building.

**Citations to Authority.** Ariz. Rev. Stat. Ann. §§ 15-341, 36-601.01–36-601.02.

**ARKANSAS**

**Coverage/Focus of the Statutes.** State statutes focus primarily on controlling smoking in public places; the statutes' effect on employment is incidental to this purpose.

**Places Where Smoking Is Prohibited.** Smoking is prohibited on school buses, in doctors' or dentists' waiting rooms, in hospital corridors, at nurses' stations in hospitals and clinics, and in all hospital rooms, except private patients' rooms.

**Exemptions/Places Where Smoking Is Permitted.** Smoking is permitted in areas designated as smoking areas. These statutes do not cover hotels, motels, and restaurants.

**Notice Requirements.** State has no statutory requirements.

**Cost-Benefit/Waiver Requirements.** State has no statutory requirements.

**Nonretaliation.** State has no statutory requirements.

**Enforcement.** Violators are guilty of a misdemeanor, punishable by a fine of $10–$100.

**Local Laws/Preemption.** State has no statutory requirements.

**Other Requirements.** Separate provisions regulate smoking in day care facilities. State government employers are required to formulate a smoking policy that considers the rights of both smokers and nonsmokers.

**Citations to Authority.** Ark. Code Ann. §§ 20-27-701 *et seq.,* 20-78-217, 25-1-102.

**CALIFORNIA**

**Coverage/Focus of the Statutes.** State statute specifically regulates smoking in enclosed places of employment.

**Places Where Smoking Is Prohibited.** No employer shall knowingly or intentionally permit, and no person shall engage in, the smoking of tobacco products in an enclosed space at a place of employment.

**Exemptions/Places Where Smoking Is Permitted.** Certain places excluded from the definition of "place of employment" include tobacco shops, certain areas of hotels and motels, bars, gaming clubs, warehouses, and private residences. Effective January 1, 1998, the exclusion of bars and gaming clubs became inoperative, thus making the statutory restrictions applicable to such establishments. An employee breakroom is the only workplace that may be a designated smoking area, and in order to allow smoking, the following requirements must be met: (1) air must be exhausted directly outside and not recirculated, (2) the employer must comply with EPA or OSHA ventilation standards, (3) the smoking room must be located in a nonwork area where no person is required to enter as part of his or her work responsibilities, (4) there are sufficient nonsmoking breakrooms to accommodate nonsmokers.

**Notice Requirements.** An employer's obligation to refrain from knowingly or intentionally permitting smoking by nonemployees is satisfied if the employer posts clear and prominent signs indicating that smoking is not permitted. An employer must also request that a nonemployee who is smoking refrain from doing so.

**Cost-Benefit/Waiver Requirements.** In order to allow smoking in a place of employment, an employer must make expenditures so as to comply with the statute, unless the existing location and ventilation of an employee breakroom already comply with the statute. See, "Exemptions/Places Where Smoking is Permitted," above.

**Enforcement.** The statute is enforced by local law enforcement agencies, including local health departments. A violation is punishable by a fine not to exceed $100 for a first violation, $200 for a second violation within one year, and $500 for a third or subsequent violation within one year.

**Local Laws/Preemption.** The statute constitutes a uniform statewide standard for regulating the smoking of tobacco products in enclosed places of employment. However, any area not defined by the statute as a "place of employment" is subject to local regulation. Furthermore, local regulations are to be suspended only as long as the 100 percent smoking prohibition provided for in the statute remains in effect. Any repeal or legislative or judicial modification of the statute revives any existing local regulations and empowers localities to enact new regulations concerning workplace smoking.

**Other Requirements.** No employer is required to reasonably accommodate a smoker, and need not designate a smoking area, even if permitted. Employers with fewer than five employees may designate a smoking area if all employees who must enter the area agree and air from the area is exhausted directly outside and not recirculated.

**Citations to Authority.** Cal. Lab. Code § 6404.5 (West).

## COLORADO

**Coverage/Focus of the Statutes.** State statutes regulate smoking in certain public places; the statutes' effect on employment is largely incidental.

**Places Where Smoking Is Prohibited.** Smoking is prohibited in schools, hospitals, theaters, state legislative buildings, and on public transportation. Other employers are encouraged to designate nonsmoking areas that are physically separate from areas where smoking is permitted and to make "every effort" to provide a nonsmoking area in employee cafeterias and lounges.

**Exemptions/Places Where Smoking Is Permitted.** Smoking is permitted in designated areas of public places and restaurants and taverns, and is specifically permitted in private offices, even if nonsmokers visit.

**Notice Requirements.** An employer must post conspicuous signs identifying smoking and nonsmoking areas.

**Cost-Benefit/Waiver Requirements.** State has no statutory requirements.

**Nonretaliation.** State has no statutory requirements.

**Enforcement.** State has no statutory requirements.

**Local Laws/Preemption.** Local governments are free to regulate smoking, and local ordinances control to the extent that they are consistent with the state statute.

**Other Requirements.** Where an employer posts a "no smoking" sign, such posting has the effect of causing that area to fall within the definition of a "public place" where smoking is prohibited.

**Citations to Authority.** Colo. Rev. Stat. §§ 25-14-101 *et seq.*

## CONNECTICUT

**Coverage/Focus of the Statutes.** State has general provisions controlling smoking in public places and has specific provisions applicable to smoking in the workplace. Only employers with 20 or more employees are subject to the provisions regarding smoking in the workplace.

**Places Where Smoking Is Prohibited.** Smoking is generally prohibited in any publicly owned building, health care institution, retail food store, nonsmoking area of a restaurant seating 75 or more persons, or public school building. Employers must establish, upon request, nonsmoking areas of sufficient size to accommodate nonsmoking employees. An employer may designate the entire work area as nonsmoking.

**Exemptions/Places Where Smoking Is Permitted.** Smoking is permitted in certain designated areas, including rooms used for private functions in restaurants and schools. In areas where smoking is permitted, an employer must utilize existing physical barriers and ventilation systems to minimize the effects of smoke on nonsmokers.

**Notice Requirements.** In areas where smoking is prohibited, the employer or person in control must conspicuously post signs stating this fact. Signs must have letters at least four inches high, except signs in elevators and restaurants.

**Cost-Benefit/Waiver Requirements.** The state labor commissioner may exempt an employer from the statutory requirements upon a showing of good-faith efforts to comply or upon a showing that compliance would be an unreasonable financial burden.

**Nonretaliation.** State has no statutory requirements.

**Enforcement.** Smokers who violate the provisions of the statute, anyone who removes a "smoking permitted" or "no smoking" sign, and employers who fail to post required signs are guilty of an (unspecified) infraction.

**Local Laws/Preemption.** Provisions of state law supersede the provisions of any municipal law relative to smoking.

**Other Requirements.** A separate statutory section prohibits smoking by operators of common carriers, including buses and trains. Any person who smokes in a bakery while performing his or her duties is subject to a fine, and even imprisonment. The use of tobacco is prohibited in any part of a milk pasteurizing plant.

**Citations to Authority.** Conn. Gen. Stat. Ann. §§ 1-21b, 21a-157, 21a-159, 22-201, 31-40q *et seq.*, 53-198.

## DELAWARE

**Coverage/Focus of the Statutes.** State statutes regulate smoking in public places and specifically address smoking in the workplace.

**Places Where Smoking Is Prohibited.** Smoking is restricted in a variety of public places. In the workplace, an employer must adopt and implement a written smoking policy that provides at a minimum a smoke-free work area to any employee who requests one and that also provides smoke-free areas in employee cafeterias, lunch rooms, and lounges that are sufficient to meet employee demand.

**Exemptions/Places Where Smoking Is Permitted.** Smoking is permitted in properly designated areas of public places, including the workplace. Restrictions do not apply to private homes, private social functions, hotel rooms, bars, and tobacco businesses.

**Notice Requirements.** Smoking or no smoking signs, or the international symbol, shall be posted in appropriate places by an employer wherever smoking is regulated by the statute.

**Cost-Benefit/Waiver Requirements.** The state Department of Labor may waive the provisions of the statute if it determines that there are compelling reasons to do so and the waiver will not significantly affect the health and comfort of nonconsumers of tobacco products.

**Nonretaliation.** Any employer who discharges an employee for filing a complaint or providing information to the Department of Labor shall be subject to a civil penalty of not less than $1,000 nor more than $5,000 for each violation.

**Enforcement.** Any person who violates the statute is subject to an administrative penalty of $25 for the first violation and not less than $50 for each subsequent violation.

**Local Laws/Preemption.** Any municipal or county ordinance or regulation adopted after June 28, 1994, is specifically preempted by the state statute.

**Other Requirements.** Smoking is prohibited on trackless trolley coaches and gasoline- or diesel-engine-propelled buses being used as public conveyances.

**Citations to Authority.** Del. Code Ann. tit. 11, § 1327; tit 16 §§ 2901 *et seq.*

## DISTRICT OF COLUMBIA

**Coverage/Focus of the Statutes.** District statute focuses on regulating smoking in public places; however, there are specific provisions for workplaces.

**Places Where Smoking Is Prohibited.** Smoking is generally prohibited in public places. In the workplace, an employer must adopt, implement, and maintain a written policy on smoking, which must be promulgated to employees. An employer may prohibit smoking in the entire building.

**Exemptions/Places Where Smoking Is Permitted.** Smoking is permitted in bars and tobacco shops. If an employer permits smoking, the employer's smoking policy must designate a specific area where smoking is permitted and provide physical barriers, separate rooms, or ventilation systems to minimize smoke in adjacent nonsmoking areas.

**Notice Requirements.** An employer must post conspicuous signs identifying smoking and nonsmoking areas. Signs must include a warning stating that smoking causes lung cancer, heart disease, and emphysema and that it may cause fetal injury in pregnant women.

**Cost-Benefit/Waiver Requirements.** State has no statutory requirements.

**Nonretaliation.** No employer may discharge or otherwise discriminate against an employee on the basis of tobacco use in compliance with the statute or the employer's smoking policy. An employee may bring a separate civil action for violation of this provision and may recover back pay, damages, reasonable attorney fees, and costs.

**Enforcement.** Fines are imposed for smoking in a nonsmoking area and for removing or defacing a sign. An aggrieved person may bring an action to enjoin violation of the statute.

**Local Laws/Preemption.** State has no statutory requirements.

**Other Requirements.** A separate section of the statute prohibits smoking on the Metro. Designation of a smoking area in a workplace is subject to collective bargaining. The mayor must establish an education program under the statute.

**Citations to Authority.** D.C. Code Ann. §§ 6-911 *et seq.*, 44-223.

## FLORIDA

**Coverage/Focus of the Statutes.** State statute focuses primarily on controlling smoking in public places; however, included in the definition of "public place" is a place of employment. Specific workplace provisions are included in the statute.

**Places Where Smoking Is Prohibited.** Smoking is generally prohibited in public places, including, but not limited to, government buildings, public transportation, hospitals, schools, day care facilities, courtrooms, grocery stores, theaters, places of employment, restaurants seating more than 50 persons, and retail stores (excluding tobacco stores).

**Exemptions/Places Where Smoking Is Permitted.** In public places, smoking is permitted only in designated areas. An employer may designate an area for smoking and must use existing physical barriers and ventilation systems to minimize smoke. In a workplace where there are smokers and nonsmokers, an employer must develop, implement, and post a smoking policy, which shall take into consideration the proportion of smokers and nonsmokers. An entire work area may be designated a smoking area if all workers agree. Smoking may be permitted in private offices and at private functions in public places.

**Notice Requirements.** An employer is required to post conspicuous signs identifying designated smoking areas. An employer may post signs elsewhere indicating that smoking is permitted only in the designated areas.

**Cost-Benefit/Waiver Requirements.** An employer is not required to modify an area physically to minimize smoke and is not required to install new ventilation systems or operate existing ventilation systems if doing so will increase electricity use. An employer may seek an exemption from the requirements of the statute based on good-faith efforts to comply or on emergency or extraordinary circumstances.

**Nonretaliation.** State has no statutory requirements.

**Enforcement.** State administrative agencies enforce the statute and may impose fines or seek injunctions against violators. No private right of action is specifically provided.

**Local Laws/Preemption.** State statute specifically preempts any municipal or county smoking ordinance.

**Other Requirements.** An employer who makes "reasonable efforts" to develop, implement, and post a smoking policy is deemed in compliance.

**Citations to Authority.** Fla. Stat. Ann. §§ 386.201 *et seq.*

## GEORGIA

**Coverage/Focus of the Statutes.** State statute prohibits smoking in certain public areas; the statutes' effect on employment is only incidental.

**Places Where Smoking Is Prohibited.** Smoking is prohibited in any area that is open to or used by the public and that is clearly designated by a no-smoking sign. Smoking is entirely prohibited in elevators, public transportation, day care centers and group and family day care homes.

**Exemptions/Places Where Smoking Is Permitted.** Smoking is permitted in any public area not designated by a no-smoking sign.

**Notice Requirements.** All nonsmoking areas must be clearly designated by posted signs.

**Cost-Benefit/Waiver Requirements.** State has no statutory requirements.

**Nonretaliation.** State has no statutory requirements.

**Enforcement.** Violators may incur fines of $10–$100.

**Local Laws/Preemption.** Statute does not preempt any local laws, rules, and regulations of state or local agencies that are more restrictive.

**Other Requirements.** Separate provision regulates smoking in day care facilities.

**Citations to Authority.** Ga. Code Ann. § 16-12-2.

## HAWAII

**Coverage/Focus of the Statutes.** State statutes focus on regulating smoking in public places; however, there are specific provisions for workplaces.

**Places Where Smoking Is Prohibited.** Smoking is generally prohibited in public places. In the workplace, an employer must adopt, implement, and maintain a written smoking policy that reasonably accommodates both smoking and nonsmoking employees by using ventilation systems, separate rooms, or partitions.

**Exemptions/Places Where Smoking Is Permitted.** Smoking is permitted in designated areas and is not regulated on property owned or leased by the federal government or in private enclosed offices, even if visited by nonsmokers. Smoking is permitted in small businesses and retail stores with less than 5,000 square feet of floor space.

**Notice Requirements.** An employer must clearly mark areas where smoking is prohibited.

**Cost-Benefit/Waiver Requirements.** No expenditures or structural alterations are required.

**Nonretaliation.** State has no statutory requirements.

**Enforcement.** The state director of health enforces the statute by requesting employers to comply or by instituting an action to enjoin compliance. Any person may request the director to enforce the statute. Violators may be fined.

**Local Laws/Preemption.** Any county may enact ordinances more stringent than the statute.

**Other Requirements.** If no reasonable accommodation between smokers and nonsmokers can be reached, a simple majority in each affected area shall determine whether smoking is or is not prohibited. Nonsmokers may appeal to the state director of health. "Employee," as defined by the statute, refers only to a person working 20 or more hours per week. Violation of the statute is not negligence per se. Separate provision regulates smoking in day care facilities.

**Citations to Authority.** Haw. Rev. Stat. §§ 328K-1 *et seq.*

## IDAHO

**Coverage/Focus of the Statutes.** State statutes regulate smoking in certain public places; the statutes' effect on employment is largely incidental.

**Places Where Smoking Is Prohibited.** Smoking is prohibited at public meetings, in restaurants seating 30 or more persons, in retail stores, elevators, schools, and hospitals, and on public transportation.

**Exemptions/Places Where Smoking Is Permitted.** Smoking is permitted in designated areas in which an employer must make a good-faith effort to minimize smoke. Bars, bowling alleys, and rooms for private functions are exempt from the statute.

**Notice Requirements.** "No smoking" signs must be posted at a public meeting. An employer must make reasonable efforts to prevent smoking by posting appropriate signs.

**Cost-Benefit/Waiver Requirements.** The director of health may waive the requirements of the statute for compelling reasons, provided the waiver will not significantly affect the health and comfort of nonsmokers.

**Nonretaliation.** State has no statutory requirements.

**Enforcement.** A violator is guilty of an infraction and may be fined $50. Any violation may be reported to a law enforcement officer.

**Local Laws/Preemption.** State has no statutory requirements.

**Other Requirements.** If a public place is a single room, the statutory requirement is deemed to have been met if one side of the room is designated nonsmoking.

**Citations to Authority.** Idaho Code §§ 18-5904–18-5906, 39-5501 *et seq.*

## ILLINOIS

**Coverage/Focus of the Statutes.** State statute focuses on controlling smoking in public places, including certain workplaces. Workplaces that are not covered include factories, warehouses, and similar places of employment not frequented by the general public.

**Places Where Smoking Is Prohibited.** Smoking is prohibited in public places, including, but not limited to, hospitals, child care centers, restaurants, retail stores, offices, commercial establishments, theaters, schools, libraries, public transportation, auditoriums, and arenas.

**Exemptions/Places Where Smoking Is Permitted.** Smoking is permitted in bars and bowling alleys, public rooms used for private social functions, and private offices, even if they are visited by nonsmokers. Smoking is also permitted in designated areas of public places. In establishing a smoking area, an employer must utilize existing barriers and ventilation systems to minimize smoke.

**Notice Requirements.** The posting of notices is not specifically required. (See "Enforcement.")

**Cost-Benefit/Waiver Requirements.** State has no statutory requirements.

**Nonretaliation.** No person may be discriminated against in any manner because of the exercise of rights under the statute.

**Enforcement.** Employers and state or local officials shall make reasonable efforts to prevent smoking in public places outside those areas designated as smoking areas by posting appropriate signs, by contacting a law enforcement officer, or by other appropriate means. Any aggrieved person may seek an injunction against a violator. A person violating the statute is guilty of a petty offense.

**Local Laws/Preemption.** The state statute preempts any local laws regulating smoking unless they were promulgated prior to October 1, 1989.

**Other Requirements.** When a public place is a single room or enclosure, the statute may be satisfied by establishing a reasonable portion of the room or enclosure as a smoking area. Separate provision regulates smoking in day care facilities.

**Citations to Authority.** 410 Ill. Comp. Stat. Ann. 80/1–80/11.

## INDIANA

**Coverage/Focus of the Statutes.** State statute controls smoking in public buildings; the statute's effect on smoking in the workplace is incidental.

**Places Where Smoking Is Prohibited.** Smoking is prohibited in public buildings, which are defined as buildings occupied by state or local government agencies, universities, public schools, and health facilities. If a public building is a single room, any part or all of the room may be reserved as a nonsmoking area.

**Exemptions/Places Where Smoking Is Permitted.** Smoking is permitted in designated areas of public buildings. A person in charge may designate an area as a smoking area and may take reasonably necessary measures to accommodate both smokers and nonsmokers.

**Notice Requirements.** A person in charge is required to post conspicuous signs warning that smoking is permitted only in designated areas.

**Cost-Benefit/Waiver Requirements.** A person in charge may be granted a waiver from the statute's requirements if there are compelling reasons and if the waiver will not significantly affect the health and comfort of nonsmokers.

**Nonretaliation.** State has no statutory requirements.

**Enforcement.** A person in charge must request that a violator refrain from smoking, and if the violator refuses to refrain, the person in charge must remove the violator from the building. Violation of the statute is a Class C infraction.

**Local Laws/Preemption.** The statute does not prohibit a local government unit from adopting more restrictive ordinances.

**Other Requirements.** The state department of health may adopt rules to restrict or prohibit smoking in public buildings where, because of the close proximity of workers, smoking affects the health and comfort of nonsmoking employees. A prison is exempt from the definition of a "public building."

**Citations to Authority.** Ind. Code Ann. §§ 16-41-37-1 *et seq.* (Burns). [*Gorman v. Moody,* 710 F. Supp. 1256 (N.D. Ind. 1989)]

## IOWA

**Coverage/Focus of the Statutes.** State regulates smoking in public places; "public place" is defined to include a place of work with over 250 square feet of space.

**Places Where Smoking Is Prohibited.** Smoking is prohibited in places including, but not limited to, retail stores, commercial establishments, offices, malls, hospitals, and schools. No public place other than a bar may be designated as a smoking area in its entirety.

**Exemptions/Places Where Smoking Is Permitted.** Smoking is permitted in designated areas. Existing physical barriers and ventilation systems must be used to minimize smoke. Tobacco stores and enclosed private offices are not "public places" where smoking is prohibited. Similarly, factories, warehouses, and similar workplaces are not covered, but a nonsmoking area must be designated in an employee cafeteria in such a place.

**Notice Requirements.** An employer must make reasonable efforts to prevent smoking by posting appropriate signs and arranging seating accordingly.

**Cost-Benefit/Waiver Requirements.** State has no specific statutory requirements.

**Nonretaliation.** State has no statutory requirements.

**Enforcement.** Fines are imposed for violations. Magistrates hear and determine violations upon prosecution by the government attorney.

**Local Laws/Preemption.** All inconsistent local laws or regulations are superseded by the statute.

**Other Requirements.** If a public place is a single room, the statutory requirement is deemed to have been met if one side of the room is designated nonsmoking.

**Citations to Authority.** Iowa Code Ann. §§ 142B.1 *et seq.*

## KANSAS

**Coverage/Focus of the Statutes.** State statutes regulate smoking in public areas; the statute's effect on employment is largely incidental.

**Places Where Smoking Is Prohibited.** Smoking is prohibited at public meetings and in public places, including elevators, school buses, and means of mass transportation. Also, smoking is prohibited in any other place as determined by the fire marshal or other law.

**Exemptions/Places Where Smoking Is Permitted.** Smoking is permitted in designated areas. Existing physical barriers and ventilation systems shall be used to minimize the toxic effect of smoke in adjacent nonsmoking areas.

**Notice Requirements.** A person in charge shall post conspicuous signs clearly stating that smoking is prohibited by state law.

**Cost-Benefit/Waiver Requirements.** State has no statutory requirements.

**Nonretaliation.** State has no statutory requirements.

**Enforcement.** The state's Department of Health and Environment may institute an action in any court to enjoin repeated violations of the statute. A violator is guilty of a misdemeanor, punishable by a fine of not more than $20 for each violation. A person in charge who fails to post signs is guilty of a misdemeanor, punishable by a fine of not more than $50.

**Local Laws/Preemption.** Any city or county may enact ordinances at least as stringent as the state statute.

**Other Requirements.** Separate provisions regulate smoking in schools and in day care and health facilities. On and after July 1, 1995, smoking is entirely prohibited in the state capitol building.

**Citations to Authority.** Kan. Stat. Ann. §§ 21-4009 *et seq.,* 72-53,107.

## KENTUCKY

**Coverage/Focus of the Statutes.** State statute focuses on regulating governmental smoking policies for the protection of government employees who smoke.

**Places Where Smoking Is Prohibited.** Any smoking policy covering state or local government buildings or workplaces must be passed in writing by the appropriate governing body and must require accessible indoor smoking areas. Any such policy must also favor allowing smoking in open public areas where ventilation and air exchange are adequate.

**Exemptions/Places Where Smoking Is Permitted.** The statute does not apply to state universities or to state-operated hospitals, mental facilities, nursing homes, or jails.

**Notice Requirements.** State has no statutory requirements.

**Cost-Benefit/Waiver Requirements.** State has no statutory requirements.

**Nonretaliation.** State has no statutory requirements.

**Enforcement.** Violation of the statute prohibiting smoking on school grounds is punishable by a fine of $1–$5.

**Local Laws/Preemption.** State has no statutory requirements.

**Other Requirements.** Smoking is generally prohibited in school buildings and on school grounds, but smoking is permitted by school employees in designated areas. The Commissioner of Prisons may prohibit or permit smoking in detention facilities.

**Citations to Authority.** Ky. Rev. Stat. Ann. §§ 61.165, 196.245, 438.050.

## LOUISIANA

**Coverage/Focus of the Statutes.** State statutes specifically regulate smoking in the office workplace and apply only to employers with 25 or more full-time employees.

**Places Where Smoking Is Prohibited.** Any employee may object to smoke in his or her office workplace. Office workplaces include, but are not limited to, hospitals, clinics, nursing homes, libraries, museums, child care facilities, and office buildings.

**Exemptions/Places Where Smoking Is Permitted.** Smoking is permitted in designated areas. An office workplace does not include a private home used as an office or a private enclosed office occupied exclusively by smokers. Employers shall use available means of ventilation or separation of office space to reach reasonable accommodation between nonsmoking and smoking employees.

**Notice Requirements.** Areas where smoking is prohibited must be clearly marked with signs. Smoking policy shall be announced and posted conspicuously in all office workplaces under the employer's jurisdiction.

**Cost-Benefit/Waiver Requirements.** State has no statutory requirements.

**Nonretaliation.** State has no statutory requirements.

**Enforcement.** State has no statutory requirements.

**Local Laws/Preemption.** No political subdivision of the state may impose ordinances or regulations more restrictive than those of the state, but state statutes do not supersede any ordinances adopted before September 1, 1993.

**Other Requirements.** Separate provisions regulate smoking in public schools and school buses.

**Citations to Authority.** La. Rev. Stat. Ann. §§ 17:240, 40:1300.22 *et seq.*

## MAINE

**Coverage/Focus of the Statutes.** State statute has separate sections regulating smoking in certain public places and includes specific provisions regulating smoking in the workplace.

**Places Where Smoking Is Prohibited.** Smoking is prohibited in schools, restaurants, hospitals, and places of employment. Smoking may be prohibited throughout an entire workplace.

**Exemptions/Places Where Smoking Is Permitted.** Smoking is permitted in designated areas. Any workplace that is also a private residence is exempted from the statute. School employees may designate a smoking area through collective bargaining.

**Notice Requirements.** An employer must establish and post a written policy prohibiting smoking and provide copies upon request. "No smoking" signs must be posted in other public places.

**Cost-Benefit/Waiver Requirements.** Where an employer and all employees have agreed privately to a smoking policy, the statute is inapplicable.

**Nonretaliation.** It is unlawful to discriminate against an employee who has assisted in supervising or enforcing the statute.

**Enforcement.** Failure by the employer to establish or post the policy is a violation punishable by a fine.

**Local Laws/Preemption.** State has no statutory requirements.

**Other Requirements.** Separate requirements control smoking in retail stores and nursing homes. Violation of the statute is not negligence per se. Upon request, the Bureau of Health must assist an employer in developing a written policy.

**Citations to Authority.** Me. Rev. Stat. Ann. tit. 22, §§ 1578 *et seq.,* 1825; tit. 25, § 2433.

## MARYLAND

**Coverage/Focus of the Statutes.** State smoking statutes and regulations were recently enacted to specifically address smoking in the workplace. Smoking is also restricted in other public places.

**Places Where Smoking Is Prohibited.** Under administrative regulation, smoking is generally banned in all enclosed places of employment. The administrative prohibition includes all indoor work areas, vehicles used in the course of employment, restaurants, bars, and hotel and motel rooms. Smoking is legislatively prohibited in public areas of retail stores employing 20 or more full-time employees, on intrastate carriers, and in certain health care facilities.

**Exemptions/Places Where Smoking Is Permitted.** The administrative regulations banning all workplace smoking were legislatively modified on July 1, 1995, to permit smoking in certain areas of the workplace. Specifically, smoking is permitted in any generally recognized bar or tavern, including those located in restaurants. Smoking is allowed in a separate, enclosed room of a restaurant, as long as the room does not exceed 40 percent of the total area of the restaurant. Smoking is also now allowed in 40 percent of the sleeping rooms of a hotel or motel. Under the newly enacted legislation, no separate ventilation is required in these smoking areas, as it had been under the regulations. However, the regulatory requirements that designated smoking areas have solid walls that tightly join the floor and ceiling, a closable door, be maintained at a negative pressure in respect to nonsmoking areas, and be located in areas where no employee is required to enter in the regular course of his or her employment are still in force. In addition, the legislative prohibition on smoking in health care facilities does not apply to certain mental health facilities, facilities where the average patient stay is 30 days or more, or physician-authorized smoking where safeguards for nonsmokers are maintained.

**Notice Requirements.** A person in charge is required to post conspicuous "no smoking" signs in areas where smoking is prohibited.

**Cost-Benefit/Waiver Requirements.** Under the new legislation, no expenditures are required to be made by employers who wish to designate smoking areas in a workplace as long as the areas conform to the requirements of the statute.

**Nonretaliation.** State has no statutory requirements.

**Enforcement.** A fine of up to $25 may be levied for violation of the smoking prohibition on intrastate carriers. Also, if adequate signs are posted, a person in charge will not be liable if employees or members of the public smoke in violation of the statute.

**Local Laws/Preemption.** The newly enacted legislation is not intended to preempt the authority of a county or municipal corporation from enacting any law or ordinance that is more restrictive of smoking in establishments open to the public in which smoking is permitted under the act.

**Other Requirements.** State has no statutory requirements.

**Citations to Authority.** Md. Health-Gen. Code Ann. §§ 24-205 *et seq.*, 24-501 *et seq.*; Md. Lab. and Emp. Code Ann. §§ 2-106, 5-314; Code of Maryland Regulations § 9.12.23 (1994).

## MASSACHUSETTS

**Coverage/Focus of the Statutes.** State statutes control smoking in public places; their effect on smoking in the workplace is incidental.

**Places Where Smoking Is Prohibited.** Smoking is prohibited in public places, including retail food stores, public transit, courthouses, schools or universities, day care centers, waiting rooms of health care facilities, restaurants seating 75 or more persons, and all public buildings.

**Exemptions/Places Where Smoking Is Permitted.** Smoking is permitted in designated areas of public places. An area may be designated as a smoking area only if nonsmoking areas are of sufficient size and capacity to accommodate nonsmokers. Completely enclosed private offices are exempted from the provisions of the statute.

**Notice Requirements.** A person in charge must post conspicuous signs indicating the smoking area and the nonsmoking area.

**Cost-Benefit/Waiver Requirements.** State has no statutory requirements.

**Nonretaliation.** State has no statutory requirements.

**Enforcement.** A complaint may be filed with a local government official by any aggrieved party; the official is responsible for enforcing the provisions of the statute.

**Local Laws/Preemption.** State has no statutory requirements.

**Other Requirements.** Separate statutes regulate smoking in nursing homes, in jury rooms, in polling places, in public transit terminals and conveyances, in certain stables for horses and mules, and on school buses. Imprisonment of up to 10 days or a fine of not more than $100, or both, are the penalties provided for violating the regulations on smoking in public transit terminals and conveyances.

**Citations to Authority.** Mass. Gen. Laws Ann. ch. 54, § 73; ch. 90, § 7B; ch. 111, § 72X; ch. 234, § 34C; ch. 270, § 22; ch. 272, §§ 43A, 86A–86C.

## MICHIGAN

**Coverage/Focus of the Statutes.** State statute controls smoking in public places, but does not apply to public places used for private functions. Bars and restaurants are covered by separate statutory provisions. The statute's effect on smoking in the workplace is incidental.

**Places Where Smoking Is Prohibited.** Smoking is prohibited in public places, including areas used by the public and as workplaces in government buildings and in privately owned schools, health care facilities, nursing homes, child care institutions, food stores, auditoriums, arenas, theaters, museums, and concert halls. Smoking is prohibited in the common area of a health care treatment office.

**Exemptions/Places Where Smoking Is Permitted.** Smoking is permitted in designated public areas. If a smoking area is designated, existing physical barriers and ventilation systems must be used to minimize the effects of smoke, and a written policy must be developed to provide, at a minimum, that nonsmokers be located closest to the source of fresh air and that special consideration be given to individuals with hypersensitivity to smoke. The written policy must provide a procedure to receive, investigate, and take action on complaints. Smoking is permitted in private offices, even if visited by nonsmokers.

**Notice Requirements.** A person in charge must post signs indicating that smoking is permitted only in designated areas.

**Cost-Benefit/Waiver Requirements.** State has no statutory requirements.

**Nonretaliation.** State has no statutory requirements.

**Enforcement.** State or local government officials may sue to enforce the provisions of the statute and impose fines as set out in the statute. Any person may seek an injunction against continued violations.

**Local Laws/Preemption.** State has no statutory requirements.

**Other Requirements.** If a public place is a single room, one half of the room must be designated as a nonsmoking area. An employer must arrange seating in a public place to provide, as nearly as practicable, a smoke-free area. A "cubicle" is not a private office such that smoking may be permitted therein. [1987 Op. Mich. Att'y Gen. No. 6460] Separate provision regulates smoking in day care facilities.

**Citations to Authority.** Mich. Comp. Laws Ann. §§ 333.12601 *et seq.,* 333.12901 *et seq.*; Mich. Stat. Ann. §§ 14.15(12601) *et seq.,* 14.15(12901) *et seq.*; 25.358 (13b), (13c), (13d).

## MINNESOTA

**Coverage/Focus of the Statutes.** State regulates smoking in any "public place," which is defined to include a place of work.

**Places Where Smoking Is Prohibited.** Smoking is prohibited in public places, including, but not limited to, retail stores, restaurants, offices, commercial establishments, hospitals, day care facilities, and other places of work.

**Exemptions/Places Where Smoking Is Permitted.** Smoking is permitted in designated areas if existing physical barriers and ventilation systems are used to minimize smoke. Factories, warehouses, and similar workplaces are not covered, but the Commissioner of Health may establish rules restricting smoking at such places. Smoking is permitted in an enclosed private office, even if visited by nonsmokers. Smoking is permitted in a bar and in public rooms used for private social functions.

**Notice Requirements.** An employer must post appropriate signs.

**Cost-Benefit/Waiver Requirements.** A waiver may be granted for compelling reasons if it will not significantly affect the health and comfort of nonsmokers.

**Nonretaliation.** No state employee complaining of smoke-induced discomfort may be disciplined for making such a complaint.

**Enforcement.** A violator is guilty of a petty misdemeanor. Any affected party may institute an action to enjoin repeated violations. A person is guilty of a misdemeanor if the person intentionally smokes in a building area in which no smoking signs have been prominently posted or when requested not to do so by the operator.

**Local Laws/Preemption.** State has no statutory requirements.

**Other Requirements.** Smoking is prohibited in the presence of explosives and in state buildings. An employer must arrange seating to provide a smoke-free area and ask smokers to refrain from smoking upon the request of a client or employee bothered by the smoke. If a public place is a single room, the statutory requirement is deemed to have been met if one side of the room is designated nonsmoking.

**Citations to Authority.** Minn. Stat. Ann. §§ 16B.24(9), 144.411 *et seq.,* 609.576, 609.681.

## MISSISSIPPI

**Coverage/Focus of the Statutes.** The state statute is very limited and only prohibits smoking on public buses.

**Places Where Smoking Is Prohibited.** See "Coverage," above.

**Exceptions/Places Where Smoking Is Permitted.** See "Coverage," above.

**Notice Requirements.** State has no statutory requirements.

**Cost-Benefit/Waiver Requirements.** State has no statutory requirements.

**Nonretaliation.** State has no statutory requirements.

**Enforcement.** Violation of the statute is a misdemeanor.

**Local Laws/Preemption.** State has no statutory requirements.

**Other Requirements.** State has no statutory requirements.

**Citations to Authority.** Miss. Code Ann. § 97-35-1.

## MISSOURI

**Coverage/Focus of the Statutes.** State statutes control smoking in public places, which are defined to include places of employment.

**Places Where Smoking Is Prohibited.** Smoking is prohibited at public meetings and in public places, including, but not limited to, retail establishments, health care facilities, public transportation and waiting rooms for public transportation, restrooms, elevators, libraries, educational facilities, day care facilities, museums, and enclosed indoor places for entertainment.

**Exemptions/Places Where Smoking Is Permitted.** Smoking is permitted in designated smoking areas, at private social functions, in retail stores where more than 50 percent of the business relates to tobacco, in bars and restaurants that seat fewer than 50 people, in billiard parlors, and in private residences. No more than 30 percent of a public space may be designated as a smoking area.

**Notice Requirements.** A person in charge must make reasonable efforts to prevent smoking by posting signs.

**Cost-Benefit/Waiver Requirements.** State has no statutory requirements.

**Nonretaliation.** State has no statutory requirements.

**Enforcement.** Violators are guilty of an infraction.

**Local Laws/Preemption.** Local political subdivisions can enact rules or ordinaces more stringent than the state statutes.

**Other Requirements.** Specific provisions regulate smoking in schools and day care facilities. A designated area where state employees may smoke during work shall be provided if such area can be adequately ventilated at minimal cost.

**Citations to Authority.** Mo. Ann. Stat. §§ 191.765 *et seq.*

## MONTANA

**Coverage/Focus of the Statutes.** State regulates smoking in public places, which are defined to include places of work.

**Places Where Smoking Is Prohibited.** Smoking is prohibited in public places, including, but not limited to, restaurants, elevators and kitchens of any establishment doing business with the general public, stores, offices, health care facilities, and state buildings. An employer may designate an entire area as a nonsmoking area.

**Exemptions/Places Where Smoking Is Permitted.** Smoking is permitted in designated areas of public places. An entire area may be designated as a smoking area if appropriate signs are posted. Smoking is also permitted in restaurants, bars, and public rooms seating 6 or fewer persons.

**Notice Requirements.** An employer must post easily readable signs designating smoking and nonsmoking areas. Signs must be posted at entrances indicating whether or not areas inside have been designated as nonsmoking areas.

**Cost-Benefit/Waiver Requirements.** State has no statutory requirements.

**Nonretaliation.** State has no statutory requirements.

**Enforcement.** Local boards of health are charged with enforcement of the statute. Penalties are provided only for persons failing to post appropriate signs.

**Local Laws/Preemption.** State has no statutory requirements.

**Other Requirements.** In state-owned buildings, an employer must designate at least one smoking area, suited to be such by architectural design. In establishing such an area, the employer shall consider the number of smoking and nonsmoking employees.

**Citations to Authority.** Mont. Code Ann. §§ 50-40-101 *et seq.*

## NEBRASKA

**Coverage/Focus of the Statutes.** State regulates smoking in any public place, which is defined to include a place of work.

**Places Where Smoking Is Prohibited.** Smoking is prohibited in public places, including, but not limited to, retail stores, restaurants, offices, commercial establishments, hospitals, and other places of work.

**Exemptions/Places Where Smoking Is Permitted.** Smoking is permitted in designated areas if existing physical barriers and ventilation systems are used to minimize smoke. Factories, warehouses, and similar workplaces are not covered, but the Commissioner of Health may establish rules restricting smoking at such places. Smoking is permitted in an enclosed private office, even if visited by nonsmokers. Smoking is permitted in a bar and in public rooms used for private social functions.

**Notice Requirements.** An employer must post appropriate signs.

**Cost-Benefit/Waiver Requirements.** A waiver may be granted for compelling reasons if it will not significantly affect the health and comfort of nonsmokers.

**Nonretaliation.** State has no statutory requirements.

**Enforcement.** A violator is guilty of a Class V misdemeanor. Any affected party may institute an action to enjoin repeated violations.

**Local Laws/Preemption.** State has no statutory requirements.

**Other Requirements.** If a public place is a single room, one side of the room must be reserved for nonsmokers. The Department of Health shall promulgate rules under the statute. An employer must arrange seating to provide a smoke-free area and must ask smokers to refrain from smoking upon the request of a client or employee bothered by the smoke.

**Citations to Authority.** Neb. Rev. Stat. §§ 71-5701 *et seq.*

## NEVADA

**Coverage/Focus of the Statutes.** State statute controls smoking in public places; the statute's effect on workplaces is incidental.

**Places Where Smoking Is Prohibited.** Smoking is generally prohibited in public places, including public buildings and the public areas of food stores.

**Exemptions/Places Where Smoking Is Permitted.** Smoking is permitted in designated areas. A public building must have a designated smoking area. A business with more than 50 percent of receipts from alcohol sales may permit smoking on the entire premises.

**Notice Requirements.** An employer must post signs in nonsmoking areas.

**Cost-Benefit/Waiver Requirements.** State has no statutory requirements.

**Nonretaliation.** State has no statutory requirements.

**Enforcement.** The county board of health enforces the statute, violation of which is a misdemeanor, punishable by a fine of $100. All funds collected due to a violation of the statute are to be deposited into the account for health education of minors.

**Local Laws/Preemption.** Local laws may not impose more stringent restrictions than are imposed by the statute.

**Other Requirements.** Separate smoking rooms may be established in licensed gaming establishments.

**Citations to Authority.** Nev. Rev. Stat. §§ 202.2485 *et seq.*, 475.050.

## NEW HAMPSHIRE

**Coverage/Focus of the Statutes.** State statutes focus on controlling smoking in public places and include specific provisions regulating smoking in public or privately owned workplaces (with four or more employees).

**Places Where Smoking Is Prohibited.** Smoking is prohibited in enclosed public places and enclosed workspaces except in "effectively segregated" smoking areas. An employer must develop a written policy stating that smoking is prohibited except in such areas (if any).

**Exemptions/Places Where Smoking Is Permitted.** If an employer permits smoking, a smoking area must be effectively segregated. Employee preferences must be determined, and the smoking areas must be physically separated by walls or distance, such that smoke does not intrude on a nonsmoking area. Smoking is permitted in restaurants and cocktail lounges.

**Notice Requirements.** An employer must post signs indicating where smoking is permitted or prohibited.

**Cost-Benefit/Waiver Requirements.** An employer may seek extra time to comply with the statute, if it can show compelling reasons and if the health and well-being of employees is not jeopardized.

**Nonretaliation.** No employer may discriminate against any employee for exercising rights under the statute.

**Enforcement.** An employee may complain to an employer, and, if the complaint is not resolved in a timely manner, an administrative adjudication may proceed. Fines are provided for violation. Any law enforcement officer may enforce the statute.

**Local Laws/Preemption.** State and local fire safety laws that prohibit smoking are not affected by the statute.

**Other Requirements.** Smoking areas must be located, if possible, by exhaust vents. An employer's written policy must be made available to employees, and employees must receive orientation regarding the policy. The policy must instruct employees to aid in enforcement and must take special consideration of an employee with a documented allergic reaction to smoke.

**Citations to Authority.** N.H. Rev. Stat. Ann. §§ 155:64 *et seq.*

## NEW JERSEY

**Coverage/Focus of the Statutes.** State regulates smoking extensively by statute, and separate statutory provisions apply to elevators, health care facilities, doctors' offices, educational institutions, food stores, indoor public places, and government buildings. There are specific statutory provisions regulating smoking in places of employment.

**Places Where Smoking Is Prohibited.** Every employer must establish a written policy on smoking in the workplace, designating certain areas as nonsmoking areas in order to protect employees from the detrimental effects of tobacco smoke.

**Exemptions/Places Where Smoking Is Permitted.** An employer may designate areas where smoking is permitted, unless smoking is otherwise prohibited by municipal ordinance or by statute.

**Notice Requirements.** In a place of employment where 50 or more employees work, the employer must post signs indicating whether smoking is permitted or prohibited. Use of the international no-smoking symbol is allowed.

**Cost-Benefit/Waiver Requirements.** A one-year phaseout period may be provided when an area is designated as a nonsmoking area.

**Nonretaliation.** No employer shall discriminate against an employee because the employee does or does not smoke, unless the employer has a rational basis that is reasonably related to the employment. An aggrieved person may bring a civil action for damages, injunction, and attorneys' fees. An employer may be penalized up to $2,000 for a first violation and $5,000 for subsequent violations.

**Enforcement.** The state department of health enforces the workplace smoking regulations. An employer is given notice of violation and must be given time to comply before further action is taken. No employer who adopts a written smoking policy may be liable in a personal injury suit based on inhalation of second-hand smoke.

**Local Laws/Preemption.** The state statute supersedes local laws regulating smoking, except for local fire safety ordinances.

**Other Requirements.** The legislature declares that while it is not public policy to deny anyone the right to smoke, in places affected by the act the right of the nonsmoker to breathe clean air should supersede the right of the smoker to smoke. The state department of health must provide consultation services to employers upon request.

**Citations to Authority.** N.J. Stat. Ann. §§ 26:3D-1 *et seq.*, 34:6B-1 *et seq.*

## NEW MEXICO

**Coverage/Focus of the Statutes.** State regulates smoking in public places owned or leased by the state, and there are specific provisions on places of employment with more than 15 state employees.

**Places Where Smoking Is Prohibited.** Smoking is prohibited in a public place except in designated areas. A public employer who has smoking and nonsmoking employees must develop and maintain a written smoking policy that provides smoke-free work areas to employees who request them.

**Exemptions/Places Where Smoking Is Permitted.** Smoking is permitted in designated areas, which may not exceed 50 percent of a public place, in public rooms for private social functions, and in private offices, even if they are visited by nonsmokers. An employer must use existing barriers and ventilation to minimize the effect of transient smoke on nonsmoking areas.

**Notice Requirements.** An employer must post "no smoking" signs, or signs with the international no-smoking symbol, in any area designated as a nonsmoking area.

**Cost-Benefit/Waiver Requirements.** An employer need not make structural changes to comply. An employer who makes "reasonable efforts" to develop a smoking policy is deemed in compliance.

**Nonretaliation.** An employer may not disadvantage an employee because the employee is a smoker or a nonsmoker. The employer may not require as a condition of employment that any employee refrain from smoking during nonworking hours. However, if smoking is a bona fide occupational qualification, an adverse action may be taken. An aggrieved employee may bring civil suit for damages and attorneys' fees, but must mitigate damages.

**Enforcement.** An employer who fails to adopt a policy, or to post appropriate signs, is in violation of the statute.

**Local Laws/Preemption.** Local laws are not preempted if they are not inconsistent with the statute.

**Other Requirements.** An employer must arrange seating so as to provide a smoke-free work area. Violation of the statute is not evidence of negligence, nor will it sustain an action for nuisance.

**Citations to Authority.** N.M. Stat. Ann. §§ 24-16-1 *et seq.*, 50-11-1 *et seq.*

## NEW YORK

**Coverage/Focus of the Statutes.** State statutes prohibit smoking in certain public areas and include provisions specifically relating to smoking in the workplace.

**Places Where Smoking Is Prohibited.** Smoking is entirely prohibited in certain public areas—for example, food stores, public transportation vehicles, and terminals. In other indoor public places, smoking is prohibited except in designated areas. Each employer must adopt and implement a written smoking policy providing nonsmoking employees with a smoke-free area. Employee demand shall be considered in setting aside nonsmoking areas in employee lounges and cafeterias. Any employer may designate the entire workplace as a nonsmoking area.

**Exemptions/Places Where Smoking Is Permitted.** Smoking restrictions do not apply to private social functions, tobacco businesses, and bars. Smoking is permitted in certain designated areas, including, but not limited to, the concourse area of a bowling alley and separate enclosed rooms not open to the public. An employer's smoking policy may set aside a work area for smoking if all employees in that area agree. Smoking is permitted in a company vehicle or in a conference or meeting room only if all occupants agree.

**Notice Requirements.** Employers shall prominently post the smoking policy in the workplace and supply a written copy upon request to any employee or prospective employee. Employers must display "no smoking" signs or the international no-smoking symbol.

**Cost-Benefit/Waiver Requirements.** An employer is not required to make expenditures or structural changes in creating a smoke-free work area. An employer may be granted a waiver if compliance would cause undue financial hardship or strict compliance would otherwise be unreasonable. An official granting a waiver must consider the adverse effects of the waiver on nonsmokers.

**Nonretaliation.** State has no statutory requirements.

**Enforcement.** An aggrieved person may file a complaint with the appropriate government official who is charged with enforcing the statute. An employer who has made good-faith efforts to comply with the regulations has an affirmative defense against enforcement. Violators are subject to penalty not to exceed $500.

**Local Laws/Preemption.** Municipalities may adopt smoking regulations more stringent than the state statute.

**Other Requirements.** A separate provision prohibits smoking in factories, except in areas designated by the Commissioner of Labor. The statute does not abrogate the common law with respect to liability for exposure to smoke.

**Citations to Authority.** N.Y. Pub. Health Law §§ 1399-n *et seq.* (McKinney); N.Y. Lab. Law § 283 (McKinney).

## NORTH CAROLINA

**Coverage/Focus of the Statutes.** State statutes regulate smoking in designated areas of buildings owned or occupied by the state; their effect on the workplace and employment is only incidental.

**Places Where Smoking Is Prohibited.** Smoking is prohibited in designated nonsmoking areas in buildings owned or occupied by the state.

**Exemptions/Places Where Smoking Is Permitted.** Facilities exempt from all provisions of the statutes include: (1) any primary or secondary school or day care center except for a teacher's lounge; (2) an enclosed elevator; (3) a public school bus; (4) a hospital, nursing home, or rest home; (5) the local health department; (6) any nonprofit organization or corporation whose primary purpose is to discourage the use of tobacco products by the general public; and (7) any tobacco manufacturing, processing, or administrative facility. These facilities may choose to regulate or not to regulate smoking as desired.

**Notice Requirements.** State has no statutory requirements.

**Cost-Benefit/Waiver Requirements.** An employer is not required to make any physical modifications to create nonsmoking areas if such modifications will add to the employer's expenses.

**Nonretaliation.** State has no statutory requirements.

**Enforcement.** A person who smokes in a nonsmoking area may be fined not more than $25.

**Local Laws/Preemption.** State statutes shall not supersede local laws regulating the use of tobacco products enacted prior to October 15, 1993. Local laws adopted on or after October 15, 1993, shall not contain more restrictive no-smoking provisions than those in state statutes.

**Other Requirements.** Employers must provide a smoking area as near as feasible to 20 percent of the interior space.

**Citations to Authority.** N.C. Gen. Stat. §§ 95-28.2, 143-595 *et seq.*

## NORTH DAKOTA

**Coverage/Focus of the Statutes.** State regulates smoking in places of public assembly and in state-owned buildings. The statutes' effect on employment is incidental.

**Places Where Smoking Is Prohibited.** Smoking is prohibited in places of public assembly, including theaters, hospitals, restaurants seating more than 50 people, public transportation, and health care facilities.

**Exemptions/Places Where Smoking Is Permitted.** Smoking is permitted in designated areas that do not exceed 50 percent of a place of public assembly and that are situated so as to minimize smoke drift. Smoking is permitted in bars and at private social functions.

**Notice Requirements.** An employer must post signs in designated smoking areas.

**Cost-Benefit/Waiver Requirements.** State has no statutory requirements.

**Nonretaliation.** State has no statutory requirements.

**Enforcement.** The state department of health enforces the statute, and other authorities may cooperate in enforcement. An employer who willfully fails to comply can be fined up to $100.

**Local Laws/Preemption.** State has no statutory requirements.

**Other Requirements.** A restaurant employer may temporarily expand a smoking area beyond 50 percent if demand so requires.

**Citations to Authority.** N.D. Cent. Code §§ 23-12-09 *et seq.*

## OHIO

**Coverage/Focus of the Statutes.** State regulates smoking in places of public assembly and other specified places. Employment is affected only incidentally.

**Places Where Smoking Is Prohibited.** Smoking is prohibited in places of public assembly, including publicly owned buildings, theaters (except the lobby), and any building open to the public that has a seating capacity of 50 or more persons.

**Exemptions/Places Where Smoking Is Permitted.** In public places where smoking is prohibited, smoking is permitted only in designated areas. An employer may designate smoking areas, but has the discretion to designate the entire building as a no-smoking area. Restaurants, bowling alleys, and bars are not places of public assembly.

**Notice Requirements.** Employers must designate no-smoking areas by posting appropriate signs and ensuring that the signs remain in place.

**Cost-Benefit/Waiver Requirements.** State has no statutory requirements.

**Nonretaliation.** State has no statutory requirements.

**Enforcement.** A person who violates the statute is guilty of a minor misdemeanor.

**Local Laws/Preemption.** State has no statutory requirements.

**Other Requirements.** Separate statutory sections prohibit smoking in child or family day care centers, in schools, and at self-service gasoline stations, on streetcars, fireworks plants, and in certain mines.

**Citations to Authority.** Ohio Rev. Code Ann. §§ 1567.65, 3313.751, 3741.14, 3791.031, 4951.51, 5104.015 (Anderson).

## OKLAHOMA

**Coverage/Focus of the Statutes.** State regulates smoking in publicly or privately owned "public places" and in places of work for public employees.

**Places Where Smoking Is Prohibited.** Smoking is prohibited in public places, including, but not limited to, schools, nursing and child care facilities, health facilities, theaters, museums, restaurants seating 50 or more persons, and workplaces for public employees.

**Exemptions/Places Where Smoking Is Permitted.** Smoking is permitted in designated areas if existing physical barriers and ventilation systems are used to minimize smoke. Smoking is permitted at private functions, in certain bars, and at licensed race tracks. Smoking is permitted in private offices, even if nonsmokers visit.

**Notice Requirements.** An employer must post signs where smoking is prohibited.

**Cost-Benefit/Waiver Requirements.** State has no specific statutory requirements.

**Nonretaliation.** State has no statutory requirements.

**Enforcement.** The state board of health promulgates rules and regulations to implement the statute. Unlawful smoking is punished by fine. Nursing and child care facility employees may be fined specifically by the state Board of Health for violating the statute.

**Local Laws/Preemption.** Local governments may not enact laws more stringent than the state statute.

**Other Requirements.** If a public place is a single room, an employer is deemed in compliance if the room is designated as nonsmoking. An employer must ask a smoker to refrain from smoking upon request of a client or an employee who is made uncomfortable by or is hypersensitive to smoke.

**Citations to Authority.** Okla. Stat. Ann. tit. 21, § 1247; tit. 63, §§ 1-1521 *et seq.*

## OREGON

**Coverage/Focus of the Statutes.** State statutes regulate smoking in public areas and in places of work for state employees.

**Places Where Smoking Is Prohibited.** Smoking is prohibited in enclosed indoor public areas, including, but not limited to restaurants, bowling centers, retail stores, banks, nursing homes, and grocery stores. State employers most provide smoke-free lounge areas. A state employer may designate an entire workplace as a nonsmoking area.

**Exemptions/Places Where Smoking Is Permitted.** Smoking is permitted in designated areas. No public place may be designated in its entirety as a smoking area except: cocktail lounges, taverns, offices exclusively occupied by smokers, rooms used for private functions, businesses primarily engaged in the sale of tobacco, and restaurants with seating capacity for 30 or fewer people or restaurants with specific air filtration systems.

**Notice Requirements.** A person in charge shall post appropriate signs.

**Cost-Benefit/Waiver Requirements.** Provisions of these statutes may be waived for valid reasons.

**Nonretaliation.** State has no statutory requirements.

**Enforcement.** A person who violates the statutes is guilty of a Class A misdemeanor.

**Local Laws/Preemption.** State has no statutory requirements.

**Other Requirements.** Separate provisions regulate smoking in hospitals.

**Citations to Authority.** Or. Rev. Stat. §§ 192.710, 243.345 *et seq.*, 433.835 *et seq.*, 441.815.

## PENNSYLVANIA

**Coverage/Focus of the Statutes.** State regulates smoking in certain public places, the workplace, and other specified locations.

**Places Where Smoking Is Prohibited.** Smoking is prohibited in any nonsmoking area of a public place, including the workplace, theaters, museums, restaurants, and concert halls.

**Exemptions/Places Where Smoking Is Permitted.** Smoking is permitted only in designated areas of a public place covered by the statute. An employer must develop, post, and implement a policy to regulate smoking in the workplace and may designate smoking and nonsmoking areas. Exempted from the definition of a "public place" are private social functions, certain restaurants, bars, tobacconists, factories, warehouses, and similar places of work not frequented by the general public.

**Notice Requirements.** Notice provisions are mandatory only for restaurants that provide nonsmoking areas.

**Cost-Benefit/Waiver Requirements.** State has no statutory requirements.

**Nonretaliation.** State has no statutory requirements.

**Enforcement.** The state department of health enforces the statute, and no employer who establishes a policy pursuant to the statute is subject to a private court action. Violation of the statute shall be punishable by a fine of not more than $50.

**Local Laws/Preemption.** Municipalities are specifically empowered to prohibit smoking in retail stores that accommodate 100 or more persons or that employ ten or more employees.

**Other Requirements.** Separate statutory sections regulate smoking in schools, in hospitals and hospital rooms, on public conveyances, and in certain areas in and around a mine. Nothing in the statute regulating smoking in the workplace affects any contractual or collective bargaining agreement between the employer and employee concerning smoking.

**Citations to Authority.** Pa. Stat. Ann. tit. 35, §§ 361, 1223.5, 1230.1; tit. 52, §§ 701-101 *et seq.*; tit. 53, § 46202(22); tit. 55, § 560.1.

## RHODE ISLAND

**Coverage/Focus of the Statutes.** State statutes focus on controlling smoking in public places and include specific provisions regulating smoking in the workplace.

**Places Where Smoking Is Prohibited.** Smoking is prohibited in public places, including theaters, museums, court buildings, supermarkets, medical offices, and hospitals. An employer may designate an entire workplace as a nonsmoking area. If an employer allows smoking in the workplace, the employer must implement and maintain a policy that represents a "reasonable accommodation" between smoking and nonsmoking employees.

**Exemptions/Places Where Smoking Is Permitted.** Smoking is permitted in designated areas only. If an area is designated, existing ventilation systems, partitions, or separate rooms must be used to reasonably accommodate employees. Smoking is permitted in home offices and in private offices occupied exclusively by smokers, even if nonsmokers visit.

**Notice Requirements.** An employer must conspicuously post signs designating all nonsmoking areas within three weeks of the adoption of the smoking policy.

**Cost-Benefit/Waiver Requirements.** No expenditures or structural changes are required under the statute.

**Nonretaliation.** An employer may not discriminate against an employee for the exercise of rights under the statute. An aggrieved employee may be awarded triple damages, injunctive relief, and costs in an action for retaliation.

**Enforcement.** An employee may complain to the department of health, which enforces the statute, by sending notice to the employer or instituting appropriate action. A violator of these provisions is subject to a fine of $50 to $500 per day that violation is committed.

**Local Laws/Preemption.** State has no statutory requirements.

**Other Requirements.** Separate sections regulate smoking in schools and in tents. The statute is not intended to provide a private right of action for smoke-related injury.

**Citations to Authority.** R.I. Gen. Laws §§ 23-20.6-1 *et seq.*, 23-20.7-1 *et seq.*, 23-20.9-1 *et seq.*, 23-28.19-11.

## SOUTH CAROLINA

**Coverage/Focus of the Statutes.** State statutes prohibit smoking in certain public areas; their effect on employment is incidental.

**Places Where Smoking Is Prohibited.** Smoking is prohibited in public schools, including preschool and day care centers, health care facilities, public areas of government buildings, elevators, public conveyances (except taxicabs), arenas, and auditoriums.

**Exemptions/Places Where Smoking Is Permitted.** Smoking is permitted in designated areas. Smoking is permitted in enclosed private offices of government buildings.

**Notice Requirements.** The owner, manager, or agent in charge of the premises or vehicle must conspicuously display signs designating smoking and nonsmoking areas.

**Cost-Benefit/Waiver Requirements.** Person in charge shall use existing physical barriers and ventilation systems to prevent smoke from designated smoking areas impinging on designated smoke-free areas.

**Nonretaliation.** State has no statutory requirements.

**Enforcement.** A violator of these provisions is guilty of a misdemeanor, punishable by a fine of $10–$25.

**Local Laws/Preemption.** State has no statutory requirements.

**Other Requirements.** No person may be required to submit to any form of testing to determine whether nicotine or other tobacco residue is present in the body. Employees of retail food stores may not smoke in areas where food is processed or where equipment/utensils are washed.

**Citations to Authority.** S.C. Code Ann. §§ 44-95-10 *et seq.*; S.C. Health & Environ. Regs. 61-26 III(D)(1).

## SOUTH DAKOTA

**Coverage/Focus of the Statutes.** State regulates smoking in public areas. Employment is affected only incidentally.

**Places Where Smoking Is Prohibited.** Smoking is prohibited in hospitals, medical or dental clinics, nursing homes, public libraries, museums, indoor theaters, concert halls, schools, public conveyances, jury rooms, and elevators.

**Exemptions/Places Where Smoking Is Permitted.** Smoking is permitted in designated smoking areas.

**Notice Requirements.** State has no statutory requirements.

**Cost-Benefit/Waiver Requirements.** State has no statutory requirements.

**Nonretaliation.** State has no statutory requirements.

**Enforcement.** A violator of these provisions is guilty of a petty offense.

**Local Laws/Preemption.** State has no statutory requirements.

**Other Requirements.** None.

**Citations to Authority.** S.D. Codified Laws Ann. §§ 22-36-2; Exec. Order 92-10.

## TENNESSEE

**Coverage/Focus of the Statutes.** The statutes regulate smoking in government buildings and in all public and private kindergartens, elementary and secondary schools, and in certain other areas where children are likely to be present.

**Places Where Smoking Is Prohibited.** In government buildings, the person in charge of each agency or department must establish a smoking policy. Nonsmoking areas must be provided if smoking is allowed by the policy. Smoking is prohibited in schools, child day-care centers, youth group-care homes, health-care facilities (except nursing homes), museums, children's residential treatment facilities, youth development facilities, and zoos.

**Exceptions/Places Where Smoking Is Permitted.** For government buildings, each smoking policy must designate at least one indoor area in each building where smoking employees are allowed to smoke. Adult employees of public and private schools may smoke outside the school building, but not within 50 feet of any entrance. Adult employees of day-care centers and other workplaces where smoking is prohibited may smoke only in designated areas of the workplace to which children are not allowed access.

**Notice Requirements.** In places where smoking is prohibited, a person in charge must post appropriate notices.

**Cost-Benefit/Waiver Requirements.** State has no statutory requirements.

**Nonretaliation.** No employee shall be discharged solely for engaging in the lawful use of an agricultural product that is not regulated by the alcoholic beverage commission and that is not otherwise proscribed by law when the employee engages in such use in a manner that complies with all applicable employer policies when the employee is working.

**Enforcement.** A violator is guilty of a class B misdemeanor, punishable only by a fine not to exceed $500.

**Local Laws/Preemption.** State has no statutory requirements.

**Other Requirements.** None.

**Citations to Authority.** Tenn. Code Ann. §§ 4-4-121; 39-17-1601 *et seq.*; 50-1-304.

## TEXAS

**Coverage/Focus of the Statutes.** State statutes regulate smoking in public places; their effect on employment is incidental.

**Places Where Smoking Is Prohibited.** Smoking is prohibited in all public primary or secondary schools, elevators, enclosed theatres or movie houses, libraries, museums, and hospitals, and on all transit system buses and intrastate buses, planes, or trains.

**Exemptions/Places Where Smoking Is Permitted.** Smoking is permitted in designated smoking areas or when participating in an authorized theatrical performance.

**Notice Requirements.** In conveyances and public places where smoking is prohibited, a notice must be prominently displayed warning that smoking is prohibited by state law and that an offense is punishable by a fine not to exceed $500.

**Cost-Benefit/Waiver Requirements.** State has no statutory requirements.

**Nonretaliation.** State has no statutory requirements.

**Enforcement.** A violator is guilty of a Class C misdemeanor.

**Local Laws/Preemption.** Local laws regulating smoking are not preempted by these statutes.

**Other Requirements.** All conveyances and public places where smoking is prohibited must be equipped with facilities for extinguishment of smoking materials.

**Citations to Authority.** Tex. Penal Code Ann. § 48.01.

## UTAH

**Coverage/Focus of the Statutes.** State statutes focus on controlling smoking extensively in all public places. Specific provisions regulate smoking in the workplace.

**Places Where Smoking Is Prohibited.** Smoking is entirely prohibited in almost all public places, including government buildings. All other employers must establish a smoking policy by February 1, 1995. The policy must be in writing if the employer has more than ten full-time employees. The policy shall: prohibit smoking entirely from the workplace, or restrict smoking to designated enclosed areas, or permit smoking in designated unenclosed areas if smoke does not migrate and 75 percent of employees agree. The local health board may ban smoking in a workplace entirely through a hearing process.

**Exemptions/Places Where Smoking Is Permitted.** Smoking is permitted only in limited areas, including private clubs, separately ventilated smoking rooms in the Salt Lake City Airport, guest rooms in hotels and motels, and properly designated smoking areas in workplaces that are not places of public access or public buildings.

**Notice Requirements.** An employer must post appropriate signs conspicuously.

**Cost-Benefit/Waiver Requirements.** State has no specific statutory requirements.

**Nonretaliation.** State has no statutory requirements.

**Enforcement.** State and local health departments enforce the statute and may adopt rules in order to do so. Such authorities may seek an injunction against repeated violations. Violators may be fined up to $100 for the first and $100–$500 for subsequent violations.

**Local Laws/Preemption.** The statute supersedes any ordinance that is not essentially identical to the restrictions found in the statute enacted by a local government body.

**Other Requirements.** Smoking is prohibited in schools, day care centers, health facilities, and restaurants. Native American ceremonies are exempt from statute.

**Citations to Authority.** Utah Code Ann. §§ 26-38-1 *et seq.*

## VERMONT

**Coverage/Focus of the Statutes.** State statutes specifically prohibit smoking in the workplace, in addition to most other public places.

**Places Where Smoking Is Prohibited.** An employer must establish, or negotiate through collective bargaining, a smoking policy that prohibits smoking entirely or limits smoking to designated areas. Smoking is entirely prohibited in government buildings, health facilities, restaurants, schools, and day care facilities.

**Exemptions/Places Where Smoking Is Permitted.** Smoking is permitted in designated areas. Up to 30 percent of an employee cafeteria or lounge may be designated as a smoking area.

**Notice Requirements.** An employer must post the smoking policy and provide copies to employees upon request. The smoking policy must be in writing if the employer has at least 10 employees who work more than 15 hours per week.

**Cost-Benefit/Waiver Requirements.** State has no statutory requirements.

**Nonretaliation.** An employer may not discipline an employee because the employee assisted in the enforcement of the statute. An aggrieved employee may be reinstated with back pay.

**Enforcement.** An aggrieved employee may file a complaint with the department of health. An employer is given a chance to comply before further action is taken.

**Local Laws/Preemption.** The statute does not supersede any municipal smoking ordinance, provided that the ordinance is at least as protective of the rights of nonsmokers as the statute.

**Other Requirements.** Smoking is separately regulated in schools. Instead of adopting a smoking policy, an employer may permit smoking in an unenclosed area if it does not irritate nonsmokers and if 75 percent of employees agree. The department of health must assist employers in developing a smoking policy. In legislation that became effective on July 1, 1995, the Vermont legislature strengthened prohibitions regarding smoking on school grounds. Smoking is now entirely prohibited on all public school grounds, as is tobacco use by students at public school events.

**Citations to Authority.** Vt. Stat. Ann. tit. 16, §§ 140, 909; tit. 18, §§ 1421 *et seq.*

## VIRGINIA

**Coverage/Focus of the Statutes.** State statute regulates smoking in public places and in other specified areas. Employment is affected only incidentally.

**Places Where Smoking Is Prohibited.** Smoking is entirely prohibited in certain public places, including interior areas in schools, hospital emergency rooms, child care centers, and cashier lines. Smoking is prohibited in any nonsmoking area of other public places, including government buildings and certain retail establishments. Smoking is prohibited in state-owned buildings and health facilities.

**Exemptions/Places Where Smoking Is Permitted.** Smoking is permitted only in designated areas of a public place. Such areas shall not be so large that they fail to provide a reasonable nonsmoking area, and employers must use existing physical barriers and ventilation systems to minimize smoke. Retail stores with less than 15,000 square feet are excluded from the definition of a public place, as are tobacco stores, tobacco warehouses, and tobacco manufacturing facilities.

**Notice Requirements.** An employer is required to post conspicuous "smoking" and "no smoking" signs. Failure to do so may result in a $25 fine.

**Cost-Benefit/Waiver Requirements.** An employer is not required to physically alter any structure in order to comply with the statute.

**Nonretaliation.** State has no statutory requirements.

**Enforcement.** Any law enforcement officer may issue a summons regarding a violation of the statute. Any person who continues to smoke in a no-smoking area after being asked to refrain is subject to a $25 fine.

**Local Laws/Preemption.** Local ordinances promulgated prior to January 1, 1990, are not invalid, but local ordinances promulgated after that date must not contain provisions that exceed those established in the state statute. In no case may a local ordinance regulate smoking in bars, retail tobacco stores, offices, or work areas not entered by the general public, or restaurants used for private functions. Local ordinances may affect certain smoking regulations in private workplaces.

**Other Requirements.** Separate statutory sections regulate smoking in workrooms and food-producing establishments.

**Citations to Authority.** Va. Code Ann. §§ 3.1-379, 15.2-2800 *et seq.*

## WASHINGTON

**Coverage/Focus of the Statutes.** State statute controls smoking in public places; the law's effect on employment is incidental. (See "Other Requirements" below.)

**Places Where Smoking Is Prohibited.** Smoking is prohibited in public places, including public conveyances, health care facilities, retail stores, financial institutions, and the state legislative chamber. An employer may prohibit smoking in an entire facility.

**Exemptions/Places Where Smoking Is Permitted.** Smoking is permitted in designated areas, and existing physical barriers and ventilation systems must be used to minimize smoke. Smoking is not regulated in private offices, even if nonsmokers visit. A bar, tobacco shop, tavern, bowling alley, or restaurant may be designated a smoking area in its entirety, but notices so stating must be posted.

**Notice Requirements.** An employer must use reasonable efforts to prevent smoking by conspicuously posting appropriate signs. Boundaries between nonsmoking and smoking areas must be clearly designated.

**Cost-Benefit/Waiver Requirements.** State has no specific statutory requirements.

**Nonretaliation.** State has no statutory requirements.

**Enforcement.** Unlawful smoking and defacing of signs are violations punishable by fine. Local law enforcement officers may issue notices of infractions much like traffic tickets. The local government attorney may seek an injunction.

**Local Laws/Preemption.** Local agencies may adopt regulations to implement the statute.

**Other Requirements.** Separate statutory sections regulate smoking on buses. The state Department of Labor and Industries recently issued a regulation that prohibited smoking entirely in indoor office areas or required designated smoking areas that shall be ventilated at a fixed rate, shall be maintained at negative pressure with respect to nonsmoking areas, shall have air exhausted directly outside and not recirculated, and shall not require the entrance of any employee while smoking is occurring. Enactment was slated for September 1, 1994, but was delayed by a court injunction. The injunction was overturned by a state court that decided that regulators had the authority to create the ban.

**Citations to Authority.** Wash. Rev. Code Ann. §§ 9.91.025, 70.160.010 *et seq.*; Wash. Admin. Code 296-62-12000 *et seq.*

## WEST VIRGINIA

**Coverage/Focus of the Statutes.** State statute regulates some smoking behavior; its effect on employment is incidental.

**Places Where Smoking Is Prohibited.** State has no statutory requirements. (See "Other Requirements.")

**Exemptions/Places Where Smoking Is Permitted.** State has no statutory requirements. (See "Other Requirements.")

**Notice Requirements.** State has no statutory requirements.

**Cost-Benefit/Waiver Requirements.** State has no statutory requirements.

**Nonretaliation.** State has no statutory requirements.

**Enforcement.** A person who smokes in a factory, mercantile mill, or workshop where a conspicuously placed sign states that no smoking is allowed is guilty of a misdemeanor. Each offense is punishable by a fine of $20–$100.

**Local Laws/Preemption.** State has no statutory requirements.

**Other Requirements.** Separate provisions regulate smoking in mines. Smoking is generally prohibited on school grounds, except by school employees in designated areas. Smoking is prohibited by employees and customers in the workroom of a tattoo parlor.

**Citations to Authority.** W. Va. Code §§ 16-9A-4, 21-3-8, 21-3-19, 22A-2-57, 30-33-4.

## WISCONSIN

**Coverage/Focus of the Statutes.** State statute regulates smoking in public places and includes specific provisions for offices and retail workplaces.

**Places Where Smoking Is Prohibited.** Smoking is prohibited in indoor public places, including publicly or privately owned offices and retail establishments, as well as schools, day care facilities, health care facilities, restaurants, and public conveyances.

**Exemptions/Places Where Smoking Is Permitted.** Smoking is permitted in designated areas of public places, unless prohibited by a fire safety law or ordinance. An employer must arrange seating to accommodate nonsmokers if they are near a designated smoking area and use existing barriers and ventilation systems to minimize smoke. An entire building may not be designated as a smoking area, but may be designated as a nonsmoking area. Smoking may be permitted in private offices occupied by smokers, at private functions, and in bars, manufacturing facilities, and correctional institutions.

**Notice Requirements.** An employer is generally required to post signs only in areas where smoking is permitted. The state Department of Health shall specify characteristics of signs and may not require use of unreasonably expensive signs.

**Cost-Benefit/Waiver Requirements.** An employer is not required to construct new physical barriers or install new ventilation systems in order to comply with the statute.

**Nonretaliation.** State has no statutory requirements.

**Enforcement.** Any affected party may institute an action to enjoin repeated violations of the statute. Fines of up to $10 are provided for violation of the rules regarding smoking and the posting of signs.

**Local Laws/Preemption.** A local government is free to adopt ordinances regulating smoking as long as they are consistent with the statute and protect the health and comfort of the public.

**Other Requirements.** Separate statutory provisions regulate ventilation in workplaces where smoking is permitted and provide for criminal penalties for any person who causes a fire by smoking tobacco.

**Citations to Authority.** Wis. Stat. Ann. §§ 101.025, 101.123, 254.76.

## WYOMING

**Coverage/Focus of the Statutes.** State smoking regulations are limited to state government employees.

**Places Where Smoking Is Prohibited.** Smoking is generally prohibited in any building under control of the Capitol Building Commission.

**Exceptions/Places Where Smoking Is Permitted.** Smoking is permitted in specially ventilated designated smoking areas.

**Notice Requirements.** State has no statutory requirements.

**Cost-Benefit/Waiver Requirements.** State has no statutory requirements.

**Nonretaliation.** State has no statutory requirements.

**Enforcement.** State has no statutory requirements.

**Local Laws/Preemption.** State has no statutory requirements.

**Other Requirements.** None.

**Citations to Authority.** Wy. State Government Nonsmoking Policy (1989).

# Table 8.2-1

## MUNICIPAL SMOKING ORDINANCES

(See also text at § 8.2.)

| | *Employers Exempted* | *Employees Covered* | *Parts of the Workplace Covered by the Ordinance* | *Nonretaliation Clause* | *Smoker and Nonsmoker Disputes* | *Enforcement* | *Other Requirements* | *Citations to Authority* |
|---|---|---|---|---|---|---|---|---|
| Chandler, AZ | Private residences that serve as places of employment; bars; pool and billiards rooms; bowling centers; nightclubs; hotel and motel rooms rented to guests; tobacco stores; hotel and motel conference or meeting rooms (when entire room used for a private function and not under the control of the proprietor of the hotel or motel); private clubs and recreation facilities; public areas of restaurants that conspicuously post notices at the entrance that the restaurant does not provide nonsmoking areas. | All employees working for direct or indirect monetary wages or profit. | *Employees' Workspaces.* Owner, operator, or manager of enclosed public place may declare entire place smoke-free. Employers have right to designate any place of employment or portion thereof a nonsmoking area. Employers must attempt to reach a reasonable accommodation of the preferences of smoking and nonsmoking employees using already available means of ventilation, separation, or partition of office space. Employer not required to make any expenditures or structural changes to the place of employment.<br><br>*Common Areas.* Smoking may be restricted in conference and meeting rooms, classrooms, auditoriums, hallways, stairways, waiting areas, and rest rooms.<br><br>*Break Rooms and Eating Facilities.* Employers must maintain separate nonsmoking areas in employee lounges, cafeterias, and lunchrooms.<br><br>*Private Offices.* "Place of employment" includes any enclosed area under the control of a private employer that is intended for occupancy by employees during the course of employment. | No employee shall be terminated or subject to disciplinary action as a result of a complaint about smoking or nonsmoking in his or her place of employment. | If no satisfactory accommodation can be reached to all affected nonsmoking employees in a given work area, the employer will prohibit smoking in that area. | Any owner, manager, operator, or employee upon observing or being advised of a violation has an obligation to report the violation and request immediate compliance. | Employers must implement and maintain a written smoking policy containing the following requirements: (1) prohibition of smoking in enclosed public places, except in designated smoking areas; (2) provision and maintenance of separate nonsmoking area in cafeterias, lunchrooms, and employee lounges; and (3) definition of work area; "No Smoking" signs must be posted in appropriate areas. | Mun. Code. Sec. 17-50. |

| | | | | | | | | |
|---|---|---|---|---|---|---|---|---|
| Phoenix, AZ | Workplaces in private homes; bars; pool halls; bowling alleys; tobacco stores; public and private meeting rooms; private clubs; recreational facilities. | All employees working for wages or profit, whether direct or indirect. | *Employees' Workspaces.* An employee may object to smoke in his or her immediate work area. Employer, using existing structure and ventilation, must use its best efforts to reasonably accommodate the preferences of smokers and nonsmokers.<br>*Common Areas.* Smoking prohibited in conference and meeting rooms, classrooms, auditoriums, restrooms, waiting areas, medical facilities, hallways, stairways, and elevators.<br>*Break Rooms and Eating Facilities.* At least half of seating capacity and floor space must be nonsmoking.<br>*Private Offices.* No statutory requirements. | No employee will be terminated or disciplined due to a smoking complaint. Violation is punishable by a $2,500 fine. Any retaliation will be redressed by reinstatement and back pay. An aggrieved person must file with the city Equal Opportunity Department within 60 days after violation. | If no accommodation can be reached between smokers and nonsmokers in a work area, the employer will prohibit smoking in that area. | Fire marshal or designee may levy a fine; any affected person may bring a civil action to abate the nuisance. | Employer must maintain a written smoking policy that defines immediate work area. The smoking policy must be announced to employees and posted conspicuously or made available upon request. Failure to implement a policy results in a prohibition of smoking on the entire premises. "Smoking" and "No Smoking" signs must be posted. Employer need not incur expenditures or make structural changes to comply. | Mun. Code ch. 23, art. IX. |
| Berkeley, CA* | Bars; tobacco retail stores; private homes used for employment, except for childcare and health care, unless employer designates as nonsmoking. | All employees working for direct or indirect monetary wages or profit. | *Employees' Workspaces.* Employers must provide a smoke-free workplace for all employees. Smoking is prohibited in *all* enclosed facilities (including private offices, common areas, cafeterias, and lounges), unless an employer choses to provide a sealed, separate smoking area with appropriate ventilation.<br>*Common Areas.* (See "Employees' Workspaces.")<br>*Break Rooms and Eating Facilities.* (See "Employees' Workspaces.")<br>*Private Offices.* (See "Employees' Workspaces.") | No employee or applicant shall be discharged or refused employment due to exercise of rights. | Rights of nonsmoker take precedence. | Enforcement is by Department of Health and Human Services; citizen may file complaint and seek to enforce; owner, manager, or employer must inform and stop violators. | "Smoking" and "No Smoking" signs must be posted. Employer may designate entire place of employment as nonsmoking. Employer may be granted a waiver on a showing of financial impracticability. | Mun. Code ch. 12.70 (see note regarding statewide legislation at end of this table). |
| Fresno, CA* | Places of business where services or goods are sold with fewer than 5 employees, bars, tobacco stores, and (*cont'd*) | All employees working for direct or indirect monetary wages. | *Employees' Workplaces.* Employees have the right to designate their immediate work area as a nonsmoking area. Existing physical barriers and ventilation systems shall be used to minimize the toxic effect of smoke on nonsmokers. (*cont'd*) | No employee shall be terminated or subject to disciplinary action as a result of exercising rights afforded by article. | Smoking policy shall establish a mechanism for resolving disputes between employees in which the health concerns of (*cont'd*) | Violation of provision shall be an infraction. A first violation shall be subject to a penalty of up to $100. (*cont'd*) | Employers must draft and implement written smoking policy and must notify all employees. "Smoking" or "No Smoking" signs (*cont'd*) | Mun. Code Article 16 § 9-1609 *et seq.* |

*(Table continues.)*

**Table 8.2-1** *(cont'd)*

MUNICIPAL SMOKING ORDINANCES

(See also text at § 8.2.)

| | *Employers Exempted* | *Employees Covered* | *Parts of the Workplace Covered by the Ordinance* | *Nonretaliation Clause* | *Smoker and Nonsmoker Disputes* | *Enforcement* | *Other Requirements* | *Citations to Authority* |
|---|---|---|---|---|---|---|---|---|
| Fresno, CA* *(cont'd)* | convention facilities or hotel convention halls when used for private functions. | | *Common Areas.* Smoking is prohibited in enclosed areas of general passage including hallways and elevators.<br>*Break Room and Eating Facilities.* Smoking in employee lounges and areas of general assembly may be permitted provided that if an employee so requests, a nonsmoking lounge of substantially equal size and amenities is made available.<br>*Private Offices.* Smoking is allowed. | | nonsmokers shall take precedence. | Any citizen can file a complaint. | shall be posted in every public place and in every place of general assembly by employees in places of employment. | |
| Hemet, CA | Private offices; hotel and motel meeting assembly rooms rented to guests; rooms used for private functions, private hospital rooms occupied exclusively by smokers; psychiatric facilities; jails; bars; tobacco stores; restaurants that seat fewer than 50 persons; private residences (unless used as child care center). | No specific provisions. | *Employees' Workspaces.* Smoking is prohibited in areas under the control of public and private employers that employees normally frequent during the course of employment. Smoking is prohibited in public places (all enclosed areas to which the public is invited). Existing physical barriers and ventilation systems shall be used to minimize the toxic effect of smoke on nonsmokers.<br>*Common Areas.* Smoking is prohibited in conference rooms, classrooms, hallways, and elevators.<br>*Break Rooms and Eating Facilities.* Smoking is prohibited in rest rooms, employee lounges, cafeterias, and lunchrooms. | No employee shall be discharged or discriminated against for exercising rights under this ordinance. | All employers must provide a smoke-free work area to any employee who requests one in writing, to the extent that existing facilities permit. | Owner, manager, or operator of any facility, business, or agency to which this ordinance applies may not provide services to anyone in violation of the ordinance. | Employer must post "No Smoking" signs in appropriate areas. | Code of the City of Hemet, Sec. 34-91–34-100. |

| | | | | | | | | |
|---|---|---|---|---|---|---|---|---|
| | | | *Private Offices.* (See "Employers Exempted.") | | | | | |
| Los Angeles, CA* | Federal, state, and municipal employers; employers with fewer than 5 employees. | All paid employees and volunteers working 10 or more hours per week. | *Employees' Workspaces.* Employer must provide smoke-free workplace to the maximum extent possible. Employer need not incur any expense to comply. Any area may be designated as nonsmoking.<br>*Common Areas.* Smoking is prohibited in elevators, restrooms, and medical facilities.<br>*Break Rooms and Eating Facilities.* At least two thirds of seating capacity and floor space must be reserved for nonsmokers in lunchrooms and lounges. Alternatively, an employer may provide a designated smoking lounge, provided any such lounge comprises no more than one half of all available lounge space. Smoking is prohibited in employee cafeterias.<br>*Private Offices.* Smoking is allowed even when nonsmokers visit. | Employer cannot discharge an employee if the dominant intent is retaliation for exercising rights under the ordinance. | Disputes must be resolved to accommodate the wishes of both smokers and nonsmokers. | Enforcement is by city attorney; smoking in nonsmoking area or destruction of "No Smoking" signs punishable by fine; employer's failure to maintain and implement smoking policy is a misdemeanor punishable by fine and/or imprisonment. | Employer must draft and implement written smoking policy and must notify all employees. Employer must post appropriate "No Smoking" signs. "Reasonable efforts" to develop and implement a smoking policy are deemed compliance. Smoking is entirely prohibited in buildings owned or leased by the city. | Mun. Code § 41.50 (amended 3/17/95). (See note regarding statewide legislation at end of this table.) |
| Mission Viejo, CA | Bars; private residences (except when used as child care or health care facility); hotel and motel rooms rented to guests; tobacco stores; rooms in restaurants; motel and hotel conference/meeting rooms and public and private assembly rooms (when being used for private functions); private enclosed office workspace oc- *(cont'd)* | Any person employed by a private employer in consideration for direct or indirect monetary wages or profit. | *Employees' Workplace.* Employers must provide smoke-free areas for nonsmokers within existing facilities to the maximum extent possible but are not required to incur any expense to make structural or other physical modifications to provide these areas. Any employee has the right to designate his immediate assigned work area, at a fixed location, as a nonsmoking area. Employers may designate any place of employment as a nonsmoking area.<br>*Common Areas.* Smoking prohibited in conference and meeting rooms, classrooms, auditoriums, rest rooms, medical facilities, hallways, and elevators.<br>*Break Rooms and Eating Facilities.* Employers must *(cont'd)* | Employers cannot discharge or retaliate against any employee in any manner for exercising any rights under this ordinance. | Health concerns of the nonsmoker are given precedence. | No specific provisions. | Employers must adopt, implement, and maintain a written nosmoking policy; employers must post "Smoking" and "No Smoking" signs in appropriate areas. | Mission Viejo Municipal Code, Chapter 6.40. |

*(Table continues.)*

# Table 8.2-1 *(cont'd)*

## MUNICIPAL SMOKING ORDINANCES

(See also text at § 8.2.)

| | *Employers Exempted* | *Employees Covered* | *Parts of the Workplace Covered by the Ordinance* | *Nonretaliation Clause* | *Smoker and Nonsmoker Disputes* | *Enforcement* | *Other Requirements* | *Citations to Authority* |
|---|---|---|---|---|---|---|---|---|
| Mission Viejo, CA (*cont'd*) | cupied exclusively by smokers; private employers with fewer than 9 employees. | | provide contiguous smoke-free areas of at least 50 percent of the seating capacity and floor spaces in employee cafeterias, lunchrooms, and lounges. Employers must consider time and place of prohibition of smoking in smaller employee lounges, where smoking could be prohibited in the entire room during normal meal hours.<br><br>*Private Offices.* Smoking is prohibited in enclosed areas under the control of private employers and which employees normally frequent during the course of employment. "Private employer" includes any person, partnership, or corporation that employs 10 or more in dividuals. | | | | | |
| Sacramento County, CA* | None. | All employees. | *Employees' Workspaces.* Smoking is prohibited in almost all employee workspaces (whether or not public is admitted), except for tobacco stores, bars, and at private functions.<br><br>*Common Areas.* Smoking is prohibited in conference and meeting rooms, classrooms, auditoriums, restrooms, medical facilities, hallways, and elevators.<br><br>*Break Rooms and Eating Facilities.* Smoking is pro- | A civil action may be brought by anyone who is retaliated against for seeking enforcement of the ordinance or for complaining about smoking. | Employer will attempt to reasonably accommodate the preferences of both smokers and nonsmokers. If no accommodation can be reached, the employer will restrict or prohibit smoking to accommodate nonsmokers. | Any person may bring an action for retaliation; the county director of health may conduct inspections and levy fines. | Employer must post "No Smoking" signs. A written smoking policy must be available and posted conspicuously at all workplaces. | County Code tit. 6, ch. 6.84. (as amended 12/31/93). (See note regarding statewide legislation at end of this table.) |

| | | | | | | | | |
|---|---|---|---|---|---|---|---|---|
| | | | hibited in on-site cafeterias, lunchrooms, and lounges.<br>*Private Offices.* Smoking is prohibited in private offices. | | | | | |
| San Francisco, CA* | Separately enclosed, owner-operated businesses with less than 500 square feet of floorspace; bars; and tobacco stores. | All employees. | *Employees' Workspaces.* Smoking is entirely prohibited.<br>*Common Areas.* (See "Employees' Workspaces.")<br>*Break Rooms and Eating Facilities.* (See "Employees' Workspaces.")<br>*Private Offices.* (See "Employees' Workspaces.") | Municipality has no statutory requirements. | No provisions are made for disputes, since smoking is entirely prohibited. | Director of Public Health is charged with enforcement and may request court action and fines up to $500 per day; violation is also a misdemeanor punishable by escalating fines up to $600 for a third or successive violation. | A violation of the ordinance is not intended to create a private cause of action for money damages by any person claiming to be injured by the violation. | Mun. Code ch. V, art. 19 (as amended 7/7/94). (See note regarding statewide legislation at end of this table.) |
| San Jose, CA* | Employers whose workplaces are located in private homes or in property leased or owned by a government agency; cocktail lounges and bars; standalone bars; card rooms of bingo facilities (20 percent of tables in card room with more than five tables must be designated as "no smoking" tables); tobacco stores; meeting and banquet rooms (when not used to serve food or beverages or for an exhibit); outdoor areas of restaurants; designated smoking areas of<br>(*cont'd*) | All paid employees. | *Employees' Workspaces.* Any employee may designate his or her "immediate area" as a no-smoking area.<br>*Common Areas.* Smoking is prohibited in conference and meeting rooms, classrooms, auditoriums, restrooms, medical facilities, hallways, and elevators.<br>*Break Rooms and Eating Facilities.* At least two thirds of seating capacity and floor space of eating facility or employee lounge must be nonsmoking; employer may alternatively provide for separate smoking lounge(s) as long as smoking area is no more than half the total square footage of all lounge areas.<br>*Private Offices.* Smoking is allowed when all occupants are smokers, even if nonsmoker visits. | No employer shall take retaliatory action against any person for asserting any rights under this ordinance. | Nonsmokers' rights must be given precedence over smokers' rights. | Health officer may exercise police powers to enforce ordinance. | Employer must post "No Smoking" signs. Employer must maintain a written smoking policy defining "immediate work area." | Mun. Code ch. 9.44 (last revised 6/24/97). (See note regarding statewide legislation at end of this table.) |

(*Table continues.*)

# Table 8.2-1 *(cont'd)*

## MUNICIPAL SMOKING ORDINANCES

(See also text at § 8.2.)

| | *Employers Exempted* | *Employees Covered* | *Parts of the Workplace Covered by the Ordinance* | *Nonretaliation Clause* | *Smoker and Nonsmoker Disputes* | *Enforcement* | *Other Requirements* | *Citations to Authority* |
|---|---|---|---|---|---|---|---|---|
| San Jose, CA* (*cont'd*) | San Jose Airport; on stage when smoking is part of performance. | | | | | | | |
| Vacaville, CA* | Bars with 3 or fewer employees; restaurants seating fewer than 50 persons; tobacco retail stores; homes used for employment, except for childcare or health care. | All employees working for direct or indirect monetary wages or profit. | *Employees' Workspaces.* Employer may designate area as nonsmoking and post this information; nonsmoker rights take precedence.<br>*Common Areas.* Smoking is prohibited in public areas, including waiting rooms, hallways, elevators, conference and meeting rooms, restrooms, medical facilities.<br>*Break Rooms and Eating Facilities.* Employer must allocate at least 40% of space to nonsmokers.<br>*Private Offices.* Smoking is permitted where all occupants are smokers, even if nonsmoker visits. | No employee or applicant shall be discharged or refused employment due to exercise of rights. | Rights of nonsmoker take precedence. | Enforcement is by City Manager or designee; citizen may file complaint with City Manager; owner, manager, or employer must inform and stop violators; enforced by fine. | Written policy, announced to all employees once a year; "Smoking" and "No Smoking" signs must be posted; employer need not incur expenses to make structural or physical modifications in making areas smoke-free. | Mun. Code ch. 9.65 (as amended 2/1/95). (See note regarding statewide legislation at end of this table.) |
| West Hollywood, CA* | Bars; retail tobacco stores; homes used for employment, except for childcare or health care. | Any person employed by employer in consideration for direct or indirect monetary wages or profit. | *Employees' Workspaces.* No employee shall be required to work in designated smoking area; smoking areas may be designated only if separated by walls, partitions, distance, or other methods so as to minimize smoke.<br>*Common Areas.* Smoking is permitted in waiting rooms, lobbies, and lounges, if separate nonsmoking area that is | No employee or applicant shall be discharged or refused employment due to exercise of rights. | Rights of nonsmoker take precedence. | Enforcement is by civil action or injunctive action; owner, manager, or employer must inform and stop violators; employer must conspicuously post appropriate signs or the international | Employee prevailing in retaliatory action entitled to attorneys' fees and costs; persons subject to law may apply for modifications or exemptions. Employer may designate the entire workplace as a no-smoking area. | Mun. Code art. IV, ch. 6. (See note regarding statewide legislation at end of this table.) |

| | | | | | | | | |
|---|---|---|---|---|---|---|---|---|
| | | | at least 50% of total area is provided.<br>*Break Rooms and Eating Facilities.* At least 50% of space must be allocated to nonsmokers in a separate and noncontiguous area.<br>*Private Offices.* Smoking allowed if fully enclosed. | | | no-smoking symbol. | | |
| Arvada, CO | Any establishment issued a license to sell fermented malt beverages, a beer or wine license, tavern license, or club license; tobacco stores; restaurants seating 30 or fewer patrons; enclosed premises occupied exclusively by smokers; meetings and assemblies not open to the public (as long as not conducted in public place); commercial licensed bingo facility (which designates at least 25 percent of bingo playing area as no-smoking area). | Any person who is paid a wage or salary and works in an enclosed area. | *Employees' Workspaces.* Smoking is prohibited in common areas, public places, and work places (any enclosed premises occupied principally by employees). Designated smoking areas may not exceed 25 percent of the total common area or 25 percent of employer's total floor area.<br>*Common Areas.* Smoking prohibited in any lobby, mall, or hallway open or accessible to members of the public.<br>*Break Room and Eating Facilities.* No statutory requirements.<br>*Private Offices.* No specific statutory requirements. | No specific provisions. | No specific provisions. | Fine between $25 and $500 for each separate violation. | Employers must post "Smoking" and "No Smoking" signs in appropriate work areas. | City of Arvada Code of Ordinances Sec. 21-65–21-73. |
| Denver, CO | Businesses with 4 or fewer employees; bars; retail tobacco stores; restaurants seating 25 or fewer people; bars; private residences (*cont'd*) | All employees. | *Employees' Workspaces.* Employers must provide a smoke-free work area for every employee who asks not to be exposed to environmental tobacco smoke.<br>*Common Areas.* Smoking is prohibited in auditoriums, classrooms, conference/ (*cont'd*) | Municipality has no statutory requirements. | Rights of nonsmoker take precedence. | Any police officer may enforce the ordinance; signs must be posted to designate no-smoking and smoking areas; employers may prohibit smok- (*cont'd*) | Every employer must implement, make known, follow, and enforce a smoking policy that meets the requirements of the ordinance. If providing a designated smoke-free (*cont'd*) | Mun. Code ch. 24, art. IX (amended 8/23/93). |

*(Table continues.)*

**Table 8.2-1** *(cont'd)*

MUNICIPAL SMOKING ORDINANCES

(See also text at § 8.2.)

| | *Employers Exempted* | *Employees Covered* | *Parts of the Workplace Covered by the Ordinance* | *Nonretaliation Clause* | *Smoker and Nonsmoker Disputes* | *Enforcement* | *Other Requirements* | *Citations to Authority* |
|---|---|---|---|---|---|---|---|---|
| Denver, CO (*cont'd*) | (except when used for commercial child care, teaching, or health care); rented hotel and motel rooms; conference/meeting rooms when used exclusively for private functions. | | meeting rooms, elevators, elevator lobbies, hallways, stairwells, escalators, medical facilities, and restrooms.<br>*Break Rooms and Eating Facilities.* Smoking is prohibited unless separate facilities are available to nonsmokers.<br>*Private Offices.* Smoking is allowed in private, enclosed office workplaces occupied exclusively by smokers, even if nonsmokers visit. | | | ing in the entire workplace. | area does not eliminate environmental tobacco smoke from an employee's work area, an employer must take steps to eliminate the ETS. | |
| Larimer County, CO | The ordinance applies only to employers within the unincorporated territory of Larimer County. Restaurants, bars, and tobacco stores are also exempt. | All employees. | *Employees' Workspaces.* Smoking is generally prohibited in all employee workspaces except for employer-designated smoking areas. In no event shall an employer fail to provide a smoke-free work area to accommodate an employee who requests it.<br>*Common Areas.* No smoking area may be designated in the common area of a nursing home, hospital, or health care facility. No more than 50% of any floor area in a workplace may be designated smoking.<br>*Break Rooms and Eating Facilities.* No smoking area may be designated in an employee restroom.<br>*Private Offices.* Smoking is permitted in fully enclosed of- | No employer shall harass, discharge, discipline, or otherwise retaliate or discriminate against an employee for the reason that such employee has requested a smoke-free area. | No specific provisions. | Violations of the ordinance are a Class 2 petty offense, and a $50 fine may be levied. The ordinance is enforced by the sheriff's department. | Signs must be posted to designate nonsmoking and smoking areas. Such signs must have letters not less than 1 inch in height or the international symbol for no-smoking not less than three inches in height. An employer may designate an entire workplace as nonsmoking. Employers are required to use all appropriate means to comply with the ordinance, including asking smokers to | Larimer County Code of Ordinances (adopted 5/2/94). |

| | | | | | | | | |
|---|---|---|---|---|---|---|---|---|
| | | | fices occupied exclusively by smokers where the public is not generally permitted, even if non-smokers sometimes visit. | | | | refrain from smoking and using physical barriers and ventilation systems to prevent secondhand smoke from migrating into nonsmoking areas. | |
| Thorton, CO | Tobacco stores; bars and taverns (when such bars and taverns are selling and serving alcohol); meetings sponsored by private persons or clubs. | No specific provisions. | *Employees' Workspaces.* Employers are not required to install physical barriers or additional ventilation equipment. Smoking may be allowed in a specific area if employer receives a petition for designation of smoking area signed by more than 50 percent of the permanent employees within the workplace and if such designation is within the physical limitations of the place of employment.<br>*Common Areas.* Smoking prohibited in enclosed areas open to use or gatherings of the public (including any lobby, hallway, mall foyer, elevator, or restroom).<br>*Break Rooms and Eating Facilities.* No specific provision.<br>*Private Offices.* Smoking not prohibited in fully enclosed private offices. | Employees requesting the designation of smoking areas or enforcement within no-smoking areas or designated smoking areas shall not be discharged, discriminated against, or otherwise retaliated against. | No specific provisions. | Code enforcement officers and Police Department personnel must enforce the provisions of this ordinance. Violators are fined between $25 and $1000. | Employers must post "No Smoking" and "Smoking" signs in appropriate areas. | Code of the City of Thorton, Sec. 38-457–38-464. |
| Atlanta, GA | Private residence (unless used as child care or health care facility); dining area of food establishment (as long as designated smoking area does not exceed 50 percent of seating); bars; hotel and motel rooms rented to<br>(*cont'd*) | No specific provisions. | *Employees' Workspaces.* Employers must provide nonsmoking employees with a smoke-free work area (where employees are routinely assigned). Employers are not required to make any expenditure or structural changes to create a smoke-free work area. Employers may prohibit smoking in areas in which smoking would otherwise be permitted under this ordinance.<br>*Common Areas.* Smoking prohibited in auditoriums,<br>(*cont'd*) | No specific provisions. | The nonsmoker's rights are given precedence. | The department of police has the ultimate responsibility for enforcement of this article. City solicitor and police officers may initiate any action seeking enforcement of this ordinance, if the violation occurs in the officer's presence. Employ-<br>(*cont'd*) | Employers must post "No Smoking" and "Smoking" signs in appropriate areas. | Atlanta Code of Ordinances Sec. 86-31–86-38. |

*(Table continues.)*

# Table 8.2-1 *(cont'd)*

## MUNICIPAL SMOKING ORDINANCES

(See also text at § 8.2.)

| | *Employers Exempted* | *Employees Covered* | *Parts of the Workplace Covered by the Ordinance* | *Nonretaliation Clause* | *Smoker and Nonsmoker Disputes* | *Enforcement* | *Other Requirements* | *Citations to Authority* |
|---|---|---|---|---|---|---|---|---|
| Atlanta, GA (*cont'd*) | guests; tobacco stores; banquet or meeting rooms used for private functions; jails and prisons; private boxes in sports arenas; limousines under private hire by corporation or individual. | | gymnasiums, rest rooms, elevators, classrooms, hallways, employee medical facilities, rooms/areas where photocopying equipment or other office equipment is used in common, company vehicles, conference and meeting rooms, lobbies, and reception halls.<br>*Break Rooms and Eating Facilities.* Employers must provide contiguous nonsmoking areas in employee cafeterias and lunchrooms.<br>*Private Offices.* No specific provisions. | | | ers must inform violators of the ordinance's provisions. | | |
| Gwinnett County, GA | Private residence (unless used as child care or health care facility); bars; hotel and motel rooms rented to guests; tobacco stores; designated smoking area in restaurant (as long as smoking area does not comprise more than 50 percent of restaurant's seating); banquet or | No specific provisions. | *Employees' Workspaces.* Employers must provide nonsmoking employees a smoke-free work area (where employees are routinely assigned). Employers are not required to make any expenditure or structural changes to create a smoke-free work area. Employers may prohibit smoking in areas in which smoking would otherwise be permitted under this ordinance.<br>*Common Areas.* Smoking prohibited in auditoriums, gymnasiums, rest rooms, elevators, classrooms, hallways, employee medical facilities, rooms/areas where photo- | No specific provisions. | The nonsmoker's rights are given precedence. | The county department of health has the ultimate responsibility for enforcement. Any police officer may initiate an action for violation of this article if the violation occurs in the officer's presence. Employers must inform violators of the ordinance's provisions. | Employers must post "No Smoking" and "Smoking" signs in appropriate areas. | Gwinnett County Code of Ordinances, Sec. 42-122–42-130. |

| | | | | | | | | |
|---|---|---|---|---|---|---|---|---|
| | meeting rooms used for private functions; jails or prisons; private boxes in indoor sports arenas; limousines under private hire. | | copying equipment or other office equipment is used in common, company vehicles, conference and meeting rooms, lobbies, and reception areas.<br>*Break Rooms and Eating Facilities.* Employers must provide contiguous nonsmoking areas in employee cafeterias and lunchrooms.<br>*Private Offices.* No specific provisions. | | | | | |
| Snellville, GA | Restaurants; bars; tobacco stores. | All employees are covered. | *Employees' Workspaces.* Smoking is generally prohibited in all employee workspaces except for employer-designated smoking areas.<br>*Common Areas.* No smoking area may be designated in an elevator, stairwell, or employee meeting room.<br>*Break Rooms and Eating Facilities.* No smoking area may be designated in an employee kitchen.<br>*Private Offices.* Smoking is permitted in offices occupied exclusively by smokers where the public is not generally permitted. | Municipality has no specific provisions. | Municipality has no specific provisions. | The city police department is charged with enforcement of the ordinance. | Signs must be posted to designate nonsmoking and smoking areas. Such signs must have letters not less than two inches in height or the international symbol for no-smoking. An employer may designate an entire workplace as nonsmoking. | Code of Ordinances §§ 14-101 *et seq.* (adopted 2/10/92). |
| Chicago, IL | Workplace in a private residence, unless childcare or health facility. | All employees. | *Employees' Workspaces.* Every employee may designate his or her work area as a nonsmoking area, unless it is a public place. Employer will make reasonable accommodations to minimize smoke from other work areas (employer need not make physical modifications).<br>*Common Areas.* No statutory requirements.<br>*Break Rooms and Eating Facilities.* No statutory requirements.<br>*Private Offices.* No statutory requirements. | No employer will retaliate against an employee or applicant for exercising rights under the ordinance. | Rights of nonsmoker take precedence. | Enforced by fine; employer must post appropriate signs. | Employer will adopt and communicate a written smoking policy to all employees. Copies must be given to employees upon request. | Mun. Code ch. 7-32-010–7-32-090 (as enacted 7/15/92). |

*(Table continues.)*

# Table 8.2-1 *(cont'd)*

## MUNICIPAL SMOKING ORDINANCES

(See also text at § 8.2.)

| | *Employers Exempted* | *Employees Covered* | *Parts of the Workplace Covered by the Ordinance* | *Nonretaliation Clause* | *Smoker and Nonsmoker Disputes* | *Enforcement* | *Other Requirements* | *Citations to Authority* |
|---|---|---|---|---|---|---|---|---|
| Denison, IA | Employers may choose whether to designate place of employment as smoking or nonsmoking. | All employees. | Employer may, but is not required to, designate one or more areas as nonsmoking areas. No designation of the place of employment as smoking is required unless nonsmoking areas are designated within the public place. | Municipality has no specific provision. | Municipality has no specific provision. | Violators of provision shall be deemed guilty of a misdemeanor punishable by a fine not to exceed $500. | Where no smoking has been designated, visible signs must be posted at each entrance. | Mun. Code ch. 11.11 |
| Rockville, MD | Bars or eating and drinking establishments being used exclusively for a private function or with a seating capacity of less than 25. | Ordinance applies only to eating and drinking establishments with a seating capacity of 25 or more. Effect on employees is incidental. | Establishments covered by article must designate a contiguous nonsmoking area that is at least 50 percent of the total seating capacity. | — | — | City attorney, county attorney, or any affected party may institute an action in a court of competent jurisdictions to enjoin repeated violations of the article. | Eating and drinking establishments not covered by article may elect to have provisions of article apply to them by notifying the County Department of Health. | City Code Chapter 13. |
| Gloucester, MA | All employers, including the City, who regularly use the services of two or more employees are covered. | All employees who perform services for an employer in return for wages or profit. | *Employees' Workspaces.* Smoking is generally prohibited in all employee workspaces except for employer-designated smoking areas. Employers must use physical barriers and ventilation to keep smoke from smoking areas out of nonsmoking areas.<br><br>*Common Areas.* No smoking area may be designated in an elevator, hallway, waiting area, stairwell, or employee meeting room.<br><br>*Break Rooms and Eating Facilities.* No smoking area may be designated in an employee restroom. | No specific provisions. | No specific provisions. | A person who smokes in a nonsmoking area is subject to a $25 fine, as is an employer who fails to comply with the regulations; any aggrieved party may apply for injunctive relief; the Board of Health is charged with enforcing the regulation. | Signs must be posted to designate nonsmoking and smoking areas. Such signs must state "Warning: Smoking is permitted in this establishment. Persons entering may be exposing themselves to undetermined levels of environmental tobacco smoke, which increases people's risk of respiratory tract infections, | City of Gloucester Board of Health Regulation (dated February 9, 1994, effective January 1, 1995). |

| | | | | | | | | |
|---|---|---|---|---|---|---|---|---|
| | | | *Private Offices.* Smoking is permitted in private offices only if they are physically separated from and separately ventilated such that smoke does not migrate. | | | | bronchitis, asthma attacks and lung cancer." Such signs must be not less than 48 inches square. Each employer must adopt a smoking policy and notify all employees of it within three weeks. An employer may designate an entire workplace as nonsmoking. | |
| Medfield, MA | Only employers with two or more employees are covered by the ordinance. Tobacco stores and bars are exempt. | All employees are covered. | *Employees' Workspaces.* Employers are required to designate any areas in the workplace where employees may smoke, and smoking is prohibited elsewhere.<br>*Common Areas.* Hallways, elevators, entranceways, stairwells, restrooms, and waiting areas may not be designated as smoking areas.<br>*Break Room and Eating Facilities.* Municipality has no specific requirements.<br>*Private Offices.* Municipality has no specific requirements. | Municipality has no specific requirements. | Municipality has no specific requirements. | Enforced by fine; employer must post appropriate signs; aggrieved employees have a cause of action for injunctive relief for continued failure to comply with the regulations. | Any area in the workplace designated as a smoking area must be segregated from nonsmoking areas by physical barriers and ventilation systems. Air from a smoking area should be exhausted directly outside and not recirculated within the building. Any employer may apply to the Board of Health for a variance if application of the regulations would be unduly burdensome. | Medfield Board of Health Regulations (adopted 10/28/92 under authority of Mass. G.L. ch. 111 § 31). |
| Detroit, MI | Only employers with two or more employees are covered by the ordinance. Property owned or leased by governmental agencies is also exempted. | All employees are covered. | *Employees' Workspaces.* Employers are required to adopt, implement, and maintain a smoking policy that prohibits smoking in the workplace, except for designated areas. Any employee may designate his or her immediate work area as a nonsmoking area and post appropriate signs.<br>*Common Areas.* Hallways, elevators, entranceways, stairwells, restrooms, and<br>*(cont'd)* | Municipality has no specific requirements. | An employer shall attempt to reach a reasonable accommodation between smoking and nonsmoking employees, but if no such accommodation can be reached, then the employer must prohibit smoking in<br>*(cont'd)* | Enforced by fine by the Director of Health; violation of the ordinance is a misdemeanor. | Employer must post appropriate signs and communicate the smoking policy to all employees. Any area in the workplace designated as a smoking area must be segregated from nonsmoking areas by physical barriers and venti-<br>*(cont'd)* | Ordinance No. 6-92, ch. 24, art. 11. |

*(Table continues.)*

## Table 8.2-1 *(cont'd)*

## MUNICIPAL SMOKING ORDINANCES

(See also text at § 8.2.)

| | *Employers Exempted* | *Employees Covered* | *Parts of the Workplace Covered by the Ordinance* | *Nonretaliation Clause* | *Smoker and Nonsmoker Disputes* | *Enforcement* | *Other Requirements* | *Citations to Authority* |
|---|---|---|---|---|---|---|---|---|
| Detroit, MI (*cont'd*) | | | waiting areas may not be designated as smoking areas.<br>*Break Rooms and Eating Facilities.* Any smoking area in an employee cafeteria, lunchroom, or lounge may not comprise more than one half of the seating capacity or floor space of such a place.<br>*Private Offices.* Smoking is permitted in private, enclosed offices, even if nonsmokers visit. | | the workplace. In any dispute, a nonsmoker is given preference. | | lation systems. However, no expenditures or structural changes are required to accommodate nonsmokers. | |
| Kansas City, MO | Workplaces in tobacco stores; restaurants (if employer so designates); bars; private residences; and designated areas in shopping malls. | All employees. | *Employees' Workspaces.* Smoking is prohibited except where a smoking area is designated by employer. Where a smoking area is designated, employer will use existing ventilation and physical barriers to minimize smoke in adjacent no-smoking area. Employer may not designate an entire establishment as a no-smoking area.<br>*Common Areas.* Smoking is not permitted in reception areas or lobbies of offices.<br>*Break Rooms and Eating Facilities.* (See "Common Areas.")<br>*Private Offices.* Smoking is allowed in private, enclosed offices occupied exclusively by smokers. | Municipality has no statutory requirements. | Rights of nonsmoker take precedence. | Enforced by fine. | Employers must post appropriate "Smoking" and "No Smoking" signs. Employers must request that violators cease smoking. | Health & Sanitation Code ch. 18, art. XII (as enacted 4/10/86). |

| | | | | | | | | |
|---|---|---|---|---|---|---|---|---|
| New York, NY | Employers with fewer than 5 employees; bars; tobacco businesses. | All employees. | *Employees' Workspaces.* Employee may designate his or her own workspace as a no-smoking area. Employer must make "reasonable accommodations" to minimize or eliminate smoke in the workspace.<br>*Common Areas.* Smoking is prohibited in all common areas except in conference and meeting rooms if all occupants so request.<br>*Break Rooms and Eating Facilities.* At least 50% of such space must be nonsmoking.<br>*Private Offices.* Smoking is allowed as long as each employee therein requests or allows it. | No retaliation for exercising rights under nonsmoking policy. | Employer must establish dispute mechanism. If disputes cannot be resolved, the rights of the nonsmoker shall be given preference. | Department of Health enforces; may impose fines for violations by employer and by individual employees. | Employer may designate a smoking room. Employer must maintain a written smoking policy and must provide it to certain municipal agencies. Employer must post "No Smoking" signs. Employer may be granted a waiver if strict compliance would be unreasonable. Smoking is prohibited at all times in both indoor and outdoor areas of daycare centers. | Admin. Code tit. 17, ch. 5 (as amended 4/9/96). |
| Suffolk County, NY | Private homes serving as offices; employer with fewer than 50 employees; bars and certain restaurants. | All paid employees. | *Employees' Workspaces.* Smoking and nonsmoking areas may be designated by the employer. Employee may designate his or her immediate area as a no-smoking area by posting appropriate signs.<br>*Common Areas.* Smoking is prohibited in conference rooms, indoor service lines, classrooms, auditoriums, restrooms, medical facilities, hallways, and elevators.<br>*Break Rooms and Eating Facilities.* At least half of contiguous seating capacity and floor space must be reserved for nonsmokers.<br>*Private Offices.* Smoking is allowed even when nonsmokers visit. | Municipality has no statutory requirements. | Rights of nonsmoker take precedence. | County Health Department may initiate action for fines. | Employee must post "No Smoking" signs in his or her work area. Employer must draft and implement written smoking policy. Ordinance addresses the problem of "tertiary smoke," defined as ingestion of smoke by the unborn fetus of a nonsmoking woman. | Local Law No. 12 (amended 6/2/95). |

*(Table continues.)*

# Table 8.2-1 *(cont'd)*

## MUNICIPAL SMOKING ORDINANCES

(See also text at § 8.2.)

| | *Employers Exempted* | *Employees Covered* | *Parts of the Workplace Covered by the Ordinance* | *Nonretaliation Clause* | *Smoker and Nonsmoker Disputes* | *Enforcement* | *Other Requirements* | *Citations to Authority* |
|---|---|---|---|---|---|---|---|---|
| Greensboro, NC | Bars and cocktail lounges; beauty parlors; retail stores that employ fewer than 25 persons regularly; restaurant employers with a seating capacity of less than 50 customers. | All employees are covered when they work in the specific areas were smoking is prohibited by the ordinance. | *Employees' Workspaces.* Smoking is prohibited in employee workspaces in retail stores designed to accommodate 200 or more people, or which regularly employ 25 or more people.<br>*Common Areas.* Smoking is prohibited in common areas of public libraries, museums, and art galleries.<br>*Breakrooms and Eating Facilities.* Employee smoking rooms and breakrooms in large retail stores are exempt from the smoking prohibition for such stores.<br>*Private Offices.* Executive offices in large retail stores are exempt from the smoking prohibition for such stores. | Municipality has no specific requirements. | Municipality has no specific requirements. | A violator is subject to a civil penalty of $25; violation of the sign posting requirement or removal of a sign is a misdemeanor and is also subject to a $25 fine. | Employers must post signs in areas where smoking is prohibited by the ordinance. Signs must be of standard size and lettering, approved by the fire inspector. Removing or defacing such signs is prohibited. | Greensboro Code § 10-6 (amended 9/20/93). |
| Guilford County, NC | Workplaces in private residences; the dining areas of certain restaurants and bars; state and federal employers; private clubs; tobacco stores or manufacturing facilities. | All employees working for direct or indirect wages, including independent contractors and any person who volunteers his or her services. | *Employees' Workspaces.* Each employer has the right to designate any place of employment as a nonsmoking place of employment. Employers shall make reasonable provisions for smoke-free air in enclosed areas for nonsmoking employees. If smoking is permitted, it must be done in specifically designated areas.<br>*Common Areas.* Hallways, elevators, entranceways, stairwells, restrooms, waiting areas, common work areas and spaces open to the pub- | No employer shall discharge, refuse to hire, or in any manner retaliate against any employee, applicant or member of the public for exercising any rights under the ordinance. | Municipality has no specific requirements. | An employer shall make reasonable efforts to prevent smoking in nonsmoking areas. Any aggrieved person may complain to an employer or person in charge, and if the complaint is not resolved, a formal complaint is to be lodged with the | Each employer must adopt a written environmental tobacco smoke control policy and post appropriate signs. All employers must make a written copy of the smoking policy available to any present or prospective employee on request. An employer must post appropriate signs | Guilford County Environmental Tobacco Smoke Control Rules. |

| | | | | | | | | |
|---|---|---|---|---|---|---|---|---|
| | | | lic in all places of employment shall not be designated smoking areas.<br>*Breakrooms and Eating Facilities.* (See "Employees' Workspaces.") If smoking is permitted, comparable nonsmoking areas of sufficient size and capacity must be provided by the employer.<br>*Private Offices.* (See "Employees' Workspaces.") | | | health director who must respond within 30 days. The County Department of Health may also enforce the rules. | or use the international symbol for no smoking. Removal or defacement of signs is prohibited. | |
| High Point, NC | Bars and cocktail lounges; beauty parlors; retail stores that employ fewer than 25 persons regularly; restaurant employers with a seating capacity of less than 50 customers. | All employees are covered when they work in the specific areas where smoking is prohibited by the ordinance. | *Employees' Workspaces.* Smoking is prohibited in employee workspaces in retail stores designed to accommodate 200 or more people, or that regularly employ 25 or more people.<br>*Common Areas.* Smoking is prohibited in common areas of public libraries, museums, and art galleries.<br>*Breakrooms and Eating Facilities.* Employee smoking rooms and breakrooms in large retail stores are exempt from the smoking prohibition for such stores.<br>*Private Offices.* Executive offices in large retail stores are exempt from the smoking prohibition for such stores. | Municipality has no specific requirements. | Municipality has no specific requirements. | Violation of any section of the ordinance is a misdemeanor and also subject to a $25 fine. | Employers must post signs in areas where smoking is prohibited by the ordinance. Signs must be of standard size and lettering approved by the fire inspector. Removing or defacing such signs is prohibited. The ordinance does not prohibit the imposition of stricter smoking controls by any employer. | High Point City Code §§ 12-5-1 *et seq.* (effective 10-1-93). |
| Raleigh, NC | Private homes serving as offices; eating establishments, hotel rooms, conference or meeting rooms rented for private functions; bowling alleys as long as one-third of spectator seating is designated as nonsmoking; tobacco stores; bars; restau-<br>*(cont'd)* | All employees, including volunteers are covered. | *Employees' Workspaces.* Smoking and nonsmoking areas may be designated by the employer's smoking policy. The required policy must make "reasonable provisions" for smoke-free air for nonsmoking employees.<br>*Common Areas.* Smoking is prohibited in elevators and restrooms.<br>*Break Rooms and Eating Facilities.* Municipality has no specific requirements.<br>*Private Offices.* Smoking is permitted in private offices. | Municipality has no specific requirements. | Municipality has no specific requirements. | Willful violation is punishable by a fine of $25. | Employer must draft and implement written smoking policy and supply it to employees on request. Employers must post appropriate signs having letters at least one inch in height or the international symbol for no-smoking. | Ord. No. 13-3000. |

*(Table continues.)*

# Table 8.2-1 *(cont'd)*

## MUNICIPAL SMOKING ORDINANCES

(See also text at § 8.2.)

| | *Employers Exempted* | *Employees Covered* | *Parts of the Workplace Covered by the Ordinance* | *Nonretaliation Clause* | *Smoker and Nonsmoker Disputes* | *Enforcement* | *Other Requirements* | *Citations to Authority* |
|---|---|---|---|---|---|---|---|---|
| Raleigh, NC (*cont'd*) | rants with a seating capacity of less than 30 are exempted. | | | | | | | |
| Cleveland, OH | Workplaces in function halls; retail tobacco stores; bars; eating establishments seating fewer than 30 people; private residences; bowling alleys. | Persons working in consideration for direct or indirect monetary wages or volunteers. | *Employees' Workspaces.* Any employee may designate his or her stationary work area as a no-smoking area. If the designation of a no-smoking area does not reduce smoke to the employee's satisfaction, the employee will take reasonable measures to minimize the effects of smoke.<br>*Common Areas.* Smoking is prohibited in hallways, elevators, indoor service lines, employee restrooms, vehicles used to transport employees, conference and meeting rooms, classrooms, auditoriums, and medical facilities. Smoking may be permitted in public lobbies if on the ground floor and if area is no greater than 20% of total floor space.<br>*Break Rooms and Eating Facilities.* A contiguous no-smoking area must be set aside to meet demand.<br>*Private Offices.* Smoking is permitted in any enclosed, indoor area used by employees, but no more than 50% of total floor space may be designated as a smoking area. | No employer will in any manner discriminate against an applicant or employee because he or she exercises rights under either the ordinance or the employer's smoking policy. | Rights of nonsmoker take precedence. | Enforcement is by the department of public health and welfare; director of the Law Department may commence civil and/or criminal proceedings. | Employer must post "No Smoking" signs in common areas. Employer must also furnish such signs to employees upon request. Ashtrays must be removed from no-smoking areas. Smoking may be prohibited in the entire workplace; employer with 10 or more employees must adopt and promulgate a written smoking policy. | Ord. No. 279-A-86. |

| | | | | | | | | |
|---|---|---|---|---|---|---|---|---|
| Pittsburgh, PA | Employers of fewer than 25 employees need not have a written smoking policy; private home used as a workplace, unless it is a childcare facility; bars; tobacco stores. | All employees and volunteers. | *Employees' Workspaces.* Any employee has the right to designate his or her work area as no-smoking area by posting appropriate signs to be provided by employer.<br>*Common Areas.* Smoking is prohibited in auditoriums, classrooms, conference and meeting rooms, elevators, medical facilities, and restrooms.<br>*Break Rooms and Eating Facilities.* At least 20% of separate and contiguous seating capacity and floor space must be reserved for nonsmokers.<br>*Private Offices.* Separate work areas occupied exclusively by smokers may be designated as smoking areas. | No employer will discharge, refuse to hire, or otherwise retaliate against any employee or applicant for exercising rights under the ordinance. | No statutory requirements. | Department of Public Health may levy fines if employer does not make good-faith effort to comply. City attorney's office may seek restraining order. Retaliation is redressed by reinstatement of all employment rights and benefits. | Employers of 25 or more employees must have a written smoking policy. No person will mutilate or destroy any "No Smoking" signs. An entire place of employment may be designated as nonsmoking. Employer may be granted a waiver on a showing of financial impracticability. | Pittsburgh Code, Title Six, art. I, ch. 617. |
| Austin, TX | Tobacco stores; certain bars, bowling alleys, and restaurants. | All paid employees. | *Employees' Workspaces.* If an employer permits smoking, all smoking areas must be: inaccessible to the general public, proportionate in size to the number of smoking employees, ventilated to prevent migration of smoke, physically enclosed and separate from nonsmoking areas, designated by appropriate signs, and furnished with ashtrays.<br>*Common Areas.* Smoking is permitted only if every person who works in that area agrees in writing.<br>*Break Rooms and Eating Facilities.* Smoking is prohibited.<br>*Private Offices.* Smoking is allowed even when nonsmoker visits. | No statutory requirements. | An employer may not require an employee to work in a designated smoking area if the employee requests to work in a no-smoking area. | It is a misdemeanor if an employee knowingly smokes in a nonsmoking area or if an employer fails to make a reasonable effort to prevent same. | Written smoking policy must be adopted and conspicuously posted at the workplace. Designated smoking areas must contain ashtrays and appropriate signs and must be physically enclosed and separately ventilated. If an employer's facility does not contain a separate HVAC system, smoking may not be permitted until one is installed. | Mun. Code ch. 12-5. |

*(Table continues.)*

# Table 8.2-1 *(cont'd)*

## MUNICIPAL SMOKING ORDINANCES

(See also text at § 8.2.)

| | *Employers Exempted* | *Employees Covered* | *Parts of the Workplace Covered by the Ordinance* | *Nonretaliation Clause* | *Smoker and Nonsmoker Disputes* | *Enforcement* | *Other Requirements* | *Citations to Authority* |
|---|---|---|---|---|---|---|---|---|
| Dallas, TX | Employers operating in a domestic residence or in a factory or warehouse where smoking is regulated by another municipal, state, or federal law; employers with fewer than 5 employees; tobacco stores; business establishments serving the public with less than 500 square feet of service space; restaurants. | All employees including an independent contractor with an assigned indoor location. | *Employees' Workspaces.* Employers must reasonably accommodate the interests of smokers and nonsmokers. Employers must designate nonsmoking areas using existing structures and ventilation to minimize exposure of nonsmokers to second-hand smoke.<br>*Common Areas.* Smoking is generally *not* prohibited in "administrative areas," defined as areas of an establishment not generally accessible to the public, including individual offices, stockrooms, employee lounges, and meeting rooms.<br>*Break Rooms and Eating Facilities.* (See "Common Areas.")<br>*Private Offices.* Smoking is permitted in an enclosed room with 1 regular occupant. | Employer will not retaliate against any employee who files a complaint, testifies in a proceeding under the ordinance, or exercises rights under the ordinance. | Employer will establish a procedure for addressing employee complaints. | Violations are punishable by fines. Employer is not liable for fines if an employee smokes in a no-smoking area when the employer is otherwise in compliance. | Employer must establish a written smoking policy. Employer may designate the entire workplace (with the exception of a single-occupant enclosed space) as nonsmoking. Employer must post signs in nonsmoking areas. | City Code, ch. 41. |
| Houston, TX | Restaurant bar if the bar is not located in an enclosed area including a dining area; lounge bar; tobacco retail store; restaurant with seating capacity of fewer than 50 persons; con- | Any person, except a domestic household servant, who is employed in consideration for direct or indirect wages; any contract employees. | *Employees' Workspaces.* No specific provisions.<br>*Common Areas.* Smoking permitted in lobbies, reception areas, and waiting rooms. Smoking prohibited in elevators, restrooms, and copy rooms.<br>*Break Rooms and Eating Facilities.* No specific provisions. | No specific provisions. | No specific provisions. | No specific provisions. | "No Smoking" signs should be posted in appropriate areas. | Houston Code of Ordinances, ch. 21, § 21-226–21-230. |

| | | | | | | | | |
|---|---|---|---|---|---|---|---|---|
| | vention center exhibition area; rooms used for private functions (only if the entire room or hall is reserved, the guests of the function are limited, and the seating arrangements for the function are under the control of the sponsor); rented hotel and motel rooms; hospitality suites at stadiums. | | *Private Offices.* No specific provisions. | | | | | |
| Irving, TX | None, including independent contractors. | All employees working for direct or indirect wages are covered. Includes independent contractor. | *Employees' Workspaces.* An employer must provide a nonsmoking workplace for a nonsmoking employee upon request, unless existing ventilation and partition make this impossible. Any employer may designate the entire workplace a nonsmoking area. Smoking permitted in workplace or physically separated section of a workplace that is not open to the public if all people in the area smoke.<br><br>*Common Areas.* (See "Employees' Workspaces.") A nonsmoking employee may be required to work in a smoking area if that area is a customer service area that is designated smoking. Smoking prohibited in any conference or meeting room open to the public, classrooms, and elevators.<br><br>*Breakrooms and Eating Facilities.* An employer must provide a nonsmoking area in all employee breakrooms and lounges, unless all employees smoke.<br><br>*(cont'd)* | No employer shall discharge, refuse to hire, or in any manner retaliate against any employee, applicant or member of the public for exercising any rights under the ordinance. | In any dispute, the health concerns of the nonsmoker shall be given precedence. | Any person violating the ordinance is punishable by a fine of not more than $2,000. Employer should make a "good faith effort" to prevent smoking in nonsmoking areas. | All employers must adopt, implement, and maintain a workplace smoking policy that meets the requirements of the ordinance, establishes a procedure for determining which areas in the workplace will be designated as nonsmoking or smoking, and establishes a procedure for addressing employee complaints. In order to make a "good faith effort," employers should post "No Smoking" signs and ask smokers to leave nonsmoking areas. | Code of Civil and Criminal Ordinances of the City of Irving, Texas §§ 48-12–48-15 (Ordinance 7/33, adopted 10/9/97). |

*(Table continues.)*

# Table 8.2-1 *(cont'd)*

## MUNICIPAL SMOKING ORDINANCES

(See also text at § 8.2.)

| | *Employers Exempted* | *Employees Covered* | *Parts of the Workplace Covered by the Ordinance* | *Nonretaliation Clause* | *Smoker and Nonsmoker Disputes* | *Enforcement* | *Other Requirements* | *Citations to Authority* |
|---|---|---|---|---|---|---|---|---|
| Irving, TX *(cont'd)* | | | *Private Offices.* Smoking permitted in completely enclosed private offices. (See "Employees' Workspaces.") | | | | | |
| San Antonio, TX | Employers operating in a domestic residence, tobacco stores; business establishments serving the public with less than 750 square feet of service space; restaurants; event in which entire room or hall is used for a social function sponsored by a private individual. | All employees are covered. | *Employees' Workspaces.* Employers may designate any workplace, or portion thereof, as a nonsmoking area. Any employer designating nonsmoking areas must have a written policy on smoking that is available to employees. The employer must also conspicuously post appropriate signs and provide a sufficient number of ashtrays. Employers are encouraged on a voluntary basis to eliminate smoking in the workplace.<br><br>*Common Areas.* Smoking is generally not regulated in "administrative areas," defined as areas of an establishment not generally accessible to the public, including individual offices, stockrooms, employee lounges, and meeting rooms. Smoking prohibited in elevators.<br><br>*Break Rooms and Eating Facilities.* (See "Common Areas.")<br><br>*Private Offices.* Smoking permitted in an enclosed room with one regular occupant. | Municipality has no specific requirements. | Municipality has no specific requirements. | Violations are punishable by a scale of increasing fines for successive convictions. | Employer must establish a written smoking policy. Employer may designate the entire workplace (with the exception of a single-occupant enclosed space) as nonsmoking. Employer must post signs in nonsmoking areas. | Code of Ordinances Chapter 36. |

| | | | | | | | | |
|---|---|---|---|---|---|---|---|---|
| Alexandria, VA | Tobacco stores; restaurants when providing banquet service or catering private parties; retail or food stores with fewer than 9 employees. | No specific requirements. | *Employees' Workspaces.* Smoking is generally prohibited except in designated areas. Prohibitions on smoking in employee workspaces do not apply to work areas of public buildings not usually entered by the general public.<br>*Common Areas.* No specific requirements.<br>*Break Rooms and Eating Facilities.* No specific requirements.<br>*Private Offices.* Smoking is permitted in private offices. | No specific requirements. | No specific requirements. | Enforcement is by the City Manager. | "No Smoking" signs must be posted; violators are subject to $25 fine. | Ord. No. 3270 (effective 4/26/88). |
| Newport News, VA | Bars and lounges; retail tobacco stores; restaurants, conference or meeting rooms used exclusively for private functions. | No specific provisions. | *Employee's Workspaces.* No specific provisions.<br>*Common Areas.* Smoking prohibited in elevators and restrooms.<br>*Break Rooms and Eating Facilities.* No specific provisions.<br>*Private Offices.* Smoking permitted in private offices that are not shared and not entered by the public during the normal course of business. | No specific provisions. | No specific provisions. | Department of public health responsible for enforcement of the ordinance. Violations of the ordinance are Class 4 misdemeanors. | Employers must post "No Smoking" and "Smoking Permitted" signs in appropriate areas. Those regulated by this chapter are encouraged to make structural modifications necessary to reduce the permeation of smoke into the nonsmoking areas. | Newport News Code of Ordinance, ch. 33.1, §§ 33.1-1–33.1-10. |
| Monongalia County, WV | Workplaces in bars; private residences; retail tobacco stores. | All paid or volunteer workers are covered. | *Employees' Workspaces.* Employers must provide smoke-free areas for nonsmoking employees within existing facilities to the maximum extent possible, but additional expense need not be incurred. Any employee may designate his or her work area as a nonsmoking area and post appropriate signs. Nonsmoking areas shall be designated such that employees would not be required to pass through smoking areas on a routine basis in order to perform the duties of the job or to reach a nonsmoking area.<br>*Common Areas.* Smoking is prohibited in all public waiting areas and lobbies.<br>*(cont'd)* | No employer shall discharge, refuse to hire, or in any manner retaliate against any employee, applicant or member of the public for exercising any rights under the ordinance. | In any dispute, the health concerns of the nonsmoker shall be given precedence. | An employer shall inform persons violating the regulation of the provisions of the ordinance, and the ultimate responsibility of enforcement lies with the County Health Department. A violator is guilty of an infraction and must pay a fine of $25 for the first violation, $50 for a second violation, and between $50 and<br>*(cont'd)* | Each employer must adopt a written smoking policy. All employers must make a written copy of the smoking policy available to any present or prospective employee on request. An employer must post appropriate signs or use the international symbol for no smoking. Removal or defacement of signs is prohibited. | Monongalia County Clean Indoor Air Regulation. (1994). |

*(Table continues.)*

**Table 8.2-1** *(cont'd)*

MUNICIPAL SMOKING ORDINANCES

(See also text at § 8.2.)

| | *Employers Exempted* | *Employees Covered* | *Parts of the Workplace Covered by the Ordinance* | *Nonretaliation Clause* | *Smoker and Nonsmoker Disputes* | *Enforcement* | *Other Requirements* | *Citations to Authority* |
|---|---|---|---|---|---|---|---|---|
| Monongalia County, WV *(cont'd)* | | | *Breakrooms and Eating Facilities.* (See "Employees' Workspaces.")<br>*Private Offices.* A private enclosed office workplace occupied by only one person or exclusively occupied by smokers, even though such an office workplace may be visited by nonsmokers is exempt from the ordinance. | | | $100 for each subsequent violation within 12 months. | | |

***NOTE:** On July 21, 1994, Gov. Pete Wilson signed into law an act to add Section 6404.5 to the California Labor Code, which would prohibit any employer from knowingly or intentionally permitting, or any person from engaging in, the smoking of tobacco products in an enclosed space at specified places of employment. The act states that its smoking prohibition "shall constitute a uniform statewide standard for regulating the smoking of tobacco products in enclosed places of employment and shall supersede and render unnecessary the local enactment or enforcement of local ordinances regulating the smoking of tobacco products in enclosed places of employment." However, the preemption provisions are rather complex and provide that any local regulation restricting smoking in a place not defined as a "place of employment" in the statute is not preempted. Furthermore, if any of the restrictions of § 6404.5 of the Labor Code are repealed or judicially or legislatively modified, suspended local ordinances dealing with workplace smoking are automatically revived.

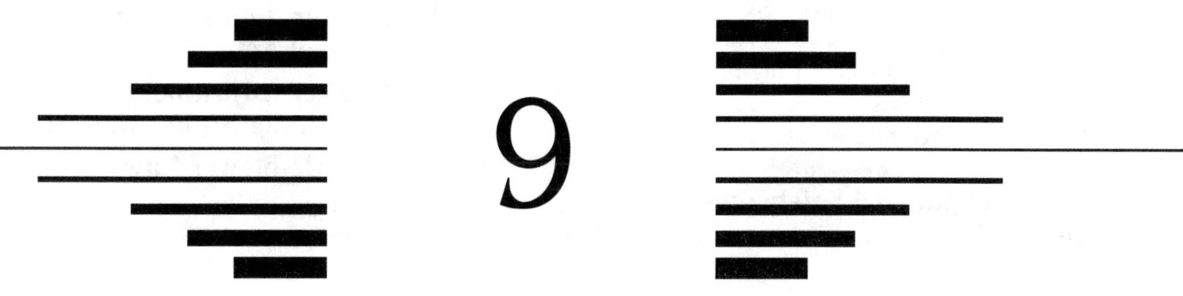

# Summary of Federal Legislation, Guidelines, and Policies on Human Resources Law

*Part 9 covers, in narrative form, federal fair employment practice statutes, the Fair Labor Standards Act, ERISA, COBRA, privacy statutes, the Occupational Safety and Health Act, the National Labor Relations Act, the Railway Act, the Immigration Reform and Control Act, the Work Adjustment Retraining Notification Act, and Whistle-blower laws.*

## § 9.1 Overview: Federal Law and Regulation of Human Resources Management

Human resources management, or personnel management, is highly regulated today. Federal, state, and local laws govern a significant percentage of the personnel decisions made in the working environment. These laws cover a broad spectrum of issues, including discrimination in the workplace, the obligation by certain employers to take affirmative action, the right of employees to join labor unions, prohibitions against the use of polygraphs in employment decisions, notification to employees of plant and facility closings, and so forth.

Because the personnel department is responsible for administering the majority of actions affecting employees, human resources professionals must be familiar with these laws to ensure that their organizations comply fully with such laws at all times.

Part 9 looks at the most significant laws on the federal level affecting human resources management. Many of these laws have state analogues, which are listed elsewhere in this book.

# § 9.2 Fair Employment Practices

## [a] Title VII of the Civil Rights Act of 1964

**General Coverage.** Title VII of the Civil Rights Act of 1964 (CRA 1964) prohibits employers from discriminating against any job applicant or employee on the basis of race, color, religion, sex, or national origin. It applies to all employers engaged in interstate commerce that have 15 or more employees, to labor unions, and to employment agencies.[1]

Title VII covers *all* areas of employment, including advertising, recruiting, hiring, promotion, compensation, benefits administration, and termination. It does, however, provide for several exceptions:

- *Bona Fide Occupational Qualification (BFOQ).* Employment decisions made on the basis of sex, national origin, or religion do not violate Title VII if the decisions are based on a BFOQ reasonably necessary to the normal operation of a particular business. This is a narrow exception that applies only if the qualification affects the employee's ability to do the job.[2]
- *Bona Fide Seniority System.* Title VII exempts discrimination that results from the operation of a bona fide seniority system. Thus, for example, a bona fide seniority system rewarding length of service under a collective bargaining agreement that has a discriminatory impact on minority employees would not violate Title VII. Again, this is a narrow exception that applies only in certain specific situations.[3]

One of the most profound developments in fair employment practices generally, and in Title VII in particular, is the Civil Rights Act of 1991 (CRA 1991).[4] CRA 1991 was designed in part to turn back the clock, reinstating the law as it existed prior to a series of significant and controversial decisions handed down by the Supreme Court between 1989 and 1991. In addition, CRA 1991 provides remedies for discrimination in employment that were previously unavailable under federal law.

CRA 1991 achieved the objectives defined by Congress through the amendment of several federal statutes, including Title VII. Specific changes brought about by the Act are discussed throughout this section.

**Procedure for Filing Charges.** To begin a proceeding under Title VII, the aggrieved individual must file a discrimination charge in writing and under oath with the Equal Employment Opportunity Commission (EEOC), the federal agency that enforces Title VII.[5] If the alleged discrimination occurs in a *deferral* state—that is, a state having its own fair employment law and investigative agency—the charge must be filed within 300 days of the occurrence. In states or localities without their own agencies, a charge must be filed with the EEOC within 180 days.[6]

**§ 9.2**

1. 42 U.S.C. §§ 2000e *et seq.*
2. 42 U.S.C. § 2000e-2(e).
3. 42 U.S.C. § 2000e-2(h).
4. Civil Rights Act of 1991, Pub. L. No. 102-166, 105, Stat. 1071 (1991).
5. 42 U.S.C. § 2000e-5.
6. 42 U.S.C. § 2000e-5(e).

If a state or local agency has been established to hear discrimination charges, the EEOC must give it the opportunity to investigate and resolve Title VII complaints. Although the findings of these agencies must be given substantial weight, the EEOC is not bound by the agencies' determinations.[7]

In addition, the EEOC itself can begin proceedings if it has reasonable cause to believe Title VII has been violated.[8] An action also may be brought on by a referral from the Office of Federal Contract Compliance Programs (OFCCP), the federal agency that enforces Executive Order 11246, the Rehabilitation Act, and the Vietnam Era Veterans Readjustment Assistance Act (see §§ 9.2[d], 9.2[i], and 9.2[k], respectively).[9] Finally, an organization, person, or agency having no affiliation with an aggrieved party may file a claim on behalf of that party.[10]

After exhausting the required administrative remedies, the aggrieved individual may also bring a court action under Title VII. (For a discussion of state court jurisdiction over Title VII claims, see "Trends and Controversies.") Prior to the adoption of CRA 1991, a trial by jury was not available for actions involving only Title VII. Further, compensatory and punitive damages were not available in such actions. Under CRA 1991, however, parties are permitted to seek a jury trial and to recover compensatory and punitive damages in addition to the traditional make-whole relief in Title VII cases where the plaintiff alleges intentional discrimination and relief is unavailable under the Civil Rights Act of 1866.[11] Although compensatory and punitive damages are capped based on the number of employees, the availability of a jury trial represents an increased risk for employers, who now face the prospect of having a jury decide whether such damages should be awarded and, if so, in what amounts.

Note that employers with 100 or more employees covered by Title VII are required to file Employer Information Reports (EEO-1) annually with the Joint Reporting Committee.[12]

7. 42 U.S.C. § 2000-e5(d).

8. 42 U.S.C. § 2000-e5(b).

9. 42 U.S.C. § 2000-e5.

10. 29 C.F.R. § 1601.7(a).

11. 42 U.S.C. § 1981a.

12. 29 C.F.R. § 1602.7.

**Discrimination Theories.** There are two types of discrimination theories under Title VII: *disparate treatment* and *disparate impact.*[13]

Disparate treatment involves the different treatment of individuals belonging to a "protected class" (i.e., different treatment based on race, color, sex, religion, or national origin). In cases involving disparate treatment, the aggrieved individual must establish a *prima facie* case of discrimination by proving intentional bias, whereas the employer alleges that its decisions are based on legitimate, nondiscriminatory reasons. The U.S. Supreme Court has ruled that for an individual to establish a *prima facie* case under the disparate treatment theory in a failure-to-hire case, for example, the individual alleging discrimination must show that he or she:

1. Belongs to a protected class;
2. Applied for a job for which the employer was seeking applicants;
3. Was qualified to perform the job; and
4. Was denied the job.

The individual must also show that the employer continued to seek applicants for the position. The model established by the U.S. Supreme Court has been adapted for use in other situations.[14]

While a failure to establish a *prima facie* case is grounds for dismissal of the suit, establishing a *prima facie* case does not automatically entitle the individual to a favorable judgment. If a *prima facie* case is established, the employer must articulate a legitimate, nondiscriminatory reason for the challenged action. If the employer meets this burden, the individual must then prove that such reason is merely a pretext for an underlying discriminatory motive.[15]

It should be noted that, in the wake of *St. Mary's Honor Center v. Hicks,*[16] a plaintiff is not necessarily entitled to judgment in his or her favor upon a showing that the employer's proffered reasons are untrue.[17] As the Supreme Court has noted, the plaintiff at all times

13. 42 U.S.C. § 2000e-2; Griggs v. Duke Power Co., 401 U.S. 424 (1971).

14. McDonnell Douglas Corp. v. Green, 411 U.S. 792 (1973); *see also* Hidalgo v. Overseas Condado Ins. Agencies, Inc., 120 F.3d 328 (1st Cir. 1997), describing burden-shifting paradigm, where plaintiff must meet a series of tests to show a prima facie case of age discrimination.

15. Id. at 802–04.

16. St. Mary's Honor Center v. Hicks, 509 U.S. 502 (1993).

17. See discussion of *St. Mary's Honor Center* case at "Trends and Controversies."

bears the ultimate burden of persuasion to show intentional discrimination. Thus, for the jury to find in the plaintiff's favor, it must not only disbelieve the employer, but must also believe the plaintiff's explanation of intentional discrimination. The Supreme Court has cautioned, however, that the jury's disbelief of the reasons put forward by the employer (particularly if disbelief is accompanied by a suspicion of mendacity), together with the elements of the *prima facie* case, will permit the jury to infer the ultimate fact of intentional discrimination.[18]

The Supreme Court's decision in *Hicks* has created some confusion regarding what the employee must show, not only to be entitled to judgment, but also to survive a motion for summary judgment brought by the employer. At the least, it is clear that an employee may no longer simply rely on the *prima facie* case set out above. It should be noted, however, that there is considerable disagreement among the courts on the precise interpretation of *Hicks.*[19]

Under the theory of disparate impact, the burden of proof rests on both the plaintiff and the defendant. CRA 1991 codified the burden of proof to be employed.[20] Under the Act, once a plaintiff demonstrates that the employer uses a particular, seemingly neutral employment practice that causes a disparate impact on a protected class, the employer must demonstrate that the challenged practice is "job related for the position in question and consistent with business necessity."

By requiring the employer to demonstrate that a practice is consistent with business necessity, the CRA 1991 shifts the burden to the employer once the plaintiff establishes disparate impact.[21] Thus, CRA 1991 reverses *Wards Cove Packing Co. v. Atonio,* in which the Supreme Court held that the burden on the employer is merely to articulate legitimate business reasons for its actions and that the burden of persuasion remains at all times with the plaintiff.[22]

Moreover, under CRA 1991, even where the employer demonstrates "business necessity," the challenged practice nevertheless may be unlawful if the plaintiff demonstrates that an "alternative employment practice" with less disparate impact exists and the employer has refused to adopt the alternative practice.[23] In effect, the Act revives the concepts of "business necessity" and "job relatedness" as enunciated by the Supreme Court in *Griggs v. Duke Power Co.*[24] The courts are left to determine the definitions of these concepts.

In 1988, the Supreme Court held that the disparate impact theory applies to subjective hiring criteria (e.g., performance evaluations) as well as to objective hiring criteria (e.g., typing tests).[25]

**Sexual Harassment Under Title VII.** Title VII prohibits employment discrimination based on an individual's sex.[26] Sexual harassment, a recognized form of sex discrimination, is broadly defined by the EEOC as any "[u]nwelcome sexual advances, requests for sexual favors, and other verbal or physical conduct of a sexual nature," which, if rejected, could affect an individual's employment status, opportunities, or work performance or create a hostile work environment.[27] Title VII requires employers to prohibit all forms of sexual harassment in the workplace and to promulgate a comprehensive policy ensuring that:

1. Complaints of sexual harassment are promptly investigated;
2. Such complaints are held in confidence and disclosed only to those with a need to know;
3. Retaliation will not be permitted against employees filing bona fide complaints; and
4. Appropriate disciplinary action will be taken against the offender.[28]

Failure to promulgate and enforce such a policy may expose the company to significant monetary liability.[29]

### [b] The Pregnancy Discrimination Act of 1978

Title VII was amended by the Pregnancy Discrimination Act of 1978, which specifically prohibits discrimination in all areas of employment on the basis of pregnancy and pregnancy-related conditions. In essence,

18. Cooper v. Paychex, Inc., 960 F. Supp. 966 (E.D. Va. 1997), citing *Hicks,* held that if the jury does not believe the defendant's proffered reason for an adverse employment action, no further evidence is required from the plaintiff.

19. See e.g., Krenik v. County of LeSuer, 47 F.3d 953 (8th Cir. 1995); Cronin v. Aetna Life Ins. Co., 46 F.3d 196 (2d Cir. 1995); Durham v. Xerox Corp, 18 F.3d 836 (10th Cir. 1994).

20. 42 U.S.C. § 2000e-2(k).

21. Id.

22. Wards Cove Packing Co. v. Atonio, 493 U.S. 802 (1989).

23. 42 U.S.C. § 2000e-2(k)(1)(A)(ii).

24. Griggs v. Duke Power Co., 401 U.S. 424 (1971).

25. Watson v. Fort Worth Bank & Trust, 487 U.S. 977 (1988).

26. 42 U.S.C. § 2000e-2(a).

27. 29 C.F.R. § 1604.11.

28. See 29 C.F.R. § 1604.11(f).

29. Meritor Sav. Bank, FSB v. Vinson, 477 U.S. 57 (1986).

this act requires employers to treat pregnant employees the same as nonpregnant workers who are disabled; this means providing pregnant workers with the same disability benefits with respect to leaves of absence, health benefits during leaves, and reinstatement after leaves.[30]

Most states and many municipalities have adopted antidiscrimination laws, many of which are broader than Title VII. To minimize liability, employers must be familiar not only with federal laws, but also with state and local laws governing each location in which offices are maintained.

### [c] The Equal Pay Act of 1963

The Equal Pay Act of 1963 (EPA), an amendment to the Fair Labor Standards Act of 1938 (FLSA), prohibits compensation discrimination on the basis of an employee's sex. In other words, an employer cannot pay employees of one sex less than employees of the other sex for performing equal work, requiring equal skill, effort, and responsibility, under similar conditions at the same establishment. The statute protects men as well as women.[31]

This provision makes an exception, however, if there is a difference among employees based on factors other than sex.[32] For example, it is not unlawful for employees to receive unequal pay if:

- A seniority system exists;
- A merit system exists; or
- A system for measuring earnings by quantity or quality of production exists.

**Procedures and Enforcement.** Complaints relating to possible EPA violations can be filed with the EEOC, which enforces the EPA. A complainant also has the right to file an EPA lawsuit in federal or state court without first exhausting the administrative remedies. Aggrieved employees may sue for damages in the form of back pay, and, if the violation is found to have been willful, they may be awarded damages in amounts equal to unpaid back pay, plus attorneys' fees and court costs. A two-year statute of limitations exists for nonwillful EPA violations; the statute of limitations is three years for willful violations.

The EEOC may receive charges from a single party alleging violations under both the EPA and Title VII of CRA 1964 (see § 9.2[a]). However, Title VII covers other types of wage discrimination not actionable under the EPA.[33]

30. 42 U.S.C. § 2000e(k).

31. 29 C.F.R. § 1620.1.

32. 29 U.S.C. § 206(d).

33. 29 C.F.R. § 1620.27.

### [d] Executive Order 11246

**General Coverage.** Executive Order 11246 (E.O. 11246) prohibits federal government contractors and subcontractors from discriminating against employees and applicants on the basis of race, color, religion, sex, or national origin.[34] E.O. 11246 obligates covered contractors with contracts exceeding $10,000 to include an equal employment opportunity (EEO) clause in each contract that states the following:

- The contractor will not discriminate against any employee or applicant and will take affirmative action for protected employees and applicants. The contractor will also conspicuously place posters at job sites outlining the provisions of this nondiscrimination clause.
- All job advertisements will state that all qualified applicants will be considered regardless of race, color, religion, sex, or national origin.
- The contractor will advise the labor unions of this nondiscrimination clause.
- The contractor will comply with E.O. 11246 provisions.
- The contractor will supply information and reports and will permit access to the books for investigators to ascertain compliance with regulations.
- The contract may be canceled, terminated, or suspended in the event of noncompliance by the contractor, and the contractor may become ineligible for further government contracts; other sanctions may also be imposed.
- These requirements will be included in every subcontract or purchase order unless specifically exempted.[35]

In addition to including an EEO clause in each contract exceeding $10,000, nonconstruction contractors with 50 or more employees and those with contracts or subcontracts exceeding $50,000 are required to develop and follow written affirmative action plans (AAPs) covering each of their establishments.[36]

**Revised Order No. 4.** The OFCCP, which administers E.O. 11246, has issued a series of detailed regulations to implement this order. Revised Order No. 4

34. Executive Order, 3 C.F.R., § 339 (1964–1965 Compilation), reprinted in 42 U.S.C. § 2000e note, issued on Sept. 24, 1965, as amended.

35. Id.

36. 41 C.F.R. § 60-1.40.

explains the written AAP requirements as well as government procedures for monitoring and auditing AAP compliance.[37]

The most important AAP requirements include:

- Listing an employer's entire workforce by race, national origin, and sex, as well as by job title within each department (workforce analysis);
- Analyzing all major job groups to determine whether minorities or women are underutilized relative to their availability in the contractor's relevant recruitment area; and
- Establishing goals and timetables to correct situations in which minorities or women are underutilized.[38]

In addition, employers must compile and maintain such support data as progression line charts, seniority rosters, applicant flow data, and applicant rejection ratios. Employers must also identify any affected class problem in the workforce and make "good faith" efforts to remedy the situation.[39]

**The Compliance Review.** Conducted by the OFCCP, the compliance review of covered contractors consists of three stages: the desk audit, the on-site review, and the off-site analysis.[40]

In the *desk audit* stage, the employer forwards a copy of its AAP and supporting documentation to the assigned OFCCP officer for initial scrutiny. The employer should be careful to identify and, if possible, excise from the AAP information that is deemed confidential, such as lists of employees, employee names, reasons for termination, and pay data. Note that this information should be coded.

In the *on-site review,* the compliance officer arranges to visit an employer's facility to review matters not fully or satisfactorily addressed in the original material. The employer must provide full access to all relevant data, including all personnel files and records as well as wage data. Managers and employees can be interviewed by the compliance officer.

The *off-site analysis* is conducted only when the compliance officer needs to study further any EEO materials.

**Procedures and Enforcement.** If the compliance review uncovers E.O. 11246 violations, the OFCCP will first issue a 30-day "show cause" notice. During this 30-day period, the employer must either show "good cause" why enforcement should not be pursued or agree to change its AAP or EEO posture.[41] Every effort will be made through conciliation to resolve the deficiencies that led to the violations findings before this period expires, but if no satisfactory result is reached, enforcement proceedings will begin.

Under E.O. 11246, either the Secretary of Labor or the appropriate contracting agency may take the following actions against the noncompliant contractor:

- Publish the names of the noncomplying contractor or union.
- Recommend a suit by the Justice Department to compel compliance.
- Recommend action by the EEOC or the Justice Department under Title VII.
- Recommend that the Justice Department bring criminal action against the offender for furnishing false information.
- Cancel, terminate, or suspend present contracts; withhold progress payments; and/or debar an employer from future government contracts until it complies.[42]

The OFCCP has not had to use these sanctions frequently. In general, it has been successful at using the compliance review process to obtain back pay for victims of discrimination and to get employers to make the necessary AAP and personnel policy and practice changes. The OFCCP has recently announced that it is officially shifting its focus from affirmative action efforts to remedial action in the form of back pay and other relief for individual employees.

### [e] Religious Discrimination Provisions of Title VII and Executive Order 11246

Both Title VII of CRA 1964 and E.O. 11246 prohibit religious discrimination.[43] Moreover, employers are under the affirmative obligation to reasonably accommodate the religious beliefs of their employees except when

37. 41 C.F.R. § 60-2.
38. 41 C.F.R. §§ 60-2.11, 60-2.12.
39. 41 C.F.R. § 60-2.12.
40. 41 C.F.R. § 60-1.20.
41. 41 C.F.R. § 60-1.28.
42. Executive Order, 3 C.F.R. § 339 (1964–1965 Compilation), reprinted in 42 U.S.C. § 2000e note, issued on Sept. 24, 1965, as amended.
43. 42 U.S.C. § 2000e-2; Executive Order, 3 C.F.R. § 339 (1964–1965 Compilation), reprinted in 42 U.S.C. § 2000e note, issued on Sept. 24, 1965, as amended.

doing so would result in undue hardship on the conduct of the employer's business.

The EEOC, which enforces Title VII, has adopted Guidelines on Religion requiring such reasonable accommodations.[44] The OFCCP, which enforces E.O. 11246, has issued regulations covering religious discrimination.[45] These regulations require that employers subject to E.O. 11246 take steps to ensure that employment decisions are made without regard to religion. The regulations specify that "[m]embers of various religions and ethnic groups, primarily but not exclusively of Eastern, Middle and Southern European ancestry, such as Jews, Catholics, Italians, Greeks and Slavic groups" are covered by these regulations.[46]

Under E.O. 11246, an employer must reasonably accommodate the religious observances and practices of an employee or prospective employee unless the employer is able to demonstrate that such accommodation would result in undue hardship to the employer.[47]

Most states prohibit employment discrimination on the basis of religion, and employers should be familiar with local laws in each state where they maintain offices or facilities.

### [f] The Civil Rights Act of 1866

**General Coverage.** The Civil Rights Act of 1866, commonly referred to as Section 1981, guarantees all persons the same right enjoyed by "white citizens" to make and enforce contracts.[48] Unlike Title VII, which applies only to employers of 15 or more persons, Section 1981 contains no statutory minimum and covers only discrimination based on race and, in some court circuits, alienage.

The definition of "race" under Section 1981 has been broadly construed by the Supreme Court to include members of any identifiable ethnic class.[49] In 1989, the Supreme Court held in *Patterson v. McLean Credit Union* that, although Section 1981 prohibits race discrimination in the making and enforcement of private employment contracts, it does not extend the prohibition to race discrimination in the carrying out of the terms of the employment contract.[50] However, CRA 1991 expressly overturned *Patterson v. McLean Credit Union,* expanding the scope of Section 1981 to conduct that occurs after the formation of an employment contract, including the "enjoyment of all benefits, privileges, terms and conditions of the contractual relationship."[51]

**Procedures and Enforcement.** Unlike Title VII, there are no administrative procedures under Section 1981 prerequisite to bringing a discrimination suit in federal court. Nor is there a federal agency to enforce this statute comparable to the EEOC for Title VII. An individual alleging a Section 1981 violation may proceed directly to federal court or to a state court.

There is no statute of limitations specifically set out in Section 1981. Instead, the courts employ the state statute most applicable to employment discrimination cases, which has been held to be the state's residual personal injury limitations period. When filing a Section 1981 action, the state statute of limitations will not be suspended by filing a Title VII discrimination charge with the EEOC.[52]

Section 1981 does not specify remedies that are available to aggrieved individuals filing suit. The courts will grant awards, which may include back pay, reinstatement, and other remedies, including compensatory and punitive damages.[53] Plaintiffs proceeding under Section 1981 may seek a jury trial.[54]

### [g] The Age Discrimination in Employment Act of 1967

**General Coverage.** The Age Discrimination in Employment Act of 1967 (ADEA) prohibits employers with 20 or more employees from discriminating on the basis of age against any individual who is 40 years of age or older.[55] Although the ADEA applies to the terms and conditions of employment, there are some conditions exempted from its provisions:

- If age is a BFOQ reasonably necessary to the normal operation of the particular business;
- If the employer differentiates on the basis of reasonable factors other than age;

---

44. 29 C.F.R. § 1605.2.
45. 41 C.F.R. § 60-50.
46. 41 C.F.R. § 60-50.1.
47. 41 C.F.R. § 60-50.3.
48. 42 U.S.C. § 1981.
49. St. Francis College v. Al-Khazraji, 481 U.S. 604 (1987); Shaare Tefila Congregation v. Cobb, 481 U.S. 615 (1987).
50. Patterson v. McLean Credit Union, 491 U.S. 164 (1989).
51. 42 U.S.C. § 1981.
52. Goodman v. Lukens Steel Co., 482 U.S. 656 (1987).
53. 42 U.S.C. § 2000e-5(g).
54. 42 U.S.C. § 1981a.
55. 29 U.S.C. §§ 621, 631.

- If the employer is observing the terms of either a bona fide seniority system or an employee benefit plan; and
- If an employer disciplines an employee for good cause, such as poor job performance.[56]

Historically, employers were not permitted to rely on age-based distinctions in the establishment of employee benefit programs, unless the distinctions could be justified on the basis of cost in compliance with EEOC regulations. Although the Supreme Court invalidated these regulations in 1989,[57] Congress responded by passing the Older Workers Benefits Protection Act of 1990 (OWBPA),[58] which prohibits age discrimination in employee benefit programs and establishes minimum standards for employees' waivers of their rights under the ADEA. Under the OWBPA, an employer must provide equal benefits to older workers unless the employer can demonstrate that the cost of providing benefits is greater for older workers.[59]

There are a few exceptions to the cost justification defense:

- A pension benefit plan may contain a minimum age requirement as a condition of eligiblity for early or normal retirement;
- A defined benefit plan may provide for a normal retirement age and for early retirement;
- Benefits may be triggered by contingent events unrelated to age, such as plant closings and layoffs.
- A benefit plan may reduce long-term disability benefits by certain amounts of pension benefits within certain requirements.[60]

In general, the ADEA prohibits mandatory retirement at any age, except for individuals who are bona fide executives or who hold high policy-making positions and who (1) are at least 65 years old, (2) have held their positions for two years immediately preceding retirement, and (3) are entitled to a retirement income of at least $44,000.[61]

**Procedures and Enforcement.** Similar to individuals filing a charge under Title VII, individuals alleging ADEA violations may bring suit in federal court. They must first file a charge with the EEOC, the enforcement agency for both the ADEA and Title VII. A charge must be filed with the EEOC within 180 days after the alleged unlawful practice occurred or, in a deferral state, within 300 days.[62] The Civil Rights Act of 1991 amended the ADEA to bring its limitations and notice provisions in line with those of Title VII. As amended, the ADEA provides that if a charge filed with the EEOC is dismissed or the EEOC otherwise terminates the proceedings, "the Commission shall notify the person aggrieved." The aggrieved person then has 90 days after the date of receipt of such notice to file a civil action against the respondent named in the charge. The wording is the same as that found in Title VII, and, thus, under the amended statute, the distinction between willful and nonwillful violations is irrelevant to the limitations period.[63]

To establish a *prima facie* case of discrimination under the ADEA, a plaintiff must set forth elements similar to those required for a Title VII case but with appropriate modifications. Similar to plaintiffs in Title VII cases as modified by CRA 1991, plaintiffs in ADEA suits may request a trial by jury,[64] which makes these claims especially troublesome for employers.

As previously noted, the OWBPA[65] amended the ADEA to provide for the regulation of employee waivers of ADEA rights. No right or claim can be waived unless the employee waiver is knowing and voluntary.[66] The OWBPA specifies the guidelines to be followed to establish the "voluntary and knowing" requirement. The provisions state that the waiver must be part of an agreement between the employer and the employee that is written in a manner calculated to be understood by the employee. The waiver must specifically refer to rights under the ADEA, and the employee may not waive rights or claims that arise after the date of the waiver.[67]

Moreover, the employee may not waive rights except for consideration in addition to the consideration to which he or she is already entitled, and the employee must be advised in writing to contact an attorney prior to signing the waiver. The OWBPA also provides that the employee must be given at least 21 days to consider the agreement

56. 29 U.S.C. § 623(f).
57. Public Employees Retirement Sys. of Ohio v. Betts, 492 U.S. 158 (1989).
58. 29 U.S.C. § 623.
59. Id.
60. 29 C.F.R. § 1625.10.
61. 29 U.S.C. § 631(c); 29 C.F.R. § 1625.12.
62. 29 U.S.C. § 626(d).
63. 29 U.S.C. § 626(e).
64. 29 U.S.C. § 626(c)(2).
65. 29 U.S.C. § 623.
66. 29 U.S.C. § 626(f)(1).
67. Id.

(45 days if in connection with an exit agreement) and that there must be a seven-day revocation period.[68]

An employer may choose to ask for an ADEA claim waiver in the context of a settlement of litigation of a discrimination charge or in the context of an agreement regarding early retirement or other termination agreement. If the waiver is in the context of the settlement of a charge, slightly different time requirements apply, and the employee may be given less time to consider or revoke the waiver.[69]

No employee waiver will affect the EEOC's right to enforce the ADEA or preclude an employee from participating in an EEOC investigation, even where the waiver conforms to the ADEA's requirements. Nor will a properly prepared waiver preclude an employee from filing an ADEA charge based on post-waiver conduct.[70]

In 1998, the EEOC issued a regulation setting out procedures for complying with the OWBPA.[71] The regulation resolves a number of issues that had arisen in the context of assessing the validity of ADEA waivers.

In the regulation, the EEOC rejected the position that a material error will invalidate a waiver agreement only if an employee proves that the error was intentional and that he or she reasonably relied on the misinformation. The EEOC takes the position that the question of materiality of an error should be judged by traditional standards without regard to intent and that reliance is not an element of proof either in the statute or the regulation. The EEOC also rejected the suggestion that the regulation require "substanial" consideration (i.e., a substantial monetary payment) as a condition of a valid waiver. In the EEOC's view, any requirement regarding the amount of the payment would be contrary to the language of the ADEA itself, which requires only "consideration in addition to anything of value to which the individual already is entitled," not "substantial" consideration.

The importance of strict adherence to the requirements of the OWBPA cannot be overemphasized. The Supreme Court recently held that an employer's failure to adhere to the applicable requirements not only invalidated the waiver, but also allowed a former employee to bring suit under the ADEA without first giving back the money received in exchange for executing the waiver.[72] Although the EEOC's 1998 regulation regarding the validity of waivers under the ADEA was approved in its final form before the Supreme Court's decision in *Oubre*, the EEOC has indicated that any requirement in a waiver agreement that the employee tender back any amount paid prior to instituting a lawsuit would be void.

A plaintiff who prevails in an ADEA suit may be awarded reinstatement and back pay or, if the violation is willful, double damages.[73]

Most states have adopted some form of protection against age discrimination. Because state statutes vary widely, employers should be familiar with local laws in each state where they maintain offices or facilities.

### [h] Individual Liability Under Title VII and the Age Discrimination in Employment Act

Although it is well established that a company may be held liable as an employer for discrimination under Title VII or under the ADEA, there is some disagreement regarding whether individuals can be held liable for employment discrimination. The confusion revolves around the definition of the term "employer" as used in Title VII and the ADEA. Under both statutes, "employer" includes any agent of the employer. Based on this definition, some courts have ruled that supervisory personnel and other agents of the employer are themselves employers for purposes of liability.[74] The District Court for the Southern District of New York has held that an individual may be liable for employment discrimination under Title VII if he or she was responsible for the challenged employment action.[75] However, the same court more recently held that individuals cannot be held liable under the ADEA.[76]

Other decisions raise some doubt about the validity of individual liability under these statutes. The Ninth Circuit Court of Appeals has reasoned that it is inconceivable that Congress would limit liability only to employers with 15 or more employees (20 or more employees under the ADEA) and still allow individual liability. The court concluded that the inclusion of "any agent" within the definitions of the term "employer" was merely designed to incorporate *respondeat superior* liability within the statutes. Thus, the court held that co-

68. Id.

69. 29 U.S.C. § 626(f)(2).

70. 29 U.S.C. § 626(f)(4).

71. 29 C.F.R. § 1625.22.

72. Oubre v. Entergy Operations, Inc., 118 S. Ct. 838 (1998).

73. 29 U.S.C. § 626(b).

74. Hamilton v. Rodgers, 791 F.2d 439 (5th Cir. 1986); Jones v. Metropolitan Denver Sewage Disposal Dist., 537 F. Supp. 966 (D. Colo. 1982).

75. Dirschel v. Speck, 1994 WL 330262 (S.D.N.Y. July, 6, 1994).

76. Wray v. Edward Blank Assoc., Inc., 924 F. Supp. 498, 503–04 (S.D.N.Y. 1996).

workers and supervisory employees may not be held liable as individuals.[77] Applying similar reasoning, the Second, Fifth, Seventh, and Eleventh Circuit Courts of Appeals have held that Title VII does not provide for the liability of individual employees who do not otherwise qualify as employers.[78]

### [i] The Rehabilitation Act of 1973

**General Coverage.** The Rehabilitation Act of 1973 applies to federal government contractors and subcontractors with contracts of $10,000 or more and to employers receiving federal assistance.[79] This Act is designed to promote the employment of otherwise qualified but handicapped individuals and to prevent discrimination against them.[80]

The Act defines a handicapped individual to include:

1. A person who has a mental or physical impairment substantially limiting one or more of his or her major life activities;
2. A person with a record of such an impairment; or
3. A person regarded as having such an impairment.[81]

Under this law, covered contractors must take affirmative action to employ and to advance in employment qualified handicapped individuals. They must also include in all contracts a paragraph with information on the following issues:

- Nondiscrimination and affirmative action employment policies;
- Compliance with implementing rules, regulations, and executive orders;
- Liability for noncompliance;
- Posting notices;
- Notification to labor representatives; and
- Implementation of affirmative action in subcontracts or purchase orders.[82]

In addition, the law requires covered contractors with contracts of $50,000 or more and those with 50 or more employees to develop written AAPs.[83] The AAPs need not include goals, timetables, or extensive employee utilization analyses, but should include such efforts as undertaking outreach programs. Unlike covered contractors, employers receiving federal funds are not obligated to develop written AAPs.

Both covered contractors and federal fund recipients must invite handicapped job applicants and employees to identify themselves.[84] These employers must also make reasonable accommodations for handicapped individuals, unless doing so would result in undue hardship to the employers. Among other measures, reasonable accommodations include making the workplace readily accessible to handicapped individuals.[85]

**Procedures and Enforcement.** The procedures for filing claims under the Rehabilitation Act, and the enforcement of the Act, are different for federal government contractors and for employers receiving federal funds.

*Federal Government Contractors.* Any applicant for a job with a federal government contractor and any employee of a federal contractor alleging discrimination may file a written complaint with the OFCCP within 180 days of the alleged violation, unless the OFCCP extends such time limit. (Note that some contractors may have an internal review procedure.) If the complaint is not resolved internally within 60 days, the OFCCP will proceed. If an investigation by the OFCCP reveals noncompliance, the agency will try to secure compliance through conciliation and persuasion within a reasonable time.[86] The statute does not provide for an express private right of action.

*Employer Receiving Federal Assistance.* The time limit for filing a complaint against an employer receiving federal assistance is specified in the funding agency's regulations, unless otherwise extended. The Department of Housing and Urban Development and the Nuclear Regulatory Commission each allows 180 days to file a complaint.[87]

77. Miller v. Maxwell's Int'l Inc., 991 F.2d 583 (9th Cir. 1993), cert. denied 510 U.S. 1109 (1994).

78. Grant v. Lone Star Co., 21 F.3d 649 (5th Cir.), cert. denied 513 U.S. 1015 (1994); Smith v. Lomax, 45 F.3d 402, 403–04 n.4 (11th Cir. 1995); EEOC v. AIC Security Investigations, Ltd., 55 F.3d 1276 (7th Cir. 1995); Tomka v. Seiler Corp., 66 F.3d 1295 (2d Cir. 1995).

79. 29 U.S.C. § 793.

80. Id.

81. 29 U.S.C. § 706.

82. 41 C.F.R. § 60-741.5.

83. 41 C.F.R. § 60-741.40–741.45.

84. 41 C.F.R. § 60-741.42.

85. 41 C.F.R. § 60-741.2(v).

86. 41 C.F.R. § 60-741.62.

87. 24 C.F.R. § 8.56 (Department of Housing and Urban Development); 10 C.F.R. § 4.332 (Nuclear Regulatory Commission).

If a hearing and investigation reveal a violation, the funding agency must notify the errant company.[88] To punish a violator, the funding agency may suspend, refuse to grant, or even terminate the violator's federal assistance.[89]

After completing the administrative process, an individual may also file action in federal court against an employer receiving federal funding. It is settled law that an aggrieved individual need not exhaust federal administrative remedies prior to filing suit in federal court.[90]

Many state laws prohibit discrimination by employers on the basis of handicap or disability. Employers should consult state law relating to handicapped employees in each location in which offices are maintained.

### [j] Americans With Disabilities Act of 1990

**General Coverage.** The Americans with Disabilities Act of 1990 (ADA) became effective for employers of 25 or more employees on July 26, 1992; the ADA became effective for employers of 15 or more employees on July 26, 1994. Covered entities include employers, employment agencies, labor organizations, and joint labor-management committees. State and local governments are covered as employers insofar as they are defined by these categories.[91]

Title I of the ADA prohibits discrimination in employment against any qualified individual with a disability. The ADA also imposes affirmative obligations to accommodate disabilities in employment. The term "disability" is defined as:

- A physical or mental impairment that substantially limits one or more of the major life activities of an individual;
- A record of such impairment; or
- Being regarded as having such an impairment.[92]

This definition follows the definition of "individual with handicap" in the Rehabilitation Act. Under the ADA, homosexuality and bisexuality are not considered disabilities.[93] Disability does not include transvestism, transsexualism, other sexual behavior disorders, compulsive gambling, kleptomania, pyromania, or psychoactive substance use disorder resulting from the current illegal use of drugs.[94] A person who is currently engaged in the illegal use of drugs is not protected by the ADA.[95] Individuals who successfully complete a drug rehabilitation program, who are participating in such a program, who are rehabilitated, or who are erroneously regarded as engaging in illegal use of drugs are not excluded if they do not currently engage in the illegal use of drugs, as defined by the Controlled Substance Act.[96]

The ADA defines a "qualified individual with a disability" as one who, with or without reasonable accommodation, can perform the essential functions of a job that he or she holds or desires.[97] The essential functions of a job include the results desired to be achieved in performing the duties of the position. Therefore, if an individual with a disability can perform specific tasks with reasonable accommodation, the individual may satisfy the definition. Although a written job description may be considered evidence of the essential functions of a job, the job description will not control.[98]

**Procedures, Damages, and Enforcement.** Since the coverage and enforcement provisions of Title VII are incorporated into the ADA, Title VII procedures that involve the EEOC are applicable. Unlike the Rehabilitation Act, the ADA gives covered individuals the right to file a civil suit after receiving a right to sue from the EEOC. CRA 1991 amended the ADA and permits individuals alleging intentional discrimination to seek jury trials and compensatory and punitive damages; however, there is an express provision in CRA 1991 applicable to the ADA that enables employers to limit their exposure to compensatory and punitive damages. In cases where the provision of a "reasonable accommodation" is involved, the employer can avoid liability for compensatory or punitive damages if it can demonstrate that "good faith efforts" were made to accommodate the individual's disability.[99]

### [k] The Vietnam Era Veterans Readjustment Assistance Act of 1974

**General Coverage.** The Vietnam Era Veterans Readjustment Assistance Act of 1974 requires federal gov-

88. 41 C.F.R. § 60-741-64.
89. Id.
90. Whitaker v. Board of Higher Educ., 461 F. Supp. 99 (E.D.N.Y. 1978); NAACP v. Medical Ctr., Inc., 599 F.2d 1247 (3d Cir. 1979).
91. 42 U.S.C. § 12111(2).
92. 42 U.S.C. § 12102(2).
93. 42 U.S.C. § 12211(2).
94. 42 U.S.C. § 12211(b).
95. 42 U.S.C. § 12114(a).
96. 42 U.S.C. §§ 12111(6), 12114; 21 U.S.C. § 812.
97. 42 U.S.C. § 12111(b)
98. Id.
99. 42 U.S.C. § 1981a(3).

ernment contractors and subcontractors with contracts of $10,000 or more to take affirmative action to employ and to advance in employment qualified disabled war veterans, including Vietnam-era veterans.[100]

Vietnam-era veterans include persons who (1) served active duty for more than 180 days, any part of which occurred between August 5, 1964, and May 7, 1975, and were not dishonorably discharged; or (2) served active duty during the above period and were discharged or released for service-connected disabilities.[101]

A "special disabled veteran" is a veteran entitled to compensation from the Veterans Administration for a disability rated at 30 percent or more or rated at 10 or 20 percent and determined to have a serious employment handicap, or a veteran who was discharged or released from active duty due to a service-connected disability.[102] A "qualified disabled veteran" is one who is capable of performing a particular job, with reasonable accommodation to his or her disability.[103]

The OFCCP, which enforces this Act, requires covered contractors with contracts of $50,000 or more and those with 50 or more employees to develop written AAPs. Unlike E.O. 11246, this law does not require that AAPs include goals, timetables, and utilization analyses but, rather, requires less stringent forms of nonquantifiable affirmative action.[104] The law also requires a covered contractor to invite veterans to identify themselves so that they may benefit under the contractor's AAP.[105]

A key provision distinguishes this statute from all others: Covered contractors must list with local state employment service offices all employment openings, except that the contractor may exclude openings for executives and top management positions, positions that are to be filled from within the contractor's organization, and positions lasting three days or less. These offices must give covered veterans priority consideration for such jobs.[106]

**Affirmative Action Clauses.** Regulations promulgated pursuant to this act require each contracting federal agency and each covered contractor to include an affirmative action clause in each government contract or subcontract. This clause must include the following information:

- Nondiscrimination and affirmative action in employment policies;
- Listing of suitable job openings at local state employment service offices;
- Reports, in certain cases, to local state employment service offices regarding job openings and new hires;
- Reports of the name and location of each hiring site statewide to the employment service system in each state where offices are maintained;
- Conditions exempted from these provisions;
- Compliance with implementing rules, regulations, and orders;
- Liability for noncompliance;
- Posting notices;
- Notification to labor representatives; and
- Implementation of the affirmative action clauses in covered subcontracts and purchase orders.[107]

**Procedure for Filing Complaints.** Any covered disabled veteran or Vietnam-era veteran who believes a covered contractor has failed or refused to comply with these provisions may file a complaint with the Veterans Employment Service of the Department of Labor through the local Veteran's Employment Representative, who will promptly investigate and take appropriate action.[108]

### [I] Employment and Reemployment Rights of Members of the Uniformed Services

**General Coverage.** The Act prohibits discrimination against persons based on their service in any uniformed service and applies to public and private employers.[109]

**Reemployment Rights.** A member of the uniformed services is entitled to reemployment and other employment benefits. As long as the person has given advance written or verbal warning of the service to the employer, the cumulative length of all previous absences from employment with this employer due to such service does not exceed five years, and the person submits for reemployment according to the provision of the Act.[110] Generally, the employee is entitled to return to his or her

100. 38 U.S.C. § 4212.
101. 38 U.S.C. § 101(29), 4211.
102. 38 U.S.C. § 4211.
103. 41 C.F.R. § 60-250.2.
104. 41 C.F.R. § 60-250.5.
105. 41 C.F.R. § 60-250.5(d).
106. 38 U.S.C. § 4212(a), 41 C.F.R. § 60-250.4.
107. 41 C.F.R. §§ 60-250.4, 60-250.5.
108. 41 C.F.R. § 60-250.26.
109. 38 U.S.C. §§ 4301, 4303(4)(A)(ii), 4303(4)(A)(iii).
110. 38 U.S.C. § 4312(a).

former position with seniority, status, pay, and benefits as if no absence had occurred.

**Employer's Defenses.** The employer is permitted to deny reemployment to a person otherwise entitled to reemployment if (1) the employer's circumstances have so changed as to make reemployment impossible or unreasonable; (2) reemployment would impose an undue hardship on the employer; or (3) the position the person left was for a brief, nonrecurrent period that carried no reasonable expectation that it would continue indefinitely.[111]

**Enforcement.** A person asserting claims under this Act may proceed by either filing a complaint with the Secretary of Labor or by filing an action directly in federal district court.[112]

### [m] The Uniform Guidelines on Employee Selection Procedures

**General Coverage.** The Uniform Guidelines on Employee Selection Procedures set forth the EEOC's position on the relationship between an employer's selection procedures and discrimination based on race, color, religion, sex, or national origin. The guidelines cover all selection devices, both objective and subjective, used by an employer to make employment decisions: written and oral testing, training programs, casual interviews, and so forth. They apply to persons subject to Title VII, E.O. 11246, or other equal employment opportunity requirements of federal law.[113]

**Adverse Impact.** The guidelines help covered employers comply with federal equal employment opportunity laws by avoiding practices resulting in an adverse impact on any "protected class" (i.e., race, sex, or ethnic group). To measure adverse impact, the guidelines use an 80-percent test that, if positive, shows "evidence" of discrimination. In other words, if the practice yields a selection rate for any race, sex, or ethnic group that is less than 80 percent of such rate for the group having the highest selection rate, evidence of discrimination exists.[114]

If an employer's selection practices are shown to have an adverse impact on minorities or women, the employer must either modify its policies to reduce such impact or attempt to justify them on the grounds of business necessity. The employer may also be required to adopt a validated, alternative procedure, with a less adverse impact than previous measures.[115]

**Record Retention Requirements.** The guidelines also specify that records of employee selection procedures must be retained and allow federal enforcement officials to infer an adverse impact from an employer's failure to maintain the required data.[116] If a selection procedure for a particular job results in what is judged to be an adverse impact, the employer must keep records for each component of the procedure.[117] If a selection procedure has no adverse impact, records need not be maintained.[118] However, employers are still advised to maintain such records in case they must demonstrate that no adverse impact exists. The guidelines do not specify how long these records must be kept.

The only other records required under the guidelines are breakdowns of the employer's workforce by sex and by specified race and/or ethnic groups, especially those for which there is extensive evidence of continuing discrimination: blacks, Hispanics, Asians, and Native Americans.[119]

### [n] The Jury System Improvement Act

The Jury System Improvement Act makes it unlawful for any employer to discharge, threaten to discharge, intimidate, or coerce an employee because of jury service.[120] Although this law contains a broad antidiscrimination provision, it does *not* require employers to pay their employees' salaries during jury duty. Employers are required, however, to (1) consider employees on a leave of absence during periods of jury service, (2) reinstate them to their positions without loss of seniority, and (3) continue their insurance and other benefits according to established leave of absence policies.[121] Employers in violation of this act may be liable for the loss of wages or other benefits, attorneys' fees, and court costs.[122] In addition, the employer may be ordered to provide other

111. 38 U.S.C. § 4312(d).

112. 38 U.S.C. § 4323.

113. 29 C.F.R. § 1607 (EEOC); 41 C.F.R. § 60-3 (OFCCP).

114. 29 C.F.R. § 1607.4(D) (EEOC); 41 C.F.R. § 60-3.4(D) (OFCCP).

115. 29 C.F.R. § 1607 (EEOC); 41 C.F.R. § 60-3 (OFCCP).

116. 29 C.F.R. § 1607.4(D) (EEOC); 41 C.F.R. § 60-3.4 (OFCCP).

117. 29 C.F.R. § 1607.4 (EEOC); 41 C.F.R. § 60-3.4(C).

118. Id.

119. 29 C.F.R. § 1607.4 (EEOC); 41 C.F.R. § 60-3.4 (OFCCP).

120. 28 U.S.C. § 1875(a).

121. 28 U.S.C. § 1875(c).

122. 28 U.S.C. § 1875(b), (d)(2).

appropriate relief including, but not limited to, reinstatement or a civil penalty of not more than $1,000 for each violation for each employee.[123]

It should be noted that a federal judge recently required an employer to pay an employee in full for jury service. Because the employer had paid its employees in the past during jury service, the court decided that the employer should pay for such service in the interests of justice.[124]

State laws vary on whether employers must pay employees summoned to serve as jurors or witnesses in state courts. Thus, employers should be familiar with the laws regarding jury and witness duty in each state in which they have employees.

### [o] The United States Bankruptcy Code

**General Coverage.** United States Bankruptcy Code Section 525(b) prohibits private employers from terminating the employment of, or discriminating against, any individual solely because that person is or has been a debtor or bankrupt.[125] There is some disagreement, however, regarding the standard of proof imposed on an employee seeking to establish a violation of the Code's antidiscrimination provision. For example, while the court in *Bell v. Sanford-Corbitt-Bruker* stated that the burden of proof should be analogous to that required in Title VII cases, the court in *Laracuente v. Chase Manhattan Bank* held that the plaintiff had to show that the discharge was due solely to bankruptcy status.[126]

123. 28 U.S.C. § 1875(b).

124. U.S. v. Adamita, 701 F. Supp. 85 (S.D.N.Y. 1988).

125. 11 U.S.C. § 525(b).

126. Bell v. Sanford-Corbitt-Bruker, 56 USLW 2231 (S.D. Ga. 1987); Laracuente v. Chase Manhattan Bank, 891 F.2d 17 (1st Cir. 1989).

**Retiree Benefits.** The Retiree Benefits Bankruptcy Protection Act of 1988 guarantees retired employees continued health and life insurance benefits in the event their former employer goes bankrupt. This law amends the Bankruptcy Code by requiring a company filing for bankruptcy to continue benefits to any retiree whose income was less than $250,000 during the year preceding the filing. Under this provision, a retiree's benefits would be categorized as part of a company's administrative expenses, which, in a bankruptcy proceeding, would place the retiree ahead of many other creditors.

These benefits are not to be modified except under specific conditions (if a company can prove, for example, that modification is necessary to avoid liquidation). Retirees can petition for an increase at a later date, however.[127]

### [p] The Consumer Credit Protection Act

The Consumer Credit Protection Act prohibits an employer from discharging any employee because his or her earnings have been subjected to garnishment for any *one* indebtedness; however, the law does not prohibit discharging an employee who is subjected to garnishment for *two* or more cases of indebtedness.[128] Nevertheless, an employer runs the risk of being charged with discrimination under the *disparate impact* theory if the individuals who are terminated for two garnishments are predominantly minorities or women (see § 9.2[a] for a detailed discussion of disparate impact).

In many cases, state laws concerning consumer credit are far more restrictive than the federal law. Hence, employers must be familiar with the applicable consumer credit protection laws in each state in which they maintain facilities.

127. 11 U.S.C. § 1114.

128. 15 U.S.C. § 1674.

## § 9.3 The Fair Labor Standards Act of 1938

**General Coverage.** Among other things, the Fair Labor Standards Act of 1938 (FLSA) establishes the minimum wage, maximum hours, and overtime pay provisions that employers must provide for covered—or nonexempt—employees.[1] The FLSA defines "employee" as any employed individual who is not specifically exempted from the law's provisions.[2] Exempt individuals include workers in bona fide executive, administrative, or professional positions, and outside salespersons. These employees are deemed "exempt" employees, whereas those within the scope of the FLSA are referred to as "nonexempt."[3]

The Small Business Job Protection Act[4] amends paragraph (1) of Section 6(a) of the FLSA, which sets out the federal minimum wage. The minimum wage, which had been at $4.25 per hour, is increased to $4.75 per hour effective October 1, 1996. On September 1, 1997, the minimum wage will increase to $5.15 per hour. Although this minimum wage will apply to most workers, an exception is created for newly hired teenage workers. For these workers, a subminimum wage of $4.25 per hour applies during the first 90 days of their employment. For tipped employees the minimum wage remains the same at $2.13 per hour.[5] In addition, any nonexempt employee required to work in excess of 40 hours a week must be compensated at a rate of not less than one and a half times the worker's regular rate.

In the public sector, the FLSA specifically permits employers to provide compensatory time off in lieu of overtime pay. The compensatory time off must be provided at a rate of not less than one and a half hours for each hour over 40 hours weekly and may be accumulated only up to 240 hours (up to 480 hours for public safety, emergency response, or seasonal work).[6] In addition, an agreement or understanding must be reached before the performance of work in order for employers to provide compensatory time in lieu of overtime payment in cash.[7] Employees with more than 240 hours (or 480 hours) of accrued compensatory time off will be paid overtime compensation for the additional hours.[8]

**Procedures and Enforcement.** The FLSA makes it unlawful for any employer to "retaliate" against an employee who files a complaint or is involved in any way in an action brought against the employer under the FLSA.[9] Employers that willfully violate the FLSA are liable for a fine of not more than $10,000, imprisonment for not more than six months, or both.[10] They are also liable for the amount of unpaid minimum wages, unpaid overtime compensation, an additional equal amount as liquidated damages,[11] court costs, and reasonable attor-

**§ 9.3**

1. 29 U.S.C. § 201.
2. 29 U.S.C. § 203(e).
3. 29 U.S.C. § 213.
4. Pub. L. No. 104-188, 110 Stat. 1755 (Aug. 10, 1996).
5. 29 U.S.C. § 206.
6. 29 C.F.R. §§ 551.21(O)(3)(a), 553.22, 553.24.
7. 29 C.F.R. § 553.23.
8. 29 C.F.R. § 551.21(O)(3)(a).
9. 29 U.S.C. § 215(3).
10. 29 U.S.C. § 216(a).
11. 29 U.S.C. § 216(b).

neys' fees. Any employer who discharges or discriminates against an employee because he files a complaint or is involved with an action against the employer brought under the FLSA is liable for relief including, without limitation, reinstatement, promotion, payment of lost wages, an additional equal amount as liquidated damages, court costs, and reasonable attorneys' fees.[12]

Under the FLSA, an action against an employer can be filed in a federal or state court by the employee or by the Secretary of Labor. Enforcement proceedings for unpaid minimum wages, unpaid overtime compensation, or liquidated damages may begin within two years after the cause of action and within three years if the action is willful.[13]

Many states have adopted their own wage and hour laws. Employers must be familiar with the wage and hour laws of each state in which they maintain facilities, as well as with federal requirements.

---

12. 29 C.F.R. § 553.23.

13. 29 U.S.C. §§ 216(b), (c), 255(a).

# § 9.4 Benefits

## [a] The Employee Retirement Income Security Act of 1974

**General Coverage.** The Employee Retirement Income Security Act of 1974 (ERISA) governs employee pension, health, and welfare benefit plans.[1] ERISA applies to all employers engaged in interstate commerce; however, federal, state, and local government employers are exempt from complying with all of ERISA's labor law provisions.

In addition to establishing participation and vesting provisions, ERISA imposes minimum funding standards, as well as fiduciary, reporting, and disclosure requirements, on employers, plan administrators, and plan trustees and fiduciaries.[2] ERISA's reporting and disclosure provisions require plan administrators to provide employees with summaries of their benefit plans, updates regarding major changes, and copies of reports on the financing of certain plans.[3]

It is unlawful for any person to discharge, discipline, or discriminate against a participant or beneficiary for exercising any right under ERISA or for anyone to interfere, in any way, with the attainment of any right to which an individual is entitled under his or her benefit plan.[4]

**Procedures and Enforcement.** Both the Internal Revenue Service and the Department of Labor are responsible for enforcing the vesting, participation, and funding requirements under ERISA. Willful violations will result in both criminal and civil penalties.[5] The Supreme Court has held that ERISA gives workers the right to sue for damages as individuals if administrators of health and retirement benefits breach their fiduciary obligation to employees by making intentional misrepresentations about plan benefits.[6]

Prior to ERISA, state laws governed the regulation of employee benefit plans. ERISA now preempts state laws as well as other federal provisions related in any way to administering employee pension and welfare benefit plans.

## [b] The Consolidated Omnibus Budget Reconciliation Act of 1986

The Consolidated Omnibus Budget Reconciliation Act of 1986 (COBRA) requires employers with more than 20 employees to offer employees and their eligible dependents a temporary extension of health coverage at group rates in certain cases in which coverage would otherwise end. Employees have the right to continue such coverage when they retire, resign, are laid off, lose group health insurance coverage as a result of changing from full-time to part-time status, or are discharged for any reason other than gross misconduct.[7]

In addition, an employee's spouse and dependents are entitled to continued coverage after these qualifying

**§ 9.4**

1. 29 U.S.C. § 1001.
2. 29 U.S.C. §§ 1021, 1052, 1053, 1082, 1101.
3. 29 U.S.C. § 1021.
4. 29 U.S.C. §§ 1140, 1141.
5. 29 U.S.C. §§ 1131, 1132.
6. Varity Corp. v. Howe, 116 S. Ct. 1065 (1996).
7. 29 U.S.C. § 1163.

events: the employee's death, a divorce or legal separation, or a dependent's loss of coverage as a result of no longer being classified as an eligible dependent under the terms of a specific plan.[8] COBRA obligates employers to inform all employees and their spouses of their right to avail themselves of continued coverage.[9]

Under COBRA, the continued coverage must be identical to that provided to current employees and to similar beneficiaries. Those individuals receiving coverage are required to pay premiums not exceeding 102 percent of the normal premium cost.[10]

### [c] The Family and Medical Leave Act of 1993

**General Coverage.** The Family and Medical Leave Act of 1993 (FMLA) requires that an employer provide leaves of absence for the birth or adoption of a child, for the care of a seriously ill family member, or for an employee's own serious health condition.[11] The FMLA applies to all employers with 50 or more employees and is available to employees who have been employed by the employer for at least 12 months and have at least 1,250 hours of service in the 12-month period preceding the leave.[12] Generally, in any case in which the necessity for leave is foreseeable, the employee must make a reasonable effort to schedule the leave to avoid undue disruption of the employer's business and must provide 30 days' notice of an intention to take leave; if the leave must take place in less than 30 days, the employee must provide such notice as is practicable.[13] The employee must be restored to the same position or an equivalent, with no loss of benefits accrued before the date leave began.[14]

The FMLA makes it unlawful for an employer to interfere with, restrain, or deny the exercise of or attempt to exercise any right provided by the FMLA, or to discharge or discriminate against any individual who opposes any practice made unlawful by the FMLA.[15] During the period of leave, the employer must continue to provide health care benefits in the same way as if the employee were still actively at work.[16]

The FMLA does not preempt state and local laws that provide greater leave rights, nor is it intended to discourage employers from offering more generous leave policies.[17]

**Procedures and Enforcement.** The FMLA enforcement procedures are similar to those under FLSA. The FMLA may be enforced by private action in either federal or state court by employees individually or on behalf of themselves and other employees similarly situated.[18] An action may also be brought by the Secretary of Labor; however, administrative requirements are not a prerequisite to a private suit.[19] The statute of limitations is two years or three years for willful violations.[20] Remedies include lost wages and benefits, any actual money losses, liquidated damages, and attorneys' fees and costs.[21]

8. Id.
9. 29 U.S.C. § 1166.
10. 29 U.S.C. §§ 1162.
11. 29 U.S.C. § 2612(a)(1).
12. 29 U.S.C. § 2611(2),(4).
13. 29 U.S.C. 2612(e).
14. 29 U.S.C. § 2614(a).
15. 29 U.S.C. § 2615.
16. 29 U.S.C. § 2614(c).
17. 29 U.S.C. §§ 2651–2653. For information regarding state laws relating to family and medical leave, see Part 5.
18. 29 U.S.C. § 2617(a)(2).
19. 29 U.S.C. § 2617(b).
20. 29 U.S.C. § 2617(c).
21. 29 U.S.C. §§ 2617(a)(1), 2617(a)(3).

# § 9.5 Privacy

### [a] The Employee Polygraph Protection Act

**General Coverage.** With limited exceptions, the Employee Polygraph Protection Act prohibits the use of lie detectors in employment decisions. This statute makes it unlawful for most employers to require, request, or even suggest that an employee or prospective employee submit to a lie detector test. Employers also may not use, refer to, or inquire about the results of any lie detector test of any employee or prospective employee. In addition, employers are prohibited from taking action or retaliating against any employee or prospective employee because that person refused to take a test, filed a complaint, or was a party to any action involving this law.[1]

Employers that are exempt from these provisions include: all U.S. state and local government employees; all government employers involved in national defense and security matters; the FBI; employers whose primary business is in the security field; employers involved in protecting facilities, materials, or operations having a significant impact on the health and safety of any state or political subdivision; employers involved in operations having a significant effect on national security; and any employer authorized to manufacture, distribute, or dispense a controlled substance.[2]

*All* employers, however, even those normally not exempt, may subject an employee to a polygraph test under these conditions:

- The test is administered in connection with an ongoing investigation involving economic loss or injury to the employer's business;
- The employee had access to property that is the subject of the investigation;
- The employer has a reasonable suspicion that the employee was involved in the incident under investigation; and
- The employer executes a statement outlining the specific incident or activity being investigated and the basis for testing the employee, shows that statement to the employee before the test, has the statement signed by an individual authorized to bind the employer,[3] and is retained by the employer for at least three years. The statement must also identify the following: the specific economic loss to the employer, an indication that the employee had access to the property that is the subject of the investigation, and a description of the basis for the employer's reasonable suspicion that the employee was involved in the incident under investigation.[4]

Throughout all phases of the polygraph test, administered in accordance with these exceptions, the examinee may terminate the test at any time.[5]

**Procedures and Enforcement.** The Secretary of Labor may bring an action to restrain violations of the statute, and employees may institute private actions within three years of the alleged violation.

**§ 9.5**

1. 29 U.S.C. §§ 2001, 2002.
2. 29 U.S.C. § 2006.
3. 29 U.S.C. § 2006(d).
4. 29 U.S.C. § 2006(d)(4).
5. 29 U.S.C. § 2007(b)(1)(A).

A court may grant both equitable and judicial relief, including but not limited to reinstatement, promotion, lost wages and benefits, and attorneys' fees. Any employer that violates this law may also be assessed a civil penalty of not more than $10,000.[6]

**State Laws.** Many states have enacted worker privacy laws also prohibiting the use of polygraph tests. To ensure that they are in compliance with federal as well as state laws regarding the administration of polygraph tests, employers should be familiar with the applicable legislation in each state in which they maintain facilities.

### [b] The Drug-Free Workplace Act of 1988

**General Coverage.** The Drug-Free Workplace Act of 1988 requires that all employers receiving federal grants, as well as certain employers entering into federal contracts, take specific steps to maintain a drug-free workplace.[7]

Specifically, this law requires covered employers to develop and disseminate policies prohibiting the manufacture, distribution, dispensation, possession, and use of controlled substances. In addition, the employers must establish "drug-free awareness programs" to inform employees about the dangers of drug abuse, about the company's drug-free workplace policy, about available counseling, rehabilitation, and employee assistance programs, and about the penalties for drug-abuse violations.[8]

Under this law, an employee who is criminally convicted of a drug violation occurring in the workplace must inform his or her employer of the conviction within five days. In turn, the employer must notify the contracting agency or the funding agency of the criminal conviction within ten days. Convicted employees may be required to participate in a drug-abuse assistance program or rehabilitation program.[9]

**Procedures and Enforcement.** Under this law, actions are initiated by an officer of the federal agency involved, pursuant to agency procedures and the Federal Acquisition Regulations.[10] The Federal Acquisition Regulations set forth the rules on suspension and debarment proceedings, on providing notice, on opportunities to respond in writing or in person, and on other procedures deemed necessary for a fair proceeding. This law also authorizes debarment of up to five years for a violation of drug-free workplace requirements.[11]

### [c] Department of Defense Drug-Free Workforce Policy

**General Coverage.** In September 1988, the Department of Defense (DOD) issued an interim rule outlining its policy for a drug-free workforce. Certain DOD contractors are required to develop and implement employee drug-testing programs on a random basis.

The DOD rule adds to all defense contracts a clause requiring contractors to "establish a program for testing for the use of illegal drugs by employees in sensitive positions." Employees in sensitive positions include those with access to classified information as well as those in positions that the contractor identifies as involving national security, health, and safety, and requiring a high degree of trust and confidence.

The rule permits the defense contractor to determine which type of program to establish, as long as the following considerations are taken into account: the employee's duties; the efficient use of contractor resources; and the potential threats to public health, safety, and national security that could result if an employee fails to discharge his or her duties. The rule also allows the contractor to decide whether to implement a drug-testing program based on reasonable suspicion of drug use in the workplace or following a worksite accident. The contractor is free to decide whether to implement the program as part of a postcounseling or rehabilitation program for employees who have tested positive for drugs or have otherwise been involved with drugs, or as part of a voluntary program. The contractor is similarly free to decide whether it will test job applicants.[12]

**Procedures for Dealing with Positive Tests.** Under the DOD rule, defense contractors must adopt procedures for dealing with employees who test positive for drugs. Covered contractors are required to remove such employees from positions with access to sensitive information or positions that might otherwise endanger the completion of contracts or the health and safety of other employees. The employer must be assured that the employee is capable of performing his or her job before allowing the employee to resume his or her previous position.

---

6. 29 U.S.C. § 2005.
7. 41 U.S.C. §§ 701–707.
8. 41 U.S.C. §§ 701, 702.
9. 41 U.S.C. §§ 701(a)(D)(ii), (E), (F), 702(a)(D)(ii), (E), (F).
10. 41 U.S.C. §§ 701(b)(2), 702(b)(2).
11. 41 U.S.C. §§ 701(b)(3), 702(b)(3).
12. 48 C.F.R. § 252.223-7004.

The DOD's drug-testing provision does not apply if it is inconsistent with state or local laws. Nor does it apply to employees covered by a collective bargaining agreement that prohibits unilateral employer adoption of a drug-testing program. In the latter case, the contractor must attempt to resolve the conflict between the collective bargaining agreement and the drug-testing rule during the next round of contract negotiations.[13]

### [d] The Fair Credit Reporting Act

**General Coverage.** The Fair Credit Reporting Act (FCRA) governs the activities of consumer credit reporting agencies as well as those of users of the information procured from such agencies. An investigative consumer report contains information about a consumer's character and reputation, as well as personal data obtained through personal interviews. A job applicant's consumer credit report is often procured by an employer for use in screening the applicant. The goal of the FCRA is to ensure that this information is used in a manner that is fair and equitable to the consumer regarding confidentiality, accuracy, and relevancy.[14]

Among other things, the FCRA prohibits the procurement of an investigative consumer report unless the procurer clearly discloses that such a report may be requested, the disclosure is made in writing, and it is mailed or otherwise delivered to the person who is the subject of the report not later than three days after the date on which the report was requested. This disclosure must also state that the subject of the report may obtain from the procurer, upon written request, a complete disclosure of the nature and scope of the investigation.[15]

If this request is made, the procurer is obligated to make a complete and accurate disclosure of the nature and scope of the investigation within five days of such request.

If an applicant is denied employment based on information in the investigative consumer credit report, the employer must so advise the applicant, supply the name and address of the consumer reporting agency, and advise the applicant of his rights to obtain a free copy of a consumer credit report on the individual from the consumer credit reporting agency employed and to challenge the accuracy or completeness of any information in the report.[16]

With limited exceptions, the FCRA prohibits a consumer reporting agency from including "adverse" information in an investigative consumer report. Adverse information pertains to paid tax liens, accounts placed for collection, arrests, indictments, criminal convictions, or any other adverse information that predates the report by more than seven years. This limitation is inapplicable if the report is to be used for screening an individual who is applying for a position paying $20,000 or more per year.[17]

**Procedures and Enforcement.** Willful noncompliance with any FCRA requirements on the part of a consumer credit reporting agency or a user of information procured from the agency results in liability to the subject of the report for an amount equal to the sum of:

- Actual damages sustained by the subject of the report;
- Punitive damages allowed by the court; and
- The costs of the action plus reasonable attorneys' fees, as determined by the court.

Civil liability for knowing noncompliance includes actual damages, the cost of the action, and reasonable attorneys' fees.[18]

In addition, any individual who knowingly and willfully obtains information from a consumer reporting agency under false pretenses will be fined under Title 18, or imprisoned not more than two years, or both.[19]

Several states have enacted their own fair credit reporting acts, which contain requirements that differ from the FCRA requirements. Employers should be aware of local law when requesting investigative reports on applicants and current employees.

13. Id.
14. 15 U.S.C. § 1681.
15. 15 U.S.C. § 1681d.
16. 15 U.S.C. § 1681m(a).
17. 15 U.S.C. § 1681c.
18. 15 U.S.C. § 1681n.
19. 15 U.S.C. § 1681q.

# § 9.6 The Occupational Safety and Health Act

**General Coverage.** The Occupational Safety and Health Act was enacted in 1970 to ensure safe and healthy working conditions for workers nationwide. The law imposes a "general duty" on employers to provide a workplace free from recognized safety and health hazards. It applies to any employer that has employees and is engaged in a business affecting commerce; however, employers with ten or fewer employees, as well as federal and state governments, are exempted from certain requirements.[1]

The requirements most applicable to employers are the Hazard Communication Standards and the general industry standards. These standards require employers to maintain clean and orderly rooms, aisles, passageways, guardrails, floors, roofs, and stairways. Other requirements pertain to recordkeeping and reporting, nondiscrimination against "whistleblowers," and notice-posting.

**Recordkeeping and Reporting Requirements.** In each location, covered employers must maintain a log and summary of all "recordable" occupational injuries and illnesses, logging each entry within six working days of the incident.[2] Injuries deemed recordable are specifically defined as: fatalities, regardless of the time between injury and death; lost workday cases; and nonfatal cases without lost workdays which result in either a transfer to another job or termination of employment or require medical treatment or involve loss of consciousness or restriction of work or motion.[3] Employers must also keep supplementary records, which must be compiled and posted annually at each location and maintained for five years.[4] Any failure to maintain required records may result in a citation and civil penalties. Employers that willfully make false statements are subject to criminal penalties as well.[5]

In addition to illness and injury records, covered employers must maintain employee medical and exposure records showing an employee's exposure to toxic substances.[6]

**Nondiscrimination Provisions.** The statute forbids any person from discharging or discriminating against any employee who either institutes a violation proceeding under this law or participates in an action instituted by another person against the employer. Employees who testify or are expected to testify in a proceeding are similarly protected from discharge or discrimination. Complaints alleging such discrimination must be filed within 30 days of the alleged violation.[7]

The statute does not provide a private right of action for individuals alleging discrimination. Instead, all complaints must be filed with the Occupational Safety and Health Agency (OSHA); awards may include reinstatement and back pay.[8] An employer violating the antidiscrimination provisions may be enjoined (formally, and in

**§ 9.6**

1. 29 U.S.C. §§ 651–678.
2. 29 U.S.C. § 657(2), 29 C.F.R. § 1904.4.
3. 29 C.F.R. § 1904.12(c).
4. 29 C.F.R. §§ 1904.5, 1904.6.
5. 29 U.S.C. § 666, 29 C.F.R. §§ 1904.5(d)(2), 1904.9.
6. 29 U.S.C. § 657(c)(3).
7. 29 U.S.C. § 660.
8. Id.

writing) from future violations and ordered to post a notice informing employees of its unlawful conduct. OSHA provides employers with notices, which must be posted.[9]

Penalties for failure to comply with these nondiscrimination provisions include civil penalties of up to $7,000 per violation.[10]

**Procedures and Enforcement.** Under this law, the Secretary of Labor is responsible for protecting worker safety. The Secretary must develop and promulgate standards of worker safety and health and monitor their application to ensure compliance. A covered employer's workplace—including machines, equipment, and materials—may be subject to inspection at any reasonable time. Anyone connected with a business undergoing inspection may also be questioned.[11]

If an investigation reveals unacceptable conditions, OSHA will issue a citation describing the violation and the proposed civil and/or criminal penalties. Citations may be contested before the Occupational Safety and Health Review Commission; hearings are presided over by an administrative law judge.[12]

9. 29 U.S.C. § 658.
10. 29 U.S.C. § 666.
11. 29 U.S.C. § 657.
12. 29 U.S.C. §§ 658–59.

# § 9.7 Labor Relations

## [a] The National Labor Relations Act

**General Coverage.** Enacted in 1935 and twice amended—in 1947 by the Taft-Hartley Act and in 1959 by the Landrum-Griffin Act—the National Labor Relations Act (NLRA) encourages the practice of collective bargaining by protecting workers' freedom of association and self-organization.[1]

More specifically, the NLRA guarantees employees the following rights:

- Self-organization;
- Forming, joining, or assisting labor organizations;
- Bargaining collectively through representatives of their own choosing; and
- Engaging in other concerted activities.[2]

Although the NLRA deals primarily with employees represented by labor unions, Section 7, the heart of this law, also protects those employees not represented by unions but who engage in protected "concerted activities."[3]

Section 8 further ensures workers' rights by prohibiting employers from engaging in the following activities:

- Interfering with any employees' rights under Section 7;
- Interfering with the formation or administration of any labor organization;
- Contributing financial or other support to any labor organization;
- Discriminating against any employee or interfering with an employee's membership in any labor organization;
- Retaliating against or dismissing employees who exercise their rights under the NLRA; and
- Refusing to bargain with the employees' representatives.

Any one of these activities may constitute an unfair labor practice by the employer.[4]

Section 8 similarly prohibits labor organizations from engaging in the following activities, any one of which may constitute an unfair labor practice by the union.[5]

- Restraining or coercing employees from exercising their rights under Section 7;
- Causing an employer to discriminate against an employee;
- Refusing to bargain collectively with an employer;
- In certain circumstances, engaging in or encouraging an employee to engage in a strike;
- Charging excessive union dues;
- Charging an employer for services not performed; and
- Picketing, unless it is lawful.

**Procedures and Enforcement.** Alleged violations of NLRA provisions must be brought to the National Labor Relations Board (NLRB) within six months of the

**§ 9.7**

1. 29 U.S.C. §§ 151 *et seq.*
2. 29 U.S.C. § 157.
3. Id.
4. 29 U.S.C. § 158(a).
5. 29 U.S.C. § 158(b).

incident. The NLRB will issue a complaint and a hearing notice not less than five days after the complaint is served.[6]

If the NLRB finds that an unfair labor practice exists, it will issue a cease and desist order and take affirmative action, which may include reinstatement of an employee with or without back pay.[7]

If no exceptions to the NLRB order are filed within 20 days, that order becomes effective. At any time, with reasonable notice, the NLRB may modify or set aside any order.[8] The NLRB can also petition any U.S. court of appeals to enforce an order or to provide appropriate temporary relief by issuing a restraining order.[9] Note that any person may petition a U.S. court of appeals to review an NLRB order.[10]

**Coordinated Enforcement.** Occasionally, violations of the NLRA may also be violations of the Americans with Disabilities Act (ADA). Recently, the Equal Employment Opportunity Commission (EEOC) and the NLRB agreed to coordinate enforcement when there are potential violations of both acts. The NLRB will consult with the EEOC whenever a charge of refusal to bargain requires interpretation of the union's ADA responsibilities or when an able-bodied person claims that an accommodation to employees with disabilities violates the NLRA. The EEOC will consult the NLRB when an employer or a union is charged with violating the ADA and it is necessary to interpret the duties of the employer or union under the NLRA.

## [b] The Railway Labor Act of 1926

**General Coverage.** The Railway Labor Act of 1926 (RLA) governs labor relations between railroad employees and their union representatives.[11] In 1936, it was extended to apply to airlines and their union representatives as well.[12] Like the NLRA, the RLA guarantees employees the right to organize and bargain collectively with representatives of their own choosing.[13] Unlike the NLRA, however, the RLA imposes mandatory mediation by a federal agency (National Mediation Board) and arbitration by boards of adjustment in contract-interpretation disputes.[14] The RLA further specifies procedures for changing pay rates, rules, and working conditions.[15]

The RLA was enacted primarily to improve the efficiency of collective bargaining through federal mediation. In contrast, other federal labor laws aim to limit disputes resulting from union efforts to organize and represent employees in collective bargaining with their employers. The RLA also provides for a negotiation process designed to minimize the use of strikes and lockouts.

**Procedures and Enforcement.** In most cases, unless the nature of the dispute is outside the National Mediation Board's jurisdiction, individuals must first exhaust the Board's administrative remedies before filing suit in court. Federal courts can review awards of arbitration boards only on limited grounds. If a court determines that part of an award is invalid and other parts are valid, the court will set aside the entire award, unless both parties agree that parts of the award are separable. Any appeal must be filed with the court of appeals within ten days after the district court decides the validity of the award; otherwise, the district court's decision stands. The determination of a court of appeals is final.[16]

---

6. 29 U.S.C. § 160(b).
7. 29 U.S.C. § 160(c).
8. 29 U.S.C. § 160(d).
9. 29 U.S.C. § 160(e).
10. 29 U.S.C. § 160(f).
11. 45 U.S.C. §§ 151 *et seq.*
12. 45 U.S.C. § 181.
13. 45 U.S.C. § 152.
14. 45 U.S.C. §§ 151, 157.
15. 45 U.S.C. § 156.
16. 45 U.S.C. § 159.

## § 9.8 Immigration Reform and Control Act

**General Coverage.** The Immigration Reform and Control Act of 1986 (IRCA), an amendment to the Immigration and Nationality Act, prohibits the knowing employment of aliens who are not legally authorized to work in the United States and/or of legal nonimmigrants whose classification does not permit employment in this country. The IRCA requires employers to certify the identity and employment eligibility of all employees hired after November 6, 1986.[1] The employer must review the employee's certification within three days of hiring.[2]

The IRCA also contains antidiscrimination provisions that make it an "unfair immigration-related employment practice" to discriminate in the recruitment, hiring, or termination of any individual on the basis of national origin or citizenship. The Immigration Act of 1990 expanded the IRCA's definition of an unfair immigration-related employment practice to include: (1) requesting more or different documents evidencing identity or work authorization than those required by Immigration and Naturalization Service (INS) regulations; (2) rejecting apparently valid identity or work authorization documents; and (3) attempting to intimidate and/or retaliate against employees for exercising rights protected by IRCA.[3] The expanded definition makes it discriminatory for employers to refuse to consider a person for employment simply because they suspect that the applicant is an unauthorized alien; employers are permitted to verify the applicant's legal status only after an offer of employment has been accepted.

**Documentation.** Each employee must complete Form I-9 issued by the INS, attesting to his or her legal status. Verifying an individual's legal status to work in the United States requires proof of both the individual's identity and the individual's authorization to work.[4] The IRCA further requires the employer to keep such documentation on file for three years following the first date of employment or for one year following the termination of employment, whichever is later.[5]

**Enforcement Procedures.** Recordkeeping and unauthorized employment violations are enforced by the INS. The INS conducts an investigation and, if appropriate, issues a notice of intent to fine. An employer receiving such a notice must request a hearing in writing and file a response within 30 days; otherwise, the employer forfeits the right to appeal any decision by the INS.[6]

**§ 9.8**

1. Employers are not required to verify the identity or employment eligibility of an independent contractor's employees or of temporary employees hired through an employment agency. If such individuals become company employees, however, the employer must then comply with IRCA requirements.

2. IRCA, §§ 274 A(a)(1), 274 A(b); 8 U.S.C. §§ 1324a, 1324b.

3. IRCA, § 274 B; 8 U.S.C. § 1324b. The IRCA's discrimination prohibition does not apply to employers with three or fewer employees. Id.

4. IRCA § 274A(b)(1)(B), (C), (D); 8 U.S.C. § 1324a(b)(1)(B), (C), (D).

5. IRCA, § 274 A(b)(3); 8 U.S.C. § 1324a(b)(3).

6. IRCA § 274A(e)(3); 8 U.S.C. § 1324a(e)(3).

Within 30 days of an administrative law judge's decision, the U.S. Attorney General may modify or vacate the decision. If the Attorney General does not act, the judge's decision is final.[7] The employer then may file a petition for review in the Court of Appeals within 45 days.[8] The Attorney General may also bring a civil action in a U.S. District Court, seeking injunctive relief against the employer.

Antidiscrimination complaints may be reported to the Special Counsel for Immigration-Related Employment Practices, the Equal Employment Opportunity Commission, or state Human Rights agencies. These agencies coordinate amongst themselves to determine the proper enforcement authority. The government has 120 days to investigate the charges and determine whether to file an administrative complaint.[9] If no complaint is filed, the complainant has an additional 90 days to pursue the charges in a private administrative action.[10]

Civil fines (from $100 to $10,000 per violation) and cease and desist orders can be imposed upon employers for violating the recordkeeping and employment requirements of the IRCA. Antidiscrimination charges can result in fines, back pay and/or front pay awards, attorneys' fees, and other damages. Criminal penalties are possible for employers who repeatedly violate the provisions of the IRCA.[11] The INS announced that it would step up enforcement efforts under the IRCA, so employers should be careful to maintain compliance with its provisions.

7. IRCA § 274A(e)(7); 8 U.S.C. § 1324a(e)(7).

8. IRCA § 274A(e)(8); 8 U.S.C. § 1324a(e)(8).

9. IRCA § 274B(d)(1); 8 U.S.C. § 1324b(d)(1).

10. IRCA § 274B(d)(2); 8 U.S.C. § 1324b(d)(2).

11. IRCA § 274B(g)(2), (h); 8 U.S.C. § 1324b(g)(2), (h).

## § 9.9 Worker Adjustment and Retraining Notification Act

**General Coverage.** The Worker Adjustment and Retraining Notification Act (WARN) provides for mandatory notices of plant closings and mass layoffs.[1] Specifically, it requires employers to provide their employees, their employees' bargaining representative (if any), and various state and local government officers with a written notice 60 days before implementing a plant closing or mass layoff.[2] WARN generally applies to all employers with 100 or more full-time employees and encompasses "any business enterprise."[3]

**Plant Closing.** Three factors must be present to establish a plant closing:

1. A "single site of employment," or one or more "facilities" or "operating units" within a single site of employment, must be permanently or temporarily shut down.
2. The shutdown at the single site must result in an "employment loss": an involuntary termination, a layoff exceeding six months, or a 50-percent reduction of monthly hours during a six-month period.
3. The shutdown must affect 50 or more full-time employees during any 30-day period.[4]

**Mass Layoff.** Under WARN, a "mass layoff" is a reduction in force resulting not from a plant closing but from an employment loss at a single employment site during any 30-day period. In addition, the reduction in force must affect either at least 33 percent of full-time employees *and* at least 50 full-time employees, or at least 500 employees.[5]

**Notice Requirement.** The central provision of WARN is the mandatory notice 60 days *prior* to a plant closing or mass layoff. The law requires covered employers to serve written notice to the following:

1. Affected workers or their exclusive bargaining representative, if any;
2. The state dislocated worker unit; and
3. The chief elected official of the local government unit in which the action will occur.

To satisfy the 60-day notice requirement when communicating with employees, WARN approves mailing the notice to an employee's last known address or enclosing the notice in the employee's paycheck.[6]

WARN permits a notice period of less than 60 days in two limited situations. Under the *faltering company* exception, an employer that is actively seeking capital or a business that, if obtained, would avoid or postpone a shutdown, need not give the full 60 days' notice if it "reasonably" and in "good faith" believes that giving notice would preclude it from obtaining the needed capital or business.[7] A shorter notice period is also permitted if the plant closing or mass layoff is caused by business

---

**§ 9.9**

1. 29 U.S.C. §§ 2101 *et seq.*
2. 29 U.S.C. § 2102.
3. 29 U.S.C. § 2101(a)(1).
4. 29 U.S.C. § 2101(a)(6). See also 29 U.S.C. § 2101(b).
5. 29 U.S.C. § 2101(3).
6. 29 U.S.C. § 2102.
7. 29 U.S.C. § 2101(b)(1).

circumstances that were not reasonably foreseeable at the time the notice would have been required.[8]

An employer that invokes either of these exceptions allowing shorter notice periods must present sufficient facts in its notice to explain why the exception applies.[9] This statement must provide affected employees an adequate and specific explanation of the underlying condition causing the shortened notice. A mere reference to the statutory exception to the notice requirement in the notice is inadequate.[10]

WARN also exempts employers from the notice requirement in a number of situations. Employers are not required to give *any* notice of a closing or mass layoff if:

1. The closing or mass layoff is due to any form of natural disaster, including flood, earthquake, or drought;[11]
2. The closing or mass layoff affects only temporary employees who knew when they were hired that their employment was limited to a temporary facility or undertaking;
3. The closing or layoff "institutes" a strike or lockout not intended to evade the notice requirements; or
4. The employees subject to the closing or mass layoff are deemed to be economic strikers under the Labor Management Relations Act of 1947 and are being permanently replaced.[12]

**Procedures and Enforcement.** WARN permits aggrieved employees, collective bargaining representatives, and local government units to bring suit, and it expressly approves class actions.[13] It also does not preclude jury trials. Although WARN does not include a statute of limitations, the Supreme Court has held that the appropriate statute of limitations for such cases is the state statute most closely analogous to WARN, not the six-month statute of limitations contained in the National Labor Relations Act.[14] In cases following this Supreme Court decision, courts have applied limitations periods for contract and tort claims.[15] The law empowers the court to award the prevailing party reasonable attorneys' fees but not to enjoin the closing or layoff.[16]

Employers that violate the provisions of WARN are liable for back pay and lost benefits, including the cost of any otherwise covered medical expenses incurred by employees during the employment loss, for a period up to 60 days. There is no provision for punitive damages.[17]

Several states and municipalities have enacted their own laws establishing notice requirements for business closings and/or large-scale layoffs. Employers should be familiar with the applicable laws and plant-closing notice requirements in each state in which facilities are maintained.

8. 29 U.S.C. § 2101(b)(2).

9. 29 U.S.C. § 2101(b)(3).

10. Alarcon v. Keller Industries, Inc., 27 F.3d 386 (9th Cir. 1994).

11. 29 U.S.C. § 210(b)(2)(B).

12. 29 U.S.C. § 2103.

13. 29 U.S.C. § 2104(a)(5).

14. North Star Steel Co. v. Thomas, 115 S. Ct. 1927 (1995).

15. Staudt v. Glastron, Inc., 92 F.3d 312 (5th Cir. 1996); Aaron v. Brown Group, Inc., 80 F.3d 1220 (8th Cir.), cert. denied 117 S. Ct. 361 (1996).

16. 29 U.S.C. 2104(a)(6).

17. 29 U.S.C. §§ 2102, 2104.

# § 9.10 Whistle-blower Laws

Many federal statutes contain whistle-blower provisions, which protect employees from retaliation for reporting employers' violations of certain statutory safety and environmental standards. The key federal statutes containing such provisions are the following:

**The Department of Defense Authorization Act of 1987 (DDAA).**[1] DDAA prohibits defense contractors from discharging, demoting, or otherwise discriminating against employees who disclose *substantial* violations of law related to defense contracts.[2] Only disclosures made to a member of Congress, an authorized official of an agency, or the Department of Justice are protected.[3] Employees may file complaints alleging a violation of this provision with the Inspector General of the Department of Defense. A contractor found to be in violation of this provision may be ordered to (1) take affirmative action to abate the reprisal, (2) reinstate the employee with compensation, back pay, and benefits, and/or (3) pay an amount equal to the aggregate amount of costs and expenses the employee incurred bringing the complaint.[4]

**The Fair Labor Standards Act of 1938 (FLSA).**[5] Employers are precluded from discharging or otherwise discriminating against employees who file complaints or institute proceedings under FLSA, testify or are about to testify in a proceeding under FLSA, or serve or are about to serve on an industry committee.[6] Employers who wilfully violate this section may be fined up to $10,000 and imprisoned up to six months. In addition, employers who retaliate against employees in violation of this provision shall be liable for legal and equitable relief including, but not limited to, employment, reinstatement, promotion, the payment of lost wages, and an additional equal amount as liquidated damages. An employee loses his right to file a complaint under this section once the Secretary of Labor files a complaint against the employer under Section 217 of FLSA.[7]

**The Federal Mines Safety and Health Act (FMSHA).**[8] The Federal Mines Safety and Health Act establishes mandatory health and safety standards to protect coal miners and other miners. FMSHA prohibits employers from discharging those employees and applicants for employment who have filed or made a complaint under FMSHA, including complaints notifying the mine operator or representatives of miners of a health or safety violation. In addition, employers are prohibited from discharging or discriminating against those miners and applicants for employment who are the subjects of medical evaluations or are potentially transferring. Employees and applicants for employment cannot be discharged or discriminated against because they have instituted or testified (or are about to testify) in a proceeding under FMSHA. Finally, employers are precluded from retaliating against employees who exercise

**§ 9.10**

1. 10 U.S.C. § 2409.
2. 10 U.S.C. § 2409(a).
3. Id.
4. Id.
5. 29 U.S.C. § 201 *et seq.*
6. 29 U.S.C. § 215(a)(3).
7. 29 U.S.C. § 216.
8. 30 U.S.C. § 815 *et seq.*

any statutory right afforded by FMSHA.[9] Miners and applicants who believe that they have been retaliated against must file a complaint with the Secretary of Labor within 60 days after the alleged violation. The Secretary refers violations to the Federal Mine Safety and Health Commission. The Commission may order the violator to take "affirmative action as to abate the violation as the Commission deems appropriate."[10] If the Secretary concludes that no violation occurred, an aggrieved employee may directly file a claim with the Commission on his own behalf.[11]

**The Longshore and Harbor Workers' Compensation Act (LHWCA).**[12] The Longshore and Harbor Workers' Compensation Act provides compensation for the disability or death of employees which results from an injury occurring on the navigable waters of the United States. LHWCA covers injuries or death occurring on a pier, wharf, dry dock, terminal, building way, or marine railway adjoining navigable water of the United States. It also covers injuries occurring in an area customarily used by an employer in loading, repairing, dismantling, or building a vessel.[13] Under LHWCA, employers are prohibited from discharging or otherwise discriminating against employees who claim or attempt to claim compensation from the employer, or testify (or are about to testify) against the employer in a proceeding under this chapter.[14] Employers in violation of the whistle-blower provision are liable for fines between $1,000 and $5,000. In addition, any employee retaliated against who is qualified to perform the duties of employment shall be restored to his employment and is entitled to lost wages.[15]

**The Migrant and Seasonal Agricultural Worker Protection Act (MSAWPA).**[16] The Migrant and Seasonal Agricultural Worker Protection Act attempts to ensure the necessary protections for migrant and seasonal agricultural workers. To carry out its purpose, MSAWPA prohibits employers from intimidating, threatening, restraining, coercing, blacklisting, discharging, or discriminating against any migrant or seasonal worker who, with just cause, files, institutes, or causes any proceeding under MSAWPA. In addition, workers who testify or are about to testify in proceedings under MSAWPA are protected from retaliatory action. Finally, retaliation against any migrant or seasonal worker exercising any right or protection afforded by the chapter is prohibited.[17] Violations of this provision must be filed with the Secretary of Labor within 180 days. If the Secretary concludes that a violation has occurred, the claim is filed in a United States district court. The court is permitted to grant "all appropriate relief," including, but not limited to, rehiring, back pay, or damages.[18]

**The Occupational Safety and Health Act of 1970 (OSHA).**[19] Under the Occupational Safety and Health Act of 1970 (OSHA), it is unlawful for employers to discharge or discriminate against employees who file any complaint or institute any proceeding "under or related" to OSHA. In addition, OSHA precludes retaliation by an employer against an employee who has testified or is about to testify in a proceeding under OSHA against the employer.[20] Employee requests for government inspection of the workplace and complaints filed with other federal and state agencies with the authority to investigate occupational safety and health are protected under this section as long as they address conditions in the workplace rather than general public safety and health concerns.[21] Finally, this provision precludes employers from firing or discriminating against those employees exercising "*any* right afforded by this chapter."[22] Therefore, employees who cooperate in government investigations and inspections or who, in good faith, refuse to work or expose themselves to hazardous conditions in the workplace are protected from subsequent discrimination.[23] Employees must file a complaint with the Secretary of Labor within 30 days following the alleged retaliation. If the Secretary concludes that a violation occurred, he must bring the action in the appropriate district court. To remedy violations of this provision, the court may order "all appropriate relief," including,

9. 30 U.S.C. § 815(c). See 30 U.S.C. § 813 for specific rights concerning inspections, investigations, and recordkeeping afforded by FMSHA.
10. Id.
11. Id.
12. 33 U.S.C. § 901 *et seq.*
13. 33 U.S.C.§ 903.
14. 33 U.S.C. § 948a.
15. Id.
16. 29 U.S.C. § 1801 *et seq.*
17. 29 U.S.C. § 1855.
18. Id.
19. 29 U.S.C. § 651 *et seq.*
20. 29 U.S.C. § 660(c)(1).
21. 29 C.F.R. § 1977.9(a), (b).
22. 29 U.S.C. § 660(c)(1).
23. 29 C.F.R. § 1977.12. See Marshall v. Whirlpool Corp., 445 U.S. 1 (1980).

but not limited to rehiring the employee to his former position with back pay.[24]

**The Surface Mining Control and Reclamation Act (SMCRA).**[25] The Surface Mining Control and Reclamation Act establishes nationwide surface mining and reclamation standards in order to protect society and the environment from the adverse effects of surface coal mining operations.[26] Employers covered by SMCRA are prohibited from discharging or discriminating against employees who file, institute, testify (or are about to testify) in proceedings under SMCRA. Violations of this provision must be filed with the Secretary of Labor within 30 days. If the Secretary concludes that a violation has occurred, the employer may be required to take "affirmative action to abate the violation."[27]

**The Surface Transportation Act (STA).**[28] The Surface Transportation Act governs employers who own or lease commercial motor vehicles used to transport passengers or cargo if the vehicle (1) has a gross vehicle weight of at least 1,000 pounds, (2) is designed to transport more than ten passengers, or (3) transports materials determined by the Secretary of Transportation to be hazardous.[29] Under STA, employers are prohibited from discharging, disciplining, or otherwise discriminating against employees who file a complaint or begin a proceeding related to a violation of commercial vehicle safety regulation or standard. Employers are also prohibited from retaliating against employees who refuse to operate a vehicle because (1) operation would violate a regulation, standard, or order of the United States (related to commercial motor vehicle safety or health) or (2) the employee has a reasonable apprehension of serious injury to the employee or the public because of the vehicle's unsafe condition. Employees must file complaints with the Secretary of Labor within 180 days of an alleged violation of this provision. If the Secretary concludes that a violation has occurred, he shall order the violator to take appropriate action to abate the violation, reinstate the employee, and pay compensatory and back pay.[30]

## [a] Employer Violation of Environmental Standards

The specific procedures for handling of discrimination complaints under the following federal employee protection statutes are described in Volume 29 of the Code of Federal Regulations, Part 24 *et seq.*

**The Clean Air Act (CAA).**[31] The Clean Air Act attempts to improve, and prevent the deterioration of, air quality by setting emission standards and limitations. In order to regulate motor vehicle and aircraft emissions and fuel standards, CAA establishes a permit system for those manufacturers and businesses that emit pollutants into the air. To encourage employees to report violations of CAA, employers are prohibited from discharging or otherwise discriminating against employees who commence, testify in, or assist in proceedings for the administration or enforcement of CAA's requirements.[32] Violations of this provision must be filed with the Secretary of Labor within 30 days after the alleged retaliation. The Secretary shall order employers in violation of this statute to take affirmative action to abate the violation and reinstate the employee to his former position with compensation, including back pay. The Secretary may order violators to pay compensatory damages and/or attorneys' fees and costs.[33]

**The Comprehensive Environmental Response Compensation and Liability Act of 1980 (CERCLA).**[34] In order to protect the environment from the dumping of hazardous materials, CERCLA prohibits employers from firing or discriminating against any employees who provide information to a state or the federal government relating to the goals of CERCLA. In addition, employers are precluded from retaliating against employees who file, institute, testify (or are about to testify) in any proceeding under CERCLA.[35] An employee must file a claim under this provision with the Secretary of Labor within thirty days of the alleged violation.[36] The Secretary shall order appropriate action in response to violations, including, but not limited to, reinstatement with compensation.[37]

24. 29 U.S.C. § 660(c)(2).
25. 30 U.S.C. § 1201 *et seq.*
26. 30 U.S.C. § 1202.
27. 30 U.S.C. § 1293.
28. 49 U.S.C. § 31101 *et seq.*
29. 49 § 31101 (1), (3).
30. 49 U.S.C. § 31105.
31. 42 U.S.C. § 7401 *et seq.*
32. 42 U.S.C. § 7622.
33. Id.
34. 42 U.S.C. § 9601 *et seq.*
35. 42 U.S.C. § 9610(a).
36. 42 U.S.C. §9610(b).
37. Id.

**The Energy Reorganization Act of 1974 (ERA).**[38] ERA prohibits employers from discharging or otherwise discriminating against employees who (1) notify the employer of alleged violations of ERA or the Atomic Energy Act of 1954 (AEA),[39] (2) refuse to engage in practices made unlawful by ERA or AEA, (3) testify before Congress or any other federal or state proceeding regarding any provision of ERA or AEA, (4) have initiated or are about to initiate a proceeding under ERA or AEA, (5) testify in any such proceeding, or (6) assist in any proceeding to carry out the purposes of ERA of AEA.[40] Claims against employers for alleged violations of this statute must be filed with the Secretary of Labor within 180 days.[41] The Supreme Court held that this whistle-blowing provision preempts state common-law actions for wrongful discharge only if the claim relates to the "radiological safety aspects involved in the . . . operation of a nuclear [facility]."[42] If an employer retaliates against an employee, the Secretary shall order the violator to take "affirmative action to abate" violations and reinstate the employee to his prior position with back pay. The Secretary may also award compensatory damages and attorneys' fees.[43]

**The Federal Water Pollution Control Act of 1972 (FWPCA).**[44] In order to encourage employees to help enforce environmental standards developed to restore and maintain the country's waterways, the Federal Water Pollution Control Act contains a provision precluding employers from firing or otherwise discriminating against employees who institute proceedings or testify against employers in violation of FWPCA.[45] Employees must file claims for violation of this provision with the Secretary of Labor within 30 days of the alleged retaliation.[46] Employers in violation of this provision shall take affirmative action to abate the violation, reinstate an employee, and pay back pay. The Secretary may also order the employer to pay court costs.[47]

**The Safe Drinking Water Act (SDWA).**[48] The Safe Drinking Water Act establishes standards for maximum contaminant levels for public water systems. Employers covered by SDWA include collection, treatment, storage and distribution facilities, and other facilities associated with water systems.[49] Employers are prohibited from discharging or otherwise discriminating against employees who (1) commence or are about to commence a proceeding for the administration or enforcement of drinking water regulations or underground injection control programs of the state, (2) have testified or are about to testify in any such proceeding, or (3) have assisted or are about to assist or participate in a proceeding or action to carry out the purposes of SDWA.[50] Alleged violations of this provision must be filed with the Secretary of Labor within 30 days.[51] Upon a finding that an employer has retaliated against an employee in violation of this provision, the Secretary may order the employer (1) to abate the violation, (2) to reinstate the employee to the prior position with back pay, (3) to pay compensatory damages, and (4) to pay exemplary damages, where appropriate.[52]

**The Solid Waste Disposal Act (SWDA).**[53] The Solid Waste Disposal Act authorizes federal financial and technical assistance in the development and application of improved methods to reduce the amount and provide for the proper and economical disposal of waste and unsalvageable materials.[54] SWDA precludes employers from firing or discriminating against employees who file, institute, or cause to be filed or instituted any proceeding under the chapter or under any applicable implementation plan. Retaliation against employees who have testified or are about to testify in any proceeding resulting from the administration or the enforcement of SWDA is also prohibited.[55] Employees who believe that their employer is in violation of this provision must file a complaint with the Secretary of Labor within 30 days of the alleged violation. Upon the finding of a violation, the Secretary shall require the employer to take affirmative action to abate the violation (including, but not

38. 42 U.S.C. § 5801 *et seq.*
39. 42 U.S.C. § 2011 *et seq.*
40. 42 U.S.C. § 5851(a)(1).
41. 42 U.S.C. § 5851(b)(1).
42. See English v. General Electric, 496 U.S. 72, 84–85 (1990).
43. 42 U.S.C. § 5851(b)(2)(B).
44. 33 U.S.C. § 1251 *et seq.*
45. 33 U.S.C. § 1367(a).
46. 33 U.S.C. § 1367(b).
47. 33 U.S.C. §§ 1367 (b), (c).
48. 42 U.S.C. § 300f *et seq.*
49. 42 U.S.C. § 300f (1), (4). Public water systems include any system that pipes water for human consumption.
50. 42 U.S.C. § 300j-9(I).
51. Id.
52. 42 U.S.C. § 300j-9(I)(2)(B)(ii).
53. 42 U.S.C. § 6901 *et seq.*
54. 42 U.S.C. § 6902.
55. 42 U.S.C. § 6971.

limited to, rehiring or reinstatement of the employee). At the request of the complainant, the Secretary may award the costs and attorneys' fees incurred in bringing the claim.[56]

**The Toxic Substances Control Act (TSCA).**[57] The Toxic Substances Control Act regulates chemical substances and mixtures that present an unreasonable risk of injury to the public health or the environment.[58] TSCA prohibits employers from discharging or discriminating against employees who (1) commence, cause, or are about to commence a proceeding under TSCA, (2) testify or are about to testify in any such proceeding, or (3) assist or participate or are about to assist or participate in a proceeding or action to carry out the purposes of TSCA. Complaints made under this provision must be filed with the Secretary of Labor within 30 days of the alleged violation. The Secretary shall order violators to (1) "take affirmative action to abate the violation," (2) reinstate the employee to his former position, with back pay, (3) pay compensatory damages, and (4) pay exemplary damages, where appropriate. The Secretary may also order violators to pay the costs and attorneys' fees accumulated in bringing the complaint.[59]

State legislatures have also enacted whistle-blower provisions. Some provisions apply to public employees only, while others apply to both private and public employees. In addition, many states have enacted laws protecting employees from being fired in retaliation for filing workers' compensation claims. Check with local jurisdictions for additional statutes.

Employers should be familiar with the federal whistle-blower laws governing their particular industry and with the whistle-blower laws in each state and local jurisdiction in which they maintain facilities. The penalties for violating such laws can be quite severe and may include back pay, compensatory damages, and recovery of attorneys' fees.

56. Id.

57. 15 U.S.C. § 2601 *et seq.*

58. 15 U.S.C. § 2601.

59. 15 U.S.C. § 2622.

# Glossary of Legal Terms

—A—

**Actual Damages** The sum of money awarded for a loss that is quantifiable and directly related in an economic sense to the loss suffered.

**Administrative Remedies** Use of an administrative agency as the place where one obtains relief following a hearing or quasi-judicial procedure. Parties are often required to "exhaust" administrative remedies before filing a lawsuit in court, which means that the parties first must complete the administrative process.

**Adverse Impact** One method of proving discrimination. An employment practice that appears neutral on its face but that operates to adversely affect a greater percentage of a protected classification as compared with a favored group (for example, blacks versus whites; females versus males). Unless the employer demonstrates that the practice serves a valid business purpose, it will be deemed unlawful.

**Affirmative Relief** Relief sought or granted to a defendant in a lawsuit. Affirmative relief often refers to such nonmonetary relief sought by either party as hiring, reinstatement, promotion, etc.

**Antiretaliatory Clause** A clause in a statute providing for protection against retaliation for exercising a right encompassed within the statute.

—B—

**Bench Trial** A trial in which a judge performs the function of a jury in making determinations of fact. *See* Jury Trial.

**Bona Fide Benefits Program** A defense to an allegation of discrimination involving benefits. A benefits program adopted by an employer that may provide unequal benefits will be termed "bona fide" or legitimate if its purpose was not discriminatory.

**Bona Fide Occupational Qualification (BFOQ)** A narrowly construed defense to allegations of sex, religious, national origin, or age discrimination that is based on a proven need to use such discriminatory criteria in setting employment policies. For example, religion may be a BFOQ for teachers at a religious school, and age is currently a BFOQ for commercial airline pilots.

**Bona Fide Seniority System** A defense to allegations of discrimination based on a functioning seniority or merit system. Employment-related decisions that adversely affect a protected classification may be defended by showing either that the seniority or merit system required the decisions or that the employer merely complied with its terms. The plaintiff must then show that the seniority or merit system was intentionally adopted to discriminate on a prohibited basis.

—C—

**Cease or Desist Order** An order from an administrative agency or court that directs a party to stop a particular course of conduct.

**Certiorari** The process by which a superior court reviews a decision from an inferior court, although the term also applies to other processes in which decisions are subject to review. The term is used most often in U.S. Supreme Court practice where parties, following an adverse appellate court decision, seek Supreme Court review by filing a petition for certiorari. Denial of such a petition has no precedential value and does not indicate Supreme Court thinking on the issues presented for review.

**Civil Action** A lawsuit filed in court that does not involve criminal sanctions but generally redresses private rights.

**Civil Damages** Money damages awarded to a party at the conclusion of a civil action.

**Claim of Appeal** A procedural requirement in which a party informs a superior court or tribunal of its intention to file an appeal of a matter decided by an inferior court or tribunal. The notice places the matter on the docket of the superior court or tribunal.

**Compensatory Damages** Money damages that exceed economic and quantifiable losses and include money for losses that are difficult or impossible to quantify with precision, such as the value of time lost or the loss associated with an emotional injury. Compensatory damages are not intended to punish but are designed to make the injured party as whole as possible.

**Criminal Sanction** Imposition of a criminal penalty, including fines and incarceration, on a party.

—D—

**Damages** The sum of money awarded to a party to compensate for a loss. The award is made against the party deemed responsible for the loss.

**Deferral State** A state that has a state or local agency designated by the Equal Employment Opportunity Commission (EEOC) to receive charges of discrimination. Rather than being subject to the regular 180-day time limit to file charges of discrimination, a party living in a deferral state has 300 days to file such charges.

**De Novo** A procedure or trial, such as a "trial de novo," that considers a matter as though it had never been the subject of a previous hearing or adjudication. Specifically, a state or local agency or the EEOC may determine whether a charge has merit following an agency investigation or hearing. If the matter proceeds to trial, the trial court will hear the case without reference to the previous determination(s). By contrast, in an appeal of a trial, the appellate court can consider only the record developed at trial; generally cannot consider new evidence; and is limited to determining whether the lower court's decision is supported by the record, the evidence admitted at trial, and a correct interpretation of the law.

**Discretionary Authority** The right of a court, agency, or individual to exercise independent judgment in the performance of an official nonministerial act. Such independent judgment, however, must comport with the duties defined by the statute, charter, or other document granting the right to exercise such judgment.

**Disparate Impact** *See* Adverse Impact.

**Disparate Treatment** Intentional discrimination. Allegations and proof that an employer's actions in a specific instance intentionally treated some people less favorably than others based on such impermissible criteria as race, color, religion, national origin, sex, and age. *Compare to* Adverse Impact, which involves facially neutral practices or policies.

—E—

**EEOC Deferral Agency** A state or local agency that has been designated by the EEOC to receive and process discrimination charges. *See* Deferral State.

**Enjoinment** A court order that prohibits a party from engaging in a specific practice. *See* Injunction.

**Equitable Relief** A broad category of relief that does not involve legal damages but may include monetary recovery for lost or back wages and injunctive relief such as an order to hire, rehire, or promote someone.

—F—

**Faltering Company** A company that, under the provisions of the Worker's Adjustment and Retraining Notification Act (WARN), is in danger of bankruptcy or other similar problem. Designation as a faltering company is a narrowly construed defense to a complaint that a company failed to provide terminated or laid-off employees with the notice of job loss that WARN requires.

—I—

**Impleading of Prior Employers** An employer's right to seek recovery of some of its payment obligations from an employee's prior employer that may be liable, in whole or in part, for the injury for which the more recent employer is providing compensation.

**Injunction** A court order directing a party to do or not do something. An injunction may be temporary, which seeks to preserve the *status quo*; preliminary, which indicates that the plaintiff will likely prevail following a hearing or trial; or permanent, which means that the plaintiff prevailed at a hearing or trial.

**Injunction Action** The lawsuit in which a party seeks injunctive relief through the issuance of an injunction.

**Investigative Consumer Report** A report concerning an individual that, under federal and state fair credit reporting acts, includes both public record information and information obtained from nonpublic sources such as interviews with employers, neighbors, etc.

—J—

**Jury Trial** A trial before a panel of the parties' peers that decides disputed matters of fact and applies the law to the facts in reaching a decision as to which of the parties prevails.

—L—

**Liquidated Damages** A sum that parties to a contract agree will constitute actual damages should one of the parties breach the contract. Liquidated damages are generally used when it may be difficult to assess actual damages. For employment purposes, liquidated damages take the place of punitive damages and constitute an additional award of damages following proof of discrimination. For example, under the federal Age Discrimination in Employment Act (ADEA), a party that proves that a defendant acted with reckless disregard of the statute may be entitled to liquidated damages in an amount equal to the actual damage recovery.

—M—

**Mandamus** An order from a court or agency to a party or inferior court or agency to perform a specific action. Such an order often involves a complaint against a government official brought by an individual seeking to compel the official to perform a ministerial act or mandatory duty that does not involve the exercise of discretion.

—N—

**Nonexclusivity of Remedies** A statute or ordinance that permits individual enforcement as well as enforcement by the government.

**Notice of Appeal** A procedural requirement in which a party informs a superior court or tribunal of its intention to file an appeal of a matter decided by an inferior court or tribunal. The notice of appeal places the matter on the docket of the appellate court or tribunal.

—O—

**Ordinances** Acts of a legislature of a municipal corporation. Ordinances are generally the laws of a local jurisdiction rather than federal or state laws.

—P—

**Petition and Bill of Particulars** A procedural termination that refers to the filing of an appeal with a superior court of a decision by an inferior court; the appeal lists the reasons why the inferior court's decision was incorrect.

**Prima Facie Evidence** The evidence needed to establish a proposition. For example, a party establishing a prima facie case of discrimination may prevail if the other party fails to counter the evidence.

**Private Cause of Action** *See* Private Right.

**Private Right** The right or ability of a person to file a civil action. Many statutes expressly provide the right of a person to file a lawsuit based on another's alleged violation of the statute. When a statute does not, however, provide such a right, courts are required to determine whether a private right of action should be inferred from the statute's language.

**Promissory Estoppel** A cause of action, based on a promise or statement made by a promisor, that the promisee relies on by acting or not acting in a way that, without the promise, it normally would. A court may enforce the promise if not doing so would cause an injustice. For employment purposes, promissory estoppel arises when an employer makes certain promises, such as a promotion, position, or salary, to applicants or current employees if they work or remain employed and then fails to fulfill such promises.

**Promulgated State Law** A state law that has been passed by a state legislature and has become law through acceptance by a governor, by operation of time, or by a veto override vote.

**Protected Class** A category of persons protected against discrimination under a fair employment statute.

**Protected Concerted Activities** Actions taken by employees, including actions of a single employee addressing a concern that involves other employees, that further their collective rights. Employers cannot adversely affect the working relationship with employees who participate in protected concerted activities.

**Punitive Damages** A sum of money awarded against a party, intended to punish the party for its actions (especially when they are reckless, wanton, and/or intentional) and to set an example for that party and others regarding the consequences of the action. Punitive damages are awarded in addition to amounts awarded to compensate a party for economic loss (*see* Actual Damages) and noneconomic loss (*see* Compensatory Damages).

—Q—

**Qualifying Formula** A calculation made to determine whether an individual is entitled to a particular benefit.

—R—

**Reprisal** *See* Retaliation.

**Restraining Order** An order prohibiting a party from engaging in a certain activity. *See* Injunction.

**Retaliation** Actions against a party for engaging in protected conduct. For example, individuals who participate in a matter under a fair employment statute may not be terminated, demoted, or otherwise adversely treated merely because of such participation.

—S—

**Sealed Record** A sealed or expunged criminal or juvenile record is one that has been closed by court order or operation of law and one to which an employer would not have access when conducting an applicant or employee investigation.

**Statute** An act of a legislative body declaring, commanding, or prohibiting something. A statute is a law governing individual and collective behavior that potentially provides for civil or criminal consequences when violated.

—T—

**Temporary Relief** Injunctive orders issued by a court at the outset of litigation to preserve the status quo.

**Trial De Novo** *See* De Novo.

—V—

**Vacate** An order by a superior court to an inferior court that sets aside, annuls, or rescinds the decision and opinion of the inferior court. On occasion, a court will vacate a decision of its own and replace it with another, rendering the first decision a nullity.

—W—

**Writ of Certiorari** *See* Certiorari.

**Writ of Error** The filing of an appeal of a decision, usually from an inferior court to a superior court. *See* Petition and Bill of Particulars.

**Writ of Review** *See* Writ of Error; Petition and Bill of Particulars.

# Topical Index

*[References are to Page numbers (xxiii–lxxviii), Section numbers (1.1–9.10), Exhibits (**E**), and Tables (**T**).]*

*[References are to Page numbers (xxiii–lxxiii), Section numbers (1.1–9.10), Exhibits (**E**), and Tables (**T**).]*

*[References are to Page numbers (xxiii–lxxiii), Section numbers (1.1–9.10), Exhibits (**E**), and Tables (**T**).]*

*[References are to Page numbers (xxiii–lxxiii), Section numbers (1.1–9.10), Exhibits (**E**), and Tables (**T**).]*

*[References are to Page numbers (xxiii–lxxiii), Section numbers (1.1–9.10), Exhibits (**E**), and Tables (**T**).]*

*[References are to Page numbers (xxiii–lxxiii), Section numbers (1.1–9.10), Exhibits (**E**), and Tables (**T**).]*

*[References are to Page numbers (xxiii–lxxiii), Section numbers (1.1–9.10), Exhibits (**E**), and Tables (**T**).]*

*[References are to Page numbers (xxiii–lxxiii), Section numbers (1.1–9.10), Exhibits (**E**), and Tables (**T**).]*

*[References are to Page numbers (xxiii–lxxiii), Section numbers (1.1–9.10), Exhibits (**E**), and Tables (**T**).]*

*[References are to Page numbers (xxiii–lxxiii), Section numbers (1.1–9.10), Exhibits (**E**), and Tables (**T**).]*

*[References are to Page numbers (xxiii–lxxiii), Section numbers (1.1–9.10), Exhibits (**E**), and Tables (**T**).]*

*[References are to Page numbers (xxiii–lxxiii), Section numbers (1.1–9.10), Exhibits (**E**), and Tables (**T**).]*



**Q**



**R**

*[References are to Page numbers (xxiii–lxxiii), Section numbers (1.1–9.10), Exhibits (**E**), and Tables (**T**).]*

*[References are to Page numbers (xxiii–lxxiii), Section numbers (1.1–9.10), Exhibits (**E**), and Tables (**T**).]*

*[References are to Page numbers (xxiii–lxxiii), Section numbers (1.1–9.10), Exhibits (**E**), and Tables (**T**).]*

*[References are to Page numbers (xxiii–lxxiii), Section numbers (1.1–9.10), Exhibits (**E**), and Tables (**T**).]*



## Y